HANDBOOK
of
PSYCHOLOGY

HANDBOOK
of
PSYCHOLOGY

VOLUME 4
EXPERIMENTAL PSYCHOLOGY

Alice F. Healy
Robert W. Proctor

Volume Editors

Irving B. Weiner

Editor-in-Chief

John Wiley & Sons, Inc.

This book is printed on acid-free paper. ♾

Published by John Wiley & Sons, Inc., Hoboken, New Jersey.
Published simultaneously in Canada.

For general information on our other products and services please contact our Customer Care Department within the United States at (800) 762-2974, outside the United States at (317) 572-3993, or fax (317) 572-4002.

Wiley also publishes its books in a variety of electronic formats. Some content that appears in print may not be available in electronic books. For more information about Wiley products, visit our web site at www.wiley.com.

Library of Congress Cataloging-in-Publication Data:

Handbook of psychology / Irving B. Weiner, editor-in-chief.
p. cm.
Includes bibliographical references and indexes.
Contents: v. 1. History of psychology / edited by Donald K. Freedheim — v. 2. Research methods in psychology / edited by John A. Schinka, Wayne F. Velicer — v. 3. Biological psychology / edited by Michela Gallagher, Randy J. Nelson — v. 4. Experimental psychology / edited by Alice F. Healy, Robert W. Proctor — v. 5. Personality and social psychology / edited by Theodore Millon, Melvin J. Lerner — v. 6. Developmental psychology / edited by Richard M. Lerner, M. Ann Easterbrooks, Jayanthi Mistry — v. 7. Educational psychology / edited by William M. Reynolds, Gloria E. Miller — v. 8. Clinical psychology / edited by George Stricker, Thomas A. Widiger — v. 9. Health psychology / edited by Arthur M. Nezu, Christine Maguth Nezu, Pamela A. Geller — v. 10. Assessment psychology / edited by John R. Graham, Jack A. Naglieri — v. 11. Forensic psychology / edited by Alan M. Goldstein — v. 12. Industrial and organizational psychology / edited by Walter C. Borman, Daniel R. Ilgen, Richard J. Klimoski.
ISBN 0-471-39262-6 (cloth : alk. paper : v. 4); ISBN 0-471-66667-X (pbk.) — ISBN 0-471-66675-0 (set : pbk.)
1. Psychology. I. Weiner, Irving B.

BF121.H1955 2003
150—dc21

2002066380

Printed in the United States of America.

10 9 8 7 6 5 4 3 2 1

Editorial Board

Handbook of Psychology Preface

Psychology at the beginning of the twenty-first century has become a highly diverse field of scientific study and applied technology. Psychologists commonly regard their discipline as the science of behavior, and the American Psychological Association has formally designated 2000 to 2010 as the "Decade of Behavior." The pursuits of behavioral scientists range from the natural sciences to the social sciences and embrace a wide variety of objects of investigation. Some psychologists have more in common with biologists than with most other psychologists, and some have more in common with sociologists than with most of their psychological colleagues. Some psychologists are interested primarily in the behavior of animals, some in the behavior of people, and others in the behavior of organizations. These and other dimensions of difference among psychological scientists are matched by equal if not greater heterogeneity among psychological practitioners, who currently apply a vast array of methods in many different settings to achieve highly varied purposes.

Psychology has been rich in comprehensive encyclopedias and in handbooks devoted to specific topics in the field. However, there has not previously been any single handbook designed to cover the broad scope of psychological science and practice. The present 12-volume *Handbook of Psychology* was conceived to occupy this place in the literature. Leading national and international scholars and practitioners have collaborated to produce 297 authoritative and detailed chapters covering all fundamental facets of the discipline, and the *Handbook* has been organized to capture the breadth and diversity of psychology and to encompass interests and concerns shared by psychologists in all branches of the field.

Two unifying threads run through the science of behavior. The first is a common history rooted in conceptual and empirical approaches to understanding the nature of behavior. The specific histories of all specialty areas in psychology trace their origins to the formulations of the classical philosophers and the methodology of the early experimentalists, and appreciation for the historical evolution of psychology in all of its variations transcends individual identities as being one kind of psychologist or another. Accordingly, Volume 1 in the *Handbook* is devoted to the history of psychology as it emerged in many areas of scientific study and applied technology.

A second unifying thread in psychology is a commitment to the development and utilization of research methods suitable for collecting and analyzing behavioral data. With attention both to specific procedures and their application in particular settings, Volume 2 addresses research methods in psychology.

Volumes 3 through 7 of the *Handbook* present the substantive content of psychological knowledge in five broad areas of study: biological psychology (Volume 3), experimental psychology (Volume 4), personality and social psychology (Volume 5), developmental psychology (Volume 6), and educational psychology (Volume 7). Volumes 8 through 12 address the application of psychological knowledge in five broad areas of professional practice: clinical psychology (Volume 8), health psychology (Volume 9), assessment psychology (Volume 10), forensic psychology (Volume 11), and industrial and organizational psychology (Volume 12). Each of these volumes reviews what is currently known in these areas of study and application and identifies pertinent sources of information in the literature. Each discusses unresolved issues and unanswered questions and proposes future directions in conceptualization, research, and practice. Each of the volumes also reflects the investment of scientific psychologists in practical applications of their findings and the attention of applied psychologists to the scientific basis of their methods.

The *Handbook of Psychology* was prepared for the purpose of educating and informing readers about the present state of psychological knowledge and about anticipated advances in behavioral science research and practice. With this purpose in mind, the individual *Handbook* volumes address the needs and interests of three groups. First, for graduate students in behavioral science, the volumes provide advanced instruction in the basic concepts and methods that define the fields they cover, together with a review of current knowledge, core literature, and likely future developments. Second, in addition to serving as graduate textbooks, the volumes offer professional psychologists an opportunity to read and contemplate the views of distinguished colleagues concerning the central thrusts of research and leading edges of practice in their respective fields. Third, for psychologists seeking to become conversant with fields outside their own specialty and for persons outside of psychology seeking information about psychological matters, the *Handbook* volumes serve as a reference source for expanding their knowledge and directing them to additional sources in the literature.

The preparation of this *Handbook* was made possible by the diligence and scholarly sophistication of the 25 volume editors and co-editors who constituted the Editorial Board. As Editor-in-Chief, I want to thank each of them for the pleasure of their collaboration in this project. I compliment them for having recruited an outstanding cast of contributors to their volumes and then working closely with these authors to achieve chapters that will stand each in their own right as valuable contributions to the literature. I would like finally to express my appreciation to the editorial staff of John Wiley and Sons for the opportunity to share in the development of this project and its pursuit to fruition, most particularly to Jennifer Simon, Senior Editor, and her two assistants, Mary Porterfield and Isabel Pratt. Without Jennifer's vision of the *Handbook* and her keen judgment and unflagging support in producing it, the occasion to write this preface would not have arrived.

IRVING B. WEINER
Tampa, Florida

Volume Preface

This volume is intended to provide thorough, accessible tutorials on the major topic areas in the field of experimental psychology. The volume should be useful not only as a reference source for professionals, being part of this *Handbook,* but also as an effective, stand-alone textbook for students. Consequently, the volume is aimed at professional psychologists, entry-level graduate students, and advanced undergraduates who have some relatively limited background in experimental psychology. Just as reading this volume does not depend on reading the other volumes in the series, reading a specific chapter in this volume is not contingent on reading any other chapters. Each chapter provides an up-to-date, state-of-the-art review of a specific subfield of experimental psychology, providing coverage of what is known and what is currently being done, along with some of the historical context.

WHAT IS EXPERIMENTAL PSYCHOLOGY?

The experimental method is defined by the manipulation of independent variables and the measurement of dependent variables. Extraneous variables are either controlled or allowed to vary randomly. In particular, care is taken to remove any variables that are confounded with the independent variables. Because of the control exerted, this method permits the investigator to isolate causal relations. Any change in the dependent variables can be viewed as caused by the manipulation of the independent variables.

Experimental psychology has a rich heritage that started when Wilhelm Wundt created the first psychology laboratory in 1879 at the University of Leipzig. Because of the unique ability to draw causal inferences with experiments, early psychology was essentially experimental psychology. Although there are certainly those who think that the experiment is the wrong methodology for many aspects of psychology, the primary methodological goal of most research in psychology has been the exertion of as much control as possible, so that the general idea of the experiment as the ideal research tool is widely accepted in psychology.

Today the term *experimental psychology* does not, however, cover all of the areas in psychology that employ the experimental method. The use of experiments is widespread, including, for example, research in biological, social, developmental, educational, clinical, and industrial psychology. Nevertheless, the term *experimental psychology* is currently limited to cover roughly the topics of perception, performance, learning, memory, and cognition. Although by definition empirical in nature, research on experimental psychology is focused on tests of theories, so that theoretical and experimental objectives and methods are necessarily intertwined. Indeed, research in experimental psychology has become progressively more interdisciplinary, with an emphasis on not only psychological theories but also theories based on other disciplines including those in the broader fields of cognitive science and neuroscience. In addition, since its inception there has been a continued growth and relevance of experimental psychology to everyday life outside of the laboratory. The potential applications of the results of psychology experiments are increasingly widespread and include, for example, implications concerning teaching and training, law, and medicine.

ORGANIZATION OF THE VOLUME

In covering the core topics of perception, performance, learning, memory, and cognition, the volume is organized approximately from the least to the most complex processes. Each of the first 23 chapters is focused on a different single or pair of psychological processes. These chapters are divided into eight sets with three chapters in each set but the last, which includes only two. The sets cover the more general topics of (a) modulatory processes, (b) sensory processes, (c) perceptual processes, (d) human performance, (e) elementary learning and memory processes, (f) complex learning and memory processes, (g) language and information processing, and (h) thinking.

Within the set of modulatory processes, we begin with the fascinating topic of consciousness (and its inverse, unconsciousness), which has deep roots in philosophy as well as in psychology. From there we delve into the topic of motivation and then the topic of mood. In addressing sensory processes, we focus on three specific senses: vision, audition, and touch. More research has been conducted on vision than on any other sense. Hence, the first chapter in this set provides an overview of the theoretical and methodological foundations of research on visual perception. Visual perception is covered from a different perspective in the following set of chapters on perceptual processes. These include chapters focused on organization and identification processes in the visual perception of objects, on depth perception and the perception of events, and on speech production and perception. For the set of chapters on performance, we progress through the topics roughly in the order in which they take place, considering first attention, then action selection, and finally motor control.

The set of chapters on elementary learning and memory processes begins with two focused on work with animals, the first on conditioning and learning and the second on animal memory and cognition, and concludes with one focused on work with humans, involving sensory and working memory. For the set of chapters on complex learning and memory processes, we include chapters on the specific topics of semantic memory and priming, episodic and autobiographical memory, and procedural memory and skill acquisition, with each of these chapters containing coverage of two different but related themes. The chapters on language and information processing address first psycholinguistics, with a focus on language comprehension and production, then reading, with a focus on word identification and eye movements, and finally the most complex of these processes, those involving text comprehension and discourse processing. We end with other complex processes, those that underlie thinking, again considering them in pairs, starting with concepts and categorization and concluding with reasoning and problem solving.

Our final chapter provides a historical and modern overview of applied experimental psychology, showing how psychological experimentation addresses practical concerns. The earlier chapters in the volume also provide some discussion of applications as well as a review of the historical development of their topic, but the emphasis on those chapters is on recent empirical results and theory.

LIMITATIONS AND ACCOMPLISHMENTS

As should be clear from this outline, the volume is quite comprehensive in scope. Nevertheless, notable gaps could not be avoided. For instance, in considering the sensory processes, we could only focus on three of the senses, ignoring the important senses of taste and smell. The length of the volume did not allow us to include separate chapters on these senses, and it proved to be unreasonable to expect one chapter to include a summary of more than one sense. There are also more subtle omissions from our coverage because chapter authors often, reasonably, chose to emphasize that aspect of their topic that was of most interest to them or for which they had the strongest background and expertise. To give just one example, the chapter on perceptual organization and identification focuses on those processes as they occur in visual perception rather than including the similar processes in audition and other senses. This is a single volume, but to provide a full, complete, and detailed coverage of experimental psychology, more than one volume would be necessary. In fact, John Wiley & Sons has just published the third edition of the classic *Stevens' Handbook of Experimental Psychology,* which is now four volumes long. The original version appeared in 1951 in a single volume, and the increase in size since then reflects the large growth of research in this area. Readers of the present volume who wish to delve more deeply into particular topics in experimental psychology are referred to the new four-volume set of the *Stevens' Handbook.*

The present volume makes up for any deficiency in quantity of coverage with its extraordinary quality of coverage. When we were asked to edit this volume, we developed a wish list of contributors including the leaders in each of the specific chapter topics. We constructed a list including two or three names of potential senior authors for each chapter. With very few exceptions, the current volume is comprised of authors from that original list. Even though we thus had extremely high expectations about the chapters in the volume from the beginning, in many cases the authors went way beyond our initial expectations because of the keen insights they introduced in their chapters. Therefore, these chapters serve not only as lucid summaries of the current state of the field but also as roadmaps leading to the most fruitful avenues of future investigation.

ACKNOWLEDGMENTS

We would like to express our deep appreciation to our team of chapter authors for their exceptional contributions. In addition, we are indebted to a number of others who have helped us in our efforts to put this volume together. First, we are indebted to Irv Weiner, the editor-in-chief for the *Handbook.* Not only did he oversee the entire project, giving us invaluable guidance at each step as we progressed from the early conception of the volume through the finished product, but he also read the draft of every chapter and offered many valuable, specific comments and suggestions. Second, we are grateful to our colleagues and collaborators, most notably Lyle Bourne and John Capaldi, for their helpful advice at many stages of this project. Third, preparation of the book and Chapter 11 benefited from the appointment of the second edition as a fellow of the Center for Behaviorial and Social Sciences, School of Liberal Arts, Purdue University during fall, 2000. The book preparation also benefited from Army Research Institute Contract DASW01-99-K-0002 to the University of Colorado, which supported the first editor during summer, 1999, 2000, and 2001. Finally but by no means least, we wish to thank our spouses, Bruce Healy and Janet Proctor, who have provided unfailing support, understanding, and encouragement as we required extra time to devote to this project on top of our normal teaching, research, and writing schedule.

ALICE F. HEALY AND ROBERT W. PROCTOR

Contents

PART FOUR
HUMAN PERFORMANCE

PART EIGHT
THINKING AND APPLICATIONS

Contributors

William P. Banks, PhD
Department of Psychology
Pomona College
Claremont, California

Kirsten R. Butcher, MA
Department of Psychology
University of Colorado at Boulder
Boulder, Colorado

E. J. Capaldi, PhD
Department of Psychological Sciences
Purdue University
West Lafayette, Indiana

Corrado Caudek, PhD
Department of Psychology
University of Trieste, Italy

Charles Clifton Jr., PhD
Department of Psychology
University of Massachusetts
Amherst, Massachusetts

Howard Egeth, PhD
Department of Psychology
Johns Hopkins University
Baltimore, Maryland

Eric Eich, PhD
Department of Psychology
University of British Columbia
Vancouver, BC, Canada

William Epstein, PhD
Department of Psychology
University of Wisconsin
Madison, Wisconsin
and
Department of Psychology
University of Virginia
Charlottesville, Virginia

Michael S. Fanselow, PhD
Department of Psychology
University of California
Los Angeles, California

Ilya Farber, PhD
Department of Philosophy
George Washington University
Washington, DC

Joseph P. Forgas, PhD
School of Psychology
University of New South Wales
Sydney, Australia

Carol A. Fowler, PhD
Haskins Laboratories
New Haven, Connecticut

Sergei Gepshtein, PhD
Vision Science Program
University of California
Berkeley, California

Bill P. Godsil, BS
Interdepartmental PhD
Program in Neuroscience
University of California
Los Angeles, California

Robert L. Goldstone, PhD
Department of Psychology
Indiana University
Bloomington, Indiana

Randolph C. Grace, PhD
Department of Psychology
University of Canterbury
Christchurch, New Zealand

Alice F. Healy, PhD
Department of Psychology
University of Colorado
Boulder, Colorado

Herbert Heuer, Dr.rer.nat
Institut für Arbeitsphysiologie
Universität Dortmund
Dortmund, Germany

Jon B. Holbrook, PhD
National Research Council
NASA Ames Research Center
Moffett Field, California

Addie Johnson, PhD
Department of Experimental and Work Psychology
University of Groningen
Groningen, The Netherlands

Alan Kersten, PhD
Department of Psychology
Florida Atlantic University
Boca Raton, Florida

Walter Kintsch, PhD, Dr.h.c.
Department of Psychology
University of Colorado
Boulder, Colorado

Roberta L. Klatzky, PhD
Department of Psychology
Carnegie Mellon University
Pittsburgh, Pennsylvania

Michael Kubovy, PhD
Department of Psychology
University of Virginia
Charlottesville, Virginia

Dominique Lamy, PhD
Department of Psychology
Tel Aviv University
Tel Aviv, Israel

Susan J. Lederman, PhD
Department of Psychology
Queen's University
Kingston, Ontario, Canada

Jacqueline P. Leighton, PhD
Department of Educational Psychology
Centre for Research in Applied Measurement and Evaluation (CRAME)
University of Alberta
Edmonton, Alberta, Canada

Elizabeth J. Marsh, PhD
Department of Psychology
Washington University
St. Louis, Missouri

Timothy P. McNamara, PhD
Department of Psychology
Vanderbilt University
Nashville, Tennessee

Antje S. Meyer, PhD
Behavioral Brain Sciences Centre
University of Birmingham
Birmingham, UK

Ralph R. Miller, PhD
Department of Psychology
State University of New York at Binghamton
Binghamton, New York

James S. Nairne, PhD
Department of Psychological Sciences
Purdue University
West Lafayette, Indiana

Raymond S. Nickerson, PhD
Psychology Department
Tufts University
Medford, Massachusetts

Stephen E. Palmer, PhD
Department of Psychology
University of California
Berkeley, California

Richard W. Pew, PhD
Distributed Systems and Logistics Department
BBN Technologies
Cambridge, Massachusetts

Alexander Pollatsek, PhD
Department of Psychology
University of Massachusetts
Amherst, Massachusetts

Robert W. Proctor, PhD
Department of Psychological Sciences
Purdue University
West Lafayette, Indiana

Dennis R. Proffitt, PhD
Department of Psychology
University of Virginia
Charlottesville, Virginia

Keith Rayner, PhD
Department of Psychology
University of Massachusetts
Amherst, Massachusetts

Henry L. Roediger III, PhD
Department of Psychology
Washington University
St. Louis, Missouri

Matthew S. Starr, PhD
Department of Psychology
University of Massachusetts
Amherst, Massachusetts

Robert J. Sternberg, PhD
PACE Center
Department of Psychology
Yale University
New Haven, Connecticut

Matthew R. Tinsley, PhD
Department of Psychology
University of California
Los Angeles, California

Rebecca Treiman, PhD
Department of Psychology
Washington University
St. Louis, Missouri

Kim-Phuong L. Vu, MS
Department of Psychological Sciences
Purdue University
West Lafayette, Indiana

Lee H. Wurm, PhD
Department of Psychology
Wayne State University
Detroit, Michigan

William A. Yost, PhD
Office of Research and the Graduate School
Loyola University Chicago
Chicago, Illinois

PART ONE

MODULATORY PROCESSES

CHAPTER 1

Consciousness

WILLIAM P. BANKS AND ILYA FARBER

Consciousness is an inclusive term for a number of central aspects of our personal existence. It is the arena of self-knowledge, the ground of our individual perspective, the realm of our private thoughts and emotions. It could be argued that these aspects of mental life are more direct and immediate than any perception of the physical world; indeed, according to Descartes, the fact of our own thinking is the only empirical thing we know with mathematical certainty. Nevertheless, the study of consciousness within science has proven both challenging and controversial, so much so that some have doubted the appropriateness of addressing it within the tradition of scientific psychology.

In recent years, however, new methods and technologies have yielded striking insights into the nature of consciousness. Neuroscience in particular has begun to reveal detailed connections between brain events, subjective experiences, and cognitive processes. The effect of these advances has been to give consciousness a central role both in integrating the diverse areas of psychology and in relating them to developments in neuroscience. In this chapter we survey what has been discovered about consciousness; but because of the unique challenges that the subject poses, we also devote a fair amount of discussion to methodological and theoretical issues and consider the ways in which prescientific models of consciousness exert a lingering (and potentially harmful) influence.

Two features of consciousness pose special methodological challenges for scientific investigation. First, and best known, is its inaccessibility. A conscious experience is directly accessible only to the one person who has it, and even for that person it is often not possible to express precisely and reliably what has been experienced. As an alternative, psychology has developed indirect measures (such as physiological measurements and reaction time) that permit reliable and quantitative measurement, but at the cost of raising new methodological questions about the relationship between these measures and consciousness itself.

The second challenging feature is that the single word *consciousness* is used to refer to a broad range of related but distinct phenomena (Farber & Churchland, 1995). *Consciousness* can mean not being knocked out or asleep; it can mean awareness of a particular stimulus, as opposed to unawareness or implicit processing; it can mean the basic functional state that is modulated by drugs, depression, schizophrenia, or REM sleep. It is the higher order self-awareness that some species have and others lack; it is the understanding of one's own motivations that is gained only after careful reflection; it is the inner voice that expresses some small fraction of what is actually going on below the surface of the mind. On one very old interpretation, it is a transcendent form of unmediated presence in the world; on another, perhaps just as old, it is the inner stage on which ideas and images present themselves in quick succession.

Where scientists are not careful to focus their inquiry or to be explicit about what aspect of consciousness they are studying, this diversity can lead to confusion and talking at cross-purposes. On the other hand, careful decomposition of the concept can point the way to a variety of solutions to the *first* problem, the problem of access. As it has turned out, the philosophical problems of remoteness and subjectivity need not always intrude in the study of more specific *forms* of consciousness such as those just mentioned; some of the more prosaic senses of consciousness have turned out to be quite amenable to scientific analysis. Indeed, a few of these—such as "awareness of stimuli" and "ability to remember and report experiences"—have become quite central to the domain of psychology and must now by any measure be considered well studied.

In what follows we provide a brief history of the early development of scientific approaches to consciousness, followed by more in-depth examinations of the two major strands in twentieth century research: the cognitive and the neuroscientific. In this latter area especially, the pace of progress has accelerated quite rapidly in the last decade; though no single model has yet won broad acceptance, it has become possible for theorists to advance hypotheses with a degree of empirical support and fine-grained explanatory power that was undreamed-of 20 years ago. In the concluding section we offer some thoughts about the relationship between scientific progress and everyday understanding.

BRIEF HISTORY OF THE STUDY OF CONSCIOUSNESS

Ebbinghaus (1908, p. 3) remarked that psychology has a long past and a short history. The same could be said for the study of consciousness, except that the past is even longer and the scientific history even shorter. The concept that the soul is the organ of experience, and hence of consciousness, is ancient. This is a fundamental idea in the Platonic dialogues, as well as the Upanishads, written about 600 years before Plato wrote and a record of thinking that was already ancient.

We could look at the soul as part of a prescientific explanation of mental events and their place in nature. In the mystical traditions the soul is conceived as a substance different from the body that inhabits the body, survives its death (typically by traveling to a supernatural realm), and is the seat of thought, sensation, awareness, and usually the personal self. This doctrine is also central to Christian belief, and for this reason it has had enormous influence on Western philosophical accounts of mind and consciousness. The doctrine of soul or mind as an immaterial substance separate from body is not universal. Aristotle considered but did not accept the idea that the soul might leave the body and reenter it (*De Anima,* 406; see Aristotle, 1991). His theory of the different aspects of *soul* is rooted in the functioning of the biological organism. The pre-Socratic philosophers for the most part had a materialistic theory of soul, as did Lucretius and the later materialists, and the conception of an immaterial soul is foreign to the Confucian tradition. The alternative prescientific conceptions of consciousness suggest that many problems of consciousness we are facing today are not inevitable consequences of a scientific investigation of awareness. Rather, they may result from the specific assumption that mind and matter are entirely different substances.

The mind-body problem is the legendary and most basic problem posed by consciousness. The question asks how subjective experience can be created by matter, or in more modern terms, by the interaction of neurons in a brain. Descartes (1596–1650; see Descartes, 1951) provided an answer to this question, and his answer formed the modern debate. Descartes's famous solution to the problem is that body and soul are two different substances. Of course, this solution is a version of the religious doctrine that soul is immaterial and has properties entirely different from those of matter. This position is termed *dualism,* and it assumes that consciousness does not arise from matter at all. The question then becomes not how matter gives rise to mind, because these are two entirely different kinds of substance, but how the two different substances can interact. If dualism is correct, a scientific program to understand how consciousness arises from neural processes is clearly a lost cause, and indeed any attempt to reconcile physics with experience is doomed. Even if consciousness is not thought to be an aspect of "soul-stuff," its concept has inherited properties from soul-substance that are not compatible with our concepts of physical causality. These include free will, intentionality, and subjective experience. Further, any theorist who seeks to understand how mind and body "interact" is implicitly assuming dualism. To those who seek a unified view of nature, consciousness under these conceptions creates insoluble problems. The philosopher Schopenhauer called the mind-body problem the "worldknot" because of the seeming impossibility of reconciling the facts of mental life with deterministic physical causality. Writing for a modern audience, Chalmers (1996) termed the problem of explaining subjective experience with physical science the "hard problem."

Gustav Fechner, a physicist and philosopher, attempted to establish (under the assumption of dualism) the relationship between mind and body by measuring mathematical relations between physical magnitudes and subjective experiences of magnitudes. While no one would assert that he solved the mind-body problem, the methodologies he devised to measure sensation helped to establish the science of psychophysics.

The tradition of structuralism in the nineteenth century, in the hands of Wundt and Titchener and many others (see Boring, 1942), led to very productive research programs. The structuralist research program could be characterized as an attempt to devise laws for the psychological world that have the power and generality of physical laws, clearly a dualistic project. Nevertheless, many of the "laws" and effects they discovered are still of interest to researchers.

The publication of John Watson's (1925; see also Watson, 1913, 1994) book *Behaviorism* marked the end of structuralism. Methodological and theoretical concerns about the current approaches to psychology had been brewing, but Watson's critique, essentially a manifesto, was thoroughgoing and seemingly definitive. For some 40 years afterward, it was commonly accepted that psychological research should study only publicly available measures such as accuracy, heart rate, and response time; that subjective or introspective reports were valueless as sources of data; and that consciousness itself could not be studied. Watson's arguments were consistent with views of science being developed by logical positivism, a school of philosophy that opposed metaphysics and argued that statements were meaningful only if they had empirically verifiable content. His arguments were consistent also with ideas (later expressed by Wittgenstein, 1953, and Ryle, 1949) that we do not have privileged access to the inner workings of our minds through introspection, and thus that subjective reports are questionable sources of data. The mind (and the brain) was considered a black box, an area closed to investigation, and all theories were to be based on examination of observable stimuli and responses.

Research conducted on perception and attention during World War II (see the chapter by Egeth and Lamy in this volume), the development of the digital computer and information theory, and the emergence of linguistics as the scientific study of mind led to changes in every aspect of the field of psychology. It was widely concluded that the behavioristic strictures on psychological research had led to extremely narrow theories of little relevance to any interesting aspect of human performance. Chomsky's blistering attack on behaviorism (reprinted as Chomsky, 1996) might be taken as the 1960s equivalent of Watson's (1913, 1994) earlier behavioristic manifesto. Henceforth, researchers in psychology had to face the very complex mental processes demanded by linguistic competence, which were totally beyond the reach of methods countenanced by behaviorism. The mind was no longer a black box; theories based on a wide variety of techniques were used to develop rather complex theories of what went on in the mind. New theories and new methodologies emerged with dizzying speed in what was termed the *cognitive revolution* (Gardner, 1985).

We could consider ourselves, at the turn of the century, to be in the middle of a second phase of this revolution, or possibly in a new revolution built on the shoulders of the earlier one. This second revolution results from the progress that has been made by techniques that allowed researchers to observe processing in the brain, through such techniques as electroencephalography (EEG), event-related electrical measures, positron-emission tomography (PET) imaging, magnetic resonance imaging (MRI), and functional MRI. This last black box, the brain, is getting opened. This revolution has the unusual distinction of being cited, in a joint resolution of the United States Senate and House of Representatives on January 1, 1990, declaring the 1990s as the "Decade of the Brain." Neuroscience may be the only scientific revolution to have the official authorization of the federal government.

Our best chance of resolving the difficult problems of consciousness, including the worldknot of the mind-body problem, would seem to come from our newfound and growing ability to relate matter (neural processing) and mind (psychological measures of performance). The actual solution of the hard problem may await conceptual change, or it may remain always at the edge of knowledge, but at least we are in an era in which the pursuit of questions about awareness and volition can be considered a task of normal science, addressed with wonderful new tools.

WHAT WE HAVE LEARNED FROM MEASURES OF COGNITIVE FUNCTIONING

Research on consciousness using strictly behavioral data has a history that long predates the present explosion of knowledge derived from neuroscience. This history includes sometimes controversial experiments on unconscious or subliminal perception and on the influences of consciously unavailable stimuli on performance and judgment. A fresh observer looking over the literature might note wryly that the research is

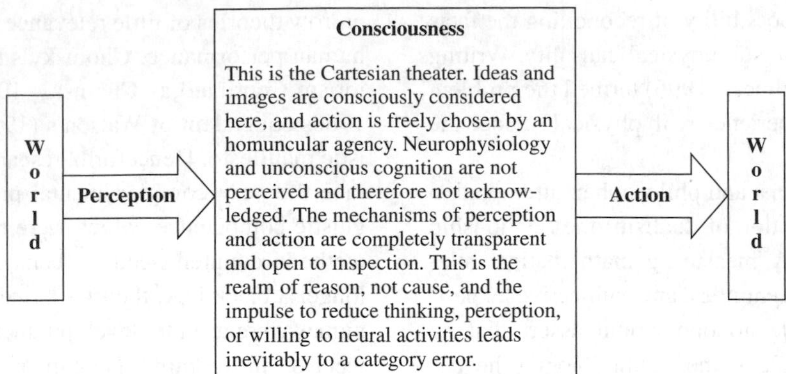

Figure 1.1 A folk model of the role of consciousness in perception and action.

more about unconsciousness than consciousness. Indeed, this is a fair assessment of the research, but it is that way for a good reason.

The motivation for this direction of research can be framed as a test of the folk theory of the role of consciousness in perception and action. A sketch of such a folk theory is presented in Figure 1.1. This model—mind as a container of ideas, with windows to the world for perception at one end and for action at the other—is consistent with a wide range of metaphors about mind, thought, perception, and intention (cf. Lakoff, 1987; Lakoff & Johnson, 1980). The folk model has no room for unconscious thought, and any evidence for unconscious thought would be a challenge to the model. The approach of normal science would be to attempt to disconfirm its assumptions and thus search for unconscious processes in perception, thought, and action.

The folk theory has enormous power because it defines common sense and provides the basis for intuition. In addition, the assumptions are typically implicit and unexamined. For all of these reasons, the folk model can be very tenacious. Indeed, as McCloskey and colleagues showed (e.g., McCloskey & Kohl, 1983), it can be very difficult to get free of a folk theory. They found that a large proportion of educated people, including engineering students enrolled in college physics courses, answered questions about physical events by using a folk model closer to Aristotelian physics than to Newtonian.

Many intuitive assumptions can be derived from the simple outline in Figure 1.1. For example, the idea that perception is essentially a transparent window on the world, unmediated by nonconscious physiological processes, sometimes termed *naive realism,* is seen in the direct input from the world to consciousness. The counterpart to naive realism, which we might call naive conscious agency, is that actions have as their sufficient cause the intentions generated in consciousness and, further, that the intentions arise entirely within consciousness on the basis of consciously available premises.

We used the container metaphor in the earlier sentence when we referred to "intentions generated in consciousness." This is such a familiar metaphor that we forget that it is a metaphor. Within this container the "Cartesian theater" so named by Dennett (1991) is a dominant metaphor for the way thinking takes place. We say that we *see* an idea (on the stage), that we have an idea *in* our mind, that we are putting something *out* of mind, that we are holding an image in our mind's eye, and so on. Perceptions or ideas or intentions are brought forth in the conscious theater, and they are examined and dispatched in the "light of reason." In another common folk model, the machine model of mental processing (Lakoff & Johnson, 1980), the "thought-processing machine" takes the place of the Cartesian stage. The transparency of perception and action is retained, but in that model the process of thought is hidden in the machine and may not be available to consciousness. Both folk models require an observer (homunculus) to supervise operations and make decisions about action.

As has been pointed out by Churchland (1986, 1996) and Banks (1993), this mental model leads to assumptions that make consciousness an insoluble problem. For example, the connection among ideas in the mind is not causal in this model, but logical, so that the reduction of cognitive processing to causally related biological processes is impossible—philosophically a category error. Further, the model leads to a distinction between reason (in the mind) and cause (in matter) and thus is another route to dualism. The homunculus has free will, which is incompatible with deterministic physical causality. In short, a host of seemingly undeniable intuitions about the biological irreducibility of cognitive processes derives from comparing this model of mind with intuitive models of neurophysiology (which themselves may have unexamined folk-neurological components).

Given that mental processes are in fact grounded in neural processes, an important task for cognitive science is to provide a substitute for the model of Figure 1.1 that is compatible with biology. Such a model will likely be as different from the folk model as relativity theory is from Aristotelian physics. Next we consider a number of research projects that in essence are attacks on the model of Figure 1.1.

Unconscious Perception

It goes without saying that a great deal of unconscious processing must take place between registration of stimulus energy on a receptor and perception. This should itself place doubt on the naive realism of the folk model, which views the entire process as transparent. We do not here consider these processes in general (they are treated in the chapters on sensation and perception) but only studies that have looked for evidence of a possible route from perception to memory or response that does not go through the central theater. We begin with this topic because it raises a number of questions and arguments that apply broadly to studies of unconscious processing.

The first experimentally controlled study of unconscious perception is apparently that of Pierce and Jastrow (1884). They found that differences between lifted weights that were not consciously noticeable were nonetheless discriminated at an above-chance level. Another early study showing perception without awareness is that of Sidis (1898), who found above-chance accuracy in naming letters on cards that were so far away from the observers that they complained that they could see nothing at all. This has been a very active area of investigation. The early research history on unconscious perception was reviewed by Adams (1957). More recent reviews include Dixon (1971, 1981), Bornstein and Pittman (1992), and Baars (1988, 1997). The critical review of Holender (1986), along with the commentary in the same issue of *Behavioral and Brain Sciences,* contains arguments and evidence that are still of interest.

A methodological issue that plagues this area of research is that of ensuring that the stimulus is not consciously perceived. This should be a simple technical matter, but many studies have set exposures at durations brief enough to prevent conscious perception and then neglected to reset them as the threshold lowered over the session because the participants dark-adapted or improved in the task through practice. Experiments that presumed participants were not aware of stimuli out of the focus of attention often did not have internal checks to test whether covert shifts in attention were responsible for perception of the purportedly unconscious material.

Even with perfect control of the stimulus there is the substantive issue of what constitutes the measure of unconscious perception. One argument would deny unconscious perception by definition: The very finding that performance was above chance demonstrates that the stimuli were not subliminal. The lack of verbal acknowledgement of the stimuli by the participant might come from a withholding of response, from a very strict personal definition of what constitutes "conscious," or have many other interpretations. A behaviorist would have little interest in these subjective reports, and indeed it might be difficult to know what to make of them because they are reports on states observable only to the participant. The important point is that successful discrimination, whatever the subjective report, could be taken as an adequate certification of the suprathreshold nature of the stimuli.

The problem with this approach is that it takes consciousness out of the picture altogether. One way of getting it back in was suggested by Cheesman and Merikle (1984). They proposed a distinction between the objective threshold, which is the point at which performance, by any measure, falls to chance, and the subjective threshold, which is the point at which participants report that they are guessing or otherwise have no knowledge of the stimuli. Unconscious perception would be above-chance performance with stimuli presented at levels falling between these two thresholds. Satisfying this definition amounts to finding a dissociation between consciousness and response. For this reason Kihlstrom, Barnhardt, and Tataryn (1992) suggested that a better term than unconscious perception would be implicit perception, in analogy with implicit memory. Implicit memory is an influence of memory on performance without conscious recollection of the material itself. Analogously, implicit perception is an effect of a stimulus on a response without awareness of the stimulus. The well-established findings of implicit memory in neurological cases of amnesia make it seem less mysterious that perception could also be implicit.

The distinction between objective and subjective threshold raises a new problem: the measurement of the "subjective" threshold. Accuracy of response can no longer be the criterion. We are then in the position of asking the person if he or she is aware of the stimulus. Just asking may seem a dubious business, but several authors have remarked that it is odd that we accept the word of people with brain damage when they claim that they are unaware of a stimulus for which implicit memory can be demonstrated, but we are more skeptical about the reports of awareness or unawareness by normal participants with presumably intact brains. There is rarely a concern that the participant is untruthful in reporting on awareness of the stimulus. The problem is more basic than honesty: It is that awareness is a state that is not directly accessible by the experimenter. A concrete consequence of this inaccessibility is that it is impossible to be sure that the experimenter's definition of awareness is shared by the participant. Simply asking the participant if he or she is aware of the stimulus amounts to embracing the participant's definition of awareness, and probably aspects of the person's folk model of mind, with all of the problems such an acceptance of unspoken assumptions entails. It is therefore important to find a criterion of awareness that will not be subject to experimental biases, assumptions by the participants about the meaning of the instructions, and so on.

Some solutions to this problem are promising. One is to present a stimulus in a degraded form such that the participant reports seeing nothing at all, then test whether some attribute of that stimulus is perceived or otherwise influences behavior. This approach has the virtue of using a simple and easily understood criterion of awareness while testing for a more complex effect of the stimulus. Not seeing anything at all is a very conservative criterion, but it is far less questionable than more specific criteria.

Another approach to the problem has been to look for a qualitative difference between effects of the same stimulus presented above and below the subjective threshold. Such a difference would give converging evidence that the subjective threshold has meaning beyond mere verbal report. In addition, the search for differences between conscious and unconscious processing is itself of considerable interest as a way of assessing the role of consciousness in processing. This is one way of addressing the important question, What is consciousness for? Finding differences between conscious and unconscious processing is a way of answering this question. This amounts to applying the contrastive analysis advocated by Baars (1988; see also James, 1983).

Holender's (1986) criticism of the unconscious perception literature points out, among other things, that in nearly all of the findings of unconscious perception the response to the stimulus—for example the choice of the heavier weight in the Pierce and Jastrow (1884) study—is the same for both the conscious and the putatively unconscious case. The only difference then is the subjective report that the stimulus was not conscious. Because this report is not independently verifiable, the result is on uncertain footing. If the pattern of results is different below the subjective threshold, this criticism has less force.

A dramatic difference between conscious and unconscious influences is seen in the exclusion experiments of Merikle, Joordens, and Stolz (1995). The exclusion technique, devised by Jacoby (1991; cf. Debner & Jacoby, 1994; Jacoby, Lindsay, & Toth, 1992; Jacoby, Toth, & Yonelinas, 1993), requires a participant *not* to use some source or type of information in responding. If the information nevertheless influences the response, there seems to be good evidence for a nonconscious effect.

The Merikle et al. (1995) experiment presented individual words, such as *spice,* one at a time on a computer screen for brief durations ranging up to 214 ms. After each presentation participants were shown word stems like *spi*—on the screen. Each time, they were asked to complete the stem with any word that had *not* just been presented. Thus, if *spice* was presented, that was the only word that they could not use to complete *spi*—(so *spin, spite, spill,* etc. would be acceptable, but not *spice*). They were told that sometimes the presentation would be too brief for them to see anything, but they were asked to do their best. When nothing at all was shown, the stem was completed 14% of the time with one of the prohibited words. This result represents a baseline percentage. The proportion at 29 ms was 13.3%, essentially the baseline level. This performance indicates that 29 ms is below the objective threshold because it was too brief for there to be any effect at all, and of course also below the subjective threshold, which is higher than the objective threshold.

The important finding is that with the longer presentations of 43 ms and 57 ms, there was an *increase* in the use of the word that was to be excluded. Finally it returned *below* baseline to 8% at 214 ms. The interpretation of this result is that at 43 ms and 57 ms, the word fell above the objective threshold, so that it was registered at some level by the nervous system and associatively primed *spice*. However, at these durations it was below the subjective threshold so that its registration was not conscious, and it could not be excluded. Finally, at the still longer duration of 214 ms, it was frequently above the subjective threshold and could be excluded.

This set of findings suggests an important hypothesis about the function of consciousness that we will see applied in many domains, namely, that with consciousness of a stimulus comes the ability to control how it is used. This could only be discovered in cases in which there was some registration of the stimulus below the subjective threshold, as was the case here.

The only concern with this experiment is that the subjective threshold was not independently measured. To make the argument complete, we should have a parallel measurement of the subjective threshold. It would be necessary to show independently that the threshold for conscious report is between 57 ms and 214 ms. This particular criticism does not apply to some similar experiments, such as Cheesman and Merikle's (1986).

Finally, whatever the definition of consciousness, or of the subjective threshold, there is the possibility that the presented material was consciously perceived, if only for an instant, and then the fact that it had been conscious was forgotten. If this were the case, the folk model in which conscious processing is necessary for any cognitive activity to take place is not challenged. It is very difficult to test the hypothesis that there was a brief moment of forgotten conscious processing that did the cognitive work being attributed to unconscious processing. It may be that this hypothesis is untestable; but testable or not, it seems implausible as a general principle. Complex cognitive acts like participating in a conversation and recalling memories take place without awareness of the cognitive processing that underlies them. If brief moments of immediately forgotten consciousness were nonetheless the motive power for all cognitive processing, it would be necessary to assume that we were all afflicted with a dense amnesia, conveniently affecting only certain aspects of mental life. It seems more parsimonious to assume that these mental events were never conscious in the first place.

Acquiring Tacit Knowledge

One of the most remarkable accomplishments of the human mind consists of learning and using extremely complex systems of knowledge and doing this without conscious effort (see chapters by Fowler and by in this volume). Natural language is a premier example of this (i.e., a system so complex that linguists continue to argue over the structure of language), but children all over the world "pick it up" in the normal course of development. Further, most adults communicate fluently with language with little or no attention to explicit grammatical rules.

There are several traditions of research on implicit learning. One example is the learning of what is often termed *miniature languages.* Braine (1963; for other examples of tacit learning see also Brooks, 1987; Lewicki & Czyzewska, 1994; Lewicki, Czyzewska, & Hill, 1997a, 1997b; Reber, 1992) presented people with sets of material with simple but arbitrary structure: strings of letters such as "abaftab." In this one example "b" and "f" can follow "a," but only "t" can follow "f." Another legal string would be "ababaf." In no case were people told that there was a rule. They thought that they were only to memorize some strings of arbitrary letters.

Braine's (1963) experimental strategy used an ingenious kind of implicit testing. In his memory test some strings of letters that had never been presented in the learning phase were assembled according to the rules he had used to create the stimulus set. Other strings in the memory test were actually presented in the learning material but were (rare) exceptions to the rules. The participants were asked to select which of these were actually presented. They were more likely to think that the legal but nonpresented strings were presented than that the illegal ones that actually had been presented were. This is evidence that they had learned a system rather than a set of strings. Postexperimental interviews in experiments of this type generally reveal that most participants had no idea that there were any rules at all.

Given the much more complex example of natural language learning, this result is not surprising, but research of this type is valuable because, in contrast to natural language acquisition, the conditions of learning are controlled, as well as the exact structure of the stimulus set. Implicit learning in natural settings is not limited to language learning. Biederman and Shiffrar (1987), for example, studied the implicit learning of workers determining the sex of day-old chicks. Chicken sexers (as they are called) become very accurate with practice without, apparently, knowing exactly how they do it (see chapter by Goldstone & Kersten in this volume).

Polanyi (1958), in discussing how scientists learn their craft, argued that such tacit learning is the core of ability in any field requiring skill or expertise (see chapter by Leighton and Sternberg in this volume). Polyani made a useful distinction between a "tool" and an "object" in thought. Knowledge of how to do something is a tool, and it is tacitly learned and used without awareness of its inner structure. The thing being thought about is the "object" in this metaphor, and this "object" is that of which we are aware. Several investigators have said the same thing using slightly different terms, namely, that we are not aware of the mechanisms of cognitive processing, only the results or objects (Baars, 1988; Peacocke, 1986). What and where are these "objects"?

Perceptual Construction

We tend to think of an object of perception—the thing we are looking at or hearing—as an entity with coherence, a single representation in the mind. However, this very coherence has become a theoretical puzzle because the brain does not represent an object as a single entity (see chapters by Palmer; Klatzky & Lederman; and Yost in this volume and the section titled "Sensory Imagery and Binding"). Rather, various aspects of the object are separately analyzed by appropriate specialists in the brain, and a single object or image is nowhere to be found. How the brain keeps parts of an object together is termed the *binding problem,* as will be discussed later in the section on neurophysiology. Here we cover some aspects of the phenomenal object and what it tells us about consciousness.

Rock (1983) presented a case for a "logic of perception," a system of principles by which perceptual objects are constructed. The principles are themselves like "tools" and are not available to awareness. We can only infer them by observing the effects of appropriate displays on perception. One principle we learn from ambiguous figures is that we can see only one interpretation at a time. There exist many bistable figures, such that one interpretation is seen, then the other (see chapter by Palmer in this volume), but never both. Logothetis and colleagues (e.g., Logothetis & Sheinberg, 1996) have neurological evidence that the unseen version is represented in the brain, but consciousness is exclusive: Only one of the two is seen at a given time.

Rock suggested that unconscious assumptions determine which version of an ambiguous figure is seen, and, by extension, he would argue that this is a normal component of the perception of unambiguous objects. Real objects seen under normal viewing conditions typically have only one interpretation, and there is no way to show the effect of interpretation so obvious with ambiguous figures. Because the "logic of perception" is not conscious, the folk model of naive realism does not detect a challenge in this process; all that one is aware of is the result, and its character is attributed to the object rather than to any unconscious process that may be involved in its representation (see chapters by Palmer, Proffitt & Caudek; and Klatzky & Lederman in this volume).

The *New Look* in perceptual psychology (Erdelyi, 1972; McGinnies, 1949) attempted to show that events that are not registered consciously, as well as unconscious expectations and needs, can influence perceptions or even block them, as in the case of perceptual defense. Bruner (1992) pointed out that the thrust of the research was to demonstrate higher level cognitive effects in perception, not to establish that there were nonconscious ones. However, unacknowledged constructive or defensive processes would necessarily be nonconscious.

The thoroughgoing critiques of the early New Look research program (Eriksen, 1958, 1960, 1962; Fuhrer & Eriksen, 1960; Neisser, 1967) cast many of its conclusions in doubt, but they had the salubrious effect of forcing subsequent researchers to avoid many of the methodological problems of the earlier research. Better controlled research by Shevrin and colleagues (Bunce, Bernat, Wong, & Shevrin, 1999; Shevrin, 2000; Wong, Bernat, Bunce, & Shevrin, 1997) suggests that briefly presented words that trigger defensive reactions (established in independent tests) are registered but that the perception is delayed, in accord with the older definition of perceptual defense.

One of the theoretical criticisms (Eriksen, 1958) of perceptual defense was that it required a "superdiscriminating unconscious" that could prevent frightening or forbidden images from being passed on to consciousness. Perceptual defense was considered highly implausible because it would be absurd to have two complete sets of perceptual apparati, especially if the function of one of them were only to protect the other from emotional distress. If a faster unconscious facility existed, so goes the argument, there would have been evolutionary pressure to have it be the single organ of perception and thus of awareness. The problem with this argument is that it assumes the folk model summarized in Figure 4.1, in which consciousness is essential for perception to be accomplished. If consciousness were not needed for all acts of perception in the first place, then it is possible for material to be processed fully without awareness, to be acted upon in some manner, and only selectively to become available to consciousness.

Bruner (1992) suggested as an alternative to the superdiscriminating unconscious the idea of a *judas eye,* which is a term for the peephole a speakeasy bouncer uses to screen out the police and other undesirables. The judas eye would be a process that uses a feature to filter perception, just as in the example all that is needed is the sight of a uniform or a badge. However, there is evidence that unconscious detection can rely on relatively deep analysis. For example, Mack and Rock (1998) found that words presented without warning while participants were judging line lengths (a difficult task) were rarely seen. This is one of several phenomena they termed "inattentional blindness." On the other hand, when the participant's name or a word with strong emotional content was presented, it was reported much more frequently than were neutral words. (Detection of one's name from an unattended auditory source has been reported in much-cited research; see Cowan & Wood, 1997; Wood & Cowan, 1995a, 1995b; and chapter by Egeth & Lamy in this volume.) Because words like "rape" were seen and visually similar words like "rope" were not, the superficial visual analysis of a judas eye does not seem adequate to explain perceptual defense and related phenomena. It seems a better hypothesis that there is much parallel processing in the nervous system, most of it unconscious, and that some products become conscious only after fairly deep analysis.

Another "object" to consider is the result of memory construction. In the model of Figure 1.1, the dominant metaphor for memory is recalling an object that is stored in memory. It is as though one goes to a "place" in memory where the "object" is "stored," and then brings it into consciousness. William James referred to the "object" retrieved in such a manner as being "as fictitious . . . as the Jack of Spades." There is an abundance of modern research supporting James. Conscious memory is best viewed as a construction based on pieces of stored information, general knowledge, opinion, expectation, and so on (one excellent source to consult on this is Schacter, 1995). Neisser (1967) likened the process of recall to the work of a paleontologist who constructs a dinosaur from fragments of fossilized bone, using knowledge derived from other reconstructions. The construction aspect of the metaphor is apt, but in memory as in perception we do not have a good model of what the object being constructed is, or what the neural correlate is. The folk concept of a mental "object," whether in perception or memory, may not have much relation to what is happening in the nervous system when something is perceived or remembered.

Subliminal Priming and Negative Priming

Current interest in subliminal priming derives from Marcel's work (1983a, 1983b). His research was based on earlier work showing that perception of one word can "prime" a related word (Meyer & Schvaneveldt, 1971; see chapter by McNamara & Holbrook in this volume). The primed word is processed more quickly or accurately than in control conditions without priming.

Marcel reported a series of experiments in which he obtained robust priming effects in the absence of perception of the prime. His conclusion was that priming, and therefore perception of the prime word, proceeds automatically and associatively, without any necessity for awareness. The conscious model (cf. Figure 1.1) would be that the prime is consciously registered, serves as a retrieval cue for items like the probe, and thus speeds processing for probe items. Marcel presented a model in which consciousness serves more as a monitor of psychological activity than as a critical path between perception and action. Holender (1986) and others have criticized this work on a number of methodological grounds, but subsequent research has addressed most of his criticisms (see Kihlstrom et al., 1992, for a discussion and review of this work).

Other evidence for subliminal priming includes Greenwald, Klinger, and Schuh's (1995) finding that the magnitude of affective priming does not approach zero as d' for detection of the priming word approaches zero (see also Draine & Greenwald, 1998). Shevrin and colleagues demonstrated classical conditioning of the Galvanic Skin Response (GSR) to faces presented under conditions that prevented detection of the faces (Bunce et al., 1999; Wong et al., 1997).

Cheesman and Merikle (1986) reported an interesting dissociation of conscious and unconscious priming effects using a variation of the Stroop (1935) interference effect. In the Stroop effect a color word such as "red" is printed in a color different from the one named, for example, blue. When presented with this stimulus ("red" printed in blue), the participant must say "blue." Interference is measured as a much longer time to pronounce "blue" than if the word did not name a conflicting color.

Cheesman and Merikle (1986) used a version of the Stroop effect in which a word printed in black is presented briefly on a computer screen, then removed and replaced with a colored rectangle that the participant is to name. Naming of the color of the rectangle was slowed if the color word named a different color. They then showed, first, that if the color word was presented so briefly that the participant reported having seen nothing, naming of the color was still slowed. This would be classified as a case of unconscious perception, but because the same direction of effect is found both consciously and unconsciously, there would be no real dissociation between conscious and unconscious processing. Holender (1986) and other critics could argue reasonably that it was only shown that the Stroop effect was fairly robust at very brief durations, and the supplementary report of awareness by the participant is unrelated to processing.

Cheeseman and Merikle (1986) devised a clever way to answer this criticism. The procedure was to arrange the pairs such that the word "red" would be followed most of the time by the color blue, the word "blue" by yellow, and so on. This created a predictive relationship between the word and the color that participants could strategically exploit to make the task easier. They apparently did use these relationships in naming the colors. With clearly supraliminal presentation of the word, a reversal in the Stroop effect was found such that the red rectangle was named faster when "blue" came before it than when "red" was the word before it.

However, this reversal was found only when the words were presented for longer than the duration needed to perceive them. When the same participants saw the same sequence of stimuli with words that were presented too briefly for conscious perception, they showed only the normal Stroop effect. The implication of this result is that the sort of interference found in the Stroop effect is an automatic process that does not require conscious perception of the word. What consciousness of the stimulus adds is control. Only when there was conscious registration of the stimulus could the participants use the stimulus information strategically.

Negative priming is an interference, measured in reaction time or accuracy, in processing a stimulus that was previously presented but was not attended. It was first discovered by Dalrymple-Alford and Budayr (1966) in the context of the Stroop effect (see also Neill & Valdes, 1996; Neill, Valdes, &

Terry, 1995; Neill & Westberry, 1987). They showed that if a participant was given, say, the word "red" printed in blue, then on the *next* pair was shown the color red, it took longer to name than other colors.

Negative priming has been found in many experiments in which the negative prime, while presented supraliminally, is not consciously perceived because it is not attended. Tipper (1985) presented overlapping line drawings, one drawn in red and the other in green. Participants were told to name only the item in one of the colors and not the other. After participants had processed one of the drawings, the one they had excluded was sometimes presented on the next trial. In these cases the previously unattended drawing was slower to name than in a control condition in which it had not been previously presented. Banks, Roberts, and Ciranni (1995) presented pairs of words simultaneously to the left and to the right ears. Participants were instructed to repeat aloud only the word presented to one of the ears. If a word that had been presented to the unattended ear was presented in the next pair to be repeated, the response was delayed.

As mentioned in the previous section (cf. Cowan & Wood, 1997; Goldstein & Fink, 1981; Mack & Rock, 1999; Rock & Gutman, 1981), material perceptually available but not attended is often the subject of "inattentional blindness"; that is, it seems to be excluded from awareness. The finding of negative priming suggests that ignored material is perceptually processed and represented in the nervous system, but is evidenced only by its negative consequences for later perception, not by any record that is consciously available.

A caveat regarding the implication of the negative priming findings for consciousness is that a number of researchers have found negative priming for fully attended stimuli (MacDonald & Joordens, 2000; Milliken, Joordans, Merikle, & Seiffert, 1998). These findings imply that negative priming cannot be used as evidence by itself that the perception of an item took place without awareness.

Priming studies have been used to address the question of whether the unconscious is, to put it bluntly, "smart" or "dumb." This is a fundamental question about the role of consciousness in processing; if unconscious cognition is dumb, the function of consciousness is to provide intelligence when needed. If the unconscious is smart—capable of doing a lot on its own—it is necessary to find different roles for consciousness.

Greenwald (1992) argued that the unconscious is dumb because it could not combine pairs of words in his subliminal priming studies. He found that some pairs of consciously presented words primed other words on the basis of a meaning that could only be gotten by combining them. For example, presented together consciously, words like "KEY" and "BOARD" primed "COMPUTER." When presented for durations too brief for awareness they primed "LOCK" and "WOOD," but not "COMPUTER." On the other hand, Shevrin and Luborsky (1961) found that subliminally presenting pictures of a pen and a knee resulted in subsequent free associations that had "penny" represented far above chance levels. The resolution of this difference may be methodological, but there are other indications that unconscious processing may in some ways be fairly smart even if unconscious perception is sometimes a bit obtuse. Kihlstrom (1987) reviews many other examples of relative smart unconscious processing.

A number of subliminal priming effects have lingered at the edge of experimental psychology for perhaps no better reason than that they make hardheaded experimentalists uncomfortable. One of these is *subliminal psychodynamic activation* (SPA; Silverman, 1983). Silverman and others (see Weinberger, 1992, for a review) have found that subliminal presentation of the single sentence, "Mommy and I are one," has a number of objectively measurable positive emotional effects (when compared to controls such as "People are walking" or "Mommy is gone"). A frequent criticism is that the studies did not make sure that the stimulus was presented unconsciously. However, many of us would be surprised if the effects were found even with clearly consciously perceived stimuli. It is possible, in fact, that the effects depend on unconscious processing, and it would be interesting to see if the effects were different when subliminal and clearly supraliminal stimuli are compared.

Implicit Memory

Neurological cases brought this topic to the forefront of memory research, with findings of preserved memory in people with amnesia (Schacter, 1987). The preserved memory is termed implicit because it is a tacit sort of memory (i.e., memory that is discovered in use), not memory that is consciously retrieved or observed. People with amnesia would, for example, work each day at a Tower of Hanoi puzzle, and each day assert that they had never seen it before, but each day show improvement in speed of completing it (Cohen, Eichenbaum, Deacedo, & Corkin, 1985). The stem completion task of Merikle et al. (1995) is another type of implicit task. After the word *spice* was presented, its probability of use would be increased even though the word was not consciously registered. In a memory experiment, people with amnesia and normals who could not recall the word *spice* would nevertheless be more likely to use it to complete the stem than if it had not been presented.

Investigation of implicit memory in normals quickly led to an explosion of research, which is covered in the chapters by

McNamara and Holbrook, Roediger and Marsh, and Johnson in this volume.

Nonconscious Basis of Conscious Content

We discussed earlier how the perceptual object is a product of complex sensory processes and probably of inferential processes as well. Memory has also been shown to be a highly inferential skill, and the material "retrieved" from memory has as much inference in it as retrieval. These results violate an assumption of the folk model by which objects are not constructed but are simply brought into the central arena, whether from perception or memory. Errors of commission in memory serve much the same evidentiary function in memory as do ambiguous figures in perception, except that they are much more common and easier to induce. The sorts of error we make in eyewitness testimony, or as a result of a number of documented memory illusions (Loftus, 1993), are particularly troublesome because they are made—and believed—with certainty. Legitimacy is granted to a memory on the basis of a memory's clarity, completeness, quantity of details, and other internal properties, and the possibility that it is the result of suggestion, association, or other processes is considered invalidated by the internal properties (Henkel, Franklin, & Johnson, 2000). Completely bogus memories, induced by an experimenter, can be believed with tenacity (cf. also Schacter, 1995; see also Roediger & McDermott, 1995, and the chapter by Roediger & Marsh in this volume).

The *Poetzl phenomenon* is the reappearance of unconsciously presented material in dreams, often transformed so that the dream reports must be searched for evidence of relation to the material. The phenomenon has been extended to reappearance in free associations, fantasies, and other forms of output, and a number of studies appear to have found Poetzl effects with appropriate controls and methodology (Erdelyi, 1992; Ionescu & Erdelyi, 1992). Still, the fact that reports must be interpreted and that base rates for certain topics or words are difficult to assess casts persistent doubt over the results, as do concerns about experimenter expectations, the need for double-blind procedures in all studies, and other methodological issues.

Consciousness, Will, and Action

In the folk model of consciousness (see Figure 1.1) a major inconsistency with any scientific analysis is the free will or autonomous willing of the homunculus. The average person will report that he or she has free will, and it is often a sign of mental disorder when a person complains that his or her actions are constrained or controlled externally. The problem of will is as much of a hard problem (Chalmers, 1996) as is the problem conscious experience. How can willing be put in a natural-science framework?

One approach comes from measurements of the timing of willing in the brain. Libet and colleagues (Libet, 1985, 1993; Libet, Alberts, & Wright, 1967; Libet et al., 1964) found that changes in EEG potentials recorded from the frontal cortex began 200 ms to 500 ms before the participant was aware of deciding to begin an action (flexion of the wrist) that was to be done freely. One interpretation of this result is that the perception we have of freely willing is simply an illusion, because by these measurements it comes after the brain has already begun the action.

Other interpretations do not lead to this conclusion. The intention that ends with the motion of the hand must have its basis in neurological processes, and it is not surprising that the early stages are not present in consciousness. Consciousness has a role in willing because the intention to move can be arrested before the action takes place (Libet, 1993) and because participation in the entire experimental performance is a conscious act. The process of willing would seem to be an interplay between executive processes, memory, and monitoring, some of which we are conscious and some not. Only the dualistic model of a completely autonomous will controlling the process from the top, like the Cartesian soul fingering the pineal gland from outside of material reality, is rejected. Having said this, we must state that a great deal of theoretical work is needed in this area (see chapters by Proctor & Vu and by Heuer in this volume).

The idea of unconscious motivation dates to Freud and before (see chapters by Eich and Forgas and by Godsil, Tinsley & Fanselow in this volume). *Freudian slips* (Freud, 1965), in which unconscious or suppressed thoughts intrude on speech in the form of action errors, should constitute a challenge to the simple folk model by which action is transparently the consequence of intention. However, the commonplace cliché that one has made a Freudian slip seems to be more of a verbal habit than a recognition of unconscious determinants of thought because unconscious motivation is not generally recognized in other areas.

Wegner (1994) and his colleagues have studied some paradoxical (but embarrassingly familiar) effects that result from attempting to suppress ideas. In what they term *ironic thought suppression,* they find that the suppressed thought can pose a problem for control of action. Participants trying to suppress a word were likely to blurt it out when speeded in a word association task. Exciting thoughts (about sex) could be suppressed with effort, but they tended to burst into awareness later. The irony of trying to suppress a thought is that the attempt at suppression primes it, and then more control is needed to keep it hidden than if it had not been suppressed in the first place. The intrusion of unconscious ideation in a modified version of the Stroop task (see Baldwin, 2001) indicates that the suppressed thoughts can be completely unconscious and still have an effect on processing (see chapters by Egeth & Lamy and by Proctor & Vu in this volume for more on these effects).

Attentional Selection

In selective attention paradigms the participant is instructed to attend to one source of information and not to others that are presented. For example, in the shadowing paradigm the participant hears one verbal message with one ear and a completely different one with the other. "Shadowing" means to repeat verbatim a message one hears, and that is what the participants do with one of the two messages. This subject has led to a large amount of research and to attention research as one of the most important areas in cognitive psychology (see chapter by Egeth & Lamy in this volume).

People generally have little awareness of the message on the ear not shadowed (Cherry, 1957; Cowan & Wood, 1997). What happens to that message? Is it lost completely, or is some processing performed on it unconsciously? Treisman (1964; see also Moray, 1969) showed that participants responded to their name on the unattended channel and would switch the source that they were shadowing if the material switched source. Both of these results suggest that unattended material is processed to at least some extent. In the visual modality Mack and Rock (1998) reported that in the "inattentional blindness" paradigm a word presented unexpectedly when a visual discrimination is being conducted is noticed infrequently, but if that word spells the participant's name or an emotional word, it is noticed much more often. For there to be a discrimination between one word and another on the basis of their meaning and not any superficial feature such as length or initial letter, the meaning must have been extracted.

Theories of attention differ on the degree to which unattended material is processed. Early selection theories assume that the rejected material is stopped at the front gate, as it were (cf. Broadbent, 1958). Unattended material could only be monitored by switching or time-sharing. Late selection theories (Deutsch & Deutsch, 1963) assumed that unattended material is processed to some depth, perhaps completely, but that limitations of capacity prevent it from being perceived consciously or remembered. The results of the processing are available for a brief period and can serve to summon attention, bias the interpretation of attended stimuli, or have other effects. One of these effects would be negative priming, as discussed earlier. Another effect would be the noticing of one's own name or an emotionally charged word from an unattended source.

An important set of experiments supports the late selection model, although there are alternative explanations. In an experiment that required somewhat intrepid participants, Corteen and Wood (1972) associated electric shocks with words to produce a conditioned galvanic skin response. After the conditioned response was established, the participants performed a shadowing task in which the shock-associated words were presented to the unattended ear. The conditioned response was still obtained, and galvanic skin responses were also obtained for words semantically related to the conditioned words. This latter finding is particularly interesting because the analysis of the words would have to go deeper than just the sound to elicit these associative responses. Other reports of analysis of unattended material include those of Corteen and Dunn (1974); Forster and Govier (1978); MacKay (1973); and Von Wright, Anderson, and Stenman (1975). On the other hand, Wardlaw and Kroll (1976), in a careful series of experiments, did not replicate the effect.

Replicating this effect may be less of an issue than the concern over whether it implies unconscious processing. This is one situation in which momentary conscious processing of the nontarget material is not implausible. Several lines of evidence support momentary conscious processing. For example, Dawson and Schell (1982), in a replication of Corteen and Wood's (1972) experiment, found that if participants were asked to name the conditioned word in the nonselected ear, they were sometimes able to do so. This suggests that there was attentional switching, or at least some awareness, of material on the unshadowed channel. Corteen (1986) agreed that this was possible. Treisman and Geffen (1967) found that there were momentary lapses in shadowing of the primary message when specified targets were detected in the secondary one. MacKay's (1973) results were replicated by Newstead and Dennis (1979) only if single words were presented on the unshadowed channel and not if words were embedded in sentences. This finding suggests that occasional single words could attract attention and give rise to the effect, while the continuous stream of words in sentences did not create the effect because they were easier to ignore.

Dissociation Accounts of Some Unusual and Abnormal Conditions

The majority of psychological disorders, if not all, have important implications for consciousness, unconscious processing, and so on. Here we consider only disorders that are primarily disorders of consciousness, that is, dissociations and other conditions that affect the quality or the continuity of consciousness, or the information available to consciousness.

Problems in self-monitoring or in integrating one's mental life about a single personal self occur in a variety of disorders. Frith (1992) described many of the symptoms that individuals with schizophrenia exhibit as a failure in attributing their actions to their own intentions or agency. In illusions of control, for example, a patient may assert that an outside force made him do something like strip off his clothes in public. By Frith's account this assertion would result from the patient's being unaware that he had willed the action, in other words, from a dissociation between the executive function and self-monitoring. The source of motivation is attributed to an outside force ("the Devil made me do it"), when it is only outside of the self system of the individual. For another example, individuals with schizophrena are often found to be subvocalizing the very voices that they hear as hallucinations (Frith, 1992, 1996); hearing recordings of the vocalizations does not cause them to abandon the illusion. There are many ways in which the monitoring could fail (see Proust, 2000), but the result is that the self system does not "own" the action, to use Kihlstrom's (1992, 1997) felicitous term.

This lack of ownership could be as simple as being unable to remember that one willed the action, but that seems too simple to cover all cases. Frith's theory is sophisticated and more general. He hypothesized that the self system and the source of willing are separate neural functions that are normally closely connected. When an action is willed, motor processes execute the willed action directly, and a parallel process (similar to feedforward in control of eye movements; see Festinger & Easton, 1974) informs the self system about the action. In certain dissociative states, the self system is not informed. Then, when the action is observed, it comes as a surprise, requiring explanation. *Alien hand syndrome* (Chan & Liu, 1999; Inzelberg, Nisipeanu, Blumen, & Carasso, 2000) is a radical dissociation of this sort, often connected with neurologic damage consistent with a disconnection between motor planning and monitoring in the brain (see chapters by Proctor & Vu and by Heuer in this volume). In this syndrome the patient's hand will sometimes perform complex actions, such as unbuttoning his or her shirt, while the individual watches in horror.

Classic dissociative disorders include fugue states, in which at the extreme the affected person will leave home and begin a new life with amnesia for the previous one, often after some sort of trauma (this may happen more often in Hollywood movies than in real life, but it does happen). In all of these cases the self is isolated from autobiographical memory (see chapter by Roediger & Marsh in this volume). *Dissociative identity disorder* is also known as multiple personality disorder. There has been doubt about the reality of this disorder, but there is evidence that some of the multiple selves do not share explicit knowledge with the others (Nissen, et al., 1994), although implicit memories acquired by one personality seem to be available to the others.

Now termed *conversion disorders,* hysterical dissociations, such as blindness or paralysis, are very common in wartime or other civil disturbance. One example is the case of 200 Cambodian refugees found to have psychogenic blindness (Cooke, 1991). It was speculated that the specific form of the conversion disorder that they had was a result of seeing terrible things before they escaped from Cambodia. Whatever the reason, the disorder could be described as a blocking of access of the self system to visual information, that is, a dissociation between the self and perception. One piece of evidence for this interpretation is the finding that a patient with hysterical analgesia in one arm reported no sensations when stimulated with strong electrical shocks but did have normal changes in physiological indexes as they were administered (Kihlstrom, et al., 1992). Thus the pain messages were transmitted through the nervous system and had many of the normal effects, but the conscious monitoring system did not "own" them and so they were not consciously felt.

Anosognosia (Galin, 1992; Ramachandran, 1995, 1996; Ramachandran, et al., 1996) is a denial of deficits after neurological injury. This denial can take the form of a rigid delusion that is defended with tenacity and resourcefulness. Ramachandran et al. (1996) reported the case of Mrs. R., a right-hemisphere stroke patient who denied the paralysis of her left arm. Ramachandran asked her to point to him with her right hand, and she did. When asked to point with her paralyzed left hand, the hand remained immobile, but she insisted that she was following the instruction. When challenged, she said, "I have severe arthritis in my shoulder, you know that doctor. It hurts."

Bisiach and Geminiani (1991) reported the case of a woman suddenly stricken with paralysis of the left side who complained on the way to the hospital that another patient had forgotten a left hand and left it on the ambulance bed. She was able to agree that the left shoulder and the upper arm were hers, but she became evasive about the forearm and continued to deny the hand altogether.

Denials of this sort are consistent with a dissociation between the representation of the body part or the function (Anton's syndrome is denial of loss of vision, for example) and the representation of the self. Because anosognosia is specific to the neurological conditions (almost always right-hemisphere damage), it is difficult to argue that the denial comes from an unwillingness to admit the deficit. Anosognosia is rarely found with equally severe paralysis resulting from left-hemisphere strokes (see the section titled "Observations from Human Pathology" for more on the neurological basis for anosognosia and related dissociations).

Vaudeville and circus sideshows are legendary venues for extreme and ludicrous effects of hypnotic suggestion, such as blisters caused by pencils hypnotically transformed to red-hot pokers, or otherwise respectable people clucking like chickens and protecting eggs they thought they laid on stage. It is tempting to reject these performances as faked, but extreme sensory modifications can be replicated under controlled conditions (Hilgard, 1968). The extreme pain of cold-pressor stimulation can be completely blocked by hypnotic suggestion in well-controlled experimental situations. Recall of a short list of words learned under hypnosis can also be blocked completely by posthypnotic suggestion. In one experiment Kihlstrom (1994) found that large monetary rewards were ineffective in inducing recall, much to the bewilderment of the participants, who recalled the items quite easily when suggestion was released but the reward was no longer available.

Despite several dissenting voices (Barber, 2000), hypnotism does seem to be a real phenomenon of extraordinary and verifiable modifications of consciousness. Hilgard's (1992) neodissociation theory treats hypnosis as a form of dissociation whereby the self system can be functionally disconnected from other sources of information, or even divided internally into a reporting self and a hidden observer.

One concern with the dissociative or any other theory of hypnosis is the explanation of the power of the hypnotist. What is the mechanism by which the hypnotist gains such control over susceptible individuals? Without a good explanation of the mechanism of hypnotic control, the theory is incomplete, and any results are open to dismissive speculation. We suggest that the mechanism may lie in a receptivity to control by others that is part of our nature as social animals. By this account hypnotic techniques are shortcuts to manipulating—for a brief time but with great force—the social levers and strings that are engaged by leaders, demagogues, peers, and groups in many situations.

What Is Consciousness For? Why Aren't We Zombies?

Baars (1988, 1997) suggested that a contrastive analysis is a powerful way to discover the function of consciousness. If unconscious perception does take place, what are the differences between perception with and without consciousness? We can ask the same question about memory with and without awareness. To put it another way, what does consciousness add? As Searle (1992, 1993) pointed out, consciousness is an important aspect of our mental life, and it stands to reason that it must have some function. What is it?

A few regularities emerge when the research on consciousness is considered. One is that strategic control over action and the use of information seems to come with awareness. Thus, in the experiments of Cheesman and Merikle (1986) or Merikle et al. (1995), the material presented below the conscious threshold was primed but could not be excluded from response as well as it could when presentation was above the subjective threshold. As Shiffrin and Schneider (1977) showed, when enough practice is given to make detection of a given target automatic (i.e., unconscious), the system becomes locked into that target and requires relearning if the target identity is changed. Automaticity and unconscious processing preserve capacity when they are appropriate, but the cost is inflexibility. These results also suggest that consciousness is a limited-capacity medium and that the choice in processing is between awareness, control, and limited capacity, on the one hand, or automaticity, unconsciousness, and large capacity, on the other.

Another generalization is that consciousness and the self are intimately related. Dissociation from the self can lead to unconsciousness; conversely, unconscious registration of material can cause it not to be "owned" by the self. This is well illustrated in the comparison between implicit and explicit memory. Implicit memory performance is automatic and not accompanied by a feeling of the sense that "I did it." Thus, after seeing a list containing the word "motorboat," the individual with amnesia completely forgets the list or even the fact that he saw a list, but when asked to write a word starting with "mo—," he uses "motorboat" rather than more common responses such as "mother" or "moth." When asked why he used "motorboat," he would say, "I don't know. It just popped into my mind." The person with normal memory who supplies a stem completion that was primed by a word no longer recallable would say the same thing: "It just popped into my head." The more radical lack of ownership in anosognosias is a striking example of the disconnection between the self and perceptual stimulation. Hypnosis may be a method of creating similar dissociations in unimpaired people, so that they cannot control their actions, or find memory recall for certain words blocked, or not feel pain when electrically shocked, all because of an induced separation between the self system and action or sensation.

We could say that consciousness is needed to bring material into the self system so that it is owned and put under strategic control. Conversely, it might be said that consciousness emerges when the self is involved with cognition. In the latter case, consciousness is not "for" anything but reflects the fact that what we call conscious experience is the product of engagement of the self with cognitive processing, which could otherwise proceed unconsciously. This leaves us with the difficult question of defining the self.

Conclusions

Probably the most important advance in the study of consciousness might be to replace the model of Figure 1.1 with something more compatible with findings on the function of consciousness. There are several examples to consider. Schacter (1987) proposed a parallel system with a conscious monitoring function. Marcel's (1983a, 1983b) proposed model is similar in that the conscious processor is a monitoring system. Baars's (1988) global workspace model seems to be the most completely developed model of this type (see Franklin & Graesser, 1999, for a similar artificial intelligence model), with parallel processors doing much of the cognitive work and a self system that has executive functions. We will not attempt a revision of Figure 1.1 more in accord with the current state of knowledge, but any such revision would have parallel processes, some of which are and some of which are not accessible to consciousness. The function of consciousness in such a picture would be controlling processes, monitoring activities, and coordinating the activities of disparate processors. Such an intuitive model might be a better starting point, but we are far from having a rigorous, widely accepted model of consciousness.

Despite the continuing philosophical and theoretical difficulties in defining the role of consciousness in cognitive processing, the study of consciousness may be the one area that offers some hope of integrating the diverse field of cognitive psychology. Virtually every topic in the study of cognition, from perception to motor control, has an important connection with the study of consciousness. Developing a unified theory of consciousness could be a mechanism for expressing how these different functions could be integrated. In the next section we examine the impact of the revolution in neuroscience on the study of consciousness and cognitive functioning.

NEUROSCIENTIFIC APPROACHES TO CONSCIOUSNESS

Data from Single-Cell Studies

One of the most compelling lines of research grew out of Nikos Logothetis's discovery that there are single cells in macaque visual cortex whose activity is well correlated with the monkey's conscious perception (Logothetis, 1998; Logothetis & Schall, 1989). Logothetis's experiments were a variant on the venerable *feature detection* paradigm. Traditional feature detection experiments involve presenting various visual stimuli to a monkey while recording (via an implanted electrode) the activity of a single cell in some particular area of visual cortex. Much of what is known about the functional organization of visual cortex was discovered through such studies; to determine whether a given area is sensitive to, say, color or motion, experimenters vary the relevant parameter while recording from single cells and look for cells that show consistently greater response to a particular stimulus type.

Of course, the fact that a single cell represents some visual feature does not necessarily imply anything about what the animal actually perceives; many features extracted by early visual areas (such as center-surround patches) have no direct correlate in conscious perception, and much of the visual system can remain quite responsive to stimuli in an animal anesthetized into unconsciousness. The contribution of Logothetis and his colleagues was to explore the distinction between what is *represented* by the brain and what is *perceived* by the organism. They did so by presenting monkeys with "rivalrous" stimuli—stimuli that support multiple, conflicting interpretations of the visual scene. One common rivalrous stimulus involves two fields of lines flowing past each other; humans exposed to this stimulus report that the lines fuse into a grating that is either upward-moving or downward-moving and that the perceived direction of motion tends to reverse approximately once per second.

In area MT, which is known to represent visual motion, some cells will respond continuously to a particular stimulus (e.g., an upward-moving grating) for as long as it is present. Within this population, a subpopulation was found that showed a fluctuating response to rivalrous stimuli, and it was shown that the activity of these cells was correlated with the monkey's behavioral response. For example, within the population of cells that responded strongly to upward-moving gratings, there was a subpopulation whose activity fluctuated (approximately once per second) in response to a rivalrous grating, and whose periods of high activity were correlated with the monkey's behavioral reports of seeing an upward-moving grating.

This discovery was something of a watershed in that it established that the activity of sensory neurons is not always explicable solely in terms of distal stimulus properties. Comparing the trials where a given neuron is highly active with those where it is less active, no difference can be found in the external stimulus or in the experimental condition. The only difference that tracks the activity of the cell is the monkey's *report* about its perception of motion. One might propose that the cells are somehow tracking the monkey's motor output or intention, but this would be hard to support given their location and connectivity. The most natural interpretation is that these neurons reflect—and perhaps form the neural basis for—the monkey's *awareness* of visual motion.

Some single-cell research seems to show a direct effect of higher level processes, perhaps related to awareness or intentionality, on lower level processes. For example, Moran and Desimone (1985) showed that a visual cell's response is modified by the monkey's attentional allocation in its receptive field.

Data from Human Pathology

One major drawback of single-cell studies is that they are only performed on nonhuman animals because the procedure is invasive and because there is little clinical use for single-cell data from a patient's visual cortex. Recent advances in neuroimaging (most notably the advent of functional MRI) have made it possible to observe the normal human brain noninvasively, at a fine scale, and in real time. Traditionally, however, most of what we know about the functional architecture of the human brain has come from the study of patients who have suffered brain damage, whether from a stroke, an injury, or degenerative disease. Data about the effects of a lesion can be gathered from clinical observation and behavioral tests, and then the location of the lesion can be discerned through simpler forms of neuroimaging or through postmortem autopsy.

It is famously difficult to use lesion data to ground claims about the localization of function because a lesion in a given area may disrupt a function even if the area itself is not "for" that function (e.g., in cases where the lesion interrupts a pathway or produces a conflicting signal). In the case of disruptions related to consciousness, however, merely coming to understand the character of the deficit itself can provide insight into the functional structure of consciousness; just seeing what sorts of breakdowns are *possible* in a system can reveal much about its architecture. Perhaps the clearest example of this has been the phenomenon of blindsight.

Blindsight occurs in some patients who have suffered damage to primary visual cortex (also known as striate cortex, or area V1). This damage produces a blind field in the patient's vision on the side opposite to the lesion; patients will report a complete absence of visual perception in this field. Nonetheless, some patients show a preserved ability to respond in certain ways to stimuli in this field. For example, patients may be able to press a button when a stimulus appears, to point reliably in the direction of the stimulus, or even to respond appropriately to the emotional content of facial expressions (de Gelder, Vroomen, Pourtois, & Weiskrantz, 1999), all while insisting that they cannot see anything and are "just guessing." Research in humans and monkeys (Weiskrantz, 1990, 1998) has supported the hypothesis that this preserved discriminatory capacity is due to extrastriate pathways that carry some visual information to areas of the brain outside of visual cortex, areas involved in functions such as sensorimotor coordination.

Blindsight relates to the study of consciousness in a number of ways. First, it provides a powerful reminder of how much work goes on "outside of" consciousness; even a form of sensory processing that *results in* a conscious reaction (e.g., the emotional response to a facial expression or the diffuse sense that "something has changed") may be quite independent of the sensory information that is available to consciousness. Second, blindsight clearly demonstrates a functional division, seen throughout the motor system, between the mechanisms involved in consciously selecting and initiating an action and the unconscious mechanisms that guide its implementation and execution (Llinás, 2001). Third, it offers the tantalizing possibility—just beginning to be realized—of using neuroimaging to investigate the differences in activity when the same task is performed with or without conscious awareness (Morris, DeGelder, Weiskrantz, & Dolan, 2001).

Another fruitful line of investigation has involved a constellation of puzzling deficits associated with unilateral damage to parietal cortex. Parietal cortex plays an essential role in coordinating action with perception and is known to contain a variety of sensory and motor maps that are integrated in complex ways. Right parietal lesions produce partial or complete paralysis of the left side of the body, and they almost always produce some degree of *hemineglect,* a tendency to ignore the side of the world opposite the lesion (i.e., the left side; hemineglect is not associated with left parietal lesions). The disorder has both sensory and motor components: Patients will fail to respond to stimuli coming from objects located on the left and will not spontaneously use their left-side limbs. This lateral bias tends to manifest itself across a variety of modalities and coordinate frames (e.g., auditory and visual, body-centered and object-centered). Many of the standard tests of hemineglect are based on paper-and-pencil tasks carried out with the right hand: For example, patients with the disorder who are asked to copy a picture (presented entirely in the patient's right field) will fill in the right half but leave the left half sketchy or blank, and if asked to bisect a horizontal line they will show a substantial rightward bias (for a review of clinical and experimental findings regarding hemineglect, see Kerkhoff, 2001).

A variety of mechanisms had been proposed for hemineglect, but the field was narrowed considerably by an ingenious experiment performed by Edoardo Bisiach and his colleagues (Bisiach & Luzzatti, 1978). To discern whether the deficit was primarily one of sense perception or of higher-level processes such as attention and representation, Bisiach designed a test that required only verbal input and output. He asked his subjects to imagine that they were standing at the north end of a well-known plaza in their city and to recount from memory all the buildings that faced on the plaza. What he found was that patients displayed hemineglect even for this imagined vista; in their descriptions, they accurately listed the buildings on the west side of the plaza (to their imaginary right) and omitted some or all of the buildings to the east. Even more strikingly, when he then asked them to repeat the same task but this time to imagine themselves at the south end of the plaza, the left-neglect persisted, meaning that they listed the buildings they had previously omitted and failed to list the same buildings that they had just described only moments before. Because the subjects were drawing on memories formed before the lesion occurred, Bisiach reasoned that the pattern of deficit could only be explained by a failure at the representational level.

This alone would be fascinating, but what makes hemineglect particularly relevant for the study of consciousness is its frequent association with more bizarre derangements of bodily self-conception. For example, some hemineglect patients suffer from misoplegia, a failure to acknowledge that the limbs on the left side of their body are their own. Patients with misoplegia often express hatred of the foreign limbs and wish to be rid of them; V. S. Ramachandran (Ramachandran & Blakeslee, 1998) reports the case of a patient who kept falling out of bed in his attempts to escape his own arm, which he thought was a cadaver's arm placed in his bed by prankish medical students. Other patients, while regarding the limb with indifference, will make bizarre and nonsensical claims such as that it "belongs to someone else" even though it is attached to their own body. It is important to emphasize that these patients are not otherwise cognitively impaired; their IQs are undiminished, and they test at or near normal on tasks that do not involve using or reasoning about the impaired hemifield.

An even stranger disorder associated with hemineglect is anosognosia, or "unawareness of deficit." This name is sometimes used more in a broader sense, to include the unawareness of other deficits such as amnesia or jargon aphasia. For present purposes we focus on anosognosia for hemineglect and hemiparesis, since it remains unclear to what extent the broader range of cases can or should be explained in a unitary fashion.

Patients with anosognosia exhibit a near-total unawareness of their paralysis. Though confined to a wheelchair, they will insist that they are capable of full normal use of their left limbs; if pressed, they may produce confabulatory excuses about being "tired" or, in one striking case, "[not] very ambidextrous" (Ramachandran, 1995). Ramachandran has shown that this unawareness extends even to unconscious decisions such as how to grasp or manipulate an object; anosognosic subjects will use their one good hand to approach tray lifting or shoe tying in a way that cannot succeed without help from the other hand and either will fail to register their failure at the task or will be surprised by it. Bisiach (Bisiach & Rusconi, 1990) has shown that anosognosia extends also to the perceptual realm; unlike patients with hemifield blindness due to retinal or occipital damage, patients with anosognosia will insist that they are fully functional even when they are demonstrably incapable of responding to stimuli in half of their visual field.

Anosognosia is a fascinating and puzzling deficit to which no brief summary will do justice. For our purposes, however, three features are most salient. First and most important is its cognitive impenetrability: Even very intelligent and cooperative patients cannot be made to understand the nature of their deficit. This qualifies the disorder as a derangement of consciousness because it concerns the subject's inability to form even an abstract representation of a particular state of affairs. Second is the bizarre, possibly hallucinatory degree of confabulation associated with the disorder. These confabulations raise deep questions about the relationship between self-perception, self-understanding, and self-description. Third, it should be noted that anosognosia is often strongly domain-specific; patients unaware of their paralysis may still admit to other health problems, and double dissociations have been demonstrated between anosognosias for different forms of neglect in single patients (e.g., sensory vs. motor neglect, or neglect for personal vs. extrapersonal space).

There are at least three major hypotheses about the mechanism of hemineglect and its associated disorders: Bisiach treats it as a systematic warping or "metric distortion" in the patient's representational space (Bisiach, Cornacchia, Sterzi, & Vallar, 1984); Heilman and Schacter attribute it to the failure of second-order monitoring systems (Heilman, Barrett, & Adair, 1998; Schacter, 1990); and Ramachandran presents a complex theory in which the left hemisphere is specialized for building coherence and the right hemisphere (damaged in these disorders) is specialized for using conflicting data to overthrow old interpretations (Ramachandran, 1995). Ramachandran's theory, while highly speculative, is the only one that accounts directly for the stranger cognitive failures of misoplegia and anosognosia. The other theories are not incompatible with the phenomena, but to provide a satisfactory explanation of patients' behavior they would (at minimum) need to be integrated with an account of the mechanisms of confabulation (see, e.g., Moscovitch & Melo, 1997). In any case, what we want to emphasize here is the way in which a lesion of a somatosensory area can produce domain-specific failures of rationality. This suggests two counterintuitive ideas about abstract reasoning, a process that has long been assumed to be a function of the frontal lobes: Either it is in fact more broadly distributed across other areas of the brain, including the temporal and parietal cortices, or coherent second-order reasoning *about* some domain may require the intact functioning of the areas that construct first-order representations *of* that domain. This second hypothesis would accord well with many recent models of the neural basis of consciousness, in particular those of Damasio and Edelman (discussed later).

An Introduction to Current Theories

Several factors have supported the current flowering of neuroscientific research into consciousness. Tremendous advances in neuroimaging have produced new insight into the functional anatomy of the brain; studies of the response properties of neurons, both *in vitro* and in computer models, have led to a deeper understanding of the principles of neurodynamics. This more sophisticated understanding of the brain has made possible more specific hypotheses about the structures that give rise to consciousness. The search for a neural theory of consciousness also conjoins naturally with the new push for large-scale theories to explain such fundamental brain functions as representation, sensorimotor integration, and executive control (Koch & Davis, 1994). These projects are ambitious, to be sure, but at this point there can be no doubting their scientific respectability.

In this section we consider a number of recent hypotheses. There has been a striking convergence among the major theories of the neural basis of consciousness, a convergence both in conceptual structure and in the choice of brain structures on which to focus. As a consequence, rather than treating individual theories one by one, each subsection is devoted to a particular concept or theoretical component that may play a role in several different theories. There is a trade-off here because in focusing on the fundamental concepts, we must necessarily gloss over some of the details of individual views. We made this choice with an eye to the balance of existing treatments: Many of the theorists covered here have recently published lucid, book-length expositions of their individual views, but we have seen almost no extended synthetic treatments. It is our hope that the approach pursued here will assist the reader both in understanding the individual views and in assessing their contributions to the overall pursuit of consciousness.

Two points about all these theories are worth noting in advance. First, their convergence affords some grounds for optimism that the broad outline of a stable, "mature" theory of consciousness may be coming into view. The specific current theories of consciousness are doubtless flawed in many respects; but it seems increasingly clear that they are at least looking in the right place, and that is a very important step in the development of a scientific subdiscipline. In a nutshell, it seems that the neuroscience of consciousness is on the cusp of moving from a revolutionary to an evolutionary mode of progress.

Second, it is worth briefly noting that all of these theories necessarily assume that consciousness is not epiphenomenal; in other words, they treat consciousness as something that plays a functional role and (presumably) confers some concrete advantage on the organisms that have it. This assumption has historically been controversial, but as these theories continue to bear empirical fruit, the assumption becomes more and more plausible.

Dynamic Activity Clusters

Arguably the first scientific approach to consciousness was that of associationist psychology, which treated consciousness as a container or space in which various ideas came and went. The two basic questions posed by the associationists remain with us today: How are ideas formed, and what principles guide the transition from one idea to another? Posing these questions within the context of neuroscience opens, for the first time, the possibility of going beyond the surface level to ask about the *mechanisms* underlying the formation and transition of ideas. Theorists of consciousness are now in a position to ask *how* and even *why* conscious experience is generated, rather than just describing *what* happens in experience.

Most current theories share the basic idea that individual percepts and concepts have as their neural correlate a dynamic "cluster" or "assembly" of neurons (Crick & Koch, 1995; Greenfield, 1995; Llinás, Ribary, Contreras, & Pedroarena, 1998; Singer, 1996; Tononi & Edelman, 1998). Cluster theories take as their starting point the challenge of distinguishing conscious mental activity from unconscious neural processing. In the sensory systems in particular, it is clear that the brain represents far more information than a person is conscious of at any given moment; for example, the entire visual field is represented in visual cortex, but conscious experience is (usually, more or less) restricted to one small part of that field. What, then, is the neural marker of this distinction? What determines *which* neural representations become, so to speak, the contents of consciousness?

Cluster theories propose that various potentially conscious percepts and/or ideas compete to enter consciousness. Each cluster is a group of neurons, often distributed across multiple areas, that collectively represent some image or sensation. As the brain processes inputs and also recursively processes its own state, different clusters may become active, and some sort of "winner-take-all" competition determines which one will be most active and (therefore) the object of consciousness. A crucial feature of this hypothesis is that clusters are dynamic and distributed—meaning that a single cluster may incorporate related feature-representations from many different areas of cortex, and a given neuron may participate in different clusters at different times.

Some of the central dynamics of cluster theories are inherited directly from classical associationism and gain plausibility from the associationist characteristics of neural networks. For example, it is a natural feature of most neural representations that activation will spread from some elements in a cluster to the others, so that activating some features of a representation will cause the network to "fill in" the missing features, eventually activating the whole cluster. Conversely, the most fundamental principle of learning at the neural level—the idea that neurons that are active at the same time become more strongly connected ("neurons that fire together wire together")—provides a mechanism for the creation of clusters on the basis of long-term regularities in experience.

In inheriting this much of the structure of associationism, however, cluster theories also inherit many of its classical problems. It is difficult to give more than a hand-waving explanation of how the various contributions of the senses, memory, and imagination interact, and the mechanism of conscious direction of thought is obscure. Perhaps most important for the present generation of theories are the problems that arise when one tries to characterize the difference between conscious and unconscious representation. Greenfield (1995) explained the difference in terms of magnitude of activation (i.e., one is conscious of whichever cluster is most active at a given time), but this is problematic because magnitude (in the form of firing rate) is already used by the brain to represent the intensity of stimuli. This is reminiscent of the problem that critics raised with Locke's claim that memories were distinguished from perception by their faintness; if true, this would mean that a memory of a bright object should be subjectively indistinguishable from a perception of a sufficiently dim object, and this is clearly not the case. If a system is to incorporate both a representation of the objective magnitude of a stimulus and a distinction between conscious and unconscious representations, that system will need separate ways of encoding these two things; a single variable such as firing rate cannot do the job by itself. In the following sections we mention some concrete proposals for what additional variables the brain might use for this purpose.

Sensory Imagery and Binding

At the neural level, one way of interpreting consciousness is as an integration or "binding" of disparate neural representations into a single, coherent percept. When we see an object, its various features such as color, shape, location, movement, and identity are represented in different areas of the brain, but our experience is still *of* a single, unified object that combines all these properties. How is this combination achieved, and how do we know which features go with which object? Christof von der Malsburg (1981) coined the term *binding problem* to refer to this puzzle in the context of models of the visual system, and it has since been broadened to refer to cross-modal and sensorimotor integration and even to the integration of perception with memory.

As von der Malsburg (1981) pointed out, one can in principle solve this problem by having the processing chain terminate in a set of object-specific neurons that stand for whole percepts. This is the type of representation often caricatured as involving "grandmother cells," since at its most extreme it would require a single cell for each possible percept (e.g., your grandmother), and that cell would fire when and only when you detect that object with any of your senses. This type of representation is highly inefficient and fragile, however; unsurprisingly, the brain does not appear to be organized this way. There is no Cartesian Theater (Dennett, 1991), no single region on which all inputs converge to produce one master representation. Recasting the binding problem, then, the challenge is to explain how a person can have a single, integrated experience of an object whose various properties are represented in different brain regions and never brought together in one place.

If not one place, how about one time? An interesting hypothesis that gained prominence in the 1990s is that temporal synchrony is what binds representations across the brain (Joliot, Ribary, & Llinás, 1994; Singer, 1996, 2001). The idea here is that all the neurons representing a given percept will produce spikes that closely coincide. This approach exploits the fact that spike frequency does not exhaust the information-carrying potential of a neuronal spike train. Even if two neurons produce the same number of spikes within a given time interval, their spike trains may differ in several important ways. Synchrony thus offers one way to encode the extra representational dimension that cluster theories need. There are also a number of good theoretical reasons to look in this direction, including the following (modified from Singer, 1996):

- The constraints of real-time perceptual processing are such that the mechanism of binding has to work on a very short timescale. It also has to allow for the dynamic creation of novel perceptual clusters involving elements that have never been associated before. Both of these requirements suggest that binding should be implemented at the level of neuronal activity rather than at the level of anatomical structure and connectivity.

- It is a robust general principle of neural dynamics that two neurons stimulating a third will have a greater total effect if both their pulses reach the target at the same time (within some small window of tolerance). From this it follows that synchronous firing would enhance the neural visibility and associative power of the disparate components of a cluster. Binding via synchrony could thus explain why a visual field containing the same set of features will call up different associations depending on how they are grouped—so, for example, seeing a purple Volkswagen might bring up memories of an old friend while seeing a purple Ford next to a green Volkswagen would not.
- Neurons in many areas can exhibit oscillatory firing patterns. Phase-locking such oscillations—coordinating them so their peaks coincide—would be a powerful and efficient means of generating synchrony across large distances in cortex. The need for a mechanism of synchrony would thus provide one (though by no means the only) possible explanation for the ubiquity of these oscillatory firing patterns.

The details of empirical studies on synchrony are beyond the scope of this chapter, but it is now widely accepted that synchronous oscillation plays an important role in visual binding and may also be crucial for attentional processes and working memory (for review and discussion, see Engel, Fries, Konig, Brecht, & Singer, 1999; Engel & Singer, 2001). Synchrony can thus be considered at least a neural precondition for consciousness because conscious attention and awareness operate within the realm of whole, bound objects (Treisman & Kanwisher, 1998).

Christof Koch and Francis Crick advanced a more specific proposal, which has come to be known as the *40-Hz hypothesis* (Koch & Crick, 1994). The central idea of this proposal was that synchronous oscillation in the so-called "gamma band" frequency range (approximately 25–55 Hz) is both necessary and sufficient for consciousness—in other words, that we are conscious of the representational contents of all neurons synchronously oscillating in this frequency band, and that all our conscious imagery is accompanied by such oscillations.

The 40-Hz hypothesis was a breakthrough in two respects. First, it led directly to clear, empirically testable claims about the neural correlate of consciousness (NCC). At the single-cell level, the hypothesis implies that the activity of a given sensory neuron should match the contents of sensory consciousness (e.g., in experiments like those of Logothetis mentioned earlier) whenever it is oscillating at frequencies in the gamma band. At the level of functional areas, it also follows that consciousness should be insensitive to differences in activity that are restricted to areas that do not exhibit significant gamma-band oscillation. This latter idea was the basis for the famous conjecture that we are not conscious of the contents of V1, the first stage of processing in visual cortex (Crick & Koch, 1995). Unfortunately, as Crick and Koch themselves pointed out, complicating factors render these seemingly simple implications problematic: How can one distinguish the neurons that are driving an oscillation from those that are merely responding to it? What about local inhibitory neurons, which play no direct role in communicating with other cortical areas—should they be considered part of the NCC if they oscillate? In recognition of these complexities, Crick and Koch now assume that the anatomical side of the NCC story will be more complex, involving (at minimum) finer-grained analysis of the contributions of different cell types and cortical layers (Crick & Koch, 1998).

The original 40-Hz hypothesis was novel in a second way that has been less widely noticed but may ultimately have more lasting consequences: Unlike previous synchrony models of binding, it provided a way to draw a distinction *within* the realm of bound representations, between those which are and are not conscious. If the 40-Hz hypothesis was correct, a neuroscientist observing the activity of a pair of sensory neurons in separate areas could place them into one of three categories based solely on the properties of their spike trains:

- If oscillating synchronously in the gamma band, the neurons must be contributing to a single conscious representation.
- If oscillating synchronously at a frequency *outside* the gamma band, they must be part of a bound representation that is *not* present to consciousness (e.g., an object in an unattended part of the visual field).
- If active but not oscillating or oscillating out of synchrony, they must be representing features which are unbound, or perhaps bound to different representations.

Even though 40-Hz oscillation itself is looking less attractive as a criterion, it would clearly be useful to have *some* means of drawing this distinction between bound representations that are and are not conscious, and another candidate for this role is discussed in the next section.

Thalamocortical Loops

The thalamus is a lower forebrain structure that is sometimes referred to as the gateway to the brain because all sensory signals except olfaction must pass through it to get to the cortex. The cortex also projects profusely back to the thalamus; for many thalamic nuclei, these downward projections outnumber the upward ones by an order of magnitude. Most nuclei of the thalamus are so-called specific nuclei, each of which connects to a relatively small area of cortex. There are also several nonspecific nuclei (including the reticular nucleus and the intralaminar nuclei), which extend diffuse, modulatory projections across most of the cortex—with a single axon synapsing in many distinct areas—and receive projections from a similarly broad swath.

The broad connectivity of the thalamus and its central role in sensation have made it a frequent target for neural theories of consciousness. One of the earliest such was Francis Crick's *thalamic searchlight hypothesis* (Crick, 1984), in which the thalamus controls which areas of cortex become the focus of consciousness. Since then, so-called *thalamocortical loop* models have been widely pursued, and this circuit now plays a role in almost all neural theories of consciousness; here we focus on the version developed by Rodolfo Llinás. During the 1990s, Llinás and his coworkers conducted a series of detailed studies of thalamocortical interactions, and out of this work Llinás has developed a theory that integrates data from waking and sleeping consciousness, addresses the binding problem, and provides a criterion for discriminating representations that can fill the hole vacated by the 40-Hz hypothesis (as discussed earlier).

First, it is important to understand how thalamocortical models in general account for binding. The common thread in these accounts is that thalamocortical interactions are necessary for the fast and precise generation of synchronous oscillations across distinct cortical regions. (This represents a minimal necessary function for the thalamus that almost all models would agree on. There are many more specific questions on which accounts vary: For example, it is not clear how crucial the thalamus is for maintaining synchrony among neurons *within* a single cortical area; and although some neurons will oscillate even in vitro, there is much debate about the extent to which oscillations observed in cortex derive from such "endogenous" oscillatory properties or from system-level interactions.)

In this respect the thalamus acts something like the conductor of a cortical symphony: It does not determine in detail what the players do, but it coordinates their activity and imposes coherence. Without this contribution from the thalamus, the brain might be able to produce local patches of synchrony, but it would not be able to bind the many different properties of a percept into a single coherent object. Incidentally, this metaphor also illustrates why it is inaccurate to describe any individual part of the brain as the seat of consciousness. A conductor and orchestra work together to produce coherent music; the conductor imposes structure on the orchestra, but in the end it is the individual musicians who produce the actual music. Likewise, the thalamus in some sense generates and directs consciousness, but only in conjunction with sensory areas that produce and embody the experienced *content* of that consciousness.

The problem of representing multiple separate-bound objects at the same time can apparently be solved at least in part by ensuring that each bound representation oscillates at a different frequency. But this still leaves open the question of what distinguishes *conscious* bound representations. What determines which of several synchronously oscillating clusters dominates a person's subjective awareness?

Llinás (Llinás & Pare, 1996) has identified a mechanism that may subserve this function. Using magnetoencephalography (MEG) in humans, he has observed waves of phase-locked activity that travel across the cortex from the front of the head to the back. Each wave takes approximately 12.5 ms to traverse the brain and is followed by a similar gap before the next wave, for a total interval of 25 ms per wave, or 40 Hz. Their presence is correlated with coherent conscious experience: They occur continuously during waking and REM sleep but vanish during non-REM sleep. These waves are apparently driven by the nonspecific nuclei of the thalamus, which send out projections that traverse the cortex from front to back.

Llinás's hypothesis is that consciousness is marked by a second type of synchrony: synchrony between an individual cluster and this nonspecific scanning wave. Thus, of all the clusters that are active at a given time, the ones that are the focus of consciousness will be those that are oscillating in phase with the scanning wave.

A crucial line of evidence for this comes from Llinás's studies of auditory perception in humans during waking, REM, and slow-wave sleep (Llinás & Ribary, 1994). In awake humans, a salient auditory stimulus (a loud click) will interrupt the scanning wave and start a new one, while in REM the stimulus will produce a cortical response but will not reset the scanning wave. This would seem to correspond to the ability of such stimuli to draw conscious attention during waking but not during REM sleep (or during nREM, where the scanning wave is absent or at least dramatically reduced).

Another set of studies (Joliot et al., 1994) showed a different sort of correlation between this "gamma reset" and conscious perception. Subjects were played a pair of clicks separated by an interval between 3 ms and 30 ms. Subjects were able to distinguish the two clicks when they were separated by approximately 13 ms or more, but with shorter intervals they perceived only one click (of normal, not double, duration). MEG revealed that intervals under 12 ms produced only a single reset, while longer intervals produced two. The authors concluded from these results that consciousness is discrete rather than continuous, with 12 ms being the "quantum of consciousness," the basic temporal unit of conscious experience. Even for the more conservatively inclined, however, these two lines of evidence do strongly suggest that there is *some* close relationship between the scanning wave and conscious experience.

Gerald Edelman and Giulio Tononi (Edelman & Tononi, 2000; Tononi & Edelman, 1998) also emphasized the thalamocortical system, although their concern was less with synchrony itself than with the functional integration that it signifies. In their model conscious neural representation is distinguished primarily by two characteristics: *integration,* the tendency of neurons within a particular representational cluster to interact more strongly with each other than with neurons outside the cluster; and *complexity,* the brain's ability to select one specific state from a vast repertoire of possible states (and to do so several times a second). They use the term *dynamic core* to refer to a functional grouping of neurons that plays this role. The word "dynamic" is crucial here: For Edelman and Tononi (as for Llinás), the "core" of consciousness is not a persistent anatomical structure but an ephemeral pattern of activity that will be present in different areas of cortex (and different neurons within those areas) at different times.

Self and Consciousness

Another major development in the study of consciousness has been the increasing degree of attention paid to the role of self-representation. Within philosophy, consciousness has often been analyzed in terms of a relation between transient mental objects or events—thoughts, ideas, sensations—and a persistent, unitary self. This approach has now been carried over into the empirical realm by neuroscientists, who are trying to determine how the brain constructs a self-representation and how this self-representation contributes to conscious experience. This is another point on which the convergence among major neural theories of consciousness is quite striking. Though we focus on the work of Antonio Damasio, self-perception and its relation to decision making are accorded a central role in Edelman and Tononi (2000) and Llinás (2001).

In *Descartes' Error,* Damasio (1994) defended the idea that conscious thought is substantially dependent on visceral self-perception. In his view conscious decision making involves not only abstract reasoning but also the constant monitoring of a body loop in which brain and body respond to each other: Physiological mechanisms such as the endocrine system and sympathetic and parasympathetic nervous systems respond to external and internal stimuli that are represented by the brain, and the brainstem monitors the body and registers the state changes wrought by these systems. This gives literal meaning to the notion of a gut instinct; in numerous studies (Bechara, Damasio, Damasio, & Anderson, 1994; Damasio, 1996) Damasio and his coworkers have shown that physiological responses may be necessary for accurate decision making and may even register the "correct" answer to a problem before the subject is consciously aware of it.

Subsequently, Damasio (1999) has extended this model to provide an account of perceptual consciousness. Visceral self-representation now constitutes the *proto-self,* a moment-to-moment sense of the presence and state of one's body. Mere perception becomes conscious experience when it is somehow integrated with or related to this proto-self, by way of second-order representations that register the body's response to a percept. *Core consciousness* is the realm of primary conscious experience, constituted by a series of these "How do I feel about what I'm seeing?" representations, and *extended consciousness* is the extension of these experiences into the past and future via the powers of memory and conceptual abstraction.

Damasio (1999) offered specific hypotheses about the neural localization of these functions. He suggested that the self-representations that constitute the proto-self are generated by a number of upper brainstem structures (including much of what is traditionally referred to as the reticular system), the hypothalamus, and cortical somatosensory areas (primarily in right parietal cortex). Core consciousness depends primarily on the cingulate cortices and on the intralaminar (nonspecific) nuclei of the thalamus, and extended consciousness relies on the temporal and prefrontal cortices.

To interpret these claims, however, it is important to understand the particular notion of localization with which Damasio is working. He is a clinical neurologist, and his primary source of evidence is observation of humans with focal brain damage. Within the tradition of clinical neurology, the claim that "function F is localized to system S" rarely means more than "damage to system S will (more or less selectively) impair function F"—and in any case, this is the strongest claim that lesion data alone can usually justify. This restricted kind of localization is important, but it is also fundamentally incomplete as an *explanation* of the function in question because it does not describe the *mechanism* by which the function is performed.

By way of illustration, consider the following statements: (a) "The lungs are the organs that oxygenate the blood" and (b) "The lungs contain a honeycomb of air vessels, and hence have a very high internal surface area. Blood is pumped directly through the lungs and is brought to the surface of these vessels, allowing for the exchange of gases with the inhaled air." Both are in some sense localizations of the function of oxygenation, but the first explains nothing about the *means* by which the function is performed. For this very reason, it is also easier to formulate and confirm—for example, by measuring the oxygen content of blood flowing into and out of the lungs.

A theory of consciousness constructed along these lines can still have important consequences: For example, it guides us in interpreting the nature and subjective character of a range of neural pathologies, from Alzheimer's disease to locked-in syndrome, and it may help to establish the parameters for more focused study of individual functions. But outside of the diagnostic realm, its utility will be limited unless and until it can be supplemented with the sort of mechanistic underpinning that supports more fine-grained prediction, testing, and explanation.

A Word on Theories at the Subneural Level

In surveying neuroscientific approaches to consciousness, we have restricted our discussion to theories at and above the single-cell level, setting aside proposals that attempt to relate consciousness to subneural structures such as microtubules and quantum particles (Eccles, 1992; Hameroff, 1998; Hameroff & Penrose, 1996; Popper & Eccles, 1977). While it is quite likely that subcellular mechanisms will play an increasing role in future theories of neural functioning, this role will be as one *piece* of a complex, multilevel theory, just as the processes described by molecular biochemistry form one piece of the explanatory structure of biology. From a methodological perspective, subcellular entities are no more sufficient for explaining consciousness than they are for explaining metabolism or immune response: There are too many other important levels of analysis, many of which are patently relevant to the functions in question. One symptom of this problem is the way in which subcellular theories tend to deal in gross correlations with just one or two properties of consciousness—for example, that (like microtubules) consciousness is affected by anesthetics, or that (as in quantum entanglement) it can change unpredictably and globally. There is certainly room under the big tent of science for a few such theories; but in our view they will not deserve serious mainstream attention unless and until they establish both a tighter integration with the intermediate levels of neuroscience and a more fine-grained, empirically testable connection with the properties of consciousness itself.

CONCLUSION: THE FUTURE OF CONSCIOUSNESS

The mind-body problem and many of the problems encountered in the study of consciousness may result from the separate mental models (or conceptual schemes) we use to think about mental events and physical events. Mental models influence our thinking profoundly, providing the structure within which we frame problems and evaluate solutions. At the same time, it is possible to distinguish properties of the model from properties of reality. As it stands, our models of the mental and the physical are distinct, but this may be more a symptom of our flawed understanding than a fact about the world itself.

One way to understand the progress described in this chapter is as a breaking down of this dualist divide. Psychologists studying consciousness have found ways to relate it to the physical behavior of the organism, forging epistemological links between mind and world. In addition, as we have learned more about the detailed structure of mental functions such as attention, perception, memory, and decision making, it has become less and less tempting to see them as parts of a transcendent consciousness. Meanwhile, neuroscience has begun to elucidate the ontological connections between mind and body, making it possible to see where our models of the mental and physical may overlap and eventually merge. These developments cause us to reflect with some amazement on the history of the scientific study of consciousness. Until the ascendancy of behaviorism in the early part of the twentieth century, it was widely considered to be the central object of the field of psychology. Then, through the behaviorist era and until late in the cognitive revolution, which began in the 1960s, it was banished entirely from study. Now it may provide a new center to integrate the diverse areas of cognition and help relate them to dramatic new findings from neuroscience.

What can be said about the future of consciousness? There is an instructive parallel here with the history of life (Farber, 2000). At the turn of the last century, there was still room for doubt about whether there would ever be a unified account of living and nonliving processes. As with consciousness, there was (and to a certain extent, still is) a division between the mental models we use to describe the behavior of animate and inanimate objects. Vitalists argued that this division was reflected in reality, while materialists argued that life was ultimately grounded in the same physical forces and entities as everything else. As it turned out, the vitalists were wrong, and the elaboration of the physical basis of life revolutionized biology and led directly to many of the greatest scientific advances of the twentieth century.

We cannot say with certainty whether psychological materialism will enjoy a similar victory; the current rate of progress certainly gives grounds for optimism, but many deep conceptual problems remain to be overcome. The real value of the parallel with the history of life is not in prediction, but in understanding the nature of the problem and how best to approach it. Vitalists posed deep philosophical problems having to do with "unique" properties of living organisms, such as self-reproduction and goal-directedness. Progress came neither from ignoring these problems nor from accepting them on their own terms, but from *reinterpreting* them as challenging scientific puzzles—puzzles that could only be solved with a combination of empirical and theoretical advances.

It is also important to notice that the victory of biological materialism did not lead to the discarding of the concept of life or to biology's becoming a branch of physics. The word "life" is still available for everyday use and remains just as respectable as it was 100 years ago, even though its meaning now depends in part on the scientific explanation that has developed during that time. Because the word "consciousness" has always been more obscure and more diverse in its meanings, it may be in for somewhat more radical change; scientists working on consciousness may rely on more technical terms (such as "attention," "awareness," and "binding"), just as biologists conduct much of their daily work without general reference to "life"; but there is no reason to presume that scientific progress will involve rejecting the very idea of consciousness or replacing mental terms with behavioral or neural ones. Explaining need not mean explaining away.

REFERENCES

Adams, J. K. (1957). Laboratory studies of behavior without awareness. *Psychological Bulletin, 54,* 383–405.

Aristotle (1991). *De anima* (R. D. Hicks, Trans.). Buffalo, NY: Prometheus Books.

Baars, B. J. (1988). *A cognitive theory of consciousness.* New York: Cambridge University Press.

Baars, B. J. (1997). *In the theater of consciousness: The workspace of the mind.* New York: Oxford University Press.

Baldwin, M. W. (2001). Relational schema activation: Does Bob Zajonc ever scowl at you from the back of your mind? In J. A. Bargh & D. K. Apsley (Eds.), *Unraveling the complexities of social life: A festschrift in honor of Robert B. Zajonc* (pp. 55–67). Washington, DC: American Psychological Association.

Banks, W. P. (1993). Problems in the scientific pursuit of consciousness. *Consciousness & Cognition: An International Journal, 2,* 255–263.

Banks, W. P., Roberts, D., & Ciranni, M. (1995). Negative priming in auditory attention. *Journal of Experimental Psychology: Human Perception & Performance, 21,* 1354–1361.

Barber, T. X. (2000). A deeper understanding of hypnosis: Its secrets, its nature, its essence. *American Journal of Clinical Hypnosis, 42,* 208–272.

Bechara, A., Damasio, A. R., Damasio, H., & Anderson, S. W. (1994). Insensitivity to future consequences following damage to human prefrontal cortex. *Cognition, 50,* 7–15.

Biederman, I., & Shiffrar, M. M. (1987). Sexing day-old chicks: A case study and expert systems analysis of a difficult perceptual-learning task. *Journal of Experimental Psychology: Learning, Memory, & Cognition, 13,* 640–645.

Bisiach, E., Cornacchia, L., Sterzi, R., & Vallar, G. (1984). Disorders of perceived auditory lateralization after lesions of the right hemisphere. *Brain, 107*(Pt 1), 37–52.

Bisiach, E., & Geminiani, G. (1991). Anosognosia related to hemiplegia and hemianopia. In G. P. Prigatano & D. L. Schacter (Eds.), *Awareness of deficit after brain injury: Clinical and theoretical issues* (pp. 17–39). New York: Oxford University Press.

Bisiach, E., & Luzzatti, C. (1978). Unilateral neglect of representational space. *Cortex, 14,* 129–133.

Bisiach, E., & Rusconi, M. L. (1990). Break-down of perceptual awareness in unilateral neglect. *Cortex, 26,* 643–649.

Boring, E. G. (1942). *Sensation and perception in the history of experimental psychology.* New York: Appleton.

Bornstein, R. F., & Pittman, T. S. (Eds.). (1992). *Perception without awareness: Cognitive, clinical, and social perspectives.* New York: Guilford Press.

Braine, M. D. S. (1963). On learning the grammatical order of words. *Psychological Review, 70,* 323–348.

Broadbent, D. E. (1958). *Perception and communication.* New York: Pergamon Press.

Brooks, L. R. (1987). Decentralized control of categorization: The role of prior processing episodes. In U. Neisser (Ed.), *Emory symposia in cognition: Vol. 1. Concepts and conceptual development: Ecological and intellectual factors in categorization* (pp. 141–174). New York: Cambridge University Press.

Bruner, J. (1992). Another look at New Look 1. *American Psychologist, 47,* 780–783.

Bunce, S. C, Bernat, E., Wong, P. S., & Shevrin, H. (1999). Further evidence for unconscious learning: Preliminary support for the conditioning of facial EMG to subliminal stimuli. *Journal of Psychiatric Research, 33,* 341–347.

Chalmers, D. J. (1996). *The conscious mind: In search of a fundamental theory.* New York: Oxford University Press.

Chan, J. L., & Liu, A. B. (1999). Anatomical correlates of alien hand syndromes. *Neuropsychiatry Neuropsychology & Behavioral Neurology, 12,* 149–155.

Cheesman, J., & Merikle, P. M. (1984). Priming with and without awareness. *Perception & Psychophysics, 36,* 387–395.

Cheesman, J., & Merikle, P. M. (1986). Distinguishing conscious from unconscious perceptual processes. *Canadian Journal of Psychology, 40,* 343–367.

Cherry, C. (1957). *On human communication: A review, a survey, and a criticism.* Cambridge, MA: MIT Press.

Chomsky, N. (1996). A review of B. F. Skinner's Verbal Behavior. In H. Geirsson & M. Losonsky (Eds.), *Readings in language and mind* (pp. 413–441). Cambridge, MA: Blackwell.

Churchland, P. S. (1986). *Neurophilosophy: Toward a unified science of the mind-brain.* Cambridge, MA: MIT Press.

Churchland, P. S. (1996). The hornswoggle problem. *Journal of Consciousness Studies, 3,* 402–408.

Cohen, N. J., Eichenbaum, H., Deacedo, B. S., & Corkin, S. (1985). Different memory systems underlying acquisition of procedural and declarative knowledge. *Annals of the New York Academy of Sciences, 444,* 54–71.

Cooke, P. (1991, June 23). They cried until they could not see. *The New York Times Magazine.*

Corteen, R. S. (1986). Electrodermal responses to words in an irrelevant message: A partial reappraisal. *Behavioral and Brain Sciences, 9,* 27–28.

Corteen, R. S., & Dunn, D. (1974). Shock-associated words in a nonattended message: A test for momentary awareness. *Journal of Experimental Psychology, 102,* 1143–1144.

Corteen, R. S., & Wood, B. (1972). Autonomic responses to shock-associated words in an unattended channel. *Journal of Experimental Psychology, 94,* 308–313.

Cowan, N., & Wood, N. L. (1997). Constraints on awareness, attention, processing, and memory: Some recent investigations with ignored speech. *Consciousness & Cognition: An International Journal, 6,* 182–203.

Crick, F. (1984). Function of the thalamic reticular complex: The searchlight hypothesis. *Proceedings of the National Academy of Science USA, 81,* 4586–4590.

Crick, F., & Koch, C. (1995). Are we aware of neural activity in primary visual cortex? *Nature, 375*(6527), 121–123.

Crick, F., & Koch, C. (1998). Constraints on cortical and thalamic projections: The no-strong-loops hypothesis. *Nature, 391*(6664), 245–250.

Dalrymple-Alford, E. C., & Budayr, B. (1966). Examination of some aspects of the stroop color-word test. *Perceptual & Motor Skills, 23*(3, Pt. 2), 1211–1214.

Damasio, A. R. (1994). *Descartes' error: Emotion, reason, and the human brain.* New York: Putnam.

Damasio, A. R. (1996). The somatic marker hypothesis and the possible functions of the prefrontal cortex. *Philosophical Transactions of the Royal Society of London B: Biological Sciences, 351*(1346), 1413–1420.

Damasio, A. R. (1999). *The feeling of what happens: Body and emotion in the making of consciousness* (1st ed.). New York: Harcourt Brace.

Dawson, M. E., & Schell, A. M. (1982). Electrodermal responses to attended and nonattended significant stimuli during dichotic listening. *Journal of Experimental Psychology: Human Perception & Performance, 8,* 315–324.

de Gelder, B., Vroomen, J., Pourtois, G., & Weiskrantz, L. (1999). Non-conscious recognition of affect in the absence of striate cortex. *Neuroreport, 10*(18), 3759–3763.

Debner, J. A., & Jacoby, L. L. (1994). Unconscious perception: Attention, awareness, and control. *Journal of Experimental Psychology: Learning, Memory, & Cognition, 20,* 304–317.

Dennett, D. C. (1991). *Consciousness explained* (1st ed.). Boston: Little Brown and Co.

Dennett, D. C. (1994). Real consciousness. In A. Revonsuo & M. Kamppinen (Eds.), *Consciousness in philosophy and cognitive neuroscience* (pp. 55–63). Hillsdale, NJ: Erlbaum.

Descartes, R. (1951). *Meditations* (L. J. Lafleur, Trans.). New York: Liberal Arts Press.

Deutsch, J. A., & Deutsch, D. (1963). Attention: Some theoretical considerations. *Psychological Review, 70,* 80–90.

Dixon, N. F. (1971). *Subliminal perception: The nature of a controversy.* London: McGraw-Hill.

Dixon, N. F. (1981). *Preconscious processing.* London: Wiley.

Draine, S. C., & Greenwald, A. G. (1998). Replicable unconscious semantic priming. *Journal of Experimental Psychology: General, 127,* 286–303.

Ebbinghaus, H. (1908). Psychology: An elementary text-book (M. Meyer, Trans.). Boston: Heath.

Eccles, J. C. (1992). Evolution of consciousness. *Proceedings of the National Academy of Science USA, 89*(16), 7320–7324.

Edelman, G. M., & Tononi, G. (2000). *A universe of consciousness: How matter becomes imagination* (1st ed.). New York: Basic Books.

Engel, A. K., Fries, P., Konig, P., Brecht, M., & Singer, W. (1999). Temporal binding, binocular rivalry, and consciousness. *Consciousness and Cognition, 8*(2), 128–151.

Engel, A. K., & Singer, W. (2001). Temporal binding and the neural correlates of sensory awareness. *Trends in Cognitive Science, 5*(1), 16–25.

Erdelyi, M. H. (1972). Role of fantasy in the Poetzl (emergence) phenomenon. *Journal of Personality & Social Psychology, 24,* 186–190.

Erdelyi, M. H. (1974). A new look at the new look: Perceptual defense and vigilance. *Psychological Review, 81,* 1–25.

Erdelyi, M. H. (1992). Psychodynamics and the unconscious. *American Psychologist, 47*(6), 784–787.

Eriksen, C. W. (1958). Unconscious processes. In M. R. Jones (Ed.), *Nebraska Symposium on motivation: 1958.* Lincoln: University of Nebraska Press.

Eriksen, C. W. (1960). Discrimination and learning without awareness: A methodological survey and evaluation. *Psychological Review, 67,* 279–300.

Eriksen, C. W. (Ed.). (1962). Behavior and awareness: A symposium of research and interpretation. *Journal of Personality, 30* (2, Suppl. No. 6), 158.

Farber, I. (2000). *Domain Integration: A Theory of Progress in the Scientific Understanding of Life and Mind.* Doctoral dissertation, University of California, San Diego.

Farber, I., & Churchland, P. S. (1995). Consciousness and the neurosciences: Philosophical and theoretical issues. In M. S. Gazzaniga (Ed.), *The cognitive neurosciences*. Cambridge, MA: MIT Press.

Festinger, L., & Easton, A. M. (1974). Inferences about the efferent system based on a perceptual illusion produced by eye movements. *Psychological Review, 81,* 44–58.

Forster, P. M., & Govier, E. (1978). Discrimination without awareness? *Quarterly Journal of Experimental Psychology, 30,* 289–295.

Franklin, S., & Graesser, A. (1999). A software agent model of consciousness. *Consciousness & Cognition: An International Journal, 8,* 285–301.

Freud, S. (1965). *The psychopathology of everyday life* (A. Tyson, Trans.). New York: Norton.

Frith, C. D. (1992). Consciousness, information processing and the brain. *Journal of Psychopharmacology, 6,* 436–440.

Frith, C. D. (1996). The role of the prefrontal cortex in self-consciousness: The case of auditory hallucinations. *Philosophical Transactions of the Royal Society: Biologic Sciences, 351,* 1505–1512.

Fuhrer, M. J., & Eriksen, C. W. (1960). The unconscious perception of the meaning of verbal stimuli. *Journal of Abnormal & Social Psychology, 61,* 432–439.

Galin, D. (1992). Theoretical reflections on awareness, monitoring, and self in relation to anosognosia. *Consciousness & Cognition: An International Journal, 1,* 152–162.

Gardner, H. (1985). The mind's new science: A history of the cognitive revolution. New York: Basic Books.

Gibson, K. R. (1992). Toward an empirical basis for understanding consciousness and self-awareness. *Consciousness & Cognition: An International Journal, 1,* 163–168.

Goldstein, E. B., & Fink, S. I. (1981). Selective attention in vision: Recognition memory for superimposed line drawings. *Journal of Experimental Psychology: Human Perception & Performance, 7,* 954–967.

Greenfield, S. (1995). *Journey to the centers of the mind: Toward a science of consciousness*. New York: Freeman.

Greenwald, A. G. (1992). New Look 3: Unconscious cognition reclaimed. *American Psychologist, 47,* 766–779.

Greenwald, A. G., & Draine, S. C. (1997). Do subliminal stimuli enter the mind unnoticed? Tests with a new method. In J. D. Cohen & J. W. Schooler (Eds.), *Carnegie Mellon symposia on cognition: Scientific approaches to consciousness* (pp. 83–108). Mahwah, NJ: Erlbaum.

Greenwald, A. G., Klinger, M. R., & Schuh, E. S. (1995). Activation by marginally perceptible ("subliminal") stimuli: Dissociation of unconscious from conscious cognition. *Journal of Experimental Psychology: General, 124,* 22–42.

Hameroff, S. (1998). Anesthesia, consciousness and hydrophobic pockets: A unitary quantum hypothesis of anesthetic action. *Toxicology Letters,* 100–101, 31–39.

Hameroff, S., & Penrose, R. (1996). Conscious events as orchestrated spacetime selections. *Journal of Consciousness Studies, 3,* 36–53.

Heilman, K. M., Barrett, A. M., & Adair, J. C. (1998). Possible mechanisms of anosognosia: A defect in self-awareness. *Philos Trans R Soc Lond B Biol Sci, 353*(1377), 1903–1909.

Henkel, L. A., Franklin, N., & Johnson, M. K. (2000). Cross-modal source monitoring confusions between perceived and imagined events. *Journal of Experimental Psychology: Learning, Memory, & Cognition, 26,* 321–335.

Hilgard, E. R. (1986). *Divided consciousness: Multiple controls in human thought and action*. New York: Wiley.

Hilgard, E. R. (1992). Divided consciousness and dissociation. *Consciousness & Cognition: An International Journal, 1,* 6–31.

Holender, D. (1986). Semantic activation without conscious identification in dichotic listening, parafoveal vision, and visual masking: A survey and appraisal. *Behavioral & Brain Sciences, 9,* 1–66.

Inzelberg, R., Nisipeanu, P., Blumen, S. C., & Carasso, R. L. (2000). Alien hand sign in Creutzfeldt-Jakob disease. *Journal of Neurology, Neurosurgery, & Psychiatry, 68,* 103–104.

Ionescu, M. D., & Erdelyi, M. H. (1992). The direct recovery of subliminal stimuli. In R. F. Bornstein & T. S. Pittman (Eds.), *Perception without awareness: Cognitive, clinical, and social perspectives* (pp. 143–169). New York: Guilford Press.

Jacoby, L. L. (1991). A process dissociation framework: Separating automatic from intentional uses of memory. *Journal of Memory & Language, 30,* 513–541.

Jacoby, L. L., Lindsay, D. S., & Toth, J. P. (1992). Unconscious influences revealed: Attention, awareness, and control. *American Psychologist, 47,* 802–809.

Jacoby, L. L., Toth, J., & Yonelinas, A. P. (1993). Separating conscious and unconscious influences of memory: Measuring recollection. *Journal of Experimental Psychology: General, 122,* 139–154.

James, W. (1983). *The principles of psychology*. Cambridge, MA: Harvard University Press. (Original work published 1890)

Joliot, M., Ribary, U., & Llinás, R. (1994). Human oscillatory brain activity near 40 Hz coexists with cognitive temporal binding. *Proc Natl Acad Sci USA, 91*(24), 11748–11751.

Kerkhoff, G. (2001). Spatial hemineglect in humans. *Progress in Neurobiology, 63*(1), 1–27.

Kihlstrom, J. F. (1987). The cognitive unconscious. *Science, 237,* 1445–1452.

Kihlstrom, J. F. (1992). Dissociation and dissociations: A comment on consciousness and cognition. *Consciousness & Cognition: An International Journal, 1,* 47–53.

Kihlstrom, J. F. (1994). Hypnosis, delayed recall, and the principles of memory. *International Journal of Clinical & Experimental Hypnosis, 42,* 337–345.

Kihlstrom, J. F. (1997). Consciousness and me-ness. In J. D. Cohen & J. W. Schooler (Eds.), *Carnegie Mellon symposia on cognition: Scientific approaches to consciousness* (pp. 451–468). Mahwah, NJ: Erlbaum.

Kihlstrom, J. F., Barnhardt, T. M., & Tataryn, D. J. (1992). Implicit perception. In R. F. Bornstein & T. S. Pittman (Eds.), *Perception without awareness: Cognitive, clinical, and social perspectives* (pp. 17–54). New York: Guilford Press.

Kihlstrom, J. F., & Hoyt, I. P. (1995). Repression, dissociation, and hypnosis. In J. L. Singer (Ed.), *The John D. and Catherine T. MacArthur Foundation series on mental health and development: Repression and dissociation: Implications for personality theory, psychopathology, and health* (pp. 181–208). Chicago: University of Chicago Press.

Koch, C., & Crick, F. (1994). Some further ideas regarding the neuronal basis of awareness. In C. Koch & J. L. Davis (Eds.), *Large-scale neuronal theories of the brain.* Cambridge, MA: MIT Press.

Koch, C., & Davis, J. L. (1994). *Large-scale neuronal theories of the brain.* Cambridge MA: MIT Press.

Lakoff, G. (1987). *Women, fire, and dangerous things: What categories reveal about the mind.* Chicago: University of Chicago Press.

Lakoff, G., & Johnson, M. (1980). *Metaphors we live by.* Chicago: University of Chicago Press.

Lakoff, G., & Johnson, M. (1999). *Philosophy in the flesh: The embodied mind and its challenge to Western thought.* New York: Basic Books.

Lewicki, P., Czyzewska, M., & Hill, T. (1997a). Cognitive mechanisms for acquiring "experience": The dissociation between conscious and nonconscious cognition. In J. D. Cohen & J. W. Schooler (Eds.), *Carnegie Mellon symposia on cognition: Scientific approaches to consciousness* (pp. 161–177). Mahwah, NJ: Erlbaum.

Lewicki, P., Czyzewska, M., & Hill, T. (1997b). Nonconscious information processing and personality. In D. C. Berry (Ed.), *How implicit is implicit learning? Debates in psychology* (pp. 48–72). New York: Oxford University Press.

Lewicki, P., Hill, T., & Czyzewska, M. (1994). Nonconscious indirect inferences in encoding. *Journal of Experimental Psychology: General, 123,* 257–263.

Libet, B. (1985). Unconscious cerebral initiative and the role of conscious will in voluntary action. *Behavioral & Brain Sciences, 8,* 529–566.

Libet, B. (1993). The neural time factor in conscious and unconscious events. In Ciba Foundation (Ed.), *Ciba Foundation symposium: Experimental and theoretical studies of consciousness: 174* (pp. 123–146). Chichester: Wiley.

Libet, B., Alberts, W. W., & Wright, E. W., Jr. (1967). Responses of human somatosensory cortex to stimuli below threshold for conscious sensation. *Science, 158*(3808), 1597–1600.

Libet, B., Alberts, W. W., Wright, E. W., Delattre, L. D., Levin, G., & Feinstein, B. (1964). Production of threshold levels of conscious sensation by electrical stimulation of human somatosensory cortex. *Journal of Neurophysiology, 27*(4), 546–578.

Llinás, R. R. (2001). *I of the vortex: From neurons to self.* Cambridge, MA: MIT Press.

Llinás, R., & Pare, D. (1996). The brain as a closed system modulated by the senses. In R. Llinas & P. S. Churchland (Eds.), *The mind-brain continuum: Sensory processes.* Cambridge, MA: MIT Press.

Llinás, R., & Ribary, U. (1994). Perception as an oneiric-like state modulated by the senses. In C. Koch & J. L. Davis (Eds.), *Large-scale neuronal theories of the brain.* Cambridge, MA: MIT Press.

Llinás, R., Ribary, U., Contreras, D., & Pedroarena, C. (1998). The neuronal basis for consciousness. *Philos Trans R Soc Lond B Biol Sci, 353*(1377), 1841–1849.

Loftus, E. F. (1993). Psychologists in the eyewitness world. *American Psychologist, 48,* 550–552.

Logothetis, N. K. (1998). Single units and conscious vision. *Philos Trans R Soc Lond B Biol Sci, 353*(1377), 1801–1818.

Logothetis, N. K., & Schall, J. D. (1989). Neuronal correlates of subjective visual perception. *Science, 245*(4919), 761–763.

Logothetis, N. K., Sheinberg, D. L. (1996). Recognition and representation of visual objects in primates: Psychophysics and physiology. In R. R. Llinás & P. S. Churchland (Eds.), *The mind-brain continuum: Sensory processes* (pp. 147–172). Cambridge, MA: MIT Press.

MacDonald, P. A., & Joordens, S. (2000). Investigating a memory-based account of negative priming: Support for selection-feature mismatch. *Journal of Experimental Psychology: Human Perception & Performance, 26,* 1478–1496.

Mack, A., & Rock, I. (1998). *Inattentional blindness.* Cambridge, MA: MIT Press.

Mackay, D. G. (1973). Aspects of the theory of comprehension, memory and attention. *Quarterly Journal of Experimental Psychology, 25,* 22–40.

Malsburg, C. von der. (1981). *The correlation theory of brain function* (Internal Report 81-2.): Department of Neurobiology, Max-Planck-Institute for Biophysical Chemistry.

Marcel, A. J. (1983a). Conscious and unconscious perception: An approach to the relations between phenomenal experience and perceptual processes. *Cognitive Psychology, 15,* 238–300.

Marcel, A. J. (1983b). Conscious and unconscious perception: Experiments on visual masking and word recognition. *Cognitive Psychology, 15,* 197–237.

McGinnies, E. (1949). Emotionality and perceptual defense. *Psychological Review, 56,* 244–251.

Merikle, P. M., & Daneman, M. (1996). Memory for events during anaesthesia: A meta-analysis. In B. Bonke & J. G. Bovill (Eds.), *Memory and awareness in anaesthesia* (Vol. 3, pp. 108–121). Assen, The Netherlands: Van Gorcum.

Merikle, P. M., Joordens, S., & Stolz, J. A. (1995). Measuring the relative magnitude of unconscious influences. *Consciousness & Cognition: An International Journal, 4,* 422–439.

Meyer, D. E., & Schvaneveldt, R. W. (1971). Facilitation in recognizing pairs of words: Evidence of a dependence between retrieval operations. *Journal of Experimental Psychology, 90,* 227–234.

Milliken, B., Joordens, S., Merikle, P. M., & Seiffert, A. E. (1998). Selective attention: A reevaluation of the implications of negative priming. *Psychological Review, 105,* 203–229.

Moran, J., & Desimone, R. (1985). Selective attention gates visual processing in the extrastriate cortex. *Science, 229,* 782–784.

Moray, N. (1969). *Listening and attention.* Baltimore: Penguin Books.

Morris, J. S., DeGelder, B., Weiskrantz, L., & Dolan, R. J. (2001). Differential extrageniculostriate and amygdala responses to presentation of emotional faces in a cortically blind field. *Brain, 124*(Pt. 6), 1241–1252.

Moscovitch, M., & Melo, B. (1997). Strategic retrieval and the frontal lobes: evidence from confabulation and amnesia. *Neuropsychologia, 35*(7), 1017–1034.

Neill, W. T., & Valdes, L. A. (1996). Facilitatory and inhibitory aspects of attention. In A. F. Kramer, M. G. H. Coles, & G. D. Logan (Eds.), *Converging operations in the study of visual selective attention* (pp. 77–106). Washington, DC: American Psychological Association.

Neill, W. T., Valdes, L. A., & Terry, K. M. (1995). Selective attention and the inhibitory control of cognition. In F. N. Dempster & C. J. Brainerd (Eds.), *Interference and inhibition in cognition* (pp. 207–261). San Diego, CA: Academic Press.

Neill, W. T., & Westberry, R. L. (1987). Selective attention and the suppression of cognitive noise. *Journal of Experimental Psychology: Learning, Memory, & Cognition, 13,* 327–334.

Neisser, U. (1967). *Cognitive psychology.* New York: Appleton-Century-Crofts.

Newstead, S. E., & Dennis, I. (1979). Lexical and grammatical processing of unshadowed messages: A re-examination of the Mackay effect. *Quarterly Journal of Experimental Psychology, 31,* 477–488.

Nissen, M. J., Ross, J. L., Willingham, D. B., Mackenzie, T. B., & Schacter, D. L. (1994). Evaluating amnesia in multiple personality disorder. In R. M. Klein & B. K. Doane (Eds.), *Psychological concepts and dissociative disorders* (pp. 259–282). Hillsdale, NJ: Erlbaum.

Peacocke, C. (1986). *Thoughts: An essay on content.* New York: Blackwell.

Pierce, C. S., & Jastrow, J. (1884). On small differences in sensation. *Memoirs of the National Academy of Sciences, 3,* 73–83.

Polanyi, M. (1958). *Personal knowledge; towards a post-critical philosophy.* Chicago: University of Chicago Press.

Popper, K. R., & Eccles, J. C. (1977). *The self and its brain.* New York: Springer International.

Proust, J. (2000). Awareness of agency: Three levels of analysis. In T. Metzinger (Ed.), *Neural correlates of consciousness: Empirical and conceptual questions* (pp. 307–324). Cambridge, MA: MIT Press.

Ramachandran, V. S. (1995). Anosognosia in parietal lobe syndrome. *Consciousness & Cognition: An International Journal, 4,* 22–51.

Ramachandran, V. S., Levi, L., Stone, L., Rogers-Ramachandran, D., et al. (1996). Illusions of body image: What they reveal about human nature. In R. R. Llinás & P. S. Churchland (Eds.), *The mind-brain continuum: Sensory processes* (pp. 29–60). Cambridge, MA: The MIT Press.

Ramachandran, V. S., & Rogers-Ramachandran, D. (1996). Denial of disabilities in anosognosia. *Nature, 382*(6591), 501. Nature Publishing Group, US, www.nature.com.

Ramachandran, V. S., & Blakeslee, S. (1998). *Phantoms in the brain: Probing the mysteries of the human mind* (1st ed.). New York: William Morrow.

Reber, A. S. (1992). The cognitive unconscious: An evolutionary perspective. *Consciousness & Cognition: An International Journal, 1,* 93–133.

Rock, I. (1983). *The logic of perception.* Cambridge, MA: MIT Press.

Rock, I., & Gutman, D. (1981). The effect of inattention on form perception. *Journal of Experimental Psychology: Human Perception & Performance, 7,* 275–285.

Roediger, H. L., & McDermott, K. B. (1995). Creating false memories: Remembering words not presented in lists. *Journal of Experimental Psychology: Learning, Memory, & Cognition, 21,* 803–814.

Ryle, G. (1949). *The concept of mind.* London: Hutchinson's University Library.

Schacter, D. L. (1987). Implicit memory: History and current status. *Journal of Experimental Psychology: Learning, Memory, & Cognition, 13,* 501–518.

Schacter, D. L. (1990). Toward a cognitive neuropsychology of awareness: Implicit knowledge and anosognosia. *Journal of Clinical and Experimental Neuropsychology, 12*(1), 155–178.

Schacter, D. L. (1995). *Memory distortion: How minds, brains, and societies reconstruct the past.* Cambridge, MA: Harvard University Press.

Searle, J. R. (1992). The rediscovery of the mind. Cambridge, MA: MIT Press.

Searle, J. R. (1993). The problem of consciousness. *Consciousness & Cognition: An International Journal, 2,* 310–319.

Shevrin, H. (2000). The experimental investigation of unconscious conflict, unconscious affect, and unconscious signal anxiety. In

M. Velmans (Ed.), *Investigating phenomenal consciousness: New methodologies and maps: Vol. 13. Advances in consciousness research* (pp. 33–65). Amsterdam, The Netherlands: Benjamins.

Shevrin, H., & Luborsky, L. (1961). The rebus technique: A method for studying primary-process transformations of briefly exposed pictures. *Journal of Nervous & Mental Disease, 133,* 479–488.

Shiffrin, R. M., & Schneider, W. (1977). Controlled and automatic human information processing: Vol. 2. Perceptual learning, automatic attending and a general theory. *Psychological Review, 84,* 127–190.

Silverman, L. H. (1983). The subliminal psychodynamic method: Overview and comprehensive listing of studies. In J. Masling (Ed.), *Empirical studies of psychoanalytic theory* (Vol. 1). Hillsdale, NJ: Erlbaum.

Singer, W. (1996). Neuronal synchronization: A solution to the binding problem? In R. Llinás & P. S. Churchland (Eds.), *The mind-brain continuum: Sensory processes.* Cambridge, MA: MIT Press.

Singer, W. (2001). Consciousness and the binding problem. *Annals of the New York Academy of Sciences,* 123–146.

Stroop, J. R. (1935). Studies of interference in serial verbal reactions. *Journal of Experimental Psychology, 18,* 643–662.

Tipper, S. P. (1985). The negative priming effect: Inhibitory priming by ignored objects. *Quarterly Journal of Experimental Psychology: Human Experimental Psychology, 37A,* 571–590.

Tononi, G., & Edelman, G. M. (1998). Consciousness and complexity. *Science, 282*(5395), 1846–1851.

Treisman, A. M. (1964). Selective attention in man. *British Medical Bulletin, 20,* 12–16.

Treisman, A. M., & Kanwisher, N. G. (1998). Perceiving visually presented objects: Recognition, awareness, and modularity. *Current Opinions in Neurobiology, 8*(2), 218–226.

Treisman, A., & Geffen, G. (1967). Selective attention: Perception or response? *Quarterly Journal of Experimental Psychology, 19,* 1–17.

Wardlaw, K. A., & Kroll, N. E. (1976). Autonomic responses to shock-associated words in a nonattended message: A failure to replicate. *Journal of Experimental Psychology: Human Perception & Performance, 2,* 357–360.

Watson, J. B. (1913). Psychology as the behaviourist views it. *Psychological Review. 20,* 158–177.

Watson, J. B. (1925). Behaviorism. New York: People's Institute.

Watson, J. B. (1994). Psychology as the behaviourist views it. *Psychological Review. 101,* 248–253.

Wegner, D. M. (1994). Ironic processes of mental control. *Psychological Review, 101,* 34–52.

Weinberger, J. (1992). Validating and demystifying subliminal psychodynamic activation. In R. F. Bornstein & T. S. Pittman (Eds.), *Perception without awareness: Cognitive, clinical, and social perspectives* (pp. 170–188). New York: Guilford Press.

Weiskrantz, L. (1990). The Ferrier lecture, 1989. Outlooks for blindsight: Explicit methodologies for implicit processes. *Proc R Soc Lond B Biol Sci, 239*(1296), 247–278.

Weiskrantz, L. (1998). Pupillary responses with and without awareness in blindsight. *Consciousness and Cognition: An International Journal, 7*(3), 324–326.

Wittgenstein, L. (1953). *Philosophical investigations* (G. E. M. Anscombe, Trans.). New York: Macmillan.

Wong, P. S., Bernat, E., Bunce, S., & Shevrin, H. (1997). Brain indices of nonconscious associative learning. *Consciousness & Cognition: An International Journal, 6,* 519–544.

Wood, N. L., & Cowan, N. (1995a). The cocktail party phenomenon revisited: Attention and memory in the classic selective listening procedure of Cherry (1953). *Journal of Experimental Psychology: General, 124,* 243–262.

Wood, N. L., & Cowan, N. (1995b). The cocktail party phenomenon revisited: How frequent are attention shifts to one's name in an irrelevant auditory channel? *Journal of Experimental Psychology: Learning, Memory, & Cognition, 21,* 255–260.

Wright, J. M. Von, Anderson, K., & Stenman, U. (1975). Generalisation of conditioned GSR's in dichotic listening. In P. M. A. Rabbitt & S. Dornic (Eds.), *Attention and performance* (Vol. 5). New York: Academic Press.

CHAPTER 2

Motivation

BILL P. GODSIL, MATTHEW R. TINSLEY, AND MICHAEL S. FANSELOW

The first two questions that a chapter on motivation must confront may betray the current status of motivational constructs in much of psychology. The first is, Why do we need motivational concepts to explain behavior? The second is, How do we define motivation? The first goal of this chapter is to answer these questions in a general way by providing a framework with which to analyze basic motivational processes. We then apply this general framework to four motivated behavior systems: feeding, fear, sexual behavior, and temperature regulation. By so doing, we hope to illustrate the power of current thinking about motivation as an organizing and predictive structure for understanding behavior.

The authors would like to thank Polar Bears Alive of Baton Rouge, LA, for the use of the polar bear photo. The authors would also like to thank M. Domjan for the quail photo, K. Hollis for the pictures of the fish, and S. Crowley for the pictures of the rats.

Why Do Theories of Behavior Need Motivational Constructs?

The goal of psychological theories is to explain and predict the variance in behavior. The two global factors to which this variance is most often attributed are genetic and learned influences. For instance, a particular species is genetically programmed to use certain sources of nourishment and not others. It is also clear that humans and other animals learn that some edible stimuli contain vital nutrients and others are toxic. Even complete knowledge of these factors and how they interact is probably not sufficient to understand all behavior; some variance is left over. Motivational constructs are invoked to explain this leftover variance. Genetically, humans need certain lipids, proteins, sugars, and vitamins to become reproductive individuals. We learn how to procure these commodities from our environment. Yet an individual may not always consume the perfect food when it is available, while at other times such food may be consumed to excess. The behavior is variable; learning and genetics alone cannot account for all of the behavior. Consequently, we invoke hunger, a motivational construct, to capture the remainder of the variance. For example, a theory of feeding might suggest that genes determine what we eat, and memory of past experiences tells us where to forage. Hunger activates foraging behavior and determines when we eat.

Any complete theory of behavior can be viewed as an analysis of variance with learning, genetics, and motivation configured to explain behavior as best as possible. Accordingly, any concept of motivation will be defined partly by the particular matrix of learning and genetics within which it is embedded. As a consequence, as our ideas about learning or behavior genetics change, so must our ideas about motivation. Indeed, our concept of motivation is dramatically different from the generalized need-based drive and the reciprocally inhibitory incentive motivation theories that characterized the earlier and later parts of the twentieth century. Although those theories have been very influential to the ideas developed here, we do not review them in this chapter. Instead, the reader is urged to consult Bolles (1975) for, arguably, the most authoritative review of those earlier approaches.

The analogy to analysis of variance highlights another important aspect of motivation, learning, and genetics. It is incorrect to think of these factors as independent "main" effects. Most of the variance in behavior is accounted for by the interactions between these factors. For example, research into constraints on learning demonstrated that even basic learning processes, such as Pavlovian and operant conditioning, have powerful and specific genetic influences that determine what information is readily acquired and what information is virtually impossible to assimilate (Seligman & Hager, 1972). Conversely, recent research on the neurobiology of learning suggests that the mechanism by which we encode information involves gene expression and that learning influences which genes are expressed (Bolhuis, Hetebrij, Den Boer-Visser, De Groot, & Zijlstra, 2001; Rosen, Fanselow, Young, Sitcoske, & Maren, 1998). Thus, learning and genetic factors affect behavior, and each other. We raise these examples to foreshadow that our explanation of motivation will also primarily reside within a description of these interactions.

A Definitional Framework for Motivation

The framework we advocate for understanding motivation is called *functional behavior systems* (Timberlake & Fanselow, 1994). Two aspects to defining a functional behavior system are common to the definition of any motivational construct: environmental cause and behavioral effect. These are the necessary components to any empirically tractable definition of an intervening variable. A functional behavior system must be anchored to objectively defined environmental causes. These are the antecedent conditions for activation of the behavior system and the things an experimenter can manipulate to turn on the system. The functional behavioral system must also have objectively observable behavioral consequences of activating the system.

Functional behavior systems have a third component to the definition that is unique to this approach. The naturally occurring problem that the system has evolved to solve is a component of the definition. This component is critical because modern views of motivation see behavior as being tightly organized around these functional concerns. Environmental causes and behavioral effects are grouped together about the naturally occurring problems that the successful organism is built to solve. This problem-oriented view focuses the analysis on how multiple behaviors relate to each other in a manner that is coordinated to solve a problem. Hunger and feeding are understood as a means to ensure that the necessary nutrients and calories are harvested from the environment. Hunger and feeding cannot be understood simply in terms of the amount eaten or the number of lever presses a rat makes for a food pellet. Nor can it be understood simply in terms of the postingestional consequences of food that satisfy some homeostatic requirement. Rather, for each species, food-related motivation is tailored to the niche that the animal occupies. An animal must search for appropriate items, procure them, prepare them, consume them, and digest them. The sequence is all-important, and a failure anywhere along the chain means that the organism fails to meet critical environmental demands. Different behaviors are necessary for each step; different rules apply to each component; and the analysis of behavior is a description of the path. A theory of motivation must capture the structure of this organization.

Impetus for the Development of Functional Behavior Systems

A metatheoretical concern in approaching motivation is how many separate motivations does a complex organism have? Freud (1915) voiced one extreme when he suggested that all motivation stemmed from a single unconscious source of energy. The instinct theorists of the early part of the twentieth century voiced another when they linked instincts directly to behaviors (e.g., Lorenz, 1937). Eventually, instinct theory crushed itself because there were no constraints on the number of instincts that could be generated. To avoid such problems, Hull (1943), like Freud (1915), argued for a single generalized source of motivation. The magnitude of this generalized drive was determined by summing all unsatisfied physiological needs; any perturbation of homeostasis resulted in an increase in a common source of behavioral energy. Empirically, Hull's generalized drive theory failed because separate sources of motivation most often do not generalize. Thirsty animals tend not to eat, and frightened animals forsake eating and drinking. It also became clear that learning was at least as important a source of motivation as was homeostatic need. Often we eat because the situation tells us to. Past experience informs us that this is the proper time or place to eat.

To account for empirical challenges to Hull's (1943) generalized drive principle, incentive motivational theories suggested that two types of motivation could be activated by Pavlovian means. Conditional stimuli (CSs; see also chapter by Miller and Grace in this volume) that predicted desirable outcomes, such as the occurrence of food or the absence of pain, activated an appetitive motivational system; CSs that predicted undesirable outcomes activated an aversive motivational system. Anything that activated the appetitive system stimulated appetitively related behaviors and suppressed aversively motivated behaviors. The opposite was true for stimuli that excited the aversive system. This explanation was an improvement because learning, in the form of Pavlovian conditioning, could provide a source of motivation. Additionally, the notion of two systems provides more selectivity than Hull's (1943) generalized drive principle. The problem with this view is that it simply does not go far enough. As we shall see, cues associated with food do not simply cause an enhancement of food-associated behaviors. Rather, the cue signals that a particular class of food-related behavior is appropriate and that others are inappropriate. On the aversive side, fear and pain are organized in an antagonistic manner. Because fear inhibits pain-related behavior, how can fear, pain, and hunger simultaneously hold mutually reciprocal relationships? As we shall see, organizing these systems around their function makes sense of the relationships between classes of behavior. By combining function, antecedent cause, and behavioral effect into our definition of a motivational system, we are also successful in limiting the number of motivational systems that can be generated.

What Is Motivation?

The idea that we eat because we are hungry seems intuitively obvious. Both lay and several formal descriptions of behavior suggest that hunger is a response to food deprivation and that hunger engenders behaviors that correct the depletion. In this way, factors such as body weight or caloric intake are regulated about some set point. This homeostatic view has directed much research, and in many situations body weight appears to be held relatively constant. However, caloric intake and body weight are influenced by many variables, such as the type and quantity of food available, activity levels, season, and palatability.

Bolles (1980) has noted that if the experimenter holds several of these variables constant, the others will come to rest at some set of values. Thus, an observed set point or consistency may be an artifact of relatively static conditions. Additionally, because all these factors are variables in an equation, the experimenter is free to solve for any of them as a function of the others. In effect, body weight may appear to be regulated simply because you have kept the other variables constant. Alternatively, if you held body weight and the other variables constant, you could solve the equation for palatability and thereby conclude that palatability is regulated. From a functional perspective what is critical is that an animal ingests the necessary substances in sufficient quantities; how that is accomplished does not matter. Natural selection favors any scheme that satisfies the goal. In this regard, regulating palatability may make a lot of sense—and is a topic to which we will return later.

This idea is a general point about motivational terminology and motivational systems. We have to recognize that motivation is organized about the evolutionary requirement that the system needs to solve (see also chapter by Capaldi in this volume). Hunger, sexual arousal, and fear really refer to a behavioral organization that is imposed on an organism when the environment demands that a particular problem be solved. Motivation is no longer conceived of as a blind force that impels an animal forward. It is something that gives form, structure, and meaning to behavior, and it is from this vantage that we will begin to analyze some exemplars of specific motivational systems.

FEEDING

The vast majority of animal species gain the nutrients they require to survive and grow by harvesting them from other living creatures. This strategy requires that animals have means to detect and capture these nutrients and that the behavioral systems governing these actions be sensitive to the availability of required nutrients and the physiological demands of the animal. Psychological examination of these requirements typically focuses on either the factors that initiate the behavior or the response topography of food-gathering behavior. We examine each of these aspects in turn.

Factors Governing Initiation of Feeding Behavior

Homeostasis

Richter (1927) observed that feeding behavior occurred in regular bouts that could be specified on the basis of their frequency, size, and temporal patterning. He suggested that finding the determinants of this regularity should be the goal of psychology and further indicated that homeostasis, the maintenance of a constant internal environment, could be one of these determinants. These observations have been supported by further research showing that animals frequently act as though defending a baseline level of intake, leading to the development of a depletion/repletion model of feeding initiation similar to homeostatic models developed to account for temperature regulation behavior (Satinoff, 1983). A great deal of evidence suggests that under relatively constant conditions, animals eat a regular amount each day and that the amount is sensitive to manipulations such as enforced deprivation or stomach preloading (Le Magnen, 1992). However, there are a number of problems with this analysis, and these problems become more intractable the more lifelike the experiment becomes. For example, initiation of feeding behavior has been demonstrated to be sensitive to a number of different factors including nutrient storage levels, food palatability, and circadian influences (Panksepp, 1974). The crucial factor in determining the influence of various manipulations on feeding behavior seems to be the nature of the experimental procedure used.

The Importance of Procedure

Collier (1987) described three different procedures that have been used to study feeding motivation. By far the most commonly used is the session procedure. Here, the animal is deprived of a required commodity for most of the day and is given repeated brief access to this commodity during a short, daily session. In such a procedure very few of the determinants of behavior are free to vary, placing most of the control of the animal's behavior into the hands of the experimenter. Features of behavior including the number of trials, the intertrial interval, session length, portion size, response contingencies, and total intake are determined by the experimenter and not the animal (Collier & Johnson, 1997). This kind of procedure changes the response characteristics of the animals by placing a premium on rapid initiation and performance of the food-rewarded behavior and does not allow analysis of feeding initiation and termination because these are also determined by the experimenter, rather than the animal.

A second class of studies uses the free-feeding procedure in which animals are offered continuous access to the commodity and their pattern of feeding is recorded. Unlike the session procedure, there is no explicit deprivation, and the animal is free to control various parameters of food consumption, including meal initiation and termination. This procedure has led to the dominant depletion/repletion model of feeding motivation. This model hypothesizes that postingestive information about the nutrient content of the meal is compared against nutrient expenditure since the last meal to determine the nutrient preference and size/duration of the next meal (Le Magnen & Devos, 1980). Correlations between length of food deprivation and subsequent meal size or the rate of responding for subsequent feeding (Bolles, 1975; Le Magnen, 1992) provide support for this interpretation. However, these correlations are influenced by a number of other factors, including the availability of other behaviors (Collier, Johnson, & Mitchell, 1999), and do not provide a complete account of feeding initiation (Castonguay, Kaiser, & Stern, 1986). Even more important, the feeding initiation and subsequent meal patterning of free-feeding animals seem to be such that they never undergo nutrient depletion: Free-feeding animals never have empty stomachs (Collier, Hirsch, & Hamlin, 1972), meaning that a near-constant stream of nutrients enters the animal. This behavior suggests either that feeding initiation must be unrelated to depletion or that it must occur prior to, but not as a consequence of, nutrient depletion.

The Cost of Feeding

One major parametric influence on feeding behavior not included in the free-feeding procedure is the cost of procuring food. In the laboratory foraging procedure (Collier, 1983) the animal is not food deprived in the conventional sense—it has constant access to food resources—but food availability is restricted by making delivery contingent on the completion of a response contingency. Unlike the session procedure, the animal is free to control the various parameters of feeding behavior. Unlike the free-feeding procedure, the animal must not only work to gain access to the commodity, but it must balance the demands of gaining access to food with other biologically important activities such as drinking and sleeping. In these studies, the cost of food procurement, and not the repletion/depletion calculation, has been demonstrated to be the crucial determinant of feeding initiation (e.g., Collier et al., 1972). Experiments manipulating the cost of food procurement have demonstrated that the number of meals an animal takes in a day is directly related to the cost of initiating a meal. By varying the number of lever presses required to initiate a meal, Collier et al. (1972) demonstrated that the daily number of meals initiated by the animal is a linear function of the log of the response requirement. The number of small meals and the frequency of short intermeal intervals decreased as the response requirement increased, leading to a smaller number of larger meals and the conservation of total intake and body weight.

Similar effects of meal-procurement cost have been demonstrated across a variety of animal species with a variety of evolutionary niches and foraging strategies (Collier & Johnson, 1990). The determination of meal cost appears to be calculated by the animal across a relatively long time window: Animals trained on alternating days of high and low cost learned to feed primarily on low-cost days (Morato, Johnson, & Collier, 1995). Animals also show a nonexclusive preference for feeding on low cost resources (Collier, 1982), on larger pellets where the cost is the same as for smaller pellets (Johnson & Collier, 1989), and on pellets with higher caloric density (Collier, Johnson, Borin, & Mathis, 1994). Animals also include risk of aversive events into the cost equation. Fanselow, Lester, and Helmstetter (1988) demonstrated that increased numbers of randomly occurring foot shocks led to changes in meal patterning similar to those induced by increased procurement costs. Characteristics of feeding demonstrated in session and free-feeding procedures, such as increased rates of responding or consumption or correlations between length of food deprivation and subsequent meal size, are not replicated in the laboratory feeding procedure (Collier & Johnson, 1997; Collier et al., 1999). This series of results has led Collier and his coworkers to suggest that the crucial determinants of feeding initiation are the costs associated with meal procurement and that physiological functions act to buffer the effects of variations in feeding initiation determined by procurement cost rather than as the instigators of feeding behavior (Collier, 1986).

The Behavioral Ecology of Feeding Cost

In the laboratory, costs are determined by the experimenter. In the real world these costs are determined by the animal's ecological niche, placing feeding behavior under the direct control of evolutionary factors. Feeding intensity can be predicted from relative predatory risk, as can be inferred from the study by Fanselow et al. (1988). For example, large predators could be expected to eat long-duration, low-intensity meals because they are not subject to threat from other animals. In contrast, small predators could be expected to eat short-duration, high-intensity meals as they are themselves potential prey. These suggestions are consistent with ethological data (Estes, 1967a, 1967b; Schaller, 1966). Meal patterning and feeding initiation can be predicted from food type. Predators could be expected to sustain high procurement costs for their nutritionally rich meals, whereas herbivores—particularly small, monogastric herbivores—could be expected to take frequent meals because of the low quality and intensive processing required by their usual foods. These suggestions have been supported by experimental data indicating that cats can eat every three to four days when procurement costs are high and maintain bodyweight, whereas guinea pigs are unable to maintain their bodyweight with fewer than two to three meals per day and are unable to sustain high procurement costs (Hirsch & Collier, 1974; Kaufmann, Collier, Hill, & Collins, 1980).

Factors Governing Variety of Intake

Alliesthesia

Food selection must provide all the nutrients necessary for survival. This task is simple for a specialized feeder that eats very few foods. However, opportunistic omnivores such as rats and humans contend with a potentially bewildering array of choices. Traditional approaches have suggested that the body detects hunger when it is deprived of a particular commodity, and this homeostatic need sets in motion behaviors directed at correcting the deficit (e.g., Rodgers, 1967). Thus, intake of various nutrients could be regulated by set points for these nutrients. Food palatability had been suggested to be an alternative mechanism (Mook, 1987). Assume that an animal (or at least an opportunistic omnivore) eats because food tastes good. If that is combined with one other assumption, that food loses its incentive value when consumed, we have a mechanism that ensures intake of a variety of substances. This phenomenon is referred to as alliesthesia (Cabanac, 1971). Cabanac demonstrated that palatability ratings of sugar solution change from positive to negative following ingestion, but not simply the taste of, sucrose.

Sensory Satiety

Despite this evidence, it is also true that sensory, rather than postingestive, stimuli associated with food play an important role in inducing variety of intake. The clearest demonstrations of these effects are those demonstrating the effects of food variety in sated animals and people. When we sit down to our holiday meal, the turkey tastes exquisite, but after two or three helpings we can barely tolerate another bite. Yet despite our satiety, we proceed to eat a large dessert. The order of courses does not matter (Rolls, Laster, & Summerfelt, 1991); the critical determinant of renewed consumption is that the food has variety (Rolls, 1979). This variety effect has been demonstrated in humans and rats (see Raynor & Epstein, 2001, for a recent review), perhaps most dramatically by the obesity of rats given a variety of highly palatable foods (Sclafani & Springer, 1976). Rats under these conditions can more than double their weight and behave similarly to animals that have obesity-inducing brain lesions.

These findings do not undermine the alliesthesia model of food selection. Rather, they suggest that exposure to the sensory aspects of food, in the absence of ingestion, is sufficient to reduce the palatability, and therefore intake, of that food. A variety of studies demonstrated just such a result. Changes in the shape of the food have an effect on intake. Rolls, Rowe, and Rolls (1982) showed that subjects would consume more pasta if it were offered as spaghetti, half hoops, and bow ties than if it were offered as spaghetti alone. Guinard and Brun (1998) demonstrated that variation in another nonnutritive dimension, food texture, can similarly lead to increases in consumption. Rolls and Rolls (1997) have demonstrated that chewing or smelling food is sufficient to induce alliesthesia-like reductions in the subsequent palatability of that food in the absence of eating that food. Thus, although ingestion may be sufficient to cause alliesthesia, it is not necessary: Sensory stimulation alone is sufficient to cause changes in palatability and to induce variety in food choice.

Factors Governing the Incentive Aspects of Foods

Cathexes

The regulation of feeding behavior through meal patterning and the regulation of food variety through alliesthesia assume that the animal knows which stimuli present in the environment are foods that will satisfy its nutritional requirements. In the case of opportunistic omnivores such as humans and rats, this knowledge must be learned. This process was described as the development of cathexes by Tolman (1949), who suggested that it involved affective, or emotional, learning that created positive affective reactions toward substances that fulfilled nutritional needs and negative affective reactions toward substances that did not or that caused unpleasant reactions such as nausea. Learning of negative cathexes has been the more fully explored of these processes through examination of conditioned taste (or flavor) aversion (CTA).

Exploration of CTA has demonstrated a distinction between aversive motivation caused by insults to the skin defense system, such as electric shock, and insults to the gut defense system caused by taste and emetic toxins (Garcia y Robertson & Garcia, 1985). This suggests that learning about the incentive value of food is based on selective associations between taste (and to a lesser extent olfactory stimuli) and postingestive consequences. However, in many cases the animal must make behavioral choices at a distance, before being in a position to taste the potentially aversive food. A great deal of research suggests that associations between the distal cues that guide behavior and the postingestive consequences of ingesting a food predicted by those cues require mediation by taste or olfactory cues (Garcia, 1989). This suggestion gives rise to a mediated-association view of food incentive learning: Postingestive consequences are associated with taste, and taste stimuli are associated with distal cues. Hence, feeding behavior is governed by a chain of distal cue–taste–postingestive consequence associations (Garcia, 1989).

The strongest evidence for this view comes from a variety of studies that emphasize the importance of taste in mediating CTA to distal cues. Rusiniak, Hankins, Garcia, and Brett (1979) demonstrated that although weak odor paired with nausea produces weak aversion to the odor, the same odor results in a much stronger aversion if presented in compound with a taste. Brett, Hankins, and Garcia (1976) demonstrated that after repeated trials, hawks rejected both black (poisoned) and white (safe) mice, but that following the addition of a distinctive taste to the black mice, the hawks began to reject the black mice and eat the white mice. Evidence also suggests that similar, though weaker, effects can be found by using the expectancy of a taste to mediate the CTA to distal cues. Holland (1981) paired a tone (distal) CS with a distinctive flavor before pairing the tone with a nausea-inducing lithium chloride injection. Subsequent testing showed decreased consumption of the tone-predicted food, indicating the development of an indirect, expectancy-based CTA. Taken together, these results indicate that learning about which foods in the environment to ingest is mediated by two different Pavlovian conditioning processes.

Incentive Learning

Although this system indicates to the animal in a general sense what is good to eat, it is not able to guide the animal's day-to-day foraging behavior because the gustatory learning system proposed to underlie cathexes is purely affective; it encodes only positive or negative values. To the extent that an animal's behavior reflects its current needs, the animal must be able to encode and act on the value of food given its current internal state. The evaluation of the incentive value of food given the animal's current internal state is called *incentive learning* (Balleine, 1992).

The study of incentive learning is complicated by the fact that the effect of internal state on feeding responses seems to differ based on the associative procedure that is used to examine those behaviors. In Pavlovian conditioning procedures, internal state (e.g., deprivation) seems to act directly to increase the animal's tendency to engage in food-reinforced behavior (Balleine, 1992). In contrast, in operant conditioning procedures, the effect of internal state on behavior depends on whether the animal has prior experience with the outcome of its behavior, the reinforcer, in that deprivation state (Dickinson & Balleine, 1994). In contrast to these effects, Davidson (1998) has shown in a Pavlovian conditioning procedure that the state of food deprivation on test had no effect on approach behavior unless the animals had had prior experience with the pellets in the undeprived state. Only rats that had previously eaten the pellets when undeprived and then tested undeprived showed a reduction in approach behavior. Just as Dickinson and Balleine (1994) interpreted their results, Davidson (1998) interpreted this as evidence that motivational control of Pavlovian food seeking by hunger has to be learned through experience of the reinforcer in both the deprived and undeprived states.

This analysis is further complicated by two additional findings. The first is that as experience with the instrumental action-outcome contingency increases, the motivational factors underlying performance also appear to shift. Increased training seems to result in a growing importance of Pavlovian incentive factors (i.e., deprivation state) and a decreasing importance of instrumental incentive learning (i.e., the incentive valuation of the outcome in the animal's current deprivation state; Dickinson, Balleine, Watt, Gonzalez, & Boakes, 1995). The second is that different instrumental actions in a chain of responding required for reinforcement appear to be governed by different motivational factors. Instrumental actions that occur earlier in a chain of responses seem to be governed by the animal's current evaluation of the reinforcer. In contrast, instrumental actions that occur immediately prior to reinforcer delivery appear to be directly regulated by the animal's current deprivation state (Balleine, Garner, Gonzalez, & Dickinson, 1995). This latter finding—of a distinction in motivational control between proximal and distal responses—mirrors the common distinction between appetitive and consummatory responding (Craig, 1918; Konorski, 1967) that is also a component of ethological (Leyhausen, 1979; Tinbergen, 1951) and psychological theories of response organization (Domjan, 1994; Timberlake, 1983, 1994).

Feeding Response Organization

Appetitive and Consummatory Behavior

The last two sections have dealt with initiation of feeding and selection of food. Another important aspect of feeding motivation concerns the topography and organization of behaviors used to obtain food. The most influential view of feeding response organization is based on Craig's (1918) distinction between appetitive and consummatory behavior. Consummatory behavior has typically been viewed as stereotyped responses that served as the endpoints of motivated sequences of behavior and could be defined by their quieting effect on the behaving animal. In contrast, appetitive behavior was conceived of as a sequence of variable but nonrandom behavior that served to increase the likelihood of the animal being able to perform the consummatory behavior by increasing the likelihood of interaction with the goal stimulus (Craig, 1918). Under this framework, specific examples of feeding consummatory behavior would include acts like chewing, swallowing, and stereotyped killing behavior such as the throat bite used by large cats. Appetitive behavior would include the typical behaviors of foraging such as motor search. These concepts were further refined by Lorenz's (1937) analysis that redefined consummatory behavior as the fixed action pattern of an instinct and suggested that it was motivated by the buildup of action-specific energy. Appetitive behavior remained undirected behavior whose function was to increase the likelihood of the animal's being able to perform the fixed action pattern by bringing it into contact with the releasing stimulus.

Parallels between the concept of the consummatory act and the reflex (Sherrington, 1906) and unconditioned response (Pavlov, 1927) led to the importation of the appetitive/consummatory distinction from ethological theorizing into the realm of learning theory (e.g., Konorski, 1967). Whereas ethologists distinguished between consummatory and appetitive behaviors on the basis of response stereotypy, learning theorists distinguished them procedurally. Consummatory behavior was investigated in Pavlovian conditioning procedures, following Pavlov's lead in examining the stimulus control of consummatory reflexes. Appetitive behavior was investigated in operant conditioning procedures that emphasized the flexibility of appetitive behavior by concentrating on arbitrary responses and arbitrary stimuli to control performance (Timberlake & Silva, 1995).

Although consummatory acts have been considered prototypically instinctive (Lorenz, 1937), careful research has demonstrated a role for learning in the development of consummatory behavior. The best demonstration of this influence comes from the work of Hogan (1973a, 1973b, 1977) on the development of feeding behavior in the Burmese red junglefowl, a close relative of the domestic chicken. Hogan (1973a) demonstrated that pecking behavior in newly hatched chicks did not discriminate between food and sand but that by 3 days of age, pecks were directed primarily at food. At that age, ingestion of food facilitated pecking, but not until 10 min to 1 hr after ingestion, and not specifically to food. Further studies (Hogan, 1973b) indicated that neither satiation nor hunger was responsible for this delayed increase and suggested instead that this effect was due to learning reinforced by the postingestive consequences of food consumption. Hogan (1977) demonstrated that only experience that involved pecking led to the development of discrimination between food and sand and that this required a postingestive delay of 2 min to 3 min, indicating that the discrimination is most likely based on short-term metabolic feedback. Hogan suggested that the behavioral control of pecking and the development of metabolic feedback develop independently, but experience is necessary for these two systems to become coordinated.

The Structure of Appetitive Behavior

The focus on using instrumental procedures to study appetitive behavior in psychology has, to a large extent, blinded it to the unlearned, underlying structure of appetitive behavior. Far from being undifferentiated activity, close examination of motivated behavior has demonstrated that appetitive behavior is organized into chains of behaviors that serve to increase the likelihood of the terminal act. The classic demonstration of this is Tinbergen's (1951) analysis of the mating behavior of the stickleback, although similar demonstrations have been made for the organization of other appetitive behavior (e.g., Leyhausen, 1979). Despite the procedural difficulty in analyzing the underlying organization of appetitive behavior in arbitrary response operant procedures, this organization has made its presence felt through various phenomena variously described as constraints on learning, misbehavior, and adjunctive learning (Staddon & Simmelhag, 1970). The constraints on learning phenomena demonstrate the underlying behavioral organization of the animal through making some responses and stimuli easier to condition to various rewards than others. One example of many is the relative inability of animals to learn an instrumental response chain that requires bar pressing on a lever proximal to the feeder prior to pressing on a lever distal to the feeder in order to be reinforced, whereas the far-near sequence is learned rapidly (Silva, Timberlake, & Gont, 1998). Perhaps the classic examples of the intrusion of the underlying structure of appetitive behavior into operant responses are the reports of misbehavior made by the Brelands (Breland & Breland, 1961, 1966) in which the typical feeding behaviors of species began to intrude into well learned, arbitrary sequences of food-reinforced behavior.

Explicit examination of the organization of appetitive behavior is a relatively recent phenomenon in learning situations and has largely taken place through the study of response topography in Pavlovian conditioning procedures and the subsequent development of behavior systems theories (Domjan, 1994; Fanselow & Lester, 1988; Timberlake, 1983). The behavioral organization of predatory foraging and feeding in the rat is the most extensively developed of these behavior systems and is presented as a specific example later. It is important to note that the precise behaviors and their organization would be expected to differ from species to species and within species based on local factors such as relative prey selection. In addition, as has been shown through operant conditioning, novel behaviors can readily be incorporated into the appetitive component of feeding behavior chains. This simple addition of new behaviors into an appetitively motivated chain of behavior can be contrasted with the relative inflexibility of aversively motivated behavior chains described in the section on aversively motivated response organization later.

A Feeding Response Organization: The Predatory Behavior System of the Rat

Timberlake (1983, 1990, 1993, 1997, 2001; Timberlake & Lucas, 1989; Timberlake & Silva, 1995) outlined a functional behavior system that describes the predatory foraging and feeding behavior of the rat in a hierarchical system that emphasizes the behavior-organizing role of motivational modes within the system. The behavior system includes selective stimulus processing mechanisms, timing and memory components, functional motor programs, and organizing motivational structures that interrelate to serve a particular function. Within that system, particular subsystems are defined by a collection of stimulus predispositions and motor outputs organized to achieve a particular goal (see Figures 2.1 and 2.2). In the case of the rat feeding system, activity in the predatory subsystem is indicated by heightened responsiveness to

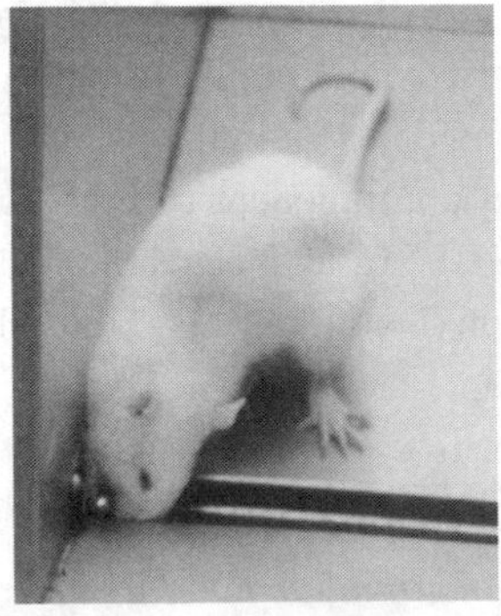

Figure 2.1 A hungry rat engages in focal search behavior directed toward a moving artificial prey stimulus (ball bearing).

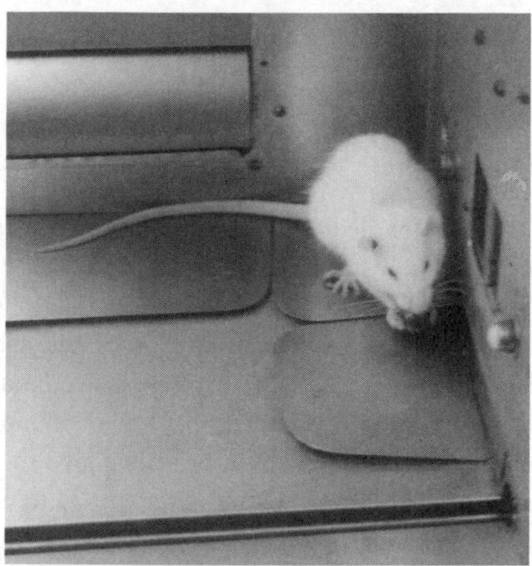

Figure 2.2 Having "captured" the ball bearing, the rat attempts to engage in consummatory behavior.

movement and the increased probability of predatory appetitive behaviors like chase and capture.

Timberlake (1993; Timberlake & Silva, 1995) suggested that within the predatory subsystem, functional behaviors are organized by motivational modes into response tendencies based on the temporal, spatial, and psychological distance to the prey. This view is complementary to the predatory imminence continuum developed by Fanselow (1989; Fanselow & Lester, 1988) in describing the functional behavior systems of defensive behavior that will be described more fully later. These modes describe the relative probability of particular responses given the appropriate environmental support stimuli and create the underlying organization of feeding behavior.

Following initiation of a predatory foraging sequence, behaviors such as motor search, visual search, target tracking, or substrate investigation are motivated by a general search mode that also specifies stimulus selectivities such as increased responding to novelty or movement. Environmental cues related to an increase in prey imminence cause a qualitative shift in stimulus and motor selectivity described as the focal search mode. Within the focal search mode, behavior patterns may shift to include responses such as chase and capture, stalking, or area-restricted search. Timberlake and Washburne (1989) investigated behavioral responses to artificial moving prey stimuli in seven different rodent species and noted that the topography of chase and capture behaviors directed toward the artificial prey stimulus were based on the subject's species-typical predatory behavior. When food is present, the animal engages in behaviors directed toward the food item and again makes a qualitative shift to the stimulus selection and motor properties organized by the handling/consuming mode. At this point, stimulus characteristics such as taste, odor, and orotactile stimulation are the predominant influences on behavior and motivation, as suggested by Garcia (1989) in his description of the factors involved in feeding cathexes, described earlier. Motor patterns are those typically described as consummatory behaviors, including the various kinds of ingestion and oral rejection behaviors.

The behavior systems model just outlined suggests that feeding response organization is governed by motivational, but not behavioral, modes. The exact nature of the behavior in any sequence is determined by the interaction of the animal's motivational mode, its behavioral repertoire, and the affordances of the stimuli in the environment. Just as ethological theories of response organization suggest that chains of behavior are organized into relatively independent subunits with their own intermediate goals (Morris, 1958; Tinbergen, 1951), this behavior systems approach also separates behavior chains into functional subunits with related stimulus and motor preparedness and particular stimulus-response transactions that function as transitions between them.

FEAR MOTIVATION

Fear motivation reverses the perspective of feeding, as we focus on prey and not predators. Because the goal of the predator is to consume the prey, the selection pressure on defense is powerful because injured or dead individuals have infinitely diminished reproductive success. Thus it is not surprising that prey species have evolved elaborate behavioral strategies to deal with such threats. Fear is a motivational system that is provoked by danger signals in the environment, and when activated this system triggers defensive reactions that protect individuals from environmental dangers. In this section we examine fear from a behavioral systems perspective.

Because of this enormous selection pressure, species have several lines of defense. Some species rely on primary defensive strategies that "operate regardless of whether or not a predator is in the vicinity" (Edmunds, 1974, p. 1). Primary defense strategies include camouflage (the animal's body color blends into environment) and Batesian mimicry (the animal's body color and form resemble another species that has dangerous or unpleasant attributes). Although primary defenses contribute to survival, these strategies are relatively inflexible and insensitive to feedback. For example, green insects avoid wild bird predation more often when they are tethered to a green environment compared to a brown environment (Di Cesnola, 1904). Thus, the insect's camouflage contributes to survival only when it rests in the matching green-colored environment, and the camouflage is ineffective elsewhere. In contrast to primary defense, secondary defensive strategies require that an animal respond to a threat with specific behaviors. Turtles withdraw into their hard shells; porcupines raise their sharp quills; and grasshoppers retreat a short distance and then become immobile when they are threatened. These behaviors can be inflexible, but they are often sensitive to feedback. Unlike primary defensive strategies, which are permanently employed, these defensive behaviors are triggered by a fear-driven motivational system.

The Pervasiveness of Fear in Motivated Behavior

Fear modulates other motivational systems. Animals that miss a meal or a mating opportunity usually live to eat or mate another day. Animals that fail to defend usually have no further reproductive chances. Therefore, fear takes precedence over other motivational systems. One of the first quantitative measures of fear was the ability to suppress food intake (Estes & Skinner, 1941). The effects of fear on feeding can also be subtle. As described earlier, Fanselow et al. (1988) demonstrated that rats adjust the size and frequency of meals in relation to shock density. Animals were housed in an environment that had a safe burrow. The burrow was attached to an area with a grid floor, and brief shock was delivered to this area on a random schedule. The rat could obtain food only if it risked venturing onto the grid floor area to eat. The results suggest that with increasing shock density, rats take fewer, but larger, meals. Thus, fear motivation seems to modulate foraging behaviors (i.e., feeding motivation). Similarly, rats cease foraging, retreat to a burrow, and delay further foraging for hours after they encounter a cat near the entrance of the burrow (Blanchard & Blanchard, 1989), and monkeys seem reluctant to reach over a snake to obtain food (Mineka & Cook, 1988). Fear also influences sexual motivation. For example, female stickleback fish produce few offspring with a male conspecific that displays inappropriate territorial aggression toward them (Hollis, Pharr, Dumas, Britton, & Field, 1997). During the aggressive act the female may be both injured and frightened by the male, and females often retreat from the vicinity when attacked. Thus, fear modulates sexual motivation by disrupting or delaying reproductive opportunities.

Factors Governing Initiation of Fear

An effective behavioral defensive strategy requires that animals identify threats with sufficient time to perform the appropriate defensive responses. Numerous types of stimuli can signal danger and activate fear motivational systems. These stimuli can be divided into three functional classes: learned fear stimuli, innate fear stimuli, and observational learning and fear stimuli.

Learned Fear Stimuli

Fear is rapidly learned and measured in the laboratory (Fanselow, 1994); it has direct clinical relevance (Bouton, Mineka, & Barlow, 2001); and it has become a standard method for exploring the behavioral processes and neural mechanisms of learning. In the prototypical laboratory experiment, a rat is placed in a chamber where it is presented with a tone that is followed by a brief aversive foot shock. Later during a test session, the rat is reexposed to either the conditioning chamber or the tone. During this reexposure the rat will engage in behaviors that are characteristic of fear. With this preparation the tone and the chamber, or context, serve as conditional stimuli (CSs). They were originally neutral stimuli, but after they were paired with an unconditional stimulus (US), the foot shock, the animal responded to the CS in a fearful manner. Such responses to the CSs are called conditional responses (CRs). These fear CRs occur specifically to the shock-paired stimuli, and these responses are used as measures of learning in Pavlovian experiments (see also chapter by Miller and Grace in this volume). To date, Pavlovian fear has been characterized with several CRs such as defensive freezing, reflex facilitation, heart rate, blood pressure, conditional suppression, conditional analgesia, and vocalizations (see Fendt & Fanselow, 1999, for review).

Animals can learn to associate a threat with numerous classes of CSs. Auditory cues, visual cues, olfactory cues, and tactile cues can all become fear CSs with the appropriate training regime. However, the nature of the CS is not arbitrary because animals are known to exhibit *selective associations*. This phenomenon is best exemplified by an experiment performed by Garcia and Koelling (1966) in which rats were presented with a compound CS. The compound CS consisted of auditory, visual, and flavor cues: a buzzing noise, a blinking light, and the taste of saccharin, respectively. During training trials the presentation of the compound CS was followed by the occurrence of footshock. During test sessions, rats exhibited fear reaction to the auditory and visual cue, and not to the flavor cue. Thus, this experiment suggests that in the rat visual and auditory cues are more readily associated with threat. Asymmetry in this sort of stimulus selection appears ubiquitous. Similar selective associations have been demonstrated in the pigeon (Foree & Lolordo, 1973). Further, tone onset is more readily associated with danger than light onset, which is more readily associated with safety

(Jacobs & LoLordo, 1980). These findings suggest that stimulus selection in the laboratory reflects phylogenetic influences on stimulus selection in the species' natural niche.

Innate Fear Stimuli

Learned fear stimuli require that an animal have previous experience with the stimuli to recognize the potential threat. In contrast, innate fear stimuli are those stimuli that can be identified as potentially threatening without previous experience. Animals display these responses without any specific training experience.

It is difficult to develop unambiguous criteria that classify innate fear stimuli. For instance, an unlearned fear stimulus could be defined as a stimulus that elicits defensive behaviors during its first presentation. With this definition a cat may be considered an unlearned fear stimulus because laboratory-reared rats exhibit robust defensive behaviors during their first encounter with the predator. This behavior suggests that the rodent's genome retains information to detect certain innate stimuli and provokes appropriate defensive reactions (Blanchard & Blanchard, 1972). However, defensive reactions to a cat could also be due to learning. In this alternative account some aspect of the cat's movement is the aversive stimulus, and the rat exhibits defensive behaviors because it is in an environment that has been paired with an aversive stimulus. Thus, the rat freezes in the presence of the cat only because its movement has been paired with other features of the cat and not because the cat itself is an innately aversive stimulus. This interpretation is supported by the observation that a moving cat, dog, or inanimate card can trigger freezing in the rat, although the sound, smell, or sight of a dead cat does not (Blanchard, Mast, & Blanchard, 1975).

Also, the fact that a defensive response follows the first presentation of a stimulus is not sufficient to classify that stimulus as an innate releaser of fear. This is nicely illustrated by the analysis of electric shock. Fear responses such as freezing, defecation, and analgesia follow the first presentation of shock. However, shock per se does not unconditionally provoke these responses. Instead, it rapidly and immediately conditions fear to the contextual cues present before shock, and it is these conditional cues that elicit the behaviors. Removing these cues before shock (Fanselow, 1986) or after shock (Fanselow, 1980) eliminates the responses. Similar patterns appear to exist (Blanchard, Fukunaga, & Blanchard, 1976). Thus, we must exert considerable caution before concluding that something is an innate trigger of fear. This pattern also raises an important question about the motivational properties of something like shock, because although it supports conditioning of fear behavior, it does not provoke fear itself. This pattern may be similar to Balleine's (1992) data, described earlier, suggesting that incentive properties of food must be learned.

Although prey species clearly react to predators in the wild with elaborate defensive responses (Coss & Owings, 1978), these studies cannot control for the ontogenetic history of the subject. Therefore, the best evidence for fear reactions to a predator comes from laboratory studies with rodents (Blanchard & Blanchard, 1972; Hirsch & Bolles, 1980; Lester & Fanselow, 1985). The strongest evidence for phylogenetic influences on defensive behavior comes from a study conducted by Hirsh and Bolles (1980). These investigators trapped two subspecies of wild deer mice that live in distinct regions of the state of Washington in the United States. *Peromyscus maniculatus austerus* comes from the moist forest regions in western Washington state, and *Peromyscus maniculatus gambeli* from an arid grassland region of eastern Washington state. These animals were bred in the laboratory, and their first generation of offspring were exposed to several predators selected from the eastern and western regions.

When tested, *P. m. gambeli* both survived more strikes and survived longer when exposed to a predatory snake from its niche compared to *P. m. austerus*. Thus, *P. m. austerus* was more vulnerable to attack by the predator alien to its niche. Moreover, *P. m. gambeli* exhibited more fear responses to the predator snake from its niche, compared to a nonpredatory snake. Thus, *P. m. gambeli* was able to discriminate between two types of snake. These results suggest that the probability of surviving an encounter with a predator is related to the evolutionary selection pressure that that predator exerts on the prey in their natural niche. Thus, animals adopt unlearned or innate defensive strategies that allow them to cope with predation in their niche.

Other observations suggest that a variety of species can innately identify predators from their own niche (see Hirsch & Bolles, 1980, for review). For example, rats exhibit robust fear reactions to cats during their first encounter with the predator, and this fear response does not seem to habituate rapidly (Blanchard et al., 1998). However, recall from our earlier discussion that cats are maximally fear provoking when they are moving. Thus, it is difficult to ascribe the fear-provoking ability to the cat "concept" when it is possible that cat-like movements are essential for provoking fear in the rat (Blanchard et al., 1975). Because a predator is a complex stimulus, research is needed to isolate what aspects of it have phylogenetic and ontogenetic fear-producing properties.

Bright light is another possible innate fear stimulus for rodents; rodents avoid it consistently. Presumably, light signals threat because rats are more visible in bright environments. Thus, negative phototaxis may be an example of defensive behavior. Walker and Davis (1997) reported that rats display enhanced startle after they have been exposed to bright light. These investigators suggested that bright light elicits fear and that this light-enhanced startle is a manifestation of that fear. Thus, this phenomenon resembles the fear-potentiated startle procedure in which startle behavior is enhanced by the presentation of learned fear stimuli (Davis, 1986).

Recent evidence has also suggested that predator odors may act as innate releasers of defensive behavior. For example, Wallace and Rosen (2000) reported that exposure to a component of fox feces, trimethylthiazoline (TMT), elicits freezing behavior in the rat. However, these results may be related to the intensity of the odor and to the test chamber's small dimensions. What is needed in all these cases is a set of criteria that unambiguously indicate that a stimulus is an innate fear stimulus. We do not have these criteria yet, but we know from the research with shock that a defensive response following the first occurrence of a stimulus is not sufficient.

Observational Learning and Fear Stimuli

This third class of fear stimuli has been developed from studies on social interactions in monkeys. Lab-reared monkeys normally do not exhibit fear reactions in the presence of a snake, whereas wild-reared monkeys do (Mineka & Cook, 1988). However, the fear of snakes can be socially transmitted by a phenomenon called *observational learning*.

In these experiments a lab-reared observer monkey can view a wild-reared cohort as it interacts with an object. The object may be a snake, a toy snake, or a flower. If the cohort is interacting with a toy snake or a flower, the animal does not exhibit any fear responses, such as fear grimacing or walking away. When this same monkey interacts with the snake, it will exhibit fear reactions. Interestingly, when an observer monkey sees its cohort engaging in fear behaviors when it encounters the snake, the observer monkey will later display fear responses to the snake. Mineka suggests that monkeys can learn about threats by observing conspecifics interact with threatening stimuli.

This phenomenon demonstrates a sophisticated means to learn about threats. Notice that the monkey can learn to fear the snake without direct experience with the snake. This phenomenon is distinct from a typical Pavlovian fear-conditioning session because the animal does not experience the US directly. It learns fear of the snake through observation. Regardless, observational learning shares selection processes that are similar to standard Pavlovian learned fear, and monkeys readily learned fear to snakes, but not to flowers, through observation. Thus, this type of fear may actually be a phylogenetically predisposed form of learning as well.

Functional Behavior Systems Analysis of Defensive Behavior

Fear elicits defensive behavior in a myriad of species (Edmunds, 1974). Each species has its own repertoire of defensive behaviors, and similar species such as the rat and hamster may react to a similar threat in very different ways. But if a species has a number of defensive behaviors in its repertoire, how does it select among them?

Throughout much of the twentieth century, the selection of fear-motivated behavior was most commonly explained with reinforcement principles. For example, Mowrer and Lamoreaux (1946) suggested that animals learn to avoid fear-provoking stimuli because the event of *not* receiving an aversive stimulus is reinforcing. Thus, rats learn to flee from predators because the tendency to flee is strengthened by negative reinforcement when they successfully avoid predation. Despite their popularity, however, theories like these provide an inadequate account of fear-motivated behavior (summarized in Bolles, 1975). Consequently, alternative accounts that use a behavioral systems approach to explain these behaviors have been developed. These explanations acknowledge that different species may use distinct defensive responses. These explanations of defensive behavior also deemphasize the importance of reinforcement in response production and emphasize the primacy of innate defensive behaviors.

The first data that led to these behavioral systems explanations came from Gibson (1952), who studied defensive behavior in the goat. She demonstrated Pavlovian conditioning of the goat's leg flexion response and noted that goats performed many different behaviors such as running away, turning around, and backing up after the shock was delivered. Gibson concluded that leg flexion itself was not a defensive reaction but that it was simply a common component of the other behaviors that she observed. Thus, leg flexion in the goat appears to be a component of several defensive responses.

Akin to Gibson's findings, Bolles (1970) proposed an explanation of avoidance behavior known as the *species-specific defensive reaction (SSDR) hypothesis.* This hypothesis suggests that every species has its own repertoire of innate defensive behaviors and that animals perform these behaviors unconditionally when they become afraid. For example, a rat's SSDRs include fleeing, freezing, fighting, and dark preference. Thus, when a rat becomes afraid, it will perform these defensive behaviors unconditionally; it does not learn to perform these responses via reinforcement. Bolles included a response selection rule in the original formulation of SSDR theory. He suggested that SSDRs were organized in a hierarchy but that the hierarchy could be rearranged by experience. If fleeing is ineffective in avoiding shock, that SSDR will be suppressed by punishment, and as a result the animal will switch to the next SSDR in the hierarchy. Upon further examination of this idea, however, Bolles and Riley (1973) concluded that freezing could not be punished by shock, and as a result the punishment rule could not explain how an animal switched between different SSDRs when threatened.

The Organization of Defensive Behavior: Predatory Imminence Theory

As an alternative to Bolles' explanation of defensive behavior, Fanselow (1989) developed the theory of the *predatory imminence continuum.* In this theory, Fanselow retains the basic tenets of the SSDR theory: Animals use innate SSDRs in defensive situations. However, Fanselow proposed a different response selection rule that determines which SSDR an animal will perform at any given moment. This rule suggests that the selection of specific defensive responses is related to a continuum of the physical and psychological distances between the predator and prey. Thus, given that danger signals elicit fear, response selection is mediated by fear directly. Specifically, high levels of imminence vigorously activate the fear motivational system, whereas low levels of imminence activate the fear system weakly. The relative activation of the fear motivational system thereby determines the selection of defensive behaviors.

Just as there are responses that are particular to each stage of predatory imminence, there are sets of stimuli that tend to be correlated with each stage. These relationships can be illustrated by considering four situations from the rat's natural environment that differ in predatory imminence.

1. *A safe burrow.* When a rat rests in a safe environment such as a burrow, predatory imminence is relatively low. In this environment the animal may not exhibit any sort of defensive behaviors because none are needed. Alternatively, the act of remaining in the burrow could itself be classified as a defensive behavior because it significantly reduces the threat of predation.
2. *A preencounter environment.* As a rat leaves its burrow to forage for food, predatory imminence increases because the probability of encountering a predator increases. Rats engage in preencounter defensive behaviors when their circumstances might lead to an encounter with a predator, but the predator has not yet been detected. These behaviors include changes in meal pattern foraging, thigmotaxis, dark preference, defensive burying, retreating to a burrow, and leaving the burrow via investigative, stretch-approach behavior.
3. *A postencounter environment.* Predatory imminence increases further when a rat encounters a threat, and it will engage in postencounter defensive behaviors. The rat's prominent postencounter defensive behavior is freezing. Rats freeze when they encounter predators, and also when they encounter aversive stimuli. Other postencounter defensive behaviors include conditional analgesia.
4. *A circa-strike situation.* When the rat's postencounter defensive behaviors have failed, a predator will typically attack. As the predator makes contact with the prey, the rat switches to circa-strike defensive behaviors. These behaviors seek to reduce predatory imminence by either escaping the attack or fending off the predator. When attacked, the rat engages in a rapid bout of flight called the activity burst, and it may also engage in defensive fighting.

Notice that two factors change across the predatory imminence continuum. First, the physical distance between predator and prey typically decreases as predatory imminence increases. Second, the psychological distance decreases as the perceived danger of the threat increases. This feature accounts for situations where the prey may fail to detect the threat, although the absolute physical distance between them is small. Thus, if a rat does not notice a cat, it may not freeze or flee despite the close proximity of the predator.

The utility of predatory imminence theory lies in its ability to predict the form of defensive behavior based on these two selection principles. One challenge of the theory lies in discovering the specific defensive behaviors for each species. It is entirely possible that similar species use different SSDRs and that these SSDRs may be organized along the predatory imminence continuum is different ways. For example, although the dominant postencounter defensive behavior for a rat is freezing, hamsters may exhibit flight when threatened (Potegal, Huhman, Moore, & Meyerhoff, 1993).

Defensive Behaviors on the Predatory Imminence Continuum

In the last section we explained the predatory imminence continuum, the basis of a functional behavior systems approach to defense. This continuum is divided into three functional classes of defensive behavior: preencounter, postencounter, and circa-strike defensive behaviors. In this section we describe and organize these behaviors according to the predatory imminence continuum. In many cases, a particular defensive behavior may fall into a single category of predatory imminence (e.g., freezing). However, the expression of some behaviors (e.g., flight) may actually reflect several different components of defensive behavior that fall into different categories.

Preencounter Defensive Behaviors

Animals display preencounter defensive behaviors in situations where a predator may be present but that predator has not yet been detected.

Meal-Pattern Adjustment. A rat may be at higher risk from predators when it leaves its burrow to forage for food. One strategy that diminishes this threat is to reduce the number of foraging excursions by increasing the size of the meal consumed on each trip. Indeed, when rats are housed in an environment that requires them to traverse a shock grid to forage for food, they modify the size and frequency of meals taken in relation to shock density. Specifically, with increasing shock density, rats take fewer, but larger, meals (Fanselow et al., 1988).

Dark Preference. Rodents have a preference for dark places. This behavior presumably has a defensive purpose because rodents are less likely to be detected by predators when they occupy a dark location (e.g., Valle, 1970). Rodents may engage in this behavior in both preencounter and postencounter defensive situations.

Thigmotaxis. Rodents have a tendency to stay near walls. This behavior contributes to successful defense because it limits the threat of attack from behind and because it may also reduce the animal's visibility (e.g., Valle, 1970). Rodents may engage in this behavior in both preencounter and postencounter defensive situations.

Burying. Rodents bury threatening objects when materials such as wood chip bedding or wooden blocks are available. For example, rats bury a metal rod that delivers shock to the animal (Pinel & Treit, 1978). The specific purpose of this behavior is disputed. Some investigators suggest that burying is fear response akin to defensive attack of the shock prod (Pinel & Treit, 1978). Other investigators have offered alternative explanations that describe burying as a manifestation of preemptive nest maintenance directed at protecting the animal from further attack (Fanselow, Sigmundi, & Williams, 1987). An interesting property of burying is that this behavior typically emerges only after rats have engaged in other defensive behaviors: Most rats freeze and flee before engaging in burying. Thus, burying is not prominent when predatory imminence is relatively high. It is also often directed at exits as much as the shock source (Modaresi, 1982). Thus, it seems likely that burying is a preencounter nest-maintenance behavior in rats. However, in some species, such as ground squirrels, it represents a higher imminence nest-defense behavior (Coss & Owings, 1978).

Stretch Approach. Stretch-approach behavior is prominent when a rodent encounters a localizable noxious object, such as a shock prod. In this situation, the level of predatory imminence is ambiguous, and this behavior may be thought of as a cautious exploratory behavior employed to collect information about potential threats. This elaborate behavioral sequence

> begins with the rat advancing slowly towards the aversive object in a low, stretched posture. As it advances, the rat periodically stops and leans forward towards the object [in a manner that] carries the rat into the vicinity of the aversive test object, from where it is able to sniff it, palpate it with its vibrissae, and occasionally contact it with its nose. (Pinel & Mana, 1989, p. 143)

Rodents exhibit stretch-attend to potential predators (Goldthwaite, Coss, & Owings, 1990), to areas of the test apparatus in which they have received shock (Van der Poel, 1979), and to objects that have been the source of an electric shock (Pinel, Mana, & Ward 1989). Pinel and Mana (1989) suggested that this behavior functions to provide information about the potentially hazardous object or location and that olfactory and tactile information via the vibrissae are important elements of this information gathering.

Leaving and Entering the Burrow. Rats often display stretch-approach behavior if there is some potential danger in the environment. Alternatively, if the rat has already left the burrow but remains nearby, a slight increase in predatory imminence will cause retreat to the burrow. This action is one form of flight. Such retreats to the burrow may be accompanied by freezing within the burrow (Blanchard & Blanchard, 1989). However, if the animal is far from the burrow, or the increase in predatory imminence is greater, the animal will enter a different stage of behavior, postencounter defense.

Postencounter Defensive Behaviors

Rodents engage in postencounter defensive behaviors when preencounter defenses have failed and a threat has been detected in the environment.

Freezing. Frightened rats display freezing behavior. This defensive behavior is prominent in but not exclusive to rodent species, and it is characterized by the absence of all movement except for breathing. In the wild, rodents often freeze when they encounter a predator. This behavior is an effective defensive strategy because many predators have difficulty detecting an immobile target, and movement can act as a releasing stimulus for predatory attack (Fanselow & Lester, 1988). In the laboratory this behavior is prevalent when rodents are presented with a CS that has been paired with foot shock (e.g., Fanselow, 1980). Rats usually freeze next to an object (thigmotaxis) such as a wall or corner. This behavior occurs even when the fear stimulus is present and the rat is not next to the object. Thus, part of the freezing response may be withdrawal to a rapidly and easily accessible location to freeze (Sigmundi, 1997). Thus, the freezing sequence contains a component of flight.

Conditional Analgesia. Rodents become analgesic when they encounter learned fear stimuli. Although triggered by fear stimuli, this analgesia becomes useful if the animal suffers injury from a predatory attack. Reduced pain sensitivity permits the animal to express defensive behaviors and forego recuperative behaviors when predatory imminence is high (Bolles & Fanselow, 1980).

Circa-Strike Defensive Behaviors

Rodents engage in circa-strike defensive behaviors when all other defensive strategies have failed. Thus, these behaviors are prominent when predatory imminence is relatively high.

Flight. Another defensive behavior that is common to rodents and many species is flight. In circa strike, flight consists of a rapid burst of activity away from the predator. If cornered, a rat will vocalize, bare its teeth, or jump beyond or at the predator (Blanchard & Blanchard, 1989). The activity burst to electric shock and the potentiated startle response of an already frightened rat to a loud noise are other examples of this behavior.

Fighting. When other defensive behaviors have failed, rodents often resort to defensive fighting when the predator attacks. In the laboratory this behavior emerges when two cohorts receive a series of inescapable foot shocks (Fanselow & Sigmundi, 1982). Fighting emerges only after many presentations of foot shock. Presumably, the attacks are an attempt to halt shock delivery, and rats attribute the delivery of shock to their cohort.

In the analysis of defense it may be important to distinguish between immediate and subsequent behaviors. Let us consider a hypothetical situation that involves a rat encountering a threat. When a rat receives a shock via a shock prod, the animal's initial response is to retreat from the shock source and then exhibit freezing behavior. Later the animal may return to the shock source's vicinity, and then it may exhibit freezing, stretch-attend, and defensive burying behaviors. The animal may also move away from the shock prod in a manner that resembles retreat to a burrow.

In the previous section we described the functional behavior systems view of defensive behavior. This view suggests that defensive behavior is organized by a continuum of perceived danger: When the threat is perceived, rats express specific sets of defensive behaviors that are qualitatively different from those expressed when the threat has not been detected. This discrimination may also vary with time if animals continually update their concept of perceived danger. This updating process may then contribute to the selection of defensive behaviors in the shock prod scenario: Initially, rats move away from the shock source and freeze, and later on they freeze, bury, and stretch-attend. Notice that the movement away from the shock prod expressed immediately differs from the flight expressed later. Thus, the immediate response to shock delivery may differ qualitatively from subsequent responses to the environment because the animal has updated its concept of perceived danger. Such updating likely depends on the basic principles of extinction, or possibly the reconsolidation phenomenon that has recently received attention (Nader, Schafe, & LeDoux, 2000).

Neural Substrates of Learned Defensive Behavior

Mammalian species share fundamentally similar brain circuits that underlie fear behavior. Indeed, in humans, rats, mice, rabbits, and monkeys the amygdala is a prominent component of the fear circuit. To date, more is known about the brain circuits that support learned fear owing to the popularity of Pavlovian fear conditioning as a model for experimental analysis. Less is known about innate fear circuitry, although evidence seems to suggest that these circuits overlap (e.g., Walker & Davis, 1997). Fendt and Fanselow (1999) have provided a comprehensive review of the neural structures of defensive behavior. Numerous brain structures mediate the acquisition and expression of Pavlovian learned fear.

The Amygdala

The amygdala consists of a cluster of interconnected nuclei that reside in the medial temporal lobe. Brown and Schaffer (1886) provided the first evidence that implicated the amygdala in emotional processing. They demonstrated that large lesions of the temporal lobe tamed previously fierce monkeys. Similarly, Kluver and Bucy (1939) described the emotional disturbances triggered by these large lesions, and Weiskrantz (1956) reported that many features of the disturbance were generated by more selective damage to the amygdala. Based on work done primarily with the Pavlovian fear conditioning paradigm, three nuclei within the amygdala are known to make major contributions to fear behavior: the lateral (LA), basal (BA), and central nuclei (CEA).

The lateral and basal nuclei comprise the *frontotemporal complex* (FTC; Swanson & Petrovich, 1998). This complex communicates most closely with the frontal and temporal lobes, and it is important in the acquisition of learned fear. Moreover, the FTC has characteristics that make it a plausible site of encoding for the learned association that is established during fear conditioning (Fanselow & LeDoux, 1999). First, the FTC receives inputs from all sensory modalities, including brain regions that are involved with nociception (Fendt & Fanselow, 1999). Thus, sensory information of the CS and pain information of the US converge in the FTC. Second, Pavlovian fear conditioning enhances the response of cells in the FTC that respond to tone CSs (Quirk, Repa, & LeDoux, 1995). Third, lesions of the FTC produce a pronounced and often total loss of many Pavlovian fear responses (e.g, Maren, 1998); fourth, chemical inactivation of this structure is similarly disruptive to fear learning (e.g., Gewirtz & Davis, 1997). Thus, the FTC is critical for the acquisition of Pavlovian fear conditioning and is a plausible site for the encoding and storage of the learned association.

The CEA may be conceived of as the output of the amygdala. It is closely tied with the striatum and is specialized to modulate motor outflow (Swanson & Petrovich, 1998). The CEA projects to a variety of structures, including the periaqueductal gray (PAG), the reticular formation, and the lateral hypothalamus. Both the lateral and basal nuclei of the amygdala project to the CEA. Lesions to the CEA disrupt the expression of a wide range of defensive behaviors (e.g., Kapp, Frysinger, Gallagher, & Haselton, 1979).

The Periaqueductal Gray

The PAG is highly interconnected with the CEA (Rizvi, Ennis, Behbehani, & Shipley, 1991). This region seems to act as a coordinator of defensive behaviors, and expression of defensive behaviors can be dissociated within the PAG. For example, electrical stimulation of the dorsal-lateral PAG (dlPAG) triggers robust activity burst–like behavior (Fanselow, 1994), whereas damage to this structure disrupts the shock-induced activity burst (Fanselow, 1994). Similarly, chemical stimulation of the caudal third of the dlPAG triggers "bursts of forward locomotion" that alternate with periods of immobility (Bandler & Depaulis, 1991, p. 183). Consequently, the dlPAG seems to coordinate overt defensive reactions, such as flight.

In contrast, similar treatments to the ventral PAG (vPAG) have very different effects. Chemical or electrical stimulation of the vPAG triggers freezing behavior, and lesions to this structure disrupt conditional freezing to aversive CSs (Fanselow, 1991). Other fear responses can also be dissociated within the vPAG. For example, the infusion of an opiate antagonist will disrupt fear-induced analgesia but spare conditioned freezing (Fanselow, 1991). Thus, the vPAG seems to coordinate conditional freezing and opiate analgesia. Based on these results, Fanselow (1994) suggested that postencounter defenses are related to the vPAG and its inputs from the amygdala, whereas circa-strike behaviors are related to the dlPAG and its inputs from the superior colliculus. At this time, little is known about the neural substrates of preencounter defenses.

Neural Substrates of Unlearned Defensive Behavior

Much less is known about the neural substrates of innate fear behavior. Walker and Davis (1997) reported that chemical inactivation of the bed nucleus of the stria terminalis (BNST) disrupts light-potentiated startle, but chemical inactivation of the CEA disrupts only fear-potentiated startle. Inactivation of the FTC disrupts both behaviors. Thus, available evidence suggests that learned and unlearned fear responses can be dissociated within a region described as the extended amygdala (Swanson & Petrovich, 1998). Wallace and Rosen (2001) reported that electrolytic lesions to the LA disrupt freezing to a predator's odor, whereas excitotoxic lesions did not. Both these lesions disrupt freezing to learned fear stimuli. This result suggests that innate and learned fear can also be dissociated within the amygdala.

SEXUAL MOTIVATION

Nothing is more closely tied to evolutionary fitness than reproductive success. The most direct measure of reproductive success is the number of offspring that survive, and therefore the terminal goal of a sexual behavior system is successful production of offspring. Animal species display a wide variety of reproductive strategies to produce offspring. *Monogamy* involves the pairing of a single male and female for the duration of the reproductive cycle. This strategy occurs mostly in species that split the burden of parental care across both parents. *Polygyny* involves the association of a single male with multiple females, and *polyandry* involves the association of a single female with multiple males. These polygamous strategies are common in species that distribute the burden of parental care unequally. These mating strategies often influence sexual motivation. Monogamous animals very often display biparental care of offspring, and sexual learning does not typically influence male competition in these species. Accordingly, sexual motivation in monogamous species is relatively similar across sexes. In contrast, species that display intense male competition typically adopt polygamy, and sexual learning and motivation vary greatly across sex (Domjan & Hollis, 1988).

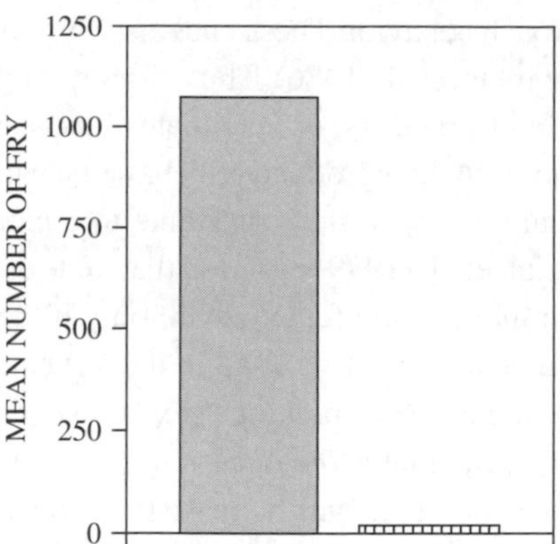

Figure 2.3 The mean number of offspring hatched in the Pavlovian-paired (black bar) and unpaired (hatched bar) groups. Fry were counted six days after spawning (adapted from Hollis et al., 1997).

Cues That Signal Reproductive Opportunity

Many species display cues that connote reproductive availability. These cues frequently are shaped by the genotype of the animal. For example, in rodent species olfaction is the primary sensory modality; rodents smell much better than they see. Accordingly, olfactory cues such as pheromones often signal a sexual opportunity in rodent species (Pfaff & Pfaffman, 1969). In contrast, birds see better than they smell, and visual cues ordinarily provide mating signals (Domjan & Hall, 1986). Females of species that undergo estrus often display overt cues that signal reproductive availability. For example, in primate species, such as the chimpanzee, females display swelling of the vaginal lips during estrus, and this cue signals reproductive availability (Mook, 1987).

Sign Stimuli

In some species the appearance of a member of the opposite gender is the dominant cue for a mating opportunity. However, often the essential cue can be reduced to an element or component of the mating partner. These components, called sign stimuli (Tinbergen, 1951), are sufficient to elicit sexual behaviors. For example, male chickens attempt to copulate with models of the torso of female conspecifics (Carbaugh, Schein, & Hale, 1962), and male quails attempt to mate with models including a female quail's head and neck (Domjan, Lyons, North, & Bruell, 1986). Thus, mere components of a whole animal are sufficient cues to elicit reproductive behavior.

Learned Cues

Learning certainly contributes to the recognition of reproductive opportunity. For instance, male blue gourami fish (*Trichogaster trichopterus*) normally display aggressive territorial behavior. These fish compete with other males for nest sites, and they attack intruders because the control of territory confers reproductive advantage. This aggressive tendency is so pronounced that males often spoil mating opportunities by mistakenly attacking female gouramis. However, male gouramis can learn to anticipate the approach of a female gourami when a cue reliably precedes her appearance during conditioning sessions (Hollis, Cadieux, & Colbert, 1989; Hollis et al., 1997). As a result of such Pavlovian conditioning, the cue acts as a CS that signals the appearance of the female. Males trained with this contingency both display less aggression toward females and spawn more offspring (Hollis et al., 1997; Figure 2.3). Thus, learning contributes to the recognition of a reproductive opportunity. Moreover, it contributes to evolutionary fitness by increasing fecundity. This result by Hollis et al. stands as the single most direct and unequivocal evidence that Pavlovian conditioning, indeed any form of learning, has a direct influence on evolutionary success (Figure 2.4).

Learning also contributes to the mating success of male Japanese quails (*Coturnix japonica*). For instance, neutral cues previously paired with a sexual encounter elicit CRs,

Figure 2.4 A male and female blue gourami.

such as approach behavior. These cues also shorten copulatory latencies (Domjan, et al., 1986). Thus, discrete Pavlovian CSs, such as red lights, buzzers, or inanimate objects, can elicit responses that facilitate reproductive behaviors in the quail.

Contextual cues may also contribute to reproductive signaling. Domjan et al. (1989) reported that male quails attempt to mate with models of a female quail only if they have previously copulated with a live quail in the test chamber. Thus, the location or context of previous sexual experience can act as a signal that facilitates the occurrence of sexual behavior. Additionally, contextual cues increase the male quail's sperm production (Domjan, Blesbois, & Williams, 1998). Notably, this demonstrates that Pavlovian learning may directly enhance reproductive success by facilitating the bird's ability to fertilize multiple eggs and produce offspring.

Sexual learning also directly influences mate selection. For example, when an orange feather is repeatedly paired with a sexual encounter, male quails display a preference for birds adorned with this cue. Males both spend more time near and display more copulatory behaviors toward these females compared to controls (Domjan, O'Vary, & Greene, 1988). Thus, Pavlovian conditioning sways attractiveness, thereby influencing mate selection.

Along with neutral cues, learning also facilitates the sexual efficacy of sign stimuli. For example, the model of a female's head and neck elicits copulatory behavior in experienced, but not in sexually naive, male quails (Domjan et al., 1989). Thus, during sexual encounters these birds may learn to identify species-typical cues, such as the plumage of female conspecifics.

Organization of the Sexual Behavior System

Sexual behavior does not begin and end with the act of copulation. Instead, species exhibit numerous behaviors that contribute to reproductive success that are not directly connected to the sex act. For example, male blue gouramis build nests used for spawning prior to contact with female conspecifics. This behavior improves reproductive success because nest occupancy increases the probability that these fish will attract a mate. Concurrently, these fish compete with male conspecifics to secure suitable nesting areas, and they display aggressive territorial behavior to defend or take control of a nest site. Thus, because these behaviors can greatly increase reproductive opportunities, sexual behavior can be linked to activities that are temporally distant from the sex act.

Domjan and associates (e.g., Domjan & Hall, 1986) described a set of behaviors that contribute to the reproductive success of Japanese quails. Males engage in general search behavior when they encounter cues distal to the female. For example, birds pace around the test chamber when they encounter a cue that has been conditioned with a long CS-US interval. This cue is relatively distal to the female because it signals that a female will appear only after a long time period elapses (Akins, Domjan, & Gutierrez, 1994). In contrast, cues conditioned with a short CS-US interval elicit focal search behavior. For instance, birds approach a red light that has previously been paired with a sexual encounter (Akins et al., 1994). This cue is relatively proximal because it signals that the female will appear after a short time period elapses. Male quails also engage in copulatory or consummatory sexual responses (Figure 2.5). These responses are elicited by cues signaling that a sexual encounter is imminent. Thus, female conspecifics or sign stimuli elicit copulatory behavior.

Figure 2.5 Two Japanese quail display mounting, one component of copulatory behavior.

Domjan and his colleagues have characterized a range of stimuli that elicit an array of sexual responses in the Japanese quail. With these observations Domjan has articulated a behavioral systems account of sexual behavior that contains both a stimulus and a response dimension. Each dimension includes three categories. The response dimension includes general search behavior, focal search behavior, and copulatory behavior. The stimulus dimension includes contextual cues, local cues, and species-typical cues.

In the model, stimuli are arranged on a temporal and spatial continuum that varies by the cue's proximity to the female quail. This continuum is similar to the spatiotemporal organization hypothesized by Timberlake (1983) in his feeding behavior system and by Fanselow (1989) in his description of defensive behavior, both discussed earlier. Prior to sexual conditioning, contextual and local cues are distal from the female and do not activate sexual behavior, whereas species-typical cues are more proximal and can elicit sexual behavior unconditionally. After a sexual conditioning event, contextual and local cues may elicit sexual behavior, and responding to species-typical cues is facilitated. Thus, according to Domjan's view, "conditioning serves to increase the range of stimuli that are effective in eliciting sexual behavior" (Domjan, 1994, p. 426). That is, learning shifts the position of cues on the continuum by increasing their proximity to the female and thereby enhancing the cues' ability to release sexual responses.

This shift on the continuum is manifested also by the change in repertoire of responses that stimuli come to elicit. Prior to conditioning, local cues elicit weak general search behavior. After conditioning they may trigger both focal search and copulatory behavior. Additionally, the strength of general search behavior is enhanced. For example, approach behavior is a form of local search behavior. Quails display approach behavior to a red light only after the cue has been paired with a sexual encounter (Domjan et al., 1986).

In the introduction we made the point that behavior is a bidirectional interaction among motivation, learning, and genetics. Perhaps nowhere is this clearer than in sexual motivation. The work of Domjan and Hollis indicates that experience strongly influences with which members of our species we prefer to mate. Because Pavlovian conditioning determines attractiveness, it also determines which sets of genes recombine. Because conditioning determines reproductive success, measured rather directly by sperm and offspring production, it also determines what genes are best represented in the next generation of many vertebrate species. Not only does the reproductive success that drives evolution influence our learning abilities, but our learning abilities drive that reproductive success as well.

TEMPERATURE MOTIVATION

Body temperature regulation is essential for the survival of animal species. Most species are adapted to the temperature range of their niche, and they can only maintain normal activity within a relatively narrow window of body temperature imposed by their genetic makeup. At extreme body temperatures critical enzymes cannot function, energy metabolism is compromised, and body systems fail. Thus, animals that fail to maintain body temperature within the critical range of their species die. Because of this stringent evolutionary selective pressure, species have adapted multiple strategies to cope with the problem of body temperature regulation.

Thermoregulatory Responses

Species utilize both physiological and behavioral means to cope with the environmental demands of body temperature regulation. These two categories of processes interact to provide an adequate temperature regulation strategy in each species and individual. Specific body temperature regulation strategies abound in the animal kingdom (e.g., Prosser & Nelson, 1981; Bartholomew, 1982). In this section we describe several strategies of thermoregulation that have evolved. Two broad categories of these strategies are *ectothermy* and *endothermy.* Ectothermic animals rely on environmental heat for body warming. Endothermic animals use metabolic heat for body warming. Animals belonging to these broad groups often display distinct behavioral tendencies because these strategies impose different thermoregulatory needs.

The Mountain Lizard

The South American mountain lizard (*Liolamus*) is both an ectotherm and a *poikilotherm.* Poikilotherms are ectothermic animals whose body temperature may vary widely at different times of the day or year. These animals often maintain body temperatures that exceed the environmental temperature during periods of activity, whereas they display relatively cold body temperatures during periods of inactivity. To accomplish these extremes, poikilotherms rely heavily on behavioral means to regulate body temperature. For example, *Liolamus* avoids freezing Andes temperatures by staying in its burrow during the night. Just after sunrise the animal emerges and moves to a position exposed to direct sunlight to absorb solar energy until its body temperature shifts from approximately 5°C to upward of 30°C. Throughout the day this lizard shuttles between sunlit and shaded microenvironments to maintain this body temperature (Bartholomew, 1982).

The Polar Bear

Polar bears live in and near the Arctic Circle. These large mammals are endotherms, and they commonly sustain activity in extreme thermal conditions that range from approximately 15°C in summer months to −30°C in winter months. Because of these drastic seasonal environmental demands, polar bears have adapted strategies that permit the animal to maintain its body temperature across the full range of environmental temperatures in its habitat.

Polar bears are genetically organized to cope with the temperature demands of their niche, and this organization is manifested in physiological adaptations. First, polar bears have a layer of blubber and fur over much of their bodies. This tissue helps insulate the animal and maintain its body temperature in winter months. Second, a polar bear's snout, ears, nose,

Figure 2.6 A polar bear lies on ice to expose its hot spots and cool off.

footpads, and inner thighs dissipate heat efficiently because they have limited insulation (Stirling, 1988). As we shall see, these physiological adaptations contribute to an effective behavioral thermoregulation scheme useful in both hot and cold environments.

As mentioned earlier, polar bears have several poorly insulated body areas, or hot spots. These hot spots are useful for behavioral thermoregulation because bears can adopt distinct postures depending on whether they need to expel or conserve heat. In warm environments, bears dissipate heat by exposing these hot spots, and in colder environments they conceal these areas (Stirling, 1988; Figure 2.6). Notice that the form of the bear's response is sensitive to environmental temperature. This thermoregulatory scheme is fairly common among endotherms.

The Rat

Rats are small mammals that live commensally with humans. These animals populate temperate zones and also live inside burrows and buildings in cold climates. Rats are endotherms that exhibit a variety of thermoregulatory behaviors (Hainsworth & Stricker, 1970). The rat's body temperature typically varies between 37°C and 38°C at neutral environmental temperatures (approximately 28°C). When environmental temperatures rise above this level, rats display a constellation of responses that promote metabolic efficiency and survival. For example, when environmental temperatures range between 36°C and 41°C, rats exhibit a sustained hyperthermia with a magnitude that exceeds the environmental temperature. This phenomenon is an adaptive and regulated response. Rats benefit from this increase in body temperature because it permits them to lose metabolic heat to the environment via conduction (Hainsworth & Stricker, 1970). Above 41°C rats are unable to sustain hyperthermia relative to the environment.

Rats also exhibit two behavioral responses to heat stress within the range that provokes hyperthermia (36°C to 41°C). At moderate levels of heat stress, rats frequently lay with a relaxed body posture often called prone extension. Much like the polar bear, the rat uses this behavior to dissipate heat by exposing body regions that conduct heat efficiently. In this case the rat's tail acts as a thermal radiator because it is both vascularized and lacking in insulation. Thus, excess body heat is readily dissipated through the tail (Rand, Burton, & Ing, 1965). Along with prone extension, rats display saliva spreading in response to moderate heat stress. This behavior exploits evaporative cooling as a means to regulate body temperature (Hainsworth, 1967), and it is characterized by the active distribution of saliva from the mouth with the forelimbs. The spreading initially focuses on the head, neck, and paw regions and later targets the ventral regions with emphasis on the scrotum and tail. Saliva spreading is prevalent in animals that lack sweat glands, such as rats, opossums, and desert rodents. Other terrestrial animals, such as humans, exploit evaporative cooling by sweating.

Above approximately 41°C, rats can no longer regulate heat exchange with controlled hyperthermia. Also, the expression of a relaxed body posture gives way to a pronounced increase in activity that is probably a manifestation of escape behavior (Hainsworth, 1967). At higher temperatures, rats also exhibit saliva spreading. The adaptive advantage of this behavior is demonstrated by the observation that desalivated rats die within 1 hr to 2 hr of high heat stress, although normal rats survive for at least 5 hr of exposure (Hainsworth, 1967).

When a pregnant rat encounters inescapable heat stress, it responds with the array of thermoregulatory responses that are typical in her species. For example, the rat will engage in both body extension and saliva spreading when heat stressed (Wilson & Stricker, 1979). However, these animals face amplified thermal demands because their body mass increases relative to the size of the available thermal windows that expel body heat via conduction. Consequently, to regulate body temperature these mothers compensate by lowering their threshold for saliva spreading, and pregnant mothers display saliva spreading at 30°C (Wilson & Stricker, 1979). Similarly, the animal's threshold for salivary secretion from the submaxillary gland decreases, thereby providing an increased saliva reservoir (Wilson & Stricker, 1979). These measures contribute to successful thermoregulation for both the mother and her offspring.

Rat mothers bear sizable litters that remain together until weaning. These pups are particularly susceptible to hypothermia because they produce little metabolic heat that is quickly lost to the environment. Moreover, pups are born with no fur and little insulation, and they do not exhibit thermogenesis via shivering behavior (Hull, 1973). Given these obstacles, rat pups may seem reliant on parental care for thermal regulation. However, when exposed to a cold environment, rat pups clump together in a manner that reduces each pups exposed body surface area. This huddling provides behavioral thermoregulation because it lessens the heat lost to the environment via conduction (Alberts, 1978).

Huddling behavior is modulated by environmental temperature. Specifically, with decreasing environmental temperature, the total surface area of the huddle diminishes. Conversely, the total surface area of the huddle increases as the environmental temperature rises (Alberts, 1978). Thus, pups act as a unit by adjusting their group's exposed surface area in a manner that defends body temperature against environmental changes.

Individual pups follow a typical movement pattern through the huddle that contributes to the changes in the whole litter's exposed surface area. These movements are competitive adjustments that position a pup in a thermally desirable location. In colder environments pups move toward the middle of the huddle, and in warm environments they shift to the periphery (Alberts, 1978). Collectively, these adjustments make the litter behave as an organized unit sensitive to the environmental temperature.

Fever

When mammals are infected by pathogens, they display an array of nonspecific "sickness" responses that include fever and fatigue. Traditionally, these symptoms were thought to result from an inability to perform normal activities because of the compromised physiological state of the sick individual. As an alternative, Bolles and Fanselow (1980) suggested that illness involving fever might be a particularly strong activator of the recuperative motivational system. Consistent with this speculation, investigators have recently suggested that sickness is an adaptive motivational response that aids recuperation (Aubert, 1999; Watkins & Maier, 2000). Importantly, part of the sickness response involves fever: a sustained hyperthermia. Thus, mammals actively modulate their body temperature as an adaptive response to pathogens. Fever and recuperation therefore may have some degree of positive feedback between them.

Learning and Thermoregulatory Responses

Earlier we described how animals learn to anticipate things like danger or to expect the appearance of a potential mating partner. What evidence exists that animals learn to anticipate thermal conditions? Most investigations in this realm have focused on escape behavior (e.g., Howard, 1962) or on the effects that environmental temperatures have on learning acquisition (e.g., Hack, 1933). In a typical escape procedure an animal is exposed to an aversive stimulus until it performs a response. For example, rats exposed to cold temperatures will press a bar to gain access to a heat lamp. Over trials, rats become very efficient at this response, and they often drive the ambient temperature up to room temperature. But what do the animals learn during these conditioning trials? Animals may learn that the bar pressing makes the chamber warm, but these studies provide little evidence for the notion that rats perform thermoregulatory responses because they *anticipate* the problem.

Very few studies demonstrate that animals will learn to perform a response that avoids hot or cold stress. Nor do many studies demonstrate that thermal cues can elicit learned CRs. Interestingly, studies that demonstrate these responses to thermal reinforcers have frequently used infant animals as subjects. For example, newborn chicks can be autoshaped to peck a bar for food (Wasserman, 1973). Newborn dogs will perform an avoidance response to avoid a cold reinforcer (Stanley, Barrett, & Bacon, 1974), and newborn rat pups exhibit tachycardia as a CR when an odor is paired with cold temperature (Martin & Alberts, 1982).

Recall that newborn animals, such as the rat pup, have little insulation and that thermoregulation requires more elaborate behavioral strategies. Perhaps we more readily observe thermal Pavlovian conditioning in the rat pup because its niche requires such learning. This suggestion may have implications for how we view thermoregulatory behavior, and it is further developed in the next section.

A Thermoregulatory Behavior System?

We have described how animals regulate body temperature with both physiological and behavioral means. Conspicuously, we have not yet provided substantial analysis of these responses. Why then would they be included in a chapter on the topic of motivation? Let us consider the traditional account of thermoregulatory behavior before we answer this question.

The Homeostatic Explanation

The concept of homeostasis has been the fundamental principle employed by traditional explanations of thermoregulatory behavior. This idea, first applied by Cannon (1932), assumes that each animal has a body temperature set point, and that thermoregulatory behavior is activated whenever the animal is perturbed from this reference. Thus, if an animal is cold, it automatically performs a series of responses to return to its set point. This explanation implies that the animal uses a "comparator" to assess the difference between its actual body temperature and its set point temperature and that whenever there is a discrepancy between these values, the system activates behaviors to remedy the discrepancy.

Santinoff (1983) provided both an eloquent review of the neural circuitry of thermoregulation and an explanation of homeostasis. The reader is advised to consult the work for both a useful historical perspective and a comprehensive analysis of the subject. Available evidence suggests that the anterior hypothalamus (AH) and the preoptic (POA) provide a significant contribution to the neural control of thermoregulatory behavior in mammals. For example, body temperature in animals with lesions to these areas has been shown to drop sharply in cold environments (e.g., Satinoff & Rutstein, 1970). Similarly, appropriate thermoregulatory responses are activated when this structure is either cooled or heated (e.g., Fusco, Hardy, & Hammel, 1961), and electrical stimulation of this region elicits prone extension (Roberts & Mooney, 1974). Additionally, the POA and AH also contain neurons that are sensitive to temperature change (Nakayama, Hammel, Hardy, & Eisenman, 1963). Thus, the AH and POA have the capacity to detect changes in temperatures; damage to this region disrupts thermoregulation; and stimulation of this region elicits appropriate responding. Together, these observations suggest that the AH and POA complex might be the neural manifestation of the comparator that detects deviance from thermal homeostasis. However, lesions to this complex do not disrupt some forms of behavioral thermoregulation. For example, rats with AH lesions are able to bar press to obtain access to a warm heat lamp in a cold environment (Satinoff & Rutstein, 1970). Thus, animals with AH lesions can both detect perturbations from their normal body temperature and perform an appropriate response to hypothermia. These and other observations argue against the hypothesis that suggests the AH and POA are the neural locus for the thermoregulatory comparator. Satinoff (1983) has developed a more sophisticated theory of thermoregulation that suggests multiple comparators linked to separate thermoregulatory behaviors and these units are organized in a hierarchical manner.

The principle of homeostatic thermoregulation suggests that regulatory responses occur whenever body temperature deviates from the set point. This homeostatic explanation does not require a motivational system, but we suggest that thermoregulation does. That is, perhaps a behavioral systems approach to thermoregulatory behavior is warranted. Let us consider several points. First, the cost of ineffective thermoregulation is significant, so there is evolutionary pressure to develop sophisticated thermoregulatory schemes. Second, numerous animal species have adapted elaborate behavioral strategies that assist in thermoregulation. Ectotherms rely almost entirely on behavioral means. Other animals, such as the rat, display an array of thermoregulatory behaviors that could be organized on a continuum of relative heat stress. Indeed, these behaviors seem to vary with the rat's niche, as neonates display a different repertoire than do adults. Third, some responses to heat stress are incompatible with the "homeostatic" account of thermoregulation. For example, rats display a controlled hyperthermia response under conditions of heat stress, and mammals exhibit fever when they are infected by pathogens. These responses actively increase the discrepancy in body temperature from the animal's set point. Thus, these responses are incompatible with the concept of a homeostasis unless resetting the reference temperature is a valid means at achieving homeostasis. Fourth, infant animals provide the best examples of learning in relation to thermal cues. These animals must cope with thermal challenge in their niche. Perhaps we detect their ability to learn about thermal cues because learning about these cues is critical to their survival. Conceivably, many animals in many systems can learn about thermal cues, and we have not detected them only because the homeostatic thermoregulatory explanation ignores the relevance of learning.

In summary, thermoregulation is crucial to survival in perhaps every niche, and many behavioral responses have been developed to cope with the problem. Given the cost of poor thermoregulation and the propensity for animals to learn and adapt, we propose that the study of thermoregulatory behavior may profit by adopting a behavior systems approach.

CONCLUSIONS

We began this chapter by suggesting that motivation accounts for that proportion of the variation in behavior not accounted for by learned and genetic influences. Why is it that an animal in the same environment presented with the same food will eat on one occasion and not on another? Given that genetic influences have been held constant and that no new information has been learned about the food or the environment, this variation must be due to changes in motivation manifested through changes in behavior. The challenge with defining motivation is to avoid merely redescribing the behavior in new and empirically intractable terms. The method we have suggested for avoiding this problem is to specify the environmental cause and behavioral effect of any changes in the hypothesized motivational construct. By defining these antecedents and consequences in terms of the ecological and evolutionary problems the animal must solve, we protect ourselves from explanations that assume an unlimited number of "motivations," as did the old theories of instinct. In addition, this focus on the functional aspects of motivational processes forces us to consider both the ecological niche that the animal occupies and the organization of the behaviors it uses to cope with the problems of the niche.

This explicitly ecological view allows the concept of motivation to make contact with behavioral ecology and evolution. Learning and genetics are not the sole determinants of behavior; an animal's ecological niche must also be considered. Animals have evolved solutions to specific environmental problems, and an understanding of these relationships can inform psychological theories of motivation and learning. Collier and Johnson (1990) suggested that appreciating that small predators are themselves potential prey gives insight into the differences in feeding rate between small and large predators. Indeed, Fanselow et al. (1988) have demonstrated that predatory risk is an important determinant in the initiation of feeding behavior. Traditional homeostatic perspectives could not contribute this insight.

In addition to highlighting the importance of ecological variables in determining motivational influences on behavior, the analyses presented in this chapter can also be used to examine similarities and differences between motivational systems. A persistent theoretical problem in theories of motivation has been specifying the number and form of motivational processes with which an animal is equipped. We have suggested that the animal is equipped with as many motivational systems as there are classes of problems in the environment for it to solve. We expect that the reader has been struck by the amount of similarity between the response organizations proposed to account for feeding and sexual behavior, and to a lesser extent between those structures and that proposed to account for the organization of defensive behavior. Each consists of a collection of motivational modes organized by some kind of imminence continuum. Each includes a set of preexisting stimulus processing and response production tendencies. The extent to which these similarities are valid remains to be determined, and this question deserves study. Just as interesting are those disparities between the response organizations. Appetitive behavior in the feeding behavior system is extremely flexible. Flexibility in sexually motivated appetitive behavior has also been demonstrated but is much less well investigated. In contrast, defensive behavior seems more rigid, perhaps due to the inherently conservative nature of defense.

The behavioral systems view suggests that motivation is a much more complex phenomenon than that described by theories of drive, incentive motivation, or opposing affective states. Any complete conception must include physiological, psychological, ecological, and evolutionary factors. Our approach attempts to address these requirements.

REFERENCES

Akins, C. K., Domjan, M., & Gutierrez, G. (1994). Topography of sexually conditioned behavior in male Japanese quail (*Coturnix japonica*) depends on the CS-US interval. *Journal of Experimental Psychology: Animal Behavior Processes, 20,* 199–209.

Alberts, J. R. (1978). Huddling by rat pups: Group behavioral mechanisms of temperature regulation and energy conservation. *Journal of Comparative & Physiological Psychology, 92,* 231–245.

Aubert, A. (1999). Sickness and behaviour in animals: A motivational perspective. *Neuroscience & Biobehavioral Reviews, 23,* 1029–1036.

Balleine, B. (1992). Instrumental performance following a shift in primary motivation depends upon incentive learning. *Journal of Experimental Psychology: Animal Behavior Processes, 18,* 236–250.

Balleine, B., Garner, C., Gonzalez, F. & Dickinson, A. (1995). Motivational control of heterogeneous instrumental chains. *Journal of Experimental Psychology: Animal Behavior Processes, 21,* 203–217.

Bandler, R., & Depaulis, A. (1991). Midbrain periaqueductal gray control of defensive behavior in the cat and rat. In A. Depauilis & R. Bandler (Eds.), *The midbrain periaqueductal gray matter: Functional, anatomical and immunohistochemical organization* (pp. 175–199). New York: Plenum Press.

Bartholomew, G. A. (1982). Body temperature and energy metabolism. In M. A. Gordon (Ed.), *Animal physiology* (pp. 333–406). New York: Macmillan.

Blanchard, R. J., & Blanchard, D. C. (1972). Effects of hippocampal lesions on the rat's reaction to a cat. *Journal of Comparative & Physiological Psychology, 78,* 77–82.

Blanchard, R. J., & Blanchard, D. C. (1989). Antipredator defensive behaviors in a visible burrow system. *Journal of Comparative Psychology, 103,* 70–82.

Blanchard, R. J., Fukunaga, K. K., & Blanchard, D. C. (1976). Environmental control of defensive reactions to a cat. *Bulletin of the Psychonomic Society, 8,* 179–181.

Blanchard, R. J., Mast, M., & Blanchard, D. C. (1975). Stimulus control of defensive reactions in the albino rat. *Journal of Comparative & Physiological Psychology, 88,* 81–88.

Blanchard, R. J., Nikulina, J. N., Sakai, R. R., McKittrick, C., McEwen, B., & Blanchard, D. C. (1998). Behavioral and endocrine change following chronic predatory stress. *Physiology & Behavior, 63,* 561–569.

Bolhuis, J. J., Hetebrij, E., Den Boer-Visser, A. M., De Groot, J. H., & Zijlstra, G. G. (2001). Localized immediate early gene expression related to the strength of song learning in socially reared zebra finches. *European Journal of Neuroscience, 13,* 2165–2170.

Bolles, R. C. (1970). Species-specific defense reactions and avoidance learning. *Psychological Review, 77,* 32–48.

Bolles, R. C. (1975). *Theory of motivation.* New York: Harper and Row.

Bolles, R. C. (1980). Some functional thoughts about regulation. In F. M. Toates & T. R. Halliday (Eds.), *Analysis of motivational processes,* (pp. 62–76). London: Academic Press.

Bolles, R. C., & Fanselow, M. S. (1980). A perceptual-defensive-recuperative model of fear and pain. *Behavioral & Brain Sciences, 3,* 291–323.

Bolles, R. C., & Riley, A. L. (1973). Freezing as an avoidance response: Another look at the operant-respondent distinction. *Learning & Motivation, 4,* 268–275.

Bouton, M. E., Mineka, S., & Barlow, D. H. (2001). A modern learning theory perspective on the etiology of panic disorder. *Psychological Review, 108,* 4–32.

Breland, K., & Breland, M. (1961). The misbehavior of organisms. *American Psychologist, 16,* 681–684.

Breland, K., & Breland, M. (1966). *Animal behavior.* New York: Academic Press.

Brett, L. P., Hankins, W. G., & Garcia, J. (1976). Prey-lithium aversions: Vol. 3. Buteo hawks. *Behavioral Biology, 17,* 87–98.

Brown, S., & Schaffer, A. (1886). An investigation into the functions of the occipital and temporal lobes of the monkey's brain. *Philosophical Transactions of the Royal Society of London, 179,* 303–327.

Cabanac, M. (1971). Physiological role of pleasure. *Science, 173,* 1103–1107.

Cannon, W. B. (1932). *The wisdom of the body*. New York: W. W. Norton.

Carbaugh, B. T., Schein, M. W., & Hale, E. B. (1962). Effects of morphological variations of chicken models on sexual responses of cocks. *Animal Behaviour, 10,* 235–238.

Castonguay, T. W., Kaiser, L., & Stern, J. S. (1986). Meal pattern analysis: Artifacts, assumptions and implications. *Brain Research Bulletin, 17,* 439–443.

Collier, G. H. (1982). Determinants of choice. In D. J. Bernstein (Ed.), *Nebraska symposium on motivation: Vol. 3. Response structure and motivation* (pp. 69–127). Lincoln: University of Nebraska Press.

Collier, G. H. (1983). Life in closed economy: The ecology of learning and motivation. In M. D. Zeiler & P. Harzem (Eds.), *Advances in the analysis of behavior* (Vol. 3, pp. 223–274). Chichester, UK: Wiley.

Collier, G. H. (1986). The dialogue between the house economist and the resident physiologist. *Nutrition and Behavior, 3,* 9–26.

Collier, G. H. (1987). Operant methodologies for studying feeding and drinking. In F. Toates & N. Rowland (Eds.), *Methods and techniques for studying feeding and drinking behavior* (pp. 37–76). Amsterdam: Elsevier.

Collier, G. H., Hirsch, E., & Hamlin, P. H. (1972). The ecological determinants of reinforcement in the rat. *Physiology & Behavior, 9,* 705–716.

Collier, G. H., & Johnson, D. F. (1990). The time window of feeding. *Physiology & Behavior*, *48,* 771–777.

Collier, G. H., & Johnson, D. F. (1997). Who is in charge? Animal versus experimenter control. *Appetite*, *29,* 159–180.

Collier, G. H., Johnson, D. F., Borin, G., & Mathis, C. E. (1994). Drinking in a patchy environment: The effect of the price of water. *Journal of the Experimental Analysis of Behavior, 63,* 169–184.

Collier, G. H., Johnson, D. F., & Mitchell, C. (1999). The relation between meal size and the time between meals: effects of cage complexity and food cost. *Physiology & Behavior, 67,* 339–346.

Coss, R. G., & Owings, D. H. (1978). Snake-directed behavior by snake naive and experienced California ground squirrels in a simulated burrow. *Zeitschrift fuer Tierpsychologie, 48,* 421–435.

Craig, W. (1918). Appetites and aversions as the constituents of instincts. *Biological Bulletin of Marine Biology, Woods Hole, MA*, *34,* 91–107.

Davidson, T. L. (1998). Hunger cues as modulatory stimuli. In N. A. Schmajuk & P. C. Hollands (Eds.), *Occasion setting: Associative learning and cognition in animals* (pp. 223–248). Washington, DC: American Psychological Association.

Davis, M. (1986). Pharmacological and anatomical analysis of fear conditioning using the fear-potentiated startle paradigm. *Behavioral Neuroscience*, *100,* 814–824.

Di Cesnola, A. P. (1904). Preliminary note on the protective value of colour in *Mantis religiosa. Biometrika, 3,* 58–59.

Dickinson, A., & Balleine, B. (1994). Motivational control of goal-directed action. *Animal Learning & Behavior, 22,* 1–18.

Dickinson, A., Balleine, B., Watt, A., Gonzalez, F., & Boakes, R. A. (1995). Motivational control after extended instrumental training. *Animal Learning & Behavior, 23,* 197–206.

Domjan, M. (1994). Formulation of a behavior system for sexual conditioning. *Psychonomic Bulletin & Review, 1,* 421–428.

Domjan, M., Blesbois, E., & Williams, J. (1998). The adaptive significance of sexual conditioning: Pavlovian control of sperm release. *Psychological Science, 9,* 411–415.

Domjan, M., Greene, P., & North, N. C. (1989). Contextual conditioning and the control of copulatory behavior by species-specific sign stimuli in male Japanese quail. *Journal of Experimental Psychology: Animal Behavior Processes, 15,* 147–153.

Domjan, M., & Hall, S. (1986). Determinants of social proximity in Japanese quail (*Coturnix coturnix japonica*): Male behavior. *Journal of Comparative Psychology, 100,* 59–67.

Domjan, M., & Hollis, K. L. (1988). Reproductive behavior: A potential model system for adaptive specializations in learning. In R. C. Bolles & M. D. Beecher (Eds.), *Evolution and learning* (pp. 213–237). Hillsdale, NJ: Erlbaum.

Domjan, M., Lyons, R., North, N. C., & Bruell, J. (1986). Sexual Pavlovian conditioned approach behavior in male Japanese quail (*Coturnix coturnix japonica*). *Journal of Comparative Psychology, 100,* 413–421.

Domjan, M., O'Vary, D., & Greene, P. (1988). Conditioning of appetitive and consummatory sexual behavior in male Japanese Quail. *Journal of the Experimental Analysis of Behavior, 50,* 505–519.

Edmunds, M. (1974). *Defence in animals: A survey of anti-predator defences*. Burnt Mill, UK: Longman.

Estes, R. D. (1967a). Predators and scavengers: Part 1. *Natural History N. Y., 76,* 20–29.

Estes, R. D. (1967b). Predators and scavengers: Part 2. *Natural History N. Y., 76,* 38–47.

Estes, W. K., & Skinner, B. F. (1941). Some quantitative properties of anxiety. *Journal of Experimental Psychology, 29,* 390–400.

Fanselow, M. S. (1980). Conditional and unconditional components of post-shock freezing in rats. *Pavlovian Journal of Biological Sciences, 15,* 177–182.

Fanselow, M. S. (1986). Associative vs. topographical accounts of the immediate-shock freezing deficit in rats: Implications for the response selection rules governing species-specific defensive reactions. *Learning & Motivation, 17,* 16–39.

Fanselow, M. S. (1989). The adaptive function of conditioned defensive behavior: An ecological approach to Pavlovian stimulus-substitution theory. In R. J. Blanchard & P. F. Brain (Eds.), *Ethoexperimental approaches to the study of behavior* (pp. 151–166). Norwell, MA: Kluwer.

Fanselow, M. S. (1991). The midbrain periaqueductal gray as a coordinator of action in response to fear and anxiety. In A. Depaulis & R. Bandler (Eds.), *The midbrain periaqueductal gray matter: Functional, anatomical and immunohistochemical organization* (pp. 151–173). New York: Plenum.

Fanselow, M. S. (1994). Neural organization of the defensive behavior system responsible for fear. *Psychonomic Bulletin & Review, 1,* 429–438.

Fanselow, M. S., & LeDoux, J. E. (1999). Why we think plasticity underlying Pavlovian fear conditioning occurs in the basolateral amygdala. *Neuron, 23,* 229–232.

Fanselow, M., & Lester, L. (1988). A functional behavioristic approach to aversively motivated behavior: Predatory imminence as a determinant of the topography of defensive behavior. In R. C. Bolles & M. D. Beecher (Eds.), *Evolution and learning* (pp.185–211). Hillsdale, NJ: Erlbaum.

Fanselow, M. S., Lester, L. S., & Helmstetter, F. J. (1988). Changes in feeding and foraging patterns as an antipredator defensive strategy: A laboratory simulation using aversive stimulation in a closed economy. *Journal of the Experimental Analysis of Behavior, 50,* 361–374.

Fanselow, M. S., & Sigmundi, R. A. (1982). The enhancement and reduction of defensive fighting by naloxone pretreatment. *Physiological Psychology, 10,* 313–316.

Fanselow, M. S., Sigmundi, R. A., & Williams, J. L. (1987). Response selection and the hierarchical organization of species-specific defense reactions: The relationship between freezing, flight, and defensive burying. *Psychological Record, 37,* 381–386.

Fendt, M., & Fanselow, M. S. (1999). The neuroanatomical basis of conditioned fear. *Neuroscience & Biobehavioral Reviews, 23,* 743–760.

Foree, D. D., & Lolordo, V. M. (1973). Attention in the pigeon: differential effects of food-getting versus shock-avoidance procedures. *Journal of Comparative & Physiological Psychology, 85,* 551–558.

Freud, S. (1953). Instincts and their vicissitudes. In J. Strachey (Ed.), *The Standard edition of the complete psychological works of Sigmund Freud* (Vol. 14, pp. 109–140). London: Hogarth Press.

Fusco, M. M., Hardy, J. D., & Hammel, H. T. (1961). Interaction of central and peripheral factors in physiological temperature regulation. *American Journal of Physiology, 200,* 572–580.

Garcia, J. (1989). Food for Tolman: Cognition and cathexis in concert. In T. Archer & L.-G. Nilsson (Eds.), *Aversion, avoidance, and anxiety: Perspectives on aversively motivated behavior* (pp. 45–85). Hillsdale NJ: Erlbaum.

Garcia, J., & Koelling, R. A. (1966). Relation of cue to consequence in avoidance learning. *Psychonomic Science, 4,* 123–124.

Garcia y Robertson, R., & Garcia, J. (1985). X-rays and learned taste aversions: Historical and psychological ramifications. In T. G. Burish, S. M. Levy, & B. E. Meyerowitz (Eds.), *Cancer, nutrition and eating behavior: A biobehavioral perspective* (pp. 11–41). Hillsdale NJ: Erlbaum.

Gewirtz, J. C., & Davis, M. (1997). Second-order fear conditioning prevented by blocking NMDA receptors in amygdala. *Nature, 388,* 471–474.

Gibson, E. J. (1952). The role of shock in reinforcement. *Journal of Comparative & Physiological Psychology, 45,* 18–30.

Goldthwaite, O., Coss, R. G., & Owings, D. H. (1990). Evolutionary dissipation of an antisnake system: Differential behavior by California and Arctic ground squirrels in above- and below-ground contexts. *Behaviour, 112,* 246–269.

Guinard, J., & Brun, P. (1998). Sensory-specific satiety: Comparison of taste and texture effects. *Appetite, 31,* 141–157.

Hack, E. R. (1933). Learning as a function of water temperature. *Journal of Experimental Psychology, 16,* 442–445.

Hainsworth, F. R. (1967). Saliva spreading, activity, and body temperature regulation in the rat. *American Journal of Physiology, 212,* 1288–1292.

Hainsworth, F. R., & Stricker, E. M. (1970). Salivary cooling in rats in the heat. In A. P. Gagge & J. A. Stolwijk (Eds.), *Physiological and behavioral temperature regulation* (pp. 611–626). Springfield, IL: Charles C. Thomas.

Hirsch, S. M., & Bolles, R. C. (1980). On the ability of prey to recognize predators. *Zeitschrift fuer Tierpsychologie, 54,* 71–84.

Hirsch, E., & Collier, G. (1974). The ecological determinants of reinforcement in the guinea pig. *Physiology & Behavior, 12,* 239–249.

Hogan, J. A. (1973a). Development of food recognition in young chicks: Vol. 1. Maturation and nutrition. *Journal of Comparative & Physiological Psychology, 83,* 355–366.

Hogan, J. A. (1973b). Development of food recognition in young chicks: Vol. 2. Learned association over long delays. *Journal of Comparative & Physiological Psychology, 83,* 367–373.

Hogan, J. A. (1977). Development of food recognition in young chicks: Vol. 4. Associative and nonassociative effects of experience. *Journal of Comparative & Physiological Psychology, 91,* 839–850.

Holland, P. C. (1981). Acquisition of representation-mediated conditioned food aversions. *Learning & Motivation, 12,* 1–18.

Hollis, K. L., Cadieux, E. L., & Colbert, M. M. (1989). The biological function of Pavlovian conditioning: A mechanism for mating success in the blue gourami (*Trichogaster trichopterus*). *Journal of Comparative Psychology, 103,* 115–121.

Hollis, K. L., Pharr, V. L., Dumas, M. J., Britton, G.B., & Field, J. (1997). Classical conditioning provides paternity advantage for territorial male blue gouramis (*Trichogaster trichopterus*). *Journal of Comparative Psychology, 111,* 219–225.

Howard, T. C. (1962). Conditioned temperature drive in rats. *Psychological Reports, 10,* 371–373.

Hull, C. L. (1943). *Principles of behavior: An introduction to behavior theory*. New York: Appleton-Century-Crofts.

Hull, D. (1973). Thermoregulation in young mammals. In C. G. Whittow (Ed.), *Comparative physiology of thermoregulation.* (Vol. 3, pp. 167–200). New York: Academic Press.

Jacobs, W. J., & LoLordo, V. M. (1980). Constraints on Pavlovian aversive conditioning: Implications for avoidance learning in the rat. *Learning & Motivation, 11,* 427–455.

Johnson, D. F., & Collier, G. (1989). Patch choice and meal size of foraging rats as a function of the profitability of food. *Animal Behaviour, 38,* 285–297.

Kapp, B. S., Frysinger, R. C., Gallagher, M., & Haselton, J. R. (1979) Amygdala central nucleus lesions: Effect on heart rate conditioning in the rabbit. *Physiology & Behavior, 23,* 1109–1117.

Kaufmann, L. W., Collier, G., Hill, W., & Collins, K. (1980). Meal cost and meal patterns in an uncaged domestic cat. *Physiology & Behavior, 25,* 135–137.

Kluver, H., & Bucy, P. C. (1939). Preliminary analysis of the temporal lobes in monkeys. *Biological Psychiatry, 42,* 461–471.

Konorski, J. (1967). *Integrative activity of the brain: An interdisciplinary approach.* Chicago: University of Chicago Press.

Le Magnen, J. (1992). *Neurobiology of feeding and nutrition.* New York: Academic Press.

Le Magnen, J., & Devos, M. (1980). Parameters of the meal pattern in rats: their assessment and physiological significance. *Neuroscience & Biobehavioral Reviews, 4,* 1–11.

Lester, L. S., & Fanselow, M. S. (1985). Exposure to a cat produces opioid analgesia in rats. *Behavioral Neuroscience, 99,* 756–759.

Leyhausen, P. (1979). *Cat behavior: The predatory and social behavior of domestic and wild cats.* New York: Garland.

Lorenz, K. (1937). The establishment of the instinct concept. *Die Naturwissenschaften, 25,* 280–300.

Maren, S. (1998). Overtraining does not mitigate contextual fear conditioning deficits produced by neurotoxic lesions of the basolateral amygdala. *Journal of Neuroscience, 18,* 3088–3097.

Martin, L. T., & Alberts, J. R. (1982). Associative learning in neonatal rats revealed by cardiac response patterns. *Journal of Comparative & Physiological Psychology, 96,* 668–675.

Mineka, S., & Cook, M. (1988). Social learning and the acquisition of snake fear in monkeys. In T. R. Zentall & B. G. Galef, Jr. (Eds.), *Social learning: Psychological and biological perspectives* (pp. 51–73). Hillsdale, NJ: Erlbaum.

Modaresi, H. A. (1982). Defensive behavior of the rat in a shock prod situation: Effects of the subjects location on preference. *Animal Learning and Behavior, 10,* 97–102.

Mook, D. G. (1987). *Motivation: the organization of action.* New York: W. W. Norton.

Morato, S., Johnson, D. F., & Collier, G. (1995). Feeding patterns of rats when food-access cost is alternately low and high. *Physiology & Behavior, 57,* 21–26.

Morris, D. (1958). The reproductive behavior of the ten-spined stickleback (*Pygosteus pungitius L.*). *Behaviour, 61,* 1–154.

Mowrer, O. H., & Lamoreaux, R. R. (1946). Fear as an intervening variable in avoidance conditioning. *Journal of Comparative Psychology, 39,* 29–50.

Nader, K., Schafe, G. E., & LeDoux, J. E. (2000). Fear memories require protein synthesis in the amygdala for reconsolidation after retrieval. *Nature, 406,* 722–726.

Nakayama, T., Hammel, H. T., Hardy, J. D., & Eisenman, J. S. (1963). Thermal stimulation of electrical single unit of the preoptic region. *American Journal of Physiology, 204,* 1122.

Panksepp, J. (1974). Hypothalamic regulation of energy balance and feeding behavior. *Federation Proceedings, 33,* 1150–1165.

Pavlov, I. P. (1927). *Conditioned reflexes.* Oxford: Oxford University Press.

Pfaff, D. W., & Pfaffman, C. (1969). Behavioral and electrophysiological responses of male rats to female rat urine odors. In C. Pfaffmann (Ed.), *Olfaction and taste* (pp. 258–267). New York: Rockefeller University Press.

Pinel, J. P., & Mana, M. (1989). Adaptive interactions of rats with dangerous inanimate objects: Support for a cognitive theory of defensive behavior. In R. J. Blanchard & P. F. Brain (Eds.), *Ethoexperimental approaches to the study of behavior* (pp. 137–150). Norwell, MA: Kluwer.

Pinel, J. P., Mana, M. J., & Ward, J. A. (1989). Stretched-approach sequences directed at a localized shock source by *Rattus norvegicus. Journal of Comparative Psychology, 103,* 140–148.

Pinel, J. P., & Treit, D. (1978). Burying as a defensive response in rats. *Journal of Comparative & Physiological Psychology, 92,* 708–712.

Potegal, M., Huhman, K., Moore, T., & Meyerhoff, J. (1993). Conditioned defeat in the Syrian golden hamster (*Mesocricetus auratus*). *Behavioral & Neural Biology, 60,* 93–102.

Prosser, C. L., & Nelson, D. O. (1981). The role of nervous systems in temperature adaptation to poikilotherms. *Annual Review of Physiology, 3,* 281–300.

Quirk, G. J., Repa, C., & LeDoux, J. E. (1995). Fear conditioning enhances short-latency auditory responses of lateral amygdala neurons: parallel recordings in the freely behaving rat. *Neuron, 15,* 1029–39.

Rand, R. P., Burton, A. C., & Ing, T. (1965). The rail of the rat in temperature regulation and acclimatization. *Canadian Journal of Physiology and Pharmacology, 43,* 257–267.

Raynor, H. A., & Epstein, L. H. (2001). Dietary variety, energy regulation, and obesity. *Psychological Bulletin, 127,* 325–341.

Richter, C. P. (1927). Animal behavior and internal drives. *Quarterly Review of Biology, 2,* 307–343.

Rizvi, T. A., Ennis, M., Behbehani, M. M., & Shipley, M. T. (1991). Connections between the central nucleus of the amygdala and the midbrain periaqueductal gray: topography and reciprocity. *Journal of Comparative Neurology, 303,* 121–31.

Roberts, W. W., & Mooney, R. D. (1974). Brain areas controlling thermoregulatory grooming prone extension, locomotion, and tail vasodilation in rats. *Journal of Comparative & Physiological Psychology, 86,* 470–480.

Rodgers, W. L. (1967). Specificity of specific hungers. *Journal of Comparative and Physiological Psychology, 64,* 49–58.

Rolls, B. J. (1979). How variety and palatability can stimulate appetite. *Nutrition Bulletin, 5,* 78–86.

Rolls, B. J., Laster, L. J., & Summerfelt, A. T. (1991). Meal order reversal: Effects of eating a sweet course first or last. *Appetite, 16,* 141–148.

Rolls, E. T., & Rolls, J. H. (1997). Olfactory sensory-specific satiety in humans. *Physiology & Behavior, 61,* 461–473.

Rolls, B. J., Rowe, E. T., & Rolls, E. T. (1982). How sensory properties of food affect human feeding behavior. *Physiology & Behavior, 29,* 409–417.

Rosen, J. B., Fanselow, M. S., Young, S. L., Sitcoske, M., & Maren, S. (1998). Immediate-early gene expression in the amygdala following footshock stress and contextual fear conditioning. *Brain Research, 796,* 132–142.

Rusiniak, K. W., Hankins, W. G., Garcia, J., & Brett, L. P. (1979). Flavor-illness aversions: Potentiation of odor by taste in rats. *Behavioral & Neural Biology, 25,* 1–17.

Satinoff, E. (1983). A reevaluation of the concept of the homeostatic organization of temperature regulation. In E. Satinoff & P. Teitelbaum (Eds.), *Handbook of behavioral neurobiology: Vol. 6. Motivation* (pp. 443–472). New York: Plenum Press.

Satinoff, E., & Rutstein, J. (1970). Behavioral thermoregulation in rats with anterior hypothalamic lesions. *Journal of Comparative & Physiological Psychology, 71,* 77–82.

Schaller, G. B. (1966). The tiger and its prey. *Natural History N. Y., 75,* 30–37.

Sclafani, A., & Springer, D. (1976). Dietary obesity in adult rats: Similarities to hypothalamic and human obesity syndromes. *Physiology & Behavior, 17,* 461–471.

Seligman, M. E., & Hager, J. L. (1972). *Biological boundaries of learning.* East Norwalk, CT: Appleton-Century-Crofts.

Sherrington, C. S. (1906). *The integrative action of the nervous system.* New York: Scribner.

Sigmundi, R. A. (1997). Performance rules for problem-specific defense reactions. In M. E. Bouton & M. S. Fanselow (Eds.), *Learning, motivation, and cognition: The functional behaviorism of Robert C. Bolles* (pp. 305–319). Washington, DC: American Psychological Association.

Silva, F. J., Timberlake, W., & Gont, R. S. (1998). Spatiotemporal characteristics of serial CSs and their relation to search modes and response form. *Animal Learning & Behavior, 26,* 299–312.

Staddon, J. E., & Simmelhag, V. L. (1970). The "supersitition" experiment: A reexamination of its implications for the principles of adaptive behavior. *Psychological Review, 78,* 3–43.

Stanley, W. C., Barrett, J. E., & Bacon, W. E. (1974). Conditioning and extinction of avoidance and escape behavior in neonatal dogs. *Journal of Comparative & Physiological Psychology, 87,* 163–172.

Stirling, I. (1988). *Polar bears.* Ann Arbor: University of Michigan Press.

Swanson, L. W., & Petrovich, G. D. (1998). What is the amygdala? *Trends in Neurosciences, 21,* 323–331.

Timberlake, W. (1983). The functional organization of appetitive behavior: Behavior systems and learning. In M. D. Zeiler & P. Harzem (Eds.), *Advances in the analysis of behavior: Vol. 3. Biological factors in learning* (pp. 177–221). Chichester, UK: Wiley.

Timberlake, W. (1990). Natural learning in laboratory paradigms. In D. A. Dewsbury (Ed.), *Contemporary issues in comparative psychology* (pp. 31–54). Sunderland, MA: Sinauer.

Timberlake, W. (1993). Behavior systems and reinforcement: An integrative approach. *Journal of the Experimental Analysis of Behavior, 60,* 105–128.

Timberlake, W. (1994). Behavior systems, associationism and Pavlovian conditioning. *Psychonomic Bulletin & Review, 1,* 405–420.

Timberlake, W. (1997). An animal-centered, causal-system approach to the understanding and control of behavior. *Applied Animal Behavior Science, 53,* 107–129.

Timberlake, W. (2001). Integrating niche-related and general process approaches in the study of learning. *Behavioural Processes, 54,* 79–94.

Timberlake, W., & Fanselow, M. S. (1994). Symposium on behavior systems: Learning, neurophysiology, and development. *Psychonomic Bulletin & Review, 1,* 403–404.

Timberlake, W., & Lucas, G. A. (1989). Behavior systems and learning: From misbehavior to general principles. In S. B. Klein & R. R. Mowrer (Eds.), *Contemporary learning theory and the impact of biological constraints on learning* (pp. 237–275). Hillsdale, NJ: Erlbaum.

Timberlake, W., & Silva, K. M. (1995). Appetitive behavior in ethology, psychology and behavior systems. In N. Thompson (Ed.), *Perspectives in ethology* (pp. 211–253). New York: Plenum Press.

Timberlake, W., & Washburne, D. L. (1989). Feeding ecology and laboratory predatory behavior toward live and artificial moving prey in seven rodent species. *Animal Learning & Behavior, 17,* 1–10.

Tinbergen, N. (1951). *The study of instinct.* Oxford, UK: Clarendon Press.

Tolman, E. C. (1949). The nature and function of wants. *Psychological Review, 56,* 357–369.

Valle, F. P. (1970). Effects of strain, sex, and illumination on open-field behavior of rats. *American Journal of Psychology, 83,* 103–111.

Van der Poel, A. M. (1979). A note on "stretched attention," a behavioural element indicative of an approach-avoidance conflict in rats. *Animal Behaviour, 27,* 446–450.

Walker, D. L., & Davis, M. (1997). Double dissociation between the involvement of the bed nucleus of the *stria terminalis* and the central nucleus of the amygdala in startle increases produced by conditioned versus unconditioned fear. *Journal of Neuroscience, 17,* 9375–9383.

Wallace, K. J., & Rosen, J. B. (2000). Predator odor as an unconditioned fear stimulus in rats: Elicitation of freezing by trimethylthiazoline, a component of fox feces. *Behavioral Neuroscience, 114,* 912–922.

Wallace, K. J., & Rosen, J. B. (2001). Neurotoxic lesions of the lateral nucleus of the amygdala decrease conditioned but not unconditioned fear of a predator odor: Comparison with electrolytic lesions. *Journal of Neuroscience, 21,* 3619–3627.

Wasserman, E. A. (1973). Pavlovian conditioning with heat reinforcement produces stimulus-directed pecking in chicks. *Science, 181,* 875–877.

Watkins, L. R., & Maier, S. F. (2000). The pain of being sick: Implications of immune-to-brain communication for understanding pain. *Annual Review of Psychology, 51,* 29–57.

Weiskrantz, L. (1956). Behavioral changes associated with ablation of the amygdaloid complex in monkeys. *Journal of Comparative & Physiological Psychology, 49,* 381–391.

Wilson, N. E., & Stricker, E. M. (1979). Thermal homeostasis in pregnant rats during heat stress. *Journal of Comparative & Physiological Psychology, 93,* 585–594.

CHAPTER 3

Mood, Cognition, and Memory

ERIC EICH AND JOSEPH P. FORGAS

Recent years have witnessed a mounting interest in the impact of happiness, sadness, and other affective states or moods on learning, memory, decision making, and allied cognitive processes. Much of this interest has focused on two phenomena: *mood-congruent cognition,* the observation that a given mood promotes the processing of information that possesses a similar affective tone or valence, and *mood-dependent memory,* the observation that information encoded in a particular mood is most retrievable in that mood, irrespective of the information's affective valence. This chapter examines the history and current status of research on mood congruence and mood dependence with a view to clarifying what is known about each of these phenomena and why they are both worth knowing about.

MOOD CONGRUENCE

The interplay between feeling and thinking, affect and cognition, has been a subject of scholarly discussion and spirited debate since antiquity. From Plato to Pascal, a long line of Western philosophers have proposed that "passions" have a potentially dangerous, invasive influence on rational thinking, an idea that re-emerged in Freud's psychodynamic theories. However, recent advances in cognitive psychology and neuroscience have promoted the radically different view that affect is often a useful and even essential component of adaptive social thinking (Adolphs & Damasio, 2001; Cosmides & Tooby, 2000).

The research to be reviewed in this section shows that affective states often produce powerful assimilative or congruent effects on the way people acquire, remember, and interpret information. However, we will also see that these effects are not universal, but depend on a variety of situational and contextual variables that recruit different information-processing strategies. Accordingly, one of the main aims of modern research, and of this review, is to clarify why mood-congruent effects emerge under certain circumstances but not others.

To this end, we begin by recapping two early theoretical perspectives on mood congruence (one based on psychoanalytic constructs, the other on principles of conditioning) and then turn to two more recent accounts (affect priming and affect-as-information). Next, we outline an integrative theory that is designed to explain the different ways in which affect can have an impact on cognition in general, and social cognition in particular. Finally, empirical evidence is examined which elucidates the essential role that different processing strategies play in the occurrence—or nonoccurrence—of mood congruence.

This chapter was prepared with the aid of grants to the first author from the National Institute of Mental Health and the Natural Sciences and Engineering Research Council of Canada and by awards to the second author from the Australian Research Council and the Alexander von Humboldt Foundation. The chapter also profited from the expert advice and assistance provided by Joseph Ciarrochi, Dawn Macaulay, Stephanie Moylan, Patrick Vargas, and Joan Webb.

Early Theories of Mood Congruence

Philosophers, politicians, and playwrights alike have recognized for centuries the capacity of moods to color the way people remember the past, experience the present, and forecast the future. Psychologists, however, were relatively late to acknowledge this reality, despite a number of promising early leads (e.g., Rapaport, 1942/1961; Razran, 1940). Indeed, it is only within the past 25 years that empirical investigations of the interplay between affect and cognition have been published with regularity in mainstream psychology journals (see LeDoux, 1996).

Psychology's late start in exploring the affect-cognition interface reflects the fact that neither behaviorism nor cognitivism—the two paradigms that dominated the discipline throughout the twentieth century—ascribed much importance to affective phenomena, whether in the form of specific, short-lived emotional reactions or more nebulous, long-lasting mood states (for detailed discussion of affect-related concepts, see Russell & Feldman Barrett, 1999; Russell & Lemay, 2000).

From the perspective of the radical behaviorist, all unobservable mental events, including those affective in nature, were by definition deemed beyond the bounds of scientific psychology. Although early behaviorist research examined the environmental conditioning of emotional responses (an issue taken up later in this chapter), later studies focused mainly on the behavioral consequences of readily manipulated drive states, such as thirst or fear. In such studies, emotion was instilled in animals through crude if effective means, such as electric shock, and so-called emotionality was operationalized by counting the number of faecal boli deposited by small, scared animals. As a result, behaviorist research and theory added little to our understanding of the interrelations between affect and cognition.

Until recently, the alternative cognitive paradigm also had little interest in affective phenomena. To the extent that the cognitive revolutionaries of the early 1960s considered affects at all, they typically envisaged them as disruptive influences on proper—read *emotionless* or *cold*—thought processes. Thus, the transition from behaviorism to cognitivism allowed psychology to reclaim its head, but did nothing to recapture its heart.

Things are different today. Affect is now known to play a critical role in how information about the world is processed and represented. Moreover, affect underlies the cognitive representation of social experience (Forgas, 1979), and emotional responses can serve as an organizing principle in cognitive categorization (Niedenthal & Halberstadt, 2000). Thus, the experience of affect—how we feel about people, places, and events—plays a pivotal role in people's cognitive representations of themselves and the world around them.

Affect also has a more dynamic role in information processing. In a classic series of studies, Razran (1940) showed that subjects evaluated sociopolitical messages more favorably when in a good than in a bad mood. Far ahead of their time, Razran's studies, and those reported by other investigators (e.g., Bousfield, 1950), provided the first empirical evidence of mood congruence, and their results were initially explained in terms of either psychodynamic or associationist principles.

Psychodynamic Account

Freud's psychoanalytic theory suggested that affect has a dynamic, invasive quality that can infuse thinking and judgments unless adequately controlled. A pioneering study by Feshbach and Singer (1957) tested the psychodynamic prediction that attempts to suppress affect should increase the "pressure" for affect infusion. They induced fear in their subjects through electric shocks and then instructed some of them to suppress their fear. Fearful subjects' thoughts about another person showed greater mood congruence, so that they perceived the other person as being especially anxious. Interestingly, indeed ironically (Wegner, 1994), this effect was even greater when subjects were trying to suppress their fear. Feshbach and Singer (1957) explained this in terms of projection and proposed that "suppression of fear facilitates the tendency to project fear onto another social object" (p. 286).

Conditioning Account

Although radical behaviorism outlawed the study of subjective experiences, including affects, conditioning theories did nevertheless have an important influence on research. Watson's work with Little Albert was among the first to find affect congruence in conditioned responses (Watson, 1929; Watson & Rayner, 1920). This work showed that reactions toward a previously neutral stimulus, such as a furry rabbit, could become affectively loaded after an association had been established between the rabbit and fear-arousing stimuli, such as a loud noise. Watson thought that most complex affective reactions acquired throughout life are established as a result of just such cumulative patterns of incidental associations.

The conditioning approach was subsequently used by Byrne and Clore (1970; Clore & Byrne, 1974) to explore affective influences on interpersonal attitudes. These researchers argued that aversive environments (as unconditioned stimuli) spontaneously produce negative affective reactions (as unconditioned responses). When another person is encountered in an aversive environment (the conditioned stimulus), the affective reaction it evokes will become associated with the new target (a conditioned response). Several studies, published in the 1970s, supported this reasoning (e.g., Gouaux, 1971; Gouaux & Summers, 1973; Griffitt, 1970). More recently, Berkowitz and his colleagues (Berkowitz, Jaffee, Jo, & Troccoli, 2000) have suggested that these early associationist ideas remain a powerful influence on current theorizing, as we shall see later.

Contemporary Cognitive Theories

Although affective states often infuse cognition, as several early experiments showed, neither the psychoanalytic nor the conditioning accounts offered a convincing explanation of the psychological mechanisms involved. In contrast, contemporary cognitive theories seek to specify the precise information-processing mechanisms responsible for these effects.

Two types of cognitive theories have been proposed to account for mood congruence: *memory-based theories* (e.g., the affect priming model; see Bower & Forgas, 2000), and *inferential theories* (e.g., the affect-as-information model; see Clore, Gasper, & Garvin, 2001). Whereas both of these accounts are chiefly concerned with the impact of moods on the content of cognition (or what people think), a third type of theory focuses on the *processing consequences* of affect (or how people think). These three theoretical frameworks are sketched in the following sections.

Memory-Based Accounts

Several cognitive theories suggest that moods exert a congruent influence on the content of cognition because they influence the memory structures people rely on when processing information. For example, Wyer and Srull's (1989) *storage-bin model* suggests that recently activated concepts are more accessible because such concepts are returned to the top of mental "storage bins." Subsequent sequential search for interpretive information is more likely to access the same concepts again. As affective states facilitate the use of positively or negatively valenced mental concepts, this could account for the greater use of mood-congruent constructs in subsequent tasks.

A more comprehensive explanation of this effect was outlined in the *associative network model* proposed by Bower (1981). In this view, the observed links between affect and thinking are neither motivationally based, as psychodynamic theories suggest, nor are they the result of merely incidental, blind associations, as conditioning theories imply. Instead, Bower (1981) argued that affect is integrally linked to an associative network of mental representations. The activation of an affective state should thus selectively and automatically prime associated thoughts and representations previously linked to that affect, and these concepts should be more likely to be used in subsequent constructive cognitive tasks. Consistent with the network model, early studies provided strong support for the concept of *affective priming,* indicating mood congruence across a broad spectrum of cognitive tasks. For example, people induced to feel good or bad tend to selectively remember more mood-congruent details from their childhood and more of the real-life events they had recorded in diaries for the past few weeks (Bower, 1981). Mood congruence was also observed in subjects' interpretations of social behaviors (Forgas, Bower, & Krantz, 1984) and in their impressions of other people (Forgas & Bower, 1987).

However, subsequent research showed that mood congruence is subject to several boundary conditions (see Blaney, 1986; Bower, 1987; Singer & Salovey, 1988). Problems in obtaining reliable mood-congruent effects were variously explained as due to (a) the lack of sufficiently strong or intense moods (Bower & Mayer, 1985); (b) the subjects' inability to perceive a meaningful, causal connection between their current mood and the cognitive task they are asked to perform (Bower, 1991); and (c) the use of tasks that prevent subjects from processing the target material in a self-referential manner (Blaney, 1986). Interestingly, mood-congruent effects tend to be more reliably obtained when complex and realistic stimuli are used. Thus, such effects have been most consistently demonstrated in tasks that require a high degree of open, constructive processing, such as inferences, associations, impression formation, and interpersonal behaviors (e.g., Bower & Forgas, 2000; Mayer, Gaschke, Braverman, & Evans, 1992; Salovey, Detweiler, Steward, & Bedell, 2001). Such tasks provide people with a rich set of encoding and retrieval cues, and thus allow affect to more readily function as a differentiating context (Bower, 1992).

A similar point was made by Fiedler (1991), who suggested that mood congruence is apt to occur only in constructive cognitive tasks, those that involve an open-ended search for information (as in recall tasks) and the active elaboration and transformation of stimulus details using existing knowledge structures (as in judgmental and inferential tasks). By contrast, tasks that do not place a premium on constructive processing, such as those requiring the simple recognition of familiar words or the reflexive reproduction of preexisting attitudes, afford little opportunity to use affectively primed information and thus tend to be impervious to mood effects.

It appears, then, that affect priming occurs when an existing affective state preferentially activates and facilitates the use of affect-consistent information from memory in a constructive cognitive task. The consequence of affect priming is *affect infusion:* the tendency for judgments, memories, thoughts, and behaviors to become more mood congruent (Forgas, 1995). However, in order for such infusion effects to occur, it is necessary for people to adopt an open, elaborate information-processing strategy that facilitates the incidental use of affectively primed memories and information. Thus, the nature and extent of affective influences on cognition should largely depend on what kind of information-processing strategy people employ in a particular situation. Later we will review the empirical evidence for this prediction and describe an integrative theory that emphasizes the role of information-processing strategies in moderating mood congruence.

Inferential Accounts

Several theorists maintain that many manifestations of mood congruence can be readily explained in terms other than affect priming. Chief among these alternative accounts is the affect-as-information (AAI) model advanced by Schwarz and Clore (1983, 1988). This model suggests that "rather than computing a judgment on the basis of recalled features of a target, individuals may . . . ask themselves: 'how do I feel about it? [and] in doing so, they may mistake feelings due to a pre-existing [*sic*] state as a reaction to the target" (Schwarz, 1990, p. 529). Thus, the model implies that mood congruence in judgments is due to an inferential error, as people misattribute a preexisting affective state to a judgmental target.

The AAI model incorporates ideas from at least three past research traditions. First, the predictions of the model are often indistinguishable from earlier conditioning research by Clore and Byrne (1974). Whereas the conditioning account emphasized blind temporal and spatial contiguity as responsible for linking affect to judgments, the AAI model, rather less parsimoniously, posits an internal inferential process as producing the same effects (see Berkowitz et al., 2000). A second tradition that informs the AAI model comes from research on misattribution, according to which judgments are often inferred on the basis of salient but irrelevant cues: in this case, affective state. Thus, the AAI model also predicts that only previously unattributed affect can produce mood congruence. Finally, the model also shows some affinity with research on judgmental heuristics (see the chapter by Wallsten & Budescu in this volume), in the sense that affective states are thought to function as heuristic cues in informing people's judgments.

Again, these effects are not universal. Typically, people rely on affect as a heuristic cue only when "the task is of little personal relevance, when little other information is available, when problems are too complex to be solved systematically, and when time or attentional resources are limited" (Fiedler, 2001, p. 175). For example, some of the earliest and still most compelling evidence for the AAI model came from an experiment (Schwarz & Clore, 1983) that involved telephoning respondents and asking them unexpected and unfamiliar questions. In this situation, subjects have little personal interest or involvement in responding to a stranger, and they have neither the motivation, time, nor cognitive resources to engage in extensive processing. Relying on prevailing affect to infer a response seems a reasonable strategy under such circumstances. In a different but related case, Forgas and Moylan (1987) asked almost 1,000 people to complete an attitude survey on the sidewalk outside a cinema in which they had just watched either a happy or a sad film. The results showed strong mood congruence: Happy theatergoers gave much more positive responses than did their sad counterparts. In this situation, as in the study by Schwarz and Clore (1983), respondents presumably had little time, motivation, or capacity to engage in elaborate processing, and hence they may well have relied on their temporary affect as a heuristic cue to infer a reaction.

On the negative side, the AAI model has some serious shortcomings. First, although the model is applicable to mood congruence in evaluative judgments, it has difficulty accounting for the infusion of affect into other cognitive processes, including attention, learning, and memory. Also, it is sometimes claimed (e.g., Clore et al., 2001; Schwarz & Clore, 1988) that the model is supported by the finding that mood congruence can be eliminated by calling the subjects' attention to the true source of their mood, thereby minimizing the possibility of an affect misattribution. This claim is dubious, as we know that mood congruence due to affect-priming mechanisms can similarly be reversed by instructing subjects to focus on their internal states (Berkowitz et al., 2000). Moreover, Martin (2000) has argued that the informational value of affective states cannot be regarded as "given" and permanent, but instead depends on the situational context. Thus, positive affect may signal that a positive response is appropriate if the setting happens to be, say, a wedding, but the same mood may have a different meaning at a funeral. The AAI model also has nothing to say about how cues other than affect (such as memories, features of the stimulus, etc.) can enter into a judgment. In that sense, AAI is really a theory of nonjudgment or aborted judgment, rather than a theory of judgment. It now appears that in most realistic cognitive tasks, affect priming rather than the affect-as-information is the main mechanism producing mood congruence.

Processing Consequences of Moods

In addition to influencing *what* people think, moods may also influence the process of cognition, that is, *how* people think. It has been suggested that positive affect recruits less effortful and more superficial processing strategies; in contrast, negative affect seems to trigger a more analytic and vigilant processing style (Clark & Isen, 1982; Mackie & Worth, 1991; Schwarz, 1990). However, more recent studies have shown that positive affect can also produce distinct processing advantages: Happy people often adopt more creative and inclusive thinking styles, and display greater mental flexibility, than do sad subjects (Bless, 2000; Fiedler, 2000).

Several theories have been advanced to explain affective influences on processing strategies. One suggestion is that the experience of a negative mood, or any affective state, gives rise to intrusive, irrelevant thoughts that deplete attentional resources, and in turn lead to poor performance in a variety of cognitive tasks (Ellis & Ashbrook, 1988; Ellis & Moore, 1999). An alternative account points to the motivational consequences of positive and negative affect. According to this view (Isen, 1984), people experiencing positive affect may try to maintain a pleasant state by refraining from any effortful activity. In contrast, negative affect may motivate people to engage in vigilant, effortful processing. In a variation of this idea, Schwarz (1990) has suggested that affects have a signaling or tuning function, informing the person that relaxed, effort-minimizing processing is appropriate in the case of positive affect, whereas vigilant, effortful processing is best suited for negative affect.

These various arguments all assume that positive and negative affect decrease or increase the effort, vigilance, and elaborateness of information processing, albeit for different reasons. More recently, both Bless (2000) and Fiedler (2000) have conjectured that the evolutionary significance of positive and negative affect is not simply to influence processing effort, but to trigger two fundamentally different processing styles. They suggest that positive affect promotes a more schema-based, top-down, assimilative processing style, whereas negative affect produces a more bottom-up, externally focused, accommodative processing strategy. These strategies can be equally vigilant and effortful, yet they produce markedly different cognitive outcomes by directing attention to internal or external sources of information.

Toward an Integrative Theory: The Affect Infusion Model

As this short review shows, affective states have clear if complex effects on both the substance of cognition (i.e., the contents of one's thoughts) and its style (e.g., whether information is processed systematically or superficially). It is also clear, however, that affective influences on cognition are highly context specific. A comprehensive explanation of these effects needs to specify the circumstances that abet or impede mood congruence, and it should also define the conditions likely to trigger either affect priming or affect-as-information mechanisms.

The *affect infusion model* or AIM (Forgas, 1995) seeks to accomplish these goals by expanding on Fiedler's (1991) idea that mood congruence is most likely to occur when circumstances call for an open, constructive style of information processing. Such a style involves the active elaboration of the available stimulus details and the use of memory-based information in this process. The AIM thus predicts that (a) the extent and nature of affect infusion should be dependent on the kind of processing strategy that is used, and (b) all things being equal, people should use the least effortful and simplest processing strategy capable of producing a response. As this model has been described in detail elsewhere (Forgas, 1995), only a brief overview will be included here.

The AIM identifies four processing strategies that vary according to both the degree of openness or constructiveness of the information-search strategy and the amount of effort exerted in seeking a solution. The *direct access* strategy involves the retrieval of preexisting responses and is most likely when the task is highly familiar and when no strong situational or motivational cues call for more elaborate processing. For example, if you were asked to make an evaluative judgment about a well-known political leader, a previously computed and stored response would come quickly and effortlessly to mind, assuming that you had thought about this topic extensively in the past. People possess a rich store of such preformed attitudes and judgments. Given that such standard responses require no constructive processing, affect infusion should not occur.

The *motivated processing* strategy involves highly selective and targeted thinking that is dominated by a particular motivational objective. This strategy also precludes open information search and should be impervious to affect infusion (Clark & Isen, 1982). For example, if in a job interview you are asked about your attitude toward the company you want to join, the response will be dominated by the motivation to produce an acceptable response. Open, constructive processing is inhibited, and affect infusion is unlikely to occur. However, the consequences of motivated processing may be more complex and, depending on the particular processing goal, may also produce a reversal of mood-congruent effects (Berkowitz et al., 2000; Forgas, 1991; Forgas & Fiedler, 1996). Recent theories, such as as Martin's (2000) configural model, go some way toward accounting for these context-specific influences.

The remaining two processing strategies require more constructive and open-ended information search strategies, and thus they facilitate affect infusion. *Heuristic processing* is most likely when the task is simple, familiar, of little personal relevance, and cognitive capacity is limited and there are no motivational or situational pressures for more detailed processing. This is the kind of superficial, quick processing style people are likely adopt when they are asked to respond to unexpected questions in a telephone survey (Schwarz & Clore, 1983) or are asked to reply to a street survey (Forgas & Moylan, 1987). Heuristic processing can lead to affect infusion as long as people rely on affect as a simple inferential cue and depend on the "how do I feel about it" heuristic to produce a response (Clore et al., 2001; Schwarz & Clore, 1988).

When simpler strategies such as direct access or motivated processing prove inadequate, people need to engage in *substantive processing* to satisfy the demands of the task at hand. Substantive processing requires individuals to select and interpret novel information and relate this information to their preexisting, memory-based knowledge structures in order to compute and produce a response. This is the kind of strategy an individual might apply when thinking about interpersonal conflicts or when deciding how to make a problematic request (Forgas, 1994, 1999a, 1999b).

Substantive processing should be adopted when (a) the task is in some ways demanding, atypical, complex, novel, or personally relevant; (b) there are no direct-access responses available; (c) there are no clear motivational goals to guide processing; and (d) adequate time and other processing resources are available. Substantive processing is an inherently open and constructive strategy, and affect may selectively prime or enhance the accessibility of related thoughts, memories, and interpretations. The AIM makes the interesting and counterintuitive prediction that affect infusion—and hence mood congruence—should be increased when extensive and elaborate processing is required to deal with a more complex, demanding, or novel task. This prediction has been borne out by several studies that we will soon review.

The AIM also specifies a range of contextual variables related to the *task,* the *person,* and the *situation* that jointly influence processing choices. For example, greater task familiarity, complexity, and typicality should recruit more substantive processing. Personal characteristics that influence processing style include motivation, cognitive capacity, and personality traits such as self-esteem (Rusting, 2001; Smith & Petty, 1995). Situational factors that influence processing style include social norms, public scrutiny, and social influence by others (Forgas, 1990).

An important feature of the AIM is that it recognizes that affect itself can also influence processing choices. As noted earlier, both Bless (2000) and Fiedler (2000) have proposed that positive affect typically generates a more top-down, schema-driven processing style whereby new information is assimilated into what is already known. In contrast, negative affect often promotes a more piecemeal, bottom-up processing strategy in which attention to external events dominates over existing stored knowledge.

The key prediction of the AIM is the *absence* of affect infusion when direct access or motivated processing is used, and the *presence* of affect infusion during heuristic and substantive processing. The implications of this model have now been supported in a number of the experiments considered in following sections.

Evidence Relating Processing Strategies to Mood Congruence

This section will review a number of empirical studies that illustrate the multiple roles of affect in cognition, focusing on several substantive areas in which mood congruence has been demonstrated, including affective influences on learning, memory, perceptions, judgments, and inferences.

Mood Congruence in Attention and Learning

Many everyday cognitive tasks are performed under conditions of considerable information overload, when people need to select a small sample of information for further processing. Affect may have a significant influence on what people will pay attention to and learn (Niedenthal & Setterlund, 1994). Due to the selective activation of an affect-related associative base, mood-congruent information may receive greater attention and be processed more extensively than affectively neutral or incongruent information (Bower, 1981). Several experiments have demonstrated that people spend longer reading mood-congruent material, linking it into a richer network of primed associations, and as a result, they are better able to remember such information (see Bower & Forgas, 2000).

These effects occur because "concepts, words, themes, and rules of inference that are associated with that emotion will become primed and highly available for use . . . [in] . . . top-down or expectation-driven processing . . . [acting] . . . as interpretive filters of reality" (Bower, 1983, p. 395). Thus, there is a tendency for people to process mood-congruent material more deeply, with greater associative elaboration, and thus learn it better. Consistent with this notion, depressed psychiatric patients tend to show better learning and memory for depressive words (Watkins, Mathews, Williamson, & Fuller, 1992), a bias that disappears once the depressive episode is over (Bradley & Mathews, 1983). However, mood-congruent learning is seldom seen in patients suffering from anxiety

(Burke & Mathews, 1992; Watts & Dalgleish, 1991), perhaps because anxious people tend to use particularly vigilant, motivated processing strategies to defend against anxiety-arousing information (Ciarrochi & Forgas, 1999; Mathews & MacLeod, 1994). Thus, as predicted by the AIM, different processing strategies appear to play a crucial role in mediating mood congruence in learning and attention.

Mood Congruence in Memory

Several experiments have shown that people are better able to consciously or explicitly recollect autobiographical memories that match their prevailing mood (Bower, 1981). Depressed patients display a similar pattern, preferentially remembering aversive childhood experiences, a memory bias that disappears once depression is brought under control (Lewinsohn & Rosenbaum, 1987). Consistent with the AIM, these mood-congruent memory effects also emerge when people try to recall complex social stimuli (Fiedler, 1991; Forgas, 1993).

Research using implicit tests of memory, which do not require conscious recollection of past experience, also provides evidence of mood congruence. For example, depressed people tend to complete more word stems (e.g., *can*) with negative than with positive words they have studied earlier (e.g., *cancer* vs. *candy;* Ruiz-Caballero & Gonzalez, 1994). Similar results have been obtained in other studies involving experimentally induced states of happiness or sadness (Tobias, Kihlstrom, & Schacter, 1992).

Mood Congruence in Associations and Interpretations

Cognitive tasks often require us to "go beyond the information given," forcing people to rely on associations, inferences, and interpretations to construct a judgment or a decision, particularly when dealing with complex and ambiguous social information (Heider, 1958). Affect can prime the kind of associations used in the interpretation and evaluation of a stimulus (Clark & Waddell, 1983). The greater availability of mood-consistent associations can have a marked influence on the top-down, constructive processing of complex or ambiguous details (Bower & Forgas, 2000). For example, when asked to freely associate to the cue *life,* happy subjects generate more positive than negative associations (e.g., *love* and *freedom* vs. *struggle* and *death*), whereas sad subjects do the opposite (Bower, 1981). Mood-congruent associations also emerge when emotional subjects daydream or make up stories about fictional characters depicted in the Thematic Apperception Test (Bower, 1981).

Such mood-congruent effects can have a marked impact on many social judgments, including perceptions of human faces (Schiffenbauer, 1974), impressions of people (Forgas & Bower, 1987), and self-perceptions (Sedikides, 1995). However, several studies have shown that this associative effect is diminished as the targets to be judged become more clear-cut and thus require less constructive processing (e.g., Forgas, 1994, 1995). Such a diminution in the associative consequences of mood with increasing stimulus clarity again suggests that open, constructive processing is crucial for mood congruence to occur. Mood-primed associations can also play an important role in clinical states: Anxious people tend to interpret spoken homophones such as *pane-pain* or *dye-die* in the more anxious, negative direction (Eysenck, MacLeod, & Mathews, 1987), consistent with the greater activation these mood-congruent concepts receive. This same mechanism also leads to mood congruence in more complex and elaborate social judgments, such as judgments about the self and others, as the evidence reviewed in the following section suggests.

Mood Congruence in Self-Judgments

Affective states have a strong congruent influence on self-related judgments: Positive affect improves and negative affect impairs the valence of self-conceptions. In one study (Forgas, Bower, & Moylan, 1990), students who had fared very well or very poorly on a recent exam were asked to rate the extent to which their test performance was attributable to factors that were internal in origin and stable over time. Students made these attributions while they were in a positive or negative mood (induced by having them watch an uplifting or depressing video) and their average ratings of internality and stability are shown in Figure 3.1. Compared to their negative-mood counterparts, students in a positive mood were more likely to claim credit for success, making more internal and stable attributions for high test scores, but less willing to assume personal responsibility for failure, making more external and unstable attributions for low test scores.

An interesting and important twist to these results was revealed by Sedikides (1995), who asked subjects to evaluate a series of self-descriptions related to their behaviors or personality traits. Subjects undertook this task while they were in a happy, sad, or neutral mood (induced through guided imagery), and the time they took to make each evaluation was recorded.

Basing his predictions on the AIM, Sedikides predicted that highly consolidated core or "central" conceptions of the self should be processed quickly using the direct-access strategy and hence should show no mood-congruent bias; in

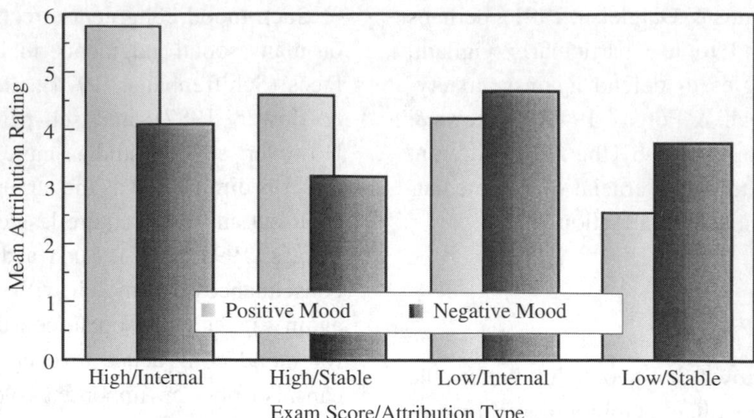

Figure 3.1 Attribution ratings made by subjects in a positive or negative mood for their performance in an earlier exam as a function of exam score (high vs. low) and attribution type (internal vs. stable). *Source:* Forgas, Bower, and Moylan, 1990.

contrast, less salient, "peripheral" self-conceptions should require more time-consuming substantive processing and accordingly be influenced by an affect-priming effect. The results supported these predictions, making Sedikides's (1995) research the first to demonstrate differential mood-congruent effects for central versus peripheral conceptions of the self, a distinction that holds considerable promise for future research in the area of social cognition.

Affect also appears to have a greater congruent influence on self-related judgments made by subjects with low rather than high levels of self-esteem, presumably because the former have a less stable self-concept (Brown & Mankowski, 1993). In a similar vein, Smith and Petty (1995) observed stronger mood congruence in the self-related *memories* reported by low rather than high self-esteem individuals. As predicted by the AIM, these findings suggest that low self-esteem people need to engage in more open and elaborate processing when thinking about themselves, increasing the tendency for their current mood to influence the outcome.

Affect intensity may be another moderator of mood congruence: One recent study showed that mood congruence is greater among people who score high on measures assessing openness to feelings as a personality trait (Ciarrochi & Forgas, 2000). However, other studies suggest that mood congruence in self-judgments can be spontaneously reversed as a result of motivated-processing strategies. Sedikides (1994) observed that after mood induction, people initially generated self-statements in a mood-congruent manner. However, with the passage of time, negative self-judgments spontaneously reversed, suggesting the operation of an "automatic" process of mood management. Recent research by Forgas and Ciarrochi (in press) replicated these results and indicated further that the spontaneous reversal of negative self-judgments is particularly pronounced in people with high self-esteem.

In summary, moods have been shown to exert a strong congruent influence on self-related thoughts and judgments, but only when some degree of open and constructive processing is required and when there are no motivational forces to override mood congruence. Research to date also indicates that the infusion of affect into self-judgments is especially likely when these judgments (a) relate to peripheral, as opposed to central, aspects of the self; (b) require extensive, time-consuming processing; and (c) reflect the self-conceptions of individuals with low rather than high self-esteem.

Mood Congruence in Person Perception

The AIM predicts that affect infusion and mood congruence should be greater when more extensive, constructive processing is required to deal with a task. Paradoxically, the more people need to think in order to compute a response, the greater the likelihood that affectively primed ideas will influence the outcome. Several experiments manipulated the complexity of the subjects' task in order to create more or less demand for elaborate processing.

In one series of studies (Forgas, 1992), happy and sad subjects were asked to read and form impressions about fictional characters who were described as being rather typical or ordinary or as having an unusual or even odd combination of attributes (e.g., an avid surfer whose favorite music is Italian opera). The expectation was that when people have to form an impression about a complex, ambiguous, or atypical individual, they will need to engage in more constructive processing and rely more on their stored knowledge about the world in order to make sense of these stimuli. Affectively primed associations should thus have a greater chance to infuse the judgmental outcome.

Consistent with this reasoning, the data indicated that, irrespective of current mood, subjects took longer to read about odd as opposed to ordinary characters. Moreover, while the former targets were evaluated somewhat more positively by happy than by sad subjects, this difference was magnified (in a mood-congruent direction) in the impressions made of atypical targets. Subsequent research, comparing ordinary versus odd couples rather than individuals, yielded similar results (e.g., Forgas, 1993).

Do effects of a similar sort emerge in realistic interpersonal judgments? In several studies, the impact of mood on judgments and inferences about real-life interpersonal issues was investigated (Forgas, 1994). Partners in long-term, intimate relationships revealed clear evidence of mood congruence in their attributions for actual conflicts, especially complex and serious conflicts that demand careful thought. These experiments provide direct evidence for the process dependence of affect infusion into social judgments and inferences. Even judgments about highly familiar people are more prone to affect infusion when a more substantive processing strategy is used.

Recent research has also shown that individual characteristics, such as trait anxiety, can influence processing styles and thereby significantly moderate the influence of negative mood on intergroup judgments (Ciarrochi & Forgas, 1999). Low trait-anxious Whites in the United States reacted more negatively to a threatening Black out-group when experiencing negative affect. Surprisingly, high trait-anxious individuals showed the opposite pattern: They went out of their way to control their negative tendencies when feeling bad, and produced more positive judgments. Put another way, it appeared that low trait-anxious people processed information about the out-group automatically and allowed affect to influence their judgments, whereas high trait anxiety combined with aversive mood triggered a more controlled, motivated processing strategy designed to eliminate socially undesirable intergroup judgments.

Mood Congruence in Social Behaviors

In this section we discuss research that speaks to a related question: If affect can influence thinking and judgments, can it also influence actual social behaviors? Most interpersonal behaviors require some degree of substantive, generative processing as people need to evaluate and plan their behaviors in inherently complex and uncertain social situations (Heider, 1958). To the extent that affect influences thinking and judgments, there should also be a corresponding influence on subsequent social behaviors. Positive affect should prime positive information and produce more confident, friendly, and cooperative "approach" behaviors, whereas negative affect should prime negative memories and produce avoidant, defensive, or unfriendly attitudes and behaviors.

Mood Congruence in Responding to Requests

A recent field experiment by Forgas (1998) investigated affective influences on responses to an impromptu request. Folders marked "please open and consider this" were left on several empty desks in a large university library, each folder containing an assortment of materials (pictures as well as narratives) that were positive or negative in emotional tone. Students who (eventually) took a seat at these desks were surreptitiously observed to ensure that they did indeed open the folders and examine their contents carefully. Soon afterwards, the students were approached by another student (in fact, a confederate) and received an unexpected polite or impolite request for several sheets of paper needed to complete an essay. Their responses were noted, and a short time later they were asked to complete a brief questionnaire assessing their attitudes toward the request and the requester.

The results revealed a clear mood-congruent pattern in attitudes and in responses to the requester: Negative mood resulted in a more critical, negative attitude to the request and the requester, as well as less compliance, than did positive mood. These effects were greater when the request was impolite rather than polite, presumably because impolite, unconventional requests are likely to require more elaborate and substantive processing on the part of the recipient. This explanation was supported by evidence for enhanced long-term recall for these messages. On the other hand, more routine, polite, and conventional requests were processed less substantively, were less influenced by mood, and were also remembered less accurately later on. These results confirm that affect infusion can have a significant effect on determining attitudes and behavioral responses to people encountered in realistic everyday situations.

Mood Congruence in Self-Disclosure

Self-disclosure is one of the most important communicative tasks people undertake in everyday life, influencing the development and maintenance of intimate relationships. Self-disclosure is also critical to mental health and social adjustment. Do temporary mood states influence people's self-disclosure strategies? Several lines of evidence suggest an affirmative answer: As positive mood primes more positive and optimistic inferences about interpersonal situations, self-disclosure intimacy may also be higher when people feel good.

In a series of recent studies (Forgas, 2001), subjects first watched a videotape that was intended to put them into either a happy or a sad mood. Next, subjects were asked to exchange e-mails with an individual who was in a nearby room, with a view to getting to know the correspondent and forming an overall impression of him or her. In reality, the correspondent was a computer that had been preprogrammed to generate messages that conveyed consistently high or low levels of self-disclosure.

As one might expect, the subjects' overall impression of the purported correspondent was higher if they were in a happy than in a sad mood. More interestingly, the extent to which the subjects related their own interests, aspirations, and other personal matters to the correspondent was markedly affected by their current mood. Happy subjects disclosed more than did sad subjects, but only if the correspondent reciprocated with a high degree of disclosure. These results suggest that mood congruence is likely to occur in many unscripted and unpredictable social encounters, where people need to rely on constructive processing to guide their interpersonal strategies.

Synopsis

Evidence from many sources suggests that people tend to perceive themselves, and the world around them, in a manner that is congruent with their current mood. Over the past 25 years, explanations of mood congruence have gradually evolved from earlier psychodynamic and conditioning approaches to more recent cognitive accounts, such as the concept of affect priming, which Bower (1981; Bower & Cohen, 1982) first formalized in his well-known network theory of emotion.

With accumulating empirical evidence, however, it has also become clear that although mood congruence is a robust and reliable phenomenon, it is not universal. In fact, in many circumstances mood either has no effect or even has an incongruent effect on cognition. How are such divergent results to be understood?

The affect infusion model offers an answer. As discussed earlier, the model implies, and the literature indicates, that mood congruence is unlikely to occur whenever a cognitive task can be performed via a simple, well-rehearsed direct access strategy or a highly motivated strategy. In these conditions there is little need or opportunity for cognition to be influenced or infused by affect. Although the odds of demonstrating mood congruence are improved when subjects engage in heuristic processing of the kind identified with the AAI model, such processing is appropriate only under special circumstances (e.g., when the subjects' cognitive resources are limited and there are no situational or motivational pressures for more detailed analysis).

According to the AIM, it is more common for mood congruence to occur when individuals engage in substantive, constructive processing to integrate the available information with preexisting and affectively primed knowledge structures. Consistent with this claim, the research reviewed here shows that mood-congruent effects are magnified when people engage in constructive processing to compute judgments about peripheral rather than central conceptions of the self, atypical rather than typical characters, and complex rather than simple personal conflicts. As we will see in the next section, the concept of affect infusion in general, and the idea of constructive processing in particular, may be keys to understanding not only mood congruence, but mood dependence as well.

MOOD DEPENDENCE

Our purpose in this second half of the chapter is to pursue the problem of mood-dependent memory (MDM) from two points of view. Before delineating these perspectives, we should begin by describing what MDM means and why it is a problem.

Conceptually, mood dependence refers to the idea that what has been learned in a certain state of affect or mood is most expressible in that state. Empirically, MDM is often investigated within the context of a two-by-two design, where one factor is the mood—typically either happy or sad—in which a person encodes a collection of to-be-remembered or target events, and the other factor is the mood—again, happy versus sad—in which retention of the targets is tested. If these two factors are found to interact, such that more events are remembered when encoding and retrieval moods match than when they mismatch, then mood dependence is said to occur.

Why is MDM gingerly introduced here as "the problem"? The answer is implied by two quotations from Gordon Bower, foremost figure in the area. In an oft-cited review of the mood and memory literature, Bower (1981) remarked that mood dependence "is a genuine phenomenon whether the mood swings are created experimentally or by endogenous factors in a clinical population" (p. 134). Yet just eight years later, in an article written with John Mayer, Bower came to a very different conclusion, claiming that MDM is an "unreliable, chance event, possibly due to subtle experimental demand" (Bower & Mayer, 1989, p. 145).

What happened? How is it possible that in less than a decade, mood dependence could go from being a "genuine phenomenon" to an "unreliable, chance event"?

What happened was that, although several early studies secured strong evidence of MDM, several later ones showed no sign whatsoever of the phenomenon (see Blaney, 1986; Bower, 1987; Eich, 1989; Ucros, 1989). Moreover, attempts to replicate positive results rarely succeeded, even when undertaken by the same researcher using similar materials, tasks, and mood-modification techniques (see Bower & Mayer, 1989; Singer & Salovey, 1988). This accounts not only for Bower's change of opinion, but also for Ellis and Hunt's (1989) claim that "mood-state dependency in memory presents more puzzles than solutions" (p. 280) and for Kihlstrom's (1989) comment that MDM "has proved to have the qualities of a will-o'-the-wisp" (p. 26).

Plainly, any effect as erratic as MDM appears to be must be considered a problem. Despite decades of dedicated research, it remains unclear whether mood dependence is a real, reliable phenomenon of memory. But is MDM a problem worth worrying about, and is it important enough to pursue? Many researchers maintain that it is, for the concept has significant implications for both cognitive and clinical psychology.

With respect to cognitive implications, Bower has allowed that when he began working on MDM, he was "occasionally chided by research friends for even bothering to demonstrate such an 'obvious' triviality as that one's emotional state could serve as a context for learning" (Bower & Mayer, 1989, p. 152). Although the criticism seems ironic today, it was incisive at the time, for many theories strongly suggested that memory should be mood dependent. These theories included the early drive-as-stimulus views held by Hull (1943) and Miller (1950), as well as such later ideas as Baddeley's (1982) distinction between independent and interactive contexts, Bower's (1981) network model of emotion, and Tulving's (1983) encoding specificity principle (also see the chapter by Roediger & Marsh in this volume). Thus, the frequent failure to demonstrate MDM reflects badly on many classic and contemporary theories of memory, and it blocks understanding of the basic issue of how context influences learning and remembering.

With respect to clinical implications, a key proposition in the prologue to Breuer and Freud's (1895/1957) *Studies on Hysteria* states that "hysterics suffer mainly from reminiscences" (p. 7). Breuer and Freud believed, as did many of their contemporaries (most notably Janet, 1889), that the grand-mal seizures, sleepwalking episodes, and other bizarre symptoms shown by hysteric patients were the behavioral by-products of earlier traumatic experiences, experiences that were now shielded behind a dense amnesic barrier, rendering them impervious to deliberate, conscious recall. In later sections of the *Studies,* Freud argued that the hysteric's amnesia was the result of repression: motivated forgetting meant to protect the ego, or the act of keeping something—in this case, traumatic recollections—out of awareness (see Erdelyi & Goldberg, 1979).

Breuer, however, saw the matter differently, and in terms that can be understood today as an extreme example of mood dependence. Breuer maintained that traumatic events, by virtue of their intense emotionality, are experienced in an altered or "hypnoid" state of consciousness that is intrinsically different from the individual's normal state. On this view, amnesia occurs not because hysteric patients do not *want* to remember their traumatic experiences, but rather, because they *cannot* remember, owing to the discontinuity between their hypnoid and normal states of consciousness. Although Breuer did not deny the importance of repression, he was quick to cite ideas that concurred with his hypnoid hypothesis, including Delboeuf's claim that "We can now explain how the hypnotist promotes cure [of hysteria]. He puts the subject back into the state in which his trouble first appeared and uses words to combat that trouble, as it now makes fresh emergence" (Breuer & Freud, 1895/1957, p. 7, fn. 1).

Since cases of full-blown hysteria are seldom seen today, it is easy to dismiss the work of Breuer, Janet, and their contemporaries as quaint and outmoded. Indeed, even in its own era, the concept of hypnoid states received short shrift: Breuer himself did little to promote the idea, and Freud was busy carving repression into "the foundation-stone on which the whole structure of psychoanalysis rests" (Freud, 1914/1957, p. 16). Nonetheless, vestiges of the hypnoid hypothesis can be seen in a number of contemporary clinical accounts. For instance, Weingartner and his colleagues have conjectured that mood dependence is a causal factor in the memory deficits displayed by psychiatric patients who cycle between states of mania and normal mood (Weingartner, 1978; Weingartner, Miller, & Murphy, 1977). In addition to bipolar illness, MDM has been implicated in such diverse disorders as alcoholic blackout, chronic depression, psychogenic amnesia, and multiple personality disorder (see Goodwin, 1974; Nissen, Ross, Willingham, MacKenzie, & Schacter, 1988; Reus, Weingartner, & Post, 1979).

Given that mood dependence is indeed a problem worth pursuing, how might some leverage on it be gained? Two approaches seem promising: one cognitive in orientation, the other, clinical. The former features laboratory studies involving experimentally induced moods in normal subjects, and aims to identify factors or variables that play pivotal roles in the occurrence of MDM. This approach is called *cognitive* because it focuses on factors—internally versus externally generated events, cued versus uncued tests of explicit retention, or real versus simulated moods—that are familiar to researchers in the areas of mainstream cognitive psychology, social cognition, or allied fields.

The alternative approach concentrates on clinical studies involving naturally occurring moods. Here the question of interest is whether it is possible to demonstrate MDM in people who experience marked shifts in mood state as a consequence of a psychopathological condition, such as bipolar illness. In the remainder of this chapter, we review recent research that has been done on both of these fronts.

Cognitive Perspectives on Mood Dependence

Although mood dependence is widely regarded as a now-you-see-it, now-you-don't effect, many researchers maintain that the problem of unreliability lies not with the phenomenon itself, but rather with the experimental methods meant to detect it (see Bower, 1992; Eich, 1995a; Kenealy, 1997). On this view, it should indeed be possible to obtain robust and reliable evidence of MDM, but only if certain conditions are met and certain factors are in effect.

What might these conditions and factors be? Several promising candidates are considered as follows.

Nature of the Encoding Task

Intuitively, it seems reasonable to suppose that how strongly memory is mood dependent will depend on how the to-be-remembered or target events are encoded. To clarify, consider two hypothetical situations suggested by Eich, Macaulay, and Ryan (1994). In Scenario 1, two individuals—one happy, one sad—are shown, say, a rose and are asked to identify and describe what they see. Both individuals are apt to say much the same thing and to encode the rose event in much the same manner. After all, and with all due respect to Gertrude Stein, a rose is a rose is a rose, regardless of whether it is seen through a happy or sad eye. The implication, then, is that the perceivers will encode the rose event in a way that is largely unrelated to their mood. If true, then when retrieval of the event is later assessed via nominally noncued or spontaneous recall, it should make little difference whether or not the subjects are in the same mood they had experienced earlier. In short, memory for the rose event should *not* appear to be mood dependent under these circumstances.

Now imagine a different situation, Scenario 2. Instead of identifying and describing the rose, the subjects are asked to recall an episode, from any time in their personal past, that the object calls to mind. Instead of involving the relatively automatic or data-driven perception of an external stimulus, the task now requires the subjects to engage in internal mental processes such as reasoning, reflection, and cotemporal thought, "the sort of elaborative and associative processes that augment, bridge, or embellish ongoing perceptual experience but that are not necessarily part of the veridical representation of perceptual experience" (Johnson & Raye, 1981, p. 70). Furthermore, even though the stimulus object is itself affectively neutral, the autobiographical memories it triggers are apt to be strongly influenced by the subjects' mood. Thus, for example, whereas the happy subject may recollect receiving a dozen roses from a secret admirer, the sad subject may remember the flowers that adorned his father's coffin. In effect, the rose event becomes closely associated with or deeply collared by the subject's mood, thereby making mood a potentially potent cue for retrieving the event. Thus, when later asked to spontaneously recall the gist of the episode they had recounted earlier, the subjects should be more likely to remember having related a vignette involving roses if they are in the same mood they had experienced earlier. In this situation, then, memory for the rose event *should* appear to be mood dependent.

These intuitions accord well with the results of actual research. Many of the earliest experiments on MDM used a simple list-learning paradigm—analogous to the situation sketched in Scenario 1—in which subjects memorized unrelated words while they were in a particular mood, typically either happiness or sadness, induced via hypnotic suggestions, guided imagery, mood-appropriate music, or some other means (see Martin, 1990). As Bower (1992) has observed, the assumption was that the words would become associated, by virtue of temporal contiguity, to the subjects' current mood as well as to the list-context; hence, reinstatement of the same mood would be expected to enhance performance on a later test of word retention. Although a few list-learning studies succeeded in demonstrating MDM, several others failed to do so (see Blaney, 1986; Bower, 1987).

In contrast to list-learning experiments, studies involving autobiographical memory—including those modeled after Scenario 2—have revealed robust and reliable evidence of mood dependence (see Bower, 1992; Eich, 1995a; Fiedler, 1990). An example is Experiment 2 by Eich et al. (1994). During the encoding session of this study, undergraduates completed a task of autobiographical event generation while they were feeling either happy (H) or sad (S), moods that had been induced via a combination of music and thought. The task required the students to recollect or generate a specific episode or event, from any time in their personal past, that was called to mind by a common-noun probe, such as *rose;* every subject generated as many as 16 different events, each elicited by a different probe. Subjects described every event in detail and rated it along several dimensions, including its original emotional valence (i.e., whether the event seemed positive, neutral, or negative when it occurred).

During the retrieval session, held two days after encoding, subjects were asked to recall—in any order and without benefit of any observable reminders or cues—the gist of as many of their previously generated events as possible, preferably by recalling their precise corresponding probes (e.g., *rose*). Subjects undertook this test of autobiographical event recall either in the same mood in which they had generated the events or in the alternative affective state, thus creating two conditions in which encoding and retrieval moods matched (H/H and S/S) and two in which they mismatched (H/S and S/H).

Results of the encoding session showed that when event generation took place in a happy as opposed to a sad mood, subjects generated more positive events (means = 11.1 vs. 6.7), fewer negative events (3.3 vs. 6.8), and about the same small number of neutral events (1.2 vs. 2.0). This pattern replicates many earlier experiments (see Bower & Cohen, 1982; Clark & Teasdale, 1982; Snyder & White, 1982), and it provides evidence of mood-*congruent* memory.

Results of the retrieval session provided evidence of mood-*dependent* memory. In comparison with their mismatched-mood counterparts, subjects whose encoding and retrieval moods matched freely recalled a greater percentage of positive events (means = 37% vs. 26%), neutral events (32% vs. 17%), and negative events (37% vs. 27%). Similar results were obtained in two other studies using moods instilled through music and thought (Eich et al., 1994, Experiments 1 & 3), as well as in three separate studies in which the subjects' affective states were altered by changing their physical surroundings (Eich, 1995b). Moreover, a significant advantage in recall of matched over mismatched moods was observed in recent research (described later) involving psychiatric patients who cycled rapidly and spontaneously between states of mania or hypomania and depression (Eich, Macaulay, & Lam, 1997). Thus, it seems that autobiographical event generation, when combined with event free recall, constitutes a useful tool for exploring mood-dependent effects under both laboratory and clinical conditions, and that these effects emerge in conjunction with either exogenous (experimentally induced) or endogenous (naturally occurring) shifts in affective state.

Recall that this section started with some simple intuitions about the conditions under which mood-dependent effects would, or would not, be expected to occur. Although the results reviewed thus far fit these intuitions, the former are by no means explained by the latter. Fortunately, however, there have been two recent theoretical developments that provide a clearer and more complete understanding of why MDM sometimes comes, sometimes goes.

One of these developments is the affect infusion model, which we have already considered at length in connection with mood congruence. As noted earlier, affect infusion refers to "the process whereby affectively loaded information exerts an influence on and becomes incorporated into the judgmental process, entering into the judge's deliberations and eventually coloring the judgmental outcome" (Forgas, 1995, p. 39). For present purposes, the crucial feature of AIM is its claim that

> Affect infusion is most likely to occur in the course of constructive processing that involves the substantial transformation rather than the mere reproduction of existing cognitive representations; such processing requires a relatively open information search strategy and a significant degree of generative elaboration of the available stimulus details. This definition seems broadly consistent with the weight of recent evidence suggesting that affect "will influence cognitive processes to the extent that the cognitive task involves the active generation of new information as opposed to the passive conservation of information given" (Fiedler, 1990, pp. 2–3). (Forgas, 1995, pp. 39–40)

Although the AIM is chiefly concerned with mood congruence, it is relevant to mood dependence as well. Compared to the rote memorization of unrelated words, the task of recollecting and recounting real-life events would seem to place a greater premium on active, substantive processing, and thereby promote a higher degree of affect infusion. Thus, the AIM agrees with the fact that list-learning experiments often fail to find mood dependence, whereas studies involving autobiographical memory usually succeed.

The second theoretical development relates to Bower's (1981; Bower & Cohen, 1982) network model of emotions, which has been revised in light of recent MDM research (Bower, 1992; Bower & Forgas, 2000). A key aspect of the new model is the idea, derived from Thorndike (1932), that in order for subjects to associate a target event with their current mood, contiguity alone between the mood and the event may not be sufficient. Rather, it may be necessary for subjects to perceive the event as enabling or causing their mood, for only then will a change in mood cause that event to be forgotten.

To elaborate, consider first the conventional list-learning paradigm, alluded to earlier. According to Bower and Forgas (2000, p. 97), this paradigm is ill suited to demonstrating MDM, because it

> arranges only contiguity, not causal belonging, between presentation of the to-be-learned material and emotional arousal. Typically, the mood is induced minutes before presentation of the learning material, and the mood serves only as a prevailing background; hence, the temporal relations are not synchronized to persuade subjects to attribute their emotional feelings to the material they are studying. Thus, contiguity without causal belonging produces only weak associations at best.

In contrast, the model allows for strong mood-dependent effects to emerge in studies of autobiographical memory, such as those reported by Eich et al. (1994). Referring to Figure 3.2, which shows a fragment of a hypothetical associative structure surrounding the concept *lake,* Bower and Forgas (2000, pp. 97–98) propose the following:

> Suppose [that a] subject has been induced to feel happy and is asked to recall an incident from her life suggested by the target word *lake*. This concept has many associations including several autobiographic memories, a happy one describing a pleasantly thrilling water-skiing episode, and a sad one recounting an episode of a friend drowning in a lake. These event-memories are connected to the emotions the events caused. When feeling happy and presented with the list cue *lake,* the subject is likely (by summation of activation) to come up with the water-skiing memory. The subject will then also associate the list context to the water-skiing memory and to the word *lake* that evoked it. These newly formed list associations [depicted by dashed lines in Figure 3.2] are formed by virtue of the subject attributing causal belonging of the word-and-memory to the experimenter's presentation of the item within the list.
>
> These contextual associations are called upon later when the subject is asked to free recall the prompting words (or the memories prompted by them) when induced into the same mood or a different one. If the subject is happy at the time of recall testing, the water-skiing memory would be advantaged because it would receive the summation of activation from the happy-mood node and the list context, thus raising it above a recall level. On the other hand, if the subject's mood at recall were shifted to sadness, that node has no connection to the water-skiing memory that was aroused during list input, so her recall of *lake* in this case would rely exclusively upon the association to lake of the overloaded, list-context node [in Figure 3.2].

Thus, the revised network model, like the AIM, makes a clear case for choosing autobiographical event generation over list learning as a means of demonstrating MDM.

Nature of the Retrieval Task

Moreover, both the AIM and the revised network model accommodate an important qualification, which is that mood dependence is more apt to occur when retention is tested in the absence than in the presence of specific, observable

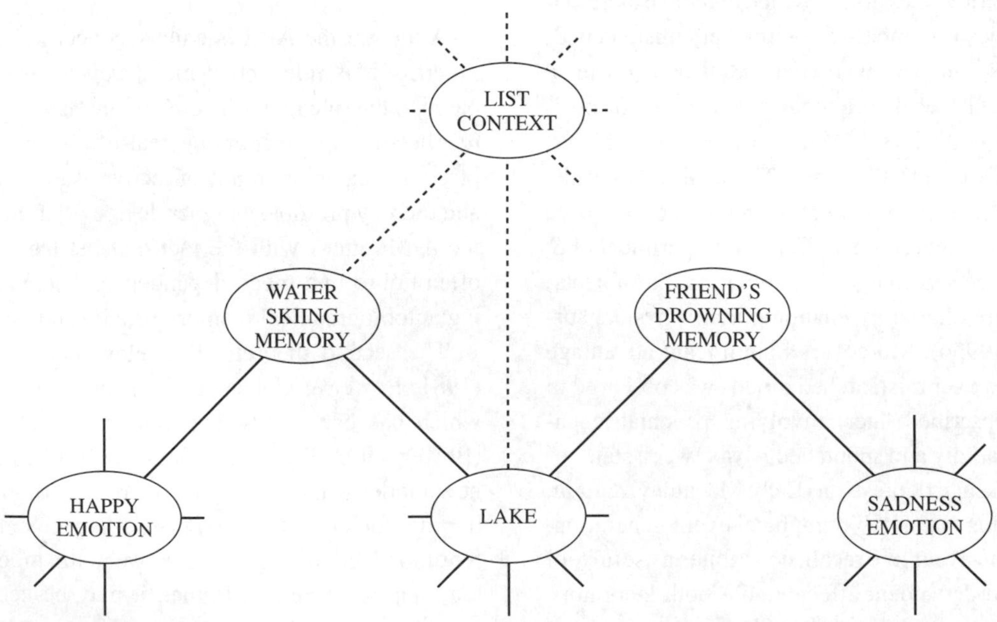

Figure 3.2 Fragment of a hypothetical person's associations involving the concept of *lake*. Lines represent associations connecting emotion nodes to descriptions of two different events, one happy and one sad. The experimental context becomes associated to experiences that were aroused by cues in that setting. *Source:* Bower and Forgas, 2000.

reminders or cues (see Bower, 1981; Eich, 1980). Thus, free recall seems to be a much more sensitive measure of MDM than is recognition memory, which is why the former was the test of choice in all three of the autobiographical memory studies reported by Eich et al. (1994).

According to the network model, "recognition memory for whether the word *lake* appeared in the list [of probes] simply requires retrieval of the *lake*-to-list association; that association is not heavily overloaded at the list node, so its retrieval is not aided by reinstatement of the [event generation] mood" (Bower & Forgas, 2000, p. 98). In contrast, the AIM holds that recognition memory entails direct-access thinking, Forgas's (1995) term for cognitive processing that is simpler, more automatic, and less affectively infused than that required for free recall.

In terms of their overall explanatory power, however, the AIM may have an edge over the revised network model on two accounts. First, although many studies have sought, without success, to demonstrate mood-dependent recognition (see Bower & Cohen, 1982; Eich & Metcalfe, 1989; for exceptions, see Beck & McBee, 1995; Leight & Ellis, 1981), most have used simple, concrete, and easily codable stimuli (such as common words or pictures of ordinary objects) as the target items. However, this elusive effect was revealed in a recent study (Eich et al., 1997; described in more detail later) in which bipolar patients were tested for their ability to recognize abstract, inchoate, Rorschach-like inkblots, exactly the kind of complex and unusual stimuli that the AIM suggests should be highly infused with affect.

Second, although the network model deals directly with differences among various explicit measures of mood dependence (e.g., free recall vs. recognition memory), it is less clear what the model predicts vis-à-vis implicit measures. The AIM, however, implies that implicit tests may indeed be sensitive to MDM, provided that the tests call upon substantive, open-ended thinking or conceptually driven processes (see Roediger, 1990). To date, few studies of implicit mood dependence have been reported, but their results are largely in line with this reasoning (see Kihlstrom, Eich, Sandbrand, & Tobias, 2000; Ryan & Eich, 2000).

Before turning to other factors that figure prominently in mood dependence, one more point should be made. Throughout both this section and the previous one, we have suggested several ways in which the affect infusion model may be brought to bear on the basic problem of why MDM occurs sometimes but not others. Figure 3.3 tries to tie these various suggestions together into a single, overarching idea—specifically, that the higher the level of affect infusion achieved both at encoding and at retrieval, the better the odds of demonstrating mood dependence.

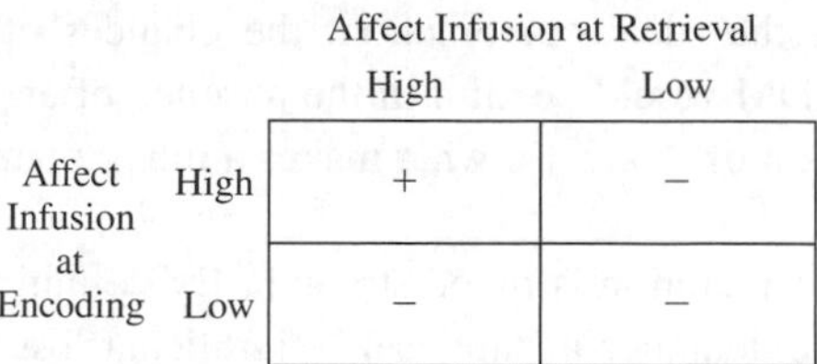

Affect Infusion at Encoding	Affect Infusion at Retrieval: High	Affect Infusion at Retrieval: Low
High	+	–
Low	–	–

Figure 3.3 Circumstances under which evidence of mood-dependent memory is likely (+) or unlikely (−) to emerge.

Although certainly simplistic, this idea accords well with what is now known about mood dependence, and, more important, it has testable implications. As a concrete example, suppose that happy and sad subjects read about and form impressions of fictional characters, some of whom appear quite ordinary and some of whom seem rather odd. As discussed earlier, the AIM predicts that atypical, unusual, or complex targets should selectively recruit longer and more substantive processing strategies and correspondingly greater affect infusion effects. Accordingly, odd characters should be evaluated more positively by happy than by sad subjects, whereas ordinary characters should be perceived similarly, a deduction that has been verified in several studies (Forgas, 1992, 1993). Now suppose that the subjects are later asked to freely recall as much as they can about the target individuals, and that testing takes place either in the same mood that had experienced earlier or in the alternative affect. The prediction is that, relative to their mismatched mood peers, subjects tested under matched mood conditions will recall more details about the odd people, but an equivalent amount about the ordinary individuals. More generally, it is conceivable that mood dependence, like mood congruence, is enhanced by the encoding and retrieval of atypical, unusual, or complex targets, for the reasons given by the AIM. Similarly, it may be that judgments about the self, in contrast to others, are more conducive to demonstrating MDM, as people tend to process self-relevant information in a more extensive and elaborate manner (see Forgas, 1995; Sedikides, 1995). Possibilities such as these are inviting issues for future research on mood dependence.

Strength, Stability, and Sincerity of Experimentally Induced Moods

To this point, our discussion of MDM has revolved around the idea that certain combinations of encoding tasks and retrieval tests may work better than others in terms of evincing robust and reliable mood-dependent effects. It stands to reason, however, that even if one were to able to identify and implement the ideal combination, the chances of demonstrating MDM would be slim in the absence of an effective manipulation of mood. So what makes a mood manipulation effective?

One consideration is mood strength. By definition, mood dependence demands a statistically significant loss of memory when target events are encoded in one mood and retrieved in another. As Ucros (1989) has remarked, it is doubtful whether anything less than a substantial shift in mood, between the occasions of event encoding and event retrieval, could produce such an impairment. Bower (1992) has argued a similar point, proposing that MDM reflects a failure of information acquired in one state to generalize to the other, and that generalization is more apt to fail the more dissimilar the two moods are.

No less important than mood strength is mood stability over time and across tasks. In terms of demonstrating MDM, it does no good to engender a mood that evaporates as soon as the subject is given something to do, like memorize a list of words or recall a previously studied story. It is likely that some studies failed to find mood dependence simply because they relied on moods that were potent initially but that paled rapidly (see Eich & Metcalfe, 1989).

Yet a third element of an effective mood is its authenticity or emotional realism. Using the autobiographical event generation and recall tasks described earlier, Eich and Macaulay (2000) found no sign whatsoever of MDM when undergraduates simulated feeling happy or sad, when in fact their mood had remained neutral throughout testing. Moreover, in several studies involving the intentional induction of specific moods, subjects have been asked to candidly assess (post-experimentally) how authentic or real these moods felt. Those who claim to have been most genuinely moved tend to show the strongest mood-dependent effects (see Eich, 1995a; Eich et al., 1994).

Thus it appears that the prospects of demonstrating MDM are improved by instilling affective states that have three important properties: strength, stability, and sincerity. In principle, such states could be induced in a number of different ways; for instance, subjects might (a) read and internalize a series of self-referential statements (e.g., *I'm feeling on top of the world* vs. *Lately I've been really down*), (b) obtain false feedback on an ostensibly unrelated task, (c) receive a post-hypnotic suggestion to experience a specified mood, or, as noted earlier, (d) contemplate mood-appropriate thoughts while listening to mood-appropriate music (see Martin, 1990). In practice, however, it is possible that some methods are better suited than others for inducing strong, stable, and sincere moods. Just how real or remote this possibly is remains to be seen through close, comparative analysis of the strengths and shortcomings of different mood-induction techniques.

Synopsis

The preceding sections summarized recent efforts to uncover critical factors in the occurrence of mood-dependent memory. What conclusions can be drawn from this line of work?

The broadest and most basic conclusion is that the problem of unreliability that has long beset research on MDM may not be as serious or stubborn as is commonly supposed. More to the point, it now appears that robust and reliable evidence of mood dependence can be realized under conditions in which subjects (a) engage in open, constructive, affect-infusing processing as they encode the to-be-remembered or target targets; (b) rely on similarly high-infusion strategies as they endeavor to retrieve these targets; and (c) experience strong, stable, and sincere moods in the course of both event encoding and event retrieval.

Taken together, these observations make a start toward demystifying MDM, but only a start. To date, only a few factors have been examined for their role in mood dependence; the odds are that other factors of equal or greater significance exist, awaiting discovery. Also, it remains to be seen whether MDM occurs in conjunction with clinical conditions, such as bipolar illness, and whether the results revealed through research involving experimentally engendered moods can be generalized to endogenous or natural shifts in affective state. The next section reviews a recent study that relates to these and other clinical issues.

Clinical Perspectives on Mood Dependence

Earlier it was remarked that mood dependence has been implicated in a number of psychiatric disorders. Although the MDM literature is replete with clinical conjectures, it is lacking in hard clinical data. Worse, the few pertinent results that have been reported are difficult to interpret.

Here we refer specifically to a seminal study by Weingartner et al. (1977), in which five patients who cycled between states of mania and normal mood were observed over several months. Periodically, the patients generated 20 discrete free associations to each of two common nouns, such as *ship* and *street,* and were tested for their recall of all 40 associations four days later. Recall averaged 35% when the mood at testing (either manic or normal) matched the mood at generation, but only 18% when there was a mismatch, a result that Bower (1981) considered "the clearest early example of mood-dependent memory" (p. 134).

Or is it? The question was raised in a review paper by Blaney (1986, p. 237), who noted that

> Weingartner et al.'s results—indicating that subjects experiencing strong mood shifts were better able to regenerate associations first generated in same as opposed to different moods—could be seen as reflecting either mood congruence or [mood] state dependence. That is, the enhanced ability of subjects to recall what they had generated when last in a given mood was (a) because what was congruent with that mood at first exposure was still congruent with it at subsequent exposure, or (b) because return to that mood helped remind subjects of the material they were thinking of when last in that mood, irrespective of content.

A study by Eich et al. (1997) sought both to resolve this ambiguity and to investigate the impact of clinical mood shifts on the performance of several different tasks. Participants were 10 patients with rapid-cycling bipolar disorder, diagnosed according to *DSM-IV* criteria (American Psychiatric Association, 1994).

Every patient was seen on at least four separate occasions, the odd-numbered occasions serving as encoding sessions and the even-numbered occasions representing retrieval sessions. Although the interval separating successive encoding and retrieval sessions varied from 2 to 7 days between patients, the interval remained constant within a given patient.

Superimposed on these sessions was a two-by-two design: mood at encoding—manic or hypomanic (M) versus depressed (D)—crossed with the same two moods at retrieval. The original plan was to vary these factors within subjects, so that every patient would participate in all four combinations of encoding and retrieval moods (viz. M/M, M/D, D/M, and D/D). This plan proved unworkable, however, as several patients quit the study prematurely for various reasons (e.g., they started a new regimen of drug therapy or they stopped cycling between moods). Of the 10 patients who took part in the study, 4 completed all four encoding and retrieval conditions, 3 completed three conditions, and 3 completed two conditions; the order of completion varied unsystematically from one patient to the next, the determining factors being which mood a patient was in when testing began and how rapidly the patient cycled from one state to the other.

During each encoding session the patients undertook a series of three tasks, summarized in subsequent paragraphs. Although the tasks remained constant from one encoding session to the next, the materials used in these tasks were systematically varied. The same applied to the tasks and materials involved in the retrieval session, which will be described shortly.

The first encoding task was *autobiographical-event generation.* Paralleling the procedures described earlier, the patients recollected a maximum of 10 specific events, from any time in the personal past, that were called to mind by neutral-noun probes. After recounting the gist of a given experience (e.g., what happened, who was involved, etc.), patients categorized the event in terms of its original affective valence.

The materials for the second encoding task, *inkblot rating,* consisted of four Rorschach-like inkblots, printed on large index cards. Patients viewed each pattern for a few seconds and then rated its aesthetic appeal.

The final encoding task was *letter-association production.* Patients were asked to name aloud 20 words beginning with one letter of the alphabet (e.g., E) and 20 words beginning with a different letter (e.g., S).

As was the case at encoding, several different tasks were administered during each retrieval session. One of these tasks, *autobiographical-event recall,* is known to show strong mood-dependent effects with experimentally induced moods, and it adhered to the procedures described earlier.

In a second task, *inkblot recognition,* patients were shown four sets of six inkblots each. Within each set, one pattern was an inkblot that the patients had seen during the immediately preceding encoding session, and the other five were perceptually similar lures. Patients were asked to select the old (previously viewed) pattern and to rate their confidence in their recognition decision on a scale ranging from 0 (guessing) to 3 (certain).

On first impression, this task seems ill advised because several studies (cited earlier) have already sought, without success, to demonstrate mood-dependent recognition. It is important to note, however, that most of these studies (a) involved experimentally induced moods (typically happiness vs. sadness) in normal subjects, and (b) investigated recognition memory for materials (usually common, unrelated nouns) that are familiar, simple, meaningful, and unemotional.

Neither these moods nor these materials may be conducive to the occurrence of mood-dependent recognition, the former because they may be too mild to have much of an impact (see Bower, 1992; Eich, 1995a), the latter because they allow little latitude for different encodings in different moods (see Bower & Cohen, 1982; Bower & Mayer, 1989). If so, then the present study may have stood a better chance than most at detecting mood-dependent recognition, given that it (a) involved moods (viz. mania or hypomania vs. depression) that can reasonably be considered strong, and (b) investigated recognition memory for novel, complex, and highly abstract stimuli (viz. Rorschach-like inkblots) that are likely to be subject to emotional biases at encoding.

The last retrieval task, *letter-association retention,* was designed with a view to clarifying the results reported by

Weingartner et al. (1977). As noted earlier, they found that word associations produced in a particular mood (either manic or normal) were especially reproducible in that mood, a finding that can be taken as evidence for either mood dependence or mood congruence.

This ambiguity in interpretation arises from an ambiguity in the test instructions that were given to the patients. Although it is clear from Weingartner et al.'s account that the patients were asked to recall their prior associations, it is unclear how the patients interpreted this request. One possibility is that they understood *recall* to mean that they should restrict their search to episodic memory—in effect, saying to themselves: "What associations did I produce the last time I saw *ship*?"—in which case the results would seem to suggest mood dependence. Alternatively, they may have taken *recall* as a cue to search semantic memory—"What comes to mind now when I think of *street,* regardless of what I said four days ago?"—in which case the data may be more indicative of mood congruence.

Seeking to avoid this ambiguity, the test of letter-association retention was divided into two phases, each entailing a different set of test instructions. The first phase involved *episodic-memory instructions:* After reminding the patients that, near the end of the last session, they had produced 20 words beginning with a particular letter (e.g., E), the experimenter asked them to freely recall aloud as many of these words as possible. Patients were dissuaded from guessing and cautioned against making intrusions. The second phase involved *semantic-memory instructions:* Patients were presented with the other letter to which they had previously responded in the immediately preceding session (e.g., S), and were asked to name aloud 20 words—any 20 words—beginning with that letter. Patients were explicitly encouraged to state the first responses that came to mind, and they were specifically told that they need not try to remember their prior associations. To get the patients into the proper frame of mind, the experimenter asked them to produce 20 associations to each of two brand-new letters before they responded to the critical semantic memory stimulus.

The reasoning behind these procedures was that if memory is truly mood dependent, such that returning to the original mood helps remind subjects of what they were thinking about when last in that mood, then performance in the episodic task should show an advantage of matched over mismatched moods. In contrast, an analogous advantage in the semantic task could be construed as evidence of mood congruence.

Disappointingly, neither task demonstrated mood dependence. On average, the patients reproduced about 30% of their prior associations, regardless of whether they intended to do so (i.e., episodic vs. semantic memory instructions) and regardless of whether they were tested under matched or mismatched mood conditions. Thus, whereas Weingartner's original study showed an effect in the reproduction of associations that could be construed as either mood congruence or mood dependence, the new study showed no effect at all.

Although this discrepancy defies easy explanation, it is worth noting that whereas Eich et al. (1997) used letters to prime the production of associative responses, Weingartner et al. (1977) used common words, stimuli that patients with clinical mood disturbance may interpret in different ways, depending on their present affective state (see Henry, Weingartner, & Murphy, 1971). It is possible that associations made to letters allow less room for state-specific interpretive processes to operate, and this in turn may lessen the likelihood of detecting either mood-congruent or mood-dependent effects (see Nissen et al., 1988).

More encouraging were the results of the test of autobiographical-event recall. Inspection of the light bars in Figure 3.4 reveals that performance was better when encoding and retrieval moods matched than when they mismatched (mean recall = 33% vs. 23%), evidence of mood dependence

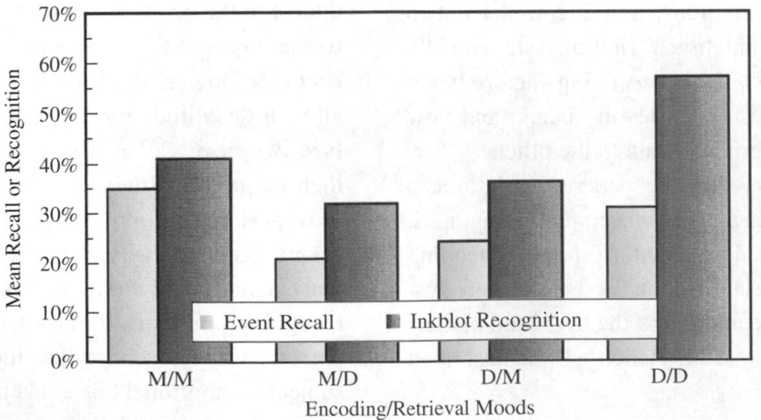

Figure 3.4 Autobiographical events recalled and inkblots recognized as a function of encoding/retrieval moods (M = manic or hypomanic, D = depressed). *Source:* Eich, Macaulay, and Lam, 1997.

that parallels the results obtained from normal subjects whose moods have been modified experimentally (see Eich et al., 1994).

The most surprising results stemmed from the test of inkblot recognition. As reflected by the dark bars in Figure 3.4, the patients were better at discriminating old inkblots from perceptually similar lures when tested under matched as opposed to mismatched mood conditions (mean correct recognition = 48% vs. 34%). Moreover, confidence ratings (made on a 5-point scale) were higher for correct than for incorrect recognition decisions (means = 1.9 vs. 1.1) in every encoding or retrieval condition. This implies that the test tapped explicit, recollective processes and that the patients did not respond to the recognition alternatives solely on the basis of an implicit feeling of familiarity. In short, the patients showed an effect—mood-dependent recognition—that is seldom seen in normals, perhaps because the former subjects experience stronger, more intense moods than do the latter. Alternatively, it may be that the key to demonstrating mood-dependent recognition is to use novel, complex, and highly abstract stimuli (e.g., Rorschach-like inkblots) that are apt to be perceived and encoded in an emotionally biased manner. What role—if any—such stimulus properties play in the occurrence of mood-dependent recognition remains to be seen, ideally through a combination of clinically relevant and laboratory-based research.

Closing Comments

In a cogent review of research on implicit memory, Schacter (1992) made a case for taking a cognitive neuroscience approach to the study of unconscious, nonintentional forms of retention. The crux of the approach is to "combine cognitive research and theory, on the one hand, with neuropsychological and neurobiological observations about brain systems, on the other, making use of data from brain-damaged patients, neuroimaging techniques, and even lesion and single-cell recording studies of nonhuman animals" (Schacter, 1992, p. 559).

To illustrate the value of this hybrid approach, Schacter identified several instances in which data derived from amnesic, alexic, or other neurologically impaired individuals provided a test bed for theories that originated in research involving the proverbial college sophomore. He also showed how studies of normal subjects could constrain neurologically inspired ideas about dissociable memory systems, such as the perceptual representation system posited by Tulving and Schacter (1990). More generally, Schacter argued that by adopting a cognitive neuroscience approach to implicit memory, one is encouraged to draw on data and ideas from diverse areas of investigation, which in turn encourages greater reliance on the logic of converging operations (Roediger, 1980, 1990).

We suggest that similar advantages would accrue through the interdisciplinary study of MDM and that mood dependence, like implicit memory, is most profitably explored through experimentation that cuts across traditional research domains. With respect to MDM, the relevant domains are cognitive, clinical, and social/personality psychology, and, even at this early stage of research, there are already several reasons to recommend their interplay.

For instance, the positive MDM results obtained in the laboratory using autobiographical-event generation and recall provided the rationale for giving the same tasks to patients with bipolar illness. By the same token, the observation that shifts between (hypo)manic and depressed states impair the recognition of nebulous, Rorschach-like patterns casts new doubt on whether mood-dependent memory is a cue-dependent phenomenon, as many cognitively oriented theorists have long maintained (e.g., Bower, 1981; Eich, 1980). Moreover, an intensive investigation of a patient with multiple personality disorder (Nissen et al., 1988) has led not only to a clearer understanding of the connection between interpersonality amnesia and MDM, but also to the intriguing prediction that both mood-congruent and mood-dependent effects in normals should be particularly potent for semantically rich materials that can be interpreted in different ways by different people in different moods. Whether or not this prediction pans out, it nicely illustrates the novel ideas that are apt to emerge when the problem of mood dependence is pursued from both a cognitive and a clinical point of view.

Recent discoveries in social/personality psychology also suggest a number of promising directions for future MDM research. For example, the concept of affect infusion, which developed out of social cognitive studies of mood congruence, has clear yet counterintuitive implications for mood dependence (e.g., that a shift in affective state should have a greater adverse impact on memory for fictional characters who seem odd rather than ordinary). Testing these implications will require MDM researchers to construct materials and tasks that are considerably more socially complex and personally engaging than anything used in the past.

A different set of implications arises from recent investigations of individual differences in mood congruence. The results of these studies suggest that that mood-congruent effects are small, even nonexistent, in people who score high on standardized measures of Machiavellianism, self-esteem, need for approval, and Type-A personality. As Bower and Forgas (2000, p. 141) have commented, high scores on these scales "probably indicate a habitual tendency to approach certain cognitive tasks from a motivated perspective, which should reduce affect infusion effects." Assuming, as we do, that affect infusion is as important to mood dependence as it is to mood congruence, individuals high in self-esteem, Type-A personality, and perhaps other personality traits should seem insusceptible to mood dependence. Tests of this assumption would likely provide new insights into the relations among affect, cognition, and personality, and aid our understanding of both mood congruence and mood dependence.

REFERENCES

Adolphs, R., & Damasio, A. R. (2001). The interaction of affect and cognition: A neurobiological perspective. In J. P. Forgas (Ed.), *Handbook of affect and social cognition* (pp. 27–49). Mahwah, NJ: Erlbaum.

American Psychiatric Association. (1994). *Diagnostic and statistical manual of mental disorders* (4th ed.). Washington, DC: Author.

Baddeley, A. D. (1982). Domains of recollection. *Psychological Review, 89,* 708–729.

Beck, R. C., & McBee, W. (1995). Mood-dependent memory for generated and repeated words: Replication and extension. *Cognition & Emotion, 9,* 289–307.

Berkowitz, L., Jaffee, S., Jo, E., & Troccoli, B. T. (2000). On the correction of feeling-induced judgmental biases. In J. P. Forgas (Ed.), *Feeling and thinking: The role of affect in social cognition* (pp. 131–152). New York: Cambridge University Press.

Blaney, P. H. (1986). Affect and memory: A review. *Psychological Bulletin, 99,* 229–246.

Bless, H. (2000). The interplay of affect and cognition: The mediating role of general knowledge structures. In J. P. Forgas (Ed.), *Feeling and thinking: The role of affect in social cognition* (pp. 201–222). New York: Cambridge University Press.

Bousfield, W. A. (1950). The relationship between mood and the production of affectively toned associates. *Journal of General Psychology, 42,* 67–85.

Bower, G. H. (1981). Mood and memory. *American Psychologist, 36,* 129–148.

Bower, G. H. (1983). Affect and cognition. *Philosophical Transactions of the Royal Society of London 302B,* 387–402.

Bower, G. H. (1987). Commentary on mood and memory. *Behavior Research and Therapy, 25,* 443–455.

Bower, G. H. (1991). Mood congruity of social judgments. In J. P. Forgas (Ed.), *Emotion and social judgments* (pp. 31–53). Oxford, UK: Pergamon.

Bower, G. H. (1992). How might emotions affect learning? In S.-A. Christianson (Ed.), *Handbook of emotion and memory* (pp. 3–31). Hillsdale, NJ: Erlbaum.

Bower, G. H., & Cohen, P. R. (1982). Emotional influences in memory and thinking: Data and theory. In M. S. Clark & S. T. Fiske (Eds.), *Affect and cognition* (pp. 291–331). Hillsdale, NJ: Erlbaum.

Bower, G. H., & Forgas, J. P. (2000). Affect, memory, and social cognition. In E. Eich, J. F. Kihlstrom, G. H. Bower, J. P. Forgas, & P. M. Niedenthal (Eds.), *Cognition and emotion* (pp. 87–168). New York: Oxford University Press.

Bower, G. H., & Mayer, J. D. (1985). Failure to replicate mood-dependent retrieval. *Bulletin of the Psychonomic Society, 23,* 39–42.

Bower, G. H., & Mayer, J. D. (1989). In search of mood-dependent retrieval. *Journal of Social Behavior and Personality, 4,* 121–156.

Bradley, P. P., & Mathews, A. M. (1983). Negative self-schemata in clinical depression. *British Journal of Clinical Psychology, 22,* 173–181.

Breuer, J., & Freud, S. (1957). *Studies on hysteria* (J. Strachey, Ed. & Trans.). New York: Basic Books. (Original work published 1895)

Brown, J. D., & Mankowski, T. A. (1993). Self-esteem, mood, and self-evaluation: Changes in mood and the way you see you. *Journal of Personality and Social Psychology, 64,* 421–430.

Burke, M., & Mathews, A. M. (1992). Autobiographical memory and clinical anxiety. *Cognition & Emotion, 6,* 23–35.

Byrne, D., & Clore, G. L. (1970). A reinforcement model of evaluation responses. *Personality, 1,* 103–128.

Ciarrochi, J. V., & Forgas, J. P. (1999). On being tense yet tolerant: The paradoxical effects of trait anxiety and aversive mood on intergroup judgments. *Group Dynamics: Theory, Research and Practice, 3,* 227–238.

Ciarrochi, J. V., & Forgas, J. P. (2000). The pleasure of possessions: Affect and consumer judgments. *European Journal of Social Psychology, 30,* 631–649.

Clark, D. M., & Teasdale, J. D. (1982). Diurnal variation in clinical depression and accessibility of memories of positive and negative experiences. *Journal of Abnormal Psychology, 91,* 87–95.

Clark, M. S., & Isen, A. M. (1982). Towards understanding the relationship between feeling states and social behavior. In A. H. Hastorf & A. M. Isen (Eds.), *Cognitive social psychology* (pp. 73–108). New York: Elsevier.

Clark, M. S., & Waddell, B. A. (1983). Effects of moods on thoughts about helping, attraction and information acquisition. *Social Psychology Quarterly, 46,* 31–35.

Clore, G. L., & Byrne, D. (1974). The reinforcement affect model of attraction. In T. L. Huston (Ed.), *Foundations of interpersonal attraction* (pp. 143–170). New York: Academic Press.

Clore, G. L., Gasper, K., & Garvin, E. (2001). Affect as information. In J. P. Forgas (Ed.). *Handbook of affect and social cognition* (pp. 121–144). Mahwah, NJ: Erlbaum.

Cosmides, L., & Tooby, J. (2000). Evolutionary psychology and the emotions. In M. Lewis & J. M. Haviland-Jones (Eds.), *Handbook of emotions* (2nd ed., pp. 91–115). New York: Guilford.

Eich, E. (1980). The cue-dependent nature of state-dependent retrieval. *Memory & Cognition, 8,* 157–173.

Eich, E. (1989). Theoretical issues in state dependent memory. In H. L. Roediger & F. I. M. Craik (Eds.), *Varieties of memory and consciousness: Essays in honour of Endel Tulving* (pp. 331–354). Hillsdale, NJ: Erlbaum.

Eich, E. (1995a). Searching for mood dependent memory. *Psychological Science, 6,* 67–75.

Eich, E. (1995b). Mood as a mediator of place dependent memory. *Journal of Experimental Psychology: General, 124,* 293–308.

Eich, E., & Macaulay, D. (2000). Are real moods required to reveal mood-congruent and mood-dependent memory? *Psychological Science, 11,* 244–248.

Eich, E., Macaulay, D., & Lam, R. W. (1997). Mania, depression, and mood dependent memory. *Cognition & Emotion, 11,* 607–618.

Eich, E., Macaulay, D., & Ryan, L. (1994). Mood dependent memory for events of the personal past. *Journal of Experimental Psychology: General, 123,* 201–215.

Eich, E., & Metcalfe, J. (1989). Mood dependent memory for internal versus external events. *Journal of Experimental Psychology: Learning, Memory, and Cognition, 15,* 443–455.

Ellis, H. C., & Ashbrook, P. W. (1988). Resource allocation model of the effects of depressed mood states on memory. In K. Fiedler & J. P. Forgas (Eds.), *Affect, cognition and social behavior* (pp. 25–43). Toronto, Canada: Hogrefe.

Ellis, H. C., & Hunt, R. R. (1989). *Fundamentals of human memory and cognition* (4th ed). Dubuque, IA: William C. Brown.

Ellis, H. C., & Moore, B. A. (1999). Mood and memory. In T. Dalgleish & M. Power (Eds.), *Handbook of cognition and emotion* (pp. 193–210). Chichester, UK: Wiley.

Erdelyi, M. H., & Goldberg, B. (1979). Let's not sweep repression under the rug: Toward a cognitive psychology of repression. In J. F. Kihlstrom & F. J. Evans (Eds.), *Functional disorders of memory* (pp. 355–402). Hillsdale, NJ: Erlbaum.

Eysenck, M. W., MacLeod, C., & Mathews, A. M. (1987). Cognitive functioning in anxiety. *Psychological Research, 49,* 189–195.

Feshbach, S., & Singer, R. D. (1957). The effects of fear arousal and suppression of fear upon social perception. *Journal of Abnormal and Social Psychology, 55,* 283–288.

Fiedler, K. (1990). Mood-dependent selectivity in social cognition. In W. Stroebe & M. Hewstone (Eds.), *European review of social psychology* (Vol. 1, pp. 1–32). New York: Wiley.

Fiedler, K. (1991). On the task, the measures and the mood in research on affect and social cognition. In J. P. Forgas (Ed.), *Emotion and social judgments* (pp. 83–104). Oxford, UK: Pergamon.

Fiedler, K. (2000). Towards an integrative account of affect and cognition phenomena using the BIAS computer algorithm. In J. P. Forgas (Ed.), *Feeling and thinking: The role of affect in social cognition* (pp. 223–252). New York: Cambridge University Press.

Fiedler, K. (2001). Affective influences on social information processing. In J. P. Forgas (Ed.), *Handbook of affect and social cognition* (pp. 163–185). Mahwah, NJ: Erlbaum.

Forgas, J. P. (1979). *Social episodes: The study of interaction routines.* London: Academic Press.

Forgas, J. P. (1990). Affective influences on individual and group judgments. *European Journal of Social Psychology, 20,* 441–453.

Forgas, J. P. (1991). Mood effects on partner choice: Role of affect in social decisions. *Journal of Personality and Social Psychology, 61,* 708–720.

Forgas, J. P. (1992). On bad mood and peculiar people: Affect and person typicality in impression formation. *Journal of Personality and Social Psychology, 62,* 863–875.

Forgas, J. P. (1993). On making sense of odd couples: Mood effects on the perception of mismatched relationships. *Personality and Social Psychology Bulletin, 19,* 59–71.

Forgas, J. P. (1994). Sad and guilty? Affective influences on the explanation of conflict episodes. *Journal of Personality and Social Psychology, 66,* 56–68.

Forgas, J. P. (1995). Mood and judgment: The affect infusion model (AIM). *Psychological Bulletin, 117,* 39–66.

Forgas, J. P. (1998). Asking nicely? Mood effects on responding to more or less polite requests. *Personality and Social Psychology Bulletin, 24,* 173–185.

Forgas, J. P. (1999a). On feeling good and being rude: Affective influences on language use and request formulations. *Journal of Personality and Social Psychology, 76,* 928–939.

Forgas, J. P. (1999b). Feeling and speaking: Mood effects on verbal communication strategies. *Personality and Social Psychology Bulletin, 25,* 850–863.

Forgas, J. P. (2001). *Affective influences on self-disclosure intimacy.* Unpublished manuscript, University of New South Wales, Sydney, Australia.

Forgas, J. P., & Bower, G. H. (1987). Mood effects on person perception judgments. *Journal of Personality and Social Psychology, 53,* 53–60.

Forgas, J. P., Bower, G. H., & Krantz, S. (1984). The influence of mood on perceptions of social interactions. *Journal of Experimental Social Psychology, 20,* 497–513.

Forgas, J. P., Bower, G. H., & Moylan, S. J. (1990). Praise or Blame? Affective influences on attributions for achievement. *Journal of Personality and Social Psychology, 59,* 809–818.

Forgas, J. P., & Ciarrochi, J. V. (2002). On managing moods: Evidence for the role of homeostatic cognitive strategies in affect regulation. *Personality and Social Psychology Bulletin, 28,* 336–345.

Forgas, J. P., & Fiedler, K. (1996). Us and them: Mood effects on intergroup discrimination. *Journal of Personality and Social Psychology, 70,* 36–52.

Forgas, J. P., & Moylan, S. J. (1987). After the movies: the effects of transient mood states on social judgments. *Personality and Social Psychology Bulletin, 13,* 478–489.

Freud, S. (1957). The history of the psychoanalytic movement. In J. Strachey (Ed.), *The standard edition of the complete psychological works of Sigmund Freud* (Vol. 14). London: Hogarth. (Original work published 1914)

Goodwin, D. W. (1974). Alcoholic blackout and state-dependent learning. *Federation Proceedings, 33,* 1833–1835.

Gouaux, C. (1971). Induced affective states and interpersonal attraction. *Journal of Personality and Social Psychology, 20,* 37–43.

Gouaux, C., & Summers, K. (1973). Interpersonal attraction as a function of affective states and affective change. *Journal of Research in Personality, 7,* 254–260.

Griffitt, W. (1970). Environmental effects on interpersonal behavior: Ambient effective temperature and attraction. *Journal of Personality and Social Psychology, 15,* 240–244.

Heider, F. (1958). *The psychology of interpersonal relations*. New York: Wiley.

Henry, G. M., Weingartner, H., & Murphy, D. L. (1971). Idiosyncratic patterns of learning and word association during mania. *American Journal of Psychiatry, 128,* 564–573.

Hull, C. L. (1943). *Principles of behavior.* New York: Appleton-Century-Crofts.

Isen, A. M. (1984). Toward understanding the role of affect in cognition. In R. S. Wyer & T. K. Srull (Eds.), *Handbook of social cognition* (Vol. 3, pp. 179–230). Hillsdale, NJ: Erlbaum.

Janet, P. (1889). *L'Automatisme psychologique* [Psychological automatism]. Paris: Alcan.

Johnson, M. K., & Raye, C. L. (1981). Reality monitoring. *Psychological Review, 88,* 67–85.

Kenealy, P. M. (1997). Mood-state-dependent retrieval: The effects of induced mood on memory reconsidered. *Quarterly Journal of Experimental Psychology, 50A,* 290–317.

Kihlstrom, J. F. (1989). On what does mood-dependent memory depend? *Journal of Social Behavior and Personality, 4,* 23–32.

Kihlstrom, J. F., Eich, E., Sandbrand, D., & Tobias, B. A. (2000). Emotion and memory: Implications for self-report. In A. A. Stone, J. S. Turkkan, C. A. Bachrach, J. B. Jobe, & V. S. Cain (Eds.), *The science of self-report: Implications for research and practice* (pp. 81–99). Mahwah, NJ: Erlbaum.

LeDoux, J. (1996). *The emotional brain.* New York: Touchstone/Simon & Schuster.

Leight, K. A., & Ellis, H. C. (1981). Emotional mood states, strategies, and state-dependency in memory. *Journal of Verbal Learning and Verbal Behavior, 20,* 251–266.

Lewinsohn, P. M., & Rosenbaum, M. (1987). Recall of parental behavior by acute depressives, remitted depressives, and nondepressives. *Journal of Personality and Social Psychology, 52,* 611–619.

Mackie, D., & Worth, L. (1991). Feeling good, but not thinking straight: The impact of positive mood on persuasion. In J. P. Forgas (Ed.), *Emotion and social judgments* (pp. 201–220). Oxford, UK: Pergamon.

Martin, L. (2000). Moods don't convey information: Moods in context do. In J. P. Forgas (Ed.), *Feeling and thinking: The role of affect in social cognition* (pp. 153–177). New York: Cambridge University Press.

Martin, M. (1990). On the induction of mood. *Clinical Psychology Review, 10,* 669–697.

Mathews, A. M., & MacLeod, C. (1994). Cognitive approaches to emotion and emotional disorders. *Annual Review of Psychology, 45,* 25–50.

Mayer, J. D., Gaschke, Y. N., Braverman, D. L., & Evans, T. W. (1992). Mood-congruent judgment is a general effect. *Journal of Personality and Social Psychology, 63,* 119–132.

Miller, N. E. (1950). Learnable drives and rewards. In S. S. Stevens (Ed.), *Handbook of experimental psychology* (pp. 435–472). New York: Wiley.

Niedenthal, P., & Halberstadt, J. (2000). Grounding categories in emotional response. In J. P. Forgas (Ed.), *Feeling and thinking: The role of affect in social cognition* (pp. 357–386). New York: Cambridge University Press.

Niedenthal, P. M., & Setterlund, M. B. (1994). Emotion congruence in perception. *Personality and Social Psychology Bulletin, 20,* 401–411.

Nissen, M. J., Ross, J. L., Willingham, D. B., MacKenzie, T. B., & Schacter, D. L. (1988). Memory and awareness in a patient with multiple personality disorder. *Brain and Cognition, 8,* 21–38.

Rapaport, D. (1961). *Emotions and memory*. New York: Science Editions. (Original work published 1942)

Razran, G. H. S. (1940). Conditioned response changes in rating and appraising sociopolitical slogans. *Psychological Bulletin, 37,* 481–493.

Reus, V. I., Weingartner, H., & Post, R. M. (1979). Clinical implications of state-dependent learning. *American Journal of Psychiatry, 136,* 927–931.

Roediger, H. L. (1980). Memory metaphors in cognitive psychology. *Memory & Cognition, 8,* 231–246.

Roediger, H. L. (1990). Implicit memory: Retention without remembering. *American Psychologist, 45,* 1043–1056.

Ruiz-Caballero, J. A., & Gonzalez, P. (1994). Implicit and explicit memory bias in depressed and non-depressed subjects. *Cognition & Emotion, 8,* 555–570.

Russell, J. A., & Feldman Barrett, L. (1999). Core affect, prototypical emotional episodes and other things called *emotion:* Dissecting the elephant. *Journal of Personality and Social Psychology, 76,* 805–819.

Russell, J. A., & Lemay, G. (2000). Emotion concepts. In M. Lewis & J. M. Haviland-Jones (Eds.), *Handbook of emotions* (2nd ed., pp. 491–503). New York: Guilford.

Rusting, C. L. (2001). Personality as a mediator of affective influences on social cognition. In J. P. Forgas (Ed.), *Handbook of affect and social cognition* (pp. 371–391). Mahwah, NJ: Erlbaum.

Ryan, L., & Eich, E. (2000). Mood dependence and implicit memory. In E. Tulving (Ed.), *Memory, consciousness, and the brain: The Tallinn conference* (pp. 91–105). Philadelphia: Psychology Press.

Salovey, P., Detweiler, J. B., Steward, W. T., & Bedell, B. T. (2001). Affect and health-relevant cognition. In J. P. Forgas (Ed.), *Handbook of affect and social cognition* (pp. 344–368). Mahwah, NJ: Erlbaum.

Schacter, D. L. (1992). Understanding implicit memory: A cognitive neuroscience approach. *American Psychologist, 47,* 559–569.

Schiffenbauer, A. I. (1974). Effect of observer's emotional state on judgments of the emotional state of others. *Journal of Personality and Social Psychology, 30,* 31–35.

Schwarz, N. (1990). Feelings as information: Informational and motivational functions of affective states. In E. T. Higgins & R. Sorrentino (Eds.), *Handbook of motivation and cognition* (Vol. 2, pp. 527–561). New York: Guilford.

Schwarz, N., & Clore, G. L. (1983). Mood, misattribution and judgments of well-being: Informative and directive functions of affective states. *Journal of Personality and Social Psychology, 45,* 513–523.

Schwarz, N., & Clore, G. L. (1988). How do I feel about it? The informative function of affective states. In K. Fiedler & J. P. Forgas (Eds.), *Affect, cognition, and social behavior* (pp. 44–62). Toronto, Canada: Hogrefe.

Sedikides, C. (1994). Incongruent effects of sad mood on self-conception valence: It's a matter of time. *European Journal of Social Psychology, 24,* 161–172.

Sedikides, C. (1995). Central and peripheral self-conceptions are differentially influenced by mood: Tests of the differential sensitivity hypothesis. *Journal of Personality and Social Psychology, 69,* 759–777.

Singer, J. A., & Salovey, P. (1988). Mood and memory: Evaluating the network theory of affect. *Clinical Psychology Review, 8,* 211–251.

Smith, S. M., & Petty, R. E. (1995). Personality moderators of mood congruency effects on cognition: The role of self-esteem and negative mood regulation. *Journal of Personality and Social Psychology, 68,* 1092–1107.

Snyder, M., & White, P. (1982). Moods and memories: Elation, depression, and the remembering of the events of one's life. *Journal of Personality, 50,* 149–167.

Thorndike, E. L. (1932). *The fundamentals of learning*. New York: Teachers College.

Tobias, B. A., Kihlstrom, J. F., & Schacter, D. L. (1992). Emotion and implicit memory. In S.-A. Christianson (Ed.), *Handbook of emotion and memory* (pp. 67–92). Hillsdale, NJ: Erlbaum.

Tulving, E. (1983). *Elements of episodic memory*. Oxford, UK: Oxford University Press.

Tulving, E., & Schacter, D. L. (1990). Priming and human memory systems. *Science, 247,* 301–306.

Ucros, C. G. (1989). Mood state-dependent memory: A meta-analysis. *Cognition & Emotion, 3,* 139–167.

Watkins, T., Mathews, A. M., Williamson, D. A., & Fuller, R. (1992). Mood congruent memory in depression: Emotional priming or elaboration. *Journal of Abnormal Psychology, 101,* 581–586.

Watson, J. B. (1929). *Behaviorism*. New York: W. W. Norton.

Watson, J. B., & Rayner, R. (1920). Conditioned emotional reactions. *Journal of Experimental Psychology, 3,* 1–14.

Watts, F. N., & Dalgleish, T. (1991). Memory for phobia related words in spider phobics. *Cognition & Emotion, 5,* 313–329.

Wegner, D. M. (1994). Ironic processes of mental control. *Psychological Review, 101,* 34–52.

Weingartner, H. (1978). Human state-dependent learning. In B. T. Ho, D. W. Richards, & D. L. Chute (Eds.), *Drug discrimination and state-dependent learning* (pp. 361–382). New York: Academic Press.

Weingartner, H., Miller, H., & Murphy, D. L. (1977). Mood-state-dependent retrieval of verbal associations. *Journal of Abnormal Psychology, 86,* 276–284.

Wyer, R. S., & Srull, T. K. (1989). *Memory and cognition in its social context.* Hillsdale, NJ: Erlbaum.

PART TWO

SENSORY PROCESSES

CHAPTER 4

Foundations of Visual Perception

MICHAEL KUBOVY, WILLIAM EPSTEIN, AND SERGEI GEPSHTEIN

This chapter contains three tutorial overviews of theoretical and methodological ideas that are important to students of visual perception. From the vast scope of the material we could have covered, we have chosen a small set of topics that form the foundations of vision research. To help fill the inevitable gaps, we have provided pointers to the literature, giving preference to works written at a level accessible to a beginning graduate student.

First, we provide a sketch of the theoretical foundations of our field. We lay out four major research programs (in the past they might have been called "schools") and then discuss how they address eight foundational questions that promise to occupy our discipline for many years to come.

Second, we discuss psychophysics, which offers indispensable tools for the researcher. Here we lead the reader from the idea of threshold to the tools of signal detection theory. To illustrate our presentation of methodology we have not focused on the classics that appear in much of the secondary literature. Rather, we have chosen recent research that showcases the current practice in the field and the applicability of these methods to a wide range of problems.

The contemporary view of perception maintains that perceptual theory requires an understanding of our environment as well as the perceiver. That is why in the third section we ask what the regularities of the environment are, how may they be discovered, and to what extent perceivers use them. Here too we use recent research to exemplify this approach.

Reviews of the research on higher visual processes are available in this volume in the chapters by Palmer and by Proffitt and Caudek.

The writing of this chapter was supported by NEI grant R01 EY 12926-06.

THEORIES AND FOUNDATIONAL QUESTIONS

Four Theories

Four theoretical approaches have dominated psychology of perception in the twentieth century: cognitive constructivism, Gestalt theory, ecological realism, and computational constructivism.

Cognitive Constructivism

According to cognitive constructivism, perceptual processing involves inductive inference or intelligent problem solving. Perceptual processing operates beyond one's awareness and attempts to construct the best description of the situation by combining the facts of occurrent stimulation with general and context-specific knowledge. These cognitive processes are not thought to be specially designed for the problems of perception; they are the same cognitive operations that are at work in conscious inference and problem solving. Accordingly, the nature and effects of these cognitive operations may be profitably studied in any setting that activates them. It is neither necessary nor desirable to reinstate the typical conditions of ordinary seeing.

Cognitive constructivism has a venerable tradition. Traces may be found in Kepler's (1604/2000) writings and in vigorous criticism of the approach in Berkeley's *Essay Towards a New Theory of Vision* (1709/2000). Among nineteenth century writers, cognitive constructivism is famously associated with Helmholtz's (1866/2000) doctrine of unconscious inference as expressed, for example, in his *Treatise on Physiological Optics.* In the twentieth century, variants of cognitive constructivism have held center stage. The transactionalists (Ittelson, 1960; Kilpatrick, 1950) Gregory (1970, 1997) and Rock (1983, 1997) are prominent proponents. Current developments of the transactionalist approach are exemplified by the view of perception as Bayesian inference (Hoffman, 1998; Knill & Richards, 1996).

Gestalt Theory

Gestalt theory proposes that the process of perception is an executive-free expression of the global properties of the brain. The organization and orderliness of the perceptual world is an emergent property of the brain as a dynamical system. Gestalt theory intends to distance itself from any position that posits an executive (a homuncular agency) that oversees the work of the perceptual system. The Gestalt theory thus recognizes regulation but will not allow a regulator. A dynamical system which instantiates a massively parallel self-organizing process satisfies is regulated but does not have a regulator. As such, the perceptual world is different from the sum of its parts and cannot be understood by an analytic investigative strategy that adopts a purely local focus. To understand perception we need to discover the principles that govern global perception. The most familiar application of this notion involves the Gestalt principles of grouping that govern perceived form (see chapter by Palmer in this volume).

Gestalt theory emerged in the early decades of the century in the writings of Wertheimer (1912), Köhler (1929, 1940), and Koffka (1935). Although Gestalt theory fell from favor after that period, its influence on modern thought is considerable. Moreover, although ardent advocacy of the original Gestalt theory may have come to an end with the death of Köhler in 1967, a new appreciation for and extension of Gestalt theory or metatheory (Epstein, 1988) has developed among contemporary students (e.g., Kubovy & Gepshtein, in press).

Ecological Realism

The ecological approach has also been called the theory of direct perception: The process of perception is nothing more than the unmediated detection of information. According to this approach, if we describe the environment and stimulation at the appropriate level, we will find that stimulation is unambiguous. In other words, stimulation carries all the information needed for perception. The appropriate level of description can be discovered by understanding the successful behavior of the whole organism in its ecological niche.

This approach appeared in embryonic form in 1950 in Gibson's *Perception of the Visual World* and in mature form in Gibson's last book (1979), in which he explicitly denied the fundamental premises of his rivals. Despite this, a significant segment of the contemporary scientific community is sympathetic to his views (Bruce, Green, & Georgeson, 1996; Nakayama, 1994).

Computational Constructivism

According to computational constructivism, the perceptual process consists of a fixed sequence of separable processing stages. The initial stage operates on the retinal image to generate a symbolic recoding of the image. Subsequent stages transform the earlier outputs so that when the full sequence has been executed the result is an environment-centered description. Computational constructivism bears a family resemblance to cognitive constructivism. Nevertheless, the computationalist is distinguished in at least three respects: (a) The canonical computationalist approach resists notions of cognitive operations in modeling perception, preferring to emphasize the contributions of biologically grounded mechanisms; (b) the computationalist approach involves stored knowledge only in the last stage of processing; (c) the computationalist aspires to a degree of explicitness in modeling the operations at each stage sufficient to support computer implementation.

Computational constructivism is the most recent entry into the field. The modern origins of computational constructivism are to be found in the efforts of computer scientists to implement machine vision (see Barrow & Tenenbaum, 1986). The first mature theoretical exercise in computational constructivism appeared in 1982 in Marr's *Vision.*

The preceding may create the impression that the vision community can be neatly segregated into four camps. In fact, many students of perception would resist such compartmentalization, holding a pragmatic or eclectic stance. In the view of the eclectic theorists, the visual system exploits a variety of processes to fulfill its functions. Ramachandran (1990a, 1990b) gives the most explicit expression of this standpoint in his utilitarian theory.

Eight Foundational Questions

The commonalities and differences among the four theories under consideration are shaped by their approaches, implicit or explicit, toward a number of basic questions.

What Is Vision For?

What is the visual system for? The answer to the question can shape both the goals of experimentation and the procedures of investigation. For most of the twentieth century one answer has been paramount: The function of the visual system is to generate or compute representations or descriptions of the world. Of course, a representation is not to be considered a picture in the mind. Nevertheless, representations serve a useful function by mirroring, even if symbolically, the organization and content of the world to be perceived.

Acceptance of the preeminence of the representational function is apparent in the Gestalt insistence that the first step in the scientific analysis of visual perception is application of the phenomenological method (Kubovy, 1999). This same endorsement is not as wholehearted in cognitive constructivist approaches (Kubovy & Gepshtein, in press). Nevertheless, a review of two of the major documents of cognitive constructivism, Rock's (1983) *The Logic of Perception* and the edited collection *Indirect Perception* (Rock, 1997), shows that in every one of the dozens of investigations reported, the dependent variables were direct or indirect measures of perceptual experience. Marr (1982) was also explicit in allying himself with the representational view. For Marr, the function of vision is "discovering from images what is present in the world." The task for the vision scientist is to discover the algorithms that are deployed by the visual system to take the raw input of sensory stimulation to the ultimate object-centered representation of the world. Given this conception of a disembodied visual system and the task for the visual system, the ideal preparation for the investigation of vision is the artificial (nonbiological) vision system realized by the computer.

The ecological realists do not join the broad consensus concerning the representational function of the visual system. For Gibson, the primary function of the visual system is to detect the information in optical structures that specifies the actions afforded by the environment (e.g., that a surface affords support, that an object affords grasping). The function of the visual system is to perceive possible action, that is, actions that may be successfully executed in particular environmental circumstances.

The representationalists also recognize that perception is frequently in the service of action. Nonetheless, the difference between the representationalists and the ecological realists is significant. For the representationalists the primary function of the visual system is description of the world. The products of the visual system may then be transmitted to the action system. The perceptual system and the action system are separate. Gibson, by contrast, dilutes the distinction between the perceptual system and the action system. The shaping of action does not await perception; action possibilities are perceived directly.

We might expect that following on the ecological realist redefinition of the function of the visual system there would be a redirection of experimental focus to emphasize action and action measures. However, a redirection along these lines is not obvious in the ecological realist literature. Although there are several notable examples of focus on action in the studies of affordances (e.g., Warren, 1984; Warren & Whang, 1987), overall, in practice it is reformulation of input that has distinguished the ecological approach. The tasks set for the subjects and the dependent measures in ecologically motivated studies are usually in the tradition established by the representationalists.

The last two decades of the twentieth century have witnessed a third answer to the question of function. According to this new view, which owes much to the work of Milner and Goodale (1995), the visual system is composed of two major subsystems supported by different biological structures and serving different functions. The proposal that there is a functional distinction between the two major projections from primary visual cortex is found in earlier writing by Schneider (1969) and Ungerleider and Mishkin (1982). These writers proposed that there were two visual systems: the "what" system designed to process information for object identification and the "where" system specialized for processing information for spatial location. The newer proposal differs from the older ones in two respects: (a) The functions attributed to the subsystems are to support object identification (the what function) and action (the how function), and (b) these functions are implemented not by processing different inputs but by processing the same input differently in accordance with the function of the system. As Milner and Goodale (1995, p. 24) noted, "we propose that the anatomical distinction between the ventral and dorsal streams corresponds to the distinction . . . between perceptual representation and visuomotor control. . . . The reason there are two cortical pathways is that each must transform incoming visual information for different purposes." The principal support for this two-vision hypothesis has been provided by findings of double dissociations between action and perception—that is, between assessments of effective action and measures of perceptual experience—in brain-damaged and intact individuals. These findings (summarized by Milner & Goodale, 1995, and by Goodale & Humphrey, 1998) imply that it will be profitable to adopt dual parallel investigative approaches to the study of vision, one deploying action-based measures, the other more traditional "perceptual" measures.

Goodale and Humphrey (1998) and Norman (in press) proposed that the two-vision model provides a framework for reconciling the ecological and computational approaches: "Marrian or 'reconstructive' approaches and Gibsonian or 'purposive animate-behaviorist' approaches need not be seen as mutually exclusive, but rather as complementary in their emphasis on different aspects of visual function" (Goodale & Humphrey, 1998, p. 181). We suspect that neither Gibson nor Marr would have endorsed this proposal. (Chapters by Heuer and by Proffitt and Caudek in this volume also discuss the distinction between the perceptual system and the action system.)

Percepts and Neurons

Perceptual processes are realized by a biological vision system that evolved under circumstances that have favored organisms (or genetic structures) that sustain contact with the environment. No one doubts that a description and understanding of the hardware of the visual system will eventually be part of an account of perception. Nevertheless, there are important differences among theories in their uses of neurophysiology.

One of the tenets of first-generation information-processing theory (e.g., Johnson-Laird, 1988; Neisser, 1967) is that the mind is an operating system that runs on the brain and that the proper business of the psychology of cognition and perception is study of the program and not the computer—the algorithm and not the hardware. Furthermore, inasmuch as an algorithm can be implemented by diverse computational architectures, there is no reason to look to hardware for constraints on algorithms. Another way of expressing this position is that the aim of information-processing theory, as a theory of perception, is to identify functional algorithms above the level of neurophysiology.

The cognitive constructivist shares many of the basic assumptions of standard information-processing theory and has adopted the independence stance toward physiology. Of course, perceptual processes are implemented by biological hardware. Nevertheless, perceptual theorizing is not closely constrained by the facts or assumptions of sensory physiology. The use of physiology is notably sparse in the principal documents of cognitive constructivism (e.g., Rock, 1983, 1997). Helmholtz may seem to be an important exception to this characterization; but, in fact, he was careful to keep his physiology and psychology separate (e.g., Helmholtz, 1866/2000, Vol. 3).

Physiological talk is also absent in the canonical works of the ecological theorists, but for different reasons. The ecologists contend that the questions that have been addressed by sensory physiologists have been motivated by tacit acceptance of a metatheory of perception that is seriously flawed: the metatheory of the cognitive constructivist. As a consequence, whereas the answers discovered by investigations of sensory physiologists may be correct, they are not very useful. For example, the many efforts to identify the properties of the neuronal structures underlying perception by recording the responses of single cells to single points of light seem to reflect the tacit belief that the perceptual system is designed to detect single points. If the specialization of the visual system is different, such as detecting spatiotemporal optical structures, the results of such studies are not likely to contribute significantly to a theory of perception. In the ecological view what is needed is a new sensory physiology informed by an ecological stance toward stimulation and the tasks of perception.

The chief integrative statement of the computational approach, Marr's (1982) *Vision,* is laced with sensory physiology. This is particularly true for the exposition of the computations of early vision. Nevertheless, in the spirit of functionalism Marr insists that the chief constraints are lodged in an analysis of the goals of perceptual computation. In theorizing about perceptual process (i.e., the study of algorithms) we should be guided by its computational goal, not by the computational capabilities of the hardware. When an algorithm can satisfy the requirements of the task, we may look for biological mechanisms that might implement it.

The Gestalt theorists (e.g., Köhler, 1929, 1940) were forthright in their embrace of physiology. For them, a plausible theory must postulate processes that are characteristic of the physical substrate, that is, the brain. Although it is in principle possible to implement algorithms in diverse ways, it is perverse to ignore the fit between the properties of the computer and the properties of the program. This view is in sharp contrast to the hardware-neutral view of the cognitive constructivist: For the Gestalt theorist, the program must be reconciled with the nature of the machine (Epstein, 1988; Epstein & Hatfield, 1994). In this respect, Gestalt theory anticipated current trends in cognitive neuroscience, such as the connectionist approaches (Epstein, 1988).

The consensus among contemporary investigators of perception favors a bimodal approach that makes a place for both the neurophysiological and the algorithmic approaches. The consensus is that the coevolution of a neurophysiology that keeps in mind the computational problems of vision and of a computational theory that keeps in mind the competencies of the biological vision system is most likely to promote good theory.

Although this bimodal approach might seem to be unexceptionable, important theoretical disagreements persist concerning its implementation. Consider, as an example, Barlow's (1972, 1995) bold proposal called the *single-neuron doctrine:* "Active high level neurons directly and simply cause the elements of our perception" (Barlow, 1972, §6.4, Fourth Dogma). In a later formulation, "Whenever two stimuli can be distinguished reliably, then some analysis of the neurological messages they cause in some *single neuron* would enable them to be distinguished with equal or greater reliability" (Barlow, 1995, p. 428). The status of the single-neuron doctrine has been reviewed by Lee (1999) and by Parker and Newsome (1998). The general experimental paradigm assesses covariation between neural activity in single cortical neurons and detection or discrimination at threshold. The single-neuron doctrine proposes that psychophysical functions should be comparable to functions describing neural activity and that decisions made near threshold should be correlated with trial-to-trial fluctuations of single cortical neurons (e.g., Britten, Shadlen, Newsome, & Movshon, 1992).

The available data do not allow a clear-cut decision concerning this fundamental prediction. However, whatever the final outcome may be, disagreements about the significance of the findings will arise from differences concerning the appropriate unit of analysis. Consider first the perceptual side that was elected for analysis. From the standpoint of the ecological realist (e.g., Gibson, 1979), the election of simple detection and discrimination at threshold is misguided. The ecological realist holds that the basic function of the visual system is to detect information in spatiotemporal optical structure that is specific to the affordances of the environment. Examining relations between neuronal activity and psychophysical functions at threshold is at the wrong level of behavior. As noted before, it is for this reason that the canonical documents of the ecological approach (Gibson, 1950, 1966, 1979) made no use of psychophysiology.

Similar reservations arise in the Gestalt approach. Since its inception, Gestalt theory (Hatfield & Epstein, 1985; Köhler, 1940) has held that only a model of underlying brain processes can stand as an explanation. In searching for the brain model, Gestalt theorists were guided by a heuristic: The brain processes and the perceptual experiences that they support have common characteristics. Consequently, a careful and epistemically honest exploration of perceptual experience should yield important clues to the correct model of the brain. According to Gestalt theory, phenomenological exploration reveals that global organization is the most salient property of the perceptual world, and it is a search for the neurophysiological correlates of global experience that will bring understanding of perception.

There are analogous differences concerning the choice of stimulation. If there is to be an examination of the neurophysiological correlates of the apprehension of affordances and global experience, then the stimulus displays must support such perceptions. Proponents of this prescription suspect that the promise of the pioneering work of Hubel and Wiesel (1962) has not been realized because investigators have opted for the wrong level of stimulation.

Concerning Information

The term *information* has many uses within psychology (Dretske, 1986). Here the term refers to putative properties of optical stimulation that could specify the environmental state of affairs (i.e., environmental properties), structures, or events that are the distal source of the optical input. To specify an environmental state is to pick out the actual state of affairs from the family of candidate states that are compatible with the given optical stimulation.

Cognitive constructivists have asserted that no properties of optical stimulation can be found to satisfy the requirements of information in this sense because optical stimulation is intractably equivocal. At best optical stimulation may provide clues—but never unequivocal information—concerning the state of the world. This assessment was already entrenched when Berkeley wrote his influential *Essay Towards a New Theory of Vision* (Berkeley, 1709/2000), and the assessment has been preserved over the ensuing three centuries. The assumption of intractable equivocality is one of the foundational premises of constructivism; it serves as a basic motivation of the enterprise. For example, the transactionalists (Ittelson, 1960; Kilpatrick, 1950, chap. 2) lay the foundation for their neo-Helmholtzian approach by showing that for any proximal retinal state there is an infinite class of distal "equivalent configurations" that are compatible with a given state of the retina. In the same vein, computational research routinely opens with a mention of the "inverse projection problem." If optical stimulation does not carry information that can specify the environment, we must look elsewhere for an account of perception.

The view of the theory of direct perception concerning information is radically different. Proponents of this theory (Rogers, 2000) vigorously reject the assumption of intractable equivocality. Following Gibson, they contend that the tenet of equivocality is false, that it is mistakenly derived from premises about the nature of the stimulation that enters into the perceptual process. The cognitive constructivist who mistakenly uses static displays of points or objects isolated from their optical context (e.g., a point of light or an illuminated object in the dark or a display presented briefly) mistakenly concludes that stimulation is informationally impoverished. But direct perception argues that this paradigm does not represent the optical environment that has shaped the visual system. Even worse, the paradigm serves to create experiments with informationally impoverished displays. Thus equivocality is only an artifact of the constructivist's favored paradigm and not a characteristic of all optical stimulation. The stimulation that the perceptual system typically encounters and to which it has been attuned by evolution is spatially and temporally distributed. These spatiotemporal optical structures, which are configurations of optical motion, *can* specify the environment. There is sufficient information in stimulation to support adaptive perception. And when pickup of information suffices to explain perception, cognitive operations that construct the perceptual world are superfluous.

The stance of the computational constructivist regarding the question of information cannot be characterized easily. If by *information* is meant a unique relationship between optical input and a distal state that is unconditional and not contingent on circumstances, then the computational constructivist must be counted among the skeptics. Optical structures cannot specify distal states noncontingently. Other conditions must be satisfied. The other conditions, which may be called *constraints,* are the regularities, covariances, and uniformities of the environment. Accordingly, assertions about the informational status of optical stimulation must include two conjoint claims: One is about properties of optical stimulation, and the other is about properties of the environment.

Moreover, from a computational constructivist stance, still more is needed to make information-talk coherent. Consideration must be given to the processes and algorithms that make explicit the relationships that are latent in the raw optical input. Whereas the advocates of the theory of direct perception talk of spatiotemporal optical structures, the computationalist sees the structure as the product of processes that operate on unstructured optical input. It is only in the tripartite context of optical input, constraints, and processing algorithms that the computationalist talks about information for perception.

The Gestalt psychologists, writing well before the foregoing theorists, also subscribed to the view that optical stimulation does not carry information. Two considerations led them to this conclusion. First, like the later computationalists, they were convinced that it was a serious error to attribute organization or structure to raw optical input. The perceptual world displays organization, and by Gestalt hypothesis the brain processes underlying perception are organized; but retinal stimulation is not organized. Second, even were it permissible to treat optical input as organized, little would be gained because optical input underdetermines the distal state of affairs. For example, even granting the status of an optical motion configuration to an aggregate of points that displace across the retina by different directions, amplitudes, and velocities (i.e., granting organization to stimulation), there are infinitely many three-dimensional structures consistent with a given configuration of optical motion. For Gestalt theory, structure and organization are the product of spontaneous dynamic interactions in the brain. Optical input is a source of constraints in determining the solution into which the brain process settles.

Concerning Representation

A representation is something that stands for something else. To stand for a represented domain the representation does not have to be a *re-presentation.* The representations that are active in theoretical formulations of the perceptual process are not iconic images of the represented domain. Rather, a representation is taken to be a symbolic recoding that preserves the information about objects and relations in the represented domain (Palmer, 1976).

Representations play a prominent role in cognitive and computational constructivism. Positing representations is a way of reconciling a sharp disparity between the phenomenology of everyday seeing and the scientific analysis of the possibilities of seeing. The experience of ordinary seeing is one of direct contact with the world. But as the argument goes, even cursory analysis shows that all that is directly available to the percipient is the light reflected from surfaces in the world onto receptive surfaces of the eye. How can this fundamental fact be reconciled with the nature of the experience of seeing? Moreover, how can the fact that only light gets in be reconciled with the fact that it is the world that we see, not light? (Indeed, what could it mean to say that we see light?) Both questions are resolved by the introduction of representations. It is representations that are experienced directly, and because the representations preserve the features, relationships, and events in the represented world, the experience of perception is one of direct contact with the world. In this way, representations get the outside inside (Epstein, 1993).

According to constructivist theory, the perceptual world is constructed or assembled from the raw material of sensory input and stored knowledge. The process of construction has been likened to inference or problem solving, and more recently the process has been characterized as computational. The representational framework serves as a superstructure for support of this conception of the perceptual process. Proponents of the computational/representational approach (e.g., Fodor, 1983; Fodor & Pylyshyn, 1981) argue that the only plausible story of perception is computational and that the only plausible computational story must assume a representational system in which the computations are executed.

It seems undeniable that if a variant of the standard constructivist/computational approach is adopted, the representational framework is needed to allow the approach to proceed smoothly. Any theory that postulates a process resembling nondemonstrative inference (Gregory, 1970; Rock, 1983, 1997; or the Bayesian approaches, e.g., Hoffman, 1998; Knill & Richards, 1996) or a process of representational transformation (e.g., Marr, 1982) must postulate a representational medium for the display of "premises" or the display of representations, that is, the output of processes (algorithms) that operate over mappings. No one has been more straightforward and exacting in promoting this approach than Marr in his *Vision*.

In contrast, the theory of direct perception makes no use of representations. Advocates of direct theory argue that the flaws of representationalism are insurmountable. Some of these flaws are logical, such as the familiar troubles with the representational theory of mind, the philosophical progenitor of the contemporary representational framework. As one example, if direct perception were only of representations, how do we come to know what external objects are like, or which representations they resemble? By hypothesis, we can only perceive representations, so that whenever we may think that we are observing external objects to compare them with representations or to discover their intrinsic nature, we are only observing other representations. In general, it is difficult to escape from the world of representations.

In addition to pointing to logical difficulties, proponents of the theory of direct perception see no need to invoke representations in the first place. According to the ecological realists, representationalism is parasitic on constructivism. If constructivism is accepted, then representationalism is compelling; but if it is rejected, then representationalism is unmotivated.

Gestalt theory developed before the age of self-conscious representationalism. There is no explicit treatment of representations in the writings of the Gestalt theorists. Nevertheless, we can infer that the Gestalt theorists would have sided with the advocates of direct perception in this matter. Considerations that support this inference emerge in the next two sections.

Representational Transformation

As a general rule, perceiving is automatic and seamless. Compare, for instance, the effortlessness of seeing with the trouble and toil of learning and reasoning. Although the characterization is unlikely to be questioned as a description of the experience of ordinary seeing, when we consider the process that underlies perceiving, important differences among theories emerge with respect to decomposability. Ignoring theoretical nuances for the present, we find that constructivist theories, both cognitive and computational, hold a common view, whereas Gestalt theory and the theory of direct perception adopt a contrasting position.

The constructivist view is that the process of perception may be decomposed into a series of operations whose function is to take the raw input to the sensory surface and by a series of transformations generate a distally correlated representation of the environment. The process of perception is a process of representational transformation. The constructivists are drawn to this position by an a priori belief that only a model of representational transformation will be sufficient as a description of the perceptual process. One form of empirical support for this belief is found in the requirements of successful algorithms for the attainment of the objectives of perception, such as generating three-dimensional structure from stereopsis. Evidence of the psychological reality of the putative intermediate representations is provided by experimental procedures that ostensibly segregate the component representations.

Neither Gestalt theory nor the theory of direct perception makes use of the model of representational transformation. They do not agree that postulation of a sequential multistage process is necessary, and they question the interpretation of the experimental data. For Gestalt theory, the perceptual process is a noncognitive, highly interactive process that automatically settles into the best fitting state (Epstein & Hatfield, 1994; Hatfield & Epstein, 1985). Any effort to parse the process into intermediate states is arbitrary. On no account should such contrived states be assigned a role in the causal story of perception. Proponents (e.g., Gibson, 1966, 1979; Turvey, Shaw, Reid, & Mace, 1981) of the theory of direct perception have been equally adamant in rejecting the model of representational transformation. They maintain that the model results from questionable premises. Once these are abandoned, the apparent need for positing intervening representational states vanishes.

Perception and Cognition

What is the relationship between perceptual processes and cognitive processes? The answers to this question have ranged widely over the theoretical landscape. The cognitive constructivists consider perception to be perfused by cognition. In the view of the cognitive constructivist, the perceptual process *is* a cognitive process. The principal distinction between perceptual processes and cognitive processes is that in the former case mental operations are applied to the transformation of representations originating in occurrent optical input, whereas in the latter case mental operations are applied to the transformation or representations drawn from the preexisting knowledge base. This attribution is clear-cut for contemporary constructivists, such as Rock (1983, 1997), who characterize perception as a process of intelligent problem solving, as it was in the classical description (Helmholtz, 1866/2000) of perception as a process of unconscious inference and in the New Look movement in North American psychology (Bruner, 1957). The assumption that perception and cognition are continuous is also commonly found in applying standard information theory to problems of perception (e.g., Lindsay & Norman, 1977; Rumelhart, 1977).

The continuity claim is central to the cognitive constructivist position. The claim rests on a diverse set of experimental observations that are said to imply the interpenetration of perception and cognition. Many of the parade cases emerged from the laboratory of Rock (1983, 1997). Despite the compelling character of some of these cases, they have not been decisive. Pylyshyn (1999) has presented a thorough airing of the controversy. In his assessment the cases featured by the cognitive constructivists do not support the claim of cognitive penetrability of perception; "rather, they show that certain natural constraints on interpretation, concerned primarily with optical and geometrical properties of the world, have been compiled into the visual system" (p. 341).

The computational constructivist takes a more restrained position. The aim of the computational approach is to advance the explanation of perception without invoking cognitive factors. Nevertheless, the full explanation of perception requires cognitive operations. In the model of representational transformation adopted by the computational approach, the sequence of operations is divided into early and late vision. The former is supposed to be free of cognitive influence. The operations are executed by modular components of the visual system that are cognitively impenetrable; that is, the modules are encapsulated, sealed off from the store of general knowledge. These operations of early vision perform vital work but do not deliver a representation sufficient to sustain adaptive behavior. A full-bodied, environment-centered representation requires activation of stored mental models and interpretation of the representations of early vision in this context. An exemplar of this stance toward cognition and perception is Marr's (1982) computational theory.

The attitudes of Gestalt theory and the theory of direct perception are opposed to the constructivist stance. Indeed, in the case of Gestalt theory the difference is particularly striking. Whereas the constructivist proposes that perception has significant cognitive components, the larger program of Gestalt theory proposes that much of cognition, such as thinking and problem solving, is best understood as an expression of fundamental principles of perception. The theory of direct perception considers the entire perceptual system to be encapsulated, and therefore uninvolved, in interaction with other information-processing operations. This position does not carry with it a rejection of influences of past experience or learning in perception, but it does require a different construal of the mechanism that supports these influences.

Modularity

Is the visual system a general-purpose processor serving all of the diverse perceptual needs of the organism, or is it a collection of independent perceptual modules that have evolved to compute domain-specific solutions, such as depth from shading, shape, or motion? The answer to this question depends on how modularity is construed. Consider three construals that vary the conditions they impose on the postulation of modularity (the terms *weak, moderate,* and *strong modularity* are ours).

Weak Modularity. Weak modularity stipulates only two conditions: (a) that a segregated bit of the biological hardware be shown to be exclusively dedicated to representation of a specific environmental feature, such as solidity; and (b) that the designated hardware be specialized for the processing of a particular form of stimulation, such as retinal disparity. Under this construal, when these two conditions are satisfied, postulation of a stereoscopic depth module is warranted. If this minimal set of features for modularity is adopted, there probably will be little disagreement that the visual system is modular.

Moderate Modularity. Moderate modularity is defined by a list of features made explicit by Fodor (1983) in his *Modularity of Mind.* To the two criteria given above, Fodor adds several others: that modules are informationally encapsulated, that modular processes are unconscious, that modular processing is very fast and obligatory, that modules have shallow outputs, that modules emerge in a characteristic ontogenetic sequence, and that following insult modules exhibit characteristic disruption.

Among cognitive psychologists, claims for modularity tend to be measured against Fodor's expanded list. Unsurprisingly, when the expanded list of criterial features is adopted, agreement on modularity is harder to reach. Much of the controversy involves encapsulation. By this test, a dedicated biological device that is uniquely sensitive to an eccentric form of stimulation will be considered to be a modular component only if under normal conditions of its operation its processes run their course uninfluenced by factors that are extraneous to the module. Neither concurrent activity in other modules nor reference to stored knowledge of past events or anticipations of future events affects the module. The module is an impenetrable encapsulated system (Fodor, 1983; Pylyshyn, 1984).

Two kinds of problems recur in assessments of encapsulation. First, it is universally accepted that performance of almost any task may be affected by a host of cognitive factors. Accordingly, the claim for encapsulation says that however these cognitive factors influence performance, they do not do so by influencing the computations of the module. Consequently, an experimental demonstration that performance is affected by cognitive factors or by the output of parallel computations does not necessarily negate modularity unless it can be shown that the effects are located in the computations that are endogenous to the putative module. This latter assertion is hard to establish (e.g., Pylyshyn, 1999).

Second, there is the problem of the practice effect. That is, performance of a task that seems unlikely to be supported by a dedicated biological device or to be dependent on access to special stimulation will exhibit many of the features of modularity when the task is highly practiced. For example, performance may become very fast, mandatory, and inaccessible to conscious monitoring. Consequently, evidence that the process underlying performance exhibits these features does not necessarily implicate modularity.

Strong Modularity. Strong modularity adds to the composite list just given the added requirement that the candidate module exhibit a distinctive style of processing. Although no one has advanced this claim explicitly, it is implicit in the writings of modularists that modules work by implementing the same process. As two examples, in Marr's (1982) approach all the modules are noncognitive computational devices, and in Fodor's (1983) canonical analysis of modularity all of the modules are inferential engines. Because the modularity stance does not seem tied to views of process, a stance on modularity does not exert strong constraints on the characterization of the perceptual process. Thus an ecological realist might also adopt modularity, holding that the modules are independent devices for detection (pickup) of information in spatiotemporal optical structure.

Although the postulation of modularity is compatible with a variety of positions regarding perceptual process, an exception to the rule must be made for cognitive constructivism. On the face of it, modularity and cognitive constructivism cannot be linked except in the weak sense of modularity (the first construal). The cognitive constructivist takes the perceptual process to be a cognitive process that ranges freely over the knowledge domain. The principal arguments for the claim that the perceptual process is a form of "hypotheses testing" or "intelligent problem solving" very often take the form of demonstrations that perception is cognitively penetrable (e.g., Rock, 1997). Certainly this is the way that the cognitive constructivist wishes to be understood.

On Illusion and Veridicality

Generally, perception is a reliable guide to action. Occasionally, however, perception misrepresents and action predicated on the implications of perception fails. Perceptual misrepresentations arise under a variety of conditions: (a) The normal link between the environmental state of affairs and optical input is severed: For example, the spatial arrangement of points on the retina and the spatial arrangement of points comprising an environmental object are normally in alignment. A straight stick will have a correspondingly straight retinal contour associated with it. However, if the stick is half immersed in water, the different refractive indices of water and air will result in a "bent" retinal contour. Under these circumstances the straight stick will look bent. (b) The normal pattern of neuronal activation engendered by exposure to a distal arrangement is modified: For example, continuous visual inspection of a line tilted in the frontal plane will modify the pattern of activity of neuronal orientation detectors. The resultant perceptual effect is an alteration of perceived orientation; a test line tilted in the same direction as the inspection line will look upright, and an upright line will look tilted in the direction opposite to the tilt of the inspection line. (c) Rules of perceptual inference are overgeneralized; that is, the rules are applied under conditions for which they are inappropriate. A widely held view (e.g., Gregory, 1970, 1997) attributes many geometric illusions of size to this sort of misapplication of rules. For example, the illusions of size in perspective renderings of a scene, such as the Ponzo illusion, are attributed to the irrepressible but inappropriate application of the putative standard rule for computing size on the basis of visual angle and perceived distance.

All cases of misrepresentation do heavy work, but the contrasting theories depend on different forms of misrepresentation to promote their aims. Consider the theories of direct perception and cognitive constructivism. The ecological realist turns for support to examples of the first kind, which break the link between the environment and optical input. By decoupling the distal state from the optical state while preserving the spatiotemporal optical structure, as in the optical tunnel (Gibson, 1979, Figure 9.2, p. 154), the ecological realist means to demonstrate that information is a property of optical structure and that perception is the pickup of information in optical structure. The advocates of the theory of direct perception are of course deeply distrustful of misrepresentations of the third kind (rules are applied under conditions for which they are inappropriate). They contend that these cases are artifacts of special situations and cannot illuminate the workings of ordinary seeing. Occasionally, advocates of direct theory have suggested that a special theory, a theory of judgment and decision making under uncertainty, is needed for perceptual misrepresentations of the third kind.

The cognitive constructivist, on the other hand, relies heavily on misrepresentations of the third kind. Indeed, these instances of misrepresentations form the core of the empirical case for cognitive constructivism. It is supposed that these perceptual misrepresentations disclose the workings of the hidden processes that govern perception. According to the cognitive constructivist, the processes that underlie veridical and illusory perception are the same, and these processes are revealed by misrepresentations of the third kind. The cognitive constructivist doubts that the demonstrations of the first kind can, in fact, be interpreted in the manner urged by the advocate of direct theory.

Although it has been often suggested that investigations of misrepresentation can be decisive for theories of perception, only infrequently do analyses of misrepresentation test competing hypotheses originating in rival general theoretical orientations. The more common practice is to offer examples of misrepresentation as elements in a confirmation strategy (Nickerson, 1998). The misrepresentations of choice serve as existence proofs of some fundamental postulate of the theoretical approach. The confirmation strategy acts as a directive influence in selecting the class of misrepresentation for investigation and a disincentive that discourages consideration of contrasting accounts generated by rival theories.

PSYCHOPHYSICAL METHODS

The purpose of the remainder of this chapter is to introduce the reader to a selection of experimental techniques and tools for theory construction. Wherever possible we do this by referring new concepts to contemporary experiments and theories. In this way, the reader will understand the ideas in context. We recommend the following textbooks and chapters for the reader who wishes to pursue topics introduced in this section: Gescheider (1997), Hartmann (1998), Link (1992), Luce and Krumhansl (1988), Macmillan and Creelman (1991), and Swets (1996).

Psychophysical methods are indispensable to the advancement of perceptual research. Baird and Noma (1978, p. 1) put it well:

> Psychophysics is commonly defined as the quantitative branch of the study of perception, examining the relations between observed stimuli and responses and the reasons for those relations. This is, however, a very narrow view of the influence it has had on much of psychology. Since its inception, psychophysics has been based on the assumption that the human perceptual system is a measuring instrument yielding results (experiences, judgments, responses) that may be systematically analyzed. Because of its long history (over 100 years [in 1978]), its experimental methods, data analyses, and models of underlying perceptual and cognitive processes have reached a high level of refinement. For this reason, many techniques originally developed in psychophysics have been used to unravel problems in learning, memory, attitude measurement, and social psychology. In addition, scaling and measurement theory have adapted these methods and models to analyze decision making in contexts entirely divorced from perception.

After Fechner (1860/1996) developed psychophysics, two kinds of questions were asked: (a) How sensitive are observers to intensities of stimulation? and (b) How intense do certain amounts of stimulation appear to observers? The first question is about *thresholds,* the second about *scaling.* Given the magnitude of these two fields of research and the number of research tools each has spawned, we have chosen to focus on the more fundamental problem of observer sensitivity.

The notion of threshold comes from Leibniz's *New Essays on Human Understanding* (1765/1981):

> I would prefer to distinguish between perception and being aware. For instance, a perception of light or colour of which we are aware is made up of many minute perceptions of which we are unaware; and a noise which we perceive but do not attend to is brought within reach of our awareness by a tiny increase or addition. If the previous noise had no effect on the soul, this minute addition would have none either, nor would the total. (book 2, chap. 9, p. 134; see also Leibniz, 1989, p. 295.)

Herbart (1824/1890) may have been the first to use the Latin term for threshold, *limen,* and its German equivalent, *schwelle,* to refer to the limit below which a given stimulus ceases to be perceptible. Although the idea of threshold appears straightforward, it turns out to be complex. We now explore the original idea of threshold and show its limitations. After that we present it in its current form: signal detection theory.

Threshold Theories

We begin with the simplest threshold theory, to which we will gradually add elements until it can be confronted with data. By that point we will have introduced two fundamental ideas: the receiver operating characteristic (ROC) and the possibility of disentangling the sensitivity of observers from their response bias.

Fixed Energy Threshold—Naive Observer

The simplest threshold theory is depicted in Figure 4.1. We look at the panels from left to right.

Panel 1: Threshold Location. This panel represents two fundamental ideas: (a) The observer can be in one of two

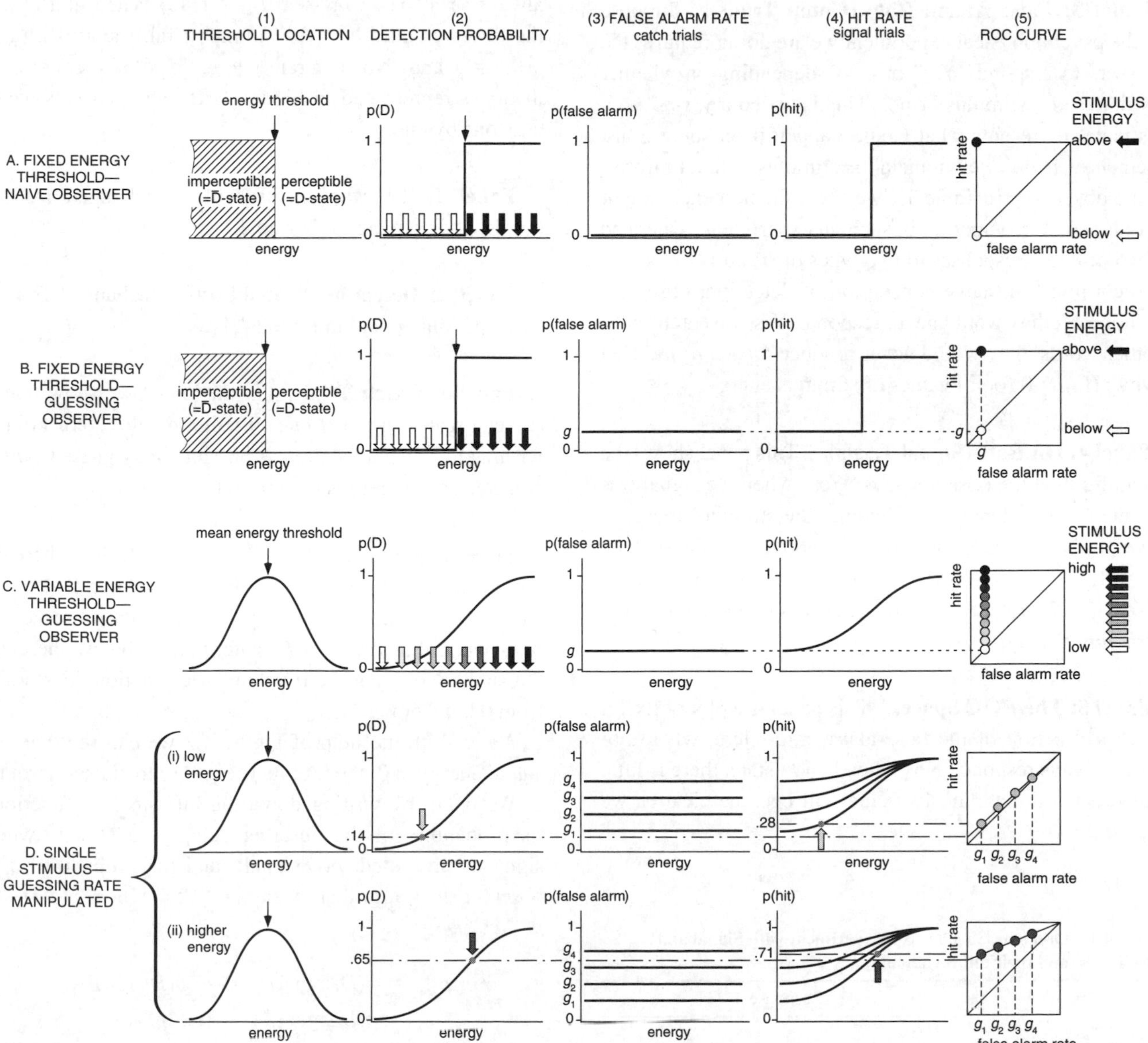

Figure 4.1 High-threshold theories: (A) Fixed energy threshold—naive observer; (B) Fixed energy threshold—sophisticated observer; (C) Variable energy threshold—sophisticated observer; (D) The effect of manipulating guessing rate: (i) Low-energy stimulus, (ii) high-energy stimulus.

states D or $\overline{D}$, and (b) on the scale of stimulus energy there is a fixed value below which observers can never detect a stimulus. Above this threshold, observers always detect it.

Panel 2: Detection Probability. This panel represents the same idea in more modern terms. This graph represents the probability of an observer being above the observer threshold—in state D—as a function of stimulus energy. As you would expect, this probability is 0 below the energy threshold and 1 above it. The multiple arrows represent stimuli; they are unfilled if they are at an energy that is below the energy threshold and filled if they are above it.

Panel 3: False Alarm Rate (Catch Trials). Suppose that the psychophysical experiment we are doing requires the observers to respond "Yes" or "No" depending on whether they detected a stimulus or not. This is called a *yes-no task.* This panel represents what would happen if on some trials, called *catch trials,* we withheld the stimulus without informing the observers. In Table 4.1 we show the nomenclature of the four possible outcomes in such an experiment, generated by two possible responses to two types of stimuli.

According to a naive conception of detection, observers are "honest"; they would never respond "Yes" on catch trials. In other words, they would never produce *false alarms.* That is why $p(\text{fa}) = 0$ for all values of stimulus energy.

Panel 4: Hit Rate (Signal Trials). This panel shows the probability that the observer says "Yes" when the signal was presented (a *hit*) depends on whether the stimulus energy is above or below threshold. If it is above threshold, then $p(\text{h}) = 1$, otherwise $p(\text{h}) = 0$. The function that relates $p(\text{"Yes"})$, or hit rate, to stimulus energy is called the *psychometric function.*

Panel 5: The ROC Space. This panel is a plot of the hit rate as a function of the false-alarm rate. Here, where observers always respond "No" when in a $\overline{D}$ state, there is little point in such a diagram. Its value will become clear as we proceed.

TABLE 4.1 Outcomes in a Yes-No Experiment with Signal and Catch Trials (and their abbreviations)

	Response	
Stimulus Class	Yes	No
Signal	Hit (h)	Miss (m)
Catch	False alarm (fa)	Correct rejection (cr)

Fixed Energy Threshold—Guessing Observer

Instead of assuming naive observers, we next assume sophisticated ones who know that some of the trials are catch trials, so some of the time they choose to guess. Let us compare this threshold theory, called *high-threshold theory,* with the most unrestricted form of two-state threshold theory (Figure 4.2). The general theory is unrestricted because it (a) allows observers to be in either a D state or a $\overline{D}$ state on both signal and catch trials and (b) imposes no restrictions on when guessing occurs.

In contrast, high-threshold theory (Figure 4.3) has three constraints: (a) During a catch trial, the observer is always in a $\overline{D}$ state: $p(D|\text{catch}) = 0$. (b) When in a D state, the observer always says "Yes": $p(\text{"Yes"}|D) = 1$. (c) When in a $\overline{D}$ state, the observer guesses "Yes" (emits a false alarm) at a rate $p(\text{fa}) = g$, and "No" at a rate $1 - g$. So $p(\text{"Yes"}|\overline{D}) = g$. The theory is represented in Figure 4.1B, whose panels we discuss one by one.

Panel 1: Threshold Location. Unchanged from the corresponding panel in Figure 4.1A.

Panel 2: Detection Probability. Unchanged from the corresponding panel in Figure 4.1A.

Panel 3: Catch Trials. In this panel we show that observers, realizing that some stimuli are below threshold and wishing to be right as often as possible, may guess when in a $\overline{D}$ state. This increases the false-alarm rate.

Panel 4: Signal Trials. The strategy depicted here does not involve guessing when the observers are in a D state. This panel shows that this strategy increases the observers' hit rates when they are in a $\overline{D}$ state, that is, below the energy threshold. Note that the psychometric function does not rise from 0 but from g.

Note: With the help of Figure 4.3 we can see that when signal energy is 0, the hit rate is equal to the false-alarm rate, g. We begin by writing down the hit rate as a function of the probability of the observer being in a D state when a signal is presented, $p(D|\text{signal})$, and the probability of the observer guessing, that is, saying "Yes" when in a $\overline{D}$ state, $p(\text{"Yes"}|\overline{D}) = g$:

$$\begin{aligned} p(\text{h}) &= p(D|\text{signal}) + [1 - p(D|\text{signal})]g \\ &= p(D|\text{signal})(1 - g) + g. \end{aligned} \quad (1)$$

When signal energy is 0, $p(D|\text{signal}) = 0$, and therefore $p(\text{h}) = g$.

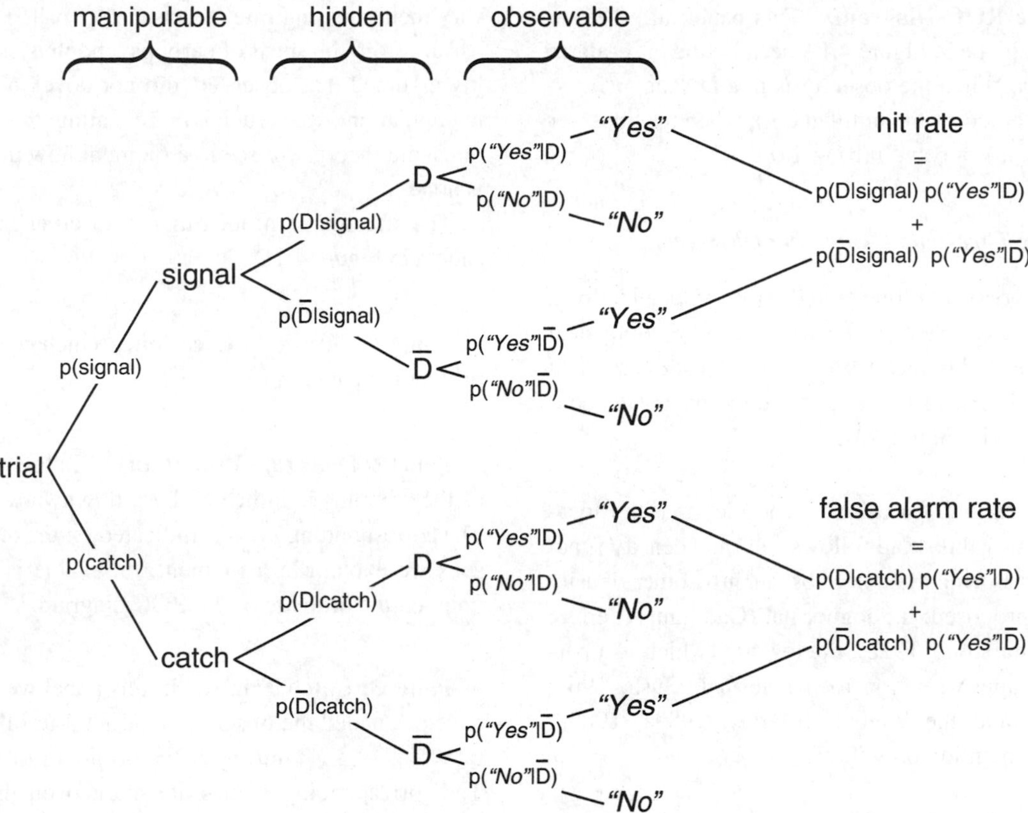

Figure 4.2 The general structure of a detection experiment, assuming two observer states.

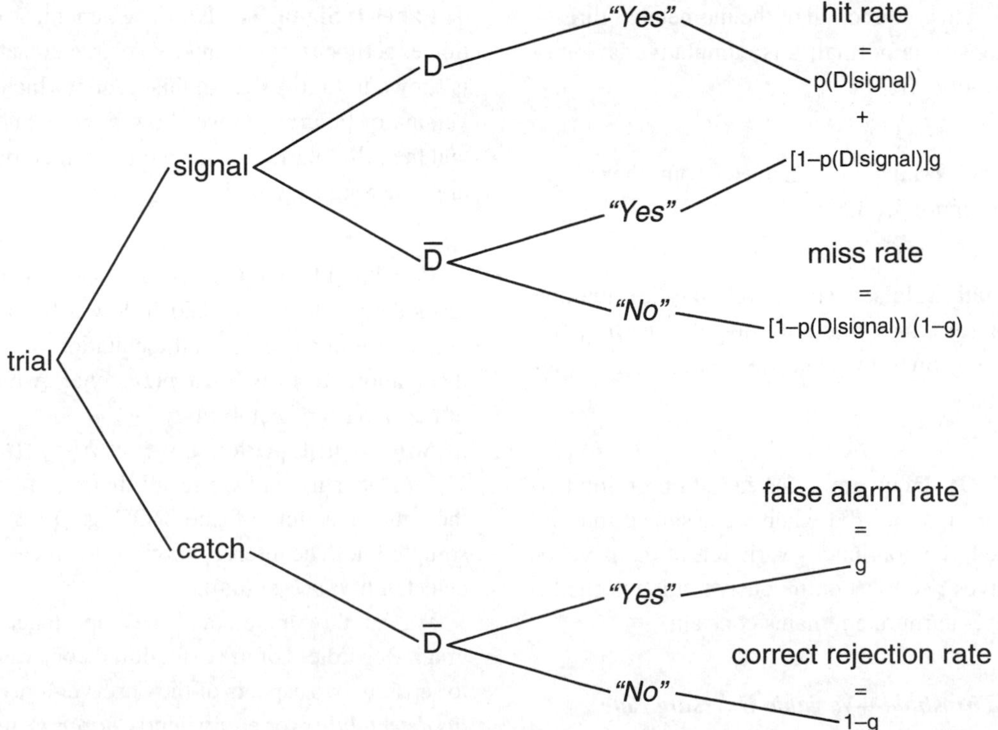

Figure 4.3 The structure of a detection experiment, assuming high-threshold theory. This is a special case of the structure shown in Figure 4.2.

Panel 5: The ROC Diagram. This panel differs from the corresponding one in Figure 4.1A because the false-alarm rate has changed. When the observer is in a $\overline{D}$ state, $p(\text{fa}) = p(\text{h}) = g$ (represented by the unfilled dot); when the observer is in a D state, $p(\text{fa}) = g$ and $p(\text{h}) = 1.0$.

Variable Energy Threshold—Guessing Observer

The preceding versions of threshold theory are idealizations; step functions are nowhere to be found in psychophysical data. In response to this realization Jastrow (1888) assumed that the threshold varies from moment to moment. This conception is depicted in Figure 4.1C.

Panel 1: Threshold Location. The idea that the location of a momentary threshold follows a normal density function comes from Boring (1917). Subsequently, other density functions were proposed: the lognormal (Gaddum, Allen, & Pearce, 1945; Thurstone, 1928), the logistic (which is a particularly useful approximation to the normal; Bush, 1963; Jeffress, 1973), and the Weibull (Marley, 1989a, 1989b; Quick, 1974), to mention only three.

Panel 2: Detection Probability. This panel shows that when the threshold is normally distributed, the probability of being in a D state follows the cumulative distribution that corresponds to the density function of the momentary threshold. When that density is normal, this cumulative is sometimes called a *normal ogive.*

Panel 3: Catch Trials. Unchanged from the corresponding panel in Figure 4.1B.

Panel 4: Signal Trials. The psychometric function shown in this panel takes on the same shape as the function that describes the growth of detection probability (Figure 4.1C, second panel).

Panel 5: The ROC Diagram. Instead of observing two points in the diagram, as we did when we assumed that the threshold was fixed, the continuous variation of the psychometric function gives rise to a continuous variation in the hit rate, while the false-alarm rate remains constant.

Variable Energy Threshold—Variable Guessing Rate

It was a major breakthrough in the study of thresholds when, in 1953–1954, psychophysicists induced their observers to vary their guessing rate (Swets, 1996, p. 15). This was a departure from the spirit of early psychophysics, which implicitly assumed that observers did not develop strategies. This manipulation was crucial in revealing the weaknesses of threshold theory. We see in a moment how this manipulation is done.

The effect of manipulating the observer's guessing rate is shown in Figure 4.1D.

Panel 1: Threshold Location. Unchanged from the corresponding panel in Figure 4.1C.

Panel 2: Detection Probability. In this panel the energy of the stimulus is indicated by a downward-pointing arrow. The corresponding $p(D)$ is indicated on the ordinate. For reasons we explain in a moment, this value is connected to a point on the ordinate of the ROC diagram.

Panel 3: Catch Trials. In this panel we assume that we have persuaded the observer to adopt four different guessing rates ($g_1, \ldots, g_4$) during different blocks of the experiment. The corresponding values are marked on the abscissa (the false-alarm rate) of the ROC diagram (Figure 4.1D, fifth panel).

Panel 4: Signal Trials. The general structure of a detection experiment, assuming two observer states, detect and $\overline{D}$, is shown in Figure 4.2. In this figure (which is an augmented version of Figure 4.3) we show how to calculate the hit rate and the false-alarm rate, as well as which parts of this model are observable and which are hidden.

Panel 5: The ROC Diagram. In this panel hit rate and false-alarm rate covary and follow a linear function. In the note that follows we give the equation of this line and show that it allows us to estimate $p(D|\text{signal})$, which is the measure of the signal's detectability.

Note: If in Equation 1 we let $b = p(D|\text{signal})$ and $m = 1 - p(D|\text{signal})$, and we recall that $g = p(\text{“Yes”}|\overline{D}) = p(\text{fa})$, then the equation of the ROC is $p(\text{hit}) = b + mp(\text{fa})$, a straight line. The intercept b gives the measure of the signal's detectability: $p(D|\text{signal})$.

We can now understand the importance of the ROC diagram. Regardless of the detection theory we hold, it allows us to separate two aspects of the observer's performance: *stimulus detectability* (or equivalently *observer sensitivity*) and *observer bias.* In high-threshold theory these measures are $p(D|\text{signal})$ and g.

TABLE 4.2 The Observer's Decision Problem in High-Threshold Theory

	Observer State	
Stimulus	D	$\overline{D}$
Signal	$p(D\mid\text{signal})$	$p(\overline{D}\mid\text{signal})$
Catch	$p(D\mid\text{catch})$	$p(\overline{D}\mid\text{catch})$

There are two ways to manipulate an observer's guessing rate: (a) Manipulate the probability of a catch trial or (b) use a payoff matrix. The observers' goal is to guess whether a signal or a catch trial occurred; according to high-threshold theory all they know is they were in D state or $\overline{D}$ state (see Table 4.2).

Observers do not know which type of trial (t_1 or t_2) caused the state they are presently experiencing (which we denote ε). Assuming that they know the probabilities of the types of trial and the probabilities of the states they could be in, they can use Bayes's rule for the probability of causes (Feller, 1968, p. 124) to determine the conditional probability of the cause (type of trial) given the evidence (their state), which is called the *posterior probability* of the cause. For example,

$$p(t_1\mid\varepsilon) = \frac{p(\varepsilon\mid t_1)p(t_1)}{p(\varepsilon\mid t_1)p(t_1) + p(\varepsilon\mid t_2)p(t_2)}, \quad (2)$$

where $p(t_1\mid\varepsilon)$ is the posterior probability of t_1, $p(\varepsilon\mid t_1)$ and $p(\varepsilon\mid t_2)$ are likelihoods (of their state given the type of trial), and $p(t_1)$ and $p(t_2)$ are the prior probabilities of the types of trial. In a different form,

$$\frac{p(t_1\mid\varepsilon)}{p(t_2\mid\varepsilon)} = \frac{p(\varepsilon\mid t_1)}{p(\varepsilon\mid t_2)}\frac{p(t_1)}{p(t_2)},$$

where $\frac{p(\varepsilon\mid t_1)}{p(\varepsilon\mid t_2)}$ is the likelihood ratio, $\frac{p(t_1)}{p(t_2)}$ is the prior odds, and $\frac{p(t_1\mid\varepsilon)}{p(t_2\mid\varepsilon)}$ is the posterior odds in favor of t_1.

In high-threshold theory, the posterior odds in favor of signal is

$$\frac{p(\text{signal}\mid D)}{p(\text{catch}\mid D)} = \frac{p(D\mid\text{signal})}{p(D\mid\text{catch})}\frac{p(\text{signal})}{p(\text{catch})}.$$

Suppose that the observers are in a D state, and they believe that half the trials are catch trials [$p(\text{signal}) = p(\text{catch}) = .5$], and that the threshold happens to be at the median of the distribution of energies [$p(D\mid\text{signal}) = p(\overline{D}\mid\text{signal}) = .5$], then

$$\frac{p(\text{signal}\mid D)}{p(\text{catch}\mid D)} = \frac{.5}{0}\frac{.5}{.5} = \infty.$$

Because the posterior odds in favor of signal are infinite, observers have no reason to guess. But if they are in a $\overline{D}$ state and hold the same beliefs, then the posterior odds are

$$\frac{p(\text{signal}\mid\overline{D})}{p(\text{catch}\mid\overline{D})} = \frac{.5}{1}\frac{.5}{.5} = .5,$$

or $p(\text{signal}\mid\overline{D}) = \frac{1}{3}$, that is, they should believe that one third of the $\overline{D}$ trials will be signal trials, and they will increase the number of correct responses by guessing.

We can use two methods to induce observers to change their guessing rate.

Prior Probabilities. In the example above, the prior odds were 1. If we change these odds, that is, increase or decrease the frequency of signal trials, the posterior probability of signal in $\overline{D}$ state will increase or decrease correspondingly. As a result the observer's guessing rate will increase or decrease.

Payoff Matrix. We can also award our observers points (which may correspond to tangible rewards) for each of the outcomes of a trial (Table 4.1), as the examples in Table 4.3 show.

We could reward them for correct responses by giving them B(h) or B(cr) points for hits or correct rejections, and punish them for errors by subtracting C(fa) or C(m) points for false alarms or a misses. To simplify Table 4.3 we set $C(\text{fa}) = C(\text{m}) = 0$. It is easy to see that when we bias the observer toward "Yes," the guessing rate will increase, and when we bias the observer toward "No," it will decrease.

The ROC curve is a particular case of a general framework for thinking about perception—the Bayesian approach to perception. It is summarized in Figure 4.4 (Mamassian, Landy, & Maloney, in press).

This diagram represents a prescriptive framework: how one should make decisions. Bayes's rule is the correct way to combine background information with present data. Furthermore, there is a considerable body of work on the correct way to combine the resulting posterior distribution with information about costs and benefits of the possible decisions (the

TABLE 4.3 Payoff Tables for Responses to Signal and Catch Trials (in points)

	General Case		Bias Toward "Yes"		Bias Toward "No"		No Bias	
	Response							
Stimulus	"Yes"	"No"	"Yes"	"No"	"Yes"	"No"	"Yes"	"No"
Signal	B(h)	C(m)	2	0	1	0	1	0
Catch	C(fa)	B(cr)	0	1	0	2	0	1

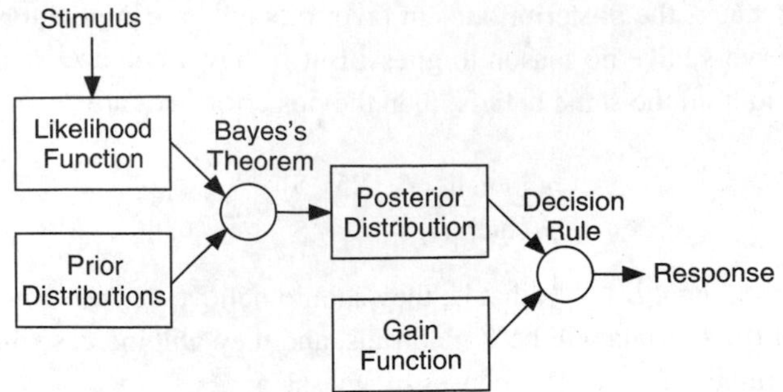

Figure 4.4 Bayesian inference (prescriptive).

gain function in Figure 4.4). When it is used as a prescriptive framework, it is called an *ideal observer.*

Observers in the laboratory, or parts of the visual system, are not subject to prescriptions. What they actually do is shown in Figure 4.5, which is a descriptive framework: how observers (or, more generally, systems) actually make decisions (Kubovy & Healy, 1980; Tanner & Sorkin, 1972).

The diagram identifies four opportunities for the observer to deviate from the normative model:

1. Observers do not know the likelihood function or the prior probabilities unless they learned them. They are unlikely to have learned them perfectly; that is why we have replaced the "likelihood function" and the "prior distributions" of Figure 4.4 with their subjective counterparts.
2. Instead of combining the "likelihood function" and the "prior distributions" by using Bayes's rule, we assume that the observer has a computer that combines the subjective counterparts of these two sources of information. This computer may not follow Bayes's rule.
3. The subjective gain function may not simply reflect the payoffs. Participants in an experiment may not only desire to maximize gain; they may also be interested in exploring the effect of various response strategies.
4. Instead of combining the "posterior distribution" with the "gain function" in a way that will maximize gain, we assume that the observer has a biaser that combines the subjective counterparts of these two sources of information.

Problems with Threshold Theories

We have seen that the ROC curve for high-threshold theory is linear. Such ROC curves are never observed. Let us consider an example. In the animal behavior literature, a widely accepted theory of discrimination was equivalent to high-threshold theory. Cook and Wixted (1997) put this theory to a test in a study of six pigeons performing a texture discrimination. On each trial the pigeons were show one of many potential texture patterns on a computer screen (Figure 4.6).

In some of these patterns all the texture elements were identical in shape and color. Such patterns were called Same (Figure 4.6D). In the other patterns some of the texture elements

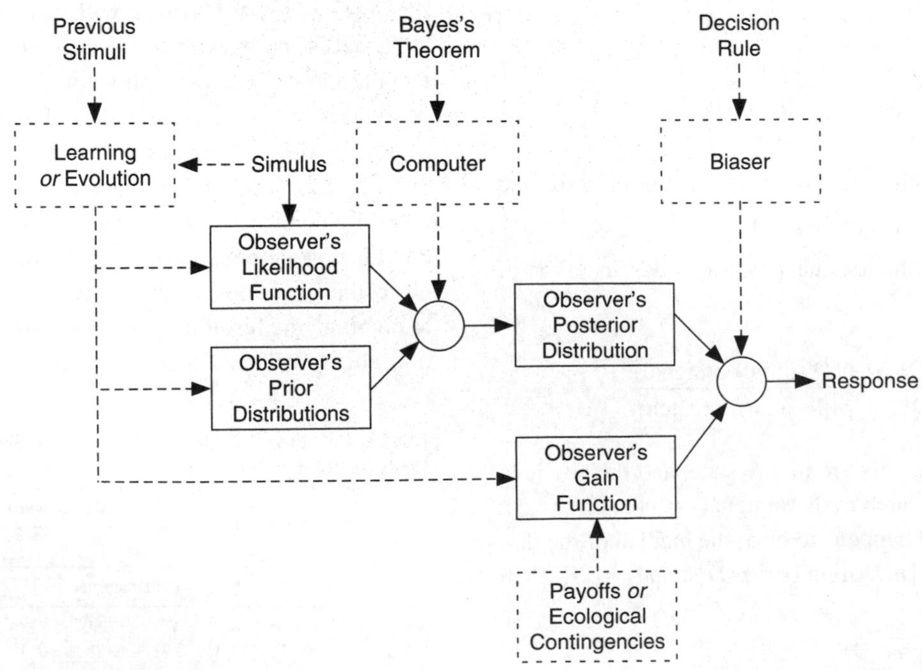

Figure 4.5 Bayesian inference (descriptive).

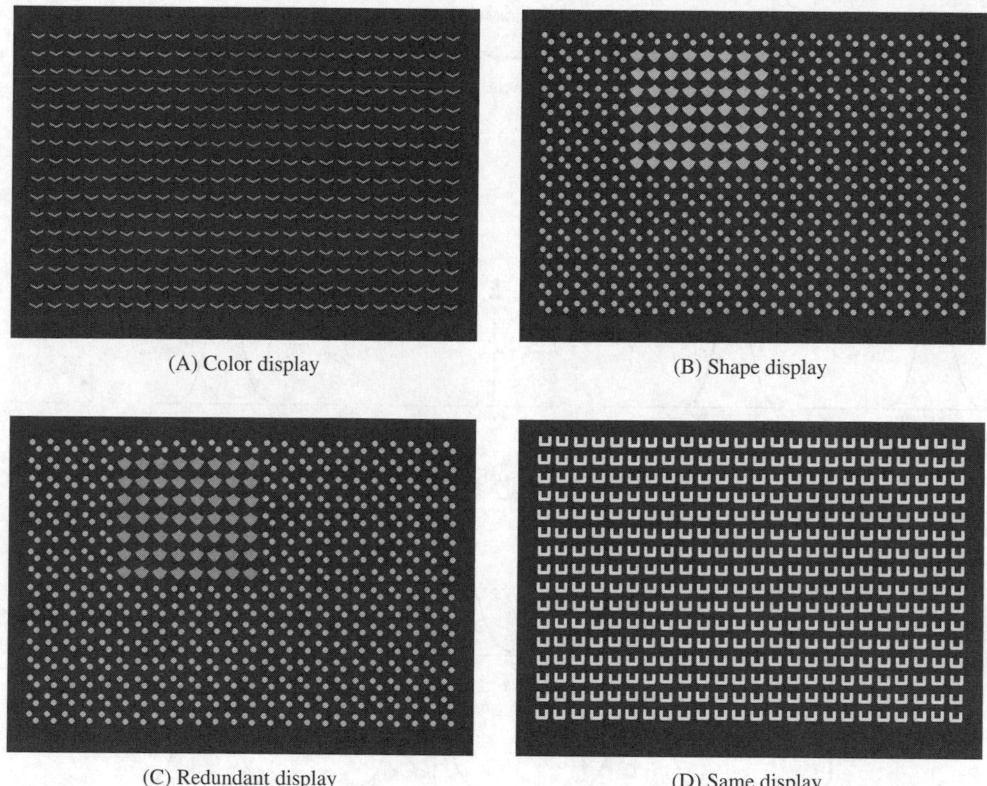

Figure 4.6 Illustrative examples of the many color, shape, and redundant Different and Same displays used in the experiments of Cook and Wixted (1997), after their Figure 4.3 and figures available at http://www.pigeon.psy.tufts.edu/jep/sdmodel/htm (accessed January 2, 2002). See insert for color version of this figure.

differed in color (Figure 4.6A), shape (Figure 4.6B), or both (Figure 4.6C); they were called Different. In the test chamber two food hoppers were available; one of them delivered food when the texture was Same, the other when the texture was Different. Choosing the Different hopper can be taken to be analogous to a "Yes" response, and choosing the Same hopper analogous to a "No" response. To produce ROC curves, Cook and Wixted (1997) manipulated the prior probabilities of Same and Different patterns. The ROC curves were nonlinear, as Figure 4.7 shows.

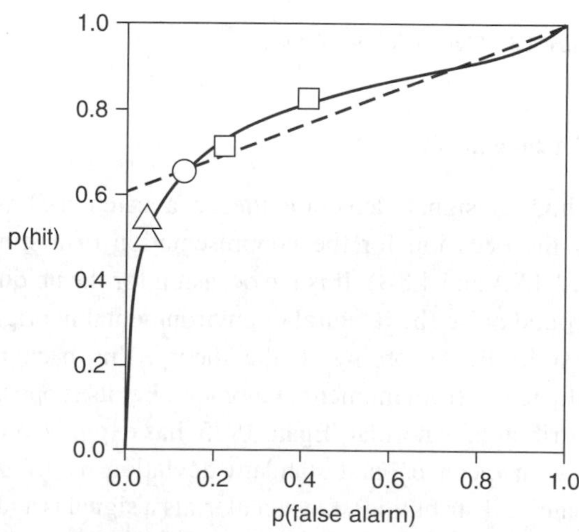

Figure 4.7 The ROC curve of shape discrimination for Ellen, one of the pigeons in the Cook and Wixted (1997) experiments. Circle: equal prior probabilities for Same and Different textures. Squares: prior probability favored Different. Triangles: prior probability favored Same. Redrawn from authors' Figure 5.

Signal Detection Theory

Nonlinear ROC curves require a different approach to the problem of detection, called *signal detection theory,* summarized in Figure 4.8. The key innovation of signal detection theory is to assume that (a) all detection involves the detection of a signal added to background noise and (b) there is no observer threshold (as we will see, this does not mean that there is no energy threshold).

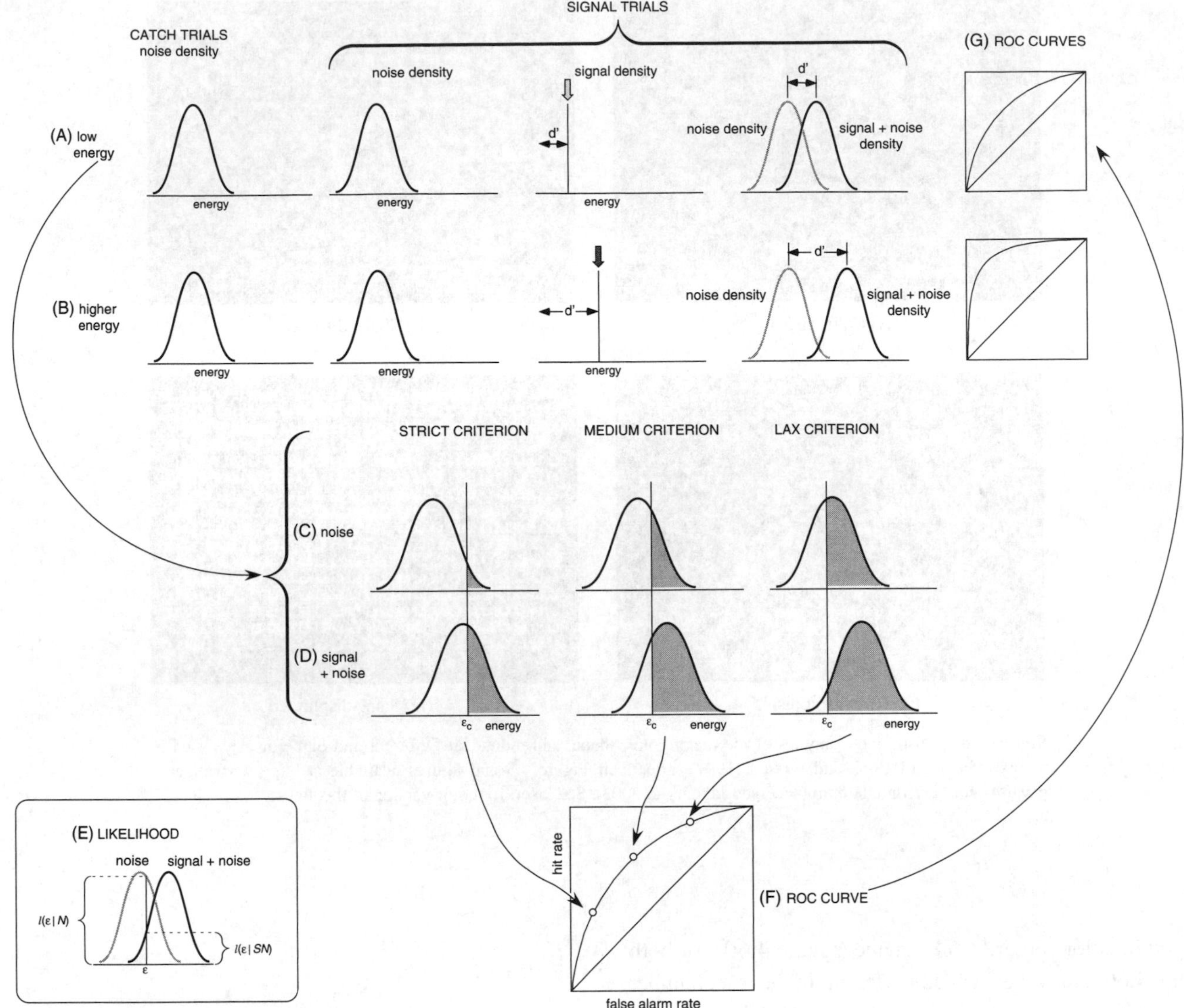

Figure 4.8 Signal detection theory.

Signal Added to Noise

According to signal detection theory a catch trial is not merely the occasion for the nonpresentation of a stimulus (Figures 4.8A and 4.8B). It is the occasion for the ubiquitous background noise (be it neural or environmental in origin) to manifest itself. According to the theory, this background noise fluctuates from moment to moment. Let us suppose that this distribution is normal (Egan, 1975, has explored alternatives), with mean μ_N and standard deviation σ_N (N stands for the noise distribution). On signal trials a signal is added to the noise. If the energy of the signal is d, its addition will produce a new fluctuating stimulus, whose distribution is also normal but whose mean is $\mu_{SN} = \mu_N + d$ (SN stands for the signal + noise distribution). The standard deviations are identical, $\sigma_{SN} = \sigma_N$. If we let $d' = \frac{d}{\sigma_N}$, then $d' = \frac{\mu_{SN} - \mu_N}{\sigma_N}$.

Variable Criterion

The observers' task is to decide on every trial whether it was a signal trial or a catch trial. The only evidence they have is the stimulus, ε, which could have been caused by N or SN. As with high-threshold theory, they could use Bayes's rule to calculate the posterior probability of SN,

$$p(SN|\varepsilon) = \frac{\ell(\varepsilon|SN)p(SN)}{\ell(\varepsilon|SN)p(SN) + \ell(\varepsilon|N)p(N)}.$$

The expressions $\ell(\varepsilon|SN)$ and $\ell(\varepsilon|N)$, explained in Figure 4.8E, are called *likelihoods*. (We use the notation $\ell(\cdot)$ rather than $p(\cdot)$, because it represent a density, not a probability.) They could also calculate the posterior odds in favor of SN,

$$\frac{p(SN|\varepsilon)}{p(N|\varepsilon)} = \frac{\ell(\varepsilon|SN)}{\ell(\varepsilon|N)} \frac{p(SN)}{p(N)}.$$

(We need not assume that observers actually use Bayes's rule, only that they have a sense of the prior odds and the likelihood ratios, and that they do something akin to multiplying them.)

Once the observers have calculated the posterior probability or odds, they need a rule for saying "Yes" or "No." For example, they could choose to say "Yes" if $p(SN|\varepsilon) \geq .5$. This strategy is by and large equivalent to choosing a value of ε below which they would say "No," and otherwise they would say "Yes." This value of ε, ε_c, is called the *criterion.*

We have already seen how we can generate an ROC curve by inducing observers to vary their guessing rates. These procedures—manipulating prior probabilities and payoffs—induce the observers to vary their criteria (Figures 4.8C and 4.8D) from lax (ε_c is low, hit rate and false-alarm rate are high) to strict (ε_c is high, hit rate and false-alarm rate are low), and produce the ROC curve shown in Figure 4.8F. Different signal energies (Figure 4.8G) produce different ROC curves. The higher *d*, the further the ROC curve is from the positive diagonal.

The ROC Curve; Estimating *d′*

The easiest way to look at signal detection theory data is to transform the hit rate and false-alarm rate into log odds. To do this, we calculate $H = k \ln \frac{p(\text{h})}{1 - p(\text{h})}$ and $F = k \ln \frac{p(\text{fa})}{1 - p(\text{fa})}$, where $k = \frac{\pi}{\sqrt{3}} = 0.55133$ (which is based on a logistic approximation to the normal). The ROC curve will often be linear after this transformation. We have done this transformation with the data of Cook and Wixted (1997; see Figure 4.9).

If we fit a linear function, $H = b + mF$, to the data, we can estimate $d = \frac{b}{m}$ and $\sigma_{SN} = \frac{1}{m}$, the standard deviation of the *SN* distribution (assuming $\sigma_N = 1$). Figure 4.9 shows these computations. (This analysis is not a substitute for more detailed and precise ones, such as Eng, 2001; Kestler, 2001; Metz, 1998; Stanislaw & Todorov, 1999.)

Energy Thresholds and Observer Thresholds

It is easy to misinterpret the signal detection theory's assumption that there are no observer thresholds (a potential misunderstanding detected and dispelled by Krantz, 1969). The assumption that there are no observer thresholds means that observers base their decisions on evidence (the likelihood ratio) that can vary continuously from 0 to infinity. It need not imply that observers are sensitive to all signal energies. To see how such a misunderstanding may arise, consider Figures 4.8A and 4.8B. Because the abscissas are labeled "energy," the panels appear to be representations of the input to a sensory system. Under such an interpretation, any signal whatsoever would give rise to a signal + noise density that differs from the noise density, and therefore to an ROC curve that rises above the positive diagonal.

To avoid the misunderstanding, we must add another layer to the theory, which is shown in Figure 4.10. Rows (a) and (c) are the same as rows (a) and (b) in Figure 4.8. The abscissas in rows (b) and (d) in Figure 4.10 are labeled "phenomenal evidence" because we have added the important but plausible assumption that the distribution of the evidence experienced by an observer may not be the same as the distribution of the signals presented to the observer's sensory system (e.g., because sensory systems add noise to the input, as Gorea & Sagi, 2001, showed). Thus in row (b) we show a case where the signal is not strong enough to cause a response in the observer: the signal is below this observer's energy threshold. In row (d) we show a case of a signal that is above the energy threshold.

Some Methods for Threshold Determination

Method of Limits

Terman and Terman (1999) wanted to find out whether retinal sensitivity has an effect on seasonal affective disorder (SAD;

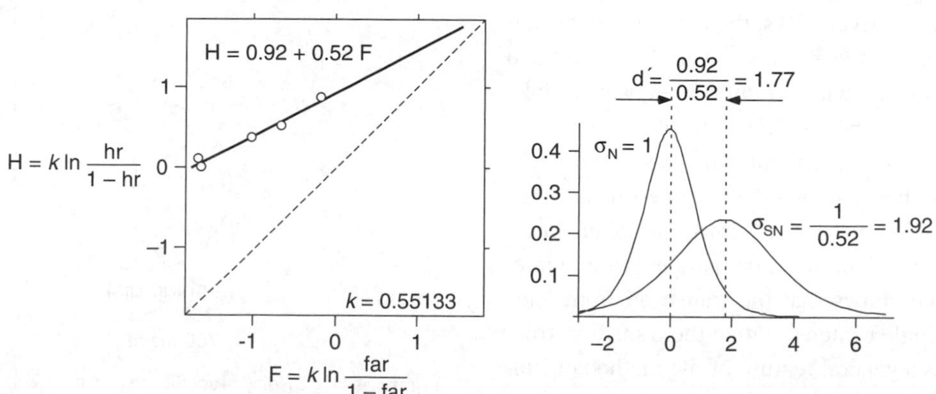

Figure 4.9 Simple analysis of the Cook and Wixted (1997) data.

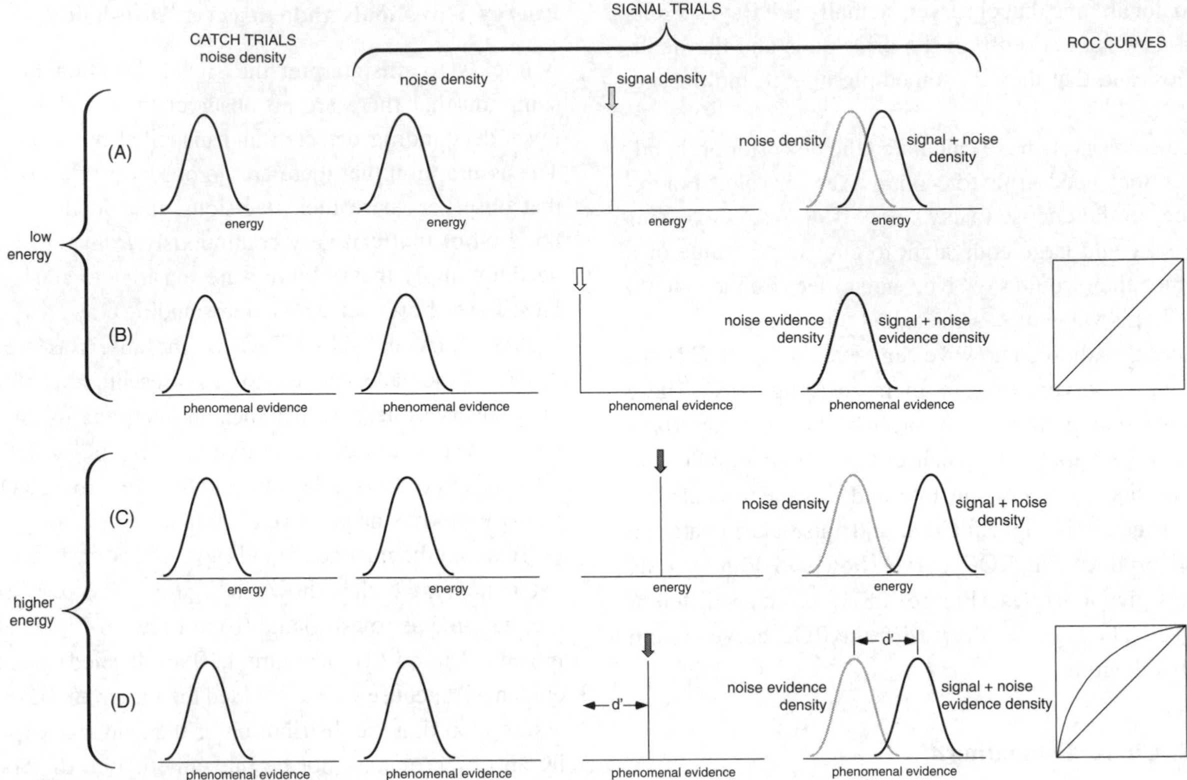

Figure 4.10 Revision of Figure 4.8 to show that energy thresholds are compatible with the absence of an observer threshold.

reviewed by Mersch, Middendorp, Bouhuys, Beersma, & Hoofdakker, 1999). To determine an individual's retinal sensitivity, they used a psychophysical technique called the *method of limits* and studied the course of their dark adaptation (for a good introduction, see Hood & Finkelstein, 1986, §4).

Terman and Terman (1999) first adapted the participants to a large field of bright light for 5 min. Then they darkened the room and turned on a dim red spot upon which the participants were asked to fix their gaze (Figure 4.11). Because they wanted to test dark adaptation of the retina at a region that contained both rods and cones, they tested the ability of the participants to detect a dim, intermittently flashing white disk below that fixation point. Every 30 s, the experimenter gradually adjusted the target intensity upward or downward and then asked the participant whether the target was visible. When target intensity was below threshold (i.e., the participant responded "no") the experimenter increased the intensity until the response became "yes." The experimenter then reversed the progression until the subject reported "no." Figure 4.12 shows the data for one patient with winter depression. The graph shows that the transition from "no" to "yes" occurs at a higher intensity than the transition from "yes" to "no." This is a general feature of the method of limits, and it is a manifestation of a phenomenon commonly seen in perceptual processes called *hysteresis*.

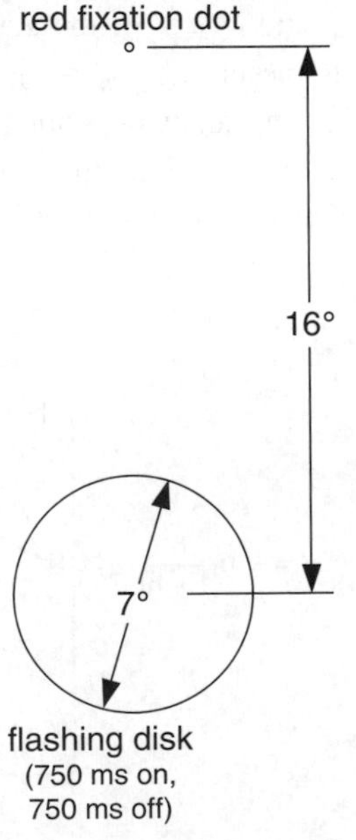

Figure 4.11 Display for the seasonal affective disorder experiment (Terman & Terman, 1999). Rules of thumb: 20° of visual angle is the width of a hand at arm's length; 2° is the width of your index finger at arm's length.

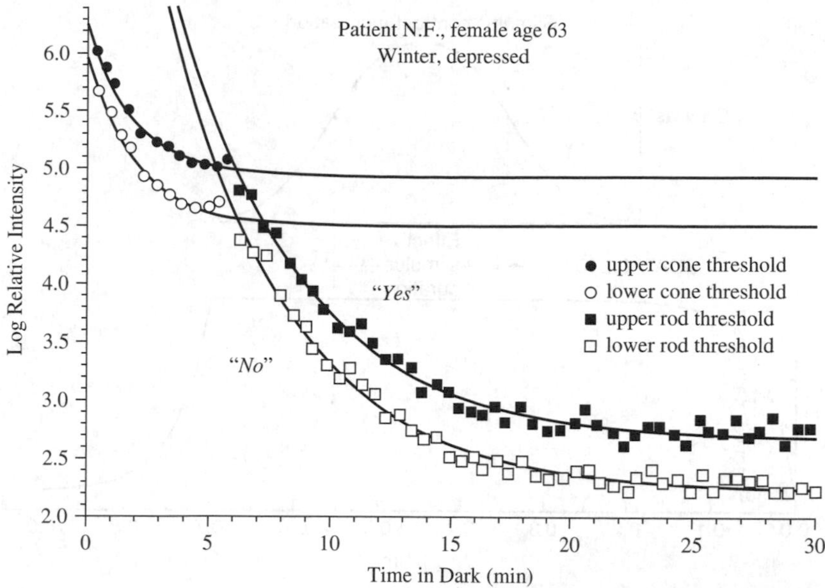

Figure 4.12 Visual detection threshold during dark adaptation for a patient with winter depression. The curves are exponential functions for photopic (cone) and scotopic (rod) segments of dark adaptation. *Source:* From "Photopic and scotopic light detection in patients with seasonal affective disorder and control subjects," by J. S. Terman and M. Terman, 1999, *Biological Psychiatry, 46,* Figure 1. Copyright 1999 by Society of Biological Psychiatry. Reprinted with permission.

Terman and Terman (1999) overcame the problem of hysteresis by taking the mean of these two values to characterize the sensitivity of the participants. The cone and rod thresholds of all the participants were lower in the summer than in the winter. However, in winter the 24 depressed participants were more sensitive than were the 12 control participants. Thus the supersensitivity of the patients in winter may be one of the causes of winter depression.

Method of Constant Stimuli

Barraza and Colombo (2001) wanted to discover conditions under which glare hindered the detection of motion. Their stimulus is one commonly used to explore motion thresholds: a drifting sinusoidal grating, illustrated in Figure 4.13 (Graham, 1989, §2.1.1, defines such gratings).

The lowest velocity at which such a grating appears to be drifting consistently is called the lower threshold of motion

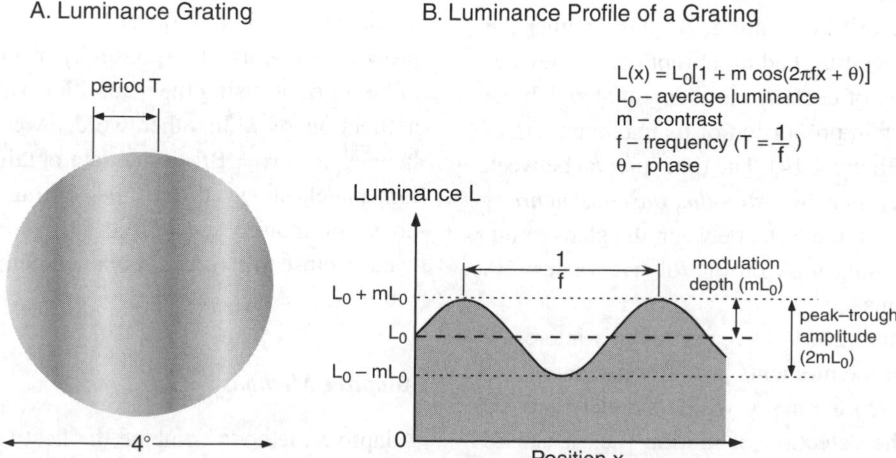

Figure 4.13 (A) The sinusoidal grating used by Barraza and Colombo (2001) drifted to the right or to the left at a rate that ranged from about one cycle per minute (0.0065 cycles per second, or Hz) to about one cycle every 3.75 s (0.0104 Hz). The grating was faded in and out, as shown in Figure 4.14. It is shown here with approximately its peak contrast. (B) The luminance profile of a sinusoidal grating, and its principal parameters.

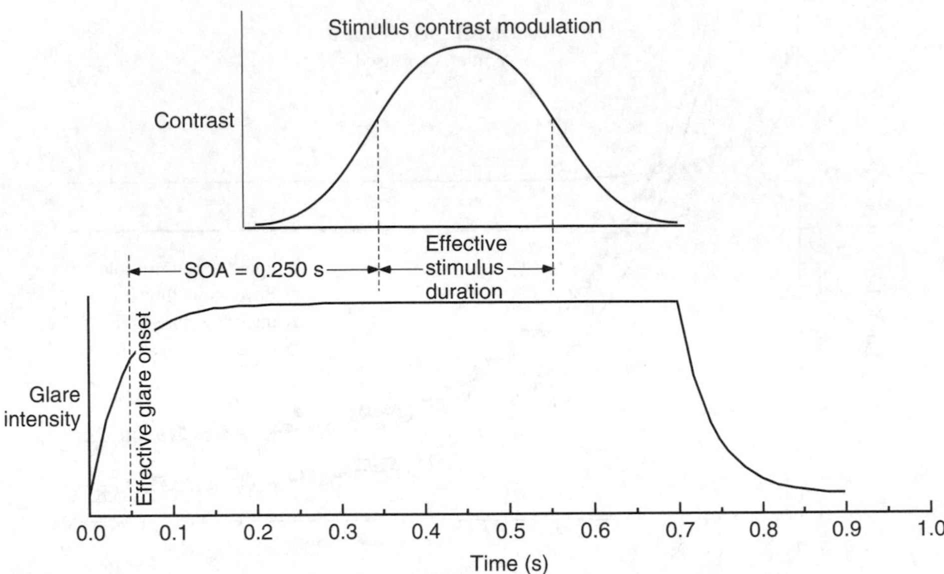

Figure 4.14 Scheme of presentation of glare and test stimulus in a trial for a 250-ms value of SOA. After Barraza and Colombo (2001, Figure 1).

(LTM). To determine the LTM, Barraza and Colombo (2001) showed the observers two gratings in succession. One was drifting to the right, and the other was drifting to the left. The observer had to report whether the first or the second interval contained the leftward-drifting grating. Such tasks are called *forced-choice tasks.* More specifically, this is an instance of a temporal two-alternative forced-choice task (2AFC; to learn more about forced-choice designs, see Macmillan & Creelman, 1991, chap. 5, and Hartmann, 1998, chap. 24).

To simulate the effect of glare, Barraza and Colombo (2001) used an incandescent lamp located 10° away from the observer's line of sight. On each trial, they first turned on the glare stimulus, and then after a predetermined interval of time, they showed the drifting grating. Because neither the glare stimulus nor the grating had an abrupt onset, they defined the *effective onset* of each as the moment at which the stimulus reached a certain proportion of its maximum effectiveness (as shown in Figure 4.14). The time interval between the onset of two stimuli is called *stimulus-onset asynchrony* (SOA). In this experiment the SOA between the glare stimulus and the drifting grating took on one of five values: 50, 150, 250, 350, or 450 ms.

Barraza and Colombo (2001) were particularly interested in determining whether the moments just after the glare stimulus was turned on were the ones at which the glare was the most detrimental to the detection of motion (i.e., it caused the LTM to rise). To measure the LTM for each condition, they used the *method of constant stimuli:* They presented the gratings repeatedly at a given drift velocity so that they could estimate the probability that the observer could discriminate between left- and right-drifting gratings.

To calculate the LTM, they plotted the proportion of correct responses for a given SOA as a function of the rate at which the grating drifted (Figure 4.15, top panel). They then fitted a Weibull function to these data and determined the LTM by finding the grating velocity that corresponded to 80% correct responses (dashed lines). Although there is no substitute for publishing the best-fitting normal, logistic, or Weibull distribution function to such data (using *logistic regression* for a logistic distribution or a *probit model* for the normal; Agresti, 1996), the easiest way to look at such data is to transform the percentage of correct data into log odds. Let us denote motion frequency by f and the corresponding proportion of correct responses by $\pi(f)$. We plot the log-odds of being right (using the natural logarithm, denoted by ln) as a function of f. In other words, we fit a linear function, $\ln \frac{\pi(f)}{1-\pi(f)} = \alpha + \beta f$, to the data obtained. Figure 4.15, bottom panel, shows the results. Fitting the linear regression does not require specialized software, and the results are usually close to estimates obtained with more complex fitting routines.

Adaptive Methods

Adaptive methods combine the best features of the method of limits and forced-choice procedures. Instead of exploring the response to many levels of the independent variable, as in the method of constant stimuli, adaptive methods quickly

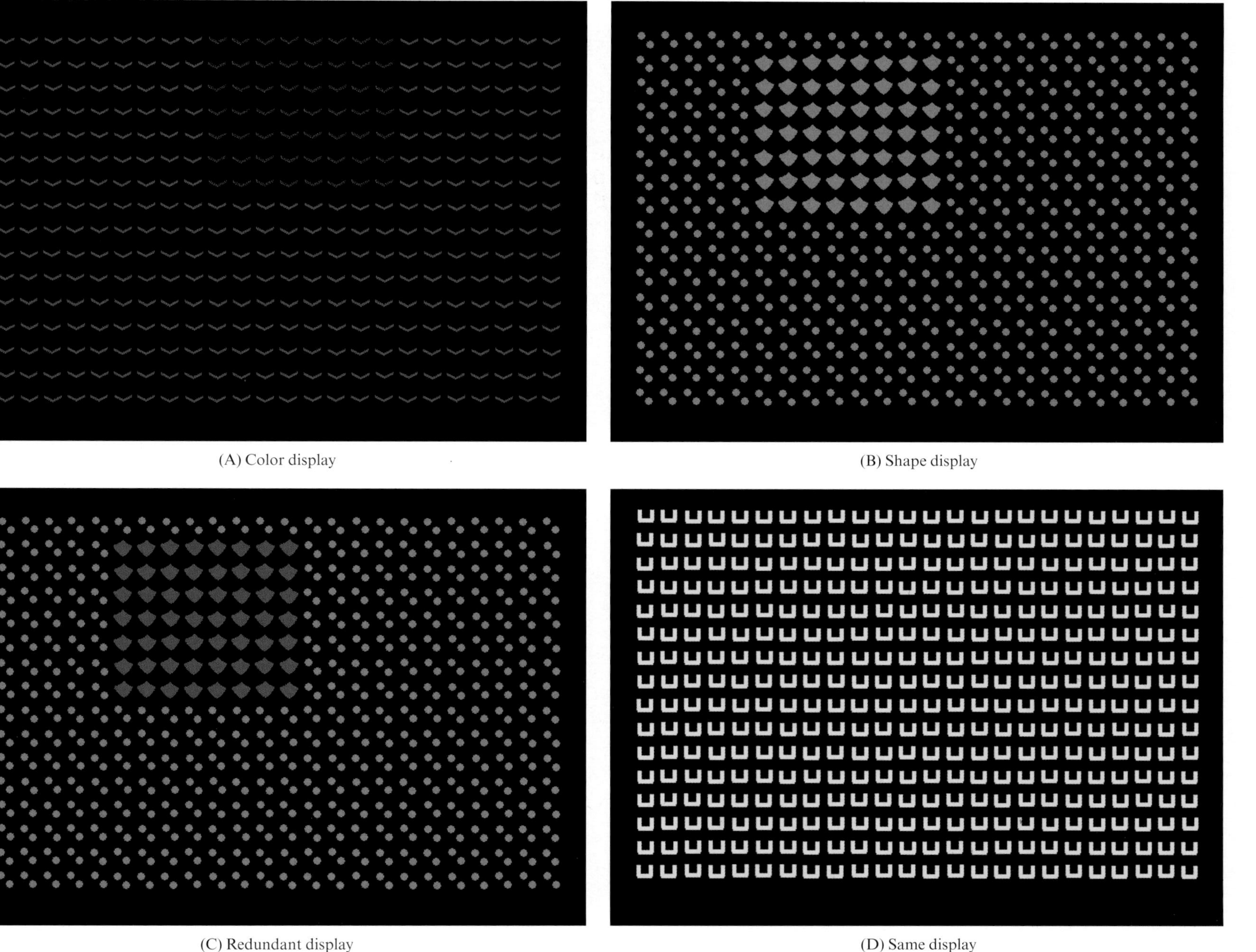

Figure 4.6 Illustrative examples of the many color, shape, and redundant Different and Same displays used in the experiments of Cook and Wixted (1977), after their Figure 4.3 and figures available at http://www.pigeon.psy.tufts.edu/jep/sdmodel/htm (accessed January 2, 2002).

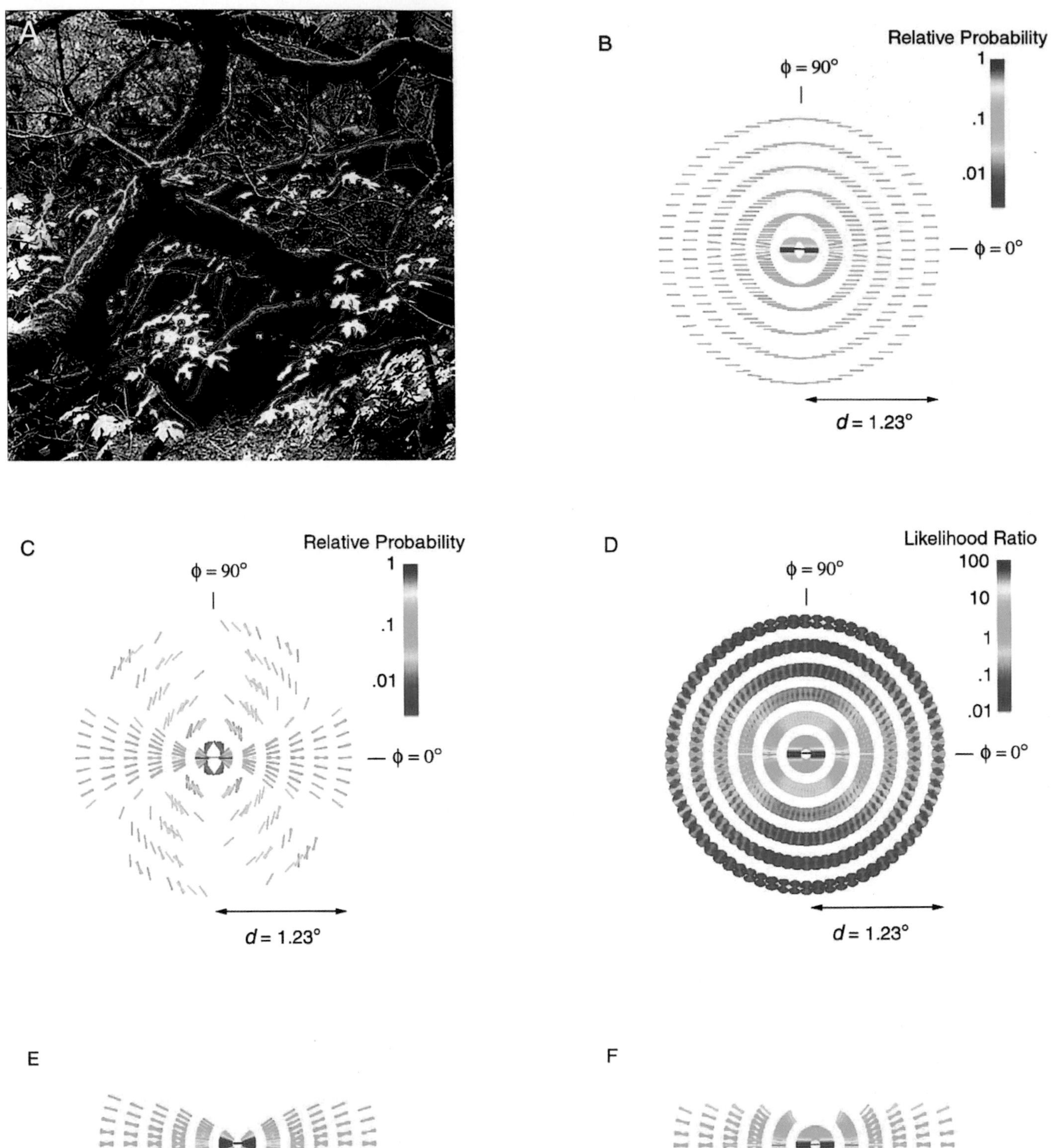

Figure 4.19 Statistics of edge co-occurrence in the sample images shown in Figure 4.18. *Source:* Copyright 2001 by Elsevier Science Ltd. Reprinted with permission.

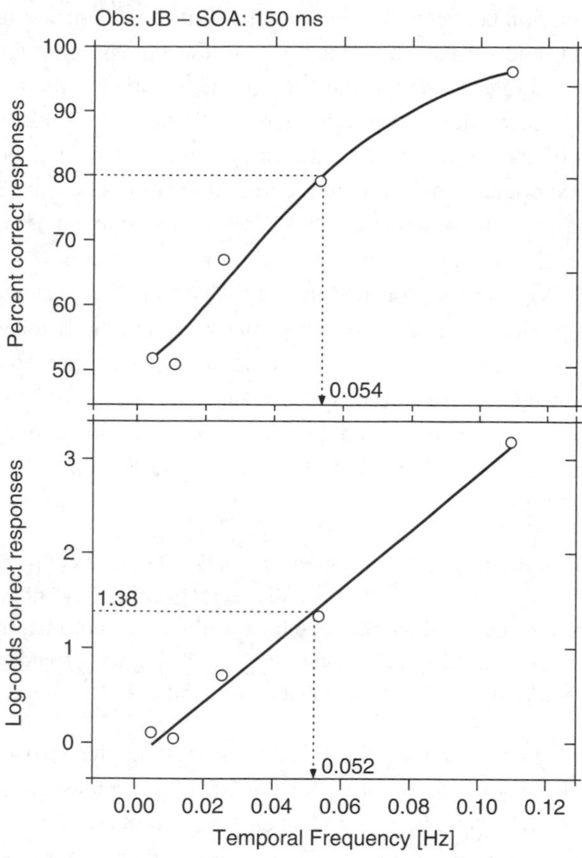

Figure 4.15 The psychometric function for one condition of the experiment and one observer: proportion of correct responses (percentage) as a function of grating-motion velocity. *Top:* The curve fitted to the data is a Weibull function. *Bottom:* The proportion of correct responses is transformed into log-odds, resulting in a function that is approximately linear. (A graph much like the one in the top panel was kindly provided by José Barraza, personal communication, July 26, 2001.)

A	B	3	1	3	5	9	0	1	1	5	8
C	D	9	6	0	2	5	4	3	9	6	6
H	E	4	9	5	0	9	9	2	5	4	7
K	N	6	0	7	5	2	0	0	5	9	8
R	S	1	8	5	0	1	8	7	1	3	0
U	V	9	4	3	3	4	5	6	9	0	8
X	Z	1	9	2	1	0	6	5	3	B	6
Stop		1	4	9	7	6	8	9	3	8	8
Resume		5	2	3	3	8	7	7	9	9	9
		8	1	6	5	1	0	5	3	4	7

Figure 4.16 The largest search array (10 × 10 characters) used by Näsänen et al. (2001). The observer was to find a letter in this array and respond by clicking on the appropriate field in the two columns on the left. *Source:* From "Effect of stimulus contrast on performance and eye movements in visual search," by R. Näsänen, H. Ojanpää, and I. Kojo, 2001, *Vision Research, 41,* Figure 1. Copyright 2001 by Elsevier Science Ltd. Reprinted with permission.

converge onto the region around the threshold. In this they resemble the method of limits. But adaptive methods do not suffer from hysteresis, which is characteristic of the method of limits.

For example, Näsänen, Ojanpää, and Kojo (2001) used a *staircase procedure* (Wetherill & Levitt, 1965) to study the effect of stimulus contrast on observers' ability to find a letter in an array of numerals (Figure 4.16). The display was first presented at a duration of 4 s. After three consecutive correct responses, its duration was reduced by a factor of 1.26 ($\log 1.26 \approx 0.1$), and after each incorrect response the duration was increased by the same factor. As a result, the duration was halved in three steps (4, 3.17, 2.52, 2.00, . . . , 0.10, . . . , s), or doubled (4, 5, 6.4, 8, . . . , s). When the sequence reversed from ascending to descending (because of consecutive correct responses) or from descending to ascending (because of an error), a *reversal* was recorded. The procedure was stopped after eight reversals. The length of the procedure ranged from 30 to 74 trials. Since the durations were on a logarithmic scale, the threshold was computed by taking the geometric mean of the eight reversal durations.

What does this staircase procedure estimate? It estimates the array duration for which the observer can correctly identify the letter among the digits 79% of the time ($p_c = .79$). Let us see why. Suppose that we are presenting the array at an observer's threshold duration. At this level, the procedure has the same chance of (a) going down after three correct responses as it has of (b) going up after one error. So $p_c^3 = 1 - p_c = .5$, which gives $p_c = \sqrt[3]{.5} \approx .79$ (for further study: Hartmann, 1998; Macmillan & Creelman, 1991).

Näsänen et al. (2001) varied the contrast of the letters and the size of the array. The measure of contrast they used is called the Michelson contrast: $c = \frac{L_{max} - L_{min}}{L_{max} + L_{min}}$, where L_{max} is the maximum luminance (in this case the background luminance), and L_{min} is the minimum luminance (the luminance of the letters). In the notation of Figure 4.14, $L_0 + mL_0 = L_{max}$ and $L_0 - mL_0 = L_{min}$. Figure 4.17 shows that search time decreased when set size was decreased and when contrast was increased. Using an eye tracker, the authors also found that the number of fixations and their durations decreased with increasing contrast, from which they concluded that "visual span, that is, the area from which information can be collected in one fixation, increases with increasing contrast" (Näsänen et al., 2001, p. 1817).

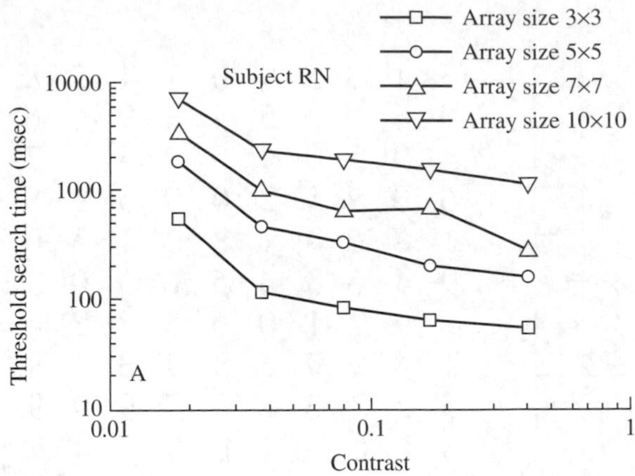

Figure 4.17 Threshold search times as a function of the contrast of the letters against the background (Näsänen et al., 2001). Each point is the mean of three threshold estimates. *Source:* From "Effect of stimulus contrast on performance and eye movements in visual search," by R. Näsänen, H. Ojanpää, and I. Kojo, 2001, *Vision Research, 41,* Figure 2 (partial). Copyright 2001 by Elsevier Science Ltd. Reprinted with permission.

THE "STRUCTURE" OF THE VISUAL ENVIRONMENT AND PERCEPTION

Regularities of the Environment

As we saw earlier, the contemporary view of perception maintains that perceptual theory requires that we understand both our environment and the perceiver. In the preceding section we reviewed some methods used to measure the perceptual capacity of perceivers. In this section we turn our attention to the environment and ask how one can determine (a) the regularities of the environment and (b) the extent to which perceivers use them.

The structure of the environment and the capacities of the perceiver are not independent. When researchers look for statistical regularities in the environment, they are guided by beliefs about the aspects of the environment that are relevant to perception. These beliefs are based on the phenomenology of perception as well as on psychophysical and neural evidence. We see that insights from the phenomenology and neuroscience of vision interact to establish a correspondence between the structure of the environment and the mechanisms of perception.

The *phenomenology* of perception, championed by Gestalt psychologists and their successors in the twentieth century (Ellis, 1936; Kanizsa, 1979; Koffka, 1935; Köhler, 1929; Kubovy, 1999; Kubovy & Gepshtein, in press; Wertheimer, 1923), is a prominent source of ideas about the kinds of information the visual system seeks in the environment. The Gestaltist program of research revealed many examples of correlation between the relational properties of visual stimulation and visual experience. The Gestalt psychologists believed that the regularities of experience arise in the brain by virtue of the intrinsic properties of the brain, independent of the regularities of the environment. On this view, the experience-environmental correlation occurs because the brain is a physical system, just as the environment is, and hence they operate along the same dynamic principles.

This Gestalt approach—known as *psychophysical isomorphism*—has been criticized by many, including Brunswik (1969), who nevertheless considered the factors of perceptual organization discovered by the Gestalt psychologists as "guides to the life-relevant properties of the remote environmental objects." Brunswik and Kamiya (1953, pp. 20–21) argued that

> the possibility of such an interpretation [of the factors of perceptual organization] hinges upon the "ecological validity" of these factors, that is, their objective trustworthiness as potential indicators of mechanical or other relatively essential or enduring characteristics of our manipulable surroundings.

Brunswik anticipated the modern interest in the statistical regularities of the environment by several decades; he was the first (Barlow, in press; Geisler, Perry, Super, & Gallogly, 2001) to propose ways of measuring these regularities (Brunswik & Kamiya, 1953).

Another prominent champion of environmental factors in perception was James J. Gibson, whose ecological realism we reviewed earlier. We will only add here that Gibson derived his ecological optics from an analysis of environment that is hard to classify as other than phenomenological. Epstein and Hatfield (1994, p. 174) put it clearly:

> We cannot shake the impression that "the world of ecological reality" is largely coextensive with the world of phenomenal reality, and that the description of ecological reality, although couched in the language of "ecological physics," nonetheless is an exercise in phenomenology. . . . Gibson's distinction between ecological reality and physical reality parallels the Gestalt distinction between the behavioral environment and geographical environment.

Besides visual phenomenology, an important source of ideas about the information relevant for visual perception is visual neuroscience. The evidence of visual mechanisms selective to particular "features" of stimulation (such as the orientation, spatial frequency, or direction of motion of luminance edges) suggests the aspects of stimulation in which the brain is most interested. As we mentioned earlier, this line of thought can be challenged by the *level of analysis* argument: Particular features could be optimal stimuli for single cells not because the low-level features themselves are of interest for perception, but because these features make convenient stepping-stones for the detection of higher order features in the stimulation.

The view of a perceptual system as a collection of devices sensitive to low-level features of stimulation raises the difficult question of how such features are combined into the meaningful entities of our visual experience. This question, known as the *binding problem,* has two aspects: (a) How does the brain know which similar features (such as edges of a contour) belong to the same object in the environment? and (b) How does the brain know which different features (e.g., pertaining to the form and the color) should be bound into the representation of a single object? These questions could not be answered without understanding the statistics of *optical covariation* (MacKay, 1986), as we argue in the next section. That the visual system uses such statistical data is suggested by physiological evidence that visual cortical cells are concurrently selective for values on several perceptual dimensions rather than being selective to a single dimension (Zohary, 1992). We now briefly review the background against which the idea of optical covariation has emerged in order to prepare the ground for our discussion of contemporary research on the statistics of natural environment.

Redundancy and Covariation

Following the development of the mathematical theory of communication and the theory of information (Shannon & Weaver, 1949; Wiener, 1948; see also chapter by Proctor and Vu in this volume), mathematical ideas about information-handling systems began to influence the thinking of researchers of perception. Although the application of these ideas to perception required a good deal of creative effort and insight, the resulting theories of perception looked much like the theories of human-engineered devices, "receiving" from the environment packets of "signals" through separable "channels." Whereas the hope of assigning precise mathematical meaning to such notions as information, feedback, and capacity was to some extent fulfilled with respect to low-level sensory processes (Graham, 1989; Watson, 1986), it gradually became clear that a rethinking of the ideas inspired by the theory of communication was in order (e.g., Nakayama, 1998).

An illuminating example of such rethinking is the evolution of the notion of *redundancy reduction* into the notion of *redundancy exploitation* (see Barlow, 2001, in press, for a firsthand account of this evolution). The notion of redundancy comes from Shannon's information theory, where it was a measure of nonrandomness of messages (see Attneave, 1954, 1959, p. 9, for a definition). In a structureless distribution of luminances, such as the snow on the screen of an untuned TV set, the are no correlations between elements in different parts of the screen. In a structure-bearing distribution there exist correlations (or redundancy) between some aspects of the distribution, so that we can to some extent predict one aspect of the stimulation from other aspects. As Barlow (2001) put it, "any form of regularity in the messages is a form of redundancy, and since information and capacity are quantitatively defined, so is redundancy, and we have a measure for the quantity of environmental regularities."

On Attneave's view, and on Barlow's earlier view, a purpose of sensory processing was to reduce redundancy and code information into the sensory "channels of reduced capacity." After this idea dominated the literature for several decades, it has become increasingly clear—from factual evidence (such as the number of neurons at different stages of visual processing) and from theoretical considerations (such as the inefficiency of the resulting code)—that the redundancy of sensory representations does not decrease in the brain from the retina to the higher levels in the visual pathways. Instead, it was proposed that the brain exploits, rather than reduces, the redundancy of optical stimulation.

According to this new conception of redundancy, the brain seeks redundancy in the optical stimulation and uses it for a variety of purposes. For example, the brain could look for a correlation between the values of local luminance and retinal distances across the scene (underwriting grouping by proximity; e.g., Ruderman, 1997), or it could look for correlations between local edge orientations at different retinal locations (underwriting grouping by continuation; e.g., Geisler et al., 2001). The idea of discovering such correlations between multiple variables is akin to performing covariational analysis on the stimulation. MacKay (1986, p. 367) explained the utility of covariational analysis:

> The power of covariational analysis—asking "what else happened when this happened?"—may be illuminated by its use in the rather different context of military intelligence-gathering. It becomes effective and economical, despite its apparent crudity, when the range of possible states of affairs to be identified is relatively small, and when the categories in terms of which covariations are sought have been selected or adjusted according to the information already gathered. It is particularly efficacious where many coincidences or covariations can be detected cheaply in parallel, each eliminating a different fraction of the set of possible states of affairs. To take an idealized example, if each observation were so crude that it eliminated only half of the range of possibilities, but the categories used were suitably orthogonalized (as in the game of "Twenty questions"), only 100 parallel analyzers would be needed in principle to identify one out of 2^{100}, or say 10^{30}, states of affairs.

In the remainder of this chapter we explore an instance of covariational analysis applied by Geisler et al. (2001) to grouping by good continuation (Field, Hayes, & Hess, 1993; Wertheimer, 1923). We see how Geisler et al. used this analysis to ask whether the statistics of contour relationships in natural images correspond to the characteristics of the perceptual processes of contour grouping in human observers.

Co-occurrence Statistics of Natural Contours

Geisler et al. (2001) used the images shown in Figure 4.18 as a representative sample of visual scenes. In these images they measured the statistics of relations between contour segments. In every image they found contour segments, called *edge elements,* using an algorithm that simulated the properties of neurons in the primary visual cortex that are sensitive to edge orientations. This produced for every image a set of locations and orientations for each edge element. Figure 4.19A shows an example of an image with the selected edge elements (discussed later). Geisler et al. submitted these data to a statistical analysis of relative orientations and distances between every possible pair of edges within every image. We now consider what relations between the edge elements the authors measured and how they constructed the distributions of these relations.

Figure 4.18 The set of sample images used by Geisler et al. (2001). *Source:* From "Effect of stimulus contrast on performance and eye movements in visual search," by R. Näsänen, H. Ojanpää, and I. Kojo, 2001, *Vision Research, 41,* Figure 2 (partial). Copyright 2001 by Elsevier Science Ltd. Reprinted with permission.

The geometric relationship between a pair of edge elements is determined by three parameters explained in Figure 4.20. The relative position of element centers is specified by two parameters: distance between element centers, d, and the direction of the virtual line connecting elements centers, ϕ. The third parameter, θ, measures the relative orientation of the elements, called *orientation difference.* For every edge element in an image, Geisler et al. (2001) considered the pairs of this element with every other edge elements in the image and, within every pair, measured the three parameters: d, θ, and ϕ. The authors repeated this procedure for every edge element in the image and obtained the probability of every magnitude of the three parameters of edge relationships. They called the resulting quantity the *edge co-occurrence (EC) statistic,* which is a three-dimensional probability density function, $p(d, \theta, \phi)$, as we explain later. Geisler et al. used two methods to obtain edge co-occurrence statistics: One was independent of whether the elements belonged to the same contour or not, whereas the other took this information into account. The authors called the resulting statistics *absolute* and *Bayesian,* respectively. We now consider the two statistics.

Absolute Edge Co-occurrence

This EC statistic is called absolute because it does not depend on the layout of objects in the image. In other words, those edge elements that belonged to different contours in the image contributed to the absolute EC statistic to the same extent as did the edge elements that belonged to the same contour. As Geisler et al. (2001) put it, this statistic was measured "without reference to the physical world."

Figures 4.19B and 4.19C show two properties of absolute EC statistic averaged across the images. Because the covariational analysis used by Geisler et al. (2001) concerns a relation between three variables, the results are easier to understand when we think of varying only one variable at a time, while keeping the two other variables constant.

Consider first Figure 4.19B, which shows the most frequent orientation differences for a set of 6 distances and 36 directions of edge-element pairs. To understand the plot, imagine a short horizontal line segment, called a *reference element,* in the center of a polar coordinate system (d, ϕ). Then imagine another line segment—a *test element*—at a radial distance d_t and direction ϕ_t from the reference element. Now rotate the test element around its center until it is aligned with the most likely orientation difference θ at this location. Then color the segment, using the color scale shown in the figure, to indicate the magnitude of the relative probability of this most likely orientation difference. (The probability is called

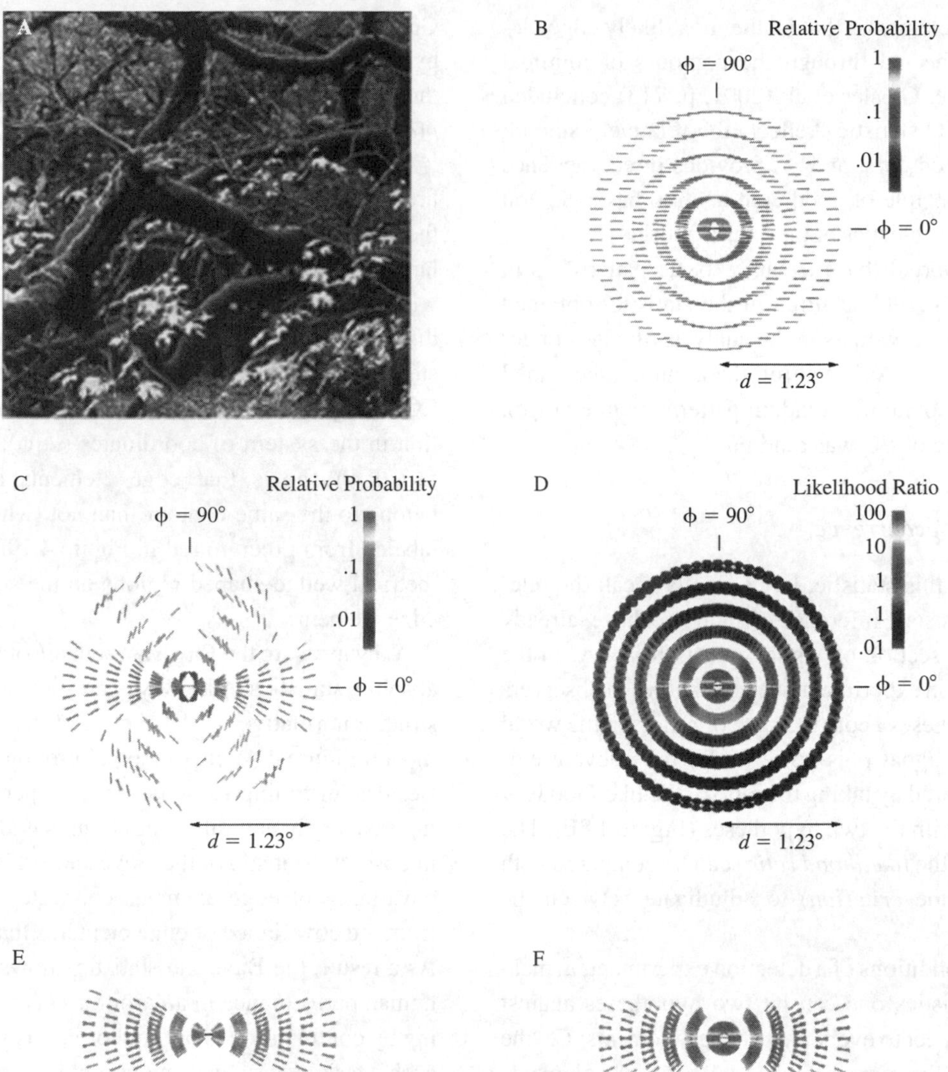

Figure 4.19 Statistics of edge co-occurrence in the sample images shown in Figure 4.18. *Source:* Copyright 2001 by Elsevier Science Ltd. Reprinted with permission. See insert for color version of this figure.

"relative" to indicate that it was normalized such that the highest probability in the plot was 1.0). Figure 4.19B, which shows such orientation differences, demonstrates that for 6 distances and 36 directions of the test element, the edge elements are likely to be roughly parallel to the reference element. Geisler et al. (2001, p. 713) concluded,

> This result shows that there is a great deal of parallel structure in natural images, presumably due to the effects of growth and erosion (e.g., the parallel sides of a branch, parallel geological strata, etc.), perspective projection (e.g., the elongation of surface markings due to slant), shading (e.g., the illumination of a branch often produces a shading contour parallel to the side of the branch), and so on.

Now consider Figure 4.19C, which shows the most frequent directions for the same set of distances and directions of edge element pairs as in Figure 4.19B. To understand this plot, imagine you choose a test element under an orientation difference θ and a distance d and rotate it around the center of polar coordinates (i.e., along a circumference with radius d) until it finds itself at the most likely direction ϕ for the given distance and orientation difference. Figure 4.19C shows that in the resulting pattern the test elements are approximately cocircular

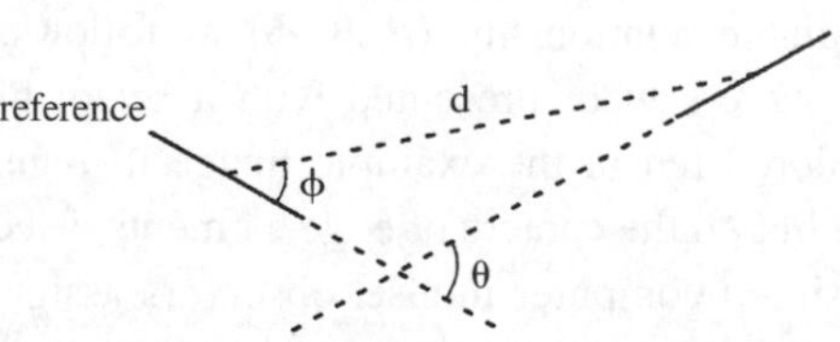

Figure 4.20 Parameters of the relationship between two edge elements: distance d, direction ϕ, and orientation difference θ. *Source:* Copyright 2001 by Elsevier Science Ltd. Reprinted with permission.

with the reference elements; that is, the most likely edge elements can be connected through the contours of minimal change of curvature. Geisler et al. (2001, p. 713) concluded that the absolute EC statistic "reflects the relatively smooth shapes of natural contours, and . . . provides direct evidence that the Gestalt principle of good continuation has a general physical basis in the statistics of the natural world."

The authors reported that the same "basic pattern" as in Figures 4.19B and 4.19C occurred in the statistics obtained from all the images, as well as in the analysis of edges under different spatial scales. As a control, the authors ascertained that in the images containing random patterns (white noise), the absolute statistic of EC was random.

Bayesian Edge Co-occurrence

Before we explain this statistic, let us briefly recall the relevant ideas of Bayesian inference, which we have already encountered in the section on signal detection theory. In the context of a detection experiment, we saw that when observers generate two hypotheses about the state of affairs in the world ("noise trial" vs. "signal plus noise trial") the relevant evidence can be measured by taking the ratio of the likelihoods of events associated with the two hypotheses (Figure 4.8E). The resulting quantity (the *likelihood ratio*) can be compared with another quantity (the *criterion*) to adjudicate between the hypotheses.

Similar to the conditions of a detection experiment, in measuring the EC statistics one can pit two hypotheses against each other with respect to every pair of edge elements: C, "the elements belong to the same contour" and $\sim C$, "the elements do not belong to the same contour." The relevant evidence can be expressed in the form of a likelihood ratio:

$$\ell(d, \theta, \phi) = \frac{p(d, \theta, \phi|C)}{p(d, \theta, \phi|\sim C)}, \tag{3}$$

where $p(d, \theta, \phi|C)$ and $p(d, \theta, \phi|\sim C)$ are the conditional probabilities of a particular relationship $\{d, \theta, \phi\}$ between edge elements to occur, when the elements belong or do not belong to the same contour, respectively. (We explain how to obtain the criterion in a moment.)

Geisler et al. (2001) measured the likelihood ratio for every available relationship $\{d, \theta, \phi\}$ as follows. In every image, observers were presented with a set of highlighted pixels (colored red in the example image in Figure 4.19A) corresponding to the centers of edge elements detected in the image. Using a computer mouse, observers assigned sets of highlighted pixels to the perceived contours in the image. Thus observers reported about the belongingness of edge elements to contours in every image. With this information Geisler et al. conditionalized the absolute probabilities of EC by whether the edge elements within every pair belonged to the same contour or not, that is, to obtain the likelihoods $p(d, \theta, \phi|C)$ and $p(d, \theta, \phi|\sim C)$.

The resulting distribution of $L(d, \theta, \phi)$ is shown in Figure 4.19D, again using a color scale, averaged across all the sample images and two observers. (The two observers largely agreed about the assignment of edges to contours, with the correlation coefficient between the two likelihood distributions equal to .98.) In contrast to the plots of absolute statistics in Figures 4.19B and 4.19C, the plot of conditional EC in Figure 4.19D shows all 36 orientations at every location in the system of coordinates (d, ϕ). The distribution of $L(d, \theta, \phi)$ shows that edge elements are more likely to belong to the same contour than not (when $L[d, \theta, \phi] > 1.0$, labeled from green to red in Figure 4.19D), within two symmetrical wedge-shaped regions on the sides of the reference edge element.

Why measure the Bayesian statistic of EC in addition to the absolute statistics? The Bayesian statistic allows one to construct a normative model (i.e., a prescriptive ideal observer model; Figure 4.4) of perceptual grouping of edge elements. Besides informing us on how the properties of element relations covary in natural images (which is already accomplished in absolute statistics), the Bayesian statistic tells us how the covariance of edge elements connected by contours differs from the covariance of edge elements that are not connected. As a result, the Bayesian statistic allows one to tell whether human performance in an arbitrary task of perceptual grouping by continuation is optimal or not. Human performance in such a task is classified as optimal if human observers assign edge elements to contours with the same likelihood as is prescribed by the Bayesian statistic. In the next section we see how Geisler et al. (2001) constructed the ideal observer model of grouping by continuation and how they compared its performance with the performance of human observers.

Predicting Human Performance from the Statistics of Natural Images

Psychophysical Evidence of Grouping by Good Continuation

To find out whether human performance in grouping by good continuation agrees with the statistics of EC in natural images, Geisler et al. (2001) conducted a psychophysical experiment. They used a stimulus pattern for which they could derive the predictions of grouping from their statistical data and pit the predictions against the performance of human observers. An example of the stimulus pattern is shown in Figure 4.21A.

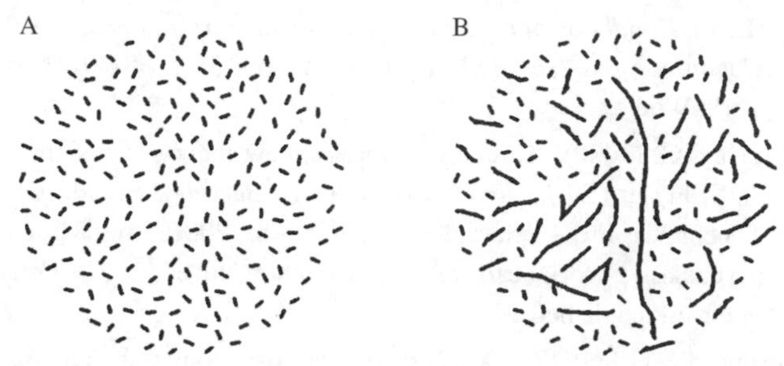

Figure 4.21 (A) An example of the path stimulus. (B) The prediction of grouping in A, from the EC statistics shown in Figure 4.19. *Source:* Copyright 2001 by Elsevier Science Ltd. Reprinted with permission.

The stimulus consists of a set of aligned line segments (arranged in this example in a nearly vertical path to the right of the vertical midline), embedded in the background of randomly oriented line segments. Observers viewed successive presentations of two patterns, one containing both the target path and the background noise and one containing only the background noise. Their order was randomized. The task was to tell which of the two presentations contained the target path.

Geisler et al. (2001) varied the length of the path, the amplitude of the path deviations from a straight line, and path noisiness (due to the range of random orientations of the line segments comprising the path) to generate up to 216 classes of random contour shape. The data from the psychophysical experiments provided the authors with a "detailed parametric measurement of human ability to detect naturalistic contours in noisy backgrounds" (p. 717).

To generate the predictions of contour grouping from the EC statistics, Geisler et al. (2001) needed a function that determines which pairs of edge elements group together. The authors derived two such *local grouping functions* (Figures 4.19E and 4.19F)—one based on the absolute statistic and one based on the Bayesian statistic—which we explore in detail in a moment. Because Geisler et al. measured EC for pairs of edge elements, they used a transitivity rule to construct contours consisting of more than two elements: "if edge element *a* binds to *b*, and *b* binds to *c*, then *a* becomes bound to *c*." Using this rule, Geisler et al. could predict which target paths are seen in their stimuli, using the local grouping functions derived from the statistics of natural images: An example of grouping by continuation from image statistics is shown in Figure 4.21B. We consider the Bayesian local grouping function first, because it requires fewer parameters than does the absolute local grouping function.

Bayesian Local Grouping Function

As we saw earlier, the likelihood ratio at every location in the (d, ϕ) space in Figure 4.19D tells, for 36 orientation differences, how likely it is that the edge elements belong to the same contour as the reference element. To decide whether two edge elements belong to the same contour, for any particular relationship d, θ, ϕ between the elements, the corresponding likelihood ratio can be compared with a criterion, which Geisler et al. (2001) called a *binding criterion,* β. As the signal detection theory prescribes, the ideal binding criterion is equal to the ratio of prior probabilities (called prior odds, as discussed earlier):

$$\beta = \frac{p(\sim C)}{p(C)} = \frac{1 - p(C)}{p(C)} \qquad (4)$$

where $p(C)$ and $p(\sim C)$ are the probabilities of two edge elements to belong or not to belong, respectively, to the same contour.

The prior odds β were available to Geisler et al. (2001) directly from the Bayesian EC statistic. In a true ideal observer model of grouping by good continuation, the local grouping function would have to completely determine which edge elements should group solely from the statistics of natural images (i.e., with no free parameters in the model). However, it turned out that Geisler et al. could not use this optimal strategy because they found that the magnitude of β varied as they varied the area of analysis in the image. In other words, the authors could not find a unique—an ideal—magnitude of β. Instead, Geisler et al. decided to leave β as a (single) free parameter in their model, just as the observer criterion is a free parameter in modeling human data obtained in a detection experiment. By fitting the single free-parameter model to human data, Geisler et al. found that the best results are achieved with $\beta = 0.38$; the Bayesian local grouping function shown in Figure 4.19F was constructed using that best-fitting magnitude of β. Thus, the local grouping function was not truly ideal.

Absolute Local Grouping Function

Because absolute EC statistics do not convey information about belongingness of edge elements to contours, Geisler et al. (2001) had to introduce a second parameter, in addition to binding criterion β, in order to derive a local grouping function from the absolute EC statistics. This new parameter, called *tolerance,* determined how sharply the probabilities of element grouping fell off around the most likely parameters of EC shown in Figure 4.19C. For example, low tolerance implies that grouping occurs only when the parameters are close to the most common values evident in the absolute EC statistics. Different values of tolerance result in different absolute local grouping functions; one is shown in Figure 4.19E. When fitting the predictions of the two-parameter absolute local grouping functions to human data, Geisler et al. were able to obtain almost as good a correlation between the predicted and the observed accuracies ($r = .87$) as they obtained in the one-parameter Bayesian local grouping function ($r = .89$).

In the conclusion of this section, we wish to emphasize the profound theoretical repercussions of the kind of analysis undertaken by Geisler et al. (2001). These authors looked for a foundation of the principles of perceptual organization in the statistics of the natural world and discovered a covariational structure in these statistics. Furthermore, Geisler et al. showed that under minimal assumptions, the regularities of environment can predict human performance in simple perceptual tasks. The findings of Geisler et al. imply that optical stimulation does contain information for perception, in contrast to the view held by the Gestaltists. The information is available for perceptual systems to develop the corresponding sensitivities and to match the perceptual capacities of the organism to the structure of the environment.

As Geisler et al. (2001) pointed out, the rapidly growing research in neural networks shows that self-organizing networks (such as in Kohonen, 1997) are sensitive to the covariational structure of their inputs. This suggests that self-organizing neural networks could provide a useful tool in guiding our search for the match between the perceptual capacities of the biological organisms and the statistical structure of their environments.

REFERENCES

Agresti, A. (1996). *An introduction to categorical data analysis.* New York: Wiley.

Attneave, F. (1954). Some informational aspects of visual perception. *Psychological Review, 61,* 183–193.

Attneave, F. (1959). *Applications of information theory to psychology: A summary of basic concepts.* New York: Holt, Rinehart and Winston.

Baird, J. C., & Noma, E. (1978). *Fundamentals of scaling and psychophysics.* New York: Wiley.

Barlow, H. (2001). Redundancy reduction revisited. *Network: Computation in Neural Systems, 12,* 241–253.

Barlow, H. (in press). The exploitation of regularities in the environment by the brain. *Behavioral and Brain Science.*

Barlow, H. B. (1972). Single units and sensation: A neuron doctrine for perceptual psychology? *Perception, 1,* 371–394.

Barlow, H. B. (1995). The neuron doctrine in perception. In M. S. Gazzaniga (Ed.), *The cognitive neurosciences* (pp. 415–435). Cambridge, MA: MIT Press.

Barraza, J. F., & Colombo, E. M. (2001). The time course of the lower threshold of motion during rapid events of adaptation. *Vision Research, 41,* 1139–1144.

Barrow, H. G., & Tenenbaum, J. M. (1986). Computational approaches to vision. In K. R. Boff, L. Kaufman, & J. P. Thomas (Eds.), *Handbook of perception and human performance: Vol. 2. Cognitive processes and performance* (pp. 38-1–38-70). New York: Wiley.

Berkeley, G. (2000). An essay towards a new theory of vision. In A. C. Fraser (Ed.), *The works of George Berkeley.* Bristol, UK: Thoemmes Press. Retrieved August 18, 2001, from http://psychclassics.yorku.ca/Berkeley/vision.htm, 4th ed., 1732. (Original work published 1709)

Boring, E. G. (1917). A chart of the psychometric function. *American Journal of Psychology, 28,* 465–470.

Britten, K. H., Shadlen, M. N., Newsome, W. T., & Movshon, J. A. (1992). The analysis of visual motion: A comparison of neuronal and psychophysical performance. *Journal of Neuroscience, 12,* 4745–4765.

Bruce, V., Green, P. R., & Georgeson, M. A. (1996). *Visual perception: Physiology, psychology, ecology* (3rd ed.). Hove, UK: Erlbaum.

Bruner, J. S. (1957). On perceptual readiness. *Psychological Review, 64,* 123–152.

Brunswik, E. (1952). *The conceptual framework of psychology.* Chicago: University of Chicago Press. (International Encyclopedia of Unified Science: Foundations of the Unity of Science, Vol. 1, No. 10)

Brunswik, E., & Kamiya, J. (1953). Ecological cue-validity of "proximity" and other Gestalt factors. *American Journal of Psychology, 66,* 20–32.

Bush, R. R. (1963). Estimation and evaluation. In R. D. Luce, R. R. Bush, & E. Galanter (Eds.), *Handbook of mathematical psychology* (Vol. 1, pp. 429–469). New York: Wiley.

Cook, R. G., & Wixted, J. T. (1997). Same-different texture discrimination in pigeons: Testing competing models of discrimination and stimulus integration. *Journal of Experimental Psychology: Animal Behavior Processes, 23,* 401–416.

Dretske, F. (1986). *Knowledge and the flow of information.* Cambridge, MA: MIT Press.

Egan, J. P. (1975). *Signal detection theory and ROC analysis.* New York: Academic Press.

Ellis, W. D. (Ed.). (1936). *A source book of Gestalt psychology.* London: Routledge & Kegan Paul.

Eng, J. (2001, February 11). *Roc curve fitting.* Retrieved August 14, 2001, from http://www.rad.jhmi.edu/jeng/javarad/roc/ JROCFITi.html.

Epstein, W. (1988). Has the time come to rehabilitate gestalt theory? *Psychological Research, 50,* 2–6.

Epstein, W. (1993). The representational framework in perceptual theory. *Perception & Psychophysics, 53,* 704–709.

Epstein, W., & Hatfield, G. (1994). Gestalt psychology and the philosophy of mind. *Philosophical Psychology, 7,* 163–181.

Fechner, G. T. (1996). *Elements of psychophysics* (H. E. Adler, Trans.). New York: Holt, Rinehart and Winston. (Original work published 1860)

Feller, W. (1968). *An introduction to probability theory and its applications.* New York: Wiley.

Field, D., Hayes, A., & Hess, R. (1993). Contour integration by the human visual system: Evidence for a local association field. *Vision Research, 33,* 173–193.

Fodor, J. (1983). *The modularity of mind.* Cambridge, MA: MIT Press.

Fodor, J., & Pylyshyn, Z. W. (1981). How direct is visual perception? Some reflections on Gibson's ecological approach. *Cognition, 9,* 139–196.

Gaddum, J. H., Allen, P., & Pearce, S. C. (1945). Lognormal distributions. *Nature, 156,* 463–466.

Geisler, W. S., Perry, J. S., Super, B. J., & Gallogly, D. P. (2001). Edge co-occurrence in natural images predicts contour grouping performance. *Vision Research, 41,* 711–724.

Gescheider, G. A. (1997). *Psychophysics: The fundamentals* (3rd ed.). Mahwah, NJ: Erlbaum.

Gibson, J. J. (1950). *The perception of the visual world.* Boston: Hougton Mifflin.

Gibson, J. J. (1966). *The senses considered as perceptual systems.* Boston: Hougton Mifflin.

Gibson, J. J. (1979). *The ecological approach to visual perception.* Boston: Houghton Mifflin.

Goodale, M. A., & Humphrey, G. K. (1998). The objects of action and perception. *Cognition, 67,* 181–207.

Gorea, A., & Sagi, D. (2001). Disentangling signal from noise in visual contrast discrimination. *Nature Neuroscience, 4,* 1146–1150.

Graham, N. V. S. (1989). *Visual pattern analyzers.* New York: Oxford University Press.

Gregory, R. L. (1970). *The intelligent eye.* New York: McGraw-Hill.

Gregory, R. L. (1997). *Eye and brain: The psychology of seeing* (5th ed.). Princeton: Princeton University Press.

Hartmann, W. M. (1998). *Signals, sound, and sensation.* New York: AIP Press & Springer Verlag.

Hatfield, G., & Epstein, W. (1985). The status of the minimum principle in the theoretical analysis of visual perception. *Psychological Bulletin, 97,* 155–186.

Helmholtz, H. L. F. von. (2000). *Helmholtz's treatise on physiological optics* (J. P. C. Southall, Trans.). Bristol, UK: Thoemmes Press. (Original work published 1866)

Herbart, J. F. (1890). Psychologie als wissenschaft [Psychology as science]. In K. Kehrbach (Ed.), *Jon. Fr. Herbart's sämtliche Werke in chronologischer Reihenfolge* (Vol. 5, Pt. 1, pp. 177–434). Langensalza, Germany: Hermann Beyer und Söhne. (Original work published 1824)

Hoffman, D. D. (1998). *Visual intelligence.* New York: Norton.

Hood, D. C., & Finkelstein, M. A. (1986). Sensitivity to light. In K. R. Boff, L. Kaufman, & J. P. Thomas (Eds.), *Handbook of perception and human performance: Vol. 1. Sensory processes and perception* (pp. 5-1–5-66). New York: Wiley.

Hubel, D. H., & Wiesel, T. N. (1962). Receptive fields, binocular interaction and functional architecture in the cat's visual cortex. *Journal of Physiology, 160,* 106–154.

Ittelson, W. H. (1960). *Visual space perception.* New York: Springer.

Jastrow, J. (1888). A critique of psycho-physic methods. *American Journal of Psychology, 1,* 271–309.

Jeffress, L. A. (1973). The logistic distribution as an approximation to the normal curve. *Journal of the Acoustical Society of America, 53,* 1296.

Johnson-Laird, P. N. (1988). *The computer and the mind.* Cambridge, MA: Harvard University Press.

Kanizsa, G. (1979). *Organization in vision: Essays on Gestalt perception.* New York: Praeger.

Kepler, J. (2000). *Optics* (W. H. Donahue, Trans.). Santa Fe, NM: Green Lion Press. (Original work published 1604)

Kestler, H. A. (2001). ROC with confidence—a Perl program for receiver operator characteristic curves. *Computer Methods & Programs in Biomedicine, 64,* 133–136.

Kilpatrick, F. P. (Ed.). (1950). *Human behavior from a transaction point of view.* Hanover, NH: Institute for Associated Research.

Knill, D. C., & Richards, W. (Eds.). (1996). *Perception as Bayesian inference.* Cambridge, UK: Cambridge University Press.

Koffka, K. (1935). *Principles of gestalt psychology.* New York: Harcourt Brace.

Köhler, W. (1929). *Gestalt psychology.* New York: Liveright.

Köhler, W. (1940). *Dynamics in psychology.* New York: Liveright.

Kohonen, T. (1997). *Self-organizing maps.* Berlin: Springer.

Krantz, D. H. (1969). Threshold theories of signal detection. *Psychological Review, 76,* 308–324.

Kubovy, M. (1999). Gestalt psychology. In R. A. Wilson & F. C. Keil (Eds.), *The MIT encyclopedia of the cognitive sciences* (pp. 346–349). Cambridge, MA: MIT Press.

Kubovy, M., & Gepshtein, S. (in press). Grouping in space and in space-time: An exercise in phenomenological psychophysics. In M. Behrmann & R. Kimchi (Eds.), *Perceptual organization in vision: Behavioral and neural perspectives.* Mahwah, NJ: Erlbaum.

Kubovy, M., & Healy, A. F. (1980). Process models of probabilistic categorization. In T. S. Wallsten (Ed.), *Cognitive processes in choice and decision behavior* (pp. 239–262). Hillsdale, NJ: Erlbaum.

Lee, B. B. (1999). Single units and sensation: A retrospect. *Perception, 28,* 1493–1508.

Leibniz, G. W. (1981). *New essays on human understanding* (P. Remnant & J. Bennett, Trans.). Cambridge, UK: Cambridge University Press. Retrieved August 5, 2001, from http://pastmasters2000.nlx.com/. (Original work published 1765)

Leibniz, G. W. (1989). *Philosophical essays* (R. Ariew & D. Garber, Trans.). Indianapolis, IN: Hackett. Retrieved August 5, 2001, from http://pastmasters2000.nlx.com/.

Lindsay, P. H., & Norman, D. A. (1977). *Human information processing: An introduction to psychology.* New York: Academic Press.

Link, S. W. (1992). *The wave theory of difference and similarity.* Hillsdale, NJ: Erlbaum.

Luce, R. D., & Krumhansl, C. L. (1988). Measurement, scaling, and psychophysics. In R. C. Atkinson, R. J. Herrnstein, & G. Lindzey (Eds.), *Stevens' handbook of experimental psychology* (2nd ed., pp. 3–74). New York: Wiley.

MacKay, D. M. (1986). Vision: The capture of optical covariation. In J. D. Pettigrew, K. J. Sanderson, & W. R. Levick (Eds.), *Visual neuroscience* (pp. 365–373). Cambridge, UK: Cambridge University Press.

Macmillan, N. A., & Creelman, C. D. (1991). *Detection theory: A user's guide.* Cambridge, UK: Cambridge University Press.

Mamassian, P., Landy, M., & Maloney, L. T. (in press). Bayesian modeling of visual perception. In R. Rao, B. Olshausen, & M. Lewicki (Eds.), *Probabilistic models of the brain and neural function.* Cambridge, UK: MIT Press.

Marley, A. A. (1989a). A random utility family that includes many of the "classical" models and has closed form choice probabilities and choice reaction times. *British Journal of Mathematical & Statistical Psychology, 42,* 13–36.

Marley, A. A. (1989b). A random utility family that includes many of the "classical" models and has closed form choice probabilities and choice reaction times: Addendum. *British Journal of Mathematical & Statistical Psychology, 42,* 280.

Marr, D. (1982). *Vision.* San Francisco: Freeman.

Mersch, P. P. A., Middendorp, H. M., Bouhuys, A. L., Beersma, D. G. M., & Hoofdakker, R. H. van den. (1999). Seasonal affective disorder and latitude: A review of the literature. *Journal of Affective Disorders, 53,* 35–48.

Metz, C. E. (1998). *Roc analysis.* Retrieved August 14, 2001, from http://www-radiology.uchicago.edu/krl/toppage11.htm.

Milner, A. D., & Goodale, M. A. (1995). *The visual brain in action.* Oxford, UK: Oxford University Press.

Nakayama, K. (1994). Gibson: An appreciation. *Psychological Review, 101,* 329–335.

Nakayama, K. (1998). Vision fin de siècle: A reductionistic explanation of perception for the 21st century. In J. Hochberg (Ed.), *Perception and cognition at century's end* (pp. 307–331). San Diego, CA: Academic Press.

Näsänen, R., Ojanpää, H., & Kojo, I. (2001). Effect of stimulus contrast on performance and eye movements in visual research. *Vision Research, 41,* 1817–1824.

Neisser, U. (1967). *Cognitive psychology.* New York: Appleton-Century-Crofts.

Nickerson, R. S. (1998). Confirmation bias: A ubiquitous phenomenon in many guises. *Review of General Psychology, 2,* 175–220.

Norman, J. (in press). Two visual systems and two theories of perception: An attempt to reconcile the constructivist and ecological approaches. *Behavioral and Brain Sciences.*

Palmer, S. E. (1976). Fundamental aspects of cognitive representation. In E. Rosch & B. B. Lloyd (Eds.), *Cognition and categorization* (pp. 259–303). Hillsdale, NJ: Erlbaum.

Parker, A. J., & Newsome, W. T. (1998). Sense and single neuron: Probing the physiology of perception. *Annual Review of Neuroscience, 21,* 227–277.

Pylyshyn, Z. (1984). *Computation and cognition.* Cambridge, MA: MIT Press.

Pylyshyn, Z. (1999). Is vision continuous with cognition? The case for cognitive impenetrability of visual perception. *Behavioral and Brain Sciences, 22,* 341–365.

Quick, R. F. (1974). A vector magnitude model of contrast detection. *Kybernetik, 16,* 65–67.

Ramachandran, V. S. (1990a). Interactions between motion, depth, color, and form: A utilitarian theory of perception. In C. Blakemore (Ed.), *Vision: Coding and efficiency* (pp. 346–360). Cambridge, UK: Cambridge University Press.

Ramachandran, V. S. (1990b). Visual perception in people and machines. In R. Blake & T. Troscianko (Eds.), *AI and the eye* (pp. 12–77). New York: Wiley.

Rock, I. (1983). *The logic of perception.* Cambridge, MA: Bradford Books/MIT Press.

Rock, I. (1997). *Indirect perception.* Cambridge, MA: MIT Press.

Rogers, S. (2000). The emerging concept of information. *Ecological Psychology, 12,* 365–375.

Ruderman, D. L. (1997). Origins of scaling in natural images. *Vision Research, 37,* 3385–3395.

Rumelhart, D. E. (1977). *Introduction to human information processing.* New York: Wiley.

Schneider, G. E. (1969). Two visual systems: Brain mechanisms for localization and discrimination are dissociated by tectal and cortical lesions. *Science, 63,* 895–902.

Shannon, C. E., & Weaver, W. (1949). *The mathematical theory of communication.* Urbana, IL: University Illinois Press.

Stanislaw, H., & Todorov, N. (1999). Calculation of signal detection theory measures. *Research Methods, Instruments, & Computers, 31,* 137–149.

Swets, J. A. (1996). *Signal detection theory and ROC analysis in psychology and diagnostics: Collected papers.* Hillsdale, NJ: Erlbaum.

Tanner, W. P., & Sorkin, R. D. (1972). The theory of signal detectability. In J. V. Tobias (Ed.), *Foundations of modern auditory theory* (pp. 65–98). New York: Academic Press.

Terman, J. S., & Terman, M. (1999). Photopic and scotopic light detection in patients with seasonal affective disorder and control subjects. *Biological Psychiatry, 46,* 1642–1648.

Thurstone, L. L. (1928). The phi-gamma hypothesis. *Journal of Experimental Psychology, 11,* 293–305.

Turvey, M. T., Shaw, R. E., Reid, E. S., & Mace, W. (1981). Ecological laws of perceiving and acting: In reply to Fodor and Pylyshyn. *Cognition, 9,* 237–304.

Ungerleider, L. G., & Mishkin, M. (1982). Two cortical visual systems. In E. J. Ingle, M. A. Goodale, & R. J. W. Mansfield (Eds.), *Analysis of visual behavior* (pp. 549–586). Cambridge, MA: MIT Press.

Warren, W. H. (1984). Perceiving affordance: Visual guidance of stair climbing. *Journal of Experimental Psychology: Human Perception and Performance, 10,* 683–703.

Warren, W. H., & Whang, S. (1987). Visual guidance of walking through aperture: Body-scaled information for affordances. *Journal of Experimental Psychology: Human Perception and Perception, 73,* 371–383.

Watson, A. B. (1986). Temporal sensitivity. In K. R. Boff, L. Kaufman, & J. P. Thomas (Eds.), *Handbook of perception and human performance* (pp. 6-1–6-43). New York: Wiley.

Wertheimer, M. (1912). Experimentelle Studien über das Sehen von Bewegung [Experimental studies on seeing motion]. *Zeitschrift für Psychologie, 61,* 161–265.

Wertheimer, M. (1923). Untersuchungen zur Lehre von der Gestalt: II. [Investigations of the principles of Gestalt: II.] *Psychologische Forschung, 4,* 301–350.

Wetherill, G. B., & Levitt, H. (1965). Sequential estimation of points on a psychometric function. *British Journal of Mathematical & Statistical Psychology, 18,* 1–10.

Wiener, N. (1948). *Cybernetics.* New York: Wiley.

Zohary, E. (1992). Population coding of visual stimuli by cortical neurons tuned to more than one dimension. *Biological Cybernetics, 66,* 265–272.

CHAPTER 5

Audition

WILLIAM A. YOST

HEARING AS SOUND SOURCE DETERMINATION

Hearing allows an organism to use sound to detect, discriminate, and segregate objects in its surrounding world (de Cheveigne, 2001). A simple nervous system could allow a primitive animal to detect the presence of the sound produced by prey on one side of the animal and to use a motor system, like a fin, on the opposite side of the animal to propel it toward the prey. Such a simple auditory detector would not be adaptive if the sound were from a predator. In this case, the system needs to be able to discriminate prey from predator and to activate a different response system (i.e., a fin on the same side of the body) to escape the predator. If the world consisted of either prey or predator, but not both, this primitive animal might survive. In the real world, however, prey and predator commingle. In the real world, the auditory system requires greater complexity in order to segregate prey from predator and then to make an appropriate neural decision to activate the proper response.

Sounds in the world do not travel from their sources to an animal along independent paths; rather, they are mixed into one complex sound wave before reaching the ears of an animal. As we will learn, the peripheral auditory system codes the spectral-temporal attributes of this complex sound wave. The rest of the auditory nervous system must interpret this code in order to reveal information about the sources of the complex sound wave in order that detection, discrimination, and especially segregation can occur (Yost, 1992a). As Bregman (1990) describes, the complex sound wave produces an auditory scene in which the images of this scene are the sound producing sources. Auditory scene analysis is based on perceptual mechanisms that process the spectral-temporal neural code laid down by the inner ear and auditory nerve.

Hearing therefore involves sound, neural structures that code for sound, and perceptual mechanisms that process this neural code. Then this information is integrated with that from other sensory systems and experiences to form a complete auditory system. This chapter begins with a discussion of sound; follows with a description of the anatomy and physiology of the auditory system, especially the auditory periphery; and concludes with a discussion of auditory detection, discrimination, and segregation.

SOURCES OF SOUND: THE PHYSICS OF THE COMPLEX SOUND WAVE

Simple Vibrations

An object that vibrates can produce sound if it and the medium through which sound travels has mass and the property of inertia. A simple mass-and-spring model can be used to describe such a vibrating system, with the spring representing the property of inertia. When the mass that is attached to the spring is moved from its starting position and let go, the mass will oscillate back and forth. A simple sinusoidal function describes the vibratory oscillation of the mass after it is set into motion: $D(t) = \sin[(\sqrt{s/m})\, t + \theta]$, where $D(t)$ is the displacement of the mass as a function of time (t), m is a measure of mass, and s a measure of the spring forces. In general, such a sinusoidal vibration is described by $D(t) = A \sin(2\pi ft + \theta)$, where f is frequency ($f = \sqrt{s/m}$) and A is peak amplitude. Thus, a sinusoidal vibration has three mutually independent parameters: frequency (f), amplitude (A), and starting phase (θ). Figure 5.1 shows two cycles of a sinusoidal relationship between displacement and time. Frequency and amplitude (also level and intensity) are the physical parameters of a vibration and sound. Pitch and loudness are the subjective and perceptual correlates of frequency and amplitude, and it is often important to keep the physical descriptions separated from the subjective. Pitch and loudness are discussed later in this chapter.

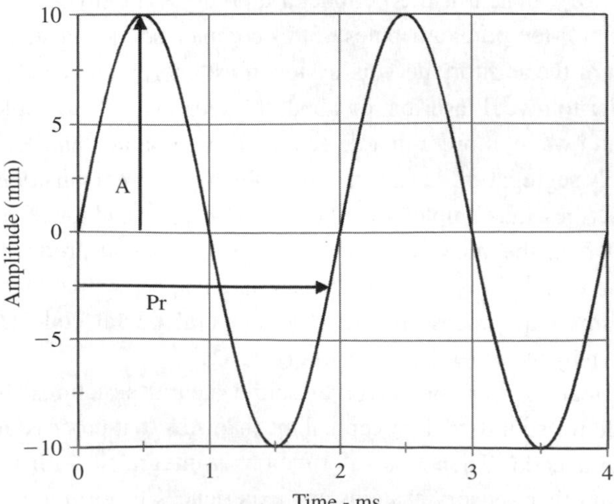

Figure 5.1 Two cycles of sinusoidal vibration, with a frequency of 500 Hz, period (Pr) of 2 ms, peak amplitude (A) of 10 mm, and 0° starting phase.

In addition to describing the vibration of the simple mass-and-spring model of a vibrating object, sinusoidal vibrations are the basic building blocks of any vibratory pattern that can produce sound. That is, any vibration may be defined as the simple sum of sinusoidal vibrations. This fact is often referred to as the Fourier sum or integral after Joseph Fourier, the nineteenth-century French chemist who formulated this relationship. Thus, it is not surprising that sinusoidal vibrations are the basis of most of what is known about sound and hearing (Hartmann, 1998).

Frequency is the number of cycles competed in one second and is measured in hertz (Hz), in which n cycles per second is n Hz. Amplitude is a measure of displacement, with A referring to peak displacement. Starting phase describes the relative starting value of the sine wave and is measured in degrees. When a sinusoid completes one cycle, it has gone through 360° (2π radians) of angular velocity, and a sinusoid that starts at time zero with an amplitude of zero has a zero-degree starting phase ($\theta = 0°$). The period (Pr) of a sine wave is the time it takes to complete one cycle, such that period and frequency are reciprocally related [$F = 1/Pr$, Pr in seconds (sec), or $F = 1000/Pr$, Pr in milliseconds (msec)]. Thus, in Figure 5.1, frequency (f) is 500 Hz ($Pr = 2$ msec), peak amplitude (A) is 10, and starting phase (θ) is 0°.

Complex Vibrations

Almost all objects vibrate in a complex, nonsinusoidal manner. According to Fourier analysis, however, such complex vibrations can be described as the sum of sinusoidal vibrations for periodic complex vibrations:

$$D(t) = \sum_{n=1}^{\infty} a_n \sin(2\pi n f_o t) + b_n \cos(2\pi n f_o t),$$

where a_n and b_n are constants and *sin* and *cos* are sinusoidal functions.

Or as the complex integral for any complex vibration:

$$f(t) = (1/2\pi)\, f(w) e^{iwt}\, dt,$$

where $w = 2\pi f$, $f(t)$ is a function of time, and $f(w)$ is a function of frequency.

Any complex vibration can be described in either the time or the frequency domain. The time domain description provides the functional relationship between the amplitude of vibration and time. The frequency domain description contains the amplitude and phase spectra of the vibration. The amplitude spectrum relates the amplitude of each frequency component of the complex vibration to its frequency. The phase spectrum provides the starting phases of each frequency component. That is, a complex vibration is the sum of sinusoidal vibrations. The amplitude spectrum describes the amplitudes of each sinusoid and the phase spectrum the starting phase of each sinusoidal component. When the instantaneous amplitudes of each sinusoidal component of the complex vibration are added point for point in time, the time domain description is determined. The time domain and the frequency domain descriptions of complex vibrations are transforms of each other, with each completely describing the vibration. Simple vibrations are sinusoidal vibrations and complex vibrations are the sum of simple or sinusoidal vibrations.

Several different complex signals are described in this chapter. Transient (click) signals are brief (usually less then 1 msec) signals that come on suddenly, stay on at a fixed level, and then go off suddenly. Transients have very broad amplitude spectra, with most of the spectral energy lying in the spectral region less than $1/T$, where T is the duration of the transient expressed in seconds (thus, $1/T$ has the units of frequency). Noise stimuli have randomly varying instantaneous amplitudes and contain all frequencies (within a certain range). If the instantaneous amplitudes vary according to the normal (Gaussian) distribution, the noise is Gaussian noise. If the average level of each frequency component in the noise is the same, the noise is white noise. Noises can be generated (filtered) to be narrow band, such that a narrowband noise contains frequency components in a limited frequency range (the bandwidth of the noise). The amplitudes or frequencies of a signal can vary as a function of time. For instance, a sinusoidal signal can have its amplitude modulated: $A(t)\sin(2\pi ft)$; or it can have its frequency modulated: $A\sin(2\pi F(t)t)$, where $A(t)$ is the amplitude-modulation pattern and $F(t)$ is the frequency-modulation pattern. In general, any signal $[x(t)]$ can be amplitude modulated: $A(t)x(t)$. In this case, $A(t)$ is often referred to as the signal envelope and $x(t)$ as the signal fine structure. Such amplitude- and frequency-modulated sounds are common in nature.

Sound Propagation

Objects vibrate and the effects of this vibration travel through the medium (e.g., air) as a sound wave that eventually reaches the ears of a listener. Air consists of molecules in constant random motion. When an object vibrates in air, it causes the air molecules to move in the direction of the vibrating object's outward and inward movements. An outward motion causes the air molecules to propagate from the source and to condense into areas of condensation where the density of molecules is greater than the average density of air molecules in the object's surrounding environment. Thus, at a condensation, the air pressure is greater than the average static air pressure, because pressure is proportional to the density of molecules. When the object moves inward, rarefaction areas of lower density are produced, generating lower pressure. These areas of condensation and rarefaction propagate away from the source in a spherical manner as the object continues to vibrate. Figure 5.2 is a schematic depiction of these areas of condensation and rarefaction at one instant in time. Eventually, the pressure wave of alternating areas of condensations and rarefactions cause the eardrum (tympanic membrane) to vibrate, and the process of hearing begins.

The distance between successive condensations (or successive rarefactions) is the wavelength (λ) of sound. Wavelength is proportional to the speed of sound in the medium (c) and inversely proportional to frequency (f): $\lambda = c/f$. The pressure of the sound wave decreases as a function of the square of the distance from the source, and this relationship is called the inverse square law of sound propagation.

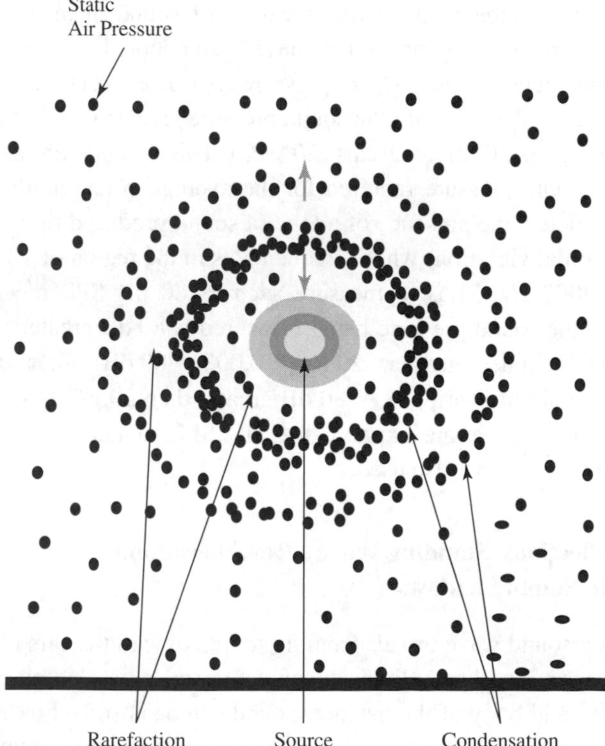

Figure 5.2 Diagram of what one might see if air molecules were photographed as a sound source vibrated. The rarefaction and condensation are shown, as well as the direction (grey arrows above the source) in which the molecules were moving at the instant the picture was taken. The wave moves out in circular manner (actually as a sphere in the three-dimensional real world). As the wave moves out from the source it occupies a greater area, and thus the density of molecules at rarefactions and condensations lessens. The area around the border of the figure represents the static air motion before the propagated wave reaches this area. *Source:* Adapted from Yost (2000).

Sound intensity (I) is proportional to pressure (p) squared: $I = p^2/p_o c$, where p_o is the density of the medium in which sound travels (e.g., air). Sound intensity is a power (P) measure of the rate at which work can be done and energy (E) is the measure of the amount of work: $I = P = E/T$, where T is time.

The Decibel

In many situations involving sound, including hearing, the range of measurable sound intensity is very large. The range of sound intensity from the softest sound that one can detect to the loudest sound one can tolerate (the dynamic range of hearing) is on the order of 10^{13}. This large range led to the decibel measure of sound intensity in which the decibel (dB) is 10 times the logarithm of the ratio of two sound intensities: $\text{dB} = 10 \log_{10}(I/I_o)$, $\log_{10}$ is the logarithm to the base 10 and I_o is a referent sound intensity. Because sound intensity is proportional to pressure squared, $\text{dB} = 20 \log_{10}(p/p_o)$, where p_o is a referent pressure. Thus, the dynamic range of hearing is approximately 130 dB.

The decibel is a relative measure of sound intensity or pressure. Several conventions have been adopted for the referent sound intensity (I_o) or pressure (p_o). The most common is the decibel measured in sound pressure level (SPL). In this case, p_o is 20 micropascals (20 μPa). This is approximately the sound pressure required for the average young adult to just detect the presence of a tone (a sound produced by a sinusoidal vibration) whose frequency is in the region of 1000 to 4000 Hz. Thus, a measure such as 80 dB SPL means that the sound pressure being measured is 80 dB greater (or 10,000 times greater, $20 \log_{10} 10{,}000 = 80$ dB) than the threshold of hearing (i.e., 80 dB greater than 20 μPa). Most often, decibels are expressed as dB SPL, but many other conventions are also used.

Reflections, Standing Waves, Reverberation, and Sound Shadows

As a sound wave travels from its source toward the ears of a listener, it will most likely encounter obstacles, including the head and body of the listener. Sound can be absorbed in, reflected from, diffracted around, or transmitted to the medium of the obstacle that the sound wave encountered. Each obstacle offers an impedance to the transmission of the sound wave to the medium of the obstacle. Impedance has three main components. The medium can offer a resistance (R) to the transmission of sound. The mass of the medium can offer a mass reactance (Xm) that impedes the sound, and the springlike inertia properties of the medium also produce spring reactance (Xs). The impedance (Z) of the medium equals $\sqrt{[R^2 + (Xm - Xs)^2]}$. Thus, each obstacle has a characteristic impedance, and the greater the difference in characteristic impedance between two objects, the more sound is reflected from and not transmitted to the new medium. The characteristic impedance of an object is proportional to $p_o c$, which is the denominator of the definition of sound intensity ($I = p^2/p_o c$). Thus, sound intensity is equal to pressure squared divided by characteristic impedance.

When sound is reflected from an object, the reflected sound wave can interact with the original sound wave, causing regions in which the two sound waves reinforce each other or at other locations cancel each other. Under the proper conditions, the reflected reinforcements and cancellations can establish a standing wave. A standing wave represents spatial locations in which the pressure is high (antinodes) due to reinforcements and spatial locations where the pressure is low nodes due to cancellations. The wavelength of a standing wave (distance between adjacent nodes or antinodes) is determined by the size of the environment in which the standing wave exists. Large areas produce long standing-wave wavelengths and hence low frequencies, and the converse is true for small areas. Thus, a standing wave in a short tube will produce a high-frequency standing wave, and a long tube will produce a low-frequency standing wave. This is the principal upon which organ pipes and horns operate to produce musical notes. Structures in the auditory system, such as the outer ear canal, can also produce standing waves.

The reflections from many surfaces can reinforce each other and sustain sound in an environment long after the sound has terminated. The time it takes this reverberation to decline by 60 dB relative to the source level is the reverberation time of the environment. Rooms can support high speech intelligibility and pleasant listening if there is some reverberation, but not if the reverberation time is too long.

If the size of an object is large relative to a sound's wavelength, most of the sound will either be reflected from the object or be transmitted to the object. Sound will be diffracted around (bypass) an object whose size is much smaller than the sound's wavelength. When the wavelength of sound is approximately the same as the size of an object, some of the sound is reflected from the object and some is diffracted around the object. The result is that there is an area on the side of the object opposite from where the sound originated where the sound pressure is lower. Thus, such an object produces a sound shadow in an area very near the object, where there is a lower sound pressure than there is in areas farther away from the object. The head, for instance, produces a sound shadow at the far ear when the frequency of sound arriving at the lead ear is generated by a sound with a wavelength that is approximately equal to or smaller than the size of the head.

AUDITORY ANATOMY AND PHYSIOLOGY

The auditory system (see Figure 5.3) has four main parts: The outer ear collects and funnels sound to the middle ear, which increases the force produced by air moving the tympanic membrane (eardrum) so that the fluid and tissues of the inner ear are efficiently vibrated; this enables the inner ear to transduce vibration into a neural code for sound, which the central auditory nervous system can process and integrate with other sensory and experiential information in order to provide motor, behavioral, and other outputs.

The Peripheral Auditory System: Transduction and Coding

Outer Ear

As sound travels from the source across the body and head, especially the pinna (see Figure 5.3), various body parts attenuate and delay the sound in a frequency-specific way caused by properties of reflection and diffraction. Thus, sound arriving at the outer ear canal is spectrally different from that leaving the source. These spectral alterations are described by head-related transfer functions (HRTFs), which specify the spectral (amplitude and phase) changes produced by the body and head for sources located at different points in space. The HRTFs may provide cues that are useful for sound localization (Wightman & Kistler, 1989a). Within the outer ear canal, resonances can be established that boost sound pressure in spectral regions near the 3000- to 5000-Hz resonant frequency of the outer ear canal (Shaw, 1974).

Middle Ear

The major function of the middle ear is to provide an increase in vibratory force so that the fluids and tissues of the inner ear can be effectively moved (Geisler, 1998; Pickles, 1988). The impedance of the inner ear structures is about 40 times greater

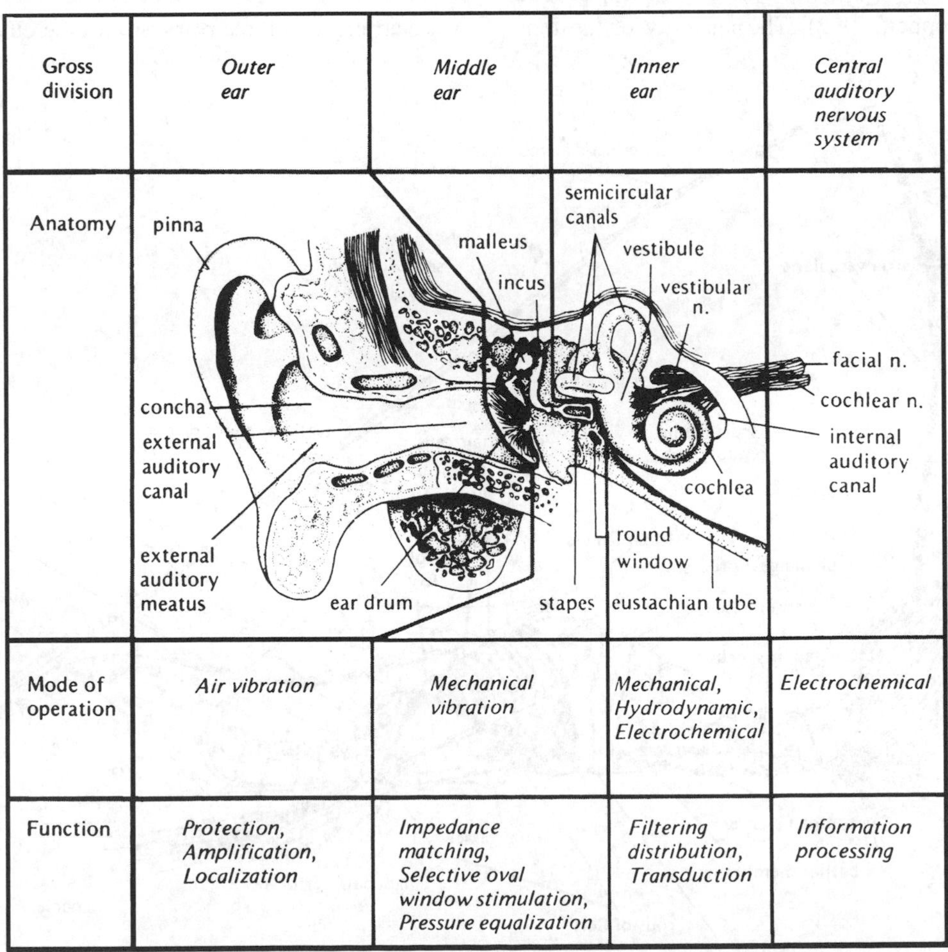

Gross division
Outer ear
Middle ear
Inner ear
Central auditory nervous system
Anatomy
pinna
concha
external auditory canal
external auditory meatus
ear drum
malleus
incus
semicircular canals
vestibule
vestibular n.
facial n.
cochlear n.
internal auditory canal
cochlea
round window
stapes
eustachian tube
Mode of operation
Air vibration
Mechanical vibration
Mechanical, Hydrodynamic, Electrochemical
Electrochemical
Function
Protection, Amplification, Localization
Impedance matching, Selective oval window stimulation, Pressure equalization
Filtering distribution, Transduction
Information processing

Figure 5.3 Cross section of human ear, showing divisions into outer, middle, and inner ears and central nervous system. Below are listed the predominant modes of operation of each division and its suggested function. *Source:* From Yost (2000), adapted from similar drawing by Ades and Engstrom (1974); Dallos (1973), with permission.

than that of air (a 32-dB change). The middle ear compensates for this impedance difference via the lever action of the ossicular chain (a chain of three bones—malleus, incus, stapes—connecting the tympanic membrane to the inner ear) in combination with the pressure increase between the large area of the malleus's connection to the tympanic membrane and the small area of the footplate of the stapes' connection to the oval window of the inner ear. Over a significant portion of the audible frequency range, the middle ear in combination with the resonances of the outer ear canal delivers the sound to the inner ear with no pressure loss due to the high impedance of the inner ear structures. The eustachian tube connects the middle ear to the nasal cavities so that pressure on each side of the tympanic membrane remains the same, a necessary condition for efficient middle- and inner-ear functioning.

Inner Ear

The inner ear contains the hearing organs and those of the vestibular (balance-equilibrium) system (Fay & Popper, 1992; Webster, Fay, & Popper, 1992). The anatomy of the inner ear differs significantly across the animal kingdom. In mammals, the cochlea, a snail-like tube that spirals on itself three to four times, is the hearing organ of the inner ear (see Figure 5.3). The cochlea contains an inner tube, the cochlear partition, which contains supporting structures and the hair cells, the biological transducers for hearing. The cochlea is thus divided into three canals or scala: scala vestibuli (above the cochlear partition), scala media (the cochlear partition), and scala tympani (below the cochlear partition). Scala vestibuli and scala tympani contain a viscous fluid, perilymph, whereas scala media contains a different fluid, endolymph. In a cross-section (see Figure 5.4), the cochlear partition is bounded above by Resiner's membrane and below by the basilar membrane. The metabolic engine for the cochlea resides within stria vascularis on the outer wall of the cochlea. Fibers from the auditory part of the VIIIth cranial nerve innervate the hair cells along the basilar membrane and course through the middle (modiolus) of the cochlea before picking up myelination on the way to the auditory brain stem. There are two types of hair cells (see Figure 5.5): outer hair cells, which in mammals are arranged in three rows toward the outside of the cochlear

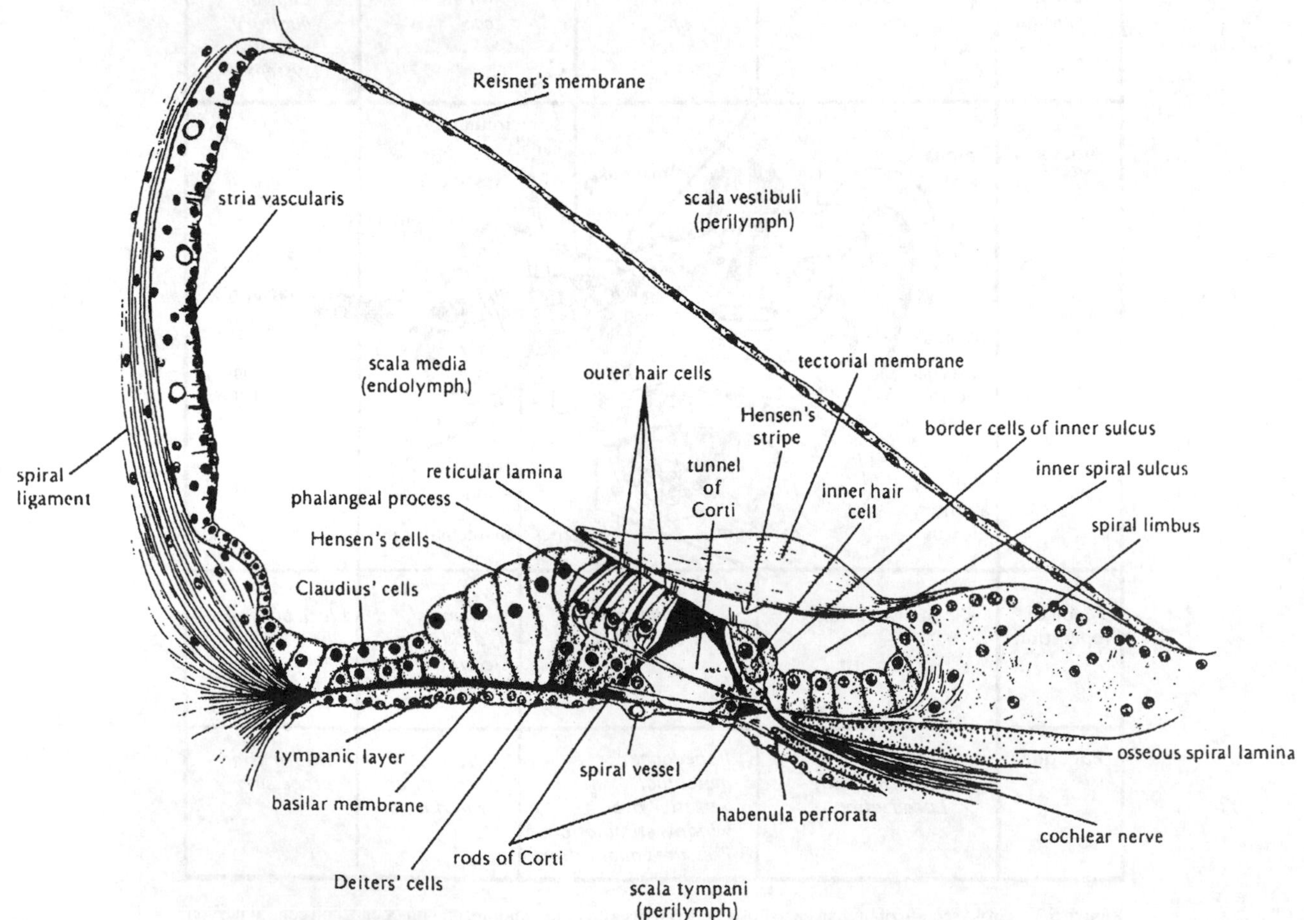

Figure 5.4 Main components of the inner ear in relation to the other structures of the ear. (From Yost, 2000, adapted from drawings by Dorland, 1965, with permission.) Schematic diagram of middle ear and partially uncoiled cochlea, showing the relationship of the various scalae. *Source:* From Yost (2000), adapted from similar drawings from Zemlin (1981), with permission.

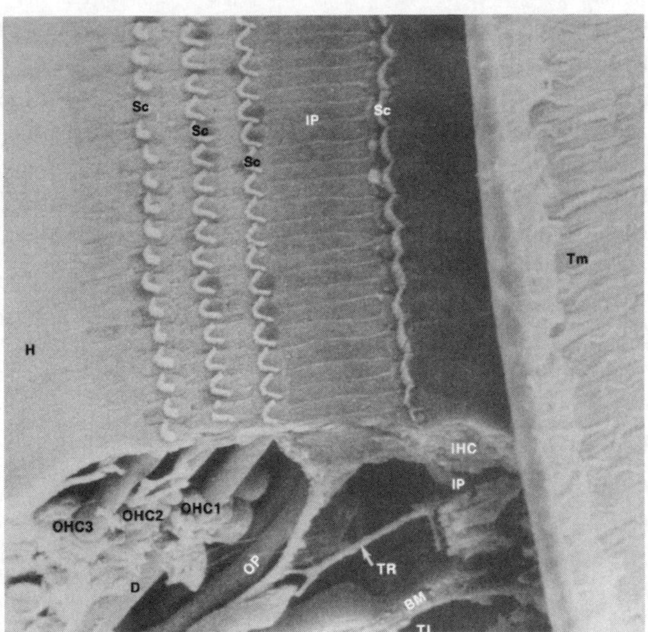

Figure 5.5 Light micrograph of a cross section of a chinchilla organ of Corti. Clearly shown are: *IHC:* inner hair cells; *OHC:* the three rows of outer hair cells. The stereocilla (Sc) of the outer and inner hair cells protrude through the recticular lamina that helps support the hair cells. Other supporting structures are shown. *Source:* From Yost (2000), photographs courtesy of Dr. Ivan Hunter-Duvar, Hospital for Sick Children, Toronto.

partition; and inner hair cells, which are aligned in a single row. Several different supporting structures buttress the hair cells on the basilar membrane.

The vibration of the stapes causes the oval window to vibrate the fluids of the cochlea (Dallos, Popper, & Fay, 1996). This vibration sets up a pressure differential across the cochlear partition, causing the cochlear partition to vibrate. This vibration causes a shearing action between the basilar membrane upon which the hair cells set, and the tectorial membrane, which makes contact with the stereocilia (the hairs, so to speak, that protrude from the top of the hair cells; see Figure 5.5) such that the stereocilia are bent. The shearing of the stereocilia opens transduction channels, presumably toward the tips of the stereocilia, which initiates a generator potential in the hair cell and a resulting action potential in the auditory nerve fiber that innervates the hair cells (Pickles, 1988). Thus, the mechanical vibration of the stereocilia is transduced into a neural signal.

The properties of the cochlear partition involving its width and tension, as well as the fact that the cochlear partition does not terminate at the end of the cochlea, all result in a particular motion being imparted to the cochlear partition when it is vibrated by the action of the stapes (Dallos et al., 1996). The cochlear partition motion is described as a traveling wave, such that the vibration of the cochlear partition is distributed across the partition in a frequency-specific manner. High-frequency sounds generate maximal displacement toward the base of the partition where the stapes is, and the vibration does not travel very far along the partition. Low-frequency sounds travel along the partition towards its apex (end opposite of the stapes), such that maximal displacement is toward the apical end of the cochlear partition. Figure 5.6 provides a schematic depiction of the traveling wave for three different frequencies. The biomechanical traveling wave, therefore, sorts frequency according to the location of maximal displacement along the cochlear partition: High frequencies cause maximal vibration at the base, low frequencies at the apex, and middle frequencies at intermediate partition locations. Thus, the place of maximal displacement codes for the frequency content of the stimulating sound wave. If a sound wave is the sum of two frequency components, then there will be two locations of maximal displacement; three frequency components would generate a maximum of three, and so forth. The hair cells are distributed along the cochlear partition as if they were sensors of the cochlear displacement. Thus, different hair cells code for the frequency content of the incoming sound.

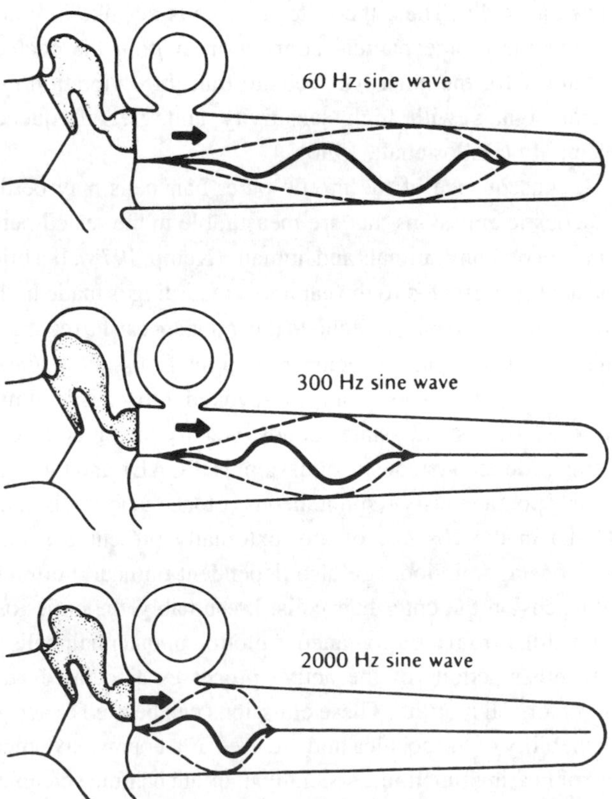

Figure 5.6 Instantaneous patterns and envelopes of traveling waves of three different frequencies shown on a schematic diagram of the cochlea. Note that the point of maximum displacement, as shown by the high point of the envelope, is near the apex for low frequencies and near the base for higher frequencies. Also note that low frequencies stimulate the apical end as well as the basal end, but that displacement from higher frequencies is confined to the base. *Source:* From Yost (2000), adapted from similar drawings Zemlin (1981), with permission.

Why should the system have two types of hair cells (inner and outer)? More than 90% of the inner hair cells are innervated by afferent auditory nerve fibers, indicating that the inner haircells are the biological transducers for sound. The outer hair cells appear to preform a very different task (Dallos et al., 1996). The outer hair cells change their size (primarily in length) in reaction to stimulation, and the change in length happens on a cycle-by-cycle basis, even for high frequencies of 20,000 Hz and above. The shearing of the stereocilia of outer hair cells causes a neural action leading to a deformation of the walls of the outer hair cells, resulting in a change in length (Brownell, Bader, Bertrand, & de Ribaupierre, 1985; Geisler, 1998; Pickles, 1988). The length change most likely alters the connections between the basilar and tectorial membranes in a dynamic fashion, which in turn affects the shearing of the inner hair cell stereocilia (Zajic & Schacht, 1991). This type of positive feedback system appears to feed energy back into the cochlea, making the haircell function as an active process. The high sensitivity, fine frequency resolution, and nonlinear properties of the biomechanical action of the cochlear partition depend on viable outer hair cells. Thus, the outer hair cells act like a motor, varying the biomechanical connections within the cochlea that allow for the inner hair cells to transduce vibration into neural signals with high sensitivity and great frequency selectivity (Dallos et al., 1996).

A consequence of the motile outer hair cells may be the otoacoustic emissions that are measurable in the sealed outer ear canal of many animals and humans (Kemp, 1978). If a brief transient is presented to the ear and a recording is made in the closed outer ear canal, an echo to the transient can be recorded. This echo or emission is cochlear in origin. Emissions occur in response to transients (transient-evoked otoacoustic emissions; TOAE), steady-state sounds (usually measured as distortion product otoacoustic emissions; DPOAE), and they can occur spontaneously (spontaneous otoacoustic emissions; SOAE) in the absence of any externally presented sound. Otoacoustic emissions are also dependent on neural efferent influences on the outer hair cells. Presumably, the emissions result either from the spontaneous motion of outer hair cells or from other actions of the active processes associated with outer hair cell motility. These emissions can be used to access the viability of the cochlea and are used as a noninvasive measure of hearing function, especially in infant hearing screening programs (Lonsbury-Martin & Martin, 1990).

Auditory Nerve

Each inner hair cell is connected to about ten auditory nerve fibers, which travel in the XIIIth cranial nerve in a topographical organization to the first synapse in the cochlear nucleus of the auditory brain stem (Webster et al., 1992). Thus, the auditory nerve fibers carry information about the activity of the inner hair cells, which are monitoring the biomechanical displacements of the cochlear partition (Fay & Popper, 1992; Geisler, 1998; Pickles, 1988). Figure 5.7 shows tuning curves for individual auditory nerve fibers. A

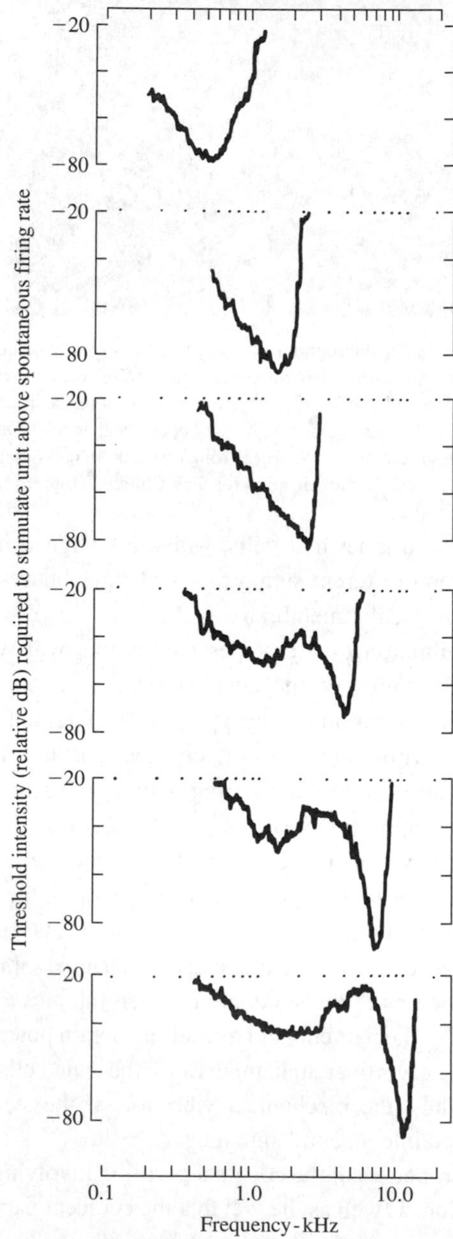

Figure 5.7 Tuning curves for six single auditory neurons with different characteristic frequencies. The stimulus level in dB SPL calibrated at the tympanic membrane needed to reach each neuron's threshold is plotted as a function of stimulus frequency. Note the steep slope on the high-frequency side of the tuning curve and the shallow slope on the low-frequency side, suggesting a high degree of frequency selectivity. *Source:* From Yost (2000), adapted from Liberman and Kiang (1978), with permission.

tuning curve represents the tonal level required for a threshold number of neural discharges as a function of the frequency of the tone. The sharp V-shape tuning curves indicate that auditory nerve fibers are highly tuned to the frequency of stimulation; thus, they reflect the biomechanical traveling wave action of the cochlear partition.

The discharges of auditory nerve fibers are also synchronized to the vibratory pattern of acoustic stimulation. Figure 5.8 shows histograms for auditory nerve fibers indicating that the timing pattern of acoustic stimulation is preserved in these fibers up to about 5000 Hz (Geisler, 1998; Pickles, 1988). The auditory nerve discharges during only one phase of the sound, and the probability of discharge is proportional to the instantaneous amplitude of the sound. Thus, the temporal pattern of neural discharges in auditory nerve fibers depicts the temporal structure of sound's pressure wave form for those frequency components that are lower in frequency than approximately 5000 Hz.

The number of discharges and number of discharging fibers increases in proportion to stimulus level. However, the discharge rate of individual auditory nerve fibers varies over only about a 40–50 dB range. Thus, although increased discharge rate does provide information about a sound's overall amplitude, a simple relationship between discharge rate and sound amplitude cannot account for the range of sound intensity that most animals are capable of processing.

Thus, auditory nerve fibers are highly frequency-selective, discharge in synchrony with the acoustic stimulus (at least up to 5000 Hz), and change their discharge rates in proportion to sound level. The discharge rate of any particular auditory

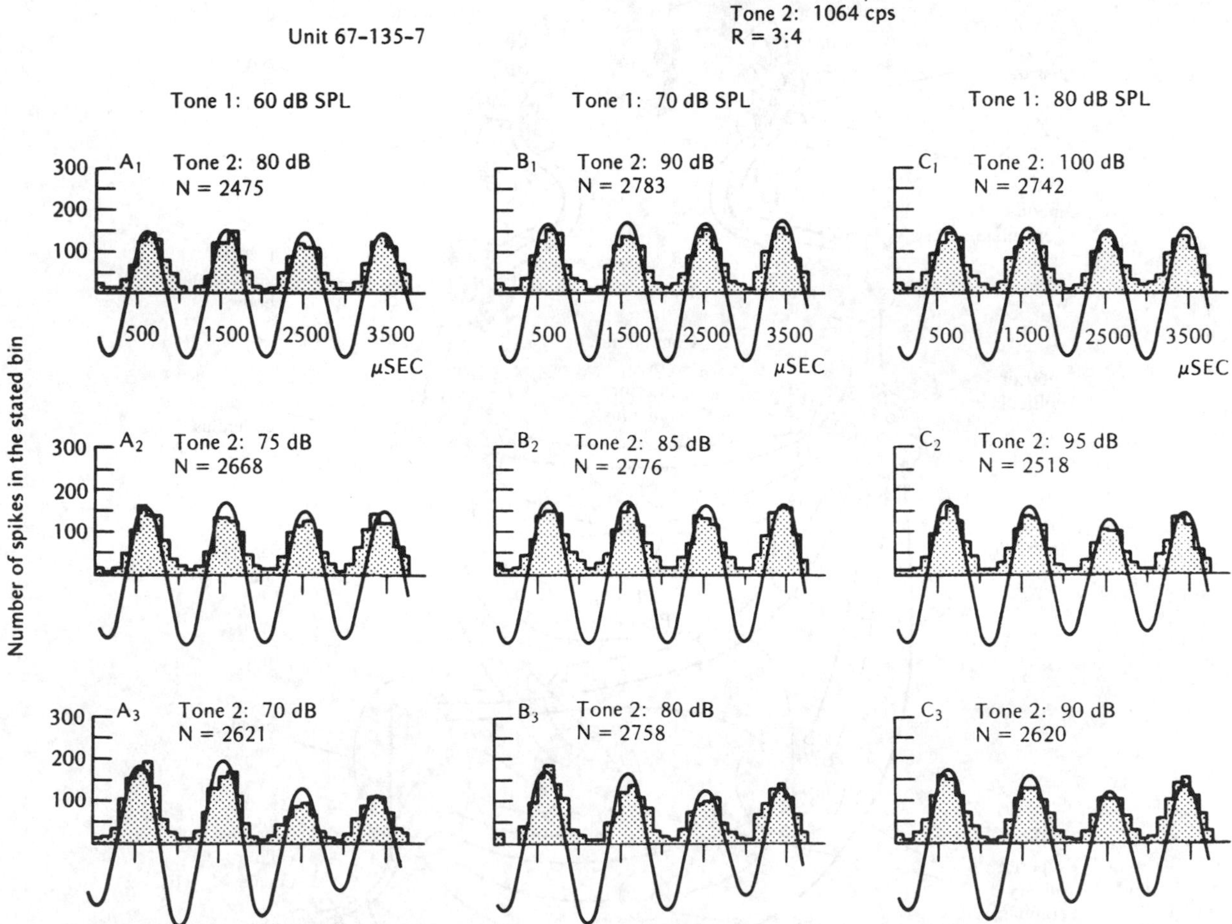

Figure 5.8 Time-locked post-stimulus-time (PST) histograms to the sum of two pure tones. In the top row, tone 2 is 20 dB more intense than tone 1. In the middle row there is a 15 dB difference between the two tones, and in the bottom row the difference is 10 dB. For all cases the time domain waveform of the summed sinusoids is superimposed on top of the PST histogram. The nerve discharges only during one phase of the waveform (the positive-going sections of the waveform). The PST histogram displays the ability of the nerve to discharge in synchrony with the period of the input stimulus envelope, at least for low-frequency stimulation. *Source:* From Yost (2000), based on a figure from Hind, Anderson, Brugge, and Rose (1967), with permission.

nerve represents the relative amplitude of a particular frequency in the sound. The temporal discharge pattern of the fiber indicates the time domain properties of the sound in this frequency region. The overall level of neural discharge rate indicates the sounds's overall amplitude. Individual auditory nerve fibers are topographically organized within the auditory nerve bundle; fibers carrying low-frequency information are toward the middle of the XIIIth bundle, and fibers carrying high-frequency information are toward the outside of the bundle. Thus, a spatial (spectral)-temporal representation of the stimulating sound is transmitted via the auditory nerve to the auditory brain stem. This spatial-temporal pattern represents the neural code for the sound waveform that is the composite of the sounds generated from all of the sources in the acoustic environment.

Central Auditory Nervous System

Figure 5.9 depicts a schematic diagram of the gross anatomy of the major components of central auditory nervous system. In addition to the afferent pathways indicated in Figure 5.9, there is a network of efferent centrifugal connections as well (Altschuler, Hoffman, Bobbin, & Clopton, 1989).

The cochlear nucleus has many different fiber types and connections in its three main subdivisions. There is evidence for lateral inhibitory networks in the cochlear nucleus that may aid it in performing different types of spectral pattern processing (Young, 1984). Processing of binaural information occurs in the olivary complex, where the first significant bilateral interactions occur. The medial superior olive is most sensitive to interaural (between the ears) time differences,

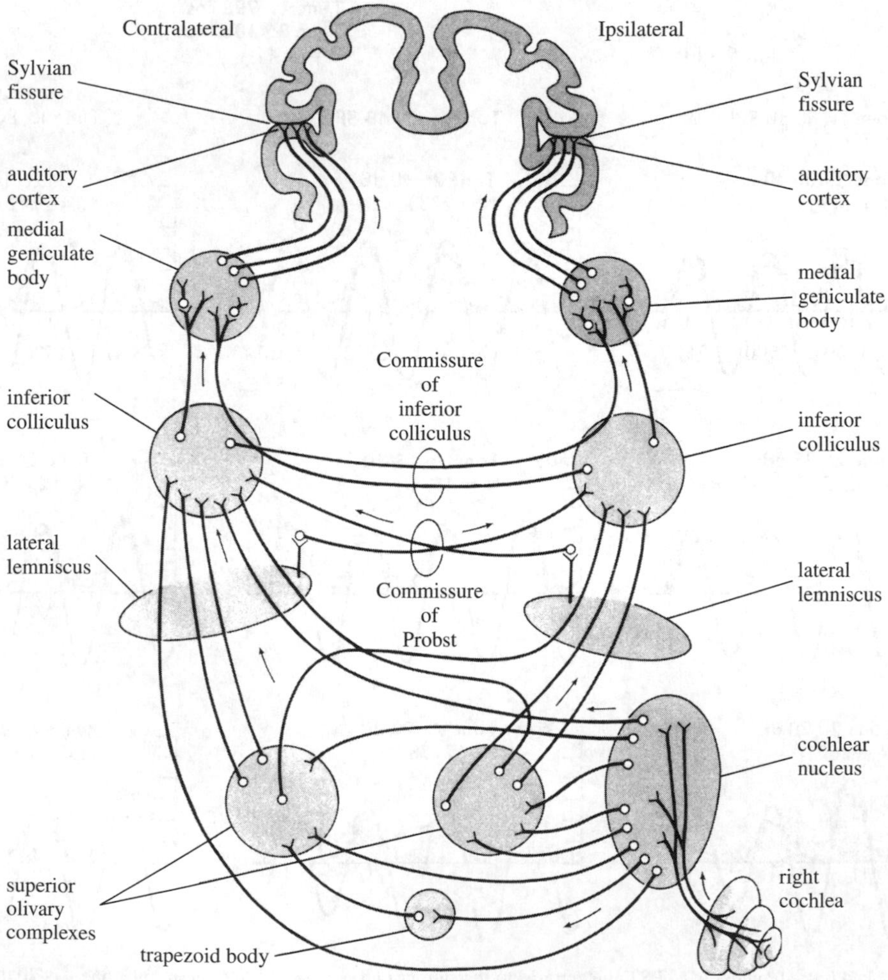

Figure 5.9 Highly schematic diagram of the ascending (afferent) pathways of the central auditory system from the right cochlea to the auditory cortex. No attempt is made to show the subdivisions and connections within the various regions, cerebellar connections, or connections with the reticular formation. *Source:* From Yost (2000), a compilation of similar diagrams by Ades (1959); Whitfield (1967); Diamond (1973); Harrison and Howe (1974).

and the lateral superior olive is most sensitive to interaural level differences. Interaural time and level differences are important cues for sound localization (Yost & Gourevitch, 1987) . The lateral limniscus is primarily a monaural pathway in many animals. The inferior colliculus appears to be a major processing nucleus for spatial hearing, modulation processing, and spectral pattern recognition (Fay & Popper, 1992). In mammalian systems, not a lot is known about the function of the medial geniculate body (Fay & Popper, 1992). The auditory cortex in primates is located deep within the Sylvian fissure, making it difficult to reach for physiological study. The auditory cortex, as are all parts of the central auditory nervous system, is tonotopically organized: Different cortical neurons are selective for different frequencies. There is evidence for modulation processing in the auditory cortex, and the auditory cortex may provide spatial maps for sound localization (Altschuler et al., 1989).

The study of animals with special adaptations for hearing, echo-locating bats (Suga, 1988), and the barn owl (Konishi, Takahashi, Wagner, Sullivan, & Carr, 1988), have provided valuable information about the functional role of the central auditory system. These studies have helped guide the study of the brain stems and cortices of other animals, including humans. The auditory nervous system is an anatomically complex system, perhaps reflecting the amount of neural computation that hearing appears to require.

DETECTION

Thresholds of Hearing

A basic measure of auditory detection is the threshold of hearing for pure tones, or the audiogram. The audiogram can be obtained in two conditions, each requiring its own calibration procedure. In the minimal audible field (MAF) process, listeners detect the presence of pure tones presented from loudspeakers, whereas in the minimal audible pressure (MAP) process, the sounds are presented over headphones. Figure 5.10 shows the thresholds of hearing (the audiogram) for the two procedures. The figure also shows estimates of the upper limit for hearing, indicating those sound levels that either are very uncomfortable or yield the sensation of pain. The thresholds of hearing have been standardized for both the MAP and MAF procedures, and the two estimates differ by on average about 6 dB. However, the differences are accounted for by calculating the diffraction of sound around the head and the resonance properties of the outer ear canal, which are substantially different in the MAP and MAF procedures (Yost & Killion, 1993). Figure 5.10 suggests that young humans can detect sounds from 20 to 20,000 Hz, and

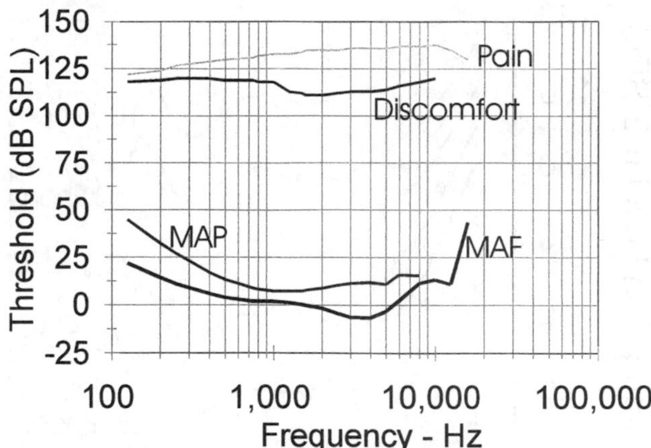

Figure 5.10 The thresholds of hearing in decibels of sound pressure level (dB SPL) are shown as a function of frequency for Minimal Audible Field (MAF) thresholds, MAP, thresholds for pain, and thresholds for discomfort. The thresholds for pain and discomfort represent estimates of the upper limit of level that humans can tolerate. *Source:* These thresholds are based on national and international standards.

the dynamic range of hearing is about 130 dB in the middle of the range of the audible frequencies. At 0 dB SPL the pressure in the outer ear canal is 20 μPa, which indicates that the tympanic membrane at auditory threshold is moving a distance equal to approximately the diameter of a hydrogen atom. Females have slightly lower thresholds of hearing than do males. The thresholds of hearing increase as a function of age in a frequency-dependent manner (presbycusis), such that the thresholds for high-frequency sounds increase at an earlier age than do those for low-frequency sounds. This frequency dependence is consistent with the operation of the traveling wave, in which all sounds excite the base of the cochlear partition, where high-frequencies are coded, but only low-frequencies sounds excite the apex. Thus, the base of the cochlear partition, where high frequencies are coded, is more likely to be fatigued over time than is the apex.

Figure 5.10 shows the threshold levels for tonal detection. The subjectively perceived loudness of sound is also a joint function of the sound's physical frequency and level. Figure 5.11 shows subjective equal-loudness contours; each contour describes the tonal levels and frequencies that are judged, in a loudness matching procedure, equally loud to a 1,000-Hz tone presented at the constant level indicated by the phon rating of the contour. Thus, all tones that have a loudness of *x* phons are judged equally loud to a 1,000-Hz tone presented at *x* dB SPL.

The thresholds of hearing are dependent on the duration of the sound—the shorter the sound, the higher the thresholds. Thresholds for tonal stimuli decrease as duration is increased until the duration is approximately 300 ms; then threshold remains constant as duration is increased further. To a first

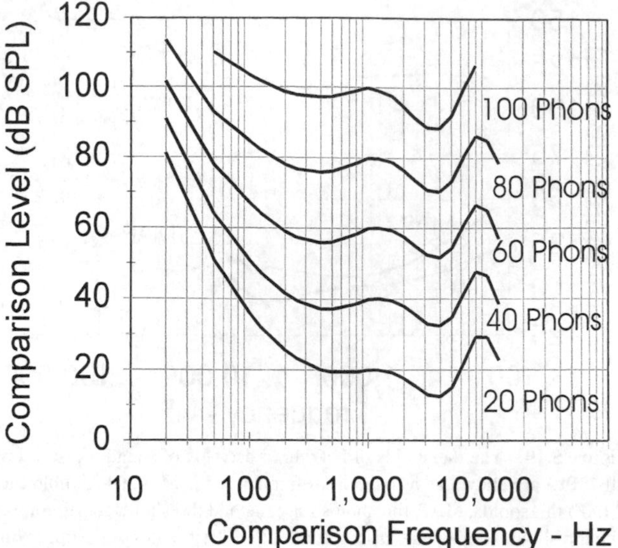

Figure 5.11 Equal loudness contours showing the level of a comparison tone required to match the perceived loudness of a 1,000-Hz standard tone presented at different levels (20, 40, 60, 80, and 100 dB SPL). Each curve is an equal loudness contour. *Source:* Based on international standards.

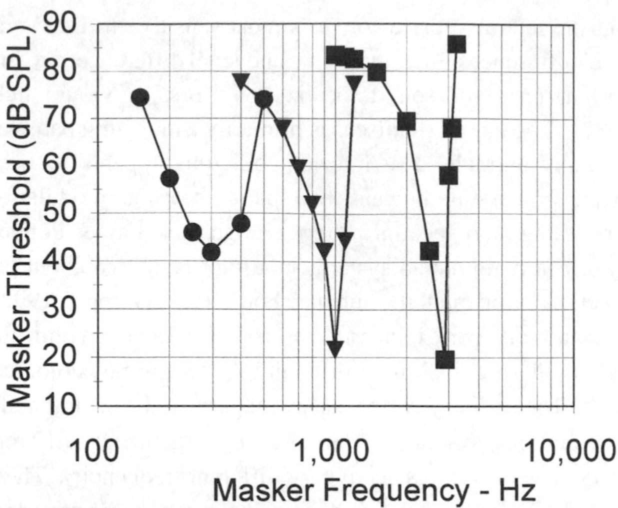

Figure 5.12 Three psychophysical tuning curves for simultaneous masking are shown. The different curves are for conditions in which the signal frequency was 300, 1000, and 3000 Hz. *Source:* From Yost (2000), adapted from data of Wightman, McGee, and Kramer (1977), with permission.

approximation and over a considerable range of durations, if the energy of the sound remains constant, detection thresholds also remain constant (equal-energy rule). The duration at which thresholds no longer change with increases in duration (i.e., at 300 ms) is referred to as the integration time for detection (Viemeister & Plack, 1993).

Masking

When the threshold for detecting sound A is increased in the presence of another sound, sound B, sound B is said to be a masker for the signal, sound A. The amount of masking is the amount of the increase in signal detection threshold due to the presence of the masker. Figure 5.12 shows the thresholds for detecting a signal tone of one frequency as a function of tonal maskers of different frequencies. For these data, listeners were asked to detect the presence of a short-duration tonal signal presented just a few decibels above its threshold of hearing. The level of the tonal masker that yielded threshold performance for detecting the signal was determined for each masker frequency. Both the similarity of the shape of the data curves in Figure 5.12 to those in Figure 5.7 and the methodological similarities result in these psychophysical data being referred to as psychophysical tuning curves. It is assumed that the frequency selectivity suggested by psychophysical tuning curves results from the frequency selectivity measured in the auditory periphery (Moore, 1997).

The observation from Figure 5.12, that masking is greatest when the frequency of the masker is near that of the signal, was studied extensively by Harvey Fletcher in the 1940s. He formed the concept of the critical band (Fletcher, 1953), stating that only a band of frequencies near that of the signal was critical for masking. He further theorized that the amount of masking of a tonal signal was proportional to the power of the critical masking band. These observations have been confirmed by many experiments since the 1940s.

The tonal psychophysical curves are one method used to measure this critical band. However, several interactions can occur between a tonal signal and a tonal masker that can complicate interpretation of some tone-on-tone masking results (Wegel & Lane, 1924). If the signal and masker frequencies differ by 20 or fewer Hz, then the tones interact to produce slow fluctuations in overall intensity that result in the perception of beats (alteration in loudness), which can be used as a cue for detecting the presence of the tonal signal. In addition, the nonlinear properties of auditory transduction can produce aural distortion products that can also provide a detection cue. The tonal masker can produce aural harmonics, which are frequencies at the harmonics of the masker frequency caused by the nonlinear process. The nonlinear properties of transduction can produce difference tones, which are frequencies equal to differences between the frequencies of the masker and signal. The psychophysical tuning curve method reduces, but does not always eliminate, the effect of many of these stimulus interactions as possible detection cues.

The preferred method for measuring the critical band is the band-reject noise paradigm as shown in Figure 5.13. A band-reject noise has a frequency region filtered out of the noise, which for masking is a frequency region surrounding the signal frequency. This band-reject, noise-masking procedure (Moore, 1986) reduces or eliminates all of the interactive

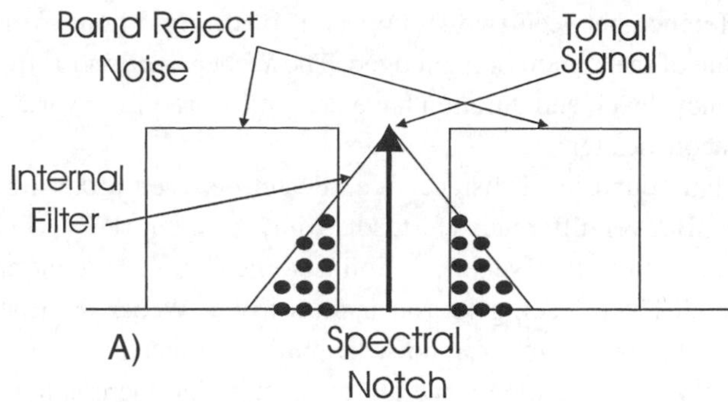

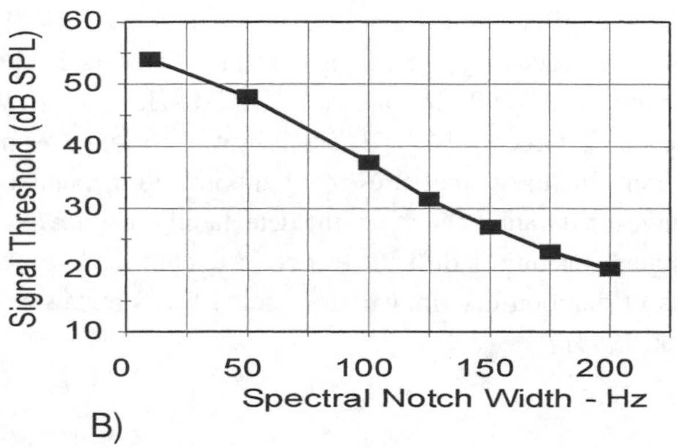

Figure 5.13 (A) A noise band with a spectral notch or gap is used to mask a signal whose frequency is in the center of the spectral gap. (B) The masked thresholds for detecting a 1,000-Hz signal are shown as a function of increasing the spectral notch of the band-reject noise. *Source:* From Yost (2000), adapted from data of Patterson and Moore (1989), with permission.

effects obtained with tonal maskers and signals. As the width of the band-reject noise increases, signal threshold is lowered because there is less power in the critical band of frequencies near that of the signal. The width of the critical band is proportional to signal frequency as is consistent with frequency tuning measured in the auditory periphery (Glasberg & Moore, 1990). That is, as the frequency content of a signal increases, the range of frequencies that are critical for masking the signal also increases proportionally.

The concept of the critical band as a measure of auditory-processing channels that are frequency tuned is closely tied to the biomechanical and neural measures of processing in the auditory periphery. This combination of physiological and psychophysical evidence for frequency-tuned channels forms a significant part of all current theories and models of auditory processing (Moore & Patterson, 1986).

Many data from masking experiments, especially those involving Gaussian noises and tonal signals, can be explained using the energy detection model (Green & Swets, 1973) from the general theory of signal detection (TSD). For instance, in an experiment in which a Gaussian noise masks a tonal signal, the energy detection model assumes that the energy of the noise is compared to that of the signal plus noise. The noise masker energy is a random variable that can be described with a distribution with a known mean and standard deviation. The addition of the signal to the noise often increases the mean of the distribution, but not the standard deviation. As signal level increases, the normalized (normalized by the common standard deviation) difference in the means of the distributions increases. On any presentation, listeners use a sample of energy to decide whether the signal plus noise or just noise was presented. If the likelihood of the sampled energy is greater than a criterion value (set by the listener's response proclivity or bias), the listener responds that the signal plus noise was presented, because high signal levels are more likely to produce high energy levels. A measure of performance (d') can be obtained from the theoretical distributions of signal-plus-noise and noise-alone conditions, and then can be compared to a similar d' measure obtained from the listener's data. Various forms of the energy model and other models based on TSD have been successful in accounting for a variety of masking results (Green & Swets, 1973).

Temporal Masking

The masking data described so far are based on conditions in which the signal and masker occur at the same time. Masking also takes place when the signal and maskers do not temporally overlap. Forward masking occurs when the signal comes on after the masker is turned off and backward masking occurs when the signal precedes the masker. For the same temporal separation between signal and masker, there is usually more forward than backward masking. In the fringe conditions, a short-duration signal is presented near the onset (forward fringe) or offset (backward fringe) of a longer-duration masker. Most often, the greatest amount of masking occurs in these fringe conditions (masking overshoot).

As has already been described, the nonlinear properties of auditory transduction can have several psychophysical consequences. The existence of aural harmonics and difference tones is one such consequence. It is also probably the case that there are suppressive effects that are a function of some form of nonlinearity. That is, the masker may suppress or inhibit the excitatory effect of the signal under different conditions. The separation of the signal and masker in temporal masking conditions allows one to potentially isolate these suppressive effects. The fact that psychophysical tuning measured in forward masking generates measures of narrower tuning (smaller critical bands) than that obtained in simultaneous masking may be consistent with such suppressive effects existing in the simultaneous conditions (Moore, 1986).

Nonlinear peripheral processing is a compressive nonlinearity in which neural output is compressively related to sound input. Thus, the same decibel change in sound level produces a smaller change in neural output at high-sound levels than at low-sound levels. This compressive nonlinearity may also be the cause of a difference between simultaneous and forward tonal masking. In simultaneous tonal masking, the signal must change by about 1 dB for each 1 dB change in masker level in order for constant signal detection to occur. In forward masking, a change of less than 1 dB for each decibel change in masker level is required for constant detection. This change in masking slopes between simultaneous and forward masking may result because in simultaneous masking, both the signal and masker undergo the same form of compression. In forward masking, the temporal separation between the masker and signal results in the lower-level signal undergoing a different form of compression than that for the higher-level masker (Moore, 1995).

Temporal Modulation Transfer Functions

Most sounds change in their overall level over time (these sounds are amplitude modulated). The temporal modulation transfer function is one measure of the auditory system's ability to detect such level changes. A noise waveform is amplitude modulated such that its overall amplitude varies from a low to a high level in a sinusoidal manner. Listeners are asked to detect whether such dynamic amplitude modulation occurs. The depth of modulation (the difference between the peak and valley levels) required for modulation detection (i.e., the ability to detect a difference between a noise with no modulation and a noise sinusoidally amplitude modulated) is determined as a function of the rate at which the amplitudes are modulated. As the modulation rate increases, the depth of modulation must increase to maintain a threshold ability to detect modulation. That is, at low rates of modulation, only a small depth of modulation is required to detect amplitude modulation. As the rate of modulation increases, the depth of modulation required for modulation detection also increases in a monotonic manner. The function relating threshold depth of modulation to the rate of modulation resembles that of a lowpass filter. The lowpass form of this function describes the temporal modulation transfer function for processing temporal amplitude changes (Dau, Kollmeier, & Kohlraush, 1997; Viemeister & Plack, 1993).

DISCRIMINATION

Measures of the ability of listeners to discern differences in frequency, level, and the timing properties of sounds is often tied to the nineteenth-century observations of Weber and Fechner. The Weber fraction states that the just-noticeable difference between two stimuli is a fixed proportion of the value of the stimuli being judged. The Weber fraction for frequency, level, and duration have been measured for a variety of acoustic signals.

For sound level, listeners can detect between a 0.5- and 1.5-dB level difference (Jesteadt, Weir, & Green, 1977). For tonal stimuli, the Weber fraction is somewhat dependent on overall level, leading to a near miss to the Weber fraction. The Weber fraction for noise stimuli is constant at about 0.5 dB as a function of overall level, such that there is not a near-miss to Weber's fraction for noise signals. The just-noticeable difference for tonal frequency is about 0.2–0.4% of the base frequency; for example, trained listeners can just discriminate a 1002-Hz tone from a 1000-Hz tone (Weir, Jesteadt, & Green, 1977). There is not a constant Weber fraction for most measures of temporal discrimination. Changes in duration can affect the detectability and loudness of sound, making it difficult to obtain unconfounded measures of duration discrimination (Abel, 1971; Viemeister & Plack, 1993).

SOUND LOCALIZATION

Sound Localization in Three-Dimensional Space

Sound has the properties of level, frequency, and time, but not space. Yet, the sound produced by an object can be used by most animals to locate that object in three-dimensional space (Blauert, 1997; Gilkey & Andersen, 1997). A different set of acoustic cues is used for sound localization in each plane. The location of a sound source is determined by neural computations based on these cues.

In the horizontal or azimuth plane, left-right judgments of sound location are most likely based on interaural differences of time and level (Wightman & Kistler, 1993; Yost & Gourevitch, 1987). The sound from a source will reach one ear (near ear) before it reaches the other ear (far ear), and the interaural difference in arrival time (or a subsequent interaural phase difference) is a cue for sound localization. However, given the small maximal interaural time difference due to the size of the head, this cue is probably only useful for low-frequency sounds. The sound level at the near ear will be greater than that at the far ear, primarily because the head produces a sound shadow at the far ear. The sound shadow is proportional to frequency, so that interaural level differences most likely provide cues for sound localization at high frequencies. The fact that interaural time provides a cue for sound location at low frequencies and interaural level differences a cue at high frequencies is referred to as the duplex theory of sound localization (Yost & Gourvitvch, 1987).

Sound localization accuracy is best at frequencies below 1000 Hz (the region where interaural time differences are useful cues) and above 2000 Hz (the region where interaural level differences are useful cues), and the transition region around 1500 Hz is consistent with the duplex theory of sound localization. Sound localization acuity is best for azimuthal judgements. Differences as small as 1° of visual angle can be discriminated when the sound sources are directly in front (discriminations of differences in sound source locations are referred to as minimal audible angles; see Mills, 1972). Differences in interaural time differences as small as 10 microseconds and differences in interaural level differences as small as 0.5 dB can be discriminated (Blauret, 1997).

All sounds that lie on cones of confusion (Mills, 1972) generate the same interaural time and level differences. One such cone is the midsagittal plane: the plane that is from directly in front, to directly overhead, to directly behind, to directly below a listener. All locations on the midsagittal plane produce zero differences of interaural time and level, and as such these interaural differences would not allow sound location within this plane. Yet, listeners can accurately locate sound sources in this plane without moving their heads (head movements would change the cone of confusion). Thus, cues other than the interaural differences are most likely used to locate sounds in the vertical plane (in the up-down direction).

The head-related transfer functions (HRTFs) discussed in relationship to the outer ear describe the spectral changes that sound undergoes as it travels from its source across the body and head of the listener toward the middle ear. The spectral characteristics of the HRTF are dependent on the location of the sound source. In particular, there are spectral peaks and valleys in frequency regions above 4000 Hz that change spectral location in a systematic and orderly manner as a function of the vertical position of the sound source (Wightman & Kistler, 1989b). Thus, the frequency location of these HRTF spectral peaks and valleys are probable cues for sound localization in the vertical direction. For instance, vertical sound localization is degraded if sound is low-passed filtered so that there is little or no energy above 4000 Hz where the spectral peaks and valleys are located. Acuity in the vertical direction is generally poorer than in the horizontal direction (Middlebrooks, 1992). The greatest number of sound localization errors occur along cones of confusions. For instance, there can be significant front-back and back-front confusions in the midsagittal plane (Wightman & Kistler, 1989b).

Sound localization accuracy of the distance of a sound source is poorer than either horizontal or vertical sound localization accuracy. The primary cues for distance perception are either the relative sound level or the ratio of reverberant to direct sound impinging on the listener (Loomis, Klatzky, Philbeck, & Golledge, 1998). If the sound source is within the near field of a listener (within about one meter), then interaural level differences may aid in distance judgements. Relative sound level is only a useful cue if there is some a priori knowledge of the level, because sound level can vary at the source, as well as a function of distance. The ratio of reflected or reverberant sound to that coming directly from the source varies as a function of distance, making this ratio a probable cue for distance judgements when there are reflective surfaces (e.g., the ground).

Models of Sound Localization

Neural coincidence networks have been suggested as one means by which the auditory system might compute interaural differences, especially interaural time differences (Colburn & Durlach, 1978). The network contains cells receiving bilateral inputs. The cells fire upon the simultaneous arrival of neural information from the two inputs. The network can serve as a neural crosscorrelator of the timing information arriving at each ear. Thus, sound arriving at the same time at each ear activates neurons in the middle of the network, whereas sound arriving at one ear ahead of that arriving at the other ear activates neurons to one side of the network. The activation of these neurons in the coincidence network could form a type of spatial neural map. Several computational models based on coincidence and crosscorrelation have been successful in accounting for a great deal of data based on manipulations of interaural time differences. There is neural evidence in some species, especially birds, for just this sort of coincidence network (Konishi et al., 1988).

Lateralization Versus Localization

When sounds are presented over headphones and interaural differences of time or level are varied, listeners report that the sounds move left and right as they do in the real world. However, the sounds are lateralized inside the head rather than in space as any real-world sound source would be located—and therefore localized. Thus, lateralization is often used to refer to headphone-delivered sounds in the study of sound localization and localization when sound sources are in the external world (Blauert, 1997; Yost & Gouervitch, 1987).

One reason that sound delivered over headphones may be lateralized rather than localized is that the headphone-delivered sounds have not undergone the spectral transformations associated with the HRTFs that naturally occurring sounds undergo. If the information about the HRTF is put back into the sound delivered over headphones, then it is possible to produce a sound over headphones (using HRTF filters) that is spectrally identical to that which would have arrived at the middle ear from a real sound source at some location in space. When such HRTF filters are used, listeners are much more likely to localize the sounds in space at a location appropriate for the specific HRTF used than they are to lateralize the sound inside the head. Thus, HRTF-filtered sound presentations over headphones can create a virtual auditory environment simulating sound localization in the real world. Under the proper conditions, sounds delivered over headphones are perceived as nearly indistinguishable from the sound delivered from actual sources (Gilkey & Andersen, 1997; Wightman & Kisltler, 1989b).

The Effects of Precedence

Although reflections from surfaces may aid distance judgements, they could also offer a confusing auditory scene for sound localization, because each reflection could be misinterpreted as a possible sound source location. In most real-world spaces, reflections do not have a significant effect on either the location or on the fidelity of the sound from the originating source. The sound from the source will reach a listener before that of any reflection due to the longer path any reflection must travel. Hence, it is as if the sound from the source takes perceptual precedence over that from reflections (Litovsky, Colburn, Yost, & Guzman, 1999).

The effects of precedence (Litovsky et al., 1999) include that fact that the reflections are rarely perceived as separate echoes (fusion), the perceived location of a sound source in a reflective environment is dominated by the location of the source and not by the location of reflections (location dominance), and information about reflections is suppressed relative to that about the source (discrimination suppression). Evidence also suggests that the effects of precedence may be influenced by a listener's prior listening experience in an acoustic environment. A common paradigm (Litovsky et al., 1999) for studying the effects of precedence involves the presentation of a transient from one loudspeaker (the lead or source sound), followed a few milliseconds later by an identical transient presented from a different loudspeaker (the lag or reflected sound). In most cases in this lead-lag paradigm, a single transient is perceived (fusion), at the location of the lead loudspeaker (localization dominance), and the spatial acuity of the lag is reduced relative to conditions when the lag was presented in isolation of the lead (discrimination suppression).

SOUND SOURCE SEGREGATION

Any animal's auditory experience probably involves processing several simultaneously or nearly simultaneously occurring sound sources. Several stimulus cues have been suggested as possibilities for segregating sound sources in the complex acoustic world: spectral separation, temporal separation, spatial separation, pitch and timbre (harmonicity and temporal regularity), spectral profiles, common onsets and offsets, and common modulation (Yost & Sheft, 1993; Yost, Popper, & Faye, 1993).

Recall from the description of the auditory periphery that the auditory nerve codes for the spectral-temporal properties of sound. Sounds from every sound source in an acoustic environment are combined into a single complex sound field that stimulates the inner ear. The auditory periphery codes for the spectral-temporal structure of this complex sound field. The spectral-temporal code must be analyzed to determine the potential sound sources. That is, the spectral-temporal neural properties must be deconvolved into subsets of spectral-temporal patterns representing the sound originating from each individual sound source. This form of analysis is presumably performed by the central auditory nervous system. Note that in order for this type of analysis to take place, computations must be made across frequency and over time (Bregman, 1990).

Spectral Separation

If two sound sources had very different and nonoverlapping spectral structures, the frequency-resolving ability of the auditory system might segregate the two sound sources very nicely into two patterns. Thus, in some cases the frequency-resolving abilities of the auditory system can aid in sound source segregation, but not in all cases. The difficulty arises when the spectra of sounds from different sources overlap in frequency and time.

Temporal Separation

Clearly, if the sound from two sources occurs at different times, and there is little, if any, temporal masking, then sound source segregation is possible. In many real-world situations, the sound from one source is intermittent and may overlap in time with sounds from other sources that are also intermittent. In addition to the question of segregation of one sound source from other sound sources, this stimulus situation also addresses the question of how an intermittent sound from a source continues to be identified as originating from that source, especially if other sounds occur at or about the same time. A series of studies referred to as auditory stream analysis investigates this type of stimulus condition (Bregman, 1990).

An early context for the study of auditory stream processing involved the presentation of two tones of different frequencies, and each tone is pulsed on and off such that when one tone is on, the other is off. Two different percepts may occur in this situation. In one case, the perception is of one sound source that is alternating in pitch. In the other case, the perception is of two sound sources, each associated with the individual frequencies and with each containing a pulsing sound. In the latter case, it as if there were two sound sources, each producing a pulsing tone occurring at the same time, like two streams running side by side (stream segregation). By determining the stimulus conditions that yield stream segregation, investigators have attempted to study those stimulus conditions that promote sound source segregation. In addition to an appropriate frequency separation between the two sounds, differences in stimulus complexity, interaural differences (i.e., spatial differences), temporal amplitude modulation differences, and level differences may promote stream segregation. The temporal structure of the stimulus context plays a crucial role in stream segregation. In general, spectral differences promote stream segregation more than other stimulus attributes do.

In another methodology involving temporal sequences of sounds, an auditory pattern of tonal sounds is generated as a model of complex sounds, such as speech (Watson, 1976). In many conditions, a pattern of 10 tones presented in succession, each with a different frequency, is used as a tonal pattern. The frequency range over which the tones vary, the duration of each tone, and the overall duration of the 10-tone pattern are often similar to that occurring for many speech sounds, like words (see the Fowler chapter of this volume). Listeners are asked to discriminate a change in the frequency of 1 of the 10 tones in the pattern. In many conditions, the patterns change from trial to trial in a random manner. In this case, frequency discrimination of one tone in a pattern of changing tones is very poor, especially for tones at the beginning and at the end of the 10-tone pattern. However, as the random variation in the patterns is reduced, frequency discrimination improves, and the differences in discrimination as function of the temporal order of the tones are also reduced. When the same 10-tone pattern is presented on each trial (i.e., there is no randomization of the pattern frequencies) and only one tone is subjected to a frequency change, frequency discrimination thresholds for any one tone in the 10-tone pattern is nearly equal to that achieved when that tone is presented in isolation. These 10-tone pattern experiments show that the uncertainty about the stimulus context can have a large effect on performance in identifying complex sounds.

Information masking is used to describe the decrease in performance attributable to the stimulus context rather than to the actual values of the stimulus parameters. Thus, the changes in performance due to certain versus uncertain contexts in the 10-tone pattern experiments for the same stimulus values is due to informational masking. Another example of informational masking involves a tonal signal and a tonal-complex masker. If the tonal complex is a 100-tone masker and all 100 tones are mixed together at one time to form the masker, a certain signal level is required for signal detection (assume the signal frequency is in the center of the range of the frequencies used for the tonal-complex masker). If only 1 of the 100 tones in the tonal-complex masker is chosen at random and presented alone on each trial and masking of the signal is measured over the random presentation of the 100 tones, then signal threshold may be elevated by 20 or more decibels relative to the case when all 100 tones were mixed together at the same time to form the single tonal-complex masker. The increase in threshold is referred to as informational masking due to the uncertainty in the masking stimulus from trial to trial, despite the fact that the frequency range over which the masker varies is the same in both conditions, and on many trials the signal should be easy to detect because its frequency would be very different from that of the masker on that trial (Neff & Green, 1987).

Spatial Separation

The section on sound localization described the ability of listeners to locate a sound source based on the sound that is produced. When sound sources are located at different locations, does this spatial separation aid sound source segregation? Cherry (1953) stated that spatial separation would aid sound source segregation when he coined the term *cocktail party effect*. That is, spatial separation was a way to segregate one sound from the concoction of other sounds at a noisy cocktail party. Spatially separating sound sources does aid in the identification of the individual sound sources, especially when there are more than two sound sources (Yost, Dye, & Sheft, 1996).

The masked threshold for detecting a signal presented with one set of interaural differences can vary greatly as a function of the interaural differences of the masker. If the signal and masker are presented with a different set of interaural differences, then signal threshold is lower than in conditions in which the signal and masker are presented with the same interaural differences. The decibel difference in masked threshold between a condition in which the signal and masker have different interaural differences compared to that in which they have the same interaural differences is the masking-level difference, MLD (Green & Yost, 1975; Yost & Dye, 1991). For instance, if the masker (M) and the signal (S) each have no interaural differences (subscript 0), the condition is

M_0S_0. If the masker is M_0, but the signal is presented with a 180° (π radians) interaural phase difference, the condition is M_0S_π. The threshold for detection of the signal in the M_0S_π condition is 15–18 dB lower than it is in the M_0S_0 condition (the MLD is 15–18 dB). The MLD has been studied for a wide variety of stimulus conditions and interaural configurations, and the MLD is always positive when the signal and masker have a different set of interaural differences, as compared to conditions in which the signal and masker have the same set of interaural differences.

Because an interaural difference is associated with a horizontal location in space, signals and maskers that have different interaural differences are similar to stimuli that are at different positions in space. Thus, the results from the MLD literature suggest that when the signal and masker are in different spatial locations (have different interaural differences), signal threshold is lower than when the signal and masker occupy the same spatial locations (have the same interaural differences). Such threshold differences do exist when signals and maskers are presented from loudspeakers in real-world spaces (Gilkey & Andersen, 1997). These results appear consistent with Cherry's observation about the role spatial separation plays in solving the cocktail party problem. Models that are variations of the coincidence models used to account for processing interaural time differences have also been successful in accounting for a great deal of the data from the MLD literature (Colburn & Durlach, 1978).

Pitch and Timbre: Harmonicity and Temporal Regularity

Pitch is that subjective attribute of sound that varies along a low-high dimension and is highly correlated with the spectral content of sound. The pitch of a target sound is often given in terms of hertz, such that the pitch of a target sound is *x* Hz, if a tone of *x* Hz is judged perceptually equal in pitch to the target sound. Musical scales, such as the 12-note scale, can also be used to denote the pitch of a sound.

Timbre is defined as that subjective attribute of a sound that differentiates two sounds that are otherwise equal in pitch, loudness, and duration. Thus, the difference between the sound from a cello playing the note G for the same duration and loudness as the sound from a violin playing the same note G, is said to be a difference in timbre. The sound of the cello differs in timbre from that of a violin. There are no units for measuring timbre, and timbre is often correlated with the spectral or temporal complexity of the sound.

Although the pitch of a sound is often highly correlated with frequencies that are the most intense in a sound's spectrum, many complex sounds produce a strong pitch in the absence of such a concentration of spectral energy. Consider a complex sound with frequency components of 300, 400, 500, and 600 Hz. This sound will often have a 100-Hz pitch, even though there is no spectral component at 100 Hz. Note that 100 Hz is the fundamental of this sound (all of the existing spectral components are harmonics of a 100-Hz fundamental), but the fundamental is missing. Thus, this type of complex pitch is referred to as the "pitch of the missing fundamental." Many sound sources (e.g., most musical instruments) contain a spectrum of harmonics. The pitches associated with these sounds are derivatives of the pitch of the missing fundamental.

The stimulus described above that leads to the pitch of the missing fundamental will often have a periodic time envelope, which in this case will have a 100-Hz repetition (a 10-ms period). Thus, the pitch may be associated with the temporal regularity in the envelope. However, stimuli with very little envelope periodicity can still produce a complex pitch like that of the pitch of the missing fundamental. Such stimuli may not have a smooth spectrum like that of the tonal complex described above. Thus, neither envelope periodicity nor a smooth spectrum appear to be necessary and sufficient conditions for producing a complex pitch. However, such stimuli without periodic temporal envelopes may contain a temporally regular, but nonperiodic, fine structure that may be the basis for complex pitch (an analysis of this stimulus, such as autocorrelation, will reveal this otherwise difficult-to-determine temporal regularity; see Yost, 1996).

In addition to influencing the pitch of complex sounds, harmonic structure also influences timbre. Thus, a complex harmonic sound with high-amplitude, high-frequency harmonics may have a brighter timbre than a complex sound with high-amplitude, low-frequency harmonics, which would have a dull timbre. Certain forms of temporal regularity (e.g., noise vs. periodic sounds) can also influence a sound's timbre.

Therefore, harmonic structure and temporal regularity are important stimulus properties that help determine the pitch and timbre of complex sounds. Complex sounds differ in pitch and timbre, and, as such, these two subjective attributes may allow for sound source segregation. Indeed, complex pitch and timbre have both been used to segregate sound sources in auditory stream experiments (Bregman, 1990). The two-vowel paradigm (Summerfield & Assmann, 1991; Yost & Sheft, 1993) is another procedure used to study the influence of harmonicity on sound source segregation. In the two-vowel procedure, two artificially generated (via computer) vowels are mixed. Often it is difficult or impossible to identify the two vowels generated in this manner. Any stimulus manipulation that allows for vowel recognition in the two-vowel stimulus is arguably a crucial stimulus condition for sound source segregation. If the fundamental voicing frequency of the two vowels is made to differ, then often vowel recognition is improved. Because a change in the fundamental voicing frequency also alters the harmonic structure of each vowel, this result suggests that harmonicity does support sound source segregation.

Spectral Profile

Most of the time, the identifiable properties of a sound source are level independent. For instance, an uttered sentence has about the same intelligibility at many different overall loudness levels. Thus, the overall spectral-temporal structure of the sound from a source, which remains constant as overall level is varied, is the important determiner of sound-source identification. An area of study referred to as profile analysis (Green, 1989) has been used to study this property of auditory perception.

In a typical profile analysis experiment, several tones that are all of the same level but of different frequencies are mixed together. The frequency spacing of the tones is usually logarithmic to avoid generating sounds with harmonic structure that may have complex pitches. The level of a tone in the spectral middle of the complex (the signal tone) is increased, and the level of this signal tone required for the complex with the signal to be just discriminable from the complex with all tones equal in level is measured in several different conditions. The key aspect of these profile studies is that the overall level of both complexes is randomly varied across stimulus presentations over a large range, such as 40 dB. The random variation would affect two possible cues for detection. If detection were based on just attending to the signal tone, the overall random-level variation would require a very large signal-level increment for discrimination. An increase in the level of the signal will increase the overall level of the complex as compared to the complex in which all tones are presented at the same level. Thus, overall level (or loudness) could be a cue for detection. However, the random overall level variation would again require a very large signal-level increment if this loudness cue were to be the basis for discrimination. If, on the other hand, listeners could use the relative change in level between the level of the signal as compared to the level of the other tones in the complex, then the random overall level variation would not affect this cue. The complex with the signal increment would have a pointed spectral profile, whereas the complex without the signal increment would have a flat profile. Thus, if this spectral profile cue were used, then discrimination between the signal and nonsignal complexes might occur for small changes in signal level.

The data in Figure 5.14 suggest that such a spectral profile cue is being used. The level of the tonal signal required for

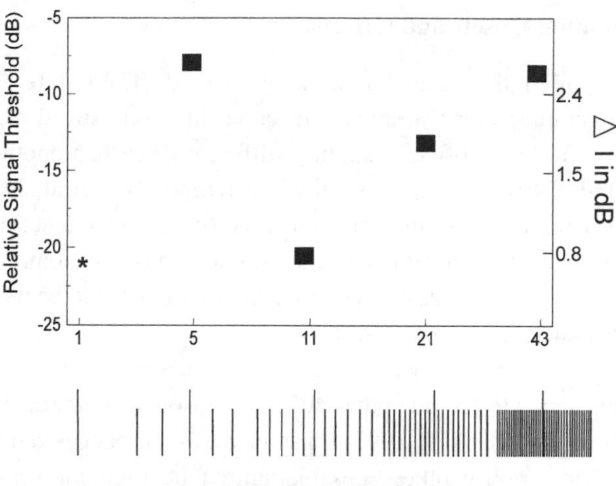

Figure 5.14 The results from a profile analysis experiment in which the number of masker frequency components surrounding a 1000-Hz signal component increased from 4 to 42. The thresholds for detecting an increment in the 1000-Hz signal component (the center component) are shown in decibels relative to that of the rest of the masker component intensity. The asterisk on the far left indicates the typical threshold for detecting a level increment of a single, 1000-Hz tone. Thresholds for the 10-masker condition are almost as low as those for the single-tone condition, and the thresholds first decrease and then increase as the number of masker components increases from 4 to 42. *Source:* From Yost (2000), based on data from Green (1989), with permission.

detection of the signal increment is shown as a function of the number of total tones in the complex. With 11 tones in the complex, the threshold is about the same as it was when the signal was presented in isolation of any flanking tones. When there are fewer or more flanking tones in the complex than 11, thresholds are higher. When a large number of tones fit into the same bandwidth, the tones are so close together that they directly interact, so that tones near that of the signal mask the signal. The increase in threshold with increases in tonal density is consistent with other masking data. When there are only a few tones in the complex, it is argued that the profile is difficult to determine; for example, there is a large spectral difference between the signal tone and its nearest neighbor, making it difficult to discern the spectral profile. A model of listener performance, based on how listeners weigh the spectral information in these tonal profile complexes, suggests that listeners do monitor the spectral profile of these stimuli as the basis for their discrimination judgments (Green, 1989).

Experiments like these profile experiments suggest that the auditory system is very sensitive to subtle changes in the spectral shape of complex signals. Thus, sounds from different sources can be segregated based on changes in spectral shape. Note that the use of spectral shape requires the auditory system to process information across a wide spectral range.

Common Onsets and Offsets

It is often the case that although sounds from different sources may occur at about the same time, one sound may come on or go off at a slightly different time than another sound. When this happens, all of the temporal-spectral characteristics of one sound come on and go off at a different time than that occurring for the other sound. Thus, the common onset or offset of these spectral-temporal cues could be used for sound source segregation.

Asynchronous onsets, and in some cases offsets, have been shown to provide powerful cues for sound source segregation (Yost & Sheft, 1993). In some cases, onset cues can be used to amplify other cues that might be used for sound source segregation. As described above in the section on pitch, a harmonic sequence can produce a complex pitch equal to the fundamental frequency of the complex. If two complexes with different fundamentals are mixed, in most conditions listeners do not perceive the two pitches corresponding to the original two fundamental frequencies. The spectral characteristics of the new complex consisting of the mixture of the two harmonic sequences appear to be analyzed as a whole (synthetically). However, if one of the harmonic complexes is turned on slightly before (50 ms) the other harmonic complex, listeners often perceive the two pitches, even though for most of the time (perhaps for a second) the two harmonic complexes occur together (Darwin, 1981).

Common Modulation

Most everyday sound sources impart a slow amplitude and frequency modulation (change) to the overall spectral-temporal properties of the sound from the source. Each sound source will produce a different pattern of modulation, and these modulation patterns may allow for sound source segregation (Yost & Sheft, 1993). When a person speaks, the vocal cords open and close in a nearly periodic manner that determines the pitch of a voice (Fowler chapter in this volume). However, the frequency of these glottal openings varies (frequency modulation, voicing vibrato) slightly, and the amplitude of air released by each opening also randomly varies (amplitude modulation, voicing jitter) over a small range. Each person has a different pattern of vibrato and jitter. Speech sounds can be artificially generated (via computer) such that the speech (see Fowler chapter in this volume) is produced with constant glottal frequency and amplitude. If two such constant speech sounds are generated and mixed, it is often difficult to segregate the two sounds into the two different speech signals. However, if random variation is introduced into the computer-generated glottal openings and closing (random vibrato and jitter), segregation can occur (McAdams, 1984).

Thus, common amplitude and frequency modulation may be possible cues for sound source segregation. However, frequency modulation per se is probably not a cue used for sound source segregation (Carylon, 1991), but amplitude modulation is most likely a useful cue. Two experimental procedures have been extensively studied to investigate the role of amplitude modulation in auditory processing: comodulation masking release (CMR) and modulation detection interference (MDI).

In a typical CMR experiment (Hall, Haggard, & Fernandes, 1984; Yost & Sheft, 1993) listeners are asked to detect a tonal signal spectrally centered in the middle of a narrow band of noise (target band). In one condition, the detection of the signal is compared to a case in which another narrow band of noise (the flanking band) is simultaneously added in another region of the spectrum. The addition of this flanking band has little effect on signal threshold in the target band, if the target and flanking bands are completely independent. This is consistent with the critical-band view of auditory processing, in that the flanking band falls outside the spectral region of the critical band of the target band and therefore should have little influence on signal detection within the target band. However, if the target and flanking band are dependent in that they have the same pattern of amplitude modulation (they are comodulated), then signal threshold for the target band is lowered by 10–15 dB. This improvement in signal threshold due to comodulation is referred to as CMR, and the results from a typical experiment are shown in Figure 5.15.

The CMR results suggest that the common modulation increases the listener's ability to detect the signal. One explanation of these results is based on the assumption that comodulation groups the flanking and target bands into one perceived sound source that contains more information than that in a single band. Independent (non-comodulated) bands of noise would not come from a single sound source and therefore would not be grouped together. The additional information in the combined (grouped) sound might aid signal detection. For instance, it might make the valleys of low amplitude in the modulated noises more obvious, increasing the ability of the auditory system to detect the tone occurring in these valleys. The addition of the signal changes the correlation between the signal-plus-masking stimuli and the masking-alone stimuli. The combined stimulus may increase this correlation, increasing signal detection.

In an MDI condition (Yost, 1992b; Yost & Sheft, 1993), listeners are asked to discriminate between two amplitude-modulated tonal carrier signals (the probe stimuli) on the basis of the depth of the amplitude modulation. Threshold performance is typically a 3% change in the depth of amplitude modulation. If a tone of a different frequency and not

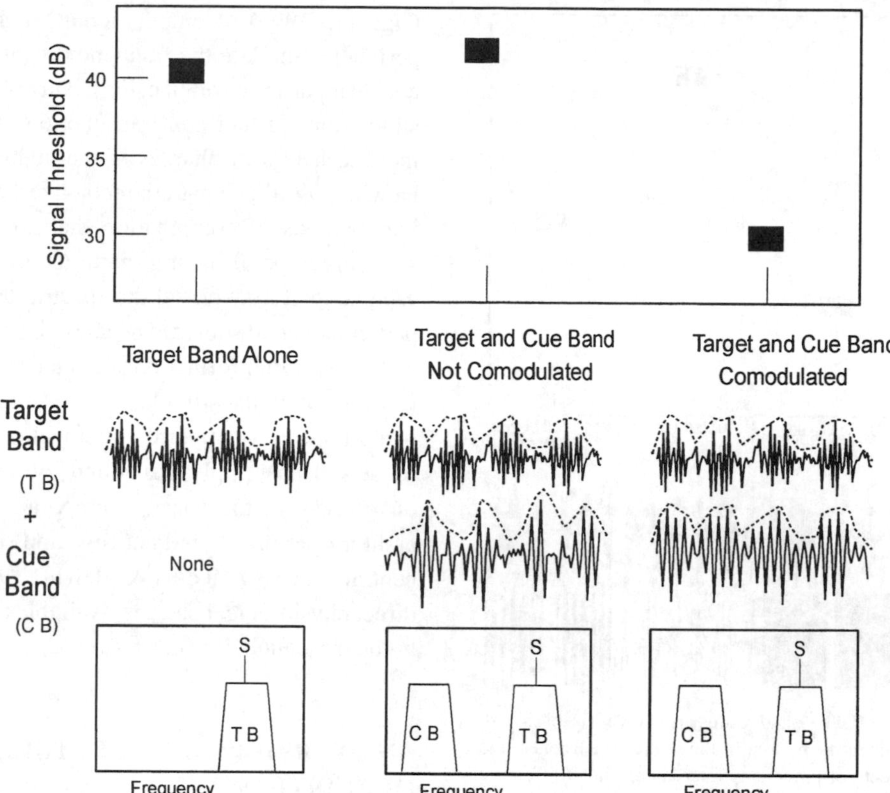

Figure 5.15 Both the basic CMR task and results are shown. At the bottom the time-domain waveforms for the narrow-band maskers (Target and Cue Bands) and the amplitude spectra for the maskers and the signal are shown in a schematic form. The dotted line above each time-domain waveform depicts the amplitude envelope of the narrow-band noises. The listener is asked to detect a signal (S) which is always added to the target band. In the target-band alone condition, the signal is difficult to detect. When a cue band is added to the target band such that it is located in a different frequency region than the target band and has an amplitude envelope that is different (not comodulated with) from the target band, there is little change in threshold from the target-band alone condition. However, when the target and cue bands are comodulated, the threshold is lowered by approximately 12 dB, indicating that the comodulated condition makes it easier for the listener to detect the signal. The waveforms are not drawn to scale. *Source:* From Yost (2000), based on data from Hall et al. (1984), with permission.

amplitude modulated (unmodulated masker) is added simultaneously to the amplitude-modulated probe, there is only a small change in the threshold for discriminating a change in modulation depth. This is consistent with the critical-band view of auditory processing in that the unmodulated masking tone's frequency is not near the carrier frequency of the probe. If the masker is now amplitude modulated with the same amplitude modulation pattern (same rate of modulation) of the probe, then threshold is increased to around 20% (a 15–16 dB increase). The increase in modulation-depth threshold due to the common pattern of modulation between the probe and masker is referred to as modulation detection interference, MDI, and typical results are shown in Figure 5.16.

One argument for why MDI occurs is that the probe and masker are grouped together as a single sound source based on the common pattern of amplitude modulation. Because the common pattern of amplitude modulation is the basis of the grouping, the auditory system has difficulty detecting changes in modulation unless it affects the pattern of modulation. Because changes in amplitude modulation depth of one tone would have a small affect on the modulation pattern of the mixture of the two tones, it is difficult for the auditory system to detect changes in the depth of amplitude modulation for the probe. One test of this argument is to make the pattern (rate) of masker modulation different from that of the probe. In this case, the masker and probe would not be grouped as a single sound source, and MDI would be less or disappear. The data shown in Figure 5.16 are consistent with this argument.

Models or Theories of Sound Source Segregation

One key aspect of accounting for sound source segregation is the recognition that such processing requires the auditory system to process sound across a wide spectral range and

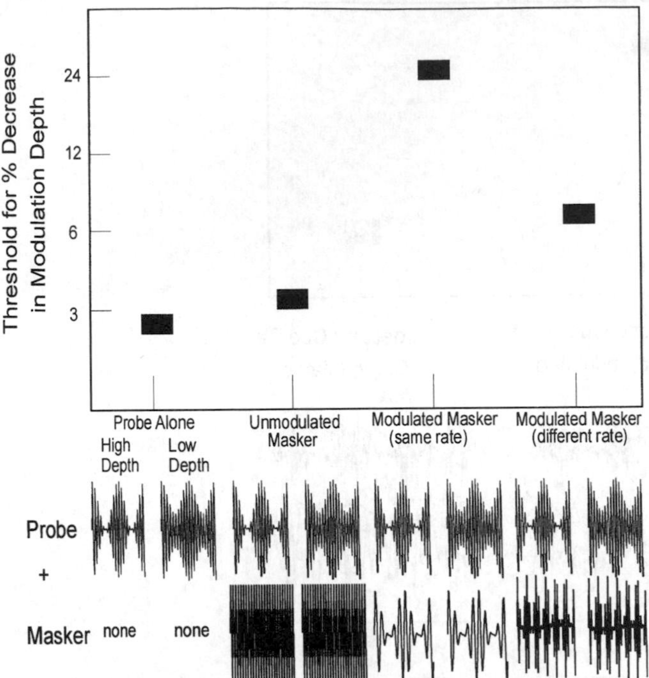

Figure 5.16 Both the basic MDI task and results are shown. The basic task for the listener is depicted along the bottom of the figure. The listener is to detect a decrement in the depth of probe amplitude modulation (difference between low and high depth). When just the probes are presented the task is relatively easy. When an unmodulated masker tone with a frequency different from that of the probe is simultaneously added to the probe, threshold for detecting a decrease in probe modulation depth is not changed much from the probe-alone condition. However, when the masker is modulated with the same rate pattern as the probe, the threshold for detecting a decrement in probe modulation depth increases greatly, indicating that modulation depth is difficult to detect when both the probe and masker are comodulated. When the masker is modulated, but with a different rate (shown as a faster rate in the figure) than the probe, then the threshold for detecting a modulation-depth decrement is lowered. The waveforms are not drawn to scale. *Source:* From Yost (2000), based on data from (Yost, 1992b), with permission.

over time. This is in contrast to the critical-band approach to explaining auditory processing, in which only a narrow region of the spectrum (in the critical band) is processed in a very short period of time. As pointed out above, explanations of profile analysis, CMR, and MDI all assume wide-band spectral processing and procedures like auditory stream segregation emphasize the importance of information integration over a long period of time.

Bregman (1990) has approached explanations of sound source segregation from a perceptual point of view, borrowing many concepts from the Gestalt school of perception. Several computational models have been developed to account for aspects of sound source segregation, especially those from auditory stream segregation experiments. These models are usually based on pattern recognition computations that interrogate spectral-temporal patterns generated by modeling the processes of the auditory periphery (Patterson, Allerhand, & Giguere, 1995). Computational models of the auditory periphery simulate the frequency-resolving properties of the cochlear partition (often using a bank of band-pass filters) and simulations of hair cell transduction of stereocilia displacement to neural discharges in the auditory nerve (Meddis & Hewitt, 1992). The pattern recognizers are neural nets or similar methods of computation that attempt to segregate the spectral-temporal neural patterns into subparts, whereby each subpart may reveal the spectral-temporal structure of a particular sound source. The cues discussed in this chapter, as well as a priori information about the stimulus context or prior learning about the stimulus context, are used to segregate the overall spectral-temporal pattern into these subparts. These models clearly imply that sound source segregation is based on processing the spectral-temporal code provided by the auditory periphery, and hence sound source segregation is a central process (Meddis & Hewitt, 1992). As of yet, little direct physiological data are available that can be used to help guide these modeling efforts.

AN OVERVIEW OF THE FUTURE STUDY OF AUDITION

A great deal of what is known about hearing comes from understanding the causes of hearing loss and its treatment. The major links in the hearing process that are most vulnerable to damage are the intricate structures of the inner ear, especially the hair cells. The study of the function of inner and outer hair cells and the exact consequences each plays in hearing will continue to be a major research focus in audition. The recent suggestions that the compressive nonlinear properties of cochlear transduction are derived from outer hair cell function have led to a better understanding of auditory perception in both people with normal hearing and those with impaired hearing. Perhaps, however, the most exciting discovery concerning hair cells is the fact that hair cells in birds, fish, and probably amphibians regenerate after damage due to overexposure to either sound or ototoxic drugs (Tsue, Osterle, & Rubel, 1994). These regenerated hair cells in birds appear to function normally in support of normal hearing, but additional work is needed to fully understand the perceptual abilities of these animals with regenerated hair cells. Hair cells in mammals do not regenerate. The quest is on to determine why hair cell regeneration occurs in some nonmammals but not in mammals. The ability to regrow hair cells could, for many different types of hearing loss, be the ultimate hearing aid.

The study of hair cell regeneration is one of many areas in which genetic techniques are supplying new and important facts about auditory function. In addition to revealing important clues for understanding normal audition, the genetic revolution has made significant strides in identifying the genetic basis for several different forms of inheritable deafness. A gene that may control the motile response of the outer hair cells has been identified (Zheng, Shen, He, Long, & Pallos, 2000), opening a whole array of possibilities (e.g., genic manipulation) for better understanding outer hair-cell function. In many areas, perceptual research should provide improved ways to determine different phenotypes in order to better define structure-function auditory relationships.

The development of better hearing aids, both amplification hearing aids and the cochlear prosthesis, has stimulated new knowledge about audition; these technologies have benefitted from the past research on hearing as well. The cochlear prosthesis in particular offers unique opportunities to study the hearing process (Miller & Spelman, 1989). The cochlear prosthesis is a wire with multiple electrodes that is surgically inserted into the cochlear partition of a patient with a hearing loss. The electrodes stimulate selected portions of the cochlear partition, based on the transduction of sound into electrical current via a sound processor worn by the patient. The success achieved by thousands of cochlear prosthetic users worldwide suggests that these devices provide a useful means of aural communication for many people with hearing impairments. Because the use of cochlear prostheses bypasses the biomechanical properties of the inner ear, understanding the auditory abilities of successful implant users provides valuable information about the early neural stages of the auditory process. Many successful users of the cochlear prostheses had been deprived of useful hearing for many years before their implantation. The significant improvement in auditory abilities achieved by these cochlear prostheses users, after implementation and training, suggests a degree of auditory plasticity that is receiving a great deal of attention. The importance of this issue has increased now that young children are being implanted.

In addition to providing potential utility for hearing aids, research on spatial hearing and the HRTF have provided improvements for devices used in many sound localization situations (Gilkey & Andersen, 1997). For instance, many traditional hearing aids (especially if only one hearing aid is used) do not allow users to accurately localize sound sources. Proper use of HRTF technology may enable hearing aid users to more accurately localize sound sources, and such accuracy may also improve their ability to detect sounds in noisy environments (the aforementioned cocktail party effect). HRTF technology has also been adopted in the audio entertainment and other industries.

The use of the HRTF offers complete control of the sound cues that are important for sound localization. Such control offers several advantages for studying hearing (Gilkey & Andersen, 1997). One interesting use of HRTF-transformed sound is in the study of auditory adaptation and neural plasticity to alterations of the normal cues for sound localization (Hofman, Van Riswick, & Van Opstal, 1998). If the HRTF is altered such that the location of a sound source is now perceived at a new location, listeners can adapt to the change and after a few days demonstrate near-normal sound localization abilities. When the nonnormal alterations are removed, listeners quickly return to being able to accurately localize as they had before the alteration. Such sound localization adaptation research with human and animal (e.g., the barn owl) listeners is revealing and will continue to reveal important insights about the plasticity of neural sound localization processes (Knudsen, Esterly, & Olsen, 1994).

In the late 1980s and early 1990s, several authors (Hartmann, 1988; Moore, 1997; Yost, 1992a), most notably Bregman (1990), suggested that our ability to determine the sources of sounds, especially in multisource acoustic environments, was a major aspect of hearing about which very little was known. Although the early history of the study of hearing suggests that so-called object identification was an important aspect of hearing, for most of the last century and a half the study of audition focused on the detection and discrimination of the attributes of sound—frequency, level, and timing—and how those attributes were coded in the auditory periphery (Yost, 1992a). While there is still not a lot known about how the auditory scene is achieved, current research in hearing is no longer focused on processing in narrow frequency bands and over very short temporal durations. Psychophysical and physiological investigators have examined and will continue to investigate auditory mechanisms that integrate acoustic information across the spectrum and over time, because such processing is crucial for sound source determination.

The progress in understanding auditory scene processing may be hindered by a lack of appropriate techniques to study these problems. New correlation techniques in psychophysics, multiple electrode technology, new physiological techniques, new ways of extracting information from neural data, and neural imaging are some of the new methods that may open up opportunities for understanding sound source determination and audition. Auditory science also knows very little about the functional purposes of the auditory nuclei in the ascending auditory pathway and within the auditory cortex. With a few notable exceptions of several animal models (e.g., bats and echo processing; barn owls and sound localization), very little is known about the roles various neural centers play in hearing. A great deal is known about the anatomy of many neural circuits and the physiological properties of many types of fibers in most neural centers, but far less is known about what function those circuits and fibers play in hearing. This is perhaps understandable because most of functional hearing is based on significant neural computation of the incoming auditory signal. The neural centers that perform the computations necessary for sound localization, especially computations for interaural time and level differences, are beginning to be sorted out, probably because a great deal is known about the type of computations that are required for accurate sound localization. Similar work for understanding the functionality of other auditory neural centers will continue to be an intense area of interest for auditory science. Progress will require a better understanding of auditory neural circuits in the central auditory system, additional knowledge about the auditory cues used for sound source determination, and testable models and theories of sound source determination.

Models of auditory processing, especially computational models, have provided significant new insights into possible mechanisms of cental auditory processing (Hawkins, McMullen, Popper, & Fay, 1996). Several computational models of the auditory periphery have been shown to produce accurate representations of the spectral-temporal code provided by the inner ear and auditory nerve. These models can be used instead of the laborious collection of physiological data to explore possible models of central mechanisms for processing sound. Additional work on these models will continue to be an active area of research in audition.

There is a growing interest in neural imaging (e.g., PET; positron-emission tomography), especially fMRI (functional magnetic resonance imaging), as a potentially potent tool for probing neural mechanisms of auditory processing. Some of the most recent work is focusing on basic auditory processing (Griffith, Buchel, Frankowiak, & Patterson, 1998), as opposed to speech and language processing based on spoken language (see Fowler chapter in this volume). Such imaging research will be most useful when the spatial and temporal scales of measurement allow one to study the individual neural circuits involved with hearing. New imaging techniques, such as cardiac triggering and sparse imaging, are just now demonstrating the promise this technology might provide for better understanding auditory processing, especially in human listeners.

Although remarkable progress has been made in understanding audition, the field really is in its infancy when one considers all that is not known. While more is to be learned about the auditory periphery and the detectability and discriminability of sounds, a major challenge facing audition is unraveling the function of the central auditory nervous system and how it supports our abilities to process the sound sources that constantly bombard us with crucial information about the world in which we live.

REFERENCES

Abel, S. M. (1971). Duration discrimination of noise and tone bursts. *Journal of the Acoustical Society of America, 51,* 1219–1224.

Ades, H. W. (1959). Central auditory mechanisms. In J. Field, H. W. Magoun, & V. E. Hall (Eds.), *Handbook of physiology: Vol. 1. Neurophysiology* (pp. 38–54). Washington, DC: American Physiological Society.

Ades, H. W., & Engstrom, H. (1974). Anatomy of the inner ear. In W. D. Keidel & W. D. Neff (Eds.), *Handbook of sensory physiology: Vol. 5. Auditory system* (pp. 199–219). New York: Springer-Verlag.

Altschuler, R., Hoffman, D., Bobbin, R., & Clopton, B. (Eds.). (1989). *Neurobiology of hearing: The central nervous system.* New York: Raven Press.

Blauert, J. (1997). *Spatial hearing.* Cambridge, MA: MIT Press.

Bregman, A. S. (1990). *Auditory scene analysis: The perceptual organization of sound.* Cambridge, MA: MIT Press.

Brownell, W. E., Bader, C. R., Bertrand, D., & Ribaupierre, Y. de. (1985). Evoked mechanical responses of isolated cochlear outer hair cells. *Science, 227,* 194–196.

Carlyon, R. P. (1991). Discriminating between coherent and incoherent frequency modulation of complex tones. *Hearing Research, 41,* 223–236.

Cherry, C. (1953). Some experiments on the recognition of speech with one and with two ears. *Journal of the Acoustical Society of America, 25,* 975–981.

Cheveigne, A. de. (2001). The auditory system as a "separation machine." In A. J. M. Houtsma, A. Kohlrausch, V. F. Prijs, & R. Schoonhoven (Eds.), *Physiological and psychophysical bases of auditory function* (pp. 393–400). Maastricht, The Netherlands: Shaker.

Colburn, H. S., & Durlach, N. I. (1978). *Handbook of perception: Vol. 4.* New York: Academic.

Dallos, P. (1973). *The auditory periphery: Biophysics and physiology.* New York: Academic.

Dallos, P., Popper, A. N., & Fay, R. R. (Eds.). (1996). *The cochlea.* New York: Springer-Verlag.

Darwin, C. J. (1981). Perceptual grouping of speech components differing in fundamental frequency and onset time. *Quarterly Journal of Expermental Psychology, 33A,* 185–207.

Dau, T., Kollmeier, B., & Kohlraush, A. (1997). Modeling auditory processing of amplitude modulation: II. Spectral and temporal integration in modulation detection. *Journal of the Acoustical Society of America, 102,* 2906–2919.

Diamond, I. T. (1973). Neuronatamony of the auditory system: Report on a workshop. *Archives of Otolaryngology, 98,* 397–413.

Dorland, A. (1965). *Dorland's illustrated medical dictionary.* London: Saunders.

Fay, R. R., & Popper, A. N. (Eds.). (1992). *The auditory pathway: Neurophysiology.* New York: Springer-Verlag.

Fletcher, H. (1953). *Speech and hearing in communication.* New York: Van Nostrans.

Geisler, C. D. (1998). *From sound to synapse: Physiology of the mammalian ear*. New York: Oxford Press.

Gilkey, R. H., & Anderson, T. A. (1997). *Binaural and spatial hearing in real and virtual environment.* New Jersey: Erlbaum.

Glasberg, B. R., & Moore, B. C. J. (1990). Deviation of auditory filter shapes from notched-noise data. *Hearing Research, 47,* 133–138.

Green, D. M. (1989). *Profile analysis*. New York: Oxford Press.

Green, D. M., & Swets, J. A. (1973). *Signal detection theory and psychophysics*. New York: Krieger.

Green, D. M., & Yost, W. A. (1974). Binaural analysis. In W. D. Keidel & W. D. Neff (Eds.), *Handbook of sensory physiology: Vol. 5. Auditory system* (pp. 461–480). New York: Springer-Verlag.

Griffiths, T. D., Buchel, C., Frankowiak, R. S. J., & Patterson, R. D. (1998). Analysis of temporal structure in sound by the human brain. *Nature Neuroscience, 1,* 422–427.

Hall, J. W., III, Haggard, M., & Fernandes, M. A. (1984). Detection in noise by spectro-temporal pattern analysis. *Journal of the Acoustical Society of America, 76,* 50–60.

Harrison, J. M., & Howe, M. E. (1974). Anatomy of the afferent auditory nervous system of mammals. In W. D. Keidel & W. D. Neff (Eds.), *Handbook of sensory physiology: Vol. 5. Auditory system* (pp. 1010–1021). New York: Springer-Verlag.

Hartmann, W. M. (1988). Pitch perception and the organization and integration of auditory entities. In G. W. Edelman, W. E. Gall, & W. M. Cowan (Eds.), *Auditory function: Neurobiological bases of hearing.* New York: Wiley.

Hartmann, W. M. (1998). *Signal, sounds and sensation*. New York: Springer-Verlag.

Hawkins, H., McMullen, T., Popper, A. N., & Fay, R. R. (Eds.). (1996). *Auditory computation.* New York: Springer-Verlag.

Hind, J., Anderson, D., Brugge, J., & Rosc, J. (1967). Coding of information of pertaining to paired low-frequency tones in single auditory nerve fibers of the squirrel monkey. *Journal of Neurophysiology, 30,* 794–816.

Hofman, P. M., Van Riswick, J. G. A., & Van Opstal, A. J. (1998). Relearning sound localization with new ears. *Nature Neuroscience, 1,* 417–422.

Jesteadt, W., Weir, C. C., & Green, D. M. (1977). Intensity discrimination as a function of frequency and sensation level. *Journal of the Acoustical Society of America, 61,* 169–177.

Kemp, D. T. (1978). Stimulated acoustic emissions from within the human auditory system. *Journal of the Acoustical Society of America, 64,* 1386–1391.

Konishi, M., Takahashi, T. T., Wagner, H., Sullivan, W. E., & Carr, C. E. (1988). Neurophysiological and anatomical substrates of sound localization in the owl. In G. W. Edelman, W. E. Gall, & W. M. Cowan (Eds.), *Auditory function: Neurobiological bases of hearing.* New York: Wiley.

Knudsen, E. I., Esterly, S. D., & Olsen, J. F. (1994). Adaptive plasticity of the auditory space map in the optic tectum of adult and baby barn owls in response to external ear modification. *Journal of Neurophysiology, 71,* 79–94.

Liberman, M. C., & Kiang, N. Y.-S. (1978). Acoustic trauma in cats. *Acta Otolaryngology, 358,* 1–63.

Litovsky, R., Colburn, S., Yost, W. A., & Guzman, S. (1999). The precedence effect. *Journal of the Acoustical Society of America, 106,* 1633–1654.

Lonsbury-Martin, B. L., & Martin, G. K. (1990). The clinical utility of distortion-product otoacoustic emissions. *Ear and Hearing, 11,* 144–154.

Loomis, J. M., Klatzky, R. L., Philbeck, J. W., & Golledge, R. G. (1998). Assessing auditory distance perception using perceptually directed action. *Perception and Psychophysics, 60,* 966–975.

McAdams, S. (1984). *Spectral fusion, spectral parsing and the formation of auditory images.* Unpublished doctoral dissertation, Stanford University.

Meddis, R., & Hewitt, M. J. (1992). Modeling the identification of concurrent vowels with different fundamental frequencies. *Journal of the Acoustical Society of America, 91,* 233–245.

Middlebrooks, J. C. (1992). Narrow-band sound localization related to external ear acoustics. *Journal of the Acoustical Society of America, 92,* 2607–2624.

Miller, J. M., & Spelman, F. A. (Eds.). (1989). *Cochlear implants: Models of the electrically stimulated ear.* New York: Springer-Verlag.

Mills, A. W. (1972). Auditory localization. In J. V. Tobias (Ed.), *Foundations of modern auditory theory: Vol. 2* (pp. 301–348). New York: Academic Press.

Moore, B. C. J. (1986). *Frequency selectivity in hearing*. London: Academic Press.

Moore, B. C. J. (1995). *Perceptual consequences of cochlear damage*. Oxford, England: Oxford University Press.

Moore, B. C. J. (1997). *An introduction to the psychology of hearing* (3rd ed.). London: Academic Press.

Moore, B. C. J., & Patterson, R. D. (Eds.). (1986). *Auditory frequency selectivity*. London: Plenum Press.

Neff, D. L., & Green, D. M. (1987). Masking produced by spectral uncertainty with multicomponent maskers. *Perception and Psychophysics, 41,* 409–415.

Patterson, R. D., Allerhand, M., & Giguere, C. (1995). Time-domain modeling of peripheral auditory processing: A modular architecture and a software platform. *Journal of the Acoustical Society of America, 98,* 1890–1895.

Patterson, R. D., & Moore, B. C. J. (1989). Auditory filters and excitation patterns as representations of frequency resolution. In B. C. J. Moore (Ed.), *Frequency selectivity in hearing* (pp. 123–178). London: Academic Press.

Pickles, J. O. (1988). *An Introduction to the physiology of hearing* (2nd ed.). London: Academic Press.

Shaw, E. A. G. (1974). The external ear. In W. D. Keidel & W. D. Neff (Eds.), *Handbook of Sensory Physiology: Vol. 5.* Auditory system. New York: Springer-Verlag.

Suga, N. (1988). Neuroethology and speech processing. In G. W. Edelman, W. E. Gall, & W. M. Cowan (Eds.), *Auditory function: Neurobiological bases of hearing* (pp. 679–721). New York: Wiley.

Summerfield, Q., & Assmann, P. F. (1991). Perception of concurrent vowel: Effects of harmonic misalignment and pitch-period asynchrony. *Journal of the Acoustical Society of America, 89,* 1364–1377.

Tsue, T. T., Osterle, E. C., & Rubel, E. W. (1994). Hair cell regeneration in the inner ear. *Otolaryngology, Head and Neck Surgery, 111,* 281–301.

Viemeister, N. V., & Plack, C. (1993). Temporal processing. In W. A. Yost, A. N. Popper, & R. R. Fay (Eds.), *Human psychoacoustics* (pp. 116–154). New York: Springer-Verlag.

Watson, C. S. (1976). Factors in the discrimination of work-length auditory patterns. In S. K. Hirsh, D. H. Eldridge, & S. R. Silverman (Eds.), *Hearing and Davis: Essays honoring Hallowell Davis* (pp. 175–190). St. Louis: Washington University Press.

Webster, D., Fay, R. R., & Popper, A. N. (Eds.). (1992). *The auditory pathway: Neuroanatomy.* New York: Springer-Verlag.

Wegel, R. L., & Lane, C. E. (1924). The auditory masking of one sound by another and its probable relation to the dynamics of the inner ear. *Physics Review, 23,* 266–285.

Weir, C. C., Jesteadt, W., & Green, D. M. (1977). Frequency discrimination as a function of frequency and sensation level. *Journal of the Acoustical Society of America, 61,* 178–183.

Whitfield, I. C. (1967). *The auditory pathway.* Baltimore: Williams & Wilkins.

Wightman, F. L., & Kistler, D. J. (1989a). Headphone simulation of free-field listening: I. Stimulus synthesis. *Journal of the Acoustical Society of America, 85,* 858–867.

Wightman, F. L., & Kistler, D. J. (1989b). Headphone simulation of free-field listening: II. Psychophysical validation. *Journal of the Acoustical Society of America, 85,* 868–887.

Wightman, F. L., & Kistler, D. J. (1993). Localization. In W. A. Yost, A. N. Popper, & R. R. Fay (Eds.), *Human psychoacoustics* (pp. 155–192). New York: Springer-Verlag.

Wightman, F., McGee, T., & Kramer, M. (1977). Factors influencing frequency selectivity in normal and hearing-impaired listeners. In E. F. Evans & J. Wilson (Eds.), *Psychophysics and Physiology of Hearing* (pp. 295–310). London: Academic Press.

Yost, W. A. (1992a). Auditory image perception and analysis. *Hearing Research, 56,* 8–19.

Yost, W. A. (1992b). Auditory perception and sound source determination. *Current Directions in Psychological Science, 1,* 12–15.

Yost, W. A. (1996). Pitch of iterated rippled noise. *Journal of the Acoustical Society of America, 100,* 511–519.

Yost, W. A. (2000). *Fundamentals of hearing: An introduction* (4th ed.). New York: Academic Press.

Yost, W. A., & Dye, R. H. (1991). Properties of sound localization by humans. In R. Altschuler, D. Hoffman, R. Bobbin, & B. Clopton (Eds.), *Neurobiology of hearing: The central nervous system.* New York: Raven Press.

Yost, W. A., Dye, R. H., & Sheft, S. (1996). A simulated "cocktail party" with up to three sound sources. *Perception and Psychophysics, 58,* 1026–1036.

Yost, W. A., & Gourevitch, G. (Eds.). (1987). *Directional hearing.* New York: Springer-Verlag.

Yost, W. A., & Killion, M. C. (1993). Quiet absolute thresholds. In M. Crocker (Ed.), *Handbook of acoustics* (pp. 1545–1554). New York: Wiley.

Yost, W. A., Popper, A. N., & Fay, R. R. (Eds.). (1993). *Human psychoacoustics.* New York: Springer-Verlag.

Yost, W. A., & Sheft, S. (1993). Auditory processing. In W. A. Yost, A. N. Popper, & R. R. Fay (Eds.), *Human psychoacoustics* (pp. 193–236). New York: Springer-Verlag.

Young, E. D. (1984). Response characteristics of neurons in the cochlear nuclei. In C. I. Berlin (Ed.), *Hearing science.* San Diego, CA: College-Hill Press.

Zajic, G., & Schacht, J. (1991). Shape changes in isolated outer hair cells: Measurements with attached microspheres. *Hearing Research, 52,* 407–411.

Zemlin, W. R. (1981). *Speech and hearing science.* Englewood Cliffs, NJ: Prentice Hall.

Zheng, J., Shen, D. Z. Z., He, K., Long, L. D., & Dallos, P. (2000). Prestin is a motor protein in cochlear outer hair cells. *Nature, 405,* 149–155.

CHAPTER 6

Touch

ROBERTA L. KLATZKY AND SUSAN J. LEDERMAN

This chapter describes a sensory modality that underlies the most common everyday activities: maintaining one's posture, scratching an itch, or picking up a spoon. As a topic of psychological research, touch has received far less attention than vision has. However, the substantial literature that is available covers topics from neurophysiology, through basic psychophysics, to cognitive issues such as memory and object recognition. All these topics are reviewed in the current chapter.

We begin by defining the modality of touch as comprising different submodalities, characterized by their neural inputs. A brief review of neurophysiological and basic psychophysical findings follows. The chapter then pursues a number of topics concerning higher-level perception and cognition. Touch is emphasized as an active modality in which the perceiver seeks information from the world by exploratory movements. We ask how properties of objects and surfaces—like roughness or size—are perceived through contact and movement. We discuss the accuracy of haptic space perception and why movement might introduce systematic errors or illusions. Next comes an evaluation of touch as a pattern-recognition system, where the patterns range from two-dimensional arrays like Braille to real, free-standing objects. In everyday perception, touch and vision operate together; this chapter offers a discussion of how these modalities interact. Higher-level cognition, including attention and memory, is considered next. The chapter concludes with a review of some applications of research on touch.

A number of common themes underlie these topics. One is the idea that perceptual modalities are similar with respect to general functions they attempt to serve, such as conveying information about objects and space. Another is that by virtue of having distinct neural structures and relying on movement for input, touch has unique characteristics. The chapter makes the point that touch and vision interact cooperatively in extracting information about the world, but that the two modalities represent different priorities, with touch emphasizing information about material properties and vision emphasizing spatial and geometric properties. Thus there is a remarkable balance between redundant and complementary functions across vision and touch. The chapter by Stephen in this volume reviews vision generally and hence provides many points of comparison with this chapter. A final theme of the present chapter is that research on touch has exciting applications to everyday problems.

TOUCH DEFINED AS AN ACTIVE, MULTISENSORY SYSTEM

The modality of touch encompasses several distinct sensory systems. Most researchers have distinguished among three systems—cutaneous, kinesthetic, and haptic—on the basis of the underlying neural inputs. In the terminology of Loomis and Lederman (1986), the cutaneous system receives sensory inputs from mechanoreceptors—specialized nerve endings that respond to mechanical stimulation (force)—that are embedded in the skin. The kinesthetic system receives sensory inputs from mechanoreceptors located within the body's muscles, tendons, and joints. The haptic system uses combined inputs from both the cutaneous and kinesthetic systems. The term *haptic* is associated in particular with active touch. In an everyday context, touch is active; the sensory apparatus is intertwined with the body structures that produce movement. By virtue of moving the limbs and skin with respect to surfaces and objects, the basic sensory inputs to touch are enhanced, allowing this modality to reveal a rich array of properties of the world.

When investigating the properties of the peripheral sensory system, however, researchers have often used passive, not active, displays. Accordingly, a basic distinction has arisen between active and passive modes of touch. Unfortunately, over the years the meaning and use of these terms have proven to be somewhat variable. On occasion, J. J. Gibson (1962, 1966) treated passive touch as restricted to cutaneous (skin) inputs. However, at other times Gibson described passive touch as the absence of motor commands to the muscles (i.e., efferent commands) during the process of information pickup. For example, if an experimenter shaped a subject's hands so as to enclose an object, it would be a case of active touch by the first criterion, but passive touch by the second one. We prefer to use Loomis and Lederman's (1986) distinctions between types of active versus passive touch. They combined Gibson's latter criterion, the presence or absence of motor control, with the three-way classification of sensory systems by the afferent inputs used (i.e., cutaneous, kinesthetic, and haptic). This conjunction yielded five different modes of touch: (a) tactile (cutaneous) perception, (b) passive kinesthetic perception (kinesthetic afferents respond without voluntary movement), (c) passive haptic perception (cutaneous and kinesthetic afferents respond without voluntary movement), (d) active kinesthetic perception, and (e) active haptic perception. The observer only has motor control over the touch process in modes d and e.

In addition to mechanical stimulation, the inputs to the touch modality include heat, cooling, and various stimuli that produce pain. Tactile scientists distinguish a person's subjective sensations of touch per se (e.g., pressure, spatial acuity, position) from those pertaining to temperature and pain. Not only is the quality of sensation different, but so too are the neural pathways. This chapter primarily discusses touch and, to a lesser extent, thermal subsystems, inasmuch as thermal cues provide an important source of sensory information for purposes of haptic object recognition. Overviews of thermal sensitivity have been provided by Sherrick and Cholewiak (1986) and by J. C. Stevens (1991). The topic of pain is not extensively discussed here, but reviews of pain responsiveness by Sherrick and Cholewiak (1986) and, more recently, by Craig and Rollman (1999) are recommended.

THE NEUROPHYSIOLOGY OF TOUCH

The Skin and Its Receptors

The skin is the largest sense organ in the body. In the average adult, it covers close to 2 m and weighs about 3–5 kg (Quilliam, 1978). As shown in Figure 6.1, it consists of two major layers: the epidermis (outer) and the dermis (inner). The encapsulated endings of the mechanoreceptor units, which are believed to be responsible for transducing mechanical energy into neural responses, are found in both layers, as well as at the interface between the two. A third layer lies underneath the dermis and above the supporting structures made up of muscle and bone. Although not considered part of the formal medical definition of skin, this additional layer (the hypodermis) contains connective tissue and subcutaneous fat, as well as one population of mechanoreceptor end organs (Pacinian corpuscles).

We focus here on the volar portion of the human hand, because the remainder of this chapter considers interactions of the hand with the world. This skin, which is described as *glabrous* (hairless), contains four different populations of cutaneous mechanoreceptor afferent units. These populations are differentiated in terms of both relative receptive field size

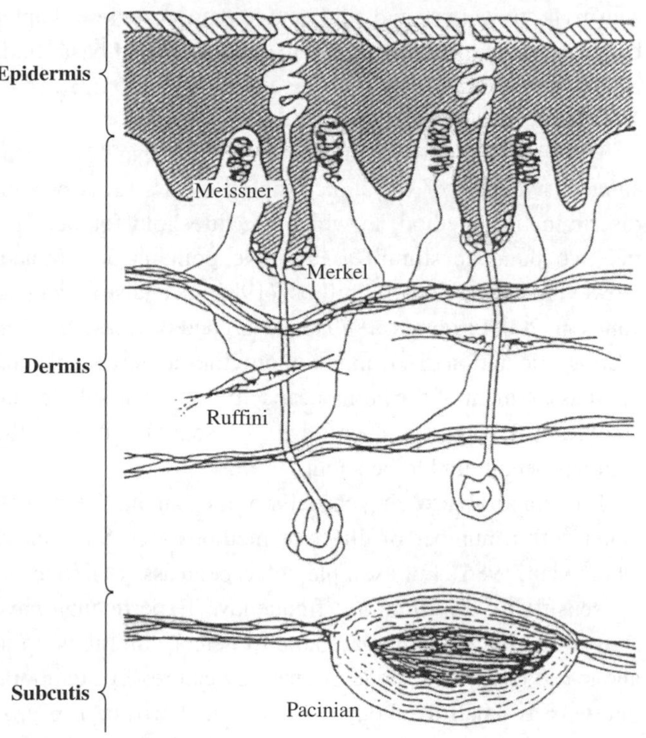

Figure 6.1 Vertical section of the glabrous skin of the human hand, schematically demonstrating the locations of the four types of mechanoreceptors; the major layers of human skin are also shown. *Source:* After Johansson & Vallbo (1983; Figure 4). Reprinted with permission.

and adaptation responses to sustained and transient stimulation (see Table 6.1).

The two fast-adapting populations (FA units) show rapid responses to the onset, and sometimes the offset, of skin deformation. In addition, FAI (fast adapting type I) units have very small, well-defined receptive fields, whereas FAII (fast adapting type II) units have large receptive fields with poorly defined boundaries. FAI units respond particularly well to rate of skin deformation, and they are presumed to end in Meisner's corpuscles. FAII units respond reliably to both the onset and offset of skin deformation, particularly acceleration and higher-derivative components, and have been shown to terminate in Pacinian corpuscles. The two

TABLE 6.1 Four Mechanoreceptor Populations in the Glabrous Skin of the Human Hand, with Their Defining Characteristics

	Adaptation Response	
Receptive Field	Fast; No response to sustained stimulation	Slow; Responds to sustained stimulation
Small, well defined	FAI	SAI
Large, diffuse	FAII	SAII

Note: FA = fast adapting; SA = slow adapting; and I and II index types within each classification.

slow-adapting populations (SA units) show a continuous response to sustained skin deformation. SAI (slow adapting type I) units demonstrate a strong dynamic sensitivity, as well as a somewhat irregular response to sustained stimulation. They are presumed to end in Merkel cell neurite complexes (see Figure 6.1). SAII (slow adapting type II) units show less dynamic sensitivity but a more regular sustained discharge, as well as spontaneous discharge sometimes in the absence of skin deformation; they are presumed to end in Ruffini endings. Bolanowski, Gescheider, Verrillo, and Checkosky (1988) have developed a four-channel model of mechanoreception, which associates psychophysical functions with the tuning curves of mechanoreceptor populations. Each of the four mechanoreceptors is presumed to produce different psychophysical responses, constituting a sensory channel, so to speak.

Response to thermal stimulation is mediated by several peripheral cutaneous receptor populations that lie near the body surface. Researchers have documented the existence of separate "warm" and "cold" thermoreceptor populations in the skin; such receptors are thought to be primarily responsible for thermal sensations. Nociceptor units respond only to extremes (noxious) in temperature (or sometimes mechanical) stimulation, but these are believed to be involved in pain rather than temperature sensation.

Response to noxious stimulation has received an enormous amount of attention. Here, we simply note that two populations of peripheral afferent fibers (high-threshold nociceptors) in the skin have been shown to contribute to pain transmission: the larger, myelinated A-delta fibers and the narrow, unmyelinated C fibers.

Mechanoreceptors in the muscles, tendons, and joints (and in the case of the hand, in skin as well) contribute to the kinesthetic sense of position and movement of the limbs. With respect to muscle, the muscle spindles contain two types of sensory endings: Large-diameter primary endings code for rate of change in the length of the muscle fibers, dynamic stretch, and vibration; smaller-diameter secondary endings are primarily sensitive to the static phase of muscle activity. It is now known that joint angle is coded primarily by muscle length. Golgi tendon organs are spindle-shaped receptors that lie in series with skeletal muscle fibers. These receptors code muscle tension. Finally, afferent units of the joints are now known to code primarily for extreme, but not intermediate, joint positions. As they do not code for intermediate joint positions, it has been suggested that they serve mainly a protective function—detecting noxious stimulation. The way in which the kinesthetic mechanoreceptor units mediate perceptual outcomes is not well understood, especially in comparison to cutaneous mechanoreceptors. For further details on kinesthesis, see reviews by Clark and Horch (1986) and by Jones (1999).

Pathways to Cortex and Major Cortical Areas

Peripheral units in the skin and muscles congregate into single nerve trunks at each vertebral level as they are about to enter the spinal cord. At each level, their cell bodies cluster together in the dorsal root ganglion. These ganglia form chains along either side of the spinal cord. The proximal ends of the peripheral units enter the dorsal horn of the spinal cord, where they form two major ascending pathways: the dorsal column-medial lemniscal system and the anterolateral system. The dorsal column-medial lemniscal system carries information about tactile sensation and limb kinesthesis. Of the two systems, it conducts more rapidly because it ascends directly to the cortex with few synapses. The anterolateral system carries information about temperature and pain—and to a considerably lesser extent, touch. This route is slower than the dorsal column-medial lemniscal system because it involves many synapses between the periphery and the cortex. The two pathways remain segregated until they converge at the thalamus, although even there the separation is preserved.

The primary cortical receiving area for the somatic senses, S-I, lies in the postcentral gyrus and in the depths of the central sulcus. It consists of four functional areas, which when ordered from the central sulcus back to the posterior parietal lobe, are known as Brodmann's areas 3a, 3b, 1, and 2. Lateral and somewhat posterior to S-I is S-II, the secondary somatic sensory cortex, which lies in the upper bank of the lateral sulcus. S-II receives its main inputs from S-I. The posterior parietal lobe (Brodmann's areas 5 and 7) also receives somatic inputs. It serves higher-level associative functions, such as relating sensory and motor processing, and integrating the various somatic inputs (for further details, see Kandel, Schwartz, & Jessell, 1991).

SENSORY ASPECTS OF TOUCH

Cutaneous Sensitivity and Resolution

Tests of absolute and relative sensitivity to applied force describe people's threshold responses to intensive aspects of mechanical deformation (e.g., the depth of penetration of a probe into the skin). In addition, sensation magnitude has been scaled as a function of stimulus amplitude, in order to reveal the relation between perceptual response and stimulus variables at suprathreshold levels. Corresponding psychophysical experiments have been performed to determine sensitivity to warmth and cold, and to pain. A review chapter by Sherrick and Cholewiak (1986) has described basic findings in this area in detail (see also Rollman, 1991; Stevens, 1991).

The spatial resolving capacity of the skin has been measured in a variety of ways, including the classical two-point discrimination method, in which the threshold for perceiving two punctate stimuli as a single point is determined. However, Johnson and Phillips (1981; see also Craig & Johnson, 2000; Loomis, 1979) have argued persuasively that grating orientation discrimination provides a more stable and valid assessment of the human capacity for cutaneous spatial resolution. Using spatial gratings, the spatial acuity of the skin has been found to be about 1 mm.

The temporal resolving capacity of the skin has been evaluated with a number of different methods (see Sherrick & Cholewiak, 1986). For example, it has been assessed in terms of sensitivity to vibratory frequency. Experiments have shown that human adults are able to detect vibrations up to about 700 Hz, which suggests that they can resolve temporal intervals as small as about 1.4 ms (e.g., Verrillo, 1963). A more conservative estimate (5.5 ms) was obtained when determining the minimum separation time between two 1-ms pulse stimuli that is required for an observer to perceive them as successive.

Overall, the experimental data suggest that the hand is poorer than the eye and better than the ear in resolving fine spatial details. On the other hand, it has proven to be better than the eye and poorer than the ear in resolving fine temporal details.

Effects of Body Site and Age on Cutaneous Thresholds

It has long been known that the sensitivity, acuity, and magnitude of tactile and thermal sensations can vary quite substantially as a function of the body locus of stimulation (for details, see van Boven & Johnson, 1994; Stevens, 1991; Weinstein, 1968; Wilska, 1954). For example, the face (i.e., upper lip, cheek, and nose) is best able to detect a low-level force, whereas the fingers are most efficient at processing spatial information. The two-point threshold is shown for various body sites in Figure 6.2.

More recently, researchers have addressed the effect of chronological age on cutaneous thresholds (for details, see Verrillo, 1993). One approach to studying aging effects is to examine the vibratory threshold (the skin displacement at which a vibration becomes detectable) as a function of age. A number of studies converge to indicate that aging particularly affects thresholds for vibrations in the range detected by the Pacinian corpuscles (i.e, at frequencies above 40 Hz; see

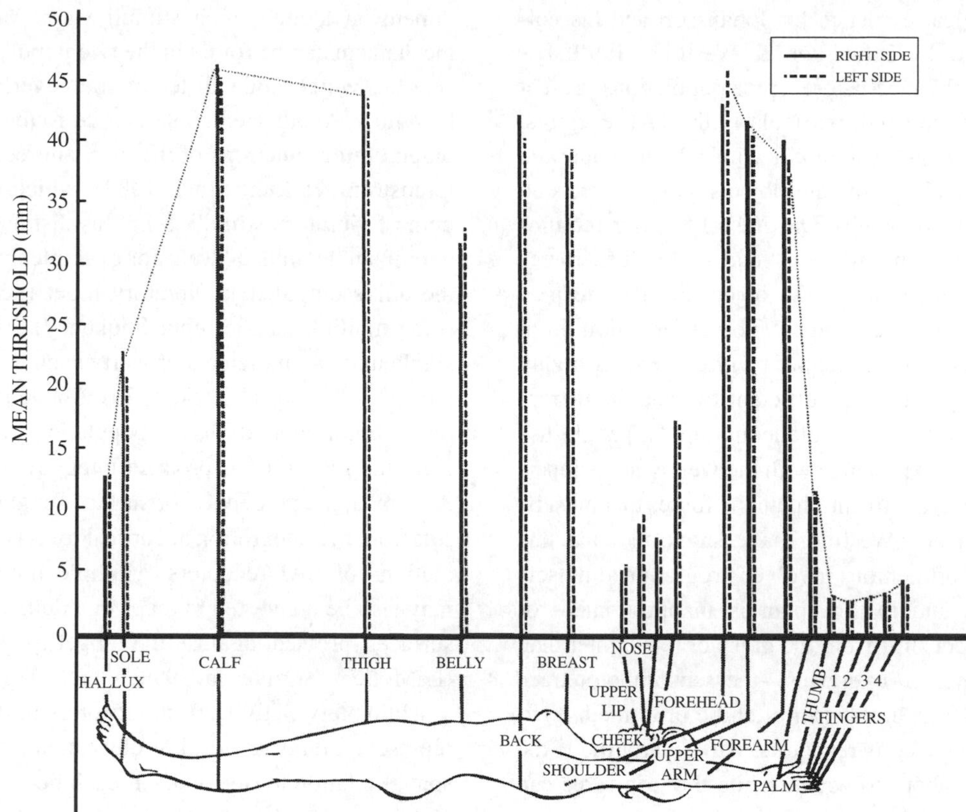

Figure 6.2 The minimal separation between two points needed to perceive them as separate (2-point threshold), when the points are applied at different sites of the body. *Source:* From Weinstein (1968), in D. R. Kenshalo, *The Skin Senses,* 1968. Courtesy of Charles C. Thomas, Publisher, Ltd., Springfield, Illinois. Reprinted with permission.

Gescheider, Bolanowski, Verrillo, Hall, & Hoffman, 1994; Verillo, 1993). The rise in the threshold with age has been attributed to the loss of receptors. By this account, the Pacinian threshold is affected more than are other channels because it is the only one whose response depends on summation of receptor outputs over space and time (Gescheider, Edwards, Lackner, Bolanowski, & Verrillo, 1996). Although the ability to detect a vibration in the Pacinian range is substantially affected by age, the difference limen—the change in amplitude needed to produce a discriminable departure from a baseline value—varies little after the baseline values are adjusted for the age-related differences in detection threshold (i.e., the baselines are equated for magnitude of sensation relative to threshold; Gescheider et al., 1996).

Cutaneous spatial acuity has also been demonstrated to decline with age. Stevens and Patterson (1995) reported an approximate 1% increase in threshold per year over the ages of 20 to 80 years for each of four acuity measures. The measures were thresholds, as follows: minimum separation of a 2-point stimulus that allows discrimination of its orientation on the finger (transverse vs. longitudinal), minimum separation between points that allows detection of gaps in lines or disks, minimum change in locus that allows discrimination between successive touches on the same or different skin site, and difference limen for length of a line stimulus applied to the skin.

The losses in cutaneous sensitivity that have been described can have profound consequences for everyday life in older persons because the mechanoreceptors function critically in basic processes of grasping and manipulation.

Sensory-Guided Grasping and Manipulation

Persons who have sustained peripheral nerve injury to their hands are often clumsy when grasping and manipulating objects. Such persons will frequently drop the objects; moreover, when handling dangerous tools (e.g., a knife), they can cut themselves quite badly. Older adults, whose cutaneous thresholds are elevated, tend to grip objects more tightly than is needed in order to manipulate them (Cole, 1991). Experiments have now confirmed what these observations suggest: Namely, cutaneous information plays a critical role in guiding motor interactions with objects following initial contact. Motor control is discussed extensively in the chapter written by Heuer in this volume.

Neurophysiological evidence by Johansson and his colleagues (see review by Johansson & Westling, 1990) has clearly shown that the mechanoreceptor populations present in glabrous skin of the hand, particularly the FAI receptors, contribute in vital ways to the skill with which people are able to grasp, lift, and manipulate objects using a precision grip (a thumb-forefinger pinch). The grasp-lift action requires that people coordinate the grip and load forces (i.e., forces perpendicular and tangential to the object grasped, respectively) over a sequence of stages. The information from cutaneous receptors enables people to grasp objects highly efficiently, applying force just sufficient to keep them from slipping. In addition to using cutaneous inputs, people use memory for previous experience with the weight and slipperiness of an object in order to anticipate the forces that must be applied. Johansson and Westling have suggested that this sensorimotor form of memory involves programmed muscle commands. If the anticipatory plan is inappropriate—for example, if the object slips from the grasp or it is lighter than expected and the person overgrips—the sensorimotor trace must be updated. Overt errors can often be prevented, however, because the cutaneous receptors, particularly the FAIs, signal when slip is about to occur, while the grip force can still be corrected.

HAPTIC PERCEPTION OF PROPERTIES OF OBJECTS AND SURFACES

Up to this point, this chapter has discussed the properties of touch that regulate very early processing. The chapter now turns to issues of higher-level processing, including representations of the perceived world, memory and cognition about that world, and interactions with other perceptual modalities. A considerable amount of work has been done in these areas since the review of Loomis and Lederman (1986). We begin with issues of representation. What is it about the haptically perceived world—its surfaces, objects, and their spatial relations—that we represent through touch?

Klatzky and Lederman (1999a) pointed out that the haptic system begins extracting attributes of surfaces and objects from the level of the most peripheral units. This contrasts with vision, in which the earliest output from receptors codes the distribution of points of light, and considerable higher-order processing ensues before fundamental attributes of objects become defined.

The earliest output from mechanoreceptors and thermal receptors codes attributes of objects directly through various mechanisms. There may be different populations of peripheral receptors, each tuned to a particular level of some dimension along which stimuli vary. An example of this mechanism can be found in the two populations of thermoreceptors, which code different (but overlapping) ranges of heat flow. Another example can be found in the frequency-based tuning functions of the mechanoreceptors (Johansson, Landstrom, & Lundstrom, 1982), which divide the continuum of vibratory stimuli. Stimulus distinctions can be made within single units as well: for example, by phase locking of the unit's output to a vibratory input (i.e., the unit fires at some multiple of the input frequency). The firing rate of a single unit can indicate a property such as the sharpness of a punctate stimulus (Vierck, 1979). Above the level of the initial receptor populations are populations that combine inputs from the receptors to produce integrative codes. As is later described, the perception of surface roughness appears to result from the integration at cortical levels of inputs from populations of SAI receptors. Multiple inputs from receptors may also be converted to maps that define spatial features of surfaces pressed against the fingertip, such as curvature (LaMotte & Srinivasan, 1993; Vierck, 1979).

Ultimately, activity from receptors to the brain leads to a representation of a world of objects and surfaces, defined in spatial relation to one another, each bound to a set of enduring physical properties. We now turn to the principal properties that are part of that representation.

Haptically Perceptible Properties

Klatzky and Lederman (1993) suggested a hierarchical organization of object properties extracted by the haptic system. At the highest level, a distinction is made between *geometric* properties of objects and *material* properties. Geometric properties are specific to particular objects, whereas material properties are independent of any one sampled object.

At the next level of the hierarchy, the geometric properties are divided into *size* and *shape*. Two natural scales for these properties are within the haptic system, differentiated by the role of cutaneous versus kinesthetic receptors, which we call micro- and macrogeometric. At the microgeometric level, an object is small enough to fall within a single region of skin, such as the fingertip. This produces a spatial deformation pattern on the skin that is coded by the mechanoreceptors (particularly the SAIs) and functions essentially as a map of the object's spatial layout. This map might be called 2-1/2 D, after Marr (1982), in that the coding pertains only to the surfaces that are in contact with the finger. The representation extends into depth because the fingertip accommodates so as to have differential pressure from surface planes lying at different depth. At the macrogeometric level, objects do not fall within a single region of the skin, but rather are enveloped in hands or limbs, bringing in the contribution of kinesthetic receptors and skin sites that are not somatotopically continuous, such as multiple fingers. Integration of these inputs must be performed to determine the geometry of the objects.

The hierarchical organization of Klatzky and Lederman further differentiates material properties into *texture, hardness* (or compliance), and apparent *temperature*. Texture comprises many perceptually distinct properties, such as roughness, stickiness, and spatial density. Roughness has been the most extensively studied, and we treat it in some detail in a following section. Compliance perception has both cutaneous and kinesthetic components, the relative contributions of which depend on the rigidity of the object's surface (Srinivasan & LaMotte, 1995). For example, a piano key is rigid on the surface but compliant, and kinesthesis is a necessary input to the perception that it is a hard or soft key to press. Although cutaneous cues are necessary, they are not sufficient, because the skin bottoms out, so to speak, whether the key is resistant or compliant. On the other hand, a cotton ball deforms as it is penetrated, causing a cutaneous gradient that may be sufficient by itself to discriminate compliance. Another property of objects is *weight,* which reflects geometry and material. Although an object's weight is defined by its total mass, which reflects density and volume, we will see that perceived weight can be affected by the object's material, shape, and identity.

A complete review of the literature on haptic perception of object properties would go far beyond the scope of this chapter. Here, we treat three of the most commonly studied properties in some detail: texture, weight, and curvature. Each of these properties can be defined at different scales, although the meaning of *scale* varies with the particular dimension of interest. The mechanisms of haptic perception may be profoundly affected by scale.

Roughness

A textured surface has protruberant elements arising from a relatively homogeneous substrate. The surface can be characterized as having macrotexture or microtexture, depending on the spacing between surface elements. Different mechanisms appear to mediate roughness perception at these two scales. In a microtexture, the elements are spaced at intervals on the order of microns (thousandths of a millimeter); in a macrotexture, the spacing is one or two orders of magnitude greater, or more. When the elements get too sparse, on the order of 3–4 mm apart or so, people tend to be reluctant to characterize the surface as textured. Rather, it appears to be a smooth surface punctuated by irregularities.

Early research determined some of the primary physical determinants of perceived roughness with macrotextures (i.e., ≥1 mm spacing between elements). For example, Lederman (Lederman, 1974, 1983; Lederman & Taylor, 1972; see also Connor, Hsaio, Philips, & Johnson, 1990; Connor & Johnson, 1992; Sathian, Goodwin, John, & Darian-Smith, 1989; Sinclair & Burton, 1991; Stevens & Harris, 1962), using textures that took the form of grooves with rectangular profiles, found that perceived roughness strongly increased with the spacing between the ridges (groove width). Increases in ridge width—that is, the size of the peaks rather than the troughs in the surface—had a relatively modest effect, tending to decrease perceived roughness. Although roughness was principally affected by the geometry of the surface, the way in which the surface was explored also had some effect. Increasing applied fingertip force increased the magnitude of perceived roughness, and the speed of relative motion between hand and surface had a small but systematic effect on perceived roughness. Finally, conditions of active versus passive control over the speed-of-hand motion led to similar roughness judgments, suggesting that kinesthesis plays a minimal role, and that the manner in which the skin is deformed is critical.

Taylor and Lederman (1975) constructed a model of perceived roughness, based on a mechanical analysis of the skin deformation resulting from changes in groove width, fingertip force, and ridge width. Their model suggested that perceived roughness of gratings was based on the total amount of skin deformation produced by the stimulus. Taylor and Lederman described the representation of roughness in terms of this proximal stimulus as "intensive" because the deformation appeared to be integrated over the entire area of contact, resulting in an essentially unidimensional percept.

The neural basis for coding roughness has been modeled by Johnson, Connor, and associates (Connor et al., 1990; Connor & Johnson, 1992). The model assumes that initial coding of the textured surface is in terms of the relative activity rates of spatially distributed SAI mechanoreceptors. The spatial map is preserved in S-I, the primary somatosensory cortex (specifically, area 3b), which computes differences in activity of adjacent (1 mm apart) SAI units. These differences in spatially distributed activity are passed along to neurons in S-II, another somatosensory cortical area that integrates the information from the primary cortex (Hsiao, Johnson, & Twombly, 1993).

Although vibratory signals exist, psychophysical studies suggest that humans tend not to use vibration to judge macrotextures presented to the bare skin. Roughness judgments were unaffected by the spatial period of stimulus gratings (Lederman, 1974, 1983) and minimally affected by movement speed (Katz, 1925/1989; Lederman, 1974, 1983), both of which should alter vibration; they were also unaffected by either low- or high-frequency vibrotactile adaptation (Lederman, Loomis, & Williams, 1982). Vibratory coding of roughness does, however, occur with very fine microtextures. LaMotte and Srinivasan (1991) found that observers could discriminate a featureless surface from a texture with height .06–.16 microns and interelement spacing ~100 microns. Subjects reported attending to the vibration from stroking the texture. Moreover, measures of mechanoreceptor activity in monkeys passively exposed to the same surfaces implicated the FAII (or PC) units, which respond to relatively high-frequency vibrations (peak response ~250 Hz; Johansson & Vallbo, 1983). Vibrotactile adaptation affected perceived roughness of fine but not coarse surfaces (Hollins, Bensmaia, & Risner, 1998).

Somewhat surprisingly, the textural scale where spatial coding of macrotexture changes to vibratory coding of microtexture appears to be below the limit of tactile spatial resolution (.5–1.0 mm). Dorsch, Yoshioka, Hsiao, and Johnson (2000) reported that SAI activity, which implicates spatial coding, was correlated with roughness perception over a range of gratings that began with a .1-mm groove width. Using particulate textures, Hollins and Risner (2000) found evidence for a transition between vibratory and spatial coding at a similar particle size.

Weight

The perception of weight has been of interest for a time approaching two centuries, since the work of Weber (1834/1978). Weber pointed out that the impression of an object's heaviness was greater when it was wielded than when it rested passively on the skin, suggesting that the perception of weight was not entirely determined by its objective value. In the late 1800s (Charpentier, 1891; Dresslar, 1894), the discovery of the size-weight illusion—that given equal objective weight, a smaller object seems heavier—pointed to the fact that multiple physical factors determine heaviness perception. Recently, Amazeen and Turvey (1996) have integrated a body of work on the size-weight illusion and weight perception by accounting for perceived weight in terms of resistance to the rotational forces imposed by the limbs as an object is held and wielded. Their task requires the subject to wield an object at the end of a rod or handle, precluding volumetric shape cues. Figure 6.3 shows the experimental setup for a wielding task. Formally, resistance to wielding is defined by an entity called the inertia tensor, a three-by-three matrix whose elements represent the resistance to rotational acceleration about the axes of a three-dimensional coordinate system that is imposed on the object around the center of rotation. Although the inertia tensor will vary with the

Figure 6.3 Experimental setup for determining the property of an object by wielding; the subject is adjusting a visible board so that its distance is the same as the perceived length of the rod. For weight judgments, the subject assigns a number corresponding to the impression of weight from wielding. *Source:* From Turvey (1996; Figure 2). Copyright © 1996 by the American Psychological Association. Reprinted with permission.

coordinate system that is imposed on the object, its eigenvalues are invariant. (The *eigenvalues* of a matrix are scalars that, together with a set of eigenvectors—essentially, coordinate axes—can be used to reconstruct it.) They correspond to the principal moments of inertia: that is, the resistances to rotation about a nonarbitrary coordinate system that uses the primary axes of the object (those around which the mass is balanced). In a series of experiments in which the eigenvalues were manipulated and the seminal data on the size-weight illusion were analyzed (Stevens & Rubin, 1970), Amazeen and Turvey found that heaviness was directly related to the product of power functions of the eigenvalues (specifically, the first and third). This finding explains why weight is not dictated simply by mass alone; the reliance of heaviness perception on resistance to rotation means that it will also be affected by geometric factors.

But the story is more complicated, it seems, as weight perception is also affected by the material from which an object is made and the way in which it is gripped. A material-weight relation was documented by Wolfe (1898), who covered objects of equal mass with different surface materials and found that objects having surface materials that were more dense were judged lighter than those with surfaces that were less dense (e.g., comparing brass to wood). Flanagan and associates (Flanagan, Wing, Allison, & Spencely, 1995; Flanagan & Wing, 1997; see also Rinkenauer, Mattes, & Ulrich, 1999) suggested that material affected perceived weight because objects that were slipperier required a greater grip force in order to be lifted, and a more forceful grip led to a perception of greater weight (presumably because heavier objects must be gripped more tightly to lift them). Ellis and Lederman (1999) reported a material-weight illusion, however, that could not be entirely explained by grip force, because the slipperiest object was not felt to be the heaviest. Moreover, they demonstrated that the effects of material on perceived heaviness vanished when (a) objects of high mass were used, or (b) even low-mass objects were required to be gripped tightly. The first of these effects, an interaction between material and mass, is a version of scale effects in haptic perception to which we previously alluded.

However, cognitive factors cannot be entirely excluded either, as demonstrated by an experiment by Ellis and Lederman (1998) that describes the so-called *golf-ball illusion,* a newly documented misperception of weight. Experienced golfers and nongolfers were visually shown practice and real golf balls that looked alike, but that were adjusted to be of equal mass. The golfers judged the practice balls to be heavier than the real balls, in contrast to the nongolfers, who judged them to be the same apparent weight. These results highlight the contribution of a cognitive component to weight perception, inasmuch as only experienced golfers would know that practice balls are normally lighter than real golf balls.

Collectively, this body of studies points to a complex set of factors that affect the perception of weight via the haptic system. Resistance to rotation is important, particularly when an object is wielded (as opposed, e.g., to being passively held). Grip force and material may reflect cognitive expectancies (i.e., the expectation that more tightly gripped objects and denser objects should be heavier), but they may also affect more peripheral perceptual mechanisms. A pure cognitive-expectancy explanation for these factors would suggest equivalent effects when vision is used to judge weight, but such effects are not obtained (Ellis & Lederman, 1999). Nor would a pure expectancy explanation explain why the effects of material on weight perception vanish when an object is gripped tightly. Still, a cognitive expectancy explanation does explain the differences in the weight percepts of the experienced golfers versus the nongolfers. As for lower-level processes that may alter the weight percept, Ellis and Lederman (1999) point out that a firm grip may saturate mechanoreceptors that usually provide information about slip. And Flanagan and Bandomir (2000) have found that weight perception is affected by the width of the grip, the number of fingers involved, and the contact area, but not the angle of the contacted surfaces; these findings suggest the presence of additional complex interactions between weight perception and the motor commands for grasping.

Curvature

Curvature is the rate of change in the angle of the tangent line to a curve as the tangent point moves along it. Holding shape constant, curvature decreases as scale increases; for example, a circle with a larger radius has a smaller curvature. Like other haptically perceived properties, the scale of a curve is important. A curved object may be small enough to fall within the area of a fingertip, or large enough to require a movement of the hand across its surface in order to touch it all. If the curvature of a surface is large (e.g., a pearl), then the entire surface may fall within the scale of a fingertip. A surface with a smaller curvature may still be presented to a single finger, but the changes in the tangent line over the width of the fingertip may not make it discriminable from a flat surface.

One clear point is that curvature perception is subject to error from various sources. One is manner of exploration. For example, when curved edges are actively explored, curvature away from the explorer may lead to the perception that the edge is straight (Davidson, 1972; Hunter, 1954). Vogels, Kappers, and Koenderink (1996) found that the curvature of a surface was affected by another surface that had been touched previously, constituting a curvature aftereffect. The apparent curvature of a surface also depends on whether it lies along or across the fingers (Pont, Kappers, & Koenderink, 1998), or whether it touches the palm or upper surface of the hand (Pont, Kappers, & Koenderink, 1997).

When small curved surfaces, which have relatively high curvature, are brought to the fingertip, slowly adapting mechanoreceptors provide an isomorphic representation of the pressure gradient on the skin (LaMotte & Srinivasan, 1993; Srinivasan & LaMotte, 1991; Vierck, 1979). This map is sufficient to make discriminations between curved surfaces on the basis of a single finger's touch. Goodwin, John, and Marceglia (1991) found that a curvature equivalent to a circle with a radius of .2 m could be discriminated from a flat surface when passively touched by a single finger.

When larger surfaces (smaller curvature) are presented, they may be explored by multiple fingers of a static hand or by tracing along the edge. Pont et al. (1997) tested three models to explain curvature perception when static, multifinger exposure was used.

To understand the models, consider a stimulus shaped like a semicircle, the flat edge of which lies on a tabletop with the curved edge pointing up. This situation is illustrated in Figure 6.4. Assume that the stimulus is felt by three fingers, with the middle finger at the highest point (i.e., the midpoint) of the curve. There are then three parameters to consider. The first is height difference: The middle finger is higher (i.e., at a greater distance from the tabletop) than the

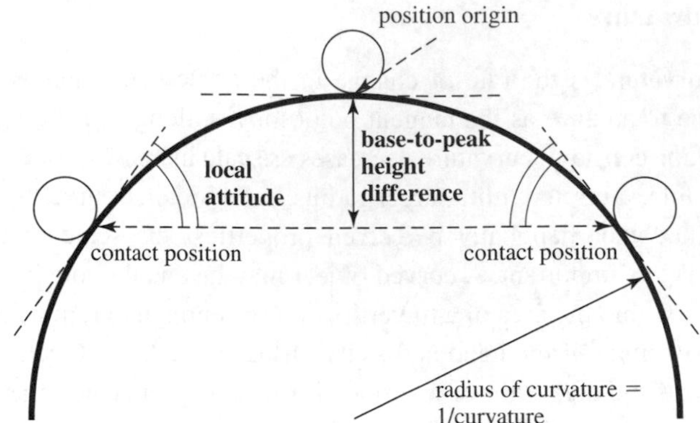

Figure 6.4 Definition of three different measures of curvature detectable from touch (Pont et al., 1999; Figure 5, top)—the height difference, the attitude of the fingers, and the radius of curvature. The circles represent three fingers touching a curved surface. Reprinted with permission.

other fingers by some height. The second is the difference in the angles at which the two outer fingers lie: These fingers' contact points have tangent lines tilted toward one another, with the difference in their slopes constituting an attitude difference, so to speak. In addition, the semicircle has some objective curvature. All three parameters will change as the semicircle's radius changes size. For example, as the radius increases and the surface gets flatter, the curvature will decrease, the difference in height between the middle and outer fingers will decrease, and the attitudes of the outer fingers approach the horizontal from opposing directions, maximizing the attitude difference. The question is, which of these parameters—height difference, attitude difference, or curvature—determines the discriminability between edges of different curvature? Pont et al. concluded that subjects compared the difference in attitudes between surfaces and used that difference to discriminate them. That is, for each surface, subjects considered the difference in the slope at the outer points of contact. For example, this model predicts that as the outer fingers are placed further apart along a semicircular edge of some radius, the value of the radius at which there is a threshold level of curvature (i.e., where a curved surface can just be discriminated from a flat one) will increase. As the fingers move farther apart, only by increasing the radius of the semicircle can the attitude difference between them be maintained.

As we report in the following section, when a stimulus has an extended contour, moving the fingers along its edge is the only way to extract its shape; static contact does not suffice. For simple curves, at least, it appears that this is not the case, and static and dynamic curvature detection is similar. Pont (1997) reported that when subjects felt a curved edge by moving their index finger along it, from one end to the other of a window of exposure, the results were similar to those with static touch. She again concluded that it was the difference in local attitudes, the changing local gradients touched by the finger as it moved along the exposed edge, that were used for discrimination. A similar conclusion was reached by Pont, Kappers, and Koenderink (1999) in a more extended comparison of static and dynamic touch. It should be noted that the nature of dynamic exploration of the stimulus was highly constrained in these tasks, and that the manner in which a curved surface is touched may affect the resulting percept (Davidson, 1972; Davidson & Whitson, 1974). We now turn to the general topic of how manual exploration affects the extraction of the properties of objects through haptic perception.

Role of Manual Exploration in Perceiving Object Properties

The sensory receptors under the skin, and in muscles, tendons, and joints, become activated not only through contact with an object but through movement. Lederman and Klatzky (1987) noted the stereotypy with which objects are explored when people seek information about particular object properties. For example, when people seek to know which of two objects is rougher, they typically rub their fingers along the objects' surfaces. Lederman and Klatzky called such an action an "exploratory procedure," by which they meant a stereotyped pattern of action associated with an object property.

The principal set of exploratory procedures they described is as follows (see Figure 6.5):

Lateral motion—associated with texture encoding; characterized by production of shearing forces between skin and object.

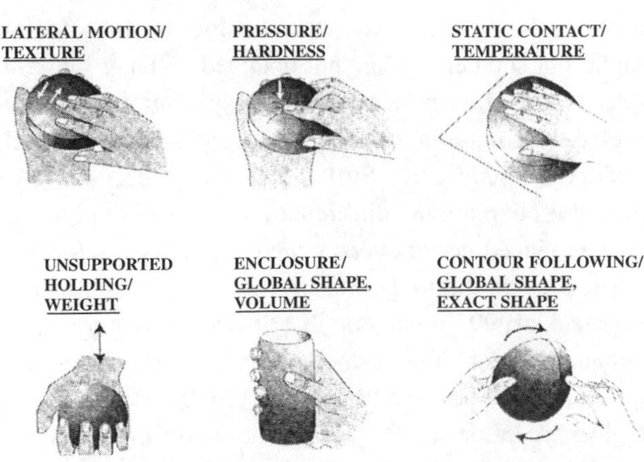

Figure 6.5 Exploratory procedures described by Lederman and Klatzky (1987; Figure 1; adapted) and the object properties with which each is associated. Reprinted with permission.

Static contact—associated with temperature encoding; characterized by contact with maximum skin surface and without movement, also without effort to mold to the touched surface.

Enclosure—associated with encoding of volume and coarse shape; characterized by molding to touched surface but without high force.

Pressure—associated with encoding of compliance; characterized by application of forces to object (usually, normal to surface), while counterforces are exerted (by person or external support) to maintain its position.

Unsupported holding—associated with encoding of weight; characterized by holding object away from supporting surface, often with arm movement (hefting).

Contour following—associated with encoding of precise contour; characterized by movement of exploring effector (usually, one or more fingertips) along edge or surface contour.

The association between these exploratory procedures and the properties they are used to extract has been documented in a variety of tasks. One paradigm (Lederman & Klatzky, 1987) required blindfolded participants to pick the best match, among three comparison objects, to a standard object. The match was to be based on a particular property, like roughness, with others being ignored. The hand movements of the participants when exploring the standard object were recorded and classified as exploratory procedures. In another task, blindfolded participants were asked to sort objects into categories defined by haptically perceptible properties, as quickly as possible (Klatzky, Lederman, & Reed, 1989; Lederman, Klatzky, & Reed, 1993; Reed, Lederman, & Klatzky, 1990). The objects were custom fabricated and varied systematically (across several sets) in shape complexity, compliance, size, hardness, and surface roughness. In both of these tasks, subjects were observed to produce the exploratory procedure associated with the targeted object property.

Haptic exploratory procedures are also observed when vision is available, although they occur only for a subset of the properties, and then only when the judgment is relatively difficult (i.e., vision does not suffice). In particular (Klatzky, Lederman, & Matula, 1993), individuals who were asked which of two objects was greater along a designated property—size, weight, and so on—used vision alone to make judgments of size or shape, whether the judgments were easy or difficult. However, they used appropriate haptic exploratory procedures to make difficult judgments of material properties, such as weight and roughness.

One might ask what kind of exploration occurs when people try to identify common objects. Klatzky, Lederman, and Metzger (1985) observed a wide variety of hand movements when participants tried to generate the names of 100 common objects, as each object was placed in their hands in turn. Lederman and Klatzky (1990) probed for the hand movements used in object identification more directly, by placing an object in the hands of a blindfolded participant and asking for its identity with one of two kinds of cues. The cue referred either to the object's basic-level name (e.g., *Is this writing implement a pencil?*) or to a name at a subordinate level (e.g., *Is this pencil a used pencil?*). An initial phase of the experiment determined what property or properties people thought were most critical to identifying the named object at each level; in this phase, a group of participants selected the most diagnostic attributes for each name from a list of properties that was provided. This initial phase revealed that shape was the most frequent diagnostic attribute for identifying objects at the basic level, although texture was often diagnostic as well. At the subordinate level, however, the set of object names was designed to elicit a wider variety of diagnostic attributes; for example, whereas shape is diagnostic to identify a food as a noodle, compliance is important when identifying a noodle as a cooked noodle. In the main phase of the experiment, when participants were given actual exemplars of the named object and probed at the basic or subordinate level, their hand movements were recorded and classified. Most identifications began with a grasp and lift of the object. This initial exploration was often followed by more specific exploratory procedures, and those procedures were the ones that were associated with the object's most diagnostic attributes.

Why are dedicated exploratory procedures used to extract object properties? Klatzky and Lederman (1999a) argued that each exploratory procedure optimizes the input to an associated property-computation process. For example, the exploratory procedure associated with the property of apparent temperature (i.e., static holding) uses a large hand surface. Spatial summation across the thermal receptors means that a larger surface provides a stronger signal about rate of heat flow. As another example, lateral motion—the scanning procedure associated with the property of surface roughness—has been found to increase the firing rates of slowly adapting receptors (Johnson & Lamb, 1981), which appear to be the input to the computation of roughness for macrotextured surfaces (see Hsaio et al., 1993, for review). (For a more complete analysis of the function of exploratory procedures, see Klatzky & Lederman, 1999a.)

The idea that the exploratory procedure associated with an object property optimizes the extraction of that property is supported by an experiment of Lederman and Klatzky

(1987, Experiment 2). In this study, participants were constrained to use a particular exploratory procedure while a target property was to be compared. Across conditions, each exploratory procedure was associated with each target property, not just the property with which the procedure spontaneously emerged. The accuracy and speed of the comparison were determined for each combination of procedure and property. When performance on each property was assessed, the optimal exploratory procedure in this forced-exploration task (based on accuracy, with speed used to disambiguate ties) was found to be the same one that emerged when subjects freely explored to compare the given property. That is, the spontaneously executed procedure was in fact the best one to use, indicating that the procedure maximizes the availability of relevant information. The use of contour following to determine precise shape was found not only optimal, but also necessary in order to achieve accurate performance.

Turvey and associates, in an extensive series of studies, have examined a form of exploration that they call "dynamic touch," to contrast it with both cutaneous sensing and haptic exploration, in which the hand actively passes over the surface of an object (for review, see Turvey, 1996; Turvey & Carello, 1995). With dynamic touch, the object is held in the hand and wielded, stimulating receptors in the tendons and muscles; thus it can be considered to be based on kinesthesis. The inertia tensor, described previously in the context of weight perception, has been found to be a mediating construct in the perception of several object properties from wielding. We have seen that the eigenvalues of the inertia tensor—that is, the resistance to rotation around three principal axes (the eigenvectors)—appear to play a critical role in the perception of heaviness. The eigenvalues and eigenvectors also appear to convey information about the geometric properties of objects and the manner in which they are held during wielding, respectively. Among the perceptual judgments that have been found to be directly related to the inertia tensor are the length of a wielded object (Pagano & Turvey, 1993; Solomon & Turvey, 1988), its width (Turvey, Burton, Amazeen, Butwill, & Carello, 1998), and the orientation of the object relative to the hand (Pagano & Turvey, 1992). A wielded object can also be a tool for finding out about the external world; for example, the gap between two opposing surfaces can be probed by a handheld rod (e.g., Barac-Cikoja & Turvey, 1993).

Relative Availability of Object Properties

Lederman and Klatzky (1997) used a variant of a visual search task (Treisman & Gormican, 1988) to investigate which haptically perceived properties become available at different points in the processing stream. In their task, the participant searched for a target that was defined by some haptic property and presented to a single finger, while other fingers were presented with distractors that did not have the target property. For example, the target might be rough, and the distractors smooth. From one to six fingers were stimulated on any trial, by means of a motorized apparatus. The participant indicated target presence or absence by pressing a thumb switch, and the response time—from presentation of the stimuli to the response—was recorded. The principal interest was in the search function; that is, the function relating response time to the number of fingers that were stimulated. Two such functions could be calculated, one for target-present trials and the other for target-absent trials. The functions were generally strongly linear.

Twenty-five variants on this task were performed, representing different properties. The properties fell into four broad classes. One was material properties: for example, rough-smooth (a target could be rough and distractors smooth, or vice versa), hard-soft, and cool-warm (copper vs. pine). A second class required subjects to search for the presence or absence of abrupt surface discontinuities, such as detecting a surface with a raised bar among flat surfaces. A third class of discriminations was based on planar or three-dimensional spatial position. For example, subjects might be asked to search for a vertical edge (i.e., a raised bar aligned along the finger) among horizontal-edge distractors, or they might look for a raised dot to the right of an indentation among surfaces with a dot to the left of an indentation (Experiments 8–11). Finally, the fourth class of searches required subjects to discriminate between continuous three-dimensional contours, such as seeking a curved surface among flat surfaces.

From the resulting response-time functions, the slope and intercept parameters were extracted. The slope indicates the additional cost, in terms of processing time, of adding a single finger to the display. The intercept includes one-time processes that do not depend on the number of fingers, such as adjusting the orientation of the hand so as to better contact the display. Note that although the processes entering the intercept do not depend on the number of fingers, they may depend on the particular property that is being discriminated. The intercept will include the time to extract information about the object property being interrogated, to the extent the process of information extraction is done in parallel and it does not use distributed capacity across the fingers (in which case, the processing time would affect the slope).

The relative values of the slope and intercept indicate the availability ordering among properties. A property whose discrimination produces a higher slope extracts a higher finger-by-finger cost and hence is slower to extract; a property producing a higher intercept takes longer for one-time processing and hence is slow to be extracted. Both the slopes and intercepts of this task told a common story about the relative availability among haptically accessible properties. There was a progression in availability from material properties, to surface discontinuities, to spatial relations. The slopes for material properties tended to be low (≤36 ms), and several were approximately equal to zero. Similarly, the intercepts of material-property search functions tended to be among the lowest, except for the task in which the target was cool (copper) and the distractors warm (pine). This exception presumably reflects the time necessary for heat to flow from the subject's skin to the stimulus, activating the thermoreceptors. In contrast, the slopes and intercepts for spatially defined properties tended to be among the highest.

Why should material properties and abrupt spatial discontinuities be more available than properties that are spatially defined? Lederman and Klatzky (1997) characterized the material and discontinuity properties as unidimensional or *intensive:* That is, they can be represented by a scalar magnitude that indicates the intensity of the perceptual response. In contrast, spatial properties are, by definition, related to the two- or three-dimensional layout of points in a reference system. A spatial discrimination task requires that a distinction be made between stimuli that are equal in intensity but vary in spatial placement. For example, a bar can be aligned with or across the fingertip, but exerts the same amount of pressure in either case.

The relative unavailability of spatial properties demonstrated in this research is consistent with a more general body of work suggesting that spatial information is relatively difficult to extract by the haptic system, in comparison both to spatial coding by the visual system and to haptic coding of nonspatial properties (e.g., Cashdan, 1968; Johnson & Phillips, 1981; Lederman, Klatzky, Chataway, & Summers, 1990).

HAPTIC SPACE PERCEPTION

Vision-based perception of space is discussed in the chapter by Proffitt and Caudek in this volume. Whereas a large body of theoretical and empirical research has addressed visual space perception, there is no agreed-upon definition of haptic space. Lederman, Klatzky, Collins, and Wardell (1987) made a distinction between manipulatory and ambulatory space, the former within reach of the hands and the latter requiring exploration by movements of the body. Both involve haptic feedback, although to different effectors. Here, we consider manipulatory space exclusively.

A variety of studies have established that the perception of manipulatory space is nonveridical. The distortions have been characterized in various ways. One approach is to attempt to determine a distance metric for lengths of movements made on a reached surface. Brambring (1976) had blind and sighted individuals reach along two sides of a right triangle and estimate the length of the hypotenuse. Fitting the hypotenuse to a general distance metric revealed that estimates departed from the Euclidean value by using an exponent less than 2. Brambring concluded that the operative metric was closer to a city block. Subsequent work suggests, however, that no one metric will apply to haptic spatial perception, because distortions arise from several sources, and perception is not uniform over the explored space; that is, haptic spatial perception is *anisotropic*.

One of the indications of anisotropy is the vertical-horizontal illusion. Well known in vision, although observed long ago in touch as well (e.g., Burtt, 1917), this illusion takes the form of vertical lines' being overestimated relative to length-matched horizontals. Typically, the illusion is tested by presenting subjects with a T-shaped or L-shaped form and asking them to match the lengths of the components. The T-shaped stimulus introduces another source of judgment error, however, in that the vertical line is bisected (making it perceptually shorter) and the horizontal is not. The illusion in touch is not necessarily due to visual mediation (i.e., imagining how the stimulus would look), because it has been observed in congenitally blind people as well as sighted individuals (e.g., Casla, Blanco, & Travieso, 1999; Heller & Joyner, 1993). Heller, Calcaterra, Burson, & Green (1997) demonstrated that the patterns of arm movement used by subjects had a substantial effect on the illusion. Use of the whole arm in particular augmented the magnitude of the illusion. Millar and Al-Attar (2000) found that the illusion was affected by the position of the display relative to the body, which would affect movement and, potentially, the spatial reference system in which the display was represented.

Another anisotropy is revealed by the radial-tangential effect in touch. This refers to the fact that movements directed toward and away from the body (radial motions) are overestimated relative to side-to-side (tangential) motions of equal extent (e.g., Cheng, 1968; Marchetti & Lederman, 1983). Like the vertical-horizontal illusion, this appears to be heavily influenced by motor patterns. The perception of distance is greater when the hand is near the body, for example (Cheng, 1968; Marchetti & Lederman, 1983). Wong (1977) found that the slower the movement, the greater the judged extent; he suggested that the difference between radial and tangential distance judgments may reflect different execution times. Indeed, when Armstrong and Marks (1999) controlled for movement duration, the difference between estimates of radial and tangential extents vanished.

A third manifestation of anisotropy in haptic space perception is the oblique effect, also found in visual perception (e.g., Appelle & Countryman, 1986; Gentaz & Hatwell, 1995, 1996, 1998; Lechelt, Eliuk, & Tanne, 1976). When people are asked to reproduce the orientation of a felt rod, they do worse with obliques (e.g., 45°) than with horizontal or vertical lines. As with the other anisotropies that have been described, the pattern in which the stimulus is explored appears to be critical to the effect. Gentaz and Hatwell (1996) had subjects reproduce the orientation of a rod when the gravitational force was either natural or nulled by a counterweight. The oblique effect was greater when the natural gravitational forces were present. In a subsequent experiment with blind subjects (Gentaz & Hatwell, 1998), it appeared that the variability of the gravitational forces, rather than their magnitude, was critical: The oblique effect was not found in the horizontal plane, even with an unsupported arm; in this plane the gravitational forces do not vary with the direction of movement. In contrast, the oblique effect was found in the frontal plane, where gravitational force impedes upward and facilitates downward movements, regardless of arm support.

A study by Essock, Krebs, and Prather (1997) points to the fact that anisotropies may have multiple processing loci. Although effects of movement and gravity point to the involvement of muscle-tendon-joint systems, the oblique effect was also found for gratings oriented on the finger pad. This is presumably due to the filtering of the cutaneous system. The authors suggest a basic distinction between low-level anisotropies that arise at a sensory level, and ones that arise from higher-level processing of spatial relations.

The influence of high-level processes can be seen in a phenomenon described by Lederman, Klatzky, and Barber (1985), which they called "length distortion." In their studies, participants were asked to trace a curved line between two endpoints, and then to estimate the direct (Euclidean) distance between them. The estimates increased directly with the length of the curved line, in some cases amounting to a 2:1 estimate relative to the correct value. High errors were maintained, even when subjects kept one finger on the starting point of their exploration and maintained it until they came to the endpoint. Under these circumstances, they had simultaneous sensory information about the positions of the fingers before making the judgment; still, they were pulled off by the length of the exploratory path. Because the indirect path between endpoints adds to both the extent and duration of the travel between them by the fingers, Lederman et al. (1987) attempted to disambiguate these factors by having subjects vary movement speed. They found that although the duration of the movement affected responses, the principal factor was the pathway extent. In short, it appears that the spatial pattern of irrelevant movement is taken into account when the shortest path is estimated.

Bingham, Zaal, Robin, and Shull (2000) suggested that haptic distortion might actually be functional: namely, as a means of compensating for visual distortion in reaching. They pointed out that although visual distances are distorted by appearing greater in depth than in width, the same appears to be true of haptically perceived space (Kay, Hogan, & Fasse, 1996). Given an error in vision, then, the analogous error in touch leads the person to the same point in space. Suppose that someone reaching to a target under visual guidance perceives it to be 25% further away than it is—for example, at 1.25 m rather than its true location of 1 m. If the haptic system also feels it to be 25% further away than it is, then haptic feedback from reaching will guide a person to land successfully on the target at 1 m while thinking it is at 1.25 m. However, the hypothesis that haptic distortions usefully cancel the effects of visual distortions was not well supported. Haptic feedback in the form of touching the target after the reach compensated to some extent, but not fully, for the visual distortion.

Virtually all of the anisotropies that have been described are affected by the motor patterns used to explore haptic space. The use of either the hand or arm, the position of the arm when the hand explores, the gravitational forces present, and the speed of movement, for example, are all factors that have been identified as influencing the perception of a tangible layout in space. What is clearly needed is research that clarifies the processes by which a representation of external space is derived from sensory signals provided by muscle-tendon-joint receptors, which in turn arise from the *kinematics* (positional change of limbs and effectors) and *dynamics* (applied forces) of exploration. This is clearly a multidimensional problem. Although it may turn out to have a reduced-dimensional solution, the solution seems likely to be relatively complex, given the evidence that high-level cognitive processes mediate the linkages between motor exploration, cutaneous and kinesthetic sensory responses, and spatial representation.

HAPTIC PERCEPTION OF TWO- AND THREE-DIMENSIONAL PATTERNS

Pattern perception in the domain of vision is presented in the chapter by Stephen in this volume. Perception of pattern by the haptic system has been tested within a number of stimulus domains. The most common stimuli are vibrotactile patterns, presented by vibrating pins. Other two-dimensional patterns that have been studied are Braille, letters, unfamiliar outlines, and outline drawings of common objects. There is also work on fully three-dimensional objects.

Vibrotactile Patterns

A vibrotactile pattern is formed by repeatedly stimulating some part of the body (usually the finger) at a set of contact points. Typically, the points are a subset of the elements in a matrix. The most commonly used stimulator, the Optacon (for optical-to-tacile converter), is a array with 24 rows and 6 columns; it measures 12.7 $*$ 29.2 mm (Cholewiak & Collins, 1990). The row vibrators are separated by approximately 1.25 mm and the column pins by approximately 2.5 mm. The pins vibrate approximately 230 times per second. Larger arrays were described by Cholewiak and Sherrick (1981) for use on the thigh and the palm.

A substantial body of research has examined the effects of temporal and spatial variation on pattern perception with vibrating pin arrays (see Craig & Rollman, 1999; Loomis & Lederman, 1986). When two temporally separated patterns are presented, they may sum to form a composite, or they may produce two competing responses; these mechanisms of temporal interaction appear to be distinct (Craig, 1996; Craig & Qian 1997). These temporal effects can occur even when the patterns are presented to spatial locations on two different fingers (Craig & Qian, 1997).

Spatial interactions between vibratory patterns may occur because the patterns stimulate common areas of skin, or because they involve a common stimulus identity but are not necessarily at the same skin locus. The term *communality* (Geldard & Sherrick, 1965) has been used to measure the extent to which two patterns have active stimulators in the same spatial location, whether the pattern identities are the same or different. The ability to discriminate patterns has been found to be inversely related to their communality at the finger, palm, and thigh (Cholewiak & Collins, 1995; see that paper also for a review). The extent to which two patterns occupy common skin sites has also been found to affect discrimination performance. Horner (1995) found that when subjects were asked to make same-different judgments of vibrotactile patterns, irrespective of the area of skin that was stimulated, they performed best when the patterns were presented to the same site, in which case the absolute location of the stimulation could be used for discrimination. As the locations were more widely separated, performance deteriorated, suggesting a cost for aligning the patterns within a common representation when they were physically separated in space.

Two-Dimensional Patterns and Freestanding Forms

Another type of pattern that has been used in a variety of studies is composed of raised lines or points. Braille constitutes the latter type of pattern. Loomis (1990) modeled the perception of characters presented to the fingertip—not only Braille patterns, but also modified Braille with adjacent connected dots, raised letters of English and Japanese, and geometric forms. Confusion errors in identifying members of these pattern sets, tactually and visually when seen behind a blurring filter (to simulate filtering properties of the skin), were compiled. The data supported a model in which the finger acts like a low-pass filter, essentially blurring the input; the intensity is also compressed. Loomis has pointed out that given the filtering imposed by the skin, the Braille patterns that have been devised for use by the blind represent a useful compromise between the spatial extent of the finger and its acuity: A larger pattern would have points whose relative locations were easier to determine, but it would then extend beyond the fingertip.

The neurophysiological mechanisms underlying perception of raised, two-dimensional patterns at the fingertip have been investigated by Hsaio, Johnson, and associates (see Hsaio, Johnson, Twombly, & DiCarlo, 1996). The SAI mechanoreceptors appear to be principally involved in form perception. These receptors have small receptive fields (about 2 mm diameter), respond better to edges than to continuous surfaces (Phillips & Johnson, 1981), and given their sustained response, collectively produce an output that preserves the shape of embossed patterns presented to the skin. Hsaio et al. (1996) have traced the processing beyond the SI mechanoreceptors to cortical areas SI and SII in succession. Isomorphism is preserved in area SI, whereas SII neurons have larger receptive fields and show more complex responses that are not consistently related to the attributes of the stimulus.

Larger two-dimensional shapes, felt with the fingers of one or more hands, have also been used to test the pattern-recognition capabilities of the haptic system. These larger stimuli introduce demands of memory and integration (see following paragraphs), and often, performance is poor. Klatzky, Lederman, and Balakrishnan (1991) found chance performance in a successive matching task with irregularly shaped planar forms (like wafers) on the order of 15 cm in diameter. Strategic exploration may be used to reduce the - memory demands and detect higher-order properties of such stimuli. Klatzky et al. found that subjects explored as symmetrically as possible, often halting exploration with one hand so that the other, slowed by a more complex contour, could catch up, so to speak, to the same height in space. Ballesteros, Manga, and Reales (1997) and Ballesteros, Millar, and Reales (1998) found that such bimanual exploration facilitated the ability to detect the property of symmetry in raised-line shapes scaled well beyond the fingertip.

Two-Dimensional Outline Drawings of Common Objects

If unfamiliar forms that require exploration beyond the fingertip are difficult to identify and compare, one might expect better performance with familiar objects. Studies that examine object-identification performance with raised, two-dimensional depictions of objects have led to the conclusion that performance is considerably below that with real objects (see following discussion), but well above chance. Lederman et al. (1990) found that sighted individuals recognized only 34% of raised-line drawings of objects, even when they were allowed up to 2 minutes of exploration. The blind participants did substantially worse (10% success). Loomis, Klatzky, and Lederman (1991) implicated memory and integration processes as limiting factors in two-dimensional haptic picture recognition. This study compared visual and tactual recognition with identical line drawings of objects. In one condition with visual presentation, the contours of the object were revealed through an aperture scaled to have the same proportion, relative to the size of the object, as the fingertip. As the participant moved his or her hand on a digital pad, the contours of the object were continuously revealed through the aperture. Under these viewing conditions, performance with visual recognition—which was completely accurate when the whole object was simultaneously exposed—deteriorated to the level of the tactual condition, despite high familiarity with the object categories.

There is evidence that given the task of recognizing a two-dimensional picture by touch, people who have had experience with sight attempt to form a visual image of the object and recognize it by visual mediation. Blind people with some visual experience do better on the task than those who lacked early vision (Heller, 1989a), and among sighted individuals, measures of imagery correlate with performance (Lederman et al., 1990). However, Heller also reported a study in which blind people with some visual experience outperformed sighted, blindfolded individuals. This demonstrates that visual experience and mediation by means of visual images are not prerequisites for successful picture identification. (Note that spatial images, as compared to visual images, may be readily available to those lacking in visual experience.) D'Angiulli, Kennedy, and Heller (1998) also found that when active exploration of raised pictures was used, performance by blind children (aged 8–13) was superior to that of a matched group of sighted children; moreover, the blind children's accuracy averaged above 50%. They suggested that the blind had better spontaneous strategies for exploring the pictures; the sighted children benefited from having their hands passively guided by the experimenter. A history of instruction for the blind individuals may contribute to this effect (Heller, Kennedy, & Joyner, 1995).

The studies just cited clearly show that persons who lack vision can recognize raised drawings of objects at levels that, although they do not approach visual recognition, nonetheless point to a strong capacity to interpret kinesthetic variation in the plane as a three-dimensional spatial entity. This ability is consistent with demonstrations that blind people often create drawings that illustrate pictorial conventions such as perspective and metaphorical indications of movement (Heller, Calcaterra, Tyler, & Burson, 1996; Kennedy, 1997).

Three-Dimensional Objects

Real, common objects are recognized very well by touch. Klatzky et al. (1985) found essentially perfect performance in naming common objects placed in the hands, with a modal response time of 2 s. This level of performance contrasts with the corresponding data for raised-line portrayals of common objects (i.e., low accuracy even with 2 minutes of exploration), raising the question as to what is responsible for the difference. No doubt there are several factors. Experience is likely to be one; note that experience is implicated in previously described studies with raised-line objects.

Another relevant factor is three-dimensionality. A two-dimensional object follows a convention of projecting variations in depth to a picture plane, from which the third dimension must be constructed. This is performed automatically by visual processes, but not, apparently, in the domain of touch. Lederman et al. (1990) found that portrayals of objects that have variations in depth led to lower performance than was found with flat objects that primarily varied in two dimensions (e.g., a bowl vs. a fork). Shimizu, Saida, and Shimura (1993) used a pin-element display to portray objects as two-dimensional outlines or three-dimensional relief forms. Ratings of haptic legibility were higher for the three-dimensional objects, and their identification by early blind individuals was also higher. Klatzky, Loomis, Lederman, Wake, and Fujita (1993) asked participants to identify real objects while wearing heavy gloves and exploring with only a single finger, which reduced the objects' information content primarily to three-dimensional contour (although some surface information, such as coefficient of friction, was no doubt available). Performance was approximately 75% accurate, well above the level achieved when exploring raised-line depictions of the same objects.

Lakatos and Marks (1999) investigated whether, when individuals explore three-dimensional objects, they emphasize the local features or the global form. The task was to make similarity judgments of unfamiliar geometric forms (e.g., cube; column) that contained distinctive local features such as grooves and spikes (see Figure 6.6). The data suggested a greater salience for local features in early processing, with global features becoming more equal in salience as processing time increased. Objects with different local features but similar in overall shape were judged less similar when explored

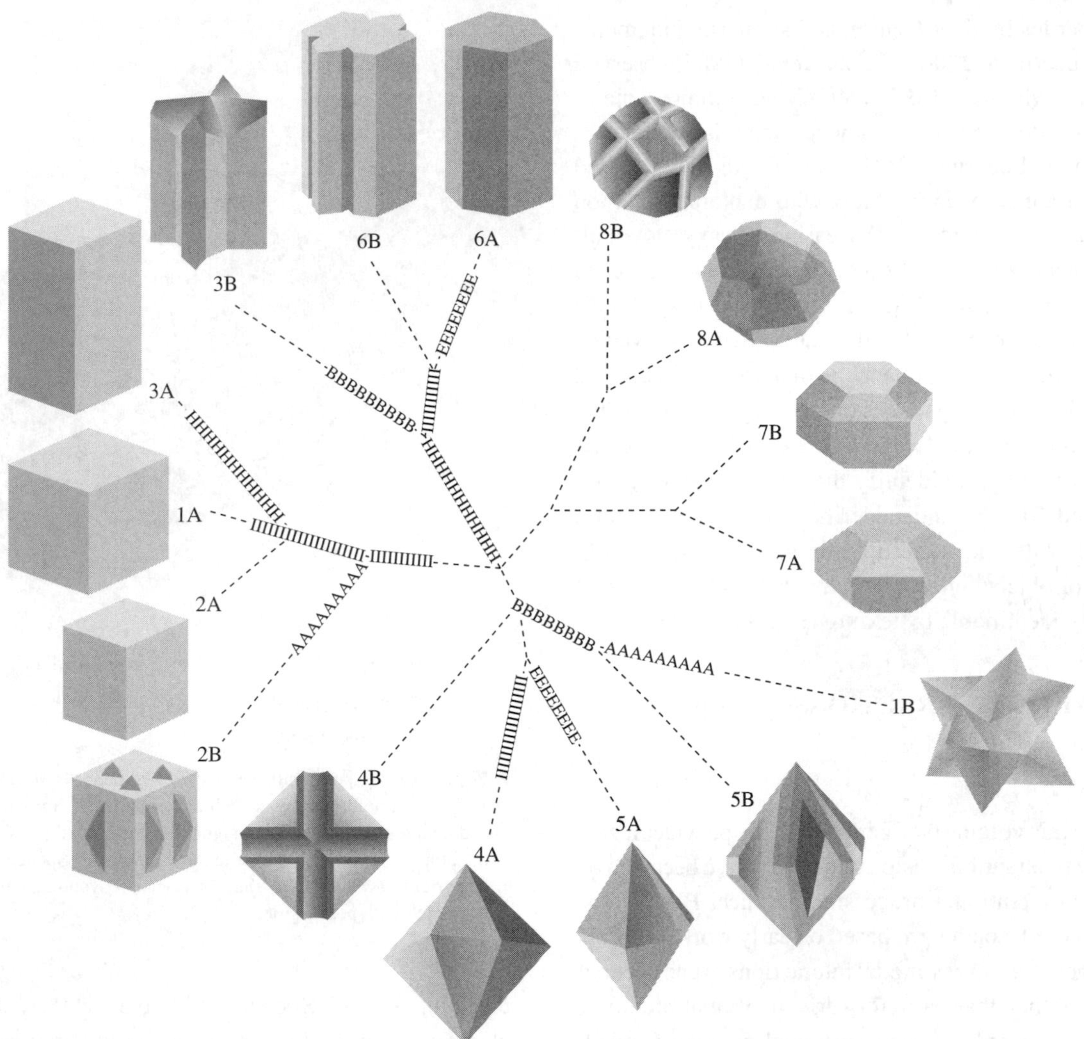

Figure 6.6 Objects used by Lakatos and Marks (1999, Figure 2) and their similarity as determined by a clustering algorithm. The algorithm distributes the objects in a tree, such that objects at the end of a common branch are similar. Letters on the branches indicate features that are found on objects falling on different branches (e.g., the letter *A* denotes sharp protrusions, as found on objects 1B and 2B).

haptically than when vision was available. Longer exposure time (increasing from 1 s to 16 s) produced greater similarity ratings for objects that were locally different but globally similar, indicating the increasing salience for global shape over time.

When people do extract local features of three-dimensional objects, they appear to have a bias toward encoding the back of the object—the reverse of vision. Newell, Ernst, Tian, and Bülthoff (2001) documented this phenomenon using objects made of Lego blocks. The participants viewed or haptically explored the objects, and then tried to recognize the ones to which they had been exposed. On some trials, the objects were rotated 180° (back-to-front) between exposure and the recognition test. When exposure and test were in the same modality (vision or touch), performance suffered if the objects were rotated. When the modality changed between exposure and test, however, performance was better when the objects were rotated as well: In this case, the surface that was felt at the back of the object was viewed at the front. Moreover, when exploration and testing were exclusively by touch, performance was better for objects explored from the back than for those explored from the front.

Although the previously described studies emphasized the role of shape, no doubt a critical factor in recognizing real, common objects by touch is material. Material is locally available, whereas extraction of the shape of an object requires following its contours or enclosing it in the hand (Lederman & Klatzky, 1987). A number of studies by Klatzky, Lederman, and associates point to the importance of material properties in identification and similarity judgments (Klatzky & Lederman, 2000). Klatzky, et al. (1985) observed that individuals who were freely identifying common objects often reported attending to the objects' material properties. Klatzky, Loomis, Lederman, Wake, and Fujita (1993) found that the performance of individuals who explored common objects with a single finger while wearing a heavy glove improved significantly when the tip of the glove was cut off to expose the object's material. Lederman and Klatzky (1990) found that when an object's identity was particularly revealed by its material (e.g., as compliance is diagnostic of a cooked noodle), people attempting to identify the object executed the exploratory procedure that was associated with the relevant material property (e.g., to identify the cooked noodle, pressing on it). And Klatzky and Lederman (1995) found that a 200-ms touch with the fingertip was sufficient to identify 25% of a set of objects selected to have large surfaces and to be particularly identifiable by texture (e.g., sandpaper).

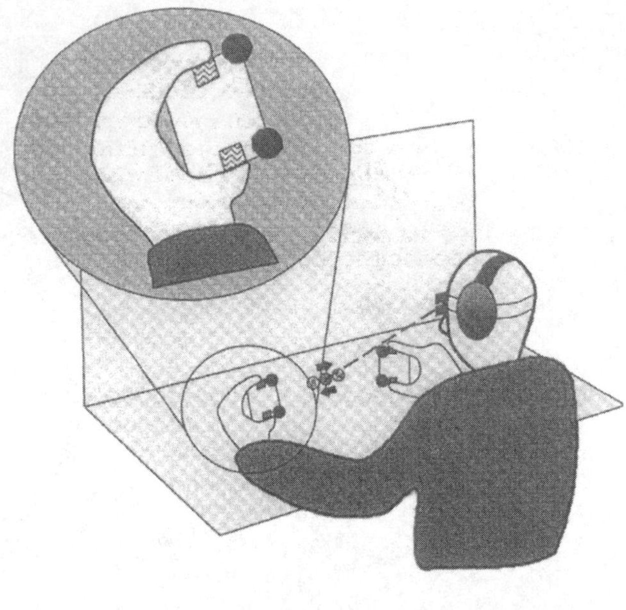

Figure 6.7 Experimental setup used by Spence et al. (2000, Figure 3). The subject holds a cube in each hand that has a vibrotactile stimulator and light, either of which can signal the required response; the arrows at fixation are used to direct attention. *Source:* Spence et al. (2000). Copyright © 2000 by the American Psychological Association. Reprinted with permission.

VISUAL-HAPTIC INTERACTIONS

Attention

The chapter in this volume by Egeth and Lamy provides a general overview of attention. Vision and touch have been shown to be linked in attentional processing. Spence, Pavani, and Driver (2000) used a paradigm based on early work of Posner (1978) to demonstrate cross-modal interactions in endogenous (self-directed rather than stimulus-driven) spatial attention. Subjects discriminated between sustained or pulsed targets that were presented either visually (by a light) or tactually (by a force to the fingertip) on the right or left side of the body. They indicated the target's form (sustained vs. pulsed), *not* its spatial location, with a foot pedal. A centralized visual precue, a right or left arrow, correctly predicted the target location on 80% of trials, which should trigger a voluntary orienting of attention to the precued location. Both visual and tactual precueing effects were obtained, in the form of facilitation when the cue was valid (correctly predicted the target location). In a subsequent experiment, shown in Figure 6.7, in each hand the participant held a foam cube, which could produce either vibrotactile stimulation or a light on the upper or lower edge. The response was to indicate elevation of the target (upper vs. lower edge), regardless of the cube on which it appeared or of its modality. Again, a central arrow cue, predicting the likely hand to be stimulated, was facilitative when it was valid. These experiments indicated that spatial attention could be endogenously directed in the visual or tactual modality.

Just as a visual cue can direct attention to a tactile stimulus, incongruent visual stimulation can interfere with tactile detection. Pavani, Spence, and Driver (2000) asked individuals to indicate the location of a tactile stimulus on the hand while it held a cube underneath a table (i.e., the hand could not be seen). Simultaneously with the tactile stimulus, a light could flash on a visible cube located on the table top. When the light flashed at one location on the cube while the tactile stimulus occurred at another location, tactile detection was slowed. This interference from an incongruent visual stimulus increased when the participants saw rubber hands holding the visible cubes on top of the table, aligned with their own hands. Moreover, some participants reported feeling that the rubber hands were their own!

Another study of Spence et al. (2000) specifically tested cross-modal cueing of attention: The target appeared in one of the two modalities (the so-called primary modality) on 73% of trials, and participants were instructed to direct their attention primarily in that modality and not in the other (the so-called secondary modality). A critical manipulation was that the cue indicating the likely spatial location of the target within the primary modality was incorrect (actually reversed by a ratio of 2:1) for the secondary one. For example, if touch was primary—that is, a tactile stimulus occurred most often—a cue predicting a right-side tactile stimulus actually implied that if a visual stimulus occurred instead, it would be on the left side. Thus, participants had countermotivation to direct their attention in the primary and secondary modalities to the same side. The results indicated that individuals responded faster when the target appeared on the side cued within the primary modality. This occurred not only for stimuli in the primary modality, in which the cue's prediction was valid, but also for the secondary modality, in which the cue was invalid most of the time—although the primary cueing effect was stronger. Thus, for example, when touch was primary and the cue indicated a right-side stimulus, a visual stimulus on the right was responded to faster than on the left—even though a right-side cue for touch implied a left-side stimulus for vision. On the whole, the results indicate that subjects did not have two dissociated attentional mechanisms that could be directed to opposite areas of space. Rather, the attentional focus directed by the primary modality applied to both modalities.

Cortical sites that may underlie these early attentional interactions between vision and touch were identified by Macaluso, Frith, and Driver (2000). They began with the observation that a touch on one hand can improve visual discrimination in nearby locations (e.g., Butter, Buchtel, & Santucci, 1989). Functional MRI was used while subjects were presented with visual stimulation alone, or visual-plus-tactile stimulation on the same or different sides. When tactile stimulation occurred on the same side as visual, there was elevated activity in the visual cortex. Visual-plus-tactile stimulation on opposite sides did not produce such an elevated response. The authors suggested that this influence of touch on early visual processing arises from pathways that arise in the parietal lobe and project backward.

Cross-Modal Integration

Visual-haptic interactions have been investigated at higher levels of stimulus processing, in which sensory inputs produce a unitary perceptual response. A common paradigm in this research uses a discrepancy between visual and haptic stimuli—sizes or textures, for example—to determine the relative weighting of the modalities under different conditions. In early work, Rock (Rock & Harris, 1967; Rock & Victor, 1964) reported total dominance of haptic percepts by visual inputs, when participants judged the size of a square that was simultaneously felt and viewed through a reducing lens. However, subsequent research has challenged the early claim of strong visual dominance. Friedes (1974) and Welch and Warren (1980) have argued that a better predictor of relative weighting of modality pairs (e.g., vision-touch, touch-audition, vision-audition) is the relative appropriateness (i.e., defined in terms of accuracy, precision, and cue availability) of the task for each modality. More recently, Heller, Calcaterra, Green, and Brown (1999) showed that the modality and precision of the response strongly influenced the weighting of the input stimuli. When subjects responded by viewing a ruler, vision dominated, whereas when they indicated size with a pinch posture, touch dominated. This suggests that the relative contributions of the modalities can be modulated by attention.

A response by age interaction was found in a size-discrepancy study by Misceo, Hershberger, and Mancini (1999). Children from 6 to 12 years of age matched a viewed and touched square to a set of comparison squares that were either felt or viewed. While visual dominance was found across age groups with the visual response, the haptic response led to an age progression from visual to haptic dominance. Thus it appears that experience, maturation, or both alter the extent to which the haptic input can be weighted.

Cognitive factors were also identified in a texture-discrepancy study by Lederman, Thorne, and Jones (1986). One group of subjects was asked to judge the so-called spatial density of a set of textured surfaces by vision, by touch, and by vision and touch together. A second group was asked to judge the same stimuli in terms of roughness, once again by vision, touch, and vision and touch together. The spatial-density instructions produced strong dominance of vision over touch, presumably because fine spatial resolution is required by the task, something that vision does considerably better than touch. In contrast, the roughness instructions produced equally strong tactual dominance over vision; this time it was argued because the sense of touch can differentiate fine differences in surface roughness better than vision can (Heller, 1989b).

Further work on visual-haptic interactions is related to representations in memory. A particularly important issue is whether the two channels converge on a common representation. Memory is reviewed in the next section.

HAPTIC MEMORY

Chapters in this volume that provide broad coverage of human memory are those by Nairne; McNamara and Holbrook; Roediger and Marsh; and Johnson. The literature in this area has tended to neglect the haptic modality, being dominated by verbal stimuli in the auditory and visual modalities. In particular, there has been little effort to build an information-processing systems approach that would identify, for example, sensory stores and different forms of long-term memory.

Research on memory within the modality of touch is also plagued by the possibility, even the likelihood, of mediating representations in the verbal or spatial domains. In an informative review, Millar (1999) has summarized a substantial body of research within the memory-systems approach. She points to evidence for the existence of short-term memory in the tactual modality with a limiting span of two to three items (Millar, 1975a; Watkins & Watkins, 1974). A counterpart to the very short-term iconic and echoic memories, found in vision and audition, has not been clearly demonstrated.

One of the general issues in memory research is the nature of the internal representation. When information is encountered through the sense of touch, one version of this question is whether the representation is intrinsic to the modality or whether it is more general (e.g., spatial). There is evidence for specifically tactual coding during early learning of small patterns like Braille forms; that is, coding that is in terms of tactual features such as texture or dot density, rather than being spatially mediated (see Millar, 1997). Millar (1999) suggested that when patterns can be organized within spatial reference frames, memory for touched patterns is further aided by spatial coding.

Another issue is whether the representation resulting from touch is cross-modal, in the sense of being accessible by other modalities—especially vision. The answer has been demonstrated to be cross-modal. Specifically, haptically presented patterns can be subsequently recognized through the visual modality, although the effect is regulated by a number of factors such as discriminability (see Millar, 1975b).

In a study with 5-year-olds, Bushnell and Baxt (1999) demonstrated that the children were virtually error-free at discriminating between previously presented and newly presented common objects, whether the modality changed between vision and touch or was held constant between presentation and test. Cross-modal recognition became less accurate (although still above chance levels) when the objects were unfamiliar, or when the old and new objects were different tokens of the same category name. The authors suggest that these decrements due to unfamiliarity and categorical similarity arise from different sources. The categorical effect is likely to be due to mediation at a conceptual level or explicit naming, which children were observed to do. Use of the same name for old and new objects would lead to misrecognitions.

On the other hand, the decrement due to using unfamiliar objects is thought to depend on the use of a perceptual code, which emphasizes different aspects of the objects under vision and touch. Such a representation is suggested by experiments on haptic object categorization, which indicate that people use different attributes to group objects, depending on whether vision is available and on whether the participants are instructed to think about what the objects feel like versus what they look like (Klatzky, Lederman, & Reed, 1987; Lederman, Summers, & Klatzky, 1996). Other research suggests that age as well as modality affects the relative emphasis of haptically accessible attributes in object categorization (Schwarzer, Kuefer, & Wilkening, 1999).

A major distinction in memory systems that has emerged in the past two decades or so is made between implicit and explicit memory. Explicit memory is indicated by conscious recollection or recognition: that is, by knowledge that memory is being tapped. Implicit memory is indicated by *priming*—a change in the performance of some task, due to prior exposure to the task materials. For example, having studied a list of words, participants may be asked to generate completions for three-letter word stems; they tend to generate more completions that match the studied words than would be expected by chance, regardless of whether they explicitly remember those words.

This paradigm has been extended to the haptic modality in several studies. Srinivas, Greene, and Easton (1997a) investigated the effects of elaborative (meaningful) processing on an implicit and explicit memory test with two-dimensional forms. In verbal learning studies, elaborative processing generally leads to better performance on explicit tests of memory, but not on implicit tests. In the Srinivas et al. experiment, participants studied the forms by feeling them and verbally describing their features. They then went on to do elaborative encoding: generating a function for the form (e.g., coat hanger)—or shallow encoding: reporting the number of horizontal and vertical lines in the form. When tested, participants either recognized whether a form was studied or new (i.e., an explicit test), or they drew the form as accurately as possible after 4 seconds of study (i.e., an implicit test). The nature of encoding, whether elaborative or shallow, substantially affected the explicit test but not the implicit test. This indicates that implicit memory extends to the haptic modality (see also Easton, Srinivas, & Greene, 1997).

A subsequent experiment (Srinivas, Greene, and Easton, 1997b) showed that both the explicit and implicit tactual memory tests were affected by changes in the orientation and size of the forms between study and test. Indeed, when the forms were left-right reversed or rescaled, the priming produced by implicit memory vanished. In contrast, a visual version of the test was affected by orientation changes but not size changes; this suggests that the basis for implicit memory in touch is not identical to that in vision, and that the functional representation in touch preserves the physical structure and scale of the touched object.

Cross-modal priming between the visual and haptic modalities has also been of interest. Such priming would indicate an implicit memory representation that is accessible multimodally. Using seen or felt words as stimuli, and with stem completion as the implicit test, Easton et al. (1997) demonstrated substantial cross-modal priming between vision and touch. Reales and Ballesteros (1999) examined implicit and explicit memory under intra- and cross-modal conditions, using common objects as stimuli. Various implicit tests were used, including the speed of object naming, the level of completeness at which a fragmented picture could be identified, and speed of deciding whether a line drawing depicted a real object. All of these showed substantial cross-modal and intramodal priming (faster responses for previously studied objects), and in some cases the magnitude of the cross- and intramodal priming effects were equivalent. Moreover, as has previously been found, explicit and implicit tests were governed by different variables: For example, when pictures were used in an implicit test, priming was greater when pictures had been studied than when real objects had been studied, but an explicit test that used pictures benefited when real objects had been studied. The authors argued that the priming effect arises from an abstract structural (cf. semantic) description of objects that is accessible by vision and touch. Data from a delayed test indicated that this representation appears to endure at least over a half hour.

APPLICATIONS OF RESEARCH ON TOUCH

Applications of experimental psychology are the topic of the chapter in this volume by Nickerson and Pew. Work on the sense of touch can be applied in many areas. A long-standing application has been to human factors, for the design of handles or knobs. Work on vibrotactile stimulation has led to development of reading aids for blind persons, like the Optacon, and speech-augmentation devices for deaf persons. Increasingly, computer-driven force stimulators have led to applications in the form of virtual reality and teleoperation. Understanding of the basic capacities and information-processing mechanisms of the haptic perceptual system is highly useful, if not necessary, for developing successful applications in these areas. Conversely, the need for application has motivated basic research.

Aids for the Visually Impaired

Printed media are an unquestioned aspect of life for sighted individuals; reading text and viewing images like maps and pictures are taken for granted. Efforts to provide tactual substitutes for text can be traced to the eighteenth century (see Millar, in press). Interest in maps for blind individuals has lagged considerably; it is noteworthy that the first international conference on maps for the blind was held only in the 1980s (Wiedel, 1983).

Millar (in press) pointed to the need for understanding basic processes in haptic perception in order to understand how advanced Braille readers succeed and to apply this understanding to Braille education. She emphasized the inaccuracy of the naive assumption that Braille patterns constitute gestalt, or wholistic, shapes that are read character by character. On the contrary, detailed observation indicates that skilled Braille reading involves interactive scanning by the two hands, which share higher-order goals. One goal is to maintain spatial orientation on the lines of text, and the other is to extract verbal content. Typically, an advanced reader will alternate these functions over the two hands, with one hand starting to find the next line of text while the other finishes the extraction of meaning from the preceding one. This scanning process is moderated by the task goal: for example, to read for meaning or to find a target letter. In order to learn Braille, then, students must master not only the decoding of individual letters, but also the monitoring and controlling of their orientation relative to the text, as well as maintaining a smooth scan.

In designing letters or graphics for the blind, the nature of the pattern is critical. With respect to letters, legibility is the principal issue. The Braille cell uses dot separations that are well within the discrimination of a typical fingerpad, although the dots may be too dense for people with lowered cutaneous acuity, like elderly or diabetic persons. The inventor of Braille designed dotted patterns in preference to embossed continuous letters, with which he had been taught. The punctate nature of Braille dots has been found preferable for matching characters (see Millar, in press). However, Loomis (1990) reported that sighted, blindfolded individuals identified continuous versions of Braille patterns as well as the original dots.

When it comes to graphical aids for the blind other than printed characters, such as icons used on maps, many factors in addition to legibility are important. In early work in this area, Heath (1958) tested a variety of symbolic patterns for discriminability, and various groups have made recommendations for the symbol system of tangible graphics on this basis (Jansson, 1972; Nolan & Morris, 1971; Edman, 1992). Another consideration is function. Golledge (1991) suggested that the blind traveler would find it particularly useful to have strip maps providing navigable routes between landmarks that are reoriented relative to the user's current perspective, rather than survey maps that convey the relative positions of the landmarks in a fixed spatial reference system. Lederman and Campbell (1982) found that the relative effectiveness of a format for raised graphs depended on the use to which the graph was put. When the ordinate value for a given abscissa value had to be determined, a raised grid aided performance, but the same grid was confusing when subjects had to find the coordinates of an intersection. Patterns of scanning also affect the utility of a display (Berlá, 1982).

Basic research on haptic perception indicates that the iconic value of a symbol may be different in touch than in vision. For example, the limited spatial resolution of the fingertip may make it difficult to determine the direction of a raised arrow, whereas a pattern that is rough in one direction and smooth in the other can be read quickly as a directional signal (Schiff, Kaufer, & Mosak, 1966). Research by Lambert and Lederman (1989) extended this notion by designing raised point symbols for designating interior landmarks of buildings, in which the three-dimensional structure inherently suggested the intended meaning of the symbol.

Technological advances have permitted increasingly sophisticated aids for blind persons. Touch tablets are an electronic means of displaying maps to visually impaired individuals. The display is divided into a matrix, and when a cell is touched, a synthesized speech message is invoked. This is the basis for the NOMAD system (Parkes, 1988). Another system, MoBIC (The MoBIC Consortium, 1997), combines a computer-based map, global positioning sensing, and speech synthesis. It can be used to preview and plan a journey (virtual travel), or it can be consulted en route by means of a keypad in order to get information about current position and a travel plan. The initial system did not include a tactual map. In an experimental test, however, Bringhammar, Jansson, and Douglas (1997) found that after planning and walking with the system, visually impaired participants had high ratings for usability and satisfaction, but augmenting the system with a tactual map increased satisfaction ratings and measures of route understanding.

The development of aids for the blind will undoubtedly benefit from a two-pronged approach, in which applied research is coupled with work on the basic capabilities of the haptic system. Sensory limitations such as spatial thresholds are important, but so are many higher-level factors. In order to develop effective displays for people without vision, one must deal with issues such as what properties of stimuli are available, how these properties emerge in perceptual processing, how exploration alters what is encoded, and how haptic information is remembered, particularly in the context of a real, multimodal environment.

Haptic Augmentation of Speech Perception

Speech perception and production are the focus of the chapter by Fowler in this volume. The use of haptic stimulation to augment speech perception is motivated in part by the success of the Tadoma method for speech communication to deaf and blind individuals (Reed et al., 1985). In this method, shown in Figure 6.8, the receiver of communication places his or her hand on the face and neck of a speaker and monitors the movements of the speech musculature. In addition to changing position of the jaw and lips, users have access to changes in air flow, temperature, and vibration. Experienced users can achieve high levels of speech understanding based on multiple sources of sensory information.

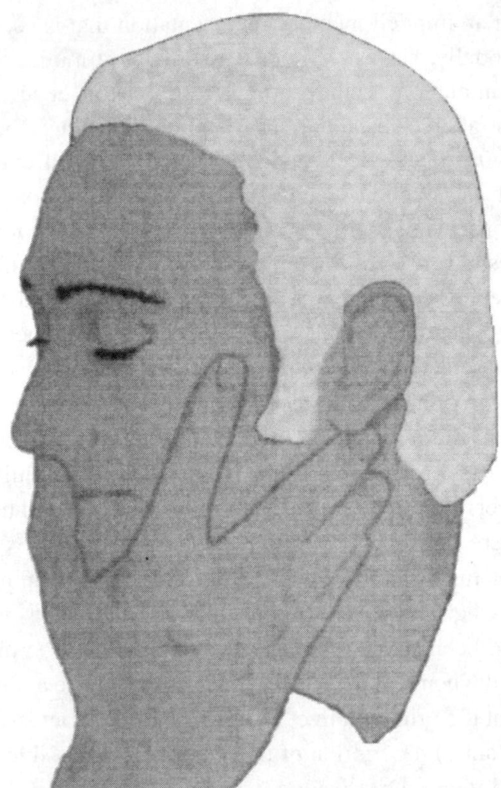

Figure 6.8 The Tadoma method for conveying speech to the blind and deaf.

Efforts to create haptic stimulators to produce similar effects have varied both with respect to the type of device and the aspect of the speech signal that they attempt to convey. The first formant of the speech signal (F0, or fundamental frequency) has been conveyed by vibration and more recently by vibration-spatial coupling (i.e., both the location and the frequency of the vibration are manipulated; see Auer, Bernstein, & Coulter, 1998, for review). An advantage of conveying F0 is that it is related to several aspects of speech, including voicing, stress, intonation (question vs. statement), and syntactic boundaries. Auer et al. found that when vision was combined with a spatio-temporal display of F0, intonation identification was augmented relative to vision alone.

Bernstein (1992) summarized data from a number of extant devices, along with Tadoma data, in terms of information transmitted (Miller & Nicely, 1955). The Tadoma method was superior to any of the aids tested. She reported it "perplexing" (p. 171) that those studies comparing tactile-visual stimulation to that of visual and tactile alone showed only modest gains when the tactile device was added to visual stimulation. Bernstein suggested this might reflect either cross-modal interactions, which would supress the contribution of one modality in the presence of the other, or redundancy in the visual and tactual speech signals.

The limitations on augmentation of speech by a haptic device reflect, of course, the device itself. Tan, Durlach, Reed, and Rabinowitz (1999) devised a haptic speech device, the Tactuator, that through vibrations and movements of the finger, combines cutaneous and kinesthetic features, hence enriching the stimulus dimensionality. Independent acutators move the fingerpads of the thumb, index finger, and middle finger; the thumb moves perpendicularly to the other fingers so that the hand posture is natural. The system has a temporal response range of up to 400 Hz and can displace the finger by 26 mm. From absolute identification tasks, the authors estimated the information transmission rate at 12 bits/s, comparable to that of Tadoma. The capabilities of the system for augmenting natural speech remain to be demonstrated.

Teleoperation and Virtual Environments

A haptic interface is a device that enables manual interaction with virtual or remote environments (Durlach & Mavor, 1994). The device feeds back information to the operator about the consequences of interaction in the remote world. Although the feedback modality is unspecified in principle, it can take the form of haptic feedback, which indicates the forces and vibrations that are imposed on the effector in the remote or simulated world. This type of feedback has been used in two contexts. One is known as *teleoperation*—that is, when a human operator controls a remote device. The other is virtual haptic environments, in which contact with computer-generated objects and surfaces is simulated. In either case, haptic feedback enhances a sense of *telepresence,* the feeling that the operator is in a physical environment.

Three types of information are potentially provided by a haptic display. One is directional force feedback, indicating forces that the remote or simulated effector encounters in the environment. Commercial force stimulators are available, such as the PHANToM™, and new laboratory models have been developed (e.g., Berkelman & Hollis, 2000). Another type of information is the sustained, distributed spatial pattern of local forces that generates skin deformation across the fingertip. To generate this information requires a stimulator in the form of a matrix of pins; such devices have been difficult for engineers to implement, although there are some examples (Kontarinis & Howe, 1993). Perhaps the most promising display for immediate application is one that produces vibrotactile stimulation (Cholewiak & Wollowitz, 1992). Vibratory stimulation can be produced relatively cheaply, and the frequency and amplitude can be set to optimally activate human mechanoreceptors. An example of this type of display is the Optacon. A more recent development is the vibrating mouse, although that does not present a spatial array of forces.

Haptic displays promise to be useful in many applications in which conveying a sense of physical interaction is important. Haptic feedback has already been found to be essential for performing some tasks, and it is highly useful for others (e.g., Kontarinis & Howe, 1995; Sheridan, 1992). Vibrations in particular, have been shown to improve performance in industrial teleoperation (Dennerlein, Millman, & Howe, 1997), in which a human operator controls a remote robot. Vibratory signals are effective cues to the moment of puncture in medical applications (Kontarinis & Howe, 1995), and they can aid remote manipulation by conveying the forces encountered by a robot effector (Murray, 1999). Other potential applications of haptic displays are to electronic commerce, in which the quality or aesthetic value of produces could be displayed, and haptic augmentation of visual displays of complex data sets (Infed et al., 1999).

Basic research on haptic perception is necessary to guide the development and use of haptic interfaces. For example, Klatzky, Lederman, and associates (Klatzky & Lederman, 1999b; Lederman, Klatzky, Hamilton, & Ramsay, 1999) investigated how people perceived the roughness of a surface composed of raised elements by rubbing it with a rigid probe. These circumstances were meant to model a haptic virtual display in which vibration is the cue to texture. The psychophysical function relating perceived roughness to the spacing of raised elements was quadratic in form, which contrasts with the function typically obtained for roughness perception via the bare skin. The obtained function has direct implications for efforts to simulate texture by altering vibrations to the hand, because it means that any vibratory roughness system must deal with nonmonotonic responses to changes in frequency, amplitude, or both.

SUMMARY AND FUTURE DIRECTIONS

This chapter has attempted to provide a view of the modality of touch as a sensory and cognitive system, one that shares many features of perceptual systems but is also, by virtue of underlying neurophysiology and linkage to the motor system, unique. The brief review of the neurophsiology of touch proves sufficient to show that this modality is based on a variety of receptors, responding to mechanical, thermal, and noxious stimulation. Classical psychophysics has described thresholds for the basic receptors and higher-level properties. Much of this chapter has focused on the role of touch in perceiving properties of objects and surfaces. It has emphasized that touch is particularly adapted for receiving and processing information about the material of which the world is made, more than its form. Nonetheless, form and space perception are performed through touch, and a wide variety of patterns can be discriminated and recognized. The latter part of the chapter portrayed touch as a fully cognitive system, playing a role in the direction of attention and providing a substrate for conscious and implicit memory. The chapter's conclusion, which identified a number of applications for touch, should make clear the many contexts in which research on human haptic capability is relevant to daily life.

Future research will no doubt characterize the neurophysiology of touch, particularly at cortical levels, much more fully. Comparative neurophysiological work, which relates human and nonhuman systems with respect to this modality, is also ongoing. Research on touch as a cognitive system appears to be just breaking stride; only 20 years ago the basic object-recognition abilities possible through touch had not been widely recognized. Forthcoming research is likely to emphasize even more, as did David Katz (1925/1989) in the early twentieth century, that the sense of touch is an active, richly informative, and highly useful perceptual modality. The burgeoning field of applied haptics will no doubt prove this further by bringing forth new applications to fields such as entertainment, electronic commerce, and telesurgery.

REFERENCES

Amazeen, E. L., & Turvey, M. T. (1996). Weight perception and haptic size-weight illusion are functions of the inertia tensor. *Journal of Experimental Psychology: Human Perception and Performance, 22,* 213–232.

Appelle, S., & Countryman, M. (1986). Eliminating the haptic oblique effect: Influence of scanning incongruity and prior knowledge of the standards. *Perception, 15,* 325–329.

Armstrong, L., & Marks, L. E. (1999). Haptic perception of linear extent. *Perception & Psychophysics, 61,* 1211–1226.

Auer, E. T., Bernstein, L. E., & Coulter, D. C. (1998). Temporal and spatio-temporal vibrotactile displays for voice fundamental frequency: An initial evaluation of a new vibrotactile speech perception aid with normal-hearing and hearing-impaired individuals. *Journal of the Acoustical Society of America, 104,* 2477–2489.

Ballesteros, S., Manga, D., & Reales, J. M. (1997). Haptic discrimination of bilateral symmetry in 2-dimensional and 3-dimensional unfamiliar displays. *Perception & Psychophysics, 59,* 37–50.

Ballesteros, S., Millar, S., & Reales, S. (1998). Symmetry in haptic and in visual perception. *Perception & Psychophysics, 60,* 389–404.

Barac-Cikoja, D., & Turvey, M. T. (1993). Haptically perceiving size at a distance. *Journal of Experimental Psychology: General, 122,* 347–370.

Berkelman, P. J., & Hollis, R. L. (2000). Lorentz magnetic levitation for haptic interaction: Device design, performance and integration with physical simulations. *The International Journal of Robotics Research, 19,* 644–667.

Berlá, E. P. (1982). Haptic perception of tangible graphic displays. In W. Schiff & E. Foulk (Eds.), *Tactual perception: A sourcebook* (pp. 364–386). Cambridge, England: Cambridge University Press.

Bernstein, L. E. (1992). The evaluation of tactile aids. In I. R. Summers (Ed.), *Tactile aids for the hearing impaired* (pp. 167–186). London: Whurr.

Bingham, G. P., Zaal, F., Robin, D., & Shull, J. A. (2000). Distortions in definite distance and shape perception as measured by reaching without and with haptic feedback. *Journal of Experimental Psychology: Human Perception and Performance, 26,* 1436–1460.

Bolanowski, S. J., Jr., Gescheider, G. A., Verrillo, R. T., & Checkosky, C. M. (1988). Four channels mediate the mechanical aspects of touch. *Journal of the Acoustical Society of America, 84,* 1680–1694.

van Boven, R. W., & Johnson, K. O. (1994). The limit of tactile spatial resolution in humans: Grating orientation discrimination at the lip, tongue, and finger. *Neurology, 44,* 2361–2366.

Brambring, M. (1976). The structure of haptic space in the blind and sighted. *Psychological Research, 38,* 283–302.

Bringhammar, C., Jansson, G., & Douglas, G. (1997). *The usefulness of a tactile map before and during travel without sight: A research report.* Birmingham, England: University of Birmingham, Research Centre for the Education of the Visually Handicapped.

Burtt, H. E. (1917). Tactual illusions of movement. *Journal of Experimental Psychology, 2,* 371–385.

Bushnell, E. W., & Baxt, C. (1999). Children's haptic and cross-modal recognition with familiar and unfamiliar objects. *Journal of Experimental Psychology: Human Perception and Performance, 25,* 1867–1881.

Butter, C. M., Buchtel, H. A., & Santucci, R. (1989). Spatial attentional shifts: Further evidence for the role of polysensory mechanisms using visual and tactile stimuli. *Neuropsychologia, 27,* 1231–1240.

Cashdan, S. (1968). Visual and haptic form discrimination under conditions of successive stimulation. *Journal of Experimental Psychology, 76,* 221–224.

Casla, M., Blanco, F., & Travieso, D. (1999). Haptic perception of geometric illusions by persons who are totally congenitally blind. *Journal of Visual Impairment & Blindness, 93,* 583–588.

Charpentier, A. (1891). Analyse experimentale de quelques elements de la sensation de poids [Experimental study of some aspects of weight perception]. *Archives de Physiologie Normales et Pathologiques, 3,* 122–135.

Cheng, M. F. H. (1968). Tactile-kinaesthetic perception of length. *American Journal of Psychology, 81,* 74–82.

Cholewiak, R. W., & Collins, A. A. (1990). The effects of a plastic-film covering on vibrotactile pattern perception with the Optacon. *Behavior Research Methods, Instruments, & Computers, 22,* 21–26.

Cholewiak, R. W., & Collins, A. A. (1995). Vibrotactile pattern discrimination and communality at several body sites. *Perception & Psychophysics, 57,* 724–737.

Cholewiak, R. W., & Sherrick, C. E. (1981). A computer-controlled matrix system for presentation to the skin of complex spatiotemporal patterns. *Behavior Research Methods & Instrumentation, 13,* 667–673.

Cholewiak, R. W., & Wollowitz, M. (1992). The design of vibrotactile transducers. In I. R. Summers (Ed.), *Tactile aids for the hearing impaired* (pp. 57–82). London: Whurr.

Clark, F. J., & Horch, K. W. (1986). Kinesthesia. In K. R. Boff, L. Kaufman, & J. P. Thomas (Eds.), *Handbook of perception & human performance: Vol. 1. Sensory processes and perception* (pp. 13-1–13-62). New York: Wiley.

Cole, K. J. (1991). Grasp force control in older adults. *Journal of Motor Behavior, 23,* 251–258.

Connor, C. E., Hsiao, S. S., Phillips, J. R., & Johnson, K. O. (1990). Tactile roughness: Neural codes that account for psychophysical magnitude estimates. *Journal of Neuroscience, 10,* 3823–3836.

Connor, C. E., & Johnson, K. O. (1992). Neural coding of tactile texture: Comparison of spatial and temporal mechanisms for roughness perception. *Journal of Neuroscience, 12,* 3414–3426.

Craig, J. C. (1996). Interference in identifying tactile patterns: Response competition and temporal integration. *Somatosensory and Motor Research, 13,* 199–213.

Craig, J. C., & Johnson, K. O. (2000). The two-point threshold: Not a measure of tactile spatial resolution. *Current Directions in Psychological Science, 9,* 29–32.

Craig, J. C., & Qian, X. (1997). Tactile pattern perception by two fingers: Temporal interference and response competition. *Perception & Psychophysics, 59,* 252–265.

Craig, J. C., & Rollman, G. B. (1999). Somesthesis. *Annual Review of Psychology, 50,* 305–331.

D'Angiulli, A., Kennedy, J. M., & Heller, M. A. (1998). Blind children recognizing tactile pictures respond like sighted children given guidance in exploration. *Scandinavian Journal of Psychology, 39,* 187–190.

Davidson, P. W. (1972). Haptic judgements of curvature by blind and sighted humans. *Journal of Experimental Psychology, 93,* 43–55.

Davidson, P. W., & Whitson, T. T. (1974). Haptic equivalence matching of curvature by blind and sighted humans. *Journal of Experimental Psychology, 102,* 687–690.

Dennerlein, J. T., Millman, P., & Howe, R. D. (1997). Vibrotactile feedback for industrial telemanipulators. In G. Rizzoni (Ed.), *Proceedings of the ASME Dynamic Systems and Control Division Meeting: Vol. 61. Symposium on haptic interfaces* (189–196). Dallas, TX: American Society of Mechanical Engineers.

Dresslar, F. B. (1894). Studies in the psychology of touch. *American Journal of Psychology, 6,* 313–368.

Durlach, N. I., & Mavor, A. S. (1994). *Virtual reality: Scientific and technical challenges.* Washington, DC: National Academy Press.

Easton, R. D., Srinivas, K., & Greene, A. J. (1997). Do vision and haptics share common representations? Implicit and explicit memory within and between modalities. *Journal of Experimental Psychology: Learning, Memory, and Cognition, 23,* 153–163.

Edman, P. (1992). *Tactile graphics.* New York: American Foundation for the Blind.

Ellis, R. E., & Lederman, S. J. (1998). The "golf-ball" illusion: Evidence for top-down processing in weight perception. *Perception, 27,* 193–202.

Ellis, R. R., & Lederman, S. J. (1999). The material-weight illusion revisited. *Perception & Psychophysics, 61,* 1564–1576.

Essock, E. A., Krebs, W. K., & Prather, J. R. (1997). Superior sensitivity for tactile stimuli oriented proximally-distally on the finger: Implications for mixed class 1 and class 2 anisotropies. *Journal of Experimental Psychology: Human Perception and Performance, 23,* 515–527.

Flanagan, J. R., & Bandomir, C. A. (2000). Coming to grips with weight perception: Effects of grasp configuration on perceived heaviness. *Perception & Psychophysics, 62,* 1204–1219.

Flanagan, J. R., & Wing, A. M. (1997). Effects of surface texture and grip force on the discrimination of hand-held loads. *Perception & Psychophysics, 59,* 111–118.

Flanagan, J. R., Wing, A. M., Allison, S., & Spenceley, A. (1995). Effects of surface texture on weight perception when lifting objects with a precision grip. *Perception & Psychophysics, 57,* 282–290.

Friedes, D. (1974). Human information processing and sensory modality: Cross-modal functions, information complexity, memory and deficit. *Psychological Bulletin, 81,* 284–310.

Geldard, F. A., & Sherrick, C. E. (1965). Multiple cutaneous stimulation: The discrimination of vibratory patterns. *Journal of the Acoustical Society of America, 37,* 797–801.

Gentaz, E., & Hatwell, Y. (1995). The haptic "oblique effect" in children's and adults' perception of orientation. *Perception, 24,* 631–646.

Gentaz, E., & Hatwell, Y. (1996). Role of gravitational cues in the haptic perception of orientation. *Perception & Psychophysics, 58,* 1278–1292.

Gentaz, E., & Hatwell, Y. (1998). The haptic oblique effect in the perception of rod orientation by blind adults. *Perception and Psychophysics, 60,* 157–167.

Gescheider, G. A., Bolanowski, S. J., Verrillo, R. T., Hall, K. L., & Hoffman, K. E. (1994). The effects of aging on information-processing channels in the sense of touch: I. Absolute sensitivity. *Somatosensory and Motor Research, 11,* 345–357.

Gescheider, G. A., Edwards, R. R., Lackner, E. A., Bolanowski, S. J., & Verrillo, R. T. (1996). The effects of aging on information-processing channels in the sense of touch: III. Differential sensitivity to changes in stimulus intensity. *Somatosensory and Motor Research, 13,* 73–80.

Gibson, J. J. (1962). Observations on active touch. *Psychological Review, 69,* 477–490.

Gibson, J. J. (1966). *The senses considered as perceptual systems.* Boston: Houghton Mifflin.

Golledge, R. G. (1991). Tactual strip maps as navigational aids. *Journal of Visual Impairment & Blindness, 85,* 296–301.

Goodwin, A. W., John, K. T., & Marceglia, A. H. (1991). Tactile discrimination of curvature by humans using only cutaneous information from the fingerpads. *Experimental Brain Research, 86,* 663–672.

Heath, W. (1958). *Maps and graphics for the blind: Some aspects of the discriminability of textural surfaces for use in areal differentiation.* Unpublished doctoral dissertation. University of Washington, Seattle.

Heller, M. A. (1989a). Picture and pattern perception in the sighted and the blind: The advantage of the late blind. *Perception, 18,* 379–389.

Heller, M. A. (1989b). Texture perception in sighted and blind observers. *Perception & Psychophysics, 45,* 49–54.

Heller, M. A., Calcaterra, J. A., Burson, L. L., & Green, S. L. (1997). The tactual horizontal-vertical illusion depends on radial motion of the entire arm. *Perception & Psychophysics, 59,* 1297–1311.

Heller, M. A., Calcaterra, J. A., Green, S. L., & Brown, L. (1999). Intersensory conflict between vision and touch: The response modality dominates when precise, attention-riveting judgments are required. *Perception & Psychophysics, 61,* 1384–1398.

Heller, M. A., Calcaterra, J. A., Tyler, L. A., & Burson, L. L. (1996). Production and interpretation of perspective drawings by blind and sighted people. *Perception, 25,* 321–334.

Heller, M. A., & Joyner, T. D. (1993). Mechanisms in the haptic horizontal-vertical illusion: Evidence from sighted and blind subjects. *Perception & Psychophysics, 53,* 422–428.

Heller, M. A., Kennedy, J. M., & Joyner, T. D. (1995). Production and interpretation of pictures of houses by blind people. *Perception, 24,* 1049–1058.

Hollins, M., Bensmaia, S., & Risner, R. (1998). The duplex theory of tactile texture perception. *Proceedings of the 14th Annual Mtg. Of the International Society for Psychophysics.* 115–120.

Hollins, M., & Risner, S. R. (2000). Evidence for the duplex theory of tactile texture perception. *Perception & Psychophysics, 62,* 695–716.

Horner, D. T. (1995). The effect of location on the discrimination of spatial vibrotactile patterns. *Perception & Psychophysics, 57,* 463–474.

Hsiao, S. S., Johnson, K. O., & Twombly, I. A. (1993). Roughness coding in the somatosensory system. *Acta Psychologica, 84,* 53–67.

Hsiao, S. S., Johnson, K. O., Twombly, A., & DiCarlo, J. (1996). Form processing and attention effects in the somatosensory system. In O. Franzen, R. Johansson, & L. Terenius, (Eds.), *Somesthesis and the neurobiology of the somatosensory cortex* (pp. 229–247). Basel, Switzerland: Birkhauser.

Hunter, I. M. L. (1954). Tactile-kinaesthetic perception of straightness in blind and sighted humans. *Quarterly Journal of Experimental Psychology, 6,* 149–154.

Infed, F., Brown, S. V., Lee, C. D., Lawrence, D. A., Dougherty, A. M., & Pao, L. Y. (1999). Combined visual/haptic rendering modes for scientific visualization. In N. Olgac (Ed.), *Proceedings of the ASME Dynamic Systems and Control Division Meeting, Nashville, TN* (Vol. 67, 93–100). NY: ASME.

Jansson, G. (1972). Symbols for tactile maps. In B. Lindquist & N. Trowald (Eds.), *European conference on educational research for the visually handicapped* (Rep. No. 31, pp. 66–77). Uppsala, Sweden: Larahogskolan i Uppsala, Pedagogiska institutionen.

Johansson, R. S., Landstrom, U., & Lundstrom, R. (1982). Responses of mechanoreceptive afferent units in the glabrous skin of the human hand to sinusoidal skin displacement. *Brain Research, 244,* 17–25.

Johansson, R. S., & Vallbo, A. B. (1983). Tactile sensory coding in the glabrous skin of the human hand. *Trends in Neuroscience, 6,* 27–32.

Johansson, R. S., & Westling, G. (1990). Tactile afferent signals in control of precision grip. In M. Jeannerod (Ed.), *Attention and performance XIII* (pp. 677–713). Mahwah, NJ: Erlbaum.

Johnson, K. O., & Lamb, G. D. (1981). Neural mechanisms of spatial tactile discrimination: Neural patterns evoked by Braille-like dot patterns in the monkey. *Journal of Physiology, 310,* 117–144.

Johnson, K. O., & Phillips, J. R. (1981). Tactile spatial resolution: I. Two-point discrimination, gap detection, grating resolution, and letter recognition. *Journal of Neurophysiology, 46,* 1177–1191.

Jones, L. A. (1999). Proprioception. In H. Choen (Ed.), *Neuroscience for rehabilitation* (2nd. ed., pp. 111–130). NY: Lippincott, Williams & Wilkins.

Kandel, E. R., Schwartz, J. H., & Jessell, T. M. (1991). *Principles of neural science* (3rd ed.). Norwalk, CT: Appleton and Lange.

Katz, D. (1989). The world of touch. (L. Krueger, Trans.). Mahwah, NJ: Erlbaum. (Original work published 1925)

Kay, B. A., Hogan, N., & Fasse, E. D. (1996). *The structure of haptic perceptual space is a function of the properties of the arm: One more time on the radial-tangential illusion.* Unpublished manuscript, Massachusetts Institute of Technology, Cambridge, Department of Mechanical Engineering.

Kennedy, J. M. (1997). How the blind draw. *Scientific American, 276,* 76–81.

Klatzky, R. L., & Lederman, S. J. (1993). Toward a computational model of constraint-driven exploration and haptic object identification. *Perception, 22,* 597–621.

Klatzky, R. L., & Lederman, S. J. (1995). Identifying objects from a haptic glance. *Perception & Psychophysics, 57,* 1111–1123.

Klatzky, R. L., & Lederman, S. J. (1999a). The haptic glance: A route to rapid object identification and manipulation. In D. Gopher & A. Koriat (Eds.), *Attention and performance XVII: Cognitive regulation of performance: Interaction of theory and application* (pp. 165–196). Mahwah, NJ: Erlbaum.

Klatzky, R. L., & Lederman, S. J. (1999b). Tactile roughness perception with a rigid link interposed between skin and surface. *Perception & Psychophysics, 61,* 591–607.

Klatzky, R. L., & Lederman, S. J. (2000). L'identification haptique des objets significatifs [The haptic identification of everyday life objects]. In Y. Hatwell, A. Streri, & E. Gentaz (Eds.), *Toucher pour connacetre: Psychologie cognitive de la perception tactile manuelle* [Touching for Knowing: Cognitive psychology of tactile manual perception] (pp. 109–128). Paris: Presses Universitaires de France.

Klatzky, R. L., Lederman, S. J., & Balakrishnan, J. D. (1991). Task-driven extraction of object contour by human haptics: I. *Robotica, 9,* 43–51.

Klatzky, R. L., Lederman, S. J., & Matula, D. E. (1993). Haptic exploration in the presence of vision. *Journal of Experimental Psychology: Human Perception and Performance, 19,* 726–743.

Klatzky, R. L., Lederman, S. J., & Metzger, V. (1985). Identifying objects by touch: An "expert system." *Perception & Psychophysics, 37,* 299–302.

Klatzky, R. L., Lederman, S. J., & Reed, C. L. (1987). There's more to touch than meets the eye: The salience of object attributes for haptics with and without vision. *Journal of Experimental Psychology: General, 116,* 356–369.

Klatzky, R. L., Lederman, S. J., & Reed, C. L. (1989). Haptic integration of object properties: Texture, hardness, and planar contour. *Journal of Experimental Psychology: Human Perception and Performance, 15,* 45–57.

Klatzky, R. L., Loomis, J. M., Lederman, S. J., Wake, H., & Fujita, N. (1993). Haptic identification of objects and their depictions. *Perception & Psychophysics, 54,* 170–178.

Kontarinis, D. A., & Howe, R. D. (1993). Tactile display of contact shape in dextrous manipulation. In H. Kazerooni, B. D. Adelstein, & J. E. Colgate (Eds.), *Proceedings of ASME Symposium on Haptic Interfaces for Virtual Environments and Teleoperator Systems, New Orleans, LA, 49,* 81–88.

Kontarinis, D. A., & Howe, R. D. (1995). Tactile display of vibratory information in teleoperation and virtual environments. *Presence, 4,* 387–402.

Lakatos, S., & Marks, L. E. (1999). Haptic form perception: Relative salience of local and global features. *Perception & Psychophysics, 61,* 895–908.

Lambert, L., & Lederman, S. (1989). An evaluation of the legibility and meaningfulness of potential map symbols. *Journal of Visual Impairment & Blindness, 83,* 397–403.

LaMotte, R. H., & Srinivasan, M. A. (1991). Surface microgeometry: Tactile perception and neural encoding. In O. Franzen & J. Westman (Eds.), *Information processing in the somatosensory system* (pp. 49–58). London: Macmillan Press.

LaMotte, R. H., & Srinivasan, M. A. (1993). Responses of cutaneous mechanoreceptors to the shape of objects applied to the primate fingerpad. *Acta Psychologica, 84,* 41–51.

Lechelt, E. C., Eliuk, J., & Tanne, G. (1976). Perceptual orientational asymmetries: A comparison of visual and haptic space. *Perception & Psychophysics, 20,* 463–469.

Lederman, S. J. (1974). Tactile roughness of grooved surfaces: The touching process and effects of macro- and microsurface structure. *Perception & Psychophysics, 16,* 385–395.

Lederman, S. J. (1983). Tactual roughness perception: Spatial and temporal determinants. *Canadian Journal of Psychology, 37,* 498–511.

Lederman, S. J., & Campbell, J. I. (1982). Tangible graphs for the blind. *Human Factors, 24,* 85–100.

Lederman, S. J., & Klatzky, R. L. (1987). Hand movements: A window into haptic object recognition. *Cognitive Psychology, 19,* 342–368.

Lederman, S. J., & Klatzky, R. L. (1990). Haptic object classification of common objects: Knowledge driven exploration. *Cognitive Psychology, 22,* 421–459.

Lederman, S. J., & Klatzky, R. L. (1997). Relative availability of surface and object properties during early haptic processing. *Journal of Experimental Psychology: Human Perception and Performance, 23,* 1680–1707.

Lederman, S. J., Klatzky, R. L., & Barber, P. (1985). Spatial and movement-based heuristics for encoding pattern information through touch. *Journal of Experimental Psychology: General, 114,* 33–49.

Lederman, S. J., Klatzky, R. L., Chataway, C., & Summers, C. D. (1990). Visual mediation and the haptic recognition of two-dimensional pictures of common objects. *Perception & Psychophysics, 47,* 54–64.

Lederman, S. J., Klatzky, R. L., Collins, A., & Wardell, J. (1987). Exploring environments by hand or foot: Time-based heuristics for encoding distance in movement space, *Journal of Experimental Psychology: Learning, Memory and Cognition, 13,* 606–614.

Lederman, S. J., Klatzky, R. L., Hamilton, C. L., & Ramsay, G. I. (1999). Perceiving roughness via a rigid stylus: Psychophysical effects of exploration speed and mode of touch. *Haptics-e, The electronic journal of haptics Research (www.haptics-e.org), 1*(1) October 8.

Lederman, S. J., Klatzky, R. L., & Reed, C. L. (1993). Constraints on haptic integration of spatially shared object dimensions. *Perception, 22,* 723–743.

Lederman, S. J., Loomis, J. M., & Williams, D. A. (1982). The role of vibration in the tactual perception of roughness. *Perception & Psychophysics, 32,* 109–116.

Lederman, W., Summers, C., & Klatzky, R. (1996). Cognitive salience of haptic object properties: Role of modality-encoding bias. *Perception, 25,* 983–998.

Lederman, S. J., & Taylor, M. M. (1972). Fingertip force, surface geometry and the perception of roughness by active touch. *Perception & Psychophysics, 12,* 401–408.

Lederman, S. J., Thorne, G., & Jones, B. (1986). The perception of texture by vision and touch: Multidimensionality and intersensory integration. *Journal of Experimental Psychology: Human Perception & Performance, 12,* 169–180.

Loomis, J. M. (1979). An investigation of tactile hyperacuity. *Sensory Processes, 3,* 289–302.

Loomis, J. M. (1990). A model of character recognition and legibility. *Journal of Experimental Psychology: Human Perception and Performance, 16,* 106–120.

Loomis, J. M., Klatzky, R. L., Lederman, S. J. (1991). Similarity of tactual and visual picture recognition with limited field of view. *Perception, 20,* 167–177.

Loomis, J. M., & Lederman, S. J. (1986). Tactual perception. In K. R. Boff, L. Kaufman, & J. P. Thomas (Eds.), *Handbook of perception and human performances Vol. 2. Cognitive processes and performance* (pp. 31/1–31/41). New York: Wiley.

Maculuso, E., Frith, C. D., & Driver, J. (2000). Modulation of human visual cortex by crossmodal spatial attention. *Science, 289,* 1206.

Marchetti, F. M., & Lederman, S. J. (1983). The haptic radial-tangential effect: Two tests of Wong's "moments of inertia" hypothesis. *Bulletin of the Psychonomic Society, 21,* 43–46.

Marr, D. (1982). *Vision.* San Francisco: W. H. Freeman.

Millar, S. (1975a). Effects of tactual and phonological similarity on the recall of Braille letters by blind children. *British Journal of Psychology, 66,* 193–201.

Millar, S. (1975b). Spatial memory by blind and sighted children. *British Journal of Psychology, 66,* 449–459.

Millar, S. (1997). *Reading by touch.* London: Routledge.

Millar, S. (1999). Memory in touch. *Psicothema, 11,* 747–767.

Millar, S. (in press). Reading by touch in blind children and adults. In P. E. Bryant and T. Nunes (Eds.), *Handbook of children's literacy.* Dotrecht, Netherlands: Kluwer.

Millar, S., & Al-Attar, Z. (2000). Vertical and bisection bias in active touch. *Perception, 29,* 481–500.

Miller, G. A., & Nicely, P. E. (1955). An analysis of perceptual confusions among English consonants. *Journal of the Acoustical Society of America, 27,* 338–352.

Misceo, G. F., Hershberger, W. A., & Mancini, R. L. (1999). Haptic estimates of discordant visual-haptic size vary developmentally. *Perception & Psychophysics, 61,* 608–614.

MoBIC Consortium (1997). *Mobility of blind and elderly people interacting with computers. Final report.* London: Royal National Society of the Blind.

Murray, A. M. (1999). *Engineering design and psychophysical evaluation of a wearable vibrotactile display.* Unpublished doctoral dissertation, Pittsburgh, PA: Carnegie Mellon University.

Newell, F. N., Ernst, M. O., Tian, B. S., & Bülthoff, H. H. (2001). Viewpoint dependence in visual and haptic object recognition. *Psychological Science, 12,* 37–42.

Nolan, C., & Morris, J. (1971). *Improvement of tactual symbols for blind children: Final report.* Louisville, KY: American Printing House for the Blind.

Pagano, C. C., & Turvey, M. T. (1992). Eigenvectors of the inertia tensor and perceiving the orientation of a hand-held object by dynamic touch. *Perception & Psychophysics, 52,* 617–624.

Pagano, C. C., & Turvey, M. T. (1993). Perceiving by dynamic touch the distances reachable with irregular objects. *Ecological Psychology, 5,* 125–151.

Parkes, D. (1988). "Nomad": An audio-tactile tool for the acquisition, use and management of spatially distributed information by visually impaired people. In A. F. Tatham & A. G. Dodds (Eds.), *Proceedings of the second international symposium on maps and graphics for visually impaired people* (pp. 24–29). London: International Cartographic Association Commission VII (Tactile and Low Vision Mapping) and Royal National Institute for the Blind.

Pavani, F., Spence, C., & Driver, J. (2000). Visual capture of touch: Out-of-the-body experiences with rubber gloves. *Psychological Science, 11,* 353–359.

Phillips, J. R., & Johnson, K. O. (1981). Tactile spatial resolution: II. Neural representation of bars, edges, and gratings in monkey afferents. *Journal of Neurophysiology, 46,* 1192–1203.

Pont, S. C. (1997). *Haptic curvature comparison.* Utrecht, The Netherlands: Helmholtz Instituut.

Pont, S. C., Kappers, A. M. L., & Koenderink, J. J. (1997). Haptic curvature discrimination at several regions of the hand. *Perception & Psychophysics, 59,* 1225–1240.

Pont, S. C., Kappers, A. M. L., & Koenderink, J. J. (1998). Anisotropy in haptic curvature and shape perception. *Perception, 27,* 573–589.

Pont, S. C., Kappers, A. M. L., & Koenderink, J. J. (1999). Similar mechanisms underlie curvature comparison by static and dynamic touch. *Perception and Psychophysics, 61,* 874–894.

Posner, M. I. (1978). *Chronometric explorations of mind.* Mahwah, NJ: Erlbaum.

Quilliam, T. A. (1978). The structure of finger print skin. In G. Gordon (Ed.), *Active touch: The mechanism of recognition of objects by manipulation* (pp. 1–15). Oxford: Pergamon.

Reales, J. M., & Ballesteros, S. (1999). Implicit and explicit memory for visual and haptic objects: Cross-modal priming depends on structural descriptions. *Journal of Experimental Psychology: Learning, Memory, and Cognition, 25,* 644–663.

Reed, C. L., Lederman, S. J., & Klatzky, R. L. (1990). Haptic integration of planar size with hardness, texture and plan contour. *Canadian Journal of Psychology, 44,* 522–545.

Reed, C. M., Rabinowitz, W. M., Durlach, N. I., Braida, L. D., Conway-Fithian, S., & Schultz, M. C. (1985). Research on the Tadoma method of speech communication. *Journal of the Acoustical Society of America, 77,* 247–257.

Rinkenauer, G., Mattes, S., & Ulrich, R. (1999). The surface-weight illusion: on the contribution of grip force to perceived heaviness. *Perception & Psychophysics, 61,* 23–30.

Rock, I., & Harris, C. S. (1967). Vision and touch. *Scientific American, 216,* 96–104.

Rock, I., & Victor, J. (1964). Vision and touch: An experimentally created conflict between the two senses. *Science, 143,* 594–596.

Rollman, G. B. (1991). Pain responsiveness. In M. A. Heller & W. Schiff (Eds.), *The psychology of touch* (pp. 91–114). Mahwah, NJ: Erlbaum.

Sathian, K., Goodwin, A. W., John, K. T., & Darian-Smith, I. (1989). Perceived roughness of a grating: Correlation with responses of mechanoreceptive afferents innervating the monkey's fingerpad. *Journal of Neuroscience, 9,* 1273–1279.

Schiff, W., Kaufer, L., & Mosak, S. (1966). Informative tactile stimuli in the perception of direction. *Perceptual and Motor Skill, 23,* 1315–1335.

Schwarzer, G., Kuefer, I., & Wilkening, F. (1999). Learning categories by touch: On the development of holistic and analytic processing. *Memory & Cognition, 27,* 868–877.

Sheridan, T. B. (1992). *Telerobotics, automation, and human supervisory control.* Cambridge: MIT Press.

Sherrick, C. E., & Cholewiak, R. W. (1986). Cutaneous sensitivity. In K. Boff, L. Kaufman, & J. Thomas (Eds.), *Handbook of perception and human performance* (Vol. 1, pp. 1–70). New York: Wiley.

Shimizu, Y., Saida, S., & Shimura, H. (1993). Tactile pattern recognition by graphic display: Importance of 3-D information for haptic perception of familiar objects. *Perception & Psychophysics, 53,* 43–48.

Sinclair, R. J., & Burton, H. (1991). Neuronal activity in the primary somatosensory cortex in monkeys (*Macaca mulatta*) during active touch of gratings. *Journal of Neurophysiology, 70,* 331–350.

Solomon, H. Y., & Turvey, M. T. (1988). Haptically perceiving the distances reachable with hand-held objects. *Journal of Experimental Psychology: Human Perception and Performance, 14,* 404–427.

Spence, C., Pavani, F., & Driver, J. (2000). Crossmodal links between vision and touch in covert endogenous spatial attention. *Journal of Experimental Psychology: Human Perception and Performance, 26,* 1298–1319.

Srinivas, K., Greene, A. J., & Easton, R. D. (1997a). Implicit and explicit memory for haptically experienced two-dimensional patterns. *Psychological Science, 8,* 243–246.

Srinivas, K., Greene, A. J., & Easton, R. D. (1997b). Visual and tactile memory for 2-D patterns: Effects of changes in size and left-right orientation. *Psychonomic Bulletin & Review, 4,* 535–540.

Srinivasan, M. A., & LaMotte, R. H. (1991). Encoding of shape in the responses of cutaneous mechanoreceptors. In O. Franzen & J. Westman (Eds.), *Information processing in the somatosensory system* (pp. 59–69). London: Macmillan.

Srinivasan, M. A., & LaMotte, R. H. (1995). Tactual discrimination of softness. *Journal of Neurophysiology, 73,* 88–101.

Stevens, J. C. (1991). Thermal sensibility. In M. A. Heller & W. Schiff (Eds.), *The psychology of touch* (pp. 61–90). Mahwah, NJ: Erlbaum.

Stevens, J. C., & Patterson, M. Q. (1995). Dimensions of spatial acuity in the touch sense: Changes over the life span. *Somatosensory and Motor Research, 12,* 29–47.

Stevens, J. C., & Rubin, L. L. (1970). Psychophysical scales of apparent heaviness and the size-weight illusion. *Perception & Psychophysics, 8,* 240–244.

Stevens, S. S., & Harris, J. R. (1962). The scaling of subjective roughness and smoothness. *Journal of Experimental Psychology: General, 64,* 489–494.

Tan, H. Z., Durlach, N. I., Reed, C. M., & Rabinowitz, W. M. (1999). Information transmission with a multifinger tactual display. *Perception & Psychophysics, 61,* 993–1008.

Taylor, M. M., & Lederman, S. J. (1975). Tactile roughness of grooved surfaces: A model and the effect of friction. *Perception & Psychophysics, 17,* 23–26.

Treisman, A., & Gormican, S. (1988). Feature analysis in early vision: Evidence from search assymmetries. *Psychological Review, 95,* 15–48.

Turvey, M. T., (1996). Dynamic touch. *American Psychologist, 51,* 1134–1152.

Turvey, M. T., Burton, G., Amazeen, E. L., Butwill, M., & Carello, C. (1998). Perceiving the width and height of a hand-held object by dynamic touch. *Journal of Experimental Psychology: Human Perception and Performance, 24,* 35–48.

Turvey, M. T., & Carello, C. (1995). Dynamic touch. In W. Epstein & S. Rogers (Eds.), *Handbook of perception and cognition: Vol. 5. Perception of space and motion* (pp. 401–490). San Diego, CA: Academic Press.

Verrillo, R. T. (1963). Effect of contactor area on the vibrotactile threshold. *Journal of the Acoustical Society of America, 35,* 1962–1971.

Verrillo, R. T. (1993). The effects of aging on the sense of touch. In R. T. Verrillo (Ed.), *Sensory research: Multimodal perspectives* (pp. 285–298). Mahwah, NJ: Erlbaum.

Vierck, C. J. (1979). Comparisons of punctate, edge and surface stimulation of peripheral, slowly-adapting, cutaneous, afferent units of cats. *Brain Research, 175,* 155–159.

Vogels, I. M. L. C., Kappers, A. M. L., & Koenderink, J. J. (1996). Haptic after-effect of curved surfaces. *Perception, 25,* 109–119.

Watkins, M. J., & Watkins, O. C. (1974). A tactile suffix effect. *Memory & Cognition, 5,* 529–534.

Weber, E. H. (1978). *The sense of touch* (H. E. Ross, Ed. & Trans.). London: Academic Press. (Original work published 1834)

Weinstein, S. (1968). Intensive and extensive aspects of tactile sensitivity as a function of body part, sex, and laterality. In D. R. Kenshalo (Ed.), *The skin senses* (pp. 195–222). Springfield, IL: Thomas.

Welch, R. B. & Warren, D. H. (1980). Immediate perceptual response to intersensory discordance. *Psychological Bulletin, 88,* 638–667.

Wiedel, J. (Ed.). (1983). *Proceedings of the first international conference on maps and graphics for the visually impaired.* Washington, DC: Association of American Geographers.

Wilska, A. (1954). On the vibrational sensitivity in different regions of the body surface. *Acta Psychologica Scandinavia, 31,* 285–289.

Wolfe, H. K. (1898). Some effects of size on judgments of weight. *Psychological Review, 5,* 25–54.

Wong, T. S. (1977). Dynamic properties of radial and tangential movements as determinants of the haptic horizontal-vertical illusion with an L figure. *Journal of Experimental Psychology: Human Perception and Performance, 3,* 151–164.

Yoshioka, T., Gibb, B., Dorsch, A. K., Hsiao, S. S., & Johnson, K. O. (2001). Neural coding mechanisms underlying perceived roughness of finely textured surfaces. *Journal of Neuroscience, 21,* 6905–6916.

PART THREE

PERCEPTUAL PROCESSES

CHAPTER 7

Visual Perception of Objects

STEPHEN E. PALMER

Visual perception begins when light entering the eye activates millions of retinal receptors. The initial sensory state of the organism at a given moment can therefore be completely described by the neural activity of each receptor. Perhaps the most astonishing thing about this description of sensory information, aside from its sheer complexity, is how enormously it differs from the nature of the visual experiences that arise from it. Instead of millions of independent points of color, we perceive a visual world structured into complex, meaningful objects and events, consisting of people, houses, trees, and cars. This transformation from receptor activity to highly structured perceptions of meaningful objects, relations, and events is the subject matter of this chapter. It is divided into two related subtopics: how people organize visual input into perceptual objects and how people identify these objects as instances of known, meaningful categories such as people, houses, trees, and cars.

This chapter describes perceptual organization and object identification in the visual modality only. This is not because either organization or identification is absent in other sensory modes—quite the contrary. But the specific stimulus information and processing mechanisms are different enough across modalities that it makes more sense to discuss them separately. Some of the issues covered in this chapter for vision are therefore also discussed in the chapter by Yost for audition, in the chapter by Fowler for speech perception, and in the chapter by Klatzky and Lederman for touch (all in this volume). Indeed, the present chapter concentrates mainly on organization and identification in static scenes because dynamic issues are considered in the chapter by Proffitt and Caudek in this volume for visual perception of depth and events.

PERCEPTUAL ORGANIZATION

The term *perceptual organization* refers somewhat ambiguously both to the structure of experiences based on sensory activity and to the underlying processes that produce that perceived structure. The importance and difficulty of achieving useful organization in the visual modality can perhaps be most easily appreciated by considering the output of the retinal mosaic simply as a numerical array, in which each number represents the neural response of a single receptor. The main organizational problem faced by the visual nervous system is to determine object *structure:* what parts of this array go together, so to speak, in the sense of corresponding to the same objects, parts, or groups of objects in the environment. This way of stating the problem implies that much of perceptual organization can be understood as the process by which a *part-whole hierarchy* is constructed for an image (Palmer, in press-b). There is more to perceptual organization than just part-whole structure, but it seems to be the single most central issue.

The first problem, therefore, is to understand what part-whole structure people perceive in a given scene and how it might be characterized. Logically, there are limitless possible organizations for any particular image, only one (or a few) of which people actually perceive. A possible part-whole structure for the leopard image in Figure 7.1 (A) is given in Figure 7.1 (C). It is represented as a hierarchical graph in which each node stands for a perceptual unit or element, and the various labels refer to the image regions distinguished in Figure 7.1 (B). The top (or root) node represents the entire image. The scene is then divided into the leopard, the branch, and the background sky. The leopard is itself a complex perceptual object consisting of its own hierarchy of parts: head, body, tail, legs, and so forth. The branch also has parts consisting of its various segments. The sky is articulated into different regions in the image, but it is perceptually uniform because it is completed behind the leopard and branches. The bottom (or terminal) nodes of the graph represent the millions of individual receptors whose outputs define this particular optical image.

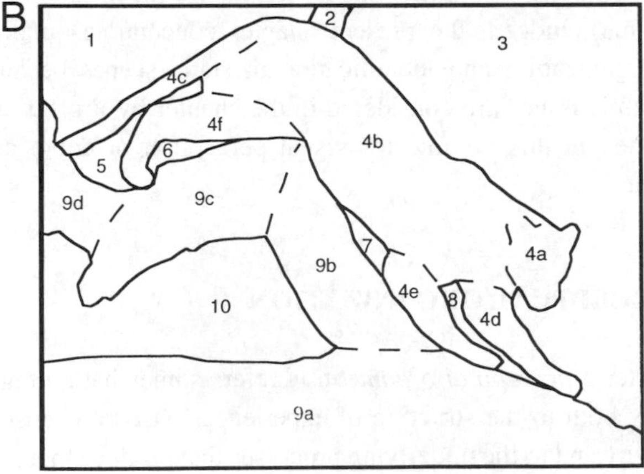

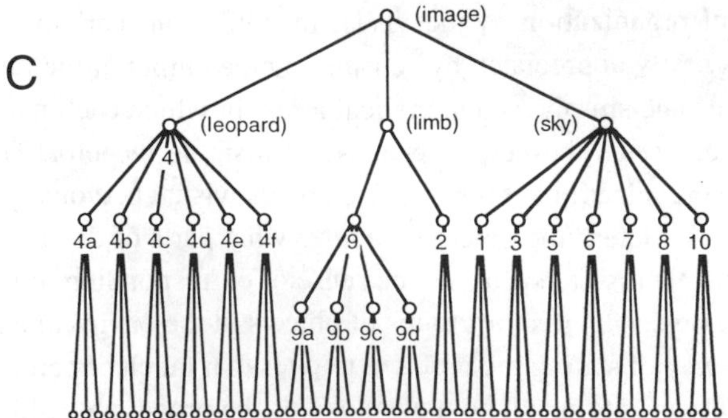

Figure 7.1 A natural image (A), its decomposition into uniform connected regions (B), and a hierarchical graph of its part-whole structure (C).
Source: From Palmer, 2002.

The second problem is how such a part-whole hierarchy might be determined by the visual system. This problem, in turn, has at least three conceptual parts. One is to understand the nature of the stimulus information that the visual system uses to organize images. This includes not only specifying the crucial stimulus variables, but also determining their ecological significance: why they are relevant to perceiving part-whole structure. It corresponds to what Marr (1982) called a "computational" analysis. The second problem is to specify the processing operations involved in extracting this information: how a particular organization is computed from an image via representations and processes. It corresponds to what Marr called an "algorithmic" analysis. The third is to determine what physiological mechanisms perform these operations in the visual nervous system. It corresponds to what Marr called an "implementational" analysis. As we shall see, we currently know more about the computational level of perceptual organization than about the algorithmic level, and almost nothing yet about the neural implementation.

Perceptual Grouping

The visual phenomenon most closely associated historically with the concept of perceptual organization is *grouping:* the fact that observers perceive some elements of the visual field as "going together" more strongly than others. Indeed, perceptual grouping and perceptual organization are sometimes presented as though they were synonymous. They are not. Grouping is one particular kind of organizational phenomenon, albeit a very important one.

Principles of Grouping

The Gestalt psychologist Max Wertheimer first posed the problem of perceptual organization in his groundbreaking 1923 paper. He then attempted a solution at what would now be called the computational level by asking what stimulus

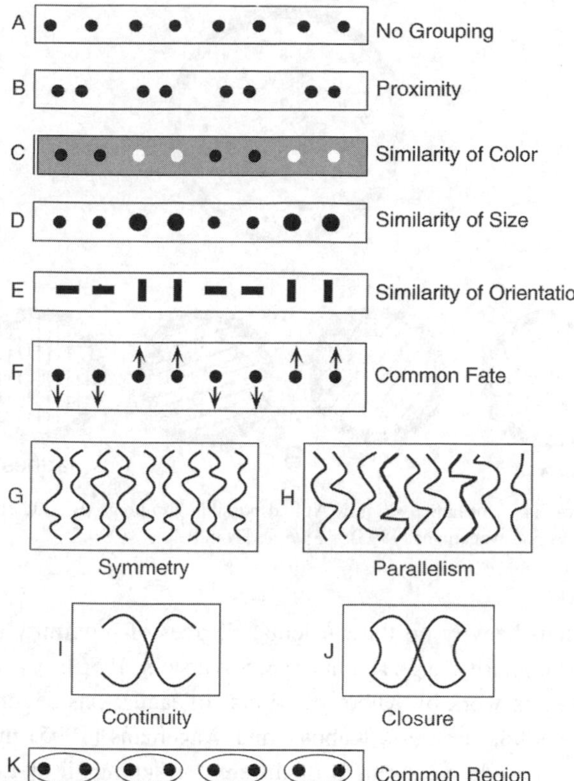

Figure 7.2 Classical principles of grouping: no grouping (A) versus grouping by proximity (B), similarity of color (C), similarity of size (D), similarity of orientation (E), common fate (F), symmetry (G), parallelism (H), continuity (I), closure (J), and common region (K).

factors influence perceived grouping of discrete elements. He first demonstrated that equally spaced dots do not group together into larger perceptual units, except the entire line (Figure 7.2; A). He then noted that when he altered the spacing between adjacent dots so that some dots were closer than others, the closer ones grouped together strongly into pairs (Figure 7.2; B). This factor of relative distance, which Wertheimer called *proximity,* was the first of his famous *laws* or (more accurately) *principles of grouping*.

Wertheimer went on to illustrate other grouping principles, several of which are portrayed in Figure 7.2. Parts C, D, and E demonstrate different versions of the general principle of *similarity:* All else being equal, the most similar elements (in color, size, and orientation for these examples) tend to be grouped together. Another powerful grouping factor is *common fate:* All else being equal, elements that move in the same way tend to be grouped together. Notice that both common fate and proximity can actually be considered special cases of similarity grouping in which the relevant properties are similarity of velocity and position, respectively. Further factors that influence perceptual grouping of more complex elements, such as lines and curves, include *symmetry* (Figure 7.2; G), *parallelism* (Figure 7.2; H), and *continuity* or *good continuation* (Figure 7.2; I). Continuity is important in Figure 7.2 (I) because observers usually perceive it as containing two continuous intersecting lines rather than as two angles whose vertices meet at a point. Figure 7.2 (J) illustrates the further factor of *closure:* All else being equal, elements that form a closed figure tend to be grouped together. Note that this display shows that closure can overcome continuity because the very same elements that were organized as two intersecting lines in part I are organized as two angles meeting at a point in part J.

Recently, two new grouping factors have been suggested: *common region* (Palmer, 1992) and *synchrony* (Palmer & Levitin, 2002). Common region refers to the fact that, all else being equal, elements that are located within the same closed region of space tend to be grouped together. Figure 7.2 (K) shows an example analogous to Wertheimer's classic demonstrations (Figures 7.2; B–F): Otherwise equivalent, equally spaced dots are strongly organized into pairs when two adjacent elements are enclosed within the same surrounding contour.

The principle of synchrony states that, all else being equal, visual events that occur at the same time tend to be perceived as grouped (Palmer & Levitin, 2002). Figure 7.3 depicts an example similar to those in Figure 7.2 (B–F). Each element in an equally spaced row of dots flickers alternately between dark and light. The arrows indicate that half the circles change color at one time and the other half at a different time. When the alternation rate is about 5–25 changes per second or fewer, observers see the dots as strongly grouped into pairs based on the synchrony of these changes. At much faster rates, there is no grouping among what appear to be chaotically flickering dots. At much slower rates, there is momentary grouping into pairs when the changes occur, but the grouping dissipates during the unchanging interval between

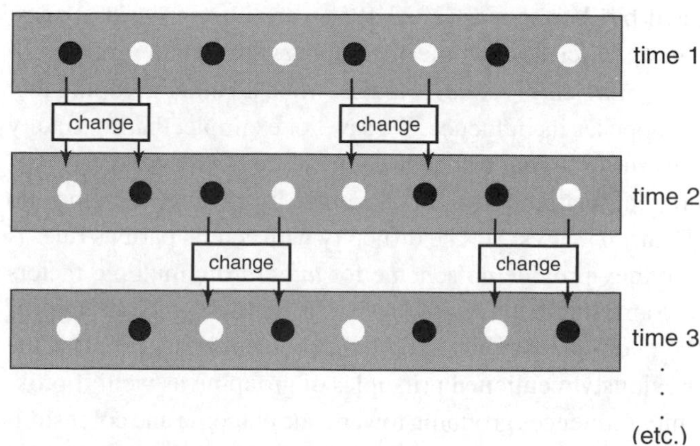

Figure 7.3 Grouping by synchrony of changes.

them. Synchrony is related to the classical principle of common fate in the sense that it is a dynamic factor, but, as this example shows, the "fate" of the elements does not have to be common: Some dots get brighter and others get dimmer. Synchrony grouping can even occur when the elements change along different dimensions, some changing brightness, others changing size, and still others changing orientation.

One might think that grouping principles are mere textbook curiosities only distantly related to anything that occurs in normal perception. On the contrary, they pervade virtually all perceptual experiences because they determine the objects and parts we perceive in the environment. Dramatic examples of perceptual organization going wrong can be observed in natural camouflage. The leopard in Figure 7.1 (A) is not camouflaged against the uniform sky, but if it were seen against a mottled, leafy backdrop, it would be very difficult to see—until it moved. Even perfect static camouflage is undone by the principle of common fate. The common motion of its markings and contours against the stationary background causes them to be strongly grouped together, providing an observer with enough information to perceive it as a distinct object against its unmoving background.

Successful camouflage also reveals the ecological rationale for the principles of grouping: finding objects. Camouflage results when the same grouping processes that would normally make an organism stand out from its environment as a separate object cause it to be grouped with its surroundings instead. This results primarily from similarity grouping of various forms, when the color, texture, size, and shape of the organism are similar enough to those of the objects in its environment to be misgrouped.

Integrating Multiple Principles of Grouping

The demonstrations of continuity and closure in Figure 7.2 (I and J) illustrate that grouping principles, as formulated by Wertheimer (1923/1950), are *ceteris paribus* rules: They predict the outcome of grouping with certainty only *when everything else is equal*—that is, when no other grouping factor opposes its influence. We saw, for example, that continuity governs grouping when the elements do not form a closed figure, but continuity can be overcome by closure when they do (Figure 7.2; I vs. J). The difficulty with ceteris paribus rules is that they provide no scheme for *integrating* multiple factors into an overall outcome—that is, for predicting the strength of their combined effects. The same problem arises for all of the previously mentioned principles of grouping as well. If proximity influences grouping toward one outcome and color similarity toward another, which grouping will be perceived

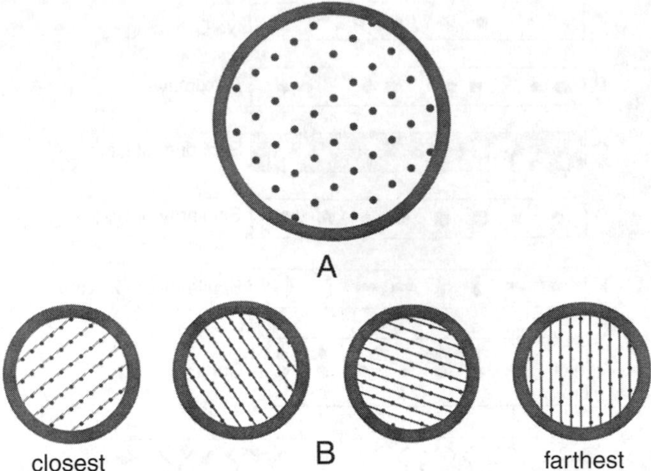

Figure 7.4 Dot lattice stimuli (A) and possible groupings (B) studied by Kubovy and Wagemans (1995). *Source:* From Palmer, 1999.

depends heavily on the particular degrees of proximity and color similarity (e.g., Hochberg & Silverstein, 1956).

Recent work by Kubovy and his colleagues has begun to address this problem. Kubovy and Wagemans (1995) measured the relative strength of different groupings in dot lattices (Figure 7.4; A) by determining the probability with which subjects reported seeing them organized into lines in each of the four orientations indicated in Figure 7.4 (B). After seeing a given lattice for 300 ms, subjects indicated which of the four organizations they perceived so that, over many trials, the probability of perceiving each grouping could be estimated. Consistent with the Gestalt principle of proximity, their results showed that the most likely organization is the one in which the dots are closest together, with other organizations being less likely as the spacing between the dots increased.

More precisely, Kubovy and Wagemans (1995) found that their data were well fit by a mathematical model in which the attraction between dots decreases exponentially as a function of distance:

$$f(v) = e^{-\alpha(v/a-1)},$$

where $f(v)$ is the attraction between two elements in the lattice as a function of the distance, v, between them, α is a scaling constant, and a is shortest distance between any pair of elements. Further experiments using lattices in which the dots differed in color similarity as well as proximity showed that the rule by which multiple grouping factors combine is multiplicative (see Kubovy & Gepstein, 2000). This finding begins to specify general laws by which multiple factors can be integrated into a combined result.

Is Grouping an Early or Late Process?

If perceptual organization is to be understood as the result of computations, the question of where grouping occurs in the stream of visual processing is important. Is it an early process that works at the level of two-dimensional image structure or does it work later, after depth information has been extracted and perceptual constancy has been achieved? (Perceptual constancy refers to the ability to perceive the unchanging properties of distal environmental objects despite variation in the proximal retinal images caused by differences in viewing conditions; see Chapter 4.) Wertheimer (1923) discussed grouping as though it occurred at a low level, presumably corresponding to what is now called image-based processing (see Palmer, 1999). The view generally held since Wertheimer's seminal paper has been that organization must occur early to provide virtually all higher level perceptual processes with discrete units as input (e.g., Marr, 1982; Neisser, 1967).

Rock and Brosgole (1964) reported evidence against the early-only view of grouping, however. They examined whether the relevant distances for grouping by proximity are defined in the two-dimensional image plane or in perceived three-dimensional space. They showed observers a two-dimensional rectangular array of luminous beads in a dark room either in the frontal plane (perpendicular to the line of sight) or slanted in depth, so that the horizontal dimension was foreshortened to a degree that depended on the angle of slant. The beads were actually closer together vertically, so that when they were viewed in the frontal plane, observers saw them grouped into vertical columns rather than horizontal rows.

The crucial question was what would happen when the same lattice of beads was presented to the observer slanted in depth so that the beads were closer together horizontally when measured in the retinal image, even though they are still closer together vertically when measured in the three-dimensional environment. When observers viewed this slanted display with just one eye, so that binocular depth information was not available, they reported that the beads were organized into rows. But when they perceived the slant of the lattice in depth by viewing the same display binocularly, their reports reversed: They now reported seeing the slanted array of beads organized into vertical columns. This finding thus supports the hypothesis that final grouping occurs after stereoscopic depth perception.

Rock, Nijhawan, Palmer, and Tudor (1992) addressed a similar issue in lightness perception. Their results showed that grouping followed the predictions of a late (postconstancy) grouping hypothesis: Similarity grouping in the presence of shadows and translucent overlays was governed by the perceived lightnesses of the elements rather than by their retinal luminances. Further findings using analogous methods have shown that perceptual grouping is also strongly affected by amodal completion (Palmer, Neff, & Beck, 1996) and by illusory contours (Palmer & Nelson, 2000), both of which are believed to depend on depth perception in situations of occlusion (see Rock, 1983). (Amodal completion is the process by which partly occluded surfaces of objects are perceived as continuing behind the occluding object, as illustrated in Figure 7.10, and illusory contours are edges that are perceived where there is no physical luminance gradient present because the occluding surface is the same color as the occluded surface, as illustrated in Figure 7.13. See section entitled "Visual Interpretation" for further information.) Such results show that grouping cannot be attributed entirely to early, preconstancy visual processing, but they are also compatible with the possibility that grouping is a temporally extended process that includes components at both early and later levels of processing (Palmer, in press-a). A provisional grouping might be determined at an early, preconstancy stage of image processing, but might be overridden if later, object-based information (from depth, lighting conditions, occlusion, etc.) required it.

Before leaving the topic of early versus late grouping, it is worth noting that Wertheimer (1923) discussed a further factor in perceptual grouping that is seldom mentioned: past experience. The idea is that elements that have been previously grouped in certain ways will tend to be seen as grouped in the same way when they are seen again. According to modern visual theory, such effects would also support the hypothesis that grouping effects can occur relatively late in perception, because they would have to happen after contact has been made between the information in the stimulus display and representations in memory.

Figure 7.5 provides a particularly strong demonstration of the effects of prior experience. People who have never seen

Figure 7.5 Effects of past experience on perceptual organization (see text). *Source:* Original photograph by R. C. James.

this image before usually perceive it as a seemingly random array of meaningless black blobs on a white background. After they have discerned the Dalmatian with its head down, sniffing along a street, however, the picture becomes dramatically reorganized, with certain of the blobs going together because they are part of the dog and others going together because they are part of the street or the tree. The interesting fact relevant to past experience is that after you have seen the Dalmatian in this picture, you will see it that way for the rest of your life! Past experience can thus have a dramatic effect on grouping and organization, especially if the organization of the image is highly ambiguous.

Region Segmentation

There is an important logical gap in the story of perceptual organization that we have told thus far. No explanation has been given of how the to-be-grouped "elements" (e.g., the dots and lines in Figure 7.2) arise in the first place. Wertheimer (1923/1950) appears simply to have assumed the existence of such elements, but notice that they are not directly given by the stimulus array. Rather, their formation requires an explanation, including an analysis of the factors that govern their existence as perceptual elements and how such elements might be computed from an optical array of luminance values. This initial organizational operation is often called *region segmentation:* the process of partitioning an image into an exhaustive set of mutually exclusive two-dimensional areas.

Uniform Connectedness

Palmer and Rock (1994a, 1994b) suggested that region segmentation is determined by an organizational principle that they called *uniform connectedness*. They proposed that the first step in constructing the part-whole hierarchy for an image is to partition the image into a set of uniformly connected (UC) regions, much like a stained glass window. A region is uniformly connected if it constitutes a single, connected subset of the image that is either uniform or slowly varying in its visual properties, such as color, texture, motion, and binocular disparity. Figure 7.1 (B) shows a plausible set of UC regions for the leopard image, bounded by the solid contours and labelled as regions 1 through 10.

Uniform connectedness is an important principle of perceptual organization because of its informational value in designating connected objects or object parts in the environment. As a general rule, if an area of the retinal image constitutes a UC region, it almost certainly comes from the light reflected from a single, connected, environmental object or part. This is not true for successful camouflage, of course, but such situations are comparatively rare. Uniform connectedness is therefore an excellent heuristic for finding image regions that correspond to parts of connected objects in the environment.

Figure 7.6 (B) shows how an image of a penguin (Figure 7.6; A) has been divided into a possible set of UC regions by a global, explicitly region-based procedure devised by Malik and his colleagues (Leung & Malik, 1998; Shi & Malik, 1997). Their "normalized cuts" algorithm is a graph theoretic procedure that works by finding the binary partition of a given region—initially, the whole image—into two sets of pixels that maximizes a particular measure of pairwise pixel similarity within the same subregion, normalized relative to the total pairwise pixel similarity within the entire region. Similarity of pixel pairs is defined in their algorithm by the weighted integration of a number of Gestalt-like

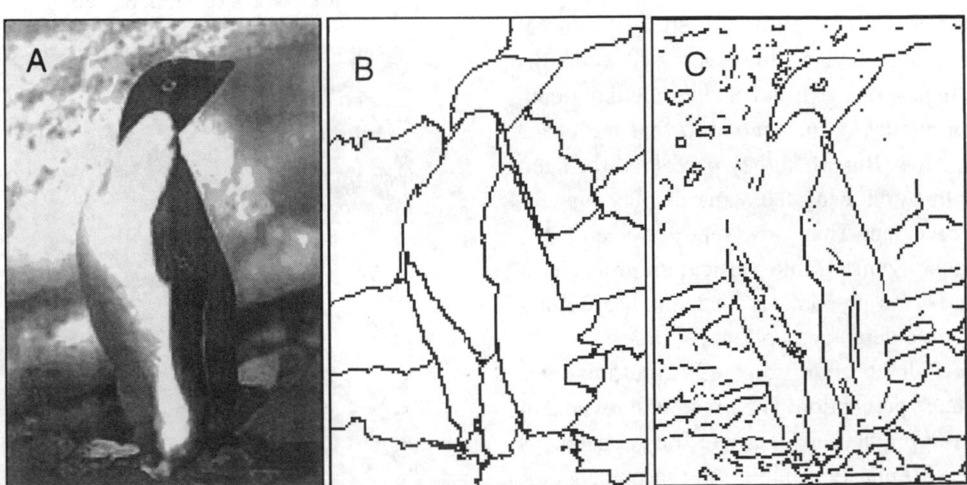

Figure 7.6 A gray-scale image of a penguin (A), a regional segmentation of that image using Malik's normalized cuts algorithm (B), and the output of the Canny edge detection algorithm (C). *Source:* Parts A and B from Shi and Malik, 1997; part C courtesy of Thomas Leung.

grouping factors, such as proximity, color similarity, texture similarity, and motion similarity. They also include a grouping factor based on evidence for the presence of a local edge between the given pair of pixels, which reduces the likelihood that they are part of the same subregion. When this normalized cuts algorithm is applied repeatedly to a given image, dividing and subdividing it into smaller and smaller regions, perceptually plausible partitions emerge rapidly (Figure 7.6; B). Notice that Malik's region-based approach produces closed regions by definition.

Another possible approach to region segmentation is to begin by detecting luminance edges. Whenever such edges form a closed contour, they define two regions: the fully bounded interior and the partly bounded exterior. An image can therefore be segmented into a set of connected regions by using an edge-detection algorithm to locate closed contours. This idea forms a theoretical bridge between the well-known physiological and computational work on edge detection (e.g., Canny, 1986; Hubel & Wiesel, 1962; Marr & Hildreth, 1980) and work on perceptual organization, suggesting that edge detection may be viewed as the first step in region segmentation. An important problem with this approach is that most edge-detection algorithms produce few closed contours, thus requiring further processing to link them into closed contours. The difficulty is illustrated in Figure 7.6 (C) for the output of Canny's (1986) well known edge-detection algorithm.

Texture Segmentation

A special case of region segmentation that has received considerable attention is texture segmentation (e.g., Beck, 1966, 1972, 1982; Julesz, 1981). In Figure 7.1(A), for example, the leopard is not very different in overall luminance from the branch, but the two can easily be distinguished visually by their different textures.

The factors that govern region segmentation by texture elements are not necessarily the same as those that determine explicit judgments of shape similarity, even for the very same texture elements when they are perceived as individual figures. For instance, the dominant texture segmentation evident in Figure 7.7 (A)—that is to say, that separating the upright *T*s and *L*s from the tilted *T*s—is the opposite of simple shape similarity judgments (Figure 7.7; B) in which a single upright *T* was judged more similar to a tilted *T* than it was to an upright *L* (Beck, 1966). From the results of many such experiments, texture segmentation is believed to result from detecting differences in feature density (i.e., the number of features per unit of area) for certain simple attributes, such as line orientation, overall brightness, color, size, and movement (Beck, 1972). Julesz (1981) later proposed a similar theory in which textures were segregated by detecting

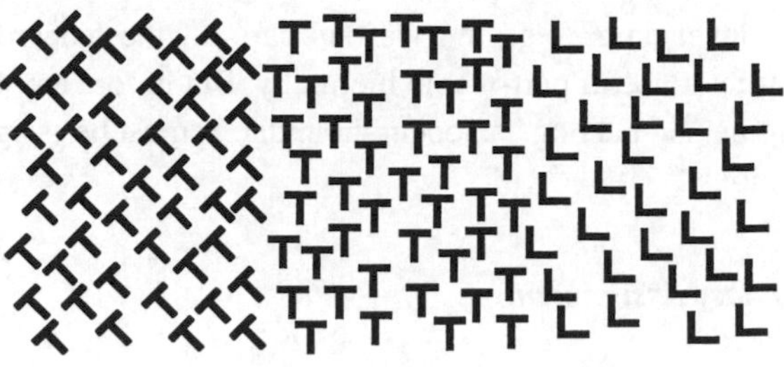

A. Texture Segregation

B. Shape Similarity

Figure 7.7 Texture segmentation of *T*s, tilted *T*s, and *L*s (A) versus shape similarity of the same letters (B). *Source:* From Palmer, 1999.

changes in the density of certain simple, local textural features that he called *textons* (Julesz, 1981), which included elongated blobs defined by their color, length, width, orientation, binocular disparity, and flicker rate, plus line terminators and line crossings or intersections.

Julesz also claimed that normal, effortless texture segmentation based on differences in texton densities was a *preattentive* process: one that occurs automatically and in parallel over the whole visual field prior to the operation of focussed attention. He further suggested that there were detectors early in the visual system that are sensitive to textons such that texture segmentation takes place through the differential activation of the texton detectors. Julesz's textons are similar to the critical features ascribed to simple cells in cortical area V1 (Hubel & Wiesel, 1962), and to some of the primitive elements in Marr's *primal sketch* (Marr, 1982; Marr & Nishihara, 1978). Computational theories have since been proposed that perform texture segmentation by detecting textural edges from the outputs of quasi-neural elements whose receptive fields are like those found in simple cells of area V1 of the visual cortex (e.g., Malik & Perona, 1990).

Figure-Ground Organization

If the goal of perceptual organization is to construct a scene-based hierarchy consisting of parts, objects, and groups, region segmentation can be no more than a very early step, because uniform connected regions in images seldom correspond directly to the projection of whole environmental objects. As is evident from Figures 7.1 (A, B, and C), some UC regions need to be grouped into higher-level units (e.g., the various patches of sky) and others need to be parsed into lower-level units (e.g., the various parts of the leopard) to construct a useful part-whole hierarchy. But before any final grouping and parsing can occur, boundaries must be assigned to regions.

Boundary Assignment

For every bounding contour in a segmented image there is a region on both sides. Because most visible surfaces are opaque, the region on one side usually corresponds to a closer, occluding surface, and the region on the other side to a farther, occluded surface that extends behind the closer one. Boundary assignment is the process of determining to which region the contour belongs, so to speak, thus determining the shape of the closer surface, but not that of the farther surface.

To demonstrate the profound difference that alternative boundary assignments can make, consider Figure 7.8. Region segmentation processes will partition the square into two UC regions, one white and the other black. But to which side does the central boundary belong? If you perceive the edge as belonging to the white region, you will see a white object with rounded fingers protruding in front of a black background. If you perceive the edge as belonging to the black region, you will see a black object with pointed claws in front of a white background. This particular display is highly ambiguous, so that sometimes you see the white fingers and other times the black claws. (It is also possible to see a mosaic organization in which the boundary belongs to both sides at once, as in the case of jigsaw puzzle pieces that fit snugly together to form a single contour. This interpretation is infrequent, probably because it does not arise very often in normal situations, except when two adjacent, parallel contours are clearly visible.) This boundary-assignment aspect of perceptual organization is known in the classical perception literature as *figure-ground organization* (Rubin, 1921). The "thing-like" region is referred to as the *figure* and the "background-like" region as the *ground*.

Figure 7.8 Ambiguous edge assignment and figure-ground organization. *Source:* From Rock, 1983.

Principles of Figure-Ground Organization

Figure 7.8 is highly ambiguous in its figure-ground organization because it is about equally easy to see the back and white regions as figure, but this is not always, or even usually, the case. The visual system has distinct preferences for perceiving certain kinds of regions as figural, and these are usually sufficient to determine figure-ground organization. Studies have determined that the following factors are relevant, all of which bias the region toward being seen as figural: surroundedness, smaller size, horizontal-vertical orientation, lower region (Vecera, Vogel, & Woodman, in press), higher contrast, greater symmetry, greater convexity (Kanisza & Gerbino, 1976), parallel contours, meaningfulness (Peterson & Gibson, 1991), and voluntary attention (Driver & Baylis, 1996). Analogous to the Gestalt principles of perceptual grouping, these principles of figure-ground organization are *ceteris paribus* rules—, rules in which a given factor has the stated effect, if all other factors are equal (i.e., eliminated or otherwise neutralized). As such, they have the same weaknesses as the principles of grouping, including the inability to predict the outcome when several conflicting factors are at work in the same display.

In terms of information processing structure, Palmer and Rock (1994a, 1994b) proposed a process model of perceptual organization in which figure-ground organization occupies a middle position, occurring after region segmentation, but before grouping and parsing (see Figure 7.9). They argued that figure-ground processing logically must occur after region-segmentation processing because segmented regions are required as input by any algorithm that discriminates figure from ground. The reason is that most of the principles of figure-ground organization—for example, surroundedness, size, symmetry, and convexity—are properties that are only

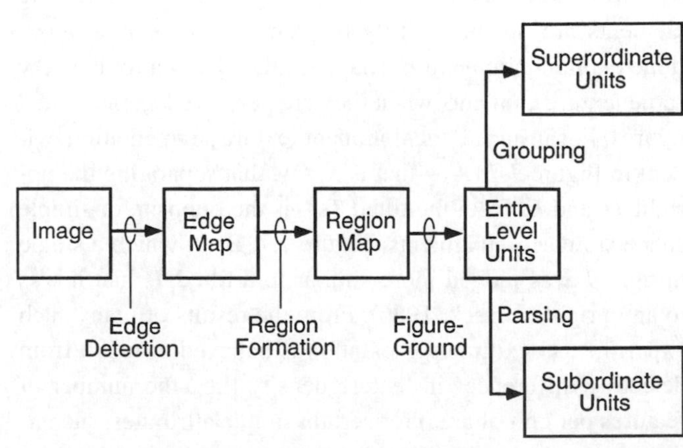

Figure 7.9 A computational theory of visual organization. *Source:* From Palmer and Rock, 1994a.

defined for two-dimensional regions, and thus require two-dimensional regions as input. More speculatively, Palmer and Rock (1994a, 1994b) also claimed that figure-ground organization must logically precede grouping and parsing. The reason is that the latter processes, which apparently depend on certain shape-based properties of the regions in question—for example, concavity-convexity, similarity of orientation, shape, size, and motion—require prior boundary assignment. Grouping and parsing thus depend on shape properties that are logically well-defined for regions only after boundaries have been assigned, either to one side or perhaps initially to both sides (Peterson & Gibson, 1991)

Parsing

Another important process involved in the organization of perception is *parsing* or *part segmentation:* dividing a single element into two or more parts. This is essentially the opposite of grouping. Parsing is important because it determines what subregions of a perceptual unit are perceived as belonging together most coherently. To illustrate, consider the leopard in Figure 7.1 (A). Region segmentation might well define it as a single region based on its textural similarity (region 4), and this conforms to our experience of it as a single object. But we also experience it as being composed of several clear and obvious parts: the head, body, tail, and three visible legs, as indicated by the dashed lines in Figure 7.1 (B). The large, lower portion of the tree limb (region 9) is similarly a single UC region, but it too can be perceived as divided (although perhaps less strongly) into the different sections indicated by dotted lines in Figure 7.1 (B).

Palmer and Rock (1994a) argued that parsing must logically follow region segmentation because parsing presupposes the existence of a unitary region to be divided. Since they proposed that region segmentation is the first step in the process that forms such region-based elements, they naturally argued that parsing must come after it. There is no logical constraint, however, on the order in which parsing and grouping must occur relative to each other. They could very well happen simultaneously. This is why the flowchart of Palmer and Rock's theory (Figure 7.9) shows both grouping and parsing taking place at the same time after regions have been defined. According to their analysis, parsing should also occur after figure-ground organization. The reason is that parsing, like grouping, is based on properties (such as concavity-convexity) that are properly attributed to regions only after some boundary assignment has been made. There is no point in parsing a background region at concavities along its border if that border does not define the shape of the corresponding environmental object, but only the shape of a neighboring object that partly occludes it.

There are at least two quite different ways to go about dividing an object into parts: *boundary rules* and *shape primitives*. The boundary rule approach is to define a set of general conditions that specify where the boundaries lie between parts. The best known theory of this type was developed by Hoffman and Richards (1984). Their key observation was that the two-dimensional silhouettes of multipart objects can usually be divided at *deep concavities:* places where the contour of an object's outer border is maximally curved inward (concave) toward the interior of the region. Formally, these points are local negative minima of curvature.

An alternative to parsing by boundary rules is the *shape primitive* approach. It is based on a set of atomic, indivisible shapes that constitute a complete listing of the most basic parts. More complex objects are then analyzed as configurations of these primitive parts. This process can be thought of as analogous to dividing cursively written words into parts by knowing the cursive alphabet and finding the primitive component letters. Such a scheme for parsing works well if there is a relatively small set of primitive components, as there is in the case of cursive writing. It is far from obvious, however, what the two-dimensional shape primitives might be in the case of parsing two-dimensional projections of natural scenes.

If the shape primitive approach is going to work, it is natural that the shape primitives appropriate for parsing the projected images of three-dimensional objects should be the projections of three-dimensional *volumetric* shape primitives. Such an analysis has been given in Binford's (1971) proposal that complex three-dimensional shapes can be analyzed into configurations of *generalized cylinders:* appropriately sized and shaped volumes that are generalized from standard cylinders in the sense that they have extra parameters that enable them to describe many more shapes. The extra parameters include ones that specify the shape of the base (rather than always being circular), the curvature of the axis (rather than always being straight), and so forth (see also Biederman, 1987; Marr, 1982). The important point for present purposes is that if one has a set of shape primitives and some way of detecting them in two-dimensional images, complex three-dimensional objects can be appropriately segmented into primitive parts. Provided that the primitives are sufficiently general, part segmentation will be possible, even for novel objects.

Visual Interpolation

With the four basic organizational processes discussed thus far—region segmentation, figure-ground organization, grouping, and parsing—it is possible to see how a rudimentary part-whole hierarchy might be constructed by some appropriate sequence of operations. One of the main further problems that the visual system must solve is how to perceive partly occluded objects as such. In Figure 7.1 (A), for example, the part of the branch above the leopard is perceived as the extension of the branch below it. This is more than simple grouping of the two corresponding image regions because the observer *completes* the branch in the sense of perceiving that it continues behind the leopard. The various patches of sky between and around the leopard and branches must likewise be perceived as parts of the uninterrupted sky behind them. The crucial ecological fact is that most environmental surfaces are opaque and therefore hide farther surfaces from view. What is needed to cope with the incomplete, piecewise, and changeable montage of visible surfaces that stimulate the retina is some way to infer the nature of *hidden* parts from visible ones.

The visual system has evolved mechanisms to do this, which will be referred to collectively as processes of *visual interpolation* (Kellman & Shipley, 1991). They have limitations, primarily because all they can do is make a best guess about something that can be only partly seen. Completely occluded objects are seldom interpolated, even if they are present, because there is no evidence from which to do so, and even partly visible objects are sometimes completed incorrectly. Nevertheless, people are remarkably adept at perceiving the nature of partly occluded objects, and this ability requires explanation.

Amodal Completion

Amodal completion is the process by which the visual system infers the nature of hidden parts of partly occluded surfaces and objects from their visible projections. It is called *amodal* because there is no direct experience of the hidden part in any sensory modality; it is thus experienced amodally. A simple example is provided in Figure 7.10 (A). Observers spontaneously perceive a full circle behind a square, as indicated in Figure 7.10 (B), even though one quarter of the circle is not visible.

Amodal completion is logically underdetermined. The real environmental state of affairs corresponding to Figure 7.10 (A) might be a square covering a whole circle (B), a mosaic, of a square abutting a three-quarter circle (or pac-man; C), or a square in front of a circle with odd protrusions (D). It might also be a pac-man in front of a square with odd protrusions (E), or an infinite number of other possibilities. The visual system therefore appears to have strong preferences about

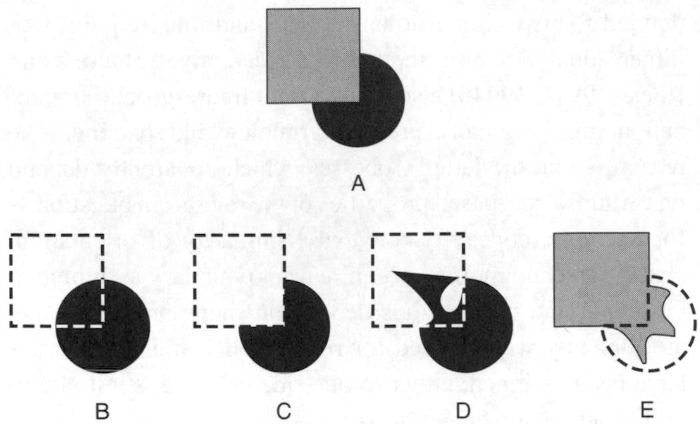

Figure 7.10 An image (A) that is perceived as a square occluding an amodally completed circle (B) rather than as a square abutting a pac-man (C), a square occluding some odd-shaped object (D), or a pac-man occluding some odd-shaped object (E). *Source:* From Palmer, 1999.

how to complete partly occluded objects, aimed at maximizing veridical perception of whole objects in the world. There are at least three general types of explanations of how this might happen.

One possibility is that the visual system completes the circle behind the square based on frequency of *prior experiences*. Although people have all seen three-quarter circles, most have probably seen a good many more full circles. Perhaps people complete partly occluded figures according to the most frequently encountered shape compatible with the visible stimulus information. Novel shapes can also be amodally completed (e.g., Gregory, 1972), however. This shows that familiarity cannot be the whole story, although it may be part of it.

A second possibility is that partly occluded figures are completed in the way that results in the *simplest* perceived figures. For example, a square occluding a complete circle in Figure 7.10 (A) is simpler than any of the alternatives in this set of completions, and the same could be true for the possible completions of novel shapes. Explaining phenomena of perceptual organization in terms of maximizing simplicity—or, equivalently, minimizing complexity—was the theoretical approach favored by Gestalt psychologists (e.g., Koffka, 1935). They called this proposal the *principle of Prägnanz,* which was later dubbed the *minimum principle* (Hochberg & McAlister, 1953): The percept will be as good or as simple, as the prevailing conditions allow.

Gestaltists were never very clear about just what constituted goodness or simplicity, but later theorists have offered explicit computational theories that are able to show that many completion phenomena can be predicted by minimizing representational complexity (e.g., Buffart & Leeuwenberg, 1981; Leeuwenberg, 1971, 1978). One problem faced by such theories is that they are only as good as the simplicity metric on which they are based. Failure to predict experimental results can thus easily be dismissed on the grounds that a better simplicity measure would bring the predictions into line with the results. This may be true, of course, but it makes a theory difficult to falsify.

A third possibility is to explain amodal completion by appealing directly to *ecological evidence* of occlusion. For example, when a contour of one object is occluded by that of another, they typically form an intersection known as a *T-junction*. The top of the T is interpreted as the closer edge whose surface occludes those surfaces adjacent to the stem of the T. The further assumptions required to account for amodal completion are that the occluded edge (and the surface attached to it) connects with another occluded edge in the scene and a set of specifications about how they are to be joined.

One such theory of completion is Kellman and Shipley's (1991) *relatability theory*. It can be understood as a more complete and well-specified extension of the classic grouping principle of good continuation (Wertheimer, 1923/1950). The basic principles of relatability theory are illustrated in Figure 7.11. The first step is to locate all *edge discontinuities,* which are discontinuities in the first derivative of the mathematical function that describes the edge over space. These are circled in Figure 7.11 (A). The second is to relate pairs of edges if and only if (a) their extensions intersect at an angle of 90° or more, and (b) they can be smoothly connected to each other, as illustrated in Figure 7.11 (B). Third, a new perceptual unit is formed when amodally completed edges form an enclosed area, as shown in Figure 7.11 (C). Finally, units are assigned positions in depth based on available depth information (see chapter in this volume by Proffitt and Caudek), as depicted in Figure 7.11 (D). In completion, for example, depth information from occlusion specifies that the amodally completed edges are behind the object at whose borders they terminate. This depth assignment is indicated in Figure 7.11 (D) by arrows that point along the edge in the direction for which the nearer region is on the right.

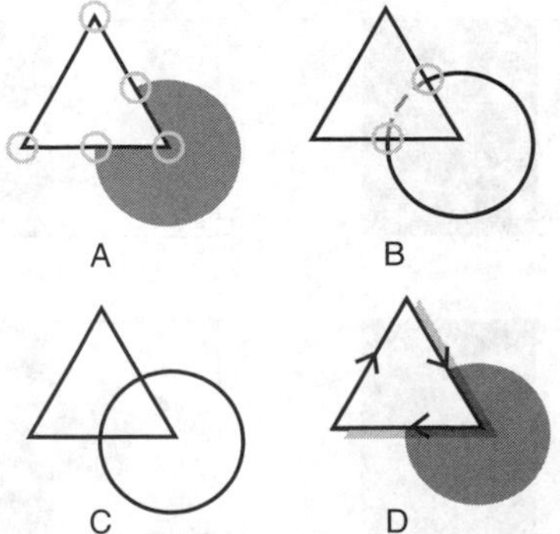

Figure 7.11 Steps in determining completion according to Kellman and Shipley's relatability theory (see text). *Source:* From Palmer, 1999.

Kellman and Shipley's (1991) relatability theory of amodal completion is couched in terms of image-based information: the existence of edge discontinuities and their two-dimensional relatability in terms of good continuation. Other, more complex approaches are possible, however. One is that completion takes place within a surface-based representation by relating two-dimensional surfaces embedded in three-dimensional space (Nakayama, He, & Shimojo, 1995). Another is that it occurs in an object-based representation when three-dimensional volumes are merged (Tse, 1999). Recent evidence supports the hypothesis that the final perception of amodal completion is based on merging volumes (Tse, 1999). Figure 7.12 provides evidence against both image-based and surface-based views. Part A shows an example in which the outer contours on the left and right side of the closest object line up perfectly, thus conforming to the requirements of edge relatability, yet they fail to support amodal completion. Figure 7.12 (B) shows the opposite situation, in which there are no relatable contours (because they are themselves occluded), yet people readily perceive amodal completion behind the cylinder. These examples thus show that relatable contours at the level of two-dimensional images are neither necessary nor sufficient for perceiving amodal completion.

Figure 7.12 (C) shows a case in which there are relatable surfaces on the left and right sides of the occluder, and yet

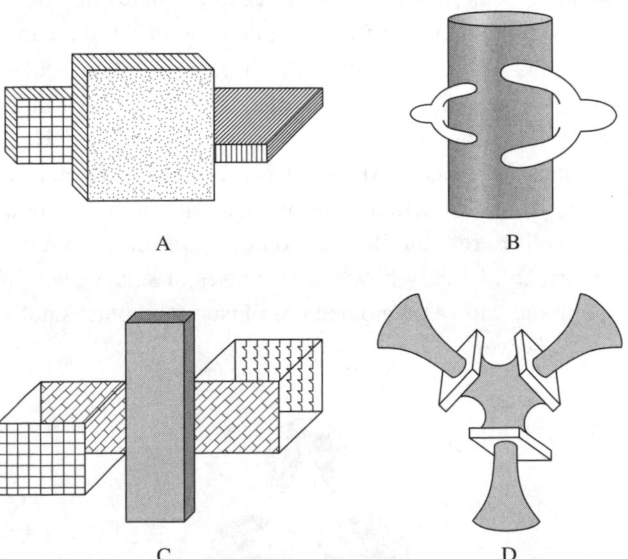

Figure 7.12 Image-based versus surface-based versus and volume-based approaches to completion (see text). *Source:* From Tse, 1999.

people perceive two distinct objects, rather than one that is completed behind it. Finally, Figure 7.12 (D) shows an example in which there are no relatable surfaces, yet amodal completion is perceived. These two example therefore show that relatable surfaces are neither necessary nor sufficient for perceiving amodal completion. Tse (1999) has argued persuasively from such examples that completion is ultimately accomplished by merging inferred three-dimensional volumes.

Illusory Contours

Another important form of visual interpolation produces a striking illusion in which contours are seen that do not actually exist in the stimulus image. This phenomenon of *illusory contours* (also called *subjective contours*) was first described almost a century ago (Schumann, 1904), but modern interest in it was sparked by the elegant demonstrations of Kanizsa (1955, 1979). One of the best known examples is the so-called *Kanizsa triangle* shown in Figure 7.13. The white triangle so readily perceived in this display is defined by illusory contours because the stimulus image consists solely of three pac-man–shaped figures. Most observers report seeing well-defined luminance edges where the contours of the triangle should be, with the interior region of the triangle appearing lighter than the surrounding ground. These edges and luminance differences simply are not present in the optical image.

Recent physiological research has identified cells in cortical area V2 that appear to respond to the presence of illusory contours. Cells in area V2 have receptive fields that do not initially appear much different from those in V1, but careful testing has shown that about 40% of the orientation selective cells in V2 also fire when presented with stimuli that induce illusory contours in human perception (von der Heydt, Peterhans, & Baumgartner, 1984; Peterhans & von der Heydt, 1991). Sometimes the orientational tuning functions of the cells to real and illusory contours are similar, but often they are not. Exactly how the responses of such cells might explain the known phenomena of illusory contours is not yet clear, however.

Figure 7.13 Illusory contours in a Kanizsa triangle. *Source:* After Kanizsa, 1955.

Perceived Transparency

Another phenomenon of visual interpolation is *perceived transparency:* the perception of objects as being viewed through a closer, translucent object that transmits some portion of the light reflected from the farther object rather than blocking it entirely. Under conditions of translucency, the light striking the retina at a given location provides information about at least *two* different external points along the same viewer-centered direction: one on the farther opaque surface and the other on the closer translucent surface (Figure 7.14; A).

Perception of transparency depends on both spatial and color conditions. Violating the proper relations of either sort is sufficient to block it. For example, transparency will be perceived if the translucent surface is positioned so that reflectance edges on the opaque surface behind it can be seen both through the translucent surface and outside it, as illustrated in Figure 7.14 (A). When this happens, a phenomenon called *color scission* or *color splitting* occurs, and the image colors in the regions of the translucent surface are perceived as a combination of one color belonging to the background and one color belonging to the translucent surface. Color scission will *not* occur, however, if the translucent surface lies completely within a single reflectance region, as illustrated in Figure 7.14 (B). It can also be blocked by destroying the unity of the translucent region (Figure 7.14; C) or merely weakening it (Figure 7.14; D).

When color scission occurs, the perceived color in each region of overlap is split into a component from the transparent

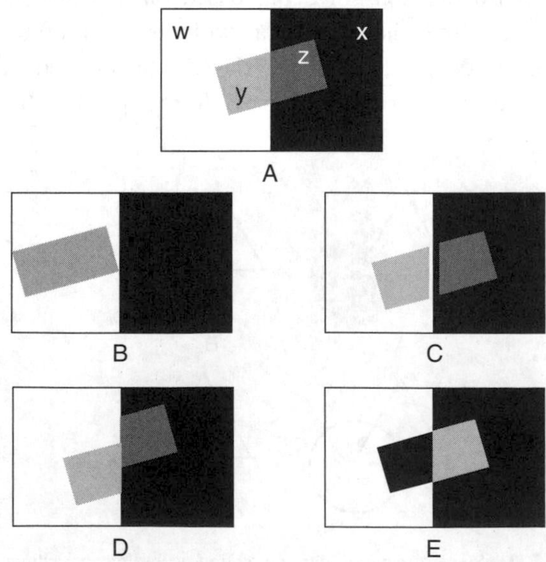

Figure 7.14 Conditions for perceiving transparency (see text). *Source:* From Palmer, 1999.

Figure 7.15 Figural scission, in which a single homogeneous region is sometimes perceptually divided into two overlapping objects, one of which partly occludes the other. *Source:* From Palmer, 1999

layer and a component from the opaque layer. For this to happen, the components due to the transparent layer must be the same. Metelli (1974), Gerbino (1994), and Anderson (1997) have precise, quantitative theories of the conditions for transparency to be perceived. Violating these constraints also blocks perceived transparency (Figure 7.14; E).

Figural Scission

Yet another example of visual interpolation is *figural scission:* the division of a single homogeneous region into two overlapping figures of the same color, one in front of and occluding the other. This phenomenon, illustrated in Figure 7.15, has many interesting features. One is that there is no local sensory information that requires the single region to be split at all. The visual system constructs illusory contours where the closer figure occludes the farther one. The visual system also *completes* the portions of the farther figure that are occluded by the closer one. But because the stimulus conditions do not determine which figure is in front and which behind, either possibility can be perceived. Indeed, if you view such displays for awhile, the depth relations of the two parts spontaneously reverse.

Parts and Wholes

Assuming that objects are indeed perceived as structured into something like a hierarchy of objects, parts, subparts, and so on (cf. Palmer, 1977; Reed & Johnsen, 1975), a question that naturally arises is whether parts are perceived before wholes or wholes before parts. Although Gestaltists never posed the question in precisely this form, their approach to perception suggests that wholes may be processed first in some important sense. Most other approaches to perception imply the opposite: that wholes are constructed by integrating local information into increasingly larger aggregations. Even physiological evidence seems to support a local-first view. Retinal receptors respond to exceedingly tiny regions of stimulation, and as one traces the path of neural information processing, synapse by synapse, deeper into the brain, the receptive fields of visual neurons become ever larger and responsive to ever more complex stimulus configurations (e.g., Van Essen & De Yoe, 1995).

There are problems in accepting this line of argument as settling anything about *perceptual experience,* however. First, the order in which processing is *initiated* may not be nearly as relevant for perceptual experience as the order in which it is *completed.* Although it is clear that neural processing is initiated in a local-to-global order, it is by no means clear that it is completed in this order. Indeed, there is strong evidence that the flow of neural information processing is not unidirectional from the sensory surface of the retina to higher centers of the brain. Massive backward projections from higher to lower cortical areas suggest that a great deal of feedback may occur, although nobody yet knows precisely what form it takes or even what functions it serves. The existence of feedback raises the possibility that the order in which perceptual experience arises is not given by the simplistic reading of the physiological facts given in the previous paragraph. Moreover, evidence from psychological experiments suggests that perception of global objects often precedes that of local parts.

Global Precedence

Navon (1976) asked about the priority of wholes versus parts by studying discrimination tasks with hierarchically structured stimuli: typically, large letters made of many appropriately positioned small letters. On some trials subjects were shown *consistent configurations* in which the global and local letters were the same, such as a large *H* made of many small *H*s or a large *S* made of many small *S*s. On others, they were shown *inconsistent configurations* in which the global and local letters conflicted, such as a large *H* made of many small *S*s or a large *S* made of many small *H*s. They were cued on each trial whether to report the identity of the letter represented at the global or the local level. Response times and error rates were measured.

The results of Navon's experiment strongly supported the predictions of *global precedence:* the hypothesis that observers perceive the global level of hierarchical stimuli before the local level. Response times were faster to global than to local letters, and global inconsistency interfered when subjects were attending to the local level, but local inconsistency did not interfere when they were attending to the global level. The data thus appear to indicate that perceptual processes proceed from global, coarse-grained analysis to local, fine-grained analysis.

Further investigation suggested a more complex story, however. Kinchla and Wolfe (1979) found that the speed of naming local versus global forms depended on their retinal sizes. Identifying global letters was faster than local ones when the global stimuli were smaller than about 8–10° of visual angle, but identifying local letters was faster than global ones when the stimuli were larger than this. Other experiments suggest that global and local levels of information are being processed simultaneously rather than sequentially. For example, when subjects were monitoring for a target letter at either the global or the local levels, their responses were faster when a target letter was present at both global and local levels than when there was a target letter present at either level alone (Miller, 1981). The findings on global versus local precedence may therefore be best understood as the result of parallel processing in different size channels, with some channels being processed slightly faster than others, rather than as reflecting a fixed global-to-local order of processing.

Further experiments by Robertson and her colleagues studying patients with brain damage have shown that global and local information is processed differently in the two cerebral hemispheres. Several lines of evidence show that there is an advantage for global processing in the right temporal-parietal lobe, whereas there is an advantage for local processing in the left temporal-parietal lobe (Robertson, Lamb, & Knight, 1988). For example, Figure 7.16 shows how patients with lesions in the left versus right temporal-parietal region copied the hierarchical stimulus shown on the left in part A (Delis, Robertson, & Efron, 1986). The patient with right

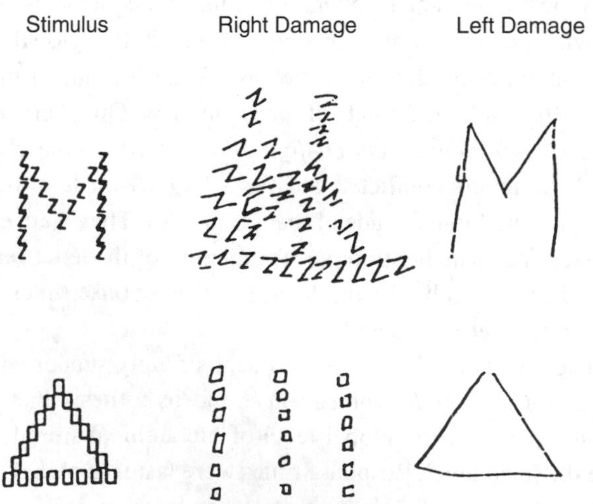

Figure 7.16 Drawings of hierarchical stimuli from patients with lesions in the right hemisphere (central column) and patients with lesions in the left hemisphere (right column). *Source:* From Delis, Robertson, and Efron, 1986.

hemisphere damage, who suffers deficits in global processing, is able to reproduce the small letters making up the global letter, but is unable to reproduce their global structure. The patient with left hemisphere damage, who suffers deficits in local processing, is able to reproduce the global letter, but not the small letters that comprise it.

Further psychological evidence that global properties are primary in human perception comes from experiments in which discrimination of parts is found to be superior when they are embedded within meaningful or well-structured wholes. Not only is performance better than in comparable control conditions in which the same parts must be discriminated within meaningless or ill-structured contexts, but it is also superior compared to discriminating the same parts in isolation. This evidence comes from several different phenomena, such as the word superiority effect (Reicher, 1969), the object superiority effect (Weisstein & Harris, 1974), the configural orientation effect (Palmer, 1980; Palmer & Bucher, 1981), and the configural superiority effect (Pomerantz, Sager, & Stover, 1977). Although space limitations do not permit discussion of these interesting experiments, their results generally indicate that perceptual performance on various simple local discrimination tasks does not occur in the local-to-global order.

Exactly how these contextual effects should be interpreted is open to debate, however. One possibility is that neural processing proceeds from local parts to global wholes, but feedback from the holistic level to the earlier part levels then facilitates processing of local elements, if they are part of coherent patterns at the global level. This is the mechanism proposed in the influential *interactive activation model* of letter and word processing (McClelland & Rumelhart, 1981; Rumelhart & McClelland, 1982). Another possibility is that although neural processing proceeds from local parts to global wholes, people may gain conscious access to the results in the opposite order, from global wholes to local parts (Marcel, 1983). Regardless of what mechanism is ultimately found to be responsible, the results of many psychological experiments rule out the possibility that the perception of local structure necessarily precedes that of global structure. The truth, as usual, is much more interesting and complex.

Frames of Reference

Another set of perceptual phenomena that support the priority of global, large-scale structure in perceptual organization is the existence of what are called *reference frame* effects (see Rock, 1990, for a review). A frame of reference in visual perception is a set of assumed reference standards with respect to which the properties of perceptual objects are encoded. Visual reference frames are often considered to be analogous to *coordinate systems* in analytic geometry (Palmer, 1989). Reference frame effects generally show that the reference frame for a given visual element is defined by the next-higher element in the perceptual part-whole hierarchy. In this section, reference frame effects in orientation and shape perception are briefly considered. Analogous effects are also present in motion perception, but these are discussed in the chapter by Proffitt and Caudek in this volume.

Orientation Perception

One of the most compelling demonstrations of reference frame effects on orientation perception occurs when you enter a tilted room, like the ones in a fun house or mystery house of an amusement park. Although you notice the slant of the floor as you first enter, you rapidly come to perceive the room as gravitationally upright. After this misperception occurs, all sorts of other illusions follow. You perceive the chandelier as hanging at a strange angle from the ceiling, for example, and you perceive yourself as leaning precariously to one side, despite the fact that both the chandelier and you are, in fact, gravitationally upright. If you try to correct your posture to align yourself with the orientation of the room, you may lose your balance or even fall.

Normally, the vertical orientation in the reference frame of the large-scale visual environment coincides with gravitational vertical, because the dominant orientations of perceived objects—due to walls, floors, tree trunks, the ground plane, standing people, and so forth—are either aligned with gravity or perpendicular to it. The heuristic assumption that the walls, floor, and ceiling of a room are vertical and horizontal thus generally serves us well in accurately perceiving the orientations of objects. When you walk into a tilted room, however, this assumption is violated, giving rise to illusions of orientation. The visual reference frame of the room, which is out of alignment with gravity, captures your sense of upright. You then perceive yourself as tilted because your own bodily orientation is not aligned with your perception of upright.

One particularly well-known reference frame effect on orientation perception is the *rod and frame effect* (Asch & Witkin, 1948a, 1948b). Subjects were shown a luminous rod within a large, tilted, luminous rectangle and were asked to set the rod to gravitational vertical. Asch and Witkin found large systematic errors in which subjects set the rod to an orientation somewhere between true vertical and alignment with the frame's most nearly vertical sides. Several experiments show that the effect of the frame is greatest when the rectangle is large, and that small ones just surrounding the line have little effect (Ebenholtz, 1977; Wenderoth, 1974). Other studies have shown that when two frames are present, one inside the other, it is the larger surrounding frame that dominates perception (DiLorenzo & Rock, 1982). These facts are consistent with the interpretation that the rectangle in a rod and frame task induces a visual frame of reference that is essentially a world surrogate, so to speak, for the visual environment (Rock, 1990). By this account, a visual structure will be more likely to induce a frame of reference when it is large, surrounding, and stable over time, like the tilted room in the previous example.

Shape Perception

Because perceived shape depends on perceived orientation, robust reference frame effects also occur in shape perception. One of the earliest, simplest, and most elegant demonstrations of this fact was Mach's (1914/1959) observation that when a square is rotated 45°, people generally perceive it as an upright diamond rather than as a tilted square. This figure can be perceived as a tilted square if the flat side at 45° is taken to be its top. But if the upper vertex is perceived as the top, the shape of the figure is seen as diamond-like and quite different from that of an upright square.

This relation suggests that the shape of an object should also be influenced by the orientation of a frame of reference, and this is indeed true. One of the earliest and most compelling demonstrations was provided by Kopferman (1930), who showed that a gravitational diamond is perceived as a square when it is enclosed within a 45° tilted rectangle. Palmer (1985) later extended Kopferman's discovery to other factors that Palmer had previously shown to influence orientation perception in the perceived pointing of ambiguous, equilateral triangles, factors such as the orientation of configural lines, the width and orientation of textural stripes, and the direction of rigid motion (Palmer & Bucher, 1982; Bucher & Palmer, 1985). In all of these cases, the claim is that the contextual factors induce a perceptual frame of reference that is aligned along the 45° axis of the diamond and that the shape of the figure is then perceived relative to that orientation, leading to the perception of a tilted square rather than an upright diamond.

Rock (1973) showed that such reference frame effects on shape perception are much more general. He presented subjects with a sequence of amorphous, novel shapes in a particular orientation during an initial presentation phase. He later tested their recognition memory for the figures in the same versus a different orientation (see Figure 7.17; A). The results showed that people were far less likely to recognize the shapes if they were tested in an orientation different from the original one. This poor recognition performance, which approached

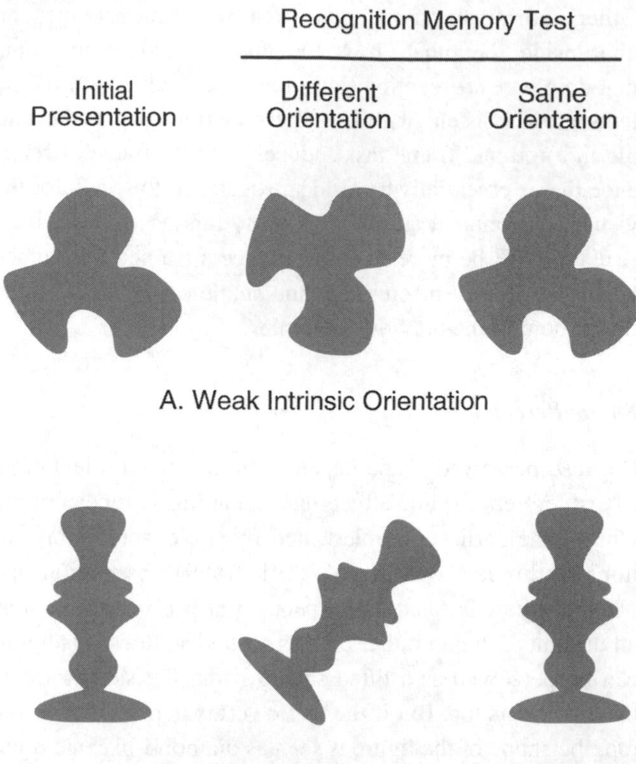

Figure 7.17 Effects of orientation on perceived shape for figures with poor intrinsic axes (A) versus figures with good intrinsic axes (B). *Source:* From Palmer, 1999.

chance for 90° rotations, indicates that subjects often fail to perceive the equivalence in shape of the presented and tested figures when they are differently oriented. Further, Rock (1973) found that tilting the observer's head reduced recognition memory less than tilting the objects within the environment. This suggests that the reference frames for these figures are environmental rather than retinal.

Why, then, do people seldom fail to recognize, say, a chair when it is seen lying on its side rather than standing up? The crucial fact appears to be that objects like chairs have enough orientational structure that they effectively carry their own intrinsic, object-centered reference frames along with them. Roughly speaking, an *object-centered reference frame* is a perceptual reference frame that is chosen on the basis of the intrinsic properties of the to-be-described object, one that is somehow made to order for that particular object (see Palmer, 1999, pp. 368–371). For example, if the orientations of two otherwise identical objects are different, such as an upright and a tipped-over chair, the orientation of each object-centered reference frame—for instance, the axis of elongation that lies in its plane of symmetry—will be defined such that both objects will have the same shape description relative to their object-centered frames.

Wiser (1981) used Rock's memory paradigm to study shape perception for objects with good intrinsic axes and found that they are recognized as well when they are presented and tested in different orientations as when they are presented and tested in the same orientation (Figure 7.17; B). In further experiments, she showed that when a well-structured figure is presented initially so that its axis is *not* aligned with gravitational vertical, subsequent recognition is actually fastest when the figure is tested in its *vertical* orientation. She interpreted this result to mean that the shape is stored in memory as though it were upright, relative to its own object-centered reference frame. This idea is important in certain theories of object identification, a topic which will be discussed in this chapter's section entitled "Theories of Object Identification."

OBJECT IDENTIFICATION

After the image has been organized into a part-whole hierarchy and partly hidden surfaces have been completed, the perceptual objects thus defined are very often identified as instances of known, meaningful types, such as people, houses, trees, and cars. This process of object identification is often also referred to as *object recognition* or *object categorization.* Its presumed goal is the perception of *function,* thereby enabling the observer to know, simply by looking, what objects in the environment are useful for what purposes. The general idea behind perceiving function via object identification is to match the perceived properties of a seen object against internal representations of the properties of known categories of objects. After the object has been identified, its function can then be determined by retrieving associations between the object category and its known uses. This will not make *novel* uses of the object available—additional problem solving processes are required for that purpose—rather, only uses that have been previously understood and stored with that category are retrieved.

Before pursuing the topic of object identification in depth, it is worth mentioning that there is an alternative approach to perceiving function. The competing view is Gibson's (1979) theory of *affordances,* in which opportunities for action are claimed to be perceived directly from visible structure in the dynamic optic array. Gibson claimed, for example, that people can literally see whether an object affords being grasped, or sat upon, or walked upon, or used for cutting without first identifying it as, say, a baseball, a chair, a floor, or a knife. This is possible only if the relation between an object's form and its affordance (the function it offers the organism) is transparent enough that the relevant properties are actually *visible*. If this is not the case, then category-mediated object identification appears to be the only route for perception of function.

Typicality and Basic-Level Categories

The first fact that must be considered about identifying objects is that it is an act of classification or categorization. Although most people typically think of objects as belonging to just one category—something is either a dog, a house, a tree, or a book—all objects are actually members of many categories. Lassie is a dog, but she is also a collie, a mammal, an animal, a living thing, a pet, a TV star, and so on. The categories of human perception and cognition are quite complex and interesting psychological structures (see chapter by Goldstone and Kersten in this volume).

One of the most important modern discoveries about human categorization is the fact that our mental categories do not seem to be defined by sets of *necessary and sufficient conditions,* but rather to be structured around so-called best examples, called *prototypes* (Rosch, 1973, 1975a, 1975b). The prototypical bird, for example, would be the "birdiest" possible bird: probably a standard bird that is average in size, has a standard neutral sort of coloring, and has the usual shape of a bird. When Rosch asked participants to rate various members of a category, like particular kinds of birds, in terms of how "good" or "typical" they were as examples of birds, she found that they systematically rated robins quite high and penguins and ostriches quite low. These *typicality* (or *goodness-of-example*) ratings turn out to be good predictors of how quickly subjects can respond "true" or "false" to verbal statements such as, "A robin is a bird," versus, "A penguin is a bird" (Rosch, 1975b). Later studies showed that it also takes longer to verify that a picture of a penguin depicts an example of a bird than to verify that a picture of a robin does (Ober-Thomkins, 1982). Thus, the time required to identify an object as a member of a category depends on how typical it is perceived to be as an example of that category.

Rosch's other major discovery about the structure of human categories concerned differences among levels within the hierarchy. For example, at which level does visual identification first occur: at some low, specific level (e.g., collie), at some high, general level (e.g., animal), or at some intermediate level (e.g., dog)? The answer is that people generally recognize objects first at an intermediate level in the categorical hierarchy. Rosch called categories at this level of abstraction *basic level categories* (Rosch, Mervis, Gray, Johnson, & Boyes-Braem, 1976). Later research, however, has shown the matter to be somewhat more complex.

Jolicoeur, Gluck, and Kosslyn (1984) studied this issue by having subjects name a wide variety of pictures with the first verbal label that came to mind. They found that objects that were *typical* instances of categories, such as robins or sparrows, were indeed identified as members of a basic level category, such as birds. *Atypical* ones, such as penguins and ostriches, tended to be classified at a lower, subordinate level. This pattern of naming was not universal for all atypical category members, however. It occurs mainly for members of basic level categories that are relatively diverse. Consider some basic level categories from the superordinate categories of fruit (e.g., apples, bananas, and grapes) versus animals (e.g., dogs, birds, and monkeys). Most people would agree that the shape variation within the categories of apples, for instance, is more constrained than that within the categories of dogs. Indeed, most people would be hard-pressed to distinguish between two different kinds of apples, bananas, or grapes from shape alone, but consider how different dachshunds are from greyhounds, penguins are from ostriches, and goldfish are from sharks. Not surprisingly, then, the atypical exemplars from diverse basic-level categories are the ones that tend to be named according to their subordinate category. Because the categories into which objects are initially classified is sometimes different from the basic level, Jolicoeur, Gluck, and Kosslyn (1984) called them *entry-level categories*.

It is worth noting that, as in the case of basic-level categories, the entry-level category of an object can vary over different observers, and perhaps over different contexts as well. To an ornithologist or even to an avid bird watcher, for instance, *bird* may be the entry-level category for very few, if any, species of bird. Through a lifetime of experience at discriminating different kinds of birds, their perceptual systems may become so finely tuned to the distinctive characteristics of different kinds of birds that they first perceive robins as robins and sparrows as sparrows rather than just as birds (Tanaka & Taylor, 1991).

Perspective Effects

One of the seemingly obvious facts about identifying three-dimensional objects is that people can do it from almost any viewpoint. The living-room chair, for example, seems to be easily perceived as such regardless of whether one is looking at it from the front, side, back, top, or any combination of these views. Thus, one of the important phenomena that must be explained by any theory of object classification is how this is possible.

But given the fact that object categorization is possible from various perspective views, it is all too easy to jump to the conclusion that object categorization is *invariant* over

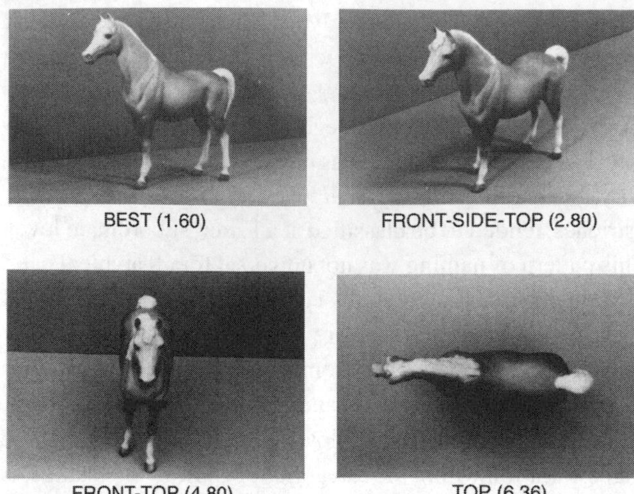

Figure 7.18 Different perspective views of a horse (see text). *Source:* From Palmer, Rosch, and Chase, 1981.

Figure 7.19 Stimuli used in an experiment on object recognition from different viewpoints. *Source:* From Bülthoff and Edelman, 1992.

perspective views. Closer study indicates that this is not true. Palmer, Rosch, and Chase (1981) systematically investigated and documented perspective effects in object identification. They began by having participants view many pictures of the same object (such as the horse series in Figure 7.18) and make subjective ratings of how much each one looked like the objects they depicted using a scale from 1 (very like) to 7 (very unlike). Participants made the average ratings indicated below the pictures. Other individuals were then asked to name the entry-level categories of these pictures, as quickly as possible, using five perspectives (from the best to the worst) based on the ratings. Pictures rated as the best (or *canonical*) perspective were named fastest, and naming latencies gradually increased as the goodness of the views declined, with the worst ones being named much more slowly than the best ones.

It seems possible that such perspective effects could be explained by familiarity: Perhaps canonical views are simply the most frequently seen views. More recent studies have examined perspective effects using identification of novel objects to control for frequency effects. For example, Edelman and Bülthoff (1992) found canonical view effects in recognition time for novel bent paper-clip objects that were initially presented to subjects in a sequence of static views that produced apparent rotation of the object in depth (Figure 7.19). Because each single view was presented exactly once in this motion sequence, familiarity effects should be eliminated. Even so, recognition performance varied significantly over viewpoints, consistent with the perspective effects reported by Palmer et al. (1981).

Further studies have shown that familiarity does matter, however. When only a small subset of views was displayed in the initial training sequence, later recognition performance was best for the views seen during the training sequence and decreased with angular distance from these training views (Bülthoff & Edelman, 1992; Edelman & Bülthoff, 1992). These results suggest that subjects may be storing specific two-dimensional views of the objects and matching novel views to them via processes that deteriorate with increasing disparity between the novel and stored views.

Further experiments demonstrated that when multiple views of the same objects were used in the training session, recognition performance improved, but the improvement depended on the relation of the test views to the training views (Bülthoff & Edelman, 1992). In particular, if the novel test views were related to the training views by rotation about the *same* axis through which the training views were related to each other, recognition was significantly better than for novel views that were rotations about an *orthogonal* axis. This suggests that people may be interpolating between and extrapolating beyond specific two-dimensional views in recognizing three-dimensional objects. This possibility will be important in this chapter's section entitled "Theories of Object Identification," in which view-based theories of object categorization are described (e.g., Poggio & Edelman, 1990; Ullman, 1996; Ullman & Basri, 1991).

A different method of study, known as the *priming paradigm,* has produced interesting but contradictory results about perspective views. The basic idea behind this experimental design is that categorizing a particular picture of an object will be faster and more accurate if the same picture is presented a second time, because the processes that accomplish it initially are in a state of heightened readiness for the second presentation (Bartram, 1974). The priming effect is defined as the difference between the naming latencies in the first block of trials and those in the second block of repeated pictures. What makes priming experiments informative about object categorization is that the repetitions in the second block of trials can differ from the initial presentation in different ways. For example, repetitions can be of the same object, but with changes in its position within the visual field (e.g., left vs. right side), its retinal size (large vs. small), its mirror-image reflection (as presented initially or left-right reversed), or the perspective from which the object is viewed.

The results of such studies show that the magnitude of the object priming effect does not diminish when the second presentation shows the same object in a different position or reflection (Biederman & Cooper, 1991) or even at a different size (Biederman & Cooper, 1992). Showing the same object from a different perspective, however, has been found to reduce the amount of priming (Bartram, 1974). This perspective effect is thus consistent with the naming latency results reported by Palmer et al. (1981) and the recognition results by Edelman and Bülthoff (1992) and Bülthoff and Edelman (1992). Later studies on priming with different perspective views of the same object by Biederman and Gerhardstein (1993), however, failed to show any significant decrease in priming effects due to depth rotations.

To explain this apparent contradiction, Biederman and Gerhardstein (1993) then went on to show that priming effects did not diminish when the same *parts* were visible in the different perspective conditions. This same-part visibility condition is not necessarily met by the views used in the other studies, which often include examples in which different parts were visible from different perspectives (see Figure 7.18). Visibility of the same versus different parts may thus explain why perspective effects have been found in some priming experiments but not in others. The results of these experiments on perspective effects therefore suggest care in distinguishing two different kinds of changes in perspective: those that do not change the set of visible parts, and those that do.

Orientation Effects

Other effects due to differences in object orientation cannot be explained in this way, however, because the same parts are visible in all cases. Orientation effects refer to perceptual differences caused by rotating an object about the observer's line of sight rather than rotating it in depth. Depth rotations of the object often change the visibility of different parts of the object, as just discussed, but orientation changes never do, and Jolicoeur (1985) has shown that subjects are faster at categorizing pictures of objects in a normal, upright orientation than when they are misoriented in the picture plane. Naming latencies increase with angular deviation from their upright orientation, as though subjects were mentally rotating the objects to upright before making their response.

Interestingly, orientation effects diminish considerably with extended practice. Tarr and Pinker (1989) studied this effect using novel objects so that the particular orientations at which subjects saw the objects could be precisely controlled. When subjects received extensive practice with the objects at *several* orientations, rather than just one, naming latencies were fast at *all* the learned orientations. Moreover, response times at novel orientations increased with distance from the nearest familiar orientation. Tarr and Pinker therefore suggested that people may actually store multiple representations of the same object at different orientations rather than a single representation that is orientation invariant. This possibility becomes particularly important in the section entitiled "Theories of Object Identification," in which view-specific theories of categorization are considered.

Part Structural Effects

The first half of this chapter developed the idea that perceptual organization is centrally related to the idea that the perceived world is structured into part-whole hierarchies. Human bodies have heads, arms, legs, and a torso; tables have a flat top surface, and legs; an airplane has a fuselage, two main wings, and several smaller tail fins. The important question is whether these parts play a significant mediating role in object identification. The most revealing studies of this question were performed by Biederman and Cooper (1991) using a version of the priming paradigm discussed in this chapter's section entitled "Perspective Effects." They showed that identification of degraded line drawings in the second (test) block of trials was facilitated when subjects had seen the *same parts* of the same objects in the initial (priming) block, but not when they had seen *different parts* of the same object in the priming block. This result implies that the process of identifying objects is mediated by perceiving their parts and spatial interrelations—because otherwise, it is not clear why more priming occurs only when the same parts were seen again.

The drawings Biederman and Cooper (1991) used were degraded by deleting half of the contours in each stimulus. In the first experiment, subjects were shown a priming series of contour-deleted drawings and then a test series in which they saw either the identical drawing (Figure 7.20; A), its line

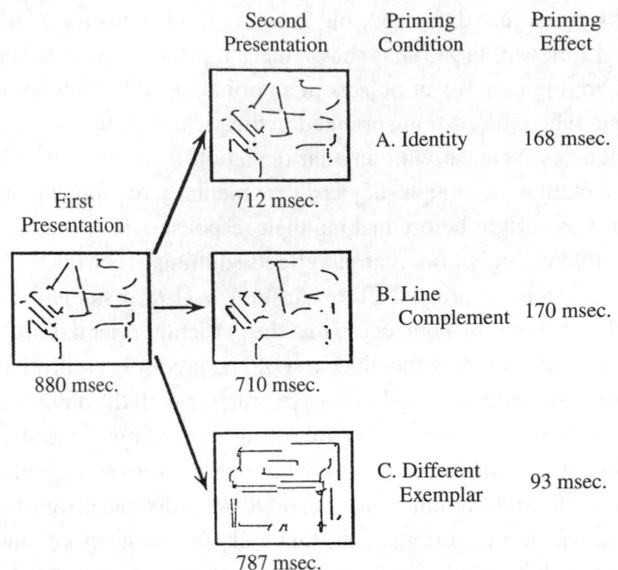

Figure 7.20 A line-complement priming experiment (see text). *Source:* From Palmer, 1999.

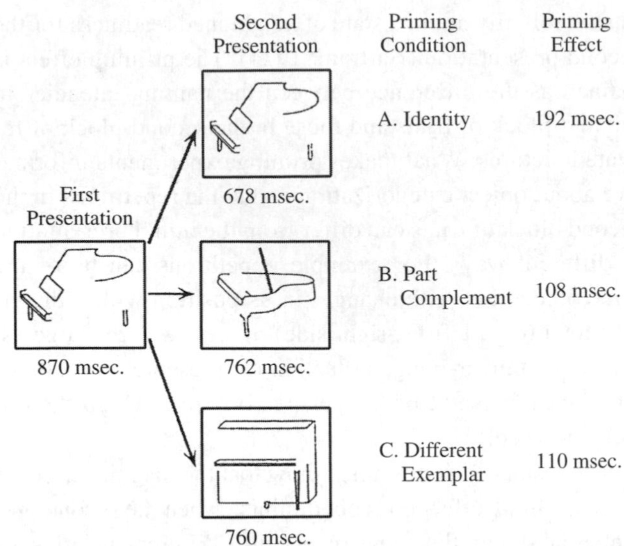

Figure 7.21 A part-complement priming experiment (see text). *Source:* From Palmer, 1999.

complement (Figure 7.20; B), or a different object from the same category (Figure 7.20; C). The results showed that the line-complement drawings produced just as much priming (170 ms) as the identical drawings (168 ms), and much more than the same-name drawings (93 ms). Biederman and Cooper (1991) argued that the stronger priming in the first two conditions was due to the fact that the same parts were perceived both in the identical and the line-complement drawings.

To be sure that this pattern was not due merely to the fact that the same object was depicted in the same pose in both of these conditions, they performed a second experiment, in which half of the parts were deleted in the initial priming block (Figures 7.21; A–C). Then, in the test block, they found that priming by the part-complement drawings was much less (108 ms) than was priming by the identical drawings (190 ms). In fact, part-complement priming was no different from that in the same-name control condition (110 ms). Thus, the important feature for obtaining significantly more priming than for mere response repetition is that the same parts must be visible in the priming and test blocks. This result supports the inference that object identification is mediated by part perception.

Contextual Effects

All of the phenomena of object identification considered thus far concern the nature of the target object itself: how typical it is of its category, the perspective from which it is viewed, and its size, position, orientation, and visible parts. But identification can also be influenced by *contextual factors:* the spatial array of objects that surround the target object. One well-known contextual effect can be demonstrated by the phrase TAE CAT, which everyone initially perceives as THE CAT. This seems entirely unproblematic—until one realizes that the central letters of both words are actually identical and ambiguous, midway between an *H* and an *A*. It is therefore possible that the letter strings could be perceived as *TAE CHT, TAE CAT,* or *THE CHT,* but this almost never happens.

There have been several well-controlled experiments documenting that appropriate context facilitates identification, whereas inappropriate context hinders it. In one such study, Palmer (1975a) presented subjects with line drawings of common objects to be identified following brief presentations of contextual scenes (Figure 7.22). The relation between the

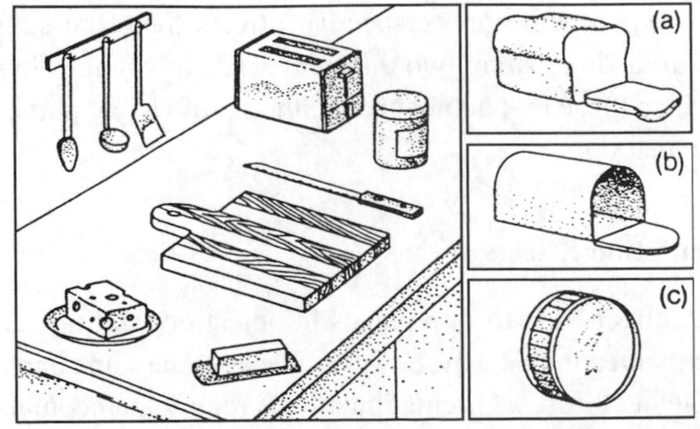

Figure 7.22 Stimuli from an experiment on contextual effects on object identification (see text). *Source:* From Palmer, 1975a.

contextual scene and the target object was studied. In the case of the kitchen counter scene, for example, the subsequently presented object could be either appropriate to the scene (a loaf of bread), inappropriate (a bass drum), or misleading in the sense that the target object was visually similar to the appropriate object (a mailbox). For the no-context control condition, the objects were presented following a blank field instead of a contextual scene. By presenting the objects and scenes in different combinations, all objects were equally represented in all four contextual conditions.

The results of this experiment showed that appropriate contexts facilitated correct categorization relative to the no-context control condition and that inappropriate contexts inhibited it. Performance was worst of all in the misleading context condition, in which participants were likely to name the visually similar object appropriate to the scene. These differences demonstrate that recognition accuracy can be substantially affected by the nature of the surrounding objects in a simple identification task.

Biederman (1972; Biederman, Glass, & Stacy, 1973) used a different method to study context effects. He had participants search for the presence of a given target object in a scene and measured their visual search times. In the first study, he manipulated context by presenting either a normal photograph or a randomly rearranged version. Participants took substantially longer to find the target object in the rearranged pictures than in the normal ones.

These contextual effects indicate that relations among objects in a scene are complex and important factors for normal visual identification. Obviously, people can identify objects correctly even in bizarre contexts. A fire hydrant on top of a mailbox may take longer to identify—and cause a major double-take after it is identified—but people manage to recognize it even so. Rather, context appears to change the efficiency of identification. In each case, the target object in a normal context is processed quickly and with few errors, whereas one in an abnormal context takes longer to process and is more likely to produce errors. Because normal situations are, by definition, encountered more frequently than are abnormal ones, such contextual effects are generally beneficial to the organism in its usual environment.

Visual Agnosia

A very different—and fascinating phenomenon of object identification is *visual agnosia,* a perceptual deficit due to brain damage, usually in the temporal lobe of cortex, in which patients are unable to correctly categorize common objects with which they were previously familiar. (*Agnosia* is a term derived from Greek that means *not knowing.*) There are many different forms of visual agnosia, and the relations among them are not well understood. Some appear to be primarily due to damage to the later stages of sensory processing (termed *apperceptive agnosia* by Lissauer, 1890/1988). Such patients appear unable to recognize objects because they do not see them normally. Other patients have fully intact perceptual abilities, yet still cannot identify the objects they see, a condition Lissauer called *associative agnosia.* Teuber (1968) described their condition as involving "a normal percept stripped of its meaning" due to an inability to categorize it correctly.

The case of a patient, known as "GL," is a good example of associative agnosia (Ellis & Young, 1988). This patient suffered a blow to his head when he was 80 years old, after which he complained that he could not see as well as before the accident. The problem was not that he was blind or even impaired in basic visual function, for he could see the physical properties of objects quite well; indeed, he could even copy pictures of objects that he could not identify. He mistook pictures for boxes, his jacket for a pair of trousers, and generally could not categorize even the simplest everyday objects correctly.

Patients with visual agnosia suffer from a variety of different symptoms. Some have deficits specific to particular classes of objects or properties. One classic example is *prosopagnosia:* the inability to recognize faces. Prosopagnosic patients can describe in detail the facial features of someone at whom they are looking, yet be completely unable to recognize the person, even if it is their spouse, their child, or their own face in a mirror. Such patients will typically react to a relative as a complete stranger—until the person speaks, at which time the patient can recognize his or her voice.

Other agnosic patients have been studied who have problems with object categories such as living things. Patient JBR, for example, was able to identify 90% of the pictures depicting inanimate objects, but only 6% of those depicting plants and animals (Warrington & Shallice, 1984). Even more selective deficits have been reported, including those confined to body parts, objects found indoors, and fruits and vegetables, although some of these deficits may be linguistic in nature rather than perceptual (Farah, 1990).

One problem for many visual agnosic persons that has been studied experimentally is their particular inability to categorize objects presented in atypical or unusual perspective views. Warrington and Taylor (1973, 1978) found that many agnosic persons who are able to categorize pictures of common objects taken from a usual perspective are unable to do so for unusual views. This phenomenon in agnosic patients bears a striking resemblance to perspective effects found in normally functioning individuals (Palmer et al., 1981), except that instead of simply taking longer to arrive at the correct answer, these patients are unable to perform the task at all, even in unrestricted viewing conditions.

There are many other visual disorders due to brain damage that are related to visual agnosia. They exhibit a wide variety of complex symptoms, are caused by a broad range of underlying brain pathologies, and are generally not well understood. Still, the case histories of such patients and their phenomenological descriptions of their symptoms make for fascinating reading, such as the patient whose agnosia led neurologist Oliver Sacks (1985) to entitle one of his books, *The Man Who Mistook His Wife for a Hat*. The interested reader is referred to Farah (1990, 2000) for discussions of these and related disorders.

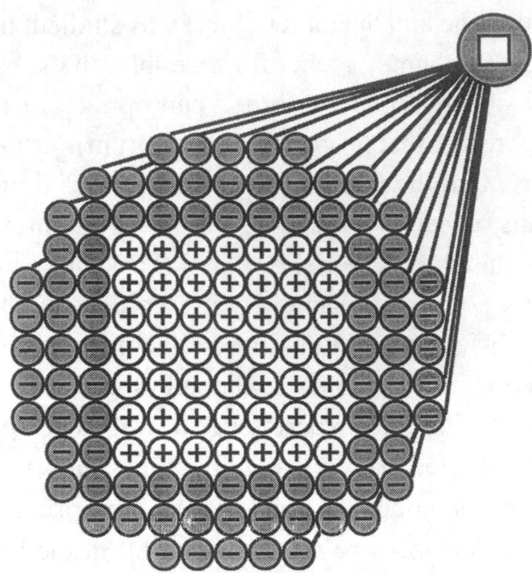

Figure 7.23 A template representation of a square. *Source:* From Palmer, 1999.

THEORIES OF OBJECT IDENTIFICATION

Given that people obviously manage to identify visually perceived objects as members of known, functional classes, how might this result be achieved? There are many possibilities, but within a modern, computational framework, all of them require four basic components: (a) The relevant characteristics of the to-be-categorized object must be perceived and represented within the visual system in an *object representation;* (b) Each of the set of possible categories must be represented in memory in a *category representation* that is accessible to the visual system; (c) There must be *comparison processes* through which the object representation is matched against possible category representations; (d) There must be a *decision process* that uses the results of the comparison process to determine the category to which a given object belongs. This section considers each of these components and then describes two contrasting types of theories that attempt to explain how object identification might be performed.

Representing Objects and Categories

The problem of how to represent objects and categories is a difficult one (cf. Palmer, 1978) that lies at the heart of most theories of object identification. Especially thorny are the representational issues pertaining to shape, which tends to be the single most important feature for object identification. Most proposals about shape representation cluster into three general classes: templates, feature lists, and structural descriptions, although various hybrids are also possible. Space limitations prohibit a detailed discussion of these issues, but the interested reader can consult the more extensive treatment by Palmer (1999, chapter 8).

Templates

The idea behind *templates* is to represent shape as shape. In standard presentations of this kind of theory, templates are specified by the conjunction of the set of receptors on which the image of the target shape would fall. A template for a square, for example, can be formed by constructing what is called a square-detector cell whose receptive field structure consists of excitation by all receptors that the square would stimulate, plus inhibition by all nearby receptors around it that it would not stimulate (Figure 7.23). A white square on a black ground would maximally excite this square detector because its spatial structure corresponds optimally to that of its receptive field.

Templates are often ridiculed as grossly inadequate for representing shape. In fact, however, they are the most obvious way to convert spatially structured images into symbolic descriptions. Line- and edge-detector theories of simple cells in cortical area V1 can be viewed as template representations for lines and edges. Each line detector cell responds maximally to a line at a specific position, orientation, and contrast (light on dark versus dark on light). Whether such a scheme can be extended to more complex shape representations is questionable (see following discussion), but recent theories of object identification have concentrated on view-specific representations that are template-like in many respects (see this chapter's section entitled "View-Specific Theories").

Some of the most difficult problems associated with templates as a general scheme for representing shapes of objects and categories are outlined in the following list:

1. *Concreteness:* There are many visual factors that have essentially no impact on perceived shape, yet strongly influence the matching of template representations, including

factors such as differences in lightness, color, texture, binocular disparity, and other low-level sensory features. A green square on a yellow ground is seen as having the same shape as a blue square on a red ground, for example, even though they will require separate templates. A general square template would thus have to be the disjunction of a huge number of very specific square templates.

2. *Spatial transformations:* Shape is largely invariant over the similarity transformations—translations, rotations, dilations, reflections, and their various combinations (Palmer, 1989)—yet comparing template representations that differ by such transformations will not generally produce good matches. Three ways to solve this problem for template representations are replication, interpolation, and normalization. *Replication* refers to the strategy of constructing a different template for each distinct shape in each position, orientation, size, and sense (reflection), as the visual system does for receptive field structures in area V1. This is feasible only if the set of template shapes is very small, however. *Interpolation* is a way of reducing the number of templates by including processes that can construct intermediate representations between a pair of stored templates, thus reducing the number of templates, but at the expense of increasing the complexity of the matching process. *Normalization* postulates processes that transform (or normalize) the input image into a canonical position, orientation, size, and sense prior to being matched against the templates so that these factors do not matter. How to normalize effectively then becomes a further problem.

3. *Part structure:* People perceive most objects as having a complex hierarchical structure of parts (see this chapter's section entitled "Perceptual Organization"), but templates have just two levels: the whole template and the atomic elements (receptors) that are associated within the template. This means that standard templates cannot be matched on a partwise basis, as appears to be required when an object is partly occluded.

4. *Three dimensionality:* Templates are intrinsically two-dimensional, whereas most objects are three-dimensional. There are just two solutions to this problem. One is to make the internal templates three-dimensional, like the objects themselves, but that means that three-dimensional templates would have to be constructed by some complex process that integrates many different two-dimensional views into a single three-dimensional representation (e.g., Lowe, 1985). The other solution is to make the internal representations of three-dimensional objects two-dimensional by representing two-dimensional projections of their shapes. This approach has the further problem that different views of the same object would then fail to match any single template. Solving this problem by replication requires different templates for each distinct perspective view, necessitating hundreds or thousands of templates for complex three-dimensional objects. Solving it by interpolation requires additional processes that generate intermediate views from two stored views (e.g., Poggio & Edelman, 1990; Ullman & Basri, 1991). Normalization is not feasible because a single two-dimensional view simply does not contain enough information to specify most objects from some other viewpoint.

Feature Lists

A more intuitively appealing class of shape representation is *feature lists:* symbolic descriptions consisting of a simple set of attributes. A square, for example, might be represented by the following set of discrete features: *is-closed, has-four-sides, has-four-right-angles, is-vertically-symmetrical, is-horizontally-symmetrical,* etc. The degree of similarity between an object shape and that of a stored category can then be measured by the degree of correspondence between the two feature sets.

In general, two types of features have been used for representing shape: *global properties,* such as symmetry, closure, and connectedness, and *local parts,* such as containing a straight line, a curved line, or an acute angle. Both types of properties can be represented either as *binary features* (e.g., a given symmetry being either present or absent) or as *continuous dimensions* (e.g., the degree to which a given symmetry is present). Most classical feature representations are of the discrete, binary sort (e.g., Gibson, 1969), but ones based on continuous, multidimensional features have also been proposed (e.g., Massaro & Hary, 1986).

One reason for the popularity of feature representations is that they do not fall prey to many of the objections that so cripple template theories. Feature representations can solve the problem of concreteness simply by postulating features that are already abstract and symbolic. The feature list suggested for a square at the beginning of this section, for example, made no reference to its color, texture, position, or size. It is an abstract, symbolic description of all kinds of squares. Features also seem able to solve the problem of part structure simply by including the different parts of an object in the feature list, as in the previously mentioned feature list for squares. Similarly, a feature representation of a human body might include the following part-based features: *having-a-head, having-a-torso, having-two-legs,* and so forth. The features of a head would likewise include *having two-eyes, having-a-nose, having-a-mouth,* etc. Features also seem capable of solving the problems resulting from three-dimensionality, at least in principle. The kinds of features that are included in a shape representation can refer to intrinsically three-dimensional qualities and parts as well as two-dimensional ones, and so can be used to capture the shape of three-dimensional as well as two-dimensional objects. For instance, the shape of an object can be described as having the feature *spherical* rather than *circular* and as *contains-a-pyramid* rather than *contains-a-triangle.* Thus, there is nothing intrinsic to the feature-list approach that limits it to two-dimensional features.

Feature theories have several important weaknesses, however. One is that it is often unclear how to determine computationally whether a given object actually *has* the features that are proposed to comprise its shape representation. Simple part-features of two-dimensional images, such as lines, edges, and blobs, can be computed from an underlying template system as discussed above, but even these must be abstracted from the color-, size-, and orientation-specific peripheral channels that detect lines, edges, and blobs. Unfortunately, these simple image-based features are just the tip of a very large iceberg. They do not cover the plethora of different attributes that feature theorists might (and do) propose in their representations of shape. Features like *contains-a-cylinder* or *has-a-nose,* for instance, are not easy to compute from gray-scale images. Until such feature-extraction routines are available to back up the features proposed for the representations, feature-based theories are incomplete in a very important sense.

Another difficult problem is specifying what the proper features might be for a shape representation system. It is one thing to propose that some appropriate set of shape features can, in principle, account for shape perception, but quite another to say exactly what those features are. Computer-based methods such as multidimensional scaling (Shepard, 1962a, 1962b) and hierarchical clustering can help in limited domains, but they have not yet succeeded in suggesting viable schemes for the general problem of representing shape in terms of lists of properties.

Structural Descriptions

Structural descriptions are graph-theoretical representations that can be considered an elaboration or extension of feature theories. They generally contain three distinct types of information: properties, parts, and relations between parts. They are usually depicted as hierarchical networks in which nodes represent the whole object and its various parts and subparts with labeled links (or arcs) between nodes that represent structural relations between objects and parts. Because of this hierarchical network format, structural descriptions are surely the representational approach that is closest to the view of perceptual organization that was presented in the first half of this chapter.

Another important aspect of perceptual organization that can be encoded in structural descriptions is information about the intrinsic reference frame for the object as a whole and for each of its parts. Each reference frame can be represented as global features attached to the node corresponding to the object or part, one each for its position, orientation, size, and reflection (e.g., Marr, 1982; Palmer, 1975b). The reference frame for a part can then be represented relative to that of its superordinate, as evidence from organizational phenomena suggests (see this chapter's section entitled "Frames of Reference").

One serious problem with structural descriptions is how to represent the global shapes of the components. An attractive solution is to postulate *shape primitives:* a set of indivisible perceptual units into which all other shapes can be decomposed. For three-dimensional objects, such as people, houses, trees, and cars, the shape primitives presumably must be three-dimensional volumes. The best known proposal of this type is Binford's (1971) suggestion, later popularized by Marr (1982), that complex shapes can be analyzed into combinations of *generalized cylinders.* As the name implies, generalized cylinders are a generalization of standard geometric cylinders in which several further parameters are introduced to encompass a larger set of shapes. Variables are added to allow, for example, a *variable base shape* (e.g., square or trapezoidal in addition to circular), a variable axis (e.g., curved in addition to straight), a *variable sweeping rule* (e.g., the cross-sectional size getting small toward one end in addition to staying a constant size), and so forth. Some of the other proposals about shape primitives are very closely related to generalized cylinders, such as *geons* (Biederman, 1987) and some are rather different, such as *superquadrics* (Pentland, 1986).

Structural descriptions with volumetric shape primitives can overcome many of the difficulties with template and feature approaches. Like features, they can represent abstract visual information, such as edges defined by luminance, texture, and motion. They can account for the effects of spatial transformations on shape perception by absorbing them within object-centered reference frames. They deal explicitly with the problem of part structure by having distinct representations of parts and the spatial relations among those parts. And they are able to represent three-dimensional shape by using volumetric primitives and three-dimensional spatial relations in representing three-dimensional objects.

One difficulty with structural descriptions is that the representations become quite complex, so that matching two such descriptions constitutes a difficult problem by itself. Another is that a sufficiently powerful set of primitives and relations must be identified. Given the subtlety of many shape-dependent perceptions, such as recognizing known faces, this is not an easy task. Further, computational routines must be devised to identify the volumetric primitives and relations from which the structural descriptions are constructed, whatever those might be. Despite these problems, structural descriptions seem to be in the right ballpark, and their general form corresponds nicely with the result of organizational processes discussed in the first section of this chapter.

Comparison and Decision Processes

After a representation has been specified for the to-be-identified objects and the set of known categories, a process has to be devised for comparing the object representation with each category representation. This could be done serially across categories, but it makes much more sense for it to be performed in parallel. Parallel matching could be implemented, for example, in a neural network that works by spreading activation, where the input automatically activates all possible categorical representations to different degrees, depending on the strength of the match (e.g., Hummel & Biederman, 1992).

Because the schemes for comparing representations are rather specific to the type of representation, in the following discussion I will simply assume that a parallel comparison process can be defined that has an output for each category that is effectively a bounded, continuous variable representing how well the target object's representation matches the category representation. The final process is then to make a decision about the category to which the target object belongs. Several different rules have been devised to perform this decision, including the *threshold, best-fit,* and *best-fit-over-threshold* rules.

The threshold approach is to set a criterial value for each category that determines whether a target object counts as one of its members. The currently processed object is then assigned to whatever category, if any, exceeds its threshold matching value. This scheme can be implemented in a neural network in which each neural unit that represents a category has its own internal threshold, such that it begins to fire only after that threshold is exceeded. The major drawback of a simple threshold approach is that it may allow the same object to be categorized in many different ways (e.g., as a fox, a dog, and a wolf), because more than one category may exceed its threshold at the same time.

The best-fit approach is to identify the target object as a member of whatever category has the highest match among a set of mutually exclusive categories. This can be implemented in a "winner-take-all" neural network in which each category unit inhibits every other category unit among some mutually exclusive set. Its main problem lies in the impossibility of deciding that a novel target object is not a member of any known category. This is an issue because there is, by definition, always *some* category that has the highest similarity to the target object.

The virtues of both decision rules can be combined—with the drawbacks of neither—using a hybrid decision strategy: the best-fit-over-threshold rule. This approach is to set a threshold below which objects will be perceived as novel, but above which the category with the highest matching value is chosen. Such a decision rule can be implemented in a neural network by having internal thresholds for each category unit as well as a winner-take-all network of mutual inhibition among all category units. This combination allows for the possibility of identifying objects as novel without resulting in ambiguity when more than one category exceeds the threshold. It would not be appropriate for deciding among different hierarchically related categories (e.g., collie, dog, and animal), however, because they are not mutually exclusive.

Part-Based Theories

Structural description theories were the most influential approaches to object identification in the late 1970s and 1980s. Various versions were developed by computer scientists and computationally oriented psychologists, including Binford (1971), Biederman (1987), Marr (1982), Marr & Nishihara (1978), and Palmer (1975b). Of the specific theories that have been advanced within this general framework, this chapter describes only one in detail: Biederman's (1987) *recognition by components theory,* sometimes called *geon theory*. It is not radically different from several others, but it is easier to describe and has been developed with more attention to the results of experimental evidence. I therefore present it as representative of this class of models rather than as the correct or even the best one.

Recognition by components (RBC) theory is Biederman's (1987) attempt to formulate a single, psychologically motivated theory of how people classify objects as members of entry-level categories. It is based on the idea that objects can be specified as spatial arrangements of a small set of volumetric primitives, which Biederman called *geons.* Object categorization then occurs by matching a geon-based structural description of the target object with corresponding geon-based structural descriptions of object categories. It was later implemented as a neural network (Hummel & Biederman, 1992), but this chapter considers it at the more abstract algorithmic level of Biederman's (1987) original formulation.

Geons

The first important assumption of RBC theory is that both the stored representations of categories and the representation of a currently attended object are volumetric structural descriptions. Recognition-by-components representations are functional hierarchies whose nodes correspond to a discrete set of three-dimensional volumes (geons) and whose links to other nodes correspond to relations among these geons. Geons are generalized cylinders that have been partitioned into discrete classes by dividing their inherently continuous parameters (see below) into a few discrete ranges that are easy to distinguish from most vantage points. From the relatively small set of 108 distinct geons, a huge number of object representations can be constructed by putting together two or more geons much as an enormous number of words can be constructed by putting together a relatively small number of letters. A few representative geons are illustrated in Figure 7.24 along with some common objects constructed by putting several geons together to form recognizable objects.

Biederman defined the set of 108 geons by making discrete distinctions in the following variable dimensions of generalized cylinders: *cross-sectional curvature* (straight vs. curved), *symmetry* (asymmetrical vs. reflectional symmetry alone vs. both reflectional and rotational symmetry), *axis curvature* (straight vs. curved), *cross-sectional size variation* (constant vs. expanding and contracting vs. expanding only), and *aspect ratio* of the sweeping axis relative to the largest dimension of the cross-sectional area (approximately equal vs. axis greater vs. cross-section greater). The rationale for these particular distinctions is that, except for aspect ratio, they are qualitative rather than merely quantitative differences that result in qualitatively different retinal projections. The image features that characterize different geons are therefore relatively (but not completely) insensitive to changes in viewpoint.

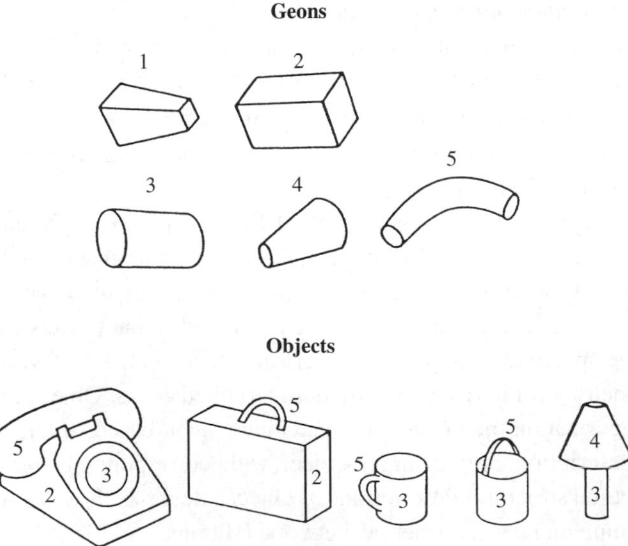

Figure 7.24 Examples of geons and their presence in objects (see text). *Source:* From Biederman, 1995.

Because complex objects are conceived in RBC theory as configurations of two or more geons in particular spatial arrangements, they are encoded as structural descriptions that specify both geons and their spatial relations. It is therefore possible to construct different object types by arranging the same geons in different spatial relations, such as the cup and pail in Figure 7.24. RBC theory uses 108 qualitatively different geon relations. Some of them concern how geons are attached (e.g., *side-connected* and *top-connected*), whereas others concern their relational properties, such as relative size (e.g., larger than and smaller than). With 108 geon relations and 108 geons, it is logically possible to construct more than a million different two-geon objects. Adding a third geon pushes the number of combinations into the billions. Clearly, geons are capable of generating a rich vocabulary of different complex shapes. Whether it is sufficient to capture the power and versatility of visual categorization is a question to which this discussion returns later.

After the shape of an object has been represented via its component geons and their spatial relations, the problem of object categorization within RBC theory reduces to the process of matching the structural description of an incoming object with the set of structural descriptions for known entry-level categories. The theory proposes that this process takes place in several stages. In the original formulation, the overall flow of information was depicted in the flowchart of Figure 7.25—(a) An *edge extraction* process initially produces a line drawing of the edges present in the visual scene; (b) The image-based properties needed to identify geons are extracted from the edge information by *detection of nonaccidental properties.* The crucial features are the nature of the edges (e.g., curved versus straight), the nature of the vertices (e.g., Y-vertices, K-vertices, L-vertices, etc.), parallelism (parallel vs. nonparallel), and symmetry (symmetric vs. asymmetric). The goal of this process is to provide the feature-based information required to identify the different kinds of geons (see Stage d); (c) At the same time as these features are being extracted, the system attempts to *parse objects at regions of deep concavity,* as suggested by Hoffman and Richards (1984) and discussed in the section of this chapter entitled "Parsing." The goal of this parsing process is to divide the object into component geons without having to match them explicitly on the basis of edge and vertex features; (d) The combined results of feature detection (b) and object parsing (c) are used to *activate the appropriate geons and spatial relations* among them; (e) After the geon description of the

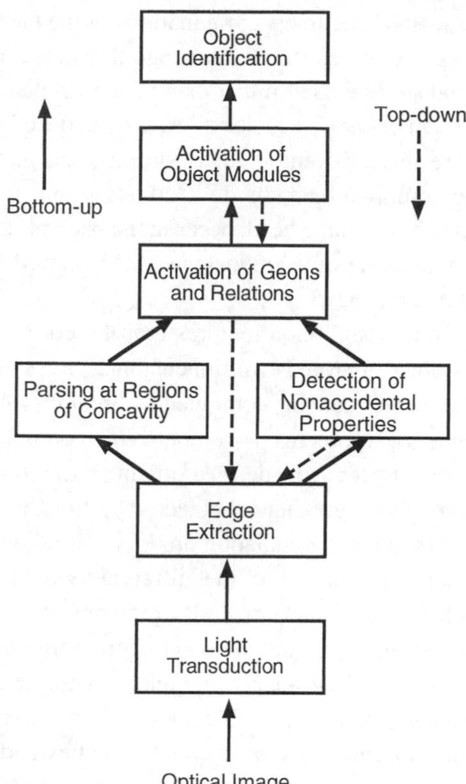

Figure 7.25 Processing stages in RBC theory (see text). *Source:* From Biederman, 1987.

input object is constructed, it automatically causes the activation of similar geon descriptions stored in memory. This matching process is accomplished by activation spreading through a network from geon nodes and relation nodes present in the representation of the target object to similar geon nodes and relation nodes in the category representations. This comparison is a fully parallel process, matching the geon description of the input object against all category representations at once and using all geons and relations at once; (f) Finally, *object identification* occurs when the target object is classified as an instance of the entry-level category that is most strongly activated by the comparison process, provided it exceeds some threshold value.

Although the general flow of information within RBC theory is generally bottom-up, it also allows for top-down processing. If sensory information is weak (e.g., noisy, brief, or otherwise degraded images) top-down effects are likely to occur. There are two points in RBC at which they are most likely to happen: feedback from geons to geon features and feedback from category representations to geons. Contextual effects could also occur through feedback from prior or concurrent object identification to the nodes of related sets of objects, although this level of processing was not actually represented in Biederman's (1987) model.

View-Specific Theories

In many ways, the starting point for view-specific theories of object identification is the existence of the perspective effects described in the section of this chapter entitled "Perspective Effects." The fact that recognition and categorization performance is not invariant over different views (e.g., Palmer et al., 1981) raises the possibility that objects might be identified by matching two-dimensional input images directly to some kind of view-specific category representation. It cannot be done with a single, specific view (such as one canonical perspective) because there is simply not enough information in any single view to identify other views. A more realistic possibility is that there might be *multiple* two-dimensional representations from several different viewpoints that can be employed in recognizing objects. These multiple views are likely to be those perspectives from which the object has been seen most often in past experience. As mentioned in this chapter's section entitled "Orientation Effects," evidence supporting this possibility has come from a series of experiments that studied the identification of two-dimensional figures at different orientations in the frontal plane (Tarr & Pinker, 1989) and of three-dimensional figures at different perspectives (Bülthoff & Edelman, 1992; Edelman & Bülthoff, 1992).

Several theories of object identification encorporate some degree of view specificity. One is Koenderink and Van Doorn's (1979) *aspect graph theory,* which is a well-defined elaboration of Minsky's (1975) *frame theory* of object perception. An aspect graph is a network of representations containing all topologically distinct two-dimensional views (or *aspects*) of the same object. Its major problem is that it cannot distinguish among different objects that have the same edge topology. All tetrahedrons are equivalent within aspect graph theory—for example, despite large metric differences that are easily distinguished perceptually. This means that there is more information available to the visual system than is captured by edge topology, a conclusion that led to later theories in which projective geometry plays an important role in matching input views to object representations.

One approach was to match incoming two-dimensional images to internal three-dimensional models by an alignment process (e.g., Huttenlocher & Ullman, 1987; Lowe, 1985; Ullman, 1989). Another was to match incoming two-dimensional images directly against stored two-dimensional views, much as template theories advocate (e.g., Poggio & Edelman, 1990; Ullman, 1996; Ullman & Basri, 1991). The latter, exclusively two-dimensional approach has the same problem that plagues template theories of recognition: An indefinitely large number of views would have to be stored.

Figure 7.26 Novel views obtained by combination of gray-scale images (see text). *Source:* From Ullman, 1996.

However, modern theorists have discovered computational methods for deriving many two-dimensional views from just a few stored ones, thus suggesting that template-like theories may be more tenable than had originally been supposed.

Ullman and Basri (1991) demonstrated the viability of deriving novel two-dimensional views from a small set of other two-dimensional views, at least under certain restricted conditions, by proving that all possible views of an object can be reconstructed as a linear combination from just three suitably chosen orthographic projections of the same three-dimensional object. Figure 7.26 shows some rather striking examples based on this method. Two actual two-dimensional views of a human face (models M1 and M2) have been combined to produce other two-dimensional views of the same face. One is an intermediate view that has been interpolated *between* the two models (linear combination LC2), and the other two views have been extrapolated *beyond* them (linear combinations LC1 and LC3). Notice the close resemblance between the interpolated view (LC2) and the actual view from the corresponding viewpoint (novel view N).

This surprising result only holds under very restricted conditions, however, some of which are ecologically unrealistic. Three key assumptions of Ullman and Basri's (1991) analysis are that (a) all points belonging to the object must be visible in each view, (b) the correct correspondence of all points between each pair of views must be known, and (c) the views must differ only by rigid transformations and by uniform size scaling (dilations). The first assumption requires that none of the points on the object be occluded in any of the three views. This condition holds approximately for wire objects, which are almost fully visible from any viewpoint, but it is violated by almost all other three-dimensional objects due to occlusion. The linear combinations of the faces in Figure 7.26, for example, actually generate the image of a mask of the facial surface itself rather than of the whole head. The difference can be seen by looking carefully at the edges of the face, where the head ends rather abruptly and unnaturally. The linear combination method would not be able to derive a profile view of the same head, because the back of the head is not present in either of the model views (M1 and M2) used to extrapolate other views.

The second assumption requires that the correspondence between points in stored two-dimensional views be known before the views can be combined. Although solving the correspondence problems is a nontrivial computation for complex objects, it can be derived off-line rather than during the process of recognizing an object. The third assumption means that the view combination process will fail to produce an accurate combination if the different two-dimensional views include plastic deformations of the object. If one view is of a person standing and the other of the same person sitting, for instance, their linear combination will not necessarily correspond to any possible view of the person. This restriction thus can cause problems for bodies and faces of animate creatures as well as inanimate objects made of pliant materials (e.g., clothing) or having a jointed structure (e.g., scissors). Computational theorists are currently exploring ways of solving these problems (see Ullman, 1996, for a wide-ranging discussion of such issues), but they are important limitations of the linear combinations approach.

The results obtained by Ullman and Basri (1991) prove that two-dimensional views can be combined to produce new views under the stated conditions, but it does not specify how these views can be used to recognize the object from an input image. Further techniques are required to find a best-fitting match between the input view and the linear combinations of the model views as part of the object recognition process. One approach is to use a small number of features to find the best combination of the model views. Other methods are also possible, but are too technical to be described here. (The interested reader can consult Ullman, 1996, for details.)

Despite the elegance of some of the results that have been obtained by theorists working within the view-specific framework, such theories face serious problems as a general explanation of visual object identification.

1. They do not account well for people's perceptions of three-dimensional structure in objects. Just from looking at an object, even from a single perspective, people generally know a good deal about its three-dimensional structure, including how to shape their hands to grasp it and what it would feel like if they were to explore it manually.

It is not clear how this can occur if their only resource is a structured set of two-dimensional views.

2. Most complex objects have a fairly clear perceived hierarchical structure in terms of parts and subparts. The view-specific representations previously considered do not contain any explicit representation of such hierarchical structure because they consist of sets of unarticulated points or low-level features, such as edges and vertices. It is not clear, then, how such theories could explain Biederman and Cooper's (1991) priming experiments on the difference between line and part deletion conditions (see section entitiled "Part Structural Effects"). Ullman (1996) has suggested that parts as well as whole objects may be represented separately in memory. This proposal serves as a reminder that part-based recognition schemes like RBC and view-based schemes are not mutually exclusive, but rather can be combined into various hybrid approaches (e.g., Hummel & Stankiewicz, 1996).
3. Finally, it is not clear how the theory could be extended to handle object identification for entry-level categories. The situations to which view-specific theories have been successfully applied thus far are limited to identical objects that vary only in viewpoint, such as recognizing different views of the same face. The huge variation among different exemplars of chairs, dogs, and houses poses serious problems for view specific theories.

One possible resolution would be that both part-based and view-based processes may be used, but for different kinds of tasks (e.g., Farah, 1992; Tarr & Bülthoff, 1995). View-specific representations seem well suited to recognizing the very same object from different perspective views because in that situation, there is no variation in the structure of the object; all the differences between images can be explained by the variation in viewpoint. Recognizing specific objects is difficult for structural description theories, because their representations are seldom specific enough to discriminate between different exemplars. In contrast, structural description theories such as RBC seem well suited to entry level categorization because they have more abstract representations that are better able to encompass shape variations among different exemplars of the same category. This is exactly where view-specific theories have difficulty.

Another possibility is that both view-based and part-based schemes can be combined to achieve the best of both worlds. They are not mutually exclusive, and could even be implemented in parallel (e.g., Hummel & Stankiewicz, 1996). This approach suggests that when the current view matches one stored in view-based form in memory, recognition will be fast and accurate; when it does not, categorization must rely on the slower, more complex process of matching against structural descriptions. Which, if any, of these possible resolutions of the current conflict will turn out to be most productive is not yet clear. The hope is that the controversy will generate interesting predictions that can be tested experimentally, for that is how science progresses.

The foregoing discussion of what is known about perceptual organization and object identification barely scratches the surface of what needs to be known to understand the central mystery of vision: how the responses of millions of independent retinal receptors manage to provide an organism with knowledge of the identities and spatial relations among meaningful objects in its environment. It is indisputable that people achieve such knowledge, that it is evolutionarily important for our survival as individuals and as a species, and that scientists do not yet know how it arises. Despite the enormous amount that has been learned about low-level processing of visual information, the higher-level problems of organization and identification remain largely unsolved. It will take a concerted effort on the part of the entire vision science community—including psychophysicists, cognitive psychologists, physiologists, neuropsychologists, and computer scientists—to reach explanatory solutions. Only then will we begin to understand how the extraordinary feat of perception is accomplished by the visual nervous system.

REFERENCES

Anderson, B. L. (1997). A theory of illusory lightness and transparency in monocular and binocular images: The role of contour junctions. *Perception, 26*(4), 419–453.

Asch, S. E., & Witkin, H. A. (1948a). Studies in space orientation: I. Perception of the upright with displaced visual fields. *Journal of Experimental Psychology, 38,* 325–337.

Asch, S. E., & Witkin, H. A. (1948b). Studies in space orientation: II. Perception of the upright with displaced visual fields and with body tilted. *Journal of Experimental Psychology, 38,* 455–477.

Bartram, D. J. (1974). The role of visual and semantic codes in object naming. *Cognitive Psychology, 6*(3), 325–356.

Beck, J. (1966). Effects of orientation and shape similarity on perceptual grouping. *Perception and Psychophysics, 1,* 300–302.

Beck, J. (1972). Similarity grouping and peripheral discriminability under uncertainty. *American Journal of Psychology, 85*(1), 1–19.

Beck, J. (1982). Textural segmentation. In J. Beck (Ed.), *Organization and representation in perception* (pp. 285–318). Hillsdale, NJ: Lawrence Erlbaum.

Biederman, I. (1972). Perceiving real-world scenes. *Science, 177* (4043), 77–80.

Biederman, I. (1987). Recognition-by-components: A theory of human image understanding. *Psychological Review, 94*(2), 115–117.

Biederman, I. (1995). Visual identification. In S. M. Kosslyn & D. N. Osherson (Eds.), *An invitation to cognitive science: Vol. 2, Visual cognition* (pp. 121–165). Cambridge, MA: MIT Press.

Biederman, I., & Cooper, E. E. (1991). Priming contour-deleted images: Evidence for intermediate representations in visual object recognition. *Cognitive Psychology, 23*(3), 393–419.

Biederman, I., & Cooper, E. E. (1992). Size invariance in visual object priming. *Journal of Experimental Psychology: Human Perception & Performance, 18*(1), 121–133.

Biederman, I., & Gerhardstein, P. C. (1993). Recognizing depth-rotated objects: Evidence and conditions for three-dimensional viewpoint invariance. *Journal of Experimental Psychology: Human Perception & Performance, 19*(6), 1162–1182.

Biederman, I., Glass, A. L., & Stacy, E. W. (1973). Searching for objects in real-world scenes. *Journal of Experimental Psychology, 97*(1), 22–27.

Binford, T. O. (1971). *Visual perception by computer.* Paper presented at the IEEE Conference on Systems and Control, Miami, FL.

Bucher, N. M., & Palmer, S. E. (1985). Effects of motion on perceived pointing of ambiguous triangles. *Perception & Psychophysics, 38*(3), 227–236.

Buffart, H., & Leeuwenberg, E. L. J. (1981). Structural information theory. In H. G. Geissler, E. L. J. Leeuwenberg, S. Link, & V. Sarris (Eds.), *Modern issues in perception.* Berlin, Germany: Lawrence Erlbaum.

Bülthoff, H. H., & Edelman, S. (1992). Psychophysical support for a two-dimensional interpolation theory of object recognition. *Proceedings of the National Academy of Science, USA, 89,* 60–64.

Canny, J. F. (1986). A computational approach to edge detection. *IEEE Transactions on Pattern Analysis and Machine Intelligence, 8,* 769–798.

Delis, D. C., Robertson, L. C., & Efron, R. (1986). Hemispheric specialization of memory for visual hierarchical stimuli. *Neuropsychologia, 24*(2), 205–214.

DiLorenzo, J. R., & Rock, I. (1982). The rod-and-frame effect as a function of the righting of the frame. *Journal of Experimental Psychology: Human Perception & Performance, 8*(4), 536–546.

Driver, J., & Baylis, G. C. (1996). Edge-assignment and figure-ground segmentation in short-term visual matching. *Cognitive Psychology, 31,* 248–306.

Ebenholtz, S. M. (1977). Determinants of the rod-and-frame effect: The role of retinal size. *Perception & Psychophysics, 22*(6), 531–538.

Edelman, S., & Bülthoff, H. H. (1992). Orientation dependence in the recognition of familiar and novel views of three-dimensional objects. *Vision Research, 32*(12), 2385–2400.

Ellis, A. W., & Young, A. W. (1988). *Human cognitive neuropsychology.* Hillsdale, NJ: Erlbaum.

Essen, D. C. Van, & DeYoe, E. A. (1995). Concurrent processing in the primate visual cortex. In M. S. Gazzaniga (Ed.), *The cognitive neurosciences* (pp. 383–400). Cambridge, MA: MIT Press.

Farah, M. J. (1990). *Visual agnosia: Disorders of object recognition and what they tell us about normal vision.* Cambridge, MA: MIT Press.

Farah, M. J. (1992). Is an object and object an object?: Cognitive and neuropsychological investigations of domain specificity in visual object recognition. *Current Directions in Psychological Science, 1,* 164–169.

Farah, M. J. (2000). *The cognitive neuroscience of vision.* Malden, MA: Blackwell Publishers.

Gerbino, W. (1994). Achromatic transparency. In A. L. Gilchrist (Ed.), *Lightness, brightness, and transparency* (pp. 215–255). Hillsdale, NJ: Lawrence Erlbaum.

Gibson, E. J. (1969). *Principles of perceptual learning and development.* New York: Appleton-Century-Crofts.

Gibson, J. J. (1979). *The ecological approach to visual perception.* Boston: Houghton Mifflin.

Gregory, R. L. (1972). Cognitive contours. *Nature, 238,* 51–52.

Heydt, R. von der, Peterhans, E., & Baumgartner, G. (1984). Illusory contours and cortical neuron responses. *Science, 224* (4654), 1260–1262.

Hochberg, J., & McAlister, E. (1953). A quantitative approach to figural "goodness." *Journal of Experimental Psychology, 46,* 361–364.

Hochberg, J., & Silverstein, A. (1956). A quantitative index for stimulus similarity: Proximity versus differences in brightness. *American Journal of Psychology, 69,* 480–482.

Hoffman, D. D., & Richards, W. A. (1984). Parts of recognition: Visual cognition [Special issue]. *Cognition, 18*(1-3), 65–96.

Hubel, D. H., & Wiesel, T. N. (1962). Receptive fields, binocular interaction, and functional architecture of the cat's visual cortex. *Journal of Physiology (London), 160,* 106–154.

Hummel, J. E., & Biederman, I. (1992). Dynamic binding in a neural network for shape recognition. *Psychological Review, 99*(3), 480–517.

Hummel, J. E., & Stankiewicz, B. J. (1996). Categorical relations in shape perception. *Spatial Vision, 10*(3), 201–236.

Huttenlocher, D. P., & Ullman, S. (1987). *Object recognition using alignment* (MIT AI Memo No. 937). Cambridge, MA: MIT.

Jolicoeur, P. (1985). The time to name disoriented natural objects. *Memory & Cognition, 13*(4), 289–303.

Jolicoeur, P., Gluck, M. A., & Kosslyn, S. M. (1984). Pictures and names: Making the connection. *Cognitive Psychology, 16*(2), 243–275.

Julesz, B. (1981). Textons, the elements of texture perception, and their interactions. *Nature, 290*(5802), 91–97.

Kanizsa, G. (1955). Margini quasi-percettivi in campi con stimolazione omogenea. *Rivista di Psicologia, 49,* 7–30.

Kanizsa, G. (1979). *Organization in vision: Essays on Gestalt perception.* New York: Praeger.

Kanizsa, G., & Gerbino, W. (1976). Convexity and symmetry in figure-ground organization. In M. Henle (Ed.), *Vision and artifact* (pp. 25–32). New York: Springer.

Kellman, P. J., & Shipley, T. F. (1991). A theory of visual interpolation in object perception. *Cognitive Psychology, 23*(2), 141–221.

Kinchla, R. A., & Wolfe, J. M. (1979). The order of visual processing: "Top-down," "bottom-up," or "middle-out." *Perception & Psychophysics, 25*(3), 225–231.

Koenderink, J. J., & van Doorn, A. J. (1979). The internal representation of solid shape with respect to vision. *Biological Cybernetics, 32,* 211–216.

Koffka, K. (1935). *Principles of Gestalt psychology.* New York: Harcourt, Brace.

Kopferman, H. (1930). Psychologishe Untersuchungen uber die Wirkung Zweidimensionaler korperlicher Gebilde. *Psychologische Forschung, 13,* 293–364.

Kubovy, M., & Gepstein, S. (2000). Gestalt: From phenomena to laws. In K. Boyer & S. Sarkar (Eds.), *Perceptual organization for artificial vision systems* (pp. 41–72). Dordrecht, the Netherlands: Kluwer Academic.

Kubovy, M., & Wagemans, J. (1995). Grouping by proximity and multistability in dot lattices: A quantitative Gestalt theory. *Psychological Science, 6*(4), 225–234.

Leeuwenberg, E. L. J. (1971). A perceptual coding language for visual and auditory patterns. *American Journal of Psychology, 84*(3), 307–349.

Leeuwenberg, E. L. J. (1978). Quantification of certain visual pattern properties: Salience, transparency, and similarity. In E. L. J. Leeuwenberg & H. F. J. M. Buffart (Eds.), *Formal theories of visual perception* (pp. 277–298). New York: Wiley.

Leung, T., & Malik, J. (1998). *Contour continuity in region based image segmentation.* Paper presented at the Proceedings of the 5th European Conference on Computer Vision, Freiburg, Germany.

Lissauer, H. (1988). A case of visual agnosia with a contribution to theory. *Cognitive Neuropsychology, 5*(2), 157–192. (Original work published 1890)

Lowe, D. G. (1985). *Perceptual organization and visual recognition.* Boston, MA: Kluwer Academic.

Mach, E. (1959). *The analysis of sensations.* Chicago: Open Court. (Original work published 1914)

Malik, J., & Perona, P. (1990). Preattentive texture discrimination with early vision mechanisms. *Journal of the Optical Society of America A, 7*(5), 923–932.

Marcel, A. J. (1983). Conscious and unconscious perceptions: An approach to the relations between phenomenal experience and perceptual processes. *Cognitive Psychology, 15,* 238–300.

Marr, D. (1982). *Vision: A computational investigation into the human representation and processing of visual information.* San Francisco: W. H. Freeman.

Marr, D., & Hildreth, E. C. (1980). Theory of edge detection. *Proceedings of the Royal Society of London: Series B, 207,* 187–217.

Marr, D., & Nishihara, H. K. (1978). Representation and recognition of the spatial organization of three-dimensional shapes. *Proceedings of the Royal Society London, 200,* 269–294.

Massaro, D. W., & Hary, J. M. (1986). Addressing issues in letter recognition. *Psychological Research, 48*(3), 123–132.

McClelland, J. L., & Rumelhart, D. E. (1981). An interactive activation model of context effects in letter perception: I. An account of basic findings. *Psychological Review, 88*(5), 375–407.

Metelli, F. (1974). The perception of transparency. *Scientific American, 230*(4), 90–98.

Miller, J. (1981). Global precedence in attention and decision. *Journal of Experimental Psychology: Human Perception & Performance, 7*(6), 1161–1174.

Minsky, M. (1975). A framework for representing knowledge. In P. H. Winston (Ed.), *The psychology of computer vision* (pp. 211–280). New York: McGraw Hill.

Nakayama, K., He, Z. J., & Shimojo, S. (1995). Visual surface representation: A critical link between lower-level and higher-level vision. In S. M. Kosslyn & D. N. Osherson (Eds.), *Visual cognition: An invitation to cognitive science* (2nd ed., Vol. 2, pp. 1–70). Cambridge, MA: MIT Press.

Navon, D. (1976). Irrelevance of figural identity for resolving ambiguities in apparent motion. *Journal of Experimental Psychology: Human Perception and Performance, 2,* 130–138.

Neisser, U. (1967). *Cognitive psychology.* Englewood Cliffs, NJ: Prentice-Hall.

Ober-Thompkins, B. A. (1982). *The effects of typicality on picture perception and memory.* Unpublished doctoral dissertation, University of California, Berkeley.

Palmer, S. E. (1975a). The effects of contextual scenes on the identification of objects. *Memory & Cognition, 3*(5), 519–526.

Palmer, S. E. (1975b). Visual perception and world knowledge: Notes on a model of sensory-cognitive interaction. In D. A. Norman & D. E. Rumelhart (Eds.), *Explorations in cognition* (pp. 279–307). San Francisco: W. H. Freeman.

Palmer, S. E. (1977). Hierarchical structure in perceptual representation. *Cognitive Psychology, 9*(4), 441–474.

Palmer, S. E. (1978). Fundamental aspects of cognitive representation. In E. Rosch & B. Lloyd (Eds.), *Cognition and categorization* (pp. 261–304). Hillsdale, NJ: Lawrence Erlbaum.

Palmer, S. E. (1980). What makes triangles point: Local and global effects in configurations of ambiguous triangles. *Cognitive Psychology, 12*(3), 285–305.

Palmer, S. E. (1985). The role of symmetry in shape perception. *Acta Psychologica, 59*(1), 67–90.

Palmer, S. E. (1989). Reference frames in the perception of shape and orientation. In B. E. Shepp & S. Ballesteros (Eds.), *Object perception: Structure and process* (pp. 121–163). Hillsdale, NJ: Lawrence Erlbaum.

Palmer, S. E. (1992). Common region: A new principle of perceptual grouping. *Cognitive Psychology, 24*(3), 436–447.

Palmer, S. E. (1999). *Vision science: Photons to phenomenology.* Cambridge, MA: Bradford Books/MIT Press.

Palmer, S. E. (2002). Perceptual organization in vision. In H. Pashler (Series Ed.) & S. Yantis (Vol. Ed.), *Stevens' Handbook of Experimental Psychology: Vol. 1. Sensation and perception* (3rd ed., pp. 177–234). New York: Wiley.

Palmer, S. E. (in press-a). Perceptual grouping: It's later than you think. *Current Directions in Psychological Science.*

Palmer, S. E. (in press-b). Understanding perceptual organization and grouping. In R. Kimchi, M. Behrman, & C. Olson (Eds.), *Perceptual organization in vision: Behavioral and neural perspectives.* Hillsdale, NJ: Erlbaum.

Palmer, S. E., & Bucher, N. M. (1981). Configural effects in perceived pointing of ambiguous triangles. *Journal of Experimental Psychology: Human Perception & Performance, 7*(1), 88–114.

Palmer, S. E., & Bucher, N. M. (1982). Textural effects in perceived pointing of ambiguous triangles. *Journal of Experimental Psychology: Human Perception & Performance, 8*(5), 693–708.

Palmer, S. E., & Levitin, D. (2002). *Synchrony: A new principle of perceptual organization.* Manuscript in preparation.

Palmer, S. E., Neff, J., & Beck, D. (1996). Late influences on perceptual grouping: Amodal completion. *Psychonomic Bulletin & Review, 3*(1), 75–80.

Palmer, S. E., & Nelson, R. (2000). Late influences on perceptual grouping: Illusory contours. *Perception & Psychophysics, 62*(7), 1321–1331.

Palmer, S. E., & Rock, I. (1994a). On the nature and order of organizational processing: A reply to Peterson. *Psychonomic Bulletin & Review, 1,* 515–519.

Palmer, S. E., & Rock, I. (1994b). Rethinking perceptual organization: The role of uniform connectedness. *Psychonomic Bulletin & Review, 1*(1), 29–55.

Palmer, S. E., Rosch, E., & Chase, P. (1981). Cannonical perspective and the perception of objects. In J. Long & A. Baddeley (Eds.), *Attention and Performance: Vol. 9.* (pp. 135–151). Hillsdale, NJ: Erlbaum.

Pentland, A. (1986). Perceptual organization and the representation of natural form. *Artificial Intelligence, 28,* 293–331.

Peterhans, E., & von der Heydt, R. (1991). Subjective contours: Bridging the gap between psychophysics and physiology. *Trends in Neurosciences, 14*(3), 112–119.

Peterson, M. A., & Gibson, B. S. (1991). The initial identification of figure-ground relationships: Contributions from shape recognition processes. *Bulletin of the Psychonomic Society, 29*(3), 199–202.

Poggio, T., & Edelman, S. (1990). A neural network that learns to recognize three-dimensional objects. *Nature, 343,* 263–266.

Pomerantz, J. R., Sager, L. C., & Stoever, R. J. (1977). Perception of wholes and of their component parts: Some configural superiority effects. *Journal of Experimental Psychology: Human Perception & Performance, 3*(3), 422–435.

Reed, S. K., & Johnsen, J. A. (1975). Detection of parts in patterns and images. *Memory & Cognition, 3*(5), 569–575.

Reicher, G. M. (1969). Perceptual recognition as a function of meaningfulness of stimulus material. *Journal of Experimental Psychology, 81*(2), 275–280.

Robertson, L. C., Lamb, M. R., & Knight, R. T. (1988). Effects of lesions of the temporal-parietal junction on perceptual and attentional processing in humans. *Journal of Neuroscience, 8,* 3757–3769.

Rock, I. (1973). *Orientation and form.* New York: Academic Press.

Rock, I. (1983). *The logic of perception.* Cambridge, MA: MIT Press.

Rock, I. (1990). The frame of reference. In I. Rock (Ed.), *The legacy of Solomon Asch: Essays in cognition and social psychology* (pp. 243–268). Hillsdale, NJ: Lawrence Erlbaum.

Rock, I., & Brosgole, L. (1964). Grouping based on phenomenal proximity. *Journal of Experimental Psychology, 67,* 531–538.

Rock, I., Nijhawan, R., Palmer, S., & Tudor, L. (1992). Grouping based on phenomenal similarity of achromatic color. *Perception, 21*(6), 779–789.

Rosch, E. (1973). Natural categories. *Cognitive Psychology, 4*(3), 328–350.

Rosch, E. (1975a). Cognitive representations of semantic categories. *Journal of Experimental Psychology: General, 104*(3), 192–233.

Rosch, E. (1975b). The nature of mental codes for color categories. *Journal of Experimental Psychology: Human Perception & Performance, 104*(1), 303–322.

Rosch, E., Mervis, C. B., Gray, W. D., Johnson, D. M., & Boyes-Braem, P. (1976). Basic objects in natural categories. *Cognitive Psychology, 8*(3), 382–439.

Rubin, E. (1921). *Visuell Wahrgenommene Figuren* [Visual perception of figures]. Kobenhaven: Glydenalske boghandel.

Rumelhart, D. E., & McClelland, J. L. (1982). An interactive activation model of context effects in letter perception: II. The contextual enhancement effect and some tests and extensions of the model. *Psychological Review, 89*(1), 60–94.

Sacks, O. W. (1985). *The man who mistook his wife for a hat and other clinical tales.* New York: Summit Books.

Schumann, F. (1904). Beitrage zur Analyse der Gesichtswahrnehmungen. *Zeitschrift fur Psychologie, 36,* 161–185.

Shepard, R. N. (1962a). The analysis of proximities: Multidimensional scaling with an unknown distance function: Part I. *Psychometrika, 27,* 125–140.

Shepard, R. N. (1962b). The analysis of proximities: Multidimensional scaling with an unknown distance function: Part II. *Psychometrika, 27*(3), 219–246.

Shi, J., & Malik, J. (1997). *Normalized cuts and image segmentation.* Paper presented at the Proceedings of the IEEE Conference on Computation: Vision and Pattern Recognition, San Juan, Puerto Rico.

Tanaka, J. W., & Taylor, M. (1991). Object categories and expertise: Is the basic level in the eye of the beholder? *Cognitive Psychology, 23*(3), 457–482.

Tarr, M. J., & Bülthoff, H. H. (1995). Is human object recognition better described by geon structural descriptions or by multiple views? Comment on Biederman and Gerhardstein (1993). *Journal of Experimental Psychology: Human Perception & Performance, 21*(6), 1494–1505.

Tarr, M. J., & Pinker, S. (1989). Mental rotation and orientation-dependence in shape recognition. *Cognitive Psychology, 21*(2), 233–282.

Teuber, H. L. (1968). Alteration of perception and memory in man: Perception. In L. Weiskrantz (Ed.), *Analysis of behavioral change* (pp. 274–328). New York: Harper and Row.

Tse, P. U. (1999). Volume completion. *Cognitive Psychology, 39,* 37–68.

Ullman, S. (1989). Aligning pictorial descriptions: An approach to object recognition. *Cognition, 32,* 193–254.

Ullman, S. (1996). *High level vision.* Cambridge, MA: MIT Press.

Ullman, S., & Basri, R. (1991). Recognition by linear combinations of models. *IEEE Transactions on Pattern Analysis and Machine Intelligence, 13*(10), 992–1006.

Vecera, S. P., Vogel, E. K., & Woodman, G. F. (in press). Lower region: A new cue for figure-ground segregation. *Journal of Experimental Psychology: General.*

Warrington, E. K., & Shallice, T. (1984). Category specific semantic impairments. *Brain, 107,* 829–854.

Warrington, E. K., & Taylor, A. M. (1973). The contribution of the right parietal lobe to object recognition. *Cortex, 9*(2), 152–164.

Warrington, E. K., & Taylor, A. M. (1978). Two categorical stages of object recognition. *Perception, 7*(6), 695–705.

Weisstein, N., & Harris, C. S. (1974). Visual detection of line segments: An object-superiority effect. *Science, 186*(4165), 752–755.

Wenderoth, P. M. (1974). The distinction between the rod-and-frame illusion and the rod-and-frame test. *Perception, 3*(2), 205–212.

Wertheimer, M. (1923). Untersuchungen zur Lehre von der Gestalt. *Psychology Forschung, 4,* 301–350.

Wiser, M. (1981). *The role of intrinsic axes in shape recognition.* Paper presented at the Third Annual Conference of the Cognitive Science Society, Berkeley, CA.

CHAPTER 8

Depth Perception and the Perception of Events

DENNIS R. PROFFITT AND CORRADO CAUDEK

Our understanding of the perception of depth and events entails a paradox. On the one hand, it seems that there is simply not enough information to make the achievement possible, yet on the other hand the amount of information seems to be overly abundant. This paradox is a consequence of evaluating information in isolation versus evaluating it in context. Berkeley (1709) noted that a point in the environment projects as a point on the retina in a manner that does not vary in any way with distance. For a point viewed in isolation, this is true. From this fact, Berkeley concluded that the visual perception of distance, from sight alone, was impossible. Visual information, he concluded, must be augmented by nonvisual information. For example, fixating a point with two eyes requires that the eyes converge in a manner that does vary with distance; thus, proprioceptive information about eye positions could augment vision to yield an awareness of depth. If our visual world consisted of a single point viewed in a void, then depth perception from vision alone would, indeed, be tough. Fortunately, this is not the natural condition for visual experience.

As the visual environment increases in complexity, the amount of information specifying its layout increases. By adding a second point to the visual scene, additional information is created. If the two points are at different depths, then they will project to different relative locations in the two eyes, thereby providing information about their relative distances to each other. If the observer fixates on one point and moves his or her head sideways, then motion parallax will be created that gives information about relative depth. Expanding the points into extended forms, placing these forms on a ground plane, having the forms move, or allowing the observer to move are some of the possible complications that create information about the depth relationships in the scene.

Complex natural environments provide lots of different kinds of information, and the perceptual system must combine all of it into the singular set of relationships that is our experience of the visual world. It is not enough to register the available information; the information must also be combined.

From this brief introduction, two fundamental questions emerge: What is the information provided for perceiving spatial relationships and how is this information combined by the perceptual system? We begin our chapter by reviewing the literature that addresses these questions. (Additional topics in visual perception are discussed in the chapter by Kubovy, Gepshtein, and Epstein in this volume.)

There is a third question that we also address: Do people perceive spatial layout accurately? The answer to this question depends upon the criteria used to define accuracy. Certainly, people act in the environment as if they represent its spatial relationships accurately; however, effective action can often be achieved without this accurate representation. This issue is developed and discussed throughout the chapter.

DEPTH PERCEPTION

Depth Cues: What Is the Information? What Information Is Actually Used?

The rules for projecting a three-dimensional object or three-dimensional layout onto a surface (for example, the retina) are unambiguously defined, whereas the inverse operation (from the image to the three-dimensional projected object or scene) is not. This is the so-called *inverse-projection problem.* Any two-dimensional projection is inherently ambiguous, and a central problem of visual science is to determine how the perceptual system is able to recover three-dimensional information from a retinal projection. This problem is usually attacked from two sides: first, by analyzing those properties of the image (hereafter called *sources of depth information,* or *cues*) that, in principle, allow for the recovery of some of the three-dimensional properties of the projected objects; second, by investigating the effectiveness of these sources of depth information for the human visual system. In this section, we discuss the problem of depth perception by clarifying what kinds of three-dimensional information can be recovered from each source of depth information in isolation, and by presenting psychophysical evidence suggesting whether and to what degree the visual system is actually able to use them. We start with the ocular motor sources of information, followed by binocular disparity, pictorial depth cues, and motion.

Ocular Motor

There are two potentially useful extraretinal sources of information for specifying egocentric distance: the vergence angle of the eyes and the state of accommodation. The vergence angle is approximately equal to the angle between the lines from the optical centers of the eyes to the fixation point and the parallel rays that would define gaze direction if the eyes were fixated at infinity. If the vergence angle and the interocular distance are known, then it is clear that the radial distance to the fixation point could in principle be recovered. This potential cue to depth, however, is limited to a restricted range of distances, because the eyes become effectively parallel (optical infinity) for fixation distances larger than 6 m. Moreover, the information content of vergence drops off rapidly with increasing distance: The variation in the vergence angle is very limited for fixation distances larger than about 0.5 m. Psychophysical evidence suggests that vergence information is not a very effective source of information about distance. Erkelens and Collewijn (1985), for example, showed that observers could make large tracking vergence eye movements without seeing any motion in depth when the expansion or contraction of the retinal projection is controlled. In such a cue-conflict situation (with ocular convergence conflicting with the absence of expansion or contraction of the retinal image), extraretinal information fails to affect perceived distance.

Accommodation is a second source of extraretinal information about distance and refers to the change in shape of the lens that the eye performs to keep in focus objects at different distances. Changes in accommodation occur between the nearest and the farthest points that can be placed in focus by the thickening and thinning of the lens. Although in principle, accommodation could be a source of depth information, psychophysical investigations suggest that the contribution of accommodation to perceived depth is minimal and that there are large individual differences (Fisher & Ciuffreda, 1988). For single point-light targets in the dark, Mon-Williams and Tresilian (1999) reported that observers were unable to provide reliable absolute-depth judgments on the basis of accommodation alone, even within a stretched-arm distance. Observers, however, were able to recover ordinal-depth information for sequentially presented targets from accommodation alone, even though the depth-order judgments were only 80% correct.

In conclusion, the ocular-motor cues are not reliable cues for perceiving absolute depth, even though they may play a more important role in the recovery of ordinal-depth information. The effectiveness of the ocular-motor cues is limited to a small range of distances, and they are easily overcome when other sources of depth information are available.

Binocular Disparity

Since Euclid, we have known that the same three-dimensional object or surface-layout projects two different images in the left and right eye. It was Wheatstone (1938), however, who provided the first empirical demonstration that disparate line drawings presented separately to the two eyes could elicit an impression of depth. Since then, binocular disparity has been considered one of the most powerful sources of optical information for depth perception, as is easily realized by anyone who has ever seen a stereogram. It is likewise easy to realize that binocular disparity—although by itself sufficient to specify relative distance—may not be sufficient to specify absolute-distance information. The problem of scaling disparity information is one of the central themes in the literature on stereopsis.

Using the small angle approximation, the geometrical relation between disparity and depth is

$$\eta \approx \frac{I\delta}{D(D - \delta)}$$

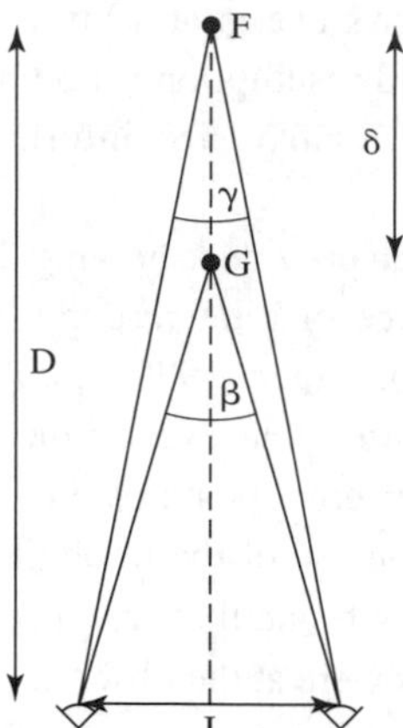

Figure 8.1 F = fixation point, I = interocular separation, δ = depth difference between F and G, γ = binocular parallax of F, and β = binocular parallax of G. The relative disparity, η, between F and G is $\beta - \gamma$.

where η is the angular binocular disparity, D is the viewing distance, δ is the depth, and I is the interocular distance. The angles and distances of stereo geometry are specified in Figure 8.1. From disparity, therefore, the depth magnitudes can be recovered as

$$\delta \approx \frac{\eta D^2}{I + \eta D}$$

The previous equation reveals that there is a nonlinear relationship between horizontal disparity (η) and depth (δ) that varies with the interocular separation (I) and the viewing distance (D). This means that disparity information by itself is not sufficient for specifying depth magnitudes, because different combinations of interocular separation, depth, and distance can generate the same disparity. In order to provide an estimate about depth, disparity must be scaled, so to speak, by some other source of information specifying the interocular separation and the viewing distance. This is the traditional *stereoscopic depth-constancy problem* (Ono & Comerford, 1977).

One proposal is that this scaling of disparity is accomplished on the basis of extraretinal sources. According to this approach, failures of veridical depth perception from stereopsis have been attributed to the misperception of the viewing distance. Johnston (1991), for example, showed random-dot stereograms to observers who decided whether they were seeing simulated cylinders that were flattened or elongated along the depth axis with respect to a circular cylinder. Johnston found that depth was overestimated at small distances (with physically circular cylinders appearing as elongated in depth) and underestimated at larger distances (with physically circular cylinders appearing as flattened). These depth distortions have been attributed to the hypothesis that observers scaled the horizontal disparities with an incorrect measure of physical distance, entailing an overestimation of close distances and an underestimation of far distances. A second proposal is that disparity is scaled on the basis of purely visual information. Mayhew and Longuet-Higgins (1982), for example, proposed that full metric depth constancy could be achieved by the global computation of vertical disparities. The psychophysical findings, however, do not support this hypothesis. It has been found, in fact, that human performance is very poor in tasks involving the estimation of metric structure from binocular disparities, especially if compared with the precision demonstrated by performance in stereo acuity tasks involving ordinal-depth discriminations, with thresholds as low as 2 s arc (Ogle, 1952).

Koenderink and van Doorn (1976) proposed a second purely visual model of stereo-depth. This model does not try to account for the recovery of absolute depth, but only for the recovery of the affine (i.e., ordinal) structure from a combination of the horizontal and vertical local disparity gradient. This model, however, is inconsistent with the psychophysical data. It predicts that the local manipulation of either horizontal or vertical disparity should have the same effects on perceived shape; however, it has been shown that the manipulation of the local horizontal disparities has reliable consequences on perceived depth, whereas the manipulation of the local vertical disparities does not (Cumming, Johnston, & Parker, 1991). Moreover, several studies have shown that vertical disparity processing is not local, but rather is performed by pooling over a large area (Rogers & Bradshaw, 1993).

In conclusion, binocular disparity in isolation gives rise to the most compelling impression of depth, and for relatively short distances provides a reliable source of relative-, but not of absolute-depth information. Although the geometric relationship between binocular disparity and depth is well understood, a plausible psychological model of stereopsis has yet to be provided.

Pictorial

Pictorial depth cues consist of those depth-relevant regularities that are manifested in pictures. There is a long list of these cues, and although we have attempted to describe the most important ones, our list is not exhaustive.

Aerial Perspective. *Aerial perspective* refers to the reduction of contrast that occurs when an object is viewed from great distances. Aerial perspective is the product of the scattering of light by particles in the atmosphere. The contrast reduction by aerial perspective is a function of both distance and the attenuation coefficient of the atmosphere. Under hazy conditions, for example, the contrast of a black object against the sky at 2000 m is only 45% of the contrast produced by the same object when it is viewed at a distance of 1 m (Fry, Bridgeman, & Ellerbrock, 1949).

Aerial perspective is an ambiguous cue about absolute distance: The recovery of distance from aerial perspective requires knowledge of both the reflectance value of the object and the attenuation coefficient of the atmosphere. It should also be noticed that the attenuation coefficient is changed by the scattering and blocking of light by pollutants. As a consequence, aerial perspective cannot be taken as providing more than ordinal-depth information, and several psychophysical investigations have indicated its effectiveness as a depth-order cue (Ross, 1971).

Height in the Visual Field and the Horizon Ratio. If an observer and an object are situated on the same ground plane, then the observer's horizontal line of sight will intersect the object at the observer's eye height. Because this line of sight also coincides with the horizon, the horizon intersects the object at the observer's eye height. The reference to the (explicit or implicit) horizon line therefore can be used to recover absolute size information as multiples of the observer's eye height. The geometry of the horizon ratio was first presented by Sedgwick (1973):

$$h = \frac{\tan \beta + \tan \gamma}{\tan \beta}$$

where γ is the visual angle subtended by the object above the horizon, and β is the visual angle subtended by the object below the horizon (see Figure 8.2). Although size information (h) is independent of the distance of the object from the observer, the object size (scaled in terms of eye height) and the visual angle are known; thus, distance itself can also be recovered. The recovery of absolute-size information from the horizon ratio requires two assumptions: (a) that both observer and target object lie on the same ground plane, and

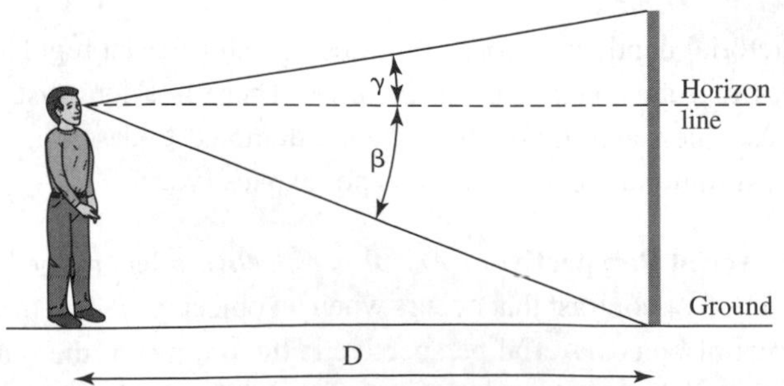

Figure 8.2 D = distance from the observer to the object, β = visual angle between the point where the object meets the ground and the horizon, and γ = visual angle between the top of the object and the horizon.

(b) that the observer's eye is at a known distance from the ground. If the second assumption is not met, then the horizon ratio still provides relative-size information about distant objects.

Evidence has been provided showing that the horizon ratio is an effective source of relative-depth information in pictures (Rogers, 1996). Wraga (1999) and Bertamini, Yang, and Proffitt (1998) reported that eye-height information is used differently across different postures. For example, Bertamini et al. investigated the use of the implicit horizon in relative-size judgments. They found that size discrimination was best when object heights were at the observers' eye height regardless of whether they were seated or standing.

Occlusion. Occlusion occurs when an object partially hides another object from view, thus providing ordinal information: The occluding object is perceived as closer and the occluded object as farther. Investigations of occlusion have focused on understanding how occlusion relationships are identified: that is, how the perceptual system decides whether a surface "owns" an image boundary or whether the boundary belongs to a second occluding surface. It is easily understood that the so-called border ownership problem is critical to correctly segmenting the spatial layout of the visual scene into surface regions at different depths. Boundaries that belong to an object are *intrinsic* to its form, whereas those that belong to an occluding object are *extrinsic* (Shimojo, Silverman, & Nakayama, 1989). Shimojo et al. (1989) created a powerful demonstration of the perceptual effect derived from changing border ownership by using the barber-pole effect. The barber-pole effect has been attributed to the propagation of motion signals generated by the contour terminators along the long sides of the aperture (Hildreth, 1984). By stereoscopically placing the contours behind aperture boundaries, Shimojo et al. caused the terminators to be classified as extrinsic to the contours (because they were generated by a near occluding surface), and the terminators to be subtracted from the integration process. As a consequence, Shimojo et al. found that the bias of the barber-pole effect was effectively eliminated.

Relative and Familiar Size. The relative-size cue to depth arises from differences in the projected angular sizes of two objects that have identical sizes and are located at different distances. If the assumption that the two objects have identical physical sizes is met, then from the ratio of their angular sizes, it is possible to determine the inverse ratio of their distances to the observer. In this way, metrically scaled relative-depth information can be specified. If the observer also knows the size of the objects, then in principle, absolute-distance information becomes available. Several reports indicate that the familiar-size cue to depth does indeed affect perceived distance in cue-reduction conditions (Sedgwick, 1986), but it does not affect perceived distance under naturalistic viewing conditions (Predebon, 1991).

Texture Gradients. Textural variations provide information about both the location of objects and the shape of their surfaces. Cutting and Millard (1984) distinguished among three textural cues to shape: *perspective, compression* (or *foreshortening*), and *density*.

Perspective: Due to perspective, the size of the individual texture elements (referred to here as *texels*) is inversely scaled with distance from the viewer. Perspective (or scaling) gradients are produced by perspective projections, in the cases of both planar and curved surfaces. To derive surface orientation from perspective gradients, it is necessary to know the size of the individual texels.

Compression: The ratio of the width to the length of the individual texels is traditionally referred to as compression. If the shape of the individual texels is known a priori, compression can in principle provide a *local* cue to surface orientation. Let us assume, for example, that the individual texels are ellipses. In such a case, if the visual system assumes that an ellipse is the projection of a circle lying on a slanted plane, then the orientation of the plane could be locally determined without the need of measuring texture gradients. In general, the effectiveness of compression requires the assumption of *isotropy* (A. Blake & Marinos, 1990). If the texture on the scene surface is indeed isotropic, then for both planar and curved surfaces, compression is informative about surface orientation under both orthogonal and perspective projections.

Density: Density refers to the spatial distribution of the texels' centers in the image. In order to recover surface orientation from density gradients, it is necessary to make assumptions about the distribution of the texels over the object surface. Homogeneity is the default assumption; that is, the texture is assumed to be uniformly distributed over the surface. Variation in texture density can therefore be used to determine the orientation of the surface. Under the homogeneity assumption, the density gradient is in principle informative about surface orientation for both planar and curved surfaces under perspective projections, and only for curved surfaces under orthographic projections.

Even if the mathematical relationship between the previous texture cues and surface orientation is well understood for both planar (Stevens, 1981) and curved surfaces (Gårding, 1992), the psychological mechanism underlying the perception of shape from texture is still debated. Investigators are trying to determine which texture gradients observers use to judge shape from texture (Cutting & Millard, 1984), and to establish whether perceptual performance is compatible with the isotropy and homogeneity assumptions (Rosenholtz & Malik, 1997).

Linear Perspective. Linear perspective is a very effective cue to depth (Kubovy, 1986), but it can be considered to be a combination of other previously discussed depth cues (e.g., occlusion, compression, density, size). Linear perspective is distinct from natural perspective by the abundant use of receding parallel lines.

Shading. Shading information refers to the smooth variation in image luminance determined by a combination of three variables: the illuminant direction, the surface's orientation, and the surface's reflective properties. Given that different combinations of these variables can generate the same pattern of shading, it follows that shading information is inherently ambiguous (for a discussion, see Todd & Reichel, 1989). Mathematical analyses have shown, however, that the inherent ambiguity of shading can be overcome if the illuminant direction is known, and computer vision algorithms relying on the estimate of the illuminant direction have been devised for reconstructing surface structure from image shading (Pentland, 1984).

Psychophysical investigations have shown that shading information evokes a compelling impression of three-dimensional shape, even though perceived shape from shading is far from being accurate. The perceptual interpretation of shading information is strongly affected by the pictorial information provided by the image boundaries (Ramachandran, 1988). Moreover, systematic distortions in perceived three-dimensional shape occur when the direction of illumination is changed in both static (Todd, Koenderink, van Doorn, & Kappers, 1996) and dynamic patterns of image shading (Caudek, Domini, & Di Luca, in press).

Thus, perceiving shape from shading presents a paradox. Shading information can, in principle, specify shape if illumination direction is known. Moreover, in some circumstances, observers recover this direction with good accuracy (Todd & Mingolla, 1983). Yet, perceived shape from shading is often inaccurate, as revealed by the studies manipulating the image boundaries and the illuminant direction.

Motion. The importance of motion information for the perception of surface layout and the three-dimensional form of objects has been known for many years (Gibson, 1950; Wallach & O'Connell, 1953). When an object or an observer moves, the dynamic transformations of retinal projections become informative about depth relationships. When one object is seen to move in front of or behind another, dynamic occlusion occurs. This information specifies depth order. When an observer moves, motion parallax occurs between objects at different depths, and when an object rotates, it produces regularities in its changing image. These events provide information about the three-dimensional structure of objects and their spatial layout.

Dynamic Occlusion. Dynamic occlusion provides effective information for determining the depth order of textured surfaces (Andersen & Braunstein, 1983). In one of the earliest studies, Kaplan (1969) showed two random-dot patterns moving horizontally at different speeds and merging at a vertical margin. Observers reported a vivid impression of depth at the margin, with the pattern exhibiting texture element deletion being perceived as the farthest surface.

It is interesting to compare dynamic occlusion and motion parallax, because in a natural setting, these two sources of depth information covary. Ono, Rogers, Ohmi, and Ono (1988) put motion parallax and dynamic occlusion in conflict and found that motion parallax determines the perceived depth order when the simulated depth separation is small (less than 25 min of equivalent disparity), and dynamic occlusion determines the perceived depth order when the simulated depth separation is large (more than 25 min of equivalent disparity). On the basis of these findings, Ono et al. proposed that motion parallax is most appropriate for specifying the depth order *within* objects (given that the depth separation among object features is usually small), whereas dynamic occlusion is more appropriate for specifying the depth order *between* objects at different distances.

Structure From Motion. The phenomenon of the perceived *structure from motion* (SFM) has been investigated at (at least) three different levels: (a) the theoretical understanding of the depth information that, in principle, can be derived from a moving projection; (b) the psychophysical investigation of the effective ability of observers to solve the SFM problem; and (c) the modeling of human performance. These different facets of the SFM literature are briefly examined in the following section.

Mathematical analyses: A way to characterize the dynamic properties of retinal projections is to describe them in terms of a pattern of moving features, often called *optic flow* (Gibson, 1979). Mathematical analyses of optic flow have shown that, if appropriate assumptions are introduced in the interpretation process, then *veridical* three-dimensional object shape can be derived from optic flow. If rigid motion is assumed, for example, then three orthographic projections of four moving points are sufficient to derive their three-dimensional metric structure (Ullman, 1979). It is important to distinguish between the *first-order* temporal properties of optic flow (*velocities*), which are produced by two projections of a moving object, and the *second-order* temporal properties of the optic flow (*accelerations*), which require three projections of a moving object. Although the first-order temporal properties of optic flow are sufficient for the recovery of affine properties (Koenderink & van Doorn, 1991; Todd & Bressan, 1990), the second-order temporal properties of optic flow are necessary for a full recovery of the three-dimensional metric structure (D. D. Hoffman, 1982).

Psychophysical investigations: A large number of empirical investigations have tried to determine whether observers actually use the second-order properties of optic flow that are needed to reconstruct the veridical three-dimensional metric shape of projected objects. The majority of these studies have come to the conclusion that, in deriving three-dimensional shape from motion, observers seem to use only the first-order properties of optic flow (e.g., Todd & Bressan, 1990). This conclusion is warranted, in particular, by two findings: (a) the metric properties of SFM are often misperceived (e.g., Domini & Braunstein, 1998; Norman & Todd, 1992), and (b) human performance in SFM tasks does not improve as the number of views is increased from two to many (e.g., Todd & Bressan, 1990).

Modeling: An interesting result of the SFM literature is that observers typically perceive a unique metric interpretation when viewing an ambiguous two-view SFM sequence (with little inter- and intraobserver variability), even though the sequence could have been produced by the orthographic projection of an infinite number of different three-dimensional rigid structures (Domini, Caudek, & Proffitt, 1997). The desire to understand how people derive such perceptions has led researchers to study the relationships between the few parameters that characterize the first-order linear velocity field and the properties of the perceived three-dimensional shapes. Several studies have concluded that the best predictor of perceived three-dimensional shape from motion is one component of the local (linear) velocity field, called deformation (*def;* see Koenderink, 1986). Domini and Caudek (1999) have proposed a probabilistic model whereby, under certain assumptions, a unique surface orientation can be derived from an ambiguous first-order velocity field according to a maximum likelihood criterion. Results consistent with this model have been provided relative to the perception of surface slant (Domini & Caudek, 1999), the discrimination between rigid and nonrigid motion (Domini et al., 1997), the perceived orientation of the axis of rotation (Caudek & Domini, 1998), the discrimination between constant and variable three-dimensional angular velocities (Domini, Caudek, Turner, & Favretto, 1998), and the perception of depth-order relations (Domini & Braunstein, 1998; Domini, Caudek, & Richman, 1998).

In summary, the research on perceived depth from motion reveals that the perceptual analysis of a moving projection is relatively insensitive to the second-order component of the velocity field (accelerations), which is necessary to uniquely derive the metric structure in the case of orthographic projections. Perceptual performance has been explained by two hypotheses. Some researchers maintain that the perceptual recovery of the metric structure from SFM displays is consistent with a heuristical analysis of optic flow (Braunstein, 1976, 1994; Domini & Caudek, 1999; Domini et al., 1997). Other researchers maintain that the perception of three-dimensional shape from motion involves a hierarchy of different perceptual representations, including the knowledge of the object's topological, ordinal, and affine properties, whereas the Euclidean metric properties may derive from processes that are more cognitive than perceptual (Norman & Todd, 1992).

Integration of Depth Cues: How Is the Effective Information Combined?

A pervasive finding is that the accuracy of depth and distance perception increases as more and more sources of depth information are present within a visual scene (Künnapas, 1968). It is also widely believed that the visual system functions normally, so to speak, only within a rich visual environment in which the three-dimensional shape of objects and spatial layout are specified by multiple informational sources (Gibson, 1979). Understanding how the visual system integrates the information provided by several depth cues represents, therefore, one of the fundamental issues of depth perception.

The most comprehensive model of depth-cue combination that has been proposed is the *modified weak fusion* (MWF) model (Landy, Maloney, Johnston, & Young, 1995). *Weak fusion* refers to the independent processing of each depth cue by a modular system that then linearly combines the depth estimates provided by each module (Clark & Yuille, 1990). *Strong fusion* refers to a nonmodular depth processing system in which the most probable three-dimensional interpretation is provided for a scene without the necessity of combining the outputs of different depth-processing modules (Nakayama & Shimojo, 1992). Between these two extremes, Landy et al. proposed a modular system made up of depth modules that interact solely to facilitate *cue promotion*. As seen previously, visual cues provide qualitatively different types of information. For example, motion parallax can in principle provide absolute depth information, whereas stereopsis provides only relative-depth information, and occlusion specifies a greater depth on one side of the occlusion boundary than on the other, without allowing any quantification of this (relative) difference. The depth estimates provided by these three cues are incommensurate, and therefore cannot be combined. According to Landy et al., combining information from different cues necessitates that all cues be made to provide absolute depth estimates. To achieve this task, some depth cues must be supplied with of one or more missing parameters. If motion parallax and stereoscopic disparity are available in the same location, for example, then the viewing distance specified by motion parallax could be used to specify this missing parameter in stereo disparity. After stereo disparity has been *promoted* so as to specify metric depth information, then the depth estimates of both cues can be combined. In conclusion, for the MWF model, interactions among depth cues are limited to what is required to place all of the cues in a common format required for integration.

In the MWF model, after the cues are promoted to the status of absolute depth cues, it becomes necessary to establish the *reliability* of each cue: "Side information which is not necessarily relevant to the actual estimation of depth, termed an *ancillary measure,* is used to estimate or constrain the reliability of a depth cue" (Landy et al., 1995, p. 398). For example, the presence of noise differentially degrading two cues present in the same location can be used to estimate their different reliability.

The final stage of cue combination is that of a weighted average of the depth estimates provided by the cues. The weights take into consideration both the reliability of the cues and the discrepancies between the depth estimates. If the cues provide consistent and reliable estimates, then their depth values are linearly combined. On the other hand, if the discrepancy between the individual depth estimates is greater than what is found in a natural scene, then complex interactions are expected.

Cutting and Vishton (1995) proposed an alternative approach. According to their proposal, the three-dimensional information specified by all visual cues is converted into an ordinal representation. The information provided by the different sources is combined at this level. After the ordinal representation has been generated, a metric sealing can then be created from the ordinal relations.

The issue of which cue-combination model best fits the psychophysical data has been much debated. Other models of cue combination, in fact, have been proposed, either linear (Bruno & Cutting, 1988) or multiplicative (Massaro, 1988), with no single model being able to fully account for the large number of empirical findings on cue integration.

A similar lack of agreement in the literature concerns two equally fundamental and related questions: How can we describe the mapping between the physical and the perceived space? What geometric properties comprise perceived space?

Several answers have been provided to these questions. According to Todd and Bressan (1990), physical and perceived spaces may be related by an affine transformation. Affine transformations preserve distance ratios in all directions, but alter the relative lengths and angles of line segments oriented in different directions. A consequence of such a position is that a depth map may not provide the common initial representational format for all sources of three-dimensional information, as was proposed by Landy et al. (1995).

The problem of how to describe the properties of perceived space has engendered many discussions and is far from being solved. According to some, the intrinsic structure of perceptual space may be Euclidean, whereas the mapping between physical and perceptual space may not be Euclidean (Domini et al., 1997). According to others, visual space may be hyperbolic (Lunenburg, 1947), or it may reflect a Lie algebra group (W. C. Hoffman, 1966). Some have proposed the coexistence of multiple representations of perceived three-dimensional shape, reflecting different ways of combining the different visual cues (Tittle & Perotti, 1997).

A final fundamental question about visual-information integration is whether the cue-combination strategies can be modified by learning or feedback. Some light has recently been shed on this issue by showing that observers can modify their cue-combination strategies through learning, and can apply each cue-combination strategy in the appropriate context (Ernst, Banks, & Bülthoff, 2000).

In conclusion, an apt summarization of this literature was provided by Young, Landy, and Maloney (1993), who stated that a description of the depth cue-combination rules "seems likely to resemble a microcosm of cognitive processing: elements of memory, learning, reasoning and heuristic strategy may dominate" (p. 2695).

Distance Perception

Turning our attention from *how* spatial perception is achieved to *what* is perceived, we are struck by the consistent findings of distortions of both perceived distance and object shape, even under full-cue conditions. For example, Norman, Todd, Perotti, and Tittle (1996) asked observers to judge the three-dimensional lengths of real-world objects viewed in near space and found that perceived depth intervals become more and more compressed as viewing distance increased. Given that many reports have found visual space to be distorted, the question arises as to why we do not walk into obstacles and misguide our reaching. Clearly, our everyday interactions with the environment are not especially error-prone. What, then, is the meaning of the repeated psychophysical findings of failures of distance perception?

We can try to provide an answer to this question by considering four aspects of distance perception. We examine (a) the segmentation of visual space, (b) the methodological issues in distance perception research, (c) the underlying mechanisms that are held responsible for distance perception processing, and (d) the role of calibration.

Four Aspects of Distance Perception

The Segmentation of Visual Space. Cutting and Vishton (1995) distinguished three circular regions surrounding the observer, and proposed that different sources of information are used within each of these regions. *Personal space* is defined as the zone within 2 m surrounding the observer's head. Within this space, distance perception is supported by occlusion, retinal disparity, relative size, convergence, and accommodation. Just beyond personal space is the *action space* of the individual. Within the action space, distance perception is supported by occlusion, height in the visual field, binocular disparity, motion perspective, and relative size. Action space extends to the limit of where disparity and motion can provide effective information about distance (at about 30 m from the observer). Beyond this range is *vista space,* which is supported only by the pictorial cues: occlusion, height in the visual field, relative size, and aerial perspective.

Cutting and Vishton (1995) proposed that different sources of information are used within each of these visual regions, and that a different ranking of importance of the sources of information may exist within personal, action, and vista space. If this is true, then the intrinsic geometric properties of these three regions of visual space may also differ.

Methodological Issues. The problem of distance perception has been studied by collecting a number of different response measures, including verbal judgments (Pagano & Bingham, 1998), visual matching (Norman et al., 1996), pointing (Foley, 1985), targeted walking with and without vision (Loomis, Da Silva, Fujita, & Fukusima, 1992), pointing triangulation (Loomis et al., 1992), and reaching (Bingham, Zaal, Robin, & Shull, 2000). Different results have been obtained by using different response measures. Investigations of targeted walking in the absence of vision, for example, have produced accurate distance estimates (Loomis et al., 1992), although verbal judgments have not (Pagano & Bingham, 1998). Reaching has been found to be accurate when dynamic binocular information was available, but not when it is guided by monocular vision, even in the presence of feedback (Bingham & Pagano, 1998). Matching responses for distance perception have typically shown that simulated distances are underestimated (Norman et al., 1996).

The fact that such a variety of results have been obtained by using different response measures suggests at least two conclusions. First, different response measures may be the expression of different representations of visual space that need not be consistent. This would mean that visual space could not be conceptualized as a unitary, internally consistent construct. In particular, motor responses and visual judgments may be informed by different visual representations. Second, there are reports indicating that accurate distance perception can be obtained, but only if the appropriate response measure is used in conjunction with the appropriate visual input. By using a reaching task, for example, Bingham and Pagano (1998) have recently reported accurate perception of distance with dynamic binocular vision (at least within what Cutting and Vishton (1995) call "personal space"), but not with monocular vision.

Conscious Representation of Distance Versus Action. Some evidence suggests that different mechanisms may mediate conscious distance perception and actions such as reaching, grasping, or ballistic targeting. This leads to the hypothesis that separate visual pathways exist for perception and action. Milner and Goodale (1995) proposed that two different pathways, each specialized for different visual functions, exist in the visual system. The projection to the temporal lobe (the ventral stream) "permit[s] the formation of perceptual and cognitive representations which embody the enduring characteristics of objects and their significance," whereas the parietal cortex (the dorsal stream) "capture[s] instead the instantaneous and egocentric features of objects, [and] mediate[s] the control of goal-directed actions" (Milner & Goodale, 1995, p. 66). In Milner and Goodale's proposal, the coding that mediates the required transformations for the visual control of skilled actions is assumed to be separate from that mediating experiential perception of the visual world. According to this proposal, the many dissociations that have been discovered between conscious distance perception and locomotion "highlight surprising instances where what we think we 'see' is not what guides our actions. In all cases, these apparent paradoxes provide direct evidence for the operation of visual processing systems of which we are unaware, but which can control our behavior" (p. 177).

The dissociations most relevant for the present discussion are examined in the later section on egocentric versus exocentric distance. In general, this research suggests that accuracy measured in action performance is usually greater than that found in visual judgment measures. It must be noticed, however, that action measures do not always produce accurate or distortion-free results (Bingham & Pagano, 1998; Bingham et al., 2000).

The Role of Calibration. It has been suggested that some response measures (such as visual matching) produce poor performance in distance perception because the task is unnatural, infrequently performed, and thus poorly calibrated. Bingham and Pagano (1998) suggest that in these circumstances, only relative-depth measures can be obtained. Conversely, absolute-distance perception may be obtained (within some tolerance limits) by using feedback to calibrate ordinally scaled distance estimates. Evidence that haptic feedback reduces the distortions of egocentric distance has indeed been provided (Bingham & Pagano, 1998; Bingham et al., 2000), although feedback does not always reduce spatial distortions, and never does so completely.

Egocentric Versus Exocentric Distance. From the point of view of the observer, the horizontal plane extends in all directions from his or her current position. The observer's body is the center of egocentric space. Objects placed on the rays that intersect this center have an egocentric distance relative to the observer, whereas objects on different rays have an exocentric distance relative to each other.

It has been repeatedly found that even in full-cue viewing conditions, distances are perceptually compressed in the egocentric direction relative to exocentric extents, with most comparisons being between egocentric distances and those in the fronto-parallel plane (Amorim, Loomis, & Fukusima, 1998; Loomis et al., 1992; Norman et al., 1996).

In a typical experiment, observers were instructed to match an egocentric extent to one in the fronto-parallel plane (Loomis et al., 1992). Observers made the extents in the egocentric direction greater in order to perceptually match them to those in the fronto-parallel direction. This inequality in perceived distance defines a basic anisotropy in the perception of space and objects. The perceptions of extents and object shapes are compressed in their depth-to-width ratio. Loomis and Philbeck (1999) showed that this anisotropy in perceived three-dimensional shape is invariant across size scales.

Paradoxically, the compression in exocentric distance does not seem to affect visually guided actions. One method to assess the accuracy of visually guided behavior is to have observers view a target in depth, and then after blindfolding the observer, have them walk to the target location. This technique is called *blindwalking*. Numerous studies have found that people are able to walk to targets without showing any systematic error (overshoot or undershoot) when viewing occurs in full-cue conditions and distances fall within about 20 m (Loomis et al., 1992; Philbeck & Loomis, 1997; Philbeck, Loomis, & Beall, 1997; Rieser, Ashmead, Talor, & Youngquist, 1990; Thomson, 1983).

Two alternative explanations could account for this discrepancy between the compression found in explicit reports of perceived distance and the accuracy observed in blindwalking to targets. By one account, the difference is attributable to two distinct streams of visual processing in the brain. From the visual cortex, there is a bifurcation in the primary cortical visual pathways, with one stream projecting to the temporal lobe and the other to the parietal. Milner and Goodale (1995) have characterized the functioning of the temporal stream as supporting conscious space perception, whereas the parietal stream is responsible for the visual guidance of action. Other researchers have characterized the functioning of these two streams somewhat differently; for a review, see Creem and Proffitt (2001). By a two-visual-systems account, the compression observed in explicit judgments of egocentric distance is a product of temporal stream processing, whereas accurate blindwalking is an achievement of the parietal stream. The second explanation posits that both behaviors are grounded in the same representation of perceived space; however, differences in the transformations that relate perceived space to distinct behaviors cause the difference in accuracy. Philbeck and Loomis (1997) showed that verbal distance judgments and blindwalking varied together under manipulations of full- and reduced-cue viewing conditions in a manner that is strongly suggestive of this second alternative.

The dissociation between verbal reports and visually guided actions depends upon whether distances are encoded in exocentric or egocentric frames of reference. Wraga, Creem, and Proffitt (2000) created large Müller-Lyer configurations that lay on a floor. Observers made verbal judgments and also blindwalked the perceived extent. It was found that the illusion influenced both verbal reports and blindwalking when the configurations were viewed from a short distance; however, the illusion only affected verbal judgments when observers stood at one end of the configurations' extent. As was suggested by Milner and Goodale (1995), accuracy in visually guided actions may depend upon the egocentric encoding of space.

Size Perception

The size of an object does not appear to change with varying viewing distance, despite the fact that retinal size depends on the distance between the object and the observer. Researchers have proposed several possible explanations for this phenomenon: the size-distance invariance hypothesis, the familiar-size hypothesis, and the direct-perception approach.

Taking Distance Into Account

The *size-distance invariance hypothesis* postulates that retinal size is transformed into perceived size after taking apparent distance into account (see Epstein, 1977, for review). If accurate distance information is available, then size perception will also be accurate. However, if distance information were unavailable, then perceived size would be determined by visual angle alone. According to the size-distance invariance hypothesis (Kilpatrick & Ittelson, 1953), perceived size (S') and perceived distance (D') stand in a unique ratio determined by some function of the visual angle (θ):

$$\frac{S'}{D'} = f(\theta)$$

The size-distance invariance hypothesis has taken slightly different forms, depending on how the function f in the previous equation has been specified. If the size-distance invariance hypothesis is simply interpreted as a geometric relation, then $f(\theta) = \tan\theta$ (Baird & Wagner, 1991). For small visual angles, $\tan\theta$ approximates θ, and so $S'/D' = \theta$. According to a psychophysical interpretation, the ratio of perceived size to perceived distance varies as a power function of visual angle: $f(\theta) = k\theta^n$, where k and n are constants. Foley (1968) and Oyama (1974) reported that the exponent of this function is approximately 1.45. According to a third interpretation, visual angle θ is replaced by perceived visual angle θ' (McCready, 1985). If θ' is a linear function of θ, then $\tan\theta' = \tan(a + b\theta)$, where a and b are constants.

The adequacy of the size-distance invariance hypothesis has often been questioned, given that the empirically determined relation between S' and D' for a given visual angle is sometimes opposite from that predicted by this hypothesis (Sedgwick, 1986). For example, observers often report that the moon at the horizon appears to be both larger and closer to the viewer than the moon at the zenith appears (Hershenson, 1989). This discrepancy has been called the *size-distance paradox*.

Familiar Size

According to the familiar-size hypothesis, the problem of size perception is reduced to a matter of object recognition for those objects that have stable and known sizes (Hershenson & Samuels, 1999). Given that familiar size does not assume information about distance, it can itself be considered a source of that information: Familiar size may determine perceived size, which, in agreement with the size-distance invariance hypothesis, may determine perceived distance (Ittelson, 1960).

The hypothesis that familiar size may determine apparent size (or apparent distance) has been denied by the *theory of off-sized perceptions* (Gogel & Da Silva, 1987). According to this theory, the distance of a familiar object under impoverished viewing conditions is determined by the egocentric reference distance, which in turn determines the size of the object according to the size-distance invariance hypothesis.

Direct Perception

Epstein (1982) summarizes the main ideas of Gibson's (1979) account of size perception as follows: "(a) there is no perceptual representation of size correlated with the retinal size of the object; (b) perceived size and perceived distance are independent direct functions of information in stimulation; (c) perceived size and perceived distance are not causally linked, nor is the perception of size mediated by operations combining information about retinal size and perceived distance. The correlation between perceived size and perceived distance is attributed to the correlation between the specific variables of stimulation which govern these percepts in the particular situation" (p. 78).

Surprisingly little research on size perception has been conducted within the direct-perception perspective. However, the available empirical evidence, consistent with this perspective, suggests that perceived size might be affected by the ground texture gradients (Bingham, 1993; Sinai, Ooi, & He, 1998) and the horizon ratio (Carello, Grosofsky, Reichel, Solomon, & Turvey, 1989).

Size in Pictures Versus Size in the World

It is sometimes assumed that illusions, especially geometrical ones, are artifacts of picture perception. This assumption is false, at least with respect to the anisotropy between vertical and horizontal extents. The perceptual bias to see vertical extents as greater than equivalent horizontal extents is even greater when viewing large objects in the world than when viewing pictures (Chapanis & Mankin, 1967; Higashiyama, 1996; Yang, Dixon, & Proffitt, 1999).

Yang et al. (1999) compared the magnitude of the vertical-horizontal illusion for scenes viewed in pictures, in the real world, and in virtual environments viewed in a head-mounted display. They found that pictures evoke a bias averaging about 6%, whereas viewing the same scenes in real or virtual worlds results in an overestimation of the vertical averaging about 12%.

Geographical Slant Perception

The perceptual bias to overestimate vertical extents pales in comparison to that seen in the perception of geographical slant. Perceived topography grossly exaggerates the geometrical properties of the world in which we live (Bhalla & Proffitt, 1999; Kammann, 1967; Ross, 1974; Proffitt, Bhalla, Gossweiler, & Midgett, 1995).

Proffitt et al. (1995; Bhalla & Proffitt, 1999) obtained two measures of explicit geographical slant perception from observers who stood at either the tops or bottoms of hills in either real or virtual worlds. Observers provided verbal judgments and also adjusted the size of a pie-shape segment of a disk so as to make it correspond to the cross-section of the hills they were observing. These two measures were nearly equivalent and revealed huge overestimations. Five-degree hills, for example, were judged to be about 20°, and 10° hills were judged to be about 30°. These huge overestimations seem odd for at least two reasons. First, people know what angles look like. Proffitt et al. (1995) asked participants to set cross-sections with the disk to a variety of angles and found that they were quite accurate in doing so. Second, when viewing a hill in cross-section, the disk could be accurately adjusted by lining up the two edges of the pie section to lines in the visual scene; however, the overestimations found for people viewing hills in cross-section do not differ from judgments taken when the hills are viewed head-on (Proffitt, Creem, & Zosh, 2001).

Proffitt and colleagues have argued that the conscious overestimation of slant is adaptive and reflective of psychophysical response compression (Bhalla & Proffitt, 1999; Proffitt et al., 2001; Proffitt et al., 1995). Psychophysical response compression means that participants' response sensitivities decline with increases in the magnitude of the stimulus. Expressed as a power function, the exponent is less than 1. Response compression promotes sensitivity to small changes in slant within the range of small slants that are of behavioral relevance for people. Overestimation necessarily results from a response compression function that is anchored at 0° and 90°. People are accurate at 0°—they can tell whether the ground is going up or down—and for similar reasons of discontinuity, they are also accurate at 90°.

All of Proffitt's and his colleagues' studies utilized a third dependent measure, which was a visually guided action in which participants adjusted the incline of a tilt board without looking at their hands. These action-based estimates of slant were far more accurate than were the explicit judgments.

It was proposed that the dissociation seen between explicit perceptions and visually guided actions were a symptom of the two visual streams of processing. The basis for this argument was a dissociation found in the influence of physiological state on the explicit versus motoric dependent measures.

Proffitt et al. (1995) found that, as assessed by verbal reports and the visual matching task employing the pie-shaped disk, hills appear steeper when people are fatigued. Bhalla and Proffitt (1999) replicated this finding; in addition, he found that hills appear steeper when people are encumbered by a heavy backpack, have low physical fitness, are elderly, or have failing health. None of these factors influenced the visually guided action of adjusting the tilt board. Thus, in the case of geographical slant, explicit judgments were influenced by the manipulation of physiological state, although the visually guided action was unaffected. This finding differs from Philbeck and Loomis's (1997) results showing that verbal reports of distance and blindwalking changed together with manipulations of reduced-cue environments.

EVENT PERCEPTION

Events are occurrences that unfold over time. We have already seen that the visual perception of space and three-dimensional form is derived from motion-carried information. The structure perceived in these cases is, of course, recovered from events. The literature in the field of visual perception, however, has partitioned the varieties of motion-carried information into distinct fields of inquiry. For example, perceiving spatial layout and three-dimensional form from motion parallax and object rotations falls under the topic of structure-from-motion. The field of event perception has historically dealt with two issues, perceptual organization (see chapter by Palmer in this volume) and perceiving dynamics.

Perceptual Organization

The law of common fate is among the Gestalt principles of perceptual organization that were proposed by Wertheimer (1923/1937). In essence, this law states that elements that move together tend to be perceived as belonging to the same group. This notion of grouping by common fate is at the heart of the event perception literature that developed as an answer to this question: *What are the perceptual rules that define what it means for elements to move together?*

In response to this question, three classes of events have received the most attention: (a) surface segregation from motion, (b) hierarchical motion organization, and (c) biological motion.

Surface Segregation From Motion

We have already discussed how dynamic occlusion specifies depth order within the section on motion-based depth cues. With respect to issues of perceptual organization, however, there are additional matters to relate to this event.

In a typical dynamic occlusion display, one randomly textured surface is placed on top of another (Gibson, Kaplan, Reynolds, & Wheeler, 1969). When the surfaces are stationary, there is no basis for seeing that two separate surfaces are, in fact, present. The instant that one of the surfaces moves, however, the distinct surfaces become apparent. The dynamic occlusion that occurs under these conditions provides an invariant related to depth order. The surface that exhibits an accretion and deletion of optical texture is behind the one that does not. Yonas, Craton, and Thompson (1987) used sparse point-light displays to show that perceptual surface segregation occurs even when optical texture elements do not actually overlap in the display. In their display, the point lights were turned on and off in a manner consistent with their being occluded by a virtual surface carrying other point lights. The surface segregation that is perceived in the presence of dynamic occlusion is different from the figure-ground segregation that is perceived in static pictures due to the lack of ambiguity of edge assignment and depth order. In dynamic occlusion displays, the edge is seen to belong to the surface that does not undergo occlusion; moreover, this surface is unambiguously perceived to be closer.

Hierarchical Motion Organization

Suppose that you observe someone bouncing a ball; the ball is seen to move up and down. Suppose next that the person who is bouncing the ball is standing on a moving wagon. In this latter case, you will likely still see the ball moving up and down and at the same time moving with the wagon. The wagon's motion has become a perceptual frame of reference for seeing the motion of the bouncing ball. This is an example of hierarchical motion organization in which the ball's motion has been perceptually decomposed into two components, that which it shares with the wagon and that which it does not.

Rubin (1927) and Duncker (1929/1937) provided early demonstrations of the perceptual system's proclivity to produce hierarchically organized motions; however, Johansson (1950) brought the field into maturity. Johansson (1950, 1973) provided a vector analysis description of the perceptual decomposition of complex motions. In the case of the ball's being bounced on a moving wagon, the motion of the ball relative to a stationary environmental reference frame is its *absolute motion,* whereas the motion shared by the ball and the wagon is the *common motion* component, and the unique motion of the ball with respect to the wagon is the *relative motion* component. It is generally assumed that relative and common motion components sum to equal the perceptually registered absolute motion; however, this assumption has rarely been tested and, in at least one circumstance, has been shown not to hold (Vicario & Bressan, 1990).

Johansson frequently used point-light displays to demonstrate the nature of hierarchical motion organization. In a case analogous to the bouncing ball example, Johansson created a display in which a single point light moved along a diagonal path, the horizontal component of which was identical to that of a set of flanking point lights moving above and below it. Observers tend to see the single point light moving vertically relative to the flankers and the whole array of point lights moving with a common back and forth motion. Here, two sorts of perceptual organization are apparent. First, perceptual grouping is achieved on the basis of common fate; second, the common motion is serving as a moving frame of reference for the perception of the event's relative motion.

Another event that has received considerable attention is the perception of a few point lights moving as if attached to a rolling wheel. Duncker (1929/1937) showed that the motions perceived in this event depend upon where the configuration of point lights is placed on the wheel. If two point lights are place on the rim of an unseen wheel, 180° apart, then the points will appear to move in a circle (relative motion) and at the same time translate horizontally (common motion). On the other hand, if the points are place 90° apart, so that the center of the configuration does not coincide with the center of the wheel, then the points will appear to tumble. The reason for this difference is that the perceptual system derives relative motions that occur around the center of the configuration, with the observed common motion being of the configural centroid (Borjesson & von Hofsten, 1975; Proffitt, Cutting, & Stier, 1979). When the configural centroid coincides with the hub of the wheel, smooth horizontal translation is seen as the common motion. If it does not coincide, then the common motion will follow a more complex wavy path (a prolate cycloid).

Attempts have been made to provide a general processing model for perceiving hierarchical motion organization; however, little success has been achieved. Johansson's (1973) perceptual vector analysis model describes well what is seen in events, but does not derive these descriptions in a principled way. Restle (1979) applied Leeuwenberg's (1971, 1978) perceptual coding theory to many of Johansson's displays. By this account, the resulting perception is a consequence of a minimization of the number of parameters required to describe the event. The analysis worked well; however, it evaluates descriptions after some other process has derived them—thus it fails to account for the process that produces the set of initial descriptions. Borjesson and von Hofsten (1975) and Cutting and Proffitt (1982) proposed models in which the perceptual system minimized relative motions. These accounts work well for wheel-generated motions, but they are not sufficiently general to account for the varieties of hierarchical motion organizations.

Not all motions are equally able to serve as perceptual frames of reference. In the case of the ball bouncing on a wagon, the common motion is a translation. Bertamini and Proffitt (2000) compared events in which the common motion was a translation, a rotation, or a divergence-convergence (radial expansion or contraction). They found that common translations and divergence-convergence evoked hierarchical motion organizations, but that rotations typically did not. In the cases in which rotations did serve as perceptual reference frames, it was found that they did so because there were also structural invariants present in the displays. A structural invariant is a spatial property that, in these cases, was revealed in motion. For example, if one point orbited around another at a constant distance, then this spatial invariant would promote a perceptual grouping. Given sufficiently strong spatial groupings, a rotational common motion can be seen as a hierarchical reference frame for the extraction of relative motions. One case in which this occurs is the class of events called biological motions.

Biological Motion

Few displays have captured the imagination of perceptual scientists as strongly as the point-light walker displays first introduced to the field by Johansson (1973; Mass, Johansson, Janson, & Runeson, 1971). These displays consist of spots of light attached to the joints of an actor, who is then filmed in the dark. When the actor is stationary, the lights appear as a disorganized array. As soon as the actor moves, however, observers recognize the human form as well as the actor's actions. In the Mass et al. movie, the actors walked, climbed steps, did push-ups, and danced to a Swedish folk song. The displays are delightful, as they demonstrate the amazing organizing power of the perceptual system under conditions of seemingly minimal information.

Following Johansson's lead, others showed that observers could recognize their friends in such point-light displays (Cutting & Kozlowski, 1977), and moreover that gender was reliably evident (Barclay, Cutting, & Kozlowski, 1978). Runeson and Frykholm (1981) filmed point-light actors lifting different weights in a box and found that observers could reliably judge the amount of weight being lifted. These are amazing perceptual feats. Upon what perceptual processes are they based?

When a point-light walker is observed, hierarchical nestings of pendular motions are observed within the figure, along with a translational common motion. Models have been proposed for extracting connectivity in these events; however, they are not sufficiently general to succeed in recovering structure in cases in which the actor rotates, as in the Mass et al. dancing sequence (D. D. Hoffman & Flinchbaugh, 1982; Webb & Aggarwal, 1982). These models look for rigid relationships in the motions between points that are not specific to biological motions. It may be that the perceptual system is attuned to other factors specific to biomechanics, such as necessary constraints on the phase relationships among the limbs (Bertenthal & Pinto, 1993; Bingham, Schmidt, & Zaal, 1999). It may also be the case that point-light walker displays are organized, at least in part, by making contact with representations in long-term memory that have been established through experiences of watching people walk. Consistent with this notion is the finding that when presented upside down, these displays are rarely identified as people (Sumi, 1984). Cats have also been found to discriminate point-light cats from foils containing the same motions in scrambled locations when the displays were viewed upright, but not when displays were upside down (R. Blake, 1993). Additional support for the proposal that experience plays a role is seen in the findings on infant sensitivities to biological motions. It has been found that infants as young as 3 months of age can extract some structure from point-light walker displays (Bertenthal, Proffitt, & Cutting, 1984; Fox & McDaniels, 1982). However, it is not until they are 7 to 9 months old that they show evidence of identifying the human form. At earlier ages, they seem to be sensitive to local structural invariants.

Perceiving Dynamics

Suppose that you are taking a walk and notice a brick lying on the ground. Now, suppose that as you approach the brick, a small gust of wind blows it into the air. You will, of course, be surprised and this surprise is a symptom of your violated expectation that the brick was much too heavy to be moved by the wind. Certainly, people form dynamical intuitions all of the time about quantities such as mass. A question that has stimulated considerable research is whether the formation of dynamical intuitions is achieved by thought or by perception.

Hume (1739/1978) argued that perception could not supply sufficient and necessary information to specify the underlying causal necessity of events. Hume wrote that we see forms and motions interacting in time, not the dynamic laws that dictate the regularities that are observed in their motions. Challenging Hume's thesis, Michotte (1963) demonstrated that people do, in fact, form spontaneous impressions about causality when viewing events that have a collision-like structure. Michotte's studies created considerable interest in the question of how much dynamic information could be perceived in events.

In this spirit, Bingham, Schmidt, and Rosenblum (1995) showed participants patch-light displays of simple events such as a rolling ball, stirring water, and a falling leaf. Participants were found to classify these events based upon similarities in their dynamics.

Runeson (1977/1983) showed that there were regularities in events that could support the visual perception of dynamical quantities. So, for example, when two balls of different mass collide, a ratio can be formed between the differences in their pre- and postcollision velocities that specifies their relative masses. Moreover, it has been shown that, when people view collision events, they can make relative mass judgments (Gilden & Proffitt, 1989; Runeson, Juslin, & Olsson, 2000; Todd & Warren, 1982). Contention exists, however, on the accuracy of these judgments and on what underlying processes are responsible for this ability. Following Todd and Warren (1982), Gilden and Proffitt (1989) provided evidence that judgments were based upon heuristics, such as *the ball that ricochets is lighter* or *the ball with greatest postcollision speed is lighter.* Like all heuristics, these judgments reflect accuracy in some contexts but not in others. On the other hand, Runeson et al. (2000) showed that people could make accurate judgments, provided that these individuals are given considerable practice with feedback.

People also perceive mass when viewing displays of point-light actors lifting weights (Bingham, 1987; Runeson & Frykholm, 1983). It has yet to be determined how accurate people are in their judgments and upon what perceptual or cognitive processes these judgments are based.

In addition to noticing dynamical quantities when viewing events, people also seem more attuned to what is dynamically appropriate when they view moving (as opposed to static) displays. For example, many studies have used static depictions to look at people's apparent inability to accurately predict trajectories in simple dynamical systems (Kaiser, Jonides, & Alexander, 1986; McCloskey, 1983; McCloskey, Caramazza, & Green, 1980). For example, when asked to predict the path of an object dropped by a moving carrier—participants were shown a picture of an airplane carrying a bomb—many people predict that it will fall straight down (McCloskey, Washburn, & Felch, 1983). However, when shown a computer animation of the erroneous trajectory that they would predict, these people viewed these paths as being anomalous and choose as correct the dynamically correct event (Kaiser, Proffitt, Whelan, & Hecht, 1992).

The ability to discriminate between dynamically correct and anomalous events is not without limit. People's ability to perceptually penetrate rotational events has been found to be severely limited. Kaiser et al. (1992) showed people computer animations of a satellite spinning in space. The satellite would open or close its solar panels; as it did so, its spinning rate would increase, decrease, or reverse direction. Rotation rate should increase as the panels contracted (and visa versa), as does a twirling ice-skater who extends or contracts his or her arms. People showed virtually no perceptual appreciation for the dynamical appropriateness of the satellite simulations. Other than when the satellite actually changed its rotational direction, the dynamically anomalous and canonical events were all judged to be equally possible. Another event that does not improve with animation is performance on the water-level task. In paper-and-pencil tests, it has been found that about 40% of adults do not draw horizontal lines when asked to indicate the surface orientation of water in a stationary tilted container (McAfee & Proffitt, 1991). Animating this event does not improve performance (Howard, 1978).

Clearly, a theory of dynamical event perception needs to specify not only what people can do, but also what they cannot. Attempts to account for the limits of our dynamical perceptions have focused on perceptual biases and on event complexity. With respect to the former, perceptual frame-of-reference biases have been used to explain certain biases in people's dynamical judgments (Hecht & Proffitt, 1995; Kaiser et al., 1992; McAfee & Proffitt, 1991; McCloskey et al., 1983). As a first approximation toward defining dynamical event complexity, Proffitt and Gilden (1989) made a distinction between particle (easy) and extended body (hard) motions. *Particle motions* are those that can be described adequately by treating the object as if it were a point particle located at the object's center of mass. Free-falling is a particle motion if air resistance is ignored. *Extended body motions* make relevant other object properties such as shape and rotations. A spinning top is an example of an extended body motion. The apparent gravity-defying behavior of a spinning top gives evidence to our inability to see the dynamical constraints that cause it to move as it does. Tops are enduring toys because their dynamics cannot be penetrated by perception.

Perceiving Our Own Motion

In this section, we consider the perception of our own motion by examining three problems: how we perceive our direction of motion (*heading*); the illusion of self-motion experienced by stationary individuals when viewing moving visual surrounds (*vection*); and the visual control of posture.

Heading

In studying how the direction of self-motion (or *heading*) is recovered, researchers have focused on the use of relevant visual information. However, vestibular information (Berthoz, Istraël, George-François, Grasso, & Tsuzuku, 1995) and feedback from eye movements (Royden, Banks, & Crowell, 1992) may also play a role in this task. Gibson (1950) proposed that the primary basis for the visual control of locomotion is *optic flow*.

In general, instantaneous optic flow can be conceptualized as the sum of a translational and a rotational component (for a detailed discussion, see Hildreth & Royden, 1998; Warren, 1998). The translational component alone generates a radial pattern of velocity vectors emanating from a singularity in the velocity field called the *focus of expansion* (FOE). A pure translational flow is generated, for example, when an observer moves in a stationary environment while looking in the direction of motion. In these circumstances, the FOE specifies the direction of self-motion. In general, however, optic flow contains a rotational component as well, such as when an observer experiences pursuit eye movement when fixating on a point not in line with the motion direction. For a pure rotational flow, equivalent to a rigid rotation of the world about the eye, both the direction and magnitude of the velocity vectors are independent of the distance between the observer and the projected features. The rotational component, therefore, is informative neither about the structure of the environment, nor about the motion of the observer. The presence of the rotational flow, however, does complicate retinal flow. When both translational and rotational components are present, a singularity still exists in the flow field, but in this case it specifies the fixation point rather than the heading direction. Thus, "if observers simply relied on the singularity in the field to determine heading, they would see themselves as heading toward the fixation point" (Warren, 1995, p. 273).

Many theoretical analyses have demonstrated how the direction of heading could be recovered from the optic flow (e.g., Regan & Beverly, 1982). However, no agreement exists on whether, in a biologically plausible model of heading, the rotational component must first be subtracted from retinal flow in order to recover the FOE from the translational flow, or whether heading can be recovered without decomposing retinal flow into its two components. Most of the theoretical analyses of the compound velocity field have been developed for computer vision applications and have followed the first of these two routes (for a review, see Hildreth & Royden, 1998). The second approach has received less attention and has been advocated primarily by Cutting and collaborators (Cutting, Springer, Braren, & Johnson, 1992). Although followers of this second proposal used more naturalistic settings, most studies on the perception of heading have used random-dot displays simulating the optical motion that would be produced by an observer moving relative to a ground plane, a three-dimensional cloud of dots, or one or more fronto-parallel surfaces at different depths.

Overall, empirical investigations on heading show that the human visual system can indeed recover the heading direction from velocity fields like those generated by the normal range of locomotion speeds. The psychophysical studies in particular have revealed the following about human perception of heading: It is remarkably robust in noisy flow fields (van den Berg, 1992); it is capable of making use of sparse clouds of motion features (Cutting et al., 1992) and of extraretinal information about eye rotation (Royden, Banks, & Crowell, 1992); and it improves in its performance when other three-dimensional cues are present in the scene (van den Berg & Brenner, 1994). Some of the proposed computational models embody certain of these features, but so far no model has been capable of mimicking the whole range of capabilities revealed by human observers.

Vection

Observers sometimes experience an illusory perception of self-motion while sitting in a stationary train and watching an adjacent train pulling out of the station. This *train illusion* is the best-known example of vection (Fisher & Kornmüller, 1930). Vection can be induced not only by visual, but also by auditory (Lackner, 1977), somatosensory (Lackner & DiZio, 1984), and combined somatosensory and kinesthetic (Bles, 1981) information. The first studies on visually induced vection can be dated back to Mach (1875) and were performed using a vertically striped optokinetic drum or an endless belt (Mach, 1922). Two kinds of vection can be distinguished: circular and linear. Circular vection typically refers to yaw motion about the vertical axis, whereas linear vection refers to translatory motion through a vertical or horizontal axis. Vection is called *saturated* when the inducing stimulus appears to be stationary and only self-motion is perceived (Wertheim, 1994).

Linear vection is typically induced about 1–2 s after the onset of stimulation (Giannopulu & Lepecq, 1998), circular vection after about 2–3 s, and saturated vection after about 10 s (Brandt, Dichgans, & Koenig, 1973). A more compelling vection is induced by faster speeds of translation or rotation (Larish & Flach, 1990), by low temporal frequencies (Berthoz, Lacour, Soechting, & Vidal, 1979), by more or larger elements (Brandt, Wist, & Dichgans, 1975); this is also the case when larger retinal areas are stimulated (Brandt et al., 1975) and when the inducing stimulus belongs to the background relative to the foreground (Nakamura & Shimojo, 1999).

Visual Control of Posture

Postural stability, or stance, is affected by visual, vestibular, and somatosensory information. Visual and somatosensory information are more effective in the low-frequency range of postural sway, whereas vestibular information is more effective in the high-frequency range (Howard, 1986). A device known as the *moving room* has been used to demonstrate that visual information can be used to control posture. In their original study, Lee and Aronson (1974) required infants to stand within a room in which the walls were detached from the floor and could slide back and forth. They reported that when the walls moved, infants swayed or staggered in spite of the fact that the floor remained stationary, a finding later replicated by many other studies (Bertenthal & Bai, 1989; for adult, see Lee & Lishman, 1975).

Two sources of visual information are available for postural control: the radial and lamellar motions of front and side surfaces, respectively, and the motion parallax between objects at different depths that is generated by the translation of the observer's head (Warren, 1995). Evidence has shown that posture is regulated by compensatory movements that tend to minimize both of these patterns of optical motion (Lee & Lishman, 1975; Warren, Kay, & Yilmaz, 1996). Three hypotheses have been proposed concerning the locus of retinal stimulation: (a) the *peripheral dominance hypothesis,* which states that the retinal periphery dominates both the perception of self-motion and the control of stance (Dichgans & Brandt, 1978); (b) the *retinal invariance hypothesis,* which states that self-motion and object motion are perceived independently of the part of the retina being stimulated (Crowell & Banks, 1993); and (c) the *functional sensitivity hypothesis,* which states that "central vision accurately extracts radial . . . and lamellar flow, whereas peripheral vision extracts lamellar flow but it is less sensitive to radial . . . flow" (Warren & Kurtz, 1992, p. 451). Empirical findings have contradicted the peripheral dominance hypothesis (Stoffregen, 1985) and the functional sensitivity hypothesis (Bardy, Warren, & Kay, 1999). Instead, they support the retinal invariance hypothesis by emphasizing the importance of the optic-flow structure for postural control, regardless of the locus of retinal stimulation.

Perceiving Approaching Objects

Time to Contact and Time to Passage

Coordinating actions within a dynamic environment often requires temporal information about events. For example, when catching a ball, we need to be able to initiate the grasp before the ball hits our hand. One might suspect that in order to plan for the ball's time of arrival, the perceptual system would have to compute the ball's speed and distance; however, this turns out not to be the case. In determining time to contact, there exists an optical invariant, *tau,* which does not require that object speed or distance be taken into account.

First derived by Hoyle (1957) in his science-fiction novel, *The Black Cloud,* and later introduced to the vision community by Lee (1974), tau relates the optical size of an object to its rate of expansion in a manner that specifies time to contact. Tau is defined as follows:

$$\text{tau} \approx \theta/\delta\theta/\delta t$$

where θ is the angular extend of the object in radians, and $\delta\theta/\delta t$ is the rate of its expansion. Tau specifies time to contact under the assumption that the object is moving with a constant velocity.

In the case in which the object and observer are not on a collision course, a similar relationship specifies time to passage (Lee, 1974, 1980). Let Φ be the angular extent between the observer's heading direction and the object, then time-to-passage, in terms of tau, is defined by

$$\text{tau} \approx \Phi/\delta\Phi/\Phi t$$

Tresilian (1991) has refined the definition of tau by distinguishing between local and global tau. Local tau can be computed solely on the basis of information about angular extents and their rate of change. Global tau is only available to a moving observer and requires that the direction of heading be computed as well.

Research on tau has taken two forms. First, researchers have investigated whether people and animals are sensitive to time to contact and time to passage. Second, they have studied whether performance is actually based upon a perceptual derivation of tau. In summary, the literature suggests that time to contact and time to passage are accurately perceived; however, whether this perceptual feat is due to an appreciation of tau is currently a point of contention.

Optical expansion, or looming, evokes defensive postures in adults, animals (Schiff, 1965), and human infants (Bower, Broughton, & Moore, 1970). The assumption is that these defensive actions are motivated by a perception that the expanding object is on an imminent collision course. Although it is tempting to think of the link between looming and impending collision as being innate, human infants do not clearly show behaviors that can be defined as defensive in these conditions until 9 months of age (Yonas et al., 1977).

Adults are quite accurate in making time-to-contact judgments (Schiff & Oldak, 1990; Todd, 1981). Todd's data show relative time-to-contact judgments to be sensitive to less than 100-ms time differences. Relative time-to-passage judgments are less accurate, requiring differences of about 500 ms (Kaiser & Mowafy, 1993).

How people actually make time-to-contact judgments is currently a topic of debate. In a review of the literature, Wann (1996) found that empirical support for the tau proposal was weak and that other optical variables, such as indexes of relative distance, could account for research findings as well as tau. Recently, Tresilian (1999) provided a revised tau hypothesis in which it is acknowledged that the effective information in time-to-contact situations is task- and context-specific, and moreover that it involves the utilization of multiple cues from diverse sources.

Intercepting a Fly Ball

In order to catch a fly ball, players must achieve two goals: First, they must get themselves to the location where the ball will land; and second, they must catch it. It seems reasonable to assume that satisfying the first goal of interception would require a determination of the ball's landing location, but this is not necessarily so. If a player looks at the ball in flight and runs so that the ball's perceived trajectory follows a straight path, then the ball will intersect the player's path on its descent (McBeath, Shaffer, & Kaiser, 1995). If players followed this simple control heuristic, then they would run along curved paths to the location of the ball's landing. If, instead, they knew where the ball would land, then they would run to that place in a straight line. In fact, outfielders run on curved paths that closely follow the predictions of the control heuristic formulation (McBeath et al., 1995). (See the chapter by Heuer in this volume for a discussion of motor control.)

This final experimental finding clearly points to the difficulty of disentangling conscious visual perceptions from the visual control of actions. Ask baseball players what they do when they catch fly balls, and they will tell you that they see the ball moving through space and run to where they can catch it. Without doubt, they perceive the ball to be moving in depth. On the other hand, the control heuristic that guides their running does not entail a representation of three-dimensional space. The heuristic applies to a two-dimensional representation of the ball's trajectory in the virtual image plan defined by their line of sight to the ball.

CONCLUSION

In perceiving depth and events, the relevant information is both limited and abundant. Viewed in isolation, visual information is almost always found lacking in its ability to uniquely specify those aspects of the environment to which it relates. However, combining different informational sources leads to a more satisfactory state of affairs. In general, the more complex the visual scene, the more well specified it becomes.

Movement- and goal-directed behaviors are complications that add considerably to the sufficiency of optical information for specifying environmental layout and events; however, their study has recently led to the following conundrum: Conscious visual perceptions and visually guided actions do not always reflect a common underlying representation. For example, geographical slant is grossly overestimated; however, a visually guided adjustment of perceived slant is accurate. When catching a baseball, players perceive themselves to be moving in a three-dimensional environment even though the visual guidance of their running path is controlled by heuristics applied to a two-dimensional representation of the scene. The disparity between awareness and action in these cases may reflect the functioning of multiple perceptual systems.

Looking to the future, we see at least three developments that should have a significant impact on research on how people perceive depth and events. These developments include (a) improvements in research technology, (b) increased breadth in the interdisciplinary nature of research, and (c) increased sophistication in the theoretical approach.

Perceptual research has benefited enormously from computer technology. For example, Johansson (1950) used computers to create moving point-light displays on an oscilloscope thereby establishing the field of event perception. Current computer systems allow researchers to create almost any imaginable scene. Over the last 10 years, immersive displays have become available. Immersive displays surround observers and allow them to move and interact within a virtual environment. Head-mounted displays present images with small screens in front of the eyes and utilize tracking systems to register the position and orientation of the head and other tracked parts of the body. Another immersive display system is the Cave Automatic Virtual Environment, CAVE, which is a room having rear-projected images. The observer's head is tracked and the projected images transform in a manner consistent with the observer's movement through a three-dimensional environment. Such immersive display systems allow researchers to control optical variables that heretofore could only be manipulated within the confines of a computer terminal. Given the increased availability of immersive display systems, we expect to see more investigations of perceptions in situations entailing the visual control of action.

Understanding the perception of space and events is of interest to a wide variety of disciplines. The current chapter has emphasized the psychophysical perspective, which relates relevant optical information to perceptual sensitivities. However, within such fields as computer science and cognitive neuroscience, there is also considerable research on this topic.

Computer scientists are often interested in automating perceptual feats, such as the recovery of three-dimensional structure from optical motion information, and comparisons of digital and biological algorithms have proven to be useful (Marr, 1982). Another area of computer science that is ripe for interdisciplinary collaboration is in the computer-graphics animation of events. Interestingly, many movies today employ methods of motion capture to create computer-animated actors. These methods entail placing sensors on the head and joints of real actors and recovering an animation of a stick figure that can be fleshed out in graphics. One cannot help but think of Johansson's point-light walker displays when viewing such a motion capture system in use. Currently, there is considerable work attempting to create synthetic actors directly with algorithms. Perceptual scientists should be able to learn a lot by studying what works and what does not in this attempt to create synthetic thespians. Just as the pictorial depth cues were first discovered by artists and then articulated by psychologists, the study of computer-simulated events should help us better understand what information is needed to evoke the perceptions of such natural motions as a person walking, and perhaps more generally, perceptions of animacy and purpose.

Research in cognitive neuroscience has had an increasing impact on perceptual theory, and this trend is likely to continue. Advances in clinical case studies, functional brain imaging, and animal research have greatly shaped our current conceptions of perceptual processing. For example, the anatomical significance of the dorsal and ventral cortical pathways is currently receiving a lot of attention (Creem & Proffitt, 2001). These two pathways are the dominant visual processing streams in the cortex; however, there are many others visual streams in the brain. We have much to learn from functional anatomy that will help us constrain and develop our theoretical conceptions.

Finally, there have been a number of recent advances in the sophistication of our theoretical approach. One of the most notable of these was made recently by Cutting and Vishton (1995). Every text on depth perception provides a list of depth cues, as does the current chapter. How these cues are combined is still much debated. Given the huge number of cues, however, an account of how depth is perceived in the context of all possible combinations of these variables is probably unattainable. On the other hand, Cutting and Vishton showed that there is much to be gained by investigating the range of efficacy of different cues. For example, binocular disparity is useful at near distances but not far ones, whereas occlusion is equally useful at all distances. Looking at the problem of depth perception from this perspective motivates a search for the conditions under which information is useful. A related theoretical approach is seen in the search for perceptual heuristics. Heuristics are simple processing rules having a precision that is no better than what is needed to effectively guide behavior. The control heuristics engaged when catching baseballs are examples (McBeath et al., 1995). From a pragmatic perspective, optical information is useful to the degree that it helps inform the requirements defined by the demands of the task at hand.

REFERENCES

Amorim, M.-A., Loomis, J. M., & Fukusima, S. S. (1998). Reproduction of object shape is more accurate without the continued availability of visual information. *Perception, 27,* 69–86.

Andersen, G. J., & Braunstein, M. L. (1983). Dynamic occlusion in the perception of rotation in depth. *Perception & Psychophysics, 34,* 356–362.

Baird, J. C., & Wagner, M. (1991). Transformation theory of size judgment. *Journal of Experimental Psychology: Human Perception and Performance, 17,* 852–864.

Barclay, C. D., Cutting, J. E., & Kozlowski, L. T. (1978). Temporal and spatial factors in gait perception that influence gender recognition. *Perception & Psychophysics, 23,* 145–152.

Bardy, B. G., Warren W. H., & Kay, B. A. (1999). The role of central and peripheral vision in postural control during walking. *Perception & Psychophysics, 61,* 1356–1368.

Berkeley, G. (1709). *An essay towards a new theory of vision.* London: J. M. Dent.

Bertamini, M., & Proffitt, D. R. (2000). Hierarchical motion organization in random dot configurations. *Journal of Experimental Psychology: Human Perception and Performance, 26,* 1371–1386.

Bertamini, M., Yang, T. L., & Proffitt, D. R. (1998). Relative size perception at a distance is best at eye level. *Perception & Psychophysics, 60,* 673–682.

Bertenthal, B. I., & Bai, D. L. (1989). Infants' sensitivity to optical flow for controlling posture. *Developmental Psychology, 25,* 936–945.

Bertenthal, B. I., & Pinto, J. (1993). Complementary processes in the perception and production of human movements. In E. Thelan & L. Smith (Eds.), *A dynamic systems approach to development: Applications* (pp. 209–239). Cambridge, MA: MIT Press.

Bertenthal, B. I., Proffitt, D. R., & Cutting, J. E. (1984). Infant sensitivity to figural coherence in biomechanical motions. *Journal of Experimental Child Psychology, 37,* 171–178.

Berthoz, A., Istraël, I., George-François, P., Grasso, R., & Tsuzuku, T. (1995). Spatial memory of body linear displacement: What is being stored? *Science, 269,* 95–98.

Berthoz, A., Lacour, M., Soechting, J. F., & Vidal, P. P. (1979). The role of vision in the control of posture during linear motion. *Progress in Brain Research, 50,* 197–209.

Bhalla, M., & Proffitt, D. R. (1999). Visual-motor recalibration in geographical slant perception. *Journal of Experimental Psychology: Human Perception and Performance, 25,* 1076–1096.

Bingham, G. P. (1987). Kinematic form and scaling: Further investigations on the visual perception of lifted weight. *Journal of Experimental Psychology: Human Perception and Performance, 13,* 155–177.

Bingham, G. P. (1993). Perceiving the size of trees: Form as information about scale. *Journal of Experimental Psychology: Human Perception and Performance, 19,* 1139–1161.

Bingham, G. P., & Pagano, C. C. (1998). The necessity of a perception-action approach to definite distance perception: Monocular distance perception to guide reaching. *Journal of Experimental Psychology: Human Perception and Performance, 24,* 145–168.

Bingham, G. P., Schmidt, R. C., & Rosenblum, L. D. (1995). Hefting for a maximum distance throw: A smart perceptual mechanism. *Journal of Experimental Psychology: Human Perception and Performance, 15,* 507–528.

Bingham, G. P., Schmidt, R. C., & Zaal, F. T. J. M. (1999). Visual perception of the relative phasing of human limb movements. *Perception & Psychophysics, 2,* 246–258.

Bingham, G. P., Zaal, F., Robin, D., & Shull, J. A. (2000). Distortions in definite distance and shape perception as measured by reaching without and with haptic feedback. *Journal of Experimental Psychology: Human Perception and Performance, 26,* 1436–1460.

Blake, A., & Marinos, C. (1990). Shape from texture: Estimation, isotropy and moments. *Journal of Artificial Intelligence, 45,* 323–380.

Blake, R. (1993). Cats perceive biological motion. *Psychological Science, 4,* 54–57.

Bles, W. (1981). Stepping around: Circular vection and Coriolis effects. In J. B. Long & A. D. Baddeley (Eds.), *Attention and performance* (Vol. 9, pp. 47–61). Hillsdale, NJ: Erlbaum.

Borjesson, E., & von Hofsten, C. (1975). A vector model for perceived object rotation and translation in space. *Psychological Research, 38,* 209–230.

Bower, T. G. R., Broughton, J. M., & Moore, M. K. (1970). The coordination of visual and tactile input in infants. *Perception & Psychophysics, 8,* 51–53.

Brandt, T., Dichgans, J., & Koenig, E. (1973). Differential effects of central versus peripheral vision on egocentric and exocentric motion perception. *Experimental Brian Research, 16,* 476–491.

Brandt, T., Wist, E. R., & Dichgans, J. (1975). Foreground and background in dynamic spatial orientation. *Perception & Psychophysics, 17,* 497–503.

Braunstein, M. L. (1976). *Depth perception through motion.* New York: Academic Press.

Braunstein, M. L. (1994). Decoding principles, heuristics and inference in visual perception. In G. Johansson, S. S. Bergstrom, &

W. Epstein (Eds.), *Perceiving events and objects* (pp. 436–446). Hillsdale, NJ: Erlbaum.

Bruno, N., & Cutting, J. E. (1988). Minimodularity and the perception of layout. *Journal of Experimental Psychology: General, 117,* 161–170.

Carello, C., Grosofsky, A., Reichel, F., Solomon, H. Y., & Turvey, M. T. (1989). Perceiving what is reachable. *Ecological Psychology, 1,* 27–54.

Caudek, C., & Domini, F. (1998). Perceived orientation of axis of rotation in structure-from-motion. *Journal of Experimental Psychology: Human Perception and Performance, 24,* 609–621.

Caudek, C., Domini, F., & Di Luca, M. (in press). Illusory 3D rotation induced by dynamic image shading. *Perception & Psychophysics.*

Chapanis, A., & Mankin, D. A. (1967). The vertical-horizontal illusion in a visually rich environment. *Perception & Psychophysics, 2,* 249–255.

Clark, J., & Yuille. A. (1990). *Data fusion for sensory information processing systems.* Boston: Kluwer.

Creem, S. H., & Proffitt, D. R. (2001). Defining the cortical visual systems: "What," "where," and "how." *Acta Psychologica, 107,* 43–68.

Crowell, J. A., & Banks, M. S. (1993). Perceiving heading with different retinal regions and types of optic flow. *Perception & Psychophysics, 53,* 325–337.

Cumming, B. G., Johnston, E. B., & Parker, A. J. (1991). Vertical disparities and perception of three-dimensional shape. *Nature, 349,* 411–413.

Cutting, J. E., & Kozlowski, L. T. (1977). Recognizing friends by their walk: Gait perception without familiarity cues. *Bulletin of the Psychonomic Society, 9,* 353–356.

Cutting, J. E., & Millard, R. T. (1984). Three gradients and the perception of flat and curved surfaces. *Journal of Experimental Psychology: General, 113,* 198–216.

Cutting, J. E., & Proffitt, D. R. (1982). The minimum principle and the perception of absolute, common, and relative motions. *Cognitive Psychology, 14,* 211–246.

Cutting, J. E., Springer, K., Braren, P. A., & Johnson, S. H. (1992). Wayfinding on foot from information in retinal, not optical, flow. *Journal of Experimental Psychology: General, 102,* 41–72, 129.

Cutting, J. E., & Vishton, P. M. (1995). Perceiving layout and knowing distances: The integration, relative potency, and contextual use of different information about depth. In W. Epstein & S. Rogers (Eds.), *Perception of space and motion* (pp. 69–117). San Diego, CA: Academic Press.

Dichgans, J., & Brandt, T. (1978). Visual-vestibular interaction: Effects on self-motion perception and postural control. In H. Leibowitz & H.-L. Teuber (Eds.), *Handbook of sensory physiology* (pp. 755–804). New York: Springer-Verlag.

Domini, F., & Braunstein, M. L. (1998). Recovery of 3-D structure from motion is neither euclidean nor affine. *Journal of Experimental Psychology: Human Perception and Performance, 24,* 1273–1295.

Domini, F., & Caudek, C. (1999). Perceiving surface slant from deformation of optic flow. *Journal of Experimental Psychology: Human Perception and Performance, 25,* 426–444.

Domini, F., Caudek, C., & Proffitt, D. R. (1997). Misperceptions of angular velocities influence the perception of rigidity in the kinetic depth effect. *Journal of Experimental Psychology: Human Perception and Performance, 23,* 1111–1129.

Domini, F., Caudek, C., & Richman, S. (1998). Distortions of depth-order relations and parallelism in structure from motion. *Perception & Psychophysics, 60,* 1164–1174.

Domini, F., Caudek, C., Turner, J., & Favretto, A. (1998). Discriminating constant from variable angular velocities in structure from motion. *Perception & Psychophysics, 60,* 747–760.

Duncker, K. (1937). Induced motion. In W. D. Ellis (Ed. and Trans.), *A source-book in Gestalt psychology.* London: Routledge. (Original work published 1929)

Epstein, W. (1977). *Stability and constancy in visual perception.* New York: Wiley.

Epstein, W. (1982). Percept-percept couplings. *Perception, 11,* 75–83.

Erkelens, C. J., & Collewijn, H. (1985). Eye movements and stereopsis during dichoptic viewing of moving random-dot stereograms. *Vision Research, 25,* 1689–1700.

Ernst, M. O., Banks, M. S., & Bülthoff, H. H. (2000). Touch can change visual slant perception. *Nature Neuroscience, 3,* 69–73.

Fisher, S. K., & Ciuffreda, K. J. (1988). Accommodation and apparent distance. *Perception, 17,* 609–621.

Fisher, M. H., & Kornmüller, A. E. (1930). Optokinetisch ausgelöste Bewegungswahrnehmungen und optokinetischer Nystagmus [The perception of movement and optokinetic nystagmus initiated by optokinesis]. *Journal für Psychologie und Neurologie, 41,* 273–308.

Foley, J. M. (1968). Depth, size and distance in stereoscopic vision. *Perception & Psychophysics, 3,* 265–274.

Foley, J. M. (1985). Binocular distance perception: Egocentric distance tasks. *Journal of Experimental Psychology: Human Perception and Performance, 11,* 133–149.

Fox, R., & McDaniels, C. (1982). The perception of biological motion by human infants. *Science, 218,* 486–487.

Fry, G. A., Bridgeman, C. S., & Ellerbrock, V. J. (1949). The effect of atmospheric scattering on binocular depth perception. *American Journal of Optometry, 26,* 8–15.

Gårding, J. (1992). Shape from texture for smooth curved surfaces in perspective projection. *Journal of Mathematical Imaging and Vision, 2,* 327–350.

Giannopulu, I., & Lepecq, J. C. (1998). Linear-vection chronometry along spinal and sagittal axes in erect man. *Perception, 27,* 363–372.

Gibson, J. J. (1950). *The perception of the visual world.* Boston: Houghton Mifflin.

Gibson, J. J. (1979). *The ecological approach to visual perception*. Boston: Houghton Mifflin.

Gibson, J. J., Kaplan, G. A., Reynolds, H. N., & Wheeler, K. (1969). The change form visible to invisible: A study of optical transition. *Perception & Psychophysics, 5,* 113–116.

Gilden, D. L., & Proffitt, D. R. (1989). Understanding collision dynamics. *Journal of Experimental Psychology: Human Perception and Performance, 15,* 372–383.

Gogel, W. C., & Da Silva, J. A. (1987). Familiar size and the theory of off-sized perceptions. *Perception & Psychophysics, 41,* 318–328.

Hecht, H., & Proffitt, D. R. (1995). The price of expertise: Effects of experience on the water-level task. *Psychological Science, 6,* 90–95.

Hershenson, M. (1989). Duration, time constant, and decay of the linear motion aftereffect as a function of inspection duration. *Perception & Psychophysics, 45,* 251–257.

Hershenson, M., & Samuels, S. M. (1999). An airplane illusion: Apparent velocity determined by apparent distance. *Perception, 28,* 433–436.

Higashiyama, A. (1996). Horizontal and vertical distance perception: The discorded-orientation theory. *Perception & Psychophysics, 58,* 259–270.

Hildreth, E. C. (1984). *The measurement of visual motion*. Cambridge, MA: MIT Press.

Hildreth, E. C., & Royden, C. S. (1998). Computing observer motion from optical flow. In T. Watanabe (Ed.), *High-level motion processing: Computational, neurobiological, and psychophysical perspectives* (pp. 269–293). Cambridge, MA: MIT Press.

Hoffman, D. D. (1982). Inferring local surface orientation from motion fields. *Journal of the Optical Society of America, 72,* 888–892.

Hoffman, D. D., & Flinchbaugh, B. E. (1982). The interpretation of biological motion. *Biological Cybernetics, 42,* 195–204.

Hoffman, W. C. (1966). The Lie algebra of visual perception. *Journal of Mathematical Psychology, 3,* 65–98.

Howard, I. P. (1978). Recognition and knowledge of the water-level problem. *Perception, 7,* 151–160.

Howard, I. P. (1986). The perception of posture, self-motion, and the visual vertical. In K. R. Boff, L. Kaufman, & J. P. Thomas (Eds.), *Handbook of perception and human performance* (pp. 18-1–18-62). New York: Wiley.

Hoyle, F. (1957). *The black cloud*. London: Heineman.

Hume, D. (1978). *A treatise on human nature*. Oxford, UK: Oxford University Press. (Original work published 1739)

Ittelson, W. H. (1960). *Visual space perception*. Berlin: Springer.

Johansson, G. (1950). *Configuration in event perception*. Uppsala, Sweden: Almqvist & Wiksell.

Johansson, G. (1973). Visual perception of biological motion and a model for its analysis. *Perception & Psychophysics, 14,* 210–211.

Johnston, E. B. (1991). Systematic distortions of shape from stereopsis. *Vision Research, 31,* 1351–1360.

Kaiser, M. K., Jonides, J., & Alexander, J. (1986). Intuitive reasoning about abstract and familiar physics problems. *Memory & Cognition, 14,* 308–312.

Kaiser, M. K., & Mowafy, L. (1993). Optical specification of time-to-passage: Observers' sensitivity to global tau. *Journal of Experimental Psychology: Human Perception and Performance, 19,* 1028–1040.

Kaiser, M. K., Proffitt, D. R., Whelan, S. M., & Hecht, H. (1992). Influence of animation on dynamical judgments. *Journal of Experimental Psychology: Human Perception and Performance, 18,* 669–690.

Kammann, R. (1967). The overestimation of vertical distance and slope and its role in the moon illusion. *Perception & Psychophysics, 2,* 585–589.

Kaplan, G. A. (1969). Kinetic disruption of optical texture: The perception of depth at an edge. *Perception & Psychophysics, 6,* 193–198.

Kilpatrick, F. P., & Ittelson, W. H. (1953). The size-distance invariance hypothesis. *Psychological Review, 60,* 223–231.

Koenderink, J. J. (1986). Optic flow. *Vision Research*, *26*, 161–179.

Koenderink, J. J., & van Doorn, A. J. (1976). Geometry of binocular vision and a model for stereopsis. *Biological Cybernetics, 21,* 29–35.

Koenderink, J. J., & van Doorn, A. J. (1991). Affine structure from motion. *Journal of the Optical Society of America, 8A,* 377–385.

Kubovy, M. (1986). *The psychology of perspective and Renaissance art*. Cambridge, UK: Cambridge University Press.

Künnapas, T. (1968). Distance perception as a function of available visual cues. *Journal of Experimental Psychology, 77,* 523–529.

Lackner, J. R. (1977). Induction of illusory self-rotation and nystagmus by a rotating sound-field. *Aviation, Space, & Environmental Medicine, 48,* 129–131.

Lackner, J. R., & DiZio, P. (1984). Some efferent and somatosensory influences on body orientation and oculomotor control. In L. Spillmann & B. R. Wooten (Eds.), *Sensory experience, adaptation, and perception*. Hillsdale, NJ: Erlbaum.

Landy, M. S., Maloney, L. T., Johnston, E. B., & Young, M. (1995). Measurement and modeling of depth cue combination: In defense of weak fusion. *Vision Research, 35,* 389–412.

Larish, J. F., & Flach, J. M. (1990). Sources of optical information useful for perception of speed of rectilinear self-motion. *Journal of Experimental Psychology: Human Perception and Performance, 16,* 295–302.

Lee, D. N. (1974). Visual information during locomotion. In R. B. McLeod & H. Pick (Eds.), *Perception: Essays in honor of J. J. Gibson* (pp. 250–267). Ithaca, NY: Cornell University Press.

Lee, D. N. (1980). Visuo-motor coordination in space-time. In G. E. Stelmach & J. Requin (Eds.), *Tutorials in motor behavior* (pp. 281–295). Amsterdam: North-Holland.

Lee, D. N., & Aronson, E. (1974). Visual proprioceptive control of standing in human infants. *Perception & Psychophysics, 15,* 529–532.

Lee, D. N., & Lishman, J. R. (1975). Visual proprioceptive control of stance. *Journal of Human Movement Studies, 1,* 224–230.

Leeuwenberg, E. L. J. (1971). A perceptual coding language for visual and auditory patterns. *American Journal of Psychology, 84,* 307–349.

Leeuwenberg, E. L. J. (1978). Quantification of certain visual pattern similarities: Salience, transparency, similarity. In E. L. J. Leeuwenberg & H. F. J. M. Buffart (Eds.), *Formal theories of visual perception* (pp. 277–298). New York: Wiley.

Loomis, J. M., Da Silva, J. A., Fujita, N., & Fukusima, S. S. (1992). Visual space perception and visually directed action. *Journal of Experimental Psychology: Human Perception and Performance, 18,* 906–921.

Loomis, J. M., & Philbeck, J. W. (1999). Is the anisotropy of perceived 3-D shape invariant across scale? *Perception & Psychophysics, 61,* 397–402.

Lunenburg, R. K. (1947). *Mathematical analysis of binocular vision*. Princeton, NJ: Princeton University Press.

Mach, E. (1875). *Grundlinien der Lehre von der Bewegungsempfindungen* [Basic principles for the study of motion perception]. Leipzig, Germany: Engelmann.

Mach, E. (1922). *Die Analyse der Empfindungen* [The analysis of sensations]. Jena, Germany: Gustav Fischer.

Marr, D. (1982). *Vision: A computational investigation into the human representation and processing of visual information*. San Francisco: W. F. Freeman.

Mass, J. B., Johansson, G., Janson, G., & Runeson, S. (1971). *Motion perception I and II* [Film]. Boston: Houghton Mifflin.

Massaro, D. W. (1988). Ambiguity in perception and experimentation. *Journal of Experimental Psychology: General, 117,* 417–421.

Mayhew, J. E., & Longuet-Higgins, H. C. (1982). A computational model of binocular depth perception. *Nature, 297,* 376–378.

McAfee, E. A., & Proffitt, D. R. (1991). Understanding the surface orientation of liquids. *Cognitive Psychology, 23,* 483–514.

McBeath, M. K., Shaffer, D. M., & Kaiser, M. K. (1995). How baseball outfielders determine where to run to catch fly balls. *Science, 268,* 569–573.

McCloskey, M. (1983). Intuitive physics. *Scientific American, 248,* 122–130.

McCloskey, M., Caramazza, A., & Green, B. (1980). Curvilinear motion in the absence of external forces: Naive beliefs about the motion of objects. *Science, 210,* 1139–1141.

McCloskey, M., Washburn, A., & Felch, L. (1983). Intuitive physics: The straight-down belief and its origin. *Journal of Experimental Psychology: Learning, Memory, & Cognition, 9,* 636–649.

McCready, D. (1985). On size, distance, and visual angle perception. *Perception & Psychophysics, 37,* 323–334.

Michotte, A. (1963). *The perception of causality* (T. R. Miles & E. Miles, Trans.). London: Methuen.

Milner, A. D., & Goodale, M. A. (1995). *The visual brain in action.* Oxford, UK: Oxford University Press.

Mon-Williams, M., & Tresilian, J. R. (1999). Some recent studies on the extraretinal contribution to distance perception. *Perception, 28,* 167–181.

Nakamura, S., & Shimojo, S. (1999). Critical role of foreground stimuli in perceiving visually induced self-motion (vection). *Perception, 28,* 893–902.

Nakayama, K., & Shimojo, S. (1992). Experiencing and perceiving visual surfaces. *Science, 257,* 1357–1363.

Norman, J. F., & Todd, J. T. (1992). The visual perception of 3-dimensional form. In G. A. Carpenter & S. Grossberg (Eds.), *Neural networks for vision and image processing* (pp. 93–110). Cambridge, MA: MIT Press.

Norman, J. F., Todd, J. T., Perotti, V. J., & Tittle, J. S. (1996). The visual perception of three-dimensional length. *Journal of Experimental Psychology: Human Perception and Performance, 22,* 173–186.

Ogle, K. O. (1952). On the limits of stereoscopic vision. *Journal of Experimental Psychology, 48,* 50–60.

Ono, H., & Comerford, T. (1977). Stereoscopic depth constancy. In W. Epstein (Ed.), *Stability and constancy in visual perception: Mechanisms and processes* (pp. 91–128). New York: Wiley.

Ono, H., Rogers, B. J., Ohmi, M., & Ono, M. E. (1988). Dynamic occlusion and motion parallax in depth perception. *Perception, 17,* 255–266.

Oyama, T. (1974). Perceived size and perceived distance in stereoscopic vision and an analysis of their causal relations. *Perception & Psychophysics, 16,* 175–182.

Pagano, C. C., & Bingham, G. P. (1998). Comparing measures of monocular distance perception: Verbal and reaching errors are not correlated. *Journal of Experimental Psychology: Human Perception and Performance, 24,* 1037–1051.

Pentland, A. P. (1984). Local shading analysis. *IEEE, Transactions on Analysis & Machine Intelligence, 6,* 170–187.

Philbeck, J. W., & Loomis, J. M. (1997). Comparison of two indicators of perceived egocentric distance under full-cue and reduced-cue conditions. *Journal of Experimental Psychology: Human Perception and Performance, 23,* 72–85.

Philbeck, J. W., Loomis, J. M., & Beall, A. C. (1997). Visually perceived location is an invariant in the control of action. *Perception & Psychophysics, 59,* 601–612.

Predebon, J. (1991). Spatial judgments of exocentric extents in an open-field situation: Familiar versus unfamiliar size. *Perception & Psychophysics, 50,* 361–366.

Proffitt, D. R., Bhalla, M., Gossweiler, R., & Midgett, J. (1995). Perceiving geographical slant. *Psychonomic Bulletin & Review, 2,* 409–428.

Proffitt, D. R., Creem, S. H., & Zosh, W. (2001). Seeing mountains in mole hills: Geographical slant perception. *Psychological Science, 12,* 418–423.

Proffitt, D. R., Cutting, J. E., & Stier, D. M. (1979). Perception of wheel-generated motions. *Journal of Experimental Psychology: Human Perception and Performance, 5,* 289–302.

Proffitt, D. R., & Gilden, D. L. (1989). Understanding natural dynamics. *Journal of Experimental Psychology: Human Perception and Performance, 15,* 384–393.

Ramachandran, V. S. (1988). Perceiving shape from shading. *Scientific American, 259,* 76–83.

Regan, D., & Beverly, K. I. (1982). How do we avoid confounding the direction we are looking and the direction we are moving? *Science, 215,* 194–196.

Restle, F. (1979). Coding theory of the perception of motion configurations. *Psychological Review, 86,* 1–24.

Rieser, J. J., Ashmead, D. H., Talor, C. R., & Youngquist, G. A. (1990). Visual perception and the guidance of locomotion without vision to previously seen targets. *Perception, 19,* 675–689.

Rogers, B. J., & Bradshaw, M. F. (1993). Vertical disparities, differential perspective and binocular stereopsis. *Nature*, 361, 253–255.

Rogers, S. (1996). The horizon-ratio relation as information for relative size in pictures. *Perception & Psychophysics, 58,* 142–152.

Rosenholtz, R., & Malik, J. (1997). Surface orientation from texture: Isotropy or homogeneity (or both)? *Vision Research, 37,* 2283–2293.

Ross, H. E. (1971). Do judgements of distance and greyness follow the physics of aerial perspective? In A. Garriga-Trillo, P. R. Minon, C. Garcia-Gallego, P. Lubin, A. Merino, & A. Villarino (Eds.), *Fechner Day '93: Proceedings of the International Society for Psychonomics* (pp. 233–238). Palma de Mallorca, Spain: International Society for Psychophysics.

Ross, H. E. (1974). *Behavior and perception in strange environments*. London: George Allen & Unwin.

Royden, C. S., Banks, M. S., & Crowell, J. A. (1992). The perception of heading during eye movements. *Nature, 360,* 583–585.

Rubin, E. (1927). Visuell whrgenommene wirkliche Bewegungen [Visually perceived actual motion]. *Zeitschrift fur Psychologie, 103,* 384–392.

Runeson, S. (1983). On visual perception of dynamic events. *Acta Universitatis Upsaliensis: Studia Psychologica Upsaliensia (Series 9).* (Original work published 1977)

Runeson, S., & Frykholm, G. (1981). Visual perception of lifted weight. *Journal of Experimental Psychology: Human Perception and Performance, 7,* 733–740.

Runeson, S., & Frykholm, G. (1983). Kinematic specification of dynamics as an informational basis for person and action perception: Expectation, gender recognition, and deceptive intention. *Journal of Experimental Psychology: General, 112,* 585–615.

Runeson, S., Juslin, P., & Olsson, H. (2000). Visual perception of dynamic properties: Cue heuristics versus direct-perceptual competence. *Psychological Review, 107,* 525–555.

Schiff, W. (1965). Perception of an impending collision: A study of visually directed avoidant behavior. *Psychological Monograph: General and Applied, 79,* (11, Whole No. 604).

Schiff, W., & Oldak, R. (1990). Accuracy of judging time-to-arrival: Effects of modality, trajectory, and gender. *Journal of Experimental Psychology: Human Perception and Performance, 16,* 303–316.

Sedgwick, H. (1973). The visible horizon: A potential source of visual information for the perception of size and distance. *Dissertation Abstracts International, 34,* 1301–1302B. (UMI No. 73-22, No. 03B 530)

Sedgwick, H. (1986). Space perception. In K. R. Boff, L. Kaufman, & J. P. Thomas (Eds.), *Handbook of perception and human performance* (Vol. 1, pp. 1–57). New York: Wiley.

Shimojo, S., Silverman, G. H., & Nakayama, K. (1989). Occlusion and the solution to the aperture problem for motion. *Vision Research, 29,* 619–626.

Sinai, M. J., Ooi, T. L., & He, Z. J. (1998). Terrain influences the accurate judgement of distance. *Nature, 395,* 497–500.

Stevens, K. A. (1981). The information content of texture gradients. *Biological Cybernetics, 42,* 95–105.

Stoffregen, T. A. (1985). Flow structure versus retinal location in the optical control of stance. *Journal of Experimental Psychology: Human Perception and Performance, 11,* 554–565.

Sumi, S. (1984). Upside down presentation of the Johansson moving light spot pattern. *Perception, 13,* 283–286.

Thomson, J. A. (1983). Is continuous visual monitoring necessary in visually guided locomotion? *Journal of Experimental Psychology: Human Perception and Performance, 9,* 427–443.

Tittle, J. S., & Perotti, V. J. (1997). The perception of shape and curvedness from binocular stereopsis and structure from motion. *Perception & Psychophysics, 59,* 1167–1179.

Todd, J. T. (1981). Visual information about moving objects. *Journal of Experimental Psychology: Human Perception and Performance, 7,* 795–810.

Todd, J. T., & Bressan, P. (1990). The perception of 3-dimensional affine structure from minimal apparent motion sequences. *Perception & Psychophysics, 48,* 419–430.

Todd, J. T., Koenderink, J. J., van Doorn, A. J., & Kappers, A. M. (1996). Effects of changing viewing conditions on the perceived structure of smoothly curved surfaces. *Journal of Experimental Psychology: Human Perception and Performance, 22,* 695–706.

Todd, J. T., & Mingolla, E. (1983). Perception of surface curvature and direction of illumination from patterns of shading. *Journal of Experimental Psychology: Human Perception and Performance, 9,* 583–595.

Todd, J. T., Reichel, F. D. (1989). Ordinal structure in the visual perception and cognition of smoothly curved surfaces. *Psychological Review, 96,* 643–657.

Todd, J. T., & Warren, W. H., Jr. (1982). Visual perception of relative mass in dynamic events. *Perception, 11,* 325–335.

Tresilian, J. R. (1991). Approximate information sources and perceptual variables in interceptive timing. *Journal of Experimental Psychology: Human Perception and Performance, 20,* 154–173.

Tresilian, J. R. (1999). Analysis of recent empirical challenges to an account of interceptive timing. *Perception & Psychophysics, 61,* 515–528.

Ullman, S. (1979). *The interpretation of visual motion*. Cambridge, MA: MIT Press.

van den Berg, A. V. (1992). Robustness of perception of heading from optic flow. *Vision Research, 32,* 1285–1296.

van den Berg, A. V., & Brenner, E. (1994). Humans combine the optic flow with static depth cues for robust perception of heading. *Vision Research, 34,* 2153–2167.

Vicario, G. B., & Bressan, P. (1990). Wheels: A new illusion in the perception of rolling objects. *Perception, 19,* 57–61.

Wallach, H., & O'Connell, D. N. (1953). The kinetic depth effect. *Journal of Experimental Psychology, 45,* 205–217.

Wann, J. P. (1996). Anticipating arrival: Is the tau-margin a specious theory? *Journal of Experimental Psychology: Human Perception and Performance, 22,* 1031–1048.

Warren, W. H. (1995). Self-motion: Visual perception and visual control. In W. Epstein & S. Rogers (Eds.), *Perception of space and motion* (pp. 263–325). San Diego, CA: Academic Press.

Warren, W. H. (1998). The state of flow. In T. Watanabe (Ed.), *High-level motion processing: Computational, neurobiological, and psychophysical perspectives* (pp. 315–358). Cambridge, MA: MIT Press.

Warren, W. H., Kay, B. A., & Yilmaz, E. H. (1996). Visual control of posture during walking: Functional specificity. *Journal of Experimental Psychology: Human Perception and Performance, 22,* 818–838.

Warren, W. H., & Kurtz, K. J. (1992). The role of central and peripheral vision in perceiving the direction of self-motion. *Perception & Psychophysics, 51,* 443–454.

Webb, J. A., & Aggarwal, J. K. (1982). Structure from motion of rigid and jointed objects. *Artificial Intelligence, 19,* 107–130.

Wertheim, A. H. (1994). Motion perception during self-motion: The direct versus inferential controversy revisited. *Behavioral & Brain Sciences, 17,* 293–355.

Wertheimer, M. (1937). Laws of organization in perceptual forms. In W. D. Ellis (Ed. & Trans.), *A source book of Gestalt psychology* (pp. 71–88). London: Routledge. (Original work published 1923)

Wheatstone, C. (1938). Contributions to the physiology of vision: I. On some remarkable and hitherto unobserved phenomena of binocular vision. *Philosophical Transactions of the Royal Society of London, 128,* 371–394.

Wraga, M. (1999). The role of eye height in perceiving affordances and object dimensions. *Perception & Psychophysics, 61,* 490–507.

Wraga, M., Creem, S. H., & Proffitt, D. R. (2000). Perception-action dissociations of a walkable Müller-Lyer configuration. *Psychological Science, 11,* 239–243.

Yang, T. L., Dixon, M. W., & Proffitt, D. R. (1999). Seeing big things: Overestimation of heights is greater for real objects than for objects in pictures. *Perception, 28,* 445–467.

Yonas, A., Bechtold, A. G., Frankel, D., Gordon, F. R., McRoberts, G., Norcia, A., & Sternfels, S. (1977). Development of sensitivity to information for impending collisions. *Perception & Psychophysics, 21,* 97–104.

Yonas, A., Craton, L. G., & Thompson, W. B. (1987). Relative motion: Kinetic information for the order of depth at an edge. *Perception & Psychophysics, 41,* 53–59.

Young, M. J., Landy, M. S., & Maloney, L. T. (1993). A perturbation analysis of depth perception from combinations of texture and motion cues. *Vision Research, 33,* 2685–2696.

CHAPTER 9

Speech Production and Perception

CAROL A. FOWLER

In order to convey linguistic messages that are accessible to listeners, speakers have to engage in activities that count in their language community as encodings of the messages in the public domain. Accordingly, spoken languages consist of forms that express meanings; the forms are (or, by other accounts, give rise to) the actions that make messages public and perceivable. Psycholinguistic theories of speech are concerned with those forms and their roles in communicative events. The focus of attention in this chapter will be on the phonological forms that compose words and, more specifically, on consonants and vowels.

As for the roles of phonological forms in communicative events, four are central to the psycholinguistic study of speech. First, phonological forms may be the atoms of word forms as language users store them in the mental lexicon. To study this is to study phonological competence (that is, knowledge). Second, phonological forms retrieved from lexical entries may specify words in a mental plan for an utterance. This is phonological planning. Third, phonological forms are implemented as vocal tract activity, and to study this is to study speech production. Fourth, phonological forms may be the finest-grained linguistic forms that listeners extract from acoustic speech signals during speech perception. The main body of the chapter will constitute a review of research findings and theories in these four domains.

Before proceeding to those reviews, however, I provide a caveat and then a setting for the reviews. The caveat is about the psycholinguistic study of speech. Research and theorizing in the domains under review generally proceed independently and therefore are largely unconstrained by findings in the other domains (cf. Kent & Tjaden, 1997, and Browman & Goldstein, 1995a, who make a similar comment). As my review will reveal, many theorists have concluded that the relevant parts of a communicative exchange (phonological competence, planning, production, and perception) fit together poorly. For example, many believe that the forms of phonological competence have properties that cannot be implemented as vocal tract activity, so that the forms of language cannot literally be made public. My caveat is that this kind of conclusion may be premature; it may be a consequence of the independence of research conducted in the four domains. The stage-setting remarks just below will suggest why we should expect the fit to be good.

Preparation of this chapter was supported by NICHD grant HD-01994 and NIH grants DC-02717 and DC-03782 to Haskins Laboratories.

In the psycholinguistic study of speech, as in psycholinguistics generally (see chapter by Treiman, Clifton, Meyer, & Wurm in this volume), the focus of attention is almost solely on the individual speaker/hearer and specifically on the memory systems and mental processing that underlie speaking or listening. It is perhaps this sole focus of attention that has fostered the near autonomy of investigations into the various components of a communicative exchange just described. Outside of the laboratory, speaking almost always occurs in the context of social activity; indeed, it is, itself, prototypically a social activity. This observation matters, and it can help to shape our thinking about the psycholinguistics of speech.

Although speaker/hearers can act autonomously, and sometimes do, often they participate in cooperative activities with others; jointly the group constitutes a special purpose system organized to achieve certain goals. Cooperation requires coordination, and speaking helps to achieve the social coordinations that get conjoint goals accomplished (Clark, 1996).

How, at the phonological level of description, can speech serve this role? Speakers speak intending that their utterance communicate to relevant listeners. Listeners actively seek to identify what a talker said as a way to discover what the talker intended to achieve by saying what he or she said. Required for successful communication is achievement of a relation of sufficient equivalence between messages sent and received. I will refer to this relation, at the phonological level of description, as *parity* (Fowler & Levy, 1995; cf. Liberman & Whalen, 2000).

That parity achievement has to be a typical outcome of speech is one conclusion that emerges from a shift in perspective on language users, a shift from inside the mind or brain of an individual speaker/listener to the cooperative activities in which speech prototypically occurs. Humans would not use speech to communicate if it characteristically did not. This conclusion implies that the parts of a communicative exchange (competence, planning, production, perception) have to fit together pretty well.

A second observation suggests that languages should have parity-fostering properties. The observation is that language is an evolved, not an invented, capability of humans. This is true of speech as well as of the rest of language. There are adaptations of the brain and the vocal tract to speech (e.g., Lieberman, 1991), suggesting that selective pressures for efficacious use of speech shaped the evolutionary development of humans.

Following are two properties that, if they were characteristic of the phonological component of language, would be parity fostering. The first is that phonological forms, here consonants and vowels, should be able to be made public and therefore accessible to listeners. Languages have forms as well as meanings exactly because messages need to be made public to be communicated. The second parity-fostering characteristic is that the elements of a phonological message should be preserved throughout a communicative exchange. That is, the phonological elements of words that speakers know in their lexicons should be the phonological elements of words that they intend to communicate, they should be units of action in speech production, and they should be objects of speech perception. If the elements are not preserved—if, say, vocal tract actions are not phonological things and so acoustic signals cannot specify phonological things—then listeners have to reconstruct the talker's phonological message from whatever they can perceive. This would not foster achievement of parity.

The next four sections of the chapter review the literature on phonological competence, planning, production, and perception. The reviews will accurately reflect the near independence of the research and theorizing that goes on in each domain. However, I will suggest appropriate links between domains that reflect the foregoing considerations.

PHONOLOGICAL COMPETENCE

The focus here is on how language users know the spoken word forms of their language, concentrating on the phonological primitives, consonants and vowels (*phonetic* or *phonological* segments). Much of what we know about this has been worked out by linguists with expertise in phonetics or phonology. However, the reader will need to keep in mind that the goals of a phonetician or phonologist are not necessarily those of a psycholinguist. Psycholinguists want to know how language users store spoken words. Phoneticians seek realistic descriptions of the sound inventories of languages that permit insightful generalizations about universal tendencies and ranges of variation cross-linguistically. Phonologists seek informative descriptions of the phonological systematicities that languages evidence in their lexicons. These goals are not psychologically irrelevant, as we will see. However, for example, descriptions of phonological word forms that are most transparent to phonological regularities may or may not reflect the way that people store word forms. This contrast will become apparent below when theories of linguistic phonology are compared specifically to a recent hypothesis raised by some speech researchers that lexical memory is a memory of word tokens (exemplars), not of abstract word types.

Word forms have an internal structure, the component parts of which are meaningless. The consonants and vowels are also discrete and permutable. This is one of the ways in which language makes "infinite use of finite means" (Von Humbolt, 1936/1972; see Studdert-Kennedy, 1998). There is no principled limit on the size of a lexicon having to do with the number of forms that can serve as words. And we do know a great many words; Pinker (1994) estimates about 60,000 in the lexicon of an average high school graduate. This is despite the fact that languages have quite limited numbers of consonants and vowels (between 11 and 141 in Maddieson's (1984) survey of 317 representative languages of the world).

In this regard, as Abler (1989) and Studdert-Kennedy (1998) observe, languages make use of a "particulate principle" also at work in biological inheritance and chemical compounding, two other domains in which infinite use is made of finite means. All three of these systems are self-diversifying in that, when the discrete particulate units of the domain (phonological segments, genes, chemicals) combine to form larger units, their effects do not blend but, rather, remain distinct. (Accordingly, words that are composed of the same phonological segments, such as "cat," "act," and "tack," remain distinct.). In language, this in part underlies the unboundedness of the lexicon and the unboundedness of what we can use language to achieve. Although some writing about speech production suggests that, when talkers coarticulate, that is, when they temporally overlap the production of consonants and vowels in words, the result is a blending of the properties of the consonants and vowels (as in Hockett's, 1955, famous metaphor of coarticulated consonants and vowels as smashed Easter eggs), this is a mistaken understanding of coarticulation. Certainly, the acoustic speech signal at any point in time is jointly caused by the production of more than one consonant or vowel. However, the information in its structure must be about discrete consonants and vowels for the particulate principle to survive at the level of lexical knowledge.

Phonetics

Feature Systems

From phonetics we learn that consonants and vowels can be described by their featural attributes, and, when they are, some interesting cross-linguistic tendencies are revealed. Feature systems may describe consonants and vowels largely in terms of their articulatory correlates, their acoustic correlates, or both. A feature system that focuses on articulation might distinguish consonants primarily by their place and manner of articulation and by whether they are voiced or unvoiced. Consider the stop consonants in English. *Stop* is a manner class that includes oral and nasal stops. Production of these consonants involves transiently stopping the flow of air through the oral cavity. The stops of English are configured as shown.

	Bilabial	Alveolar	Velar
oral stops: voiced	b	d	g
unvoiced	p	t	k
nasal stops: voiced	m	n	N

The oral and nasal voiced stops are produced with the vocal folds of the larynx approximated (adducted); the oral voiceless stops are produced with the vocal folds apart (abducted). When the vocal folds are adducted and speakers exhale as they speak, the vocal folds cyclically open and close releasing successive puffs of air into the oral cavity. We hear a voicing buzz in consonants produced this way. When the vocal folds are abducted, air flows more or less unchecked by the larynx into the oral cavity, and we hear such consonants as unvoiced.

Compatible descriptions of vowels are in terms of height, backing, and rounding. Height refers to the height of the tongue in the oral cavity, and backing refers to whether the tongue's point of closest contact with the palate is in the back of the mouth or the front. Rounding (and unroundedness) refers to whether the lips are protruded during production of the vowel as they are, for example, in the vowel in *shoe*.

Some feature systems focus more on the acoustic realizations of the features than on the articulatory realizations. One example of such a system is that of Jakobson, Fant, and Halle (1962), who, nonetheless, also provide articulatory correlates of the features they propose. An example of a feature contrast of theirs that is more obviously captured in acoustic than articulatory terms is the feature [±grave]. Segments denoted as [+grave] are described as having acoustic energy that predominates in the lower region of the spectrum. Examples of [+grave] consonants are bilabials with extreme front articulations and uvulars with extreme back places of articulation. Consonants with intermediate places of articulation are [−grave]. Despite the possible articulatory oddity of the feature contrast [±grave], Jakobson, Fant, and Halle had reason to identify it as a meaningful contrast (see Ohala, 1996, for some reasons).

Before turning to what one can learn by describing consonants and vowels in terms of their features, consider two additional points that relate back to the stage-setting discussion above. First, many different feature systems have been proposed. Generally they are successful in describing the range of consonants and vowels in the world's languages and in capturing the nature of phonological slips of the tongue that speakers make (see section titled "Speech Errors"). Both of these observations are relevant to a determination of how language users know the phonological forms of words. Nonetheless, there are differences among the systems that may have psychological significance. One relates back to the earlier discussion of parity. I suggested there that a parity-fostering property of languages would be a common currency in which messages are stored, formulated, sent, and received so that the phonological form of a message is preserved throughout a communicative exchange. Within the context of that discussion, a proposal that the features of consonants and vowels as language users know them are articulatory implies that the common currency is articulatory. A proposal that featural correlates are acoustic suggests that the common currency is acoustic.

A second point is that there is a proposal in the literature that the properties of consonants and vowels on which language knowledge and use depends are not featural. Rather, the phonological forms of words as we know them consist of "gestures" (e.g., Browman & Goldstein, 1990). Gestures are linguistically significant actions of the vocal tract. An example is the bilabial closing gesture that occurs when speakers of English produce /b/, /p/, or /m/. Gestures do not map 1:1 onto either phonological segments or features. For example, /p/ is produced by appropriately phasing two gestures, a bilabial constriction gesture and a devoicing gesture. Because Browman and Goldstein (1986) propose that voicing is the default state of the vocal tract producing speech, /b/ is achieved by just one gesture, bilabial constriction. As for the sequences /sp/, /st/, and /sk/, they are produced by appropriately phasing a tongue tip (alveolar) constriction gesture for /s/ and another constriction gesture for /p/, /t/, or /k/ with a single devoicing gesture that, in a sense, applies to both consonants in the sequence.

Browman and Goldstein (e.g., 1986) have proposed that words in the lexicon are specified as sequences of appropriately phased gestures (that is, as *gestural scores*). In a parity-fostering system in which these are primitives, the common currency is gestural. This is a notable shift in perspective because the theory gives primacy to public phonological forms (gestures) rather than to mental representations (features) with articulatory or acoustic correlates.

Featural Descriptions and the Sound Inventories of Languages

Featural descriptions of the sound inventories of languages have proven quite illuminating about the psychological factors that shape sound inventories. Relevant to our theme of languages' developing parity-fostering characteristics, researchers have shown that two factors, perceptual distinctiveness and articulatory simplification (Lindblom, 1990), are major factors shaping the consonants and vowels that languages use to form words. Perceptual distinctiveness is particularly important in shaping vowel inventories. Consider two examples.

One is that, as noted earlier, vowels may be rounded (with protruded lips) or unrounded. In Maddieson's (1984) survey of languages, 6% of front vowels were rounded, whereas 93.5% of back vowels were rounded. The evident reason for the correlation between backing and rounding is perceptual distinctiveness. Back vowels are produced with the tongue's constriction location toward the back of the oral cavity. This makes the cavity in front of the constriction very long. Rounding the lips makes it even longer. Front vowels are produced with the tongue constriction toward the front of the oral cavity so that the cavity in front of the constriction is short. An acoustic consequence of backing/fronting is the frequency of the vowel's second formant (i.e., the resonance associated with the acoustic signal for the vowel that is second lowest in frequency [F2]). F2 is low for back vowels and high for front vowels. Rounding back vowels lowers their F2 even more, enhancing the acoustic distinction between front and back vowels (e.g., Diehl & Kluender, 1989; Kluender, 1994).

A second example also derives from the study of vowel inventories. The most frequently occurring vowels in Maddieson's (1984) survey were /i/ (a high front unrounded vowel as in *heat*), /a/ (a low central unrounded vowel as in *hot*) and /u/ (a high back rounded vowel as in *hoot*), occurring in 83.9% (/u/) to 91.5% (/i/) of the language sample. Moreover, of the 18 languages in the survey that have just three vowels, 10 have those three vowels. Remarkably, most of the remaining 8 languages have minor variations on the same theme. Notice that these vowels, sometimes called the point vowels, form a triangle in vowel space if the horizontal dimension represents front-to-back and the vertical dimension vowel height:

```
i       u
    a
```

Accordingly, they are as distinct as they can be articulatorily and acoustically. Lindblom (1986) has shown that a principle of perceptual distinctiveness accurately predicts the location of vowels in languages with more than three vowels. For example, it accurately predicts the position of the fourth and fifth vowels of five-vowel inventories, the modal vowel inventory size in Maddieson's survey.

Consonants do not directly reflect a principle of perceptual dispersion as the foregoing configuration of English stop consonants suggests. Very tidy patterns of consonants in voicing, manner, and place space are common, yet such patterns mean that phonetic space is being densely packed. An important consideration for consonants appears to be articulatory complexity. Lindblom and Maddieson (1988) classified consonants of the languages of the world into basic, elaborated, and complex categories according to the complexity of the articulatory actions required to produce them. They found that languages with small consonant inventories tend to restrict themselves to basic consonants. Further, languages with elaborated consonants always have basic consonants as well. Likewise, languages with complex consonants (for example, the click consonants of some languages of Africa) always also have both basic and elaborated consonants as well. In short, language communities prefer consonants that are easy to produce.

Does the foregoing set of observations mean that language communities value perceptual distinctiveness in vowels but articulatory simplicity in consonants? This is not likely. Lindblom (1990) suggests that the proper concept for understanding popular inventories both of vowels and of consonants is that of "sufficient contrast." Sufficient contrast is the equilibrium point in a tug-of-war between goals of perceptual distinctiveness and articulatory simplicity. The balance shifts toward perceptual distinctiveness in the case of vowel systems, probably because vowels are generally fairly simple articulatorily. Consonants vary more in that dimension, and the balance point shifts accordingly.

The major global observation here, however, is that the requirements of efficacious public language use clearly shape the sound inventories of language. Achievement of parity matters.

Features and Contrast: Onward to Phonology

An important concept in discussions of feature systems is contrast. A given consonant or vowel can, in principle, be exhaustively described by its featural attributes. However, only some of those attributes are used by a language community to distinguish words. For example, in the English *till,* the first consonant is /t/, an unvoiced, alveolar stop. It is also "aspirated" in that there is a longish unvoiced and breathy interval from the time that the alveolar constriction by the tongue tip is released until voicing for the following vowel begins. The /t/ in *still* is also an unvoiced, alveolar stop, but it is unaspirated. This is because, in the sequence /st/, although both the /s/ and the /t/ are unvoiced, there is just one devoicing gesture for the two segments, and it is phased earlier with respect to the tongue constriction gesture for /t/ than it is phased in *till.* Whereas a change in any of the voicing, manner, or place features can create a new word of English (voicing: *dill;* manner: *sill;* place: *pill*), a change in aspiration does not. Indeed, aspiration will vary due to rate of speaking and emphasis, but the /t/ in *till* will remain a /t/.

Making a distinction between contrastive and noncontrastive features historically allowed a distinction to be made also in how consonants and vowels were characterized. Characterizing them as *phonological segments* (or phonemes) involved specifying only their contrastive features. Characterizing them as *phonetic segments* (or phones) involved specifying fairly exactly how they were to be pronounced. To a first approximation, the contrastive/noncontrastive distinction evolved into another relating to predictability that has had a significant impact on how modern phonologists have characterized lexical word forms. Minimally, lexical word forms have to specify unpredictable features of words. These are approximately contrastive features. That is, that the word meaning "medicine in a small rounded mass to be swallowed whole" (Mish, 1990) is *pill,* not, say, *till,* is just a fact about English language use. It is not predictable from any general phonological or phonetic properties of English. Language users have to know the sequence of phonological segments that compose the word. However, the fact that the /p/ is aspirated is predictable. Stressed-syllable initial unvoiced stops are aspirated in English. An issue for phonologists has been whether lexical word forms are abstract, specifying only unpredictable features (and so giving rise to differences between lexical and pronounced forms of words), or whether they are fully specified.

The mapping of contrastive/noncontrastive onto predictable/unpredictable is not exact. In context, some contrastive features of words can be predictable. For example, if a consonant of English is labiodental (i.e., produced with teeth against lower lip as in /f/ or /v/), it must be a fricative. And if a word begins /skr/, the next segment must be [+vocalic]. An issue in phonology has been to determine what should count as predictable and lexically unspecified. Deciding that determines how abstract in relation to their pronounced forms lexical entries are proposed to be.

Phonology

Most phonologists argue that lexical forms must be abstract with respect to their pronunciations. One reason that has loomed large in only one phonology (Browman & Goldstein's, e.g., 1986, Articulatory Phonology) is that we do not pronounce the same word the same way on all occasions. Particularly, variations in speaking style (e.g., from formal to casual) can affect how a word is pronounced. Lexical forms, it seems (but see section titled "Another Abstractness Issue"), have to be abstracted away from detail that distinguishes those different pronunciations. A second reason given for abstract word forms is, as noted above, that some properties of word forms are predictable. Some linguists have argued that lexical entries should include just what is phonologically unpredictable about a word. Predictable properties can be filled in another way, by rule application, for example. A final reason that words in the lexicon may be phonologically abstract is that the same morpheme may be pronounced differently in different words. For example, the prefixes on *inelegant* and *imprecise* are etymologically the same prefix, but the alveolar /n/ becomes labial /m/ before labial /p/ in *imprecise*. To capture in the lexicon that the morpheme is the same in the two words, some phonologists have proposed that they be given a common form there.

An early theory of phonology that focused on the second and third reasons was Chomsky and Halle's (1968) generative phonology. An aim there was to provide in the lexicon only the unpredictable phonological properties of words and to generate surface pronunciations by applying rules that provided the predictable properties. In this phonology, the threshold was rather low for identifying properties as predictable, and underlying forms were highly abstract.

A recent theory of phonology that appears to have superseded generative phonology and its descendents is optimality theory, first developed by Prince and Smolensky (1993). This theory accepts the idea that lexical forms and spoken forms are different, but it differs markedly from generative phonology in how it gets from the one to the other.

In optimality theory, there are no rules mediating lexical and surface forms. Rather, from a lexical form, a large number of candidate surface forms are generated. These are evaluated relative to a set of universal constraints. The constraints are ranked in language-particular ways, and they are violable. The surface form that emerges from the competition is the one that violates the fewest and the lowest ranked constraints. One kind of constraint that limits the abstractness of underlying forms is called a *faithfulness constraint*. One of these specifies that lexical and surface forms must be the same. (More precisely, every segment or feature in the lexical entry must have an identical correspondent in the surface form, and vice versa.) This constraint is violated in *imprecise,* the lexical form of which will have an /n/ in place of the /m/. A second constraint (the identical cluster constraint in Pulleyblank, 1997) requires that consonant clusters share place of articulation. It is responsible for the surface /m/.

On the surface, this model is not plausible as a psychological one. That is, no one supposes that, given a word to say, the speaker generates lots of possible surface forms and then evaluates them and ends up saying the optimal one. But there are models that have this flavor and are considered to have psychological plausibility. These are network models. In those models (e.g., van Orden, Pennington, & Stone, 1990), something input to the network (say, a written word) activates far more in the phonological component of the model than just the word's pronunciation. Research suggests that this happens in humans as well (e.g., Stone, Vanhoy, & Van Orden, 1997). The activation then settles into a state reflecting the optimal output, that is, the word's actual pronunciation. From this perspective, optimality theory may be a candidate psychological model of the lexicon.

Another theory of phonology, articulatory phonology (Browman & Goldstein, 1986), is markedly different from both of those described above. It does not argue from predictability or from a need to preserve a common form for the same morpheme in the lexicon that lexical entries are abstract. Indeed, in the theory, they are not very abstract. As noted earlier, primitive phonological forms in the theory are gestures. Lexical entries specify gestural scores. The lexical entries are abstract only with respect to variation due to speaking style. An attractive feature of their theory, as Browman and Goldstein (1995a) comment, is that phonology and phonetics are respectively macroscopic and microscopic descriptions of the same system. In contrast to this, in most accounts, phonology is an abstract, cognitive representation, whereas phonetics is its physical implementation. In an account of language production incorporating articulatory phonology, therefore, there need be no (quite mysterious) translation from a mental to a physical domain (cf. Fowler, Rubin, Remez, & Turvey, 1980); rather, the same domain is at once physical and cognitive (cf. Ryle, 1949). Articulatory phonology is a candidate for a psychological model.

Another Abstractness Issue: Exemplar Theories of the Lexicon

Psychologists have recently focused on a different aspect of the abstractness issue. The assumption has been until recently that language users store word types, not word tokens, in the lexicon. That is, even though listeners may have heard the word *boy* a few million times, they have not stored memories of those few million occurrences. Rather, listeners have just one word *boy* in their lexicon.

In recent years, this idea has been questioned, and some evidence has accrued in favor of a token or exemplar memory (see chapter by Goldstone & Kersten in this volume). The idea comes from theories of memory in cognitive psychology. Clearly, not all of memory is a type memory. We can recall particular events in our lives. Some researchers have suggested that exemplar memory systems may be quite pervasive. An example theory that has drawn the attention of speech researchers is Hintzman's (e.g., 1986) memory model, MINERVA. In the model, input is stored as a trace, which consists of feature values along an array of dimensions. When an input is presented to the model, it not only lays down its own trace, but it activates existing traces to the extent that they are featurally similar to it. The set of activated traces forms a composite, called the echo, which bears great resemblance to a type (often called a prototype in this literature). Accordingly, the model can behave as if it stores types when it does not.

In the speech literature, researchers have tested for an exemplar lexicon by asking whether listeners show evidence of retaining information idiosyncratic to particular occurrences of words, typically, the voice characteristics of the speaker. Goldinger (1996) provided an interesting test in which listeners identified words in noise. The words were spoken in 2, 6, or 10 different voices. In a second half of the test (after a delay that varied across subjects), he presented some words that had occurred in the first half of the test. The tokens in the second half were produced by the same speaker who produced them in the first half (and typically they were the same token) or were productions by a different speaker. The general finding was that performance identifying words was better if the words were repeated by the speaker who had produced them in the first half of the test. This across–test-half priming persisted across delays between test halves as long as one week. This study shows that listeners retain token-level memories of words (see also Goldinger, 1998). Does it show that these token-level memories constitute word forms in the mental lexicon? Not definitively. However, it is now incumbent on theorists who retain the claim that the lexicon is a type memory to provide distinctively positive evidence for it.

PHONOLOGICAL PLANNING

Speakers are creators of linguistic messages, and creation requires planning. This is in part because utterances are syntactically structured so that the meaning of a sentence is different from the summed meanings of its component words. Syntactic structure can link words that are distant in a sentence. Accordingly, producing a syntactically structured utterance that conveys an intended message requires planning units larger than a word. Planning may also be required to get the phonetic, including the prosodic, form of an utterance right.

For many years, the primary source of evidence about planning for language production was the occurrence of spontaneous errors of speech production. In approximately the last decade other, experimentally generated, behavioral evidence has augmented that information source.

Speech Errors

Speakers sometimes make mistakes that they recognize as errors and are capable of correcting. For example, intending to say *This seat has a spring in it,* a speaker said *This spring has a seat in it* (Garrett, 1980), exchanging two nouns in the intended utterance. Or intending to say *It's the jolly green giant,* a speaker said *It's the golly green giant* (Garrett, 1980), anticipating the /g/ from *green.* In error corpora that researchers have collected (e.g., Dell, 1986; Fromkin, 1973; Garrett, 1980; Shattuck-Hufnagel, 1979), errors are remarkably systematic and, apparently, informative about planning for speech production.

One kind of information provided by these error corpora concerns the nature of planning units. Happily, they appear to be units that linguists have identified as linguistically coherent elements of languages. However, they do not include every kind of unit identified as significant in linguistic theory. In the two examples above, errors occurred on whole words and on phonological segments. Errors involving these units are common, as are errors involving individual morphemes (e.g., *point outed;* Garrett, 1980). In contrast, syllable errors are rare and so are feature errors (as in Fromkin's, 1973, *glear plue sky*). Rime (that is, the vowel and any postvocalic consonants of a syllable) errors occur, but consonant-vowel (CV) errors are rare (Shattuck-Hufnagel, 1983). This is not to say that syllables and features are irrelevant in speech planning. They are relevant, but in a different way from words and phonemes.

Not only are the units that participate in errors tidy, but the kinds of errors that occur are systematic too. In the word error above, quite remarkably, two words exchanged places. Sometimes, instead, one word is anticipated, but it also occurs in its intended slot (*This spring has a spring in it*) or a word is perseverated (*This seat has a seat in it*). Sometimes, noncontextual substitutions occur in which a word appears that the speaker did not intend to say at all (*This sheep has a spring in it*). Additions and deletions occur as well. To a close approximation, the same kinds of errors occur on words and phonological segments.

Errors have properties that have allowed inferences to be drawn about planning for speech production. Words exchange, anticipate, and perseverate over longer distances than do phonological segments. Moreover, word substitutions appear to occur in two varieties: semantic (e.g., saying *summer* when meaning to say *winter*) and form-based (saying *equivocal when* meaning to say *equivalent*). These observations suggested to Garrett (1980) that two broad phases of planning occur. At a functional level, lemmas (that is, words as semantic and syntactic entities) are slotted into a phrasal structure. When movement errors occur, lemmas might be put into the wrong phrasal slot, but because their syntactic form class determines the slots they are eligible for, when words anticipate, perseverate, or exchange, they are members of the same syntactic category. Semantic substitution errors occur when a semantic neighbor of an intended word is mistakenly selected. At a positional level, planning concerns word forms rather than their meanings. This is where sound-based word substitutions may occur.

For their part, phonological segment errors also have highly systematic properties. They are not sensitive, as word movement errors are, to the syntactic form class of the words involved in the errors. Rather, they are sensitive to phonological variables. Intended and erroneous segments in errors tend to be featurally similar, and their intended and actual slots are similar in two ways. They tend to have featurally similar segments surrounding them, and they come from the same syllable position. That is, onset (prevocalic) consonants move to other onset positions, and codas (postvocalic consonants) move to coda positions.

These observations led theorists (e.g., Dell, 1986; Shattuck-Hufnagel, 1979) to propose that, in phonological planning, the phonemes that compose words to be said are slotted into syllabic frames. Onsets exchange with onsets, because, when an onset position is to be filled, only onset consonants are candidates for that slot. There is something intuitively displeasing about this idea, but there is evidence for it, theorists have offered justifications for it, and there is at least one failed attempt to avoid proposing a frame (Dell, Juliano, & Govindjee, 1993). The idea of slotting the phones of a word into a structural frame is displeasing, because it provides the opportunity for speakers to make errors, but seems to accomplish little else. The phones of words must be serially ordered in the lexical entry. Why reselect and reorder them in the frame? One justification has to do with productivity (e.g., Dell, 1986; Dell, Burger, & Svec, 1997). The linguistic units that most frequently participate in movement errors are those that we use productively. That is, words move, and we create novel sentences by selecting words and ordering them in new ways. Morphemes move, and we coin some words (e.g., *videocassette*) by putting morphemes together into novel combinations. Phonemes move, and we coin words by selecting consonants and vowels and ordering them in new ways (e.g., *smurf*). The frames for sentences (that is, syntactic structure) and for syllables permit the coining of novel sentences and words that fit the language's constraints on possible sentences and possible words.

Dell et al. (1993; see also Dell & Juliano, 1996) developed a parallel-distributed network model that allowed accurate sequences of phones to be produced without a frame-content distinction. The model nonetheless produced errors hitherto identified as evidence for a frame. (For example, errors were phonotactically legal the vast majority of the time, and consonants substituted for consonants and vowels for vowels.) However, the model did not produce anticipations, perseverations, or exchanges, and, even with modifications that would give rise to anticipations and perseverations, it would not make exchange errors. So far, theories and models that make the frame-content distinction have the edge over any that lack it.

Dell (1986) more or less accepted Garrett's (1980) two-tiered system for speech planning. However, he proposed that the lexical system in which planning occurs has both feedforward (word to morpheme to syllable constituent to phone) links and feedback links, with activation of planned lexical units spreading bidirectionally. The basis for this idea was a set of findings in speech error corpora. One is that, although phonological errors do create nonwords, they create words at a greater than chance rate. Moreover, in experimental settings, meaning variables can affect phonological error rates (see, e.g., Motley, 1980). Accordingly, when planning occurs at the positional level, word meanings are not irrelevant, as Garrett had supposed. The feedforward links in Dell's network provide the basis for this influence. A second finding is that semantic substitutions (e.g., the *summer/winter* error above) tend to be phonologically more related than are randomly re-paired intended and error words. This implies activation that spreads along feedback links.

In the last decade, researchers developed new ways to study phonological planning. One reason for these developments is concern about the representativeness of error corpora. Error collectors can only transcribe errors that they hear. They may fail to hear errors or mistranscribe them for a variety of reasons. Some errors occur that are inaudible. This has been shown by Mowrey and MacKay (1990), who measured activity in muscles of the vocal tract as speakers produced tongue twisters (e.g., *Bob flew by Bligh Bay*). In some utterances, Mowrey and MacKay observed tongue muscle activity for /l/ during production of *Bay* even though the word sounded error free to listeners. The findings show that errors occur that transcribers will miss. Mowrey and MacKay also suggest that their data show that subphonemic errors occur, in particular, in activation of single muscles. This conclusion is not yet warranted by their data, because other, unmonitored muscles for production of an intruding phoneme might also have been active. However, it is also possible that errors may appear to the listener tidier than they are.

We know, too, that listeners tend to "fluently restore" (Marslen-Wilson & Welsh, 1978) speech errors. They may not hear errors that are, in principle, audible, because they are focusing on the content of the speaker's utterance, not its form. These are not reasons to ignore the literature on speech errors; it has provided much very useful information. However, it is a reason to look for converging measures, and that is the next topic.

Experimental Evidence About Phonological Planning

Some of the experimental evidence on phonological planning has been obtained from procedures that induce speech errors (e.g., Baars, Motley, & MacKay, 1975; Dell, 1986). Here, however, the focus is on findings from other procedures in which production response latencies constitute the main dependent measure.

This research, pioneered by investigators at the Max Planck Institute for Psycholinguistics in the Netherlands, has led to a theory of lexical access in speech production (Levelt, Roelofs, & Meyer, 1999) that will serve to organize presentation of relevant research findings. The theory has been partially implemented as a computational model, WEAVER (e.g., Roelofs & Meyer, 1998). However, I will focus on the theory itself. It begins by representing the concepts that a speaker might choose to talk about, and it describes processes that achieve selection of relevant linguistic units and ultimately speech motor programs. Discussion here is restricted to events beginning with word form selection.

In the theory, selection of a word form provides access to the word's component phonological segments, which are abstract, featurally underspecified segments (see section titled "Features and Contrast: Onward to Phonology"). If the word does not have the default stress pattern (with stress on the syllable with the first full vowel for both Dutch and English speakers), planners also access a metrical frame, which specifies the word's number of syllables and its stress pattern. For words with the default pattern, the metrical frame is constructed online. In this theory, as in Dell's, the segments are types, not tokens, so that the /t/ in *touch* is the very /t/ in *tiny*. This allows for the possibility of form priming. That is, preparing to say a word that shares its initial consonant with a prime word can facilitate latency to produce the target word. In contrast to Dell's (1986) model, however, consonants are not exclusively designated either onset consonants or coda consonants. That is, the /t/ in *touch* is also the very /t/ in *date*.

Accessed phonological segments are spelled out into phonological word frames. This reflects an association of the phonological segments of a word with the metrical frame, if there is an explicit one in the lexical entry, or with a frame computed on line. This process, called prosodification, is proposed to be sequential; that is, segments are slotted into the frame in an early-to-late (left-to-right) order.

Meyer and Shriefers (1991) found evidence of form priming and a left-to-right process in a picture-naming task. In one experiment, at some stimulus onset asynchrony (SOA) before or after presentation of a picture, participants heard a monosyllabic word that overlapped with the monosyllabic picture name at the beginning (the initial CV), at the end (the VC), or not at all. On end-related trials, the SOA between word and picture was adjusted so that the VC's temporal relation to the picture was the same as that of the CV of begin-related words. On some trials no priming word was presented. The priming stimulus generally slowed responses to the picture, but, at some SOAs, it did so less if it was related to the target. For words that overlapped with the picture name in the initial CV, the response time advantage (over response times to pictures presented with unrelated primes) was significant when words were presented 150 ms before the pictures (but not 300 ms before) and continued through the longest lagging SOA tested, when words were presented 150 ms after the picture. For words overlapping with the picture name in the final VC, priming began to have an effect at 0 ms SOA and continued through the 150-ms lag condition. The investigators infer that priming occurs during phonological encoding, that is, as speakers access the phonological segments of the picture name. Perhaps at a 300-ms lead the activations of phonological segments shared between prime and picture name have decayed by the time the picture is processed. However, by a 150-ms lead, the prime facilitates naming the picture, because phonemes activated by its presentation are still active and appropriate to the picture. The finding that end-related primes begin facilitating later than begin-related items, even though the overlapping phonemes in the prime bore the same temporal relation to the picture's presentation as did the overlapping CVs or initial syllables, suggests an early-to-late process.

Using another procedure, Meyer (1990, 1991) also found form priming and evidence of a left-to-right process. Meyer (1990) had participants learn word pairs. Then, prompted by the first word of the pair, they produced the second. In homogeneous sets of word pairs, disyllabic response words of each pair shared either their first or their second syllable. In heterogeneous sets, response words were unrelated. The question was whether, across productions of response words in homogeneous sets, latencies would be faster than to response words in heterogeneous sets, because segments in the overlapping syllables would remain prepared for production. Meyer found shorter response latencies only in the homogeneous sets in which the first syllable was shared across response words. In a follow-up study, Meyer (1991) showed savings when word onsets were shared but not when rimes were shared. On the one hand, these studies provide evidence converging with that of Meyer and Shriefers (1991) for form priming and left-to-right preparation. However, the evidence appears to conflict in that Meyer (1990, 1991) found no end-overlap priming, whereas Meyer and Shriefers did. Levelt et al. (1999) suggested, as a resolution, that the latter results occur as the segments of a lexical item are activated, whereas the results of Meyer reflect prosodification (that is, merging of those segments with the metrical frame).

The theory of Levelt et al. (1999) makes a variety of predictions about the prosodification process. First, the phonological segments and the metrical frame are retrieved as separate entities. Second, the metrical frame specifies only the number of syllables in the word and the word's stress pattern; it does not specify the CV pattern of the syllables. Third, for words with the default stress pattern, no metrical frame is retrieved; rather, it is computed online.

Roelofs and Meyer (1998) tested these predictions using the implicit priming procedure. In the first experiment, in homogeneous sets, response words were disyllables with second-syllable stress that shared their first syllables; heterogeneous sets had unrelated first syllables. Alternatively, homogeneous (same first syllables) and heterogeneous (unrelated first syllables) response words had a variable number of syllables (2–4) with second-syllable stress. None of the words in this and the following experiments had the default stress pattern, so that, according to the theory, a metrical frame had to be retrieved. Priming (that is, an advantage in response latency for the homogeneous as compared to the heterogeneous sets) occurred only if the number of syllables was the same across response words. This is consistent with the prediction that the metrical frame specifies the number of syllables. A second experiment confirmed that, with the number of syllables per response word held constant, the stress pattern had to be shared for priming to occur. A third experiment tested the prediction that shared CV structure did not increase priming. In this experiment, response words were monosyllables that, in homogeneous sets, shared their initial consonant clusters (e.g., *br*). In one kind of homogeneous set, the words shared their CV structure (e.g., all were CCVCs); in another kind of homogeneous set, they had different CV structures. The two homogeneous sets produced equivalent priming relative to latencies to produce heterogeneous responses. This is consistent with the claim of the theory that the metrical frame only specifies the number of syllables, but not the CV structure of each syllable. Subsequent experiments showed that shared number of syllables with no segmental overlap and shared stress pattern without segmental overlap give rise to no priming. Accordingly, it is the integration of the word's phonological segments with the metrical frame that underlies the priming effect.

Finally, in a study by Meyer, Roelofs, and Schiller, described by Levelt et al. (1999), Meyer et al. examined words with the default stress pattern for Dutch. In this case, no metrical frame should be retrieved and so none can be shared across response words. Meyer et al. found that for words that shared their initial CVs and that had the default stress pattern for Dutch, shared metrical structure did not increase priming.

The next process in the theory is phonetic encoding in which talkers establish a gestural score (see section titled "Feature Systems") for each phonological word. This phase of talking is not well worked out by Levelt et al. (1999), and it is the topic of the next major section ("Speech Production"). Accordingly, I will not consider it further here.

Disagreements Between the Theories of Dell, 1986, and Levelt et al., 1999

Two salient differences between the theory of Dell (1986), developed largely from speech error data, and that of Levelt et al. (1999), developed largely from speeded naming data, concern feedback and syllabification. Dell's model includes feedback. The theory of Levelt et al. and Roelof and Meyer's (1998) model WEAVER do not. In Dell's model, phones are slotted into a syllable frame, whereas in the theory of Levelt et al., they are slotted into a metrical frame that specifies the number of syllables, but not their internal structure.

As for the disagreement about feedback, the crucial error data supporting feedback consist of such errors as saying *winter* for *summer,* in which the target and the error word share both form and meaning. In Dell's (1986) model, form can affect activation of lexical items via feedback links in the network. Levelt et al. (1999) suggest that these errors are monitoring failures. Speakers monitor their speech, and they often correct their errors. Levelt et al. suggest that the more phonologically similar the target and error words are, the more likely the monitor is to fail to detect the error.

The second disagreement is about when during planning phonological segments are syllabified. In Dell's (1986) model, phones are identified with syllable positions in the lexicon, and they are slotted into abstract syllable frames in the course of planning for production. In the theory of Levelt et al. (1999), syllabification is a late process, as it has to be to allow resyllabification to occur. There is evidence favoring both sides. As described earlier, Roelofs and Meyer (1998) reported that implicit priming occurs across response words that share stress pattern, number of syllables, and phones at the beginning of the word, but shared syllable structure does not increase priming further. Sevald, Dell, and Cole (1995) report apparently discrepant findings. Their task was to have speakers produce a pair of nonwords repeatedly as quickly as possible in a 4-s interval. They measured mean syllable production time and found a 30-ms savings if the nonwords shared the initial syllable. For example, the mean syllable production time for KIL KIL.PER (where the "." signals the syllable boundary) was shorter than for KILP KIL.PER or KIL KILP.NER. Remarkably, they also found shorter production times when only syllable structure was shared (e.g., KEM TIL.PER). These findings show that, at whatever stage of planning this effect occurs, syllable structure matters, and an abstract syllable frame is involved. This disagreement, like the first, remains unresolved (see also Santiago & MacKay, 1999).

SPEECH PRODUCTION

Communication by language use requires that speakers act in ways that count as linguistic. What are the public events that count as linguistic? There are two general points of view. The more common one is that speakers control their actions, their movements, or their muscle activity. This viewpoint is in common with most accounts of control over voluntary activity (see chapter by Heuer in this volume). A less common view, however, is that speakers control the acoustic signals that they produce. A special characteristic of public linguistic events is that they are communicative. Speech activity causes an acoustic signal that listeners use to determine a talker's message.

As the next major section ("Speech Perception") will reveal, there are also two general views about immediate objects of speech perception. Here the more common view is that they are acoustic. That is, after all, what stimulates the perceiver's auditory perceptual system. A less common view, however, is that they are articulatory or gestural.

An irony is that the most common type of theory of production and the most common type of theory of perception do not fit together. They have the joint members of communicative events producing actions, but perceiving acoustic structure. This is unlikely to be the case. Communication requires prototypical achievement of parity, and parity is more likely to be achieved if listeners perceive what talkers produce. In this section, I will present instances of both types of production theory, and in the next section, both types of perception theory. The reader should keep in mind that considerations of parity suggest that the theories should be linked. If talkers aim to produce particular acoustic patternings, then acoustic patterns should be immediate perceptual objects. However, if talkers aim to produce particular gestures, then that is what listeners should perceive.

How Acoustic Speech Signals Are Produced

Figure 9.1 shows the vocal tract, the larynx, and the respiratory system. Articulators of the vocal tract include the jaw, the tongue (with relatively independent control of the tip or blade and the tongue body), the lips, and the velum. Also involved in speech is the larynx, which houses the vocal folds, and the lungs. In prototypical production of speech, acoustic energy is generated at a source, in the larynx or oral cavity. In production of vowels and voiced consonants, the vocal folds are adducted. Air flow from the lungs builds up pressure beneath the folds, which are blown apart briefly and then close again. This cycling occurs at a rapid rate during voiced speech. The pulses of air that escape whenever the folds are blown apart are filtered by the oral cavity. Vowels are produced by particular configurations of the oral cavity achieved by positioning the tongue body toward the front (e.g., for /i/) or back (e.g., for /a/) of the oral cavity, close to the palate (e.g., /i/, /u/) or farther away (e.g., /a/), with lips rounded (/u/) or not. In production of stop consonants, there is a complete

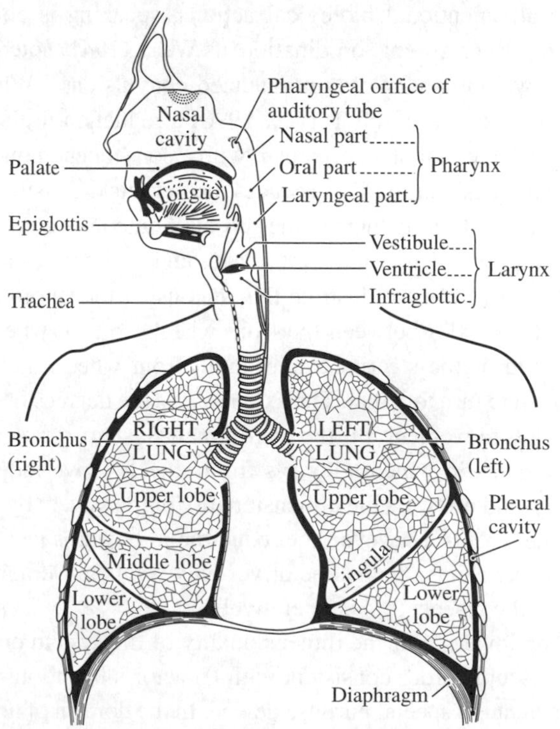

Figure 9.1 The speech sound producing system (from Borden, Harris, & Raphael, 1994). Reprinted with permission.

stoppage of airflow through the oral cavity for some time due to a constriction that, in English, occurs at the lips (/b/, /p/, /m/), with the tongue tip against the alveolar ridge of the palate (/d/, /t/, /n/) or with the tongue body against the velum (/g/, /k/, /ŋ/). For the nasal consonants, /m/, /n/, and /ŋ/, the velum is lowered, allowing airflow through the nose. For fricatives, the constriction is not complete, so that airflow is not stopped, but the constriction is sufficiently narrow to cause turbulent, noisy airflow. This occurs in English, for example, in /s/, /f/, and /θ/ (the initial consonant of, e.g., *theta*). Consonants of English can be voiced (vocal folds adducted) or unvoiced (vocal folds abducted).

The acoustic patterning caused by speech production bears a complex relation to the movements that generate it. In many instances the relation is nonlinear, so that, for example, a small movement may generate a marked change in the sound pattern (as, for example, when the narrow constriction for /s/ becomes the complete constriction for /t/). In other instances, a fairly large change in vocal tract configuration can change the acoustic signal rather little. Stevens (e.g., 1989) calls these "quantal regions," and he points out that language communities exploit them, for example, to reduce the requirement for extreme articulatory precision.

Some Properties of Speech That a Production Theory Needs to Explain

Like all intentional biological actions, speaking is coordinated action. Absent coordination, as Weiss (1941) noted, activity would consist of "unorganized convulsions." What is coordination? It is (cf. Turvey, 1990) a reduction in the degrees of freedom of an organism with a consequent reduction in its dimensionality. This reduces the outputs the system can produce, restricting them to the subset of outcomes consistent with the organism's intentions. Although it is not (wholly) biological, I like to illustrate this idea using the automobile. Cars have axles between the front wheels so that, when the driver turns the steering wheel, both front wheels are constrained to turn together. The axle reduces the degrees of freedom of movement of the car-human system, preventing movements in which the car's front wheels move independently, and it lowers the dimensionality of the system by linking the wheels. However, the reduction in power is just what the driver wants; that is, the driver only wants movements in which the wheels turn cooperatively.

The lowering of the dimensionality of the system creates macroscopic order consistent with an actor's intentions; that is, it creates a special purpose device. In the domain of action, these special purpose devices are sometimes called "coordinative structures" (Easton, 1972) or synergies. In the vocal tract, they are linkages among articulators that achieve coordinated action. An example is a transient linkage between the jaw and two lips that achieves lip closure for /b/, /p/, and /m/ in English.

An important characteristic of synergies is that they give rise to motor equivalence: that is, the ability to achieve the same goal (e.g., lip closure in the example above), in a variety of ways. Speakers with a bite block held between their teeth to immobilize the jaw (at a degree of opening too wide for normal production of /i/, for example, or too closed for normal production of /a/) produce vowels that are near normal from the first pitch pulse of the first vowel they produce (e.g., Lindblom, Lubker, & Gay, 1979). An even more striking finding is that speakers immediately compensate for on-line articulatory perturbations (e.g., Abbs & Gracco, 1984; Kelso, Tuller, Vatikiotis-Bateson, & Fowler, 1984; Shaiman, 1989). For example, in research by Kelso et al. (1984), on an unpredictable 20% of trials, a jaw puller pulled down the jaw of a speaker producing *It's a bab again* as the speaker was closing his lips for the final /b/ of *bab*. Within 20–30 ms of the perturbation, extra activity of an upper lip muscle (compared to its activity on unperturbed trials) occurred, and closure for /b/ was achieved. When the utterance was *It's a baz again,* jaw pulling caused extra activity in a muscle of the tongue, and the appropriate constriction was achieved. These responses to perturbation are fast and functional (cf. Löfquist, 1997).

These immediate and effective compensations contrast with others. When Savariaux, Perrier, and Orliaguet (1995) had talkers produce /u/ with a lip tube that prevented rounding, tongue backing could compensate for some acoustic consequences of the lip tube. Of 11 participants in the study, however, 4 showed no compensation at all (in about 20 attempts); 6 showed a little, but not enough to produce a normal acoustic signal for /u/; just 1 achieved full compensation. Similarly, in research by Hamlet and Stone (e.g., 1978; Hamlet, 1988), after one week's experience, speakers failed to compensate fully for an artificial palate that changed the morphology of their vocal tract. What is the difference between the two sets of studies that explains the differential success of compensation? Fowler and Saltzman (1993) suggest that the bite block and on-line perturbation studies may use perturbations that approximately occur in nature, whereas the lip tube and the artificial palate do not. That is, competing demands may be placed on the jaw because gestures overlap in time. For example, the lip-closing gesture for /b/ may overlap with the gestures for an open vowel. The vowel may pull down the jaw so that it occupies a more open position for /b/ than it does when /b/ gestures overlap with those for the high vowel /i/. Responses to the bite block and to on-line perturbations of the jaw may be immediate and effective because talkers develop flexible synergies for producing vowels with a range of possible openings of the jaw and consonants with a range of jaw closings. However, nothing prevents lip protrusion in nature, and nothing changes the morphology of the vocal tract. Accordingly, synergies to compensate for those perturbations do not develop.

Indeed, gestural overlap (that is, coarticulation) is a pervasive characteristic of speech and therefore is a characteristic that speakers need to learn both to achieve and to compensate for. Coarticulation is a property of action that can only occur when discrete actions are sequenced. Coarticulation has been described in a variety of ways: as spreading of features from one segment to another (as when rounding of the lips from /u/ occurs from the beginning of a word such as *strew*) or as assimilation. However, most transparently, when articulatory activity is tracked, coarticulation is a temporal overlap of articulatory activity for neighboring consonants and vowels. Overlap occurs both in an anticipatory (right-to-left) and a carryover (perseveratory, left-to-right) direction. This characterization in terms of gestural overlap is sometimes called *coproduction*. Its span can be segmentally extensive as when vowel-to-vowel coarticulation occurs over intervening consonants (e.g., Fowler & Brancazio, 2000; Öhman, 1966; Recasens, 1984). However, it is not temporally very extensive, spanning perhaps no more than about 250 ms (cf. Fowler & Saltzman, 1993). According to the frame theory of coarticulation (e.g., Bell-Berti & Harris, 1981), in anticipatory coarticulation of such gestures as lip rounding for a rounded vowel (e.g., Boyce, Krakow, Bell-Berti, & Gelfer, 1990) or nasalization for a nasalized consonant (e.g., Bell-Berti & Krakow, 1991; Boyce et al., 1990) the anticipating gesture is not linked to the gestures for other segments with which it overlaps in time; rather, it remains tied to other gestures for the segment, which it anticipates by an invariant interval.

An interesting constraint on coarticulation is coarticulation resistance (Bladon & Al-Bamerni, 1976). This reflects the differential extent to which consonants or vowels resist coarticulatory encroachment by other segments. Recasens's research (e.g., 1984) suggests that resistance to vowels among consonants varies with the extent to which the consonants make use of the tongue body, also required for producing vowels. Accordingly, a consonant such as /b/ that is produced with the lips is less resistant than one such as /d/, which uses the tongue (cf. Fowler & Brancazio, 2000). An index of coarticulation resistance is the slope of the straight-line relation between F2 at vowel midpoint of a CV and F2 at syllable onset for CVs in which the vowel varies but the consonant is fixed (see many papers by Sussman, e.g., Sussman, Fruchter, Hilbert, & Sorish, 1999a). Figure 9.2 shows data from Fowler (1994).

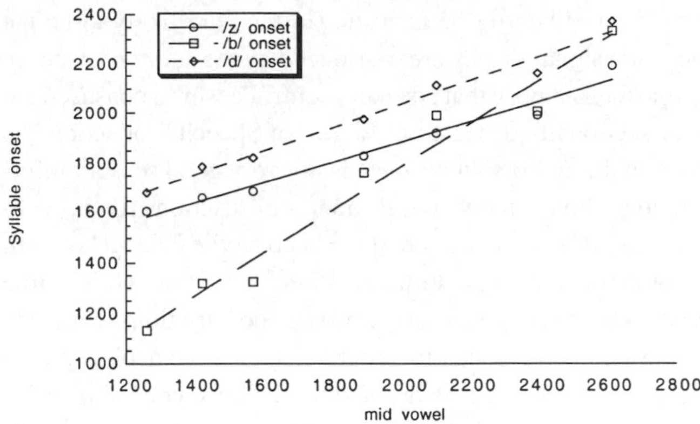

Figure 9.2 Data from Fowler (1994). Plots for /b/, /d/ and /z/ of F2 at vowel midpoint by F2 at syllable onset.

The low resistant consonant /b/ has a high slope, indicating considerable coarticulatory effect of the vowel on /b/'s acoustic manifestations at release; the slope for /d/ is much shallower; that for /z/ is slightly shallower than that for /d/. Fowler (1999) argues that the straight-line relation occurs because a given consonant resists coarticulation by different vowels to an approximately invariant extent; Sussman et al. (1999a; Sussman, Fruchter, Hilbert, & Sirosh, 1999b) argue that speakers produce the straight-line relation intentionally, because it fosters consonant identification and perhaps learning of consonantal place of articulation.

A final property of speech that will require an account by theories of speech production is the occurrence of *phase transitions* as rate is increased. This was first remarked on by Stetson (1951) and has been pursued by Tuller and Kelso (1990, 1991). If speakers begin producing /ip/, as rate increases, they shift to /pi/. Beginning with /pi/ does not lead to a shift to /ip/. Likewise, Gleason, Tuller, and Kelso (1996) found shifts from *opt* to *top*, but not vice versa, as rate increased. Phase transitions are seen in other action systems; for example, they underlie changes in gait from walk to trot to canter to gallop. They are considered hallmarks of nonlinear dynamical systems (e.g., Kelso, 1995). The asymmetry in direction of the transition suggests a difference in stability such that CVs are more stable than VCs (and CVCs than VCCs).

Acoustic Targets of Speech Production

I have described characteristics of speech production, but not its goals. Its goals are in contention. Theories that speakers control acoustic signals are less common than those that they control something motoric; however, there is a recent example in the work of Guenther and colleagues (Guenther, Hampson, & Johnson, 1998). Guenther et al. offer four reasons why targets are likely to be acoustic (in fact, are likely to be the acoustic signal as they are transduced by the auditory system). Opposing a theory that speakers control gestural constrictions (see section titled "Gestural Targets of Speech Production") is that, in the authors' view, there is not very good sensory information about many vocal tract constrictions (e.g., constrictions for vowels where there is no tactile contact between the tongue and some surface). Moreover, although it is true that speakers achieve nearly invariant constrictions (e.g., they always close their lips to say /b/), this can be achieved by a model in which targets are auditory. Third, control over invariant constriction targets would limit the system's ability to compensate when perturbations require new targets. (This is quite right, but, in the literature, this is exactly where compensations to perturbation are not immediate or generally effective. See the studies by Hamlet & Stone, 1978; Hamlet, 1988; Savariaux et al., 1995; Perkell, Matthies, Svirsky, & Jordan, 1993.) Finally, whereas many studies have shown directly (Delattre & Freeman, 1968) or by suggestive acoustic evidence (Hagiwara, 1995) that American English /r/ is produced differently by different speakers and even differently by the same speaker in different phonetic contexts, all of the gestural manifestations produce a similar acoustic product.

In the DIVA model (Guenther et al., 1998), planning for production begins with choice of a phoneme string to produce. The phonemes are mapped one by one onto target regions in auditory-perceptual (speech-sound) space. The maps are to regions rather than to points in order to reflect the fact that the articulatory movements and acoustic signals are different for a given phoneme due to coarticulation and other perturbations. Information about the model's current location in auditory-perceptual space in relation to the target region generates a planning vector, still in auditory-perceptual space. This is mapped to a corresponding articulatory vector, which is used to update articulatory positions achieved over time.

The model uses mappings that are learned during a babbling phase. Infant humans babble on the way to learning to speak. That is, typically between the ages of 6 and 8 months, they produce meaningless sequences that sound as if they are composed of successive CVs. Guenther et al. propose that, during this phase of speech development, infants map information about their articulations onto corresponding configurations in auditory-perceptual space. The articulatory information is from orosensory feedback from their articulatory movements and from copies of the motor commands that the infant used to generate the movements. The auditory perceptual information is from hearing what they have produced. This mapping is called a *forward model;* inverted, it generates movement from auditory-perceptual targets. To this end, the babbling model learns two additional mappings, from speech-sound space, in which (see above) auditory-perceptual target regions corresponding to phonemes are represented as vectors through the space that will take the model from its current location to the target region, and from those trajectories to trajectories in articulatory space.

An important idea in the model is that targets are regions rather than points in acoustic-auditory space. This allows the model to exhibit coarticulation and, with target regions of appropriate ranges of sizes, coarticulation resistance. The model also shows compensation for perturbations, because if one target location in auditory-perceptual space is blocked, the model can reach another location within the target region. Successful phoneme production does not require achievement of an invariant configuration in either auditory-perceptual or articulatory space. This property of the model underlies its failure to distinguish responses to perturbation that are immediately effective from those that require some relearning. The model shows immediate compensations for both kinds of perturbation. It is silent on phase transitions.

Gestural Targets of Speech Production

Theories in which speakers control articulation rather than acoustic targets can address all or most of the reasons that underlay Guenther et al.'s (1998) conclusion that speakers control perceived acoustic consequences of production. For example, Guenther et al. suggest that if talkers controlled constrictions, it would unduly limit their ability to compensate for perturbations where compensation requires changing a constriction location, rather than achieving the same constriction in a different way. A response to this suggestion is that talkers do have more difficulty when they have to learn a new constriction. The response of gesture theorists to /r/ as a source of evidence that acoustics are controlled will be provided after a theory has been described.

Figure 9.3 depicts a model in which controlled primitives are the gestures of Browman and Goldstein's (e.g., 1986) articulatory phonology (see section titled "Feature Systems").

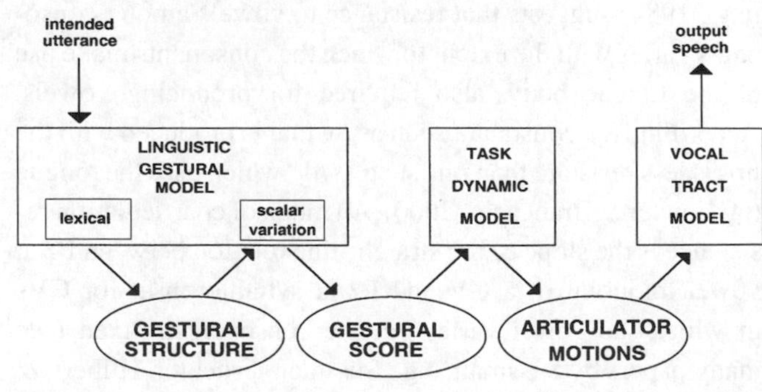

Figure 9.3 Haskins' Computational Gestural Model.

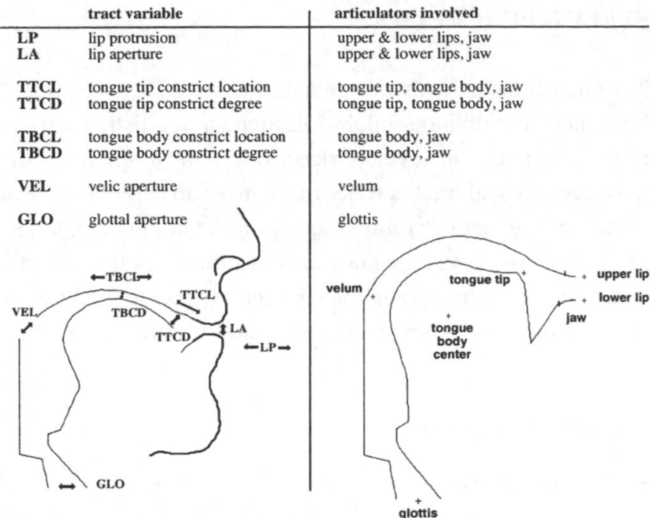

tract variable
articulators involved
LP lip protrusion
upper & lower lips, jaw
LA lip aperture
upper & lower lips, jaw
TTCL tongue tip constrict location
tongue tip, tongue body, jaw
TTCD tongue tip constrict degree
tongue tip, tongue body, jaw
TBCL tongue body constrict location
tongue body, jaw
TBCD tongue body constrict degree
tongue body, jaw
VEL velic aperture
velum
GLO glottal aperture
glottis
TBCL
TTCL
VEL
TBCD
TTCD
LA
LP
GLO
velum
tongue tip
upper lip
lower lip
jaw
tongue body center
glottis

Figure 9.4 Tract Variables for gestures and the articulators comprising their coordinative structures.

Gestures create and release constrictions in the vocal tract. Figure 9.4 displays the tract variables that are controlled when gestures are produced and the gestures' associated articulators. In general, tract variables specify constriction locations (CLs) and constriction degrees (CD) in the vocal tract. For example, to produce a bilabial stop, the constriction location is a specified degree of lip protrusion and the constriction degree is maximal; the lips are closed. The articulators that achieve these values of the tract variables are the lips and the jaw.

The linguistic gestural model of Figure 9.3 generates *gestural scores* such as that in Figure 9.5. The scores specify the gestures that compose a word and their relative phasing. Gestural scores serve as input to the task dynamic model (e.g., Saltzman, 1991; but see Saltzman, 1995; Saltzman & Byrd, 1999). Gestures are implemented as two-tiered dynamical (mass-spring) systems. At an initial level the systems refer to tract variables, and the dynamics are of point attractors. These dynamics undergo a one-to-many transformation to articulator space. Because the transformation is one-many,

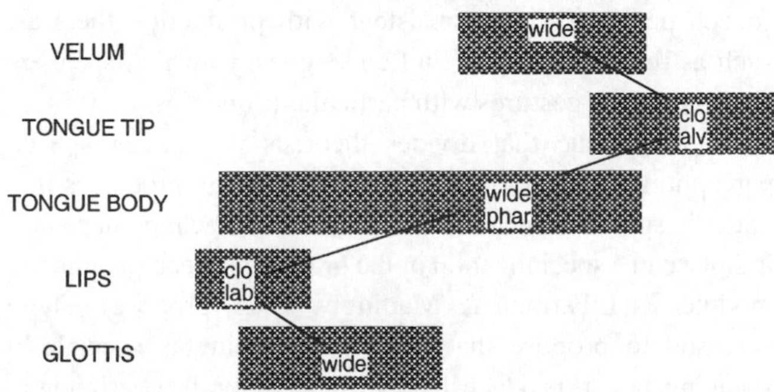

Figure 9.5 Gestural score for the word *pan.*

tract variable values can be achieved flexibly. Because the gestural scores specify overlap between gestures, the model coarticulates; moreover (e.g., Saltzman, 1991), it mimics some of the findings in the literature on coarticulation resistance. In particular, the high resistant consonant /d/ achieves its target constriction location regardless of the vowels with which it overlaps; the constriction location of the lower resistant /g/ moves with the location of the vowel gesture. The model also compensates for the kinds of perturbations to which human talkers compensate immediately (bite blocks and on-line jaw or lip perturbations in which invariant constrictions are achieved in novel ways). It does not show the kinds of compensations studied by Hamlet and Stone (1978), Savariaux et al. (1995), or Perkell et al. (1993), in which new constrictions are required. (The model, unlike that of Guenther et al., 1998, does not learn to speak; accordingly, it cannot show the learning that, for example, Hamlet and Stone find in their human talkers.) The model also fails to exhibit phase transitions although it is in the class of models (nonlinear dynamical systems) that can.

Evidence for Both Models: The Case of /r/

One of the strongest pieces of evidence convincing Guenther et al. (1998) that targets of production are acoustic is the highly variable way in which /r/ is produced. This is because of claims that acoustic variability in /r/ production is less than articulatory variability. Ironically, /r/ also ranks as strong evidence favoring gestural theory among gesture theorists. Indeed, in this domain, /r/ contributes to a rather beautiful recent set of investigations of composite phonetic segments.

The phoneme /r/ is in the class of multigestural (or *composite*) segments, a class that also includes /l/, /w/, and the nasal consonants. Krakow (1989, 1993, see also 1999) was the first to report that two salient gestures of /m/ (velum lowering and the oral constriction gesture) are phased differently in onset and coda positions in a syllable. In onset position, the velum reaches its maximal opening at about the same time as the oral constriction is achieved. In coda position, the velum reaches maximum opening as the oral articulators (the lips for /m/) begin their closing gesture. Similar findings have been reported for /l/. Browman and Goldstein (1995b), following earlier observations by Sproat and Fujimura (1993; see also Gick, 1999), report that in onset position, the terminations of tongue tip and tongue dorsum raising were simultaneous, whereas the tongue dorsum gesture led in coda position. Gick (1999) found a similar relation between lip and tongue body gestures for /w/.

As Browman and Goldstein (1997) remark, in multigestural consonants, in coda position, gestures with wider constriction degrees (that is, more open gestures) are phased earlier with respect to gestures having more narrow constriction degrees; in onset position, the gestures are more synchronous. Sproat and Fujimura (1993) suggest that the component gestures of composite segments can be identified, indeed, as vocalic (V; more open) or consonantal (C). This is interesting in light of another property of syllables. They tend, universally, to obey a sonority gradation such that more vowel-like (sonorous) consonants tend to be closer to the syllable nucleus than less sonorous consonants. For example, if /t/ and /r/ are going to occur before the vowel in a syllable of English, they are ordered /tr/. After the vowel, the order is /rt/. The more sonorous of /t/ and /r/ is /r/. Gestures with wider constriction degrees are more sonorous than those with narrow constriction degrees, and, in the coda position, they are phased so that they are closer to the vocalic gesture than are gestures with narrow constriction degrees. A reason for the sonority gradient has been suggested; it permits smooth opening and closing actions of the jaw in each syllable (Keating, 1983).

Goldstein (personal communication, October 19, 2000) suggests that the tendency for /r/ to become something like /ɔi/ in some dialects of American English (Brooklyn; New Orleans), so that *bird* (whose /r/-colored vowel is /ɚ/) is pronounced something like *boid,* may also be due to the phasing characteristics of coda C gestures. The phoneme /r/ may be produced with three constrictions: a pharyngeal constriction made by the tongue body, a palatal constriction made by the tongue blade, and a constriction at the lips. If the gestures of the tongue body and lips (with the widest constriction degrees) are phased earlier than the blade gesture in coda position, the tongue and lip gestures approximate those of /ɔ/, and the blade gesture against the palate is approximately that for /i/.

But what of the evidence of individual differences in /r/ production that convinced Guenther et al. (1998) that speech production targets are auditory-perceptual? One answer is that the production differences can look smaller than they have been portrayed in the literature if the gestural focus on vocal tract configurations is adopted. The striking differences that researchers have reported are in tongue shape. However, Delattre and Freeman (1968), characteristically cited to underscore the production variability of /r/, make this remark: "Different as their tongue shapes are, the six types of American /r/'s have one feature in common—they have two constrictions, one at the palate, another at the pharynx" (p. 41). That is, in terms of constriction location, a gestural parameter of articulatory phonology, there is one type of American English /r/, not six.

SPEECH PERCEPTION

The chapter began with the language knower. Then it explored how such an individual might formulate a linguistic message at the phonological level of description and implement the message as vocal tract activity that causes an acoustic speech signal. For an act of communication to be completed, a perceiver (another language knower) must intercept the acoustic signal and use it to recover the speaker's message. In this section, the focus is on how perception takes place.

Phonetic Perception

Preliminary Issues

I have suggested that a constraint on development of theories of phonological competence, planning, production, and perception should be an understanding that languages are likely to be parity fostering. Two parity-fostering characteristics are phonological forms that can be made public, and preservation of those forms throughout a communicative exchange. If theorists were to hew to expectations that languages have these properties, then we would expect to find perception theories in which perceptual objects are planned and produced phonological forms. We do not quite find that, because, as indicated in the introduction, research on perception, production, planning, and phonological description all have progressed fairly independently.

However, there is one respect in which perception theories intersect fairly neatly with production theories. They partition into two broad classes that divide according to the theorists' claims about immediate objects of speech perception. The majority view is that objects are acoustic. This is not an implausible view, given that acoustic signals are stimuli for speech perception. The minority view is that objects are gestural. Considerations of parity suggest a pairing of acoustic theories of speech perception with production theories like that of Guenther et al. (1998) in which speakers aim to produce acoustic signals with required properties. Gestural theories of speech perception are consistent with production theories, such as that of Saltzman and colleagues, in which speakers aim to produce gestures with particular properties.

Another issue that divides theorists is whether speech perception is special—that is, whether mental processes that underlie speech perception are unique to speech, perhaps taking place in a specialization of the brain for speech (a phonetic module, as Liberman & Mattingly, 1985, propose). There is reason to propose that speech processing is special. In speaking, talkers produce discrete, but temporally overlapping, gestures that correspond in some way to the phonological forms that listeners must recover. Coarticulation ensures that there is no temporally discrete, phone-sized segmental structure in the acoustic signal corresponding to phonological forms and that the acoustic signal is everywhere context sensitive. If listeners do recover phonological forms when they listen, this poses a problem. Listeners have to use the continuous acoustic signal to recover the discrete context-invariant phonological forms of the talker's message. Because, in general, acoustic signals are not caused by sequences of discrete, coarticulated mechanical events, speech does appear to pose a unique problem for listeners.

However, there is also a point of view that the most conservative or parsimonious first guess should be that processing is not special. Until the data demand postulating a specialization, we should attempt to explain speech perception by invoking only processes that are required to explain other kinds of auditory perception. It happens that acoustic theorists generally take this latter view. Some gestural theorists take the former.

Acoustic Theories of Speech Perception

There are a great many different versions of acoustic theory (e.g., Diehl & Kluender, 1989; Kuhl, 1987; Massaro, 1987, 1998; Nearey, 1997; Stevens & Blumstein, 1981; Sussman et al., 1999a). Here, Diehl and Kluender's auditory enhancement theory will illustrate the class.

Acoustic theories are defined by their commitment to immediate perceptual objects that are acoustic (or auditory—that is, perceived acoustic) in nature. One common idea is that auditory processing renders an acoustic object that is then classified as a token of a particular phonological category. Auditory enhancement theory makes some special claims in addition (e.g., Diehl & Kluender, 1989; Kluender, 1994). One is that there is lots of covariation in production of speech and in the consequent acoustic signal. For example, as noted earlier, rounding in vowels tends to covary with tongue backness. The lips and the tongue are independent articulators; why do their gestures covary as they do? The answer from auditory enhancement theory is that both the rounding and the tongue backing gestures lower a vowel's second formant. Accordingly, having the gestures covary results in back vowels that are acoustically highly distinct from front (unrounded) vowels. In this and many other examples offered by Diehl and Kluender, pairs of gestures that, in principle, are independent conspire to make acoustic signals that maximally distinguish phonological form. This should benefit the perceiver of speech.

Another kind of covariation occurs as well. Characteristically, a given gesture has a constellation of distinct acoustic consequences. A well-known example is voicing in stop consonants. In intervocalic position (as in *rapid* vs. *rabid*), voiced and voiceless consonants can differ acoustically in 16 different ways or more (Lisker, 1978). Diehl and Kluender (1989) suggest that some of those ways, in phonological segments that are popular among languages of the world, are mutually enhancing. For example, voiced stops have shorter closure intervals than do voiceless stops. In addition, they tend to have voicing in the closure, whereas voiceless stops do not. Parker, Diehl, and Kluender (1986) have shown that low-amplitude noise in an otherwise silent gap between two square waves makes the gap sound shorter than it sounds in the absence of the noise (as it indeed is). This implies that, in speech, voicing in the closure reinforces the perception of a shorter closure for voiced than voiceless consonants. This is an interesting case, because, in contrast to rounding and backing of vowels where two gestures reinforce a common acoustic property (a low F2), in this case, a single gesture—approximation of the vocal folds during the constriction gesture for the consonant—has two or more enhancing acoustic consequences. Diehl and Kluender (1989; see also Kluender, 1994) suggest that language communities "select" gestures that have multiple, enhancing acoustic consequences.

A final claim of the theory is that speech perception is not special and that one can see the signature of auditory processing in speech perception. A recent example of such a claim is provided by Lotto and Kluender (1998). In 1980, Mann had reported a finding of "compensation for coarticulation." She synthesized an acoustic continuum of syllables that ranged from a clear /da/ to a clear /ga/ with many more ambiguous tokens in between. The syllables differed only in the direction of the third formant transition, which fell for /da/ and rose for /ga/. She asked listeners to identify members of the continuum when they were preceded by either of the two precursor syllables /al/ or /ar/. She predicted and found that listeners identified more ambiguous continuum members as /ga/ in the context of precursor /al/ than /ar/. The basis for Mann's prediction was the likely effect of coarticulation by /l/ and /r/ on /d/ and /g/. The phoneme /l/ has a tongue tip constriction that, coarticulated with /g/, a back consonant, is likely to pull /g/ forward; /r/ has a pharyngeal constriction that, coarticulated with /d/, is likely to pull /d/ back. When listeners reported more /g/s after /al/ and more /d/s after /ar/, they appeared to compensate for the fronting effects that /l/ should have on /g/ and the backing effects of /r/ on /d/.

Lotto and Kluender (1998) offered a different account. They noticed that, in Mann's stimulus set, /l/ had a very high ending frequency of F3, higher than the starting F3s of any members of the /da/-to-/ga/ continuum. The phoneme /r/ had a very low ending frequency of F3, lower than the starting frequency of any members of the continuum. They proposed that the ending F3 frequencies of /al/ and /ar/ were exerting a contrast effect on the starting F3s of the continuum members. Contrast effects are pervasive in perception research across the sensory modalities (e.g., Warren, 1985, who, however, does not refer to them as contrast effects). For example, when individuals judge the heaviness of weights (Guilford & Park, 1931), they judge an intermediate weight lighter if they have just hefted a heavier weight than if they have just hefted a lighter weight. Lotto and Kluender suggested that the very high ending F3 of /l/ made following F3 onsets of continuum members effectively lower (and so more /g/-like) than they were; the very low F3 of /r/ made onset F3s effectively higher and more /d/-like.

They tested their hypothesis by substituting high and low sinewave tones for the precursor /al/ and /ar/ syllables of Mann (1980), and they found more /g/ judgments following the high than the low precursor tone. This cannot be compensation for coarticulation. It is, rather, according to Lotto and Kluender (1998), a signature of auditory processing showing up in speech perception judgments.

Comparisons like this between perception of speech and of nonspeech analogues has provided one way of testing claims of auditory theories. Parker et al. (1986) tested whether two acoustic properties were mutually enhancing. The test by Lotto and Kluender tested for evidence of auditory processing in speech perception. Generally, investigators have used speech/nonspeech comparisons as a way to test whether speech processing is specialized and distinct from auditory processing. Many tests have found closely similar response patterns to speech and closely similar nonspeech signals (e.g., Sawusch & Gagnon, 1995). As we will see, however, not all have.

Another test of auditory theories has been to compare responses by humans and nonhumans to speech signals. Clearly, nonhumans do not have specializations for human speech perception. If they show some of the markers of human speech perception, then it is not necessary to suppose that a specialization is responsible for the markers in humans. There are some striking findings here. Kuhl and Miller (1978) trained chinchillas in a go–no go procedure to move to a different compartment of a cage when they heard one endpoint of an acoustic voice onset time (VOT) continuum, but not when they heard a syllable at the other end. Following training, they were tested on all continuum members between the two endpoints as well as on the endpoints themselves. This allowed Kuhl and Miller to find a boundary along the continuum at which the chinchillas' behavior suggested that a voiced percept had replaced a voiceless one. Remarkably, the boundaries were close to those of humans, and there was an even more remarkable finding. In human speech, VOTs are longer for farther back places of articulation. That is, in English, /pa/ has a shorter VOT than /ta/, which has a shorter VOT than /ka/ (e.g., Zue, 1980). This may be because voicing cannot resume following a voiceless consonant until there is a sufficient drop in pressure across the larynx. With back places of constriction, the cavity above the larynx is quite small and the pressure correspondingly higher than for front constrictions. English listeners place VOT boundaries at shorter values for /pa/ than for /ta/ and for /ta/ than for /ka/, as do chinchillas (Kuhl & Miller, 1978). It is not known what stimulus property or auditory system property might underlie this outcome. However, most investigators are confident that chinchillas are not sensitive to transglottal pressure differences caused by back and front oral constrictions in human speech.

Another striking finding, now with quail, is that of Lotto, Kluender, and Holt (1997) that quail show "compensation for coarticulation" given stimuli like those used by Mann (1980).

Readers may be asking why anyone is a gesture theorist. However, gesture theories, like acoustic theories, derive from evidence and from theoretical considerations. Moreover, theorists argue that many of the claims and findings of acoustic theories are equally compatible with gesture theories. For example, findings that language communities gravitate toward phones that have mutually distinctive acoustic signals is not evidence that perceptual objects are acoustic. In gesture theories, the acoustic signal is processed; it is used as information for gestures. If the acoustic signals for distinct gestures are distinct, that is good for the gesture perceiver.

The most problematic findings for gesture theorists may be on the issue of whether speech perception is special. The negative evidence is provided by some of the speech/ nonspeech and human/nonhuman comparisons. Here, there are two lines of attack that gesture theorists can mount. One is to point out that not all such comparisons have resulted in similar response patterns (for speech/nonspeech, see below; for human/nonhuman, see, e.g., range effects in Waters & Wilson, 1976; see also Sinnott, 1974, cited in Waters & Wilson, 1976). If there are real differences, then the argument against a specialization weakens. A second line of attack is to point out that the logic of the research in the two domains is weak. It is true that if humans and nonhumans apply similar processes to acoustic speech signals (and if experiments are designed appropriately), the two subject groups should show similar response patterns to the stimuli. However, the logic required by the research is the reverse of that. It maintains that if humans and nonhumans show similar response patterns, then the processes applied to the stimuli are the same. This need not hold (cf. Trout, 2001). The same can be said of the logic of speech/nonspeech comparisons.

Gesture Theories of Speech Perception

There are two gesture theories in the class, both largely associated with theorists at Haskins Laboratories. Gesture theories are defined by their commitment to the view that immediate objects of perception are gestural. One of these theories, the motor theory (e.g., Liberman & Mattingly, 1985; Liberman & Whalen, 2000), also proposes that speech perception is special. The other, direct realist theory (Best, 1995; Fowler, 1986, 1996), is agnostic on that issue.

The motor theory of speech perception was the first gesture theory. It was developed by Liberman (1957, see also 1996) when he obtained experimental findings that, in his view, could not be accommodated by an acoustic theory. He and his colleagues were using two complementary pieces of technology, the sound spectrograph and the pattern playback, to identify the acoustic cues for perception. They used the spectrograph to make speech visible in the informative ways that it does, identified possible cues for a given consonant or vowel, and reproduced those cues by painting them on an acetate strip that, input to the pattern playback, was transformed to speech. If the acoustic structure preserved on acetate was indeed important for identifying the phone, it could be identified as a cue.

One very striking finding in that research was that, due to coarticulation, acoustic cues for consonants especially were highly context sensitive. Figure 9.6 provides a schematic spectrographic display of the syllables /di/ and /du/. Although natural speech provides a much richer signal than that in Figure 9.6, the depicted signals are sufficient to be heard as

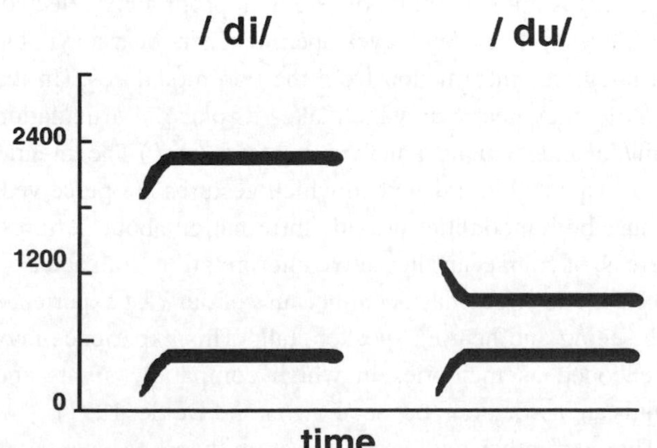

Figure 9.6 Schematic depiction of the synthetic syllables, /di/ and /du/.

/di/ and /du/. The striking finding was that the information critical to identification of these synthetic syllables was the transition of the second formant. However, that transition is high in frequency and rising in /di/, but low and falling in /du/. In the context of the rest of each syllable, the consonants sound alike to listeners. Separated from context, they sound different, and they sound the way they look like they should sound: two "chirps," one high in pitch and one lower.

Liberman (e.g., 1957) recognized that, despite the context sensitivity of the acoustic signals for /di/ and /du/, naturally produced syllables do have one thing in common. They are produced in the same way. In both syllables, the tongue tip makes a constriction behind the teeth. Listeners' percepts appeared to track the speaker's articulations.

A second striking finding was complementary. Stop consonants can be identified based on their formant transitions, as in the previous example, or based on a burst of energy that, in natural speech, precedes the transitions and occurs as the stop constriction is released. Liberman, Delattre, and Cooper (1952) found that a noise burst centered at 1440 Hz and placed in front of the vowels /i/ or /u/ was identified predominantly as /p/. However in front of /a/, it was identified as /k/. In this case, an invariant bit of acoustic structure led to different percepts. To produce that bit of acoustic structure before /i/ or /u/, a speaker has to make the constriction at the lips; to produce it before /a/, he or she has to make the constriction at the soft palate. These findings led Liberman to ask: "when articulation and the sound wave go their separate ways, which way does the perception go?" (Liberman, 1957, p. 121). His answer was: "The answer so far is clear. The perception always goes with articulation."

Although the motor theory was developed to explain unexpected research findings, Liberman and colleagues proposed a rationale for listeners' perception of gestures. Speakers have to coarticulate. Liberman and colleagues (e.g., Liberman, Cooper, Shankweiler, & Studdert-Kennedy, 1967) suggested that coarticulation is necessary to evade the limits of the temporal resolving power of the listener's ear. These limits were proposed to underlie the failure of Haskins researchers more than 50 years ago to train people to use an acoustic alphabet intended for use in a reading machine for the blind (see Liberman, 1996). Listeners could not perceive sequences of discrete sounds at anything close to the rates at which they perceive speech. Coarticulation provides a continuous signal evading the temporal resolving power limits of the ear, but it creates a new problem. The relation between phonological forms and acoustic speech structure is opaque. Liberman et al. (e.g., 1967) suggested that coarticulation required a specialization of the brain to achieve it. What system would be better suited to deal with the acoustic complexities to which coarticulation gives rise than the system responsible for generating coarticulated speech? In later versions of the motor theory, this hypothesized specialization was identified as a phonetic module (cf. Fodor, 1983).

There is an independent route to a conclusion that speech perception yields gestures. Fowler's (e.g., 1986, 1996; see also Best, 1995; Rosenblum, 1987) direct realist theory derived that claim by developing a theory of speech perception in the context of a universal theory of perceptual function. That theory, developed by James Gibson (e.g., 1966, 1979), notes that perceptual systems constitute the only means that animals have to know their world. By hypothesis, they serve that function in just one general way. Stimulus structure at the sense organs is not perceived itself. Rather, it serves as information for its causal source in the environment, and the environment is thereby perceived. In vision, for example, light that reflects from objects in the environment is structured by the properties of the objects and takes on structure that is distinctive to those properties. Because the structure is distinctive to the properties, it can serve as information for them. Environmental events and objects, not the reflected light, are perceived. Fowler (1996) argued that, if even speech perception were wholly unspecial, listeners would perceive gestures, because gestures cause the structure in stimulation to the ear. And the auditory system (or the phonetic module), no less than the visual system, uses information in stimulation at the sense organ to reveal the world of objects and events to perceivers.

What does the experimental evidence show? An early finding that Liberman (1957) took to be compatible with his findings on /di/-/du/ and /pi/-/ka/-/pu/ was categorical perception. This was a pair of findings obtained when listeners made identification and discrimination judgments of stimuli along an acoustic continuum. Figure 9.7 displays schematic findings for a /ba/-to-/da/ continuum. Although the stimuli form a smooth continuum (in which the second formant transition is gradually shifted from a trajectory for /ba/ to one for /da/), the identification function is very sharp. Most stimuli along the continuum are heard either as a clear /ba/ or as a clear /da/. Only one or two syllables in the middle of the continuum are ambiguous. The second critical outcome was obtained when listeners were asked to discriminate pairs of syllables along the continuum. The finding was that discrimination was near chance among pairs of syllables both members of which listeners identified as /ba/ or both /da/, but it was good between pair members that were equally acoustically similar as the /ba/ pairs and the /da/ pairs, but in which listeners heard one as /ba/ and the other as /da/. In contrast, say, to colors, where perceivers can easily discriminate colors that they uniformly label as *blue,* to a first approximation,

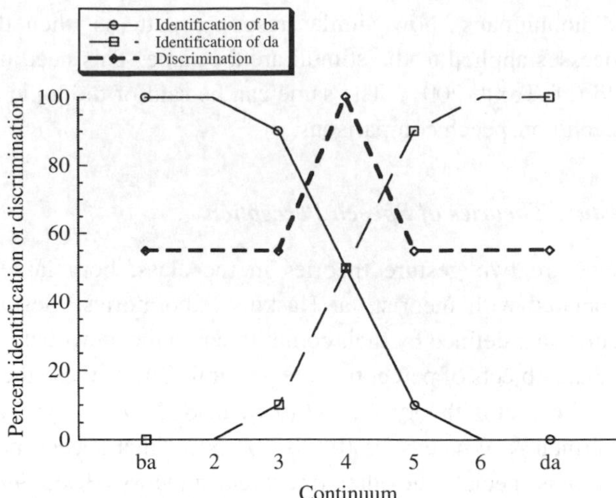

Figure 9.7 Schematic depiction of categorical identification and discrimination.

listeners could only discriminate what they labeled distinctively. The early interpretation of this finding was that it revealed perception of gestures, because the place of articulation difference between /ba/ and /da/, unlike the acoustic difference, is categorical.

This interpretation was challenged, for example, by Pisoni (e.g., Pisoni & Tash, 1974). In their study, Pisoni and Tash showed that *same* responses to pairs of syllables that were labeled the same but that differed acoustically were slower than to identical pairs of syllables. Accordingly, listeners have at least fleeting access to within-category differences. Despite this and other findings, the name *categorical perception* has endured, but now it is typically used only to refer to the data pattern of Figure 9.7, not to its original interpretation.

A set of findings that has a natural interpretation in gesture theories is the *McGurk effect* (named for one of its discoverers; McGurk and MacDonald, 1976). This effect is obtained when a videotape of a speaker mouthing a word or syllable (say, /da/) is dubbed with a different, appropriately selected, syllable (say, /ma/). With eyes open, listeners hear a syllable that integrates information from the two modalities. (In the example, they hear /na/, which takes its place of articulation from /da/ and its manner and voicing from /ma/.) The integration is expected in a theory in which gestures are perceived, because both modalities provide information about gestures. There is, of course, an alternative interpretation from acoustic theories. The effect may occur because of our vast experience both seeing and hearing speakers talk. This experience may be encoded as memories in which compatible sights and sounds are associated (but see Fowler and Dekle, 1991).

There are other findings that gesture theorists have taken to support their theory. For example, researchers have shown that performance discriminating pairs of syllables can be better for stimuli that differ in one acoustic cue for a gesture than for stimuli that differ in that cue and one other for the same gesture (e.g., Fitch, Halwes, Erickson, & Liberman, 1980). This is unexpected on acoustic grounds. It occurs just when the two cues are selected so that the stimuli of a pair are identified as the same gesturally, whereas the pair differing in one cue are not always. Another finding is that people are remarkably rapid shadowers of speech under some conditions (e.g., Porter & Castellanos, 1980; Porter & Lubker, 1980). This has been interpreted as evidence that perceiving speech is perceiving gestures that constitute the instructions for the shadowing response. A third kind of finding has been research designed to show that listeners parse acoustic speech signals along gestural lines (e.g., Fowler & Smith, 1986; Pardo & Fowler, 1997). For example, when two gestures, say devoicing a preceding stop consonant and production of intonational accent, have convergent effects on the fundamental frequency (F0) pattern on a vowel, listeners do not hear the combined effects as the vowel's intonation or pitch. They hear the contribution to F0 made by the devoicing gesture as information for devoicing (Pardo & Fowler, 1997). Finally, Fowler, Brown, and Mann (2000) have recently disconfirmed the contrast account of compensation for coarticulation offered by Lotto and Kluender (1998). They used the McGurk effect to show that, when the only information distinguishing /al/ from /ar/ was optical, and the only information distinguishing /da/ from /ga/ was acoustic, participants provided more /ga/ responses in the context of precursor /al/ than /ar/. This cannot be a contrast effect. Fowler et al. concluded that the effect is literally compensation for coarticulation.

Motor theorists have also attempted to test their idea that speech perception is achieved by a phonetic module. Like acoustic theorists, they have compared listeners' responses to speech and to similar nonspeech signals, now with the expectation of finding differences. One of the most elegant demonstrations was provided by Mann and Liberman (1983). They took advantage of duplex perception, in which, in their version, components of a syllable were presented dichotically. The base, presented to one ear, included steady-state formants for /a/ preceded by F1 and F2 transitions consistent with either /d/ or /g/. An F3 transition, presented to the other ear, distinguished /da/ from /ga/. Perception is called *duplex* because the transitions are heard in two different ways at the same time. At the ear receiving the base, listeners hear a clear /da/ or a clear /ga/ depending on which transition was presented to the other ear. At the ear receiving the transition, listeners hear a nonspeech chirp. On the one hand, this can be interpreted as evidence for a speech module, because how

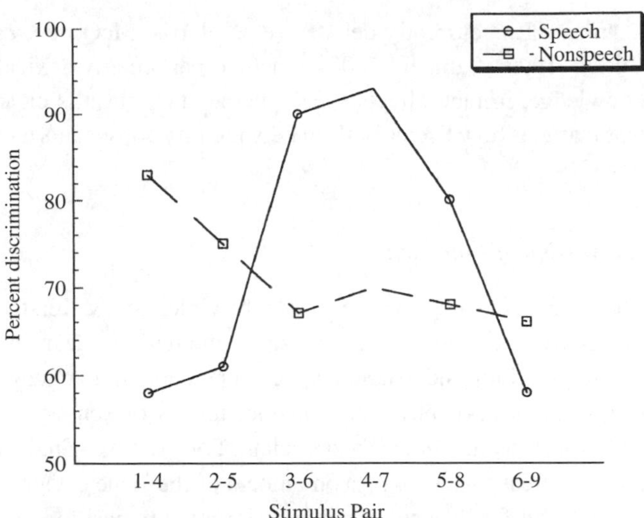

Figure 9.8 Results of speech and nonspeech discriminations of syllables and chirps (Mann & Liberman, 1983).

else, except with a separate perceptual system, can the same acoustic fragment be heard in two different ways at once? (However, see Fowler & Rosenblum, 1990, for a possible answer to the question.) On the other hand, it can provide the means of an elegant speech/nonspeech comparison, because listeners can be asked to attend to the syllable and make phonetic judgments that will vary as the critical formant transition varies, and they can be asked to attend to the chirps and make analogous judgments about them. Presented with a continuum of F3 transitions to one ear and the base to the other, and under instructions to discriminate syllable pairs or chirp pairs, listeners responded quite differently depending on the judgment, even though both judgments were based on the same acoustic pattern. Figure 9.8 shows that their speech discrimination judgments showed a sharply peaked pattern similar to that in Figure 9.7. Their chirp judgments showed a nearly monotonically decreasing pattern. This study, among others, shows that not all comparisons of speech and nonspeech perception have uncovered similarities.

Learning and Speech Perception

So far, it may appear as if speech perception is unaffected by a language user's experience talking and listening. It is affected, however. Experience with the language affects how listeners categorize consonants and vowels, and it affects the internal structure of native language phonological categories. It also provides language users with knowledge of the relative frequencies with which consonants and vowels follow one another in speech (e.g., Pitt & McQueen, 1998; Vitevitch & Luce, 1999) and with knowledge of the words of the language. It is currently debated (e.g., Norris, McQueen, & Cutler, 1999; Samuel, 2000) whether particularly lexical knowledge, in fact, affects speech perception, but it is clear that it affects how listeners ultimately identify consonants and vowels.

Knowledge of Categories

The concept of category (see chapter by Goldstone & Kersten in this volume) remains rather fuzzy, although it is clear that it is required for understanding speech perception. Language users treat sets of physically distinct tokens of consonants and vowels as functionally equivalent. For example, English listeners treat tokens of /t/ as members of the same category when /t/s differ in aspiration due to variation in position in a syllable or stress, and when they differ due to speaking rate, coarticulatory context, dialect, foreign accent, and idiosyncratic speaker characteristics. (They treat them as functionally equivalent, for example, when they count physically distinct /t/s before /ap/ all as consonants of the word *top*.) The concept of category is meant to capture this behavior. Functional equivalence of physically distinct tokens may or may not imply that listeners represent consonants and vowels as abstract types. The section titled "Another Abstractness Issue: Exemplar Theories of the Lexicon" described exemplar theories of linguistic knowledge in which clusters of relevantly similar tokens underlie behaviors suggestive of type memories. Accordingly, the reader should interpret the following discussion of categories as neutral between the possibilities that abstract types are or are not components of linguistic competence.

From the earliest ages at which they are tested, infants show evidence of categorization. On the one hand, they exhibit something like categorical perception. Eimas, Siqueland, Jusczyk, and Vigorito (1971) pioneered the use of a high-amplitude sucking technique to test infants as young as one month of age. Infants sucked on a nonnutritive nipple. If they sucked with sufficient vigor they heard a speech syllable, for example, /ba/. Over time, infants increased their sucking rate under those conditions, but eventually they showed habituation: Their sucking rate declined. Following that, Eimas et al. presented different syllables to all infants except those in the control group. They presented a syllable that adult listeners heard as /pa/ or one that was acoustically as distant from the original /ba/ as the /pa/ syllable but that adults identified as /ba/. Infants dishabituated to the first syllable, showing that they heard the difference, but they did not dishabituate to the second.

Kuhl and colleagues (e.g., Kuhl & Miller, 1982) have shown that infants classify by phonetic type syllables that they readily discriminate. Kuhl and Miller trained 6-month-old infants to turn their head when they heard a phonetic change in a repeating background vowel (from /a/ to /i/). Then they increased the difficulty of the task by presenting as background /a/ vowels spoken by different speakers or with different pitch contours. These vowels are readily discriminated by infants, but adults would identify all of them as /a/. When a change occurred, it was to /i/ vowels spoken by the different speakers or produced with the different pitch contours. Infants' head turn responses demonstrated that they detected the phonetic identity of the variety of /a/ vowels and the phonetic difference between them and the /i/ vowels.

We know, then, that infants detect phonetic invariance over irrelevant variation. However, with additional experience with their native language, they begin to show differences in what they count as members of the same and different categories. For example, Werker and Tees (1984) showed that English-learning infants at 6–8 months of age distinguished Hindi dental and retroflex voiceless stops. However, at 10–12 months they did not. English- (non-Hindi-) speaking adults also had difficulty making the discrimination, whereas Hindi adults and three Hindi 10–12 month olds who were tested made the discrimination readily. One way to understand the English-learning infants' loss in sensitivity to the phonetic distinction is to observe that, in English, the distinction is not contrastive. English alveolar stops are most similar to the Hindi dental and retroflex stops. If an English speaker (perhaps due to coarticulation) were to produce a dental stop in place of an alveolar one, it would not change the word being produced from one word into another. With learning, categories change their structure to reflect the patterning of more and less important phonetic distinctions of the language to which the learner is exposed.

In recent years, investigators have found that categories have an internal structure. Whereas early findings from categorical perception implied that all category members, being indiscriminable, must be equally acceptable members of the category, that is not the case, as research by Kuhl (e.g., 1991) and by Miller has shown.

Kuhl (e.g., 1987) has suggested that categories are organized around best instances or prototypes. When Grieser and Kuhl (1989) created a grid of vowels, all identified as /i/ by listeners (ostensibly; but see Lively & Pisoni, 1995) but differing in their F1s and F2s, listeners gave higher goodness ratings to some tokens than to others. Kuhl (1991) showed, in addition, that listeners (adults and infants aged 6–7 months, but not monkeys) showed poorer discrimination of /i/ vowels close to the prototype (that is, the vowel given the highest goodness rating) than of vowels from a nonprototype (a vowel given a low goodness rating), an outcome she called the "magnet effect." Kuhl, Williams, Lacerda, Stevens, and Lindblom (1992) showed that English and Swedish infants show magnet effects around different vowels, reflecting the different vowel systems of their languages.

We should not think of phonological categories as having an invariant prototype organization, however. Listeners identify different category members as best exemplars in different contexts. This has been shown most clearly in the work of Joanne Miller and colleagues. Miller and colleagues (e.g., Miller & Volaitis, 1989) have generated acoustic continua ranging, for example, from /bi/ to /pi/ and beyond to a very long VOT /p/ designated */p/. Listeners make goodness judgments to the stimuli (in the example, they rate the goodness of the consonants as /p/s), and Miller and colleagues get data like those in Figure 9.9. (The VOT continuum is truncated at the long end in the figure.) The functions have a peak and graded sides. Miller and collaborators have shown that the location of the best rated consonant along an acoustic continuum can vary markedly with rate of production, syllable structure, and other variables. An effect of rate is shown in Figure 9.9 (where the legend's designations "125 ms" and "325 ms" are syllable durations for fast and slow productions, respectively). Faber and Brown (1998) showed a change in the prototype with coarticulatory context. These findings suggest that the categories revealed by these studies have a dynamical character (cf. Tuller, Case, & Kelso, 1994).

How should the findings of Kuhl and colleagues and of Miller and colleagues be integrated? It is not yet clear. Kuhl (e.g., Kuhl & Iverson, 1995) acknowledges that her findings are as consistent with a theory in which there are actual prototypes in memory as with one in which prototypicality is an emergent property of an exemplar memory. It may be easier in an exemplar theory to understand how categories can change their structure dynamically.

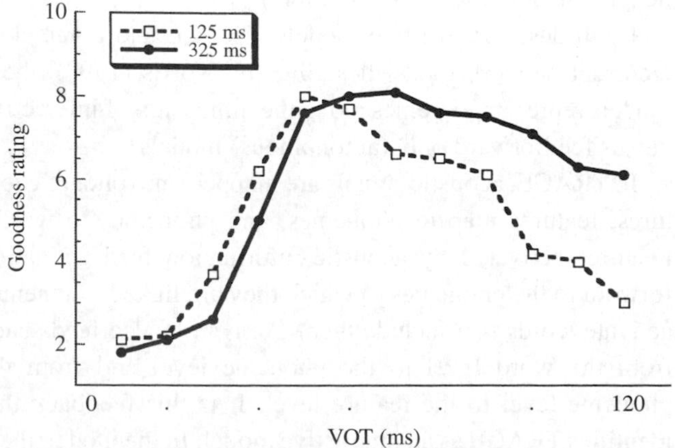

Figure 9.9 Goodness ratings along a /bi/-/pi/-*/pi/ continuum. Data similar to those of Miller and Volaitis (1989).

Possibly, Kuhl's magnet effect can also be understood from the framework of Miller's (e.g., Miller & Volaitis, 1989) findings if both sets of findings are related to Catherine Best's perceptual assimilation model (PAM; e.g., Best, 1994). PAM is a model that captures consequences of perceptual speech learning. In the model, experience with the language eventuates in the formation of language-specific categories. When listeners are given two nonnative consonants or two vowels to discriminate, and they fall into the same native category, discrimination is very poor if the phones are equally good exemplars of the category. Discrimination is better if one is judged a good and one a poor exemplar. This can be understood by looking at Figure 9.9. Tokens that fall near the peak of the goodness function sound very similar to listeners, and they sound like good members of the category. However, one token at the peak and one over to the left or right side of the function sound different in goodness and therefore presumably in phonetic quality. Functions with flat peaks and accelerating slopes to the sides of the function would give rise to a magnet effect. That is, tokens surrounding the peak would be difficult to discriminate, but equally acoustically similar tokens at the sides of the function (so a nonprototype and a token near to it) would differ considerably in goodness and be easily discriminable.

Lexical and Phonotactic Knowledge

Word knowledge can affect how phones are identified, as can knowledge of the frequencies with which phones follow one another in speech. Ganong (1980) showed that lexical knowledge can affect how a phone is identified. He created pairs of continua in which the phone sequence at one end was a word but the sequence at the other end was a nonword. For example, in one pair of continua, VOT was varied to produce a *gift*-to-*kift* continuum and a *giss*-to-*kiss* continuum. Ganong found that listeners provided more *g* responses in the *gift-kift* continuum than in the *giss-kiss* continuum. That is, they tended to give responses suggesting that they identified real words preferentially. This result has recently been replicated with audiovisual speech. Brancazio (submitted) has shown that participants exhibit more McGurk integrations if they turn acoustically specified nonwords into words (e.g., acoustic *besk* dubbed onto video *desk,* with the integrated McGurk response being *desk*) than if they turn acoustically specified words into nonwords (e.g., acoustic *bench* dubbed on to video *dench*).

Ganong's (1980) result has at least two interpretations. One is that lexical information feeds down and affects perceptual processing of consonants and vowels. An alternative is that perceptual processing of consonants and vowels is encapsulated from such feedback; however, when the processor yields an ambiguous output, lexical knowledge is brought to bear to resolve the ambiguity. In the first account, the effect of the lexicon is on perceptual processing; in the second it is on processing that follows perception of phones. The Ganong paradigm has been used many times in creative attempts to distinguish these interpretations (e.g., Fox, 1984; Miller & Dexter, 1988; Newman, Sawusch, & Luce, 1997). However, it remains unresolved.

A second finding of lexical effects is phonemic restoration (e.g., Samuel, 1981, 1996; Warren, 1970). When the acoustic consequences of a phoneme are excised from a word (in Warren's classic example, the /s/ noise of *legislature*) and are replaced with noise that would mask the acoustic signal if it were present, listeners report hearing the missing phoneme and mislocate the noise. Samuel (1981) showed that when two versions of these words are created, one in which the acoustic consequences are present in the noise and one in which they are absent, listeners asked to make a judgment whether the phone is present or absent in the noise show lower perceptual sensitivity to phones in words than in nonwords. That the effect occurs on the measure of perceptual sensitivity (d′) suggests that, here, lexical knowledge is exerting its effect on phoneme perception itself. (However, that d′ can be so interpreted in word recognition experiments has been challenged; see Norris, 1995.)

A final lexical effect occurs in experiments on compensation for coarticulation. Mann and Repp (1981) found compensation for /s/ and /ʃ/ on members of a /ta/-to-/ka/ continuum such that the more front /s/ fostered /ka/ responses, and the more back /ʃ/ fostered /ta/ responses. Elman and McClelland (1988) used compensation for coarticulation in a study that seemingly demonstrated lexical feedback on perceptual processing of consonants. They generated continua ranging from /d/ to /g/ (e.g., *dates* to *gates*) and from /t/ to /k/ (e.g., *tapes* to *capes*). Continuum members followed words such as *Christmas* and *Spanish* in which the final fricatives of each word (or, in another experiment, the entire final syllables) were replaced with the same ambiguous sound. Accordingly, the only thing that made the final fricative of *Christmas* an /s/ was the listeners' knowledge that *Christmas* is a word and *Christmash* is not. Lexical knowledge, too, was all that made the final fricative of *Spanish* an /ʃ/. Listeners showed compensation for coarticulation appropriate for the lexically specified fricatives of the precursor words.

This result is ascribed to feedback effects on perception, because compensation for coarticulation is quite evidently an effect that occurs during perceptual processing of phones. However, Pitt and McQueen (1998) challenged the feedback interpretation with findings appearing to show that the effect is not really lexical. It is an effect of listeners' knowledge of the relative frequencies of phone sequences in the language, an effect that they identify as prelexical and at the same level of processing as that on which phonemes are perceived. Pitt and McQueen note that in English, /s/ is more likely to follow the final vowel of *Christmas* than is /ʃ/, and /ʃ/ is more common than /s/ following the final vowel of *Spanish*. (If readers find these vowels—ostensibly /ə/ and /I/ according to Pitt and McQueen—rather subtly distinct, they are quite right.) These investigators directly pitted lexical identity against phone sequence frequency and found compensation for coarticulation fostered only by the transition probability variable. Lately, however, Samuel (2000) reports finding a true lexical effect on phoneme perception. The clear result is that lexical knowledge affects how we identify consonants and vowels. It is less clear where in processing the lexical effect comes in.

Pitt and McQueen's study introduces another knowledge variable that can affect phone identification: knowledge of the relative transition frequencies between phones. Although this logically could be another manifestation of our lexical knowledge, Pitt and McQueen's findings suggest that it is not, because lexical and transition-probability variables dissociate in their effects on compensation for coarticulation. A conclusion that transition probability effects arise prelexically is reinforced by recent findings of Vitevitch and Luce (1998, 1999).

There are many models of spoken-word recognition. They include the pioneering TRACE (McClelland & Elman, 1986), Marslen-Wilson's (e.g., 1987) cohort model, the neighborhood activation model (NAM; Luce, 1986; Luce & Pisoni, 1998), the fuzzy logical model of perception (FLMP; e.g., Massaro, 1987, 1998), and shortlist (e.g., Norris, 1994). (A more recent model of Norris et al., 1999, Merge, is currently a model of phoneme identification; it is not a full-fledged model of word recognition.)

I will describe just two models, TRACE and a nameless recurrent network model described by Norris (1993); these models represent extremes along the dimension of interactive versus feedforward only (autonomous) models.

In TRACE, acoustic signals are mapped onto phonetic features, features map to phonemes, and phonemes to words. Features activated by acoustic information feed activation forward to the phonemes to which they are linked. Phonemes activate words that include them. Activation also feeds back from the word level to the phoneme level and from the phoneme level to the feature level. It is this feedback that identifies TRACE as an interactive model. In the model, there is also lateral inhibition; forms at a given level inhibit forms at the same level with which they are incompatible. Lexical effects on phoneme identification (e.g., the Ganong effect and phonemic restoration) arise from lexical feedback. Given an ambiguous member of a *gift*-to-*kift* continuum, the word *gift* will be activated at the lexical level and will feed activation back to its component phonemes, including /g/, thereby fostering identification of the ambiguous initial consonant as /g/. Lexical feedback also restores missing phonemes in the phonemic restoration effect.

In TRACE, knowledge of transition probabilities is the same as knowledge of words. That is, words and nonwords with high transition probabilities include phoneme sequences that occur frequently in words of the lexicon. TRACE cannot generate the dissociations between effects of lexical knowledge and transition probabilities that both Pitt and McQueen (1998) and Vitevitch and Luce (1998) report. A second shortcoming of TRACE is its way of dealing with the temporally extended character of speech. To permit TRACE to take in utterances over time, McClelland and Elman (1986) used the brute force method of replicating the entire network of feature, phone, and word nodes at many different points in modeled time.

Norris's (1993) recurrent network can handle temporally extended input without massive replication of nodes and links. The network has input nodes that receive as input sets of features for phonemes. The feature sets for successive phonemes are input over time. Input units link to hidden units, which link to output units. There is one set of output units for words and one for phonemes. The hidden units also link to one another over delay lines. It is this aspect of the network that allows it to learn the temporally extended phoneme sequences that constitute words. The network is trained to activate the appropriate output unit for a word when its component phonemes' feature sets are presented over time to the input units and to identify phonemes based on featural input. The network has the notable property that it is feedforward only; that is, in contrast to TRACE, there is no top-down feedback from a lexical to a prelexical level. Recurrent networks are good at learning sequences, and the learning resides in the hidden units. Accordingly, the hidden units have probabilistic phonotactic knowledge. Norris has shown that this model can exhibit the Ganong effect and compensation for coarticulation; before its time, it demonstrated findings like those of Pitt and McQueen (1998) in which apparently top-down lexical effects on compensation for coarticulation in fact arise prelexically and depend on knowledge of transition probabilities. This type of model (see also Norris et al., 1999) is remarkably successful in simulating findings that had previously been ascribed to top-down feedback. However, the debate about feedback is ongoing (e.g., Samuel, 2000).

SUMMARY

Intensive research on language forms within experimental psychology has only a 50-year history, beginning with the work by Liberman and colleagues at Haskins Laboratories. However, this chapter shows that much has been learned in that short time. Moreover, the scope of the research has broadened considerably, from an initial focus on speech perception only to current research spanning the domains of competence, planning production, and perception. Additionally, in each domain, the experimental methodolgies developed by investigators have expanded and include some remarkably useful ways of probing the psychology of phonology.

Theoretical developments have been considerable, too. Within each domain, competing theoretical views have grown that foster efforts to sharpen the theories and to distinguish them experimentally. Moreover, we now have theories in domains, such as planning, where earlier there were none. The scope and depth of our understanding of language forms and their role in language use has grown impressively. A relatively new development that is proving very useful is the use of models that implement theories. The models of Dell (1986) and Levelt et al. (1999) of phonological planning, of Guenther et al. (1998) and Saltzman (1991) on speech production, and of McClelland and Elman (1986) and Norris (1994), among others, of speech perception all help to make theoretical differences explicit and theoretical claims testable.

We have much more to learn, of course. My own view, made clear in this chapter, is that enduring advances depend on more cross-talk across the domains of competence, planning, production, and perception.

REFERENCES

Abbs, J., & Gracco, V. (1984). Control of complex gestures: Orofacial muscle responses to load perturbations of the lip during speech. *Journal of Neurophysiology, 51,* 705–723.

Abler, W. (1989). On the particulate principle of self-diversifying systems. *Journal of Social and Biological Structures, 12,* 1–13.

Baars, B., Motley, M., & MacKay, D. G. (1975). Output editing for lexical status from artificially elicited slips of the tongue. *Journal of Verbal Learning and Verbal Behavior, 14,* 382–391.

Bell-Berti, F., & Harris, K. (1981). A temporal model of speech production. *Phonetica, 38,* 9–20.

Bell-Berti, F., & Krakow, R. (1991). Anticipatory velar lowering: A coproduction account. *Journal of the Acoustical Society of America, 90,* 112–123.

Best, C. T. (1994). The emergence of native-language phonological influences in infants: A perceptual assimilation model. In J. Goodman & H. Nusbaum (Eds.), *The development of speech perception: The transition from speech sounds to spoken words* (pp. 167–224). Cambridge, MA: MIT Press.

Best, C. T. (1995). A direct realist perspective on cross-language speech perception. In W. Strange & J. J. Jenkins (Eds.), *Cross-language speech perception* (pp. 171–204). Timonium, MD: York Press.

Bladon, A., & Al-Bamerni, A. (1976). Coarticulation resistance in English /l/. *Journal of Phonetics, 4,* 137–150.

Boyce, S., Krakow, R., Bell-Berti, F., & Gelfer, C. (1990). Converging sources of evidence for dissecting articulatory movements into gestures. *Journal of Phonetics, 18,* 173–188.

Brancazio, L. (2002). *Lexical influences in audiovisual speech perception.* Manuscript submitted for publication.

Browman, C., & Goldstein, L. (1986). Towards an articulatory phonology. *Phonology Yearbook, 3,* 219–252.

Browman, C., & Goldstein, L. (1990). Tiers in articulatory phonology, with some implications for casual speech. In J. Kingston & M. Beckman (Eds.), *Papers in laboratory phonology: Vol. 1. Between the grammar and the physics of speech* (pp. 341–376). Cambridge, England: Cambridge University Press.

Browman, C., & Goldstein, L. (1995a). Dynamics and articulatory phonology. In R. Port & T. van Gelder (Eds.), *Mind as motion: Explorations in the dynamics of cognition* (pp. 175–193). Cambridge, MA: MIT Press.

Browman, C., & Goldstein, L. (1995b). Gestural syllable position effects in American English. In F. Bell-Berti & L. Raphael (Eds.), *Producing speech: Contemporary issues.* (pp. 19–33). New York: American Institute of Physics.

Browman, C., & Goldstein, L. (1997). The gestural phonology mode. In W. Hulstijn, H. F. M. Peters, & P. H. H. Van Lieshout (Eds.), *Speech production: Motor control, brain research and fluency disorders* (International Congress Series, No. 1146). Amsterdam: Elsevier.

Chomsky, N., & Halle, M. (1968). *The sound pattern of English.* New York: Harper and Row.

Clark, H. (1996). *Using language.* Cambridge, England: Cambridge University Press.

Delattre, P., & Freeman, D. (1968). A dialect study of American r's by x-ray motion picture. *Linguistics, 44,* 29–68.

Dell, G. S. (1986). A spreading-activation theory of retrieval in speech production. *Psychological Review, 93,* 283–321.

Dell, G. S., Burger, L., & Svec, W. (1997). Language production and serial order: A functional analysis and a model. *Psychological Review, 104,* 127–147.

Dell, G. S., & Juliano, C. (1996). Computational models of phonological encoding. In T. Dijkstra & K. DeSmedt (Eds.), *Computational psycholinguistics: AI and connectionist models of language processing* (pp. 328–359). Philadelphia: Taylor & Francis.

Dell, G. S., Juliano, C., & Govindjee, A. (1993). Structure and content in language production: A theory of frame constraints. *Cognitive Science, 17,* 149–195.

Diehl, R., & Kluender, K. (1989). On the objects of speech perception. *Ecological Psychology, 1,* 121–144.

Easton, T. (1972). On the normal use of reflexes. *American Scientist, 60,* 591–599.

Eimas, P., Siqueland, E., Jusczyk, P., & Vigorito, J. (1971). Speech perception in infants. *Science, 171,* 303–306.

Elman, J. & McClelland, J. (1988). Cognitive penetration of the mechanisms of perception: Compensation for coarticulation of lexically restored phonemes. *Journal of Memory and Language, 27,* 143–165.

Faber, A., & Brown, J. (1998). The effect of consonant context on vowel goodness rating [Abstract]. *Journal of the Acoustical Society of America, 104,* 1759 (abstract).

Fitch, H., Halwes, T., Erickson, D., & Liberman, A. (1980). Perceptual equivalence of two acoustic cues for stop-consonant manner. *Perception and Psychophysics, 27,* 343–350.

Fodor, J. A. (1983). *The modularity of mind: An essay on faculty psychology.* Cambridge, MA: MIT Press.

Fowler, C. A. (1986). An event approach to the study of speech perception from a direct-realist perspective. *Journal of Phonetics, 14,* 3–28.

Fowler, C. A. (1994). Invariants, specifiers cues: An investigation of locus equations as information for place of articulation. *Perception & Psychophysics, 55,* 597–610.

Fowler, C. A. (1996). Listeners do hear sounds, not tongues. *Journal of the Acoustical Society of America, 99,* 1730–1741.

Fowler, C. A. (1999). The orderly output constraint is not wearing any clothes. *Behavioral and Brain Science, 21,* 265–266.

Fowler, C. A., & Brancazio, L. (2000). Coarticulation resistance of American English consonants and its effects on transconsonantal vowel-to-vowel coarticulation. *Language and Speech, 43,* 1–41.

Fowler, C. A., Brown, J., & Mann, V. (2000). Contrast effects do not underlie effects of preceding liquid consonants on stop identification in humans. *Journal of Experimental Psychology: Human Perception and Performance, 26,* 877–888.

Fowler, C. A., & Dekle, D. J. (1991). Listening with eye and hand: Crossmodal contributions to speech perception. *Journal of Experimental Psychology: Human Perception and Performance, 17,* 816–828.

Fowler, C. A., & Levy, E. (1995). Talker-listener attunements to speech events. *Journal of Contemporary Legal Studies, 6,* 305–328.

Fowler, C. A., & Rosenblum, L. D. (1990). Duplex perception: A comparison of monosyllables and slamming doors. *Journal of Experimental Psychology: Human Perception and Performance, 16,* 742–754.

Fowler, C. A., Rubin, P., Remez, R., & Turvey, M. (1980). Implications for speech production of a general theory of action. In

B. Butterworth (Ed.), *Language production: Vol. 1. Speech and talk* (Vol. 1, pp. 373–420). London: Academic Press.

Fowler, C. A., & Saltzman, E. (1993). Coordination and coarticulation in speech production. *Language and Speech, 36,* 171–195.

Fowler, C. A., & Smith, M. (1986). Speech perception as "vector analysis": An approach to the problems of segmentation and invariance. In J. Perkell & D. Klatt (Eds.), *Invariance and variability of speech processes* (pp. 123–136). Hillsdale, NJ: Lawrence Erlbaum.

Fox, R. (1984). Effect of lexical status on phonetic categorization. *Journal of Experimental Psychology: Human Perception and Performance, 10,* 526–540.

Fromkin, V. (1973). *Speech errors as linguistic evidence.* The Hague, the Netherlands: Mouton.

Ganong, W. F. (1980). Phonetic categorization in auditory word perception. *Journal of Experimental Psychology: Human Perception and Performance, 6,* 110–125.

Garrett, M. (1980). Levels of processing in speech production. In B. Butterworth (Ed.), *Language production: Vol. 1. Speech and talk* (pp. 177–220). London: Academic Press.

Gibson, J. J. (1966). *The senses considered as perceptual systems.* Boston: Houghton Mifflin.

Gibson, J. J. (1979). *The ecological approach to visual perception.* Boston: Houghton Mifflin.

Gick, B. (1999). *The articulatory basis of syllable structure: A study of English glides and liquids.* Unpublished doctoral dissertation. Yale University, New Haven, CT.

Gleason, P., Tuller, B., & Kelso, J. A. S. (1996). Syllable affiliation of final consonant clusters undergoes a phase transition over speaking rates. *Proceedings of the International Conference on Speech and Language Processing* (pp. 276–278). Philadelphia, PA.

Goldinger, S. D. (1996). Words and voices: Episodic traces in spoken word identification and recognition memory. *Journal of Experimental Psychology: Learning, Memory and Cognition, 22,* 1166–1183.

Goldinger, S. D. (1998). Echoes of echoes? An episodic theory of lexical access. *Psychological Review, 105,* 251–279.

Grieser, D., & Kuhl, P. (1989). Categorization of speech by infants: Support for speech-sound prototypes. *Developmental Psychology, 25,* 577–588.

Guenther, F., Hampson, M., & Johnson, D. (1998). A theoretical investigation of reference frames for the planning of speech. *Psychological Review, 105,* 611–633.

Guilford, J., & Park, D. (1931). The effect of interpolated weights upon comparative judgments. *American Journal of Psychology, 43,* 589–599.

Hagiwara, R. (1995). Acoustic realizations of American /r/ as produced by women and men. *UCLA Working Papers in Phonetics, 90.*

Hamlet, S. (1988). Speech compensation for prosthodontially created palatal asymmetries. *Journal of Speech and Hearing Research, 31,* 48–53.

Hamlet, S., & Stone, M. (1978). Compensatory alveolar consonant production induced by wearing a dental prosthesis. *Journal of Phonetics, 6,* 227–248.

Hintzman, D. (1986). "Schema abstraction" in a multiple trace memory model. *Psychological Review, 93,* 411–428.

Hockett, C. (1955). *A manual of phonetics.* Bloominton: Indiana University Press.

Humbolt, W. Von. (1972). *Linguistic variability and intellectual development.* (G. C. Buck & F. A. Raven, Trans.) Philadelphia: University of Pennsylvania Press. (Original work published 1836)

Jakobson, R., Fant, G., & Halle, M. (1962). *Preliminaries to speech analysis.* Cambridge, MA: MIT Press.

Keating, P. (1983). Comments on the jaw and syllable structure. *Journal of Phonetics, 11,* 401–406.

Kelso, J. A. S. (1995). *Dynamic patterns: The self-organization of brain and behavior.* Cambridge, MA: MIT Press.

Kelso, J. A. S., Tuller, B., Vatikiotis-Bateson, E., & Fowler, C. A. (1984). Functionally-specific articulatory cooperation following jaw perturbation during speech: Evidence for coordinative structures. *Journal of Experimental Psychology: Human Perception and Performance, 10,* 812–832.

Kent, R., & Tjaden, K. (1997). Brain functions underlying speech. In W. Hardcastle & J. Laver (Eds.), *The handbook of phonetic sciences* (pp. 221–255). Oxford, England: Blackwell Publishers.

Kluender, K. (1994). Speech perception as a tractable problem in cognitive science. In M. A. Gernsbacher (Ed.), *Handbook of Psycholinguistics* (pp. 173–217). San Diego, CA: Academic Press.

Krakow, R. (1989). *The articulatory organization of syllables: A kinematic analysis of labial and velar gestures.* Unpublished doctoral dissertation. Yale University, New Haven, CT.

Krakow, R. (1993). Nonsegmental influences on velum movement patterns: Syllables, segments, stress and speaking rate. In M. Huffman & R. Krakow (Eds.), *Phonetics and phonology: Vol. 5. Nasals, nasalization and the velum* (pp. 87–116). New York: Academic Press.

Krakow, R. (1999). Physiological organization of syllables: A review. *Journal of Phonetics, 27,* 23–54.

Kuhl, P. (1987). The special-mechanisms debate in speech research: Categorization tests on animals and infants. In S. Harnad (Ed.), *Categorical perception: The groundwork of cognition* (pp. 355–386). Cambridge, England: Cambridge University Press.

Kuhl, P. (1991). Human adults and human infants show a "perceptual magnet effect" for the prototypes of speech categories, monkeys do not. *Perception & Psychophysics, 50,* 93–107.

Kuhl, P., & Iverson, P. (1995). Linguistic experience and the perceptual magnet effect. In W. Strange (Ed.), *Speech perception and linguistic experience: Issues in cross-language research* (pp. 121–154). Baltimore: York Press.

Kuhl, P., & Miller, J. D. (1978). Speech perception by the chinchilla: Identification functions for synthetic VOT stimuli. *Journal of the Acoustical Society of America, 63,* 905–917.

Kuhl, P., & Miller, J. D. (1982). Discrimination of auditory target dimensions in the presence or absence of variation in a second dimension by infants. *Perception & Psychophysics, 31,* 279–292.

Kuhl, P., Williams, K., Lacerda, F., Stevens, K., & Lindblom, B. (1992). Linguistic experience alters phonetic perception in infants by six months of age. *Science, 255,* 606–608.

Levelt, W. J. M., Roelofs, A., & Meyer, A. (1999). A theory of lexical access in speech production. *Behavioral and Brain Sciences, 22,* 1–38.

Liberman, A. M. (1957). Some results of research on speech perception. *Journal of the Acoustical Society of America, 29,* 117–123.

Liberman, A. M. (1996). *Speech: A special code.* Cambridge, MA: Bradford Books.

Liberman, A. M., Cooper, F., Shankweiler, D., & Studdert-Kennedy, M. (1967). Perception of the speech code. *Psychological Review, 74,* 431–461.

Liberman, A. M., Delattre, P., & Cooper, F. (1952). The role of selected stimulus variables in the perception of the unvoiced-stop consonants. *American Journal of Psychology, 65,* 497–516.

Liberman, A. M., & Mattingly, I. (1985). The motor theory revised. *Cognition, 21,* 1–36.

Liberman, A. M., & Whalen, D. H. (2000). On the relation of speech to language. *Trends in Cognitive Sciences, 4,* 187–196.

Lieberman, P. (1991). *Uniquely human: Speech, thought and selfless behavior.* Cambridge, MA: Harvard University Press.

Lindblom, B. (1986). Phonetic universals in vowel systems. In J. Ohala & J. Jaeger (Eds.), *Experimental phonology* (pp. 13–44). Orlando, FL: Academic Press.

Lindblom, B. (1990). On the notion of "possible speech sound." *Journal of Phonetics, 18,* 135–142.

Lindblom, B., Lubker, J., & Gay, T. (1979). Formant frequencies of some fixed mandible vowels and a model of speech motor programming by predictive simulation. *Journal of Phonetics, 7,* 147–161.

Lindblom, B., & Maddieson, I. (1988). Phonetic universals in consonant systems. In L. Hyman & C. N. Li (Eds.), *Language, speech and mind* (pp. 62–78). London: Routledge.

Lisker, L. (1978). Rapid vs rabid: A catalogue of acoustic features that may cue the distinction. *Haskins Laboratories Status Report on Speech Research, 54,* 127–132.

Lively, S. & Pisoni, D. (1995). On prototypes and phonetic categories: A critical assessment of the perceptual magnet effect in speech perception. *Journal of Experimental Psychology: Human Perception and Performance, 23,* 1665–1679.

Löfquist, A. (1997). Theories and models of speech production. In W. Hardcastle & J. Laver (Eds.), *The handbook of phonetic sciences* (pp. 405–426). Oxford, England: Blackwell.

Lotto, A., & Kluender, K. (1998). General contrast effects in speech perception: Effect of preceding liquid on stop consonant identification. *Perception & Psychophysics, 60,* 602–619.

Lotto, A., Kluender, K., & Holt, L. (1997). Perceptual compensation for coarticulation by Japanese quail (*coturnix coturnix japonica*). *Journal of the Acoustical Society of America, 102,* 1134–1140.

Luce, P. (1986). *Neighborhoods of words in the mental lexicon.* Unpublished doctoral dissertation. Indiana University. Bloomington, Indiana.

Luce, P., & Pisoni, D. (1998). Recognizing spoken words: The neighborhood activation model. *Ear and Hearing, 19,* 1–36.

Maddieson, I. (1984). *Patterns of sounds.* Cambridge, England: Cambridge University Press.

Mann, V. (1980). Influence of preceding liquid on stop-consonant perception. *Perception & Psychophysics, 28,* 407–412.

Mann, V., & Liberman, A. (1983). Some differences between phonetic and auditory modes of perception. *Cognition, 14,* 211–235.

Mann, V., & Repp, B. (1981). Perceptual assessment of fricative-stop coarticulation. *Journal of the Acoustical Society of America, 69,* 1153–1169.

Marslen-Wilson, W. (1987). Functional parallelism in spoken word recognition. *Cognition, 25,* 71–102.

Marslen-Wilson, W., & Welsh, A. (1978). Processing interactions and lexical access during word recognition in continuous speech. *Cognitive Psychology, 10,* 29–63.

Massaro, D. (1987). *Speech perception by ear and eye: A paradigm for psychological inquiry.* Hillsdale, NJ: Lawrence Erlbaum.

Massaro, D. (1998). *Perceiving talking faces.* Cambridge, MA: MIT Press.

McClelland, J., & Elman, J. (1986). The TRACE model of speech perception. *Cognitive Psychology, 18,* 1–86.

McGurk, H., & MacDonald, J. (1976). Hearing lips and seeing voices. *Nature, 264,* 746–748.

Meyer, A. (1990). The time course of phonological encoding in language production: The encoding of successive syllables of a word. *Journal of Memory and Language, 29,* 524–545.

Meyer, A. (1991). The time course of phonological encoding in language production: Phonological encoding inside a syllable. *Journal of Memory and Language, 30,* 69–89.

Meyer, A., & Schrieffers, H. (1991). Phonological facilitation in picture-word interference experiments: Effects of stimulus onset asynchrony and types of interfering stimuli. *Journal of Experimental Psychology: Learning, Memory and Cognition, 17,* 1146–1160.

Miller, J. L., & Dexter, E. R. (1988). Effects of speaking rate and lexical status on phonetic perception. *Journal of Experimental Psychology: Human Perception and Performance, 14,* 369–378.

Miller, J. L., & Volaitis, L. (1989). Effect of speaking rate on the perceptual structure of a phonetic category. *Perception & Psychophysics, 46,* 505–512.

Mish, Frederick C. (1990). *Webster's Ninth New Collegiate Dictionary.* Springfield, MA: Merriam-Webster, Inc.

Motley, M. (1980). Verification of "Freudian slips" and semantically prearticulatory editing via laboratory-induced spoonerisms. In V. Fromkin (Ed.), *Errors in linguistic performance: Slips of the tongue, ear, pen, and hand* (pp. 133–147). New York: Academic Press.

Mowrey, R., & MacKay, I. (1990). Phonological primitives: Electromyographic speech error evidence. *Journal of the Acoustical Society of America, 88,* 1299–1312.

Nearey, T. (1997). Speech perception as pattern recognition. *Journal of the Acoustical Society of America, 101,* 3241–3254.

Newman, R., Sawusch, J., & Luce, P. (1997). Lexical neighborhood effects in phonemic processing. *Journal of Experimental Psychology: Human Perception and Performance, 23,* 873–889.

Norris, D. (1993). Bottom up connectionist models of "interaction." In G. Altmann & R. Shillcock (Eds.), *Cognitive models of speech processing: The second Sperlonga meeting* (pp. 211–234). Hillsdale, NJ: Lawrence Erlbaum.

Norris, D. (1994). Shortlist: A connectionist model of continuous word recognition. *Cognition, 52,* 189–234.

Norris, D. (1995). Signal detection theory and modularity: On being sensitive to the power of bias models of semantic priming. *Journal of Experimental Psychology: Human Perception and Performance, 21,* 935–939.

Norris, D., McQueen, J., & Cutler, A. (1999). Merging information in speech recognition: Feedback is never necessary. *Behavioral and Brain Sciences, 23,* 299–370.

Ohala, J. (1996). Listeners hear sounds not tongues. *Journal of the Acoustical Society of America, 99,* 1718–1728.

Ohman, S. (1966). Coarticulation in VCV utterances: Spectrographic measurements. *JASA, 39,* 151–168.

Orden, G. van, Pennington, B., & Stone, G. (1990). Word identification in reading and the promise of subsymbolic psycholinguistics. *Psychological Review, 97,* 488–522.

Pardo, J., & Fowler, C. A. (1997). Perceiving the causes of coarticulatory acoustic variation: Consonant voicing and vowel pitch. *Perception & Psychophysics, 59,* 1141–1152.

Parker, E. M., Diehl, R. L., & Kluender, K. R. (1986). Trading relations in speech and nonspeech. *Perception & Psychophysics, 39,* 129–142.

Perkell, J., Matthies, M., Svirsky, M., & Jordan, M. (1993). Trading relations between tongue-body raising and lip rounding in production of the vowel /u/: A pilot "motor equivalence" study. *Journal of the Acoustical Society of America, 93,* 2948–2961.

Pinker, S. (1994). *The language instinct.* New York: William Morrow.

Pisoni, D. B., & Tash, J. (1974). Reaction times to comparisons within and across phonetic boundaries. *Perception & Psychophysics, 15,* 285–290.

Pitt, M., & McQueen, J. (1998). Is compensation for coarticulation mediated by the lexicon? *Journal of Memory and Language, 39,* 347–370.

Porter, R., & Castellanos, F. X. (1980). Speech production measures of speech perception: Rapid shadowing of VCV syllables. *Journal of the Acoustical Society of America, 67,* 1349–1356.

Porter, R., & Lubker, J. (1980). Rapid reproduction of vowel-vowel sequences: Evidence for a fast and direct acoustic-motoric linkage. *Journal of Speech and Hearing Research, 23,* 593–602.

Prince, A., & Smolensky, P. (1993). *Optimality theory: Constraint interaction and satisfaction.* Unpublished manuscript, Rutgers University, New Brunswick, NJ, University of Colorado, Boulder.

Pulleyblank, D. (1997). Optimality theory and features. In D. Archangeli & D. T. Langendoen (Eds.), *Optimality theory: An overview* (pp. 59–101). Malden, MA: Blackwell.

Recasens, D. (1984). V-to-C coarticulation in Catalan VCV sequences: An articulatory and acoustical study. *Journal of Phonetics, 12,* 61–73.

Roelofs, A., & Meyer, A. (1998). Metrical structure in planning the production of spoken words. *Journal of Experimental Psychology: Learning, Memory and Cognition, 24,* 922–939.

Rosenblum, L. D. (1987). Towards an ecological alternative to the motor theory. *Perceiving-acting workshop, 2,* 25–28.

Ryle, G. (1949). *The concept of mind.* New York: Barnes and Noble.

Saltzman, E. (1991). The task dynamic model in speech production. In H. F. M. Peters, W. Hulstijn, & C. W. Starkweather (Eds.), *Speech motor control and stuttering* (pp. 37–52). Amsterdam: Elsevier Science.

Saltzman, E. (1995). Intergestural timing in speech production: Data and modeling. *Proceedings of the XIIIth International Congress of Phonetic Sciences, Stockholm, 2,* 84–88.

Saltzman, E., & Byrd, D. (1999). Dynamic simulations of a phase window model of relative timing. *Proceedings of the XIVth International Congress of Phonetic Sciences, San Francisco, 3,* 2275–2278.

Samuel, A. (1981). Phonemic restoration: Insights for a new methodology. *Journal of Experimental Psychology: General, 110,* 474–494.

Samuel, A. (1996). Does lexical information influence the perceptual restoration of phonemes. *Journal of Experimental Psychology: General, 125,* 28–51.

Samuel, A. (2000). Some empirical tests of Merge's architecture. In A. Cutler, J. McQueen, & R. Zondervan (Eds.), *Proceedings of the workshop on spoken word access processes* (pp. 51–54). Nijmegen: Max-Planck-Institute for Psycholinguistics.

Santiago, J., & MacKay, D. G. (1999). Constraining production theories: Principled motivation, consistency, homunculi, underspecification, failed predictions and contrary data. *Behavioral and Brain Sciences, 22,* 55–56.

Savariaux, C., Perrier, P., & Orliaguet, J. P. (1995). Compensation strategies for the perturbation of the rounded vowel [u] using a lip tube: A study of the control space in speech production. *Journal of the Acoustical Society of America, 98,* 2428–2442.

Sawusch, J., & Gagnon, D. (1995). Auditory coding, cues and coherence in phonetic perception. *Journal of Experimental Psychology: Human Perception and Performance, 21,* 635–652.

Sevald, C. A., Dell, G. S., & Cole, J. S. (1995). Syllable structure in speech production: Are syllables chunks or schemas. *Journal of Memory and Language, 34,* 807–820.

Shaiman, S. (1989). Kinematic and electromyographic responses to perturbation of the jaw. *Journal of the Acoustical Society of America, 86,* 78–88.

Shattuck-Hufnagel, S. (1979). Speech errors as evidence for a serial-ordering mechanism in sentence production. In W. Cooper & E. Walker (Eds.), *Sentence processing: Psycholinguistic studies presented to Merrill Garrett* (pp. 295–342). Hillsdale, NJ: Lawrence Erlbaum.

Shattuck-Hufnagel, S. (1983). Sublexical units and suprasegmental structure in speech production planning. In P. MacNeilage (Ed.), *The production of speech* (pp. 109–136). New York: Springer-Verlag.

Sinnott, J. M. (1974). *A comparison of speech sound discrimination in humans and monkeys.* Unpublished doctoral dissertation, University of Michigan.

Sproat, R., & Fujimura, O. (1993). Allophonic variation in English /l/ and its implications for phonetic implementation. *Journal of Phonetics, 21,* 291–311.

Stetson, R. H. (1951). *Motor phonetics.* Amsterdam: North Holland.

Stevens, K. (1989). On the quantal nature of speech. *Journal of Phonetics, 17,* 3–45.

Stevens, K., & Blumstein, S. (1981). The search for invariant correlates of phonetic features. In P. Eimas & J. Miller (Eds.), *Perspectives on the study of speech* (pp. 1–38). Hillsdale, NJ: Lawrence Erlbaum.

Stone, G., Vanhoy, M., & Van Orden, G. (1997). Perception is a two-way street: Feedforward and feedback in visual word recognition. *Journal of Memory and Language, 36,* 337–359.

Studdert-Kennedy, M. (1998). The particulate origins of language generativity: From syllable to gesture. In J. Hurford, M. Studdert-Kennedy, & C. Knight (Eds.), *Approaches to the evolution of language* (pp. 202–221). Cambridge, England: Cambridge University Press.

Sussman, H., Fruchter, D., Hilbert, J., & Sirosh, J. (1999a). Linear correlates in the speech signal: The orderly output constraint. *Behavioral and Brain Sciences, 21,* 287–299.

Sussman, H., Fruchter, D., Hilbert, J., & Sirosh, J. (1999b). Human speech: A tinkerer's delight. *Behavioral and Brain Sciences, 21,* 287–299.

Trout, J. D. (2001). The biological basis of speech: What to infer from talking to the animals. *Psychological Review, 108,* 523–549.

Tuller, B., Case, P., & Kelso, J. A. S. (1994). The nonlinear dynamics of speech categorization. *Journal of Experimental Psychology: Human Perception and Performance, 20,* 3–16.

Tuller, B., & Kelso, J. A. S. (1990). Phase transitions in speech production and their perceptual consequences. In M. Jeannerod (Ed.), *Attention and performance: Vol. 13. Motor representation and control* (pp. 429–452). Hillsdale, NJ: Lawrence Erlbaum.

Tuller, B., & Kelso, J. A. S. (1991). The production and perception of syllable structure. *Journal of Speech and Hearing Research, 34,* 501–508.

Turvey, M. T. (1990). Coordination. *American Psychologist, 45,* 938–953.

Vitevitch, M., & Luce, P. (1998). When words compete: Levels of processing in perception of spoken words. *Psychological Science, 9,* 325–329.

Vitevitch, M., & Luce, P. (1999). Probabilistic phonotactics and neighborhood activation in spoken word recognition. *Journal of Memory and Language, 40,* 374–408.

Warren, R. M. (1970). Perceptual restoration of missing speech sounds. *Science, 167,* 392–393.

Warren, R. M. (1985). Criterion shift rule and perceptual homeostasis. *Psychological Review, 92,* 574–584.

Waters, R. S., & Wilson, W. A., (1976). Speech perception by rhesus monkeys: The voicing distinction in synthesized labial and velar stop consonants. *Perception & Psychophysics, 19,* 285–289.

Weiss, P. (1941). Self differentiation of the basic pattern of coordination. *Comparative Psychology Monograph, 17,* 21–96.

Werker, J., & Tees, R. (1984). Cross-language speech perception: Evidence for perceptual reorganization during the first year of life. *Infant Behavior and Development, 7,* 49–63.

Zue, V. (1980). *Acoustic characteristics of stop consonants: A controlled study.* Bloomington: Indiana University Linguistics Club.

PART FOUR

HUMAN PERFORMANCE

CHAPTER 10

Attention

HOWARD EGETH AND DOMINIQUE LAMY

We live in a sea of information. The amount of information available to our senses vastly exceeds the information-processing capacity of our brains. How we deal with this overload is the topic of this chapter—*attention.* Consider your experience as you read this page. You are focused on just a word or two at a time. The rest of the page is available but is not being actively processed at this time. Indeed, quite apart from the other words on the page, there are many stimuli impinging on you that you are probably not aware of, such as the pressure of your chair against your back. Of course, as soon as that pressure is mentioned you probably shifted your attention to that source of stimulation, at which point you most likely stopped reading briefly. Some external stimuli do not need to be pointed out to you in order for you to become aware of them—for example, a mosquito buzzing around your face or the backfire of a car outside your window. These simple observations point to the selectivity of attention, its ability to shift quickly from one stimulus or train of thought to another, the difficulty we have in attending to more than one thing at a time, and the ability of some stimuli to capture attention. These are all important aspects of the topic of attention that will be explored in this chapter.

Perhaps the most fundamental point about attention is its selectivity. Attention permits us to play an active role in our interaction with the world; we are not simply passive recipients of stimuli. A great deal of the theoretical focus of research on attention has been concerned with how we come to select some information while ignoring the rest. Work in the years immediately following World War II led to the development of a theory that holds that information is filtered at an early stage in perceptual processing (Broadbent, 1958). According to this approach, there is a bottleneck in the sequence of processing stages involved in perception. Whereas physical properties such as color or spatial position can be extracted in parallel with no capacity limitations, further perceptual analysis (e.g., identification) can be performed only on selected information. Thus, unattended stimuli, which are filtered out as a result of attentional selection, are not fully perceived.

Subsequent research was soon to call filter theory into question. One striking result comes from Moray's (1959) studies using the dichotic listening paradigm, in which headphones are used to present separate messages to the two ears. The subject is instructed to shadow one message (i.e., repeat it back as it is spoken); the other message is unattended. Ordinarily, there is little awareness of the contents of the unattended message (e.g., Cherry, 1953). However, Moray found that when a message in the unattended ear is preceded by the subject's own name, the likelihood of reporting the unattended message is increased. This suggests that

The preparation of this chapter was supported in part by grants to Howard Egeth from NIMH (R01MH57388) and the FAA (2001-G-020). The authors would like to thank Alice Healy, Andy Leber, Melanie Palomares, Robert Proctor, Irving Weiner, and Steve Yantis for helpful comments, Robert Rauschenberger for preparation of the figures, and Terri Dannettel for technical help in the preparation of the manuscript.

the unattended message had not been entirely excluded from further analysis. Treisman (1960) proposed a modification of the filter model that was designed to handle this problem. She assumed the existence of a filter that attenuated the informational content of an unattended input without eliminating it entirely. This model was capable of predicting the occasional intrusion of meaningful material from an unattended message. However, the discrepant data that led Treisman to propose an attenuator instead of an all-or-none filter led other theorists in quite another direction. Thus, according to the late-selection view (e.g., Deutsch & Deutsch, 1963), perceptual processing operates in parallel and selection occurs after perceptual processing is complete (e.g., after identification), with capacity limitations arising only from later, response-related processes.

After nearly three decades of intensive research and debate, recent reviews have suggested that the apparent controversy between the two views may stem from the fact that the empirical data in support of each of them has typically been drawn from different paradigms.

For instance, Yantis and Johnston (1990) noted that evidence favoring the existence of late selection was typically obtained with divided-attention paradigms (e.g., Duncan, 1980; Miller, 1982). These findings showed only that there *can* be selection after identification, rather than entailing that selection *must* occur after identification. Yantis and Johnston (1990) set out to determine whether early selection is at all possible. By creating optimal conditions for the focusing of attention, they showed that subjects were able to ignore irrelevant distractors, thus demonstrating the perfect selectivity that is diagnostic of early selection. Yantis and Johnston proposed a hybrid model with a flexible locus for visual selection—namely, an early locus when the task involves filtering out irrelevant objects, and a late locus, after identification, when the task requires processing multiple objects.

Kahneman and Treisman (1984) noted that whereas the early-selection approach initially gained the lion's share of empirical support (e.g., von Wright, 1968), later studies presented mounting evidence in favor of the late-selection view (e.g., Duncan, 1980). They attributed this dichotomy to a change in paradigm that took place in the field of attention beginning in the late 1970s. Specifically, early studies used the *filtering paradigm,* in which subjects are typically overloaded with relevant and irrelevant stimuli and required to perform a complex task. Later studies used the *selective-set paradigm,* in which subjects are typically presented with few stimuli and required to perform a simple task. Thus, based on the observation that the conditions prevailing in the two types of study are very different, Kahneman and Treisman cautioned against any generalization across these paradigms.

Lavie and Tsal (1994) elaborated on this idea by proposing that perceptual load may determine the locus of selection. They showed that early selection is possible only under conditions of high perceptual load (viz., when the task at hand is demanding or when the number of different objects in the display is large), whereas results typical of late selection are obtained under conditions of low perceptual load. In other words, when the task is not demanding, the spare capacity that is unused by that task is automatically diverted to the processing of irrelevant stimuli.

The idea of a fixed locus of selection (whether early or late) implies a distinction between a preattentive stage, in which all information receives a preliminary but superficial analysis, followed by an attentive stage, in which only selected parts of the information receive further processing (Neisser, 1967). The preattentive stage has been further characterized as being automatic (i.e., triggered by external stimulation), spatially parallel, and unlimited in capacity, whereas the attentive stage is controlled (i.e., guided by the observer's goals and intentions), spatially restricted to a limited region, and limited in capacity. Within this framework, an important question becomes, *To what extent are stimuli processed during the preattentive stage?*

One implication of the proposed resolutions of the early-versus-late debate (Kahneman & Treisman, 1984; Lavie & Tsal, 1994; Yantis & Johnston, 1990) is that one cannot draw inferences from findings concerning the locus of selection to the question of how extensive preattentive processing is. That is, how efficient selection can be and what is accomplished during the preattentive stage are separate issues. For instance, the idea of a flexible locus of selection advanced by Yantis and Johnston (1990) implies that the level at which selection can be accomplished does not reveal intrinsic capacity limitations but depends only on task demands, and thus does not tell anything about preattentive processing. Similarly, the finding that perceptual load is a major determinant of selection efficiency (Lavie & Tsal, 1994) makes a useful methodological contribution, because it shows that a failure of selectivity does not reveal how extensively unattended objects are processed, but may instead reflect the mandatory allocation of unused attentional resources to irrelevant objects.

EFFICIENCY OF SELECTION

Failures of Selectivity

Various factors affect the efficiency of attentional selection. As was mentioned earlier, Lavie and Tsal (1994) proposed that low perceptual load may impair selectivity because spare attentional resources are automatically allocated to irrelevant distractors. Similarly, grouping between target and distractors may impair attentional selectivity. Another case of selectivity failure is evident in the ability of certain known-to-be-irrelevant stimuli to capture attention automatically.

Effects of Grouping on Selection

The principles of perceptual organization articulated by the Gestalt psychologists at the beginning of the last century (e.g., proximity, similarity, good continuation) correlate certain stimulus characteristics with the tendency to perceive certain parts of the visual field as belonging together—that is, as forming the same perceptual object. (For a fuller discussion of the Gestalt principles see the chapter by Palmer in this volume.) Kahneman and Henik (1981) considered the possibility that such grouping principles may impose strong constraints on visual selection, with attention selecting whole objects rather than unparsed regions of space. Beginning in the early 1980s, this object-based view of selection has gained increased empirical support from a variety of experimental paradigms.

Rock and Gutman (1981) showed object-specific attentional benefits in an early study. Subjects were presented with a sequence of 10 stimuli, each of which consisted of two overlapping outline drawings of novel shapes, one drawn in red and one in green. Thus, in each of the overlapping pairs, the two shapes occupied essentially the same overall location in space. Subjects were required to make aesthetic judgments concerning only those stimuli in one specific color (e.g., the red stimuli). At the end of the sequence, they were given a surprise recognition test. Subjects were much more likely to report attended items (those about which they had rendered aesthetic judgments) as old than to report unattended items as old. In fact, unattended items were as likely to be recognized as were new items.

This finding shows that attention can be directed to one of two spatially overlapping items. Note, however, that object-based selection was required by the task, which leaves open the possibility that object-based selection may not be mandatory. Moreover, the fact that the unattended stimulus was not recognized does not necessarily entail that it was not perceived; in particular, it may have been forgotten during the interval between presentation and the recognition test.

In a later article, Duncan (1984) explicitly laid out the distinction between space-based and object-based views of attention and tested them with a perceptual version of the Rock and Gutman (1981) memory task. In Duncan's study, object-based selection was no more task relevant than space-based selection. Subjects were presented with displays containing

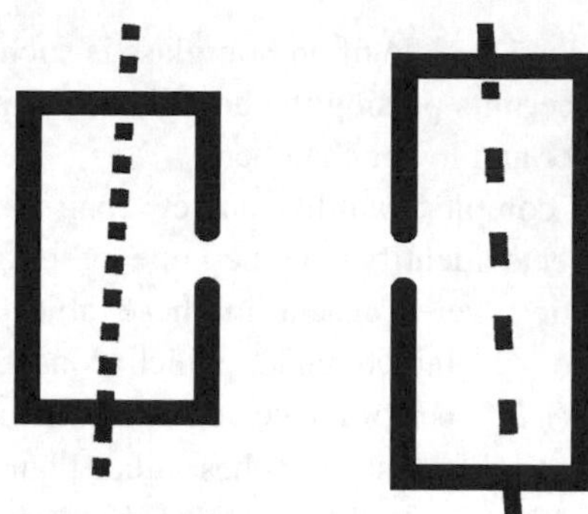

Figure 10.1 Two sample stimuli used in the study of object-based attention. Each stimulus consisted of two objects (a box and a line passing through the box). See text for further details. *Source:* Reprinted from Duncan (1984), with permission from the American Psychological Association.

two objects: an outline box and a line that was struck through the box (see Figure 10.1). The box was either short or tall, and had a gap on either its left or right side. The line was dashed or dotted and was slanted either to the right or to the left. Subjects were found to judge two properties of the same object as readily as one property. However, there was a decrement in performance when they had to judge two properties belonging to two different objects. These results showed a difficulty in dividing attention between objects that could not be accounted for by spatial factors, because the objects were superimposed in the same spatial region.

This very influential study has generated a whole body of research concerned with the issue of *object-based selection,* although it has been criticized by several authors (e.g., Baylis & Driver, 1993). Later studies where the problems associated with Duncan's study were usually overcome also demonstrated a cost in dividing attention between two objects (e.g., Baylis & Driver, 1993; but see Davis, Driver, Pavani, & Shepherd, 2000, for a spatial interpretation of object-based effects obtained using divided attention tasks).

Recently, Watson and Kramer (1999) added an important contribution to this line of research by attempting to specify a priori the stimulus characteristics that define the objects upon which selection takes place. They proposed a framework that allows one to predict whether object-based effects will be found, depending on stimulus characteristics. Borrowing from Palmer and Rock's (1994) theory of perceptual organization, they distinguished among three hierarchically organized levels of representation: (a) single, uniformly connected (UC) regions, defined as connected regions with uniform visual properties such as color or texture; (b) grouped-UC regions, which are larger representations made up of multiple single-UC regions grouped on the basis of Gestalt principles; and (c) parsed-UC regions, which are smaller representations segregated by parsing single-UC regions at points of concavity (e.g., the pinched middle of an hourglass is such a region of concavity; it permits parsing the hourglass into its two main parts, the upper and lower chambers).

They used complex familiar objects (pairs of wrenches) and had subjects identify whether one or two predefined target properties were present in these objects (see Figure 10.2). They examined under which conditions object-based effects (i.e., a performance cost for trials in which two targets belong to different wrenches rather than to the same wrench) could be obtained for each of the three representational levels. They found that (a) object-based effects are obtained when the to-be-judged object parts belong to the same single-UC region, but not when they are separate single-UC regions, and concluded that the default level at which selection occurs is the single-UC level; and (b) selection may occur at the grouped-UC level when it is beneficial to performing the task or when this level has been primed.

The finding that it is easier to divide attention between two properties when these belong to the same object suggests that perceptual organization affects the distribution of attention. Another empirical strategy used to reveal these effects is to show that subjects are unable to ignore distractors when these are grouped with the to-be-attended target (e.g., Banks & Prinzmetal, 1976). Other studies following this line of reasoning used the Eriksen response competition paradigm (Eriksen & Hoffman, 1973), where the presence of distractors flanking the target and associated with the wrong response is shown to slow choice reaction to the target (see the chapter by Proctor and Vu in this volume). They demonstrated that distractors grouped with the target (e.g., by common color or contour) slow response more than do distractors that are not grouped with it, even when target-distractor distance is the same in the two conditions (Kramer & Jacobson, 1991).

Perhaps the strongest support for the idea that attention selects perceptual groups rather than unparsed locations was provided by Egly, Driver, and Rafal's (1994) spatial cueing study. Subjects had to detect a luminance change at one of the four ends of two outline rectangles (see Figure 10.3). One end was precued. On valid-cue trials, the target appeared at the cued end of the cued rectangle, whereas on invalid-cue trials, it appeared either at the uncued end of the cued rectangle, or in the uncued rectangle. The distance between the cued location and the location where the target appeared was identical in both invalid-cue conditions. On invalid-cue trials, targets were detected faster when they belonged to the same object as the cue, rather than to the other object. Several replications were reported, with detection (e.g., Lamy & Tsal, 2000; Vecera, 1994) as well as identification tasks (e.g., Lamy & Egeth, 2002; Moore, Yantis, & Vaughan, 1998).

Although some individual studies have been criticized or proved difficult to replicate and limiting conditions for object-based selection have been identified (Lamy & Egeth, in press; Watson & Kramer, 1999), the overall picture that emerges from this selective review is that the segmentation of

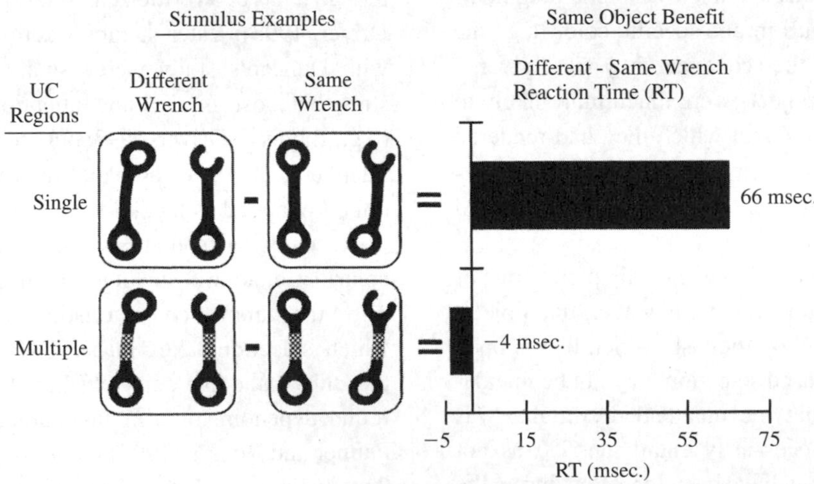

Figure 10.2 Sample stimuli and results from Experiment 1 of Watson and Kramer (1999). Each wrench in the two upper panels is homogeneously colored, and thus, according to Palmer and Rock (1994), may be characterized as a single uniformly connected (UC) region. The wrenches in the two lower panels, having stippled handles between solid black ends, each consist of multiple (i.e., three) UC regions. Subjects searched the display for the presence of two targets: an open end (shown as the upper right end in each panel), and a bent end (shown on the upper left end on the different-wrench examples, and the lower right end of the same-wrench examples). Mean reaction-time differences are shown on the right of the figure. They show a same-object effect for the single-UC wrenches, but not for the wrenches composed of multiple UC regions. *Source:* Reprinted from Watson and Kramer (1999), with permission of the Psychonomic Society.

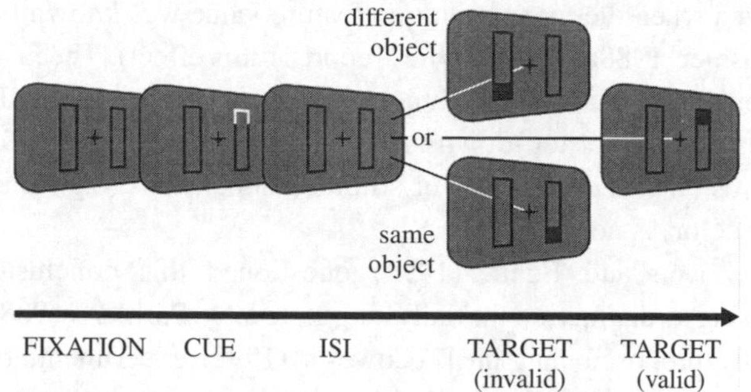

Figure 10.3 Examples of typical sequences of events in Experiments 1 and 2 of the study by Egly, Driver, and Rafal (1994). The white lines in the cue display represent the cue. The filled end of a bar represents the target. The target for the valid trial is in the same spatial location (upper right) as the cue. There are two types of invalid trials. In one, the target is the on the same bar as the cue, but at the opposite end, and thus requires a within-object shift of attention from the preceding cue. In the other, the target is on the uncued bar; this target requires a between-objects switch of attention from the cue. Note that the distance between the target and the cue is equal in the two types of invalid trial.

the visual field into perceptual groups imposes constraints on attentional selection. It is important to note, however, that this conclusion does not necessarily imply that grouping processes are preattentive. Indeed, in all the studies surveyed above, at least one part of the relevant object (i.e., of the perceptual group for which object-based effects were measured) was attended. As a result, one may conceive of the possibility that attending to an object part causes other parts of this object to be attended.

For this reason, a safer avenue to investigate whether grouping requires attention may be to measure grouping effects when the relevant perceptual group lies entirely outside the focus of attention. The studies pertaining to this issue will be discussed in the section on "Preattentive and Attentive Processing."

Capture of Attention by Irrelevant Stimuli

Goal-directed or *top-down* control of attention refers to the ability of the observer's goals or intentions to determine which regions, attributes, or objects will be selected for further visual processing. Most current models of attention assume that top-down selectivity is modulated by *stimulus-driven* (or *bottom-up*) factors, and that certain stimulus properties are able to attract attention in spite of the observer's effort to ignore them. Several models, such as the guided search model of Cave and Wolfe (1990), posit that an item's overall level of attentional priority is the sum of its bottom-up activation level and its top-down activation level. *Bottom-up activation* is a measure of how different an item is from its neighbors. *Top-down activation* (Cave & Wolfe, 1990) or *inhibition* (Treisman & Sato, 1990) depends on the degree of match between an item and the set of target properties specified by task demands. However, the relative weight allocated to each factor and the mechanisms responsible for this allocation are left largely unspecified. Curiously enough, no particular effort has been made to isolate the effects on visual search of bottom-up and top-down factors, which were typically confounded in the experiments held to support these theories (see Lamy & Tsal, 1999, for a detailed discussion). For instance, the fact that search for feature singletons is efficient has been demonstrated repeatedly (e.g., Egeth, Jonides, & Wall, 1972; Treisman & Gelade, 1980) and has been termed *pop-out search* (or *parallel feature search*). It is often assumed that this phenomenon reflects automatic capture of attention by the feature singleton. However, in typical pop-out search experiments, the singleton target is both task relevant and unique. Thus, it is not possible to determine in these studies whether efficient search stems from top-down factors, bottom-up factors, or both (see Yantis & Egeth, 1999).

Recently, new paradigms have been designed that allow one to disentangle bottom-up and top-down effects more rigorously. The general approach has been to determine the extent to which top-down factors may modulate the ability of an irrelevant salient item to capture attention. Discontinuities, such as uniqueness on some dimension (e.g., color, shape, orientation) or abrupt changes in luminance, are typically used as the operational definition of *bottom-up factors* or *stimulus salience*. Based on the evidence that has accumulated in the last decade or so, two opposed theoretical proposals have emerged. Some authors have suggested that preattentive processing is driven exclusively by bottom-up factors such as salience, with a role for top-down factors only later in processing (e.g., M. S. Kim & Cave, 1999; Theeuwes, Atchley, & Kramer, 2000). Others have proposed that attentional allocation is always ultimately contingent on top-down attentional settings (e.g., Bacon & Egeth, 1994; Folk, Remington, & Johnston, 1992). A somewhat intermediate viewpoint is that pure, stimulus-driven capture of attention is produced only by the abrupt onset of new objects, whereas other salient stimulus properties do not summon attention when they are known to be irrelevant (e.g., Jonides & Yantis, 1988). Several sets of findings have shaped the current state of the literature on how bottom-up and top-down factors affect attentional priority.

Beginning in the early 1990s, Theeuwes (e.g., 1991, 1992; Theeuwes et al., 2000) carried out several experiments suggesting that attention is captured by the element with the highest bottom-up salience in the display, regardless of whether this element's salient property is task relevant. *Capture* was measured as slower performance in parallel search

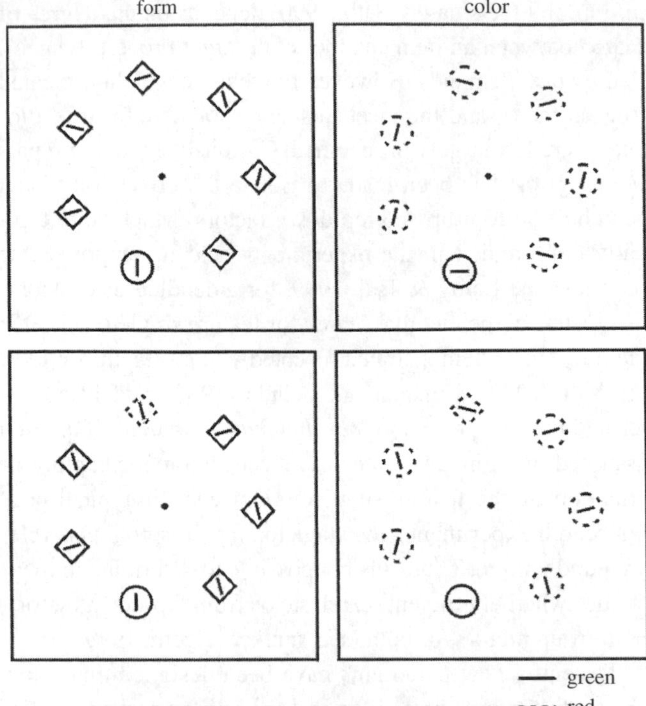

Figure 10.4 Sample stimuli from the studies of Theeuwes (1991, 1992). The subject always searched for a green circle among green diamonds (two left panels; form condition), or among red circles (two right panels; color condition), either without a distractor (top panels), or with a distractor (bottom panels). The line segment within the target element was horizontal or vertical (subjects had to indicate which); the line segments in the other forms were tilted 22.5 deg from horizontal or vertical. *Source:* Reprinted from Theeuwes (1992), with permission of the Psychonomic Society.

when an irrelevant salient object was present. For instance, Theeuwes (1991, 1992) presented subjects with displays consisting of varying numbers of colored circles and diamonds arranged on the circumference of an imaginary circle (see Figure 10.4). A line segment varying in orientation appeared inside each item, and subjects were required to determine the orientation of the line segment within a target item. In one condition, the target item was defined by its unique form (e.g., it was the single green diamond among green circles). In another condition, it was defined as the color singleton (e.g., it was the single red square among green squares). On half of the trials, an irrelevant distractor unique on an irrelevant dimension might be present. For instance, when the target item was a green diamond among green circles, a red circle was present. Theeuwes (1991) found that the presence of the irrelevant singleton slowed reaction times (RTs) significantly. However, this effect occurred only when the irrelevant singleton was more salient than the singleton target, suggesting that items are selected by order of salience. In a later study, Theeuwes (1992) reported distraction effects even when the target's unique feature value was known (see Pashler, 1988a, for an earlier report of this effect). Theeuwes concluded that when subjects are engaged in a parallel search, perfect top-down selectivity based on stimulus features (e.g., red or green) or stimulus dimensions (e.g., shape or color) is not possible.

Bacon and Egeth (1994) questioned this conclusion. Using a distinction initially suggested by Pashler (1988a), they proposed that in Theeuwes's (1992) experiment, two search strategies were available: (a) *singleton detection mode,* in which attention is directed to the location with the largest local feature contrast, and (b) *feature search mode,* which entails directing attention to items possessing the target visual feature. Indeed, the target was defined as being a singleton *and* as possessing the target attribute. If subjects used singleton detection mode, both relevant and irrelevant singletons could capture attention, depending on which exhibited the greatest local feature contrast. To test this hypothesis, Bacon and Egeth (1994) designed conditions in which singleton detection mode was inappropriate for performing the task. As a result, the disruption caused by the unique distractor disappeared. They concluded that irrelevant singletons may or may not cause distraction during parallel search for a known target, depending on the search strategy employed.

Another set of experiments revealed that abrupt onsets do produce involuntary attentional capture (Hillstrom & Yantis, 1994; Jonides & Yantis, 1988), whereas feature singletons on dimensions such as color and motion do not (e.g., Jonides & Yantis, 1988). These authors concluded that (a) abrupt onsets are unique in their ability to summon attention to their location automatically, and (b) feature singletons do not capture attention when they are task irrelevant.

The idea that the ability of a salient stimulus to capture attention depends on top-down settings—specifically, on whether subjects use singleton detection mode or feature search mode—is consistent with the contingent attentional capture hypothesis (e.g., Folk et al., 1992). According to this theory, attentional capture is ultimately contingent on whether a salient stimulus property is consistent with top-down attentional control settings. The settings are assumed to reflect current behavioral goals determined by the task to be performed. Once the attentional system has been configured with appropriate control settings, a stimulus property that matches the settings will produce "on-line" involuntary capture to its location. Stimuli that do not match the top-down attention settings will not capture attention.

Folk et al. (1992) provided support for this claim using a novel spatial cuing paradigm. In Experiment 3, for instance, subjects saw a cue display followed by a target display (see Figure 10.5). They were required to decide whether the target

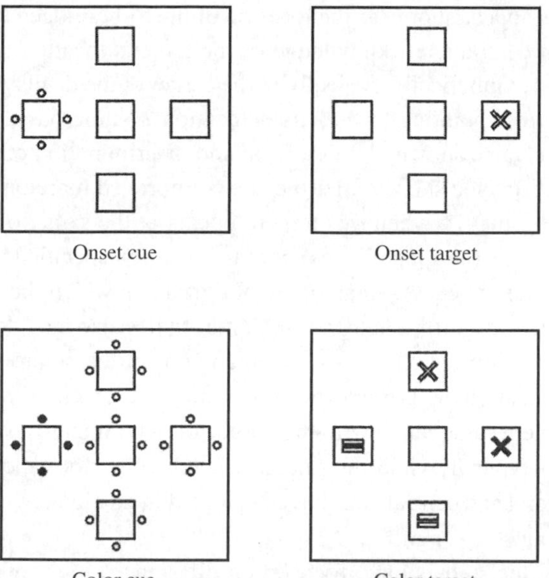

Figure 10.5 Sample cue displays and target displays used to investigate contingent attentional capture. In these examples, the cues appear in the left-hand location and the targets in the right-hand location (thus any trials composed from these particular components would be considered invalid trials). See text for further details. *Source:* Reprinted from Folk, Remington, and Johnston (1992), with permission of the American Psychological Association.

was an *x* or an "=" sign. The target was defined either as a color singleton target (e.g., the single red item among white items) or as an onset target (i.e., a unique abruptly onset item in the display). Two types of distractors were used. A color distractor consisted of four colored dots surrounding a potential target location, and arrays of white dots surrounded the remaining three locations. An onset distractor consisted of a unique array of four white dots surrounding one of the potential target locations. The two distractor types were factorially combined with the two target types, with each combination presented in a separate block. The locations of the distractor and target were uncorrelated. The authors reasoned that if a distractor were to capture attention, a target sharing its location would be identified more rapidly than a target appearing at a different location. Thus, they measured capture as the difference in performance between conditions in which distractors appeared at the target location versus nontarget locations. The question was whether capture would depend on the match between the salient property of the distractor and the property defining the target. The results showed that it did: Whereas capture was found when the distractor and target shared the same property, virtually no capture was observed when they were defined by different properties.

The foregoing discussion of attentional capture suggests that the conditions under which involuntary capture occurs remain controversial. Studies that reached incompatible conclusions usually presented numerous procedural differences. For instance, Folk (e.g., Folk et al., 1992) and Yantis (e.g., Yantis, 1993) disagree on what status should be assigned to new (or abruptly onset) objects. Yantis claims that abrupt onsets capture attention irrespective of the observer's intentions, whereas Folk argues that involuntary capture by abrupt onsets happens only when subjects are set to look for onset targets. Note, however, that Yantis's experiments typically involved a difficult search, for instance, one in which the target was a specific letter among distracting letters (e.g., Yantis & Jonides, 1990) or a line differing only slightly in orientation from surrounding distractors (e.g., Yantis & Egeth, 1999). In contrast, Folk's subjects typically searched for, say, a red target among white distractors—that is, for a target that sharply differed from the distractors on a simple dimension (e.g., Folk et al., 1992). Thus, the two groups of studies differed as to how much top-down guidance was available to find the target. This factor may possibly account for the better selectivity obtained in Folk's studies. Further research is needed to settle this issue.

The main point of agreement seems to be that an irrelevant feature singleton will not capture attention automatically when the task does not involve searching for a singleton target. This finding has been obtained using three different paradigms, under which attentional capture was gauged using different measures: a difference between distractor-present versus distractor-absent trials (Bacon & Egeth, 1994); a difference between trials in which the target and cue occupy the same versus different locations in spatial cueing tasks (e.g., Folk et al., 1992); and the difference between trials in which the target and salient item do versus do not coincide (e.g., Yantis & Egeth, 1999). Although most of the evidence provided by Theeuwes (e.g., 1992) for automatic capture was drawn from studies in which the target was a singleton, his position on whether capture occurs when the target is not a singleton is not entirely clear (see, e.g., Theeuwes & Burger, 1998).

Note, however, that in the current state of the literature, the implied distinction between *singleton detection mode,* in which any salient distractor will capture attention, and *feature search mode,* in which only singletons sharing a task-relevant feature will capture attention, suffers from two problems.

First, it is based on the yet-untested assumption that the singleton detection mode of processing is faster or less cognitively demanding than is the feature search mode. Indeed, one observes that subjects will use the feature search mode only if the singleton detection mode is not an option. For instance, when the strategy of searching for the odd one out is not available (e.g., Bacon & Egeth, 1994, Experiments 2 & 3), an irrelevant singleton does not capture attention. However, the same irrelevant singleton does capture attention when subjects search for a singleton target with a known feature (e.g., Bacon & Egeth, 1994, Experiment 1). Capture by the irrelevant singleton occurs despite the fact that using the singleton detection mode will tend to guide attention first toward a salient nontarget on 50% of the trials (or even on 100% of the trials; see M. S. Kim & Cave, 1999), whereas using the feature search mode will tend to guide attention directly to the target on 100% of the trials. The intuitive explanation for the fact that subjects use a strategy that is nominally less efficient is that the singleton-detection processing mode itself must be structurally more efficient. Yet, no study to date has put this assumption to test.

Second, in studies in which subjects must look for a unique target with a known feature, there is often an element of circularity in inferring from the data which processing mode subjects use. Indeed, if an irrelevant singleton captures attention, then the conclusion is that subjects used the singleton detection mode. If, in contrast, no capture is observed, the conclusion is that they used the feature search mode. However, the factors that induce subjects to use one mode rather than the other when both modes are available remain unspecified.

Selection by Location and Other Features

The foregoing section was concerned with factors that limit selectivity. Next, we turn to a description of the mechanisms underlying the different ways by which attention can be directed toward to-be-selected or relevant areas or objects.

Selection by Location

"Attention is quite independent of the position and accommodation of the eyes, and of any known alteration in these organs; and free to direct itself by a conscious and voluntary effort upon any selected portion of a dark and undifferenced field of view" (von Helmholtz, 1871, p. 741, quoted by James, 1890/1950, p. 438). Since this initial observation was made, a large body of research has investigated people's ability to shift the locus of their attention to extra-foveal loci without moving their eyes (e.g., Posner, Snyder, & Davidson, 1980), a process called *covert visual orienting* (Posner, 1980).

Covert visual orienting may be controlled in one of two ways, one involving peripheral (or exogenous) cues, and the other, central (or endogenous) cues. Peripheral cues traditionally involve abrupt changes in luminance—usually, abrupt object onsets, which on a certain proportion of the trials appear at or near the location of the to-be-judged target. With central cues, knowledge of the target's location is provided symbolically, typically in the center of the display (e.g., an arrow pointing to the target location). Numerous experiments have shown that detection and discrimination of a target displayed shortly after the cue is improved more on valid trials—that is, when this target appears at the same location as the cue (peripheral cues) or at the location specified by the cue (central cues)—than on invalid trials, in which the target appears at a different location. Some studies also include *neutral trials* or *no-cue trials,* in which none of the potential target locations is primed (but see Jonides & Mack, 1984, for problems associated with the choice of neutral cues). Neutral trials typically yield intermediate levels of performance. Peripheral and central cues have been compared along two main avenues.

Some studies have focused on differences in the way attention is oriented by each type of cue. The results from this line of research have suggested that peripheral cues capture attention automatically (but see the earlier section, "Capture of Attention by Irrelevant Stimuli," for a discussion of this issue), whereas attentional orienting following a central cue is voluntary (e.g., Müller & Rabbitt, 1989; Nakayama & Mackeben, 1989). Moreover, attentional orienting to the cued location was found to be faster with peripheral cues than with central cues. For instance, in Muller and Rabbitt's (1989) study, subjects had to find a target (*T*) among distractors (+) in one of four boxes located around fixation. The central cue was an arrow at fixation, pointing to one of the four boxes. The peripheral cue was a brief increase in the brightness of one of the boxes. With peripheral cues, costs and benefits grew rapidly and reached their peak magnitudes at cue-to-target onset asynchronies (SOAs) in the range of 100–150 ms. With central cues, maximum costs and benefits were obtained for SOAs of 200–400 ms.

Other studies have focused on differences in information processing that occur as a consequence of the allocation of attention by peripheral versus central cues. Two broad classes of mechanisms have been proposed to describe the effects of spatial cues. According to the *signal enhancement hypothesis* (e.g., Henderson, 1996), attention strengthens the stimulus representation by allocating the limited capacity available for perceptual processing. In other words, attention facilitates perceptual processing at the cued location. According to the uncertainty or noise reduction hypothesis (e.g., Palmer, Ames, & Lindsay, 1993) spatial cues allow one to exclude distractors from processing by monitoring only the relevant location rather than all possible ones. Thus, cueing attention to a specific location reduces statistical uncertainty or noise effects, which stem from information loss and decision limits, not from changes in perceptual sensitivity or limits of information-processing capacity.

In order to test the two hypotheses against each other, several investigators have sought to determine whether spatial cueing effects would be observed when the target appears in an otherwise empty field. The signal enhancement hypothesis predicts such effects, as the allocation of attentional resources at the cued location should facilitate perceptual processing at that location, even in the absence of noise. In contrast, the noise reduction hypothesis predicts no cueing effects with single-element displays, because no spatial uncertainty or noise reduction should be required in the absence of distractors.

This line of research has generated conflicting findings, with reports of small effects (Posner, 1980), significant effects (e.g., Henderson, 1991) or no effect (e.g., Shiu & Pashler, 1994). Relatively subtle methodological differences have turned out to play a crucial role. For instance, Shiu and Pashler (1994) criticized earlier single-target studies (Henderson, 1991) on the grounds that the masks presented at each potential location after the target display may have been confusable with the target, thus making the precue useful in reducing the noise associated with the masks. They compared a condition in which masks were presented at all potential locations vs. a condition with a single mask at the target location. Precue effects were found only in the former condition, supporting the idea that these reflect noise reduction rather than perceptual enhancement. However, recent evidence showed that spatial cueing effects can be found with a single target and mask, and are larger with additional distractors or masks. These findings suggest that attentional allocation by spatial precues leads both to signal enhancement at the cued location and noise reduction (e.g., Cheal & Gregory, 1997; Henderson, 1996).

Most of the reviewed studies employed informative peripheral cues, which precludes the possibility of determining whether the observed effects of attentional facilitation should be attributed to the exogenous or to the endogenous component of attentional allocation, or to both. Studies that employed non-informative peripheral cues (Henderson, 1996; Luck & Thomas, 1999) showed that these lead to both perceptual enhancement and noise reduction. Recently, Lu and Dosher (2000) directly compared the effects of peripheral and central cues and reported results suggesting a noise reduction mechanism of central precueing and a combination of noise reduction and signal enhancement for peripheral cueing.

To conclude, the current literature points to notable differences in the way attention is oriented by peripheral vs. central cues, as well as differences in information processing when attention is directed by one type of spatial cue vs. the other.

Is Location Special?

The idea that location may deserve a special status in the study of attention has generated a considerable amount of research, and the origins of this debate can be traced back to the notion that attention operates as a spotlight (e.g., Broadbent, 1982; Eriksen & Hoffman, 1973; Posner et al., 1980), which has had a major influence on attention research. According to this model, attention can be directed only to a small contiguous region of the visual field. Stimuli that fall within that region are extensively processed, whereas stimuli located outside that region are ignored. Thus, the spotlight model—as well as models based on similar metaphors, such as zoom lenses (e.g., Eriksen & Yeh, 1985) and gradients (e.g., Downing & Pinker, 1985; LaBerge & Brown, 1989)—endows location (or space) with a central role in the selection process. Later theories making assumptions that markedly depart from spotlight theories also assume an important role for location in visual attention (see Schneider, 1993 for a review). These include for instance Feature Integration Theory (Treisman & Gelade, 1980), the Guided Search model (Cave & Wolfe, 1990; Wolfe, 1994), van der Heidjen's model (1992, 1993), and the FeatureGate model (Cave, 1999).

A comprehensive survey of the debate on whether or not location is special is beyond the scope of the present endeavor (see for instance, Cave & Bichot, 1999; Lamy & Tsal, 2001, for reviews of this issue). Here, two aspects of this debate will be touched on, which pertain to the efficiency of selection. First, we shall briefly review the studies in which selectivity using spatial vs. non-spatial cues is compared. Then, the idea that selection is always ultimately mediated by space, which entails that selection by location is intrinsically more direct, will be contrasted with the notion that attention selects space-invariant object-based representations.

Selection by Features Other Than Location. Numerous studies have shown that advance knowledge about a non-spatial property of an upcoming target can improve performance (e.g., Carter, 1982). Results arguing against the idea that attention can be guided by properties other than location are typically open to alternative explanations (see Lamy & Tsal, 2001, for a review). For instance, Theeuwes (1989) presented subjects with two shapes that appeared simultaneously on each side of fixation. The target was defined as the shape containing a line segment, whereas the distractor was the empty shape. Subjects responded to the line's orientation. The target was cued by the form of the shape within which it appeared, or by its location. Validity effects were obtained with the location cue but not with the form cue. The author concluded that advance knowledge of form cannot guide attention. Note however, that it may have been easier for subjects to look for the filled shape, that is, to use the "defining attribute" (Duncan, 1985), rather than to use the form cue. In this case, subjects may simply not have used the cue, which would explain why it had no effect. According to this logic, using the location cue was easier than looking for the filled shape, but looking for the filled shape was easier than using the form cue. Thus, whereas Theeuwes's finding indicates that location cueing may be more efficient than form cueing, it does not preclude the possibility that form cues may effectively guide attention when no other, more efficient strategy is available.

Whereas it is generally agreed that spatial cueing is more efficient than cueing by other properties, there has been some debate as to whether qualitative differences exist between attentional allocation using one type of cue vs. the other (e.g., Duncan, 1981; Tsal, 1983). It seems that non-spatial cues differ from peripheral spatial cues in that they only prioritize the elements possessing the cued property rather than improving their perceptual representation. Moore and Egeth (1998) recently presented evidence showing that "feature-based attention failed to aid performance under 'data-limited' conditions (i.e., those under which performance was primarily affected by the sensory quality of the stimulus), but did affect performance under conditions that were not data-limited." Moreover, in several physiological studies that compared the event-related potentials (ERP) elicited by stimuli attended on the basis of location vs. other features, a qualitatively different pattern of activity was found for the two types of cues, which was taken to indicate that selection by location may occur at an earlier stage than selection by other properties (e.g., Hillyard & Munte, 1984; Näätänen, 1986).

Is Selection Mediated by Space? The idea that selection is always ultimately mediated by space, as is assumed in numerous theories of attention, has been challenged by research showing that attention is paid to space-invariant object-based representations rather than to spatial locations. Studies favoring the space-based view typically manipulated only spatial factors. The reasoning was that if spatial effects can be found when space is task irrelevant, then selection must be mediated by space, and does not therefore operate on space-invariant representations. In contrast, in studies supporting the space-invariant view, spatial factors were usually kept constant and objects were separated from their spatial location via motion. In spite of intensive investigation, no consensus has yet emerged.

It is important to make it clear that the body of research concerned with the effects of Gestalt grouping on the distribution of attention that was reviewed earlier is not relevant here. Both issues are generally conflated under the general term of "object-based selection." However, whether attention selects spatial or spatially-invariant representations concerns the medium of selection, whereas effects of grouping on attention speak to the efficiency of selection (see Lamy & Tsal, 2001; Vecera, 1994; Vecera & Farah, 1994, for further explication of this distinction).

One of the most straightforward methods used to investigate whether selection is fundamentally spatial is to have subjects attend to an object that happens to occupy a certain location in a first display and then attend to a different object occupying either the same or a different location in a subsequent display. With this procedure, sometimes referred to as the "post-display probe technique" (e.g., Kramer, Weber, & Watson, 1997), an advantage in the same-location condition is taken to support the idea that selection is space-based. The crux of this method is that it shows spatial effects in tasks where space is utterly irrelevant to the task at hand. For instance, Tsal and Lavie (1993, Experiment 4) showed that when subjects had to attend to the color of a dot (its location being task irrelevant), they responded faster to a subsequent probe when it appeared in the location previously occupied by the attended dot than in the alternative location (see M. S. Kim & Cave, 1995, for similar results).

Following a related rationale, other authors used rapid serial visual presentation (RSVP) tasks (e.g., McLean, Broadbent, & Broadbent, 1983) or partial report tasks (e.g., Butler, Mewhort, & Tramer, 1987) and showed that when subjects have to report an item with a specific color, near-location errors are the most frequent. In the same vein, Tsal and Lavie (1988) showed that when required to report one letter of a specified color and then any other letters they could remember from a visual display, subjects tended to report letters adjacent to the first-reported letter more often than letters of the same (relevant) color (see van der Heijden, Kurvink, de Lange, de Leeuw, & van der Geest, 1996, for a criticism and Tsal & Lamy, 2000, for a response). These results suggest that selecting an object by any of its properties is mediated by a spatial representation.

Other investigators attempted to demonstrate that selection is mediated by space by showing effects of distance on attention. In early studies, interference was found to be reduced as the distance between target and distractors increased (e.g., Gatti & Egeth, 1978). Attending to two stimuli was also found to be easier when these were close together rather than distant from each other (e.g., Hoffman & Nelson, 1981). More recent studies showed that distance modulates same- vs.-different object effects, as the difficulty in attending to two objects increases with the distance between these objects (e.g., Kramer & Jacobson, 1991; Vecera, 1994. See Vecera &

Farah, 1994, for a failure to find distance effects on object selection, and Kramer et al., 1997; Vecera, 1997, for a discussion of these results). There is some contrary evidence, suggesting that performance gets better as the separation between attended elements increases (e.g., Bahcall & Kowler, 1999; Becker, 2001) and still other findings showing that performance is unaffected by the separation between attended stimuli (e.g., Kwak, Dagenbach, & Egeth, 1991).

The experimental strategy of manipulating distance to demonstrate that selection is mediated by space has been criticized on several grounds. For instance, distance effects in divided attention tasks may only reflect the effects of grouping by proximity. That is, when brought closer together, two objects may be perceived as a higher-order object (e.g., Duncan, 1984). Accordingly, distance effects are attributed to effects of grouping on the distribution of attention and say nothing about whether or not the medium of attention is spatial. In tasks involving a shift of attention over small vs. large distances, the assumption underlying the use of a distance manipulation is that attention moves in an analog fashion through visual space, the time needed for attention to move from one location to another being proportional to the distance between them. However, this assumption may be unwarranted (e.g., Sperling & Weichselgartner, 1995).

Support for the Space-Invariant View. Whether attention may select from space-invariant object-based representations has been investigated by separating objects from their locations via motion. Kahneman, Treisman, and Gibbs (1992) found that the focusing of attention on an object selectively activates the recent history of that object (i.e., its previous states) and facilitates recognition when the current and previous states of the object match. They found this matching process, called "reviewing," to be successful only when the objects in the preview and probing displays shared the same "object-file," namely, when one object was perceived to move smoothly from one display to the other. This finding is typically taken to show that attention selects object-files, that is, representations that maintain their continuity in spite of location changes (e.g., Kanwisher & Driver, 1992).

Further support for the idea that attention operates in object-based coordinates comes from experiments by Tipper and his colleagues. They used the inhibition of return paradigm (e.g., Tipper, Weaver, Jerreat, & Burak, 1994) and the negative priming paradigm (Tipper, Brehaut, & Driver, 1990), as well as measurements of the performance of neglect patients (Behrmann & Tipper, 1994). Inhibition of return studies show that it is more difficult to return one's attention to a previously attended location. (Immediately after a spatial location is cued, a stimulus is relatively easy to detect at the cued location. However, after a cue-target SOA of about 300 ms, target detection is relatively difficult at the cued location. This is known as inhibition of return.) Negative priming experiments demonstrate that people are slower to respond to an item if they have just ignored it. (For a further discussion of negative priming, see the chapters by Proctor & Vu and McNamara & Holbrook in this volume.) Finally, the neurobiological disorder called *unilateral neglect* is characterized by the patients' failure to respond or orient to stimuli on the side contralateral to a lesion. Although early studies suggested that all three phenomena are associated with spatial locations (e.g., Posner & Cohen, 1984; Tipper, 1985; and Farah, Brunn, Wong, Wallace, & Carpenter, 1990, respectively), recent studies using moving displays showed that the attentional effects revealed by each of these experimental methods can be associated with object-centered representations.

Lamy and Tsal (2000, Experiment 3) used a variant of Egly et al.'s (1994) task. Subjects had to detect a target at one of the four ends of two objects, differing in color and shape. A precue appeared at one of the four ends and indicated the location where the target was most likely to show up. To dissociate the cued object from its location, the two objects were made to exchange locations between the cueing and target displays, by moving smoothly, on half of the trials. Reaction times were faster at the uncued location within the cued object than at an equally distant location within the uncued object, thus indicating that attention followed the cued object-file.

Conclusions. To summarize, in studies that measured only space-based effects using either the distance manipulation or the post-display probe technique, it was typically found that selection is mediated by space. In studies that measured the cost of redirecting attention to the same vs. a different object-file using moving objects while keeping spatial factors constant, attention was typically found to follow the object initially attended as it moved. Note that the strongest support for the view that selection is mediated by space comes from studies in which response to a new object was found to be faster if this object occupied the location of a previously attended object even when space was irrelevant to the task. Thus, in these studies, the object initially attended was no longer present in the subsequent display, where attentional effects were measured: A different object typically replaced it. Such findings may therefore only indicate that space-based selection prevails when the task is such that object continuity is systematically disrupted. In other words, selection may be space-based only under this specific condition, which does not abound in a natural environment.

On the other hand, support for the idea that selection operates on space-invariant representations of objects comes from studies showing that attending to an object entails that attentional effects remain associated with this object as it moves. However, space and object-file effects may not be as antithetical as is usually assumed. Finding that attention follows the cued object-file as it moves does not necessarily argue against the idea that selection is mediated by space. Attention may simply accrue to the locations successively occupied by the moving object (e.g., Becker & Egeth, 2000). As yet, no empirical data have been reported that preclude this possibility.

PREATTENTIVE AND ATTENTIVE PROCESSING

As was mentioned in the introductory part of this chapter, inquiring which processes are not contingent on capacity limitations for their execution amounts to inquiring which processes are preattentive, that is, do not require attention. "What does the preattentive world look like? We will never know directly, as it does not seem that we can inquire about our perception of a thing without attending to that thing" (Wolfe, 1998, p. 42). Therefore, it takes ingenious experimental designs to investigate the extent to which unattended portions of the visual field are processed.

Two general empirical strategies have traditionally been used to address this question, and differ somewhat in the underlying definition of "preattentiveness" they adopt. In some paradigms (e.g., visual search), whatever processes do not require focused attention and can be performed in parallel with attention widely distributed over the visual field are considered to be preattentive. In other paradigms (e.g., dual task), preattentive processes are those processes that can proceed without attention, that is, when attentional resources are exhausted by some other task. As we shall see, interpreting results obtained pertaining to preattentive processing has proved to be tricky.

Distributed Attention Paradigms

Visual Search

In a standard visual search experiment, the subject might be asked to indicate whether a specified target is present or absent, or which of two possible targets is present among an array of distractors. The total number of items in the display, known as the *set size* or *display size,* usually varies from trial to trial. The target is typically present on 50% of the trials, the display containing only distractors on the remaining trials. On each trial, subjects have to judge whether a target is present. In studies measuring reaction times, the search display remains visible until subjects respond. Of chief interest is the way reaction times vary as a function of set size on target-present and target-absent trials. In studies measuring accuracy, search displays are presented briefly and then masked. Accuracy can be plotted as a function of set size to reveal the processes underlying search. A common alternative approach is to determine the *exposure duration* (typically, the asynchrony between the onsets of the search display and of a subsequent masking display) required to achieve some fixed level of accuracy (e.g., 75% correct).

If finding the target (i.e., distinguishing it from the distractors) involves processes that do not require attention and are performed in parallel over the whole display, one expects to observe *parallel search.* With studies measuring reaction time, this means that the number of distractors present in the display should not affect performance; with studies measuring accuracy, this means that beyond a relatively short SOA, increasing the time available to inspect the display should not improve performance. Thus, parallel search is held to be diagnostic of preattentive (i.e., parallel, resource-free) processing. If, in contrast, distinguishing the target from the distractors involves processes that do require attention, then attention must be directed to the items one at a time (or perhaps to one subset of them at a time), until the target is found. In this case, the time required to find the target increases as the number of distractors increases. Moreover, if search is terminated as soon as the target is found, the target should be found, on average, halfway through the search process. Thus, search slopes for target-absent trials should be twice as large as for target-present trials (Sternberg, 1969). In studies measuring accuracy, if search requires attention, the more items in the display the longer the exposure time necessary to find the target.

This rationale was criticized very early on (Luce, 1986; Townsend, 1971; Townsend & Ashby, 1983). On the one hand, slopes are usually shallow, perhaps 10 ms per item, rather than null. In principle, they could reflect the operation of a serial mechanism that processes 100 items every second. However, such fast scanning is held to be physiologically not feasible (Crick, 1984).

On the other hand, linear search functions do not necessarily reflect serial processing. They are consistent with capacity-limited parallel processing, in which all items are processed at once, although the rate at which information accumulates at each location for the presence of the target or of a nontarget item decreases as the number of additional comparisons concurrently performed increases (Murdock, 1971; Townsend & Ashby, 1983).

Linear search functions are also compatible with unlimited-capacity parallel processing, in which set size affects the discriminability of elements in the array rather than processing speed per se. According to this view, the risk of confusing the target with a distractor increases as the number of elements increases, due to decision processes or to sensory processes (Palmer et al., 1993).

Finally, it has been argued that even the steepest serial slopes cannot reflect serial item-by-item attentional scanning. Whereas these range from 40 to 100 ms per item, Duncan, Ward, and Shapiro (1994) have claimed that attention must remain focused on an object for several hundred milliseconds before being shifted to another object. They referred to this period as the attentional dwell time. However, Moore, Egeth, Berglan, and Luck (1996) have shown that the long estimates of dwell time were caused, at least in part, by the use of masked targets.

Simultaneous versus Successive Presentation

Considering the complexities involved in interpreting search slopes, several investigators have explored the ability of individuals to discriminate between two targets in displays of a fixed size in which the critical manipulation involves the way the stimuli are presented over time. These experiments compare a condition in which all of the stimuli are presented simultaneously with a condition in which they are presented sequentially. (They may be presented one at a time or in larger groups.) Each stimulus is followed by a mask. The logic is that if capacity is limited, then it should be more difficult to detect a target when all of the stimuli are presented at the same time than when they are presented in smaller groups, which would permit more attention to be devoted to each item.

Shiffrin and Gardner (1972) showed that when a fairly simple discrimination was involved, such as indicating whether a *T* or an *F* target was present in a display (the nontargets here were hybrid *T-F* characters), and the number of display elements was small (four), then there was good evidence of parallel processing with unlimited capacity (see also Duncan, 1980). However, when the number of elements in the display was increased (e.g., Fisher, 1984) or the complexity of the stimuli was increased, advantages for successive presentation have been observed (e.g., Duncan, 1987; see also Kleiss & Lane, 1986).

Change Blindness

In an interesting variant of a search task, subjects are presented with a display that is replaced with a second display after a delay filled with a blank field, and have to indicate what, if anything, is different about the second display. The displays can be of any sort, from random displays of dots (Pollack, 1972) to real-life visual events (e.g., Simons & Levin, 1998). These conditions lead to a wide deployment of attention over the visual field. The striking result is that subjects show very poor performance in detecting the change, an effect that has been dubbed *change blindness*.

The change blindness effect is reminiscent of subjects' failure to detect changes that occur during a saccadic eye movement (e.g., Bridgeman, Hendry, & Stark, 1975). However, subsequent research has shown that it may occur independently of saccade-specific mechanisms (Rensink, O'Regan, & Clark, 1997). The two paradigms that are most frequently used to investigate the change blindness phenomenon are the *flicker paradigm* (Rensink et al., 1997) and the *forced-choice detection paradigm* (e.g., Pashler, 1988b; Phillips, 1974).

In the forced-choice detection paradigm, each trial consists of one presentation each of an original and a modified image. Only some of the trials contain changes, which makes it possible to use signal detection analyses in addition to measuring response latency and accuracy. For instance, Phillips (1974) presented matrices that contained abstract patterns of black and white squares and asked subjects to detect changes between the first and second displays. When the interstimulus interval was short (tens of milliseconds) the task was easy because subjects saw either flicker or motion at the location where a change was made. However, when the interstimulus interval was longer the task became very difficult because offset and onset transients occurred over the entire visual field and thus could not be used to localize the matrix locations that had been changed.

In the flicker paradigm, the original and the modified image are presented in rapid alternation with a blank screen between them. Subjects respond as soon as they detect the modification. The results typically show that subjects almost never detect changes during the first cycle of alternation, and it may take up to 1 min of alternation before some changes are detected (Rensink et al., 1997), even though the changes are usually substantial in size (typically about 20 $deg.^2$) and once pointed out or detected are extremely obvious to the observers. Moreover, changes to objects in the center of interest of a scene are detected more readily than peripheral, or marginal-interest, changes (Rensink et al.). Rensink et al. concluded that "visual perception of change in an object occurs only when that object is given focused attention; in the absence of such attention, the contents of visual memory are simply overwritten (i.e., replaced) by subsequent stimuli, and so cannot be used to make comparisons" (p. 372). Based on the change blindness finding and the results from studies of visual integration (e.g., Di Lollo, 1980), Rensink (2000) speculated that the preattentive representation of a scene "formed at any fixation can be highly detailed, but will have little coherence, constantly regenerating as long as the light continues to enter the eyes, and being created anew after each eye movement" (p. 22).

However, as was noted by Simons (2000), there are other possible accounts for the change blindness effect. "For example, we might retain all of the visual details across views, but never compare the initial representation to the current percept. Or, we might simply lack conscious access to the visual representation (or to the change itself) thereby precluding conscious report of the change" (p. 7). Thus, the finding of change blindness does not necessarily imply that the representation of the initial scene is absent. Further research using implicit measures to evaluate the extent to which this representation is preserved will be useful in order to expand our knowledge not only concerning the change blindness phenomenon but more generally, concerning preattentive vision and the role of attention.

Inattention Paradigms: Dual-Task Experiments

In *dual-task experiments* designed to explore what processes are preattentive, subjects have to execute a primary task and a secondary task. In some cases (e.g., Mack, Tang, Tuma, Kahn, & Rock, 1992; Rock, Linnett, Grant, & Mack, 1992), the primary task is assumed to exhaust subjects' processing capacities or to ensure optimal focusing of attention. If subjects can successfully perform the secondary task, then it is concluded that the processes involved in that task do not require attention and are therefore preattentive. The studies using this logic usually suffered from memory confounds, as subjects were typically requested to overtly report what they had seen in the secondary task displays after performing the primary task.

In other cases (e.g., Joseph, Chun, & Nakayama, 1997; Braun & Sagi, 1990, 1991), performance is compared between a condition in which subjects have to perform both the primary and the secondary task (a dual-task condition) and a condition in which subjects are required to perform only the secondary task (a single-task condition). Sometimes an additional single-task control condition is used, in which subjects are required to perform only the primary task. When a given task is performed equally well in the single- and dual-task conditions, this performance is taken to indicate that processes involved in the secondary task are preattentive, whereas poorer performance in the dual-task condition is held to show that these processes require attention. A caveat that is sometimes associated with this rationale is that the performance impairment produced by the addition of the primary task may reflect the cost of making two responses versus only one, rather than the inability to process the secondary task preattentively. (The results of the studies cited above are discussed later in this chapter.)

We now proceed to present a few examples of efforts to distinguish between processes that require attention and processes that are preattentive.

Further Explorations of Preattentive Processing

Grouping

Is perceptual grouping accomplished preattentively? This has proven difficult to answer, in part because grouping itself is a complex concept. For example, Trick and Enns (1997), following Koffka (1935, pp. 125–127), distinguish between *element clustering* and *shape formation*. Their research suggests that the former is preattentive, whereas the latter requires attention. Consider the stimuli in Figure 10.6. In two panels the stimuli consist of small diamond shapes made up of continuous lines, while in the other two panels the diamonds are made up of four small dots. Subjects had to determine the number of diamonds present in a display; reaction time was the dependent variable of chief interest. The two panels on the left yielded essentially identical results. The fact that clusters of dots can be counted as quickly as continuous line forms, even for small numbers of elements in the *subitizing* range (1–3 or 4 items), is consistent with the idea that the dots composing the diamonds were clustered preattentively. For related results, see Bravo and Blake (1990). Interestingly, when shape discrimination was required (counting the diamonds in the face of square distractors, as shown on the right side of Figure 10.6), the continuous line forms were counted more efficiently than the stimuli made of dots. This suggests that the shape formation process may not be preattentive.

That the shape formation component of grouping may require attention is consistent with a number of experiments that suggest grouping outside the focus of attention is not perceived (e.g., Ben-Av, Sagi, & Braun, 1992; Mack et al., 1992; Rock et al., 1992), suggesting that attention selects unparsed areas of the visual field and that grouping requires attention. Ben-Av et al. showed that subjects' performance in discriminating between horizontal and vertical grouping, or in simply detecting the presence or absence of grouping in the display background, was severely impaired when attention was engaged in a concurrent task of form identification of a target situated in the center of the screen. Mack et al. obtained similar results with grouping by proximity and similarity of lightness.

However, the dependent measure in these studies was subjects' conscious report of grouping. The fact that grouping cannot be overtly reported when attention is engaged in a demanding concurrent task does not necessarily imply that grouping requires attention. For instance, failure to report

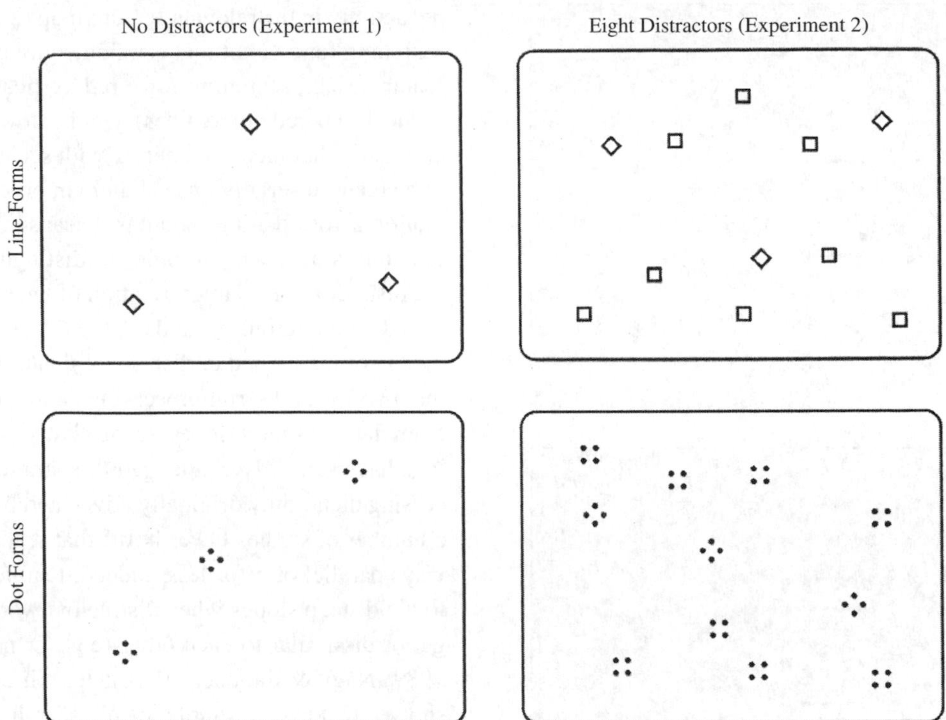

Figure 10.6 Sample stimuli of the kind used by Trick and Enns (1997) to investigate grouping.

grouping may result from memory failure. That is, grouping processes may occur preattentively, with grouping being perceived yet not remembered. In order to test this possibility, Moore and Egeth (1997) conducted a study with displays consisting of a matrix of uniformly scattered white dots on a gray background, in the center of which were two black horizontal lines (see Figure 10.7). Some of the dots were black, and on critical trials they were grouped and formed either the Ponzo illusion (Experiments 1 & 2) or the Müller-Lyer illusion (Experiment 3). Subjects attended to the two horizontal lines and reported which one was longer. Responses were clearly influenced by the two illusions. Therefore, the fact that elements lying entirely outside the focus of attention formed a group did affect behavior, indicating that grouping does not require attention. In a subsequent recognition test, subjects were unable to recognize the illusion patterns. This result confirmed the authors' hypothesis that implicit measures may reveal that subjects perceive grouping, whereas explicit measures may not. (For a further discussion of the consequences of inattention, see the chapter by Banks in this volume.)

Visual Processing of Simple Features versus Conjunctions of Features

Treisman's *feature integration theory* (FIT; e.g., Treisman & Gelade, 1980; Treisman & Schmidt, 1982) has inspired much of the research on visual search ever since its inception in the early 1980s. According to the theory, input from a visual display is processed in two successive stages. During the preattentive stage, a set of spatiotopically organized maps is extracted in parallel across the visual field, with each map coding the presence of a particular elementary stimulus attribute or feature (e.g., red or vertical). In the second stage, attention becomes spatially focused and serves to glue features occupying the same location into unified objects.

The phenomenon of *illusory conjunctions* (e.g., Treisman & Schmidt, 1982; Prinzmetal, Presti, & Posner, 1986; Briand & Klein, 1987) provides empirical support for the FIT. In the experiments of Treisman and Schmidt displays consisted of several shapes with different colors flanked by two black digits. The primary task was to report the digits, and the secondary task was then to report the colored shapes. Subjects tended to conjoin the different colors and forms erroneously. For instance, they might report seeing a red square and a blue circle when in fact a red circle and a blue square had been present. This finding is thus consistent with the idea that features are "free-floating" at the preattentive stage and that focused attention is needed to correctly conjoin them. However, the fact that subjects were unable to remember how the forms and colors were combined does not necessarily entail that such unified representations were not extracted in the absence of attention. Indeed, an alternative explanation is that illusory

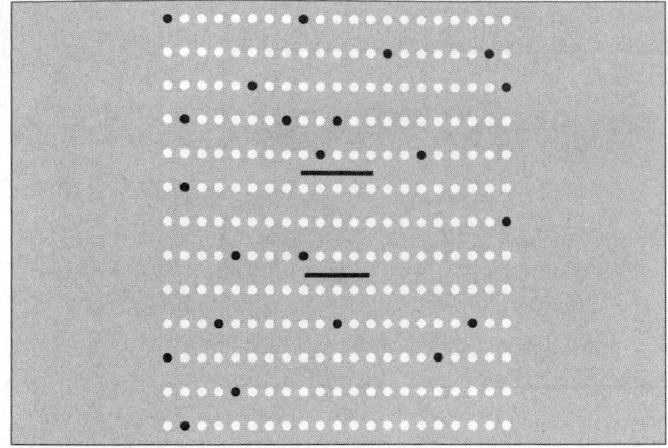

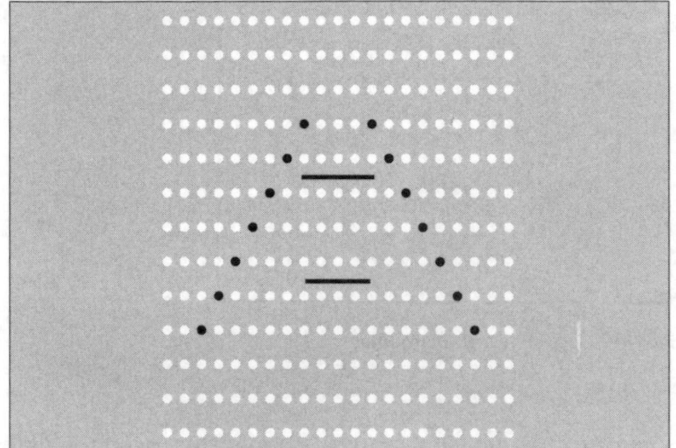

Figure 10.7 Sample stimuli used Moore and Egeth (1997). Subjects had to judge whether the upper or lower solid black line was longer. On the top is a typical noncritical trial, on the bottom a typical critical trial in which the black dots are arranged in such a manner as to induce the Ponzo illusion. *Source:* Reprinted from Moore and Egeth (1997), with permission of the American Psychological Association.

conjunctions may not reflect separate coding of different features at the preattentive stage but rather the tendency of memorial representations of unified objects to quickly disintegrate, and more so when no attention is available to maintain these representations in memory (Virzi & Egeth, 1984; Tsal, 1989). More recent studies suggest that rather than deriving from imperfect binding of correctly perceived features, illusory conjunctions may stem from target-nontarget confusions (Donk, 1999), uncertainty about the location of visual features (Ashby, Prinzmetal, Ivry, & Maddox, 1996) or post-perceptual factors (Navon & Ehrlich, 1995).

A central source of support for FIT also resides in the finding that searching for a target that is unique in some elementary feature (e.g., searching for a red target among green and blue distractors) yields fast reaction times and low error rates that are largely unaffected by set size (e.g., Treisman & Gelade, 1980; see also Egeth et al., 1972). According to the theory, features can be detected by monitoring in parallel the net activity in the relevant feature map (e.g., red). In contrast, searching for a target that is unique only in its conjunction of features (e.g., searching for a red vertical line among green vertical and red tilted lines) yields slower RTs and higher error rates that increase linearly with set size. Attention needs to be focused serially on each item in order to integrate information across feature modules, because correct feature conjunction is necessary in order to distinguish the target from the distractors. This interpretation of the results has been criticized on numerous grounds.

As we mentioned earlier, several alternative models show that parallel and serial processing cannot be directly inferred from flat and linear slopes, respectively. Moreover, new findings have seriously challenged the parallel versus serial processing dichotomy originally advocated by FIT. For instance, a number of studies have shown that feature search is not always parallel or effortless. Indeed, feature search was found to yield steep slopes when distractors were similar to the target or dissimilar to each other (e.g., Duncan & Humphreys, 1989; Nagy & Sanchez, 1990). Joseph et al. (1997) further showed that even a simple feature search (detecting an orientation singleton) that produces flat slopes when executed on its own may be impaired by the addition of a primary task with high attentional demands; the data for this experiment appear in the right panel of Figure 10.8. Although Braun (1998; see also Braun & Sagi, 1990) did not replicate Joseph et al.'s (1997) results when subjects were well practiced rather than naive, the Joseph et al. findings nevertheless, "seem to rule out a conceivable architecture for the visual system in which all feature differences are processed along a pathway that has a direct route to awareness, without having to pass through an attentional bottleneck" (Joseph et al., 1997, p. 807). Thus, Joseph et al.'s results do not challenge the idea that certain feature differences may be extracted preattentively and only overrule the notion that these differences may be reported without attention.

Other studies demonstrated that some conjunction searches are parallel (e.g., Duncan & Humphreys, 1989; Egeth, Virzi, & Garbart, 1984; Wolfe, Cave, & Franzel, 1989). For instance, Egeth et al. (1984) showed that subjects were able to limit their searches to items of a specific color or specific form. Wolfe et al. (1989) reported shallow search slopes for targets defined by conjunctions of color and form. Duncan and Humphreys (1989) showed that when target-distractor and distractor-distractor similarity are equated between feature and conjunction search tasks, performance on these tasks behaves no differently, and concluded that there is nothing intrinsically different between feature and conjunction search (see Duncan & Humphreys, 1992, and Treisman, 1992, for a discussion of this idea). Recently, McElree and

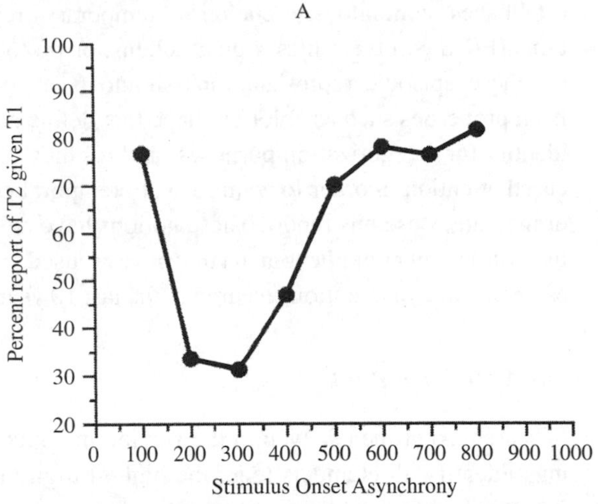

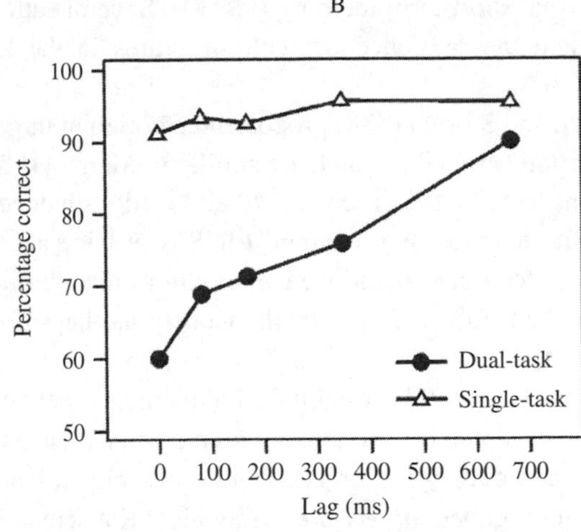

Figure 10.8 These figures show two different forms of the attentional blink. Left panel: Percentage of correct identifications of the second target as a function of the temporal lag from the onset of the first target to the onset of the second. Performance at the shortest lag exhibits what has been called *lag-1 sparing*. Reprinted from Chun and Potter (1995), with permission of the American Psychological Association. Right panel (filled symbols): Same as for left panel, except that performance at the shortest lag does not exhibit lag-1 sparing. The open symbols represent control condition performance on the "second" target when it was the only target in the display. Reprinted from Joseph, Chun, and Nakayama (1997), with permission of *Nature.* Visser, Bischof, and DiLollo (1999) discuss in detail the conditions that determine whether the attentional blink will be nonmonotonic or monotonic in form.

Carrasco (1999) used the response-signal speed-accuracy trade-off (SAT) procedure in order to distinguish between the effects of set size on discriminability and processing speed in both feature and conjunction search, and concluded that both feature and conjunctions are detected in parallel.

As a result of this spate of inconsistent findings, FIT has undergone several major modifications and alternative models have been developed, the most influential of which are the guided search model proposed by Cave and Wolfe (1990) and periodically revised by Wolfe (e.g., 1994, 1996) and Duncan and Humphreys'(1989) engagement theory, sometimes known as similarity theory. (The guided search model was described briefly in the section on "Capture of Attention by Irrelevant Stimuli.")

Stimulus Identification

When a subject searches through a display for a target, the nontarget items obviously must be processed deeply enough to allow their rejection, but this does not necessarily mean that they are fully identified. For example, in search for a digit among letters, one does not necessarily have to know that a character is a *G* to know that it is not a digit. Thus, it is possible that some evidence for parallel processing (e.g., Egeth et al., 1972) may not indicate the ability to *identify* several characters in parallel.

Pashler and Badgio (1985) designed a search task not subject to this shortcoming; they showed several digits simultaneously and asked subjects to name the highest digit. This task clearly requires identification of all of the elements. To assess whether processing was serial or parallel, they did not simply vary the number of stimuli in the display, they also manipulated the quality of the display. That is, on some trials the digits were bright and on others they were dim. The logic of this experimental paradigm, introduced by Sternberg (1967), is as follows: Let us suppose that a dim digit requires k ms longer to encode than does a bright digit. If the subject performs the task by serially encoding each item in the display, then the reaction time to a dim display with d digits should take kd ms longer than if the same display were bright. In other words, the effect of display size should interact multiplicatively with the visual quality manipulation. However, if encoding of all the digits takes place simultaneously, then the k ms should be added in just once regardless of display size. In other words, display size and visual quality should be additive. It was this latter effect that Pashler and Badgio actually observed in their experiment, suggesting that the identities of several digits could be accessed in parallel.

Attention: Types and Tokens

Recently, the notion that attention acts on the outputs of early filters dedicated to processing simple features such as motion, color, and orientation has been challenged by the idea that the units on which attention operates are temporary structures stored in a capacity-limited store usually referred to as the visual short-term memory (vSTM). Several authors have invoked the existence of such structures in the last 10 years or so.

Pylyshyn and Storm (1988) proposed the notion of fingers of instantiation (FINSTs), which are similar to Marr's (1983) place tokens because they represent filled locations independently of the features they contain. FINSTs provide access paths to attended objects, and we can monitor only a limited number of them (about five) simultaneously as they move across the visual field.

Kahneman et al. (1992) established a distinction between representations stored in long-term memory, which are used in identifying and classifying objects, and temporary episodic representations called *object-files* (see also Kahneman & Treisman, 1984). An object-file is a spatiotemporal structure in which the information about a particular object is stored and continually updated. Consequently, an object, the various properties of which change over time, retains its identity so long as the information about its successive states is assigned to the same temporary object-file. When the changes are large enough to disrupt the object's spatiotemporal continuity, a new object-file is set up. According to the theory, the information contained in an object-file becomes available when attention is allocated to it. Borrowing from this notion, Wolfe and Bennett (1997) suggested that preattentive object-files are loose collections of basic features, with focused attention needed to appreciate the relationships among features.

The distinction between types and tokens later proposed by Kanwisher (e.g., Kanwisher, 1987; Kanwisher & Driver, 1992) is essentially similar to Kahneman and Treisman's (1984) distinction between nodes stored in a long-term recognition network and temporary object-files, respectively. Kanwisher suggested that the activation of visual types and the processing of spatiotemporal token information are independent processes performed in parallel, and that attention is required to integrate the information they provide about events occurring in the visual field over space and time.

Finally, Rensink and colleagues (e.g., Rensink, 2000; Rensink et al., 1997) suggested that prior to focused attention, low-level *proto-objects* are formed in parallel across the visual field. Proto-objects are fairly complex preattentive representations with limited spatiotemporal coherence, and as such, they are inherently volatile. Unless a proto-object becomes the focus of attention, it is easily overwritten by a stimulus that subsequently occupies its location or disintegrates within a few hundred milliseconds, losing its continuity over time.

Although the various conceptualizations described above may differ along important aspects, they share a number of common assumptions, namely, that (a) the visual system establishes continuously changing temporary representations (FINSTs, object-files, object tokens, or proto-objects); (b) these episodic representations should be distinguished from properties such as color or shape that define an object's identity for categorization purposes; and (c) they require focused attention in order to acquire spatiotemporal continuity or mediate conscious report. These notions have helped shed light on a number of phenomena that have aroused great interest in the field of attention research in the last 10 years.

The Attentional Blink

In search experiments, even in the version in which subjects must identify all elements (e.g., the highest digit task), subjects typically must report only a single target on a trial. Do we have the capacity to report several targets when those targets are presented simultaneously or in temporal proximity? Duncan (1980) used the simultaneous-successive version of the visual search task described earlier. On each trial, four characters were shown at the ends of an imaginary plus sign. The characters at 9:00 and 3:00 made up the horizontal limb, those at 12:00 and 6:00 the vertical limb. The displays consisted of digit targets and letter nontargets. The occurrence of targets in the two limbs was independent. Thus, on a trial there might be a target in one or the other limb or in both limbs (however, there was never more than one target in a given limb). In the successive condition the two characters in one limb appeared briefly and were then masked; 500 ms later the two characters from the other limb were presented briefly and then masked. When only a single target was present on a trial there was no advantage for the successive-presentation condition. However, when there were two targets present, accuracy in the simultaneous condition was significantly worse than in the successive condition. This decrement cannot be attributed to the need to make two separate overt responses; when subjects simply had to count the number of targets (one vs. two targets present), the advantage in the successive condition remained. Note also that the same results were obtained when a simple orientation discrimination was required to find the targets.

Recently, an interesting extension of this double-detection task has been explored intensively and has provided new insights into what mechanisms may underlie the limits revealed by double-detection experiments. It turns out that after a subject has identified one target, it takes a surprisingly long time for the system to recover to the point that it can efficiently identify a second target (e.g., Broadbent & Broadbent, 1987; Weichselgartner & Sperling, 1987). This refractory period has been dubbed the *attentional blink* (Raymond, Shapiro, & Arnell, 1992) or *attentional dwell time* (Duncan et al., 1994).

In a typical attentional blink experiment, subjects are presented with an RSVP stream of stimuli displayed sequentially at fixation at a rate of about 10 per sec. They are required to respond to two targets (by detecting or identifying them, depending on the studies). When the SOA (or lag) between these targets ranges between 100 and 500 ms, performance on the second target, given that the first target was correctly reported, is severely impaired relative to that in a control condition in which the first target is ignored. Performance may or may not be spared at short SOAs, but in any event recovers to its baseline level at longer SOAs (see Figure 10.8). The attentional blink effect does not require that the targets be embedded in an RSVP stream. Duncan et al. (1994) obtained the effect using only two masked targets appearing at different spatial locations in the visual field.

Although the underlying mechanisms postulated by various researchers may differ (e.g., Chun & Potter, 1995; Raymond et al., 1992), the prevailing view is that the attentional blink phenomenon reveals the effects of insufficient attentional resources' being allocated to the second target. It is assumed that whereas the second target receives some initial processing, it does not reach the state at which it can be reported accurately. Shapiro, Driver, Ward, and Sorensen (1997) used a variant of the attentional blink paradigm in which subjects had to report three targets rather than two. They showed that performance on the third target (presented at an SOA long enough to allow recovery from the blink) was facilitated when it was semantically related to the second target, although the latter was poorly reported. They concluded that the attentional blink may reveal a failure to extract visual tokens, which mediate conscious perception, but not visual types, the activation of which underlies the priming effects found in their study (see also Chun, 1997, for the similar notion that the attentional blink may reflect a general limitation in the binding of correctly identified types to object tokens). For a further and more general discussion of refractory effects, see the chapter by Proctor and Vu in this volume.

Repetition Blindness

In typical *repetition blindness* experiments (e.g., Kanwisher, 1987; Mozer, 1989), subjects are required to report two targets embedded in an RSVP stream. Performance on the second target is worse when it is identical to the first target than when it is different, even when the two targets are separated by intervening stimuli. Similar results are obtained when the targets are presented simultaneously rather than sequentially (e.g., J. Kim & Kwak, 1990; Santee & Egeth, 1980). Kanwisher as well as several other investigators (e.g., Hochhaus & Marohn, 1991; Mozer, 1989) accounted for this phenomenon by proposing that the second occurrence of a repeated item is recognized as a visual type, but is not individuated as a distinct event. In other words, repetition blindness is assumed to reflect a failure in token individuation. In the absence of a separate token providing the spatiotemporal information necessary to distinguish between successive activations of the same type, the percept of the second instance becomes assimilated into the percept of the first instance. Consistent with this hypothesis, Chun (1997) showed that enhancing the episodic distinctiveness of the two targets by presenting them in different colors causes the repetition blindness effect to disappear, at least when subjects are given enough practice and learn to use the color cue.

The Aftermath of Attention

One might wonder about the aftermath of attention. If attending to an object binds together its features and permits the detection of a change in the object, for how long do these benefits last? Rensink (2000) suggests not very long. Based on the assumption that only one object can be represented at a time, if attention is switched to another object, the previously attended parts of the visual field revert to their original status as volatile proto-objects. Wolfe, Klempen, and Dahlen (2000) used a standard visual search task in which subjects looked for a target item among distractors. In one condition, a new search display was presented on each trial. In another condition, the same display was used repeatedly. The striking result was that search did not become more efficient with extensive use of the same display. Wolfe et al. concluded that the effects of attention have no cumulative effect on visual perception. As they put it, "attention to one object after another may cause an observer to learn what is in a visual display, but it does not cause that observer to see the visual display in any different manner" (p. 693). In short, to the extent that preattentive vision consists of "shapeless bundles of basic features" (Wolfe & Bennett, 1997), then so does postattentive vision.

CLOSING COMMENTS

In this chapter we have explored a large number of behavioral paradigms. We have considered what captures attention, and how attention behaves over space and time (and over objects situated in space and time). Although much has been learned about attention in the past century, and although the pace of discovery is (if anything) accelerating, there are many more questions that need to be answered. This review has been necessarily brief. For a more complete discussion of the topics covered in this chapter the reader is directed to the books by Pashler (1998) and van der Heijden (1992). It is worth noting explicitly that the present discussion has been almost entirely concerned with behavioral studies. We have barely touched on some of the other approaches that have been taken to the study of attention. In particular, readers wishing to learn about the neural bases of attention, as uncovered through studies using single-cell recordings in awake, behaving monkeys, through brain imaging or evoked potential studies of humans, or through the study of patients with neuropsychological disorders, should consult the book edited by Parasuraman (1998).

REFERENCES

Ashby, F. G., Prinzmetal, W., Ivry, R., & Maddox, W. T. (1996). A formal theory of feature binding in object perception. *Psychological Review, 103,* 165–192.

Bacon, W. F., & Egeth, H. E. (1994). Overriding stimulus-driven attentional capture. *Perception & Psychophysics, 55,* 485–496.

Bahcall, D. O., & Kowler, E. (1999). Attentional interference at small spatial separations. *Vision Research, 39,* 71–86.

Banks, W. P., & Prinzmetal, W. (1976). Configurational effects in visual information processing. *Perception & Psychophysics, 19,* 361–367.

Baylis, G. C., & Driver, J. (1993). Visual attention and objects: Evidence for hierarchical coding of location. *Journal of Experimental Psychology: Human Perception and Performance, 19,* 451–470.

Becker, L. (2001). *Attending over space and objects.* Unpublished doctoral dissertation, Johns Hopkins University, Baltimore, MD.

Becker, L., & Egeth, H. (2000). Mixed reference frames for dynamic inhibition of return. *Journal of Experimental Psychology: Human Perception and Performance, 26,* 1167–1177.

Behrman, M., & Tipper, S. P. (1994). Object-based attentional mechanisms: Evidence from patients with unilateral neglect. In L. Umilta & M. Moscovitch (Eds.), *Attention and performance XV: Conscious and nonconscious information processing* (pp. 351–375). Hillsdale, NJ: Erlbaum.

Ben-Av, M. B., Sagi, D., & Braun, J. (1992). Visual attention and perceptual grouping. *Perception & Psychophysics, 52,* 277–294.

Braun, J. (1998). Vision and attention: The role of training. *Nature, 393,* 424–425.

Braun, J., & Sagi, D. (1990). Vision outside the focus of attention. *Perception & Psychophysics, 52,* 277–294.

Braun, J., & Sagi, D. (1991). Texture-based tasks are little affected by second tasks requiring peripheral or central attentive fixation. *Perception, 20,* 483–500.

Bravo, M., & Blake, R. (1990). Preattentive vision and perceptual groups. *Perception, 19,* 515–522.

Briand, K. A., and R. M. Klein (1987). Is Posner's "beam" the same as Treisman's "glue"? On the relation between visual orienting and feature integration theory. *Journal of Experimental Psychology: Human Perception and Performance, 13,* 228–241.

Bridgeman, B., Hendry, D., & Stark, L. (1975). Failure to detect displacement of the visual world during saccadic eye movements. *Vision Research, 15,* 719–722.

Broadbent, D. E. (1958). *Perception and communication.* London: Pergamon Press.

Broadbent, D. E. (1982). Task combination and selective intake of information. *Acta Psychologica, 50,* 253–290.

Broadbent, D. E., & Broadbent, M. H. (1987). From detection to identification: Response to multiple targets in rapid serial visual presentation. *Perception & Psychophysics, 42,* 105–113.

Butler, E., Mewhort, D. J., & Tramer, S. C. (1987). Location errors in tachistoscopic recognition: Guesses, probe errors, or spatial confusions? *Canadian Journal of Experimental Psychology, 41,* 339–350.

Carter, R. C. (1982). Visual search with color. *Journal of Experimental Psychology: Human Perception and Performance, 8,* 127–136.

Cave, K. R. (1999). The FeatureGate model of visual selection. *Psychological Research, 62,* 182–194.

Cave, K. R., & Bichot, N. P. (1999). Visuo-spatial attention: Beyond a spotlight model. *Psychonomic Bulletin & Review, 6,* 204–223.

Cave, K. R., & Wolfe, J. M. (1990). Modeling the role of parallel processing in visual search. *Cognitive Psychology, 22,* 225–271.

Cheal, M., & M. Gregory (1997). Evidence of limited capacity and noise reduction with single-element displays in the location-cuing paradigm. *Journal of Experimental Psychology: Human Perception and Performance, 23,* 51–71.

Cherry, E. C. (1953). Some experiments on the recognition of speech with one and with two ears. *Journal of the Acoustical Society of America, 25,* 975–979.

Chun, M. M. (1997). Temporal binding errors are redistributed by the attentional blink. *Perception & Psychophysics, 59,* 1191–1199.

Chun, M. M., & M. C. Potter (1995). A two-stage model for multiple target detection in rapid serial visual presentation. *Journal of Experimental Psychology: Human Perception and Performance, 21,* 109–127.

Crick, F. H. C. (1984). The function of the thalamic reticular complex: The searchlight hypothesis. *Proceedings of the National Academy of Sciences USA, 81,* 4586–4590.

Davis, G., Driver, J., Pavani, F., & Shepherd, A. (2000). Reappraising the apparent costs of attending to two separate visual objects. *Vision Research, 40,* 1323–1332.

Deutsch, J. A., & Deutsch, D. (1963). Attention: Some theoretical considerations. *Psychological Review, 70,* 80–90.

DiLollo, V. (1980). Temporal integration in visual memory. *Journal of Experimental Psychology: General, 109,* 75–97.

Donk, M. (1999). Illusory conjunctions are an illusion: The effects of target-nontarget similarity on conjunction and feature errors. *Journal of Experimental Psychology: Human Perception and Performance, 25,* 1207–1233.

Downing, C. J., & Pinker, S. (1985). The spatial structure of visual attention. In M. I. Posner & O. S. M. Marin (Eds.), *Attention and performance XI* (pp. 171–187). Hillsdale, NJ: Erlbaum.

Duncan, J. (1980). The locus of interference in the perception of simultaneous stimuli. *Psychological Review, 87,* 272–300.

Duncan, J. (1981). Directing attention in the visual field. *Perception & Psychophysics, 30,* 90–93.

Duncan, J. (1984). Selective attention and the organization of visual information. *Journal of Experimental Psychology: General, 113,* 501–517.

Duncan, J. (1985). Visual search and visual attention. In M. I. Posner & O. S. M. Marin (Eds.), *Attention and performance XI* (pp. 85–105). Hillsdale, NJ: Erlbaum.

Duncan, J. (1987). Attention and reading: Wholes and parts in shape recognition—A tutorial review. In M. Coltheart (Ed.), *Attention and performance XII: The psychology of reading* (pp. 39–61). Hillsdale, NJ: Erlbaum.

Duncan, J., & Humphreys, G. W. (1989). Visual search and stimulus similarity. *Psychological Review, 96,* 433–458.

Duncan, J., & Humphreys, G. W. (1992). Beyond the search surface: Visual search and attentional engagement. *Journal of Experimental Psychology: Human Perception and Performance, 18,* 578–588.

Duncan, J., Ward, R., & Shapiro, K. L. (1994). Direct measurement of attentional dwell time in human vision. *Nature, 369,* 313–315.

Egeth, H., Jonides, J., & Wall, S. (1972). Parallel processing of multielement displays. *Cognitive Psychology, 3,* 674–698.

Egeth, H. E., Virzi, R. A., & Garbart, H. (1984). Searching for conjunctively defined targets. *Journal of Experimental Psychology: Human Perception and Performance, 10,* 32–39.

Egly, R., Driver, J., & Rafal, R. D. (1994). Shifting visual attention between objects and locations: Evidence from normal and parietal lesion subjects. *Journal of Experimental Psychology: General, 123,* 161–177.

Eriksen, C. W., & Hoffman, J. E. (1973). The extent of processing of noise elements during selective encoding from visual displays. *Perception & Psychophysics, 14,* 155–160.

Eriksen, C. W., & Yeh, Y. Y. (1985). Allocation of attention in the visual field. *Journal of Experimental Psychology: Human Perception and Performance, 11,* 583–597.

Farah, M. J., Brunn, J. L., Wong, A. B., Wallace, M. A., & Carpenter, P. (1990). Frames of reference for allocating attention to space: Evidence from the neglect syndrome. *Neuropsychologia, 28,* 335–347.

Fisher, D. L. (1984). Central capacity limits in consistent mapping, visual search tasks: Four channels or more? *Cognitive Psychology, 16,* 449–484.

Folk, C. L., Remington, R. W., & Johnston, J. C. (1992). Involuntary covert orienting is contingent on attentional control settings. *Journal of Experimental Psychology: Human Perception and Performance, 18,* 1030–1044.

Gatti, S. V., & Egeth, H. E. (1978). Failure of spatial selectivity in vision. *Bulletin of the Psychonomic Society, 11,* 181–184.

Helmholtz, H. von. (1871). Ueber die Zeit welche notig ist, damit ein Gesichtseindruck zum Bewusstsein kommt. *Berliner Monatsberichte, June 8,* 333–337.

Henderson, J. M. (1991). Stimulus discrimination following covert attentional orienting to an exogenous cue. *Journal of Experimental Psychology: Human Perception and Performance, 17,* 91–106.

Henderson, J. M. (1996). Spatial precues affect target discrimination in the absence of visual noise. *Journal of Experimental Psychology: Human Perception and Performance, 22,* 780–787.

Hillstrom, A. P., & Yantis, S. (1994). Visual motion and attentional capture. *Perception & Psychophysics, 55,* 399–411.

Hillyard, S. A., & Munte, T. F. (1984). Selective attention to color and location: An analysis with event-related brain potentials. *Perception & Psychophysics, 36,* 185–198.

Hochhaus, L. & Marohn, K. M. (1991). Factors in repetition blindness. *Journal of Experimental Psychology: Human Perception and Performance, 17,* 422–432.

Hoffman, J. E., & Nelson, B. (1981). Spatial selectivity in visual search. *Perception & Psychophysics, 30,* 283–290.

James, W. (1950). *The principles of psychology* (Vol. 1). New York: Dover. (Original work published 1890)

Jonides, J., & Mack, R. (1984). On the cost and benefit of cost and benefit. *Psychological Bulletin, 96,* 29–44.

Jonides, J., & Yantis, S. (1988). Uniqueness of abrupt visual onset in capturing attention. *Perception & Psychophysics, 43,* 346–354.

Joseph, J. S., Chun, M. M., & Nakayama, K. (1997). Attentional requirements in a preattentive feature search task. *Nature, 387,* 805–807.

Kahneman, D., & Henik, A. (1981). Perceptual organization and attention. In M. Kubovy & J. R. Pomerantz (Eds.), *Perceptual organization* (pp. 181–211). Hillsdale, NJ: Erlbaum.

Kahneman, D., & Treisman, A. (1984). Changing views on automaticity. In R. Parasuraman & R. Davies (Eds.), *Varieties of attention* (pp. 29–62). New York: Academic Press.

Kahneman, D., Treisman, A., & Gibbs, B. J. (1992). The reviewing of object files: Object-specific integration of information. *Cognitive Psychology, 24,* 175–219.

Kanwisher, N. G. (1987). Repetition blindness: Type recognition without token individuation. *Cognition, 27,* 117–143.

Kanwisher, N., & Driver, J. (1992). Objects, attributes, and visual attention: Which, what, and where. *Current Directions in Psychological Science, 1,* 26–31.

Kim, J., & Kwak, H. (1990). Stimulus repetition effects and the dimension-feature distinction in alternative targets. *Journal of Experimental Psychology: Human Perception and Performance, 16,* 857–868.

Kim, M. S., & Cave, K. R. (1995). Spatial attention in visual-search for features and feature conjunctions. *Psychological Science, 6,* 376–380.

Kim, M. S., & Cave, K. R. (1999). Top-down and bottom-up attentional control: On the nature of the interference from a salient distractor. *Perception & Psychophysics, 61,* 1009–1023.

Kleiss, J. A., & Lane, D. M. (1986). Locus and persistence of capacity limitations in visual information processing. *Journal of Experimental Psychology: Human Perception and Performance, 12,* 200–210.

Koffka, K. (1935). *Principles of Gestalt psychology*. New York: Harcourt Brace.

Kramer, A. F., & Jacobson, A. (1991). Perceptual organization and focused attention: The role of objects and proximity in visual processing. *Perception & Psychophysics, 50,* 267–284.

Kramer, A. F., Weber, T. A., & Watson, S. E. (1997). Object-based attentional selection: Grouped arrays or spatially invariant representations?: Comment on Vecera and Farah (1994). *Journal of Experimental Psychology: General, 126,* 3–13.

Kwak, H. W., Dagenbach, D., & Egeth, H. E. (1991). Further evidence for a time-independent shift of the focus of attention. *Perception & Psychophysics, 49,* 473–480.

LaBerge, D., & Brown, V. (1989). Theory of attentional operations in shape identification. *Psychological Review, 96,* 101–124.

Lamy, D., & Egeth, H. E. (2002). Object-based selection: The role of attentional shifts. *Perception & Psychophysics, 64,* 52–66.

Lamy, D., & Tsal, Y. (1999). A salient distractor does affect conjunction search. *Psychonomic Bulletin & Review, 6,* 93–98.

Lamy, D., & Tsal, Y. (2000). Object features, object locations and object-files: Which does selective attention activate and when? *Journal of Experimental Psychology: Human Perception and Performance, 26,* 1387–1400.

Lamy, D., & Tsal, Y. (2001). On the status of location in visual selective attention. *European Journal of Psychology, 13*(3), 305–342.

Lavie, N., & Tsal, Y. (1994). Perceptual load as a major determinant of the locus of selection in visual attention. *Perception & Psychophysics, 56,* 183–197.

Lu, Z. L., & Dosher, B. A. (2000). Spatial attention: Different mechanisms for central and peripheral temporal precues? *Journal of Experimental Psychology: Human Perception and Performance, 26,* 1534–1548.

Luce, R. D. (1986). *Response times: Their role in inferring elementary mental organization*. New York: Oxford University Press.

Luck, S. J., & Thomas, S. J. (1999). What variety of attention is automatically captured by peripheral cues? *Perception & Psychophysics, 61,* 1424–1435.

Mack, A., Tang, B., Tuma, R., Kahn, S., & Rock, I. (1992). Perceptual organization and attention. *Cognitive Psychology, 24,* 475–501.

Marr, D. (1983). *Vision*. San Francisco: W. J. Freeman.

McElree, B., & Carrasco, M. (1999). The temporal dynamics of visual search: Evidence for parallel processing in feature and conjunction searches. *Journal of Experimental Psychology: Human Perception and Performance, 25,* 1517–1539.

McLean, J. P., Broadbent, D. E., & Broadbent, M. H. (1983). Combining attributes in rapid serial visual presentation tasks. *Quarterly Journal of Experimental Psychology: Human Experimental Psychology, 35A,* 171–186.

Miller, J. (1982). Divided attention: Evidence for coactivation with redundant signals. *Cognitive Psychology, 14,* 247–249.

Moore, C. M., & Egeth, H. E. (1997). Perception without attention: Evidence of grouping under conditions of inattention. *Journal of Experimental Psychology: Human Perception and Performance, 23,* 339–352.

Moore, C. M., & Egeth, H. E. (1998). How does feature-based attention affect visual processing? *Journal of Experimental Psychology: Human Perception and Performance, 24,* 1296–1310.

Moore, C. M., Egeth, H. E., Berglan, L. R., & Luck, S. J. (1996). Are attentional dwell times inconsistent with serial visual search? *Psychonomic Bulletin & Review, 3,* 360–365.

Moore, C. M., Yantis, S., & Vaughan, B. (1998). Object-based visual selection: Evidence from perceptual completion. *Psychological Science, 9,* 104–110.

Moray, N. (1959). Attention in dichotic listening: Affective cues and the influence of instructions. *Quarterly Journal of Experimental Psychology, 11,* 56–60.

Mozer, M. C. (1989). Types and tokens in visual letter perception. *Journal of Experimental Psychology: Human Perception and Performance, 15,* 287–303.

Müller, H. J., & Rabbitt, P. M. A. (1989). Reflexive and voluntary orienting of visual attention: Time course of activation and resistance to interruption. *Journal of Experimental Psychology: Human Perception and Performance, 15,* 315–330.

Murdock, B. B. (1971). A parallel-processing model for scanning. *Perception & Psychophysics, 10,* 289–291.

Näätänen, R. (1986). The neural-specificity theory of visual selective attention evaluated: A commentary on Harter and Aine. *Biological Psychology, 23,* 281–295.

Nagy, A. L., & Sanchez, R. R. (1990). Critical color differences determined with a visual search task. *Journal of the Optical Society of America, 7,* 1209–1217.

Nakayama, K., & Mackeben, M. (1989). Sustained and transient components of focal visual attention. *Vision Research, 29,* 1631–1647.

Navon, D., & Ehrlich, E. (1995). Illusory conjunctions: Does inattention really matter? *Cognitive Psychology, 29,* 59–83.

Neisser, U. (1967). *Cognitive psychology*. New York: Appleton-Century-Crofts.

Palmer, J., Ames, C. T., & Lindsey, D. T. (1993). Measuring the effect of attention on simple visual search. *Journal of Experimental Psychology: Human Perception and Performance, 19,* 108–130.

Palmer, S., & Rock, I. (1994). Rethinking perceptual organization: The role of uniform connectedness. *Psychonomic Bulletin & Review, 1,* 29–55.

Parasuraman, R. (Ed.). (1998). *The attentive brain.* Cambridge, MA: MIT Press.

Pashler, H. (1988a). Cross-dimensional interaction and texture segregation. *Perception & Psychophysics, 43,* 307–318.

Pashler, H. (1988b). Familiarity and visual change detection. *Perception & Psychophysics, 44,* 369–378.

Pashler, H. (1998). *The psychology of attention.* Cambridge, MA: MIT Press.

Pashler, H., & Badgio, P. C. (1985). Visual attention and stimulus identification. *Journal of Experimental Psychology: Human Perception and Performance, 11,* 105–121.

Phillips, W. A. (1974). On the distinction between sensory storage and short-term visual memory. *Perception & Psychophysics, 16,* 283–290.

Pollack, I. (1972). Detection of changes in spatial position: Short-term visual memory or motion perception. *Perception & Psychophysics, 11,* 17–27.

Posner, M. I. (1980). Orienting of attention. *Quarterly Journal of Experimental Psychology, 32,* 3–25.

Posner, M. I., & Cohen, Y. A. (1984). Components of visual orienting. In H. Bouma & D. G. Bouwhuis (Eds.), *Attention and performance X: Control of language processes* (pp. 531–554). Hillsdale, NJ: Erlbaum.

Posner, M. I., Snyder, C. R., & Davidson, B. J. (1980). Attention and the detection of signals. *Journal of Experimental Psychology: General, 109,* 160–174.

Prinzmetal, W., Presti, D., & Posner, M. I. (1986). Does attention affect visual feature integration? *Journal of Experimental Psychology: Human Perception and Performance, 12,* 361–369.

Pylyshyn, Z. W., & Storm, R. W. (1988). Tracking multiple independent targets: Evidence for a parallel tracking mechanism. *Spatial Vision, 3,* 179–197.

Raymond, J. E., Shapiro, K. L., & Arnell, K. M. (1992). Temporary suppression of visual processing in an RSVP task: An attentional blink? *Journal of Experimental Psychology: Human Perception and Performance, 18,* 849–860.

Rensink, R. A. (2000). The dynamic representation of scenes. *Visual Cognition, 7,* 17–42.

Rensink, R. A., O'Regan, J. K., & Clark, J. J. (1997). To see or not to see: The need for attention to perceive changes in scenes. *Psychological Science, 8,* 368–373.

Rock, I., & Gutman, D. (1981). The effect of inattention on form perception. *Journal of Experimental Psychology: Human Perception and Performance, 7,* 275–285.

Rock, I., Linnett, C. M., Grant, P., & Mack, A. (1992). Perception without attention: Results of a new method. *Cognitive Psychology, 24,* 502–534.

Santee, J. L., & Egeth, H. E. (1980). Selective attention in the speeded classification and comparison of multidimensional stimuli. *Perception & Psychophysics, 28,* 191–204.

Schneider, W. X. (1993). Space-based visual attention models and object selection: Constraints, problems and possible solutions. *Psychological Research, 56,* 35–43.

Shapiro, K., Driver, J., Ward, R., & Sorensen, R. E. (1997). Priming from the attentional blink: A failure to extract visual tokens but not visual types. *Psychological Science, 8,* 95–100.

Shiffrin, R. M., & Gardner, G. T. (1972). Visual processing capacity and attentional control. *Journal of Experimental Psychology, 93,* 72–82.

Shiu, L., & Pashler, H. (1994). Negligible effect of spatial precuing on identification of single digits. *Journal of Experimental Psychology: Human Perception and Performance, 20,* 1037–1054.

Simons, D. J. (2000). Current approaches to change blindness. *Visual Cognition, 7,* 1–15.

Simons, D. J., & Levin, D. T. (1998). Failure to detect changes to people in a real-world interaction. *Psychonomic Bulletin and Review, 5,* 644–649.

Sperling, G., & Weichselgartner, E. (1995). Episodic theory of the dynamics of spatial attention. *Psychological Review, 102,* 503–532.

Sternberg, S. (1967). Two operations in character recognition: Some evidence from reaction time measurements. *Perception & Psychophysics, 2,* 45–53.

Sternberg, S. (1969). The discovery of processing stages: Extensions of Donders' method. In W. G. Koster (Ed.), *Attention and Performance II, Acta Psychologica, 30,* 276–315. Amsterdam: North Holland.

Theeuwes, J. (1989). Effects of location and form cuing on the allocation of attention in the visual field. *Acta Psychologica, 72,* 177–192.

Theeuwes, J. (1991). Cross-dimensional perceptual selectivity. *Perception & Psychophysics, 50,* 184–193.

Theeuwes, J. (1992). Perceptual selectivity for color and form. *Perception & Psychophysics, 51,* 599–606.

Theeuwes, J., Atchley, P., & Kramer, A. F. (2000). On the time course of top-down and bottom-up control of visual attention. In S. Monsell & J. Driver (Eds.), *Attention and performance XVIII: Control of cognitive processes* (pp.105–124). Cambridge, MA: MIT Press.

Theeuwes, J., & Burger, R. (1998). Attentional control during visual search: The effect of irrelevant singletons. *Journal of Experimental Psychology: Human Perception and Performance, 24,* 1342–1353.

Tipper, S. P. (1985). The negative priming effect: Inhibitory priming by ignored objects. *Quarterly Journal of Experimental Psychology: Human Experimental Psychology, 37A,* 571–590.

Tipper, S. P., Brehaut, J. C., & Driver, J. (1990). Selection of moving and static objects for the control of spatially directed action. *Journal of Experimental Psychology: Human Perception and Performance, 16,* 492–504.

Tipper, S. P., Weaver, B., Jerreat, L. M., & Burak, A. L. (1994). Object-based and environment-based inhibition of return of visual attention. *Journal of Experimental Psychology: Human Perception and Performance, 20,* 478–499.

Townsend, J. T. (1971). A note on the identifiability of parallel and serial processes. *Perception & Psychophysics, 10,* 161–163.

Townsend, J. T., & Ashby, F. G. (1983). *The Stochastic modeling of elementary psychological processes*. New York: Cambridge University Press.

Treisman, A. (1960). Contextual cues in selective listening. *Quarterly Journal of Experimental Psychology, 12,* 242–248.

Treisman, A. (1992). Spreading suppression or feature integration? A reply to Duncan and Humphreys (1992). *Journal of Experimental Psychology: Human Perception and Performance, 18,* 589–593.

Treisman, A., & Gelade, G. (1980). A feature-integration theory of attention. *Cognitive Psychology, 12,* 97–136.

Treisman, A., & Sato, S. (1990). Conjunction search revisited. *Journal of Experimental Psychology: Human Perception and Performance, 16,* 459–478.

Treisman, A., & Schmidt, H. (1982). Illusory conjunctions in the perception of objects. *Cognitive Psychology, 14,* 107–141.

Trick, L. M., & Enns, J. T. (1997). Clusters precede shapes in perceptual organization. *Psychological Science, 8,* 124–129.

Tsal, Y. (1983). Movement of attention across the visual field. *Journal of Experimental Psychology: Human Perception and Performance, 9,* 523–530.

Tsal, Y. (1989). Do illusory conjunctions support the feature integration theory? A critical review of theory and findings. *Journal of Experimental Psychology: Human Perception and Performance, 15,* 394–400.

Tsal, Y., & Lamy, D. (2000). Attending to an object's color entails attending to its location: Support for location-special views of visual attention. *Perception & Psychophysics, 62,* 960–968.

Tsal, Y., & Lavie, N. (1988). Attending to color and shape: The special role of location in selective visual processing. *Perception & Psychophysics, 44,* 15–21.

Tsal, Y., & Lavie, N. (1993). Location dominance in attending to color and shape. *Journal of Experimental Psychology: Human Perception and Performance, 19,* 131–139.

van der Heijden, A. H. C. (1992). *Selective attention in vision*. New York: Routledge.

van der Heijden, A. H. C. (1993). The role of position in object selection in vision. *Psychological Research, 56,* 44–58.

van der Heijden, A. H. C., Kurvink, A. G., de Lange, F., de Leeuw, F., & van der Geest, J. N. (1996). Attending to color with proper fixation. *Perception & Psychophysics, 58,* 1224–1237.

Vecera, S. P. (1994). Grouped locations and object-based attention: Comment on Egly, Driver, and Rafal (1994). *Journal of Experimental Psychology: General, 123,* 316–320.

Vecera, S. P. (1997). Grouped arrays versus object-based representations: Reply to Kramer, Weber, and Watson (1997). *Journal of Experimental Psychology: General, 126,* 14–18.

Vecera, S. P., & Farah, M. J. (1994). Does visual attention select objects or locations? *Journal of Experimental Psychology: General, 123,* 146–160.

Virzi, R. A., & Egeth, H. E. (1984). Is meaning implicated in illusory conjunctions? *Journal of Experimental Psychology: Human Perception and Performance, 10,* 573–580.

Visser, R. A. W., Bischof, W. F., & Di Lollo, V. (1999). Attentional switching in spatial and nonspatial domains: Evidence from the attentional blink. *Psychological Bulletin, 125,* 458–469.

von Wright, J. M. (1968). Selection in visual immediate memory. *Quarterly Journal of Experimental Psychology, 20,* 62–68.

Watson, S. E., & Kramer, A. F. (1999). Object-based visual selective attention and perceptual organization. *Perception & Psychophysics, 61,* 31–49.

Weichselgartner, E., & Sperling, G. (1987). Dynamics of automatic and controlled visual attention. *Science, 238,* 778–780.

Wolfe, J. M. (1994). Guided Search 2.0. A revised model of visual search. *Psychonomic Bulletin & Review, 1,* 202–238.

Wolfe, J. M. (1998). Visual search. In H. Pashler (Ed.), *Attention* (pp. 13–74). Hove, East Sussex, UK: Psychology Press Ltd.

Wolfe, J. M. (1997), & Bennett, S. C. (1997). Preattentive object files: Shapeless bundles of basic features. *Vision Research, 37,* 25–43.

Wolfe, J. M., Cave, K. R., & Franzel, S. L. (1989). Guided search: An alternative to the feature integration model for visual search. *Journal of Experimental Psychology: Human Perception and Performance, 15,* 419–433.

Wolfe, J. M., Klempen, N. L., & Dahlen, K. A. (2000). Postattentive vision. *Journal of Experimental Psychology: Human Perception and Performance, 26,* 693–716.

Yantis, S. (1993). Stimulus-driven attentional capture and attentional control settings. *Journal of Experimental Psychology: Human Perception and Performance, 19,* 676–681.

Yantis, S., & Egeth, H. E. (1999). On the distinction between visual salience and stimulus-driven attentional capture. *Journal of Experimental Psychology: Human Perception and Performance, 25,* 661–676.

Yantis, S., & Johnston, J. C. (1990). On the locus of visual selection: Evidence from focused attention tasks. *Journal of Experimental Psychology: Human Perception and Performance, 16,* 135–149.

Yantis, S., & Jonides, J. (1990). Abrupt visual onsets and selective attention: Voluntary vs. automatic allocation. *Journal of Experimental Psychology: Human Perception and Performance, 16,* 121–134.

CHAPTER 11

Action Selection

ROBERT W. PROCTOR AND KIM-PHUONG L. VU

Action selection refers to how a decision is made, typically under speeded response conditions, regarding which of two or more actions to take in response to perceptual events. It is usually studied using choice-reaction tasks in which subjects make assigned responses to stimuli as quickly and accurately as possible, and reaction time (RT) and response accuracy are measured. Action selection is often called response selection, but the term *action selection* has come to be used more frequently in recent years to emphasize that responses in choice-reaction tasks are goal-directed actions (Prinz, 1997).

A recent example of the importance of action selection concerns the notorious butterfly ballot used in Palm Beach County, Florida, for the 2000 U.S. presidential election. The ballot, shown in Figure 11.1, listed the names of candidates in two columns, with the appropriate response being to insert a stylus into a punch hole assigned to the candidate of choice among a centered column of holes. Although there was no fixed time limit for responding, the voters' task was speeded in the sense that a limited number of voting booths were available, with many voters needing to use them. With this ballot, some voters apparently selected the second punch hole on the list, voting for Pat Buchanan, rather than the third punch hole, which was assigned to Al Gore, for whom they intended to vote. This selection error occurred because Gore was listed in the second position of the left-hand column, immediately below the major opposing candidate, George W. Bush. Punch ballots most often list all candidates on the left-hand side, and their corresponding punch holes in the same order on the right. Because the relative location of Gore's position in the left-hand candidate list was second, previous experience would lead voters to expect that the second hole should be punched to vote for him. Moreover, this expectancy is consistent with the general principle that people tend to make the response whose relative location corresponds to that of the stimulus. Consequently, it is not surprising that some voters would incorrectly punch the second hole instead of the third one, even though arrows were used to mark the designated punch holes for the candidates. The poor design of the ballot caused a sufficient number of unintended votes for Buchanan, as well as discarded ballots for which the second and third holes were punched, costing Gore the election.

As this example illustrates, the topic of action selection is undoubtedly important. However, action selection tends to be viewed as peripheral to mainstream cognitive psychology in the United States, as reflected in the fact that the topic is rarely mentioned in undergraduate cognitive psychology

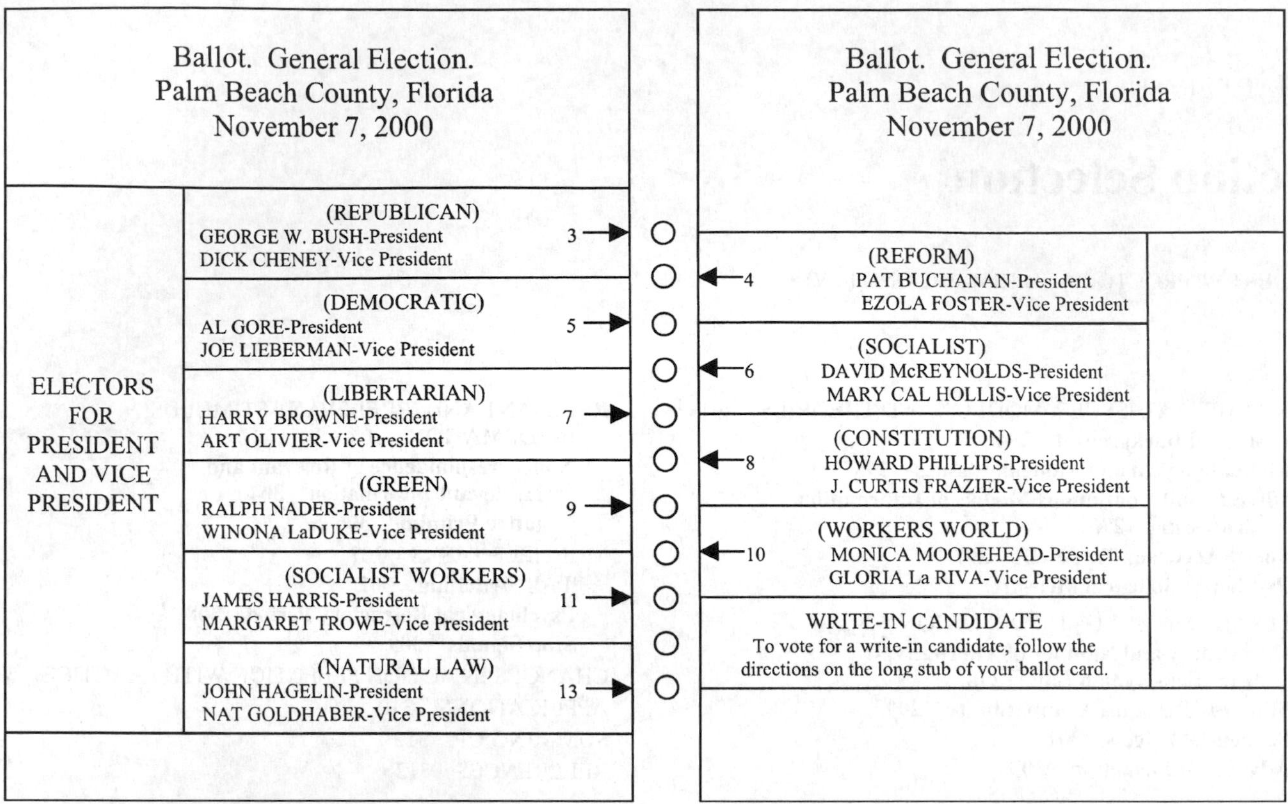

Figure 11.1 Sample Palm Beach County, Florida, butterfly ballot in the 2000 U.S. presidential election.

texts. The view of many cognitive psychologists seems to be that input and central processes can be investigated without one's having to be concerned with the translation of the outcome of these processes into output. This view is ironic, given that a major impetus to the rise of contemporary cognitive psychology was research on human performance conducted by Paul Fitts (see Fitts & Posner, 1967), Donald Broadbent (1958), and others in the 1950s. Outside of the United States, more recognition has been given to the importance of selection and execution of action in human information processing. Action selection is seen as fundamental because it involves the interface between perception and action. It is the theme of this chapter that action selection is of vital importance to many of the phenomena studied in contemporary cognitive psychology.

FUNDAMENTAL ISSUES, MODELS, AND THEORIES

Historical Background

Astronomers in the first half of the nineteenth century made the initial contribution to the measurement of RT by estimating the time it took a star to reach the midline of a grid of vertical lines relative to when it first entered the grid (see Woodworth, 1938). Although this was a clever method of measuring RT, individual differences in the judgment of when the star entered and reached the midline resulted in unreliable readings from one astronomer to another. In an attempt to compensate for individual differences, a personal equation was developed in which a constant correction was made in order to equate the readings of astronomers. However, later investigations showed that the difference between two individuals was not constant after all.

The study of action selection was of central concern in the last half of the nineteenth century. Interest arose out of issues concerning the speed of nerve transmission. Most physiologists thought that nerve transmission occurred too rapidly to be measured. However, Helmholtz (1850) conducted an experiment in which he stimulated motor nerves of frogs and measured the time between the presentation of the stimulus and muscular contraction. He estimated the rate of nerve transmission to be 26 m/s. One important contribution of this work was to demonstrate that the durations of nervous systems' processes are measurable. Helmholtz was also the first to measure RT in a procedure intended to calculate the speed of nerve transmission in humans. This procedure involved measuring RT as a function of the distance away from the brain by applying a shock to the skin. However, Helmholtz concluded that this procedure does not yield an accurate measure of nerve conduction because the measurements "suffer from the unfortunate fact that a part of the measured time depends on mental processes" (Helmholtz, 1867, p. 228).

The research of Helmholtz and others using RT to estimate the speed of nerve conduction stimulated Donders and his students to pursue the use of RT as a means for measuring mental processes. De Jagger's dissertation (1865/1970) provided the first account of the experiments conducted in Donders's lab. The first part of De Jagger's study continued Helmholtz's notion of measuring the speed of nerve conduction, but the second part focused on measuring the time required to identify a stimulus and select a motor response. In one set of experiments, subjects were required to respond to a red light with the right hand and a white light with the left hand. The mean RT was 356 ms, which was 172 ms longer than a simple reaction (executing a single response when a stimulus is presented) to the same stimuli. De Jagger interpreted this time as the duration of the central processes involving stimulus discrimination and response initiation.

Donders (1868/1969) formalized the subtractive method used by De Jagger, emphasizing specifically that the time for a particular process could be estimated by adding that process to a task and taking the difference in RT between the two tasks. He distinguished three types of reactions: type a (simple reaction), type b (choice reaction), and type c (go or no-go reaction; responding to one stimulus but not another). These types of reactions allowed separate measures of the stimulus identification and decision processes that were assessed together by De Jagger. The difference between the type-c and type-a reactions was presumed to reflect the time for stimulus identification, and the difference between the type-b and type-c reactions the time for "expression of the will" (p. 424).

Reaction time research in general, and the study of action selection in particular, continued to flourish throughout the remainder of the nineteenth century (see Jastrow, 1890). Wundt (1883) criticized Donders for using the type-c reaction as a measure of stimulus identification, reasoning that subjects must distinguish whether to respond, and suggested using the type-d reaction instead as a pure measure. The type-d reaction is measured by presenting subjects with the same stimuli and having them make the same response every time, as in the type-a reaction, with the difference being that they are instructed not to respond until they have identified the stimulus. However, Wundt's type-d reaction quickly fell out of favor because it is subjective and highly variable, and after practice, the type-d reaction time does not differ from the type-a reaction time. Criticisms of the subtractive method in general led to its demise in the early twentieth century.

Methodological and Modeling Issues

With the advent of the information processing approach in the 1950s and 1960s, the subtractive method was resurrected. This method, and the stage analysis of RT data on which it is based, came to be seen as sufficiently important to establish Donders as a major figure in the history of human performance. One influential use of the subtractive method was to estimate the rate of mental rotation by varying the amount that one stimulus was rotated relative to another to which it was to be compared, and measuring the slope of the RT function (Cooper & Shepard, 1973). Mean RT increased by approximately 240 ms for each 20° increase in angle of rotation, suggesting a continuous transformation in which each degree of rotation took about 12 ms.

A major advance in stage analysis of RT data was the development of the additive factors method by Sternberg (1969). Like the subtractive method, the additive factors method assumes discrete serial processing stages. However, whereas the subtractive method provides duration estimates for assumed stages, the additive factors method provides a way to discover the stages themselves. Sternberg showed that if two or more factors each influence the durations of distinct stages, then the effect of one of the factors on total duration will be invariant across the levels of the other factors: That is, the effects of the variables on RT will be additive. If two factors have interactive effects on RT, then they must influence at least one common stage. Thus, Sternberg advocated the use of multifactor experiments in which the presence or absence of interactions among variables is used to determine the processing stages involved in task performance.

Numerous limitations of the additive factors method have been enunciated, including problems of accepting the null hypothesis for additivity, assuming serial processing stages with no feedback loops, and assuming constant output from each stage (see Pachella, 1974). Despite these limitations, the method has proven to be a useful tool for analyzing the structure of information processing in a variety of tasks (see Sternberg, 1998) because, as Sanders (1998) states, "the method appears to provide a successful summary of a large amount of experimental data" (p. 65). One criterion for evaluating the additive factors method is stage robustness: The relations between two factors should not change as a function of levels of other factors. Although there are exceptions, stage robustness has generally been found to hold (Sanders, 1998).

Discrete and Continuous Models of Information Processing

Sternberg's (1969) additive factors method is based on a view of human information processing that assumes that the processing sequence between stimulus and response consists of a series of discrete stages, with each stage completing its processing before the next stage begins (see Figure 11.2, left side). Other models allow for parallel or overlapping operation of the different processing stages. McClelland (1979) proposed the cascade model of information processing in which partial information at one subprocess, or stage, is transferred to the next (see Figure 11.2, right side). The model assumes that each stage is continuously active and its output is a continuous value that is always available to the next stage. As in the discrete stage model, it is also assumed that each stage operates only on the output from the preceding stage. The output of the final stage indicates which of the alternative responses to execute.

In the cascade model, an experimental manipulation may affect a stage by altering the rate of activation or the asymptotic level of activation. The asymptotic level is equivalent to the stage output in the discrete stage model, which is assumed to be constant, and the activation rate determines the speed at which the final output is attained. Although the assumptions of the cascade model are different from those of the discrete stage model from which the additive factors method was derived, the patterns of interactivity and additivity can be interpreted similarly. For the cascade model, if two variables affect the rate parameter of the same stage, their effects on RT will be interactive; if each variable affects the rate parameter of a different stage, their effects on RT will be additive. In sum, as long as it is assumed that the final output of a stage does not vary as a function of the manipulations, then use of the additive factors logic to interpret the RT patterns does not require an assumption of discrete stages.

Miller (1988) argued that the discrete versus continuous categorization should not be viewed as dichotomous but as extremes on a quantitative dimension called *grain size*. In his words, "a variable is more continuous to the extent that it has a small grain size and more discrete to the extent that it has a large one" (p. 195). Miller suggested that there are three different senses in which models of human information processing can be characterized as discrete or continuous: representation, transformation, and transmission.

Representation refers to the discrete/continuous nature of the input and output codes for the processing stage. For example, if the locations of stimuli and responses in two-choice spatial reaction tasks are coded as left or right in terms of relative position, as is often assumed, the spatial codes are discrete. However, if the locations are represented in terms of absolute positions in physical space, then the representations are continuous. Transformation refers to the nature of the operation that the processing stage performs. The transformation of

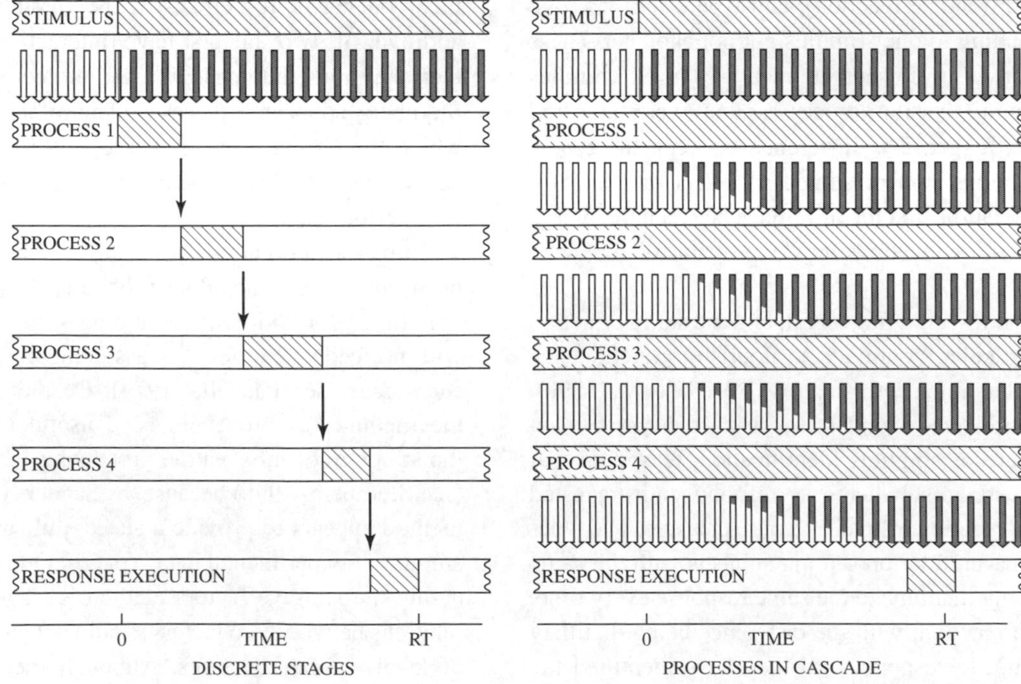

Figure 11.2 Illustration of discrete stage model (left) and cascade model (right). *Source:* From McClelland (1979).

the stage that performs mental rotation is typically characterized as continuous, in the sense that the mentally rotated object passes through a continuum of intermediate states from its initial orientation to the final orientation (Cooper & Shepard, 1973). A completely discrete transformation would be to generate the final orientation in a single step. For transmission, a model is discrete if the processing of successive stages cannot have temporal overlap; that is, the next stage in the sequence must wait until processing of the immediately preceding stage is completed. The discrete stage model underlying Sternberg's (1969) additive factors method postulates discrete representation and transmission. McClelland's (1979) cascade model, on the other hand, postulates continuous representation and transmission, as well as transformation.

A variety of models exist that are intermediate to these two extremes. One such model is Miller's (1982, 1988) asynchronous discrete coding model. This model assumes that most stimuli are composed of features, and these features are identified separately. The processing is discrete in that each feature must be identified before output about it can be passed to the response-selection stage. However, the identity of one feature may be passed to response selection while stimulus identification processes are still operating on other features.

Speed-Accuracy Trade-Off

The subtractive and additive factors methods are usually based solely on RT data. However, RT in any specific task situation is related to the number of errors that one is willing to make. A person can respond rapidly and make many errors or slowly and make few errors. This relation is called the speed-accuracy trade-off, and the function plotting speed versus accuracy is known as the speed-accuracy operating characteristic. For RT research, two aspects are crucial. First, if slower RT is accompanied by lower error rate, then the RT difference cannot be attributed unambiguously to differences in processing efficiency. Second, under conditions in which accuracy is relatively high, as in most choice-reaction studies, a small difference in error rate can translate into a large difference in RT.

Because of this close relation between speed and accuracy, some researchers have advocated conducting experiments in which the speed-accuracy criterion is varied between blocks of trials (Dosher, 1979; Pachella, 1974). There are numerous ways to vary the speed-accuracy criterion: payoffs, instructions, deadlines, time bands (responding within a certain time interval), and response signals (responding when the response signal is presented; see Wickelgren, 1977, for details). When a speed-accuracy function is obtained, information is provided about the intercept (time at which accuracy exceeds chance), asymptote (the maximal accuracy), and rate of ascension from the intercept to the asymptote, each of which may reflect different processes. Thus, a speed-accuracy study has the potential to be more informative than one based solely on RT. However, speed-accuracy studies require 5–10 times more data than RT studies and, in many circumstances, do not provide better insight into the phenomenon of interest.

In addition to looking at the macro trade-off produced by varying speed-accuracy emphasis across trial blocks, it is also possible to examine the micro trade-off between speed and accuracy of responding within a particular speed-accuracy emphasis block of the macro function. Models of the macro speed-accuracy trade-off can be differentiated on their predictions regarding the micro trade-off (Pachella, 1974). Osman et al. (2000) presented strong empirical evidence that the macro and micro functions are independent. In their experiment, which used psychophysiological measures as well as behavioral measures, the effect of the macro trade-off manipulation on RT was independent of that of the micro trade-off, with the micro trade-off affecting the part of the RT interval prior to the lateralized readiness potential (an indicator of readiness to make a left or right response, described later) and the macro trade-off affecting the part of the RT interval after the lateralized readiness potential.

The best models currently for characterizing both RT and accuracy data are sequential sampling models, which assume that information gradually accumulates until a response criterion is reached (Van Zandt, Colonius, & Proctor, 2000). In random walk models, a single counter records evidence as being toward one response criterion and away from another, or vice versa. In race models, separate counters accumulate evidence for each response alternative until the winner reaches criterion. Sequential sampling models explain the speed-accuracy trade-off by assuming that the response criteria are placed further from or closer to the starting point of the accumulation process. They explain biases toward one response over another in terms of asymmetric settings of the response criteria for the respective alternatives. Although continuous models of this general type describe the relation between speed and accuracy well, discrete models that allow pure guesses on a certain percentage of trials can also explain this relation.

Psychophysiological Measures

In recent years, there has been increasing use of psychophysiological measures to supplement RT data (Rugg & Coles, 1995). One of the most popular methods is to record electroencephalograms (EEG), which measure voltage changes in the brain over time from electrodes placed on the scalp. Of particular concern are event-related potentials (ERPs); these are voltage changes in the EEG elicited by a specific event (e.g., a stimulus onset), averaged across many trials to remove background EEG activities. One reason for the popularity of ERPs is that, while a task is being performed, they provide continuous measures of brain activity presumed to be systematically related to cognitive processes. By comparing the effects of task manipulations on various ERP components, their onset latencies, and their scalp distributions, one can make relatively detailed inferences about the cognitive processes. These inferences can be used, along with behavioral measures, to evaluate alternative information processing models.

There are a number of different ERP components, or features, that are indicators of different aspects of processing. These are labeled according to their polarity, positive (P) or negative (N), and their sequence or latency. Early components such as P1 and N1 (the first positive and negative components, respectively) are associated with early perceptual processes. They are called *exogenous components* because they occur in close temporal proximity to the stimulus event and have a stable latency with respect to it. Later components such as P3 (or P300) reflect cognitive processes such as attention. These components are called *endogenous* because they are a function of the task demands and have a more variable latency than the exogenous components. For example, when an occasional target stimulus is interspersed in a stream of standards, the P3 is observed in response to targets, but not to standards.

A measure that has been used extensively in studies of action selection is the lateralized readiness potential (LRP; Eimer, 1998), mentioned previously. This potential can be recorded in choice-reaction tasks that require a response with the left or right hand. It is a measure of differential activation of the lateral motor areas of the visual cortex that occurs shortly before and during execution of a response. The asymmetric activation favors the motor area contralateral to the hand making the response, because this is the area that controls the hand. Of importance, the LRP has been obtained in situations in which no overt response is ever executed, allowing it to be used as an index of covert, partial response activation. The LRP is thus a measure of the difference in activity from the two sides of the brain that can be used as an indicator of covert reaction tendencies, to determine whether a response has been prepared even when it is not actually executed. It can also be used to determine whether the effects of a variable are prior or subsequent to response preparation, as Osman et al. (2000) did. Falkenstein, Hohnsbein, and Hoormann (1994) suggested that the latency of the LRP is linked most closely to central decision processes (i.e., action selection), whereas the peak is more closely related to central motor processes.

Electrophysiological measurements and recordings of magnetic fields do not have the spatial resolution needed to provide precise information about the brain structures that produce the recorded activity. Recently developed neuroimaging methods, including positron-emission tomography (PET) and functional magnetic resonance imaging (fMRI), measure changes in blood flow associated with neuronal activity in different regions of the brain. These methods have poor temporal resolution but much higher spatial resolution than the electrophysiological methods. Combined use of neuroimaging and electrophysiological methods provides the greatest degree of both spatial and temporal resolution (Mangun, Hopfinger, & Heinze, 1998).

RELEVANT STIMULUS INFORMATION

Uncertainty and Number of Alternatives: The Hick-Hyman Law

Merkel (1885), described in Woodworth (1938), provided the initial demonstration that RT increases as a function of the number of possible alternatives. In Merkel's experiment, the Arabic numerals 1–5 were assigned to the left hand and the Roman numerals I–V to the right hand, in left-to-right order. Results showed that when the number of alternatives increased from 2 to 10 choices, mean RT increased from approximately 300 ms to a little over 600 ms.

Contemporary research dates from Hick's (1952) and Hyman's (1953) studies in which the increase in RT with number of alternatives was tied to information theory, which quantifies information in terms of uncertainty (for N equally likely alternatives, the number of bits of information is $\log_2 N$). The stimuli in Hick's study were 10 lamps arranged in an irregular circle, and responses were 10 keys on which the fingers of the two hands were placed. In Hyman's study, the stimuli were eight lights corresponding to the eight corners of inner and outer squares, and each light was assigned a spoken name. In both studies, RT increased as a logarithmic function of the number of alternatives. Moreover, RT also varied systematically as a function of the relative proportions of the stimulus-response (S-R) alternatives, the sequential dependencies, and speed-accuracy trade-off, as expected on the basis of information theory. This relation between RT and the stimulus information that is transmitted in the responses is known as the Hick-Hyman law:

$$RT = a + bH_T,$$

where a is basic processing time and b is the amount that RT increases with increases in the amount of information transmitted (H_T; $\log_2 N$ for equally likely S-R pairs with no errors).

The slope of the Hick-Hyman function is negatively correlated with measures of intelligence, which several researchers have claimed to reflect ability to process information rapidly (see Jensen, 1980). However, the fact that the slope of the function is highly dependent on the amount of practice (described later) and other factors severely limits any conclusions that can be drawn from the negative correlation with intelligence tests. A recent study by Vickrey and Neuringer (2000) showed that the Hick-Hyman function has a lower slope for pigeons than for humans, even when they are tested in similar circumstances, which, if the relation to intelligence were accepted, would imply that pigeons are more intelligent than humans.

One criticism of the Hick-Hyman law is that the function relating RT to number of alternatives is not logarithmic. Kvälseth (1980) introduced a variety of laws, including a power law for the case of equally likely alternatives and an exponential law for cases in which the alternatives are not equally probable. Longstreth, El-Zahhar, and Alcorn (1985) claimed that the specific power law, $RT = a + b(1 - N^{-1})$, provides a better fit to data for equiprobable alternatives than the logarithmic function. Longstreth et al.'s main argument for the power law is that as the number alternatives increases beyond 8, the function is no longer linear with respect to the logarithm, but becomes curvilinear (see Longstreth, 1988). Although theoretically derived from an attentional model, Longstreth et al.'s power law is a special case of the more general power law proposed by Kvälseth (1980). In addition, Kvälseth (1989) and Welford (1987) pointed out that Longstreth et al.'s power law has several problems. Kvälseth (1989) captures the status of the Hick-Hyman law, stating, "Although, on purely empirical grounds, Hick-Hyman's law may not be uniformly superior to other lawful relationships, it has been clearly established that it does provide a good summary description of a substantial amount of data" (p. 358).

Stimulus-Response Compatibility

Stimulus-response compatibility (SRC) is one of the principal factors affecting efficiency of action selection. SRC refers to the fact that performance is better with some mappings of stimuli to responses than with others. SRC effects are ubiquitous and occur with a variety of stimulus and response sets, although much of the research has focused on spatial SRC effects.

Spatial Compatibility Effects

Paul Fitts is given credit for formalizing the concept of SRC. Fitts and Seeger (1953) examined performance of eight-choice tasks using all combinations of three stimulus arrangements and three response arrangements. They found that responses were faster and more accurate when the stimulus and response arrangements corresponded spatially than when they did not. Fitts and Deininger (1954) showed that for conditions in which the stimulus and response arrangements were the same, responses were much slower with an arbitrary mapping of S-R locations than with one in which the corresponding response was made to each stimulus. Even more interesting, performance was also much better with a mirror-reverse mapping of stimulus locations to response locations than with a random mapping, although performance was still inferior to that of the spatially corresponding mapping.

The spatial SRC effect is robust in that it is obtained with auditory and tactual stimuli and with key presses, joystick movements, and unimanual aimed movements (see Proctor & Reeve, 1990, and Hommel & Prinz, 1997, for edited volumes on SRC). The slope of the function for the Hick-Hyman law, relating RT to the number of alternatives, is inversely related to SRC (Smith, 1968), approaching zero for highly compatible S-R mappings (Teichner & Krebs, 1974). In other words, SRC effects increase in magnitude as the number of S-R alternatives increases.

Many studies have used a two-choice task in which a left or right key press is made to a left or right stimulus. In two-choice tasks, responses are typically 50–100 ms faster when the S-R mapping is spatially compatible than when it is not, regardless of whether the stimuli are visual or auditory. Moreover, PET scans show increased bloodflow for incompatible mappings compared to compatible mappings in the same brain regions (left rostral dorsal premotor and posterior parietal areas) for both visual and auditory modalities (Iacoboni, Woods, & Mazziotta, 1998). This spatial SRC effect is a function of relative position of the stimuli and responses: It occurs even when the stimulus display or hands are shifted to the left or right of center (Nicoletti, Anzola, Luppino, Rizzolatti, & Umiltà, 1982). Moreover, the SRC effect is found when the hands are crossed so that the left hand operates the right key and the right hand the left key (Roswarski & Proctor, 2000), as well as when the responses are made with two fingers on the same hand (Heister, Schroeder-Heister, & Ehrenstein, 1990). The dependence of the effect on the spatial relations of the stimuli and responses has led most accounts of spatial SRC to focus on spatial coding as its basis. The spatial codes are based on the task goals, as illustrated in a study by Riggio, Gawryszewski, and Umiltà (1986) in which subjects operated the left key with a stick held in the right hand and the right key with a stick held in the left hand. Even though the hands were on their normal sides, responses were faster with the S-R mapping in which the stimuli corresponded to the location of the response key and not the hand used for responding.

Conceptual, Perceptual, and Structural Similarity

A variety of SRC effects in addition to spatial compatibility have been demonstrated. Kornblum, Hasbroucq, and Osman (1990) and Kornblum and Lee (1995) have argued that SRC effects will occur for any situation in which the stimulus and response sets have dimensional overlap (i.e., are similar). Dimensional overlap is presumed to include both conceptual and perceptual similarity. The role of conceptual similarity is illustrated in the findings that spatial SRC effects, broadly defined, occur when location words are spoken in response to physical location stimuli, as well as when left-right key presses are made to the words *left* and *right* or to left- and right-pointing arrows. The role of perceptual similarity is shown by the finding that SRC effects are larger within the spatial-manual and verbal-vocal modes, that is, for physical locations mapped to key presses and location words mapped to naming responses, than between the modes (Wang & Proctor, 1996).

SRC effects are also obtained when the S-R sets do not share conceptual or perceptual similarity but have structural similarity. When an ordered set of stimuli (e.g., A, B, C, D) is mapped to an ordered set of responses (e.g., 1, 2, 3, 4), RT is shorter for a mapping that preserves or reverses this order than for one that does not. Another type of structural compatibility effect occurs when a symbolic two-dimensional stimulus set is mapped to index and middle finger responses on each hand. When two letters (O, Z) of two sizes (large or small) are mapped to the responses, the left-to-right mapping of O, o, z, Z is easier than one of O, z, o, Z (Miller, 1982; Proctor & Reeve, 1985). Proctor and Reeve presented evidence that this difference is due to the letter identity distinctions being salient for the stimulus set and the distinctions between the two left and two right responses being salient for the response set. Performance is best for the condition in which the salient stimulus feature maps directly onto the salient response feature. In other words, translation of the specific stimulus into a response can occur more quickly when salient features correspond. Salient features coding has been shown to determine the compatibility effects obtained for a variety of situations in which the stimulus and response sets have structural similarity, but no conceptual or perceptual similarity (Proctor & Reeve, 1990).

Compatibility Effects in Two Dimensions

Umiltà and Nicoletti (1990) examined compatibility along two dimensions in a two-choice task by varying the stimulus and response locations for a set of trials along a diagonal (see Figure 11.3). They found that the compatibility effect was larger for the horizontal dimension than for the vertical dimension, a phenomenon they called right-left prevalence. Vu and Proctor (2001) showed that this right-left prevalence effect can be reversed to top-bottom prevalence by increasing the relative salience of the vertical dimension. This was accomplished by using response sets that emphasized the top-bottom distinction. In one experiment that showed top-bottom prevalence, subjects responded with anatomical top-bottom effectors, a hand and foot. In another experiment, top-bottom prevalence was obtained when one hand was placed over the other so that the top-bottom distinction was salient. Thus, although right-left prevalence typically is obtained when left-right effectors are used, and top-bottom prevalence when top-bottom effectors are used, the prevalence effects do not seem to have an anatomical

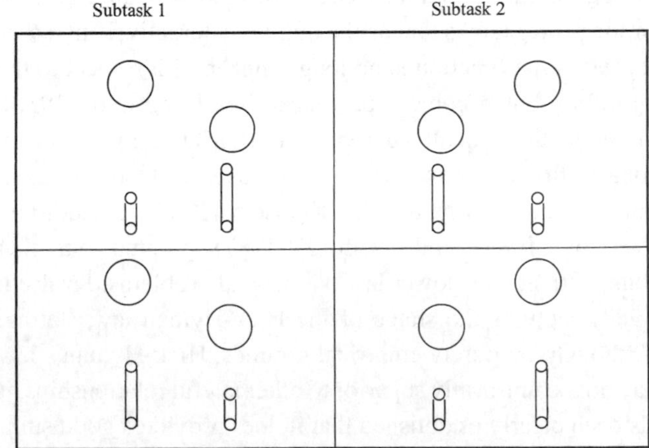

Figure 11.3 Illustration of the S-R compatibility conditions and subtasks in Umiltà and Nicoletti's (1990) two-dimensional compatibility experiments. The stimuli (depicted by circles) and response keys (depicted by cylinders) were arranged along the same (bottom row) or different (top row) diagonals. By varying the mapping of stimuli to responses for each of the four cells, mappings could be generated that were compatible on both dimensions, compatible on the vertical dimension but not the horizontal dimension and vice versa, or incompatible on both dimensions.

basis, but are by-products of the relative salience of the two dimensions.

Compatibility effects can occur as well when the spatial dimension along which the stimulus locations vary is orthogonal to that along which the response alternatives vary. For top-bottom stimuli mapped to left-right key press or vocal responses, the mapping of top-right and bottom-left yields faster responding than the alternative mapping (Cho & Proctor, 2001). A variant of salient features coding can also explain this mapping effect (Weeks & Proctor, 1990). Specifically, evidence indicates that the two alternatives on the vertical and horizontal dimensions are coded asymmetrically, with top and right being the polar referents for their respective dimensions. Consequently, the salient features coding explanation is that action selection occurs faster for the top-right/bottom-left mapping than for the alternative mapping because it is the one for which the salient features correspond. Adam, Boon, Paas, and Umiltà (1998) proposed that this asymmetric coding is a property of verbal codes but not spatial codes. However, Cho and Proctor provided evidence that it is a general property of spatial coding.

With unimanual movements of a joystick or finger, the top-right/bottom-left mapping is also typically more compatible than the alternative mapping. In this case, though, the mapping preference is affected by the location of the response apparatus. The top-right/bottom-left advantage is enhanced when responding in the right hemispace, but it reverses to a top-left/bottom-right advantage when responding in the left hemispace (Weeks, Proctor, & Beyak, 1995). Lippa (1996) provided evidence that the mapping preference is also affected by hand posture. According to her referential coding hypothesis, the finger-to-wrist axis provides a reference frame that allows the response set to be coded parallel to the stimulus set. For example, when left-right responses are made with the right hand held at a comfortable 45–90°, the left response can be coded as top and right response as bottom. Referential coding can explain many results obtained with unimanual responses, but it cannot explain why the mapping preferences described above occur when the hand and finger are in a neutral posture that allows only left-right deflections perpendicular to the sagittal body midline (Michaels & Schilder, 1991).

Because of this deficiency of the referential coding hypothesis, Lippa and Adam (2001) proposed an end-state comfort hypothesis. Similar to referential coding, the end-state comfort hypothesis views orthogonal compatibility as a correspondence effect. However, it assumes that the response dimension is mentally rotated, according to relative hand posture, to bring it into alignment with the stimulus dimension. The direction of rotation, clockwise or counterclockwise, is determined by physical constraints of the body. The response dimension is mentally rotated in the direction that would yield the most comfortable end-state posture if the hand were actually rotated (inward movement for the left or right hand when positioned at centered or ipsilateral locations, and outward movement when positioned at contralateral locations). The end-state comfort hypothesis can account for more results obtained with unimanual responses than the referential coding hypothesis, but both hypotheses are not directly applicable to the orthogonal compatibility effects obtained with bimanual or vocal response sets.

Dual-Route Models

Virtually all explanations of SRC effects agree that at least part of the difference in RT between compatible and incompatible mappings involves the time to translate the stimulus into its assigned response based on the instructions provided for the task. Translation is presumed to be fastest when an identity rule can be applied (i.e., make the response corresponding to the stimulus), intermediate when some other rule can be used (e.g., make the response that is the mirror opposite of the stimulus), and slowest when the response must be retrieved via the specific S-R associations defined for the task. Although some models rely exclusively on intentional translation (e.g., Rosenbloom & Newell, 1987), dual-route models that propose an additional direct (or automatic) response-selection route have come to be favored (e.g., Kornblum et al., 1990; see Figure 11.4). The basic idea is that when a stimulus occurs it tends to produce activation of its corresponding response by way of long-term S-R associations, regardless of the S-R mapping defined for the task. The resulting activation produces a benefit in responding when the corresponding response is correct, but a cost when it is not. The major reason that dual-route models have become popular is that correspondence effects often occur for irrelevant stimulus dimensions (see Lu & Proctor, 1995), as discussed in a subsequent section.

Sequential Effects

Repetition Benefit

Bertelson (1961) was the first to formally investigate sequential effects on performance. He showed that for a two-choice task, in which left-right stimuli were mapped compatibly to left-right keys, the total response time for a set of trials was less when the proportion of repetitions was .75 than when it was .25. This repetition benefit was evident when the

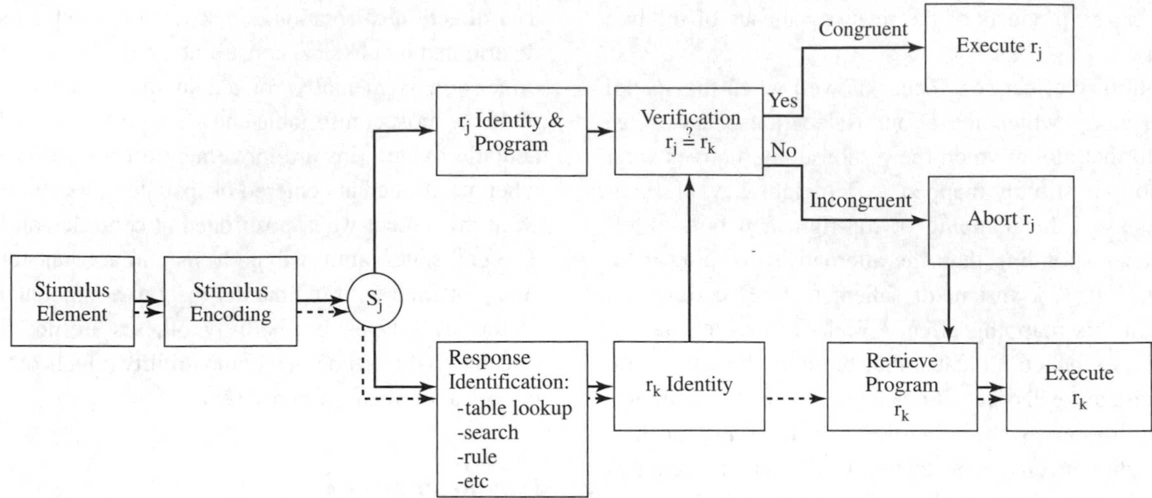

Figure 11.4 Illustration of the dimensional overlap model by Kornblum et al. (1990). The top route depicts automatic activation of the corresponding response, and the bottom route depicts identification of the assigned response by intentional S-R translation. *Source:* From Kornblum, Hasbroucq, & Osman (1990).

response-stimulus interval (RSI) was 50 ms but not when it was 500 ms.

Since Bertelson's (1961) study, numerous, more detailed investigations of sequential effects in choice-reaction tasks have been conducted. First-order sequential effects are those that involve the relation of the current trial to the immediately preceding trial. The most common first-order effect is that the response to a stimulus is faster when the S-R pair for a trial is a repetition of the preceding S-R pair than when it is not. In two-choice tasks, this repetition benefit is obtained only when the RSI is short. At RSIs of 500 ms or longer, a benefit for alternations over repetitions is typically found instead. The repetition benefit is larger in tasks with more than two choices, being an increasing function of the number of S-R alternatives, and in these tasks a repetition benefit is found even at long RSIs (Soetens, 1998). The first-order sequential effects have been attributed to two processes, much like those proposed for priming effects (Neely, 1977; chapter by McNamara & Holbrook in this volume). At short RSIs, residual activation from the preceding trial produces automatic facilitation when the current trial is identical to it; at long RSIs, strategic expectancy regarding the nature of the next trial produces faster responses for expected than unexpected stimuli (Soetens, 1998). This expectancy is for the alternative S-R pair in two-choice tasks, but for repetition of the same pair in tasks with more alternatives.

Pashler and Baylis (1991) evaluated the locus of the repetition benefit for tasks in which two stimuli were assigned to left, middle, and right response keys operated by index, middle, and ring fingers of the right hand. Two of the stimuli were digits, two were letters, and two were nonalphanumeric symbols (e.g., & and #). Stimuli were mapped to responses in a categorizable (e.g., digits-to-left response, letters-to-middle response, and symbols-to-right response) or uncategorizable (e.g., a digit and a letter to the left response, etc.) manner. For both mappings, the repetition benefit occurred primarily when the same stimulus was repeated and not when only the response was repeated. This repetition benefit for the same stimulus was not found when responses on alternate trials were vocal and manual. Consequently, Pashler and Baylis concluded that the repetition effects were at the stage of response selection, with the normal response-selection process being bypassed when the stimulus and response were repeated.

In Pashler and Baylis's (1991) experiments, a benefit for response repetition alone tended to occur with categorizable but not uncategorizable S-R mappings. Campbell and Proctor (1993) verified this effect, showing a benefit of approximately 40 ms for response repetition alone with categorizable mappings but not uncategorizable mappings. Their remaining experiments showed that this response repetition benefit, as well as the additional benefit for repeating the same stimulus, could be obtained when the responses on successive trials were made with different hands. In the critical conditions, the stimuli were presented to the left or right of fixation on alternate trials, with responses to the left stimulus made with the three fingers on the left hand and responses to the right stimulus made with the three fingers on the right hand. A cross-hand repetition benefit was obtained when either spatial or finger information was consistent across hands, but not when both consistencies were eliminated. These results imply that the response sets can be coded in terms of locations or effectors and that response selection benefits from repetition of the stimulus category when it maps onto a salient feature of the response sets.

Soetens (1998) examined sequential effects for tasks in which subjects responded to four stimuli located at the corners of an imaginary square by pressing the left key if the stimulus was to one side and the right key if it was to the other. When left-right stimulus locations were mapped compatibly to left-right responses, the repetition benefit at the short RSI (50 ms) was primarily associated with the response (i.e., the benefit was evident when the stimulus side was the same as on the previous trial, but the location was different). At the long RSI (1,000 ms), a small alternation benefit was evident. With an incompatible S-R mapping (i.e., left side to right response), the results were similar, but with an increased benefit for repeating the same stimulus, particularly at the short RSI. When up-down responses were made to the left-right stimulus locations, response and stimulus repetition benefits of similar magnitudes were found at the short RSI. At the long RSI, the only effect was a repetition benefit for the same stimulus. Soetens concluded that automatic facilitation shifted toward stimulus-related processes as the mapping became less compatible. Together, the studies of Pashler and Baylis (1991), Campbell and Proctor (1993), and Soetens indicate that response repetition, without stimulus repetition, is beneficial when there is a structural relation between the stimulus and response sets and that repetition of the stimulus is more important when the mapping is arbitrary.

Although first-order sequential effects have been most widely studied, second- and third-order repetition effects, involving the sequence of the preceding two or three stimuli, respectively, are larger and more consistent (Soetens, 1998). For two-choice tasks, at short RSIs, RT benefits from multiple repetitions, regardless of whether the present trial is a repetition or an alternation. For example, responses on the current trial tend to be faster if the three preceding trials were repetitions than if they were alternations. At long RSIs, however, a prior string of repetition trials is beneficial if the current trial is also a repetition, but a prior string of alternation trials is beneficial if the current trial is an alternation. These two patterns of results can be attributed to automatic activation and subjective expectancies, respectively. The higher order effects in Soeten's study also showed the patterns indicative of automatic facilitation at the short RSI and subjective expectancy at the long RSI.

Is the Hick-Hyman Law an Artifact of Repetition Effects?

Kornblum (1967, 1968) noted that, unless explicitly controlled, the proportion of repetition trials decreases as set size increases. Therefore, he proposed that the Hick-Hyman law is an artifact of repetition effects. Kornblum (1968) used a four-choice task in which four lights were mapped to four response keys and information was varied by manipulating stimulus probabilities. For three levels of information, conditions were constructed in which the probability of repetition was high or low. RT was shorter for the high-repetition conditions than for the corresponding low-repetition conditions, and these latter conditions showed only a nonsignificant effect of information on RT. Kornblum (1967) conducted a similar experiment in which the number of alternatives was two, four, or eight. For four- and eight-choice tasks, RT was shorter on repetition than on nonrepetition trials, with the slope being less for repetition trials. Within these tasks, RT for repetition trials increased as the amount of stimulus information increased, but RT for nonrepetitions did not.

Hyman and Umiltà (1969) noted that the RSI in Kornblum's (1967, 1968) experiments was approximately 140 ms, a short interval that would maximize repetition effects and minimize preparation for the subsequent trial. They replicated three of Kornblum's (1968) conditions, but used an average RSI of 7.5 s. Although RT was faster for repetition than nonrepetition trials, the slopes of the two functions were approximately equal. Hyman and Umiltà concluded, "There seems little doubt that the information hypothesis is much more compatible with our results than those of Kornblum's" (p. 47). In other words, the Hick-Hyman function is not an artifact of the proportion of repetition trials when there is adequate preparation time.

Advance Information

Warning Effects

Preparation is usually studied by presenting a neutral warning signal at various intervals prior to the onset of the imperative stimulus. Bertelson (1967) had subjects press a right key to a right light and a left key to a left light. The warning signal was an auditory click that, in different blocks, occurred 0, 20, 50, 100, 150, 200, or 300 ms prior to the visual stimulus. At the 0-ms warning interval, RT was approximately 265 ms. It decreased to a minimum of 245 ms at the 150-ms interval and then increased slightly to 250 ms at the two longest intervals. However, the error rate increased from about 7% at the shorter intervals to 12% at the 100- and 150-ms intervals, and decreased slightly to 9% at the longer intervals. Thus, the effect of the warning signal was to increase readiness to respond quickly, but at the expense of accuracy.

Posner, Klein, Summers, and Buggie (1973) obtained similar results for a two-choice task in which the compatibility of the mapping of the stimulus locations to responses was manipulated. Each trial was preceded by no warning or a 50-ms warning tone, followed at intervals of 50, 100, 200, 400, and 800 ms by a stimulus to the left or right of fixation. RT was a U-shaped function of foreperiod, reaching a minimum at the 200-ms interval. Error rate showed an opposing, inverted U-shaped function, being highest at the 100-ms interval. The main effect of compatibility was significant in the RT and error data, but compatibility did not interact with foreperiod. These results suggest that the warning tone altered alertness, or readiness to respond, but did not affect the rate at which the information built up in the response-selection system.

RT continues to increase as the foreperiod increases beyond 800 ms, up to at least 5 s. Sanders and Wertheim (1973) failed to find an effect of foreperiod between 1 and 5 s for auditory stimuli, although they found the standard increase in RT for visual stimuli. However, Sanders (1975) demonstrated that the critical factor seems to be stimulus intensity: Auditory stimuli below 70 dB showed foreperiod effects similar to those shown by visual stimuli, and there was a trend toward smaller effects for high-intensity visual signals.

Precuing Effects

Leonard (1958) was the first to demonstrate that subjects can use advance information to prepare for a subset of S-R alternatives. He tested himself in a six-choice reaction task in which six stimulus lights were mapped compatibly to six response keys pressed by the fingers of each hand. In the six-choice condition, all six stimuli were lit, and the target light went off 100 ms later. In a three-choice condition, only the left or right set of three stimuli was used. Of most interest was a precue condition in which the subject did not know whether the choice would involve the three left locations or the three right locations until the lights designating those locations were lit (i.e., those locations were precued). RT decreased as a function of the precuing interval, with RT at the 500-ms interval being equivalent to that of the three-choice task.

Subsequent studies using four-choice tasks have obtained similar results, in which the benefit for precuing the two left or two right locations occurs within the first 500 ms of precue onset (Miller, 1982; Reeve & Proctor, 1984). However, when other pairs such as alternate locations are precued, the maximal benefit is not evident until a longer interval. Reeve and Proctor (1984) showed that the advantage for precuing the two left or two right locations does not depend on the fact that they typically involve responses from different hands. With an overlapped hand placement in which the index and middle fingers from the two hands are alternated, the two left or right locations show a similar precuing advantage relative to other pairs of locations. These and other findings imply that the time needed to obtain the maximal benefit from a precue varies as a function of how long it takes to translate the precue information. Proctor and Reeve (1986) attributed this pattern of differential precuing benefits to the salience of the left-right distinction.

Kantowitz and Sanders (1972) distinguished between two types of precue: *utility* and *necessity*. Utility precues, as in the studies just discussed, are helpful in reducing the number of alternatives, but do not provide information that is necessary for responding. Necessity precues tell subjects what information is relevant for the current trial (e.g., whether they are to respond to stimulus color or shape). RT is longer when the precue is a necessity than when it is only useful. Because the information provided by necessity precues must be used at all intervals, it is more difficult to respond at shorter ISIs. With utility precues, subjects use the information at longer intervals but not shorter ones.

RELEVANT AND IRRELEVANT STIMULUS INFORMATION

Noncorrespondence of Relevant and Irrelevant Information

Effects of irrelevant information on performance have been studied extensively in many areas of experimental psychology. Three such effects studied in the choice reaction literature—the Stroop color-naming effect, the Eriksen flanker effect, and the Simon effect—involve correspondence of relevant and irrelevant stimulus information.

The Stroop Effect

The best-known example of irrelevant information affecting response selection is the Stroop color-naming task (see MacLeod, 1991, for a review). In this task, color words are presented in different ink colors, and subjects are instructed to name the ink color while ignoring the color word. In Stroop's (1935/1992) study, subjects took 110 s to name a list of 100 colors presented in incongruent color words, compared to 63 s to name a list of 100 colors presented in solid squares. Thus, conflicting color words nearly doubled the naming time, a phenomenon known as the Stroop effect. Stroop also reported that the time to read 100 color words in incongruent ink colors was 43 s, compared to 41 s when the words were presented in black ink. Thus, the interference with color naming was asymmetric: Irrelevant words interfered with naming ink colors, but irrelevant ink colors did not interfere with reading color words.

This asymmetric pattern of interference has been reported in numerous subsequent studies, including versions of the task in which RTs to individual stimuli are recorded. An important finding is that the pattern of asymmetry is dependent on the response mode. When the task involves pointing to a matching color, responses to color words are delayed by incongruent colors, but responses to colors are not delayed by irrelevant color words (Durgin, 2000). Similarly, in spatial versions of the task, in which the word *left* or *right* is presented in left or right locations or with an arrow pointing to the left or right, the words produce interference when the responses are made vocally, but the locations or arrows produce interference when the responses are key presses (Lu & Proctor, 1995).

Stroop (1935/1992) showed in his Experiment 3 that a dimension that does not produce interference (e.g., ink colors when the task is word reading) can be made to do so with practice. In his experiment, subjects practiced four lists of 50 words in the color-naming task for 8 days. The average time to read the list decreased from 50 s on the first day to 33 s on the last day, but this was still longer than the 25 s to name a neutral list of colored swastikas. Subjects also performed the word-reading task prior and subsequent to practicing the color-naming task. The time to perform the word-reading task was nearly twice as long (35 s) after the color-naming practice as before (19 s). Thus, the practice increased the strengths of the associations between colors and names, and the colors now produced interference with reading color words.

More generally, relative strength of association is a good predictor of whether an irrelevant stimulus dimension will affect responding to a relevant stimulus dimension. Lu and Proctor (2001) classified the association of stimulus dimensions to key presses as high if they were both conceptually and perceptually similar (e.g., arrows are spatial and nonverbal, as are key presses), intermediate if they were only conceptually similar (e.g., location words are spatial but verbal), and low if they were neither (e.g., colors and color words are not similar to key presses). Across several experiments using various combinations of relevant and irrelevant stimulus dimensions, the relative magnitudes of effect size were predictable based on relative association strength. Baldo, Shimamura, and Prinzmetal (1998) obtained similar results varying response modalities in addition to stimulus dimensions: Robust Stroop effects to location word/arrow stimuli were observed when responding manually to location words or vocally to arrows, but not for the reverse relations. The results of Lu and Proctor and of Baldo et al. are generally consistent with Kornblum et al.'s (1990) emphasis on response activation varying as a function of dimensional overlap and with parallel distributed processing models of the type proposed by Cohen, Dunbar, and McClelland (1990), which rely on relative association strength.

The Eriksen Flanker Effect

Another widely studied effect of irrelevant information is the Eriksen flanker effect (Eriksen & Eriksen, 1974). In the typical experiment examining this effect, one or more stimuli are assigned to left-right responses. The target letter for each trial is presented at a known, centered location and is flanked by instances of a distractor letter. In Eriksen and Eriksen's experiment, the letters H and K were assigned to one response and the letters S and C to the other response. The flanking letters could be the same as the target (HHHHHHH), the letter assigned to the same responses as the target (congruent; KKKHKKK), or a letter assigned to the opposite response (incongruent; SSSHSSS or CCCHCCC). When the letters were in close spatial proximity, responses were faster when the flanking letters were identical to or congruent with the target than when they were incongruent. This congruency effect decreased as the spatial separation between the letters increased.

Because distractors that are not potential targets produce little or no interference, the results suggest that the effects reflect response activation. That is, the flanking letters activate the response to which they are assigned, producing response competition when that response is not the one signaled by the target. This competition is evident in a tendency for the lateralized readiness potential to show initial activation of the wrong response 150 to 250 ms after onset of the target and incongruent distractors (Gratton, Coles, Sirevaag, Eriksen, & Donchin, 1988). Eriksen and Schultz (1979) proposed a continuous flow account of the flanker effect, much like McClelland's cascade model, in which stimulus information gradually accumulates in the visual system and continuously flows into the response system. Initially, a wide range of responses is activated, but as the output from the perceptual system becomes more exact, the response activation becomes increasingly restricted to the appropriate response. This account assumes that after a flanking letter is fully identified, it will no longer produce response activation. However, if it is assumed that fully identified flankers may still contribute to response activation, then discrete stage models can account for the results as well (Mordkoff, 1996).

The Simon Effect

The Simon effect is another close relative of the Stroop effect (Lu & Proctor, 1995). In the typical Simon task, stimulus location is irrelevant and the responses, most often left-right key presses, vary along a location dimension. The relevant stimulus dimension typically involves a distinction other than location (e.g., color or letter identity). The Simon effect is that responses are faster when the location of the stimulus and response correspond than when they do not. The effect typically is larger when responses are fast than when they are slow, implying that activation of the location information occurs quickly and then decreases because it is irrelevant to the task (Hommel, 1993b). Consistent with this view, when the correct response is not the one that corresponds with the location of the stimulus, the lateralized readiness potential shows evidence of slight, initial activation of the spatially corresponding response, which then shifts to activation of the correct, noncorresponding response (De Jong, Liang, & Lauber, 1994).

Considerable research on the Simon effect has focused on why stimulus location is coded when it is irrelevant to the task. Stoffer and Umiltà (1997) attribute the Simon effect to shifts of attention associated with eye movements. According to them, the position of the object attended at stimulus onset, typically a fixation point, provides a frame of reference. The location of the stimulus relative to the focus of attention is coded only when attention is shifted to the stimulus. This code specifies the direction and amplitude of the saccade program to shift fixation to the stimulus. The types of evidence they have presented in support of the attention-shifting hypothesis are that the Simon effect is absent when attention shifts are prevented by the need to report a stimulus presented at fixation and reversed when an attention shift back from the stimulus location to the fixation point is required.

Hommel (1993b) has argued instead that spatial coding occurs with respect to various frames of reference, of which the focus of attention may be one. Perhaps the best evidence for his referential coding hypothesis is that the Simon effect can vary as a function of multiple frames of reference. In a procedure used by Lamberts, Tavernier, and D'Ydewalle (1992) and Roswarski and Proctor (1996), a stimulus can occur in one of eight locations, four to the left of fixation and four to the right. Initially, four boxes appear to one or the other side to designate the possible locations for that trial. Then the two left or two right boxes disappear, and the imperative stimulus is presented in one of the remaining boxes. In this case, a Simon effect occurs with respect to three frames of reference: Left-right side of fixation; two left versus two right on a side; and the left-right location within the final pair. The largest difference between corresponding and noncorresponding responses occurs when the stimulus is in the far left or far right location, for which all three spatial codes are in agreement (e.g., all left or all right).

As with compatibility for relevant stimulus information, the Simon effect varies as a function of task goals. Hommel (1993a) had subjects respond to a high or low pitch tone, presented to the left or right side, by pressing a left or right key. The key closed a circuit that lit a light on the opposite side. When instructed to press the left key to the high pitch tone and the right key to the low pitch tone, a typical Simon effect occurred. However, when instructed to turn on the right light to the high pitch tone and the left light to the low pitch tone, the Simon effect was a function of light location. That is, in this case, responses were faster when the stimulus was on the side opposite the responding hand, rather than on the same side. Guiard (1983) obtained a similar finding in an experiment in which subjects responded to tone pitch by turning a steering wheel clockwise or counterclockwise. In the condition of most interest, the subject's hands were placed at the bottom of the wheel, and a clockwise turn moved a cursor to a right target location and a counter-clockwise turn moved it to the left. Because of the hand placement, when the wheel was turned clockwise the hands moved to the left, and vice versa when the wheel was turned counter-clockwise. A Simon effect was obtained as a function of the direction of wheel rotation, rather than as a function of the direction in which the hands moved.

Another goal-related phenomenon is the Hedge and Marsh (1975) reversal, in which the Simon effect reverses to favor noncorresponding locations when the response keys are labeled according to the same dimension as the relevant stimulus information, and subjects are instructed to respond in an incompatible manner (e.g., press the green key to the red stimulus and vice versa). The explanation proposed by Hedge and Marsh, and which has continued to be the most widely accepted, is that of logical recoding. The basic idea is that a *respond opposite* rule is applied both to the relevant stimulus dimension and, inadvertently, to the irrelevant location dimension, leading to activation of the noncorresponding response.

Negative Priming

For the Stroop color-naming task, and related tasks with irrelevant stimulus information, the target stimulus value on a trial can not only be a repetition or nonrepetition of the relevant value on the previous trial, but also the same as the value of the irrelevant information. When the value of the relevant stimulus dimension is the same as that of the irrelevant dimension on the preceding trial, an effect called negative priming is often observed. This effect was first demonstrated by Dalrymple-Alford and Budayr (1966) for the Stroop color-naming task. Subjects had to name the ink colors for lists of Stroop color words that differed in the relation between successive stimuli. For the control list, there was no relation between the word or ink color for successive stimuli. For the ignored repetition list, however, the irrelevant color word for one stimulus was the relevant color for the next stimulus. In other words, if the color word for stimulus n-1 was red, then the ink color for stimulus n was red. The finding of interest was that the time to name the colors for the ignored repetition list was much longer than that for the control list. This slowing of responses when the to-be-ignored information on the previous trial is relevant on the current trial is the phenomenon of negative priming.

Negative priming has subsequently been studied most often using a method in which responses to individual stimuli are measured. In that situation, the trials are often presented as pairs, with the first trial called a prime and the second a probe. Negative priming is shown when responses are slower for trials in which the previously irrelevant information is now relevant than for neutral trials. The negative priming effect has been found in a variety of tasks for which irrelevant information is present (Fox, 1995; May, Kane, & Hasher, 1995), including not only tasks that require identification of an object but also those that require localization.

The most straightforward interpretation of negative priming effects is that of selective inhibition: The irrelevant information must be inhibited in order to respond to the relevant information, and this inhibition carries forward to the next trial. Consequently, the response will be slowed if the inhibited information is now relevant. Although numerous findings are consistent with the selective inhibition hypothesis, they can also be accounted for without assuming inhibition. Moreover, the situation has been shown to be much more complex than the selective inhibition hypothesis suggests, and alternative explanations have been proposed. The two most prominent alternatives are feature mismatching and episodic retrieval. According to the feature mismatch hypothesis (Park & Kanwisher, 1994), symbol identities are bound to objects and locations, and any change in the bindings from the previous trial will produce negative priming. The episodic retrieval hypothesis (Neill & Valdes, 1992) states that presentation of a stimulus evokes retrieval of previous episodes involving the stimulus. Because recent episodes are most likely to be retrieved, if the target stimulus was a distractor on the previous trial, the episode retrieved will include an *ignore* tag.

One problematic finding for the inhibition account is that negative priming effects do not appear to be short-lived. DeSchepper and Treisman (1996) found negative priming after a delay of 30 days between the prime and probe trials. In addition, negative priming depends on the relation between the prime and probe trials. For example, for the Stroop task, the effect is not found if the probe stimulus that follows the prime Stroop stimulus is a color patch and not a colored word (Lowe, 1979). A simple inhibition account would seem to predict negative priming in this situation as well as in that for which the probe stimulus was a colored word.

MULTIPLE TASKS

Task Switching

In his classic monograph, "Mental Set and Shift," Jersild (1927) began by saying, "The fact of mental set is primary in all conscious activity. The same stimulus may evoke any one of a large number of responses depending upon the contextual setting in which it is placed" (p. 5). Jersild conducted experiments in which subjects made a series of judgments regarding each stimulus in a list as a function of whether a single task was performed for all stimuli or two tasks were performed in alternating order. The major finding was that in many situations the time to complete the list was longer for mixed lists than for pure lists of a single task.

Beginning in the mid-1990s, there has been a resurgence of interest in task switching. Research conducted on task switching, in which two tasks are presented in a fixed order (e.g., on alternate trials), has suggested that there are two components associated with changing the task set from the previous trial. One component involves voluntary preparation for the forthcoming trial, with responses for the next trial becoming progressively faster as the RSI increases. However, time to prepare for the new task cannot be the only factor contributing to the switching cost, because the cost is still evident when the RSI is long (Allport, Styles, & Hsieh, 1994; Rogers & Monsell, 1995). A second component, which Allport et al. (1994) called task set inertia and Rogers and Monsell (1995) called exogenous task set reconfiguration, is not under the subject's control. Apparently only a single trial with the new task is necessary to complete configuration for that task. Rogers and Monsell (Experiment 6) used sequences of four task repetitions and then a switch to the alternate task for four consecutive trials, and so on, and found that the switch costs were eliminated after the first trial of the new task.

Shaffer (1965) conducted a study in which trials with compatible and incompatible spatial mappings were randomly mixed. The stimulus to which the subject was to respond occurred in a left or right location, and a centered horizontal or vertical line signaled whether the mapping for the trial was compatible or incompatible. When the mapping signal occurred simultaneously with the stimulus, the standard spatial compatibility effect was eliminated. Vu and

Proctor (2001) used stimulus color to designate the mapping and obtained similar results with left-right physical-location stimuli, as Shaffer used, as well as with left-right pointing arrows. These findings are consistent with the fact that, in a variety of situations, performance of the easier of two tasks is harmed more by mixing (Los, 1996). However, Vu and Proctor found that when the stimuli were the words *left* and *right,* the advantage for the compatible mapping was enhanced compared to pure blocks of one trial type. These results, along with many others, suggest that words are processed differently than physical locations and arrows.

Proctor and Vu (2002) also showed that mixing location-relevant and location-irrelevant trials within a trial block alters the stimulus-response compatibility (SRC) effects obtained for each task. When physical location stimuli were used to convey the location information, the standard SRC effect was eliminated for location-relevant trials. However, the SRC effect was not affected with arrow stimuli and was enhanced with location word stimuli. Mixing the two trial types also affects the Simon effect obtained for the location-irrelevant trials. For all stimulus types, when the location-relevant mapping was compatible, the Simon effect was enhanced compared to pure blocks of Simon trials; when the location-relevant mapping was incompatible, a reverse Simon effect was obtained. With arrows and words, the reverse effect was smaller than the positive effect. However, with physical locations, the reverse Simon effect was at least as large as the positive effect obtained with the compatible location-relevant mapping. This outcome implies that there was no automatic activation of the corresponding response. The reversal for physical location stimuli obtained when the location-relevant mapping was incompatible was evident even when the trial type was precued by up to 2.4 s before presentation of the stimulus. This outcome indicates that the reversal does not reflect only a strategy of preparing the noncorresponding response in anticipation that location may be relevant to the trial.

Psychological Refractory Period

In a common dual-task procedure, subjects perform two different choice-reaction tasks, Task 1 (T1) and Task 2 (T2), on a single trial. The stimulus onset asynchrony (SOA) between the stimuli for T1 (S1) and T2 (S2) is varied. The typical finding is that RT for the second task (RT2) is slowed as the SOA decreases. Telford (1931) called this phenomenon the psychological refractory period (PRP) effect. Extensive research on the PRP effect has been conducted over the past 50 years, and explanations have been proposed in terms of information-processing bottlenecks, demands on limited capacity resources,

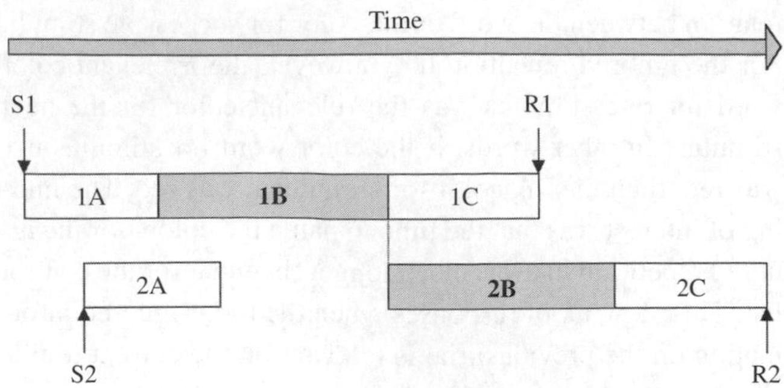

Figure 11.5 Illustration of response selection bottleneck model. Stage A is stimulus identification, Stage B is response selection, and Stage C is response initiation. Response selection for Task 2 (Stage 2B) is delayed until response selection for Task 1 (Stage 1B) is completed. S1 and R1 are the stimuli and responses for Task 1, and S2 and R2 are the stimuli and responses for Task 2.

and strategies adopted to satisfy task constraints (Meyer & Kieras, 1997; Pashler, 1998). The most widely accepted account in recent years is a response-selection bottleneck model advocated by Pashler and colleagues (see Figure 11.5). According to this model, stimulus identification and response execution occur in parallel for the two tasks. However, response selection operates serially because it requires a single-channel mechanism.

The evidence for the response-selection bottleneck model comes primarily from using locus of slack logic (Schweickert, 1983) to interpret the patterns of additive and interactive effects produced by variables presumed to selectively affect stimulus identification, response selection, and response execution. According to the model, identification of S2 commences immediately upon its presentation, regardless of the SOA. At long SOAs response selection can begin as soon as stimulus identification is completed, but at short SOAs it cannot begin until response selection for T1 is finished. Consequently, there is slack in the processing sequence for T2 between the completion of stimulus identification and initiation of response selection. At short SOAs, the slack can absorb, at least in part, an increase in time to identify S2. This leads to the effect of the stimulus-difficulty manipulation being smaller at the short SOAs than at the long SOAs. In contrast, for variables that affect response selection or response execution, which have their influence after the bottleneck, the extra time cannot be absorbed by the slack, and, therefore, their effects should be additive with those of SOA. These predicted patterns of results have been found for several variables of the respective types.

Meyer and Kieras (1997) have mounted a challenge to the response-selection bottleneck model, arguing that evidence supporting it reflects a strategy adopted by subjects when the instructions state or imply that the response for T1 must be made before that for T2. They propose that there is no capacity limitation in processing other than a bottleneck for response execution when the tasks require responses from the same output system (e.g., key presses for T1 and T2). According to their strategic response deferment model, different lock out strategies are adopted in specific situations to permit performance of T1 and T2 in the manner requested. Whether the response-selection bottleneck is due to a structural limitation on information processing or a strategy adopted to satisfy task demands is an issue that remains to be resolved.

According to response-selection bottleneck accounts of the PRP effect, whether structural or strategic, response selection for T2 does not begin until that for T1 is completed. However, several recent studies have shown cross-talk effects between T1 and T2 that imply that the T2 response is activated before the response for T1 is selected. Hommel (1998) had subjects make a left or right key press to the color of a red or green rectangle for T1 and say "red" or "green" to the letter S or H for T2. RT for both tasks showed correspondence effects at short SOAs, with the response for each task being faster when the color-naming response for T2 corresponded to the color for T1. Lien and Proctor (2000) obtained similar results when T1 involved left-right key presses with the left hand to low or high pitch tones and T2 left-right key presses with the right hand to left-right arrow directions. Also, Logan and Schulkind (2000) reported correspondence effects for the categories of T1 and T2 stimuli for a variety of tasks. For example, when both tasks required letter-digit classifications with left-right key presses on the left and right hands, respectively, RT was shorter when the two stimuli were from the same category (e.g., letters) than when they were not. The fact that, in all studies, the correspondence effects are evident in RT1, as well as RT2, implies that the stimulus for T2 is translated into response activation prior to T1 response selection. Hommel has proposed that such translation of stimulus information into response activation is automatic, with the bottleneck being only in the final decision about which response to make for each task.

Stop Signals

A goal may change during the course of action selection so that the action being selected is no longer relevant. Such situations have been studied in the stop-signal paradigm (Logan, 1994). In this paradigm, a choice-reaction task is administered, but a stop signal occurs at a variable interval after the imperative stimulus on occasional trials to indicate that a response should not be made. Of concern is whether the subject is able to inhibit the response for the choice task. The response is more likely to be inhibited the shorter the interval between the go and stop signals and the longer the choice RT.

Performance on the stop-signal task has been interpreted in terms of a stochastic race model: The go process and stop process engage in a race. The response is executed if the go process finishes before the stop process and is inhibited if the stop process finishes first. This model predicts many features of the results obtained in the stop-signal task, including the probability that the response will be inhibited as a function of go RT and stop-signal delay. The race model has been applied to a variety of stimulus and response modes, suggesting that it captures basic principles of action inhibition. However, it does not provide a detailed account of the processes underlying performance of specific tasks.

Logan and Irwin (2000) compared the processes involved in inhibiting left-right key presses and left-right eye movements. Subjects responded to peripheral left-right stimuli or central left-right pointing brackets, with hand movements or eye movements, using a compatible or incompatible S-R mapping. Estimates of stop-signal RT for hand movements were similar for the two stimulus types and mappings. Stop-signal RT for eye movements was shorter than that for the hands, being shortest for the condition in which a compatible movement was made to a peripheral stimulus. These results suggest that the inhibition processes for hand and eye movements are different, although they follow the same basic principles.

Research has focused on trying to identify the point of no return, or the stage beyond which the response cannot be stopped. De Jong, Coles, Logan, and Gratton (1990) examined this issue using left-right squeezing responses (to a criterion) to measure partial responses, the lateralized readiness potential (LRP) to measure central response activation, and the electromyogram (EMG) to measure muscle activation. LRP, EMG, and squeeze activity were found to occur on stop-signal trials for which the response was successfully inhibited (i.e., did not reach criterion), which they interpreted as suggesting that no stage of response preparation is ballistic. However, Osman, Kornblum, and Meyer (1986) argued that the point of no return should be defined as the point at which the response cannot be stopped from beginning. Using this criterion, the partial squeezes in De Jong et al.'s study are cases of unsuccessful inhibition, indicating that muscle activation is the point of no return. The evidence in De Jong et al.'s study favored two inhibitory mechanisms: Inhibition of central activation processes was implicated because the LRP was truncated on successful stop trials, but several findings suggested that there was also a more peripheral mechanism of inhibition that affected the transmission of activation from central to peripheral structures.

CHANGES IN ACTION SELECTION WITH PRACTICE

Choice RT decreases with practice at a task, with equivalent amounts of practice producing larger changes earlier in practice than later. Teichner and Krebs (1974) reviewed numerous studies of visual choice reactions and concluded that the stage of processing that benefits most from practice is response selection. Newell and Rosenbloom (1981) proposed that the changes in RT with practice follow a power function:

$$RT = BN^{-\alpha},$$

where N is the number of practice trials, B is RT on the first trial, and α is the learning rate. The power function has come to be regarded as a law to which any model that is intended to explain practice effects must conform. Although the power law provides a good description of changes in RT with practice averaged across subjects, Heathcote, Brown, and Mewhort (2000) contend that it does not fit the functions for individual performers adequately. They demonstrated that exponential functions provided better fits than power functions to the data for individuals in 40 data sets, and proposed a new exponential law of practice.

Beginning with Merkel (1885), several investigators have shown that the slope of the Hick-Hyman function decreases with practice (e.g., Hyman, 1953; Mowbray & Rhoades, 1959). Seibel (1963) used all combinations of 10 lights assigned directly to 10 keys. After more than 75,000 trials had been performed, the RT for the 1,023-alternative task was only approximately 25 ms slower than that for a 31-alternative task. Practice also is typically more beneficial for incompatible than compatible mappings. However, SRC effects do not disappear even with considerable practice (Dutta & Proctor, 1992; Fitts & Seeger, 1953).

Proctor and Dutta (1993) had subjects perform two-choice tasks for 10 blocks of 42 trials each. In the critical conditions, they performed with the hands uncrossed and crossed in alternate blocks. Whether compatible or incompatible, when the spatial mapping of left-right stimulus locations to left-right response locations remained constant, there was no cost associated with alternating the hand placements: Overall RT and changes with practice with the alternating placements were comparable to those of subjects who practiced with the same hand placement for all blocks. In contrast, when the mapping of stimulus to response locations was switched between blocks so that the same hand was used to respond to a stimulus when the hands were crossed or uncrossed, there was a substantial cost for participants who alternated hand placements compared to those who did not. These results imply that the S-R associations that are strengthened through practice involve spatial response codes.

Practice with an incompatible spatial mapping alters the influence of stimulus location on performance when location becomes irrelevant to the task. Proctor and Lu (1999) had subjects perform a two-choice task for 3 days using an incompatible spatial mapping. On the 4th day, they performed a task for which stimulus location was irrelevant. For this task, the Simon effect was reversed, with RT faster for noncorresponding responses. Tagliabue, Zorzi, Umiltà, and Bassignani (2000) found a similar effect of prior practice with an incompatible mapping and showed it to be present even when subjects were tested a week later. Thus, a limited amount of practice produces new spatial S-R associations that persist at a sufficient strength to override the preexisting associations between corresponding locations.

Nissen and Bullemer (1987) demonstrated that when the trials in a compatibly mapped four-choice spatial reaction task follow a sequence that repeats regularly (every 10 trials in their study), performance improves more with practice than when the trial order is random. Considerable effort has been devoted subsequently to determining whether this sequence learning is implicit or explicit, and to examining the nature of what is learned. Because this research is summarized in the chapter by Johnson in this volume, we restrict mention here to a study by Koch and Hoffmann (2000). Across four experiments, they varied whether the stimuli were spatial or symbolic and whether the responses were spatial or symbolic. Their results showed that the effect of sequence repetition and structure on performance was much stronger for spatial sequences than for symbolic sequences, regardless of whether the stimulus or response set was involved. Koch and Hoffmann also speculated that learning of the response sequence is greater for incompatible S-R mappings (e.g., random mappings of digits to response locations) than for compatible S-R mappings. Regardless, they emphasized, "the selective impact of S-R compatibility on learning stimulus and response sequences in SRT [serial reaction tasks] seems to us an important issue . . . that has not received much attention" (p. 879).

APPLICATIONS

Contemporary research on action selection has its roots in display-control design issues. Paul Fitts, who formalized the concept of SRC and conducted much of the groundbreaking research on action selection, was the founder of what is now the Fitts Human Engineering Division of the Armstrong Laboratory of the U.S. Air Force and made many contributions to human factors. Although most of the research on action selection has been basic in nature, the results obtained from this research are of considerable relevance to applications involving interface design. It is widely accepted that a user-friendly design must adhere to principles of action selection in general and SRC in particular (see Andre & Wickens, 1990).

In a classic study of stove configurations, Chapanis and Lindenbaum (1959) evaluated four control-burner arrangements (see Figure 11.6a). The experimenter demonstrated the individual pairings of burners to controls for one of the four stoves, and then instructed subjects to push the assigned control to the burner that was lit. Subjects showed shorter RT for Design 1 than Designs 2–4, for which RT did not differ initially. Furthermore, no errors were made for the mappings of Design 1, whereas the overall error rate was 6%, 10%, and 11% for Designs 2–4, respectively. Practice significantly reduced RT and errors for Design 2 compared to Designs 3 and 4, but performance was still worse than with Design 1. When naive subjects were asked which control-burner configuration was the best, most selected Design 1. However, they were equally divided about whether Design 2, 3, or 4 was second best. Thus, although after practice performance was better with Design 2 than Designs 3 and 4, naive subjects did not anticipate this difference.

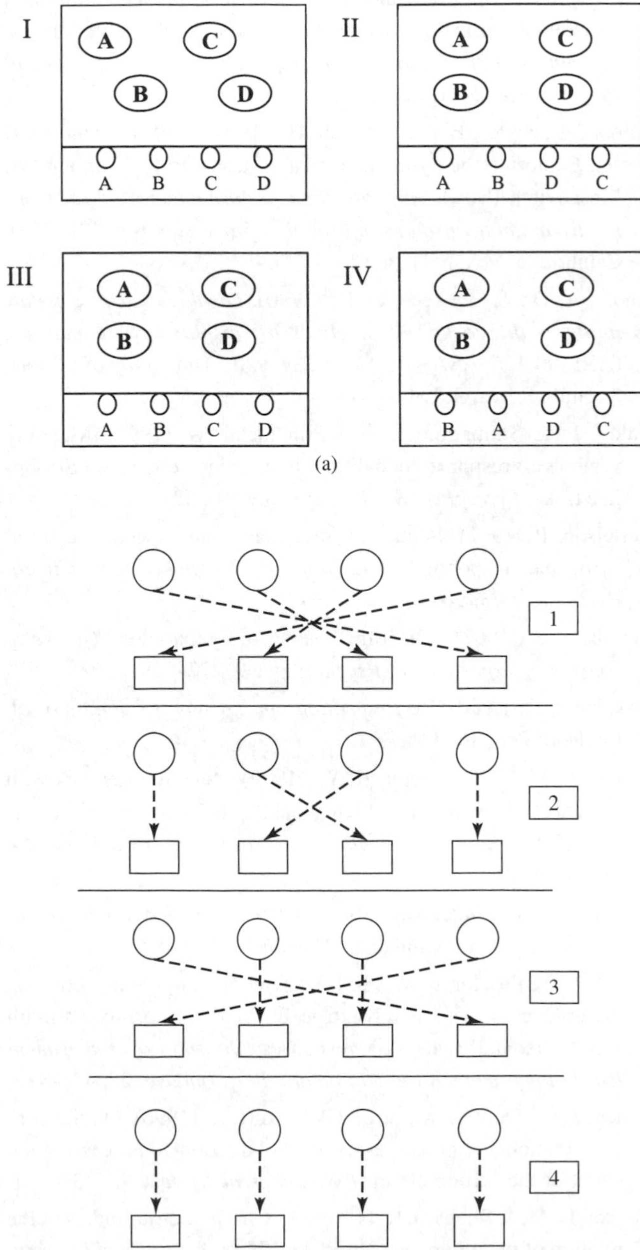

Figure 11.6 Illustration of various display-control mapping configurations for (a) stove tops (with specific burner-control pairings indicated by letters) and (b) Duncan's (1977) four-choice tasks (with specific S-R pairings indicated by arrows).

In a more recent study, Payne (1995) asked naive subjects to rank from easiest to hardest the four mappings of a four-choice SRC task in which the inner or outer pairs are mapped compatibly or incompatibly (Duncan, 1977; see Figure 11.6b). He compared the subjective rankings to RT measures obtained by Duncan. Similar to the results of the stove study, subjects had little difficulty identifying Design 4 as the easiest mapping because it was a direct mapping. However, more subjects rated Design 1 (in which both inner and outer pairs were mapped incompatibly) as being harder than Designs 2 and 3 (in which only one pair was mapped compatibly and the other incompatibly), even though actual performance was second best on Design 1.

The deleterious effect of mixed mappings illustrated in Duncan's (1977) study, as well as in that of Shaffer (1965), discussed in the "Task Switching" section, indicates that the context in which the display-control configuration is placed affects performance. Most compatibility studies evaluate performance of specific S-R mappings in isolation. However, when more than one S-R mapping is used, the benefit that one might expect from a compatible mapping is not always evident. Moreover, if two tasks must be performed simultaneously, it may be easier to perform them together when they have the same incompatible mapping than when one has a compatible mapping and the other does not (Duncan, 1979). Andre and Wickens (1990) refer to this benefit as one of global consistency and note that it may sometimes be more important than local compatibility.

Because the amount of experience with specific S-R mappings is a major factor in efficiency of action selection, designers must take into account the stereotypic behavior of the specific population for whom a product or system is being designed. For example, from years of experience, Americans are more likely to flick a light switch down when they intend to turn a light off, whereas Englishmen are more likely to flick the switch up. One of the most widely studied population stereotypes is that of direction of motion. Operators of systems that require control of direction of motion must make decisions regarding which direction to move a control in order to move the system or display indicator in a particular direction. Across populations of individuals, many arrangements show preferred relations between the direction of control action and outcome of system output (see Loveless, 1962).

Obviously, when a linear control is in the same orientation as a linear display, the stereotype is to expect the display to move in the same direction as the control. More interesting, when a linear display is oriented perpendicularly to the linear control, right is paired with upward movement and left is paired with downward movement. With control knobs, clockwise rotation tends to be associated with up or right movements (see Hoffman, 1990a, 1990b). In addition, there is a stereotype, called Warrick's principle, that the display is expected to move in the same direction as the part of the control that is nearest to the display. With a vertical display, a clockwise rotation would be preferred if the control were located to the right of the display and a counter-clockwise rotation if it were located to the left.

Hoffman (1990a, 1990b) evaluated the relative strength of the stereotypes for two- and three-dimensional display and control relationships. He found that different populations (in this case, engineers and psychologists) differed in their preference. Engineers were more likely to follow Warrick's principle, most likely because it has a mechanical basis, whereas psychologists tended to follow the stereotype of preferring clockwise for up and right movement. This difference emphasizes not only that the specific experience of individuals is important, but also that the preferred relations are based on the individual's mental model for the task.

SUMMING UP

Action selection is an important part of behavior inside and outside of the laboratory because choices among alternative actions are required in virtually all situations. Action selection has been a topic of interest in human experimental psychology since Donders's (1868/1969) seminal work, with contemporary research on the topic being at the forefront of the cognitive revolution in the 1950s. S-R compatibility, which is the quintessential action-selection topic, saw a surge in research in the 1990s, with significant advances made in the development of theoretical frameworks for explaining a variety of phenomena in terms of common mechanisms. As we move into the twenty-first century, the range of tasks and environments in which compatibility effects play a significant role, and the significant insights these effects provide regarding human performance, is only now coming to be fully appreciated.

REFERENCES

Adam, J. J., Boon, B., Paas, F. G. W. C., & Umiltà, C. (1998). The up-right/down-left advantage for vertically oriented stimuli and horizontally oriented responses: A dual-strategy hypothesis. *Journal of Experiment Psychology: Human Perception and Performance, 24,* 1582–1597.

Allport, A., Styles, E. A., & Hsieh, H., (1994). Shifting intentional set: Exploring the dynamic control of tasks. In C. Umiltà & M. Moscovitch (Eds.), *Attention and performance: Vol. 15. Conscious and nonconscious information processing* (pp. 421–452). Cambridge, MA: MIT Press.

Andre, A. D., & Wickens, C. D. (1990). *Display-control compatibility in the cockpit: Guidelines for display layout analysis.* (ARL-90-12/NASA-A^{3}I-90-1). Savoy, IL: University of Illinois, Aviation Research Laboratory.

Baldo, J. V., Shimamura, A., & Prinzmetal, W. (1998). Mapping symbols to response modalities: Interference effects on Stroop-like tasks. *Perception & Psychophysics, 60,* 427–437.

Bertelson, P. (1961). Sequential redundancy and speed in a serial two-choice responding task. *Quarterly Journal of Experimental Psychology, 13,* 90–102.

Bertelson, P. (1967). The time course of preparation. *Quarterly Journal of Experimental Psychology, 19,* 272–279.

Broadbent, D. E. (1958). *Perception and communication.* Oxford, England: Pergamon Press.

Campbell, K. C., & Proctor, R. W. (1993). Repetition effects with categorizable stimulus and response sets. *Journal of Experimental Psychology: Learning, Memory, and Cognition, 19,* 1345–1362.

Chapanis, A., & Lindenbaum, L. E. (1959). A reaction time study of four control-display linkages. *Human Factors, 1*(4), 1–7.

Cho, Y. S., & Proctor, R. W. (2001). Effect of an initiating action on the up-right/down-left advantage for vertically arrayed stimuli and horizontally arrayed responses. *Journal of Experiment Psychology: Human Perception and Performance, 27,* 472–484.

Cohen, J. D., Dunbar, K., & McClelland, J. L. (1990). On the control of automatic processes: A parallel distributed processing account of the Stroop effect. *Psychological Review, 97,* 332–361.

Cooper, L. A., & Shepard, R. N. (1973). Chronometric studies of the rotation of mental images. In W. G. Chase (Ed.), *Visual information processing* (pp. 75–176). New York: Academic Press.

Dalrymple-Alford, E. C., & Budayr, B. (1966). Examination of some aspects if the Stroop color-word test. *Perceptual and Motor Skills, 23,* 1211–1214.

De Jagger, J. J. (1970). *Reaction time and mental processes* (J. Brozek & M. S. Sibinga, Translators). Nieuwkoop, The Netherlands: B. De Graf. (Original work published 1865)

De Jong, R., Coles, M. G. H., Logan, G. D., & Gratton, G. (1990). Searching for the point of no return: The control of response processes in speeded choice reaction performance. *Journal of Experimental Psychology: Human Perception and Performance, 16,* 164–182.

De Jong, R., Liang, C.-C., & Lauber, E. (1994). Conditional and unconditional automaticity: A dual-process model of effects of spatial stimulus-response compatibility. *Journal of Experimental Psychology: Human Perception and Performance, 20,* 731–750.

DeSchepper, B., & Treisman, A. (1996). Visual memory for novel shapes: Implicit coding without attention. *Journal of Experimental Psychology: Learning, Memory, and Cognition, 22,* 27–47.

Donders, F. C. (1969). On the speed of mental processes. In W. G. Koster (Ed.), *Acta Psychologica, 30: Vol. 2. Attention and Performance* (pp. 412–431). Amsterdam: North-Holland. (Original work published 1868)

Dosher, B. A. (1979). Empirical approaches to information processing: Speed-accuracy tradeoff functions or reaction time—A reply. *Acta Psychologica, 43,* 347–359.

Duncan, J. (1977). Response selection rules in spatial choice reaction tasks. In S. Dornic (Ed.). *Attention and performance: Vol. 6* (pp. 49–71). Hillsdale, NJ: Erlbaum.

Duncan, J. (1979). Divided attention: The whole is more than the sum of the parts. *Journal of Experimental Psychology: Human Perception and Performance, 5,* 216–228.

Durgin, F. H. (2000). The reverse Stroop effect. *Psychonomic Bulletin & Review, 7,* 121–125.

Dutta, A., & Proctor, R. W. (1992). Persistence of stimulus-response compatibility effects with extended practice. *Journal of Experimental Psychology: Learning, Memory, and Cognition, 18,* 801–809.

Eimer, M. (1998). The lateralized readiness potential as an on-line measure of central response activation processes. *Behavior Research Methods, Instruments, & Computers, 30,* 146–156.

Eriksen, B. A., & Eriksen, C. W. (1974). Effects of noise letters upon the identification of a target letter in a nonsearch task. *Perception & Psychophysics, 16,* 143–149.

Eriksen, C. W., & Schultz, C. W. (1979). Information processing in visual search: A continuous flow conception and experimental results. *Perception & Psychophysics, 25,* 249–263.

Falkenstein, M., Hohnsbein, J., & Hoormann, J. (1994). Effects of choice complexity on different subcomponents of the late positive complex of the event-related potential. *Electoencephalography and Clinical Neurophysiology, 92,* 148–160.

Fitts, P. M., & Deininger, R. L. (1954). S-R compatibility: Correspondence among paired elements within stimulus and response codes. *Journal of Experimental Psychology, 48,* 483–492.

Fitts, P. M., & Posner, M. I. (1967). *Human performance*. Belmont, CA: Brooks/Cole.

Fitts, P. M., & Seeger, C. M. (1953). S-R compatibility: Spatial characteristics of stimulus and response codes. *Journal of Experimental Psychology, 46,* 199–210.

Fox, E. (1995). Negative priming from ignored distractors in visual selection: A review. *Psychonomic Bulletin and Review, 2,* 145–173.

Gratton, G., Coles, M. G. H., Sirevaag, E. J., Eriksen, C. W., & Donchin, E. (1988). Pre- and poststimulus activation of response channels: A psychophysiological analysis. *Journal of Experimental Psychology: Human Perception and Performance, 14,* 331–344.

Guiard, Y. (1983). The lateral coding of rotations: A study of the Simon effect with wheel-rotation responses. *Journal of Motor Behavior, 15,* 331–342.

Heathcote, A., Brown, S., & Mewhort, D. J. K. (2000). The power law repealed: The case for an exponential law of practice. *Psychonomic Bulletin & Review, 7,* 185–207.

Hedge, A., & Marsh, N. W. A. (1975). The effect of irrelevant spatial correspondences on two-choice reaction time. *Acta Psychologica, 39,* 427–439.

Heister, G., Schroeder-Heister, P., & Ehrenstein, W. H. (1990). Spatial coding and spatio-anatomical mapping: Evidence for a hierarchical model of spatial stimulus-response compatibility. In R. W. Proctor & T. G. Reeve (Eds.), *Stimulus-response compatibility: An integrated perspective* (pp. 117–143). Amsterdam: North-Holland.

Helmholtz, H. (1850). Messungen über den zeitlichen Verlauf der Zuckung animalischer Muskeln und die Fortpflanzungsgeschwindigkeit der Reizung in den Nerven [Measurement of the time course of the muscles and the transmission speed of nerve stimulation]. *Archiv für Anatomie und Phsysiologie,* 276–364.

Helmholtz, H. (1867). Mittheilung, betreffend Versuche über die Fortpflanzungsgeschwindigkeit der Reizung in den motorischen Nerven des Menschen, welche Herr. N. Baxt aus Petersburg im Physiologischen Laboratorium zu Heidelberg ausgeführt hat [Communication concerning experiments about the transmission speed of stimulation in the motor nerves of humans, which Mr. N. Baxt from Petersburg in the Physiology Laboratories at Heidelberg has performed]. *Monatsberichte der Akademie der Wissenschaften zu Berlin, 29,* 228–234.

Hick, W. E. (1952). On the rate of gain of information. *Quarterly Journal of Experimental Psychology, 4,* 11–26.

Hoffman, E. R. (1990a). Strength of component principles determining direction-of-turn stereotypes for horizontally moving displays. *Proceedings of the Human Factors Society 34th Annual Meeting,* 457–461.

Hoffman, E. R. (1990b). Strength of component principles for direction-of-turn stereotypes of three-dimensional display/control arrangements. *Proceedings of the Human Factors Society 34th Annual Meeting,* 462–466.

Hommel, B. (1993a). Inverting the Simon effect with intention: Determinants of detection and extent of effects of irrelevant spatial information. *Psychological Research, 55,* 270–279.

Hommel, B. (1993b). The role of attention for the Simon effect. *Psychological Research, 55,* 208–222.

Hommel, B. (1998). Automatic stimulus-response translation in dual-task performance. *Journal of Experimental Psychology: Human Perception and Performance, 24,* 1368–1384.

Hommel, B., & Prinz, W. (Eds.). (1997). *Theoretical issues in stimulus-response compatibility.* Amsterdam: North-Holland.

Hyman, R. (1953). Stimulus information as a determinant of reaction time. *Journal of Experimental Psychology, 45,* 188–196.

Hyman, R., & Umiltà, C. (1969). The information hypothesis and non-repetitions. *Acta Psychologica, 30,* 37–53.

Iacoboni, M., Woods, R. P., & Mazziotta, J. C. (1998). Bimodal (auditory and visual) left frontoparietal circuitry for sensorimotor integration and sensoimotor learning. *Brain, 121,* 2135–2143.

Jastrow, J. (1890). *The time-relations of mental phenomena.* New York: N.D.C. Hodges.

Jensen, A. R. (1980). Chronometric analysis of intelligence. *Journal of Social Biological Structure, 3,* 103–122.

Jersild, A. T. (1927). Mental set and shift. *Archives of Psychology, 14,* (Whole No. 89).

Kantowitz, B. H., & Sanders, M. S. (1972). Partial advance information and stimulus dimensionality. *Journal of Experimental Psychology, 92,* 412–418.

Koch, I., & Hoffmann, J. (2000). The role of stimulus-based and response-based spatial information on sequence learning. *Journal of Experimental Psychology: Learning, Memory, and Cognition, 26,* 863–882.

Kornblum, S. (1967). Choice reaction time for repetitions and non-repetitions. *Acta Psychologica, 27,* 178–187.

Kornblum, S. (1968). Serial-choice reaction time: Inadequacies of the information hypothesis. *Science, 159,* 432–434.

Kornblum, S., Hasbroucq, T., & Osman, A. (1990). Dimensional overlap: Cognitive basis for stimulus-response compatibility—A model and taxonomy. *Psychological Review, 97,* 253–270.

Kornblum, S., & Lee, J.-W. (1995). Stimulus-response compatibility with relevant and irrelevant stimulus dimension that do and do not overlap with the response. *Journal of Experimental Psychology: Human Perception and Performance, 21,* 855–875.

Kvälseth, T. O. (1980). An alternative to the Hick-Hyman's and Sternberg's Law. *Perceptual and Motor Skills, 50,* 1281–1282.

Kvälseth, T. O. (1989). Longstreth et al.'s reaction time model: Some comments. *Bulletin of the Psychonomic Society, 27,* 358–360.

Lamberts, K., Tavernier, G., & D'Ydewalle, G. (1992). Effects of multiple reference points in spatial stimulus-response compatibility. *Acta Psychologica, 79,* 115–130.

Leonard, J. A. (1958). Partial advance information in a choice reaction task. *British Journal of Psychology, 49,* 89–96.

Lien, M.-C., & Proctor, R. W. (2000). Multiple spatial correspondence effects on dual-task performance. *Journal of Experimental Psychology: Human Perception and Performance, 26,* 1260–1280.

Lippa, Y. (1996). A referential-coding explanation for compatibility effects of perceptually orthogonal stimulus and response dimensions. *Quarterly Journal of Experimental Psychology, 49A,* 950–971.

Lippa, Y., & Adam, J. J. (2001). An explanation of orthogonal S-R compatibility effects that vary with hand or response position: The end-state comfort hypothesis. *Perception & Psychophysics, 63,* 156–174.

Logan, G. D. (1994). On the ability to inhibit thought and action: A users' guide to the stop signal paradigm. In D. Dagenbach & T. H. Carr (Eds.), *Inhibitory processes in attention, memory, and language* (pp. 189–239). San Diego, CA: Academic Press.

Logan, G. D., & Irwin, D. E. (2000). Don't look! Don't touch! Inhibitory control of hand and eye movements. *Psychonomic Bulletin & Review, 7,* 107–112.

Logan, G. D., & Schulkind, M. D. (2000). Parallel memory retrieval in dual-task situations: Semantic memory. *Journal of Experimental Psychology: Human Perception and Performance, 26,* 1072–1090.

Longsteth, L. E. (1988). Hick's law: Its limit is 3 bits. *Bulletin of the Psychonomic Society, 26,* 8–10.

Longstreth, L. E., El-Zahhar, N., & Alcorn, M. B. (1985). Exceptions to Hick's Law: Explorations with a response duration measure. *Journal of Experimental Psychology: General, 114,* 41–74.

Los, S. A. (1996). On the origin of mixing costs: Exploring information processing in pure and mixed blocks. *Acta Psychologica, 94,* 145–188.

Loveless, N. E. (1962). Direction-of-motion stereotypes: A review. *Ergonomics, 5,* 357–383.

Lowe, D. G. (1979). Strategies, context and the mechanisms of response inhibition. *Memory & Cognition, 7,* 382–389.

Lu, C.-H., & Proctor, R. W. (1995). The influence of irrelevant location information on performance: A review of the Simon effect and spatial Stroop effects. *Psychonomic Bulletin & Review, 2,* 174–207.

Lu, C.-H., & Proctor, R. W. (2001). Influence of irrelevant information on human performance: Effects of S-R association strength and relative timing. *Quarterly Journal of Experimental Psychology, 54A,* 95–136.

MacLeod, C. M. (1991). Half a century of research on the Stroop effect: An integrative review. *Psychological Bulletin, 109,* 163–203.

Mangun, G. R., Hopfinger, J. B., & Heinze, H.-J. (1998). Integrating electrophysiology and neuroimaging in the study of human cognition. *Behavior Research Methods, Instruments, & Computers, 30,* 118–130.

May, C. P., Kane, M. J., & Hasher, L. (1995). Determinants of negative priming. *Psychological Bulletin, 118,* 35–54.

McClelland, J. L. (1979). On the time relations of mental processes: A framework for analyzing processes in cascade. *Psychological Review, 88,* 375–407.

Merkel, J. (1885). Die zeitliche Verhaltnisse de Willenstatigkeit [The temporal relations of activities of the will]. *Philosophische Studien, 2,* 73–127.

Meyer, D. E., & Kieras, D. E. (1997). A computational theory of executive cognitive processes and multiple-task performance: Part 2. Accounts of psychological refractory-period phenomena. *Psychological Review, 104,* 749–791.

Michaels, C. F., & Schilder, S. (1991). Stimulus-response compatibilities between vertically oriented stimuli and horizontally oriented responses. *Perception & Psychophysics, 49,* 342–348.

Miller, J. (1982). Discrete versus continuous stage models of human information processing: In search of partial output. *Journal of Experimental Psychology: Human Perception and Performance, 8,* 273–296.

Miller, J. (1988). Discrete and continuous models of human information processing: Theoretical distinctions and empirical results. *Acta Psychologica, 67,* 191–257.

Mordkoff, J. T. (1996). Selective attention and internal constraints: There is more to the flanker effect than biased contingencies. In A. F. Kramer, M. G. H. Coles, & G. D. Logan (Eds.), *Converging operations in the study of visual selective attention* (pp. 483–502). Washington D C: American Psychological Association.

Mowbray, G. H., & Rhoades, M. V. (1959). On the reduction of choice reaction times with practice. *Quarterly Journal of Psychology, 11,* 16–23.

Neely, J. H. (1977). Semantic priming and retrieval from lexical memory: Roles of inhibitionless spreading activation and limited-capacity attention. *Journal of Experimental Psychology: General, 106,* 226–254.

Neill, W. T., & Valdes, L. A. (1992). Persistence of negative priming: Steady state or decay? *Journal of Experimental Psychology: Learning, Memory, and Cognition, 18,* 565–576.

Newell, A., & Rosenbloom, P. S. (1981). Mechanisms of skill acquisition and the law of practice. In J. R. Anderson (Ed.), *Cognitive skills and their acquisition* (pp. 1–55). Hillsdale, NJ: Erlbaum.

Nicoletti, R., Anzola, G. P., Luppino, G., Rizzolatti, G., & Umiltà, C. (1982). Spatial compatibility effects on the same side of the body midline. *Journal of Experimental Psychology: Human Perception and Performance, 8,* 644–673.

Nissen, M. J., & Bullemer, P. (1987). Attentional requirements of learning: Evidence from performance measures. *Cognitive Psychology, 19,* 1–32.

Osman, A., Kornblum, S., & Meyer, D. E. (1986). The point of no return in choice reaction time: Controlled and ballistic stages of response preparation. *Journal of Experimental Psychology: Human Perception and Performance, 12,* 243–258.

Osman, A., Lou, L., Muller-Gethmann, H., Rinkenauer, G., Mattes, S., & Ulrich, R. (2000). Mechanisms of speed-accuracy tradeoff: Evidence from covert motor processes. *Biological Psychology, 51,* 173–199.

Pachella, R. G. (1974). The interpretation of reaction time in information-processing research. In B. H. Kantowitz (Ed.), *Human information processing: Tutorials in performance and cognition* (pp. 41–82). Hillsdale, NJ: Erlbaum.

Park, J., & Kanwisher, N. (1994). Negative priming for spatial locations: Identity mismatching, not distractor inhibition. *Journal of Experimental Psychology: Human Perception and Performance, 20,* 613–623.

Pashler, H. (1998). *The psychology of attention*. Cambridge, MA: MIT Press.

Pashler, H., & Baylis, G. (1991). Procedural learning: 2. Intertrial repetition effects in speeded choice task. *Journal of Experimental Psychology: Learning, Memory, and Cognition, 17,* 33–48.

Payne, S. J. (1995). Naïve judgments of stimulus-response compatibility. *Human Factors, 37,* 495–506.

Posner, M. I., Klein, R., Summers, J., & Buggie, S. (1973). On the selection of signals. *Memory & Cognition, 1,* 2–12.

Prinz, W. (1997). Why Donders has led us astray. In B. Hommel & W. Prinz (Eds.), *Theoretical issues in stimulus-response compatibility* (pp. 247–267). Amsterdam: North-Holland.

Proctor, R. W., & Dutta, A. (1993). Do the same stimulus-response relations influence choice reactions initially and after practice? *Journal of Experimental Psychology: Learning, Memory, and Cognition, 19,* 922–930.

Proctor, R. W., & Lu, C.-H. (1999). Processing irrelevant location information: Practice and transfer effects in choice-reaction tasks. *Memory & Cognition, 27,* 63–77.

Proctor, R. W., & Reeve, T. G. (1985). Compatibility effects in the assignment of symbolic stimuli to discrete finger response. *Journal of Experimental Psychology: Human Perception and Performance, 11,* 623–639.

Proctor, R. W., & Reeve, T. G. (1986). Salient-feature coding operations in spatial precuing tasks. *Journal of Experimental Psychology: Human Perception & Performance, 12,* 277–285.

Proctor, R. W., & Reeve, T. G. (Eds.). (1990). *Stimulus-response compatibility: An integrated perspective*. Amsterdam: North-Holland.

Proctor, R. W., & Vu, K.-P. L. (2002). Eliminating, magnifying, and reversing spatial compatibility effects with mixed location-relevant and irrelevant trials. In W. Prinz & B. Hommel (Eds.), *Common mechanisms in perception and action: Attention and performance, XIX* (pp. 443–473). New York: Oxford University Press.

Reeve, G. T., & Proctor, R. W. (1984). On the advance preparation of discrete finger responses. *Journal of Experimental Psychology: Human Perception and Performance, 10,* 541–553.

Riggio, L., Gawryszewski, L. G., & Umiltà, C. (1986). What is crossed in crossed-hand effects? *Acta Psychologica, 62,* 89–100.

Rogers, R. D., & Monsell, S. (1995). Cost of a predictable switch between simple cognitive tasks. *Journal of Experimental Psychology: General, 124,* 207–231.

Rosenbloom, P. S., & Newell, A. (1987). An integrated computational model of stimulus-response compatibility and practice. In

G. H. Bower (Ed.), *The psychology of learning and motivation* (Vol. 21, pp. 1–52). San Diego, CA: Academic Press.

Roswarski, T. E., & Proctor, R. W. (1996). Multiple spatial codes and temporal overlap in choice-reaction tasks. *Psychological Research, 59,* 196–211.

Roswarski, T. E., & Proctor, R. W. (2000). Auditory stimulus-response compatibility: Is there a contribution of stimulus-hand correspondence? *Psychological Research, 63,* 148–158.

Rugg, M. D., & Coles, M. G. H. (Eds.). (1995). *Electrophysiology of mind: Event-related brain potentials and cognition.* Oxford, England: Oxford University Press.

Sanders, A. F. (1975). The foreperiod effect revisited. *Quarterly Journal of Experimental Psychology, 27,* 591–598.

Sanders, A. F. (1998). *Elements of human performance.* Mahwah, NJ: Erlbaum.

Sanders, A. F., & Wertheim, A. H. (1973). The relation between physical stimulus properties and the effect of foreperiod duration on reaction time. *Quarterly Journal of Experimental Psychology, 25,* 201–206.

Schweickert, R. (1983). Latent network theory: Scheduling of processes in sentence verification and the Stroop effect. *Journal of Experimental Psychology: Learning, Memory, and Cognition, 9,* 353–383.

Seibel, R. (1963). Discrimination reaction time for a 1,023-alternative task. *Journal of Experimental Psychology, 66,* 215–226.

Shaffer, L. H. (1965). Choice reaction with variable S-R mapping. *Journal of Experimental Psychology, 70,* 284–288.

Smith, E. E. (1968). Choice reaction time: An analysis of the major theoretical positions. *Psychological Bulletin, 69,* 77–110.

Soetens, E. (1998). Localizing sequential effects in serial choice reaction time with the information reduction procedure. *Journal of Experimental Psychology: Human Perception and Performance, 24,* 547–568.

Sternberg, S. (1969). The discovery of processing stages: Extensions of Donders' method. In W. G. Koster (Ed.), *Attention and performance II. Acta Psychologica, 30,* 276–315.

Sternberg, S. (1998). Discovering mental processing stages: The method of additive factors. In D. Scarborough & S. Sternberg (Eds.), *An invitation to cognitive science: Methods, models, and conceptual issues* (2nd ed., Vol. 4, pp. 703–863). Cambridge, MA: MIT Press.

Stoffer, T. H., & Umiltà, C. (1997). Spatial stimulus coding and the focus of attention in S-R compatibility and the Simon effect. In B. Hommel & W. Prinz (Eds.), *Theoretical issues in stimulus-response compatibility* (pp. 181–208). Amsterdam: North-Holland.

Stroop, J. R. (1992). Studies of interference in serial verbal reactions. *Journal of Experimental Psychology: General, 121,* 15–23. (Original work published 1935)

Tagliabue, M., Zorzi, M., Umiltà, C., & Bassignani, F. (2000). The role of LTM links and STM links in the Simon effect. *Journal of Experimental Psychology: Human Perception and Performance, 26,* 648–670.

Teichner, W., & Krebs, M. J. (1974). Laws of visual choice reaction time. *Psychological Review, 81,* 75–98.

Telford, C. W. (1931). The refractory phase of voluntary and associative responses. *Journal of Experimental Psychology, 14,* 1–36.

Umiltà, C., & Nicoletti, R. (1990). Spatial stimulus-response compatibility. In R. W. Proctor & T. G. Reeve (Eds.), *Stimulus-response compatibility: An integrated perspective* (pp. 89–116). Amsterdam: North-Holland.

Van Zandt, T., Colonius, H., & Proctor, R. W. (2000). A comparison of two response time models applied to perceptual matching. *Psychonomic Bulletin & Review, 7,* 208–256.

Vickrey, C., & Neuringer, A. (2000). Pigeon reaction time, Hick's law, and intelligence. *Psychonomic Bulletin & Review, 7,* 284–291.

Vu, K.-P. L., & Proctor, R. W. (2001). Determinants of right-left and top-bottom prevalence for two-dimensional spatial compatibility. *Journal of Experimental Psychology: Human Perception and Performance, 27,* 813–828.

Vu, K.-P. L., & Proctor, R. W. (2002). *Mixing compatible and incompatible mappings: Elimination, reduction, and enhancement of spatial compatibility effects.* Manuscript submitted for publication.

Wang, H., & Proctor, R. W. (1996). Stimulus-response compatibility as a function of stimulus code and response modality. *Journal of Experimental Psychology: Human Perception and Performance, 22,* 1201–1217.

Weeks, D. J., & Proctor, R. W. (1990). Salient-features coding in the translation between orthogonal stimulus and response dimensions. *Journal of Experimental Psychology: General, 119,* 355–366.

Weeks, D. J., Proctor, R. W., & Beyak, B. (1995). Stimulus-response compatibility for vertically oriented stimuli and horizontally oriented responses: Evidence for spatial coding. *Quarterly Journal of Experimental Psychology, 48,* 367–383.

Welford, A. T. (1987). Comment on "Exceptions to Hick's law: Explorations with a response duration measure" (Longstreth, El-Zahhar, & Alcorn, 1985). *Journal of Experimental Psychology: General, 116,* 312–314.

Wickelgren, W. A. (1977). Speed-accuracy tradeoff and information processing dynamics. *Acta Psychologica, 41,* 67–85.

Woodworth, R. S. (1938). *Experimental psychology.* New York: Holt.

Wundt, W. (1883). Über psychologische Methoden [Over psychological methods]. *Philosophische Studien, 10,* 1–38.

CHAPTER 12

Motor Control

HERBERT HEUER

Motor control is a cross-disciplinary field of research in which the boundaries between established academic disciplines like psychology, physiology, neurology, engineering, and physical education are blurred. Within psychology, motor behavior tended to be a rather marginal topic for various reasons. When psychology is conceived as a science of the mind, movement is more or less beyond its scope. Less obviously, even when psychology is conceived as a science of behavior, issues of motor control do not become focal; for example, behaviorism was more concerned with "what is done" questions than with "how is it done" questions. Finally, although the first well-known psychology paper on motor control appeared at the end of the nineteenth century (Woodworth, 1899), and although James (1890, 1950) devoted a chapter to "The Production of Movement," touching on the topic in several other chapters, the founding fathers of psychology did not stamp motor control as an essential ingredient of the emerging academic discipline.

The field of motor control gains in importance as soon as one envisages that the human mind and brain may have evolved primarily to support action, not to contemplate the world. Then the question of how goals can be reached becomes critically important. This question alludes to problems of control, and motor control deals with particular goals that can be reached by moving one's limbs.

In this chapter I first introduce the core problem of motor control and discuss different ways that it can be solved. Basically, there are two such ways: open-loop and closed-loop control. Open-loop processes are initiated before a movement is actually executed, so they are described under the heading of *motor preparation*. The next section then deals with closed-loop processes, the exploitation of sensory feedback from an ongoing movement in the service of motor control, but also with other uses of sensory information. After the discussion of these rather fundamental issues, the perspective is enlarged somewhat. Many motor skills require coordinated movements of different limbs, which opens the topic of motor coordination. Finally, I shall address the flexibility of motor control which enables us to operate various tools and machines and to handle objects of various masses.

THE PROBLEM OF MOTOR CONTROL

An Outline of the Problem

Movements result from an interplay of passive and active forces. Passive forces are due to our own movements as well as to environmental factors like gravity. For example, in the swing phase of the walking cycle the thigh is rotated forward;

initially the knee is flexed, followed by extension. This forward rotation of the shank results largely from passive forces of different origins. The deceleration of the knee extension, however, is largely a result of active muscular forces, with only a small contribution of passive ones (Winter & Robertson, 1978). Thus, with the exception of a few very simple tasks, the production of movement requires not only the generation of appropriate active forces, but in addition passive forces have to be taken into account.

Figure 12.1 illustrates a joint with two opposing muscles, a kind of minimal movement device. Muscles are designated as agonist and antagonist with respect to their function in a particular movement. For example, when the movement is a flexion of the joint, the flexor is the agonist and the extensor is the antagonist; for an extension, the functional roles of flexors and extensors are reversed. Of course, Figure 12.1 is extremely simplified, both with respect to the mechanical characteristics and with respect to the number of muscles acting on the joint.

Muscles are complicated force generators. They contract when they are activated via the motor nerves. Each axon of a motor nerve innervates a smaller or larger bundle of muscle fibers; the axon together with its muscle fibers is called a motor unit. The activation can be recorded. Needle electrodes, which are inserted in the muscle tissue, allow one to record from single motor units, while surface electrodes pick up averaged and filtered electrical activity of motor units within a certain area below the electrodes. For isometric contractions, there is a systematic relation between electromyographically recorded muscle activity (EMG) and force. In particular, the relation between the integrated EMG signal and force is linear (Lippold, 1952). However, for movements for which phasic bursts of muscle activity are typical (at least when the movements are rapid), the relation is more complex.

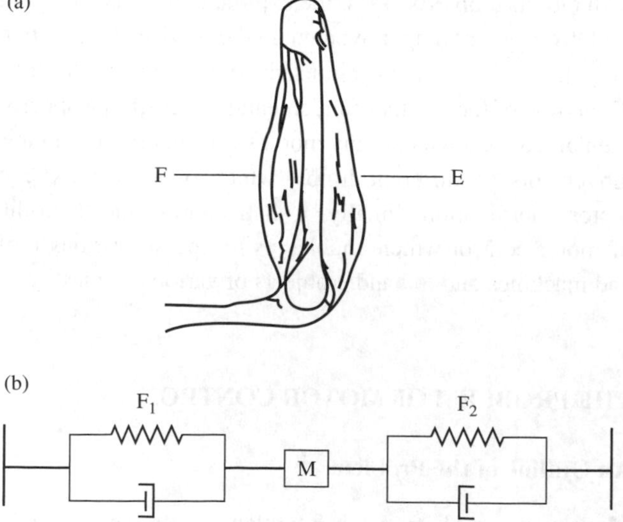

Figure 12.1 (a) A joint with two opposing muscles, flexor (F) and extensor (E); (b) mechanical analogue of two damped springs acting on a single mass (M); the mass is stationary when the two opposing forces F_1 and F_2 cancel each other. Reprinted with permission.

Complications arise, first, from the temporal relations between bursts of muscle activity and forces, which can be fairly variable. In general, forces develop only with a delay when a muscle is activated, and after the end of the burst there is a gradual decay. Complications arise also from fatigue-induced changes, with fatigue being developed in the course of repeated or prolonged activity. In addition, for a given activation level, muscle force depends on the length of the muscle and on the rate of its contraction. In particular, the length-tension relation of muscle is important for models of motor control: Muscle force increases with increasing muscle length, and the slope becomes steeper the stronger the activation of the muscle is (e.g., Rack & Westbury, 1969). Although the length-tension relation is not really linear, a linear approximation is useful, at least for certain ranges of muscle length. Thus, one can think of a muscle as being mechanically similar to a damped spring (cf. Figure 12.1).

A muscle can actively contract, but not stretch. (A rubber band would perhaps be a better analogue than a spring.) Therefore at least two opposing muscles are needed for a simple joint. From Figure 12.1 it is apparent that, as the one muscle contracts, the other one will be stretched. This implies that, with given activations of the opposing muscles, the force of the contracting muscles declines while that of the stretched muscles increases. At a certain joint angle, and at a certain relation between the lengths of the opposing muscles, the forces developed by them will be equal, but in opposite directions, and thus cancel each other. The net force is zero, and the joint position at which this is the case is called the equilibrium position. There is considerable evidence that equilibrium positions are important for motor control (cf. Kelso & Holt, 1980; Polit & Bizzi, 1979). In the simplest version of a mass-spring model, movements come about simply by the specification of a new equilibrium position (e.g., Cooke, 1980), but experiments have revealed that the equilibrium position shifts continuously and not stepwise (Bizzi, Accornero, Chapple, & Hogan, 1984).

Movement results from the net force of opposing muscles (and, of course, from passive forces). Thus, at first glance there seems not to be much sense in cocontractions, in which opposing muscles are active simultaneously. Nevertheless, cocontractions can be observed in particular early during

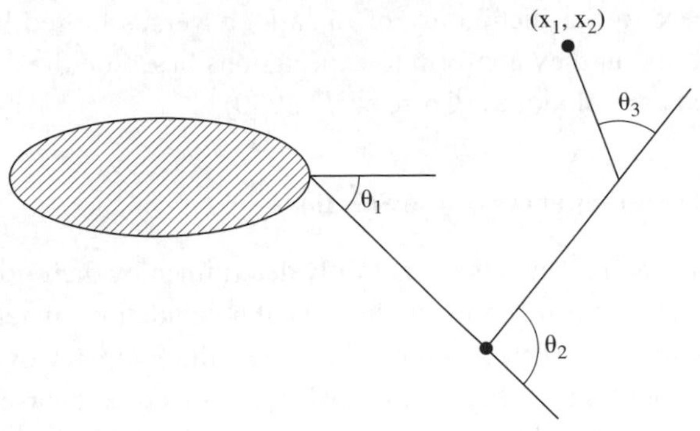

Figure 12.2 A three-jointed arm with joint angles θ_1, θ_2, and θ_3, which are associated with spatial position (x_1, x_2) of the end-effector.

practice (e.g., Metz, 1970) and in tasks requiring high precision. Even when no net forces result from cocontractions, they modulate the mechanical characteristics of the joint like friction.

Saying that joint movement results from the net force of opposing muscles (in addition to passive forces) is not the whole story. More precisely, joint rotation results from the torque, which again is related to the net force in a fairly complicated way, with the relation being dependent on the joint angle. Even with the movement of the joint, the sequence of transformations from muscle activation to movement has not yet reached its end, because in general the goals for our movements are not defined in terms of joint angles.

Figure 12.2 illustrates a three-jointed arm with the end-effector pointing to a target. The goals of many movements are defined in terms of reaching for some spatial target; for other movements, as in catching a ball, there are temporal targets in addition; for still other movements, as in writing, goals are defined in terms of movement traces (or paths). From Figure 12.2 it is apparent that a particular configuration of joint angles is associated with a particular spatial position of the end-effector.

Thus far I have sketched the transformation of muscle activation to the spatial position of an end-effector like the tip of the index finger. The purpose was to give some impression of the complexity of this transformation without going into too much detail. Sometimes different components of the transformation are discussed separately, in particular the kinematic transformation (from joint angles to end-effector positions) and the dynamic transformation (from torques to movements of the joints). As a more general term, I shall use *motor transformation* to refer to the total transformation or some part of it.

Given the complexity and the time-varying characteristics of the motor transformation, one may wonder that humans—at least after the first few months of their life—are able to produce purposeful movements at all, and not only random-appearing ones. This requires that humans be able to determine the pattern of muscular activity that is required to produce a particular movement of a particular end-effector. The very fact that humans can produce purposeful movements indicates that nature has solved this core problem of motor control; what remains for the movement scientist is to gain an understanding of what the solution is.

An Outline of Possible Solutions

The core problem of motor control can be stated in a very simple and general way. Let T be a transformation of an input signal x into an output signal y. For example, y shall be a particular time-varying position of an end-effector, and x a vector that captures time-varying muscle activity. Then the general problem of control, and that of motor control in particular, is to determine an input signal x such that the output signal y becomes identical to the desired output signal y^*. The problem is solved when the inverse of the transformation T can be determined, such that $T^{-1}T = 1$. Thus, control requires the inversion of a transformation, and there are two fundamentally different ways to achieve this (see Jordan, 1996, for a detailed discussion).

Figure 12.3a illustrates an open-loop solution which requires an internal model $\hat{T}^{-1}$ of the transformation, or, more precisely, of its inverse. There are different ways of implementing such a model formally (e.g., Jordan, 1996). Of

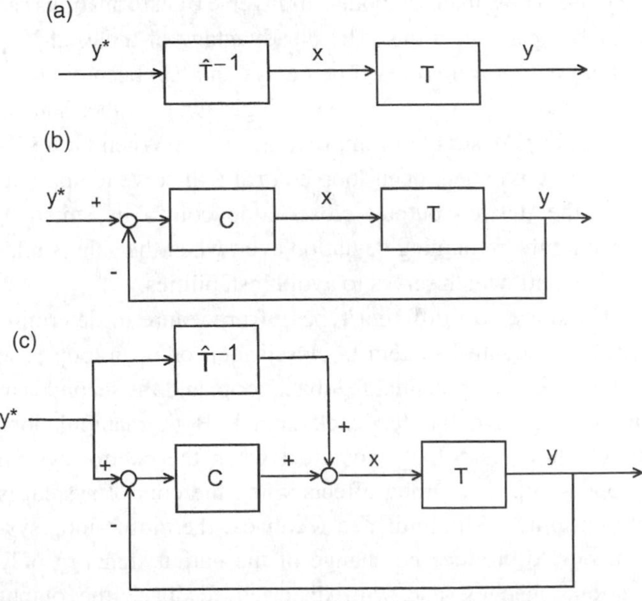

Figure 12.3 Possible solutions to a control problem. (a) Open-loop solution with an internal model $\hat{T}^{-1}$ of the (inverse) transformation; (b) closed-loop solution, with C as controller; (c) combination of open-loop and closed-loop solution.

course, such an internal model is not necessarily a kind of entity, located in some part of the brain, but it can result from the activity of a network that is distributed widely across both central and more peripheral levels of the motor system (e.g., Kalveram, 1991).

Figure 12.3b illustrates a closed-loop solution for which no internal model $\hat{T}^{-1}$ is required. Instead, the inversion of the transformation results from the structure of the loop. (This is shown formally by Jordan, 1996.) Intuitively this becomes clear from the following consideration. A closed-loop system can reduce the deviation between the output y and the desired output y^*. To the extent that this is successful, y and y^* become similar. This then implies, because $y = T(x)$, that x approximates $T^{-1}(y^*)$.

For some years, open-loop and closed-loop models of motor control were contrasted (cf. Stelmach, 1982). However, by now it is clear that nature combines both types of solution, roughly in a way illustrated in Figure 12.3c. This combination maintains the advantages of both types of solution and avoids the disadvantages of each of them. In addition, the combination exhibits some characteristics that match characteristics of human movements (Cruse, Dean, Heuer, & Schmidt, 1990).

The disadvantage of an open-loop solution is its limited precision. The motor transformation is complex, and it has time-varying characteristics. When we use tools or operate machines, there are additional transformations that must be taken into account, like the transformation of a steering-wheel rotation into a change of the direction in which a vehicle is heading. Thus, internal models of inverse transformations can only be approximations. The disadvantage of a closed-loop system is that it involves time delays and can become instable, in particular when the gain is high. On the other hand, a high gain is desirable to improve accuracy. When both systems are combined, open-loop control will serve to approximate the desired output; closed-loop control is suited to reducing the remaining deviation even when the gain is relatively small, which serves to avoid instabilities.

There are two different types of procedure to determine whether a control system is closed-loop or open-loop. The first is to cut the potential feedback loop, and the second is to distort the potential feedback signal. Both manipulations should have essentially no effect when the control system is open-loop, but strong effects when the control system is closed-loop; with eliminated feedback, the closed-loop system should produce no change of the output signal or only random changes, and with distorted feedback the output should be distorted. Human movements are often little affected by elimination of feedback, but strongly affected by its distortion. Such results do not give a clear answer with respect to the dichotomy of open-loop versus closed-loop control, but they conform to expectations based on the combined control modes (Cruse et al., 1990).

Indeterminateness of the Solutions

Typically movements are not fully determined by their goals. An example is reaching, with the goal being defined in terms of a spatial target position. Thus, only the endpoint of the movement is specified by the goal, but not its time-course. In spite of this indeterminateness a solution is reached, which takes additional task constraints as well as organismic constraints into account.

Perhaps the most extensively studied task constraint is the size of the spatial target, which affects movement duration and the shape of velocity-time curves (e.g., MacKenzie, Marteniuk, Dugas, Liske, & Eickmeier, 1987). Basically, for smaller targets humans choose to produce slower movements. The relation of movement time not only to target width, but also to the distance of the target from the start position, is of a particular kind known as Fitts' law. The early 1950s, when Fitts (1954) first described the relation, saw the rise of information theory in psychology. Thus, the relation was formulated in terms of information measures, and the tradition has left it in that form. Fitts' law states that movement time is a linear function of the index of difficulty, which is defined as $\log_2(2A/W)$, A being the movement amplitude and W the width of the target.

Fitts' law describes a particular kind of speed-accuracy trade-off: Faster movements have a larger scatter of their end-positions than slower movements, so when a small scatter is required because the target is small, slower movements have to be chosen. The law is astonishingly robust (cf. Keele, 1986), and it has given rise to various theoretical accounts (Crossman & Goodeve, 1963/1983; Fitts, 1954; Meyer, Abrams, Kornblum, Wright, & Smith, 1988), but also to alternative formulations (cf. Plamondon & Alimi, 1997) and to contrasting observations (e.g., Schmidt, Zelaznik, Hawkins, Frank, & Quinn, 1979), in particular for situations that require a certain movement duration, rather than reading a spatial target of a particular width. (Wright & Meyer, 1983; Zelaznik, Mone, McCabe, & Thaman, 1988).

Although they have received much less attention, other task constraints than target size affect the chosen movement trajectory. For example, it makes a difference whether the spatial target has to be hit or whether an object in the same position has to be grasped, and in the latter case it makes a difference whether the object is a tennis ball or a light bulb. The movement to the light bulb takes more time than the movement to the tennis ball; in particular, the deceleration of the movement toward the bulb is more gradual and extended in time (Marteniuk, MacKenzie, Jeannerod, Athènes, & Dugas, 1987). Another task constraint has been reported recently: The time it takes to move a mug to the mouth depends in a particular way on the diameter of the mug and the distance from the level of water to the edge (Latash & Jaric, in press). Such task constraints are at least to some degree reflected by our everyday experience.

A second type of constraints, which are taken into account when movement trajectories are indeterminate, is of a more organismic nature and related to the costs of movements. Although the general notion of cost minimization—as far as this is possible with the given task constraints—has a high degree of plausibility, it poses more of a problem than a solution. There are many different kinds of costs that can potentially be minimized. For example, Nelson (1983) analyzed the consequences of minimizing five different kinds of costs for the trajectories of movements aimed at a target. Other criteria have been added (e.g., Cruse, 1986; Cruse & Brüwer, 1987; Rosenbaum, Slotta, Vaughan, & Plamondon, 1991; Rosenbaum, Vaughan, Barnes, & Jorgensen, 1992; Uno, Kawato, & Suzuki, 1989), and perhaps any list will be incomplete.

A fairly general principle seems to be that movement trajectories are selected by the criterion of smoothness. Although in principle smoothness can be defined in different ways, one of the possible criteria is minimization of jerk, that is, minimization of the integral of the squared third derivative of end-effector position with respect to time (Flash & Hogan, 1985). The principle can be extended and used to model complex movement patterns, as in handwriting (cf. Teulings, 1996). In addition, for drawing-like movements, it produces a particular relation between curvature and tangential velocity, which is known as the two-thirds power law (Viviani & Flash, 1995). Basically, with a larger radius of curvature, velocity tends to be higher than with a smaller radius of curvature even when the instruction is to maintain a constant velocity (Figure 12.4). The dependency of velocity on curvature is particularly conspicuous in drawing ellipses for which the radius of curvature varies continuously. Although the reverse relation has received less attention, variations of velocity do also induce variations of curvature; for example, when one attempts to draw circles with a pattern of smaller-higher-smaller-higher velocity within each cycle, the result is likely to be ellipses (Derwort, 1938).

Indeterminateness does exist even when the goal of a movement specifies a trajectory of the end-effector in every detail. Of course, in such cases the movement trajectory is not indeterminate, but the input to the motor transformation is. The origin of the indeterminateness is apparent from

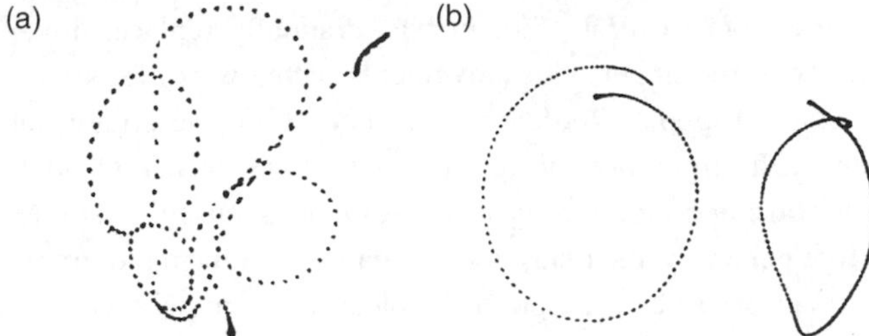

Figure 12.4 (a) A complex movement pattern produced under the instruction to maintain a constant velocity; (b) circles produced under the instruction of a constant velocity (left) and a time-varying velocity (right). These examples are taken from Derwort (1938). Recordings were made with a light placed on the index finger. The shutter of a camera was opened about 60 times per second; distance between dots thus represents distance covered in $1/60$ s, smaller distances indicating smaller, and larger distances higher, velocity.

Figure 12.2, where the target position is specified in terms of two spatial dimensions, but it can be reached with different configurations of three joints. More generally, the output of the motor transformation has a lower dimensionality than the input, so that the inversion of the motor transformation has no unique solution. The problem of how to deal with the many dimensions of the input is often called the degrees-of-freedom problem. A consequence is motor equivalence: The same movement can be performed in many different ways.

Again, cost minimization can be considered as a way to reach a unique solution (cf. Cruse, 1986; Cruse & Brüwer, 1987; Rosenbaum et al., 1991). Another possibility is the freezing of degrees of freedom. For example, in handwriting adults mainly use the wrist and the fingers, and hardly or not at all the elbow and the shoulder joints. When one observes preschoolers at their first attempts to write (which might not be the appropriate term for the result, but perhaps for the intention), one can notice that the wrist and fingers are largely immobilized, and that mainly the more proximal joints, which are closer to the trunk, are used (Blöte & Dijkstra, 1989). This can also be observed when adult right-handers write with their left hand (Newell & van Emmerik, 1989). Finally, the high dimensionality of an input vector can be reduced to a small number of degrees of freedom by way of introducing covariations. A somewhat trivial example again can be seen in handwriting: With a normal tripod grip, thumb, index finger, and middle finger are mechanically coupled (because of holding the pen) and can no longer be moved independently.

Motor equivalence implies not only the existence of criteria for selecting one of the many options, but also that different options can be chosen in case that it is desirable or necessary. For example, when one asks people to tap with their index finger as rapidly as possible, and to do so as long as they can, several of them will gradually replace movements of the finger with movements of the wrist. Less incidentally, Lippold, Redfearn, and Vučo (1960) describe what they call "migration of activity" from one muscle to other ones during prolonged activity that induces muscular fatigue. More generally, the many-to-few mapping of the motor transformation leaves the option to select different subsets from the many input dimensions when some of them are functionally impaired, be it a fatigued muscle or an immobilized joint.

MOTOR PREPARATION

The initiation of a movement is a gradual and continuous process. In Figure 12.5 an example recording of a rapid index-finger flexion of about 20° amplitude is shown, as are in particular the position-time curve, the velocity-time curve, the acceleration-time curve, and the EMG of a finger flexor (agonist) and an extensor (antagonist). Faced with such recordings, it becomes somewhat difficult to answer the question of when the movement starts. Typically the start of a movement is defined in terms of a threshold for one of the kinematic signals. From Figure 12.5 it is apparent that definitions based on the acceleration signal generally lead to earlier initiation times than definitions based on the position signal: There can be a sizeable acceleration while position has hardly changed. Thus, any definition of the start of a movement is to some degree arbitrary.

Muscle activity can be observed in advance of changes of kinematic signals, and the definition of the start of a movement can also be based on EMG traces. In many instances the agonist burst is over before a change of position can be seen. Thus, it is not too remarkable that the agonist burst is hardly or not at all affected when the overt movement is unexpectedly blocked. More remarkable is that the later bursts, which normally serve to decelerate the limb and to stabilize the end-position, still occur, although they serve no obvious purpose any more (Wadman, Denier van der Gon, Geuze, & Mol, 1979).

The overt movement is preceded not only by muscle activity, but also by various kinds of preparatory processes which can be evidenced at different levels of the motor system (see Brunia, 1999, and Brunia, Haagh, & Scheirs, 1985, for overviews of psychophysiological findings). For example, in the electroencephalogram, movement-related activity can be seen when the start of the movement is used as a trigger for averaging. Even such simple voluntary movements as keypresses are preceded by a slowly increasing negativity that starts in the order of 1 s before the overt movement. This readiness potential or *Bereitschaftspotential* was first described by Kornhuber and Deecke (1965). Initially it is symmetrical, but in the last 100 or 200 ms it becomes asymmetrical, being stronger over the hemisphere contralateral to the responding hand. This kind of asymmetry can also be observed in reaction-time tasks. Called the lateralized readiness potential, it has become an important tool in information-processing research (see chapter by Proctor & Vu in this volume).

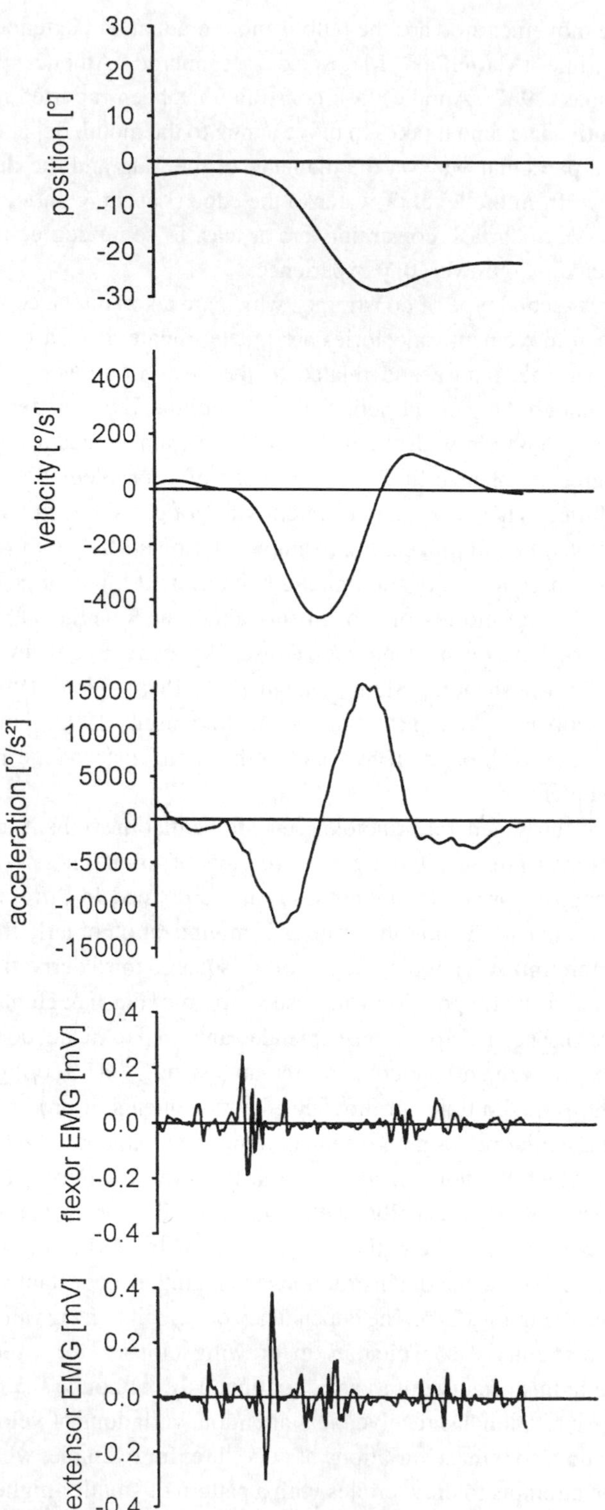

Figure 12.5 Example recording of a rapid finger flexion.

The Anticipatory Nature of Motor Preparation

The psychophysiological data indicate the existence of motor preparation, but they are more or less silent to the question of what goes on in functional terms. What they tell, of course, is that at least to some degree preparatory processes are specific for the forthcoming movement in that the data reflect some of its characteristics, like the hand used. Näätänen and Merisalo (1977) suggested that the essence of motor preparation is that everything is done in advance of the overt response that can be done, which amounts to activating the response up to a level close to the motor action limit. This characterization of motor preparation may be appropriate for simple movements like keypresses, but it falls short of capturing essential characteristics of motor preparation preceding a more complex movement.

Preparatory activities in general can anticipate the future to varying degrees. For example, in preparing for a vacation, one might book a hotel in advance for only the first night, or one might book hotels in different places for several nights to come. Activating a response close to the action limit means preparing only for movement initiation (like booking a hotel for the first night). However, motor preparation is also concerned with the future of the response (like booking hotels for several nights to come). There are at least three kinds of evidence for this.

The first kind of evidence is from reaction-time experiments. When the task is to perform a sequence of simple movements, simple reaction time increases with the length of the sequence. The seminal study was by Henry and Rogers (1960), who found increasing reaction times for (a) lifting a finger from a key, (b) lifting the finger from the key and grasping a tennis ball at a certain distance, and (c) lifting the finger from the key, touching the ball with the back of the hand, pressing another key, and hitting a second tennis ball. More systematic explorations of the sequence-length effect have been reported by Sternberg and coworkers (see Monsell, 1986, for an overview). With more homogeneous elements like keypresses, letter names, or words with a certain number of syllables, reaction time increases linearly with the number of sequence elements. At some length of about 6–12 elements, the increase of reaction time levels off, earlier for longer elements (like trisyllabic words) and later for shorter elements (like monosyllabic words).

The second kind of evidence is from studies of anticipatory postural adjustments (see Massion, 1992, for review). When a forthcoming movement threatens balance, the voluntary action is preceded by the appropriate postural adjustments. For example, Cordo and Nashner (1982) observed EMG activity of postural muscles in the leg of their standing subjects which preceded by about 40 ms the activity of arm muscles involved in the task of pulling a hand-held lever in response to an auditory signal. In a control condition with a passive support, the preparatory postural activity was absent, and arm-muscle activity had a shorter latency. Thus, anticipatory postural adjustments are not only specific with respect to the forthcoming voluntary movement (e.g., Zattara & Bouisset, 1986), but also with respect to context characteristics.

The third kind of evidence, finally, shows that earlier parts of a motor pattern are adapted to later parts. Evidence for this can be found in many skills (cf. Rosenbaum & Krist, 1996), but I shall focus here on a particularly basic kind of observation, the effect of end-state comfort (Rosenbaum & Jorgensen, 1992; Rosenbaum et al., 1992). Figure 12.6a illustrates the task of Rosenbaum et al. (1992, Exp. 1). The standing subject had to grasp a bar with a pointer, which had different initial orientations, the pointer pointing upward, downward, to the left or to the right. With the pointer upward or to the left, it is quite comfortable to grasp the bar with the thumb toward the pointer, but with the other two initial orientations this is less comfortable. Under speed instructions

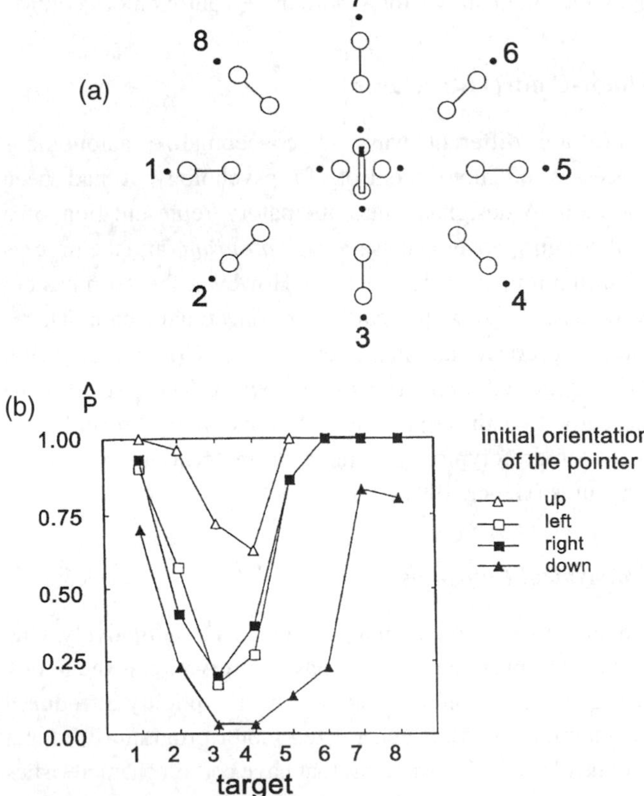

Figure 12.6 (a) Response panel used by Rosenbaum et al. (1992). The bar with pointer had to be grasped and to be placed on one of the eight targets with the pointer toward the LED (black dots). (b) Relative frequency of grasping the bar with the thumb toward the pointer as a function of the final orientation (targets 1–8), shown separately for four different initial orientations.

the subjects had not only to grasp the bar, but also to place it in one of eight target positions with the pointer toward the LED that signaled the target position in each trial; thus, there were differences in final orientation. For targets 6–8 and 1–2, holding the bar in the final orientation with the thumb toward the pointer is more or less comfortable, but for targets 3–5, holding the bar with the thumb away from the pointer is more comfortable. In Figure 12.6b the relative frequency of grasping the bar in its initial position with the thumb toward the pointer is shown. These data reveal not only an effect of the initial orientation of the bar, but also a clear effect of the final orientation. Thus, the effect of end-state comfort can be evidenced at the very start of the action, and it clearly indicates that motor preparation embraces anticipation.

The anticipatory nature of motor preparation implies that there is some kind of representation of the forthcoming movement before it begins. The existence of such a representation also implies that open-loop processes of motor control are of a particular nature in that they are predictive. In fact, the answer to the question of what goes on during motor preparation in functional terms may be largely that this kind of internal representation of the forthcoming movement is set up, which then allows for a more or less autonomous control.

Motor-Control Structures

There are different ways to conceptualize autonomous processes of motor control. In psychology it had been common to designate the anticipatory representation of a forthcoming movement as a *motor program* (and the process of setting it up as *programming*). However, this term has become associated with a particular conceptualization. Therefore, as a broader and more neutral term, Cruse et al. (1990) have suggested *motor-control structures*. There seem to be basically two different ways of modeling them, either in terms of prototypical functions or in terms of generative structures (Heuer, 1991).

Prototypical Functions

Movements vary qualitatively as well as quantitatively. One of the attempts to capture this basic observation is the notion of a generalized motor program, most explicitly introduced by Schmidt (1975). A generalized motor program is thought to control a set of movements that have certain characteristics in common. The specifics of each particular movement are thought to be determined by the program's parameters. Thus, for a certain type of movement there should be invariant characteristics, which represent the signature of the program, and variable characteristics, which reflect the variable settings of its parameters. Of course, such a concept requires that the invariant characteristics of movements of a certain type be identified.

The theoretical problem of identifying invariant characteristics met with observations of an invariance of relative timing in different motor skills (see Gentner, 1987, for a review), which led Schmidt (1980, 1985) to propose that the relative timing is an invariant feature of movements that are controlled by a single generalized motor program. In addition, relative force was hypothesized to be a second invariant characteristic. With these assumptions, a generalized motor program can be described by way of a prototypical force-time function $\varphi(\vartheta)$, which can be scaled in time by a rate parameter and in amplitude by a force parameter.

The notion of a prototypical force-time function, which can be scaled in time as well as in amplitude, is reminiscent of the way we use coordinate systems to represent force-time curves. Thus one might suspect that the concept is related more to how we plot force as a function of time than to how the brain controls movement. Nevertheless, the notion is not biologically implausible. One can think of a spatially organized representation that is read at a certain rate and thus transformed into a temporally organized movement (cf. Lashley, 1951). The speed of reading would correspond to the rate parameter. Similarly, as the read signal is channeled to the muscles, it could be amplified to variable degrees (cf. von Holst, 1939). Thus, in principle, the notion of prototypical functions implies a certain degree of independence of temporal control and force control.

The most detailed application of prototypical force-time functions has been in models of the speed-accuracy tradeoff in rapid aimed movements. These so-called impulse-variability models account for the trade-off in terms of noise in the motor system (Meyer, Smith, & Wright, 1982; Schmidt, Sherwood, Zelaznik, & Leikind, 1985; Schmidt et al., 1979). However, it is not really necessary that prototypical curves specify forces; instead, they can also be thought of as specifying kinematic characteristics (e.g., Heuer, Schmidt, & Ghodsian, 1995; Kalveram, 1991). In fact, formal models of the autonomous processes of motor control are generally somewhat diverse or even indeterminate with respect to their output variables.

The motor transformation involves a number of different variables, and in principle any of these can be taken as output variable for models of motor-control structures. Ultimately, of course, muscles must be activated. In fact, the concept of a motor program has often been associated with a prestructured sequence of muscle commands (Keele, 1968). At the other extreme, motor-control structures can be modeled with the trajectory of the end-effector as the output. In the first case, the inversion of the motor transformation is assumed to be an integrated component of a motor-control structure. In the second case, it is left to additional and separate processes. Although the choice may be somewhat arbitrary, it implies an assumption about whether the internal model of the inverse motor transformation is specific for a particular type of movement governed by a particular motor-control structure, or whether it is generalized and thus applicable to different types of movement.

There are some considerations and data that favor the modeling of motor-control structures with end-effector kinematics as output. One consideration starts with the observation that both perception and action are externalized. For example, we do not see the image on the retina, but objects and their locations in the world. Similarly, awareness of our own movements is typically not in terms of muscular contractions and joint angles. Visual distances and movement amplitudes in the external world are commensurate, whereas proximal visual stimuli and patterns of muscular activity are not (cf. Prinz, 1992). Thus, to be compatible with how we perceive the world around us, movement should be represented in terms of world coordinates.

Another consideration starts with the assumption that the variables used in motor preparation or planning should reveal themselves by the possibility of describing them concisely as well as by their consistency. For example, for pointing in a two-dimensional plane as in Figure 12.2, the movement paths approximate straight lines, whereas the relations between joint-angles can be fairly complex. More specifically, plotting the y coordinates of the end-effector as a function of the x coordinates results in straight lines at least approximately, whereas plotting the elbow angle as a function of the shoulder angle results in strongly curved lines. This suggests that motor-control structures deal with the trajectory of the end-effector, and that the time-courses of joint angles are a consequence thereof (cf. Hollerbach & Atkeson, 1987). Similarly, kinematic characteristics of single-joint movements are highly similar for movements with and against gravity, whereas the patterns of muscular activity are grossly different (Virjii-Babul, Cooke, & Brown, 1994).

No matter for which kind of variable prototypical functions are defined, the notion is intimately related to the invariance of relative timing. The invariance is never really perfect, but often. It can be taken as a reasonable approximation. However, there are also clear deviations from invariance. For example, when the target size is reduced or accuracy rather than speed is emphasized, the relative duration of the deceleration phase of aimed movements tends to increase (Fisk & Goodale, 1989; MacKenzie et al., 1987). Moreover, the concept of a prototypical function takes a particular relative timing as a mandatory characteristic of a certain type of movement which cannot easily be changed; however, when after some practice in a particular temporal pattern the relative timing is changed, humans do not encounter particular difficulties (Heuer & Schmidt, 1988). Thus, prototypical functions do not represent a valid type of model for motor-control structures in general, but nevertheless they can capture important characteristics of some types of movement.

Generative Structures

Whereas a conceptualization of motor-control structures in terms of prototypical functions posits stored trajectories, conceptualizations in terms of generative structures posit networks that generate the trajectories. An example is a model by Saltzman and Kelso (1987) that belongs to a class they called the "task-dynamic approach." For an aimed movement, Saltzman and Kelso defined a reach axis that runs through the target and the current position of the end-effector as well as an axis orthogonal to it. These axes define an abstract task space in which the end-effector is represented by a "task mass." The target position is located in the origin of the task space and is assumed to have the characteristics of a point attractor. Thus, wherever the task mass is in task space, it will move toward the target governed by a set of simple equations of motion; for the reach axis x it is $m_T\ddot{x} + b_T\dot{x} + k_Tx = 0$, with the index T designating parameters of the task space.

The task-dynamic approach goes beyond advance specifications of movements in task space. For example, joint movements are derived by way of coordinate transforms. However, for the present purpose only the highest level of the scheme is important. At first glance there does not seem to be much difference between describing a motor-control structure in terms of a differential equation that governs a generative structure or in terms of a solution of such an equation that could be stored as a prototypical function. However, there are differences. First, the parameterizations are different. Whereas the prototypical function has a rate and an amplitude parameter, the particular generative structure at hand has abstract mass, m_T, friction, b_T, and stiffness, k_T, parameters. Variation of these parameters, for example, does not necessarily result in relative-timing invariance. Second, and perhaps more important, the generative structure is less susceptible to the effects of transient perturbations. It implements a movement characteristic called equifinality: Movements tend to reach their target even when they are transiently perturbed (Kelso & Holt, 1980; Polit & Bizzi, 1979; Schmidt & McGown, 1980).

Although the model of Saltzman and Kelso (1987) seems to be more mathematically than physiologically inspired, this

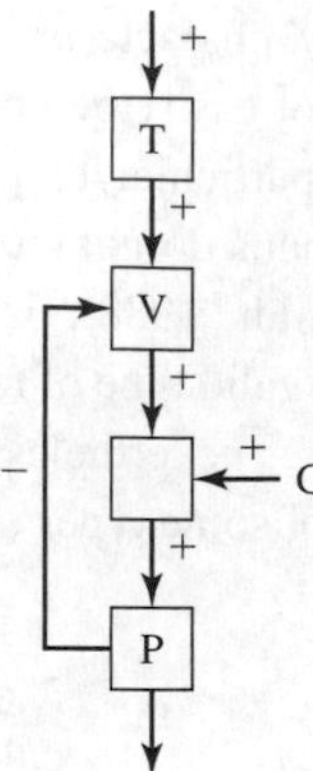

Figure 12.7 Variables of the VITE model of Bullock and Grossberg (1988) and their interrelations.

is different with the VITE model of Bullock and Grossberg (1988). (VITE stands for *vector-integration-to-endpoint.*) The formal structure of an element of the model is illustrated in Figure 12.7. The variable P is an internal representation of the position of an effector, and T represents a target position. The variable V represents the (delayed) difference, and G the Go signal. In principle, the structure of Figure 12.7 is thought to be multiplied for different muscles that are involved in a voluntary movement, with $V \geq 0$ for each particular muscle.

Without going into mathematical details, it is worth noting that the difference V in the case of aimed movements is again governed by a second-order differential equation (provided that G is a constant). In spite of this similarity, there are several basic differences from the model of Saltzman and Kelso (1987), in addition to the differences with respect to the role of physiological and psychological considerations in justifying the mathematics. The structure of Figure 12.7 is a kind of central closed-loop system. This system, however, is inoperative as long as the Go signal is zero; it is energized by the Go signal, which in addition can change across time so that the system is no longer linear. Bullock and Grossberg (1988) refer to a "factorization of pattern and energy." Basically, the Go signal allows a separation of movement planning from movement initiation (cf. Gielen, van den Heuvel, & van Gisbergen, 1984), which implies that processes of motor preparation can be temporally separated from execution of the movement, but also that movements can be initiated before advance specification is finished.

Generative structures are not restricted to aimed movements. In fact, models of generative structures for periodic movements as they occur in locomotion are historically older. Network models of central pattern generators had already been proposed early in the twentieth century (Brown, 1911), and more elaborate versions continue to be developed (e.g., Grossberg, Pribe, & Cohen, 1997). In more abstract models, of course, point attractors can be replaced by limit-cycle attractors which produce stable oscillations (e.g., Kay, Kelso, Saltzman, & Schöner, 1987).

The Advance Specification of Movement Characteristics

During motor preparation an anticipatory representation of the forthcoming movement is constructed. This representation can be described as a motor-control structure, which allows (relatively) autonomous control of the movement independent of sensory feedback. In addition to being set up, the structure must be specified, with the appropriate parameters. This is a time-consuming process. Thus, variations in necessary preparatory activities are reflected in reaction times. In addition, when the available time is varied, it is possible to trace the time course of the specification of movement characteristics. Thus far, almost all studies on the advance specification of movement characteristics have employed aimed movements or isometric contractions with different quantitative characteristics, yet qualitatively different movements have hardly been used. Therefore, little can be said about setting up different motor-control structures, but more can be said about the advance specification of parameters.

Figure 12.8 gives an example for the gradual specification of movement direction, adapted from Georgopoulos, Lurito, Petrides, Schwartz, and Massey (1989). These data are from a monkey who had been trained to perform a movement to one of eight potential targets arranged on a circle. When the target was dimly illuminated, the monkey had to reach for it directly, but when the luminance of the target was high, the monkey had to perform a movement that was rotated by 90° counterclockwise relative to the target. What is shown in Figure 12.8 is the gradual rotation of the population vector in

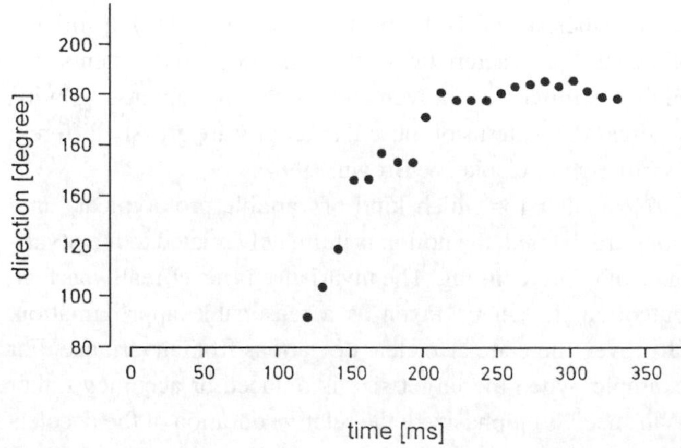

Figure 12.8 Change of the direction of the population vector as a function of the time since presentation of an imperative stimulus (after Georgopoulos et al., 1989).

such trials from the direction of the target (90°) to the direction of the movement (180°). The population vector is computed from the activity of directionally tuned neurons of the motor cortex and generally points in the direction of movement. Basically it is a weighted mean of the preferred directions of a sufficiently large sample of cortical units, with the weights being derived from the spike frequencies. The rotation of the population vector starts with a certain delay and proceeds with an almost constant slope until the target direction is reached. In human subjects this kind of rotation presumably gives rise to a systematic increase of reaction time when the angle between target and required direction of movement is increased (Georgopoulos & Massey, 1987).

The timed-response procedure allows one to trace the gradual specification of movement parameters from behavioral data. The method has been introduced for the study of the speed-accuracy trade-off in choice reaction time experiments (Schouten & Becker, 1967), and it has been adapted to the study of the advance specification of characteristics of isometric contractions and movements by Ghez and coworkers (Ghez et al., 1997; Hening, Favilla, & Ghez, 1988). Basically the method specifies a moment for the start of the movement; typically the movement has to be initiated in synchrony with the last of four tones which are presented in regular intervals. At a variable time before the last tone the target is presented, so the time available for motor specifications can be varied. The method is only suited for rapid movements or isometric contractions with short durations, so that the movement characteristics are largely determined in advance and little changed during execution.

Ghez and coworkers demonstrated the gradual specification of peak forces of isometric contractions as well as amplitudes and directions of movements with a time course similar to that of the neuronal population vector (cf. Figure 12.8). In addition, they showed that the gradual specifications break down when the differences between the alternative targets become too large (Ghez et al., 1997). When the difference between target directions is about 90° or larger, or the ratio of target amplitudes is about 12:1 or larger, the intermediate values between the two targets are no longer observed, and the choice between movement parameters becomes discrete. Thus, there seem to be two qualitatively different modes of parameter specification, namely gradual adjustments and discrete choices.

While the timed-response procedure provides a window into the gradual or discrete specification of movement characteristics, it has not been used as extensively as chronometric procedures. The latter type of studies is largely based on the movement precuing rationale of Rosenbaum (1980, 1983). Consider a set of four responses that differ on two dimensions like direction and amplitude. In a reaction time task, before presentation of the response signal, there is thus uncertainty with respect to both direction and amplitude, and after presentation of the response signal–during the reaction-time interval–both response characteristics have to be specified. When one of the dimensions is precued, it can be specified in advance of the response signal, and only one dimension remains to be specified after its presentation. Reaction time should be reduced by the time it takes to specify the precued dimension. When both dimensions are precued, both can be specified in advance, and reaction time should be reduced even more. In principle, if the rationale were fully valid, the times needed to specify various movement characteristics or combinations thereof could be estimated.

There are some broad conclusions that can be drawn from the results obtained, but there are also a number of problems that sometimes cast doubt on the general validity of the rationale (cf. Goodman & Kelso, 1980; Zelaznik, Shapiro, & Carter, 1982). Among the broad conclusions were that movement features are specified sequentially and in variable rather than fixed order (Rosenbaum, 1983). The first of these two broad conclusions can be doubted because the time needed to specify two dimensions can be smaller than the sum of the times needed to specify each of these dimensions (e.g., Lépine, Glencross, & Requin, 1989). In addition, timed-response studies show essentially parallel specifications of amplitude and direction, perhaps accompanied by some slowing when two response characteristics are specified in parallel (Favilla & De Cecco, 1996; Favilla, Hening, & Ghez, 1989).

Exceptions to the second broad conclusion seem to be rare. Fixed order of specifications is indicated by a shortening of reaction time when a movement dimension A is precued, which can be observed only when movement dimension B is precued as well, but not otherwise. This implies that the specification of dimension B is a prerequisite for specifying A. Such a result would be expected when dimension B embraces qualitatively different movements, related to different motor-control structures rather than to different parameters of a single control structure. Qualitative variations of movement characteristics, however, have rarely been studied, but some results of Roth (1988) indeed suggest that precuing the direction and the force for throwing a ball does not result in systematic reaction time benefits as long as the type of throw is not known.

THE USE OF SENSORY INFORMATION

The use of sensory information for the control of voluntary movement was among the historically early questions addressed by experimental psychology. Woodworth (1899) asked his subjects to produce reciprocal movements between two target lines in the pace of a metronome. With the participants' eyes closed, accuracy was only little affected by frequency, but with the participants' eyes open, accuracy increased relative to that found with closed eyes as soon as less than about two movements per second were produced. A next major step was a study by Keele and Posner (1968) with discrete movements. Movement times were instructed, and the movements were performed with full vision or in the dark, with the room light being switched off at the start of the movements. Except for the shortest movement time of about 190 ms, the percentage of movements that hit the target was larger with than without vision. Subsequent studies showed that the minimal duration at which accuracy gains from the availability of vision becomes shorter—about 100 ms—when conditions with and without vision are blocked rather than randomized (Elliott & Allard, 1985; Zelaznik, Hawkins, & Kisselburgh, 1983). This minimal duration reflects processing delays, but it also reflects the time it takes until a change of the pattern of muscular activity has an effect on the movement.

Woodworth (1899) distinguished between two phases of a rapid aimed movement, an "initial adjustment" and a second phase of "current control." This distinction seems to imply that accuracy should profit mainly when vision becomes available toward the end of aimed movements. However, even early vision can increase accuracy (Paillard, 1982), and accuracy increases when both initial and terminal periods of vision increase in duration (Spijkers, 1993). Thus, the view that vision is important only in the late parts of an aimed movement seems to be overly simplified.

From the basic findings it is clear that, in general, vision is not really necessary for the production of movements, but that it serves to improve accuracy. The same kind of generalization holds for the second important type of sensory information for motor control, proprioception. (For tasks that involve head movements, including stance and locomotion, the sensors of the inner ear also become important, although I shall neglect them here.) Regarding the role of proprioception for motor control, classic observations date back to Lashley (1917). Due to a spinal-cord lesion, the left knee joint of his patient was largely anesthetic and without cutaneous and tendon reflexes. In particular, the patient did not experience passive movements of the joint, nor could he reproduce them; only fairly rapid movements were noted, but the experienced direction of movement appeared random. However, when the patient was asked to move his foot by a certain distance specified in inches, the movements were surprisingly accurate, as were the reproductions of active movements; the latter reached the accuracy of a control subject. The basic finding that aimed movements are possible without proprioception (and, of course, without vision also) has been confirmed both in monkeys (e.g., Polit & Bizzi, 1979; Taub, Goldberg, & Taub, 1975) and—with local transient anesthesia—in humans (e.g., Kelso & Holt, 1980), although, of course, without proprioception there tends to be a reduction of accuracy.

The very fact that movements are possible without vision and proprioception proves that motor control is not just a closed-loop process but involves autonomous processes that do not depend on afferent information. The very fact that accuracy is generally increased when sensory information becomes available proves that motor-control structures also integrate this type of information. Beyond these basic generalizations, however, the use of sensory information becomes a highly complicated research issue because sensory information can be of various types and serves different purposes in motor control.

As a first example of some complexities, consider a task like writing or drawing. Normally we have no problems writing with our eyes closed, except that the positioning of the letters and words tends to become somewhat irregular in both dimensions of the plane. This is illustrated in Figure 12.9b. Figure 12.9a shows the writing of a deafferented patient both with and without vision (Teasdale et al., 1993). The patient had suffered a permanent loss of myelinated sensory fibers following episodes of sensory neuropathy, which resulted in

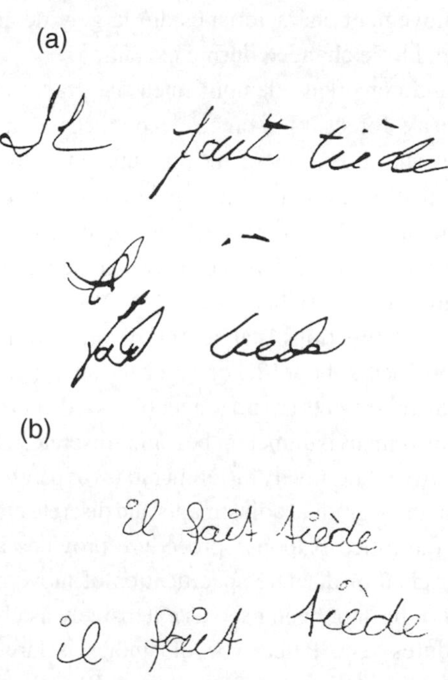

Figure 12.9 Examples of handwriting with (upper example) and without (lower example) vision in (a) a deafferented patient (from Teasdale et al., 1993) and (b) a healthy girl.

a total loss of sensitivity to touch, vibration, pressure, and kinesthesia as well as an absence of tendon reflexes, although the motor nerve conduction velocities were normal. With vision, the writing of "*Il fait tiède*" seems rather normal, but without vision the placement of words, letters, and parts of letters is severely impaired, while individual letters remain largely intact. Similarly, in drawing ellipses with eyes closed, single ellipses appeared rather normal, but successive ellipses were displaced in space. Thus, absence of sensory information affects different aspects of the skill differently, and impairments are less severe when proprioception can serve as a substitute for absent vision.

Target Information

Vision and proprioception serve at least two different functions in motor control, which are not always clearly distinguished. First, they provide information about the desired movement or target information, and, second, they provide information about the actual movement or feedback information. In the typical case, target information is provided by vision only, and feedback information both by proprioception and by vision. Thus, vision provides both kinds of information, and the effects of absent vision can be attributed to either of them. The obvious question of whether target information or feedback information is more important for movement accuracy, as straightforward as it appears, cannot unequivocally be answered. In the literature, contrasting findings have been reported. For example, Carlton (1981) found vision of the hand to be more important, whereas Elliott and Madalena (1987) found vision of the target to be crucial for high levels of accuracy. Perhaps the results depend on subtle task characteristics. However, for throwing-like tasks, vision of the target seems to be critical in general (e.g., Whiting & Cockerill, 1974), and dissociating the direction of gaze from the direction of the throw or shot seems to be a critical element of successful penalties.

Specification of Spatial Targets

Targets for voluntary movements are typically defined in extrinsic or extrapersonal space, whereas movements are produced and proprioceptively sensed in personal space. Both kinds of space must be related to each other; they must be calibrated so that positions in extrinsic space can be assigned to positions in personal space and vice versa. When we move around, the calibration must be updated because personal space is shifted relative to extrinsic space. Even when we do not move around, the calibration tends to be labile. This lability can be evidenced from the examples of handwriting in Figure 12.9: With the writer's eyes closed, calibration gets lost with the passage of time, so positions of letters or parts of them exhibit drift or random variation. This effect is much stronger when no proprioception is available.

An interesting example of failures that are at least partly caused by miscalibrations of extrinsic and personal space are unintended accelerations (cf. Schmidt, 1989). These occur in automatic-transmission cars when the transmission selector is shifted to the drive or reverse position, typically when the driver has just entered the car; when he or she is not familiar with the car, this is an additional risk factor. In manual-transmission cars, incidents of unintended acceleration are essentially absent. According to all that is known, unintended accelerations are caused by a misplacement of the right foot on the accelerator pedal rather than on the brake pedal without the driver's being aware of this. Thus, when the car starts to move, he or she will press harder, which then has the unexpected effect of accelerating the car.

The position of the brake pedal is defined in the extrinsic space of the car, whereas the foot placement is defined in the personal space of the driver. In particular upon entering a car, and more so when it is an unfamiliar car, there is the risk of initial miscalibration. Thus, when extrinsic and personal space are not properly aligned, the correct placement of the foot in personal space might reach the wrong pedal in extrinsic space. Manual-transmission cars, in contrast, have a kind of built-in safeguard against such an initial miscalibration, because shifting gears requires that the clutch be operated beforehand. Thus, before the car is set into motion, the proper relation between foot placements and pedal positions is established.

Calibration, in principle, requires that objects, the locations of which are defined in world coordinates, be simultaneously located in personal space. Mostly it is vision that serves this purpose. However, personal space embraces not only vision: In addition to visual space, there are also a proprioceptive and a motor space, and these different spaces must be properly aligned with each other. For example, in order for us to reach to a visually located target, its location must be transformed into motor space, that is, into the appropriate parameters of a motor control structure. In addition, its location must be transformed into proprioceptive space, so that we can see and feel the limb in the same position. In a later section I shall discuss the plasticity of these relations; here I shall focus on the question of how a visually located spatial target is transformed into motor space.

An object can be localized visually both with respect to an observer (egocentrically) and with respect to another object (allocentrically or exocentrically; cf. the chapter by Proffitt & Caudek in this volume). Geometrically the location of the

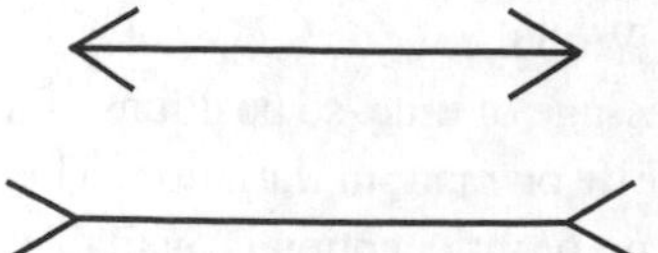

Figure 12.10 The Müller-Lyer illusion.

object can be described in terms of a vector. The length of the vector corresponds to the distance from the reference to the object; for egocentric location the reference is a point between the eyes (the *cyclopean eye*), and for allocentric location it is another object in the visual field. The direction is usually specified by angles both in a reference plane and orthogonal to it, but for the following its specification is of little importance. The available data suggest that both egocentric and allocentric localizations are used in the visual specification of targets. Which one dominates seems to depend on task characteristics.

Figure 12.10 shows a well-known optical illusion, the Müller-Lyer illusion. Although the length of the shaft is the same in both figures, it appears longer in the figure with outgoing fins than in the figure with ingoing fins. Elliott and Lee (1995) used one of the intersections as the start position and the other intersection as the target position for aimed movements. Corresponding to the difference in perceived distance between the intersections in the two figures, movement amplitudes were longer with outgoing fins than with ingoing fins (cf. Gentilucci, Chiefi, Daprati, Saetti, & Toni, 1996). In contrast to this result, Mack, Heuer, Villardi, and Chambers (1985) found no effect or only a very small effect of the illusion on pointing responses.

Perhaps the critical difference to the study of Elliott and Lee (1995) was that the participants in the study of Mack et al. (1985) pointed not from one intersection to the other, but from a start position in their lap to one or the other of the two intersections. The difference between the two tasks suggests that the movements were based on allocentric (visual distance) and egocentric (visual location) information, respectively. In fact, when psychophysical judgments of the length of the shaft are replaced by judgments of the positions of the intersections, the illusion also disappears (Gillam & Chambers, 1985). Thus, although physically a distance is the difference between two positions on a line, this is not necessarily true for perceived distances and positions. This distinction between perception of location and perception of distance matches a distinction between different types of parameters for motor control structures, namely target positions versus distances (cf. Bock & Arnold, 1993; Nougier et al., 1996; Vindras & Viviani, 1998).

Specification of spatial targets in terms of distances implies a kind of relative reference system for a single movement: Wherever it starts, this position constitutes the origin. A visually registered distance (and direction) is then used to specify a movement in terms of distance (and direction) from the start position. This way of specifying movement characteristics has a straightforward consequence: Spatial errors should propagate across a sequence of movements. In contrast, with a fixed reference system as implied by the specification of target locations in terms of (egocentric) positions, spatial errors should not propagate. In studies based on this principle, Bock and Eckmiller (1986) and Bock and Arnold (1993) provided evidence for relative reference systems, that is, for amplitude specifications. The movements they studied were pointing movements with the invisible hand to a series of visual targets. However, Bock and Arnold also noted that error propagation was less than perfect. Heuer and Sangals (1998) used different analytical procedures, but these were based on the same principle of error propagation or the lack thereof. As would be expected, when only amplitudes and directions were indicated to the subjects, only a relative reference system was used. However, when sequences of target positions were shown, there was some influence of a fixed reference system, although the movements were performed on a digitizer and thus displaced from the target presentation in a manner similar to the way a computer mouse is used.

Gordon, Ghilardi, and Ghez (1994) provided evidence for a reference system with the origin in the start position based on a different rationale, again with a task in which targets were presented on a monitor and movements were performed on a digitizer. Targets were located on circles around the start position. The distribution of end-positions of movements to a single target typically has an elliptical shape. Under the assumption that the target position is specified in terms of direction and distance from the origin of the reference system, the axes of the elliptical error distributions, determined by principal component analysis, should be oriented in a particular way: The axes (one from each endpoint distribution) should cross in the origin. It turned out that the long axes of the error ellipses all pointed to the start position, as shown in Figure 12.11. Corresponding findings were reported by Vindras and Viviani (1998), who kept the target position constant but varied the start position.

Amplitude specifications allow accurate movements even when visual space and proprioceptive-motor space are not precisely aligned. Specifically, they do not require absolute calibration, but only relative calibration: It must be possible to map distances correctly from one space to another, but not positions. Of course, without absolute calibration, movements may drift away from that region of space where the targets are, as is typical with the use of a computer mouse. Without proprioception it seems that absolute calibration is essentially missing. In the case of the deafferented patient

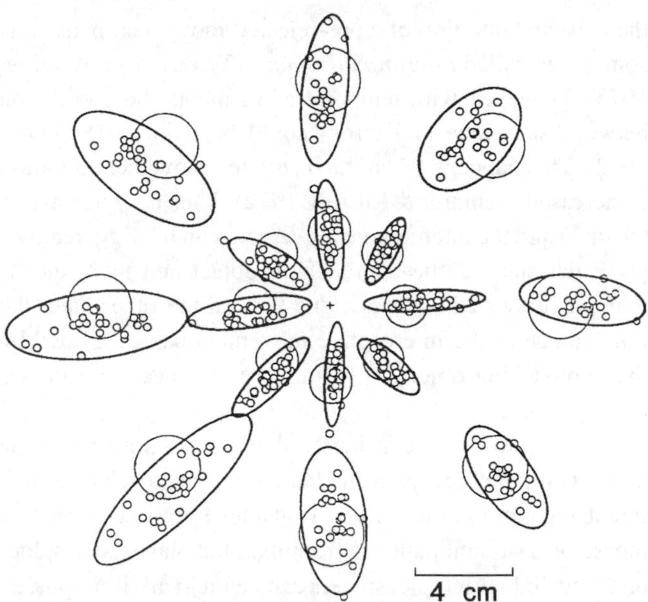

Figure 12.11 Elliptical end-position distributions of movements from a start position to concentrically arranged targets; circles mark the target areas (after Gordon et al., 1994).

mentioned above, Nougier et al. (1996) found basically correct amplitude specifications in periodic movements between two targets, although there were gross errors in the actual end-positions relative to the targets.

Contrasting with the evidence for amplitude specifications or relative reference systems in tasks of the type "reaching from one object to another," in tasks of the type "reaching out for an object" there is evidence for a reference system that is fixed, with the origin being at the shoulder or at a location intermediate between head and shoulder (Flanders, Helms Tillery, & Soechting, 1992). The analyses that led to this conclusion were again based on the assumption that errors of amplitude and direction should be essentially independent. However, when the start position of the hand is varied, an influence can again be seen, but not as dominant an influence as in the task of Gordon et al. (1994). Thus, McIntyre, Stratta, and Lacquaniti (1998) concluded that there is a mixture of different reference systems; in addition, errors of visual localization are added to errors of pointing.

Taken together, the evidence suggests that target information in general is specified both in terms of (egocentric) positions and in terms of (allocentric) distances and directions. Localization in terms of egocentric positions requires that, to perform a movement, the visual reference system be transformed to a proprioceptive-motor reference system, the first having its origin at the cyclopean eye, the latter having its origin at the shoulder, at least for certain types of arm movements. Localization in terms of allocentric distances and directions requires that the visual reference system be aligned with the proprioceptive-motor reference system in a way that the origin is in the current position of the end-effector. The relative importance of the two reference systems depends on task characteristics. In addition, there is also evidence that it can be modulated intentionally (Abrams & Landgraf, 1990).

Although spatial targets are mostly specified visually, they can also be specified proprioceptively, and again there is evidence for target specifications in terms of both position and amplitude, with the relative importance of these being affected both by task characteristics and intentions. In these experiments, participants produce a movement to a mechanical stop and thereafter reproduce this movement. When the start position is different for the second movement, participants can be instructed to reproduce either the amplitude of the first movement or its end-position. The general finding is a bias toward the target amplitude when the task is to reproduce the end-position, and a bias toward the end-position when the task is to reproduce the amplitude (Laabs, 1974). Although typically the reproduction of the end-position is more accurate than the reproduction of the amplitude, this is more so for longer movements, less so for shorter ones, and it may even be reversed for very short ones (Gundry, 1975; Stelmach, Kelso, & Wallace, 1975).

Specification of Temporal Targets

In tasks like catching, precisely timed movements are required: The hand must be in the proper place at the proper time and be closed with the proper timing to hold the ball. In very simple experimental tasks, finger taps have to be synchronized with pacing tones. Although the specification of temporal targets is fairly trivial in such tasks, the findings reveal to which aspects of the movements temporal goals are related. A characteristic finding is negative asynchrony, a systematic lead of the taps in the range of 20–50 ms, which, for example, is longer for tapping with the foot than for tapping with the finger (e.g., Aschersleben & Prinz, 1995).

The negative asynchrony is taken to indicate that the temporal target is not related to the physical movement itself, but rather to its sensory consequences, proprioceptive and tactile ones in particular, but also additional auditory ones if they are present. For example, because of the longer nerve-conduction times, sensory consequences of foot movements should be centrally available only later than sensory consequences of hand movements; thus negative asynchrony is larger in the former case than in the latter. When auditory feedback is added to the taps, negative asynchrony can be manipulated by varying the delay of the auditory feedback relative to the taps (Aschersleben & Prinz, 1997): Negative asynchrony declines when feedback tones are added without delay and increases as the delay becomes longer. With impaired tactile feedback, sensory consequences should also be delayed centrally, and negative asynchrony is increased (Aschersleben, Gehrke, & Prinz, 2001).

Synchronization of movements with discrete tones is necessarily anticipatory, provided that the interval between successive tones is sufficiently short (Engström, Kelso, & Holroyd, 1996). This is different in interceptive tasks. For example, when an object is approaching and one has to perform a frontoparallel movement that reaches the intersection of the object path and the movement path at the same time as the object does (cf. Figure 12.12a), it is possible in principle to continuously adjust the distance of the hand from the intersection to the distance of the object. In fact, this may actually happen if both the target object and the hand move slowly. At least, it is true that slower movements are adjusted more extensively to the approaching target after their start than rapid movements.

Let the start time be the time interval between the start of the interceptive movement and the time the target object reaches the intersection, and the temporal error be the time between the hand's and the target object's reaching the intersection (Figure 12.12b). Then, when the movement is started and runs off without further adjustments of its timing, the start time should be highly correlated with the temporal error. This strategy, in which the start time is selected according to

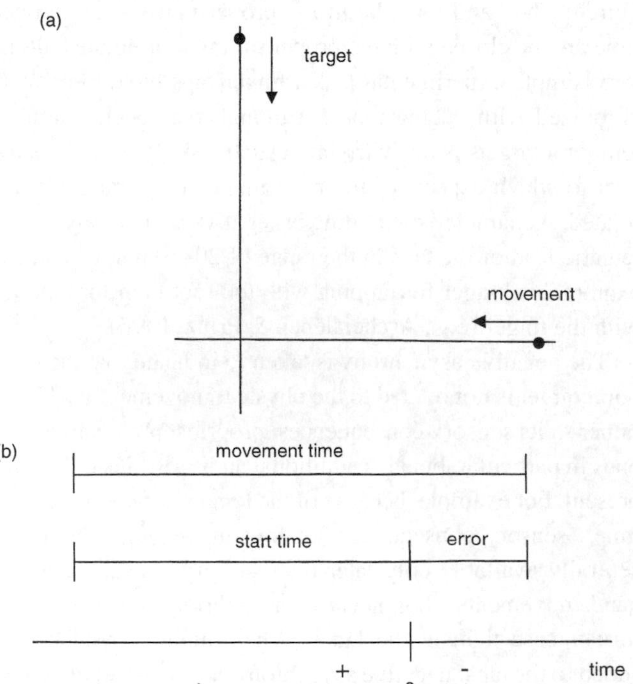

Figure 12.12 (a) Spatial layout of a simple interceptive task. (b) Variables in the analysis of the task; time zero is defined by the target's reaching the intersection.

the expected duration of a pre-selected movement pattern, is sometimes called *operational timing* (Tyldesley & Whiting, 1975). However, with temporal adjustments the correlation between start time and error should be reduced (Schmidt, 1972). This happens when the instructed movement duration is increased (Schmidt & Russell, 1972). Thus it seems that on the one hand the interceptive movement can be triggered by a particular state of the approaching object and then run off without further adjustments, and that on the other hand the time course of the interceptive movement can be guided by the approaching object, with mixtures of these two modes being possible.

In the simple task considered thus far the position of the intersection of object path and hand path is given. This is different for more natural tasks. Consider hitting a target that moves on a straight path in a frontoparallel plane like a spider on the wall. In principle, spiders can be hit in arbitrary places, but nevertheless the direction of the hitting movement has to be adjusted to an anticipated position of the moving target. A robust strategy is to adjust the lateral position of the hand to continuously updated estimates of the target position at the time the hand will reach the target plane; this requires an estimate of the time that remains until the hand reaches the plane and an estimate of the target's velocity, which, however, need not really be correct (Smeets & Brenner, 1995).

The situation is somewhat different when balls have to be intercepted in a lateral position, either for catching them or for hitting them. According to Peper, Bootsma, Mestre, and Bakker (1994), the hand will be in the correct position in the plane of interception at the right time when its lateral velocity is continuously adjusted to the current difference between the lateral position of the hand and the approaching target, divided by the time that remains until the target reaches the plane of intersection. Proper lateral adjustments, which imply temporal adjustments as well, are evident even in high-speed skills like table tennis, although the relevant information is less clear (Bootsma & van Wieringen, 1990).

What is the basis for anticipations of temporal targets? For example, when we view an approaching ball, what allows us to predict when it will be in some position where we can intercept it (cf. the chapter by Proffitt & Caudek in this volume)? The time it takes until a moving object reaches a certain position is given by the distance of the object divided by its velocity. This ratio has time as unit, and it specifies time to contact with the position, provided the object moves on a straight path with constant velocity. As noted by Lee (1976), the information required to determine time to contact with an approaching object, or with an object the observer is approaching, is available even without determining distance and velocity, namely by the ratio of the size of the retinal image of the object and its rate of change. This variable, called τ, has become quite popular. There can be little doubt that it contributes both to temporal judgments (e.g., Schiff & Detwiler, 1979) and precisely timed actions (e.g., Savelsbergh, Whiting, & Bootsma, 1991). However, it is not the only relevant information; other kinds of information, for example binocular distance information, are used as well (Bennett, van der Kamp, Savelsbergh, & Davids, 1999; Heuer, 1993a). In a recent overview, Tresilian (1999) notes that the relation between rapid interceptive actions and the kind of information used is rather flexible and in no way invariant. There is a degree of task dependence that at present does not allow firm generalizations about how rapid interceptive actions are adjusted to their temporal targets.

Feedback Information

Although movements can be performed in the absence of afferent information from the moving limb with an astonishing degree of accuracy, the use of feedback information is indicated by the effects of perturbations of feedback on performance. For example, proprioceptive information can be distorted by way of tendon vibration with a vibrator placed in the proper position on the skin. The effect is a tonic excitation of muscle spindles, which under normal conditions corresponds to a longer muscle and correspondingly different joint angle. If, for example, the biceps tendon is vibrated, the elbow angle is registered as being too large. When the elbow angle has to be matched to the elbow angle of the other arm, the matched angle is too small, corresponding to the distorted proprioceptive feedback on joint angles (Goodwin, McCloskey, & Matthews, 1972).

Regarding the effects of distorted visual feedback, a particularly striking example has been reported by Nielsen (1963). The participant's task was to move one hand along a vertical line, but the visible gloved hand was that of the experimenter and followed a curved path rather than a straight one. Subjects attempted to correct the error so that they deviated from the target line in the opposite direction. In spite of the strong discrepancies between intended and felt movement on the one hand and visual feedback on the other hand it took several trials before participants came to realize that the visible gloved hand could not be their own.

In simple movements, feedback information is functionally of little importance because autonomous processes of motor control can operate on the basis of a sufficiently accurate internal model of the motor transformation, so that only little error remains for closed-loop control to operate on (except, of course, when feedback information is distorted). However, in tasks in which a sufficiently accurate internal model is not available, the availability of visual feedback gains critical importance. This is the case when we operate sufficiently complex machines or tools which effectively add to the normal motor transformation. Experimentally tracking tasks are suited to exploring the role of visual feedback (Poulton, 1957).

For example, when the movement of the hand is proportional to the motion of the cursor on a screen, tracking performance is rather robust against short periods of eliminated visual feedback. However, with velocity control–with which the position of the hand is proportional to the velocity of the cursor on the screen–even short periods of eliminated feedback can bring performance down to an almost chance level (e.g., Heuer, 1983, p. 54). Thus, visual feedback gains in importance the less accurate the internal model of the transformation by a machine is. Internal models of sufficiently complex transformations seem not to be developed, so that practice does not reduce the critical importance of visual feedback (Davidson, Jones, Sirisena, & Andreae, 2000).

Feedback information does not only serve to guide an ongoing movement; it is also required to learn and to maintain an internal model of a transformation (cf. Jordan, 1996), provided it is not too complex. For example, Sangals (1997) had his subjects practice a nonlinear relation between the amplitude of the movement of a computer mouse and the amplitude of the cursor movement. When visual feedback during each movement of a sequence was eliminated and only terminal feedback at the end of each movement was provided, the relation between (visual) target amplitudes and movement amplitudes remained nonlinear. However, when visual feedback was completely eliminated for a sequence of several movements, the relation between (visual) target amplitudes and movement amplitudes became linear, which is likely to be a kind of default relation (cf. Koh & Meyer, 1991).

Feedback information can be processed at various levels of control; that is, it can be integrated with autonomous control processes in different ways. Consider the simple task of sine tracking: Subjects control the motion of a cursor on the screen, with the target following a sinusoidal time course. In principle, subjects could function like a position servo, minimizing the deviation between the position of the cursor and the position of the target. In fact, with a low frequency of target motion this may actually be the case. However, with higher frequencies, which approach the range where performance breaks down, human subjects produce a sinusoidal movement and seem to adjust its frequency and phase (Noble, Fitts, & Warren, 1955). Similar indications for the processing of parametric feedback rather than positional feedback have been reported by Pew (1966), but in general the processing of parametric rather than positional feedback has received very little attention. In everyday tasks like driving a car it may be of critical importance; perhaps it is not the position of the car on the road that is controlled but, rather, parameters like the curvature of the path.

In tasks like tracking there is not only visual feedback, but also proprioceptive feedback, and both types of feedback are related to different objects: proprioceptive feedback to one's own movements, but visual feedback to the motions of a controlled object. The relation between both types of feedback depends on the transformation implemented by the controlled machine. Only when the transformation is simple or well-learned, or both, can proprioceptive feedback replace visual feedback, but in general such intermodal matching is associated with some loss of accuracy as compared with intramodal matching of target and feedback information (e.g., Legge, 1965). On the other hand, when visual and proprioceptive feedback are different but nevertheless refer to the same object, as in the classical task of mirror drawing, the absence of proprioceptive feedback can actually enhance performance (Lajoie et al., 1992).

Even when visual and proprioceptive feedback refer to the same object, they are not necessarily redundant. For example, when we use a knife, both vision and proprioception provide information about its current position with respect to the object to be cut. Of course, visual information is more accurate in this respect, and as far as the spatiotemporal characteristics of the movement are concerned, proprioceptive information is not really needed. However, it provides information that is not available visually, in particular about the resistance of the cut object. Thus, although vision is critical for registering spatiotemporal characteristics, proprioception is critical for registering force characteristics. The lack of this latter kind of information is a problem in remote control and other tasks that followed from recent technological developments (cf. the chapter by Klatzky & Lederman in this volume).

An example is minimally invasive surgery (cf. Tendick, Jennings, Tharp, & Stark, 1993). Such operations are performed by means of an endoscope and instruments that are pivoted roughly at their place of insertion into the tissue. Although the facts that movements of the hand result in movements of the tip of the instrument in the opposite direction and that the gain of lateral movements depends on translational movements seem not to pose severe practical problems, the lack of appropriate force feedback seems to be more critical. In particular, there is only poor proprioceptive information about reactive forces at the tip of the instrument, so there is the risk of damage to the tissue operated on.

Sensory Information for Motor Control and Perception

Much of the sensory information that is involved in the control of movements apparently has no access to consciousness. Folklore knows that one just has to do it without attending too much to how it is done. In fact, Wulff, Höß, and Prinz (1998) found better learning of gross motor skills when the attention of the learners was focused on the effects of the movements rather than on the movements themselves, for example on a stabilometer platform rather than on the feet (for review, see Wulf & Prinz, 2001). It is not only that we do not perceive our movements in all details—for example, in skills like the long jump we do not normally perceive the details of the movements of our extremities (Voigt, 1933)—but, in addition, our movements can be more precise than would be expected from the limits of our perceptual skills. This was not only one of the major claims of a motor branch of the so-called Ganzheitspsychologie (Klemm, 1938), but it has also been emphasized in more recent times. For example, McLeod, McLaughlin, and Nimmo-Smith (1985) ascribed the very small temporal variability in batting of only a few milliseconds to the functioning of a dedicated special-purpose mechanism. In any case, hitting a falling ball at a certain position of its path is more precise than pressing a key when the ball reaches the same position (Bootsma, 1989).

Clinical cases illustrate that humans can reach to visual targets that they do not perceive, provided that the blind areas of the visual field (scotoma) are caused by certain lesions (e.g., Campion, Latto, & Smith, 1983; Perenin & Jeannerod, 1978). This phenomenon has become known as *blindsight*. In addition, clinical data give evidence of double dissociations. For example, some patients can identify and describe objects, but they cannot use the information about size, form, and orientation of the objects to grasp them; other patients, in contrast, cannot perceive these features of objects, but nevertheless can grasp them (Goodale & Milner, 1992).

The dissociability of visual information for perception and for motor control supports a theoretical distinction that has received much attention during the last 20 years. Basing their idea mainly on lesion studies, Ungerleider and Mishkin (1982) proposed the distinction between two cortical visual systems, one involving the inferotemporal cortex and the other the posterior parietal cortex (*ventral stream* and *dorsal stream,* respectively). In functional terms, these two systems have been characterized as the *what* system and the *where* system, the former serving object identification and the latter space perception. Alternatively, they are characterized functionally as the *what* system and the *how* system, the former being in the service of perception and the latter in the service of motor control (e.g., Goodale & Humphrey, 1998; Goodale & Milner, 1992). This latter functional characterization does largely coincide with a distinction between a *cognitive* and a *sensorimotor* system (Bridgeman, Kirch, & Sperling, 1981; Bridgeman, Lewis, Heit, & Nagle, 1979).

The evidence for the functional separation of a cognitive and a sensorimotor system is based on differences between psychophysical judgments and motor responses to identical stimuli. For example, Bridgeman, Peery, and Anand (1997) exploited the long-known effect of asymmetric stimuli in the visual field on the perceived direction of a target. They presented targets within a frame which was centered or shifted to the left or to the right. The target could appear in five different positions, and participants had to give their judgments by pressing one of five keys immediately after the stimulus had disappeared. For these perceptual judgments there was a clear effect of the position of the frame: When the frame was shifted to the left, judgments were shifted to the right, and vice versa. In contrast, when participants had to rotate a pointer so that it pointed to the target just presented, about half the participants exhibited no effect of the position of the frame. This was so although the response mode varied randomly and was cued only after the target had disappeared.

When delays of a few seconds between the disappearance of the target and the response were introduced, all participants showed effects of the frame position on pointing. Bridgeman et al. (1997) took their findings to indicate that the sensorimotor representation of the target is short-lived and overridden by the cognitive representation when the delay between disappearance of the target and response becomes sufficiently long. In some subjects the sensorimotor representation might even be so short-lived that it hardly survives the target presentation.

Although the *what* versus *how* distinction currently has a dominant influence, it is most likely a simplification. Processing of visual information is widely distributed across the brain, and so is motor control. Thus, it is easy to conceive of a set of systems that for different kinds of responses make use of different combinations of the various neural representations of the visual world. From such a perspective, there would be a multiplicity of perception-action systems, for which there is indeed evidence in other primates than humans (cf. Goodale & Humphrey, 1998).

MOTOR COORDINATION

In a general sense, coordination is a characteristic of almost any skilled movement, in that skilled performance requires fairly precise relations between various kinematic, kinetic, and physiological variables. For example, in cranking (and related tasks like pedaling), force pulses need to be precisely timed to occur during a certain phase of the rotation of the crank or pedal (cf. Glencross, 1970); in rapid finger tapping, muscle activity of flexors and extensors must be timed to occur at certain phases of the movement cycle (Heuer, 1998); in reaching for an object, the opening of the fingers must be related to the movement of the hand toward the object (e.g., Jeannerod, 1984); and so on. With this broad meaning, the term *coordination* becomes almost equivalent to *motor control*. However, for this section I use a narrower meaning in that I focus on the coordinated movements of different effectors, mainly the two arms (interlimb coordination).

Task Constraints and Structural Constraints

Coordinated movements of the two hands are largely determined by the task constraints. For example, the coordination pattern for sweeping with a broom is different from that for bathing a baby. This certainly is not a fact that deserves elaboration. However, there are more subtle consequences of task constraints. Perhaps the most important of these is compensatory covariation.

As an example, consider the lip aperture in speaking. A particular lip aperture can be achieved by various combinations of the positions of the upper lip, the lower lip, and the jaw. These positions exhibit compensatory covariation such that, for example, a high position of the upper lip will be accompanied by higher positions of the lower lip and/or the jaw, and a low position of the upper lip by lower positions of the lower lip and/or the jaw (Abbs, Gracco, & Cole, 1984). Compensatory covariation can be observed not only when lip positions vary spontaneously, but also when they are perturbed by means of some mechanical device (Kelso, Tuller, Vatikiotis-Bateson, & Fowler, 1984). A task similar to reaching a certain lip aperture is that of grasping an object with a precision grip, wherein there is compensatory covariation of the positions of thumb and index finger (Darling, Cole, & Abbs, 1988).

Compensatory covariation can be seen as a way to reduce the degrees of freedom in motor control. In addition, compensatory covariation contributes to solving the problem of achieving a stable movement outcome in spite of variable components. For example, with the appropriate covariation of lip and jaw positions, lip aperture will hardly vary. In fact, the principle of compensatory covariation seems to be a general principle of stabilizing movement outcomes (Müller, 2001) which is not restricted to tasks in which different limbs are involved.

A highly illustrative task for compensatory covariations is throwing a ball a certain distance. For physical reasons, when the initial flight angle varies, the initial velocity of the ball has to covary to reach a certain target distance. In particular, with an initial angle of 45° the initial velocity has to be smallest, and it has to be increased as the initial flight angle deviates from 45°, provided that the height at which the ball is released is also the height at which the target is located. Conforming to these task constraints, Stimpel (1933) observed positive correlations across series of throws to a certain target position between initial velocity and the absolute deviation of the initial flight angle from 45°. It is not fully clear how the particular covariation is established, but there is the possibility that subjects produce *equifinal trajectories* of the hand such that across time initial flight angle and velocity covary in the proper way; thereby the proper relation is established independent of the precise time at which the ball is released (Müller & Loosch, 1999).

The plot of the relation between initial velocities and initial flight angles required for a certain outcome of the throws can be thought of as an equal-outcome curve (Heuer, 1989). Figure 12.13 gives an example for a particular dart-throwing task, which also shows that with a target of a certain width, deviations from the bull's-eye-outcome curve have different consequences for accuracy depending on where on the curve subjects operate. In principle, equal-outcome curves can be determined for all sorts of tasks and for various sets of component variables. They specify how components of a skill must be related to each other in the service of satisfying the task constraints. In fact, this kind of analysis can become considerably more complex than what can be represented in terms of equal-outcome curves (or perhaps areas). An example is the analysis of juggling by Beek (1989).

The very fact that components of a motor pattern covary in the service of achieving particular outcomes has been taken as evidence for the existence of *movement Gestalts (Bewegungsgestalten)* by Stimpel (1933) and his advisor Klemm (1938),

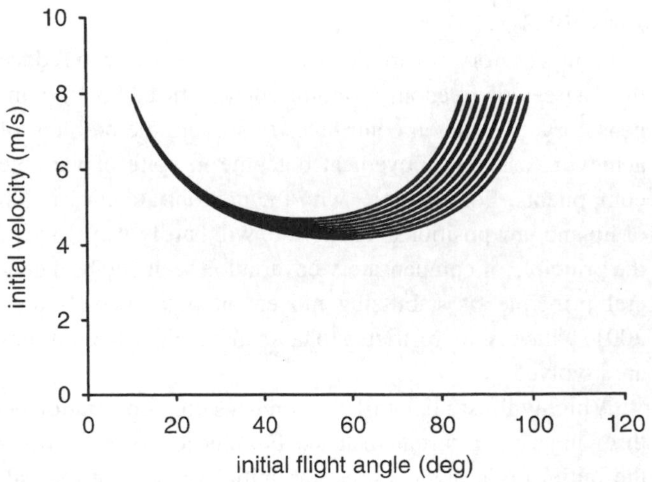

Figure 12.13 Equal-outcome curve for a particular dart-throwing task. When the target is an area rather than a point, deviations from the curve are permitted, so that it becomes an area in which initial velocity and flight angle of successful throws must be located (after Müller, 2001).

a notion that is analogous to perceptual Gestalts (see the chapter by Palmer in this volume). The core of the notion of a *Bewegungsgestalt* is the idea that the whole dominates its components and is more precise than expected from the components' variabilities. Although these notions appear fairly outdated now, it cannot be overlooked that they anticipate synergetic concepts (Haken, 1982) that currently play an important role in the study of motor coordination (cf. Kelso, 1994; Schöner, 1994). One of the core concepts is that of an order parameter (or collective variable) that enslaves the component variables, so that higher level variables are not simply the result of lower level variables, but dominate the lower level variables instead. This general idea is captured by models like the task-dynamic model of Saltzman and Kelso (1987) and the knowledge model of Rosenbaum, Loukopoulos, Meulenbroek, Vaughan, and Engelbrecht (1995).

Coordination in the service of satisfying task constraints is flexible: That is, patterns of covariation between certain effectors that can be observed when one task is performed may be absent when a different task is performed (e.g., Kelso et al., 1984). Nevertheless, for biologically important tasks like standing, locomotion, eating, and so on, there may be more rigid coordination patterns that not only support these tasks, but may also impede performance of sufficiently different tasks. Although it is not certain that such more rigid coordination patterns for biologically important tasks are indeed the origin of structural constraints on coordination, it is certain that structural constraints do exist. Basically, they limit the range of task-specific coordination patterns; while they support the production of certain patterns, they tend to impede the production of deviating patterns.

Structural constraints support symmetrical movements of the two arms. Thus, mirror writing with the left hand becomes a fairly simple task when it is performed concurrently with normal writing of the right hand (Jung & Fach, 1984). The other side of the coin is the difficulty we encounter when we attempt to produce different spatiotemporal patterns concurrently with the two hands. Although it is certainly not true that both hands are constrained to act as a unit in the sense of having a common timing (Kelso, Southard, & Goodman, 1979; Schmidt et al., 1979), bimanual movements tend toward identical durations, and only with strictly required different target durations can this tendency be overcome (Spijkers, Tachmatzidis, Debus, Fischer, & Kausche, 1994). Other deviations from strict symmetry are easier to achieve, but nevertheless there is a widespread tendency for different movements with the two hands not to be as different as they should be; the systematic errors here point to the symmetric patterns that are the ones supported by structural constraints.

The nature of structural constraints on coordination and their combination with task constraints or task-related intentions is nicely captured by perhaps the most influential model of motor coordination and its developments (Haken, Kelso, & Bunz, 1985). This model applies to tasks that require concurrent oscillations of at least two effectors, for example, the two hands. When these oscillatory movements are produced symmetrically, there is essentially no difficulty in speeding them up as far as this is possible. However, when they are produced asymmetrically, the phase relation between the oscillations is less stable, and occasionally symmetric movement cycles intrude (Cohen, 1971). When the asymmetric movements are speeded up, stability is reduced even more, provided that subjects are instructed to maintain the asymmetric phase relation (Lee, Blandin, & Proteau, 1996). However, with a "let it go" instruction, subjects tend to switch to symmetric movements at a certain critical frequency (Kelso, 1984).

Haken et al. (1985) modeled these phenomena in terms of what came later to be called an intrinsic coordination dynamics. The model was formulated at two levels, the level of actual movements and the level of an order parameter that captures the relation between the periodic movements. Basically, at the kinematic level two nonlinear oscillators were posited, one for each effector, with a nonlinear coupling in addition. Relative phase ϕ was chosen as the order parameter (or collective variable); this is the phase difference between the two oscillatory movements. For this variable the dynamics were specified based mainly on formal considerations: $\dot{\phi} = -a \sin \phi - 2b \sin 2\phi$. Better known is the formulation in terms of a potential function V with $\dot{\phi} = dV/d\phi$, $V = -a \cos \phi - b \cos 2\phi$. This potential, which is illustrated in Figure 12.14, has stable equilibria at $\phi = n\pi, n = 0, \pm 1, \pm 2, \ldots$, provided the parameters a and b are within certain ranges. Stable equilibria are characterized by $\dot{\phi}$'s being positive for smaller values of ϕ and negative for larger values, so that relative phase will drift back to the equilibrium angle whenever it deviates as a consequence of some perturbation; in the potential function, stable equilibria are characterized by minima.

The ratio of the parameters a and b is hypothesized to depend on movement frequency, b becoming relatively smaller as frequency increases. When it becomes sufficiently small, the stable equilibria at $\phi = m\pi, m = \pm 1, \pm 3, \pm 5, \ldots$ disappear (cf. Figure 12.14). This corresponds to the observation that, as the frequency increases, only symmetric oscillations (in-phase oscillations in formal terms) are maintained while asymmetric oscillations (anti-phase oscillations) tend to switch to symmetric ones.

This account of the switch is based pretty much on formal considerations, and other models are available with stronger reference to physiological or psychological considerations or

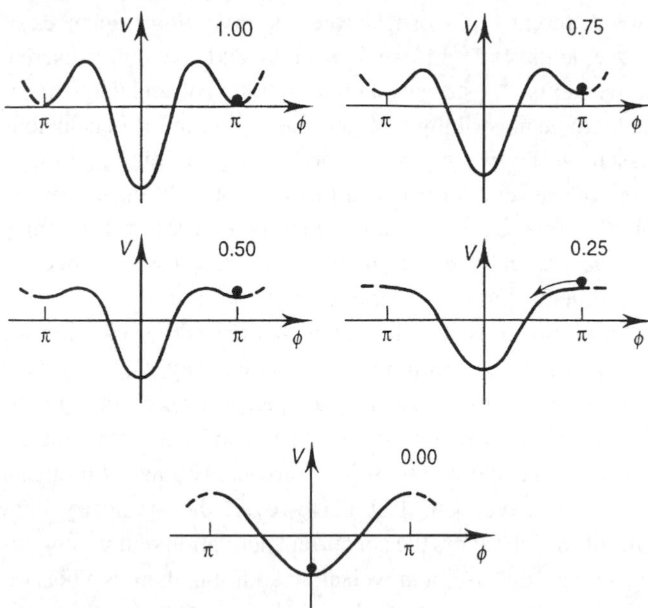

Figure 12.14 Potentials $V(\phi)$ as specified by Haken et al. (1985) for different ratios of b/a of the parameters.

both (Grossberg et al., 1997; Heuer, 1993b). In addition, the prediction that the switch should be associated with reduced movement amplitudes (Haken et al., 1985) is not necessarily correct (Peper & Beek, 1998). Nevertheless, the model captures nicely the soft nature of structural constraints, and an extension of it illustrates how structural constraints bias performance when they deviate from task constraints or task-related intentions.

Yamanishi, Kawato, and Suzuki (1980) asked their subjects to produce bimanual sequences of finger taps at various phase relations. The stability of phasing was highest with synchronous taps (relative phase of 0°), second highest with alternating taps (relative phase of 180°), and lower at all other relative phases. In addition the mean relative phases were biased toward the stable relative phases at 0° and 180°. Schöner and Kelso (1988) modeled these effects by way of adding a term to the intrinsic dynamics that reflects the "intention" to reach a target relative phase ψ, so that the potential becomes $V = -a \cos \phi - b \cos 2\phi - c \cos((\phi - \psi)/2)$. When the intended relative phase ψ differs from $\psi = 0°$ and $\psi = 180°$, the minima of this potential are broader, corresponding to an increased variability, and shifted away from the intended relative phase, corresponding to the observed systematic biases.

Basic Structural Constraints on Coordination

Structural constraints on coordination are indicated by systematic errors. They have been studied mainly by means of two different types of task, the one involving sequences of movements with different effectors and the other discrete movements, mostly of short duration. By and large there seem to be no striking discrepancies between the conclusions based on the two types of experimental paradigm, although the precise relation between them is not fully clear. For example, one cannot exclude that certain constraints may evolve gradually so that they are effective for sequences of movements, but not for brief discrete ones.

A highly consistent finding is that periodic oscillations of the upper limbs are more stable when they are performed symmetrically than when they are performed asymmetrically. The same kind of observation has also been made for bimanual circle drawing (e.g., Carson, Thomas, Summers, Walkers, & Semjen, 1997). However, the symmetry constraint, which favors the concurrent activation of homologous muscle groups, is not universal; in addition, there is a bias toward identical movement directions (e.g., Serrien, Bogaerts, Suy, & Swinnen, 1999). This is particularly obvious for periodic movements with nonsymmetric effectors. For example, Baldissera, Cavallari, and Civaschi (1982) and Baldissera, Cavallari, Marini, and Tassone (1991) found that concurrent up-and-down movements of foot and hand in identical directions are more precisely coordinated than concurrent movements in opposite directions. Thus, although essentially there is always a preferred phase relation for periodic movements of different effectors, which phase relation this is depends on the particular effectors chosen and their plane of motion.

A second highly consistent finding is related to the timing of bimanual response sequences. Such sequences are simple when they have the same frequency, and they are also fairly accurately produced when the frequencies are harmonically related, that is, by integer ratios. However, for polyrhythms performance deteriorates (e.g., Klapp, 1979). For this it is not essential that the polyrhythms are produced by the two hands, but poor or even chance performance can also be observed in vocal-manual tasks (Klapp, 1981). There seems to be a general rule that the variability of the temporal errors of individual responses increases as the product mn for $m : n$ rhythms increases (Deutsch, 1983); for example, variability is higher with a 2 : 5 ($mn = 20$) than with a 2 : 3 ($mn = 6$) rhythm. When the overall rate of polyrhythms is increased, not only does performance become poorer, but in addition complex rhythms may switch to less complex ones, like 2 : 5 to 1 : 2 (e.g., Peper, 1995).

The observations on polyrhythms have been taken to suggest the existence of a unitary timing-control mechanism for movements of the two hands (Deutsch, 1983). In fact, formal analyses of polyrhythm production in terms of timer models (cf. Vorberg & Wing, 1996) generally reveal integrated control, in which the timing of a response with the one hand can be relative to a preceding response with the other hand (Jagacinski, Marshburn, Klapp, & Jones, 1988; Klapp et al., 1985; Summers, Rosenbaum, Burns, & Ford, 1993). The difficulty in the production of polyrhythms is then basically related to the complexity of the integrated timing control structure. Only recently evidence has been reported according to which professional pianists can exhibit parallel timing control for the two hands when they produce polyrhythms at rapid rates (Krampe, Kliegl, Mayr, Engbert, & Vorberg, 2000). Except for such a select population, however, temporal coupling appears to be so tight that tasks that apparently require decoupling are performed in a way that maintains a unitary timing control.

Relatively little research effort has been invested in the study of sequences of bimanual movements with different amplitudes. Franz, Zelaznik, and McCabe (1991) studied the concurrent production of periodic lines and circles with the two hands. Drawing circles with one hand requires periodic oscillations with the same amplitudes along both axes of the plane, while drawing lines with the other hand requires a periodic oscillation along only one axis; however, for the other axis, one can think of a periodic oscillation with zero amplitude. Franz et al. found that both the lines and the circles became elliptical (Figure 12.15). Thus, the different amplitudes of the oscillations became more similar in the bimanual task: The larger amplitude oscillations in drawing circles were reduced in amplitude, and the zero-amplitude oscillations in drawing lines were enhanced in amplitude. More straightforwardly, such an amplitude assimilation for periodic movements was shown by Spijkers and Heuer (1995) and by Franz (1997), both for lines (that is, one-dimensional oscillations) and for circles (that is, two-dimensional oscillations). In addition, Spijkers and Heuer (1995) found that the amplitude assimilation became stronger as the frequency of oscillations was increased.

Kelso, Tuller, and Harris (1983) had their subjects oscillate a finger and concurrently repeat the syllable *stock*. When every second syllable had to be stressed, there was an involuntary increase of the amplitude of the accompanying finger movement; similarly, voluntarily increased finger amplitudes were accompanied by involuntary stresses of the syllable. These findings, which have been confirmed by Chang and Hammond (1987), suggest that, in addition to amplitude assimilation, changes of amplitude might overflow to other effectors.

For a more systematic exploration of the contralateral effects of large-to-small or small-to-large amplitude changes,

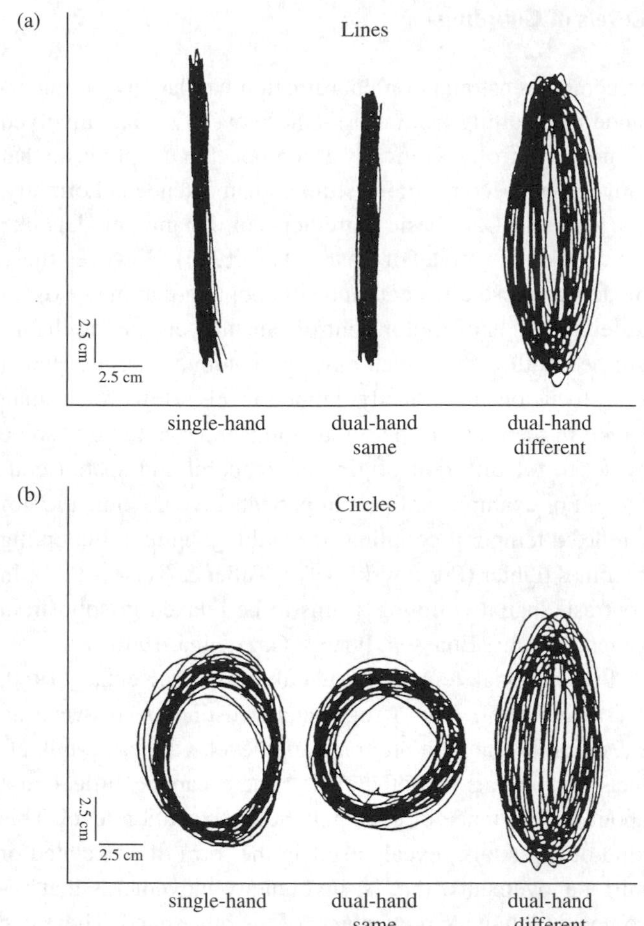

Figure 12.15 (a) Periodic lines drawn with one hand when with the other nothing was done or lines and circles were drawn concurrently; (b) periodic circles drawn with one hand when with the other hand nothing was done or circles and lines were drawn concurrently (after Franz et al., 1991).

Spijkers and Heuer (1995; Heuer, Spijkers, Kleinsorge, & Steglich, 2000) studied conditions in which one hand had to produce constant-amplitude oscillations and the other hand oscillations with alternating short and long amplitudes. They found that the requirement to change the amplitude in the one hand produced a contralateral effect in addition to the one observed with constant-amplitude oscillations. Specifically, after a change from a short to a long amplitude, the amplitude of the contralateral hand was larger than when only long amplitudes were repeated, and after a change from a long to a short amplitude the amplitude of the contralateral hand was smaller than when only short amplitudes were repeated. These findings indicate that cross-manual effects result not only from concurrent execution of different amplitudes, but perhaps also from cross-talk between processes of amplitude specifications. This is also indicated by the observation that contralateral involuntary amplitude modulations can be produced not only by movements of alternating short and long amplitudes, but also by the imagery of such movements (Heuer, Spijkers, Kleinsorge, & van der Loo, 1998).

Discrete-movement studies give clear evidence of a tight temporal coupling in that movements of different amplitude and accuracy requirements tend to be of (almost) the same duration (Kelso et al., 1979; Marteniuk, MacKenzie, & Baba, 1984). However, amplitude assimilation is only weak and tends to be asymmetrical in that the amplitude of a shorter movement is increased, while the amplitude of the concurrent longer movement is only slightly or not at all reduced (Heuer, Spijkers, Kleinsorge, van der Loo, & Steglich, 1998; Marteniuk et al., 1984; Sherwood, 1991). The tighter temporal than spatial coupling is also indicated by the typical finding that movement durations are more strongly correlated across trials than movement amplitudes (e.g., Sherwood, 1991).

Structural constraints on coordination are double-faced: On the one hand, they support the performance of certain tasks, like the production of strictly symmetric movements of the upper limbs, and on the other hand they impede the performance of other tasks, like the production of asymmetric movements. Together with the basically soft nature of structural constraints, this suggests that their strength might be modulated depending on task requirements. In particular, their strength might be enhanced when this is appropriate for the task at hand, and it might be reduced when this is appropriate. Such a task-related modulation of structural constraints on coordination does indeed exist.

Sherwood (1991) found higher intermanual correlations between the amplitudes of discrete rapid reversal movements when same amplitudes rather than different amplitudes were required. The same result was reported by Heuer, Spijkers, Kleinsorge, van der Loo, and Steglich (1998), who in addition found aftereffects such that the intermanual amplitude correlation was higher subsequent to same-amplitude movements than following different-amplitude movements, and by Steglich, Heuer, Spijkers, and Kleinsorge (1999) for peak forces of isometric contractions with same and different target forces for the two hands.

Rinkenauer, Ulrich, and Wing (2001) showed for isometric contractions that the requirement to produce different peak forces is associated not only with a reduction of the intermanual correlation between peak forces, but also with a reduction of the intermanual correlation between rise times. Similarly, when different rise times were to be produced in another experiment, both the correlations between rise times and between amplitudes were reduced. These findings indicate that the decoupling, which can be observed when different movements or isometric contractions are to be produced with the two hands, is a generalized phenomenon which is not restricted to the movement characteristic, that is actually different. In addition, coupling with respect to peak forces can be more easily modulated than temporal coupling; in fact, peak forces can be fully decoupled, but timing cannot.

In right-handed people, the right and left hands take different roles in bimanual actions: The typical function assigned to the left hand is holding, while the right hand performs manipulations relative to the left one. Generalizing this typical assignment of functions, Guiard (1987) characterized the left and right hand as *macrometric* and *micrometric,* respectively. Whereas the left hand is specialized for large-amplitude and low-frequency movements, the right hand is specialized for accurate small-amplitude and high-frequency movements. This characterization of the two hands, together with the typical functions assigned to them in bimanual tasks, suggests that structural constraints on coordination may be asymmetric. Although the results on lateral asymmetries in bimanual tasks tend to be somewhat unreliable, there seem to be at least two consistent findings.

The first finding is that bimanual tasks are easier when lower-frequency movements are assigned to the left hand and higher-frequency movements to the right hand than with the opposite assignment of movements to hands. This is true for oscillatory movements (Gunkel, 1962) and discrete finger taps (Ibbotson & Morton, 1981; Peters, 1981). An example is tapping a steady beat with the left hand and a certain rhythm with the right hand. With the opposite assignment the task is harder, and when performance breaks down, it is typically in the right hand, which also starts to produce the rhythm assigned to the left hand. Thus, conforming to Guiard's (1987) notion of macrometric and micrometric functional specializations of the two hands, task assignments that conform to these specializations are easier than task assignments that violate them. Also conforming to Guiard's notion, Spijkers and Heuer (1995) observed stronger assimilations of movement amplitudes when large-amplitude oscillations were produced with the right hand and small-amplitude oscillations with the left hand than with the opposite assignment of amplitudes to hands.

A second rather consistent finding is a lead of the right hand in bimanual tasks like circle drawing (Stucchi & Viviani, 1993; Swinnen, Jardin, & Meulenbroek, 1996). Stucchi and Viviani (1993) hypothesized that in particular the timing of bimanual movements might originate from the hemisphere contralateral to the dominant hand. This hypothesis has received some support from a PET study (Viviani, Perani, Grassi, Bettinardi, & Fazio, 1998), and it is consistent with the evidence for tight temporal coupling (or unitary timing mechanisms) in bimanual tasks.

Levels of Coupling

Structural constraints on coordination can largely be understood as resulting from cross-talk between signals involved in motor control, specifically as a product of coupling, so that movements become more similar than intended. Formally, coupling terms are basic ingredients of dynamic models like the well-known model of Haken et al. (1985). However, these models collapse different kinds of coupling that may exist at different levels of motor control. Such levels can be distinguished both in functional and in anatomical terms. Here I shall focus on functionally defined levels. However, it may be worth mentioning that in anatomical terms there is some evidence for different origins of temporal and spatial coupling. For example, split-brain patients give no indication of a relaxed temporal coupling; if anything, temporal coupling becomes tighter (Preilowski, 1972; Tuller & Kelso, 1989). In contrast, spatial coupling seems to be relaxed in split-brain patients (Franz, Eliassen, Ivry, & Gazzaniga, 1996).

In functional terms, Marteniuk and MacKenzie (1980; Marteniuk et al., 1984) suggested a distinction between an execution level and a programming level, with cross-talk effects originating at both levels. There can be little doubt about the existence of cross-talk at the execution level. This kind of cross-talk reveals itself in the form of associated or mirror movements, that is, involuntary movements that accompany voluntary movements of the other hand. These can be observed in healthy adults (e.g., Durwen & Herzog, 1989, 1992; Todor & Lazarus, 1986), but they tend to be more conspicuous under a variety of neurological conditions or in children when inhibitory mechanisms, which serve to focus the basic bilateral innervation unilaterally, are impaired or not yet fully developed (McDowell & Wolff, 1997; Schott & Wyke, 1981). Models that rely on cross-talk at the execution level can account for several observations on, for example, bimanual circle drawing (Cattaert, Semjen, & Summers, 1999). Nevertheless, there are some results that strongly favor the notion of coupling during motor programming (or parametric cross-talk) in addition to cross-talk at the execution level.

Figure 12.16 shows some data obtained with the timed-response procedure (Heuer, Spijkers, Kleinsorge, van der Loo, & Steglich, 1998). The task of the participants was to produce bimanual reversal movements with short or long amplitudes. Movements were to be initiated in synchrony with the last of four pacing tones, and cues were presented at variable cuing intervals before the last tone. The cues indicated the amplitudes of the movements, which could be short-short, long-long, short-long, and long-short. Participants had been instructed to prepare for movements with intermediate

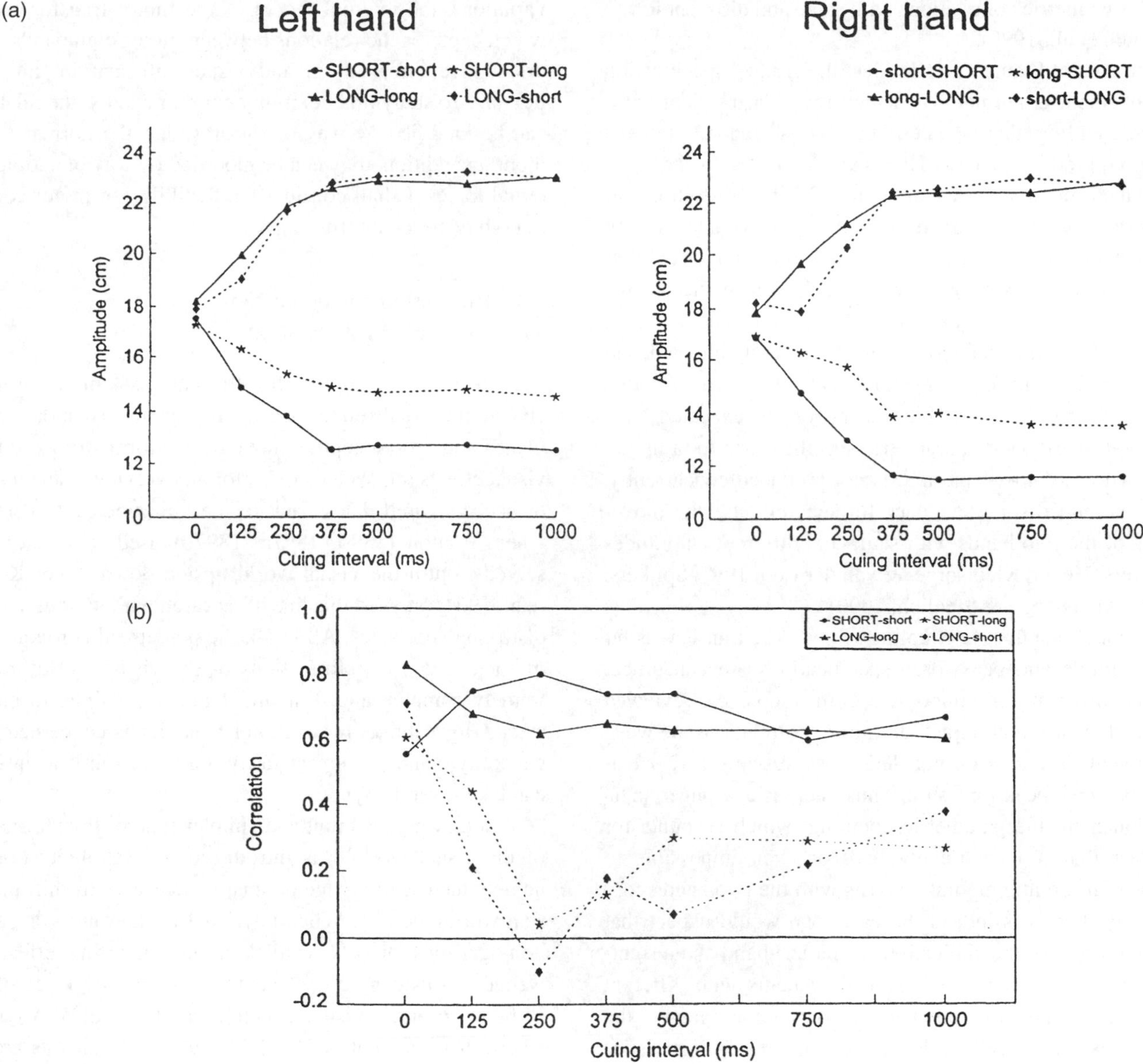

Figure 12.16 (a) Mean amplitudes of short and long reversal movements as a function of the cuing interval in a timed-response experiment, shown separately for the left and right hand and the target amplitude of the other hand. (b) Correlations between amplitudes of bimanual reversal movements for the four different amplitude combinations (after Heuer, Spijkers, Kleinsorge, van der Loo, & Steglich, 1998).

amplitudes and then to produce amplitudes according to the cues as far as this was possible.

The continuous lines in Figure 12.16a show how, with increasing preparation time, short and long movements reach their final amplitudes, beginning at an intermediate default amplitude. Broken lines show the temporal evolution of the short and long movement amplitudes when the target amplitude for the other hand was different, long and short, respectively. With long cuing intervals the already described asymmetric amplitude assimilation was found in that the amplitude of the short movement was enhanced by the concurrent requirement to produce a long-amplitude movement with the other hand, whereas the long-amplitude movement was not affected by the concurrent short-amplitude movement of the other hand. However, at short intervals there was also a transient reduction of the long amplitude, although the amplitude difference of the two hands was actually smaller than at long cuing intervals. In Figure 12.16b the correlations between the amplitudes of the two hands are shown: They stay at a high level for same-amplitude movements as the cuing interval increases, but they are rapidly reduced for different-amplitude movements. These basic findings have been replicated for different amplitude differences of the two hands (Heuer, Kleinsorge, Spijkers, & Steglich, 2001) and also for isometric contractions with same and different forces (Steglich et al., 1999).

The data of Figure 12.16a reflect the gradual specification of movement amplitudes, and they reveal a transient parametric coupling, that is, a coupling that is gradually relaxed when required by the task. This is also indicated by the intermanual correlations shown in Figure 12.16b. Parametric coupling does apply to concurrent specifications of movement parameters, but not to the time-varying force signals or other execution-related signals during actual performance of the movements. Thus it should also show up in reaction time, that is, before bimanual movements are actually initiated, and it should show up even in unimanual tasks, provided that parametric specifications for the movement executed have temporal overlap with parametric specifications for a movement with the other hand that is not produced concurrently. There is indeed some evidence for such effects with movements of the two hands with same and different amplitudes (Spijkers, Heuer, Kleinsorge, & van der Loo, 1997; Spijkers, Heuer, Kleinsorge, & Steglich, 2000).

Although parametric coupling seems to be transient as far as amplitude and peak-force specifications are concerned, this is different for temporal specifications. As reviewed above, for different target durations correlations between movement durations do not decline as strongly as correlations between peak forces do. Thus, there is a stronger static component to the parametric coupling, which accounts for the fact that it is extremely hard or even impossible to produce different temporal patterns with the two hands concurrently. If this is indeed the case, one would expect that reaction time for the choice between a left-hand and a right-hand movement is longer when movements with different rather than same temporal characteristics are assigned to the two hands. The reason is that same temporal characteristics can be prepared concurrently in advance of the response signal (or perhaps immediately after presentation as long as the choice of the correct response is not yet finished), whereas this is impossible for different temporal characteristics. Such reaction-time differences do exist (see Heuer, 1990, for a review; Heuer, 1995).

FLEXIBILITY OF MOTOR CONTROL

The motor transformation, the relation between motor commands and resulting movements, is variable. On a short time scale, variations arise when we handle objects, tools, and machines, and when we move in different directions relative to gravity. On a longer time scale, variations result from body growth and other bodily changes. As a consequence of such variations, the internal model of the motor transformation, which captures the relations between motor commands, proprioceptive information, and visual information, must be flexible. To study this flexibility experimentally, the relations can be modified by way of transforming the normal visual input; in addition, they can be modified by way of adding external forces. I shall consider the flexibility of motor control in both respects in turn.

Adapting and Adjusting to New Visuo-Motor Transformations

Various kinds of optical transformations can be used to change the usual relation between movements (motor commands and proprioceptive movement information) and their visual effects (cf. Welch, 1978, for an overview). The history of such research dates back to the late nineteenth century, when Stratton (1896, 1897a, 1897b) used spectacles that served to turn the visual world upside down. Later Kohler (e.g., 1964) pursued this line of research with various sorts of distorting spectacles. All in all, the perceptual consequences of such severe transformations of the visual world are extremely complex and difficult, if not impossible, to understand. However, as far as motor behavior is concerned, this generally comes to appear fairly normal, even if adaptation can take several days.

A somewhat different and simpler type of transformation of the visual world was introduced by Helmholtz (1867), namely the use of wedge prisms, which serve to shift the visual world laterally. When no visual background (or only a homogeneous one) is available, the distorting effects of wedge prisms can be neglected and the consequence of the shifted egocentric visual direction can be studied. A typical lateral displacement is 11°. Thus, when participants are instructed to point to a target that is visually displaced to the right, their movements will end to the right of the physical target. When they receive feedback on the pointing errors, these will gradually disappear in the course of a series of movements. In principle the disappearance of the systematic pointing errors could be due to strategic corrections, that is, to simply pointing to the left of the perceived target. Alternatively, it can be due to a change of the internal model of the visuo-motor transformation. More revealing than the disappearance of the pointing error in the exposure phase is the negative aftereffect that can be observed after removal of the wedge prisms. Now, without visual feedback, subjects tend to point in the opposite direction, that is, to the left of the target when it had been visually displaced to the right. Negative aftereffects can also be observed when the prism strength is gradually increased in the exposure period with concurrent displacements of the physical target so that it remains in a constant egocentric direction; with this procedure, systematic pointing errors are masked by random errors and are not noticed by the subjects (Howard, 1968).

Prism adaptation implies some kind of change of the internal model of the motor transformation. What is the nature of this change? A first point to note is that it is generalized and not restricted to the particular movement performed during prism exposure. Instead, an exposure period with a single visual target results in negative aftereffects not only for this particular target, but for a range of targets in different directions, and when prismatic displacement is different for targets in different directions, aftereffects reveal a kind of linear interpolation for targets in between (Bedford, 1989). Beyond the generalization across the work space, the aftereffect is not even restricted to pointing at visual targets. In many cases it is approximately the sum of two components, a proprioceptive aftereffect and a visual aftereffect (Hay & Pick, 1966), with the relative size of the two components depending on exposure conditions (e.g., Kelso, Cook, Olson, & Epstein, 1975). A test of the proprioceptive aftereffect is pointing straight ahead, whereas a test for the visual aftereffect is to align a visual stimulus with the straight-ahead position. Thus, what is changed is not the specific relation between visual and proprioceptive direction, but rather the directional meaning of visual and/or proprioceptive signals.

Some findings suggest that the adaptation during prism exposure does not involve a modification of a single internal model of the motor transformation, but some kind of addition, so that the original model remains in existence. On the one hand, negative aftereffects decay even when participants remain in darkness (e.g., Dewar, 1971); on the other hand, even when participants are confronted with the normal visual world between experimental sessions, long-term effects of prismatic adaptation can be observed as soon as they are brought back to the experimental setup (McGonigle & Flook, 1978). In addition, with repeated alternations of periods with and without lateral displacement, or with different lateral displacements, aftereffects tend to disappear, and switching between different visuo-motor transformations becomes almost instantaneous (e.g., Kravitz, 1972; Welch, 1971). These and other results (cf. Welch, Bridgeman, Anand, & Browman, 1993) strongly suggest that multiple models of visuo-motor transformations can be learned and, when required by the task, selectively be put to use, although little is known about the nature of the cues that mediate the retrieval of stored internal models.

In a certain way, the situation when wearing laterally displacing prisms is similar to a situation that has become quite common during the last one or two decades, namely the operation of a computer mouse with concurrent movements of a cursor on a laterally displaced monitor. Although in the first case there are aftereffects, we encounter no difficulties in operating the mouse with different lateral displacements of the screen. There seem to be mainly two reasons for this difference: First, movements performed with the computer mouse are parameterized in terms of (allocentric) distances, whereas movements produced in experiments with laterally displacing prisms are parameterized in terms of (egocentric) locations. Second, and perhaps of less importance, is that with the computer mouse proprioceptive and visual information indicate different egocentric directions of different objects, the hand and the cursor, while in prism-adaptation studies they refer to the same object, the hand. Object identity is a factor that affects the size of negative aftereffects (Welch, 1972).

Visuo-motor transformations can also be changed such that the relations between (allocentric) visual distances and/or directions and (hand-centered) movement amplitudes and/or directions are modified. The basic findings seem to parallel those obtained in prism-adaptation studies to a remarkable degree. For example, aftereffects occur and multiple models of visuo-motor transformations can be learned and selectively accessed when appropriate (Cunningham & Welch, 1994). When a certain internal model has been learned, there seems to follow a kind of labile period in which the learning of a new transformation results in a modification of the model, but after a period of consolidation the learning of a new transformation results in the development of a new model rather than the overriding of the old one (Krakauer, Ghilardi, & Ghez, 1999). With sufficient delays between learning periods, it seems that repeated alternation between different transformations is not needed to acquire multiple internal models.

When discussing visual feedback, I have pointed to the limitations in acquiring internal models of additional transformations of one's own movements. Whereas adjustments to changes of visuo-motor gains require only one or a few discrete movements (Young, 1969), adjustments to new relations between the directions of hand movements and cursor motions require more trials (e.g., Krakauer et al., 1999). Adjustments to nonlinear transformations require even longer experience, and for too complex transformations internal models can no longer be developed. Although the mastery of added transformations is typically not associated with their awareness (who could tell the gain factor of his or her computer mouse?), the difficulty of such transformations is affected by higher level cognitive processes. This is nicely illustrated by a little-known study of Merz, Kalveram, and Huber (1981), and additional evidence from reaction-time studies is reported in the chapter by Proctor and Vu in this volume.

In the experiment of Merz et al. (1981), participants controlled the movement of a cursor on an oscilloscope screen by means of lateral pressure on a knob. Their task was a tracking task in which they had to keep the cursor aligned with a moving target. For two groups of participants the cursor moved to the right when the knob was pressed to the right (compatible relation), and for two groups of participants the relation was reversed (incompatible). One group with each of the two levels of compatibility had the knob placed at the bottom of a steering wheel, while for the other two groups the steering wheel was covered by a piece of cardboard. In the incompatible conditions there was a strong practice effect. More important, however, is that the performance deficit in the incompatible conditions disappeared when the steering wheel was visible; performance in this condition was as good as in the compatible conditions. Thus, the visibility of the steering wheel enabled the subjects to change the incompatible relation to a compatible one in associating clockwise rotation of the wheel, which is consequent upon leftward pressure, with a rightward motion of the cursor on the screen.

Adjusting and Adapting to External Forces

When external forces vary, motor commands for intended movements have to be modulated accordingly. Except for movements with different directions relative to gravity, perhaps the most frequent adjustments are required when we deal with objects of different masses. Here, depending on the mass, the kinematic characteristics vary. Specifically, with increasing mass, peak acceleration and peak deceleration as well as peak velocity tend to decline, while movement duration tends to increase. This is true both for lifting objects (Gachoud, Mounoud, Hauert, & Viviani, 1983) and for moving them in a horizontal plane (Gottlieb, Corcos, & Agarwal, 1989). Thus, for objects with different masses, peak forces are not perfectly scaled, which would result in an invariant acceleration profile; instead, with increasing mass, acceleration and deceleration become smaller, but an increasing duration serves to avoid a shortening of the amplitude of the movements. In spite of these mass-dependent variations, the basic shape of the velocity profile remains invariant; that is, with the proper scaling of time and velocity, the profiles become identical (Bock, 1990; Ruitenbeek, 1984).

In lifting an object, it is not only the so-called load force which has to be adjusted to the mass (and weight) of the object, but also the grip force (cf. Johansson, 1996, for review). When the grip force is too weak, the object may slip; when it is too strong, the object may break; and, in addition, too high

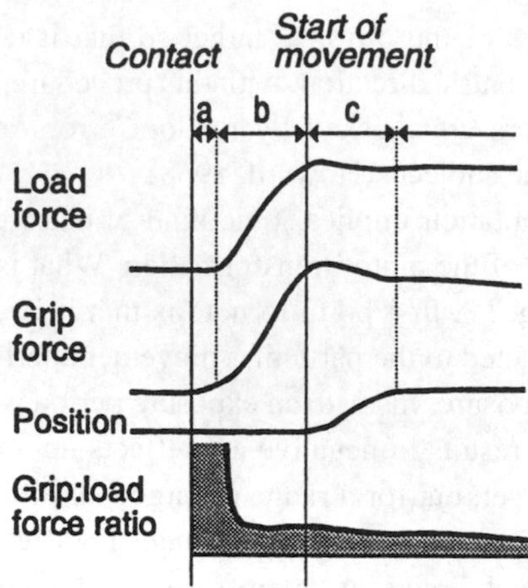

Figure 12.17 Lifting an object. Period a is the preload phase, b the loading phase, c the transitional phase, in which the object is actually lifted, followed by the static or hold phase (after Johansson, 1996).

forces are uneconomical. Figure 12.17 shows the buildup of both types of force when an object is lifted. First, grip force starts to develop (preload phase), then load force (loading phase). When the load force is sufficiently strong, the object is lifted (transitional phase) and thereafter held in a certain position.

During the loading phase a certain relation between grip force and load force is established, which is generally somewhat higher than the minimal value required to prevent the object from slipping; this safety margin is typically in the range of 10–40%. Of course, the proper adjustment of the grip force depends not only on the object, but also on its surface characteristics. In fact, there is a delicate grip-force adjustment to the friction between fingers and object surface that depends not only on the surface characteristics of the object, but also on those of the skin, which change, for example, after washing one's hands.

Adjustment of grip force is required not only when an object is lifted, but also when it is moved around, so that there is an inertial load in addition to the gravitational load. In a manner similar to the way load force and grip force increase in parallel when an object is lifted, grip force is modulated in parallel to inertial load while an object is moved (Flanagan, Tresilian, & Wing, 1993; Flanagan & Wing, 1995). In moving an object, there is an important difference between periodic horizontal and vertical movements. In horizontal movements, inertial load is orthogonal to gravitational load; inertial load reaches maxima both at the left and right movement reversals, and grip force reaches maxima at these points as well. Thus, there is a 1:2 ratio of the frequencies of periodic movements and grip-force modulations. In contrast, for vertical movements inertial and gravitational load add, so that total load is particularly strong at the lower movement reversal, but it can be close to zero at the upper movement reversal. In this case the frequency ratio becomes 1 : 1. This difference between horizontal and vertical movements disappears under conditions of microgravity because of the absence of gravitational load, and subjects adapt rapidly (during parabolic flights) to produce the appropriate 1:2 ratio also with vertical movements (Hermsdörfer et al., 2000).

Force adjustments are both predictive and reactive. This basic principle is evident already from the everyday observation that when someone hands an object to someone else, the latter can normally hold it without difficulties; only when the object is unexpectedly light or heavy, short-lived difficulties arise. Without knowing about the change of the mass of a moved object, the first movement is perturbed, but the next movement is properly adjusted to the new load (Bock, 1993). In fact, corrections for the unexpected mass set in as early as during the first movement, which, in the case of an unexpectedly high load, results mainly in a prolonged movement duration (Bock, 1993; Smeets, Erkelens, & Denier van der Gon, 1995). It seems that under conditions of microgravity, when objects are weightless but nevertheless have normal mass and thus inertial load, movements exhibit characteristics of movements with an unexpectedly high mass even for weeks (Sangals, Heuer, Manzey, & Lorenz, 1999).

Motor commands for active movements are most likely among the information that is involved in predictive force adjustments, as can be evidenced from the grip-force adjustments while moving a hand-held object. Of course, this kind of prediction can work only when force adjustments are required as a consequence of self-generated activity. When force adjustments are required to accommodate variations in load, which are independent of self-generated activity, predictions must rely on other kinds of information. Obviously, proper force adjustments depend on experience; the first movement after an unnoticed change of the load is performed with an initially maladjusted force, but not the second one. In addition, seen object size plays a role, although force adjustment is not necessarily related to estimates of weight. Gordon, Forssberg, Johansson, and Westling (1991) examined the lifting of boxes of identical weight but different sizes. Although subjects judged the smaller boxes to be heavier than the larger ones, peak grip and load forces were stronger for the larger ones. However, this difference was present only during lifting and disappeared during subsequent holding of the object, when force adjustments were perhaps related to the actual weight and no longer to the visually mediated predictive mechanisms.

Adjustments to objects of different masses seem to be comparatively simple achievements, similar to adjustments to different visuo-motor gains. When the external forces which act on a moving limb are transformed in a more complex way, similarities between adjustments to modified visuo-motor transformations and modified external force fields become more conspicuous. Shadmehr and Mussa-Ivaldi (1994) introduced such forces while the participants moved a robot arm. For example, forces were proportional to hand velocity and nearly orthogonal to the direction of hand movement, so that initially the paths of the hand were strongly curved. With continued experience the paths became again approximately straight lines, which—as an aside—can be taken as additional evidence for the claim that motor planning refers to end-effector kinematics. After removal of the external forces there were negative aftereffects: The paths of the hand were curved again, but in the opposite direction. The aftereffects indicate that the adjustments were based on a new internal model of the dynamic transformation.

Similar to the findings with modified visuo-motor transformations, multiple internal models of dynamic transformations can be acquired (Shadmehr & Brashers-Krug, 1997). Again there seems to be a labile period after a new model has been learned, during which it will be unlearned when another dynamic transformation is experienced, but after a period of consolidation this is no longer the case. Once an internal model has survived the labile period, it can be put to efficient use even months later.

Adjustments to new dynamic transformations generalize across different types of movement (Condit, Gandolfo, & Mussa-Ivaldi, 1997) and also across the work space (Shadmehr & Mussa-Ivaldi, 1994). When movements are performed in a different region of the workspace from during the practice period, external forces can remain invariant either with respect to the movement of the end-effector in coordinates of extrinsic space or with respect to the joint movements. Generalizations across the work space turned out to be approximate in joint coordinates. This is consistent with a particularly intriguing parallel between adaptation to shifted visual directions and additional external forces.

Prism adaptation involves modified relations between proprioceptive and/or visual signals and their meaning in terms of egocentric directions. Adaptation to a modified external force field seems to involve a modified relation between muscle activations (or motor commands) and the directions of consequent movements (Shadmehr & Moussavi, 2000). For example, the EMG signal from an elbow flexor can be plotted as a function of movement direction (more precisely, it is the EMG signal integrated across a certain time interval around the start of the movement); this results in a directional tuning curve of a muscle. Of course, the peak of this curve is shifted when the shoulder joint is moved. However, there is also a shift induced by the adaptation to a new force field, and this shift is more or less additive to shifts associated with rotations at the shoulder. This adaptation-induced shift allows one to predict the generalization across the work space.

MOVING ON

Research on the adaptive capabilities of human motor control can serve to illustrate some fairly general characteristics of the field: First, different phases or waves can be distinguished; second, different lines of research come together and trigger new waves; third, research on applied problems often precedes more theoretically minded research; and fourth, new concepts enter the field, often coming from other academic disciplines. At present, research on adapting to visual distortions and to added transformations, as in tracking tasks, is combined; research on the latter has a strong applied history related, for example, to vehicle control. The new theoretical concepts come largely from modern control theory and robotics. On top of such developments are new measurement technologies, which have made the recording of movements easier and which open progressively wider windows onto the activity of the brain while it controls movement.

Science seems to be driven largely by practical needs and by the apparent human desire to have coherent ideas of oneself and the world one lives in. Perhaps some of the findings reported in this chapter challenge ideas humans tend to have about themselves, but as far as motor control is concerned, the more important driving forces seem to be practical, related to technical developments as in robotics, to the control of complex machines, and to new challenges for manual skills, as in minimally invasive surgery. Perhaps future developments will result in tighter links of the (functional) theoretical concepts of the field to the solution of applied problems on the one hand and to the neuronal substrates on the other hand.

REFERENCES

Abbs, J. H., Gracco, V. L., & Cole, K. J. (1984). Control of multimovement coordination: Sensorimotor mechanisms in speech motor programming. *Journal of Motor Behavior, 16,* 195–232.

Abrams, R. A., & Landgraf, J. Z. (1990). Differential use of distance and location information for spatial localization. *Perception & Psychophysics, 47,* 349–359.

Aschersleben, G., Gehrke, J., & Prinz, W. (2001). Tapping with peripheral nerve block. A role for tactile feedback in the timing of movements. *Experimental Brain Research, 136,* 331–339.

Aschersleben, G., & Prinz, W. (1995). Synchronizing actions with events: The role of sensory information. *Perception & Psychophysics, 57,* 305–317.

Aschersleben, G., & Prinz, W. (1997). Delayed auditory feedback in synchronization. *Journal of Motor Behavior, 29,* 35–46.

Baldissera, F., Cavallari, P., & Civaschi, P. (1982). Preferential coupling between voluntary movements of ipsilateral limbs. *Neuroscience Letters, 34,* 95–100.

Baldissera, F., Cavallari, P., Marini, G., & Tassone, G. (1991). Differential control of in-phase and anti-phase coupling of rhythmic movements of ipsilateral hand and foot. *Experimental Brain Research, 83,* 375–380.

Bedford, F. L. (1989). Constraints on learning new mappings between perceptual dimensions. *Journal of Experimental Psychology: Human Perception and Performance, 15,* 232–248.

Beek, P. J. (1989). *Juggling dynamics*. Amsterdam: Free University Press.

Bennett, S., van der Kamp, J., Savelsbergh, G. J., & Davids, K. (1999). Timing a one-handed catch. I. Effects of telestereoscopic viewing. *Experimental Brain Research, 129,* 362–368.

Bizzi, E., Accornero, N., Chapple, W., & Hogan, N. (1984). Posture control and trajectory formation during arm movement. *Journal of Neuroscience, 4,* 2738–2744.

Blöte, A. W., & Dijkstra, J. F. (1989). Task effects on young children's performance in manipulating a pencil. *Human Movement Science, 8,* 515–528.

Bock, O. (1990). Load compensation in human goal-directed movements. *Behavioural Brain Research, 41,* 167–177.

Bock, O. (1993). Early stages of load compensation in human aimed arm movements. *Behavioural Brain Research, 55,* 61–68.

Bock, O., & Arnold, K. (1993). Error accumulation and error correction in sequential pointing movements. *Experimental Brain Research, 95,* 111–117.

Bock, O., & Eckmiller, R. (1986). Goal-directed arm movements in absence of visual guidance: Evidence for amplitude rather than position control. *Experimental Brain Research, 62,* 451–458.

Bootsma, R. J. (1989). Accuracy of perceptual processes subserving different perception-action systems. *Quarterly Journal of Experimental Psychology, 41A,* 489–500.

Bootsma, R. J., & van Wieringen, P. C. W. (1990). Timing an attacking forehand drive in table tennis. *Journal of Experimental Psychology: Human Perception and Performance, 16,* 21–29.

Bridgeman, B., Kirch, M., & Sperling, A. (1981). Segregation of cognitive and motor aspects of visual function using induced motion. *Perception & Psychophysics, 29,* 336–342.

Bridgeman, B., Lewis, S., Heit, G., & Nagle, M. (1979). Relation between cognitive and motor-oriented systems of visual position perception. *Journal of Experimental Psychology: Human Perception and Performance, 5,* 692–700.

Bridgeman, B., Peery, S., & Anand, S. (1997). Interaction of cognitive and sensorimotor maps of visual space. *Perception & Psychophysics, 59,* 456–469.

Brown, T. G. (1911). The intrinsic factors in the act of progression in the mammal. *Proceedings of the Royal Society, 84B,* 308–319.

Brunia, C. H. M. (1999). Neural aspects of anticipatory behavior. *Acta Psychologica, 101,* 213–242.

Brunia, C. H. M., Haagh, S. A. V. M., & Scheirs, J. G. M. (1985). Waiting to respond: Electrophysiological measurements in man during preparation for a voluntary movement. In H. Heuer, U. Kleinbeck, & K.-H. Schmidt (Eds.), *Motor behavior: Programming, control, and acquisition* (pp. 35–78). Berlin, Germany: Springer.

Bullock, D., & Grossberg, S. (1988). Neural dynamics of planned arm movements: Emergent invariants and speed-accuracy properties during trajectory formation. *Psychological Review, 95,* 49–90.

Campion, J., Latto, R., & Smith, Y. M. (1983). Is blindsight an effect of scattered light, spared cortex, and near-threshold vision? *Behavioral and Brain Sciences, 6,* 423–486.

Carlton, L. G. (1981). Visual information: The control of aiming movements. *Quarterly Journal of Experimental Psychology, 33A,* 87–93.

Carson, R. G., Thomas, J., Summers, J. J., Walters, M. R., & Semjen, A. (1997). The dynamics of bimanual circle drawing. *Quarterly Journal of Experimental Psychology, 50A,* 664–683.

Cattaert, D., Semjen, A., & Summers, J. J. (1999). Simulating a neural cross-talk model for between-hand interference during bimanual circle drawing. *Biological Cybernetics, 81,* 343–358.

Chang, P., & Hammond, G. R. (1987). Mutual interactions between speech and finger movements. *Journal of Motor Behavior, 19,* 265–274.

Cohen, L. (1971). Synchronous bimanual movements performed by homologous and nonhomologous muscles. *Perceptual and Motor Skills, 32,* 639–644.

Condit, M. A., Gandolfo, F., & Mussa-Ivaldi, F. (1997). The motor system does not learn the dynamics of the arm by role memorizations of past experience. *Journal of Neurophysiology, 78,* 554–560.

Cooke, J. D. (1980). The organization of simple, skilled movements. In G. E. Stelmach & J. Requin (Eds.), *Tutorials in motor behavior* (pp. 199–212). Amsterdam: North-Holland.

Cordo, P. J., & Nashner, L. M. (1982). Properties of postural adjustments associated with rapid arm movements. *Journal of Neurophysiology, 47,* 287–302.

Crossman, E. R. F. W., & Goodeve, P. J. (1963/1983). Feedback control of hand-movement and Fitts' law. *Quarterly Journal of Experimental Psychology, 35A,* 251–278 (originally presented at the Meeting of the Experimental Psychology Society, Oxford, 1963).

Cruse, H. (1986). Constraints for joint angle control of the human arm. *Biological Cybernetics, 54,* 125–132.

Cruse, H., & Brüwer, M. (1987). The human arm as a redundant manipulator: The control of path and joint angles. *Biological Cybernetics, 57,* 137–144.

Cruse, H., Dean, J., Heuer, H., & Schmidt, R. A. (1990). Utilization of sensory information for motor control. In O. Neumann & W. Prinz (Eds.), *Relationships between perception and action: Current approaches* (pp. 43–79). Berlin, Germany: Springer.

Cunningham, H. A., & Welch, R. B. (1994). Multiple concurrent visual-motor mapping: implications for models of adaptation. *Journal of Experimental Psychology: Human Perception and Performance, 20,* 987–999.

Darling, W. G., Cole, K. J., & Abbs, J. H. (1988). Kinematic variability in grasp movements as a function of practice and movement speed. *Experimental Brain Research, 73,* 225–235.

Davidson, P. R., Jones, R. D., Sirisena, H. R., & Andreae, J. H. (2000). Detection of adaptive inverse models in the human motor system. *Human Movement Science, 19,* 761–795.

Derwort, A. (1938). Untersuchungen über den Zeitablauf figurierter Bewegungen beim Menschen [Studies of the timing of figured movements in man]. *Pflügers Archiv für die gesamte Physiologie, 240,* 661–675.

Dewar, R. (1971). Adaptation to displaced vision: Variations in the shaping technique. *Perception & Psychophysics, 9,* 155–157.

Deutsch, D. (1983). The generation of two isochronous sequences in parallel. *Perception & Psychophysics, 34,* 331–337.

Durwen, H. F., & Herzog, A. G. (1989). Electromyographic investigation of mirror movements in normal adults: Variation of frequency with side of movements, handedness, and dominance. *Brain Dysfunction, 2,* 84–92.

Durwen, H. F., & Herzog, A. G. (1992). Electromyographic investigation of mirror movements in normal adults: Variation of frequency with site, effort, and repetition of movement. *Brain Dysfunction, 5,* 310–318.

Elliott, D., & Allard, F. (1985). The utilization of visual feedback information during rapid pointing movements. *Quarterly Journal of Experimental Psychology, 37A,* 407–425.

Elliott, D., & Lee, T. D. (1995). The role of target information on manual-aiming bias. *Psychological Research, 58,* 2–9.

Elliott, D., & Madalena, J. (1987). The influence of premovement visual information on manual aiming. *Quarterly Journal of Experimental Psychology, 39A,* 541–559.

Engström, D. A., Kelso, J. A. S., & Holroyd, T. (1996). Reaction-anticipation transitions in human perception-action patterns. *Human Movement Science, 15,* 809–832.

Favilla, M., & De Cecco, E. (1996). Parallel direction and extent specification of planar reaching arm movements in humans. *Neuropsychology, 34,* 609–613.

Favilla, M., Hening, W., & Ghez, C. (1989). Trajectory control in targeted force impulses. VI. Independent specification of response amplitude and direction. *Experimental Brain Research, 75,* 280–294.

Fisk, J. D., & Goodale, M. A. (1989). The effects of instructions to subjects on the programming of visually directed reaching movements. *Journal of Motor Behavior, 21,* 5–19.

Fitts, P. M. (1954). The information capacity of the human motor system in controlling the amplitude of movement. *Journal of Experimental Psychology, 47,* 381–391.

Flanagan, J. R., Tresilian, J., & Wing, A. M. (1993). Coupling of grip force and load force during arm movements with grasped objects. *Neuroscience Letters, 152,* 53–56.

Flanagan, J. R., & Wing, A. M. (1995). The stability of precision grip forces during cyclic arm movements with a hand-held load. *Experimental Brain Research, 105,* 455–464.

Flanders, M., Helms Tillery, S. I., & Soechting, J. F. (1992). Early stages in a sensorimotor transformation. *Behavioral and Brain Sciences, 15,* 309–362.

Flash, T., & Hogan, N. (1985). The coordination of arm movements: An experimentally confirmed mathematical model. *Journal of Neuroscience, 5,* 1688–1703.

Franz, E. A. (1997). Spatial coupling in the coordination of complex actions. *Quarterly Journal of Experimental Psychology, 50A,* 684–704.

Franz, E. A., Eliassen, J. C., Ivry, R. B., & Gazzaniga, M. S. (1996). Dissociation of spatial and temporal coupling in the bimanual movements of callosotomy patients. *Psychological Science, 7,* 306–310.

Franz, E. A., Zelaznik, H. N., & McCabe, G. (1991). Spatial topological constraints in a bimanual task. *Acta Psychologica, 77,* 137–151.

Gachoud, J. P., Mounoud, P., Hauert, C. A., & Viviani, P. (1983). Motor strategies in lifting movements: A comparison of adult and child performance. *Journal of Motor Behavior, 15,* 202–216.

Gentilucci, M., Chiefi, S., Daprati, E., Saetti, M. C., & Toni, I. (1996). Visual illusion and action. *Neuropsychologia, 34,* 369–376.

Gentner, D. R. (1987). Timing of skilled motor performance: Tests of the proportional duration model. *Psychological Review, 94,* 255–276.

Georgopoulos, A. P., Lurito, J. T., Petrides, M., Schwartz, A. B., & Massey, J. T. (1989). Mental rotation of the neuronal population vector. *Science, 243,* 234–236.

Georgopoulos, A. P., & Massey, J. T. (1987). Cognitive spatial-motor processes. 1. The making of movements at various angles from a stimulus direction. *Experimental Brain Research, 65,* 361–370.

Ghez, C., Favilla, M., Ghilardi, M. F., Gordon, J., Bermejo, R., & Pullman, S. (1997). Discrete and continuous planning of hand movements and isometric force trajectories. *Experimental Brain Research, 115,* 217–233.

Gielen, S. C. A. M., van den Heuvel, P. J. M., & van Gisbergen, J. A. M. (1984). Coordination of fast eye and arm movements in a tracking task. *Experimental Brain Research, 56,* 154–161.

Gillam, B., & Chambers, D. (1985). Size and position are incongruous: Measurements on the Müller-Lyer figure. *Perception & Psychophysics, 37,* 549–556.

Glencross, D. J. (1970). Serial organization and timing in a motor skill. *Journal of Motor Behavior, 2,* 229–237.

Goodale, M. A., & Humphrey, G. K. (1998). The objects of action and perception. *Cognition, 67,* 181–207.

Goodale, M. A., & Milner, A. D. (1992). Separate visual pathways for perception and action. *Trends in Neuroscience, 15,* 20–25.

Goodman, D., & Kelso, J. A. S. (1980). Are movements preparated in parts? Not under compatible (naturalized) conditions. *Journal of Experimental Psychology: General, 109,* 475–495.

Goodwin, G. M., McCloskey, D. I., & Matthews, P. B. C. (1972). The contribution of muscle afferents to kinaesthesia shown by vibration induced illusions of movement and by the effects of paralysing joint afferents. *Brain, 95,* 705–748.

Gordon, A. M., Forssberg, H., Johansson, R. S., & Westling, G. (1991). Visual size cues in the programming of manipulative forces during precision grip. *Experimental Brain Research, 83,* 477–482.

Gordon, J., Ghilardi, M. F., & Ghez, C. (1994). Accuracy of planar reaching movements. I. Independence of direction and extent variability. *Experimental Brain Research, 99,* 97–111.

Gottlieb, G. L., Corcos, D. M., & Agarwal, G. C. (1989). Organizing principles for single joint movements. I: A speed-insensitive strategy. *Journal of Neurophysiology, 62,* 342–357.

Grossberg, S., Pribe, C., & Cohen, M. A. (1997). Neural control of interlimb oscillations: I. Human bimanual coordination. *Biological Cybernetics, 77,* 131–140.

Guiard, Y. (1987). Asymmetric division of labor in human skilled bimanual action: The kinematic chain as a model. *Journal of Motor Behavior, 19,* 486–517.

Gundry, J. (1975). The use of location and distance in reproducing different amplitudes of movement. *Journal of Motor Behavior, 7,* 91–100.

Gunkel, M. (1962). Über relative Koordination bei willkürlichen menschlichen Gliederbewegungen [On relative coordination in voluntary human limb movements]. *Pflügers Archiv für die gesamte Physiologie, 275,* 472–477.

Haken, H. (1982). *Synergetik: Eine Einführung* [Synergetics: An introduction]. Berlin, Germany: Springer.

Haken, H., Kelso, J. A. S., & Bunz, H. (1985). A theoretical model of phase transitions in human hand movements. *Biological Cybernetics, 51,* 347–356.

Hay, J. C., & Pick, H. (1966). Visual and proprioceptive adaptation to optical displacement of the visual stimulus. *Journal of Experimental Psychology, 71,* 150–158.

Helmholtz, H. von. (1867). *Handbuch der Physiologischen Optik* [Handbook of Physiological Optics]. Leipzig, Germany: Voss.

Hening, W., Favilla, M., & Ghez, C. (1988). Trajectory control in targeted force impulses. V. Gradual specification of response amplitude. *Experimental Brain Research, 71,* 116–128.

Henry, F. M., & Rogers, D. E. (1960). Increased response latency for complicated movements and a "memory drum" theory of neuromotor reaction. *Research Quarterly, 31,* 448–458.

Hermsdörfer, J., Marquardt, C., Philipp, J., Zierdt, A., Nowak, D., Glasauer, S., & Mai, N. (2000). Moving weightless objects. Grip force control during microgravity. *Experimental Brain Research, 132,* 52–64.

Heuer, H. (1983). *Bewegungslernen* [Motor learning]. Stuttgart, Germany: Kohlhammer.

Heuer, H. (1989). Movement strategies as points on equal-outcome curves. *Behavioral and Brain Sciences, 12,* 220–221.

Heuer, H. (1990). Rapid responses with the left or right hand: Response-response compatibility effects due to intermanual interactions. In R. W. Proctor & T. G. Reeve (Eds.), *Stimulus-response compatibility: An integrated perspective* (pp. 311–342). Amsterdam: North-Holland.

Heuer, H. (1991). Invariant relative timing in motor-program theory. In J. Fagard & P. H. Wolff (Eds.), *The development of timing control and temporal organization in coordinated action: Invariant relative timing, rhythms, and coordination* (pp. 37–68). Amsterdam: North-Holland.

Heuer, H. (1993a). Estimates of time to contact based on changing size and changing target vergence. *Perception, 22,* 549–563.

Heuer, H. (1993b). Structural constraints on bimanual movements. *Psychological Research, 55,* 83–98.

Heuer, H. (1995). Models for response-response compatibility: The effects of the relation between responses in a choice task. *Acta Psychologica, 90,* 315–332.

Heuer, H. (1998). Blocking in rapid finger tapping: The role of variability in proximo-distal coordination. *Journal of Motor Behavior, 30,* 130–142.

Heuer, H., Kleinsorge, T., Spijkers, W., & Steglich, C. (2001). Static and phasic cross-talk effects in discrete bimanual reversal movements. *Journal of Motor Behavior, 33,* 67–85.

Heuer, H., & Sangals, J. (1998). Task-dependent mixtures of coordinate systems in visuomotor transformations. *Experimental Brain Research, 119,* 224–236.

Heuer, H., & Schmidt, R. A. (1988). Transfer of learning among motor patterns with different relative timing. *Journal of Experimental Psychology: Human Perception and Performance, 14,* 241–252.

Heuer, H., Schmidt, R. A., & Ghodsian, D. (1995). Generalized motor programs for rapid bimanual tasks: A two-level multiplicative-rate model. *Biological Cybernetics, 73,* 343–356.

Heuer, H., Spijkers, W., Kleinsorge, T., & Steglich, C. (2000). Parametrische Kopplung bei Folgen beidhändiger Umkehrbewegungen mit gleichen und unterschiedlichen Weiten [Parametric coupling in sequences of bimanual reversal movements with same and different amplitudes]. *Zeitschrift für experimentelle Psychologie, 47,* 34–49.

Heuer, H., Spijkers, W., Kleinsorge, T., & van der Loo, H. (1998a). Period duration of physical and imaginary movement sequences affects contralateral amplitude modulation. *Quarterly Journal of Experimental Psychology, 51A,* 755–779.

Heuer, H., Spijkers, W., Kleinsorge, T., van der Loo, H., & Steglich, C. (1998b). The time course of cross-talk during the simultaneous specification of bimanual movement amplitudes. *Experimental Brain Research, 118,* 381–392.

Hollerbach, J. M., & Atkeson, C. G. (1987). Deducing planning variables from experimental arm trajectories: Pitfalls and possibilities. *Biological Cybernetics, 56,* 279–292.

Holst, E. von (1939). Die relative Koordination als Phänomen und als Methode zentralnervöser Funktionsanalyse [Relative coordination as phenomenon and as a method for the functional analysis of the central nervous system]. *Ergebnisse der Physiologie, 42,* 228–306.

Howard, I. P. (1968). Displacing the optical array. In S. J. Freedman (Ed.), *The neuropsychology of spatially oriented behavior* (pp. 19–36). Homewood, IL: Dorsey Press.

Ibbotson, N. R., & Morton, J. (1981). Rhythm and dominance. *Cognition, 9,* 125–138.

Jagacinski, R. J., Marshburn, E., Klapp, S. T., & Jones, M. R. (1988). Tests of parallel versus integrated structure in polyrhythmic tapping. *Journal of Motor Behavior, 20,* 416–442.

James, W. (1950). *The principles of psychology*. New York: Dover. (Original work published 1890)

Jeannerod, M. (1984). The timing of natural prehension movements. *Journal of Motor Behavior, 16,* 235–254.

Johansson, R. S. (1996). Sensory and memory information in the control of dexterous manipulation. In F. Lacquaniti & P. Viviani (Eds.), *Neural bases of motor behaviour* (pp. 205–260). Dordrecht, The Netherlands: Kluwer.

Jordan, M. I. (1996). Computational aspects of motor control and motor learning. In H. Heuer & S. W. Keele (Eds.), *Handbook of perception and action: Vol. 2. Motor skills* (pp. 71–120). London: Academic Press.

Jung, R., & Fach, C. (1984). Spiegelschrift und Umkehrschrift bei Linkshändern und Rechtshändern: Ein Beitrag zum Balkentransfer und Umkehrlernen [Mirrorscript and invalid script in left-handers and righthanders: A contribution to colossal transfer and learned inversion]. In L. Spillmann & B. R. Wooten (Eds.), *Sensory experience, adaptation, and perception: Festschrift for Ivo Kohler* (pp. 377–399). Hillsdale, NJ: Erlbaum.

Kalveram, K.-T. (1991). Pattern generating and reflex-like processes controlling aiming movements in the presence of inertia, damping and gravity. *Biological Cybernetics, 64,* 413–419.

Kay, B. A., Kelso, J. A. S., Saltzman, E., & Schöner, G. (1987). Space-time behavior of single and bimanual rhythmical movements: Data and limit cycle model. *Journal of Experimental Psychology: Human Perception and Performance, 13,* 178–192.

Keele, S. W. (1968). Movement control in skilled motor performance. *Psychological Bulletin, 70,* 387–403.

Keele, S. W. (1986). Motor control. In K. R. Boff, L. Kaufman, & J. P. Thomas (Eds.), *Handbook of perception and performance: Vol. 2. Cognitive processes and performance* (pp. 30-1–30-60). New York: Wiley.

Keele, S. W., & Posner, M. I. (1968). Processing of visual feedback in rapid movements. *Journal of Experimental Psychology, 77,* 155–158.

Kelso, J. A. S. (1984). Phase transitions and critical behavior in human bimanual coordination. *American Journal of Physiology: Regulatory, Integrative, and Comparative, 246,* R1000–R1004.

Kelso, J. A. S. (1994). Elementary coordination dynamics. In S. P. Swinnen, H. Heuer, J. Massion, & P. Casaer (Eds.), *Interlimb coordination: Neural, dynamical, and cognitive constraints* (pp. 301–318). San Diego, CA: Academic Press.

Kelso, J. A. S., Cook, E., Olson, M. E., & Epstein, W. (1975). Allocation of attention and the locus of adaptation to displaced vision. *Journal of Experimental Psychology: Human Perception and Performance, 1,* 237–245.

Kelso, J. A. S., & Holt, K. G. (1980). Exploring a vibratory system analysis of human movement production. *Journal of Neurophysiology, 43,* 1183–1196.

Kelso, J. A. S., Southard, D. L., & Goodman, D. (1979). On the coordination of two-handed movements. *Journal of Experimental Psychology: Human Perception and Performance, 5,* 229–238.

Kelso, J. A. S., Tuller, B., & Harris, K. S. (1983). A "dynamic pattern" perspective on the control and coordination of movement. In P. F. MacNeilage (Ed.), *The production of speech* (pp. 137–173). Berlin, Germany: Springer.

Kelso, J. A. S., Tuller, B., Vatikiotis-Bateson, E., & Fowler, C. A. (1984). Functionally specific articulatory cooperation following jaw perturbation during speech: Evidence for coordinative structures. *Journal of Experimental Psychology: Human Perception and Performance, 10,* 812–832.

Klapp, S. T. (1979). Doing two things at once: The role of temporal compatibility. *Memory and Cognition, 7,* 375–381.

Klapp, S. T. (1981). Temporal compatibility in dual motor tasks II: simultaneous articulation and hand movements. *Memory and Cognition, 9,* 398–401.

Klapp, S. T., Hill, M., Tyler, J., Martin, Z., Jagacinski, R., & Jones, M. (1985). On marching to two different drummers: Perceptual aspects of the difficulties. *Journal of Experimental Psychology: Human Perception and Performance, 11,* 814–828.

Klemm, O. (1938). Zwölf Leitsätze zu einer Psychologie der Leibesübungen [Twelve guiding principles for a psychology of gymnastics]. *Neue Psychologische Studien, 9,* 351–382.

Koh, K., & Meyer, D. E. (1991). Function learning: Induction of continuous stimulus-response relations. *Journal of Experimental Psychology: Learning, Memory and Cognition, 17,* 811–836.

Kohler, I. (1964). The formation and transformation of the perceptual world. *Psychological Issues, 3,* 1–173.

Kornhuber, H. H., & Deecke, L. (1965). Hirnpotentialänderungen bei Willkürbewegungen und passiven Bewegungen des Menschen: Bereitschaftspotential und reafferente Potentiale [Changes of brain potentials in voluntary and passive movements of man: Bereitschaftspotential and reafferente potentiale]. *Pflügers Archiv für die gesamte Physiologie, 284,* 1–17.

Krakauer, J. W., Ghilardi, M. F., & Ghez, C. (1999). Independent learning of internal models for kinematic and dynamic control of reaching. *Nature Neuroscience, 2,* 1026–1031.

Krampe, R. T., Kliegl, R., Mayr, U., Engbert, R., & Vorberg, D. (2000). The fast and the slow of skilled bimanual rhythm production: Parallel versus integrated timing. *Journal of Experimental Psychology: Human Perception and Performance, 26,* 206–233.

Kravitz, J. H. (1972). Conditioned adaptation to prismatic displacement. *Perception & Psychophysics, 11,* 38–42.

Laabs, G. J. (1974). The effect of interpolated motor activity on the short-term retention of movement distance and end-location. *Journal of Motor Behavior, 6,* 279–288.

Lajoie, Y., Paillard, J., Teasdale, N., Bard, C., Fleury, M., Forget, R., & Lamarre, Y. (1992). Mirror drawing in a deafferented patient and normal subjects: Visuoproprioceptive conflict. *Neurology, 42,* 1104–1106.

Lashley, K. S. (1917). The accuracy of movement in the absence of excitation from the moving organ. *American Journal of Physiology, 43,* 169–194.

Lashley, K. S. (1951). The problem of serial order in behavior. In L. A. Jeffress (Ed.), *Cerebral mechanism in behavior* (pp. 112–131). New York: Wiley.

Latash, M. L., & Jaric, S. (in press). The organization of drinking: Postural characteristics of the arm-head coordination. *Journal of Motor Behavior.*

Lee, D. N. (1976). A theory of visual control of braking based on information about time-to-collision. *Perception, 5,* 437–459.

Lee, T. D., Blandin, Y., & Proteau, L. (1996). Effects of task instructions and oscillation frequency on bimanual coordination. *Psychological Research, 59,* 100–106.

Legge, D. (1965). Analysis of visual and proprioceptive components of motor skill by means of a drug. *British Journal of Psychology, 56,* 243–254.

Lépine, D., Glencross, D., & Requin, J. (1989). Some experimental evidence for and against a parametric conception of movement programming. *Journal of Experimental Psychology: Human Perception and Performance, 15,* 347–362.

Lippold, O. C. J. (1952). The relation between integrated action potentials in a human muscle and its isometric tension. *Journal of Physiology, 117,* 492–499.

Lippold, O. C. J., Redfearn, J. W. T., & Vučo, j. (1960). The electromyography of fatigue. *Ergonomics, 3,* 121–131.

Mack, A., Heuer, F., Villardi, K., & Chambers, D. (1985). The dissociation of position and extent in Müller-Lyer figures. *Perception & Psychophysics, 37,* 335–344.

MacKenzie, C. L., Marteniuk, R. G., Dugas, C., Liske, D., & Eickmeier, B. (1987). Three-dimensional movement trajectories in Fitts' task: Implications for control. *Quarterly Journal of Experimental Psychology, 39A,* 629–647.

Marteniuk, R. G., & MacKenzie, C. L. (1980). A preliminary theory of two-hand co-ordinated control. In G. E. Stelmach & J. Requin

(Eds.), *Tutorials in motor behavior* (pp. 185–197). Amsterdam: North-Holland.

Marteniuk, R. G., MacKenzie, C. L., & Baba, D. M. (1984). Bimanual movement control: Information processing and interaction effects. *Quarterly Journal of Experimental Psychology, 36A,* 335–365.

Marteniuk, R. G., MacKenzie, C. L., Jeannerod, M., Athènes, S., & Dugas, C. (1987). Constraints on human arm movement trajectories. *Canadian Journal of Psychology, 41,* 365–378.

Massion, J. (1992). Movement, posture, and equilibrium: Interactions and coordination. *Progress in Neurobiology, 38,* 35–56.

McDowell, M. J., & Wolff, P. H. (1997). A functional analysis of human mirror movements. *Journal of Motor Behavior, 29,* 85–96.

McGonigle, B. O., & Flook, J. (1978). Long-term retention of single and multistate prismatic adaptation by human. *Nature, 272,* 364–366.

McIntyre, J., Stratta, F., & Lacquaniti, F. (1998). Short-term memory for reaching to visual targets: Psychophysical evidence for body-centered reference frames. *Journal of Neuroscience, 18,* 8423–8435.

McLeod, P., McLaughlin, C., & Nimmo-Smith, I. (1985). Information encapsulation and automaticity: Evidence from the visual control of finely timed actions. In M. I. Posner & O. S. M. Marin (Eds.), *Attention and performance XI* (pp. 391–406). Hillsdale, NJ: Erlbaum.

Merz, F., Kalveram, K.-T., & Huber, K. (1981). Der Einfluß kognitiver Faktoren auf Steuerleistungen [The role of cognitive factors in manual tracking]. In L. Tent (Ed.), *Erkennen–Wollen–Handeln* (pp. 327–335). Göttingen, Germany: Hogrefe.

Metz, A. M. (1970). Änderungen der myoelektrischen Aktivität während eines sensomotorischen Lernprozesses [Changes of myoelectric activity during motor learning]. *Zeitschrift für Psychologie, 178,* 51–88.

Meyer, D. E., Abrams, R. A., Kornblum, S., Wright, C. E., & Smith, J. E. K. (1988). Optimality in human motor performance: Ideal control of rapid aimed movements. *Psychological Review, 95,* 340–370.

Meyer, D. E., Smith, J. E. K., & Wright, C. E. (1982). Models for the speed and accuracy of aimed movements. *Psychological Review, 89,* 449–482.

Monsell, S. (1986). Programming of complex sequences: Evidence from the timing of rapid speech and other productions. In H. Heuer & C. Fromm (Eds.), *Generation and modulation of action patterns* (pp. 72–86). Berlin, Germany: Springer.

Müller, H. (2001). *Ausführungsvariabilität und Ergebniskonstanz* [Variability of execution and constancy of outcomes]. Lengerich: Pabst Science Publishers.

Müller, H., & Loosch, E. (1999). Functional variability and an equifinal path of movement during targeted throwing. *Journal of Human Movement Studies, 36,* 103–126.

Näätänen, R., & Merisalo, A. (1977). Expectancy and preparation in simple reaction time. In S. Dornic (Ed.), *Attention and performance VI* (pp. 115–138) Hillsdale, NJ: Erlbaum.

Nelson, W. L. (1983). Physical principles for economies of skilled movements. *Biological Cybernetics, 46,* 135–147.

Newell, K. M., & van Emmerik, R. E. A. (1989). The acquisition of coordination: Preliminary analysis of learning to write. *Human Movement Science, 8,* 17–32.

Nielsen, T. I. (1963). Volition: A new experimental approach. *Scandinavian Journal of Psychology, 4,* 225–230.

Noble, M., Fitts, P. M., & Warren, C. E. (1955). The frequency response of skilled subjects in a pursuit tracking task. *Journal of Experimental Psychology, 49,* 249–256.

Nougier, V., Bard, C., Fleury, M., Teasdale, N., Cole, J., Forget, R., Paillard, J., & Lamarre, Y. (1996). Control of single-joint movements in deafferented patients: Evidence for amplitude coding rather than position control. *Experimental Brain Research, 109,* 473–482.

Paillard, J. (1982). The contribution of peripheral and central vision to visually guided reaching. In D. J. Ingle, M. A. Goodale, & R. J. W. Mansfield (Eds.), *Analysis of visual behavior* (pp. 367–385). Cambridge, MA: MIT Press.

Peper, C. E. (1995). *Tapping dynamics*. Unpublished doctoral dissertation, Free University Amsterdam.

Peper, C. E., & Beek, P. J. (1998). Are frequency-induced transitions in rhythmic coordination mediated by a drop in amplitude? *Biological Cybernetics, 79,* 291–300.

Peper, L., Bootsma, R. J., Mestre, D. R., & Bakker, F. C. (1994). Catching balls: How to get the hand to the right place at the right time. *Journal of Experimental Psychology: Human Perception and Performance, 20,* 591–612.

Perenin, M. T., & Jeannerod, M. (1978). Visual function within the hemianopic field following early cerebral hemidecortication in man: I. Spatial localization. *Neuropsychologia, 16,* 1–13.

Peters, M. (1981). Attentional asymmetries during concurrent bimanual performance. *Quarterly Journal of Experimental Psychology, 33A,* 95–103.

Pew, R.W. (1966). Acquisition of hierarchical control over the temporal organization of skill. *Journal of Experimental Psychology, 71,* 764–771.

Plamondon, R., & Alimi, A. M. (1997). Speed/accuracy trade-offs in target-directed movements. *Behavioral and Brain Sciences, 20,* 279–349.

Polit, A., & Bizzi, E. (1979). Characteristics of motor programs underlying arm movements in monkeys. *Journal of Neurophysiology, 42,* 183–194.

Poulton, E. C. (1957). On the stimulus and response in pursuit tracking. *Journal of Experimental Psychology, 53,* 189–194.

Preilowski, B. (1972). Possible contribution of the anterior forebrain commissures to bilateral motor coordination. *Neuropsychologia, 10,* 267–277.

Prinz, W. (1992). Why don't we perceive our brain states? *European Journal of Cognitive Psychology, 4,* 1–20.

Rack, P. M. H., & Westbury, D. R. (1969). The effects of length and stimulus rate on tension in the isometric cat soleus muscle. *Journal of Physiology, 204,* 443–460.

Rinkenauer, G., Ulrich, R., & Wing, A. (2001). Brief bimanual force phases: Correlations between the hands in force and time. *Journal of Experimental Psychology: General, Human Perception and Performance, 27,* 1485–1497.

Rosenbaum, D. A. (1980). Human movement initiation: Specification of arm, direction, and extent. *Journal of Experimental Psychology: General, 109,* 444–474.

Rosenbaum, D. A. (1983). The movement precuing technique: Assumptions, applications, and extensions. In R. A. Magill (Ed.), *Memory and control of action* (pp. 231–274). Amsterdam: North-Holland.

Rosenbaum, D. A., & Jorgensen, M. J. (1992). Planning macroscopic aspects of manual control. *Human Movement Science, 11,* 61–69.

Rosenbaum, D. A., & Krist, H. (1996). Antecedents of action. In H. Heuer & S. W. Keele (Eds.), *Handbook of perception and action: Vol. 2. Motor skills* (pp. 3–69). London: Academic Press.

Rosenbaum, D. A., Loukopoulos, L. D., Meulenbroek, R. G. J., Vaughan, J., & Engelbrecht, S. E. (1995). Planning reaches by evaluating stored postures. *Psychological Review, 102,* 28–67.

Rosenbaum, D. A., Slotta, J. D., Vaughan, J., & Plamondon, R. (1991). Optimal movement selection. *Psychological Science, 2,* 86–91.

Rosenbaum, D. A., Vaughan, J., Barnes, H. J., & Jorgensen, M. J. (1992). Time course of movement planning: Selection of handgrips for object manipulation. *Journal of Experimental Psychology: Learning, Memory, and Cognition, 18,* 1058–1073.

Roth, K. (1988). Investigations on the basis of the generalized motor programme hypothesis. In O. G. Meijer & K. Roth (Eds.), *Complex movement behaviour: "The" motor-action controversy* (pp. 261–288). Amsterdam: North-Holland.

Ruitenbeek, J. C. (1984). Invariants in loaded goal directed movements. *Biological Cybernetics, 51,* 11–20.

Saltzman, E., & Kelso, J. A. S. (1987). Skilled actions: A task-dynamic approach. *Psychological Review, 94,* 84–106.

Sangals, J. (1997). *Der Einfluß der Bewegungsrückmeldung auf das Erlernen nichtlinearer Werkzeugtransformationen* [The effect of movement feedback on the learning of nonlinear transformations]. Unpublished doctoral dissertation, Philipps-Universitat, Marburg, Marburg, Germany.

Sangals, J., Heuer, H., Manzey, D., & Lorenz, B. (1999). Changed visuomotor transformations during and after prolonged microgravity. *Experimental Brain Research, 129,* 378–390.

Savelsbergh, G. J. P., Whiting, H. T. A., & Bootsma, R. J. (1991). Grasping tau. *Journal of Experimental Psychology: Human Perception and Performance, 17,* 315–322.

Schiff, W., & Detwiler, M. L. (1979). Information used in judging impending collision. *Perception, 8,* 647–658.

Schmidt, R. A. (1972). The Index of Preprogramming (IP): A statistical method for evaluating the role of feedback in simple movements. *Psychonomic Science, 27,* 83–85.

Schmidt, R. A. (1975). A schema theory of discrete motor skill learning. *Psychological Review, 82,* 225–260.

Schmidt, R. A. (1980). On the theoretical status of time in motor-program representations. In G. E. Stelmach & J. Requin (Eds.), *Tutorials in motor behavior* (pp. 145–165). Amsterdam: North-Holland.

Schmidt, R. A. (1985). The search for invariance in skilled movement behavior. *Research Quarterly for Exercise and Sport, 56,* 188–200.

Schmidt, R. A. (1989). Unintended acceleration: A review of human factors contributions. *Human Factors, 31,* 345–364.

Schmidt, R. A., & McGown, C. (1980). Terminal accuracy of unexpectedly loaded rapid movements: Evidence for a mass-spring mechanism in programming. *Journal of Motor Behavior, 12,* 149–161.

Schmidt, R. A., & Russell, D. G. (1972). Movement velocity and movement time as determinants of degree of preprogramming in simple movements. *Journal of Experimental Psychology, 96,* 315–320.

Schmidt, R. A., Sherwood, D. E., Zelaznik, H. N., & Leikind, B. J. (1985). Speed-accuracy tradeoffs in motor behavior: Theories of impulse variability. In H. Heuer, U. Kleinbeck, & K.-H. Schmidt (Eds.), *Motor behavior: Programming, control, and acquisition* (pp. 79–123). Berlin, Germany: Springer.

Schmidt, R. A., Zelaznik, H. N., Hawkins, B., Frank, J. S., & Quinn, J. T. (1979). Motor-output variability: A theory for the accuracy of rapid motor acts. *Psychological Review, 86,* 415–451.

Schöner, G. (1994). From interlimb coordination to trajectory formation: Common dynamical principles. In S. P. Swinnen, H. Heuer, J. Massion, & P. Casaer (Eds.), *Interlimb coordination. Neural, dynamical, and cognitive constraints* (pp. 339–368). San Diego, CA: Academic Press.

Schöner, G., & Kelso, J. A. S. (1988). A synergetic theory of environmentally-specified and learned patterns of movement coordination. I: Relative phase dynamics. *Biological Cybernetics, 58,* 71–80.

Schott, G. D., & Wyke, M. A. (1981). Congenital mirror movements. *Journal of Neurology, Neurosurgery, & Psychiatry, 44,* 586–599.

Schouten, J. F., & Becker, J. A. M. (1967). Reaction time and accuracy. *Acta Psychologica, 27,* 143–153.

Serrien, D. J., Bogaerts, H., Suy, E., & Swinnen, S.P. (1999). The identification of coordination constraints across planes of motion. *Experimental Brain Research, 128,* 250–255.

Shadmehr, R., & Brashers-Krug, T. (1997). Functional stages in the formation of human long-term motor memory. *Journal of Neuroscience, 17,* 409–419.

Shadmehr, R., & Moussavi, Z. M. K. (2000). Spatial generalization from learning dynamics of reaching movements. *Journal of Neuroscience, 20,* 7807–7815.

Shadmehr, R., & Mussa-Ivaldi, F. A. (1994). Adaptive representation of dynamics during learning of a motor task. *Journal of Neuroscience, 14,* 3208–3224.

Sherwood, D. E. (1991). Distance and location assimilation in rapid bimanual movement. *Research Quarterly for Exercise and Sport, 62,* 302–308.

Smeets, J. B. J., & Brenner, E. (1995). Perception and action are based on the same visual information: Distinction between position and velocity. *Journal of Experimental Psychology: Human Perception and Performance, 21,* 19–31.

Smeets, J. B. J., Erkelens, C. J., & Denier van der Gon, J. J. (1995). Perturbations of fast goal-directed arm movements: Different behavior of early and late EMG responses. *Journal of Motor Behavior, 27,* 77–88.

Spijkers, W. (1993). *Sehen und Handeln: Die Rolle visueller Information bei zielgerichteten Bewegungen* [Perception and action: The role of visual information in aimed movements]. Aachen, Germany: Shaker.

Spijkers, W., & Heuer, H. (1995). Structural constraints on the performance of symmetrical bimanual movements with different amplitudes. *Quarterly Journal of Experimental Psychology, 48A,* 716–740.

Spijkers, W., Heuer, H., Kleinsorge, T., & Steglich, C. (2000). The specification of movement amplitudes for the left and right hand: Evidence for transient parametric coupling from overlapping-task performance. *Journal of Experimental Psychology: Human Perception and Performance, 26,* 1091–1105.

Spijkers, W., Heuer, H., Kleinsorge, T., & van der Loo, H. (1997). Preparation of bimanual movements with same and different amplitudes: Specification interference as revealed by reaction time. *Acta Psychologica, 96,* 207–227.

Spijkers, W., Tachmatzidis, K., Debus, G., Fischer, M., & Kausche, I. (1994). Temporal coordination of alternative and simultaneous aiming movements of constrained timing structure. *Psychological Research, 57,* 20–29.

Steglich, C., Heuer, H., Spijkers, W., & Kleinsorge, T. (1999). Bimanual coupling during the specification of isometric forces. *Experimental Brain Research, 129,* 302–316.

Stelmach, G. E. (1982). Motor control and motor learning: The closed-loop perspective. In J. A. S. Kelso (Ed.), *Human motor behavior: An introduction* (pp. 93–115). Hillsdale, NJ: Erlbaum.

Stelmach, G. E., Kelso, J. A. S., & Wallace, S. A. (1975). Preselection in short-term motor memory. *Journal of Experimental Psychology: Human Learning and Memory, 1,* 745–755.

Stimpel, E. (1933). Der Wurf [The throw]. *Neue Psychologische Studien, 9,* 105–138.

Stratton, G. M. (1896). Some preliminary experiments in vision without inversion of the retinal image. *Psychological Review, 3,* 611–617.

Stratton, G. M. (1897a). Upright vision and the retinal image. *Psychological Review, 4,* 182–187.

Stratton, G. M. (1897b). Vision without inversion of the retinal image. *Psychological Review, 4,* 341–360, 463–481.

Stucchi, N., & Viviani, P. (1993). Cerebral dominance and asynchrony between bimanual two-dimensional movements. *Journal of Experimental Psychology: Human Perception and Performance, 19,* 1200–1220.

Summers, J. J., Rosenbaum, D. A., Burns, B. D., & Ford, S. K. (1993). Production of polyrhythms. *Journal of Experimental Psychology: Human Perception and Performance, 19,* 416–428.

Swinnen, S. P., Jardin, K., & Meulenbroek, R. (1996). Between-limb asynchronies during bimanual coordination: Effects of manual dominance and attentional cueing. *Neuropsychologica, 34,* 1203–1213.

Taub, E., Goldberg, I. A., & Taub, P. (1975). Deafferentation in monkeys: Pointing at a target without visual feedback. *Experimental Neurology, 46,* 178–186.

Teasdale, N., Forget, R., Bard, C., Paillard, J., Fleury, M., & Lamarre, Y. (1993). The role of proprioceptive information for the production of isometric forces and for handwriting tasks. *Acta Psychologica, 82,* 179–191.

Tendick, F., Jennings, R. W., Tharp, G., & Stark, L. (1993). Sensing and manipulation problems in endoscopic surgery: experiment, analysis, and observation. *Presence, 2,* 66–81.

Teulings, H.-L. (1996). Handwriting movement control. In H. Heuer & S. W. Keele (Eds.), *Handbook of perception and action: Vol. 2. Motor skills* (pp. 561–613). London: Academic Press.

Todor, J. I., & Lazarus, J. C. (1986). Exertion level and the intensity of associated movements. *Developmental Medicine & Child Neurology, 28,* 205–212.

Tresilian, J. R. (1999). Analysis of recent empirical challenges to an account of interceptive timing. *Perception & Psychophysics, 61,* 515–528.

Tuller, B., & Kelso, J. A. S. (1989). Environmentally-specified patterns of movement coordination in normal and split-brain subjects. *Experimental Brain Research, 75,* 306–316.

Tyldesley, D. A., & Whiting, H. T. A. (1975). Operational timing. *Journal of Human Movement Studies, 1,* 172–177.

Ungerleider, L. G., & Mishkin, M. (1982). Two cortical visual systems. In D. J. Ingle, M. A. Goodale, & R. J. W. Mansfield (Eds.), *Analysis of visual behavior* (pp. 549–586). Cambridge, MA: MIT Press.

Uno, Y., Kawato, M., & Suzuki, R. (1989). Formation and control of optimal trajectory in human multijoint arm movement: Minimum torque-change model. *Biological Cybernetics, 61,* 89–101.

Vindras, P., & Viviani, P. (1998). Frames of reference and control parameters in visuo manual pointint. *Journal of Experimental Psychology: Human Perception and Performance, 24,* 569–591.

Virjii-Babul, N., Cooke, J. D., & Brown, S. H. (1994). Effects of gravitational forces on single joint arm movements in humans. *Experimental Brain Research, 99,* 338–346.

Viviani, P., & Flash, T. (1995). Minimum-jerk, two-thirds power law, and isochrony: Converging approaches to movement planning. *Journal of Experimental Psychology: Human Perception and Performance, 21,* 32–53.

Viviani, P., Perani, D., Grassi, F., Bettinardi, V., & Fazio, F. (1998). Hemispheric asymmetries and bimanual asynchrony in left- and right-handers. *Experimental Brain Research, 120,* 531–536.

Voigt, E. (1933). Über den Aufbau von Bewegungsgestalten [On the composition of movement Gestalts]. *Neue Psychologische Studien, 9,* 1–32.

Vorberg, D., & Wing, A. M. (1996). Modeling variability and dependence in timing. In H. Heuer & S. W. Keele (Eds.), *Handbook of perception and action: Vol. 2. Motor skills* (pp. 181–262). London: Academic Press.

Wadman, W. J., Denier van der Gon, J. J., Geuze, R. H., & Mol, C. R. (1979). Control of fast goal-directed arm movements. *Journal of Human Movement Studies, 5,* 3–17.

Welch, R. B. (1971). Discriminative conditioning of prism adaptation. *Perception & Psychophysics, 10,* 90–92.

Welch, R. B. (1972). The effect of experienced limb identity upon adaptation to simulated displacement of the visual field. *Perception & Psychophysics, 12,* 453–456.

Welch, R. B. (1978). *Perceptual modification. Adapting to altered sensory environments.* New York: Academic Press.

Welch, R. B., Bridgeman, B., Anand, S., & Browman, K. E. (1993). Alternating prism exposure causes dual adaptation and generalization to a novel displacement. *Perception & Psychophysics, 54,* 195–204.

Whiting, H. T. A., & Cockerill, I. M. (1974). Eyes on hand—eyes on target? *Journal of Motor Behavior, 6,* 27–32.

Winter, D. A., & Robertson, D. G. E. (1978). Joint torque and energy patterns in normal gait. *Biological Cybernetics, 29,* 137–142.

Woodworth, R. S. (1899). The accuracy of voluntary movement. *Psychological Review, 3* (Monograph Suppl. 3).

Wright, C. E., & Meyer, D. E. (1983). Conditions for a linear speed-accuracy trade-off in aimed movements. *Quarterly Journal of Experimental Psychology, 35A,* 279–296.

Wulf, G., Höß, M., & Prinz, W. (1998). Instructions for motor learning: differential effects of internal vs. external focus of attention. *Journal of Motor Behavior, 30,* 169–179.

Wulf, G., & Prinz, W. (2001). Directing attention to movement effects enhances learning: A review. *Psychonomic Bulletin and Review, 8,* 648–660.

Yamanishi, J., Kawato, M., & Suzuki, R. (1980). Two coupled oscillators as a model of the coordinated finger tapping by both hands. *Biological Cybernetics, 37,* 219–225.

Young, L. R. (1969). On adaptive manual control. *Ergonomics, 12,* 635–675.

Zattara, M., & Bouisset, S. (1986). Chronometric analysis of the posturo-kinetic programming of voluntary movement. *Journal of Motor Behavior, 18,* 215–223.

Zelaznik, H. N., Hawkins, B., & Kisselburgh, L. (1983). Rapid visual feedback processing in single-aiming movements. *Journal of Motor Behavior, 15,* 217–236.

Zelaznik, H. N., Mone, S., McCabe, G. P., & Thaman, C. (1988). Role of temporal and spatial precision in determining the nature of the speed-accuracy trade-off in aimed hand movements. *Journal of Experimental Psychology: Human Perception and Performance, 14,* 221–230.

Zelaznik, H. N., Shapiro, D. C., & Carter, M. C. (1982). The specification of digit and duration during motor programming: A new method of precueing. *Journal of Motor Behavior, 14,* 57–68.

PART FIVE

ELEMENTARY LEARNING AND MEMORY PROCESSES

CHAPTER 13

Conditioning and Learning

RALPH R. MILLER AND RANDOLPH C. GRACE

Earth's many microenvironments change over time, often creating conditions less hospitable to current life-forms than conditions that existed prior to the change. Initially, life-forms adjusted to these changes through the mechanisms now collectively called *evolution.* Importantly, evolution improves a life-form's functionality (i.e., so-called biological fitness as measured in terms of reproductive success) in the environment across generations. It does nothing directly to enhance an organism's fit to the environment within the organism's life span. However, animals did evolve a mechanism to improve their fit to the environment within each animal's life span. Specifically, animals have evolved the potential to change their behavior as a function of experienced relationships among events, with *events* here referring to both events under the control of the animal (i.e., responses) and events not under the direct control of the animal (i.e., stimuli). Changing one's behavior as a function of prior experience is what we mean by *conditioning* and *learning* (used here synonymously). The observed behavioral changes frequently are seemingly preparatory for an impending, often biologically significant event that is contingent upon immediately preceding stimuli, and sometimes the behavioral changes serve to modify the impending event in an adaptive way.

In principle, there are many possible sets of rules by which an organism might modify its behavior to increase its biological fitness (preparing for and modifying impending events) as a result of prior exposure to specific event contingencies. However, organisms use only a few of these sets of rules; these constitute what we call *biological intelligence.* Here we summarize, at the psychological level, the basic principles of elementary biological intelligence: conditioning and elementary learning. At the level of the basic learning described here, research has identified a set of rules (laws) that appear to apply quite broadly across many species, including humans. Moreover, within subjects these laws appear to apply, with only adjustments of parameters being required, across motivational systems and tasks (e.g., Domjan, 1983;

Support for the preparation of this manuscript was provided by NIMH Grant 33881. We thank Francisco Arcediano, Raymond Chang, Martha Escobar, and Steven Stout for their comments on an earlier version of the manuscript. Communication concerning this chapter should be addressed to Ralph R. Miller, Department of Psychology, SUNY-Binghamton, Binghamton, NY 13902-6000, USA; rmiller@binghamton.edu.

Logue, 1979). Obviously, as we look at more complex behavior, species and task differences have greater influence, which seemingly reflects the differing parameters previously mentioned interacting with one another. For example, humans as well as dogs readily exhibit conditioned salivation or conditioned fear, whereas social interactions are far more difficult to describe through a general set of laws.

Learning is the intervening process that mediates between an environmental experience and a change in the behavior of the organism. More precisely, learning is ordinarily defined as a relatively permanent change in a subject's response potential, resulting from experience, that is specific to the presence of stimuli similar to those from that experience, and cannot be attributed entirely to changes in receptors or effectors. Notably, the term *response potential* allows for learning that is not necessarily immediately expressed in behavior (i.e., latent learning), and the requirement that a stimulus from the experience be present speaks to learning being stimulus specific as opposed to a global change in behavior. Presumably, more complex changes in behavior are built from a constellation of such elementary learned relationships (hereafter called *associations*). See chapters in this volume by Capaldi; Nairne; McNamara and Holbrook; Roediger and Marsh; and Johnson for various descriptions of how complex cognition might arise from basic learning, just as a house can be built from bricks.

Interest in the analysis of basic learning began a century ago with its roots in several different controversies. Among these was the schism between *empiricism,* represented by the British empiricist philosophers, Hume and J. S. Mill, and *rationalism,* represented by Descartes and Kant. The empiricists assumed that knowledge about the world was acquired through interaction with events in the world, whereas rationalists argued that knowledge was inborn (at least in humans) and experience merely helped us organize and express that knowledge. Studies of learning were performed in part to determine the degree to which beliefs about the world could be modified by experience. Surely demonstrations of behavioral plasticity as a function of experience were overtly more compatible with the empiricist view, but the rationalist position never denied that experience influenced knowledge and the behavior. It simply held that knowledge arose within the organism, rather than directly from the experiencing of events. Today, this controversy (reflected in more modern terms as the nature vs. nurture debate) has faded due to the realization that experience provides the content of knowledge about the world, but extracting relationships between events from experience requires a nervous system that is predisposed to extract these relationships. Predispositions to identify relationships between events, although strongly modulated during development by experience, are surely influenced by genetic composition. Hence, acquired knowledge, as revealed through a change in behavior, undoubtedly reflects an interaction of genes (rationalism-nature) and experience (empiricism-nurture).

The second controversy that motivated studies of learning was a desire to understand whether acquired thought and behavior could better be characterized by *mechanism,* which left the organism as a vessel in which simple laws of learning operated, or by *mentalism,* which often attributed to the organism some sort of conscious control of its thought and behavior. The experimental study of learning that began in the early twentieth century was partly in reaction to the mentalism implicit in the introspective approach to psychology that prevailed at that time (Watson, 1913). Mechanism was widely accepted as providing a compelling account of simple reflexes. The question was whether it also sufficed to account for behaviors that were more complex and seemingly volitional. Mechanism has been attacked for ignoring the (arguably obvious) active role of the organism in determining its behavior, whereas mentalism has been attacked for passing the problem of explaining behavior to a so-called homunculus. Mentalism starts out with a strong advantage in this dispute because human society, culture, and religion are all predicated on people's being free agents who are able to determine and control their behavior. In contrast, most theoretical accounts of learning (see Tolman, e.g., 1932, as an exception) are mechanistic and try to account for acquired behavior uniquely in terms of (a) past experience, which is encoded in neural representations; (b) present stimulation; and (c) genetic predispositions (today at least), notably excluding any role for free will. To some degree, the mechanism-mentalism controversy has been confounded with levels of analysis, with mechanistic accounts of learning tending to be more molecular. Obviously, different levels of analysis may be complementary rather than contradictory.

The third controversy that stimulated interest in learning was the relationship of humans to other species. Human culture and religion has traditionally treated humans as superior to animals on many dimensions. At the end of the nineteenth century, however, acceptance of Darwin's theory of evolution by natural selection challenged the uniqueness of humans. Defenders of tradition looked at learning capacity as a demonstration of the superiority of humans over animals, whereas Darwinians looked to basic learning to demonstrate continuity across species. A century of research has taught us that, although species do differ appreciably in behavioral plasticity, with parametric adjustment a common set of laws of learning appears to apply across at least all warm-blooded animals (Domjan, 1983). Moreover, these parametric adjustments do not always reflect a greater learning capacity in humans than in other species. As a result of evolution in concert with species-specific experience during maturation, each species is adept at dealing with the tasks that the environment commonly presents to that particular species in its ecological niche. For example, Clark's nutcrackers (birds that cache food) are able to remember where they have stored thousands of edible items (Kamil & Clements, 1990), a performance that humans would be hard-pressed to match.

The fourth factor that stimulated an interest in the study of basic learning was a practical one. Researchers such as Thorndike (1949) and Guthrie (1938) were particularly concerned with identifying principles that might be applied in our schools and toward other needs of our society. Surely this goal has been fulfilled at least in part, as can be seen for example in contemporary use of effective procedures for behavior modification.

Obviously, the human-versus-animal question (third factor listed) required that nonhuman animals be studied, but the other questions in principle did not. However, animal subjects were widely favored for two reasons. First, the behavior of nonhuman subjects was assumed by some researchers to be governed by the same basic laws that apply to human behavior, but in a simpler form which made them more readily observable. Although many researchers today accept the assumption of evolutionary continuity, research has demonstrated that the behavior of nonhumans is sometimes far from simple. The second reason for studying learning in animals has fared better. When seeking general laws of learning that obtain across individuals, individual differences can be an undesirable source of noise in one's data. Animals permit better control of irrelevant differences in genes and prior experience, thereby reducing individual differences, than is ethically or practically possible with humans.

The study of learning in animals within simple Pavlovian situations (stimulus-stimulus learning) had many parallels with the study of simple associative learning in humans that was prevalent from the 1880s to the 1960s. The so-called cognitive revolution that began in the 1960s largely ended such research with humans and caused the study of basic learning in animals to be viewed by some as irrelevant to our understanding of human learning. The cognitive revolution was driven largely by (a) a shift from trying to illuminate behavior with the assistance of hypothetical mental processes, to trying to understand mental processes through the study of behavior, and (b) the view that the simple tasks that were being studied until that time told us little about learning and memory in the real world (i.e., lacked ecological validity). However, many of today's cognitive psychologists often return to the constructs that were initially developed before the advent of the field now called cognitive psychology (e.g., McClelland, 1988). Of course, issues of ecological validity are not to be dismissed lightly. The real question is whether complex behavior in natural situations can better be understood by reducing the behavior into components that obey the laws of basic learning, or whether a more molar approach will be more successful. Science would probably best be served by our pursuing both approaches. Clearly, the approach of this chapter is reductionist. Representative of the potential successes that might be achieved through application of the laws of basic learning, originally identified in the confines of the sterile laboratory, are a number of quasi-naturalistic studies of seemingly functional behaviors. Some examples are provided by Domjan's studies of how Pavlovian conditioning improves the reproductive success of Japanese quail (reviewed in Domjan & Hollis, 1988), Kamil's studies of how the laws of learning facilitate the feeding systems of different species of birds (reviewed in Kamil, 1983), and Timberlake's studies of how different components of rats' behavior, each governed by general laws of learning, are organized to yield functional feeding behavior in quasi-naturalistic settings (reviewed in Timberlake & Lucas, 1989).

Although this chapter focuses on the content of learning and the conditions that favor its occurrence and expression rather than the function of learning, it is important to emphasize that the capacity for learning evolved because it enhances an animal's biological fitness (reviewed in Shettleworth, 1998). *The vast majority of instances of learning are clearly functional.* However, there are many documented cases in which specific instances of learned behavior are detrimental to the well-being of an organism (e.g., Breland & Breland, 1961; Gwinn, 1949). Typically, these instances arise in situations with contingencies contrary to those prevailing in the animal's natural habitat or inconsistent with its past experience (see this chapter's section entitled "Predispositions: Genetic and Experiential"). An increased understanding of when learning will result in dysfunctional behavior is currently contributing to contemporary efforts to design improved forms of behavior therapy.

This chapter selectively reviews research on both Pavlovian (i.e., stimulus-stimulus) and instrumental (response-stimulus) learning. In many respects, an organism's response may be functionally similar to a discrete stimulus, as demonstrated by the fact that most phenomena identified in Pavlovian conditioning have instrumental counterparts. However, one important difference is that Pavlovian research has generally studied qualitative relationships (e.g., whether the frequency or magnitude of an acquired response increases or decreases with a specific treatment). In contrast, much instrumental research has sought quantitative relations between the frequency of a response and its (prior) environmental consequences. Readers interested in the preparations that have traditionally been used to study acquired behavior should consult Hearst's (1988) excellent review, which in many ways complements this chapter.

EMPIRICAL LAWS OF PAVLOVIAN RESPONDING

Given appropriate experience, a stimulus will come to elicit behavior that is not characteristic of responding to that stimulus, but is characteristic for a second stimulus (hereafter called an *outcome*). For example, in Pavlov's (1927) classic studies, dogs salivated at the sound of a bell if previously the bell had been rung before food was presented. That is, the bell acquired *stimulus control* over the dogs' salivation. Here we summarize the relationships between stimuli that promote such acquired responding, although we begin with changes in behavior that occur to a single stimulus.

Single-Stimulus Phenomena

The simplest type of learning is that which results from exposure to a single stimulus. For example, if you hear a loud noise, you are apt to startle. But if that noise is presented repeatedly, the startle reaction will gradually decrease, a process called *habituation.* Occasionally, responding may increase with repeated presentations of a stimulus, a phenomenon called *sensitization.* Habituation is far more common than sensitization, with sensitization ordinarily being observed only with very intense stimuli. Habituation is regarded as a primitive form of learning, and is sometimes studied explicitly because researchers thought that its simplicity might allow the essence of the learning process to be observed more readily than in situations involving multiple stimuli. Consistent with this view, habituation exhibits many of the same characteristics of learning seen with multiple stimuli (Thompson & Spencer, 1966). These include (a) decelerating acquisition per trial over increasing numbers of trials; (b) a so-called spontaneous loss of habituation over increasing retention intervals; (c) more rapid reacquisition of habituation over repeated series of habituation trials; (d) slower habituation over trials if the trials are spaced, but slower spontaneous loss of habituation thereafter (rate sensitivity); (e) further habituation trials after behavioral change over trials has ceased retard spontaneous loss from habituation (i.e., overtraining results in some sort of initially latent learning); (f) generalization to other stimuli in direct relation to the similarity of the habituated stimulus to the test stimulus; and (g) temporary masking by an intense stimulus (i.e., strong responding to a habituated stimulus is observed if the stimulus is presented immediately following presentation of an intense novel stimulus). As we shall see, these phenomena are shared with learning involving multiple events.

Traditionally, sensitization was viewed as simply the opposite of habituation. But as noted by Groves and Thompson (1970), habituation is highly stimulus-specific, whereas sensitization is not. Stimulus specificity is not an all-or-none matter; however, sensitization clearly generalizes more broadly to relatively dissimilar stimuli than does habituation. Because of this difference in stimulus specificity and because different neural pathways are apparently involved, Groves and Thompson suggested that habituation and sensitization are independent processes that summate for any test stimulus. Habituation is commonly viewed as nonassociative. However, Wagner (1978) has suggested that long-term habituation (that which survives long retention intervals) is due to an association between the habituated stimulus and the context in which habituation occurred (but see Marlin & Miller, 1981).

Phenomena Involving Two Stimuli: Single Cue–Single Outcome

Factors Influencing Acquired Stimulus Control of Behavior

Stimulus Salience and Attention. The rate at which stimulus control by a conditioned stimulus (CS) is achieved (in terms of number of trials) and the asymptote of control attained are both positively related to the *salience* of both the CS and the outcome (e.g., Kamin, 1965). Salience here refers to a composite of stimulus intensity, size, contrast with background, motion, and stimulus change, among other factors. Salience is not only a function of the physical stimulus, but also a function of the state of the subject (e.g., food is more salient to a hungry than a sated person). Ordinarily, the salience of a cue has greater influence on the rate at which stimulus control of behavior develops (as a function of number of training trials), whereas the salience of the outcome has greater influence on the ultimate level of stimulus control that is reached over many trials. Clearly, the hybrid construct of salience as used here has much in common with what is commonly called attention, but we avoid that construct because of its additional implications. Stimulus salience is not only important during training; conditioned responding is directly influenced by the salience of the test stimulus, a point long ago noted by Hull (1952).

Predispositions: Genetic and Experiential. The construct of salience speaks to the ease with which a cue will come to control behavior, but it does not take into account the nature of the outcome. In fact, some stimuli more readily become cues for a specific outcome than do other stimuli. For example, Garcia and Koelling (1966) gave thirsty rats access to flavored water that was accompanied by sound and light stimuli whenever they drank. For half the animals, drinking was immediately followed with foot shock, and for the other half it was followed by an agent that induced gastric distress. Although all subjects received the same audiovisual-plus-flavor compound stimulus, the subjects that received the foot shock later exhibited greater avoidance of the audiovisual cues, whereas the subjects that received the gastric distress exhibited greater avoidance of the flavor. These observations cannot be explained in terms of the relative salience of the cues. Although Garcia and Koelling interpreted this *cue-to-consequence effect* in terms of genetic predispositions reflecting the importance of flavor cues with respect to gastric consequences and audiovisual cues with respect to cutaneous consequences, later research suggests that pretraining experience interacts with genetic factors in creating predispositions that allow stimulus control to develop for some stimulus dyads more readily than for others. For example, Dalrymple and Galef (1981) found that rats forced to make a visual discrimination for food were more apt to associate visual cues with an internal malaise.

Spatiotemporal Contiguity (Similarity). Stimulus control of acquired behavior is a strong direct function of the proximity of a potential Pavlovian cue to an outcome in space (Rescorla & Cunningham, 1979) and time (Pavlov, 1927). Contiguity is so powerful that some researchers have suggested that it is the only nontrivial determinant of stimulus control (e.g., Estes, 1950; Guthrie, 1935). However, several conditioning phenomena appear to violate the so-called law of contiguity. One long-standing challenge arises from the observation that simultaneous presentation of a cue and outcome results in weaker conditioned responding to the cue than when the cue slightly precedes the outcome. However, this *simultaneous conditioning deficit* has now been recognized as reflecting a failure to express information acquired during simultaneous pairings rather than a failure to encode the simultaneous relationship (i.e., most conditioned responses are anticipatory of an outcome, and are temporally inappropriate for a cue that signals that the outcome is already present). For example, Matzel, Held, and Miller (1988) demonstrated that simultaneous pairings do in fact result in robust learning, but that this information is behaviorally expressed only if an assessment procedure sensitive to simultaneous pairings is used.

A second challenge to the law of contiguity has been based on the observation that conditioned taste aversions yield stimulus control even when cues (flavors) and outcome (internal malaise) are separated by hours (Garcia, Ervin, & Koelling, 1966). However, even with conditioned taste aversions, stimulus control (i.e., aversion to the flavor) decreases as the interval between the flavor and internal malaise increases. All that differs here from other conditioning preparations is the rate of decrease in stimulus control as the interstimulus interval in training increases. Thus, conditioned taste aversion is merely a parametric variation of the law of contiguity, not a violation of it.

Another challenge to the law of contiguity that is not so readily dismissed is based on the observation that the effect of interstimulus interval is often inversely related to the average interval between outcomes (e.g., an increase in the CS-US interval has less of a decremental effect on conditioned responding if the intertrial interval is correspondingly increased). That is, stimulus control appears to depend not so much on the absolute interval between a cue and an outcome (i.e., absolute temporal contiguity) as on the ratio of this interval to that between outcomes (i.e., relative contiguity; e.g., Gibbon, Baldock, Locurto, Gold, & Terrace, 1977). A further challenge to the law of contiguity is discussed in this chapter's section entitled "Mediation."

According to the British empiricist philosophers, associations between elements were more readily formed when the elements were similar (Berkeley, 1710/1946). More recently, well-controlled experiments have confirmed that development of stimulus control is facilitated if paired cues and outcome are made more similar (e.g., Rescorla & Furrow, 1977). The neural representations of paired stimuli seemingly include many attributes of the stimuli, including their temporal and spatial relationships. This is evident in conditioned responding reflecting not only an expectation of a specific outcome, but the outcome occurring at a specific time and place (e.g., Saint Paul, 1982; Savastano & Miller, 1998). If temporal and spatial coordinates are viewed as stimulus attributes, *contiguity* can be viewed as *similarity* on the temporal and spatial dimensions, thereby subsuming spatiotemporal contiguity within a general conception of similarity. Thus, the law of similarity appears able to encompass the law of contiguity.

Objective Contingency. When a cue is consistently followed by an outcome and these pairings are punctuated by intertrial intervals in which neither the cue nor the outcome occurs, stimulus control of behavior ordinarily develops over

2x2 Contingency Table:

	Outcome present	Outcome absent
Cue present	Type 1 *a*	Type 2 *b*
Cue absent	Type 3 *c*	Type 4 *d*

Figure 13.1 Two-by-two contingency table for dichotomous variables; *a*, *b*, *c*, and *d* are the frequencies of trial types 1, 2, 3, and 4. See text for details.

trials. However, when cues or outcomes sometimes occur by themselves during the training sessions, conditioned responding to the cue (reflecting the outcome) is often slower to develop (measured in number of cue-outcome pairings) and is asymptotically weaker (Rescorla, 1968).

There are four possibilities for each trial in which a dichotomous cue or outcome might be presented, as shown in Figure 13.1:

1. Cue–outcome.
2. Cue–no outcome.
3. No cue–outcome.
4. No cue–no outcome.

The frequencies of trials of type 1, 2, 3, and 4 are *a*, *b*, *c*, and *d*, respectively. The objective contingency is usually defined in terms of the difference in conditional probabilities of the outcome in the presence ($a/[a + b]$) and in the absence ($c/[c + d]$) of the cue. If the conditional probability of the outcome is greater in the presence rather than absence of the cue, the contingency is positive; conversely, if the conditional probability of the outcome is less in the presence than absence of the cue, the contingency is negative. Alternatively stated, contingency increases with the occurrence of *a*- and *d*-type trials and decreases with *b*- and *c*-type trials. In terms of stimulus control, excitatory responding is observed to increase and behavior indicative of conditioned inhibition (see this chapter's later section on that topic) is seen to decrease with increasing contingency, and vice versa with decreasing contingency. Empirically, the four types of trials are seen to have unequal influence on stimulus control, with Type 1 trials having the greatest impact and Type 4 trials having the least impact (e.g., Wasserman, Elek, Chatlosh, & Baker, 1993). Note that although we previously described the effect of spaced versus massed cue-outcome pairings as a qualifier of contiguity, such trial spacing effects are readily subsumed under objective contingency because long intertrial intervals are the same as Type 4 trials, provided these intertrial intervals occur in the training context.

Conditioned responding can be attenuated by presentations of the cue alone before the cue-outcome pairings, intermingled with the pairings, or after the pairings. If they occur before the pairings, the attenuation is called the *CS-preexposure* (also called *latent inhibition*) *effect* (Lubow & Moore, 1959); if they occur during the pairings, they (in conjunction with the pairings) are called *partial reinforcement* (Pavlov, 1927); and if they occur after the pairings, the attenuation is called *extinction* (Pavlov, 1927). Notably, the operations that produce the CS-preexposure effect and habituation (i.e., presentation of a single stimulus) are identical; the difference is in how behavior is subsequently assessed. Additionally, based on the two phenomena being doubly dissociable, Hall (1991) has argued that habituation and the CS-preexposure effect arise from different underlying processes. That is, a change in context between treatment and testing attenuates the CS-preexposure effect more than it does habituation, whereas increasing retention interval attenuates habituation more than it does the CS-preexposure effect.

Conditioned responding can also be attenuated by presentations of the outcome alone before the cue-outcome pairings, with the pairings, or after the pairings. If they occur before the pairings, the attenuation is called the *US-preexposure effect* (e.g., Randich & LoLordo, 1979); if they occur during the pairings, it (in conjunction with the pairings) is called the *degraded contingency effect* (in the narrow sense, as any presentation of the cue or outcome alone degrades the objective contingency, Rescorla, 1968); and if they occur after the pairings, it is an instance of *retrospective revaluation* (e.g., Denniston, Miller, & Matute, 1996). The retrospective revaluation effect has proven far more elusive than any of the other five means of attenuating excitatory conditioned responding through degraded contingency, but it occurs at least under select conditions (Miller & Matute, 1996).

If compounded, these different types of contingency-degrading treatments have a cumulative effect on conditioned responding that is at least summative (Bonardi & Hall, 1996) and possibly greater than summative (Bennett, Wills, Oakeshott, & Mackintosh, 2000). A prime example of such a compound contingency-degrading treatment is so-called learned irrelevance, in which cue and outcome presentations truly random with respect to one another precede a series of cue-outcome pairings (Baker & Mackintosh, 1977). This pretraining treatment has a decremental effect on conditioned responding greater than either CS preexposure or US preexposure.

Objective contingency effects are not merely a function of the frequency of different types of trials depicted in Figure 13.1. Two important factors that influence contingency effects are (a) trial order and spacing, and (b) modulatory stimuli. When contingency-degrading Type 2 and 3 trials are administered phasically (rather than interspersed with cue-outcome pairings), *recency* effects are pronounced. The trials that occur closest to testing have a relatively greater impact on responding; such recency effects fade with time (i.e., longer retention intervals, or at least as a function of the intervening events that occur during longer retention intervals). Additionally, if there are stimuli that are present during the pairings but not the contingency-degrading treatments (or vice versa), presentation of these stimuli immediately prior to or during testing with the target cue causes conditioned responding to better reflect the trials that occurred in the presence of the stimuli. These modulatory stimuli can be either contextual stimuli (i.e., the static environmental cues present during training: the so-called *renewal* effect, Bouton & Bolles, 1979) or discrete stimuli (e.g., Brooks & Bouton, 1993). Such modulatory stimuli appear to have much in common with so-called priming cues in cognitive research (see chapter in this volume by McNamara and Holbrook; Neely, 1977).

Modulatory effects can be obtained even when the cue-outcome pairings are interspersed with the contingency degrading events. For example, if stimulus A always precedes pairings of cue X and an outcome, and does not precede presentations of cue X alone, subjects will come to respond to the cue if and only if it is preceded by stimulus A; this effect is called *positive occasion setting* (Holland, 1983a). If stimulus A only precedes the nonreinforced presentations of cue X, subjects will come to respond to cue X only when it has not been preceded by stimulus A; this effect is called *negative occasion setting*. Surprisingly, behavioral modulation by contexts appears to be acquired in far fewer trials than with discrete stimuli, perhaps reflecting the important role of contextual modulation of behavior in each species' ecological niche.

Attenuation of stimulus control through contingency-degrading events is often at least partially reversible without further cue-outcome pairings. This is most evident in the case of extinction, for which (so-called) spontaneous recovery from extinction and external disinhibition (i.e., temporary release from extinction treatment as a result of presenting an unrelated intense stimulus immediately prior to the extinguished stimulus) are examples of recovery of behavior indicative of the cue-outcome pairings without the occurrence of further pairings (e.g., Pavlov, 1927). Similarly, spontaneous recovery from the CS-preexposure effect has been well documented (e.g., Kraemer, Randall, & Carbary, 1991). These phenomena suggest that the pairings of cue and outcome are encoded independently of the contingency-degrading events, but the behavioral expression of information regarding the pairings can be suppressed by additional learning during the contingency-degrading events.

Cue and Outcome Duration. Cue and outcome durations have great impact on stimulus control of behavior. The effects are complex, but generally speaking, increased cue or outcome duration reduces behavioral control (provided one controls for any greater hedonic value of the outcome due to increased duration). What makes these variables complex is that different components of a stimulus can contribute differentially to stimulus control. The onset, presence, and termination of a cue can each influence behavior through its own relationship to the outcome; this tendency towards fragmentation of behavioral control appears to increase with the length of the duration of the cue (e.g., Romaniuk & Williams, 2000). Similarly, outcomes have components that can differentially contribute to control by a stimulus. As an outcome is prolonged, its later components are further removed in time from the cue and presumably are less well-associated to the cue.

Response Topology and Timing

The hallmark of conditioned responding is that the observed response to the cue reflects the nature of the outcome. For example, pigeons peck an illuminated key differently depending on whether the key signals delivery of food or water, and their manner of pecking is similar to that required to ingest the specific outcome (Jenkins & Moore, 1973). However, the nature of the signal also may qualitatively modulate the conditioned response. For instance, Holland (1977) has described how rats' conditioned responses to a light and an auditory cue differ, despite their having been paired with the same outcome.

Conditioned responding not only indicates that the cue and outcome have been paired, but also reflects the spatial and temporal relationships that prevailed between the cue and outcome during those pairings (giving rise to the mentalistic view that subjects anticipate, so to speak, when and where the outcome will occur). If a cue has been paired with a rewarding outcome in a particular location, subjects are frequently observed to approach the location at which the outcome had been delivered (so-called *goal tracking*). For example, Burns and Domjan (1996) observed that Japanese quail, as part of their conditioned response to a cue for a potential mate, oriented to the absolute location in which the mate would be introduced, independent of their immediate location in the experimental apparatus. The temporal relationship between a cue and outcome that existed in training is evidenced in two ways. First, with asymptotic training, the conditioned response ordinarily is emitted just prior to the time at which the outcome would occur based on the prior pairings (Pavlov, 1927). Second, the nature of the response often changes with different cue-outcome intervals. In some instances, when an outcome (e.g., food) occurs at regular intervals, during the intertrial interval subjects emit a sequence of behaviors with a stereotypic temporal structure appropriate for that outcome in the species' ecological niche (e.g., Staddon & Simmelhag, 1970; Timberlake & Lucas, 1991).

Pavlovian conditioned responding often closely resembles a diminished form of the response to the unconditioned outcome (e.g., conditioned salivation with food as the outcome). Such a response topology is called *mimetic*. However, conditioned responding is occasionally diametrically opposed to the unconditioned response (e.g., conditioned freezing with pain as the outcome, or a conditioned increase in pain sensitivity with delivery of morphine as the outcome; Siegel, 1989). Such a conditioned response topology is called *compensatory.* We do not yet have a full understanding of when one or the other type of responding will occur (but see this chapter's section entitled "What Is a Response?").

Stimulus Generalization

No perceptual event is ever exactly repeated because of variation in both the environment and in the nervous system. Thus, learning would be useless if organisms did not generalize from stimuli in training to stimuli that are perceptually similar. Therefore, it is not surprising that conditioned responding is seen to decrease in an orderly fashion as the physical difference between the training and test stimuli increases. This reduction in responding is called *stimulus generalization decrement.* Response magnitude or frequency plotted as a function of training-to-test stimulus similarity yields a symmetric curve that is called a *generalization gradient* (e.g., Guttman & Kalish, 1956). Such gradients resulting from simple cue-outcome pairings can be made steeper by introducing trials with a second stimulus that is not paired with the outcome. Such discrimination training not only steepens the generalization gradient between the reinforced stimulus and nonreinforced stimulus, but often shifts the stimulus value at which maximum responding is observed from the reinforced cue in the direction away from the value of the nonreinforced stimulus (the so-called *peak shift;* e.g., Weiss & Schindler, 1981). With increasing retention intervals between the end of training and a test trial, stimulus generalization gradients tend to grow broader (e.g., Riccio, Richardson, & Ebner, 1984)

Phenomena Involving More Than Two Stimuli: Competition, Interference, Facilitation, and Summation

When more than two stimuli are presented in close proximity during training, one might expect that the representation of each stimulus-outcome dyad would be treated independently according to the laws described above. Surely these laws do apply, but the situation becomes more complex because interactions between stimuli also occur. That is, when stimuli X, Y, and Z are trained together, behavioral control by X based on X's relationship to Y is often influenced by the presence of Z during training. Although these interactions (described in the following sections) are often appreciable, they are neither ubiquitous (i.e., they are more narrowly parameter dependent) nor generally as robust as any of the phenomena described under "Phenomena Involving Two Stimuli."

Multiple Cues With a Common Outcome

Cues Trained Together and Tested Apart: Competition and Facilitation. For the last 30 years, much attention has been focused on *cue competition* between cues trained in compound, particularly *overshadowing* and *blocking.* Overshadowing refers to the observed attenuation in conditioned responding to an initially novel cue (X) paired with an outcome in the presence of an initially novel second cue (Y), relative to responding to X given the same treatment in the absence of Y (Pavlov, 1927). The degree that Y will overshadow X depends on their relative saliences; the more salient Y is compared to X, the greater the degree of overshadowing of X (Mackintosh, 1976). When two cues are equally salient, overshadowing is sometimes observed, but is rarely a large effect. Blocking refers to attenuated responding to a cue (X) that is paired with an outcome in the presence of a second cue (Y) when Y was previously paired with the same outcome in the absence of X, relative to responding to X when Y had not been pretrained (Kamin, 1968). That is, learning as a result of the initial Y-outcome association blocks (so to speak) responding to X that the XY-outcome pairings would otherwise support. (Thus, observation of blocking requires good responding to X by the control group, which necessitates the use of parameters that minimize overshadowing of X by Y in the control group.)

Both overshadowing and blocking can be observed with a single compound training trial (e.g., Balaz, Kasprow, & Miller, 1982; Mackintosh & Reese, 1979), are usually greatest with a few compound trials, and tend to wane with many compound trials (e.g., Azorlosa & Cicala, 1988). Notably, recovery from each of these cue competition effects can sometimes be obtained without further training trials through various treatments including (a) lengthening the retention interval (i.e., so-called spontaneous recovery; Kraemer, Lariviere, & Spear, 1988); (b) administration of so-called reminder treatments, which consists of presentation of either the outcome alone, the cue alone, or the training context (e.g., Balaz, Gutsin, Cacheiro, & Miller, 1982); and (c) posttraining massive extinction of the overshadowing or blocking stimulus (e.g., Matzel, Schachtman, & Miller, 1985). The theoretical implications of such recovery (paralleling the recovery often observed following the degradation of contingency in the two-stimulus situation) are discussed later in this chapter (see sections entitled "Expression-Focused Models" and "Accounts of Retrospective Revaluation").

Although competition is far more commonly observed, under certain circumstances the presence of a second cue during training has exactly the opposite effect; that is, it enhances (i.e., facilitates) responding to the target cue. When this effect is observed within the overshadowing procedure, it is called *potentiation* (Clarke, Westbrook, & Irwin, 1979); and when it is seen in the blocking procedure, it is called *augmentation* (Batson & Batsell, 2000). Potentiation and augmentation are most readily observed when the outcome is an internal malaise (usually induced by a toxin), the target cue is an odor, and the companion cue is a taste. However, enhancement is not restricted to these modalities (e.g., J. S. Miller, Scherer, & Jagielo, 1995). Another example of enhancement, although possibly with a different underlying mechanism, is *superconditioning,* which refers to enhanced responding to a cue that is trained in the presence of a cue previously established as a conditioned inhibitor for the outcome, relative to responding to the target cue when the companion cue was novel. In most instances, enhancement appears to be mediated at test by the companion stimulus that was present during training, in that degrading the associative status of the companion stimulus between training and testing often attenuates the enhanced responding (Durlach & Rescorla, 1980).

Cues Trained Apart and Tested Apart. Although theory and research in learning over the past 30 years have focused on the interaction of cues trained together, there is an older literature concerning the interaction of cues with common outcomes trained apart (i.e., X→A, Y→A). This research was conducted largely in the tradition of associationistic studies of human verbal learning that was popular in the mid-twentieth century. A typical example is the attenuated responding to cue X observed when X→A training is either preceded (proactive interference) or followed (retroactive interference) by Y→A training, relative to subjects receiving no Y→A training (e.g., Slamecka & Ceraso, 1960). The stimuli used in the original verbal learning studies were usually consonant trigrams, nonsense syllables, or isolated words. However, recent research using nonverbal preparations has found that such interference effects occur quite generally in both humans (Matute & Pineño, 1998) and nonhumans (Escobar, Matute, & Miller, 2001). Importantly, Y→A presentations degrade the X→A objective contingency because they include presentations of A in the absence of X. This degrading of the X-A contingency sometimes does contribute to the attenuation of responding based on the X→A relationship (as seen in subjects who receive A-alone as the disruptive treatment relative to subjects who receive no disruptive treatment). However, Y→A treatment ordinarily produces a larger deficit, suggesting that, in addition to contingency effects, associations with a common element interact to reduce target stimulus control (e.g., Escobar et al., 2001). Although interference is the more frequent result of the X→A, Y→A design, facilitation is sometimes observed, most commonly when X and Y are similar (e.g., Osgood, 1949).

Cues Trained Apart and Tested Together. When two independently trained cues are compounded at test, responding is usually at least as or more vigorous than when only one of the cues is tested (see Kehoe & Gormezano, 1980). When the response to the compound is greater than to either element, the phenomenon is called *response summation.* Presumably, a major factor limiting response summation is that compounding two cues creates a test situation different from that of training with either cue; thus, attenuated responding to the compound due to generalization decrement is expected. The question is under what conditions will generalization decrement counteract the summation of the tendencies to respond to the two stimuli. Research suggests that when subjects treat the compound as a unique stimulus in itself, distinct from the original stimuli (i.e., *configuring*), summation will be minimized (e.g., Kehoe, Horne, Horne, & Macrae, 1994). Well-established rules of perception (e.g., gestalt principles; Köhler, 1947) describe the conditions that favor and oppose configuring.

Multiple Outcomes With a Single Cue

Just as Y→A trials can interact with behavior based on X→A training, so too can X→B trials interact with behavior based on X→A training.

Multiple Outcomes Trained Together With a Single Cue. When a cue X is paired with a compound of outcomes (i.e., X→AB), responding on tests of the X→A relationship often yield less responding than that of a control group for which B was omitted, provided A and B are sufficiently different. Such a result might be expected based on either distraction during training or response competition at test, both of which are well-established phenomena. However, some studies have been designed to minimize these two potential sources of outcome competition. For example, Burger, Mallemat, and Miller (2000) used a sensory preconditioning procedure (see this chapter's section entitled "Second-Order Conditioning and Sensory Preconditioning") in which the competing outcomes were not biologically significant; and only just before testing did they pair A with a biologically significant stimulus so that the subjects' learning could be assessed. As neither A nor B was biologically significant during training, (a) distraction by B from A was less apt to occur (although it cannot be completely discounted), and (b) B controlled no behavior that could have produced response competition at test. Despite minimization of distraction and response competition, Burger et al. still observed competition between outcomes (i.e., the presence of B during training attenuated responding based on X and A having been paired). To our knowledge, no one to date has reported facilitation from the presence of B during training. But analogy with the multiple-cue case suggests that facilitation might occur if the two outcomes had strong within-compound links (i.e., A and B were similar or strongly associated to each other).

Multiple Outcomes Trained Apart With a Single Cue: Counterconditioning. Just as multiple cues trained apart with a common outcome can result in an interaction, so too can an interaction be observed when multiple outcomes are trained apart with a common cue. Alternatively stated, responding based on X→A training can be disrupted by X→B training. The best known example of this is *counterconditioning* (e.g., responding to a cue based on cue→food training is disrupted by cue→footshock training). The interfering training (X→B) can occur before, among, or after the target training trials (X→A). Although response competition is a likely contributing factor, there is good evidence that such interference effects are due to more than simple response competition (e.g., Dearing & Dickinson, 1979). Just as interference produced by Y→A in the X→A, Y→A situation can be due in part to degrading the X-A contingency, so attenuated responding produced by X→B in the X→A, X→B situation can arise in part from the degrading of the X-A contingency that is inherent in the presentations of X during X→B trials. However, research has found that the response attenuation produced by the X→B trials is sometimes greater than that produced by X-alone presentations; hence, this sort of interference cannot be treated as simply an instance of degraded contingency (Escobar, Arcediano, & Miller, 2001).

Resolving Ambiguity

The magnitude of the interference effects described in the two previous sections is readily controlled by conditions at the time of testing. If the target and interfering treatments have been given in different contexts (i.e., competing elements trained apart), presentation at test of contextual cues associated with the interfering treatment enhances interference, whereas presentation of contextual cues associated with target training reduces interference. These contextual cues can be either diffuse background cues or discrete stimuli that were presented with the target (Escobar et al., 2001). Additionally, more recent training experience typically dominates behavior (i.e., a recency effect), all other factors being equal. Such recency effects fade with increasing retention intervals, with the consequence that retroactive interference fades and, correspondingly, proactive interference increases when the posttraining retention interval is increased (Postman, Stark, & Fraser, 1968).

Notably, the contextual and temporal modulation of interference effects is highly similar to the modulation observed with degraded contingency effects (see this chapter's section entitled "Factors Influencing Aquired Stimulus Control of Behavior"). This similarity is grounds for revisiting the issue of whether interference effects are really different from degraded contingency effects. We previously cited grounds for rejecting the view that interference effects were no more than degraded contingency effects (see this chapter's section on that topic). However, if the training context is regarded as an element that can become associated with a cue on a cue-alone trial or with an outcome on an outcome-alone trial, contingency degrading trials could be viewed as target cue-context or context-outcome trials that interfere with behavior promoted by target cue-outcome trials much as Y-outcome or target-B trials do within the interference paradigm. In principle, this allows degraded contingency effects to be viewed as a subset of interference effects. However, due to the vagueness of *context* as a stimulus, this approach has not received widespread acceptance.

Mediation

Mediated changes in control of behavior by a stimulus refers to situations in which responding to a target cue is at least partially a function of the training history of a second cue that has at one time or another been paired with the target. Depending on the specific situation, mediational interaction between the target and the companion cues can occur either at the time that they are paired during training (e.g., aversively motivated second-order conditioning, see section entitled "Second-Order Conditioning and Sensory Preconditioning"; Holland & Rescorla, 1975) or at test (e.g., sensory preconditioning, see same section; Rizley & Rescorla, 1972). As discussed below, the mediated control transferred to the target can be either consistent with the status of the companion cue (e.g., second-order conditioning) or inverse to the status of the companion cue (e.g., conditioned inhibition, blocking). Testing whether a mediational relationship between two cues exists usually takes the form of presenting the companion cue with or without the outcome in the absence of the target and seeing whether that treatment influences responding to the target. This manipulation of the companion cue can be done before, interspersed among, or after the target training trials. However, sometimes posttarget-training revaluation of the companion does not alter responding to the target, suggesting that the mediational process occurs during training (e.g., aversively motivated second-order conditioning).

Second-Order Conditioning and Sensory Preconditioning

If cue Y is paired with a biologically significant outcome (A) such that Y comes to control responding, and subsequently cue X is paired with Y (i.e., Y→A, X→Y), responding to X will be observed. This phenomenon is called *second-order conditioning* (Pavlov, 1927). Cue X can similarly be imbued with behavioral control if the two phases of training above are reversed (i.e., X→Y, followed by Y→A). This latter phenomenon is called *sensory preconditioning* (Brogden, 1939). Second-order conditioning and sensory preconditioning are important for two reasons. First, these phenomena are simple examples of mediated responding—that is, acquired behavior that depends on associations between stimuli that are not of inherent biological significance. Second, these phenomena pose a serious challenge to the principle of contiguity. For example, consider sensory preconditioning: A light is paired with a tone, then the tone is paired with an aversive event (i.e., electric shock); at test, the light evokes a conditioned fear response. Thus, the light is controlling a response appropriate for the aversive event, despite its never having been paired with that event. This is a direct violation of contiguity in its simplest form. Based on the observation of mediated behavior, the law of contiguity must be either abandoned or modified. Given the enormous success of contiguity in describing the conditions that foster acquired behavior, researchers generally have elected to redefine contiguity as spatiotemporal proximity between the cue *or its surrogate* and the outcome *or its surrogate,* thereby incorporating mediation within the principle of contiguity.

Mediation appears to occur when two different types of training share a common element (e.g., X→Y, Y→A). Importantly, the mediating stimulus ordinarily does not simply act as a (weak) substitute for the outcome (as might be expected of a so-called simple surrogate). Rather, the mediating stimulus (i.e., first-order cue) carries with it its own spatiotemporal relationship to the outcome, such that the second-order cue supports behavior appropriate for a summation of the mediator-outcome spatiotemporal relationship and the second-order cue-mediator spatiotemporal relationship (for spatial summation, see Etienne, Berlie, Georgakopoulos, & Maurer, 1998; for temporal summation, see Matzel, Held et al., 1988). In effect, subjects appear to integrate the two separately experienced relationships to create a spatiotemporal relationship between the second-order cue and the outcome, despite their never having been physically paired.

The mediating process that links two stimuli that were never paired could occur in principle either during training or during testing. To address this issue, researchers have asked what happens to the response potential of a second-order cue X when its first-order cue is extinguished between training and testing. Rizley and Rescorla (1972) reported that such post-training extinction of Y did not degrade responding to a second-order cue (X), but subsequent research has under some conditions found attenuated responding to X (Cheatle & Rudy, 1978). The basis for this difference is not yet completely clear, but Nairne and Rescorla (1981) have suggested that it depends on the valence of the outcome (i.e., appetitive or aversive).

Conditioned Inhibition

Conditioned inhibition refers to situations in which a subject behaves *as if* it has learned that a particular stimulus (a so-called inhibitor) signals the omission of an outcome. Conditioned inhibition is ordinarily assessed by a combination of (a) a *summation test* in which the putative inhibitor is presented in compound with a known conditioned excitor (different from any excitor that was used in training the inhibitor) and seen to reduce responding to the excitor; and (b) a *retardation test* in which the inhibitor is seen to be slow in coming to serve as a conditioned excitor in terms of required number of pairings with the outcome (Rescorla, 1969). Because the standard tests for conditioned excitation and conditioned inhibition are operationally distinct, stimuli sometimes can pass tests for both excitatory and inhibitory status after identical treatment. The implication is that conditioned inhibition and conditioned excitation are not mutually exclusive (e.g., Matzel, Gladstein, & Miller, 1988), which is contrary to some theoretical formulations (e.g., Rescorla & Wagner, 1972).

There are several different procedures that appear to produce conditioned inhibition (LoLordo & Fairless, 1985). Among them are (a) explicitly unpaired presentations of the cue (inhibitor) and outcome (described in objective contingency on pp. 361–363); (b) Pavlov's (1927) procedure in which a training excitor (Y) is paired with an outcome, interspersed with trials in which the training excitor and intended inhibitor (X) are presented in nonreinforced compound; and (c) so-called backward pairings of a cue with an outcome (outcome→X; Heth, 1976). What appears similar across these various procedures is that the inhibitor is present at a time that another cue (discrete or contextual) signals that the outcome is apt to occur, but in fact it does not occur. Conditioned inhibition is stimulus-specific in that it generates relatively narrow generalization gradients, similar to conditioned excitation (Spence, 1936). Additionally, it is outcome-specific in that an inhibitor will transfer its response-attenuating influence on behavior between different cues for the same outcome, but not between cues for different outcomes (Rescorla & Holland, 1977). Hence, conditioned inhibition, like conditioned excitation, is a form of stimulus-specific learning about a relationship between a cue and an outcome. But because it is necessarily mediated (the cue and outcome are never paired), conditioned inhibition is more similar to second-order conditioning than it is to simple (first-order) conditioning. Moreover, just as responding to a second-order conditioned stimulus not only appears *as if* the subject expects the outcome at a time and place specified conjointly by the spatiotemporal relationships between X and Y and between Y and the outcome (e.g., Matzel, Held et al., 1988), so too does a conditioned inhibitor seemingly signal not only the omission of the outcome but also the time and place of that omission as well (e.g., Denniston, Blaisdell, & Miller, 1998).

One might ask about the behavioral consequences for conditioned inhibition of posttraining extinction of the mediating cue. Similar to corresponding tests with second-order conditioning, the results have been mixed. For example, Rescorla and Holland (1977) found no alteration of behavior indicative of inhibition, whereas others (e.g., Best, Dunn, Batson, Meachum, & Nash, 1985; Hallam, Grahame, Harris, & Miller, 1992) observed a decrease in inhibition. Yin, Grahame, and Miller (1993) suggested that the critical difference between these studies is that massive posttraining extinction of the mediating stimulus is necessary to obtain changes in behavioral control by an inhibitor.

Despite these operational and behavioral similarities of conditioned inhibition and second-order conditioning, there is one most fundamental difference. Responding to a second-order cue is appropriate for the occurrence of the outcome, whereas responding to an inhibitor is appropriate for the omission of the outcome. In sharp contrast to second-order conditioning (and sensory preconditioning), which are examples of *positive mediation* (seemingly passing information, so to speak, concerning an outcome from one cue to a second cue), conditioned inhibition is an example of *negative mediation* (seemingly inverting the expectation of the outcome conveyed by the first-order cue as the information is passed to the second-order cue). Why positive mediation should occur in some situations and negative mediation in other apparently similar situations is not yet fully understood. Rashotte, Marshall, and O'Connell (1981) and Yin, Barnet, and Miller (1994) have suggested that the critical variable may be the number of nonreinforced X-Y trials. A second difference between inhibition and second-order excitation that is likely related to the aforementioned one is that nonreinforced exposure to an excitor produces extinction, whereas nonreinforced exposure to an inhibitor not only does not reduce its inhibitory potential, but also sometimes increases it (DeVito & Fowler, 1987).

Retrospective Revaluation

Mediated changes in stimulus control of behavior can often be achieved by treatment (reinforcement or extinction) of a target cue's companion stimulus either before, during, or after the pairings of the target and companion stimuli (reinforced or nonreinforced). Recent interest has focused on treatment of the companion stimulus alone *after* the completion of the compound trials, because in this case the observed effects on responding to the target are particularly problematic to most conventional associative theories of acquired behavior. A change in stimulus control following the termination of training with the target cue is called *retrospective revaluation.* Importantly, both positive and negative mediation effects have been observed with the retrospective revaluation procedure. Sensory preconditioning is a long-known but frequently ignored example of retrospective revaluation in its simplest form. It is an example of positive retrospective revaluation because the posttarget-training treatment with the companion stimulus produces a change in responding to the target that mimics the change in control by the companion stimulus. Other examples of positive retrospective revaluation include the decrease in responding sometimes seen to a cue trained in compound when its companion cue is extinguished (i.e., mediated extinction; Holland & Forbes, 1982). In contrast, there are also many reports of negative retrospective revaluation, in which the change in control by the target is in direct opposition to the change produced in the companion during retrospective revaluation. Examples of negative retrospective revaluation include recovery from overshadowing as a result of extinction of the overshadowing stimulus (e.g., Matzel et al., 1985), decreases in conditioned inhibition as a result of extinction of the inhibitor's training excitor (e.g., DeVito & Fowler, 1987), and backward blocking (AX→outcome, followed by A→outcome, e.g., Denniston et al., 1996).

The occurrence of both positive and negative mediation in retrospective revaluation parallels the two opposing effects that are observed when the companion cue is treated before or during the compound stimulus trials. In the section entitled "Multiple Cues With a Common Outcome," we described not only overshadowing but also potentiation, which, although operationally similar to overshadowing, has a converse behavioral result. Notably, the positive mediation apparent in potentiation can usually be reversed by posttraining extinction of the mediating (potentiating) cue (e.g., Durlach & Rescorla, 1980). Similarly, the negative mediation apparent in overshadowing can sometimes be reversed by massive posttraining extinction of the mediating (overshadowing) cue (e.g., Kaufman & Bolles, 1981; Matzel et al., 1985). However, currently there are insufficient data to specify a rule for the changes in control by a cue that will be observed when its companion cue is reinforced or extinguished. That is to say, we do not know the critical variables that determine whether mediation will be positive or negative. As previously mentioned (see section titled "Conditioned Inhibition"), the two prime candidates for determining the direction of mediation are the number of pairings of the target with the mediating cue and whether those pairings are simultaneous or serial. Whatever the outcome of future studies, research on retrospective revaluation has clearly demonstrated that the previously accepted view—that the response potential of a cue cannot change if it is not presented—was incorrect.

MODELS OF PAVLOVIAN RESPONDING: THEORY

Here we turn from our summary of variables that influence acquired behavior based on cue-outcome (Pavlovian) relationships to a review of accounts of this acquired behavior. In this section, we contrast the major variables that differentiate among models, and we refer back to our list of empirical variables (see section titled "Factors Influencing Acquired Stimulus Control of Behavior") to ask how the different families of models account for the roles of these variables. Citations are provided for the interested reader wishing to pursue the specifics of one or another model.

Units of Analysis

What Is a Stimulus?

Before we review specific theories, we must briefly consider how an organism perceives a stimulus and processes its representation. Different models of acquired behavior use different definitions of stimuli. In some models, the immediate perceptual field is composed of a vast number of microelements (e.g., we learn not about a tree, but each branch, twig, and leaf; Estes & Burke, 1953; McLaren & Mackintosh, 2000). In other models, the perceptual field at any given moment consists of a few integrated sources of receptor stimulation (e.g., the oak tree, the maple tree; Rescorla & Wagner, 1972; Gallistel & Gibbon, 2000). For yet other models, the perceptual field at any given moment is fully integrated and contains only one so-called configured stimulus, which consists of all that immediately impinges on the sensorium (the forest; Pearce, 1987). Although each approach offers its own distinct merits and demerits, they have all proven viable. Generally speaking, the larger the number of elements assumed, the more readily can behavior be explained post hoc, but the more difficult it is to make testable a priori predictions. By increasing the number of stimuli, each of which can have its own associative status, one is necessarily increasing the number of variables and often the number of parameters. Thus, it may be difficult to distinguish between models that are correct in the sense that they faithfully represent some fundamental relationship between acquired behavior and events in the environment, and models that succeed because there is enough flexibility in the model's parameters to account for virtually any result (i.e., curve fitting). Most models assume that subjects process representations of a small number of integrated stimuli at any one time. That is, the perceptual field might consist of a tone and a light and a tree, each represented as an integrated and inseparable whole.

Worthy of special note here is the McLaren and Mackintosh (2000) model with its elemental approach. This model not only addresses the fundamental phenomena of acquired behavior, but also accounts for perceptual learning, thereby providing an account of how and by what mechanism organisms weave the stimulation provided by many microelements into the perceptual fabric of lay usage. In other words, the model offers an explanation of how experience causes us to merge representations of branches, twigs, and leaves into a compound construct like a tree.

What Is a Response?

In Pavlovian learning, the conditioned response reflects the nature of the outcome, which is ordinarily a biologically significant unconditioned stimulus (but see Holland, 1977). However, this is not sufficient to predict the form of conditioned behavior. Although responding is often of the same form as the unconditioned response to the unconditioned stimulus (i.e., mimetic), it is sometimes in the opposite direction (i.e., compensatory). Examples of mimetic conditioned responding include eyelid conditioning, conditioned salivation, and conditioned release of endogenous endorphins with aversive stimulation as the unconditioned stimulus. Examples of compensatory conditioned responding include conditioned freezing with foot shock as the unconditioned stimulus, and conditioned opiate withdrawal symptoms with opiates as the unconditioned stimulus. The question of under what conditions will conditioned responding be compensatory as opposed to mimetic has yet to be satisfactorily answered. Eikelboom and Stewart (1982) argued that all conditioned responding is mimetic, and that compensatory instances simply reflect our misidentifying the unconditioned stimulus—that is, for unconditioned stimuli that impinge primarily on efferent neural pathways of the peripheral nervous system, the real reinforcer is the feedback to the central nervous system. Thus, what is often called the unconditioned response precedes a later behavior that constitutes the effective unconditioned response. This approach is stimulating, but encounters problems: Most unconditioned stimuli impinge on both afferent and efferent pathways, and there are complex feedback loops at various anatomical levels between these two pathways.

Conditioned responding is not just a reflection of past experience with a cue indicating a change in the probability of an outcome. Acquired behavior reflects not only the likelihood *that* a reinforcer will occur, but *when* and *where* the reinforcer will occur. This is evident in most learning situations (see "Response Topology and Timing"). For example, Clayton and Dickinson (1999) have reported that scrub jays, which cache food, remember not only what food items have been stored, but where and when they were stored. Additionally, there is evidence that subjects can integrate temporal and spatial information from different learning experiences to create spatiotemporal relationships between stimuli that were never paired in actual experience (e.g., Etienne et al., 1998; Savastano & Miller, 1998). Alternatively stated, in mediated learning, not only does the mediating stimulus become a surrogate for the occurrence of the outcome, it carries with it information concerning where and when the outcome will occur, as is evident in the phenomenon of goal tracking (e.g., Burns & Domjan, 1996).

What Mental Links Are Formed?

In the middle of the twentieth century, there was considerable controversy about whether cue-outcome, cue-response, or response-outcome relationships were learned (i.e., associations, links). The major strategies used to resolve this question were to either (a) use test conditions that differed from those of training by pitting one type of association against another (e.g., go towards a specific stimulus, or turn right); or (b) degrade one or another component after training (e.g., satiation or habituation of the outcome or extinction of the eliciting cue) and observe its effect on acquired behavior. The results of such studies indicated that subjects could readily learn all three types of associations, and ordinarily did to various degrees, depending on which allowed the easiest solution of the task facing the subject (reviewed by Kimble, 1961). That is, subjects are versatile in their information processing strategies, opportunistic, and ordinarily adept at using whichever combination of environmental relationships is most adaptive.

Although much stimulus control of behavior can be described in terms of simple associations among cues, responses, and outcomes, *occasion setting* (described under the section entitled "Objective Contingency") does not yield to such analyses. One view of how occasion setting works is that occasion setters serve to facilitate (or inhibit) the retrieval of associations (e.g., Holland, 1983b). Thus, they involve hierarchical associations; that is, they are associated with associations rather than with simple representations of stimuli or responses (cf. section entitled "Hierarchical Associations"). Such a view introduces a new type of learning, thereby adding complexity to the compendium of possible learned relationships. The leading alternative to this view of occasion setting is that occasion setters join into configural units with the stimuli that they are modulating (Schmajuk, Lamoureux, & Holland, 1998). This latter approach suffices to explain behavior in most occasion-setting situations, but to date has led to few novel testable predictions. Both approaches appear strained when used to account for transfer of modulation of an occasion setter from the association with which they were trained to another association. Such transfer is successful only if the transfer association itself was previously occasion set (Holland, 1989).

Acquisition-Focused (Associative) Models

All traditional models of acquired behavior have assumed that critical processing of information occurs exclusively when target stimuli occur—that is, at training, at test, or at both. The various contemporary models of acquired behavior can be divided into those that emphasize processing that occurs during training (hereafter called *acquisition-focused* models) and those that emphasize processing that occurs during testing (hereafter called *expression-focused* models). For each of these two families of models in their simplest forms, there are phenomena that are readily explained and other phenomena that are problematic. However, theorists have managed to explain most observed phenomena within acquired behavior in either framework (see R. R. Miller & Escobar, 2001) when allowed to modify models after new observations are reported (see section entitled "Where Have the Models Taken Us?").

The dominant tradition since Thorndike (1932) has been the acquisition-focused approach, which assumes that learning consists of the development of associations. In theoretical terms, each association is characterized by an *associative strength* or value, which is a kind of *summary statistic* representing the cumulative history of the subject with the associated events. Hull (1943) and Rescorla and Wagner (1972) provide two examples of acquisition-focused models, with the latter being the most influential model today (see R. R. Miller, Barnet, & Grahame, 1995, for a critical review of this model). Contemporary associative models today are perhaps best represented by that of Rescorla and Wagner, who proposed that time was divided into (training) trials and on each trial for which a cue of interest was present, there was a change in that cue's association to the outcome equal to the product of the saliences of the cue and outcome, times the difference between the outcome experienced and the expectation of the outcome based on all cues present on that trial. Notably, in acquisition-focused models, subjects are assumed not to recall specific experiences (i.e., training trials) at test; rather they have accessible only the current associative strength between events. Models within this family differ primarily in the rules used to calculate associative strength, and whether other summary statistics are also computed. For example, Pearce and Hall (1980) proposed that on each training trial, subjects not only update the associative strength between stimuli present on that trial, but also recalculate the so-called associability of each stimulus present on that trial. What all contemporary acquisition-focused models share is that new experience causes an updating of associative strength; hence, recent experience is expected to have a greater impact on behavior than otherwise equivalent earlier experience. The result is that these models are quite adept at accounting for those trial-order effects that can be viewed as recency effects; conversely, they are challenged by primacy effects (which, generally speaking, are far less frequent than recency effects; see chapters by Nairne, and by Roediger & Marsh in this volume). In the following section, we discuss some of the major variables that differentiate among the various acquisition-focused models. Specifics of individual models are not described here, but relevant citations are provided.

Addressing Critical Factors of Acquired Behavior

Stimulus Salience and Attention

Nearly all models (acquisition- and expression-focused) represent the saliencies of the cue and outcome through one conjoint (e.g., Bush & Mosteller, 1951) or two independent parameters (one for the cue and the other for the outcome, e.g., Rescorla & Wagner, 1972). A significant departure from this standard treatment of salience-attention is Pearce and Hall's (1980) model, which sharply differentiates between *salience,* which is a constant for each cue, and *associability,* which changes with experience and affects the rate (per trial) at which new information about the cue is encoded.

Predispositions: Genetic and Experiential. Behavioral predispositions, which depend on evolutionary history, specific prior experience, or both, are very difficult to capture in models meant to have broad generality across individuals within a species and across species. In fact, most models of acquired behavior (acquisition- and expression-focused) have ignored the issue of predispositions. However, those models that use a single parameter to describe the conjoint associability (growth parameter) for both the cue and outcome (as opposed to separate associabilities for the cue and outcome) can readily incorporate predispositions within this parameter. For example, in the well-known Garcia and Koelling (1966) demonstration of flavors joining into association with gastric distress more readily than with electric shock and audiovisual cues entering into association more readily with electric shock than with gastric distress, separate (constant) associabilities for the flavor, audiovisual cue, electric shock, and gastric distress cannot account for the observed predispositions. In contrast, this example of cue-to-consequence effects is readily accounted for by high conjoint associabilities for flavor–gastric distress and for audiovisual cues–electric shock, and low conjoint associabilities for flavor–electric shock and for audiovisual cues–gastric distress. However, to require a separate associability parameter for every possible cue-outcome dyad creates a vastly greater number of parameters than simply having a single parameter for each cue and each outcome with changes in behavior being in part a function of these two parameters (usually their product). Hence, we see here the recurring trade-off between oversimplifying (separate parameters for each cue and each outcome) and reality (a unique parameter for each cue-outcome dyad).

An alternative to models aiming for broad generality over tasks and species is to develop separate models for each task (e.g., foraging, mating, defense, shelter from the elements) and species, consistent with the view that the mind is modular (e.g., Garcia, Lasiter, Bermudez-Rattoni, & Deems, 1985). This approach has been championed by some researchers (Cosmides & Tooby, 1994), but faces challenges because the resulting models can become very complex and are limited in their potential to generate unambiguous testable predictions.

Spatiotemporal Contiguity (Similarity). Despite the empirical importance of contiguity as a determinant of acquired behavior, it is surprising that many associative models give short shrift to this critical variable. One common tactic has been to incorporate contiguity indirectly through changes in the predictive status of the context that on subsequent trials modulates the associative status of the cue (e.g., Mackintosh, 1975; Pearce & Hall, 1980; Rescorla & Wagner, 1972). The associative models that do squarely address the effects of temporal contiguity are real-time models (see Temporal Window of Analysis on p. 374; e.g., McLaren & Mackintosh, 2000; Sutton & Barto, 1981; Wagner; 1981).

Objective Contingency. The attenuation of acquired behavior through degradation of contingency has rarely been addressed as a unified problem. Most associative models of acquired behavior have accounted for extinction through either (a) weakening of the cue-outcome association (e.g., Rescorla & Wagner, 1972), or (b) the development of an inhibitory relationship between the cue and outcome that opposes the expression of the initial excitatory association (e.g., Hull, 1952; Pearce & Hall, 1980; Wagner, 1981). Attenuated responding due to partial reinforcement (i.e., nonreinforced cues interspersed among the cue-outcome pairings) is ordinarily explained through mechanisms similar to those used to account for extinction. The CS-preexposure effect has been explained both in terms of (a) a decrease in the associability (attention) to the cue as a result of nonreinforced pretraining exposure (e.g., Pearce & Hall, 1980); and (b) the development of a strong context-cue association that attenuates acquisition of the cue-outcome association (e.g., Wagner, 1981). The context specificity of the CS-preexposure effect seemingly lends support to this latter view, but at least one attentional approach can also accommodate it (Lubow, 1989). Notably, some prominent models simply fail to account for the CS-preexposure effect (e.g., Rescorla & Wagner, 1972).

Attenuated responding achieved by degrading contingency through unsignaled USs interspersed among the CS-US pairings and the US-preexposure effect are both explained by most associative models in terms of context-outcome associations, which then compete with the cue-outcome association. This is consistent with the context specificity of these effects (i.e., CS preexposure in one context retards subsequent stimulus control during cue-outcome pairings much less if the preexposure occurred outside of the training context). However, habituation to the outcome can also contribute to the effect in certain cases (Randich & LoLordo, 1979). Only a few associative models can account for reduced responding as a result of unsignaled outcome exposures after the termination of cue training (Dickinson & Burke, 1996; Van Hamme & Wasserman, 1994). However, confirmation of this prediction is only a limited success because the effect is difficult to obtain experimentally (see Denniston et al., 1996).

Cue and Outcome Durations. Models that parse time into trials usually account for the generally weaker stimulus control observed when cue duration is increased by changing the cue's associability-salience parameter (e.g., Rescorla & Wagner, 1972). This mechanism is largely post hoc. Changes in outcome duration might be addressed in the same manner, but they have received little attention because results of studies that have varied outcome duration are mixed, presumably because the motivational properties of the outcome changed with the duration of its presentation. A far better account of cue and outcome durations is provided by real-time associative models (McLaren & Mackintosh, 2000; Sutton & Barto, 1981; Wagner, 1981). According to these models, the associative strength of a cue changes continuously when it is present, depending on the activity of the outcome representation.

Reinforcement Theory. For the first 60 years of the twentieth century, various forms of reinforcement theory dominated the study of acquired behavior. The history of reinforcement theory can be traced from Thorndike's strong law of effect (1911; see section entitled "Instrumental Responding") through Hull's several models (e.g., 1952). The basic premise of reinforcement theory was that learning did not occur without a biologically significant reinforcer. Although this view was long dominant, as early as Tolman (1932) there were objections, often framed in terms of reinforcement's having more impact on the expression of knowledge than on the encoding of it. Although reinforcement during training may well accelerate the rate at which a cue-outcome relationship is learned, encoding of stimulus relationships does occur in the absence of reinforcement (unless one insists on making esoteric arguments that every stimulus about which organisms can learn has some minimal reinforcing value). This is readily demonstrated in Pavlovian situations by the sensory preconditioning effect (X→A training followed by A→US training SPC, with a subsequent test on X; Brogden, 1939) and in instrumental situations by latent learning effects in which the subject is not motivated when exposed to the learning relationships (Tolman & Honzik, 1930).

Conditioned Inhibition. The operations and consequent changes in behavior indicative of conditioned inhibition were described previously in this chapter. At the theoretical level, there are three different ways that acquisition-focused models have accounted for conditioned inhibition. Konorski (1948) suggested that inhibitory cues elevate the activation threshold of the US representation required for generation of a conditioned response. Later, Konorski (1967) proposed that inhibitory cues activated a no-US representation that countered activation of a US representation by excitatory associations to that stimulus or other stimuli present at test. Subsequently, Rescorla and Wagner (1972) proposed that conditioned inhibitors were cues with negative associative strength. According to this view, for a specific stimulus conditioned inhibition and excitation are mutually exclusive. This position has been widely adopted, perhaps in part because of its simplicity. However, considerable data (e.g., Matzel, Gladstein, et al., 1988) demonstrate that inhibition and excitation are not mutually exclusive (i.e., a given stimulus can pass tests for both excitation and inhibition without intervening training). Most acquisition-focused theories other than the Rescorla-Wagner model allow stimuli to possess both excitatory and inhibitory potential simultaneously (e.g., Pearce & Hall, 1980; Wagner, 1981).

Response Rules. Any model of acquired behavior must include both learning rules (to encode experience) and response rules (to express this encoded information). Acquisition-focused models, by their nature, generally have simple response rules and leave accounts of behavioral phenomena largely to differences in what is learned during training. For example, the Rescorla-Wagner (1972) model simply states that responding will be a monotonic function of associative strength. In practice, most researchers who have tried to test the model quantitatively have assumed that response magnitude is proportional to associative strength. The omission of a specific response rule in the Rescorla-Wagner model was not an oversight. They wanted to focus attention on acquisition processes and did not want researchers to be distracted by concerns that were not central to their model. However, the lack of a specific response rule leaves the Rescorla-Wagner model less of a quantitative model than is sometimes acknowledged.

Information Value. The view that cues acquire associative strength to the extent that they are informative about (i.e., predict) an outcome was first suggested by Egger and Miller (1963), who observed less responding to X after A→X→US trials than after equivalent training in the absence of A (X→US; i.e., serial overshadowing). Kamin (1968) developed the position, and it was later formalized in the Rescorla-Wagner (1972) model. Rescorla and Wagner's primary concern was competition between cues trained in compound (e.g., overshadowing and blocking). They argued that a cue would acquire associative strength with respect to an outcome to the extent that the outcome was not already predicted (i.e., was surprising). If another cue that was present during training of the target already predicted the outcome, there was no new information about the outcome to be provided by the cue, and hence no learning occurred. This position held sway for several decades, became central to many subsequent models of learning (e.g., Mackintosh, 1975; Pearce, 1987; Pearce & Hall, 1980; Wagner, 1981), and is still popular today. The informational hypothesis has been invoked to account for many observations, including the weak responding observed to cues presented simultaneously with an outcome (i.e., the simultaneous conditioning deficit). But it has been criticized for failing to distinguish between learning and expression of what was learned. Demonstrations of recovery (without further training) from competition between cues trained in compound challenge the informational hypothesis (e.g., reminder cues; Kasprow, Cacheiro, Balaz, & Miller, 1982; extinction of the competing cue; Kaufman & Bolles, 1981; and spontaneous recovery; J. S. Miller, McKinzie, Kraebel, & Spear, 1996). Similarly problematic is the observation that simultaneous presentations of a cue (X) and outcome appear to result in latent learning that can later be revealed by manipulations that create a forward relationship to a stimulus presented at test (e.g., X and US simultaneous, Y→X, test on Y; Matzel, Held et al., 1988). Thus, both cue competition and the simultaneous conditioning deficit appear to be, at least in part, deficits in expression of acquired knowledge rather than deficits in acquisition, contrary to the informational hypothesis. Certainly, predictive power (the focus of the informational hypothesis) is the primary *function* of learning, but the *process* underlying learning appears to be dissociated from this important function.

Element Emphasized

Contemporary associative models of acquired behavior were designed in large part to account for cue competition between cues trained in compound. Although there is considerable reason to think that cue competition is due to factors other than deficient acquisition (see "Multiple Cues With a Common Outcome"), most contemporary associative models have attempted to account for cue competition through either the outcome's or the cue's becoming less effective in supporting new learning. *Outcome-limited* associative models are ordinarily based on the informational hypothesis, and assume that the outcome becomes less effective in promoting new learning because it is already predicted by the competing cues that are presented concurrently with the target (e.g., Rescorla & Wagner, 1972). In contrast, *cue-limited* models assume that attention to (or associability of) the target cue decreases as a result of the concurrent presence of competing cues that are better predictors of the outcome than is the target (e.g., Pearce & Hall, 1980).

As both outcome- and cue-limited models have their advantages, some theorists have created hybrid models that employ both mechanisms (e.g., Mackintosh, 1975; Wagner, 1981). Obviously, such hybrid models tend to be more successful in providing post hoc accounts of phenomena. But because they incorporate multiple mechanisms, their a priori predictions tend to be dependent on specific parameters. Thus, in some cases their predictions can be ambiguous unless extensive preliminary work is done to determine the appropriate parameters for the specific situation.

Temporal Window of Analysis

A central feature of any model of acquired behavior is the frequency with which new perceptual input is integrated with previously acquired knowledge. Most acquisition-focused models of learning are *discrete-trial* models, which assume that acquired behavior on any trial depends on pretrial knowledge, and that the information provided on the trial is integrated with this knowledge immediately after the trial (i.e., after the occurrence or nonoccurrence of the outcome; e.g., Mackintosh, 1975; Pearce & Hall, 1980; Rescorla & Wagner, 1972). Such an assumption contrasts with *real-time* models, which assume that new information is integrated continuously with prior knowledge (e.g., McLaren & Mackintosh, 2000; Sutton & Barto, 1981; Wagner, 1981). In practice, most implementations of real-time models do not integrate information instantaneously, but rather do so very frequently (e.g., every 0.1 s) throughout each training session. A common weakness of all discrete-trial models (expression- as well as acquisition-focused) is that they cannot account for the powerful effects of cue-outcome temporal contiguity. Parsing an experimental session into trials in which cues and outcomes do or do not occur necessarily implies that temporal information is lost. In contrast, real-time models (expression- as well as acquisition-focused) can readily account for temporal contiguity effects. Real-time models are clearly more realistic, but discrete-trial models are more tractable, hence less ambiguous, and consequently stimulate more research.

Expression-Focused Models

In contrast to acquisition-focused models, in which summary statistics representing prior experience are assumed to be all that is retained, expression-focused models assume that a more or less veridical representation of past experience is retained, and that on each test trial subjects process all (or a sample) of this large store of information to determine their immediate behavior (R. R. Miller & Escobar, 2001). Hence, these models can be viewed more as response rules rather than rules for learning per se. This approach makes far greater demands upon memory, but perhaps there is little empirical reason to believe that limits on long-term memory capacity constrain how behavior is modified as a function of experience. In many respects, this difference between acquisition- and expression-focused models is analogous (perhaps homologous) to the distinction between prototype and exemplar models in category learning (e.g., chapter by Goldstone & Kersten in this volume; Ross & Makin, 1999). A consistent characteristic of contemporary expression-focused models of acquired behavior is that they all involve some sort of comparison between the likelihood of the outcome in the presence of the cue and the likelihood of the outcome in the absence of the cue.

Contingency Models

One of the earliest and best known contingency models is that of Rescorla (1968; also see Kelley, 1967). This discrete-trial model posits that subjects behave *as if* they record the frequencies of (a) cue-outcome pairings, (b) cues alone, (c) outcomes alone, and (d) trials with neither (see Figure 13.1). Based on these frequencies, conditioned responding reflects the difference between the conditional probability of the outcome given the presence of the cue, and the conditional probability of the outcome in the absence of the cue (i.e., the base rate of the outcome). Alternatively stated, stimulus control is assumed to be directly related to the change in outcome probability signaled by the cue. A conditioned excitor is a cue that signals an increase in the probability of the outcome, whereas a conditioned inhibitor is a cue that signals a decrease in that probability. This model is often quite successful in describing conditioned responding (and causal inference, which appears to follow much the same rules as Pavlovian conditioning; see Shanks, 1994, for a review). However, researchers have found that differentially weighting the four types of trial frequencies (with Type 1 receiving the greatest weight and Type 4 the least), provides an improved description of the data (e.g., Wasserman et al., 1993).

Rescorla's contingency (1968) model is elegant in its simplicity (e.g., contingency effects are explained as increases in trial types 2 and 3), but suffers from several problems. Unlike most associative models, it cannot account for (a) the powerful effects of trial order (e.g., recency effects) because it ignores the order in which trials occur; or (b) cue competition effects (e.g., blocking) because it addresses only single cue situations. For these reasons, Rescorla abandoned his contingency model in favor of the Rescorla-Wagner (1972) model. However, other researchers have addressed these deficits by proposing variants of Rescorla's contingency model. For example, Cheng and Novick (1992) developed a contingency model that, rather than incorporating all trials, includes selection rules for which trials contribute to the frequencies used to compute the conditional probabilities. Their *focal set* model succeeds in accounting for cue competition. Additionally, if trials are differentially weighted as a function of recency, contingency models are able to address trial-order effects (e.g., Maldonado, Cátena, Cándido, & García, 1999). Finally, although simple contingency models cannot explain cue-outcome contiguity effects, this problem is shared with most models (acquisition- as well as expression-focused) that decompose experience into discrete trials.

Comparator Models

Comparator models are similar to contingency models in emphasizing a comparison at the time of testing between the likelihood of the outcome in the presence and absence of the cue. However, these models are not based on computation of event frequencies. Currently, there are two types of comparator models. One focuses exclusively on comparisons of temporal relationships (e.g., rates of outcome occurrence), whereas the other assumes that comparisons occur on many dimensions, with time as only one of them.

The best-known timing model of acquired behavior is Gibbon and Balsam's (1981; also see Balsam, 1984) *scalar-expectancy theory* (SET). According to SET, conditioned responding is directly related to the average interval between outcomes during training (i.e., an inverse measure of the prediction of the outcome based on the context), and inversely related to the interval between cue onset and the outcome (i.e., a measure of the prediction of the outcome based on the cue. See chapter by Capaldi in this volume for models of how temporal information might be represented cognitively; here, our concern is the use of temporal information in modulating behavior). Like all timing models (in contrast to the other expression-focused models), SET is highly successful in explaining cue-outcome contiguity effects and also does well in predicting the effects of contingency degradation that occur when the outcome is presented in the absence of the cue. Although the model accounts for the CS-preexposure effect if context exposure is held constant, it fails to explain extinction, because latencies to the outcome are assumed to be updated only when an outcome occurs. Scalar-expectancy theory also fails to account for stimulus competition-interference effects.

A recent expression-focused timing model proposed by Gallistel and Gibbon (2000), called *rate-expectancy theory* (RET), incorporates many of the principles of SET, but emphasizes rates of outcome occurrence (in the presence and absence of the cue), rather than latencies between outcomes. This inversion from waiting times (i.e., latencies) to rates allows the model to account for stimulus competition-interference effects because rates of reinforcement associated with different cues are assumed to summate; in contrast to SET, RET considers outcome rates attributed to nontarget discrete cues as well as background cues. Moreover, reinforcement rates are assumed to change continuously with exposure to the cue or to the background stimuli in the absence of as well as with the occurrence of the outcome, thereby accounting for extinction as well as the CS-preexposure effect and partial reinforcement.

A comparator model that does not focus exclusively on timing is the *comparator hypothesis* of R. R. Miller and Matzel (1988; also see Denniston, Savastano, & Miller, 2001). In this model, responding is also assumed to be directly related to the degree to which the target cue predicts the outcome and inversely related to the degree to which background (discrete and contextual) cues present *during training* of the cue predict the outcome. The down-modulating effect of the background cues on acquired responding depends on the similarity of the outcome (in all aspects, including temporal and spatial attributes) that these cues predict relative to the outcome that the target cue predicts. Thus, this model (along with contingency theory) brings to acquired responding the principle of relativity that is seen in many other subfields concerned with information processing by organisms (e.g., Fechner's law, the marginal value theorem of economics, contrast effects in motivational theory, the matching law of behavioral choice as discussed in this chapter's section entitled "Instrumental Responding"). The timing expression-focused models also emphasize relativity (so-called time-scale invariance), but only in the temporal domain. The comparator hypothesis accounts for both contingency degradation and cue competition effects through links between the cue and background stimuli (discrete and contextual) and links between these background stimuli and the outcome.

Conditioned Inhibition. In all of the comparator models, a conditioned inhibitor is viewed as a stimulus that signals a reduction in the rate or probability of reinforcement relative to the baseline occurrence of the reinforcer *during training* in the absence of the cue. This position avoids the theoretical quandary faced by the associative views of conditioned inhibition concerning the representation of (a) no-outcome, or (b) a below-zero expectation of the outcome.

Acquisition Rules. As previously stated (Acquisition-Focused (Associative) Models), models of acquired behavior must include both acquisition rules and response rules. In contrast to acquisition-focused models, which generally have simple response rules and leave accounts of behavioral differences largely to differences in what is encoded during training, expression-focused models have simple rules for acquisition and rely on response rules for an account of most behavioral differences. Thus, the attenuated responding to a target cue observed, for example, in a blocking or contingency-degrading treatment is assumed to arise not from a failure to encode the target cue-outcome pairings, but rather from a failure to express this information in behavior.

Accounts of Retrospective Revaluation

In the section entitled "Retrospective Revaluation," we described retroactive revaluation of response potential, in which, after training with a target cue in the presence of other stimuli (discrete or contextual), treatment of the companion stimuli (i.e., presentation of a companion stimulus with or without the outcome) can alter responding to the target cue. Examples include such mediational phenomena as sensory preconditioning—in which the mediating stimulus is paired with the outcome; see section entitled "Second-Order Conditioning and Sensory Preconditioning"—and recovery from overshadowing as a result of extinguishing the overshadowing cue (e.g., Dickinson & Charnock, 1985; Kaufman & Bolles, 1981; Matzel et al., 1985).

Expression-focused models that accommodate multiple cues (e.g., the comparator hypothesis and RET) generally have no difficulty accounting for retrospective revaluation because new experience with a companion stimulus changes its predictive value, and responding to the cue is usually assumed to be inversely related to the response potential of companion stimuli. Thus, a retrospective change in a cue's response potential does not represent new learning about the absent cue, but rather new learning concerning the companion stimuli.

In contrast, empirical retrospective revaluation is problematic to most traditional acquisition-focused models. This is because these models assume that responding reflects the associative status of the target cue, which is generally assumed not to change during retrospective revaluation trials (on which the cue is absent). But given growing evidence of empirical retrospective revaluation, several researchers have proposed models that allow changes in the associative status of a cue when it is absent. One of the first of these was a revision of the Rescorla-Wagner (1972) model by Van Hamme and Wasserman (1994), which allows changes in the associative strength of an absent target cue, provided that some associate of the target cue was present. This simple modification successfully accounts for most instances of retrospective revaluation, but otherwise has the same failings and successes as the Rescorla-Wagner model (see R. R. Miller et al., 1995). An alternative associative approach to retrospective revaluation is provided by Dickinson and Burke (1996), who modified Wagner's (1981) SOP model to allow new learning about absent stimuli. As might be expected, the Dickinson and Burke model has many of the same successes and problems as Wagner's model (see section entitled "Where Have the Models Taken Us?"). A notable problem for these associative accounts of retrospective revaluation is that other researchers have attempted to explain mediated learning (e.g., sensory-preconditioning and mediated extinction) with similar models, except that absent cues have an associability of opposite sign than that assumed by Van Hamme and Wasserman and by Dickinson and Burke (Hall, 1996; Holland, 1981, 1983b). Without a principled rule for deciding when mediation will be positive (e.g., second-order conditioning) as opposed to negative (e.g., recovery from overshadowing achieved through extinction of the overshadowing cue), there seems to be an arbitrariness to this approach. In contrast, the expression-focused models unambiguously predict negative mediation (and fail to account for positive mediation when it is observed). That is, a change in the response potential of a companion stimulus is always expected to be inversely related to the resulting change in the response potential of the target cue.

Where Have the Models Taken Us?

As previously noted (in our discussion of acquisition-focused models), theorists have been able to develop models of acquired behavior that can potentially account for many observations after the fact. Any *specific* model can, in principle, be refuted, but classes of models, such as the families of acquisition-focused or expression-focused models, allow nearly unlimited possibilities for future models within that family (R. R. Miller & Escobar, 2001). If the goal is to determine precisely how the mind processes information at the psychological level, contemporary theories of learning have not been successful because viable post hoc alternatives are often possible and in retrospect may appear as plausible as the a priori model that inspired the research.

Nevertheless, models have succeeded in stimulating experiments that identify new empirical relationships. The models most successful in this respect are often among the least successful in actually accounting for behavioral change. This is because a model stimulates research only to the extent that it makes unambiguous predictions. Models with many parameters and variables (e.g., McLaren & Mackintosh, 2000; Wagner, 1981) can be tuned post hoc to account for almost any observation; hence, few attempts are made to test such models, however plausible they might appear. In contrast, oversimplified models such as Rescorla and Wagner (1972) make unambiguous predictions that can be tested, with the result that the model is often refuted. For the foreseeable future, a dialectical path towards theory development, in which relatively simple models are used to generate predictions which, when refuted, lead to the development of relatively complex models that are more difficult to test, is likely to persist.

INSTRUMENTAL RESPONDING

This chapter has so far focused almost exclusively on Pavlovian (i.e., stimulus-outcome) conditioning. By definition, in a Pavlovian situation the contingency between a subject's responding and an outcome is zero, but in many situations outcomes are in fact dependent upon specific responses. That is, behavior is sensitive to the contingency between a response and an outcome. It is obvious that such sensitivity is often adaptive. For example, a rat will quickly learn to press a lever for food pellets; conversely, a child who touches a hot stove will rarely do so again. A situation in which an organism's behavior changes after exposure to a response-outcome contingency is termed *instrumental conditioning*. After reviewing Thorndike's early work on the law of effect and some basic definitions, this section considers research on instrumental conditioning from three different perspectives: associationistic, functional, and ecological-economic.

Law of Effect: What Is Learned?

Although the idea that rewards and punishments control behavior dates back to antiquity, the modern scientific study of instrumental conditioning was begun by Thorndike (1898). He placed hungry cats in so-called puzzle boxes in which the animal had to perform a response (e.g., pulling a loop of cord) in order to open a door and gain access to food. Over repeated trials, he found that the time necessary to escape gradually decreased. To explain this result, Thorndike (1911) proposed the *law of effect,* which states that stimulus-response (S-R) connections are strengthened by a "satisfying consequence" that follows the response. Thus, the pairing of the cats' escape response with food increased the likelihood that the cats would subsequently perform the response. Aversive consequences have symmetric but opposite effects; S-R connections would be weakened if an "annoying consequence" (e.g., shock) followed a response. The law of effect represents the most important *empirical* generalization of instrumental conditioning, but its theoretical significance remains in dispute. The three perspectives considered in this section (associationistic, functional, and ecological-economic) provide different interpretations of the law of effect.

The Three-Term Contingency

Unlike the contingencies used in Pavlovian conditioning, which depend on two stimuli (the cue and outcome) scheduled independently of the subjects' behavior, the contingencies considered here depend on the occurrence of a response. Such contingencies are called *instrumental* (i.e., the subjects' behavior is instrumental in producing the outcome) or *operant* (i.e., the subjects' behavior operates on the environment). Because different stimuli can be used to signal particular contingencies (i.e., illumination of a light above a lever signals that a rat's pressing the lever will result in the delivery of food), *the three-term contingency* has been proposed as the fundamental unit of instrumental behavior: In the presence of a particular stimulus (*discriminative stimulus*), a response produces an outcome (*reinforcer;* Skinner, 1969).

In an instrumental situation, the environmentally imposed reinforcement contingency defines a response and, not surprisingly, the frequency of that response ordinarily changes in a functional manner. Instrumental behavior can sometimes be dysfunctional (i.e., a different response is observed than that defined by the functional contingency), but this is the exception rather than the rule. When dysfunctional acquired behavior is observed, it usually reflects a prevailing contingency that is unusual to the subject's ecological niche or contrary to its prior experience. Two good examples of dysfunctional responding are vicious circle behavior (Gwinn, 1949) and negative automaintenance (D. R. Williams & Williams, 1969). In the former case, a previously learned response obstructs the subject from coming in contact with a newly introduced contingency, and in the latter case the reinforcement contingency (reward omission) imposed by the experiment is diametrically opposed by a species-specific predisposition that is highly functional in the natural habitat.

Such dysfunctional behaviors may provide models of select instances of human psychopathology.

Instrumental Contingencies and Schedules of Reinforcement

There are four basic types of instrumental contingencies, depending on whether the response either produces or eliminates the outcome and whether the outcome is of positive or negative hedonic value. *Positive reinforcement* (i.e., reward) is a contingency in which responding produces an outcome with the result that there is an increase in response frequency—for example, when a rat's lever press results in food presentation, or a student's studying before an exam produces an *A* grade. *Punishment* is a contingency in which responding results in the occurrence of an aversive outcome with the result that there is a decrease in response frequency—for example, when a child is scolded for reaching into the cookie jar or a rat's lever press produces foot shock. *Omission* (or positive punishment) describes a situation in which responding cancels or prevents the occurrence of a positive outcome with the result that there is a decrease in response frequency. Finally, *escape* or *avoidance conditioning* (also called *negative reinforcement*) is a contingency in which responding leads to the termination of an ongoing or prevention of an expected aversive stimulus with the result that there is an increase in response frequency—for example, if a rat's lever presses cancel a scheduled shock. Both positive and negative reinforcement contingencies by definition result in increased responding, whereas omission and punishment-avoidance contingencies by definition lead to decreased responding. For various reasons, including obvious ethical concerns, it is desirable whenever possible to use alternatives to punishment for behavior modification. For this reason and practical considerations, there has been an increasing emphasis in the basic and applied research literature on positive reinforcement; research on punishment and aversive conditioning is not discussed here (for reviews, see Ayres, 1998; Dinsmoor, 1998).

A reinforcement schedule is a rule for determining whether a particular response by a subject will be reinforced (Ferster & Skinner, 1957). There are two criteria that have been widely studied: the number of responses emitted since the last reinforced response (ratio schedules), and the time since the last reinforced response (interval schedules). Use of these criteria provide for four basic schedules of reinforcement, which depend on whether the contingency is fixed or variable: fixed interval (FI), fixed ratio (FR), variable interval (VI), and variable ratio (VR). Under an FI x schedule, the first response after x seconds have elapsed since the last reinforcement is reinforced. After reinforcement there is typically a pause in responding, which then begins, increasing slowly, and about two-thirds of the way through the interval increases to a high rate (Schneider, 1969). The temporal control evidenced by FI performance has led to extensive use of these schedules in research on timing (e.g., the *peak procedure;* Roberts, 1981). With an FR x schedule, the xth response is reinforced. After a postreinforcement pause, responding begins and generally continues at a high rate until reinforcement. When x is large enough, responding may cease entirely with FR schedules (*ratio strain;* Ferster & Skinner, 1957). Under a VI x schedule, the first response after y seconds have elapsed is reinforced, where y is a value sampled from a distribution that has an average of x seconds. Typically, VI schedules generate steady, moderate rates of responding (Catania & Reynolds, 1968). When a VR x schedule is arranged, the yth response is reinforced, where y is a value sampled from a distribution with an arithmetic mean of x. Variable ratio schedules maintain the highest overall rates of responding of these four common schedule types, even when rates of reinforcement are equated (e.g., Baum, 1993).

Reinforcement schedules have been a major focus of research in instrumental conditioning (for review, see Zeiler, 1984). Representative questions include why VR schedules maintain higher response rates than comparable VI schedules (the answer seems to be that short interresponse times are reinforced under VR schedules; Cole, 1999), and whether schedule effects are best understood in terms of momentary changes in reinforcement probability or of the overall relationship between rates of responding and reinforcement (i.e., molecular vs. molar level of analysis; Baum, 1973). In addition, because of the stable, reliable behaviors they produce, reinforcement schedules have been widely adopted for use in related disciplines as baseline controls (e.g., behavioral pharmacology, behavioral neuroscience).

Comparing Pavlovian and Instrumental Conditioning

Many of the phenomena identified in Pavlovian conditioning have instrumental counterparts. For example, the basic relations of acquisition as a result of response-outcome pairings and extinction as a result of nonreinforcement of the response, as well as spontaneous recovery from extinction, are found in instrumental conditioning (see Dickinson, 1980; R. R. Miller & Balaz, 1981, for more detailed comparisons). Blocking and overshadowing may be obtained for instrumental responses (St. Claire-Smith, 1979; B. A. Williams, 1982). Stimulus generalization and discrimination characterize instrumental conditioning (Guttman & Kalish, 1956). Temporal contiguity is important for instrumental conditioning; response rate decreases rapidly as the response-reinforcer delay increases, so long as an explicit stimulus does not fill the interval (e.g., B. A. Williams, 1976). If a stimulus does fill the interval, it may function as a conditioned reinforcer and acquire reinforcing power in its own right (e.g., Schaal & Branch, 1988; although under select conditions it can attenuate [i.e., overshadow] the response, e.g., Pearce & Hall, 1978). This provides a parallel to second-order Pavlovian conditioning. *Latent learning,* in which learning occurs in the absence of explicit reinforcement (Tolman & Honzik, 1930), is analogous to sensory preconditioning. *Learned helplessness,* in which a subject first exposed to inescapable shock later fails to learn an escape response (Maier & Seligman, 1976), provides a parallel to learned irrelevance. Instrumental conditioning varies directly with the response-outcome contingency (e.g., Hammond, 1980). Cue-response-consequence specificity (Foree & LoLordo, 1975) is similar to cue-to-consequence predispositions in Pavlovian conditioning (see Predispositions on p. 371). Overall, the number of parallels between Pavlovian and instrumental conditioning encourages the view that an organism's response can function like a stimulus, and that learning fundamentally concerns the development of associative links between mental representations of events (responses and stimuli).

Associationistic Analyses of Instrumental Conditioning

Researchers have attempted to determine what kind of associations are formed in instrumental conditioning situations. From an associationistic perspective, the law of effect implies that stimulus-response (S-R) associations are all that is learned. However, this view was challenged by Tolman (1932), who argued that S-R associations were insufficient to account for instrumental conditioning. He advocated a more cognitive approach in which the organism was assumed to form expectancies about the relation between the response and outcome. Contemporary research has confirmed and elaborated Tolman's claim, showing that in addition to S-R associations, three other types of associations are formed in instrumental conditioning: response-outcome, stimulus-outcome, and hierarchical associations.

Response-Outcome Associations

Several studies using outcome devaluation procedures have found evidence for response-outcome associations. For example, Adams and Dickinson (1981) trained rats to press a lever for one of two outcomes (food or sugar pellets, counterbalanced across groups), while the other outcome was delivered independently of responding (i.e., noncontingent). After responding had been acquired, they devalued one of the outcomes by pairing it with induced gastric distress. In a subsequent extinction test, rats for which the response-contingent outcome had been devalued responded less compared with rats for which the noncontingent outcome had been devalued. Because the outcomes were never presented during testing, Adams and Dickinson argued that the difference in responding must have been mediated by learning of the response-outcome contingency. However, substantial residual responding was still observed for the groups with the devalued contingent outcome, leading Dickinson (1994, p. 52) to conclude that instrumental training "established lever pressing partly as a goal-directed action, mediated by knowledge of the instrumental relation, and partly as an S-R habit impervious to outcome devaluation."

Stimulus-Outcome Associations

Evidence for (Pavlovian) stimulus-outcome (S-O) associations has been obtained in studies that have shown greater transfer of stimulus control to a new response that has been trained with the same outcome than with a different outcome. Colwill and Rescorla (1988) trained rats to make a common response (nose poking) in the presence of two different stimuli (light and noise). Nose poking produced different outcomes, depending on the stimulus (food pellets or sucrose solution, counterbalanced across groups). The rats were then trained to make two new responses (lever press and chain pull), each of which produced either food or sucrose. Finally, a transfer test was conducted in which rats could choose between lever pressing and chain pulling in the presence of the light and noise stimuli. Colwill and Rescorla found that the response that led to the outcome signaled by the stimulus in the original training with the nose-poke response occurred more frequently during test. Thus, rats were more likely to make whichever response led to the outcome that had been experienced in the presence of the stimulus during the nose-poke training, which suggests they had formed stimulus-outcome associations during that training.

Hierarchical Associations

In addition to binary associations involving the stimulus, response, and outcome, there is evidence that organisms encode a hierarchical association involving all three elements. Rescorla (1991) trained rats to make two responses (lever press and chain pull) for two different outcomes (food and sucrose) in the presence of a stimulus (light or noise). Rats were also trained with the opposite response-outcome relations in the presence of a different stimulus. Subsequently, one of the outcomes was devalued by pairing with LiCl. The rats were then given a test in which they could perform either response in the presence of each of the stimuli. The result was that responding was selectively suppressed; the response that led to the devalued outcome in the presence of the particular stimulus occurred less frequently. This result cannot be explained in terms of binary associations because individual stimuli and responses were paired equally often with both outcomes. It suggests that the rats had formed hierarchical associations, which encoded each three-term contingency [i.e., S − (R-O)]. Thus, the role of instrumental discriminative stimuli may be similar to occasion setters in Pavlovian conditioning (Davidson, Aparicio, & Rescorla, 1988).

Incentive Learning

Associations between stimuli, responses, and outcomes may comprise part of what is learned in instrumental conditioning, but clearly the organism must also be motivated to perform the response. Although motivation was an important topic for the neobehaviorists of the 1930s and 1940s (e.g., Hull, 1943), the shift towards more cognitively oriented explanations of behavior in the 1960s led to a relative neglect of motivation. More recently, however, Dickinson and colleagues (see Dickinson & Balleine, 1994, for review) have provided evidence that in some circumstances, subjects must learn the incentive properties of outcomes in instrumental conditioning.

For example, Balleine (1992) trained sated rats to press a lever for a novel food item. Half of the rats were later exposed to the novel food while hungry. Subsequently, an extinction test was conducted in which half of the rats were hungry (thus generating four groups, depending on whether the rats had been preexposed to the novel food while hungry, and whether they were hungry during the extinction test). The results were that the rats given preexposure to the novel food item while hungry and tested in a deprived state responded at the highest rate during the extinction test. This suggests that exposure to the novel food while in the deprived state contributed to that food's serving as an effective reinforcer. However, Dickinson, Balleine, Watt, Gonzalez, and Boakes (1995) found that the magnitude of the incentive learning effect diminished when subjects received extended instrumental training prior to test. Thus, motivational control of behavior may change, depending on experience with the instrumental contingency.

In summary, efforts to elucidate the nature of associative structures underlying instrumental conditioning have found evidence for all the possible binary associations (e.g., stimulus-response, response-outcome, and stimulus-outcome), as well as for a hierarchical association involving all three elements (stimulus: response-outcome). Additionally, in some situations, whether an outcome has incentive value is apparently learned. From this perspective, it seems reasonable to assume that these associations are acquired in the same fashion as stimulus-outcome associations in Pavlovian conditioning. In this view, instrumental conditioning may be considered an elaboration of fundamental associative processes.

Functional Analyses of Instrumental Conditioning

A second approach to instrumental conditioning is derived from Skinner's (1938) interpretation of the law of effect. Rather than construe the law literally in terms of S-R connections, Skinner interpreted the law of effect to mean only that *response strength* increases with reinforcement and decreases with punishment. Exactly how response strength could be measured thus became a major concern. Skinner (1938) developed an apparatus (i.e., experimental chambers called Skinner boxes and cumulative recorders) that allowed the passage of time as well as lever presses and reward deliveries to be recorded. This allowed a shift in the dependent variable from the probability of a response's occurring on a particular trial to the rate of that response over a sustained period of time. Such procedures are sometimes called *free-operant* (as opposed to discrete-trial). The ability to study intensively the behavior of individual organisms has led researchers in the Skinnerian tradition to emphasize molar rather than molecular measures of responding (i.e., response rate aggregated over several sessions), to examine responding at stability (i.e., asymptote) rather than during acquisition, and to use a relatively small number of subjects in their research designs (Sidman, 1960). This research tradition, often called the *experimental analysis of behavior,* has led to an emphasis on various formal arrangements for instrumental conditioning—for example, reinforcement schedules and the export of technologies for effective behavior modification (e.g., Sulzer-Azaroff & Mayer, 1991).

Choice and the Matching Law

Researchers have attempted to quantify the law of effect by articulating the functional relationships between behavior (measured as response rate) and parameters of reinforcement (specifically, the rate, magnitude, delay, and probability of reinforcement). The goal has been to obtain a quantitative expression that summarizes these relationships and that is broadly applicable to a range of situations. Interestingly, this pursuit has been inspired by research on choice—situations in which more than one reinforced instrumental response is available at the same time.

Four experimental procedures have figured prominently in research on the quantitative determiners of instrumental responding. In the *single-schedule procedure,* the subject may make a specific response that produces a reinforcer according to a given schedule. In *concurrent schedules,* two or more schedules are available simultaneously and the subject is free to allocate its behavior across the alternatives. In *multiple schedules,* access to different reinforcement schedules occurs successively, with each schedule signaled by a distinctive (discriminative) stimulus. Finally, in the *concurrent-chains procedure* (and a discrete-trial variant, the *adjusting-delay procedure*), subjects choose between two discriminative stimuli that are correlated with different reinforcement schedules.

A seminal study by Herrnstein (1961) was the first parametric investigation of concurrent schedules. He arranged two VI schedules in a Skinner box for pigeons, each schedule associated with a separate manipulandum (i.e., plastic pecking key). Reinforcement was a brief period (3 s) of access to grain. Pigeons were given extensive training (often 30 or more sessions) with a given pair of schedules (e.g., VI 1-min, VI 3-min schedules) until response allocation was stable. The schedules were then changed across a number of experimental conditions, such that the relative rate of reinforcement provided by responding to the left and right keys was varied while keeping constant the overall programmed reinforcement rate (40/hr). Herrnstein found that the relative rate of responding to each key was approximately equal to the relative rate of reinforcement associated with each key. His data, shown in Figure 13.2, demonstrate what has come to be known as the *matching law:*

$$\frac{B_L}{B_R} = \frac{R_L}{R_R} \text{ or alternatively stated } \frac{B_L}{B_L + B_R} = \frac{R_L}{R_L + R_R} \tag{13.1}$$

In Equation 13.1, B_L and B_R are the number of responses made to the left and right keys, and R_L and R_R are the reinforcements earned by responding at those keys. Although Equation 13.1 might appear tautological, it is important to note that the matching relation was not forced in Herrnstein's study, because responses substantially outnumbered reinforcers. Subsequent empirical support for the matching law has been obtained with a variety of different species, responses, and reinforcers, and thus it may represent a general principle of choice (for reviews, see Davison & McCarthy, 1988; B. A. Williams, 1988, 1994a). The matching law seems

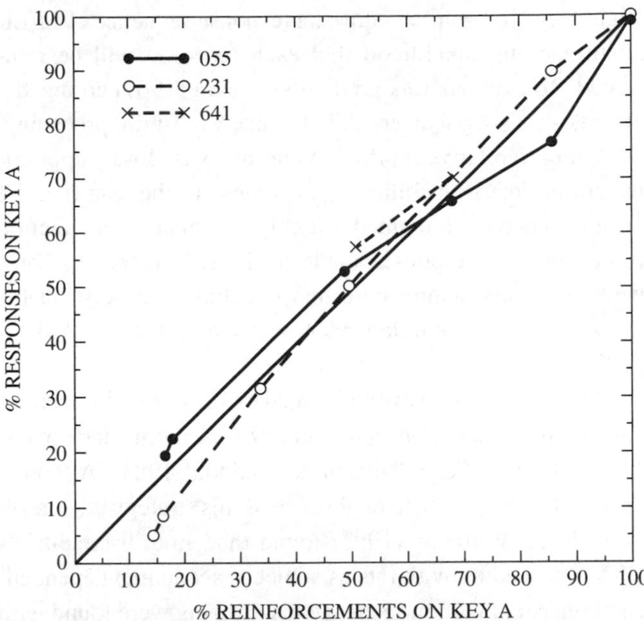

Figure 13.2 The proportion of responses made to one of two keys as a function of the reinforcers obtained on that key, for three pigeons responding on concurrent VI, VI schedules. The diagonal line indicates perfect matching (Equation 13.1). *Source:* From Herrnstein (1961). Copyright 1961 by the Society for the Experimental Analysis of Behavior, Inc.

to embody a relativistic law of effect: The relative strength of an instrumental response depends on the relative rate of reinforcement maintaining it, which parallels the relativism evident in most expression-focused models of Pavlovian conditioning (see this chapter's section entitled, "Expression-Focused Models") and probability matching in the decision-making literature.

Why Does Matching Occur?

Many investigators have accepted the matching relation as an empirical rule for choice under concurrent VI-VI schedules. An important goal, then, is to discover exactly why matching should occur. Because an answer to this question might provide insight into the fundamental behavioral processes determining choice, testing different theories of matching has been a vigorous topic of research over the past 35 years.

Shimp (1966, 1969) showed that if subjects always responded to the alternative with the immediate higher probability of reinforcement, then matching would be obtained. According to his theory, called *momentary maximizing,* responses should show a definite sequential dependence. The reason is that both schedules run concurrently, so eventually a response to the leaner alternative is more likely to be reinforced. For example, with concurrent Left Key VI 1-min,

Right Key VI 3-min schedules, a response sequence of LLLR maximizes the likelihood that each response will be reinforced. To evaluate this prediction, Nevin (1969) arranged a discrete-trials concurrent VI 1-min, VI 3-min procedure. Matching to relative reinforcement rate was closely approximated, but the probability of a response to the lean (i.e., VI 3-min) schedule remained roughly constant as a function of consecutive responses made to the rich schedule. Thus, Nevin's results demonstrate that matching can occur in the absence of sequential dependency (see also Jones & Moore, 1999).

Other studies, however, obtained evidence of a local structure in time allocation consistent with a momentary maximizing strategy (e.g., Hinson & Staddon, 1983). Although reasons for the presence or absence of this strategy are not yet clear, B. A. Williams (1992) found that, in a discrete-trials VI-VR procedure with rats as subjects, sequential dependencies consistent with momentary maximizing were found with short intertrial intervals (ITIs), but data that approximated matching without sequential dependencies were found with longer ITIs. The implication seems to be that organisms use a maximizing strategy if possible, depending on the temporal characteristics of the procedure; otherwise matching is obtained.

A second explanation for matching in concurrent schedules was offered by Rachlin, Green, Kagel, and Battalio (1976). They proposed that matching was a by-product of overall reinforcement rate maximization within a session. According to Rachlin et al., organisms are sensitive to the reinforcement obtained from both alternatives, and they distribute their responding so as to obtain the maximum overall reinforcement rate. This proposal is called *molar maximizing* because it assumes that matching is determined by an adaptive process that yields the outcome with the overall greatest utility for the organism (see section in this chapter entitled "Behavioral Economics"). In support of their view, Rachlin et al. presented computer simulations demonstrating that the behavior allocation yielding maximum overall reinforcement rate coincided with matching for concurrent VI schedules (cf. Heyman & Luce, 1979).

A large number of studies have evaluated predictions of matching versus molar maximizing. Several studies have arranged concurrent VI-VR schedules (e.g., Herrnstein & Heyman, 1979). To optimize overall reinforcement rate on concurrent VI-VR, subjects should spend most of their time responding on the VR schedule, occasionally switching over to the VI to obtain reinforcement. This implies that subjects should show a strong bias towards the VR schedule. However, such a bias has typically not been found. Instead, Herrnstein and Heyman (1979) reported that their subjects approximately matched without maximizing. Similar data with humans were reported by Savastano and Fantino (1994). Proponents of molar maximizing (e.g., Rachlin, Battalio, Kagel, & Green, 1981) have countered that Herrnstein and Heyman's results can be explained in terms of the value of *leisure time.* When certain assumptions are made about the value of leisure and temporal discounting of delayed reinforcers, it may be difficult, if not impossible, to determine whether matching is fundamental or a by-product of imperfect maximizing (Rachlin, Green, & Tormey, 1988).

A recent experiment by Heyman and Tanz (1995) shows that under appropriate conditions, both matching and molar maximizing may characterize choice. In their experiment, pigeons were exposed to a concurrent-schedules procedure in which the overall rate of reinforcement depended on the response allocation in the recent past (last 360 responses). Heyman and Tanz found that when no stimuli were differentially correlated with overall reinforcement rates, the pigeons approximately matched rather than maximized. However, when the color of the chamber house-light signaled when response allocation was increasing the reinforcement rate, the pigeons maximized, deviating from matching apparently without limit. In other words, when provided with an analogue instructional cue, the pigeons maximized. Heyman and Tanz's results strongly suggest that organisms maximize when they are able to do so, but match when they are not, implying that maximizing and matching are complementary rather than contradictory accounts of choice.

A third theory of matching, *melioration,* was proposed by Herrnstein and Vaughan (1980). The basic idea of melioration (meaning *to make better*) is that organisms switch their preference to whichever alternative provides the higher local reinforcement rate (i.e., the number of reinforcers earned divided by the time spent responding at the alternative). Because the local reinforcement rates change depending on how much time is allocated to the alternatives, matching is eventually obtained when the local reinforcement rates are equal. Although the time window over which local reinforcement rates are determined is left unspecified, it is understood to be a relatively brief duration (e.g., 4 min; Vaughan, 1981). Thus, melioration occupies essentially an intermediate level between momentary and molar maximizing in terms of the time scale over which the variable determining choice is calculated. Applications of melioration to human decision making have been particularly fruitful. For example, Herrnstein and Prelec (1992) proposed a model for drug addiction based on melioration, which has been elaborated by Heyman (1996) and Rachlin (1997).

Several studies have attempted to test the prediction of melioration that local reinforcement rates determine preference by arranging two pairs of concurrent schedules within each session and then testing preference for stimuli between pairs from different concurrent schedules in probe tests. For example, B. A. Williams and Royalty (1989) conducted several experiments in which probes compared stimuli correlated with different local and overall reinforcement rates. However, they found that the overall, not local, reinforcement rates correlated with stimuli-determined preference in the probes. In a similar study, Belke (1992) arranged a procedure with VI 20-s, VI 40-s schedules in one component and VI 40-s, VI 80-s schedules in the other component. After baseline training, pigeons' preference approximately matched relative reinforcement rate in both components (i.e., a 2 : 1 ratio). Belke then presented the two VI 40-s stimuli together in occasional choice probes. The pigeons demonstrated a strong (4 : 1) preference for the VI 40-s stimulus paired with the VI 80-s. This result is contrary to the predictions of melioration, because the VI 40-s paired with VI 20-s is correlated with a greater local reinforcement rate (see also Gibbon, 1995).

Gallistel and Gibbon (2000) have argued that the results of Belke (1992) pose a serious challenge not only to melioration, but also to the matching law as empirical support for the law of effect. They described a model for instrumental choice that was based on Gibbon (1995; see also Mark & Gallistel, 1994). According to their model, pigeons learn the interreinforcement intervals for responding on each alternative and store these intervals in memory. Decisions to switch from one alternative to another are made by a sample-and-comparison process that operates on the stored intervals. They showed that their model could predict Belke's (1992) and Gibbon's (1995) probe results. However, these data may not be decisive evidence against melioration, or indeed against any theory of matching. According to Gallistel and Gibbon, when separately trained stimuli are paired in choice probes, the same changeover patterns that were established in baseline training to particular stimuli are carried over. If carryover of baseline can account for probe preference, then the probes provide no new information beyond baseline responding. The implication is that any theory that can account for matching in baseline can potentially explain the probe results of Belke (1992) and Gibbon (1995).

Extensions of the Matching Law

Generalized Matching. Since Herrnstein's (1961) original study, the matching law has been extended in several ways to provide a quantitative framework for describing data from various procedures. Baum (1974) noted that some deviations from the strict equality of response and reinforcement ratios required by the matching law could be described by Equation 13.2, a power function generalization of Equation 13.1:

$$\frac{B_L}{B_R} = b\left(\frac{R_L}{R_R}\right)^a \tag{13.2}$$

Equation 13.2 is known as the generalized matching law. There are two parameters: bias (b), which represents a constant proportionality in responding unrelated to reinforcement rate (e.g., position preference); and an exponent (a), which represents sensitivity to reinforcement rate. Typically, a logarithmic transformation of Equation 13.2 is used, resulting in a linear relation in which sensitivity and bias correspond to the slope and intercept, respectively. Baum (1979) reviewed over 100 data sets and found that the generalized matching law commonly accounted for over 90% of the variance in behavior allocation (for a review of comparable human research, see Kollins, Newland, & Critchfield, 1997). Thus, in the generalized form represented in Equation 13.2, the matching law provides an excellent description of choice in concurrent schedules. Although undermatching (i.e., $a < 1$) is the most common result, this may result from a variety of factors, including imperfect discriminability of the contingencies (Davison & Jenkins, 1985).

Matching in Single and Multiple Schedules. If the law of effect is a general principle of behavior, and the matching law is a quantitative expression of the law of effect, then the matching principle should apply to situations other than concurrent schedules. Herrnstein (1970) proposed an extension of the matching law that applied to single and multiple schedules. His starting point was Catania and Reynolds' (1968) data showing that response rate was an increasing, negatively accelerated function of reinforcement rate on single VI schedules (see Figure 13.3).

Herrnstein (1970) reasoned that when a single schedule was arranged, a variety of behaviors other than the target response were available to the organism (e.g., grooming, pacing, defecating, contemplation). Presumably, these so-called extraneous behaviors were maintained by extraneous (i.e., unmeasured) reinforcers. Herrnstein then made two assumptions: (a) that the total amount of behavior in any situation was constant—that is, the frequencies of target and extraneous behaviors varied inversely; and (b) that "all behavior is choice" and obeys the matching law. The first assumption implies that the target and extraneous response rates sum to a

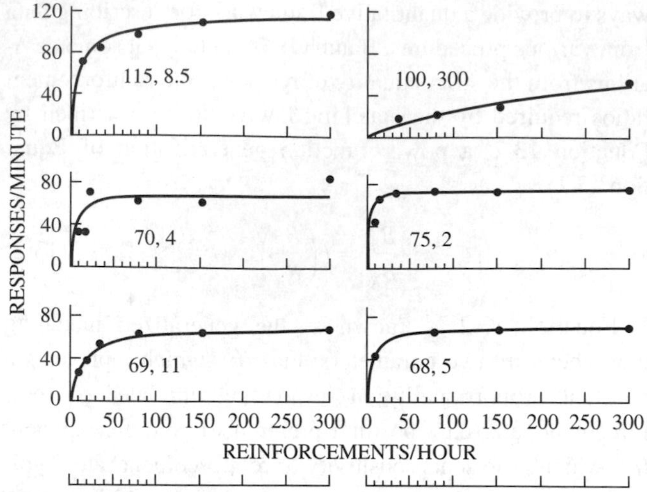

Figure 13.3 Response rate as a function of reinforcement rate for six pigeons responding under VI schedules. The numbers in each panel are the estimates of k and Re for fits of Equation 13.3. *Source:* From Herrnstein (1970).

constant ($B + Be = k$), and are maintained by rates of scheduled and extraneous reinforcement (R and Re), respectively. Based on the second assumption,

$$\frac{B}{B + Be} = \frac{R}{R + Re} \Rightarrow B = \frac{kR}{R + Re} \qquad (13.3)$$

Equation 13.3 defines a hyperbola, with two parameters, k and Re. The denominator represents the *context of reinforcement* for a particular response—the total amount of reinforcement in the situation. De Villiers and Herrnstein (1976) fit Equation 13.3 to a large number of data sets and found that it generally gave an excellent description of response rates under VI schedules. Subsequent research has generally confirmed the hyperbolic relation between response rate and reinforcement rate, although lower-than-predicted response rates are sometimes observed at very high reinforcement rates (Baum, 1993). In addition, Equation 13.3 has been derived from a number of different theoretical perspectives (Killeen, 1994; McDowell & Kessel, 1979; Staddon, 1977).

Herrnstein (1970) also developed a version of the matching law that was applicable to multiple schedules. In a multiple schedule, access to two (or more) different schedules occur successively and are signaled by discriminative stimuli. A well-known result in multiple schedules is *behavioral contrast:* Response rate in a component that provides a constant rate of reinforcement varies inversely with the reinforcement rate in the other component (see B. A. Williams, 1983, for review). Herrnstein suggested that the reinforcement rate in the alternative component served as part of the reinforcement context for behavior in the constant component. However, the contribution of alternative component reinforcement was attenuated by a parameter (m), which describes the degree of interaction at a temporal distance,

$$B_1 = \frac{kR_1}{R_1 + mR_2 + Re} \qquad (13.4)$$

with subscripts referring to the components of the multiple schedule. Equation 13.4 correctly predicts most behavioral contrast, but has difficulties with some other phenomena (see McLean & White, 1983, for review). Alternative models for multiple-schedule performance also based on the matching law have been proposed that alleviate these problems (McLean, 1995; McLean & White, 1983; B. A. Williams & Wixted, 1986).

Matching to Relative Value. The effects of variables other than reinforcement rate were examined in several early studies, which found that response allocation in concurrent schedules obeyed the matching relation when magnitude (i.e., seconds of access to food; Catania, 1963) and delay of reinforcement (Chung & Herrnstein, 1967) were varied. Baum and Rachlin (1969) then proposed that the matching law might apply most generally to *reinforcement value,* with value being defined as a multiplicative combination of reinforcement parameters,

$$\frac{B_L}{B_R} = \frac{R_L}{R_R} \cdot \frac{1/D_L}{1/D_R} \cdot \frac{M_L}{M_R} = \frac{V_L}{V_R} \qquad (13.5)$$

with M being reinforcement magnitude, D being delay, and V being value.

Equation 13.5 represents a significant extension of the matching law, enabling it to apply to a broader range of choice situations (note that frequently a generalized version of Equation 13.5 with exponents, analogous to Equation 13.2, has been used here; e.g., Logue, Rodriguez, Pena-Correal, & Mauro, 1984). One of the most important of these is *self-control,* which has been a major focus of research because of its obvious relevance for human behavior. In a self-control situation, subjects are confronted with a choice between a small reinforcer available immediately (or after a short delay), and a larger reinforcer available after a longer delay. Typically, overall reinforcement gain is maximized by choosing the delayed, larger reinforcer, which is defined as self-control (Rachlin & Green, 1972; see Rachlin, 1995, for review). By contrast, choice of the smaller, less delayed reinforcer is termed *impulsivity.* For example, if pigeons are given a choice between a small reinforcer (2-s access to grain) delayed by 1 s or a large reinforcer (6-s access to grain) delayed by 6 s, then Equation 13.5 predicts that 67% of the choice responses will be for the small reinforcer (i.e., the

6:1 delay ratio is greater than the 2:6 magnitude ratio). However, if the delays to both the small and large reinforcers are increased by the same amount, then Equation 13.5 predicts a reversal of preference. For example, if the delays are both increased by 10 s, then predicted preference for the small reinforcer is only 33% (16:11 delay ratio is no longer enough to compensate for the 2:6 magnitude ratio). Empirical support for such preference reversals has been obtained in studies of both human and nonhuman choice (Green & Snyderman, 1980; Kirby & Herrnstein, 1995). These data suggest that the temporal discounting function—that is, the function that relates the value of a reward to its delay—is not exponential, as assumed by normative economic theory, but rather hyperbolic in form (Myerson & Green, 1995).

Choice Between Stimuli of Acquired Value

Concurrent Chains. A more complex procedure that has been widely used in research on choice is *concurrent chains,* which is a version of concurrent schedules in which responses are reinforced not by food but by stimuli that are correlated with different schedules of food reinforcement. In concurrent chains, subjects respond during a choice phase (*initial links*) to obtain access to one of two reinforcement schedules (*terminal links*). The stimuli that signal the onset of the terminal links are analogous to Pavlovian CSs and are often called *conditioned reinforcers,* as their potential to reinforce initial-link responding derives from a history of pairing with food. Conditioned reinforcement has been a topic of long-standing interest because it is recognized that many of the reinforcers that maintain human behavior (e.g., money) are not of inherent biological significance (see B. A. Williams, 1994b, for review). Preference in the initial links of concurrent chains is interpreted as a measure of the relative value of the schedules signaled by the terminal links.

Herrnstein (1964) found that ratios of initial-link response rates matched the ratios of reinforcement rates in the terminal links, suggesting that the matching law might be extended to concurrent chains. However, subsequent studies showed that the overall duration of the initial and terminal links—the temporal context of reinforcement—affected preference in ways not predicted by the matching law. To account for these data, Fantino (1969) proposed the *delay-reduction hypothesis,* which states that the effectiveness of a terminal-link stimulus as a conditioned reinforcer depends on the reduction in delay to reinforcement signaled by the terminal link. According to Fantino's model, the value of a stimulus depends inversely on the reinforcement context in which it occurs (i.e., value is enhanced by a lean context, and vice versa). Fantino (1977) showed that the delay-reduction hypothesis provided an excellent qualitative account of preference in concurrent chains. Moreover, there is considerable evidence for the generality of the temporal context effects predicted by the model, as shown by the delay-reduction hypothesis's having been extended to a variety of different situations (see Fantino, Preston, & Dunn, 1993, for a review).

Preference for Variability, Temporal Discounting, and the Adjusting-Delay Procedure. Studies with pigeons and rats have consistently found evidence of preference for variability in reinforcement delays: Subjects prefer a VI terminal link in concurrent chains over an FI terminal link that provides the same average reinforcement rate. This implies that animals are risk-prone when choosing between different reinforcement delays (e.g., Killeen, 1968). Interestingly, when given a choice between a variable or fixed amount of food, animals are often risk-averse, although this preference appears to be modulated by deprivation level as predicted by risk-sensitive foraging theory from behavioral ecology (see Kacelnik & Bateson, 1996, for a review). For example, Caraco, Martindale, and Whittam (1980) found that juncos' preference for a variable versus constant number of seeds increased when food deprivation was greater.

Mazur (1984) introduced an adjusting-delay procedure that has become widely used to study preference for variability. His procedure is similar to concurrent chains in that the subject chooses between two stimuli that are correlated with different delays to reward, but the dependent variable is an indifference point—a delay to reinforcement that is equally preferred to a particular schedule. Mazur determined fixed-delay indifference points for a series of variable-delay schedules, and found that the following model (Equation 13.6) gave an excellent account of his results:

$$V = \frac{1}{n}\sum_{i=1}^{n}\frac{1}{1 + Kdi} \tag{13.6}$$

In Equation 13.6, V is the conditioned *value* of the stimulus that signals a delay to reinforcement, $d_1, \ldots, d_n$, and K is a sensitivity parameter. Equation 13.6 is called the hyperbolic-decay model because it assumes that the value of a delayed reinforcer decreases according to a hyperbola (see Figure 13.4). The hyperbolic-decay model has become the leading behavioral model of *temporal discounting*, and has been extensively applied to human choice between delayed rewards (e.g., Kirby, 1997).

General Models for Choice

Recently, several general models for choice have been proposed. These models may be viewed as extensions of the

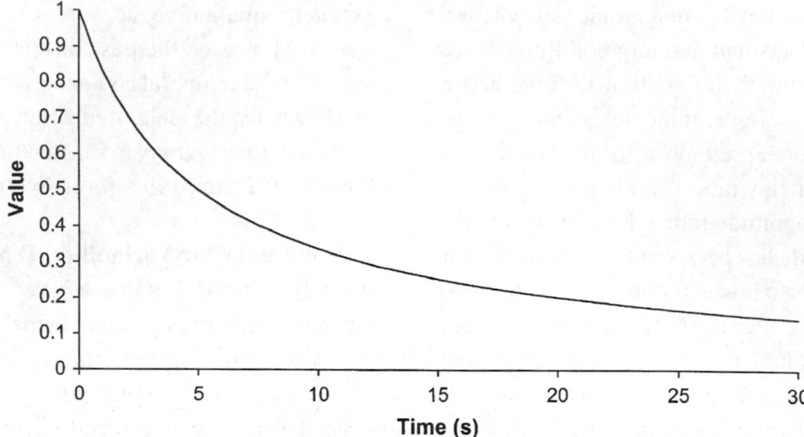

Figure 13.4 Hyperbolic discounting function. This figure shows how the value of a reward (in arbitrary units) decreases as a function of delay according to the Mazur's (1984) hyperbolic-decay model (Equation 13.6, with $K = 0.2$).

matching law, and they are integrative in the sense that they provide a quantitative description of data from a variety of choice procedures. Determining the optimal choice model may have important implications for a variety of issues, including how conditioned value is influenced by parameters of reinforcement, as well as the nature of the temporal discounting function.

Grace (1994, 1996) showed how the temporal context effects predicted by Fantino's delay-reduction theory could be incorporated in an extension of the generalized matching law. His contextual choice model can describe choice in concurrent schedules, concurrent chains, and the adjusting-delay procedure, on average accounting for over 90% of the variance in data from these procedures. The success of Grace's model as applied to the nonhuman-choice data suggests that temporal discounting may be best described in terms of a model with a power function component; moreover, such a model accounts for representative human data at least as well as the hyperbolic-decay model does (Grace, 1999). However, Mazur (2001) has recently proposed an alternative model based on the hyperbolic-decay model. Mazur's hyperbolic value-addition model is based on a principle similar to delay-reduction theory, and it provides an account of the data of comparable accuracy to that of Grace's model. Future research will determine which of these models (or whether an entirely different model) provides the best overall account of behavioral choice and temporal discounting.

Resistance to Change: An Alternative View of Response Strength

Although response rate has long been considered the standard measure of the strength of an instrumental response, it is not without potential problems. Response strength represents the product of the conditioning process. In terms of the law of effect, it should vary directly with parameters that correspond to intuitive notions of hedonic value. For example, response strength should be a positive function of reinforcement magnitude. However, studies have found that response rate often decreases with increases in magnitude (Bonem & Crossman, 1988). In light of this and other difficulties, researchers have sought other measures of response strength that are more consistently related to intuitive parameters of reinforcement.

One such alternative measure is *resistance to change.* Nevin (1974) conducted several experiments in which pigeons responded in multiple schedules. After baseline training, he disrupted responding in both components by either home-cage prefeeding or extinction. He found that responding in the component that provided the relatively richer reinforcement—in terms of greater rate, magnitude, or immediacy of reinforcement—decreased less compared with baseline responding for that component than did responding in the leaner component. Based on these results and others, Nevin and his colleagues have proposed *behavioral momentum theory,* which holds that resistance to change and response rate are independent aspects of behavior analogous to mass and velocity in classical physics (Nevin, Mandell, & Atak, 1983). According to this theory, reinforcement increases a mass-like aspect of behavior which can be measured as resistance to change.

From a procedural standpoint, the components in multiple schedules resemble terminal links in concurrent chains because differential conditions of reinforcement are signaled by distinctive stimuli and are available successively. Moreover, the same variables (e.g., reinforcement rate, magnitude, and immediacy) that increase resistance to change also increase preference in concurrent chains (Nevin, 1979). Nevin and Grace (2000) proposed an extension of behavioral momentum theory in which behavioral mass (measured as resistance to change) and value (measured as preference in concurrent chains) are different expressions of a single construct representing the reinforcement history signaled by a particular stimulus. Their model describes how stimulus-reinforcer (i.e., Pavlovian) contingencies determine the strength of an instrumental response, measured as resistance to change. Thus, it complements Herrnstein's (1970) quantitative law of effect, which describes how response strength measured as response rate depends on response-reinforcer (i.e., instrumental) contingencies.

Ecological-Economic Analyses of Instrumental Conditioning

A third approach towards the study of instrumental behavior was inspired by criticisms of the apparent circularity of the law of effect: If a reinforcer is identified solely through its effects on behavior, then there is no way to predict in advance what outcomes will serve as reinforcers (Postman, 1947). Meehl (1950) suggested that this difficulty could be overcome if reinforcers were transsituational; an outcome identified as a reinforcer in one situation should also act as a reinforcer in other situations. However, Premack (1965) demonstrated experimentally that transsituationality could be violated. Central to Premack's analysis is the identification of the reinforcer with the consummatory response, and the importance of obtaining a free-operant baseline measure of allocation among different responses. His results led to several important reconceptualizations of instrumental behavior, which emphasize the wider ecological or economic context of reinforcement in which responding—both instrumental (e.g., lever press) and contingent (e.g., eating)—occurs. According to this view, reinforcement is considered to be a molar adaptation to the constraints imposed by the instrumental contingency, rather than a molecular strengthening process as implied by the law of effect. Two examples of such reconceptualizations are behavior regulation theory and behavioral economics.

Behavior Regulation

Timberlake and Allison (1974) noted that the increase in responding associated with reinforcement occurred only if the instrumental contingency required that the animal perform more of the instrumental response in order to restore the level of the contingent (consummatory) response to baseline levels. For example, consider a situation in which a rat is allowed free access to a running wheel and drinking tube during baseline. After recording the time allocated to these activities when both were freely available, a contingency is imposed such that running and drinking must occur in a fixed proportion (e.g., 30 s of running gives access to a brief period of drinking). If the rat continued to perform both responses at baseline levels, it would spend far less time drinking—a condition Timberlake and Allison (1974) termed *response deprivation.* Because of the obvious physiological importance of water intake, the solution is for the rat to increase its rate of wheel running so as to maintain, as far as possible, its baseline level of drinking. Thus, reinforcement is viewed as an adaptive response to environmental constraint.

According to behavior regulation theory (Timberlake, 1984), there is an ideal combination of activities in any given situation, which can be assessed by an organism's baseline allocation of time across all possible responses. The allocation defines a *set point* in a behavior space. The determiners of set points may be complex and depend on the feeding ecology of the particular species (e.g., Collier, Hirsch, & Hamlin, 1972). The effect of the instrumental contingency is to constrain the possible allocations in the behavior space. For example, the reciprocal ratio contingency between running and drinking previously described implies that the locus of possible allocations is a straight line in the two-dimensional behavior space (i.e., running and drinking). If the set point is no longer possible under the contingency, the organism adjusts its behavior so as to minimize the distance between obtained allocation and the set point. Similar regulatory theories have been proposed by Allison, Miller, and Wozny (1979), Staddon (1979), and Rachlin and Burkhard (1978). Although regulatory theories have been very successful at describing instrumental performance at the molar level, they have proven somewhat controversial. For example, the critical role of deviations from the set point seems to imply that organisms are able to keep track of potentially thousands of different responses made during the session, and able to adjust their allocation accordingly. Opponents of regulatory theories (e.g., see commentaries following Timberlake, 1984) claim this is unlikely and that the effects of reinforcement are better understood at a more molecular level. Perhaps the most likely outcome of this debate is that molar and molecular accounts of instrumental behavior will prove complementary, not contradictory.

Behavioral Economics

An alternative interpretation of set points is that they represent the combination of activities with the highest subjective value or utility to the organism (e.g., so-called bliss points). One of the fundamental assumptions of economic choice theory is that humans maximize utility when allocating their resources among various commodities. Thus, perhaps it is not surprising that economics would prove relevant for the study of instrumental behavior. Indeed, over the last 25 years researchers have systematically applied the concepts of microeconomic theory to laboratory experiments with both human and nonhuman subjects. The result has been the burgeoning field of behavioral economics (for review, see Green & Freed, 1998). Here, we consider the application of two important economic concepts—demand and substitutability—to instrumental behavior.

Demand. In economics, demand is the amount of a commodity that is purchased at a given price. The extent to which consumption changes as a function of price is a demand curve. When consumption of a particular commodity shows little or no change when its price is increased, demand is said to be inelastic. Conversely, elastic demand refers to a situation in which consumption falls with increases in price. Researchers have studied elasticity of demand in nonhumans by manipulating price in terms of reinforcement schedules. For instance, if rats' lever pressing is reinforced with food according to an FR 10 schedule, changing the schedule to FR 100 represents an increase in price.

For example, Hursh and Natelson (1981) trained rats to press a lever for food reinforcement; a second lever was also available that produced a train of pulses to electrodes implanted in the lateral hypothalamus (ESB). Responses to both levers were reinforced by concurrent (and equal) VI, VI schedules. As the VI schedule values were increased, consumption of food remained constant, whereas the number of ESB reinforcers earned decreased dramatically (see Figure 13.5). Thus, demand for food was inelastic, whereas

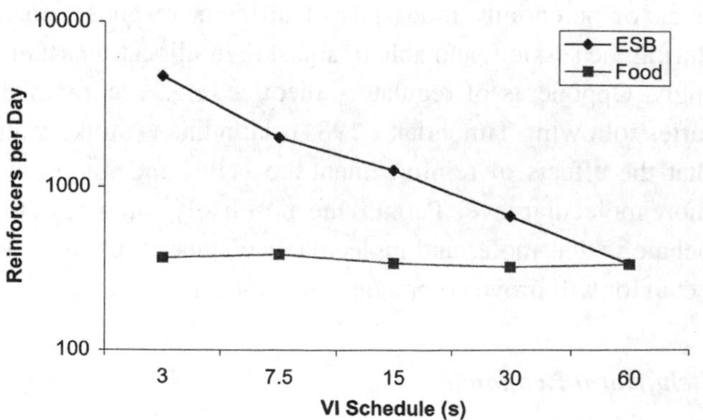

Figure 13.5 Number of food (square) and ESB (diamond) reinforcers earned per day by rats responding under concurrent (and equal) VI, VI schedules. Consumption of ESB reinforcers decrease as schedule values increase, indicating elastic demand. In contrast, number of food reinforcers remains approximately constant, showing inelastic demand. *Source:* After Hursh and Natelson (1981).

demand for ESB was highly elastic. In economic terms, differences in elasticity can be used to identify necessities (i.e., food) and luxuries (i.e., ESB).

Substitutability. Another concept from economics that has proven useful for understanding instrumental behavior is substitutability. In Herrnstein's (1961) original research leading to the matching law and in many subsequent studies (see this chapter's section titled "Choice and the Matching Law"), the reinforcers delivered by the concurrently available alternatives were identical and therefore perfectly substitutable. However, organisms must often choose between alternatives that are qualitatively different and perhaps not substitutable. In economics, substitutability is assessed by determining how the consumption of a given commodity changes when the price of another commodity is increased. To the extent that the commodities are substitutable, consumption should increase. For example, Rachlin et al. (1976) trained rats to press two levers for liquid reinforcement (root beer, or a nonalcoholic Tom Collins mix) on concurrent FR 1, FR 1 schedules. Rats were given a budget of 300 lever presses that they could allocate to either lever. Baseline consumption for one rat is shown in the left panel of Figure 13.6, together with the budget line (heavy line) indicating the possible range of choices that the rat could make. Rachlin et al. then doubled the price of root beer (by reducing the amount of liquid per reinforcer) while cutting the price of the Tom Collins mix in half (by increasing the amount). Simultaneously they increased the budget of lever presses so that rats could still obtain the same quantity of each reinforcer as in baseline. Under these conditions, the rats increased their consumption of Tom Collins mix relative to root beer. Next, the investigators cut the price of root beer in half and doubled the price of Tom Collins mix, and the rats increased consumption of root beer. This shows that root beer and Tom Collins mix were highly substitutable as reinforcers; rats' choice shifted towards whichever commodity was cheaper. In a second baseline condition, the rats chose between food and water. Rachlin et al. then increased the price of food by 67% by reducing the number of pellets per reinforcer. Again the budget of lever presses was increased so that the rats could continue to earn the same quantities as in baseline. However, as the right panel of Figure 13.6 shows, increasing the price of food had little effect on consumption. Although water was now relatively cheaper, the rats continued to earn approximately the same amount of food, demonstrating that food and water are nonsubstitutable as reinforcers. Thus, the concept of substitutability is useful for understanding choice between qualitatively different reinforcers, as it helps to specify how allocation will shift when the instrumental contingencies (i.e., prices) are changed.

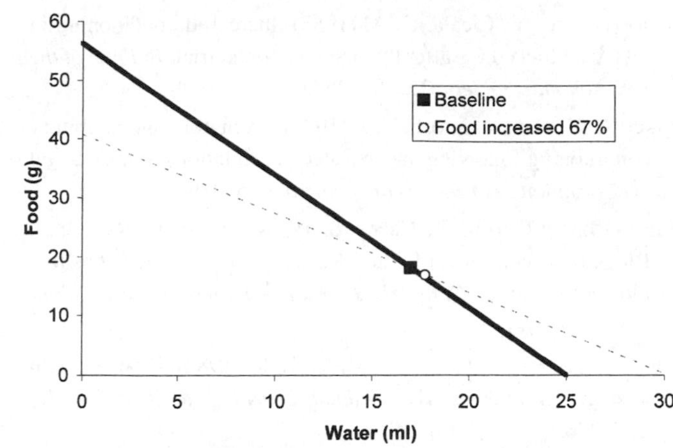

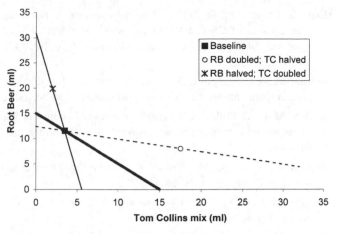

Figure 13.6 The left panel shows consumption of root beer and Tom Collins mix for one rat given a budget of 300 lever presses in baseline (square). When the price of root beer or Tom Collins mix was changed, consumption shifted towards the now-cheaper commodity, demonstrating that the outcomes were substitutable. The right panel shows results for the same rat's choosing between food and water reinforcers. In contrast, a price manipulation had little effect on consumption, demonstrating that food and water were nonsubstitutable. See text for more explanation. *Source:* After Rachlin et al. (1976).

Summary

As noted in the introduction to this section, Thorndike's pioneering studies with cats in puzzle boxes were the first systematic investigation of instrumental conditioning. Research on instrumental conditioning since then may be viewed as attempts to understand the empirical generalization of positive reinforcement that Thorndike expressed as the law of effect. The associationistic tradition (see this chapter's section titled "Associative Analyses of Instrumental Conditioning") describes the content of learning in instrumental situations in terms of associations that develop according to similar processes as Pavlovian conditioning. The experimental analysis of behavior (see this chapter's section titled "Functional Analyses of Instrumental Conditioning"), derived from the work of B. F. Skinner, represents a more functional approach and attempts to describe the relations between behavior and its environmental determiners, often in quantitative terms. A third perspective is offered by research that has emphasized the importance of the wider ecological or economic context of the organism for understanding instrumental responding (see this chapter's section titled "Ecological-Economic Analyses of Instrumental Conditioning"). These research traditions illuminate different aspects of instrumental behavior and demonstrate the richness and continued relevance of the apparently simple contingencies first studied by Thorndike over a century ago.

CONCLUSIONS

The study of learning and conditioning—basic information processing—is less in the mainstream of psychology today than it was 30–50 years ago. Yet progress continues, and there are unanswered questions of considerable importance to many other endeavors, including treatment of psychopathology (particularly behavior modification), behavioral neuroscience, and education, to name but a few. New animal models of psychopathology are the starting points of most new forms of therapeutic psychopharmacology. In behavioral neuroscience, researchers are attempting to identify the neural substrates of behavior. Surely this task demands an accurate description of the behavior to be explained. Thus, the study of basic behavior sets the agenda for much of neuroscience. Additionally, the study of basic learning and information processing has many messages for educators. For example, research has repeatedly demonstrated that distractor events, changes in context during training, and spacing of training trials all attenuate the rate at which behavior is initially altered (e.g., see chapter by Johnson in this volume). But these very procedures also result in improved retention over time and better transfer to new test situations. These are but a few of the continuing contributions stemming from the ongoing investigation of the principles of learning and basic information processing.

REFERENCES

Adams, C. D., & Dickinson, A. (1981). Instrumental responding following reinforcer devaluation. *Quarterly Journal of Experimental Psychology, 33B,* 109–122.

Allison, J., Miller, M., & Wozny, M. (1979). Conservation in behavior. *Journal of Experimental Psychology: General, 108,* 4–34.

Ayres, J. J. B. (1998). Fear conditioning and avoidance. In W. T. O'Donohue (Ed.), *Learning and behavior therapy* (pp. 122–145). Boston: Allyn & Bacon.

Azorlosa, J. L., & Cicala, G. A. (1988). Increased conditioning in rats to a blocked CS after the first compound trial. *Bulletin of the Psychonomic Society, 26,* 254–257.

Baker, A. G., & Mackintosh, N. J. (1977). Excitatory and inhibitory conditioning following uncorrelated presentations of the CS and UCS. *Animal Learning & Behavior, 5,* 315–319.

Balaz, M. A., Gutsin, P., Cacheiro, H., & Miller, R. R. (1982). Blocking as a retrieval failure: Reactivation of associations to a blocked stimulus. *Quarterly Journal of Experimental Psychology, 34B,* 99–113.

Balaz, M. A., Kasprow, W. J., & Miller, R. R. (1982). Blocking with a single compound trial. *Animal Learning & Behavior, 10,* 271–276.

Balleine, B. (1992). Instrumental performance following a shift in primary motivation depends upon incentive learning. *Journal of Experimental Psychology: Animal Behavior Processes, 18,* 236–250.

Balsam, P. D. (1984). Relative time in trace conditioning. In J. Gibbon & L. Allan (Eds.), *Annals of the New York Academy of Sciences: Timing and Time Perception* (Vol. 243, pp. 211–227). Cambridge, MA: Ballinger.

Batson, J. D., & Batsell, W. R., Jr. (2000). Augmentation, not blocking, in an A+/AX+ flavor-conditioning procedure. *Psychonomic Bulletin & Review, 7,* 466–471.

Baum, W. M. (1973). The correlation-based law of effect. *Journal of the Experimental Analysis of Behavior, 20,* 137–153.

Baum, W. M. (1974). On two types of deviation from the matching law: Bias and undermatching. *Journal of the Experimental Analysis of Behavior, 22,* 231–242.

Baum, W. M. (1979). Matching, undermatching, and overmatching in studies of choice. *Journal of the Experimental Analysis of Behavior, 32,* 269–281.

Baum, W. M. (1993). Performances on ratio and interval schedules of reinforcement: Data and theory. *Journal of the Experimental Analysis of Behavior, 59,* 245–264.

Baum, W. M., & Rachlin, H. C. (1969). Choice as time allocation. *Journal of the Experimental Analysis of Behavior, 12,* 861–874.

Belke, T. W. (1992). Stimulus preference and the transitivity of preference. *Animal Learning & Behavior, 20,* 401–406.

Bennett, C. H., Wills, S. J., Oakeshott, S. M., & Mackintosh, N. J. (2000). Is the context specificity of latent inhibition a sufficient explanation of learned irrelevance? *Quarterly Journal of Experimental Psychology, 53B,* 239–253.

Berkeley, G. (1946). *A treatise concerning the principles of human knowledge.* La Salle, IL: Open Court Publication Co. (Reprinted from 1710, Dublin, Ireland: Jeremy Pepyat)

Best, M. R., Dunn, D. P., Batson, J. D., Meachum, C. L., & Nash, S. M. (1985). Extinguishing conditioned inhibition in flavour-aversion learning: Effects of repeated testing and extinction of the excitatory element. *Quarterly Journal of Experimental Psychology, 37B,* 359–378.

Bonardi, C., & Hall, G. (1996). Learned irrelevance: No more than the sum of CS and US preexposure effects? *Journal of Experimental Psychology: Animal Behavior Processes, 22,* 183–191.

Bonem, M., & Crossman, E. K. (1988). Elucidating the effects of reinforcement magnitude. *Psychological Bulletin, 104,* 348–362.

Bouton, M. E., & Bolles, R. C. (1979). Contextual control of the extinction of conditioned fear. *Learning and Motivation, 10,* 445–466.

Breland, K., & Breland, M. (1961). The misbehavior of organisms. *American Psychologist, 16,* 681–684.

Brogden, W. J. (1939). Sensory pre-conditioning. *Journal of Experimental Psychology, 25,* 323–332.

Brooks, D. C., & Bouton, M. E. (1993). A retrieval cue for extinction attenuates spontaneous recovery. *Journal of Experimental Psychology: Animal Behavior Processes, 19,* 77–89.

Burger, D. C., Mallemat, H., & Miller, R. R. (2000). Overshadowing of subsequent events and recovery thereafter. *Quarterly Journal of Experimental Psychology, 53B,* 149–171.

Burns, M., & Domjan, M. (1996). Sign tracking versus goal tracking in the sexual conditioning of male Japanese quail (*Coturnix japonica*). *Journal of Experimental Psychology: Animal Behavior Processes, 22,* 297–306.

Bush, R. R., & Mosteller, F. (1951). A mathematical model for simple learning. *Psychological Review, 58,* 313–323.

Caraco, T., Martindale, S., & Whittam, T. S. (1980). An empirical demonstration of risk-sensitive foraging preferences. *Animal Behaviour, 28,* 820–830.

Catania, A. C. (1963). Concurrent performances: A baseline for the study of reinforcement magnitude. *Journal of the Experimental Analysis of Behavior, 6,* 299–300.

Catania, A. C., & Reynolds, G. S. (1968). A quantitative analysis of responding maintained by interval schedules of reinforcement. *Journal of the Experimental Analysis of Behavior, 11,* 327–383.

Cheatle, M. D., & Rudy, J. W. (1978). Analysis of second-order odor-aversion conditioning in neonatal rats: Implications for Kamin's blocking effect. *Journal of Experimental Psychology: Animal Behavior Processes, 4,* 237–249.

Cheng, P. W., & Novick, L. R. (1992). Covariation in natural causal induction. *Psychological Review, 99,* 365–382.

Chung, S.-H., & Herrnstein, R. J. (1967). Choice and delay of reinforcement. *Journal of the Experimental Analysis of Behavior, 10,* 67–74.

Clarke, J. C., Westbrook, R. F., & Irwin, J. (1979). Potentiation instead of overshadowing in the pigeon. *Behavioral and Neural Biology, 25,* 18–29.

Clayton, N. S., & Dickinson, A. (1999). Scrub jays (*Aphelocoma coerulescens*) remember the relative time of caching as well as the location and content of their caches. *Journal of Comparative Psychology, 113,* 403–416.

Cole, M. R. (1999). Molar and molecular control in variable-interval and variable-ratio schedules. *Journal of the Experimental Analysis of Behavior, 71,* 319–328.

Collier, G., Hirsch, E., & Hamlin, P. H. (1972). The economic determinants of reinforcement in the rat. *Physiology and Behavior, 9,* 705–716.

Colwill, R. M., & Rescorla, R. A. (1988). Associations between the discriminative stimulus and the reinforcer in instrumental learning. *Journal of Experimental Psychology: Animal Behavior Processes, 14,* 155–164.

Cosmides, K., & Tooby, J. (1994). Origins of domain-specificity: The evolution of functional organization. In L. A. Hirschfeld & S. A. Gelman (Eds.), *Mapping the mind: Domain specificity in cognition and culture* (pp. 85–116). New York: Cambridge University Press.

Dalrymple, A. J., & Galef, B. G. (1981). Visual discrimination pretraining facilitates subsequent visual cue/toxicosis conditioning in rats. *Bulletin of the Psychonomic Society, 18,* 267–270.

Davidson, T. L., Aparicio, J., & Rescorla, R. A. (1988). Transfer between Pavlovian facilitators and instrumental discriminative stimuli. *Animal Learning & Behavior, 16,* 285–291.

Davison, M., & Jenkins, P. E. (1985). Stimulus discriminability, contingency discriminability, and schedule performance. *Animal Learning & Behavior, 13,* 77–84.

Davison, M. & McCarthy, D. (1988). *The matching law: A research review.* Hillsdale, NJ: Erlbaum.

Dearing, M. F., & Dickinson, A. (1979). Counterconditioning of shock by a water reinforcer in rabbits. *Animal Learning & Behavior, 7,* 360–366.

Denniston, J. C., Blaisdell, A. P., & Miller, R. R. (1998). Temporal coding affects transfer of serial and simultaneous inhibitors. *Animal Learning & Behavior, 26,* 336–350.

Denniston, J. C., Miller, R. R., & Matute, H. (1996). Biological significance as a determinant of cue competition. *Psychological Science, 7,* 235–331.

Denniston, J. C., Savastano, H. I., & Miller, R. R. (2001). The extended comparator hypothesis: Learning by contiguity, responding by relative strength. In R. R. Mowrer & S. B. Klein (Eds.), *Handbook of contemporary learning theories* (pp. 65–117). Hillsdale, NJ: Erlbaum.

de Villiers, P. A., & Herrnstein, R. J. (1976). Toward a law of response strength. *Psychological Bulletin, 33,* 1131–1153.

DeVito, P. L., & Fowler, H. (1987). Enhancement of conditioned inhibition via an extinction treatment. *Animal Learning & Behavior, 15,* 448–454.

Dickinson, A. (1980). *Contemporary animal learning theory.* Cambridge, UK: Cambridge University Press.

Dickinson, A. (1994). Instrumental conditioning. In N. J. Mackintosh (Ed.), *Animal learning and cognition* (pp. 45–79). New York: Academic Press.

Dickinson, A., & Balleine, B. (1994). Motivational control of goal-directed action. *Animal Learning & Behavior, 22,* 1–18.

Dickinson, A., Balleine, B., Watt, A., Gonzalez, F., & Boakes, R. A. (1995). Motivational control after extended instrumental training. *Animal Learning & Behavior, 23,* 197–206.

Dickinson, A., & Burke, J. (1996). Within-compound associations mediate the retrospective revaluation of causality judgments. *Quarterly Journal of Experimental Psychology, 49B,* 60–80.

Dickinson, A., & Charnock, D. J. (1985). Contingency effects with maintained instrumental reinforcement. *Quarterly Journal of Experimental Psychology, 37B,* 397–416.

Dinsmoor, J. A. (1998). Punishment. In W. T. O'Donohue (Ed.), *Learning and behavior therapy* (pp. 188–204). Boston: Allyn & Bacon.

Domjan, M. (1983). Biological constraints on instrumental and classical conditioning: Implications for general process theory. In G. H. Bower (Ed.), *The psychology of learning and motivation* (Vol. 17, pp. 215–277). New York: Academic Press.

Domjan, M., & Hollis, K. L. (1988). Reproductive behavior: A potential model system for adaptive specializations in learning. In R. C. Bolles & M. D. Beecher (Eds.), *Evolution and learning* (pp. 213–237). Hillsdale, NJ: Erlbaum.

Durlach, P. J., & Rescorla, R. A. (1980). Potentiation rather than overshadowing in flavor-aversion learning: An analysis in terms of within-compound associations. *Journal of Experimental Psychology: Animal Behavior Processes, 6,* 175–187.

Egger, M. D., & Miller, N. E. (1963). When is a reward reinforcing? An experimental study of the information hypothesis. *Journal of Comparative and Physiological Psychology, 56,* 132–137.

Eikelboom, R., & Stewart, J. (1982). Conditioning of drug-induced psychological responses. *Psychological Review, 89,* 507–528.

Escobar, M., Arcediano, F., & Miller, R. R. (2001). Conditions favoring retroactive interference between antecedent events and between subsequent events. *Psychonomic Bulletin & Review, 8,* 691–697.

Escobar, M., Matute, H., & Miller, R. R. (2001). Cues trained apart compete for behavioral control in rats: Convergence with the associative interference literature. *Journal of Experimental Psychology: General, 130,* 97–115.

Estes, W. K. (1950). Toward a statistical theory of learning. *Psychological Review, 57,* 94–170.

Estes, W. K., & Burke, C. J. (1953). A theory of stimulus variability in learning. *Psychological Review, 60,* 276–286.

Etienne, A. S., Berlie, J., Georgakopoulos, J., & Maurer, R. (1998). Role of dead reckoning in navigation. In S. Healy (Ed.), *Spatial representation in animals* (pp. 54–68). Oxford, UK: Oxford.

Fantino, E. (1969). Choice and rate of reinforcement. *Journal of the Experimental Analysis of Behavior, 12,* 723–730.

Fantino, E. (1977). Conditioned reinforcement: Choice and information. In W. K. Honig & J. E. R. Staddon (Eds.), *Handbook of operant behavior* (pp. 313–339). Englewood Cliffs, NJ: Prentice-Hall.

Fantino, E., Preston, R. A., & Dunn, R. (1993). Delay reduction: Current status. *Journal of the Experimental Analysis of Behavior, 60,* 159–169.

Ferster, C. B., & Skinner, B. F. (1957). *Schedules of reinforcement.* New York: Appleton-Century-Crofts.

Foree, D. D., & LoLordo, V. M. (1975). Stimulus-reinforcer interactions in the pigeon: The role of electric shock and the avoidance contingency. *Journal of Experimental Psychology: Animal Behavior Processes, 1,* 39–46.

Gallistel, C. R., & Gibbon, J. (2000). Time, rate and conditioning. *Psychological Review, 107,* 219–275.

Garcia, J., & Koelling, R. A. (1966). Relation of cue to consequence in avoidance learning. *Psychonomic Science, 4,* 123–124.

Garcia, J., Ervin, F. R., & Koelling, R. A. (1966). Learning with prolonged delay of reinforcement. *Psychonomic Science, 5,* 121–122.

Garcia, J., Lasiter, P. S., Bermudez-Rattoni, F., & Deems, D. A. (1985). A general theory of aversion learning. *Annals of the New York Academy of Sciences, 443,* 8–21.

Gibbon, J. (1995). Dynamics of time matching: Arousal makes better seem worse. *Psychonomic Bulletin & Review, 2,* 208–215.

Gibbon, J., & Balsam, P. (1981). Spreading association in time. In C. M. Locurto, H. S. Terrace, & J. Gibbon (Eds.), *Autoshaping and conditioning theory* (pp. 219–253). New York: Academic Press.

Gibbon, J., Baldock, M. D., Locurto, C., Gold, L., & Terrace, H. S. (1977). Trial and intertrial durations in autoshaping. *Journal of Experimental Psychology: Animal Behavior Processes, 3,* 264–284.

Grace, R. C. (1994). A contextual model of concurrent-chains choice. *Journal of the Experimental Analysis of Behavior, 61,* 113–129.

Grace, R. C. (1996). Choice between fixed and variable delays to reinforcement in the adjusting-delay procedure and concurrent chains. *Journal of Experimental Psychology: Animal Behavior Processes, 22,* 362–383.

Grace, R. C. (1999). The matching law and amount-dependent exponential discounting as accounts of self-control choice. *Journal of the Experimental Analysis of Behavior, 71,* 27–44.

Green, L., & Freed, D. E. (1998). Behavioral economics. In W. O'Donohue (Ed.), *Learning and behavior therapy* (pp. 274–300). Boston: Allyn & Bacon.

Green, L., & Snyderman, M. (1980). Choice between rewards differing in amount and delay: Toward a choice model of self control. *Journal of the Experimental Analysis of Behavior, 34,* 135–147.

Groves, P. M., & Thompson, R. F. (1970). Habituation: A dual-process theory. *Psychological Review, 77,* 419–450.

Guthrie, E. R. (1935). *The psychology of learning.* New York: Harper.

Guthrie, E. R. (1938). *The psychology of human conflict.* New York: Harper.

Guttman, N., & Kalish, H. I. (1956). Discriminability and stimulus generalization. *Journal of Experimental Psychology, 51,* 79–88.

Gwinn, G. T. (1949). The effects of punishment on acts motivated by fear. *Journal of Experimental Psychology, 39,* 260–269.

Hall, G. (1991). *Perceptual and associative learning.* Oxford, UK: Oxford University Press.

Hall, G. (1996). Learning about associatively activated stimulus representations: Implications for acquired equivalence in perceptual learning. *Animal Learning & Behavior, 24,* 233–255.

Hallam, S. C., Grahame, N. J., Harris, K., & Miller, R. R. (1992). Associative structures underlying enhanced negative summation following operational extinction of a Pavlovian inhibitor. *Learning and Motivation, 23,* 43–62.

Hammond, L. J. (1980). The effect of contingency upon the appetitive conditioning of free-operant behavior. *Journal of the Experimental Analysis of Behavior, 34,* 297–304.

Hearst, E. (1988). Fundamentals of learning and conditioning. In R. C. Atkinson, R. J. Herrnstein, G. Lindzey, & R. D. Luce (Eds.), *Stevens' handbook of experimental psychology: Vol. 2. Learning and cognition* (pp. 3–109). New York: Wiley.

Herrnstein, R. J. (1961). Relative and absolute strength of response as a function of frequency of reinforcement. *Journal of the Experimental Analysis of Behavior, 4,* 267–272.

Herrnstein, R. J. (1964). Secondary reinforcement and rate of primary reinforcement. *Journal of the Experimental Analysis of Behavior, 7,* 27–36.

Herrnstein, R. J. (1970). On the law of effect. *Journal of the Experimental Analysis of Behavior, 13,* 243–266.

Herrnstein, R. J., & Heyman, G. M. (1979). Is matching compatible with reinforcement maxmization on concurrent variable interval, variable ratio? *Journal of the Experimental Analysis of Behavior, 31,* 209–223.

Herrnstein, R. J., & Prelec, D. (1992). A theory of addiction. In G. Loewenstein & J. Elster (Eds.), *Choice over time* (pp. 331–360). New York: Russell Sage.

Herrnstein, R. J., & Vaughan, W. (1980). Melioration and behavior allocation. In J. E. R. Staddon (Ed.), *Limits to action* (pp. 143–176). New York: Academic Press.

Heth, C. D. (1976). Simultaneous and backward fear conditioning as a function of number of CS-UCS pairings. *Journal of Experimental Psychology: Animal Behavior Processes, 2,* 117–129.

Heyman, G. M. (1996). Resolving the contradictions of addiction. *Behavioral and Brain Sciences, 19,* 561–610.

Heyman, G. M., & Luce, R. D. (1979). Operant matching is not a logical consequence of maximizing reinforcement rate. *Animal Learning & Behavior, 7,* 133–140.

Heyman, G. M., & Tanz, L. (1995). How to teach a pigeon to maximize overall reinforcement rate. *Journal of the Experimental Analysis of Behavior, 64,* 277–297.

Hinson, J. M., & Staddon, J. E. R. (1983). Hill-climbing by pigeons. *Journal of the Experimental Analysis of Behavior, 39,* 25–47.

Holland, P. C. (1977). Conditioned stimulus as a determinant of the form of the Pavlovian conditioned response. *Journal of Experimental Psychology: Animal Behavior Processes, 3,* 77–104.

Holland, P. C. (1981). Acquisition of representation-mediated conditioned food aversions. *Learning and Motivation, 12,* 1–18.

Holland, P. C. (1983a). Occasion setting in Pavlovian feature positive discriminations. In M. L. Commons, R. J. Herrnstein, & A. R. Wagner (Eds.), *Quantitative analyses of behavior: Discrimination processes* (pp. 183–206). Cambridge, MA: Ballinger.

Holland, P. C. (1983b). Representation-mediated overshadowing and potentiation of conditioned aversions. *Journal of Experimental Psychology: Animal Behavior Processes, 9,* 1–13.

Holland, P. C. (1989). Feature extinction enhances transfer of occasion setting. *Animal Learning & Behavior, 17,* 269–279.

Holland, P. C., & Forbes, D. T. (1982). Representation-mediated extinction of conditioned flavor aversions. *Learning and Motivation, 13,* 454–471.

Holland, P. C., & Rescorla, R. A. (1975). The effect of two ways of devaluing the unconditioned stimulus after first- and second-order appetitive conditioning. *Journal of Experimental Psychology: Animal Behavior Processes, 1,* 355–363.

Hull, C. L. (1943). *Principles of behavior: An introduction to behavior theory.* New York: Appleton-Century.

Hull, C. L. (1952). *A behavior system: An introduction to behavior theory concerning the individual organism.* New Haven, CT: Yale University Press.

Hursh, S. R., & Natelson, B. H. (1981). Electrical brain stimulation and food reinforcement dissociated by demand elasticity. *Physiology & Behavior, 26,* 509–515.

Jenkins, H. M., & Moore, B. R. (1973). The form of the autoshaped response with food or water reinforcers. *Journal of the Experimental Analysis of Behavior, 20,* 163–181.

Jones, J. R., & Moore, J. (1999). Some effects of intertrial-duration on discrete-trial choice. *Journal of the Experimental Analysis of Behavior, 71,* 375–393.

Kacelnik, A., & Bateson, M. (1996). Risky theories—the effects of variance on foraging decisions. *American Zoologist, 36,* 402–434.

Kamil, A. C. (1983). Optimal foraging theory and the psychology of learning. *American Zoologist, 23,* 291–302.

Kamil, A. C., & Clements, K. C. (1990). Learning, memory, and foraging behavior. In D. A. Dewsbury (Ed.), *Contemporary issues in comparative psychology* (pp. 7–30). Sunderland, MA: Sinauer.

Kamin, L. J. (1965). Temporal and intensity characteristics of the conditioned stimulus. In W. F. Prokasy (Ed.), *Classical conditioning* (pp. 118–147). New York: Appleton-Century-Crofts.

Kamin, L. J. (1968). "Attention-like" processes in classical conditioning. In M. R. Jones (Ed.), *Miami Symposium on the Prediction of Behavior: Aversive stimulation* (pp. 9–33). Miami, FL: University of Miami Press.

Kasprow, W. J., Cacheiro, H., Balaz, M. A., & Miller, R. R. (1982). Reminder-induced recovery of associations to an overshadowed stimulus. *Learning and Motivation, 13,* 155–166.

Kaufman, M. A., & Bolles, R. C. (1981). A nonassociative aspect of overshadowing. *Bulletin of the Psychonomic Society, 18,* 318–320.

Kehoe, E. J., & Gormezano, I. (1980). Configuration and combination laws in conditioning with compound stimuli. *Psychological Bulletin, 87,* 351–378.

Kehoe, E. J., Horne, A. J., Horne, P. S., & Macrae, M. (1994). Summation and configuration between and within sensory modalities in classical conditioning of the rabbit. *Animal Learning & Behavior, 22,* 19–26.

Kelley, H. H. (1967). Attribution theory in social psychology. In D. Levine (Ed.), *Nebraska Symposium on Motivation* (Vol. 15, pp. 192–240). Lincoln: University of Nebraska Press.

Killeen, P. (1968). On the measurement of reinforcement frequency in the study of preference. *Journal of the Experimental Analysis of Behavior, 11,* 263–269.

Killeen, P. (1994). Mathematical principles of reinforcement. *Behavioral and Brain Sciences, 17,* 105–172 (includes commentary).

Kimble, G. A. (1961). *Hilgard and Marquis' "Condition and Learning."* New York: Appleton-Century-Crofts.

Kirby, K. N. (1997). Bidding on the future: Evidence against normative discounting of delayed rewards. *Journal of Experimental Psychology: General, 126,* 54–70.

Kirby, K. N., & Herrnstein, R. J. (1995). Preference reversals due to myopic discounting of delayed reward. *Psychological Science, 6,* 83–89.

Köhler, W. (1947). *Gestalt psychology: An introduction to new concepts in modern psychology.* New York: Liveright Publication Co.

Kollins, S. H., Newland, M. C., & Critchfield, T. S. (1997). Human sensitivity to reinforcement in operant choice: How much do consequences matter? *Psychonomic Bulletin & Review, 4,* 208–220.

Konorski, J. (1948). *Conditioned reflexes and neuron organization.* Cambridge, UK: Cambridge University Press.

Konorski, J. (1967). *Integrative activity of the brain: An interdisciplinary approach.* Chicago: University of Chicago Press.

Kraemer, P. J., Lariviere, N. A., & Spear, N. E. (1988). Expression of a taste aversion conditioned with an odor-taste compound: Overshadowing is relatively weak in weanlings and decreases over a retention interval in adults. *Animal Learning & Behavior, 16,* 164–168.

Kraemer, P. J., Randall, C. K., & Carbary, T. J. (1991). Release from latent inhibition with delayed testing. *Animal Learning & Behavior, 19,* 139–145.

Logue, A. W. (1979). Taste aversion and the generality of the laws of learning. *Psychological Bulletin, 86,* 276–296.

Logue, A. W., Rodriguez, M. L., Pena-Correal, T. E., & Mauro, B. C. (1984). Choice in a self-control paradigm: Quantification of experience-based differences. *Journal of the Experimental Analysis of Behavior, 41,* 53–67.

LoLordo, V. M., & Fairless, J. L. (1985). Pavlovian conditioned inhibition: The literature since 1969. In R. R. Miller & N. E. Spear (Eds.), *Information processing in animals: Conditioned inhibition* (pp. 1–49). Hillsdale, NJ: Erlbaum.

Lubow, R. E. (1989). *Latent inhibition and conditioned attention theory.* Cambridge, UK: Cambridge University Press.

Lubow, R. E., & Moore, A. U. (1959). Latent inhibition: The effect of nonreinforced preexposure to the conditioned stimulus. *Journal of Comparative and Physiological Psychology, 52,* 415–419.

Mackintosh, N. J. (1975). A theory of attention: Variations in the associability of stimuli with reinforcement. *Psychological Review, 82,* 276–298.

Mackintosh, N. J. (1976). Overshadowing and stimulus intensity. *Animal Learning & Behavior, 4,* 186–192.

Mackintosh, N. J., & Reese, B. (1979). One-trial overshadowing. *Quarterly Journal of Experimental Psychology, 31,* 519–526.

Maier, S. F., & Seligman, M. E. P. (1976). Learned helplessness: Theory and evidence. *Journal of Experimental Psychology: General, 105,* 3–46.

Maldonado, A., Cátena, A., Cándido, A., & García, I. (1999). The belief revision model: Asymmetrical effects of noncontingency on human covariation learning. *Animal Learning & Behavior, 27,* 168–180.

Mark, T. A., & Gallistel, C. R. (1994). Kinetics of matching. *Journal of Experimental Psychology: Animal Behavior Processes, 20,* 79–95.

Marlin, N. A., & Miller, R. R. (1981). Associations to contextual stimuli as a determinant of long-term habituation. *Journal of Experimental Psychology: Animal Behavior Processes, 7,* 313–333.

Matute, H., & Pineño, O. (1998). Stimulus competition in the absence of compound conditioning. *Animal Learning & Behavior, 26,* 3–14.

Matzel, L. D., Gladstein, L., & Miller, R. R. (1988). Conditioned excitation and conditioned inhibition are not mutually exclusive. *Learning and Motivation, 19,* 99–121.

Matzel, L. D., Held, F. P., & Miller, R. R. (1988). Information and expression of simultaneous and backward associations: Implications for contiguity theory. *Learning and Motivation, 19,* 317–344.

Matzel, L. D., Schachtman, T. R., & Miller, R. R. (1985). Recovery of an overshadowed association achieved by extinction of the overshadowed stimulus. *Learning and Motivation, 16,* 398–412.

Mazur, J. E. (1984). Tests for an equivalence rule for fixed and variable reinforcer delays. *Journal of Experimental Psychology: Animal Behavior Processes, 10,* 426–436.

Mazur, J. E. (2001). Hyperbolic value addition and general models of animal choice. *Psychological Review, 108,* 96–112.

McClelland, J. L. (1988). Connectionist models and psychological evidence. *Journal of Memory and Language, 27,* 107–123.

McDowell, J. J., & Kessel, R. (1979). A multivariate rate equation for variable-interval performance. *Journal of the Experimental Analysis of Behavior, 31,* 267–283.

McLaren, I. P. L., & Mackintosh, N. J. (2000). An elemental model of associative learning. I. Latent inhibition and perceptual learning. *Animal Learning & Behavior, 28,* 211–246.

McLean, A. P. (1995). Contrast and reallocation of extraneous reinforcers as a function of component duration and baseline rate of reinforcement. *Journal of the Experimental Analysis of Behavior, 63,* 203–224.

McLean, A. P., & White, K. G. (1983). Temporal constraint on choice: Sensitivity and bias in multiple schedules. *Journal of the Experimental Analysis of Behavior, 39,* 405–426.

Meehl, P. E. (1950). On the circularity of the law of effect. *Psychological Bulletin, 47,* 52–75.

Miller, J. S., McKinzie, D. L., Kraebel, K. S., & Spear, N. E. (1996). Changes in the expression of stimulus selection: Blocking represents selective memory retrieval rather than selective associations. *Learning and Motivation, 27,* 307–316.

Miller, J. S., Scherer, S. L., & Jagielo, J. A. (1995). Enhancement of conditioning by a nongustatory CS: Ontogenetic differences in the mechanisms underlying potentiation. *Learning and Motivation, 26,* 43–62.

Miller, R. R., & Balaz, M. A. (1981). Differences in adaptiveness between classically conditioned responses and instrumentally acquired responses. In N. E. Spear & R. R. Miller (Eds.), *Information processing in animals: Memory mechanisms* (pp. 49–80). Hillsdale, NJ: Erlbaum.

Miller, R. R., Barnet, R. C., & Grahame, N. J. (1995). Assessment of the Rescorla-Wagner model. *Psychological Bulletin, 117,* 363–386.

Miller, R. R., & Escobar, M. (2001). Contrasting acquisition-focused and performance-focused models of behavior change. *Current Directions in Psychological Science, 10,* 141–145.

Miller, R. R., & Matute, H. (1996). Biological significance in forward and backward blocking: Resolution of a discrepancy between animal conditioning and human causal judgment. *Journal of Experimental Psychology: General, 125,* 370–386.

Miller, R. R., & Matzel, L. D. (1988). The comparator hypothesis: A response rule for the expression of associations. In G. H. Bower (Ed.), *The psychology of learning and motivation* (Vol. 22, pp. 51–92). San Diego, CA: Academic Press.

Myerson, J., & Green, L. (1995). Discounting of delayed rewards: Models of individual choice. *Journal of the Experimental Analysis of Behavior, 64,* 263–276.

Nairne, J. S., & Rescorla, R. A. (1981). Second-order conditioning with diffuse auditory reinforcers in the pigeon. *Learning and Motivation, 12,* 65–91.

Neely, J. H. (1977). Semantic priming and retrieval from lexical memory: Roles of inhibitionless spreading activation and limited-capacity attention. *Journal of Experimental Psychology: General, 106,* 226–254.

Nevin, J. A. (1969). Interval reinforcement of behavior in discrete trials. *Journal of the Experimental Analysis of Behavior, 12,* 875–885.

Nevin, J. A. (1974). Response strength in multiple schedules. *Journal of the Experimental Analysis of Behavior, 21,* 389–408.

Nevin, J. A. (1979). Reinforcement schedules and response strength. In M. D. Zeiler & P. Harzem (Eds.), *Reinforcement and the organization of behaviour* (pp. 117–158). Chichester, UK: Wiley.

Nevin, J. A., & Grace, R. C. (2000). Behavioral momentum and the law of effect. *Behavioral and Brain Sciences, 23,* 73–130 (includes commentary).

Nevin, J. A., Mandell, C., & Atak, J. R. (1983). The analysis of behavioral momentum. *Journal of the Experimental Analysis of Behavior, 39,* 49–59.

Osgood, C. E. (1949). The similarity paradox in human learning: A resolution. *Psychological Review, 56,* 132–143.

Pavlov, I. P. (1927). *Conditioned reflexes.* London: Oxford University Press.

Pearce, J. M. (1987). A model for stimulus generalization in Pavlovian conditioning. *Psychological Review, 94,* 61–73.

Pearce, J. M., & Hall, G. (1978). Overshadowing the instrumental conditioning of a lever press response by a more valid predictor of reinforcement. *Journal of Experimental Psychology: Animal Behavior Processes, 4,* 356–367.

Pearce, J. M., & Hall, G. (1980). A model for Pavlovian learning: Variations in the effectiveness of conditioned but not of unconditioned stimuli. *Psychological Review, 87,* 532–552.

Postman, L. (1947). The history and present status of the law of effect. *Psychological Bulletin, 44,* 489–563.

Postman, L., Stark, K., & Fraser, J. (1968). Temporal changes in interference. *Journal of Verbal Learning and Verbal Behavior, 7,* 672–694.

Premack, D. (1965). Reinforcement theory. In D. Levine (Ed.), *Nebraska Symposium on Motivation* (Vol. 18, pp. 123–180). Lincoln: University of Nebraska Press.

Rachlin, H. (1995). Self-control: Beyond commitment. *Behavioral and Brain Sciences, 18,* 101–159 (includes commentary).

Rachlin, H. (1997). Four teleological theories of addiction. *Psychonomic Bulletin & Review, 4,* 462–473.

Rachlin, H., Battalio, R., Kagel, J., & Green, L. (1981). Maximization theory in behavioral psychology. *Behavioral and Brain Sciences, 4,* 371–417 (includes commentary).

Rachlin, H., & Burkhard, B. (1978). The temporal triangle: Response substitution in instrumental conditioning. *Psychological Review, 85,* 22–47.

Rachlin, H., & Green, L. (1972). Commitment, choice and self-control. *Journal of the Experimental Analysis of Behavior, 17,* 15–22.

Rachlin, H., Green, L., Kagel, J. H., & Battalio, R. C. (1976). Economic demand theory and psychological studies of choice. In G. Bower (Ed.), *The psychology of learning and motivation* (Vol. 10, pp. 129–154). New York: Academic Press.

Rachlin, H., Green, L., & Tormey, B. (1988). Is there a decisive test between matching and maximizing? *Journal of the Experimental Analysis of Behavior, 50,* 113–123.

Randich, A., & LoLordo, V. M. (1979). Associative and nonassociative theories of the UCS preexposure phenomenon. *Psychological Bulletin, 86,* 523–548.

Rashotte, M. E., Marshall, B. S., & O'Connell, J. M. (1981). Signaling functions of the second-order CS: Partial reinforcement during second-order conditioning of the pigeon's keypeck. *Animal Learning & Behavior, 9,* 253–260.

Rescorla, R. A. (1968). Probability of shock in the presence and absence of CS in fear conditioning. *Journal of Comparative and Physiological Psychology, 66,* 1–5.

Rescorla, R. A. (1969). Pavlovian conditioned inhibition. *Psychological Bulletin, 72,* 77–94.

Rescorla, R. A. (1991). Associative relations in instrumental learning: The Eighteenth Bartlett Memorial Lecture. *Quarterly Journal of Experimental Psychology, 43B,* 1–23.

Rescorla, R. A., & Cunningham, C. L. (1979). Spatial contiguity facilitates Pavlovian second-order conditioning. *Journal of Experimental Psychology: Animal Behavior Processes, 5,* 152–161.

Rescorla, R. A., & Furrow, D. R. (1977). Stimulus similarity as a determinant of Pavlovian conditioning. *Journal of Experimental Psychology: Animal Behavior Processes, 3,* 203–215.

Rescorla, R. A., & Holland, P. C. (1977). Associations in Pavlovian conditioned inhibition. *Learning and Motivation, 8,* 429–447.

Rescorla, R. A., & Wagner, A. R. (1972). A theory of Pavlovian conditioning: Variations in the effectiveness of reinforcement and non-reinforcement. In A. H. Black & W. F. Prokasy (Eds.), *Classical conditioning: Vol. 2. Current theory and research* (pp. 64–99). New York: Appleton-Century-Crofts.

Riccio, D. C., Richardson, R., & Ebner, D. L. (1984). Memory retrieval deficits based upon altered contextual cues: A paradox. *Psychological Bulletin, 96,* 152–165.

Rizley, R. C., & Rescorla, R. A. (1972). Associations in second-order conditioning and sensory preconditioning. *Journal of Comparative and Physiological Psychology, 81,* 1–11.

Roberts, S. (1981). Isolation of an internal clock. *Journal of Experimental Psychology: Animal Behavior Processes, 7,* 242–268.

Romaniuk, C. B., & Williams, D. A. (2000). Conditioning across the duration of a backward conditioned stimulus. *Journal of Experimental Psychology: Animal Behavior Processes, 26,* 454–461.

Ross, B. H., & Makin, V. S. (1999). Prototype versus exemplar models in cognition. In R. J. Sternberg (Ed.), *The nature of cognition* (pp. 206–241). Cambridge, MA: MIT press.

St. Claire-Smith, R. (1979). The overshadowing and blocking of punishment. *Quarterly Journal of Experimental Psychology, 31,* 51–61.

Saint Paul, U. v. (1982). Do geese use path integration for walking home? In F. Papi & H. G. Wallraff (Eds.), *Avian navigation* (pp. 298–307). New York: Springer.

Savastano, H. I., & Fantino, E. (1994). Human choice in concurrent ratio-interval schedules of reinforcement. *Journal of the Experimental Analysis of Behavior, 61,* 453–463.

Savastano, H. I., & Miller, R. R. (1998). Time as content in Pavlovian conditioning. *Behavioural Processes, 44,* 147–162.

Schaal, D. W., & Branch, M. N. (1988). Responding of pigeons under variable-interval schedules of unsignaled, briefly signaled, and completely signaled delays to reinforcement. *Journal of the Experimental Analysis of Behavior, 50,* 33–54.

Schmajuk, N. A., Lamoureux, J. A., & Holland, P. C. (1998). Occasion setting: A neural network approach. *Psychological Review, 105,* 3–32.

Schneider, B. (1969). A two-state analysis of fixed-interval responding in the pigeon. *Journal of the Experimental Analysis of Behavior, 12,* 667–687.

Shanks, D. R. (1994). Human associative learning. In N. J. Mackintosh (Ed.), *Animal learning and cognition* (pp. 335–374). San Diego, CA: Academic Press.

Shettleworth, S. J. (1998). *Cognition, evolution, and behavior.* New York: Oxford.

Shimp, C. P. (1966). Probabilistically reinforced choice behavior in pigeons. *Journal of the Experimental Analysis of Behavior, 9,* 433–455.

Shimp, C. P. (1969). Optimum behavior in free-operant experiments. *Psychological Review, 76,* 97–112.

Sidman, M. (1960). *Tactics of scientific research.* New York: Basic Books.

Siegel, S. (1989). Pharmacological conditioning and drug effects. In A. J. Goudie & M. W. Emmet-Oglesby (Eds.), *Psychoactive drugs: Tolerance and sensitization* (pp. 115–185). Clifton, NJ: Humana Press.

Skinner, B. F. (1938). *The behavior of organisms.* New York: Appleton-Century-Crofts.

Skinner, B. F. (1969). *Contingencies of reinforcement: A theoretical analysis.* New York: Appleton-Century-Crofts.

Slamecka, N. J., & Ceraso, J. (1960). Retroactive and proactive inhibition of verbal learning. *Psychological Bulletin, 57,* 449–475.

Spence, K. W. (1936). The nature of discrimination learning in animals. *Psychological Review, 43,* 427–449.

Staddon, J. E. R. (1977). On Herrnstein's equation and related forms. *Journal of the Experimental Analysis of Behavior, 28,* 163–170.

Staddon, J. E. R. (1979). Operant behavior as adaptation to constraint. *Journal of Experimental Psychology: General,* 108, 48–67.

Staddon, J. E. R., & Simmelhag, V. L. (1970). The "superstition" experiment: A reexamination of its implications for the principles of adaptive behavior. *Psychological Review, 78,* 3–43.

Sulzer-Azaroff, B., & Mayer, R. G. (1991). *Behavior analysis for lasting change.* Ft. Worth, TX: Holt, Rinehart, & Winston.

Sutton, R. S., & Barto, A. G. (1981). Toward a modern theory of adaptive networks: Expectation and prediction. *Psychological Review, 88,* 135–170.

Thompson, R. F., & Spencer, W. A. (1966). Habituation: A model phenomenon for the study of neuronal substrates of behavior. *Psychological Review, 73,* 16–43.

Thorndike, E. L. (1898). Animal intelligence: An experimental study of the associative processes in animals. *Psychological Monographs, 2,* No. 8.

Thorndike, E. L. (1911). *Animal intelligence: Experimental studies.* New York: Macmillan.

Thorndike, E. L. (1932). *Fundamentals of learning.* New York: Columbia University.

Thorndike, E. L. (1949). *Selected writings from a connectionist's psychology.* East Norwalk, CT: Appleton-Century-Crofts.

Timberlake, W. (1984). Behavior regulation and learned performance: Some misapprehensions and disagreements. *Journal of the Experimental Analysis of Behavior, 41,* 355–375.

Timberlake, W., & Allison, J. (1974). Response deprivation: An empirical approach to instrumental performance. *Psychological Review, 81,* 146–164.

Timberlake, W., & Lucas, G. A. (1989). Behavior systems and learning: From misbehavior to general principles. In S. B. Klein & R. R. Mowrer (Eds.), *Contemporary learning theories: Instrumental conditioning theory and the impact of biological constraints in learning* (pp. 237–275). Hillsdale, NJ: Erlbaum.

Timberlake, W., & Lucas, G. A. (1991). Periodic water, interwater interval, and adjunctive behavior in a 24-hour multiresponse environment. *Animal Learning & Behavior, 19,* 369–380.

Tolman, E. C. (1932). *Purposive behavior in animals and men.* London: Century/Random House.

Tolman, E. C., & Honzik, C. H. (1930). Introduction and removal of reward, and maze performance in rats. *University of California Publications in Psychology, 4,* 257–275.

Van Hamme, L. J., & Wasserman, E. A. (1994). Cue competition in causality judgments: The role of nonpresentation of compound stimulus elements. *Learning and Motivation, 25,* 127–151.

Vaughan, W. (1981). Melioration, matching, and maximization. *Journal of the Experimental Analysis of Behavior, 36,* 141–149.

Wagner, A. R. (1978). Expectancies and the priming of STM. In S. H. Hulse, H. Fowler, & W. K. Honig (Eds.), *Cognitive processes in animal behavior* (pp. 177–209). Hillsdale, NJ: Erlbaum.

Wagner, A. R. (1981). SOP: A model of automatic memory processing in animal behavior. In N. E. Spear & R. R. Miller (Eds.), *Information processing in animals: Memory mechanisms* (pp. 5–47). Hillsdale, NJ: Erlbaum.

Wasserman, E. A., Elek, S. M., Chatlosh, D. L., & Baker, A. G. (1993). Rating causal relations: Role of probability in judgments of response-outcome contingency. *Journal of Experimental Psychology: Learning, Memory, and Cognition, 19,* 174–188.

Watson, J. B. (1913). Psychology as a behaviorist views it. *Psychological Review, 20,* 158–177.

Weiss, S. J., & Schindler, C. W. (1981). Generalization peak shift in rats under conditions of positive reinforcement and avoidance. *Journal of the Experimental Analysis of Behavior, 35,* 175–185.

Williams, B. A. (1976). The effects of unsignalled delayed reinforcement. *Journal of the Experimental Analysis of Behavior, 26,* 441–449.

Williams, B. A. (1982). Blocking the response-reinforcer association. In M. L. Commons, R. J. Herrnstein, & A. R. Wagner (Eds.), *Quantitative analyses of behavior: Vol. 3. Acquisition* (pp. 427–447). Cambridge, MA: Ballinger.

Williams, B. A. (1983). Another look at contrast in multiple schedules. *Journal of the Experimental Analysis of Behavior, 39,* 345–384.

Williams, B. A. (1988). Reinforcement, choice, and response strength. In R. C. Atkinson, R. J. Herrnstein, G. Lindzey, & R. D. Luce (Eds.), *Stevens' handbook of experimental psychology: Vol. 2. Learning and cognition* (2nd ed., pp. 167–244). New York: Wiley.

Williams, B. A. (1992). Dissociation of theories of choice via temporal spacing of choice opportunities. *Journal of Experimental Psychology: Animal Behavior Processes, 18,* 287–297.

Williams, B. A. (1994a). Reinforcement and choice. In N. J. Mackintosh (Ed.), *Animal learning and cognition* (pp. 81–108). San Diego, CA: Academic Press.

Williams, B. A. (1994b). Conditioned reinforcement: Neglected or outmoded explanatory construct? *Psychonomic Bulletin & Review, 1,* 457–475.

Williams, B. A., & Royalty, P. (1989). A test of the melioration theory of matching. *Journal of Experimental Psychology: Animal Behavior Processes, 15,* 99–113.

Williams, B. A., & Wixted, J. T. (1986). An equation for behavioral contrast. *Journal of the Experimental Analysis of Behavior, 45,* 47–62.

Williams, D. R., & Williams, H. (1969). Auto-maintenance in the pigeon: Sustained pecking despite contingent non-reinforcement. *Journal of the Experimental Analysis of Behavior, 12,* 511–520.

Yin, H., Barnet, R. C., & Miller, R. R. (1994). Second-order conditioning and Pavlovian conditioned inhibition: Operational similarities and differences. *Journal of Experimental Psychology: Animal Behavior Processes, 20,* 419–428.

Yin, H., Grahame, N. J., & Miller, R. R. (1993). Extinction of comparator stimuli during and after acquisition: Differential facilitative effects on Pavlovian responding. *Learning and Motivation, 24,* 219–241.

Zeiler, M. D. (1984). The sleeping giant: Reinforcement schedules. *Journal of the Experimental Analysis of Behavior, 42,* 485–493.

CHAPTER 14

Animal Memory and Cognition

E. J. CAPALDI

Animal cognition is of concern not only to psychologists but to numerous other scientists in diverse fields. It may be said that there has been an explosion of interest in animal cognition in recent years. Two of the major but independent factors responsible for this increase in interest are a dissatisfaction with "simpler" associative approaches to animal behavior and the application of evolutionary thinking to an increasing number of problem areas. Rejecting associationism is not new (see, e.g., Lashley, 1951). Nor is applying evolution to cognition new, Darwin (1871) himself being a devotee of that approach. Increasingly, however, biologists and psychologists, among others, are turning to the study of animal behavior, if not animal cognition, within the context of evolution.

Behaviorism was an early dominant movement in American psychology. It suggested that the subject matter of psychology was behavior, and that behavior was best investigated employing animals, particularly in learning situations. Moreover, behavior was to be explained by eschewing mental states as explanatory devices while emphasizing learned associations, particularly associations between stimuli and responses. Two prominent exceptions to these more or less orthodox behavioristic views were those of Edward Chase Tolman (1932) and B. F. Skinner (1938). Tolman (1948) saw himself as a cognitive or purposive behaviorist and considered forms of explanations in addition to associations—for example, cognitive representations such as maps of spatial relations in the environment. For Skinner (a radical behaviorist), on the other hand, even associations were too mentalistic: Skinner rejected all forms of mentalistic explanation. Clark Hull's (1943) form of behaviorism, developed from the 1930s to the 1950s, was quite popular. In Hull's system, internal processes mediated between external stimuli and overt responses, but mediational events were not mental states. Rather, they were internal stimuli (e.g., stimuli arising from response feedback) and fractional forms of overt responses (e.g., small chewing movements).

Two basic learning processes were favored by the early behaviorists; these processes remain popular today. In one, *Pavlovian conditioning,* stimuli are presented without regard to the animal's behavior. For example, a tone might be presented for a brief period, followed by food. Learning would be indexed by salivation, initially elicited by food, but later occurring to the tone. Interestingly, many Pavlovian phenomena obtained in birds and rats appear to take a similar form in humans (e.g., Wasserman & Berglan, 1998). In the other popular procedure, *instrumental conditioning,* reinforcement is contingent on responding in the presence of some stimulus. For example, a tone might signal a hungry rat to receive food by pressing a bar. Pavlovian and instrumental conditioning are treated at length by Miller and Grace; see their chapter in this volume.

In the 1970s there arose within animal psychology a renewed concern with animal cognition (see, e.g., Hulse, Fowler, & Honig, 1978). This movement had several characteristics worth mentioning. It was concerned with problems not emphasized, or even recognized, within the broad conventional behavioristic approach to animal behavior—for example, how animals manage to get from one place to another (spatial learning). It was also concerned in considerable part with either augmenting, or in some cases replacing (see, e.g., Hulse & Dorsky, 1977), interpretations that stress associations between stimuli and responses with more cognitively slanted views. For example, in learning to go from one spatial location to another, do animals form a representation or map of the environment à la Tolman's cognitive map? Finally, it was concerned with investigation in animals' problems often investigated in people, for example, concept learning, list learning, numerical abilities, and so on.

Although the previously described approach to animal cognition has produced much in the way of useful data and theory, it can be said to be incomplete in some important respects. For one, the approach tended to emphasize behaviors acquired on the basis of an individual animal's experience. Accordingly, it tended to ignore interesting behaviors shared by most (if not all) members of a particular species that appear to have relatively little in common in the way of a learning component. As we shall see, many such behaviors are controlled by internal mind-brain states normally associated with behaviors that are commonly classified as cognitive. In considering such species-characteristic behaviors, it would be well to keep in mind that all behaviors are the result of an interaction of environmental and genetic components. Progress in understanding animal cognition, if not cognition generally, may have much to gain by better understanding the processes controlling the behavior of sonar (for example) using bats, dancing bees, and bower-building birds, to mention only a few species that display interesting species-specific behaviors.

Other movements arising outside orthodox psychology have contributed substantially to our understanding of animal behavior and cognition. These include ethology, cognitive ethology, and evolutionary biology and psychology. *Ethology,* at its inception in the 1930s, was initially concerned with investigating the so-called "species-typical behavior" of animals in their normal environments in the wild. As ethology developed, it subsequently came to embrace laboratory studies as well, at least in some instances. An example of an initial concern in ethology would include filial imprinting in, say, ducklings, in which baby ducklings learn to follow their parents and parents learn to recognize their own progeny (e.g., Hoffman, 1978). As an example of the subsequent laboratory concern, we could mention lab studies of song acquisition in various species of birds (e.g., Marler, 1987; Marler & Peters, 1989). Both sorts of studies have contributed to our understanding of animal behavior. For example, the imprinting studies indicate that receptivity to certain classes of events has a developmental basis. The song-learning studies indicate, among other things, that some bird species can more easily learn the songs of their own species than those of some other species.

Cognitive ethology, influenced considerably by the work of the biologist Donald Griffin (1992), who pioneered work on echolocation in bats, emphasized (contrary to behaviorism) animal consciousness, awareness, and intentions. For example, when a plover leads a fox away from its nest and eggs by dragging a wing on the ground and then flies away vigorously when the fox is some distance from the nest, does the bird knowingly intend to deceive the fox? According to Griffin (1992), in stark disagreement with Skinner, a proper understanding of animal behavior necessarily entails inquiring into questions of subjective awareness. Consider the bat *myotis.* While cruising for food at night it emits ultrasonic vocalizations in particular directions. At cruising speed it emits about 10 clicks/s. On detecting an insect the bat homes in on its prey, raising its clicking rate to as many as 200 clicks/s. As the bat emits pulses at such high rates and considerable intensity, it in effect turns off its ears as the sound goes out—otherwise its ears would be injured. The bat's ear muscles relax at the cessation of outputting the pulses so as to be sensitive to the returning echo. This process of send signal (tense muscles) and receive signal (relax muscles) can go as high as 50 cycles/s. A bat can determine the distance of its prey as well as its direction of movement, and can distinguish its own cries from those of its numerous hunting companions. Some insects have developed the capacity to take evasive action when detected by the bats, by going into dives and the like, yet they are often captured nevertheless. Clearly, the sonar system of some bats is extremely complicated, involving precise information processing on a split-second basis (see, e.g., Dawkins, 1996). As in the case of the plover, cognitive ethologists want to know how much of the complex information processing of the bat is under conscious, intentional control. As many have indicated, however, it may not be possible to determine what is going on in the mind of another species.

Ecologists are concerned with determining the interrelationship between an organism and its environment, often integrating experimental psychology with evolutionary biology to do so. An ecologist might investigate whether two closely related bird species have similar or different patterns of behaviors ranging from mating to food storage. In investigating such problems, ecologists pay close attention to such processes as perception, learning, and cognition, and in these respects have much in common with experimental psychologists.

Evolutionary biologists and *psychologists* are distinguished from some others concerned with animal cognition, most prominently by their particular conception of the mind-brain mechanisms controlling behavior. Their view is that the

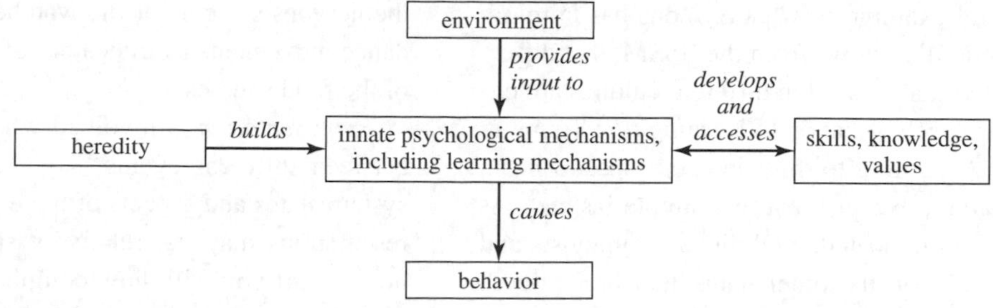

Figure 14.1 From Pinker's (1994) book *The Language Instinct,* which shows how heredity, environment, skills, knowledge, and values interact to influence the innate psychological mechanisms that cause behavior.

brain is composed of numerous specific mechanisms, often called *modules,* that are designed by evolution to solve specific problems. This theory of modularity is more or less universally accepted at the sensory level (e.g., eyes to solve the problem of sight) and at the level of organs (e.g., the heart to solve the problem of pumping blood), but is controversial at the level of higher order central processes (e.g., a module in the brain for the preference for one's own kin) (see, e.g., Fodor, 1983).

One informative view of how various environmental factors interact with mental modules or specific problem-solving devices was proposed by Pinker (1994) (see Figure 14.1). The mental modules, which are built by heredity to solve some specific problem (e.g., speaking with others), are modified by the environment (e.g., hearing English rather than French) and by skills, knowledge, and values (e.g., knowing to speak when important information is to be conveyed). The approach shown in Figure 14.1 contrasts with a view of mind that is widespread in psychology in general and with a view of evolution held by many psychologists. Many psychologists tend to favor the idea that the mind is best conceptualized as a general problem-solving device, a device that can be applied to many different problems. As for evolution, many psychologists believe, implicitly if not explicitly, in what is known as *continuity*—for example, some process such as intelligence increases gradually and progressively from (say) birds to humans.

A compromise between the general computer versus specific models view is sometimes suggested. For example, Mithen (1996)—an archeologist—believes, on the basis of the fossil evidence and evidence from comparing various species of animals, that in humans the mental modules, rather than being completely independent or encapsulated, are capable of interacting with each other. In any event, evolutionary psychology rejects what has come to be known as the *standard social science model,* or SSSM. The SSSM, in brief, suggests that while animals may be controlled by biology, humans are responsive to culture. Dominated by learning, humans are molded by culture through a system of rewards and punishments, according to the SSSM. Whether some animals can be said to possess culture will be considered in the final section of this chapter.

The belief of evolutionary biologists and psychologists is that the mind consists (to use an analogy) of numerous specialized computers, each designed to solve some particular problem. This approach rules out, as is perhaps apparent, continuity in favor of the idea that animals that face particular problems evolve specialized learning and cognitive mechanisms to deal with those problems. To put the matter bluntly, a rat, a monkey, and a chimpanzee do not represent, only or necessarily, animals of increasing intelligence approaching that of a human being. There may indeed be some gain in learning ability over these species, but each at the same time has evolved specialized mechanisms to deal with the particular problems it faces in its own environment. For example, bees, which in some respects lack the learning abilities of rats, seem nevertheless to be better able to communicate the location of a food source to their conspecific than are rats. Bees, of course, communicate the distance and direction of a food source to their conspecifics by doing what is called a *dance* in the hive. To use another example closer to home, language, rather than having evolved slowly over many different species, may be a specialized ability in humans lacking in any significant respect in any other species. Most notably the much-investigated chimpanzee. If this is the case, then the considerable effort expended to teach dolphins, gorillas, and especially chimpanzees language may be less worthwhile, theoretically speaking, than the trainers of these animals might hope.

As the previous example may imply, evolutionary biologists and psychologists believe that at least some problems investigated by social scientists, who have an outdated conception of evolution, are a waste of time and effort. As Symons (1987, 1992) has noted, social scientists sometimes postulate explanatory mechanisms that could not possibly have survived if current evolutionary thinking is correct. As a more-or-less general example of what Symons has in mind, we might cite a belief that flows from the SSSM, that differences between individuals reared in different cultures are entirely due to culture itself—that is, to learning (see Tooby & Cosmides, 1992). According to this view, our species has a nature, but that nature, except for a few simple instincts, is entirely malleable. As indicated, evolutionary biologists and psychologists suggest, on the other hand, that brains, both human and animal, consist of many special-purpose devices, some of which may be widely shared over species, others of which may be common to only a few species, but that in any case constrain how experience (culture in humans) will affect the behavior of that species (see Figure 14.1).

WHAT IS ANIMAL COGNITION?

The question *What is animal cognition?* has at least two answers. One is that it consists of all those topics treated in the last few chapters of animal-learning textbooks that are otherwise primarily concerned with Pavlovian and instrumental conditioning. This would include such topics as serial learning counting, language acquisition, concept learning, and the like. Another answer is that cognition may be identified with particular processes such as information processing, internal representations, attention, memory, and so on. Whatever one's approach to animal cognition, it is the case (as we will attempt to demonstrate in this section) that distinguishing between the cognitive versus the noncognitive is difficult and in some cases perhaps even arbitrary.

Consider the idea that cognition involves the internal processing of information—a very reasonable suggestion. Keep in mind, however, that there are behaviors under the control of complex information processing that are not normally classified as cognitive. For example, the hunting behavior of bats, briefly described earlier, involves real-time computations of the prey's distance, its speed of movement, its direction of movement, its moment-by-moment evasive actions, and the like. Surely some of the bat's hunting behavior is learned: It may learn with experience to identify the prey's species by the configuration of the returning echo. Yet equally surely, much of the bat's complex, rapid information process is "hardwired" into its brain. Nor is the bat an exception. Bees, as indicated, after locating a food source must fly back to the hive where they communicate to their sisters the direction and distance of the desired commodity by doing what is called a dance that their sisters "comprehend". Not only are the bees engaging in complex information processing, but the dance symbolizes or represents such parameters as the direction and distance of the food source. Essentially, the nervous systems of the watcher bees interpret particular dance movements as indicators of the distance and direction of the food sources.

Representation is involved when an isomorphism occurs between different events, say, between brain or nervous-system states and aspects of the environment. The bees' representations may be, relatively speaking, simple. Imagine, however, if you will, how complex the bat's auditory representations of its prey must be. In real time it computes and updates its prey's location, speed, direction of movement, and so on. As Dawkins (1976) has indicated, were bats able to do so they might find our species' reliance on visual processing as strange and mysterious as we find their reliance on auditory processing. Many researchers may be reluctant to consider such behaviors as involving cognition, however, for the following reasons. A hallmark of cognition according to some, is that it allows animals to modify their behaviors to deal with a changing and unpredictable environment. Cognition, according to this view, allows animals to behave in a flexible manner in novel environments. Responses that are hardwired, so to speak, cannot, properly speaking, be considered cognitive. Consider language in people, however. According to some of the major authorities in the field the capacity to acquire language is innate in humans and can be described as an *instinct* (e.g., Bickerton, 1998; Pinker, 1994). Thus it is possible that understanding of, say, sonar use in bats may contribute to better understanding of language acquisition in humans, or, indeed, vice versa. On this basis, one may suggest that too sharp a distinction between hardwired behaviors, particularly complicated and elaborate ones, and cognition may not be useful.

Decision making and problem solving may properly be regarded as cognitive activities—but who can doubt that bats and bees (to use our familiar examples) are making numerous decisions (to dive when prey dives) and solving significant problems (to forage for food and return to hive to dance) when engaged in their normal activities? Consider another example of decision making. Male bower birds build large, elaborate nests that they decorate with brightly colored objects in the hope of attracting a female. If the nest fails in this regard, the male bird tears down the nest and builds a new one. Nest building by bower birds improves with experience, older birds building better nests than younger birds. Is bower building, therefore, an instance of flexible decision-making behavior in the face of novel circumstances, or is it merely hardwired? In any event, a cognitive ethologist might impute purpose and awareness to the bower birds' nest building, perhaps more purpose and awareness than some might find reasonable. Yet, might we be equally unreasonable in going to the other extreme, dismissing the male bower bird's nest-building activity as totally irrelevant to matters of animal cognition?

As indicated, current animal-learning textbooks often treat Pavlovian and instrumental conditioning separately from animal cognition. However, there are interpretations of Pavlovian conditioning in terms of attention (e.g., Mackintosh, 1975) and information processing (e.g., Pearce & Hall, 1980). To mention a final example, many orthodox instrumental learning phenomena, ranging from reward schedule effects to brightness discrimination learning, have been said to involve complex memorial processes (e.g., Capaldi, 1994). Thus, just as the distinction between hardwired behavior and cognition may be too sharply drawn, so too might the distinction between learning and cognition.

COGNITIVE PROCESSES

Perception

Interestingly, built into the perceptual systems of animals are decision processes of the sort that could otherwise be mediated by learning or cognition. For example, the eye of a vertebrate is a complicated mechanism shaped by evolution to solve problems of importance to a given species in its particular environment. The senses, therefore, may be regarded as information-processing devices. Consider some examples. Frogs have retinal "bug detectors." The retina of the rabbit contains several specialized mechanisms, including a "hawk detector." Different species of birds have different retinal distributions of photoreceptors shaped by their particular environments. As one example, birds of prey, which tend to hunt from above, have the densest array of photoreceptors in the section of the retina that views the ground. Moreover, the placement of eyes in the head varies according to an animal's lifestyle. In some animals, our species included, the eyes face toward the front. In other species, the eyes are placed more to the side of the head so as to better view stimuli from the sides and behind. To consider still another example, bees and some species of birds are able to detect ultraviolet light.

Some ant species send out foragers who follow more or less random paths in their explorations. On the way out the scouts lay down a train of scent molecules, or *pheromones*. When a scout finds food it returns to the colony. A scout finding more nearby food returns to the nest sooner and thus lays down a stronger scent path. Other ants follow the stronger path. A longer path leading to food, discovered by any other scout, gets less traffic and its scent fades as the pheromones evaporate. This apparently simple sensory solution to a problem of importance to the survival of ants has, according to Peterson (2000), suggested to engineers and computer scientists "powerful computational methods for finding alternative traffic routes over congested telephone lines and novel algorithms for governing how robots operating independently would work together" (p. 314). Moreover, some computer scientists have devised software to solve complex problems by mimicking the pheromone-following behavior of ants.

All of the previously cited examples, from ants to bees to frogs to birds to rabbits (not to mention echolocating in bats), indicate that sensory systems of animals have evolved to solve significant problems. Thus these systems, if not cognitive themselves, are at least in some instances the gateways to cognition, and they solve problems that would otherwise involve cognition. Moreover, a better understanding of these sensory systems, whether it be of pheromone-sensing ants, or of echolocation-using bats, may provide important clues to the operation of higher level cognitive processes.

Discrimination Learning and Categorization

In a *discrimination learning* study a hungry rat might be rewarded with food for responding to one stimulus, say, black (B), and nonrewarded for responding to another stimulus, say, white (W). The two stimuli may be presented separately on different trials (*successive training*) or together in the same trial (*simultaneous training*). In successive training, discrimination learning might be indexed by more vigorous responding to B (called the *positive cue,* in this case, B+) than to W (called the *negative cue,* W−). In simultaneous training, B might appear irregularly on the left (B+W−) on half the trials and on the right (W−B+) on the remaining half. Discrimination learning might be indexed by the animal's selection of B+ when it is either to the left or to the right of W−.

Discrimination learning has been and continues to be a major battleground between theories that stress associations and theories that stress other processes such as cognition or perception. Spence's (1936, 1937) theory of discrimination learning is a good example of a more or less orthodox associative theory that has battled successfully with various nonassociative views. Spence's theory suggests that all stimuli falling on the receptors when a response is made become excitatory when rewarded (i.e., such stimuli elicit responding) and that all stimuli falling on the receptors when a response is made become inhibitory when nonrewarded (e.g., such stimuli oppose responding). Both excitation and inhibition generalize to similar stimuli (*stimulus generalization*), and *net excitation* (excitation minus inhibition) regulates responding. This deceptively straightforward and simple theory is quite powerful. First, it can explain many discrimination learning phenomena. Second, the theory is general and can be used, for example, to explain the acquisition of concepts or categories, as will be explained shortly.

Spence's theory, as indicated, suggests that a variety of stimuli simultaneously become excitatory when rewarded and inhibitory when nonrewarded . Lashley (1929) opposed Spence on this score, suggesting instead the more cognitive view that animals selectively attend to stimuli. Discrimination learning, according to Lashley, consists of successively eliminating, one by one, stimuli that fail to predict successfully, the animal ultimately fastening on the relevant stimulus dimension. Lashley's attentional-cognitive view was not supported by experiments showing that reversal of the positive and negative cues (i.e., B+W− to W+B−) while animals were still responding at a chance level (50% correct) on the original problem (B+W−) produced serious retardation in learning the reversal (W+B−). Such retardation should not occur, according to Lashley, because animals responding at a chance level have not (by definition) isolated the relevant stimulus dimension; thus, reversing the S+ and S− cues should not influence the final solution, which is contrary to fact. Attentional theories that assume animals can attend to two or more stimuli simultaneously are better able to deal with the reversal findings described previously (see, e.g., Sutherland & Mackintosh, 1971). Spence's theory predicts, of course, that reversing the S+ and S− cues when the animal is responding at a 50% level will have a deleterious effect on discriminative responding. This is because animals responding at a 50% (or chance) level have nevertheless learned something about the S+ and S− cues, enough to retard reversal learning.

Gestalt psychology, which emphasized perception, explained discrimination learning in terms of learning relationships between stimuli. In a B+W− discrimination, for example, the animal would not learn that B is excitatory and W is inhibitory, as Spence suggested, but rather would learn to select the darker of the two stimuli. Offered as support for the Gestalt view was the phenomenon of *transposition*. For example, an animal that learned to select medium gray (positive) over light gray (negative) might, in a subsequent test phase, when given a choice between the medium gray and a newly introduced dark gray, actually select the novel dark gray because it is the darker of the two stimuli.

Spence's arguments with Lashley and the Gestalt psychologists illustrate an important point suggested earlier: Discrimination learning has been and continues to be an important battleground for testing the adequacy of associative versus various nonassociative approaches to animal cognition and learning. Spence's theory is able to explain transposition in associative terms without appealing to the learning of

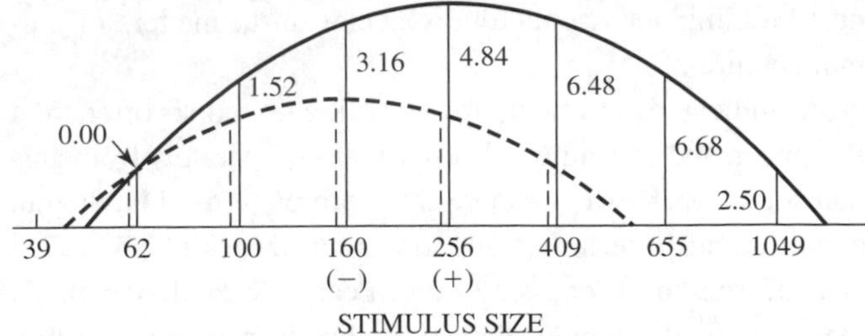

Figure 14.2 From Spence (1937). Excitation at S+ (solid line) and inhibition at S− (dotted line) and their generalization to other stimuli. As explained in the text, more net excitation (excitation minus inhibition) exists at S+ than at S−, thus producing discriminative responding, and more excitation exists at a stimulus to the right of S+ (stimulus 409) than at S+ itself, producing transposition.

relationships. This is shown graphically in Figure 14.2. The figure shows inhibition and its generalization associated with the negative (S−) cue (dotted line) and excitation and its generalization associated with the positive (S+) cue (solid line). Net excitation is shown by the length of the solid vertical lines above various stimulus points. Note that greater net excitation is associated with the S+ cue rather than with the S− cue, and so the animal will select the S+ cue. However, greater net excitation is associated with the cue to the right of the S+ cue, and so the animal will select that, novel untrained stimulus in preference to the S+ cue—the transposition phenomenon. In sum, Spence's theory is able to explain transposition by employing rather orthodox associative concepts.

More recently, individuals concerned with evaluating the role of cognition have employed categorization experiments that are, essentially, elaborate discrimination learning investigations. In these, pigeons might be shown numerous photographic slides containing (say) trees and numerous other slides lacking trees (e.g., Herrnstein, 1979). The pigeon might be rewarded for pecking the "tree" slides (S+ cue) but not reinforced for pecking the non-tree slides (S− cue). The pigeons readily learn this sort of discrimination, which they transfer well to novel stimuli. The meaning of results of this sort remains unclear. For example, one might think it is easier to learn a category (trees vs. non-trees) than to learn 80 unrelated slides (40+ and 40−). Vaughan and Greene (1984), however, employing 160+ slides and 160− slides, uncategorized, showed that pigeons more or less easily came to master the discrimination and even performed well after a 2-year rest. Although pigeons perform better with categorical than with noncategorical grouping of stimuli, this may not indicate that they learned a concept (see Watanabe, Lea, & Dittrich, 1993). It is the case that category slides will have more in common with each other than will noncategory slides. Thus more excitatory stimulus generalization will occur between category slides than between noncategory slides. An associative approach can explain much of the available category data (Wasserman & Astley, 1994). *Feature theory*, the view that a set of conjoined features separates category members from nonmembers, has been applied to category data (Watanabe et al., 1993). Feature theory, too, is compatible with an associative analysis.

In categorization experiments animals may come to form a *prototype,* an exemplar representing the central tendency of all of the individual exemplars. For example, a robin is a better prototype of bird than is, say, a penguin. There is no compelling evidence that animals form prototypes (see, e.g., Mackintosh, 1995). Rather, available data in animals can be interpreted in terms of exemplars. An extensive discussion of the use of concepts and categories by humans is to be found in the Goldstone and Kersten chapter in this volume.

Serial Learning

The specific experiments cited in the previous section, as well as many other types, are explicitly recognized instances of discrimination learning. However, there are many other types of investigations that are clear instances of discrimination learning but are not generally considered under that heading. A case in point is *serial learning,* a procedure popular in animal and human learning alike. In one type of serial learning task, items are presented successively in a particular order (e.g., A-B-C-D) and the animal's task is to learn both the items and the specific order in which they occur. People master many sorts of successive serial tasks: days of the week, months of the year, the alphabet, and so on. In a serial learning task in which items are presented successively, the animal must learn to respond differentially to different stimuli; thus serial learning is a variety of discrimination learning.

Not surprisingly, the issues raised in animal serial learning are quite similar to those raised in connection with explicitly recognized instances of discrimination learning. In some respects, however, contrary to popular opinion, serial learning data are more germane to the issue of animal cognition than are currently available, explicitly recognized instances of discrimination learning, including category learning. For one thing, there can be little doubt that serial learning, as investigated using animals, involves cognition of some sort, particularly memory, as we shall see. For another, it is clear that categorization (called *chunking*) is involved in serial learning, and it apparently cannot be explained in terms of stimulus generalization.

Consider an animal that learned to respond appropriately to a progressively decreasing series of reward magnitudes terminating in nonreward (e.g., large reward, medium reward, small reward, nonreward). Appropriate responding might consist of progressively weaker responding over the series. What has an animal learned in such a case? Consider three different interpretations. The animal may, as the Gestalt psychologists have suggested, have learned a relationship among the items; that is, it may be that reward magnitude decreases monotonically over trials (e.g., Hulse & Dorsky, 1977). The animal may learn an association between the item and its position in the series—that is, that Position 1 signals large reward, Position 2 signals medium reward, and so on (Burns, Dunkman, & Detloff, 1999). The animal may also learn an association between the memory of one or more prior items and the current item; that is, the memory of Item A (large reward) signals B (medium reward), the memories of Items A and B signal C (small reward), and so on (see Capaldi, 1994). Recent evidence suggests that rats are able to employ either item cues or position cues in learning a successively presented series of food items (Burns et al., 1999; Capaldi & Miller, 2001a). The conditions under which rats may tend to employ either position cues or item cues or both have yet to be isolated and identified clearly.

In the sort of serial learning task examined in this section, items are separated by a retention interval. For example, a given item, say, A, may be presented and removed minutes or hours before the participant is asked to respond to the next item, B. Appropriate serial responding under retention interval conditions necessarily involves employing the memory or representation of some prior event (item memory, position memory, or both) in order to anticipate the current event correctly. Series may be employed such that the memory or representation involved is necessarily that of one or more prior items. As an example, consider rats that have received two slightly different series in irregular order: XNY and ZNN (Capaldi & Miller, 1988a). X, Y, and Z are discriminably different food items; N is nonreward. Items of each series were separated by shorter intervals than that separating the series themselves. Rats trained XNY and ZNN learn to respond correctly to the third item of the series—that is, to respond more vigorously to Y than to N. Trial 3 running cannot be mediated by the Trial 2 event because it is the same in both series, N. Whatever else may be the case, therefore, discriminative responding on Trial 3 requires that the rat remember on Trial 3 the item presented on Trial 1; that is, the rat must respond more vigorously when X occurred on Trial 1 than when Z occurred on Trial 1. Further implicating memory, rats have responded more vigorously on rewarded (R) than nonrewarded (N) trials when the R and N trials were alternated (R, N, R, N, etc.) and the retention interval was 24 hr (e.g., Capaldi & Lynch, 1966; Capaldi & Minkoff, 1966).

A *chunk* consists of lower order functional elements (e.g., letters of the alphabet) combined to form higher order elements (e.g., words). If items of a series are grouped—say some on the left, others on the right—rats may tend to chunk items similarly grouped (see Capaldi, 1992). Chunking is clearly a form of categorization. Grouping cues that lead to chunking in people have been used with rats and shown to be similarly effective. These include the presentation of items under different brightness conditions, in different spatial locations, and at different temporal intervals (see, e.g., Capaldi, 1992, 1994).

Another method employed in investigating serial learning is the displaying of all items simultaneously rather than successively. The participants' task is to respond to the items in a particular order. One of the more interesting findings obtained employing the simultaneous presentation of items is that monkeys appear to have a better grasp of an overall sequence of events than do pigeons. For example, pigeons make more errors than monkeys to interior items of, say, a five-item series (see D'Amato & Colombo, 1988; Terrace, 1986).

A *reward schedule investigation* consists of presenting rewards according to some rule. For example, food reward might occur on a random half of all trials, nonreward on the other half. A reward schedule of this sort, called a *50% irregular partial reward schedule,* is clearly of major concern to various orthodox theories of animal learning. We might ask what, theoretically speaking, the difference is between a 50% irregular schedule of partial reward and a serial learning task in which, say, reward magnitudes become progressively smaller over successive trials (a decreasing monotonic schedule). It is the case that the two sorts of situation have been treated differently in that many theories that attempt to deal with 50% irregular schedules do not attempt to deal with monotonic schedules, and vice versa. Recent evidence suggests that treating the two sorts of schedules differently appears to be unjustified (Capaldi & Miller, in 2001b). That is, memory, which is clearly a major factor controlling performance in orthodox cases of serial learning (e.g., the monotonic schedule) is also a major factor in controlling performance in orthodox reward schedule cases (e.g., the 50% irregular schedule). Capaldi and Miller (2001b) demonstrated, essentially, that similar variables, such as the number of nonrewarded trials that occur in succession, have identical effects in the two situations. The general implication of such findings is as follows. If a clearly cognitive process such as memory is intimately involved in regulating performance under 50% irregular schedules, it is probably a factor in regulating instrumental learning generally. Put somewhat differently, the usual distinction between orthodox learning tasks (e.g., varieties of instrumental conditioning) and orthodox cognitive tasks (e.g., complex serial learning) may be artificial, cognition being involved in both.

The investigation of chunking in serial learning provides a window into the ability of an animal such as the rat to organize separately presented items into wholes. Evidence has been presented indicating that rats can form three different sorts of chunks of varying degrees of complexity (see Capaldi, 1992; Haggbloom, Birmingham, & Scranton, 1992). Consider a rat trained in a runway—an apparatus in which the animal must run from one end of a confined path to the other end to obtain food. The first (and lowest order) chunk formed is what is called the *trial chunk.* A trial chunk consists of the animal's combining into a single whole the separate events of the trial—for example the opening of a door to allow the animal access to the runway, to the animal's running in the middle section of the runway, to its entering the goal box at the end of the runway. The next highest chunk is called a *series chunk,* which consists of the animal's combining trial chunks into a higher level chunk. For example, a rat trained under four nonrewarded trials followed by a rewarded trial responds as follows: It begins by running slowly to the initial nonrewarded trial, the progressively increases its running speed over the successive nonreward trials, until by the terminal nonrewarded trial, the animal runs about as fast as it is able. Such responding indicates that the rat is treating the five trials, four nonrewarded followed by a reward, as a single organized whole or a chunk. The third chunk, a *list chunk,* consists of the animal's using a series chunk as a discriminative stimulus or signal for a subsequent series chunk. For example, rats have learned that a particular series of perhaps three trials (say, two rewards followed by a nonreward) will signal, some 1 to 20 min later, another distinctive subsequent series of, say, three trials. This only reliable signal of the subsequent series is the *initial series*. Under these conditions, rats have correctly anticipated the trials of the subsequent series (e.g., running fast, fast, slow, respectively, over the three trials consisting of two rewards followed by a nonreward). List chunks indicate that rats possess a fairly high capacity to organize discrete events into wholes (see Haggbloom et al., 1992).

An explanation of how chunks are formed in serial tasks stresses *overshadowing* (Capaldi, Birmingham, & Miller, 1999). Overshadowing may occur when two stimuli, A and B, signal some event, X, when one of the stimuli is a more valid or reliable signal than the other. In a case of this sort the more valid or reliable signal becomes the stronger signal for X. In a serial task, item validity may be reduced when similar or identical items signal different items. For example, in the series A-B-C-B-D-E, the validity of B is reduced because it signals both C and D. Thus, if some novel cue were to signal D exclusively, it would be more valid than B, and it (rather than B) would become the better signal for D. This would result in the formation of the series A-B-C-B-D-E into two chunks, A-B-C-B and D-E.

Numerical Abilities

In recent years, much experimental effort has been invested in detecting numerical abilities in animals, most notably birds, rats, monkeys, and chimpanzees (see, e.g., Boysen & Capaldi, 1993). At a relatively simple level, animals may be asked to discriminate between two quantities, more versus less—a relative numerousness discrimination. At a more complicated level, animals may be asked to perform some operation on numbers, such as addition or subtraction. In between these extremes animals may be asked to count—that is, to enumerate items explicitly. The accumulating evidence reveals that animals may be able to do each of these things, although operating on numbers has as yet been demonstrated only in the chimpanzee (Boysen & Berntson, 1989). In that study a chimpanzee that visited a number of food sites, each containing a different number of food items, was able at the end of the circuit to select an Arabic numeral corresponding to the total number of items seen. The animal had not been explicitly trained to add items, only to enumerate them.

In *explicit counting* studies, items have been presented either simultaneously or successively. In such investigations a variety of stimuli are confounded with number of items, and these confounds must be removed. For example, all else being equal, it takes longer to present three items than two items. Contemporary counting studies (e.g., Capaldi, 1998) have gone to great lengths to eliminate these confounds successively. Those studies and others have found that animals such as birds, rats, and monkeys can make discriminations based upon the number of items. One of the major issues in counting studies is whether animals count reluctantly and only when the number of items is the only discriminative cue available (Davis & Pérusse, 1988). Furthermore, do animals count routinely and rather easily, employing the number of items as a discriminative cue even when number is confounded with other variables (e.g., Capaldi & Miller, 1988b)?

An animal may be said to be counting if its behavior suggests conformance with three principles. The items to be counted or enumerated should be arrayed in one-to-one correspondence to internal number tags, which in the case of people are conventional symbols such as one, two, three, and so on. The tags should be applied to events in a stable order. Thus we may not enumerate items one, two, three in one occasion and one, three, two on another occasion. The *order irrelevance principle* suggests that items may be enumerated in any order. For example, in enumerating three different items X, Y, and Z we may do so in any order: X first and Z last, or Z first and X last, and so on. In experiments reported by Capaldi and collaborators (see, e.g., Capaldi, 1993; Capaldi & Miller, 1988b), rats were shown to be able to enumerate successively presented food items according to the three principles just outlined. In those experiments, control was exercised over variables confounded with number of successively presented food items, such as amount eaten, time spent eating, response effort expended in obtaining food items, and so on (see Capaldi, 1993, 1998).

Gelman and Gallistel (1978) suggested that children count effortlessly and as a matter of course. One might say that counting is an instinct in humans (see, e.g., Spelke, 2001). Capaldi and Miller (1988b; see also Capaldi, 1993) suggested that rats also enumerate items as a matter of course and will do so even when number of items is confounded with other variables. In one experiment, Capaldi and Miller (1988b) trained rats such that number of food items was confounded with a number of other variables, among them, time and effort. When the confounds were removed and only number of food items was a valid cue, the rats continued to behave appropriately, indicating that counting occurred even when other valid cues were simultaneously available.

Highly interesting data relevant to this important issue were recently reported by Brannon and Terrace (2000). In that investigation, rhesus monkeys were trained to enumerate items (such as geometrical forms) that were presented visually. In initial training sessions the animals enumerated 1 to 4 items. Having mastered 1 to 4 items, the monkeys were now asked to enumerate 5 to 9 items without explicit training. The monkeys quickly did so. Brannon and Terrace suggested that these findings indicated that monkeys count even when not forced to do so.

The interests of investigators concerned with counting in animals vary. Some seem interested in animal counting for its own sake. Some seem interested in similarities and differences between human and animal cognition (see, e.g., Brannon & Terrace, 2000). Still others have suggested that counting is of interest because it is routinely involved in many learning situations ranging from irregular reward schedule to serial learning (e.g., Capaldi, 1994; Capaldi & Miller, 1988b).

Theory of Mind

As applied to humans, having a *theory of mind* means that we attribute behavior—our own as well as that of others—to beliefs and desires. Baron-Cohen (1995) has suggested that humans have an innate "theory of mind module." According to Baron-Cohen, autistic children, some of whom seem not to be aware of others (as evidenced by their sitting alone, rocking back and forth, and in other respects living in a private world), lack a theory of mind.

Premack and Woodruff (1978) asked whether the chimpanzee has a theory of mind. This question has sparked considerable research and much controversy over the last 20 years or so. C. M. Heyes (1998) concluded that no convincing evidence has been produced to suggest that chimpanzees have a theory of mind. Reaction to her criticisms has been varied. At one extreme, Gordon (1998) suggested that the question itself is ill conceived and thus not worth asking. Byrne (1998) suggests, on the other hand, that Hayes misrepresents findings and that the theory-of-mind approach is a useful one.

Heyes (1998) identified six areas of investigations emphasized in theory-of-mind research: imitation, self-recognition, social relationships, rule taking, deception, and perspective taking. In this chapter, two of these areas will be discussed in enough detail to give, hopefully, an adequate idea of what is intended by the term *theory of mind*. These are *self-recognition* and *imitation*.

Self-Recognition

Gordon Gallup (1970) presented chimpanzees with mirrors. Initially the chimpanzees reacted to the mirror images as though they were other chimpanzees. Following hours of experience with mirrors, the chimpanzees dropped other-directed behavior in favor of what Gallup termed *self-directed behavior*. These self-directed behaviors were interpreted by Gallup to indicate that a chimpanzee recognized the image in the mirror as itself. To provide better evidence for self-recognition, Gallup devised the *mark test*: He anesthetized the animals and marked then with an undetectable (i.e., odorless) dye over one eye and the opposite ear—areas that could not be seen without the aid of the mirror. The basic finding was that chimpanzees that had mirror experience showed mark-directed behavior, whereas control chimpanzees lacking mirror experience did not.

Gallup's (1970) initial conclusion was that chimpanzees are capable of recognizing themselves and therefore have a sense of self-awareness. Subsequently, Gallup (1977) extended his conclusions. The ability to self-recognize, Gallup suggested, implied consciousness and self-consciousness, the latter encompassing the ability to think about thinking and to be aware of one's own state. In 1982, Gallup went still further. An animal that is self-aware, he suggested, has a mind, and having a mind includes having empathy and the ability to deceive.

Human children, of course, have passed the mark test, as have some orangutans. After several failures, gorillas have been shown to pass the mark test. In general, monkeys fail the mark test, and even in instances in which behavior has been directed at the mark, the observation is equivocal. A variety of additional findings have been reported: Not all chimpanzees pass the mark test; young chimpanzees (below age 3 years, 6 months) may prove likely to fail the mark test. Epstein, Lanza, and Skinner (1981) claim to have trained a pigeon to pass the mark test, a claim that has been disputed (e.g., Gallup, 1982).

Criticism of the self-recognition claim ranges from the observation that failing the mark test may not imply a diminished mental capacity, to the observation that passing the mark test may not indicate advanced mental capacity. As an example of the former, it has been observed that monkeys may not look in the mirror because eye-contact is a threatening gesture. As an example of the latter, mirror recognition may imply no more than that the animal has a "body concept," one that is used in, say, ordinary locomotion.

A test similar to the mark test has been employed with children; it is called the *rouge test*. Children are given a small rouge mark below the right eye that can be recognized only by using a mirror. By about 19 months of age, 52% of children immediately direct behavior to the rouge, indicting self-recognition (Asendorpf, Warkentin, & Baudonniere, 1996).

Imitation and Social Learning

By observing another engage in some extended act that involves a number of different and discrete steps, a person may learn in a matter of minutes what might otherwise require hours or days of individual effort without guidance. Any number of such activities comes to mind, ranging from changing a tire to setting a VCR. Perhaps because learning by observing others is so important and widespread in the human species, some have taken it to be a hallmark of intelligence in other species. For example, Romanes (1882) provided a number of rich examples of animals' engaging in quite complex behaviors established by imitation. The problem is that Romanes's examples were based on anecdotes and thus his data by modern and entirely reasonable standards are deficient.

Determining the extent to which other species learn by imitation is a more difficult problem than it appears to be at first blush. For example, what sort of behaviors should be selected for analysis? Well-fed chickens can be induced to continue to eat by watching other chickens feed. It would seem that species-typical behavior, such as chickens' pecking for food, would provide relatively unconvincing evidence for true imitation. The idea of learning by imitation would seem to require three things to be entirely convincing: The behavior to be imitated should be stored as a representation by the observer; the observer's behavior should be a more or less faithful copy of the demonstrator's behavior; and the behavior imitated should be reasonably complex and not a species-typical behavior such as pecking by a chicken. A useful experimental design to study imitation is called the *two-action test.* In this design, a given result may be accomplished in two different ways. Observers should be shown to engage in the particular behavior that they were allowed to observe rather than the one not observed (Heyes, 1996).

Rats prefer foods their mothers ingested during pregnancy and after birth. Nursing rats come to prefer foods ingested by their mothers. Rats also come to prefer foods eaten by their conspecific; one way they determine what this is food is is by smelling the breath of their conspecific. It has been shown that a group of rats that has come to prefer a specific flavor will pass on that preference to new members of the group.

Roof rats have come to occupy the pine forests of Israel, where they subsist on pine seeds, which are rendered difficult to extract because of the tough scales that must be removed. To remove the scales, the rat must begin chewing on them at the base of the cone, removing them scale by scale by following the spiral pattern that goes to the top of the cone. Rats have failed to learn this if left to their own devices. If raised with a mother who is an efficient stripper they do acquire the knack of getting to the seeds—but not, apparently, through imitation. They acquire the behavior by getting access to cones that have already been partially stripped, even if they have been partially stripped by the experimenter.

In a noteworthy case of observational conditioning, monkeys have acquired fear of snakes by observing a demonstrator monkey exhibiting such fear (Mineka & Cook, 1988). Fear is acquired even by merely observing a demonstrator on video showing fear to a toy snake. Monkeys have observed demonstrators on video showing an apparent fear of flowers that had been spliced into the film in place of the snake. Fear of snakes is acquired more readily by naive monkeys than fear of flowers.

In addition to observational conditioning, three others categories of learning have been distinguished: stimulus enhancement, emulation, and imitation. In *stimulus enhancement,* the demonstrator's behavior simply directs the observer to stimuli that makes copying the demonstrated behavior more likely. *Emulation* occurs when behavior is copied in a more or less general way by employing techniques different from that of the demonstrator. *Imitation* involves faithful copying of the demonstrator's behavior. Children appear to imitate behavior more faithfully than chimpanzees (see, e.g., Whiten & Boesch, 1999).

Interest in imitation or learning from others has a long history (e.g., Romanes, 1882; Thorndike, 1911), and over that long period of time scores of observational and experimental reports have been published. Nevertheless, we know little about imitation. One problem is the lack of a useful theory of imitation that can direct our efforts into useful channels. Another is that only in relatively recent times have we developed useful experimental procedures for investigating learning by observation. Two examples here would include the video techniques mentioned earlier for examining fear acquisition in monkeys, and the two-action experimental design. It may not be too optimistic to conclude that our understanding of imitation may undergo rapid and significant development over the next few years.

Interval Timing

The ability of animals to time arbitrary events has been intensively investigated in recent years through a variety of procedures. How animals time intervals is seen as important for understanding learning and cognition generally. For example, according to one view, animals employ the same mechanisms to time events as to count them. Even more generally, timing events has been seen as fundamental to understanding all varieties of learning and cognition (Gallistel & Gibbon, 2000). That is, both Pavlovian and instrumental procedures are seen as involving the learning of temporal intervals. For example, in the Pavlovian preparation the animal responds most vigorously at the termination of the conditioned stimulus in delayed conditioning. This finding suggests that the animals are sensitive to the time elapsed since the stimulus was presented. In instrumental conditioning, it has been suggested that the animals compared the time to reinforcement in the trial to the overall time between reinforcements (but see Capaldi, Alptekin, & Birmingham, 1996).

Most studies explicitly concerned with timing have used instrumental conditioning. In the *peak procedure,* animals receive many daily trials in which reinforcement occurs after a fixed time following the onset of a signal (Roberts, 1981). A major finding is that animals respond most at approximately the time that reinforcement is due. For example, if the interval is 20 s, most responding occurs at about 20 s. Another major finding using the peak procedure is that maximum response rate is reached at a certain proportion of the way into this interval regardless of the interval's length.

In tests of *temporal generalization,* an animal is reinforced for responding to one signal duration but not others. A major finding using this procedure is that a typical generalization gradient is obtained with maximum responding confined to the reinforced duration (Church & Gibbon, 1982).

In the *bisection procedure,* two levers may be inserted into an operant box; the rat is reinforced for pressing the left lever after a tone of one duration and the right lever after a tone of another duration (Church & Deluty, 1977). In the test condition, the rat is presented with tones of intermediate duration. Of special interest is the duration at which they choose each lever half the time (50% responding). It develops that the interval used by rats is the geometric mean of the two intervals not the arithmetic mean. For example, if the intervals are 4 s and 16 s, respectively, the arithmetic mean is 10 ([4+16]/2), whereas the geometric mean is 8 ($\sqrt{4 \times 16}$). In this example, 50% responding would occur closer to 8 s than to 10 s.

Other experiments indicate that animals time linearly and that they can start and stop their interval clocks. How animals time has produced much theorizing. It has been variously suggested that rats time by employing a pacemaker (e.g., Church, Meck, & Gibbon, 1994), by using oscillators (e.g., Gallistel, 1994), or by using behaviors that predictably fill given intervals (e.g., Killeen & Fetterman, 1988).

Gallistel and Gibbon (2000) have presented a timing theory that is highly ambitious in that it attempts to explain a wide range of phenomena. The theory has been used to explain phenomena as different as delayed classical conditioning to extinction following different reward schedules in instrumental conditioning. Whatever the fate of this theory, it is clear that animals such as rats and pigeons have well-developed capacities for timing events. How extensively this timing capacity enters into learning and cognition appears to be a major issue that will occupy investigators over the near future.

Memory

Memory is among the most intensively investigated topics in animal cognition. Animal memory may be studied either in its own right or as a mechanism controlling learning and performance. Determining under what conditions forgetting occurs is an example of the former; examining the capacity of the memory of nonreward stored on one trial to be retrieved on the next trial so as to correctly anticipate the reward outcome on that trial is an example of the latter.

It is now recognized that animals can retain information over long temporal periods. This was not always known. In the early days of the investigation of animal learning, laboratory data suggested that animals possessed only fleeting memory. A popular procedure devised by W. S. Hunter (1913) in the early 1900s is a case in point. In Hunter's procedure, called *delayed reaction,* animals that were retained in a delay chamber could determine which of three doors lead to food because a light was flashed in front of the correct door. After the light went off animals ran from the delay chamber to the doors after varying retention intervals. Rats failed at this task with delays of as little as 10 s. Raccoons were able to respond correctly following a delay of up to 25 s.

Contrast such poor performance with some subsequent findings obtained under both field conditions and in the laboratory. A certain bird, Clark's nutcracker, stores the seeds of pine cones in individual caches in the late summer and early spring when food is plentiful, recovering the seeds months later when food is scarce. It is estimated that the bird stores many thousands of seeds in caches of a few seeds each. A high percentage of seeds is recovered by the bird. Skinner (1950) trained pigeons to peck for food at a spot on an illuminated key. Following a 4 year retention interval the pigeons were tested and immediately pecked the correct key. Wendt (1937) trained a dog to withdraw its foot at the sound of a tone paired with shock. After a 30 month retention period, foot withdrawal to the tone occurred on 80% of the test trials, only a slight drop from the prior training session.

A currently debated topic concerns whether memory is a unitary system or is composed of two or more subsystems. Some examples of currently postulated subsystems are procedural versus declarative memory, semantic versus episodic memory, and long-term versus short-term memory (see, e.g., Spear & Riccio, 1994). In the animal area one of the most popular distinctions is that between working memory and reference memory. *Working memory* is concerned with keeping track of information that may change from one trial to the next. *Reference memory* is concerned with isolating important relationships in the situation that are stable over trials. As an example, consider rats rewarded for a running response on every other trial, under a single alternation schedule of rewarded and nonrewarded trials. Rats so trained may eventually come to run faster on rewarded than on nonrewarded trials. In this situation working memory would be used to determine whether reward or nonreward occurred on the prior trial and thus whether reward or nonreward is to occur on the current trial. Reference memory would be employed to learn that rewards and nonrewards occur according to a particular rule or schedule—a single alternating one.

Working memory, unlike short-term memory, may be effective following long retention intervals. In the single-alternation situation, as indicated earlier, rats have employed the memory of the reward outcome on the prior trial to anticipate the reward outcome correctly on the current trials when trials were separated by 24 hr (see, e.g., Capaldi, 1994). The single-alternation situation is useful for understanding a second popular distinction between memories in the animal area as well as in human memory: that between retrospective and prospective memory. In the case of the single-alternation schedule, *retrospective memory* would consist of retaining the memory of poor reward or nonreward over the retention interval, utilizing that memory to determine whether responding on the current trial should be fast or slow. Employing *prospective memory,* the animal would determine at the time of reward or nonreward whether it should run fast or slow on the subsequent trial, thus making it unnecessary to retain the memory of reward or nonreward over the retention interval.

Memory may be analyzed in terms of three stages. The first, *encoding,* refers to the stage in which the memory is formed. The second, *retention,* refers to the persistence of the memory over time. The third, *retrieval,* refers to recall of the stored memory. We may fail to remember because of poor retrieval cues. This occurs when the cues at retrieval differ from the cues that accompany storage. *Interference* may also be responsible for forgetting. In proactive interference, memory for material learned earlier may interfere with material learned later. In retroactive interference, material learned later may interfere with material learned earlier.

A popular procedure employed to study animal memory (it is sometimes used with people as well) is *delayed matching to sample* (*DMTS*). In this procedure a subject (say, a pigeon) is initially trained to peck each of three keys arranged in a horizontal row on the wall of an apparatus called an *operant chamber*. A typical trial begins by exposing a stimulus—the sample stimulus, say, a horizontal line on a white background—on the center key, with the side keys being blank. After the pigeon has observed the horizontal line, or sample stimulus, for some period (or has pecked it), the center key goes blank. There then ensues the retention interval in which all three keys remain blank. When the appropriate retention interval has elapsed the side keys are illuminated, one with the horizontal line and the other with a vertical line. These are called the *comparison stimuli*. A correct response, which may produce food reward, consists of pecking the side key that contains the comparison stimulus matching the sample—in the present example, the horizontal line. The horizontal and vertical lines may be presented equally often as samples in an irregular fashion over trials. The positions of the comparison stimuli are varied irregularly over trials such that each may appear equally often on the right key and on the left key.

Both retroactive and proactive interferences have been demonstrated in the DMTS situation. Retroactive interference has been investigated as follows. Typically the chamber is dark during the retention interval of a DMTS task. If, after the sample stimulus is removed, the chamber is illuminated, correct responding may decrease substantially. Proactive interference is a major factor in DMTS (see, e.g., Wright, Urcuioli, & Sands, 1986). For example, memory is much better when many rather than few sample stimuli are used. This is because presenting only a few sample stimuli increases proactive interference. In an interesting experiment employing monkeys, when trial unique stimuli were employed, retention was good even at a 24 hr interval.

Several models of Pavlovian conditioning emphasized memory. In an early model suggested by Wagner (1976), rehearsal of the conditioned stimulus was stressed. According to Wagner, surprising events are better rehearsed and thus better remembered than expected events. For example, on the first trial, a surprising tone may be strongly rehearsed together with the subsequent shock because of surprise. This would lead to a strong increment in the capacity of the tone to signal shock. On subsequent trials in which shock is expected following tone, and thus surprise is reduced, little or no increase in learning may occur.

A person may be asked to remember, say, 12 items consisting of 3 items in each of four different categories: flowers, foods, furniture, and animals. On outputting the items the person may do so by category: 3 flowers, followed by 3 animals, and so on. Organization processes of this sort are of concern in animal memory. For example, in a study by Roberts (1998), a 12-arm radial maze, which consists of a central platform with a number of arms branching out at equal angles, was baited with four each of three different types of food, always in the same arms over successive trials. For example, cheese might be placed in arms 1, 3, 5, and 8 on successive trials. The rats learned to take the food items in a particular order, each of the four preferred foods first, the four least preferred foods last. The ability of rats to employ one entire series of items to predict another series of items correctly, as considered earlier, is another example of complex organization processes in rats.

Animals such as birds, rats, and monkeys have been shown to possess highly impressive memories—impressive from the standpoint of retaining a considerable amount of information over long intervals (consider Clark's nutcracker), and from that of being able to organize discrete events into useful wholes (identified as *chunks* in the "Serial Learning" section). Memory investigations are perhaps as illuminating as any other in suggesting that animals are not merely passive learners but actively process information.

Spatial Learning

Animals may have to move around in space for a variety of reasons: to find mates, to forage for food, to escape predators. Thus, spatial learning is of vital importance to a wide variety of animals. Spatial learning is an area of intense investigation under both laboratory and field conditions and includes a variety of topics, ranging from the navigational abilities of birds to maze learning in rats. Accordingly, spatial learning occupies the attention of an equally diverse array of investigators, ranging from evolutionary biologists to experimental psychologists.

Consider an application of evolutionary thinking to spatial learning. Gaulin and Fitzgerald (1989) reasoned that spatial abilities would be genetically selected-for more often in males than in females of polygymous species of meadow voles, because the male maintains a larger home range in which to seek potential mates or resources to attract mates. They compared the polygamous meadow voles to the monogamous pine voles. They found, first of all, that sex difference in favor of a larger home range occurred in male meadow voles but not male pine voles. They compared the two species on a variety of mazes of increasing difficulty, finding that males outperformed females in meadow voles but not in pine voles. Moreover, the hippocampus, which is considered to be of importance in spatial learning, was found to be larger in meadow voles than in pine voles (Jacobs, Gaulin, Sherry, & Hoffman, 1990).

Sex differences in spatial learning occur in a variety of species, including humans. Human males outperform human females in a variety of spatial learning tasks ranging from mental rotation of objects to map reading. Human females outperform human males in recalling the locations of objects interspersed in a room, and the difference is larger for incidental learning than for direct learning. Silverman and Eals (1992) interpret these sex differences in humans in evolutionary terms. It is believed that in the Pleistocene (the period in which much human evolution is considered to have occurred), males tended to hunt, and so traveled greater distances than females (favoring male spatial learning), whereas females gathered items such as vegetables (which favored learning the location of items by females).

Spatial learning thus provides a good illustration of the evolutionary approach to animal and human cognition. The *evolutionary approach* assumes that the cognitive ability possessed by a species was designed by evolution to meet the demands of its particular environment. Thus the evolutionary approach is fully prepared to discover that a given species may possess a unique adaptation. Unique adaptations are hardly rare, and several have already been mentioned: echolocation in bats, dancing in bees, language in humans. That each of these has been considered to be instinctive by some does not necessarily lessen their importance to cognition. For example, although our species' ability to master language may be instinctive to a great degree, there is reason to suppose that language development was a major factor in human problem solving, tool using, and related cognitive activities (see, e.g., Bickerton, 1998).

The radial maze mentioned earlier is an important tool used to investigate spatial learning and other problems in the laboratory. A pellet of food is placed at the end of each arm of the maze. The rat is placed on the central platform and is free to enter the arms. Rats easily master radial mazes, as indicated by their entering each arm only once. Efficient performance of this sort may itself have an instinctive or unlearned basis. It has long been known that in, say, a T-maze, the rats, having obtained food in one arm, typically avoid that arm in favor of responding to the other arm, a behavior sometimes called *win-shift*. In foraging in the wild it may be of benefit to animals such as rats to avoid going back to a location in which food was obtained because the availability of food at that source may be less likely than at some new source.

Not only are eight-arm radial mazes solved efficiently by rats, but so, too, are mazes containing a greater number of arms. The most impressive of these was a hierarchical maze employed by Roberts (1998). That maze consisted of eight primary arms. At the end of each primary arm were three branching secondary arms. The rats performed very well in this maze under a variety of conditions. For example, under one condition the rats were allowed to enter the primary arms with some of the secondary arms blocked off. In a subsequent test phase the rats entered the previously blocked secondary arms with a high degree of accuracy. This finding indeed suggests that the rat's memory for spatial location is well developed. Another indication of the rat's impressive memory in this situation is the difficulty of producing retroactive inhibition. In retroactive inhibition, as indicated earlier, memory of an initial task is reduced by provision of a subsequent task prior to testing of the initial task. Various means of producing retroactive inhibition in the radial maze have been used, including learning another maze in a different room. In an impressive experiment by Beatty and Shavalia (1980), rats exhibited little to no retroactive interference when they were required to enter four arms of a different radial maze within a 4 hr retention interval.

Rats can learn radial mazes by employing either *distal cues,* such as the shape of the room, *landmark cues,* such as objects in the environment, or *intramaze cues,* such as light differences in the appearance of the maze in different areas. In a very interesting experiment Williams and Meck (1991) reported that in the radial maze distal cues were used more often by males than by females, with landmarks cues being used more often by females than by males.

How animals represent spatial conditions is a topic of great interest. According to one view, animals such as rats may possess a *cognitive map* of the environment that consists of both a general framework, within which objects are located relative to each other, and general features of the environment, such as its shape (O'Keefe & Nadel, 1978). Gallistel (1990) provides a somewhat different definition of a cognitive map, in that it is evidenced by any orientation based upon computing distance. Others suggest that the concept of a cognitive map is not necessary to explain spatial learning. According to this view, animals acquire a set of memories of local views of the environment associated with the particular movements that take them from one place to another (e.g., Leonard & McNaughton, 1990).

As much as any topic, the ability of animals to go from one place to another brings together the topics of instinct and cognition. Consider the indigo bunting, a bird studied by Emlen (1970). The bird migrates over great distances. Yet, although migration is a species-typical behavior, specific migratory routes are learned by the bird by its exposure to the star pattern in the sky. In what follows it is possible to describe only a few examples of the many procedures that have been used to study map like learning in various species of animals.

In going from one place to another, do animals learn to make specific responses or do they acquire more general, cognitively informed spatial information? An early and hotly contested attempt to resolve this issue involved what came to be known as the *place versus response controversy*. This may be illustrated by considering the two cross mazes shown in Figure 14.3. Two groups of rats might be used, both being trained to traverse the maze from each of two different start locations, S_1 and S_2. The difference is this: The group on the left is rewarded for making a specific response (turning left), going from S_1 to G_1 and from S_2 to G_2; the group on the right is rewarded for going to a specific place, from S_1 to G_1 and from S_2 to G_1. Thus the response group is rewarded for going to two different places whereas the place group is rewarded for making two different responses, left (S_1–G_1) and right (S_2–G_1). As a review (Restle, 1957) of the extensive literature in this area indicated, rats learn to do both. If trained in a visually rich, well-illuminated environment, the place group is superior to the response group. In an impoverished, dimly illuminated environment the response group is superior to the place group.

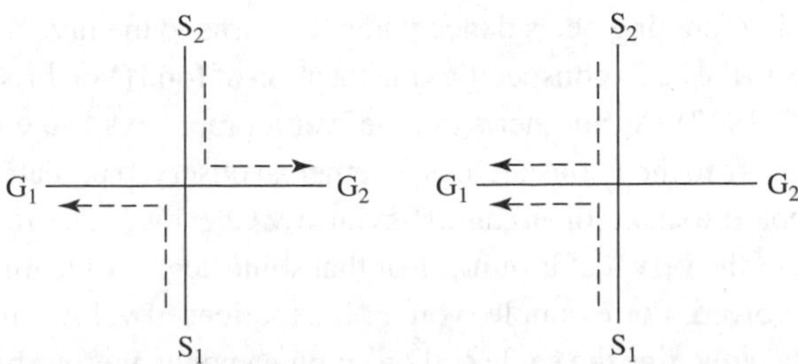

Figure 14.3 In the cross maze on the left, arrows indicate that animals starting at S_1 are reinforced for going to G_1 and animals starting at S_2 are reinforced for going to G_2, thus learning a left-turn response. In the cross maze on the right, animals starting at either S_1 or S_2 are reinforced for going to G_1 and thus learn to go to a place (a place response).

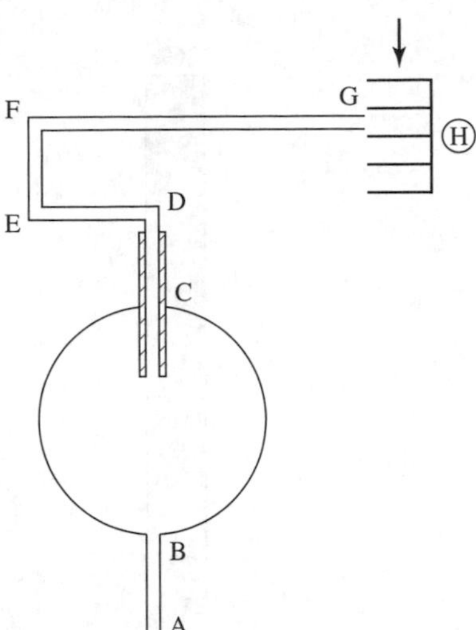

Figure 14.4 An apparatus employed by Tolman, Ritchie, and Kalish (1946). In preliminary training, rats were reinforced for running along the path A-B-C-D-E-F-G to H.

Another of the various procedures employed to determine whether rats learn specific responses or more general spatial information involved the maze shown in Figure 14.4. Path AB was the starting path. The rats ran along the paths B-C-D-E-F-G. H was a dim light. Figure 14.5 shows how the rats were tested. Path AD was blocked. Path 5 led to the original goal and the dim light, H. If the animals were learning a specific response, then presumably they would begin by going left, selecting paths 10 to 18. If they were learning to go to a

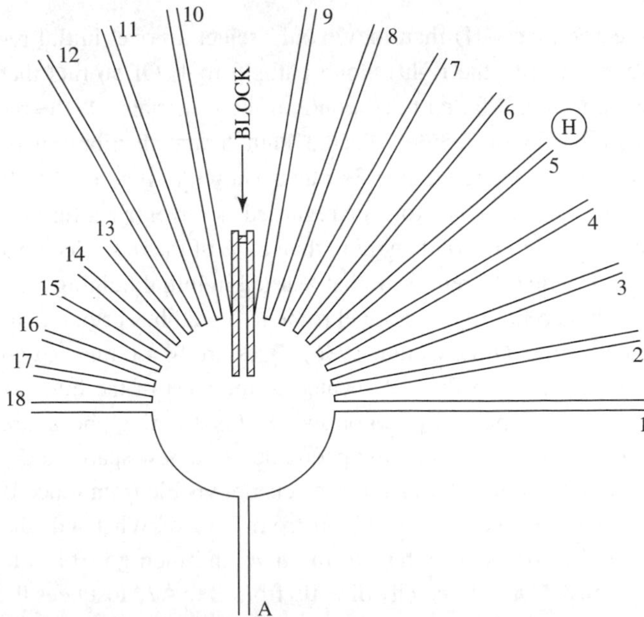

Figure 14.5 The apparatus employed in the test phase of the Tolman et al. (1946) experiment. The most frequently selected path was Path 6 (see Figure 14.6), indicating that the rats learned to go to a place rather than learn a specific response.

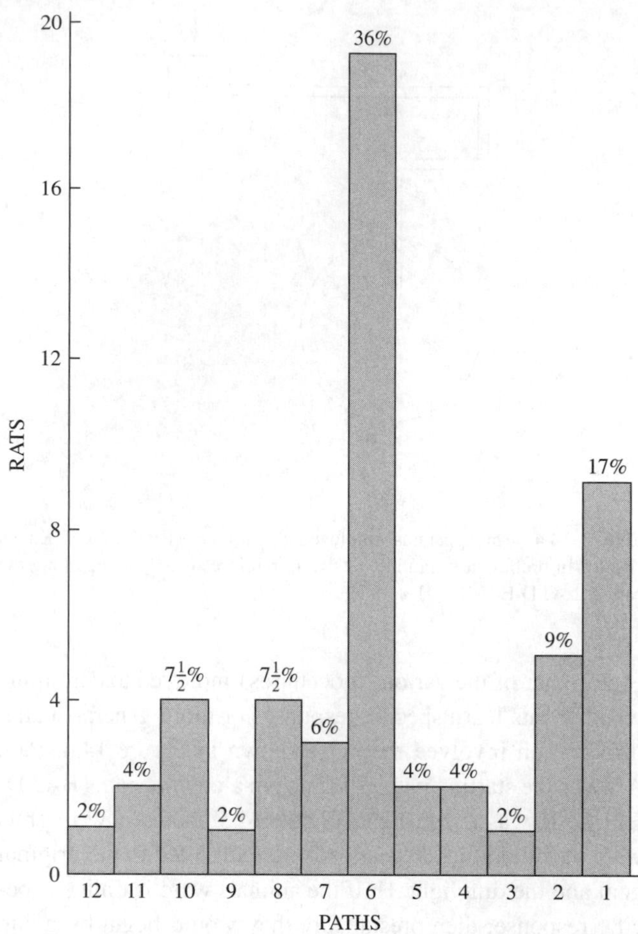

Figure 14.6 The distribution of choices in the test phase of the Tolman et al. (1946) experiment.

specific place (H) then they would select a novel initial response (go to the right) along paths 9 to 1. Of 56 rats that were tested, 3 failed to respond on the test trials. Of the remaining 53 rats, 36% selected Path 5; the distribution of choices for the remaining 34 rats is shown in Figure 14.6. If choices from paths 9 to 1 are regarded as novel (right turn instead of a left turn), then more than 87% of the rats selected a novel route different from that learned in initial training.

This ability to use a novel route to a goal has been examined in bees (J. L. Gould, 1986). Bees are first trained to go from the hive to Place A located to the west of the hive, as shown in Figure 14.7. Following this training, bees are caught and removed in an opaque box to a new spatial location to the south, Place B. Place A is not visible from Place B and the bees have never flown from B to A. What will the bees do? Will they return to the hive and then go from the hive to A? Or will they fly directly from B to A? Most bees fly directly from Place B to Place A. This behavior, Gould suggests, indicates that the bee is using a map-like representation of its environment.

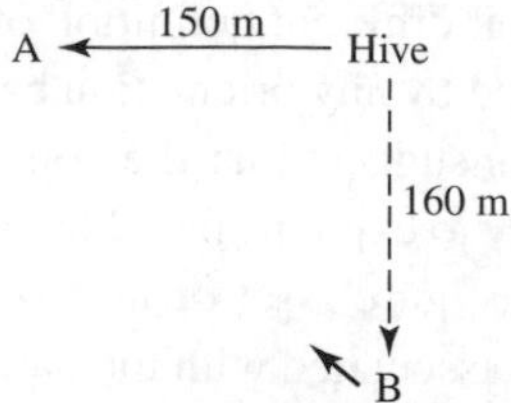

Figure 14.7 The figure shows that bees trained to go from the hive to Place A when moved to a new location (Place B) go from B to A, rather than from B to the hive to A.

Since bees and rats can employ novel routes to reach a goal, it is perhaps not surprising that the chimpanzee can do the same. In an interesting experiment by Menzel (1973), a chimpanzee was carried on the shoulders of one experimenter around a large area (4,000 m^2) while a second experimenter hid food in each of 18 randomly selected locations. The chimpanzees, when released, were highly successful in locating the hidden food, retrieving an average 13 of the 18 items. In so retrieving the hidden items, the animals neither followed the routes along which they had been taken, nor responded haphazardly and at random. Rather, they followed efficient routes that minimized the distance to the items.

Another indication that chimpanzees can form a map-like representation of the environment comes from a study by Menzel, Premack, and Woodruff (1978). In that study, chimpanzees were shown an impoverished TV picture of where food was hidden in a rather complicated area containing trees, hills, and large objects. They were more successful in reaching the goal than were control animals given no information. Thus chimpanzees can match the information provided on a flat TV screen to spatial locations in the three-dimensional environment.

Language Learning in Animals

It is quite clear that animals communicate in the sense that certain behaviors in one animal are capable of producing specific and predictable behaviors in another animal. Thus, as indicated, a foraging bee's dance when it returns to the hive indicates to the bee's conspecifics the location of food (Von Frisch, 1950, 1967). As another example, vervet monkeys can communicate to their conspecifics whether an observed predator is a leopard, a snake, or an eagle (Seyfarth & Cheney, 1990). In the case of the vervet, it is quite clear that some degree of learning is involved. For example, young, inexperienced vervets may mistakenly give the eagle call on spying a nondangerous bird.

Hockett (1960) identified 13 characteristics of human language that can be presented in any system of communication. These are shown in Table 14.1.

TABLE 14.1 The Thirteen Design Features of Language

Number	Design Feature
1.	Vocal auditory channel.
2.	Broadcast transmission and directional reception.
3.	Rapid fading (transitoriness).
4.	Interchangeability (a speaker can reproduce any linguistic message he or she can understand).
5.	Total feedback (the speaker of a language hears everything of linguistic relevance in what he or she says).
6.	Specialization (sound waves of speech serve only as signals).
7.	Semanticity.
8.	Arbitrariness.
9.	Discreteness.
10.	Displacement.
11.	Productivity.
12.	Traditional transmission.
13.	Duality of patterning.

Source: Hockett, 1960.

Hockett (1960) suggests that characteristics 1 through 5 (vocal auditory channel, broadcast transmission and directional reception, rapid fading [transitoriness], interchangeability, and total feedback) are common to a variety of animal species, including some birds and many mammals. Characteristics 6 through 8 (specializing, semanticity, arbitrariness) are to be found in primates. *Displacement,* the ability to consider things that are remote in either space or time, can be found only in humans. Other particularly human characteristics are *productivity* (the ability to say novel things), *duality of patterning* (which refers to making words from phonemes), and *arbitrariness* (the fact that words do not resemble the objects they signify in any physical sense).

Although animals are capable of communication, that they are capable of acquiring language is another matter, and one fraught with continuing controversy. On the one hand, there can be little doubt that many of the investigators of ape language, such as the Rumbaughs (e.g., Rumbaugh, 1977) and the Gardners (e.g., 1969), are quite convinced that chimpanzees possess the capacity to acquire language or some aspects of language. On the other hand, other investigators of ape language such as Terrace (1979) are equally convinced that no such thing has been demonstrated. To complete the picture, importantly, many linguists and other language experts are strongly of the opinion that no animal has come even close to demonstrating the sort of language ability displayed by humans (see, e.g., Healy, 1980; Pinker, 1994). They point out, among other things, that although children acquire complex language skills practically effortlessly, heroics and extensive training efforts are required to get chimpanzees to master relatively simple skills that may, at best, approximate language.

Some early unsuccessful attempts to teach language to animals involved raising chimpanzees or other primates at home and tutoring them in spoken English (C. Hayes, 1951; K. J. Hayes & Hayes, 1952). It came to be realized that the chimpanzees' vocal apparatus is not designed for speaking. Beatrice and Allen Gardner (1969) overcame the difficulty by teaching sign language to an infant, female chimpanzee named Washoe. After 51 months of training, Washoe had acquired 122 signals. It was asserted by the Gardners that Washoe could combine signals into phrases of some two to four items. An often-cited example is that Washoe gave two signs on seeing a swan: the sign for *water* followed by the sign for *bird.*

Another approach was to get Sarah, a now famous chimpanzee, to place symbols for objects on a board (Premack & Premack, 1983). Sarah was then thought to write sentences on the board. For example, Sara was given an apple if she placed on the board the symbols for *give* and *apple.*

Still another approach provided chimpanzees with keys on a computer exhibiting lexigrams. The lexigrams were different geometric patterns, each of which represented something such as a request (*please*) or an item (*banana*). Lana, one of the chimpanzees employed in this research, could request items by pressing the lexigrams in a particular order: *please machine give banana.*

Terrace (1979) trained a young chimpanzee named Nim Chimpsky (a play on the name of the famous linguist Noam Chomsky). Nim was taught sign language. As a result of his research, Terrace concluded that there was no evidence suggesting that Nim had learned language. Nim, it was concluded, was either imitating his trainer or was merely exhibiting a rather straightforward form of serial learning. Terrace's criticisms brought into question any attempt to teach language to an animal that evolved stringing together items, such as gestures or lexigrams, because these could easily be interpreted as forms of serial learning based on learning simple associations.

Following Terrace's telling criticisms, a new tactic was adopted by the Rumbaughs (e.g., Savage-Rumbaugh et al., 1993). Instead of attempting only to get animals to reproduce items such as signals or gestures, they also required the animals to comprehend items. For example, Kanzi, a pigmy chimpanzee (or bonobo), might be told "Kanzi go out to the hall and get the ball." By teaching Kanzi many words, presenting him with many sentences, and issuing commands to him using different word orders (e.g., Savage-Rumbaugh et al., 1993), the researchers concluded that Kanzi had acquired language in a meaningful sense. Indeed, in terms of sentence compression Kanzi was said to rival a child, Alia, up until the time she became 2 years old, after which age Alia increasingly surpassed Kanzi. The approach involving the ability to comprehend language has also been employed with the dolphin (e.g., Herman, 1986).

If children are more or less totally deprived of language experience when quite young, they exhibit serious deficiencies in language use later in life (Bickerton, 1998; Candland, 1993). On the other hand, if children are provided with minimum language experienced they use language normally later in life. Indeed, as Bickerton (1998) has described, children deprived of normal language manage on their own to create a fully functional language in a single generation. This has occurred, for example, when people who speak many different languages are thrown together (as on plantations) and communicate by means of what is called a *pidgin*. Pidgins are very simple ways of communicating that consist of two to three words. Children exposed to a pidgin, in the absence of explicit instruction, create a much more sophisticated language called a *Creole*. A similar thing happens when deaf children are exposed to parents or others who may use sign language badly. These facts and others (see Pinker, 1994) have caused language experts to suggest that the language gulf between humans and other animals is a matter of kind and not of degree.

From an evolutionary standpoint, there is no particular reason that our closest relative, the chimpanzee, should possess even a rudimentary language ability. Humans and chimpanzees separated from each other—that is, no longer shared a common ancestor—about 5 to 7 million years ago. Language ability may have evolved in the human line after we separated from the chimpanzee. Perhaps species more closely related to ours, such as the extinct *Homo erectus,* possessed language, or at least something approximating human language. Whatever the truth may be, the language gulf between humans and extant animals such as the chimpanzee is very large and may be one of kind, not degree.

Pidgins, as indicated, are very simple ways of communicating and consist of a few words being strung together like beads on a string. Bickerton (1998) has suggested that animals such as chimpanzees and bonobos are capable, at most, of acquiring a pidgin. According to Bickerton, children under 2 years of age use a pidgin, which is acquired on the basis of general intellectual capacity. At above 2 years of age, children begin to acquire language on the basis of a mechanism specifically shaped by evolution for this purpose, and often called a *language acquisition device*. In Bickerton's view, the language capacities of both mature apes and children under 2 years of age are on a par and do not represent true language. Interestingly, as indicated before, Kanzi, a bonobo, was able to follow verbal commands as well as Alia, a child, up until Alia was 2 years of age, whereupon Alia increasingly surpassed Kanzi in comprehension.

Experts are not agreed on many important aspects of language that may bear upon animal abilities along this line. To consider merely one line of disagreement, Pinker (1994) is of the opinion that language evolved slowly and in stages over the 350,000 or so generations separating our species from the chimpanzee. Bickerton (1998) believes that language evolved in two stages, a pidgin stage followed by a Creole-type stage. Pinker's view allows that we might find in animals some intermediate language stage(s) between that of a pidgin and a Creole. Bickerton's view does not allow this and suggests we will never observe in animals a form of language more complicated than a pidgin. Both Pinker and Bickerton think that language is a hardwired capacity of our species, independent of general intelligence. If, as some (e.g., S. J. Gould, 1987) think, language is a result of an increase of intelligence in humans, then it should be possible to find in animals increasingly better forms of language correlated with better intelligence. Although these are interesting speculations, definite and secure knowledge concerning animal language ability lies in future research.

Still another view suggesting that language in humans is fundamentally different from that in animals was suggested by Dunbar (1993). Dunbar suggests that language evolved in three principle stages. *Australopithecus cines,* an early ancestor, had a primate system of vocalization similar to that seen in present-day apes such as chimpanzees. This could not be called *language*. With *Homo erectus,* a close relative of our species, a simple kind of language evolved that prompted bonding between individuals. About 50,000 or so years ago, our own species, Homo sapiens, developed fully modern language that was employed for more than social boding. Essential language developed into a useful means for communicating abstract ideas. Thus Dunbar, like Bickerton and Pinker, is of the opinion that as far as language is concerned, the gulf between man and other animas is one of kind and not degree.

Evolution and Cognition

Several characteristics of the approach to animal and human cognition currently employed within experimental psychology are noteworthy. Workers in human cognition all but ignore animal learning and cognition. Workers in animal cognition, for the most part, employ a limited number of species, most notably rats and pigeons. The cognitive capacities isolated for examination in animal cognition are often those similar to those possessed in abundance by humans. Do animals possess numerical abilities? Can animals make inferences of the sort *If* $A = B$ *and* $B = C$, *then* $A = C$? To what extent do human theories of serial learning apply to animals? Are animals, like humans, capable of self-recognition? By virtue of examining these and other questions much useful information has been provided for better understanding both animal and human cognition. Furthermore, there is ample reason for believing that at least in some cases similar processes are in operation over a broad range of animal species. The prime example of this is the sort of associative learning examined in Pavlovian and instrumental conditioning.

It is probably the case that most (if not all) experimental psychology and perhaps most social scientists accept evolution. This being so, Symons (1987) wrote a paper entitled "If we're Darwinians, what's the fuss about?" The fuss, according to Symons, is about this: "Perhaps the central issue of psychology is whether the mechanisms of the mind are few, general and simple, on the one hand, or numerous, specific and complex on the other" (p. 126). As indicated previously, and speaking generally, many experimental psychologists tend toward the former assumptions whereas many evolutionary biologists and psychologist tend toward the latter, and some incline toward the view that the modules are in communication with each other (Mithen, 1996). To employ metaphors, experimental psychologists might compare the mind to a general-purpose computer, whereas evolutionary biologists and psychologists often compare the mind to a Swiss army knife, a general-purpose tool having a diversity of different functions.

Evolution and Cognition: Implications

At one time, unlike now, animal and human learning and cognition were seen as highly related (see, e.g., McGeoch & Irion, 1952). Workers in the two areas shared a variety of important assumptions and considered, very probably, that choosing animals or humans for study involved little more than a strategic decision. If an attitude of common purpose was once the rule of the day, then it appears to be no more. On the one hand, many workers in human learning and cognition do not appear to regard animal learning and cognition as especially relevant to their concerns. It may be that many workers in human learning and cognition see the intellectual gap between our species and others to be very wide, so wide as to be one of kind and not of degree. According to this view, animal cognition has little to offer human cognition.

Interestingly, and perhaps ironically, many workers in animal learning and cognition may hold a contrary opinion, that is, that humans and animals differ cognitively, but only in degree. This inference seems to make sense when one examines some of the concerns popular in the study of animal cognition. As we have seen, workers in animal cognition are interested in determining the extent to which animals possess language, can use numerical information, imitate others, and so on. What these concerns have in common, of course, is that they are things that are done by humans and done very well. Needless to say, perhaps, these are legitimate problems, ones well worth studying.

The attitudes of workers in animal and human cognition may stem from the same source: an incorrect understanding of how evolution shapes cognitive adaptations. Both camps appear to accept some version of a *continuity view,* that as we go from so-called "lower" to "higher" animals, intellectual capacity increases. Workers in human learning and cognition, as indicated, appear to believe for whatever reason (e.g., that intermediate species became extinct) that human intellectual capacity, at least in some significant respects, differs from that of animals in kind and therefore that animal cognition may be ignored. Workers in animal learning and cognition also accept some version of the continuity view but appear to believe, generally speaking, that intellectual development of various sorts has progressed far enough in animals to make them useful objects of study. If the foregoing analysis is correct, then new more useful approaches to learning and cognition are being ignored by both animal and human workers.

There are certain implications that follow from an evolutionary approach embracing both discontinuity and continuity of intellectual development over species, which may well result in a closer, if not close, reuniting of animal and human learning and cognition. On the one hand, although there may well be some capacities unique to humans (e.g., the capacity for language), there are undoubtedly others that are widely shared over species and that, accordingly, should benefit from a comparative approach. A prime example here is spatial learning. As we saw, spatial learning is well developed in many species, and in some species (including our own), males seem better at spatial learning than females. This difference seems related to the different demands placed on males and females in the environment in which they evolved.

Thus, animals that had to move about a good deal, that had to go from place to place to find food or mates or to escape danger, would be expected to be better at spatial learning than animals that had fewer such demands. Note the difference between the emphasis here and that previously described as shared by many workers in human and animal cognition: The emphasis is not on the degree of correspondence between the cognitive capacity of humans versus other animals, but on the relation between particular animals and the specific demands of the environment in which those animals evolved. That is, to better understand the degree or kind of cognitive capacity an animal might possess, a first step might well involve a better acquaintance with the problems that animals faced in the environment in which it evolved.

In Pavlovian conditioning, as indicated, a tone may be presented a few seconds prior to food, and the relation between these events may be learned as indicated by the animal's coming, with training, to salivate to the tone. Pavlovian learning of this sort appears to be common in a variety of species (see, e.g., Wasserman & Berglan, 1998). Presumably this is because learning such Pavlovian relationships is important to survival in many species. That is, it is hardly uncommon for events of biological significance to be reliably signaled by other events—a rustle of leaves indicating an approaching predator, circling vultures indicating a dead animal and a potential meal, and so on. If this is so, then as expected, learning Pavlovian relations is common to a wide variety of species.

If, as indicated, regularities in the environment play an important role in shaping an animal's cognitive capacities, then it becomes incumbent upon investigations to obtain knowledge about regularities and behavior in that environment. We have already seen how our understanding of spatial learning in animals and humans has benefited from such an approach. To suggest another familiar example, we have seen how our understanding of language has benefited from examining real-life situations in which children exposed to a pidgin develop on their own, within a single generation, a more complex form of language called a *Creole*. As another example, observations of chimpanzees in the wild suggest that they possess a high level of cognitive capacity that might otherwise go unnoticed. Field observation of 14 different groups of widely separated chimpanzees suggests that they may be characterized as possessing a culture (Whiten & Boesch, 1999). By *culture* it is meant that the various groups of chimpanzees engage in complex behaviors that are obviously learned and, in addition, are passed on from one generation to the next.

An outstanding example of such complex behavior is termite fishing, in which chimpanzees insert thin, flexible strips of bark into termite mounds to extract the insects, which they eat. This behavior is practiced by 8 of the 14 groups of chimpanzees observed. However, it is practiced differently by different groups. For example, once the insects have swarmed up the stick, 3 of the 8 groups pull the stick through their fists and eat the gathered prey. This technique is used by some other groups of chimpanzees who also pull the stick through their mouths. To cite another complex behavior, 3 of the 14 groups of chimpanzees use small sticks to remove bone marrow inside the bones of monkeys they have killed. The point here, at least as suggested by Whiten and Boesch (1999), is not merely that termite fishing and removing bone marrow with sticks are complex learned behaviors, but that they are passed on from one generation to the next, and so, in the opinion of some, indicate that chimpanzees possess a culture. Whiten and Boesch (1999) indicate that still other animals may possess a culture, as (for example) populations of whales that sing in different dialects and hunt in different ways. Are the sorts of behaviors engaged by chimpanzees and possibly other animals, such as whales, really manifestations of culture, on par in some respects with human culture as suggested by Whiten and Boesch (1999)—or is it something simpler? It may be, for example, that termite fishing is composed of many component behaviors, gradually and accidentally learned over time by one or two members of a chimpanzee group, which are then acquired by other members according to the same principles that explain other forms of instrumental learning. Laboratory studies that, for example, compare learning by imitation in chimpanzees with such learning in a variety of other animals, including humans and birds, can help determine whether ascribing culture to chimpanzees is valid and useful. The plain implication of the previous analysis is that experimental psychologists, if they are to better understand learning and cognition, must supplement laboratory studies of learning and cognition with real-life field studies of animals dealing with problems of evolutionary adaptation in their environments.

Although the strategy just outlined is already being followed in some cases, unfortunately, the practice is less widespread than is desirable. However, it does seem to be growing. For example, the behavior system approach assumes that in Pavlovian conditioning, an *unconditioned stimulus* (*UCS*) such as food or shock activates an underlying organization of behavior appropriate to that UCS (for the food UCS, the feeding system, for shock, the defensive system). According to this view, a *conditioned stimulus* (*CS*) will come to elicit responses that are components of the behavior system activated by the UCS. Thus, not only must preorganized response systems be considered but also a particular species' sensitivity to different stimuli and its underlying motivational system. The usefulness of this approach has been demonstrated in a variety of laboratory experiments that were cognizant of the animals' species-typical behaviors. As merely one example, Timberlake and Washburne (1989) examined predation in seven different species of rodents. Characteristic differences in prey-capture of crickets by the rodents were related to species-typical behavior (e.g., more carnivorous species captured prey more quickly and reliably), and the response of each species to a CS, a rolling ball bearing, resembled that particular species' typical response to actual prey.

Felial imprinting (e.g., baby ducklings' following a parent) is another example of how an understanding of species-typical behavior may be profitably used to conduct and illuminate laboratory studies. Some of the so-called "attributes" of imprinting based on field studies have been shown by laboratory studies not to be entirely correct. For example, the supposed irreversibility of imprinting was questioned by Salzen and Meyer (1968), who showed that chicks imprinted on one ball could be shifted to another ball and reversed. Other important characteristics ascribed to imprinting (e.g., that imprinting is a specialized form of learning, differing in several important respects from other forms of learning) seem more feasible (see, e.g., Bateson, 1990). For example, imprinting occurs more readily to species-typical stimuli than to artificial stimuli.

Of course, it is not only the study of animal cognition that can benefit from a better understanding of species-typical behavior. We have seen, for example, that children exposed to a pidgin convert it to a more complex Creole in a single generation, supplying a good reason for believing, as Pinker (1994) asserts, that language is an instinct. Perhaps we will come to better understand this language instinct as we learn more about other complex (or even simple) instincts in humans and other animals. That is, similar processes may underlie various complex instincts, such as the language instinct in humans and echolocation in bats.

What the future may hold is difficult to say. However, there are signs that the current divide between animal and human learning and cognition may diminish, returning us to a view more commonly held in the 1930s, 40s, and 50s. This time around it may be a much better informed view. It should benefit from three areas that are much more sophisticated today than in the past: cognitive neuroscience (e.g., Rapp, 2001), behavior genetics (e.g., Bailey, 1998), and evolutionary psychology (e.g., Crawford & Krebs, 1998). Some would argue that opening laboratory psychology up to these more biologically informed influences should help to place the field in a more proper, and thus more useful, perspective. That is, it should moderate what some see as the extreme environmentalism that has dominated psychology during the past 75 years or so (see, e.g., Pinker, 1994; Tooby & Cosmides, 1992), replacing it with a more balanced view. This more balanced view would hold that environmental influences are indeed important, but that these work through evolved mechanisms to determine behavior. Two prime examples of such evolved mechanisms cited in this chapter are the language acquisition device of humans, and mechanisms of echolocation in bats.

REFERENCES

Asendorpf, S. B., Warkentin, V., & Baudonniere, P. M. (1996). Social awareness and other awareness: Vol. 2. Mirror self-recognition, social contingency awareness and synchronic imitation. *Developmental Psychology, 32,* 313–321.

Bailey, J. M. (1998). Can behavior genetics contribute to evolutionary behavioral science? In C. Crawford & D. L. Krebs (Eds.), *Handbook of evolutionary psychology: Ideas, issues, and applications* (pp. 211–233). Mahwah, NJ: Erlbaum.

Baron-Cohen, S. (1995). *Mindblindness.* Cambridge, MA: MIT Press.

Bateson, P. P. G. (1990). Is imprinting such a special case? *Philosophical Transaction of the Royal Society of London, 329B,* 125–131.

Beatty, W. W., & Shavalia, D. A. (1980). Spatial memory in rats: Time course of working memory and effects of anesthetics. *Behavioral and Neural Biology, 28,* 454–462.

Bickerton, D. (1998). The creation and re-creation of language. In C. Crawford & D. L. Krebs (Eds.), *Handbook of evolutionary psychology: Ideas, issues, and applications* (pp. 613–634). Mahwah, NJ: Erlbaum.

Boysen, S. T., & Berntson, G. G. (1989). Numerical competence in a chimpanzee (*Pan Troglodytes*). *Journal of Comparative Psychology, 103,* 23–31.

Boysen, S. T., & Capaldi, E. J. (Eds.). (1993). *The development of numerical competence: Animal and human models.* Hillsdale, NJ: Erlbaum.

Brannon, E. M., & Terrace, H. S. (2000). Representation of numerosities 1–9 by Rhesus Macaques (*Macaca mulatta*). *Journal of Experimental Psychology: Animal Behavior Processes, 26,* 31–49.

Burns, R. A., Dunkman, J. A., & Detloff, S. L. (1999). Ordinal position in the serial learning of rats. *Animal Learning & Behavior, 27,* 272–279.

Byrne, R. W. (1998). So much easier to attract straw men. *Behavior and Brain Sciences, 21,* 116–117.

Candland, D. K. (1993). *Feral children and clever animals.* New York: Oxford University Press.

Capaldi, E. J. (1992). The organization of behavior. *Journal of Applied Behavior Analysis, 25,* 575–577.

Capaldi, E. J. (1993). Animal number abilities: Implications for a hierarchical approach to instrumental learning. In S. T. Boysen & E. J. Capaldi (Eds.), *The development of numerical competence: Animal and human models* (pp. 191–209). Hillsdale, NJ: Erlbaum.

Capaldi, E. J. (1994). The sequential view: From rapidly fading stimulus traces to the organization of memory and the abstract concept of number. *Psychonomic Bulletin & Review, 1,* 156–181.

Capaldi, E. J. (1998). Counting behavior. In G. Greenberg & M. M. Haraway (Eds.), *Comparative psychology: A handbook* (pp. 817–822). New York: Garland Publishing.

Capaldi, E. J., Alptekin, S., & Birmingham, K. M. (1996). Instrumental performance and time between reinforcements: Intimate relation to learning or memory retrieval? *Animal Learning & Behavior, 24,* 211–220.

Capaldi, E. J., Birmingham, K. M., & Miller, R. M. (1999). Forming chunks in instrumental learning: The role of overshadowing. *Animal Learning & Behavior, 27,* 221–228.

Capaldi, E. J., & Lynch, D. (1966). Patterning at 24-hour ITI: Resolution of a discrepancy more apparent than real. *Psychonomic Science, 6,* 229–230.

Capaldi, E. J., & Minkoff, R. (1966). Reward schedule effects at a relatively long intertrial interval. *Psychonomic Science, 6,* 321–322.

Capaldi, E. J., & Miller, D. J. (1988a). Counting in rats: Its functional significance and the independent cognitive processes that constitute it. *Journal of Experimental Psychology: Animal Behavior Processes, 14,* 3–17.

Capaldi, E. J., & Miller, D. J. (1988b). Number tags applied by rats to reinforcers are general and exert powerful control over responding. *Quarterly Journal of Experimental Psychology, 40B,* 279–297.

Capaldi, E. J., & Miller, R. M. (2001a). Molar vs. molecular approaches to reward schedule and serial learning phenomena. *Learning and Motivation, 32,* 22–35.

Capaldi, E. J., & Miller, R. M. (2001b). Stimulus control of anticipatory responding in instrumental learning. *Animal Learning & Behavior, 29,* 165–175.

Church, R. M., & Deluty, M. Z. (1977). Bisection of temporal intervals. *Journal of Experimental Psychology: Animal Behavior Processes, 3,* 216–228.

Church, R. M., & Gibbon, J. (1982). Temporal generalization. *Journal of Experimental Psychology: Animal Behavior Processes, 8,* 165–186.

Church, R. M., Meck, W. H., & Gibbon, J. (1994). Application of scalar timing theory to individual trials. *Journal of Experimental Psychology: Animal Behavior Processes, 20,* 135–155.

Crawford, C., & Krebs, D. L. (Eds.). (1998). *Handbook of evolutionary psychology: Ideas, issues, and applications.* Mahwah, NJ: Erlbaum.

D'Amato, M. R., & Colombo, M. (1988). Representation of serial order in monkeys (*Cebus apella*). *Journal of Experimental Psychology: Animal Behavior Processes, 14,* 131–139.

Darwin, C. (1871). *The descent of man and selection in relation to sex.* London: John Murray.

Davis, H., & Pérusse, R. (1988). Numerical competence in animals: Definitional issues, current evidence, and a new research agenda. *Behavioral and Brain Sciences, 11,* 561–579.

Dawkins, R. (1976). *The selfish gene.* London: Oxford University Press.

Dawkins, R. (1996). *The blind watchmaker: Why the evidence of evolution reveals a universe without design.* New York: W. W. Norton.

Dunbar, R. I. M. (1993). Coevolution of neocortical size, group size, and language in humans. *Behavioral and Brain Sciences, 16,* 681–737.

Emlen, S. T. (1970). Celestial rotation: Its importance in the development of migratory orientation. *Science, 170,* 1198–1201.

Epstein, R., Lanza, R. P., & Skinner, B. F. (1981). "Self-awareness" in the pigeon. *Science, 212,* 695–696.

Fodor, J. (1983). *The modularity of mind.* Cambridge, MA: MIT Press.

Gallistel, C. R. (1990). *The organization of learning.* Cambridge, MA: The MIT Press.

Gallistel, C. R. (1994). Space and time. In N. J. Mackintosh (Ed.), *Animal learning and cognition* (pp. 221–253). San Diego, CA: Academic Press.

Gallistel, C. R., & Gibbon, J. (2000). Time, rate and conditioning. *Psychological Review, 107,* 289–344.

Gallup, G. G. (1970). Chimpanzees: Self-recognition. *Science, 167,* 86–87.

Gallup, G. G. (1977). Self-recognition in primates. *American Psychologist, 32,* 329–338.

Gallup, G. G. (1982). Self-awareness and the emergence of mind in primates. *American Journal of Primatology, 2,* 237–248.

Gardner, R. A., & Gardner, B. T. (1969). Teaching sign language to a chimpanzee. *Science, 165,* 664–672.

Gaulin, S. J. C., & Fitzgerald, R. W. (1989). Sexual selection for spatial-learning ability. *Animal Behavior, 37,* 322–331.

Gelman, R., & Gallistel, C. R. (1978). *The child's understanding of number.* Cambridge, MA: Harvard University Press.

Goldstone, R. L., & Kersten, A. (in press). Concepts and categorization. In A. F. Healy & R. W. Proctor (Eds.), *Comprehensive handbook of psychology: Vol. 4. Experimental sychology.* New York: Wiley.

Gordon, R. M. (1998). The prior question: Do primates have a theory of mind? *Behavior and Brain Sciences, 21,* 120–121.

Gould, J. L. (1986). The locale map of honey bees: Do insects have cognitive maps? *Science, 232,* 861–863.

Gould, S. J. (1987). *The limits of adaptation: Is language a spandrel of the human brain?* Paper presented at the Cognitive Science Seminar for Cognitive Science, Cambridge, MA, MIT.

Griffin, D. R. (1992). *Animal minds.* Chicago: University of Chicago Press.

Haggbloom, S. J., Birmingham, K. M., & Scranton, D. L. (1992). Hierarchical organization of series information by rats: Series chunks and list chunks. *Learning and Motivation, 23,* 183–199.

Hayes, C. (1951). *The ape in our house.* New York: Harper.

Hayes, K. J., & Hayes, C. (1952). Imitation in a home-raised chimpanzee. *Journal of Comparative and Physiological Psychology, 45,* 450–459.

Healy, A. F. (1980). Can chimpanzees learn a phonemic language? In T. A. Sebeok & J. Umiker-Sebeok (Eds.), *Speaking of apes: A critical anthology of two-way communication with man* (pp. 141–143). New York: Plenum Press.

Herman, L. M. (1986). Cognition and language competencies of bottlenosed dolphins. In R. J. Schusterman, J. A. Thomas, & F. G. Wood (Eds.), *Dolphin behavior and cognition: Comparative and ecological aspects* (pp. 221–252). Hillsdale, NJ: Erlbaum.

Herrnstein, R. J. (1979). Acquisition, generalization, and discrimination reversal of a natural concept. *Journal of Experimental Psychology: Animal Behavior Processes, 5,* 116–129.

Heyes, C. M. (1998). Theory of mind in nonhuman primates. *Behavior and Brain Sciences, 21,* 101–168.

Heyes, C. M. (1996). Genuine imitation. In C. M. Heyes & B. Galef (Eds.), *Social learning in animals: The roots of culture* (pp. 53–71). San Diego, CA: Academic Press.

Hockett, C. F. (1960). Logical considerations in the study of animal communication. In W. E. Lanyon & W. N. Tavolga (Eds.), *Animal sounds and communication* (pp. 392–430). Washington, DC: American Institute of Biological Sciences.

Hoffman, H. S. (1978). Experimental analysis of imprinting and its behavioral effects. *The Psychology of Learning and Motivation, 12,* 1–37.

Hull, C. L. (1943). *Principles of behavior: An introduction to behavior theory.* New York: Appleton-Century.

Hulse, S. H., & Dorsky, N. P. (1977). Structural complexity as a determinant of serial pattern learning. *Learning and Motivation, 8,* 488–506.

Hulse, S. H., Fowler, H., & Honig, W. K. (Eds.). (1978). *Cognitive processes in animal behavior.* Hillsdale, NJ: Erlbaum.

Hunter, W. S. (1913). The delayed reaction in animals and children. *Behavior Monographs, 2,* 1–86.

Jacobs, L. F., Gaulin, S. J. C., Sherry, D., & Hoffman, G. E. (1990). Evolution of spatial cognition: Sex-specific patterns of spatial behavior predict hippocampal size. *Proceedings of the National Academy of Sciences, USA, 87,* 6349–6352.

Killeen, P. R., & Fetterman, J. G. (1988). A behavioral theory of timing. *Psychological Review, 95,* 274–295.

Lashley, K. S. (1929). *Brain mechanisms and intelligence.* Chicago: University of Chicago Press.

Lashley, K. S. (1951). The problem of serial order in behavior. In L. A. Jeffries (Eds.), *Cerebral mechanisms in behavior* (pp. 112–136). New York: Wiley.

Leonard, B., & McNaughton, B. L. (1990). Spatial representation in the rat: Conceptual, behavior, and neurophysiological perspectives. In R. P. Kesner & D. S. Olton (Eds.), *Neurobiology of comparative cognition* (pp. 363–422). Hillsdale, NJ: Erlbaum.

Mackintosh, N. J. (1975). A theory of attention: Variations in the associability of stimuli with reinforcement. *Psychological Review, 82,* 276–298.

Mackintosh, N. J. (1995). Categorization by people and by pigeons: The twenty-second Bartlett memorial lecture. *Quarterly Journal of Experimental Psychology, 48B,* 193–214.

Marler, P. (1987). Sensitive periods and the roles of specific and generally sensory stimulation in birdsong learning. In J. P. Rauschecker & P. Marler (Eds.), *Imprinting and cortical plasticity* (pp. 99–135). New York: Wiley.

Marler, P., & Peters, P. (1989). Species differences in auditory responsiveness in early vocal learning. In R. J. Dooling & S. H. Hulse (Eds.), *The comparative psychology of audition: Perceiving complex sounds* (pp. 243–273). Hillsdale, NJ: Erlbaum.

McGeoch, J. A., & Irion, A. L. (1952). *The psychology of human learning* (2nd ed.). New York: Longmans, Green.

Menzel, E. W. (1973). Chimpanzee spatial memory. *Science, 182,* 943–945.

Menzel, E. W., Premack, D., & Woodruff, G. (1978). Map reading by chimpanzees. *Folia Primatologica, 29,* 241–249.

Miller, R. R., & Grace, R. C. (in press). Conditioning and learning. In A. F. Healy & R. W. Proctor (Eds.), *Comprehensive handbook of psychology: Vol. 4: Experimental psychology.* New York: Wiley.

Mineka, S., & Cook, M. (1988). Social learning and the acquisition of snake fear in monkeys. In T. Zentall & B. G. Galef, Jr. (Eds.), *Social learning* (pp. 51–73). Hillsdale, NJ: Erlbaum.

Mithen, S. (1996). *The prehistory of the mind.* London: Thames and Hudson.

O'Keefe, J., & Nadel, L. (1978). *The hippocampus as a cognitive map.* Oxford, UK: Clarendon Press.

Pearce, J. M., & Hall, G. (1980). A model for Pavlovian learning: Variations in the effectiveness of conditioned but not of unconditioned stimuli. *Psychological Review, 87,* 532–552.

Peterson, I. (2000). Calculating swarms: Ant teamwork suggest models for computing faster and organizing better. *Science News, 158,* 314–316.

Pinker, S. (1994). *The language instinct: How the mind creates language.* New York: William Morrow.

Premack, D., & Premack, A. J. (1983). *The mind of an ape.* New York: W. W. Norton.

Premack, D., & Woodruff, G. (1978). Does the chimpanzee have a theory of mind? *Behavioral and Brain Sciences, 4,* 515–526.

Rapp, B. (Ed.). (2001). *The handbook of cognitive neuropsychology: What deficits reveal about the human mind.* Philadelphia: Psychology Press.

Restle, F. (1957). Discrimination of cues in mazes: A resolution of the place vs. response question. *Psychological Review, 64,* 217–228.

Roberts, W. A. (1981). Retroactive inhibition in rat spatial memory. *Animal Learning & Behavior, 9,* 566–574.

Roberts, W. A. (1998). *Principles of animal cognition.* New York: McGraw-Hill.

Romanes, G. J. (1882). *Animal intelligence.* New York: Appleton.

Rumbaugh, D. M. (Ed.). (1977). *Language learning by a chimpanzee.* New York: Academic Press.

Salzen, E. A., & Meyer, C. C. (1968). Reversibility of imprinting. *Journal of Comparative and Physiological Psychology, 66,* 269–275.

Savage-Rumbaugh, E. S., Murphy, J., Sevcik, R. A., Brakke, K. E., Williams, S. L., & Rumbaugh, D. M. (1993). Language comprehension in ape and child. *Monographs of the Society for Research in Child Development, 58*(3–4).

Seyfarth, R., & Cheney, D. (1990). The assessment by vervet monkeys of their own and another species' alarm calls. *Animal Behaviour, 40,* 754–764.

Silverman, I., & Eals, M. (1992). Sex differences in spatial abilities: Evolutionary theory and data. In J. H. Barkow, L. Cosmides, & J. Tooby (Eds.), *The adapted mind: Evolutionary psychology and the generation of culture* (pp. 533–549). New York: Oxford University press.

Skinner, B. F. (1938). *The behavior of organisms.* New York: Appleton-Century-Crofts.

Skinner, B. F. (1950). Are theories of learning necessary? *Psychological Review, 57,* 193–216.

Spear, N. E., & Riccio, D. C. (1994). *Memory: Phenomena and principles.* Boston: Allyn & Bacon.

Spelke, E. S. (2001). Core knowledge. *American Psychologist, 55,* 1233–1243.

Spence, K. W. (1936). The nature of discrimination learning in animals. *Psychological Review, 43,* 427–449.

Spence, K. W. (1937). The differential response in animals to stimuli varying within a single dimension. *Psychological Review, 44,* 430–444.

Sutherland, N. S., & Mackintosh, N. J. (1971). *Mechanisms of animal discrimination learning.* New York: Academic Press.

Symons, D. (1987). If we're all Darwinians, what's the fuss about? In C. B. Crawford, M. F. Smith, & D. L. Krebs (Eds.), *Sociobiology and psychology* (pp. 121–146). Hillsdale, NJ: Erlbaum.

Symons, D. (1992). On the use and misuse of Darwinism in the study of human behavior. In J. H. Barkow, L. Cosmides, & J. Tooby (Eds.), *The adapted mind: Evolutionary psychology and the generation of culture* (pp. 137–159). New York: Oxford University Press.

Terrace, H. S. (1979). *Nim: A chimpanzee who learned sign language.* New York: Knopf.

Terrace, H.S. (1986). A nonverbal organism's knowledge of ordinal position in a serial learning task. *Journal of Experimental Psychology: Animal Behavior Processes, 12,* 203–214.

Thorndike, E. L. (1911). *Animal intelligence: Experimental studies.* New York: Macmillan.

Timberlake, W., & Washburne, D. L. (1989). Feeding ecology and laboratory predatory behavior toward live and artificial moving prey in seven rodent species. *Animal Learning & Behavior, 17,* 2–11.

Tolman, E. C. (1932). *Purposive behavior in animals and men.* New York: Appleton-Century-Crofts.

Tolman, E. C. (1948). Cognitive maps in rats and men. *Psychological Review, 55,* 189–208.

Tolman, E. C., Ritchie, B. F., & Kalish, D. (1946). Studies in spatial learning: Vol. 1. Orientation and the short-cut. *Journal of Experimental Psychology, 36,* 13–24.

Tooby, J., & Cosmides, L. (1992). The psychological foundations of culture. In J. H. Barkow, L. Cosmides, & J. Tooby (Eds.), *The adapted mind: Evolutionary psychology and the generation of culture* (pp. 19–136). New York: Oxford University Press.

Vaughan, W., Jr., & Greene, S. L. (1984). Pigeon visual memory capacity. *Journal of Experimental Psychology: Animal Behaviour Processes, 10,* 256–271.

Von Frisch, K. (1950). *Bees, their vision, chemical senses and language.* Oxford, UK: Oxford University Press.

Von Frisch, K. (1967). *The dance language and orientation of bees.* Cambridge, MA: Belknap Press of Harvard University Press.

Wagner, A. R. (1976). Priming in STM: An information processing mechanism for self-generated and retrieval-generated depression in performance. In T. J. Tighe & R. N. Leaton (Eds.), *Habituation: Perspectives from child development, animal behavior, and neurophysiology* (pp. 95–128). Hillsdale, NJ: Erlbaum.

Wasserman, E. A., & Astley, S. L. (1994). A behavioral analysis of concepts: Its application to pigeons and children. *Psychology of Learning and Motivation, 31,* 73–132.

Wasserman, E. A., & Berglan, L. R. (1998). Backward blocking and recovery from overshadowing in human causal judgement: The role of within-compound associations. *Quarterly Journal of Experimental Psychology, 51B,* 121–138.

Watanabe, S., Lea, S. E. G., & Dittrich, W. H. (1993). What can we learn from experiments on pigeon concept discrimination? In H. P. Zeigler & H.-J. Bischof (Eds.), *Vision, brain, and behavior in birds* (pp. 351–376). Cambridge, MA: MIT Press.

Wendt, G. R. (1937). Two and one-half year retention of a conditioned response. *Journal of General Psychology, 17,* 178–180.

Whiten, A. J., & Boesch, C. (1999). Chimps employ culture to branch out. *Sciences News, 155,* 13–15.

Williams, C. L., & Meck, W. H. (1991). The organizational effects of gonadal steroids on sexually dimorphic spatial ability. *Psychoneuroendocrinology, 16,* 155–176.

Wright, A. A., Urcuioli, P. J., & Sands, S. F. (1986). Proactive interference in animal memory. In D. F. Kendrick, M. E. Rilling, & M. R. Denny (Eds.), *Theories of animal memory* (pp. 101–125). Hillsdale, NJ: Erlbaum.

CHAPTER 15

Sensory and Working Memory

JAMES S. NAIRNE

To remember is to conjure up an image of the distant past, or perhaps a reflection from hours or days previous. Yet we remember over the very short term as well—over time periods lasting minutes, seconds, and even milliseconds. Consider language: We need to remember the early parts of a spoken phrase, or the particular sequence of phonemes in a word, for periods lasting beyond their physical presentation. Such short-lived memories are widely believed to be adaptive components of on-line cognitive processing. They help us produce and interpret spoken language, remember telephone numbers, reason, solve problems, and even think. The purpose of this chapter is to review and comment on the psychology of these transient memories.

Traditionally, memory researchers have distinguished between two types of transient memories: sensory memories and short-term memories. *Sensory memories* are faithful, veridical records of initiating stimuli. You can think of a sensory memory as a kind of continuation of the actual event—the same information simply removed in time (Crowder & Surprenant, 2000). By definition, then, sensory memories are modality specific: Visual stimuli lead to visual sensory memories, auditory stimuli lead to auditory sensory memories, tactile stimuli produce tactile sensory memories, and so on. Sensory memories tend to last for only a second or two, at best, and are widely thought to accrue from the processes involved in normal sensation and perception.

Short-term memories are the active, but analyzed, contents of mind. Any time that we form a conscious idea, or process incoming information from the world, we activate existing long-term memory structures; as a collective set, this activated knowledge defines what most psychologists currently mean by short-term memory (e.g., Cowan, 1995; Shiffrin, 1999). Short-term memories, unlike sensory memories, need not accurately reflect a just-presented stimulus. Instead, they usually represent meaningful interpretations of what has just occurred. For example, we might see a string of visual forms representing the letters P U M P K I N, but actively maintain a short-term memory for the word *pumpkin* and perhaps even a visual image of the orange object itself. Evidence suggests that short-term memories are often represented in the form of an acoustic code—an inner voice—which probably plays a vital role in the interpretation and production of spoken language (e.g., Baddeley, Gathercole, & Papagno, 1998).

Psychologists use an additional term, *working memory,* to refer to the set of processes, or systems, that control and maintain activation of short-term memories (Baddeley, 1986; Miyake & Shah, 1999). Activation is assumed to be inherently fragile, so short-term memories are quickly lost in the absence of some kind of maintenance process. The working memory system is thought to contribute to virtually all aspects of cognitive processing (e.g., reading, reasoning, problem solving, etc.), but this chapter focuses solely on the task of remembering over the short term. What are the characteristics of memory over the short term? How does memory over the short term differ from long-term memory? Are different systems or mnemonic principles needed to explain short- and long-term remembering? To begin, I turn to the briefest of memories: the lingering aftereffects of event presentation.

PROLONGING THE PRESENT: SENSORY MEMORY

It is easy to demonstrate that the internal experience of a briefly presented event outlasts the event itself. Twirl a sparkler on a warm summer night and you'll see a trail of the light, perhaps enough to form a rough circle or to attempt the outlines of a name. The abrupt ending of a symphony, experienced in a quiet room, leaves an echo that contributes to the drama of the musical piece. The briefest of touches can linger, leaving behind a record of the preceding impression. These are sensory memories: fleeting, raw records of experience.

There is nothing in the concept of a sensory memory that is necessarily tied to the passage of time. We can recognize the sound of a person's voice, or call to mind two viewings of the same visual scene, even though months or years might have passed. Most psychologists, however, use the term *sensory memory* to refer to stimulus persistence, a kind of prolonging of the present. Longer term modality-specific memories, such as the long-term recall or recognition of a person's voice, are generally classified as *perceptual* memories to distinguish them from sensory persistence per se (e.g., Cowan, 1984, 1988; Massaro, 1975; Massaro & Loftus, 1996). There may be different forms of short-term sensory persistence. For example, some have suggested that there are two distinct phases of sensory storage, one lasting only a few hundred milliseconds and a second lasting up to 20 s (e.g., Coltheart, 1980; Cowan, 1984; Massaro, 1975).

Unfortunately, the distinction between the various forms of sensory persistence and perceptual memory is not a clean one and has led to some interpretive problems in the sensory memory literature. For example, many of the tasks that have traditionally been used to study sensory persistence may, in fact, be measuring perceptual memory (see Loftus & Irwin, 1998). Questions have also been raised about the adaptive value of the persistence process itself (Haber, 1983). In theory, a prolonging process seems clearly adaptive: To perceive a spoken word, it is necessary to integrate across phonemic information that is presented sequentially in time (Cowan, 1984; Darwin, 1976); integrating two visual images successfully, such as those produced by a rapidly moving object, may require one to maintain a relatively intact memory for the initially presented image (Eriksen & Collins, 1967). However, it is uncertain how much of a role sensory persistence actually plays in these situations, or whether it plays a role at all. Some researchers have suggested that sensory persistence may result from the fact that neural responses are simply extended in time (Loftus & Irwin, 1998; Francis, 1999). The fact that the subjective experience of persistence—even its very presence—depends on factors such as the duration and intensity of the physical stimulus supports this kind of explanation.

Measuring Sensory Persistence

As with most psychological phenomena, our understanding of sensory persistence has been largely defined by measurement techniques. One relatively direct technique, known as a *synchrony judgment task,* asks observers to adjust the timing of an index stimulus, such as an auditory click, until it coincides with the onset or offset of a target stimulus, such as a light (e.g., Bowen, Pola, & Matin, 1974; Efron, 1970). Observers are quite accurate at deciding when the target stimulus first appears—its onset—but overestimate its offset by around 150 ms; in other words, observers think the stimulus continues for a brief period after it has physically disappeared. Again, the extent of the persistence depends on the intensity and presentation duration of the target stimulus, but seems to be largely independent of presentation modality. For brief target presentations, both visual and auditory stimuli show sensory persistence effects lasting somewhere between 100 and 200 ms.

Comparable results are obtained using a technique called *backward masking* (e.g., Massaro, 1970; Turvey, 1973). Here, visual or auditory stimuli are presented and then followed closely by an interfering "mask" from the same presentation modality. The task is to identify or recognize the target stimulus. For example, in a simple auditory backward masking task a high- or low-pitched tone might be presented, followed at some variable time by another irrelevant but masking tone; the subject's task is simply to categorize the pitch of the first tone (high or low). The common finding is that recognition or identification performance improves as the interval between the end of the target stimulus and presentation of the mask increases, until an asymptote is reached at around 250 ms (Massaro, 1970; see Figure 15.1). After 250 ms, further delays in presentation of the mask do not affect performance very much (see also Massaro & Loftus, 1996).

The 250-ms asymptote is commonly interpreted as the point beyond which the stimulus no longer persists—that is, the duration of the sensory memory. Alternatively, 250 ms could simply represent the point at which the subject has extracted all the relevant information that he or she needs.

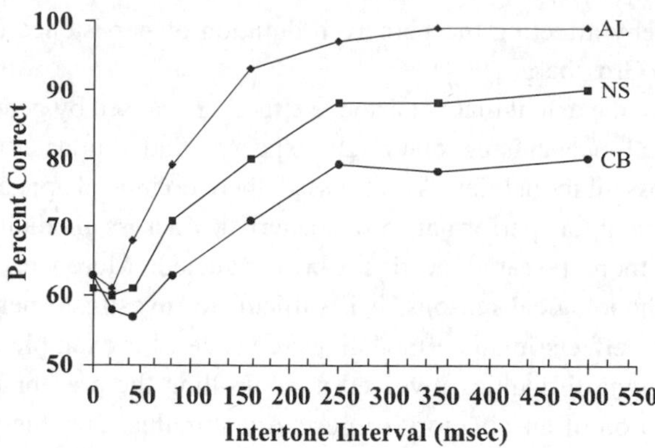

Figure 15.1 Percent correct identification performance in a simple auditory backward masking experiment, plotted as a function of the delay of the masking tone. The data are shown separately for three individual subject (after Massaro, 1970). Reprinted with permission.

Many researchers find it compelling that similar masking functions are found for visual and auditory stimuli (Cowan, 1995; Massaro, 1975); furthermore, the estimated duration derived from backward masking—250 ms—roughly corresponds to the phenomenological duration tapped by the synchrony judgment task. Other persistence tasks yield similar duration estimates. For example, in a *temporal integration task,* subjects are asked to identify a missing element in an array of elements (e.g., Di Lollo, Hogben, & Dixon, 1994). Presentation of the array unfolds over time: Subjects receive a random half of the elements at Time 1 and the second half after a brief, but variable, delay. Successful performance requires perceptual integration of the two halves, which seems to occur only if the two halves are separated by fewer than 100–200 ms.

The Partial Report Technique

The measurement technique most commonly associated with sensory memory, particularly visual sensory memory, is the partial report procedure developed by Sperling (1960; see also Averbach & Coriell, 1961). When people are presented with a visual display of letters—for example, a three-by-four array of 12 letters—for a very brief duration—say, around 50 ms—roughly 3 or 4 letters can be reported correctly. People can presumably process only a limited amount of information in 50 ms, so this result may not seem surprising. However, people report the clear sensation of seeing the entire display, with all 12 letters, but the display fades before all the letters can be reported. Sperling (1960) set out to measure the persistence of the display, which he believed tapped a form of visual sensory memory.

Sperling's first challenge was to document that people do, in fact, have more than three or four letters available following the offset of the display. He devised a partial report condition, which required the reporting of only part of the display rather than all 12 letters (hence the name *partial report*). After the display was turned off, one of three auditory cues sounded—a high-, medium-, or low-pitched tone—which signaled the subject to recall only one of the three rows of letters. Because the cue was presented after the display was physically terminated, average row performance could be used to estimate availability of the display as a whole. Sperling discovered that, indeed, people have much more display information available than the three to four letters tapped by whole report.

The partial over whole report advantage is important, but it does not, by itself, establish the presence of sensory memory. For one thing, fewer items need to be recalled under partial report (4 instead of 12 letters), so some kind of recall (or output) interference could be contributing to the condition differences. Of main interest is the finding that the partial report advantage declines rapidly with the insertion of a delay between display offset and the occurrence of the recall cue. Sperling found that the advantage was eliminated if the recall cue was delayed for 1 s after offset of the display, and it was sharply reduced after a few hundred milliseconds. The inference is that the visual display persists, as a sensory or iconic memory, for a brief period following offset, allowing the subject to continue processing its contents. Note that the estimate of duration derived from the partial report technique is slightly longer than, but in the same ballpark as, the estimates of persistence derived from the other procedures described previously.

Considerable work has been conducted using the partial report task over the past 40 years (see Greene, 1992; Massaro, 1975; Neath, 1998, for general reviews). Auditory versions of the task indicated initially that auditory sensory memory might last considerably longer than visual sensory memory (on the order of seconds rather than milliseconds; e.g., Darwin, Turvey, & Crowder, 1973), but methodological concerns cloud this conclusion (see Massaro, 1975). Other influential work has studied the particulars of the errors that occur in the task as the recall cue is delayed. It turns out that people primarily make location errors with delay: That is, the identities of the letter are not lost, but, rather, people become confused about the row the letters occupied (Mewhort, Campbell, Marchetti, & Campbell, 1981).

The Characteristics of Sensory Persistence

It is not yet certain whether each of the tasks just described really measures the same psychological construct—that is, a decaying sensory memory. Each has somewhat different task requirements, so it is reasonable to expect differences. For example, a synchrony judgment task does not require one to extract meaningful information from the display, such as letter identities, and the partial report technique requires one to allocate attention selectively to the cued location in the visual display (Dixon, Gordon, Leung, & Di Lollo, 1997). Few studies have attempted to compare the different techniques directly, but there is some indication that the partial report technique may be measuring something qualitatively different from what is tapped by the other techniques (Loftus & Irwin, 1998).

Inverse Effects

Most forms of sensory persistence, at least as studied by the majority of measurement techniques, do show common characteristics. For example, the duration of persistence is inversely related to target stimulus *duration* and *intensity*. Efron (1970) found that people were quite accurate at judging stimulus offset as long as the target stimulus was presented for at least 150 ms. In general, as the duration of the target stimulus increases, people experience less persistence. The duration of persistence also shortens as the intensity of the target stimulus increases: For example, brighter stimuli lead to shorter persistence effects. One interpretation of these results is that the target stimulus, at onset, initiates a period of neural activity that lasts for a few hundred milliseconds. If the physical stimulus is removed prior to the completion of this neural response, the stimulus will appear to persist until the response function is complete. If the duration of the stimulus itself exceeds the neural response time, or if some other factor, such as intensity, effectively shortens the neural response time, then no persistence effects will be found.

Neural Dynamics

At present, there is no consensus on the proper interpretation of these persistence effects. However, the idea that people have special sensory memory stores, designed to maintain literal copies of sensory input as an aid to subsequent perceptual processing, is losing favor among researchers. Instead, persistence effects are widely believed to result from the dynamics of neural processing, perhaps simply as an artifact of systems that are designed to accomplish more general ends. For example, Francis (1999) has proposed that visual persistence effects accrue from a general mechanism of excitatory feedback in cortical neural circuits; the duration of persistence, in turn, is driven by cortical "reset" signals that dampen, or inhibit, the feedback. Increases in stimulus duration or intensity increase the strength of the reset signals, thereby affecting the perceived duration of persistence (see also Grossberg, 1994).

To the extent that persistence effects are caused by general neural mechanisms, one might expect to find similar effects across all modalities. As discussed, there do indeed appear to be common performance characteristics across modalities, but more research needs to be conducted. Moreover, for methodological reasons, it is difficult to investigate persistence effects in some modalities; consider, for example, the inherent difficulties involved in controlling the presentation duration of an olfactory or gustatory stimulus. For this reason, little work has been conducted on modalities other than vision and audition. New techniques are in development, particularly techniques designed to tap neural processing (see Näätänen & Winkler, 1999), so answers may be on the horizon.

Modality and Suffix Effects

The evidence gleaned from the partial report technique, as well as the other measures of persistence, was used in the 1960s and 1970s to support the proposal of specialized sensory memory stores—that is, iconic memory for visual stimuli and echoic memory for auditory memory. These memory stores, in turn, were widely believed to contribute to performance in a number of perceptual and mnemonic tasks. In immediate serial recall, for example, a persisting auditory, or echoic, trace was thought to underlie the modality effect, which is the large recency advantage that one typically sees for lists presented aloud (Corballis, 1966). An extensive literature developed to explain how factors influenced the size of the modality effect, purportedly for the reason of understanding the characteristics of auditory sensory memory.

Precategorical Acoustic Storage

Crowder and Morton (1969) proposed that lingering echoic information was held in precategorical acoustic storage (PAS), a limited-capacity sensory store capable of holding a few auditory items. Unlike visual sensory memory, which decayed very rapidly, the contents of PAS were believed to last for several seconds, allowing a subject time to give the last one or two items in a memory list a kind of once-over prior to recall. This provided an end-of-the list advantage for aurally presented items because the subject could use the echoic information in PAS to correct selective information in short-term (or working) memory (see Crowder, 1976). A related empirical phenomenon, the suffix effect, provided supporting evidence: If an auditory list is followed by another redundant spoken item, such as the word *recall,* the auditory recency advantage is reduced or eliminated. In this case it was assumed that the suffix, because of the limited capacity of PAS, interfered with the echoic traces for the last list item or two, eliminating the recency boost.

Initially, a great deal of evidence accumulated supporting the PAS account. For example, delaying the suffix by a few seconds typically reduces its interfering effect, supporting the proposal that the contents of PAS have a useful lifetime of only a few seconds. In addition, the destructive power of the suffix depends importantly on its acoustic, rather than its semantic or categorical, similarity to the list items (J. Morton, Crowder, & Prussin, 1971). What is stored in PAS, according to the model, is a raw, uncategorized sensory trace; consequently, one would expect the modality and suffix effects to show sensitivity only to acoustic variables. Crowder (1978) further showed that if list items are comprised of homophones presented aloud (plus visually for identification), such as *pare, pair, pear,* no enhanced recency is found. In this case the lingering echoic information, although still stored in PAS, is nondiscriminative acoustically: It cannot be used selectively to correct the short-term memory records for recency items (see Nairne, 2001, for a fuller discussion).

In the 1980s, however, support for the PAS model was weakened considerably by the demonstration of modality effect patterns for nonacoustic presentation modes. For example, sharp recency effects were obtained for lip-read stimuli (Campbell & Dodd, 1980) and occurred when subjects silently mouthed visual stimuli (Greene & Crowder, 1984; Nairne & Walters, 1983). Neither lipreading nor mouthing involves sound, thus precluding a role for PAS, yet both produced serial position curves that mimicked those found for auditory presentation. The suffix effect was also discovered to be sensitive in some cases to conceptual attributes (Ayres, Jonides, Reitman, Egan, & Howard, 1979; Neath, Surprenant, & Crowder, 1993), and to last over intervals considerably longer than a few seconds (Watkins & Watkins, 1980). Although various attempts were made to rescue the PAS model from conflicting data (see Greene, 1992), the account generally has fallen into disfavor (see Neath, 1998). Instead, both the modality and suffix effects are now widely believed to be short-term memory phenomena, although some form of residual perceptual memory may play an important role (see Nairne, 1988, 1990).

SHORT-TERM OR WORKING MEMORY

Whereas sensory memories tend to be veridical copies of the environment, short-term memories comprise the stuff of immediate experience. Consider the process of remembering a telephone number as you cross the room. The numbers, no longer physically present, remain active in consciousness because you engage in a process of internal repetition (in what appears to be a kind of inner voice). If you are distracted prior to reaching the phone, or fail to rehearse, the numbers are likely to vanish, leaving you with considerable uncertainty—a number here or there perhaps, but little or no confidence about the final order.

This description, which corresponds to subjective experience, actually represents the standard way that most memory researchers think about remembering over the short term (see Nairne, 2002). Permanent knowledge structures are activated, creating short-term memories, which renders the activated information immediately and directly recallable. Because of inherent attentional and resource limitations (see the chapter by Egeth & Lamy in this volume), only a certain number of items can be refreshed, through rehearsal, prior to loss, creating the familiar limitations in memory span (e.g., Miller, 1956). The whole process is somewhat akin to a juggler's attempt to maintain a set of plates in the air: The capacity of the juggler is determined by how well he or she can counteract the forces of gravity by effectively retossing each plate before it hits the ground (also see Nairne, 1996).

The standard model of short-term memory successfully explains a wide range of empirical data, everything from the recency effect in free recall to the intricacies of immediate serial recall (see Healy & McNamara, 1996, for a review). In recent years, various researchers have attempted to formalize the mechanics of how storage is controlled in the form of computer simulation models, and I review some of these models later in the chapter. However, questions remain about the proper interpretation of how we remember over the short term. Not all researchers accept the standard juggler model of short-term memory, choosing instead to opt for general mnemonic principles that apply over both the short and the long term (e.g., Melton, 1963; Nairne, 2002). In the following sections, I review the empirical data base on short-term retention with an eye toward shedding light on these controversies.

Forgetting Over the Short Term

Any discussion of short-term memory is properly begun with the topic of forgetting. As noted previously, it is the fact that we forget rapidly over the short term that produces the familiar limitations in memory span. The concept of a short-term memory capacity, in effect, is meaningful only because we typically fail to remember certain portions of a presented memory list. For many years, immediate retention was largely ignored by memory researchers. Instead, the focus was placed on multitrial learning, particularly paired-associate and serial learning, in the interest of specifying the conditions of transfer and interference (see Osgood, 1953). Single-trial immediate serial recall, which today reigns as the prototype of the short-term memory task, went largely unstudied for the first half of the twentieth century.

The situation changed dramatically around 1960 with the introduction of the Brown-Peterson technique, developed independently by John Brown (1958) and Lloyd and Margaret Peterson (Peterson & Peterson, 1959). In the original Peterson procedure, trials consisted of the presentation and recall of single consonant trigrams (e.g., CHJ) following a distractor-filled retention interval. Retention intervals varied randomly from 3 to 18 seconds and, importantly, the subject was required to count backwards aloud (by threes) throughout the interval to prevent rehearsal. The striking finding was that consonant trigrams, presented singly, were essentially forgotten after a retention interval of 18 s. Murdock (1961) extended the procedure to word recall and found similar results: nearly complete forgetting of a list of three words after approximately 18 s of counting (see Figure 15.2).

The Peterson finding was newsworthy for a number of reasons: First, most researchers were surprised to find any significant forgetting after such a short retention interval, especially given that the memory load was well below span. Second, the activity filling the retention interval—counting backward—lacked formal similarity to the to-be-remembered stimulus items (letters or words). Circa 1960, the main mechanism for forgetting was assumed to be interference, and not much interference was expected to occur between highly dissimilar materials. (There was some phonemic similarity between the letters and the digits, although this fact was not widely appreciated at the time.) Finally, the negatively accelerated form of the short-term forgetting curve showed a marked similarity to long-term forgetting functions (Ebbinghaus, 1885/1964), suggesting that it might be possible to study retention at a more fine-grained level (Slamecka, 1967).

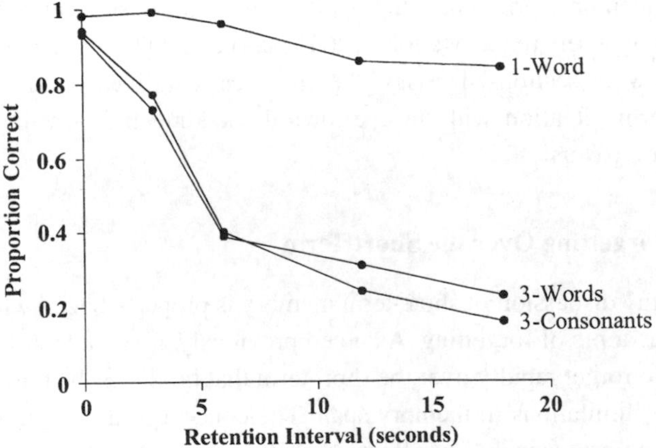

Figure 15.2 Proportion correct recall performance in a Brown-Peterson short-term retention task. The data are shown separately for lists containing one word, three words, or three consonants and are plotted as a function of the length of the distractor period (after Murdock, 1961).

Decay Versus Interference

Among the more interesting implications of this rapid short-term forgetting, as noted by J. Brown (1958) and others (e.g., Broadbent, 1958), was the possibility that autonomous decay might be responsible for the loss. The notion that mnemonic information is lost spontaneously with the passage of time (e.g., as in Thorndike's law of disuse) had largely fallen out of favor among psychologists, at least for long-term retention, because (a) memory sometimes improves with the passage of time (e.g., spontaneous recovery, reminiscence, or both) and (b) forgetting depends so critically on the nature of interfering material. John McGeoch's famous analogy was of an iron bar left out to rust in open air: Rust accumulates with time, but it is the processes that operate in time (i.e., oxidation), not time per se, that are ultimately responsible for the changes (McGeoch, 1932). The fact that significant forgetting could occur in the absence of interference resurrected the concept of decay and bolstered the novel idea that short-term retention might be mediated by its own unique operating system.

As noted, retroactive interference could be easily dismissed as the source of short-term forgetting in the Brown-Peterson task, because counting and letters or words are highly dissimilar, but proponents of decay were forced to acknowledge that proactive interference might be responsible for at least some of the loss. Proactive interference is the interference that prior information, such as the items on trial $N - 1$, imposes on the retention of current trial information (trial N). Peterson and Peterson (1959) checked for proactive interference in their experiments but failed to find any support for it (in fact, performance actually improved from early to late in the session). However, in a landmark study, Keppel and Underwood (1962) eliminated practice trials and focused only on the very first trial. No proactive interference is possible on the first trial in a session, because there is no prior trial information, and Keppel and Underwood found almost no forgetting, regardless of the length of the retention interval. Differences between a short and a long retention interval began to emerge only on the second or third trial in the session, when, presumably, proactive interference was able to kick in.

Theoretically, the Keppel and Underwood (1962) findings are critical: If you believe in a separate short-term memory system, distinct from long-term memory, then it is important to show that short-term memory follows its own unique operating laws or solves problems that cannot be solved by the mechanisms governing long-term retention. The suggestion that most, if not all, short-term forgetting is caused by proactive interference—the same kind of interference that controls much of long-term retention—diminishes the rationale for rejecting a single-system view (see Melton, 1963). Other early work further supported the case for interference. Murdock (1961) found less forgetting when one word, rather than three, was used as the to-be-remembered stimulus (see Figure 15.2); in addition, Melton reported dramatically different short-term forgetting functions for lists varying from one to five consonants (a form of within-trial interference that he termed "intra-unit" interference). Others went on to show that even retroactive interference could play a role under some circumstances: For instance, more forgetting is found when items are presented aloud and the intervening distractor activity is also auditory (e.g., Proctor & Fagnani, 1978).

However, the fact that interference is operative in short-term memory environments does not rule out decay; both decay and interference might be involved. Indeed, this was the position advocated a decade later by Baddeley and Scott (1971). They noted that in the Keppel and Underwood (1962) study, as well as in other studies documenting little effect of forgetting on the first trial (e.g., Cofer & Davidson, 1968), performance tended to hover near or at the ceiling. Thus, they argued, there might have been forgetting, but it was masked by the high performance levels. To get performance off the ceiling, they increased the length of the memory list from the standard three items to five items in one condition and seven in another. Under these conditions, significant forgetting was found on the first trial, but it appeared to reach asymptotic levels by around 5 or 6 s. Moreover, no differences were found in the slope of the forgetting curves as a function of list length, and the asymptotic levels of performance were significantly above the levels normally found when multiple trials are tested in a session. This suggested that some sort of decay operates early in the retention interval but is complete by around 5 s; it also suggested that interference, particularly from prior trials, must cause the bulk of the forgetting found later in the retention interval.

The conclusions reached by Baddeley and Scott (1971) have largely dominated the field for the past three decades. Most researchers believe that interference plays a significant role in short-term forgetting—in fact, interference is acknowledged to cause most, if not all, of the forgetting in the Brown-Peterson task—but few have completely rejected the concept of decay. As I discuss later, the case for decay was strengthened initially by the discovery of time-dependent limitations in short-term memory capacity (the word length effect; Baddeley, Thomson, & Buchanan, 1975). Moreover, it was subsequently shown that short-term forgetting is nearly complete after only a second or two if the recall test appears unexpectedly; in the traditional Brown-Peterson procedure, subjects expect the recall test and, consequently, may engage in elaborative processes that enhance long-term memory for the list items (see Healy & Cunningham, 1995; Muter, 1980; Sebrechts, Marsh, & Seamon, 1989). In the absence of elaborative processing, which enables a kind of back-up recall from long-term memory, one is forced to rely exclusively on the fragile activity trace, which decays rapidly—in a second or two—in the absence of rehearsal.

Temporal Distinctiveness

According to the standard model, as just discussed, decay of the activity trace is largely complete after only a few seconds. Interference, particularly proactive interference, is then largely responsible for any further forgetting that occurs during a retention interval. But what specific interference mechanisms are involved? One common assumption is that subjects are able to retrieve just-presented items from long-term memory, after the activity trace has decayed, but successful retrieval requires discriminating correct list targets from incorrect alternatives. Items from earlier trials, as well as extraexperimental items to a certain extent, form a noisy background against which the correct item must be selected.

There is a reasonable amount of evidence indicating that the mechanism for trace discrimination involves temporal or positional information (see G. D. A. Brown, McCormack, & Chater, 2001; Neath & Crowder, 1990). After all, time-of-occurrence information, when available, provides a foolproof method for distinguishing items from Trial N from those occurring on the previous trial, N − 1. Various studies have shown that forgetting in short-term memory environments depends importantly on the temporal spacing of items within a list, the length of the retention interval, and the temporal spacing between trials in the session. It is not time per se that predicts retention, but rather the temporal relations among the items in the experimental session.

In a slight variation of the typical Brown-Peterson task, Turvey, Brick, and Osborn (1970) asked different groups of subjects to count backward as distractor activity for either 10, 15, or 20 s. Remarkably, no retention differences were found among these groups, despite the retention interval differences (see also Greene, 1996). Of main interest, though, was a critical trial in which all groups were switched to the same 15-s distractor interval. Correct recall dropped in the 10-s group (from .33 to .20), stayed roughly constant in the 15-s group (.30 to .28), and actually *improved* in the 20-s group (.30 to .38). Notice that the passage of time—and therefore the opportunity for decay—was equated across the groups on the critical 15-s trial, yet performance depended critically on the timing of prior trials.

According to distinctiveness accounts, memory improves to the extent that target items can be easily discriminated from the memories created by prior trials. As with most perceptual comparisons, the discrimination process is assumed to be relative: As time passes, temporally distant items seem more similar and become harder to discriminate, just as telephone poles watched from a moving car appear to merge together with increasing distance traveled (Crowder, 1976). Thus, two items separated by 5 s become harder to discriminate after 20 s than after 10 s. This relationship can be expressed easily in terms of a ratio: Discriminability is proportional to the interitem interval (the period separating the two items in question) divided by the retention interval (the time separating the most recent item from the point of test).

Now reconsider performance in the Turvey et al. (1970) experiment (see Figure 15.3). Prior to the 15-s critical trial, the intertrial intervals remained constant within the session (10, 15, or 20 s), creating a discriminability ratio of 1.0 for each group. As noted above, no retention differences were actually found among these groups, despite the different retention intervals, providing strong support for the distinctiveness account. On the critical trial, however, the ratios change differentially across the groups, in the direction predicted by the data. More specifically, the discriminability ratio declines in the 10-s group (10/15 = 0.67), leading to poorer retention performance, and increases in the 20-s condition (20/15 = 1.33), leading to improved performance; the ratio remains at 1.0 in the 15-s condition, and no performance changes were recorded (15/15 = 1.0).

The Turvey et al. (1970) data are particularly important because they show that short-term memory performance can decrease, stay the same, or even increase depending on timing variables. Comparable results have been found in other contexts: Neath and Knoedler (1994), for example, found that memory for early items in a list sometimes improves as

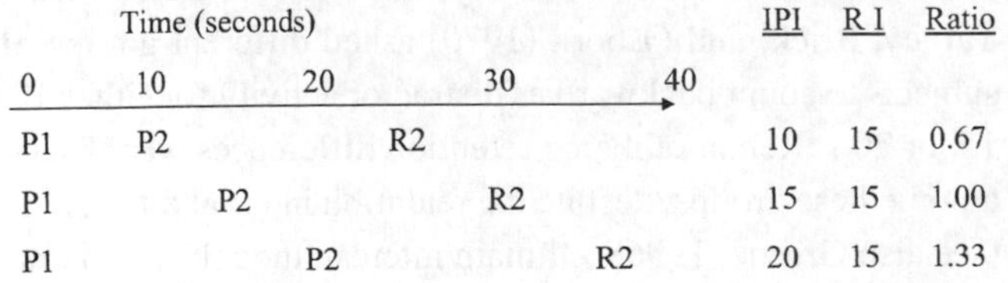

Time (seconds) 0	10	20	30	40	IPI	R I	Ratio
P1	P2		R2		10	15	0.67
P1		P2		R2	15	15	1.00
P1		P2		R2	20	15	1.33

Figure 15.3 A schematic outline of the three conditions in the Turvey, Brick, and Osborn (1970) study. P1 represents list items presented on trial N; P2 represents list items presented on trial N + 1; R2 represents the point of recall for items presented on trial N + 1. Recall improves as the ratio of the interpresentation interval (P1–P2) to the retention interval (P2–R2) increases (see text).

the length of the retention interval increases (see also Wright, Santiago, Sands, Kendrick, & Cook, 1985). According to distinctiveness accounts, early items become relatively more discriminable as all list items recede backward into the past (see also Bjork, 2001). No simple version of decay theory can handle such findings; the passage of time, it turns out, fails as a general predictor of short-term memory performance (except, perhaps, for the first few seconds of a retention interval).

Capacity Limitations

Obviously, to the extent that items are rapidly forgotten over the short term, for whatever reason, there will appear to be fundamental limitations in memory capacity. From the perspective of the standard juggler model outlined earlier, the storage capacity of short-term memory is determined by the trade-off between decay and the rate of internal rehearsal. The number of items that can be recalled correctly, in order, on at least half of the trials (i.e., memory span) is determined by the number of items that can be rehearsed within the time-limited decay window. That number, as noted by Ebbinghaus (1885/1964) and others (e.g., Miller, 1956), tends to be around seven plus or minus two unrelated items.

It is misleading, though, to think about capacity limitations in short-term memory simply in terms of items, particularly in terms of a number such as seven plus or minus two. First, as Miller (1956) showed, it is not really the number of nominal items but rather the number of functional "chunks" that influences span. We can remember seven unrelated letters, seven unrelated words, or even seven unrelated sentences with somewhat comparable degrees of efficiency (although see Cowan, 2001, for evidence that the limit may actually be closer to four). More importantly, though, a strong argument can be made that some other variable—perhaps time—truly controls retention. Holding the number of to-be-remembered chunks constant, immediate retention can vary dramatically as a function of item characteristics. For example, it turns out that memory span is well predicted by the length of time needed to say items aloud or repeat items aloud in succession.

The Limits of Time

In a seminal article, Baddeley et al. (1975) found that lists of short words lead to better immediate serial recall than lists of long words, even though the number of chunks (i.e., words) is constant across conditions. Of course, short and long words can differ in a number of ways (e.g., number of letters, syllables, and so on), so intraunit interference could conceivably account for this word length effect (e.g., Melton, 1963). However, Baddeley et al. (1975) found that the performance differences remained when all factors other than pronunciation time—or articulation rate—were controlled. For example, the words *bishop* and *Friday* have the same number of letters and syllables but differ in pronunciation time (*Friday* takes longer to say); lists of long words, defined solely in terms of duration, still yielded poorer recall than lists of matched short words.

As has been noted, the standard model assumes that decay is the main culprit behind forgetting, and the word length effect is certainly consistent with this view. The longer it takes to rehearse a set of items, the greater the chances that some of the items will be lost prior to refreshing. Pronunciation time, or articulation rate, is simply assumed to correlate with the speed of internal rehearsal. Specifying capacity in terms of items, then, is correct only in the sense that it usually takes more time to rehearse a large number of items. Baddeley et al. (1975) reported that the useful lifetime of a short-term activity trace is around 2 s (see also Schweickert & Boruf, 1986); consequently, memory span should be roughly equal to the amount of material that can be rehearsed in 2 s. On average, not surprisingly, we can rehearse somewhere around seven plus or minus two items in 2 s.

This relationship between pronunciation time and immediate memory span generally holds at the level of group data as well as for individual subjects. In fact, it is possible to predict individual differences in memory span, for both children and adults, by measuring overt articulation rate (see Hulme, Thomson, Muir, & Lawrence, 1984; Tehan & Lalor, 2000). Developmental changes in memory span are also associated with rehearsal rate, to a certain extent, as are some differences that occur in span cross-culturally. For instance, digit span tends to be higher in English and Chinese than in Arabic or Welsh, presumably because it takes longer to say digit names in the latter languages (see Ellis & Hennelly, 1980; Naveh-Benjamin & Ayres, 1986).

Recent data, however, are qualifying these conclusions somewhat. For example, it turns out that span differences sometimes remain even when pronunciation times are held constant. Memory span is typically lower for phonologically similar lists of words, compared to phonologically dissimilar lists, but similarity has little, if any, effect on pronunciation rate (Hulme & Tordoff, 1989; Schweickert, Guentert, & Hersberger, 1990). Hulme, Maughan, and Brown (1991) found that words can produce higher memory spans than nonwords, even when articulation rates are matched for the item types; similar dissociations between articulation rate and span have been found for concrete versus abstract words (Walker & Hulme, 1999) and for high- and low-frequency words (Hulme et al., 1997; Roodenrys, Hulme, Alban, & Ellis, 1994). Any model that appeals simply to time-based limits in storage capacity—for example, the standard rehearsal plus decay model—has no clear way of explaining these data.

Even more troubling are recent reports suggesting that one of the major conclusions of Baddeley et al. (1975)—namely, that duration-based span differences exist for word sets matched on all variables other than spoken duration—may apply only to restricted sets of words. Caplan, Rochon, and Waters (1992) found no memory advantage for short-duration words in lists containing short- and long-duration words matched for number of syllables and phonemes; instead, they reported a reverse word length effect (long better than short) when duration was implemented by using "lax" vowels of short duration (e.g., carrot) and "tense" vowels of long duration (e.g., spider). Caplan et al. (1992) suggested that the phonological structure of a word, not its spoken duration, determines the magnitude of the word length effect. A similar conclusion was reached by Service (1998) using Finnish stimuli, which allow one to vary duration by manipulating combinations of the same articulatory and acoustic features. Lastly, Lovatt, Avons, and Masterson (2000) varied spoken duration in disyllabic words, holding constant a host of potentially confounding factors (e.g., frequency, familiarity, number of phonemes) and found no advantage for short-duration words across several experiments; word duration effects emerged only when the original word sets used by Baddeley et al. (1975) were used as the to-be-remembered stimuli.

The Limits of Attention

In retrospect, it is not surprising that factors other than time contribute to limitations in immediate retention. Even within the standard model, storage capacity is not fixed, but rather arises from the trade-off between decay—which is purely time-based—and a controlled process of rehearsal. Successful retention depends on one's ability to keep list items in an active and recallable state, but also on the ability to counteract distraction and eliminate interference from nontarget information in memory. Errors in immediate retention, for example, often turn out to be intrusions from immediately preceding trials (e.g., Estes, 1991; Wickelgren, 1967).

Some researchers believe that limits in immediate memory arise, at least in part, from the ability to use controlled attention to ignore or filter out potentially interfering material (see Dempster, 1992; Kane & Engle, 2000). There is some evidence to suggest that individuals with low memory spans are more susceptible to proactive interference than high-span subjects: Rosen and Engle (1998), for instance, found that low-span subjects were more likely to intrude previously learned items into a current paired-associate recall task. It is also possible to get high-span subjects, who presumably possess more capacity for controlled attention, to mimic low-span subjects' susceptibility to interference by having them perform an additional concurrent task (Kane & Engle, 2000). The greater the amount of controllable attention, the easier it is to inhibit or reject interfering material as well as to keep target items active in memory through rehearsal.

It is also worth noting that some measures of capacity correlate reasonably well with other cognitive measures, such as reading comprehension, vocabulary learning, and even intelligence. For example, Engle and colleagues developed the operation span task, in which the presentation of to-be-remembered items is interspersed with a requirement to solve simple addition problems (e.g., Turner & Engle, 1989). The number of words recalled is still of main interest, but the dual task conditions (arithmetic plus immediate retention) seem to tap attentional capacity to a greater extent than simple span measures. The operation span task, as well as related measures (e.g., Daneman & Carpenter, 1980), turns out to predict higher order cognitive abilities such as general fluid intelligence or the verbal scholastic aptitude score (see Engle, Kane, & Tuholski, 1999, for a review).

What emerges is a view proposing that the storage capacity of short-term memory, as defined generally by a measure such as memory span, is determined by a variety of factors, not a single factor such as a magic number of seven plus or minus two. The capacity to focus and sustain attention, engage in strategic rehearsal, and even recall quickly (Dosher & Ma, 1998) modulates the number of items that can be remembered over the short term. The characteristics of the items also matter: Word frequency, imageability, and lexical status all influence memory span, as does the similarity among the items presented together in a list. Another important factor is the rhythm and timing of stimulus presentation: If temporal gaps occur predictably within list presentation, immediate memory can improve substantially (e.g., Hitch, Burgess, Towse, & Culpin, 1996; Ryan, 1969). All of these factors need to be explained by a complete model of immediate retention.

It is also the case that any act of remembering will be influenced by the nature of the retrieval environment, regardless of whether the remembering occurs over the short or long term. As I discuss in the next section, retrieval from short-term memory, like long-term memory, is essentially cue-driven. Moreover, the effectiveness of cues depends on how target information has been encoded, as well as the extent to which the cue uniquely specifies the to-be-remembered item. This means that even with unlimited amounts of time, or an unlimited amount of attentional capacity, there can still be forgetting and, therefore, apparent limitations in storage capacity. Although there may be a relatively fixed amount of resource or attentional capacity available at any moment in time (see the chapter by Egeth & Lamy in this volume), understanding this limit will not explain, or effectively predict, all instances of short-term retention.

Retrieval of Short-Term Memories

As defined earlier, short-term memories are the active, but analyzed, contents of mind. By virtue of their activation, some researchers have assumed that they are immediately available for recall—that is, short-term memories exist in a state that allows for direct and effortless retrieval (e.g., McElree, 1998; Wickens, Moody, & Dow, 1981). On reflection, however, it is difficult to see how such a mechanism for remembering might actually work. For one thing, multiple short-term memories exist concurrently (short-term memory, as a whole, is often described as the set of activated knowledge), so a mechanism is needed to select a particular activated item for recall. More importantly, as just noted, the success of immediate retention seems to depend critically on the nature and extent of retrieval cues that are available.

Most recent models of short-term retention assume that the short-term activity trace forms the basis of immediate memory, but the trace needs to be interpreted, or deblurred, prior to actual recall. Interference, or possibly decay, degrades the activity trace over time, rendering its identity equivocal. The term *redintegration* is widely used to describe the interpretation process, which is assumed to rely on information stored in long-term memory. It is here, during the redintegration stage, that item characteristics such as word frequency or concreteness probably exert their effects. For example, one can assume that time-dependent rehearsal affects the intactness of the activity trace at the point of recall, but item-based characteristics (e.g., concreteness) affect the ease of redintegration (see Schweickert, 1993). Separating the status of the activity trace itself from its interpretation prior to recall allows one to explain, for instance, how immediate recall differences can occur despite the equating of pronunciation time.

Retrieval Dynamics

Assuming that a set of activated information exists at any moment in time, how does one select an appropriate candidate to recall? In the 1960s, Saul Sternberg developed a task to investigate the retrieval process. In Sternberg's task, subjects are presented with short, below-span lists of items (e.g., words, letters, digits) followed immediately by the presentation of a single probe; this probe either matches, or not, one of the just-presented items (e.g., Sternberg, 1966). Obviously, a task of this kind is relatively easy, and people rarely make mistakes. Of main interest is the latency, or reaction time, of correct responses, usually as a function of a variable like list length.

Sternberg found that mean reaction time increased linearly with list length, but the slopes of the reaction time functions were roughly equivalent for positive and negative responses. This suggested that people search short-term memory in a serial, or item-by-item, fashion looking for a match to the recognition probe; the more items that need to be searched, the longer the reaction times. Equal positive and negative slopes suggested as well that the search process was exhaustive, meaning that all the items in the set were compared regardless of when (or whether) a match was found. The proposed serial exhaustive search process seemed to rule out other plausible search procedures—for example, self-terminating (in which the search process stops once a match is found) or parallel processing (in which all activated items are compared simultaneously with the probe).

However, it turns out that mean reaction time cannot be used to discriminate definitively between serial and parallel search processes; it is possible to mimic the reaction time patterns noted by Sternberg (1966), for example, using a parallel processing mechanism with certain additional assumptions (e.g., Townsend & Ashby, 1983). More diagnostic evidence comes from either a fuller analysis of reaction time distributions (e.g., Ratcliff, 1978; Reed, 1976) or from techniques that examine the full time course of processing during recognition decisions. In the latter instance, the response-signal procedure cues the subject to respond at particular times after the appearance of the recognition probe: For example, the cue to respond might appear almost immediately after appearance of the probe, which yields performance near chance levels, or seconds later, which allows for the most accurate performance. One can then determine how accuracy unfolds over time—so-called retrieval dynamics—which allows for a more sensitive analysis of possible retrieval mechanisms (see Dosher & McElree, 1992; McElree & Dosher, 1989).

Application of the response-signal technique to the retrieval of short-term memories in the Sternberg task supports a parallel, direct-access retrieval process. Retrieval dynamics seem not to vary much with list length, or serial position, which is consistent with a parallel matching process (Ratcliff, 1978). The nature of the retrieval process may change, however, depending on the type of information that must be retrieved. McElree and Dosher (1993) report that the recovery of order information—which of two list items occurred more recently?—is accomplished through a slow serial retrieval process; again, this conclusion is based on the finding that the retrieval dynamics for the order judgment differ systematically from those found in item recognition (i.e., the Sternberg task). The fact that the retrieval dynamics vary in this way undermines the simple notion that activity traces exist in a state of immediate availability. Even if items exist in a special focus of attention (e.g., Cowan, 1995), by virtue of their activation, various kinds of retrieval-based selection processes are clearly needed to satisfy the demands of differing tasks.

It is possible, however, that there is something special about retrieval of the very last item, or item chunk, in a short list. The last item is recognized faster than other items, but more importantly, the retrieval dynamics appear different as well (McElree & Dosher, 1989; Wickelgren, Corbett, & Dosher, 1980). This finding has been interpreted to mean that the last item remains active in awareness and, thus, can be matched directly with the recognition probe; the item essentially remains in consciousness, eliminating the need for a retrieval mechanism to move it from a passive to an active state. McElree (1998) recently showed that up to three items at the end of the list can show these special properties, as long as they are members of the same category (forming, presumably, a category chunk). However, alternative interpretations of the data pattern are possible. For example, one could argue that the contextual cues available at the point of probe presentation especially match the cues associated with the last list item; this, in turn, could affect the ease and quality of the retrieval process.

Cue-Driven Retention

One of the troubling features of direct access (or cueless retrieval) is the idea that items can be remembered without considering the nature of the retrieval environment. As Tulving (1983) has argued, there is no justification for making absolute statements about the memorability of items—for example, based on their inherent characteristics or encoding properties—because remembering always depends on an interaction between encoding conditions and retrieval conditions. It is possible that short-term memories represent a special case, violating Tulving's dictum, but the available evidence suggests otherwise.

Direct access received some early support from studies showing that immediate retention, tested without a distractor interval, can show immunity to proactive interference (Halford, Mayberry, & Bain, 1988; Tehan & Humphreys, 1995; Wickens et al., 1981). In the Tehan and Humphreys (1995) experiments, trials consisted of the presentation of either one or two short four-item lists; the subject's task was to recall the last presented list, so on two-list trials subjects were told to ignore the first list. Of main interest was the effect of the first list on recall of the second list—that is, proactive interference. On interference trials, one or more items in the first list were drawn from the same taxonomic category as items in the second list; on control trials the items were unrelated across the lists. When subjects were tested immediately, Tehan and Humphreys found no evidence for proactive interference (recall of control trials was equal to interference trials), but a significant control advantage emerged when a 2-s distractor task (reading digits aloud) occurred prior to recall.

If short-term memories are immediately available in consciousness, requiring no cue-based retrieval, then there is no reason to expect interference from a prior trial: One does not need to discriminate current items from previous items because the former are still active in awareness. However, immunity from interference turns out to be illusory. Semantic similarity between the first and second lists fails to hurt performance only because, on immediate tests, subjects can use residual phonemic information from the second list as a cue to help discriminate second- from first-list items. If the first and second lists contain items that rhyme, immunity disappears and significant proactive interference is found on the immediate test (see Tehan & Humphreys, 1995, 1996, 1998). Presumably, these subjects still have residual phonemic information available at test, but that information no longer uniquely specifies items from the second list.

Existing evidence strongly supports the idea that immediate retention is cue-driven. First, as described earlier, immediate recall is very sensitive to item characteristics, such as word frequency, lexicality, and concreteness. Most researchers assume, as a result, that the short-term activity trace must be interpreted prior to recall—that is, the short-term activity trace acts essentially as a cue to guide retrieval. Second, there is a considerable literature on release from proactive interference that confirms the importance of cues in immediate retention. In a typical release experiment, successive lists are drawn from the same conceptual class (e.g., fruit). Recall gets worse over trials, presumably because people have a difficult time discriminating items on the current trial from conceptually similar items that occurred on previous trials. On the release trial, however, list items are drawn from a new conceptual class (e.g., moving from fruit to animals) and performance improves substantially (see Wickens, 1970).

This effect is most commonly interpreted to mean that people are using conceptual class as a cue to guide short-term recall; the effectiveness of this cue, in turn, hinges on its ability to predict current trial information. When successive lists are presented from the same conceptual class, the cue becomes overloaded (Watkins & Watkins, 1975) which means it starts to predict many items, especially those from previous trials. On release trials, however, the distinctive power of the cue is regained: It now uniquely specifies information from the current trial, and performance improves. Particularly strong support for this interpretation comes from experiments in which the nature of the retrieval cue is manipulated at test, after the critical list has actually been presented. It is possible to record significant levels of release, at test, if discriminating cues are provided (see Dillon & Bittner, 1975; Gardiner, Craik, & Birtwistle, 1972).

Diagnostic evidence for cue-driven retention also comes from the study of errors in immediate recall. When mistakes are made, the errors that occur tend not to be random, but rather follow certain patterns. For example, when a list item is recalled in an incorrect serial position, it is typically placed in a nearby position (e.g., the third item on the list is placed incorrectly in the second or fourth serial position). Recorded error gradients are systematic, showing that incorrect item placements drop off regularly as distance from the original position of occurrence increases (e.g., Healy, 1974). If lists are grouped, and people wrongly place an item from one group into another group, the item tends to be put in an identical relative serial position (e.g., Henson, 1999). Finally, when people intrude an item from a previous list, it is likely to have occurred at the same serial position in that list (Estes, 1991; Henson, 1996). Data of this sort indicate that people are not simply outputting activated items from short-term memory, but rather may be using some kind of position cue to help decide what occurred on the just-presented list.

Clearly, any full understanding of short-term memory will require some specification of how short-term memories are retrieved and translated into performance. The idea that immediate retention is cue-driven is appealing, in particular, because it is consistent with how most researchers conceive of long-term retention (see the chapter by Roediger & Marsh in this volume). All forms of remembering are cue-driven, although the nature of the cues, as well as the mechanics of the retrieval process, may differ between the short and the long term. This means that any empirical dissociations between short- and long-term retention, by themselves, will not be diagnostic of separate short- and long-term memory systems. One could still hold to a single system view, in which all forms of remembering are guided by the same set of general operating principles, and simply attribute the dissociations to differences in the composition of active retrieval cues (see Nairne, 2002).

The Working Memory Model

In the remainder of the chapter, I discuss some popular theoretical conceptions of the short-term memory system, beginning with the working memory model championed by Alan

Baddeley (e.g., Baddeley, 2000; Baddeley & Logie, 1999). The working memory model was developed initially to counter the view that short-term memory is a unitary storage system: a single place, or store, where complex forms of cognitive processing (e.g., reasoning or language comprehension) occur concurrently with temporary storage. Baddeley and Hitch (1974) argued instead for a multicomponent system with separate subsystems designed to handle particular kinds of processing, such as the temporary storage of visual versus phonological information. The working memory model maintains a strong distinction between short- and long-term memory, but it fractionates short-term memory into separate parts.

Baddeley and Hitch (1974) noted, for example, that remembering a span-length list of items produces little disruption of a concurrent reasoning or problem-solving task. If both temporary storage and on-line cognitive processing are controlled by the same processing machinery—the same processing store—then significant interference should have occurred between the two. The fact that little interference is found suggests that temporary storage and attention-based central processing may be controlled by separate mechanisms. Data from the study of brain-damaged patients proved troubling as well: It was discovered, for example, that patients with severely impaired short-term memory can show relatively intact long-term memory (e.g., Shallice & Warrington, 1970); a view proposing that both temporary storage and long-term learning are controlled by the same system has trouble accounting for this pattern.

The working memory model has undergone significant changes since its inception, but its core architecture still consists of three basic components: the central executive, the phonological loop, and the visuo-spatial sketchpad. The *central executive,* as the name suggests, controls and coordinates the actions of the remaining subsystems. It is assumed to be a limited-capacity attentional system that directs the focusing and switching of attention, and it may play a role in activating structures in long-term memory as well (see Baddeley, 1996). The central executive plays no role in storage per se, except as the controller of the loop and the sketchpad. The central executive is the least well-specified working memory component and, as Baddeley readily admits, it often serves as a kind of theoretical "grab bag" for intractable problems (see Baddeley, 2000).

The Phonological Loop

The bulk of the empirical effort on working memory has been spent on the phonological loop, which is the system assumed to control the temporary storage of acoustic and verbal information. The loop is divided into two components: a phonological store, which is the actual storage location for to-be-used information, and a rehearsal/recoding device called the articulatory control process. Information residing in the phonological store decays in roughly 2 s, although it can be refreshed, via rehearsal, through the articulatory control process. Capacity limitations in immediate retention—for example, the magic number seven—are assumed to arise from trade-offs between decay and loop-based rehearsal. In essence, the phonological loop account is a prototypical instantiation of the standard juggler model described earlier in the chapter (see Nairne, 1996, 2002).

The success of the working memory account hinges on its ability to explain a wide range of standard empirical phenomena. For example, the loop provides a nice account of the word length effect, discussed earlier, by assuming that there are inherent limitations in the operation of the articulatory control process. Memory span is limited to roughly what a person can rehearse within the time window established by decay—that is, about 2 s. When words are long, fewer can be refreshed before decay renders the short-term memory traces unreadable. The model also successfully predicts that the word length effect should be eliminated under conditions of articulatory suppression (Baddeley et al., 1975). Articulatory suppression—repeating a redundant item (e.g., *the*) aloud—acts to block rehearsal, thereby eliminating the mechanism that produces the word length effect.

In addition to refreshing decaying activity traces, the articulatory rehearsal mechanism serves an additional recoding function: It translates verbal material into phonological form. Representing stored traces phonologically, in the phonological store, enables the model to handle the phonological similarity effect, the finding that lists containing similar-sounding items (e.g., *g, c, b, t*) are harder to recall than lists of dissimilar-sounding items (Conrad, 1964). Moreover, by linking the phonological translation process to rehearsal, the model generates the unique prediction that the phonological similarity effect should be eliminated under articulatory suppression, at least for visually presented material. Preventing rehearsal blocks the recoding function, forcing one to rely on nonphonological forms of storage. In fact, articulatory suppression does seem to eliminate the phonological similarity effect when materials are presented visually (e.g., Murray, 1968). When list items are presented aloud, the effect remains under suppression, presumably because auditory materials are automatically registered in the phonological store (see Baddeley, 1986).

Along with its temporary storage functions, the phonological loop is also assumed to play a very important role in language processing, particularly the learning of new phonological material. Variables known to affect the functioning of the phonological loop, such as articulatory suppression and the word length effect, also affect one's ability to learn novel phonological forms, such as those required in the learning of a second language (see Baddeley et al., 1998). The learning of new words by children can also be predicted reasonably well by nonword repetition, a task that is assumed to tap functioning of the phonological loop. Finally, patients who show severe impairments in short-term memory tasks but show generally intact long-term memory and learning appear to have a selective deficit in the long-term learning of phonological information (Papagno, Valentine, & Baddeley, 1991). Baddeley et al. (1998) argue that the phonological loop may have evolved primarily to store unfamiliar sound patterns during time periods when more permanent memory records are being constructed.

The Visuo-Spatial Sketchpad

Whereas the phonological loop handles the temporary storage of verbal and acoustic information, the visuo-spatial sketchpad controls short-term processing and retention of visuospatial material. Like the phonological loop, the sketchpad probably has separable components, controlling visual, spatial, and possibly kinesthetic information (Baddeley, 2000; Baddeley & Logie, 1999). The visual component, which helps to retain visual patterns, is known as the visual *cache;* the capacity to remember sequences of spatial movements is attributed to an inner *scribe* (see Logie, 1995).

Most of the research investigating the sketchpad has employed dual-task methodologies. The goal is to demonstrate selective interference, thereby dissociating the capacity to retain visual, spatial, or verbal information, or combinations of these types of information. If subjects are asked to learn a list of words using an imagery mnemonic, which presumably taps the sketchpad more than the phonological loop, performance is hurt by the concurrent requirement to track a moving spot of light; the same tracking task has little, if any, effect on performance when subjects use a verbal-based rote learning strategy (Baddeley & Lieberman, 1980). Changing, but irrelevant, visual materials have been shown to disrupt the short-term retention of visual information (e.g., Quinn & McConnell, 1996); the retention of spatial patterns can also be selectively disrupted by spatial movements during a retention interval (see Baddeley & Logie, 1999). Collectively, these dissociations bolster the case for proposing separate storage mechanisms for verbal, spatial, and visual information.

However, at this point, there is no firm consensus on the inner workings of the sketchpad. It is unclear how dissociable the visual cache and the inner scribe will turn out to be, or the extent to which the different components draw on the same cognitive resources. Questions have also been raised about the relationship between mental imagery, in general, and operation of the sketchpad. Some evidence suggests that the two are dissociable. For instance, patients have been discovered who perform poorly on mental imagery tasks (such as mental rotation) but handle the short-term retention of visuo-spatial information quite well (N. Morton & Morris, 1995). In addition, some concurrent tasks, such as arm movements, that selectively disrupt the retention of spatial patterns have little effect on the performance of mental imagery tasks (Baddeley & Logie, 1999).

The Episodic Buffer

The working memory model has been enormously influential as an explanatory heuristic. It successfully ties together a wide range of standard laboratory phenomena, as well as data gathered from developmental and neurological studies. The model does have inherent problems, however, which it shares with other implementations of the standard juggler model (see Nairne, 2002, for a full discussion). For example, as noted earlier, word duration is probably not the important controlling factor in the word length effect. Words matched for pronunciation duration, but differing along other dimensions such as lexicality, regularly lead to memory span differences. The working memory model has no obvious mechanism to handle such effects. Moreover, the phonological similarity effect is assumed to result from confusions among representations in the phonological store, but no mechanism has ever been offered to explain exactly how these confusions arise. If items are immediately available by virtue of their residence in the store, why do the confusions occur? Is there some cue-based retrieval mechanism in place that can explain phonological confusions as well as other cue-driven immediate retention effects?

Another issue that has particularly troubled Baddeley is the question of how verbal information is stored temporarily when the phonological loop is unavailable. For example, under articulatory suppression, immediate memory performance is impaired, but only slightly: That is, performance might drop from a span of seven items to a span of five (Baddeley, Lewis, & Vallar, 1984). Given that the phonological loop is filled to capacity by the suppression activity, how are these items being stored? One possibility is the central executive, but Baddeley has assumed that the central executive performs no storage function (see Baddeley, 2000). Another possibility is the sketchpad, but verbal materials show little sensitivity to visual similarity under articulatory suppression. As Baddeley has recently stated, "the data suggest the need for some kind of 'back-up' store that is capable of supporting serial recall, and

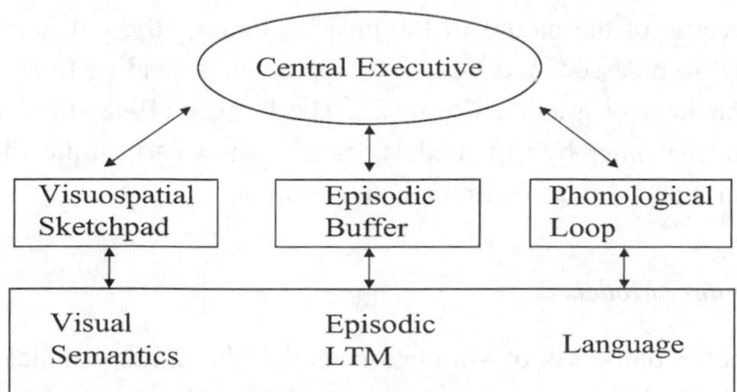

Figure 15.4 The multicomponent working memory model proposed by Baddeley (2000). The central executive controls three slave systems (visuospatial sketchpad; episodic buffer; phonological loop); each interacts with long-term memory and knowledge to improve on-line performance.

presumably of integrating phonological, visual, and possibly other types of information" (Baddeley, 2000, p. 419).

To solve these and other problems, Baddeley recently proposed a new working memory component—the episodic buffer—to serve as a limited capacity temporary storage system (see Figure 15.4). Controlled by the central executive, the episodic buffer differs from the loop and the sketchpad in performing both a storage and an integrative function; information from many different sources can be tied together in the buffer, including semantic information, and the result is a multidimensional episodic code. Presumably, the buffer enables one to store material when the loop or the sketchpad is unavailable, and it helps to explain how certain item characteristics (e.g., lexicality or imageability) might affect remembering over the short term. It is difficult to judge the merits of this new component of working memory at this point, however, because it has little, if any, unique empirical support.

Simulation Models of Short-Term Memory

Over the years, a number of formal simulation models (either mathematical or computer-based) have been proposed to explain the particulars of short-term retention. Probably the best known is the Atkinson and Shiffrin (1968) buffer model, which maintained a distinction between the structural features of a memory system (e.g., a limited-capacity short-term store) and the strategic control processes that operate within those structures (e.g., rehearsal, coding, or both). The buffer model established the mold for many subsequent modeling attempts, but most current models possess a decidedly different flavor. For example, whereas little attention was given in the Atkinson and Shiffrin model to the retrieval of short-term memories (items were simply dumped out of the short-term store), most current efforts focus extensively on the retrieval and interpretation of activity traces.

Virtually all current models maintain the distinction between short- and long-term memory, but they differ in whether similar processes are assumed to operate in the two cases. For example, some models essentially mimic the standard juggler model and attribute many of the standard immediate memory phenomena to a trade-off between rehearsal and decay (e.g., Burgess & Hitch, 1999; Henson, 1998; Page & Norris, 1998). Other so-called unitary models reject the concept of decay and offer little role for rehearsal, assuming instead that short-term retention is controlled by the same processes that control all forms of remembering—that is, both short- and long-term (e.g., Anderson & Matessa, 1997; G. D. A. Brown, Preece, & Hulme, 2000; Nairne, 1990). Space does not permit a full accounting of these models, but I very briefly outline some of their main features in the following two sections.

Hybrid Models

I use the term *hybrid* to classify the first set of models, because most acknowledge the important role that cue-driven retrieval processes play in short-term retention. Thus, items are not dumped out of a short-term buffer or loop; instead, recall candidates are chosen through some kind of item selection mechanism. This is a characteristic shared by unitary models that assign no special properties to remembering over the short term. In most other respects, though, hybrid models are simply implementations of the standard juggler model: Performance is based on short-term activity traces that are subject to immediate decay in the absence of continued internal rehearsal.

In the primacy model of Page and Norris (1998), immediate retention of serial order is controlled by the relative activation levels of list item traces. Activation level is determined by a primacy gradient, such that the trace for the first list item is assumed to be more active than the second list item, and so on. At the point of recall, items are selected for output based on their activation level, which means that the first list item tends to be output first and then suppressed. The output selection process is noisy, so there is a certain probability that items will be selected for output out of their proper sequence (leading to errors). Page and Norris (1998) have shown how these simple assumptions, along with standard assumptions about the trade-off between decay and rehearsal, can produce serial position functions and error gradients that mimic the patterns normally found in short-term serial recall.

In many respects, the primacy model attempts to formalize the main features of Baddeley's phonological loop. By adding specific mechanisms—for example, primacy-based activation gradients, noisy selection processes, suppression—it becomes possible to generate precise and sometimes novel predictions. For example, the primacy model predicts a unique and interesting kind of output error called a *fill-in error*. It turns out that when people miss an item in the recall sequence, as when they fail to recall the letter B in the second serial position, there is a significant tendency to report the missed item in the next serial position (i.e., as occurring in Position 3). Page and Norris (1998) argue that the assumptions of the primacy model correctly predict this tendency, whereas other models do not (although see Neath, Kelley, & Surprenant, 2001).

The connectionist model of Burgess and Hitch (1999) also attempts to formalize the operation of the phonological loop. Serial recall is more clearly cue-driven in this model, rather than based on activation levels, and the cues in this case are elements of a moving or drifting context signal. List items are associated with a snapshot of the context, which is set at the moment an item is presented. Adjacent items, because the context signal is slow-moving, tend to be associated to similar contextual cues, which helps to explain, in part, why people tend to transpose adjacent items in recall output. At the point of recall, the context signal is reset, and a competitive selection process proceeds based partly on the activations that items receive via their connections with the context.

The Burgess and Hitch (1999) model also assumes that connections exist between phonemic information and to-be-recalled items. This phonemic layer, when activated, serves essentially as the analogue for the phonological store in the working memory model. Rehearsal strengthens otherwise decaying connections between the phonemic layer and items, thereby helping to account for phenomena such as the word length effect. Again, the details are beyond the scope of this chapter, but the model nicely handles a variety of phenomena in immediate retention, including the occurrence of sound-based errors, the effects of articulatory suppression, and even temporal grouping effects (see also Hitch et al., 1996).

Another recently developed hybrid model is the Start-End model of Henson (1998). Once again, the major assumptions of the standard juggler model are reproduced in the form of decaying representations that are refreshed through internal rehearsal. The locus of the word length effect, and the general relationship between articulation rate and span, is placed in the trade-off between rehearsal and decay. The unique aspect of the Start-End model is its machinery for handling the recovery of serial order. Henson (1998) assumes that, during presentation, list items are coded relative to the start and end of the list. Items near the beginning of the list are associated more strongly with a beginning-of-the-list start marker, and recency items more strongly with an end marker. These position codes are then reinstated at test and used to activate associated items, and an item is selected for recall. Because of the nature of the position codes, adjacent items tend to be associated with overlapping cues, leading to systematic error gradients in recall. The Henson (1998) model, like the other hybrid models, can be shown to mimic the major phenomena of immediate retention.

Unitary Models

The second class of simulation model, the unitary models, typically rejects decay and rehearsal as the major determinants of immediate memory performance. As noted earlier in the chapter, there are both empirical and theoretical reasons to question whether decay and rehearsal are viable explanatory constructs in immediate retention. Although people certainly do rehearse, and rehearsal can play a role in unitary models, its role in unitary models is not to refresh otherwise decaying representations. Instead, rehearsal is typically viewed as another kind of stimulus presentation, which can, depending on the circumstance, either facilitate or interfere with subsequent retention (see G. D. A. Brown et al., 2000; Tan & Ward, 2000).

In the OSCAR model (which stands for OSCillator-based Associative Recall), forgetting is caused entirely by various forms of interference (G. D. A. Brown et al., 2000). By relying on interference and rejecting decay, OSCAR shares an important property with most conceptions of how forgetting occurs in long-term memory (see Crowder, 1976; Neath, 1998). In a fashion similar to the Burgess and Hitch (1999) model, associations are formed between to-be-recalled items and snapshots of a moving context signal (instantiated through sets of slow and fast temporal oscillators). The context is reset for recall, and there is cue-driven competition for output. Interference in the model occurs because of response competition during the selection process, output interference, and inherent capacity limitations in the storage mechanism that is employed (see Brown et al. for details).

Regarding rehearsal, the OSCAR model includes no active mechanism for the rehearsal of items during list presentation. Although its authors did consider the possibility of strategic rehearsal, the concept was rejected because, essentially, "we have found no need for it in accounting for the phenomena under consideration" (G. D. A. Brown et al., 2000, p. 172). With regard to decay, the concept is rejected for many of the same reasons discussed earlier in the chapter—that is, certain data seem antagonistic to the proposal of decay—but also because OSCAR is designed to explain data from both short- and long-term retention environments. Indeed, OSCAR fits data from retention intervals lasting seconds as well as it fits data from intervals lasting hours, without changing any of its main assumptions.

A similar characteristic is found in the perturbation model of Estes (1972, 1997), an early simulation model that strongly influenced the development of OSCAR. In the perturbation model, items are effectively represented as values along dimensions, such as temporal or spatial position. The organization can be hierarchical, meaning that an item might be represented in terms of its position along an ordered list, within-list, or within-group dimension (see Lee & Estes, 1981; Nairne, 1991). The crux of the model is the assumption that the position values are subject to random perturbations over time: That is, there is a certain probability that each represented value will drift along its position dimension. The probability that a perturbation will occur can be specified mathematically, and the model has been shown to generate precise predictions about correct and incorrect performance.

For example, the model does an excellent job of explaining the nature of errors in immediate serial recall. As noted earlier, when people make errors in ordered recall, items tend to be placed incorrectly in nearby positions, and there is a regular gradient found as distance increases from the item's original position (see Healy, 1974). The perturbation model not only generates these errors, but it also specifies exactly how the gradients should change as retention intervals increase. The model also nicely handles empirical dissociations between item and order memory, particularly the different forms of the serial position curve that have been reported (see Healy, 1974). Moreover, as Nairne (1991, 1992) has shown, essentially the same assumptions that handle data from immediate serial recall can also fit data across retention intervals lasting minutes or hours (although see Healy & McNamara, 1996, for some qualifying arguments). Thus, the perturbation model can be viewed as a unitary model, explaining both short- and long-term memory performance, and neither rehearsal nor fixed decay assumptions are needed to fit the data (Estes, 1997; Nairne, 1991).

The final model that I discuss is my own feature model (Nairne, 1988, 1990, 2001; Neath & Nairne, 1995). All forgetting in the feature model is attributed to interference, either from feature overwriting or from incorrect interpretation of the primary memory trace. Rehearsal can play a role in the model, as a mechanism for effectively re-presenting list items, but rehearsal plays no real role in producing standard immediate memory phenomena such as the word length effect or even the effects of articulatory suppression on performance (see also Neath, 2000). The model assumes that residual remnants of perceptual processing remain in primary memory after list presentation. These primary memory traces are represented as vectors of features and can be overwritten, based on similarity, by subsequent list items. At the point of recall, surviving traces exist in a degraded or blurry form and must be interpreted prior to recall. Most of the interesting effects of immediate retention arise out of the interpretation process.

The feature model has been applied successfully to most of the standard phenomena of immediate memory, including the modality and suffix effects. One of its most important assumptions is the idea that the trace interpretation process is guided by the presence or absence of distinctive features. Correct performance hinges on the presence of features in the degraded trace that uniquely specify one of the possible recall candidates. To the extent that primary memory traces contain features that are matched in all of the presented items, such as a common sound or phoneme, performance suffers. It is this characteristic of the model that explains the phonological similarity effect, as well as long-standing phenomena such as the von Restorff effect (see Kelley & Nairne, 2001). More importantly, the trace interpretation process is assumed to resemble the kinds of cue-driven retrieval processes that guide all forms of remembering, regardless of the time scales involved (see Nairne, 2002). The feature model, like the other unitary models discussed, assigns no special mnemonic laws or properties (such as decay) to remembering over the short term.

CONCLUSIONS

Transient memories, discussed here in the form of sensory and short-term memory, clearly serve highly adaptive functions in human cognitive processing. Sensory memories enable us to prolong the present, for the briefest of intervals; short-term memories comprise the ingredients of conscious awareness and play a vital role, among other things, in the comprehension and production of spoken language. Compared to the study of long-term retention, studying transient memories is a relatively recent enterprise, commencing with full vigor only in the second half of the twentieth century. As we have seen, many issues remain unresolved, and fundamental controversies continue. Does short-term retention follow its own unique operating laws? Is it necessary to propose processes, such as decay, that apply uniquely to remembering over the short term? Is sensory persistence truly an evolved form of remembering, serving its own special function, or is it simply an artifact of the properties of neural networks?

Despite these controversies, few questions remain about the data to be explained. In the presence of distractor activity, we can still remember only a handful of unrelated items for more than 10 or 20 s; when an array of unrelated letters is briefly flashed, a partial reporting of the array is still dramatically better than reporting of the whole. Whatever form the final accounting of these phenomena takes, it will undoubtedly provide insight into far more than simply remembering over the short term. The study of transient memories is likely to provide a clear window for understanding all forms of memory, both short and long.

REFERENCES

Anderson, J. R., & Matessa, M. (1997). A production system theory of serial memory. *Psychological Review, 104,* 728–774.

Atkinson, R. C., & Shiffrin, R. M. (1968). Human memory: A proposed system and its control processes. In K. W. Spence & J. T. Spence (Eds.), *The psychology of learning and motivation* (Vol. 2, pp. 89–105). New York: Academic Press.

Averbach, E., & Coriell, H. S. (1961). Short-term memory in vision. *Bell Systems Technical Journal, 40,* 309–328.

Ayres, T. J., Jonides, J., Reitman, J. S., Egan, J. C., & Howard, D. A. (1979). Differing suffix effects for the same physical suffix. *Journal of Experimental Psychology: Human Learning and Memory, 5,* 315–321.

Baddeley, A. D. (1986). *Working memory.* Oxford, UK: Oxford University Press.

Baddeley, A. D. (1996). Exploring the central executive. *Quarterly Journal of Experimental Psychology, 49A,* 5–28.

Baddeley, A. D. (2000). The episodic buffer: A new component of working memory? *Trends in Cognitive Sciences, 4,* 417–423.

Baddeley, A. D., Gathercole, S. E., & Papagno, C. (1998). The phonological loop as a language learning device. *Psychological Review, 105,* 158–173.

Baddeley, A. D., & Hitch. G. (1974). Working memory. In G. H. Bower (Ed.), *The psychology of learning and motivation* (Vol. 8, pp. 47–89). New York: Academic Press.

Baddeley, A. D., Lewis, V. J., & Vallar, G. (1984). Exploring the articulatory loop. *Quarterly Journal of Experimental Psychology, 36,* 233–252.

Baddeley, A. D., & Lieberman, K. (1980). Spatial working memory. In R. Nickerson (Ed.), *Attention and performance VIII* (pp. 521–539). Hillsdale, NJ: Erlbaum.

Baddeley, A. D., & Logie, R. H. (1999). Working memory: The multicomponent model. In A. Miyake & P. Shah (Eds.), *Models of working memory* (pp. 28–61). Cambridge, UK: Cambridge University Press.

Baddeley, A. D., & Scott, D. (1971). Short term forgetting in the absence of proactive interference. *Quarterly Journal of Experimental Psychology, 23,* 275–283.

Baddeley, A. D., Thomson, N., & Buchanan, M. (1975). Word length and the structure of short-term memory. *Journal of Verbal Learning and Verbal Behavior, 14,* 575–589.

Bjork, R. A. (2001). Recency and recovery in human memory. In H. L. Roediger, J. S. Nairne, I. Neath, & A. Surprenant (Eds.), *The nature of remembering: Essays in honor of Robert G. Crowder* (pp. 211–232). Washington, DC: American Psychological Association.

Bowen, R. W., Pola, J., & Matin, L. (1974). Visual persistence: Effects of flash luminance, duration and energy. *Vision Research, 14,* 295–303.

Broadbent, D. E. (1958). *Perception and communication.* London: Pergamon Press.

Brown, G. D. A., McCormack, T., & Chater, N. (2001). The chronological organisation of memory: Common psychological foundations for remembering and time. In C. Hoerl & T. McCormack (Eds.), *Time and memory: Issues in philosophy and psychology.* Oxford, UK: Oxford University Press.

Brown, G. D. A., Preece, T., & Hulme, C. (2000). Oscillator-based memory for serial order. *Psychological Review, 107,* 127–181.

Brown, J. (1958). Some tests of the decay theory of immediate memory. *Quarterly Journal of Experimental Psychology, 10,* 12–21.

Burgess, N., & Hitch, G. J. (1999). Memory for serial order: A network model of the phonological loop and its timing. *Psychological Review, 106,* 551–581.

Campbell, R., & Dodd, B. (1980). Hearing by eye. *Quarterly Journal of Experimental Psychology, 32,* 85–99.

Caplan, D., Rochon, E., & Waters, G. S. (1992). Articulatory and phonological determinants of word-length effects in span tasks. *Quarterly Journal of Experimental Psychology, 45A,* 177–192.

Cofer, C. N., & Davidson, E. H. (1968). Proactive interference in STM for consonant units of two sizes. *Journal of Verbal Learning and Verbal Behavior, 7,* 268–270.

Coltheart, M. (1980). Iconic memory and visual persistence. *Perception & Psychophysics, 27,* 183–228.

Conrad, R. (1964). Acoustic confusion in immediate memory. *British Journal of Psychology, 55,* 75–84.

Corballis, M. C. (1966). Rehearsal and decay in immediate recall of visually and aurally presented items. *Canadian Journal of Psychology, 20,* 43–51.

Cowan, N. (1984). On short and long auditory stores. *Psychological Bulletin, 96,* 341–370.

Cowan, N. (1988). Evolving conceptions of memory storage, selective attention, and their mutual constraints within the human information processing system. *Psychological Bulletin, 104,* 163–191.

Cowan, N. (1995). *Attention and memory: An integrated framework.* New York: Oxford University Press.

Cowan, N. (2001). The magical number 4 in short-term memory: A reconsideration of mental storage capacity. *Behavioral and Brain Sciences, 24,* 87–185.

Crowder, R. G. (1976). *Principles of learning and memory.* Hillsdale, NJ: Erlbaum.

Crowder, R. G. (1978). Memory for phonologically uniform lists. *Journal of Verbal Learning and Verbal Behavior, 17,* 73–89.

Crowder, R. G., & Morton, J. (1969). Precategorical acoustic storage (PAS). *Perception & Psychophysics, 5,* 365–373.

Crowder, R. G., & Surprenant, A. M. (2000). Sensory memory. In A. E. Kazdin (Ed.), *Encyclopedia of psychology* (Vol. 7, pp. 227–229). New York: Oxford University Press and American Psychological Association.

Daneman, M., & Carpenter, P. A. (1980). Individual differences in working memory and reading. *Journal of Verbal Learning and Verbal Behavior, 19,* 450–466.

Darwin, C. J. (1976). The perception of speech. In E. C. Carterette & M. P. Friedman (Eds.), *Handbook of perception* (Vol. 7, pp. 175–218). New York: Academic Press.

Darwin, C. J., Turvey, M. T., & Crowder, R. G. (1973). An auditory analogue of the Sperling partial-report procedure. *Cognitive Psychology, 3,* 255–267.

Dempster, F. N. (1992). The rise and fall of the inhibitory mechanism: Toward a unified theory of cognitive development and aging. *Developmental Review, 12,* 45–75.

Dillon, R. F., & Bittner, L. A. (1975). Analysis of retrieval cues and release from proactive inhibition. *Journal of Verbal Learning and Verbal Behavior, 14,* 616–622.

Di Lollo, V., Hogben, J. H., & Dixon, P. (1994). Temporal integration and segregation of brief visual stimuli: Patterns of correlation in time. *Perception & Psychophysics, 55,* 373–386.

Dixon, P., Gordon, R. D., Leung, A., & Di Lollo, V. (1997). Attentional components of partial report. *Journal of Experimental Psychology: Human Perception and Performance, 23,* 1253–1271.

Dosher, B. A., & Ma, J.-J. (1998). Output loss or rehearsal loop? Output-time versus pronunciation-time limits in immediate recall for forgetting-matched materials. *Journal of Experimental Psychology: Learning, Memory, and Cognition, 24,* 316–335.

Dosher, B. A., & McElree, B. (1992). Memory search: Retrieval processes in short-term and long-term retention. In L. R. Squire (Ed.), *Encyclopedia of learning and memory* (pp. 398–405). New York: Macmillan.

Ebbinghaus, H. (1964). *Memory: A contribution to experimental psychology.* New York: Dover. (Original work published 1885)

Efron, R. (1970). Effect of stimulus duration on perceptual onset and offset latencies. *Perception & Psychophysics, 8,* 231–234.

Ellis, N. C., & Hennelley, R. A. (1980). A bilingual word-length effect: Implications for intelligence testing and the relative ease of mental calculation in Welsh and English. *British Journal of Psychology, 71,* 43–52.

Engle, R. E., Kane, M. J., & Tuholski, S. W. (1999). Individual differences in working memory capacity and what they tell us about controlled attention, general fluid intelligence, and functions of the prefrontal cortex. In A. Miyake & P. Shah (Eds.), *Models of working memory* (pp. 102–134). Cambridge, UK: Cambridge University Press.

Eriksen, C. W., & Collins, J. F. (1967). Some temporal characteristics of visual pattern perception. *Journal of Experimental Psychology, 74,* 476–484.

Estes, W. K. (1972). An associative basis for coding and organization in memory. In A. W. Martin & E. Martin (Eds.), *Coding processes in human memory* (pp. 161–190). Washington, DC: Winston.

Estes, W. K. (1991). On types of item coding and source of recall in short-term memory. In W. E. Hockley & S. Lewandowsky (Eds.), *Relating theory and data: Essays on human memory in honor of Bennet B. Murdock* (pp. 155–174). Hillsdale, NJ: Erlbaum.

Estes, W. K. (1997). Processes of memory loss, recovery, and distortion. *Psychological Review, 104,* 148–169.

Francis, G. (1999). Spatial frequency and visual persistence: Cortical reset. *Spatial Vision, 12,* 31–50.

Gardiner, J. M., Craik, F. I. M., & Birtwistle, J. (1972). Retrieval cues and release from proactive inhibition. *Journal of Verbal Learning and Verbal Behavior, 11,* 778–783.

Greene, R. L. (1992). *Human memory: Paradigms and paradoxes.* Hillsdale, NJ: Erlbaum.

Greene, R. L. (1996). The influence of experimental design: The example of the Brown-Peterson paradigm. *Canadian Journal of Experimental Psychology, 50,* 240–242.

Greene, R. L. & Crowder, R. G. (1984). Modality and suffix effects in the absence of auditory stimulation. *Journal of Verbal Learning and Verbal Behavior, 23,* 371–382.

Grossberg, S. (1994). 3-D vision and figure-ground separation by the visual cortex. *Perception & Psychophysics, 55,* 48–120.

Haber, R. N. (1983). The impending demise of the icon: A critique of the concept of iconic storage in visual information processing. *Behavioral and Brain Sciences, 6,* 1–10.

Halford, G. S., Mayberry, M. T., & Bain, J. D. (1988). Set-size effects in primary memory: An age-related capacity limitation? *Memory & Cognition, 16,* 480–487.

Healy, A. F. (1974). Separating item from order information in short-term memory. *Journal of Verbal Learning and Verbal Behavior, 13,* 644–655.

Healy, A. F., & Cunningham, T. F. (1995). Very rapid forgetting: A reply to Muter. *Memory & Cognition, 23,* 387–392.

Healy, A. F., & McNamara, D. S. (1996). Verbal learning and memory: Does the modal model still work? *Annual Review of Psychology, 47,* 143–172.

Henson, R. N. A. (1996). *Short-term memory for serial order.* Unpublished doctoral dissertation, University of Cambridge, Cambridge, UK.

Henson, R. N. A. (1998). Short-term memory for serial order: The start-end model. *Cognitive Psychology, 36,* 73–137.

Henson, R. N. A. (1999). Positional information in short-term memory: Relative or absolute? *Memory & Cognition, 27,* 915–927.

Hitch, G. J., Burgess, N., Towse, J. N., & Culpin, V. (1996). Temporal grouping effects in immediate recall: A working memory analysis. *Quarterly Journal of Experimental Psychology, 49A,* 116–139.

Hulme, C., Maughan, S., & Brown, G. D. A. (1991). Memory for familiar and unfamiliar words: Evidence for a long-term memory contribution to short-term memory span. *Journal of Memory and Language, 30,* 685–701.

Hulme, C., Roodenrys, S., Schweickert, R., Brown, G. D. A., Martin, S., & Stuart, G. (1997). Word frequency effects on short-term memory tasks: Evidence for a multinomial processing tree model of immediate serial recall. *Journal of Experimental Psychology: Learning, Memory, and Cognition, 23,* 1217–1232.

Hulme, C., Thomson, N., Muir, C., & Lawrence, A. (1984). Speech rate and the development of short-term memory span. *Journal of Experimental Child Psychology, 38,* 241–253.

Hulme, C., & Tordoff, V. (1989). Working memory development: The effects of speech rate, word length, and acoustic similarity on serial recall. *Journal of Experimental Child Psychology, 47,* 72–87.

Kane, M. J., & Engle, R. W. (2000). Working-memory capacity, proactive interference, and divided attention: Limits on long-term memory retrieval. *Journal of Experimental Psychology: Learning, Memory, and Cognition, 26,* 336–358.

Kelley, M. R., & Nairne, J. S. (2001). von Restorff revisited: Isolation, generation, and memory for order. *Journal of Experimental Psychology: Learning, Memory, and Cognition, 27,* 54–66.

Keppel, G., & Underwood, B. J. (1962). Proactive inhibition in short-term retention of single items. *Journal of Verbal Learning and Verbal Behavior, 1,* 153–161.

Lee, C. L., & Estes, W. K. (1981). Item and order information in short-term memory: Evidence for multilevel perturbation processes. *Journal of Experimental Psychology: Human Learning and Memory, 7,* 149–169.

Loftus, G. R., & Irwin, D. E. (1998). On the relations among different measures of visible and informational persistence. *Cognitive Psychology, 35,* 135–199.

Logie, R. H. (1995). *Visuo-spatial working memory.* Hove, UK: Erlbaum.

Lovatt, P., Avons, S. E., & Masterson, J. (2000). The word-length effect and disyllabic words. *Quarterly Journal of Experimental Psychology, 53A,* 1–22.

Massaro, D. W. (1970). Perceptual processes and forgetting in memory tasks. *Psychological Review, 77,* 557–567.

Massaro, D. W. (1975). *Experimental psychology and information processing.* Chicago: Rand-McNally.

Massaro, D. W., & Loftus, G. R. (1996) Sensory and perceptual storage. In E. L. Bjork & R. A. Bjork (Eds.), *Handbook of perception and cognition* (Vol. 10, pp. 67–99). New York: Academic Press.

McElree, B. (1998). Attended and non-attended states in working memory: Accessing categorized structures. *Journal of Memory and Language, 38,* 225–252.

McElree, B., & Dosher, B. A. (1989). Serial position and set size in short-term memory: Time course of recognition. *Journal of Experimental Psychology: General, 118,* 346–373.

McElree, B., & Dosher, B. A. (1993). Serial retrieval processes in the recovery of order information. *Journal of Experimental Psychology: General, 122,* 291–315.

McGeoch, J. A. (1932). Forgetting and the law of disuse. *Psychological Review, 39,* 352–370.

Melton, A. W. (1963). Implications of short-term memory for a general theory of memory. *Journal of Verbal Learning and Verbal Behavior, 2,* 1–21.

Mewhort, D. J. K., Campbell, A. J., Marchetti, F. M., & Campbell, J. I. D. (1981). Identification, localization, and "iconic memory:" An evaluation of the bar-probe task. *Memory & Cognition, 9,* 50–67.

Miller, G. A. (1956). The magical number seven plus or minus two: Some limits on our capacity for processing information. *Psychological Review, 63,* 81–97.

Miyake, A., & Shah, P. (1999). *Models of working memory.* Cambridge, UK: Cambridge University Press.

Morton, J., Crowder, R. G., & Prussin, H. A. (1971). Experiments with the stimulus suffix effect. *Journal of Experimental Psychology, 91,* 169–190.

Morton, N., & Morris, R. G. (1995). Image transformation dissociated from visuospatial working memory. *Cognitive Neuropsychology, 12,* 767–791.

Murdock, B. B., Jr. (1961). The retention of individual items. *Journal of Experimental Psychology, 62,* 618–625.

Murray, D. J. (1968) Articulation and acoustic confusability in short-term memory. *Journal of Experimental Psychology, 78,* 679–684.

Muter, P. (1980). Very rapid forgetting. *Memory & Cognition, 8,* 174–179.

Näätänen, R., & Winkler, I. (1999). The concept of auditory stimulus representation in cognitive neuroscience. *Psychological Bulletin, 125,* 826–859.

Nairne, J. S. (1988). A framework for interpreting recency effects in immediate serial recall. *Memory & Cognition, 16,* 343–352.

Nairne, J. S. (1990). A feature model of immediate memory. *Memory & Cognition, 18,* 251–269.

Nairne, J. S. (1991). Positional uncertainty in long-term memory. *Memory & Cognition, 19,* 332–340.

Nairne, J. S. (1992). The loss of positional certainty in long-term memory. *Psychological Science, 3,* 199–202.

Nairne, J. S. (1996). Short-term/working memory. In E. L. Bjork & R. A. Bjork (Eds.), *Memory* (pp. 101–126). New York: Academic Press.

Nairne, J. S. (2001). A functional analysis of primary memory. In H. L. Roediger, J. S. Nairne, I. Neath, & A. M. Surprenant (Eds.), *The nature of remembering: Essays in honor of Robert G. Crowder* (pp. 282–296). Washington, DC: American Psychological Association.

Nairne, J. S. (2002). Remembering over the short-term: The case against the standard model. *Annual Review of Psychology, 53,* 53–81.

Nairne, J. S., & Walters, V. L. (1983). Silent mouthing produces modality- and suffix-like effects. *Journal of Verbal Learning and Verbal Behavior, 22,* 475–483.

Naveh-Benjamin, M., & Ayres, T. J. (1986). Digit span, reading rate, and linguistic relativity. *Quarterly Journal of Experimental Psychology, 38A,* 739–751.

Neath, I. (1998). *Human memory: An introduction to research, data, and theory.* Pacific Grove, CA: Brooks/Cole.

Neath, I. (2000). Modelling the effects of irrelevant speech on memory. *Psychonomic Bulletin & Review, 7,* 403–423.

Neath, I., & Crowder, R. G. (1990). Schedules of presentation and temporal distinctiveness in human memory. *Journal of Experimental Psychology: Learning, Memory, and Cognition, 16,* 316–327.

Neath, I., Kelley, M. R., & Surprenant, A. M. (2001). *Fill-in and infill errors in immediate serial recall.* Manuscript submitted for publication.

Neath, I., & Knoedler, A. J. (1994). Distinctiveness and serial position effects in recognition and sentence processing. *Journal of Memory and Language, 33,* 776–795.

Neath, I., & Nairne, J. S. (1995). Word-length effects in immediate memory: Overwriting trace-decay theory. *Psychonomic Bulletin & Review, 2,* 429–441.

Neath, I., Surprenant, A. M., & Crowder, R. G. (1993). The context dependent stimulus suffix effect. *Journal of Experimental Psychology: Learning, Memory, and Cognition, 19,* 698–703.

Osgood, C. E. (1953). *Method and theory in experimental psychology.* New York: Oxford University Press.

Page, M. P. A., & Norris, D. (1998). The primacy model: A new model of immediate serial recall. *Psychological Review, 105,* 761–781.

Papagno, C., Valentine, T., & Baddeley, A. D. (1991). Phonological short-term memory and foreign-language vocabulary learning. *Journal of Memory and Language, 30,* 331–347.

Peterson, L. R., & Peterson, M. J. (1959). Short-term retention of individual verbal items. *Journal of Experimental Psychology, 58,* 193–198.

Proctor, R. W., & Fagnani, C. A. (1978). Effects of distractor-stimulus modality in the Brown-Peterson distractor task. *Journal of Experimental Psychology: Human Learning and Memory, 4,* 676–684.

Quinn, J. G., & McConnell, J. (1996). Irrelevant pictures in visual working memory. *Quarterly Journal of Experimental Psychology, 49A,* 200–215.

Ratcliff, R. (1978). A theory of memory retrieval. *Psychological Review, 85,* 59–108.

Reed, A. V. (1976). The time course of recognition in human memory. *Memory & Cognition, 4,* 16–30.

Roodenrys, S., Hulme, C., Alban, J., & Ellis, A. W. (1994). Effects of word frequency and age of acquisition on short-term memory span. *Memory & Cognition, 22,* 695–701.

Rosen, V. M., & Engle, R. W. (1998). Working memory capacity and suppression. *Journal of Memory and Language, 39,* 418–436.

Ryan, J. (1969). Grouping and short-term memory: Different means and patterns of groups. *Quarterly Journal of Experimental Psychology, 21,* 137–147.

Schweickert, R. (1993). A multinomial processing tree model for degradation and redintegration in immediate recall. *Memory & Cognition, 21,* 167–175.

Schweickert, R., & Boruff, B. (1986). Short-term memory capacity: Magic number or magic spell? *Journal of Experimental Psychology: Learning, Memory, and Cognition, 12,* 419–425.

Schweickert, R., Guentert, L., & Hersberger, L. (1990). Phonological similarity, pronunciation rate, and memory span. *Psychological Science, 1,* 74–77.

Sebrechts, M. M., Marsh, R. L., & Seamon, J. G. (1989). Secondary memory and very rapid forgetting. *Memory & Cognition, 17,* 693–700.

Service, E. (1998). The effect of word length on immediate serial recall depends on phonological complexity, not articulatory duration. *Quarterly Journal of Experimental Psychology, 51A,* 283–304.

Shallice, T., & Warrington, E. K. (1970). Independent functioning of verbal memory stores: A neuropsychological study. *Quarterly Journal of Experimental Psychology, 22,* 261–273.

Shiffrin, R. M. (1999). 30 years of memory. In C. Izawa (Ed.), *On human memory: Evolution, progress, and reflections on the 30th anniversary of the Atkinson-Shiffrin model* (pp. 17–33). Mahwah, NJ: Erlbaum.

Slamecka, N. J. (1967). *Human memory and learning: Selected readings.* New York: Oxford University Press.

Sperling, G. (1960). The information available in brief visual presentation. *Psychological Monographs, 74,* 1–29.

Sternberg, S. (1966). High-speed scanning in human memory. *Science, 153,* 652–654.

Tan, L., & Ward, G. (2000). A recency-based account of the primacy effect in free recall. *Journal of Experimental Psychology: Learning, Memory, and Cognition, 26,* 1589–1625.

Tehan, G., & Humphreys, M. S. (1995). Transient phonemic codes and immunity to proactive interference. *Memory & Cognition, 23,* 181–191.

Tehan, G., & Humphreys, M. S. (1996). Cuing effects in short-term recall. *Memory & Cognition, 24,* 719–732.

Tehan, G., & Humphreys, M. S. (1998). Creating proactive interference in immediate recall: Building a dog from a dart, a mop and a fig. *Memory & Cognition, 26,* 477–489.

Tehan, G., & Lalor D. M. (2000). Individual differences in memory span: The contribution of rehearsal, access to lexical memory and output speed. *Quarterly Journal of Experimental Psychology, 53A,* 1012–1038.

Townsend, J. T., & Ashby, F. G. (1983). *The stochastic modeling of elementary psychological processes.* Cambridge, UK: Cambridge University Press.

Tulving, E. (1983). *Elements of episodic memory.* New York: Oxford University Press.

Turner, M. L., & Engle, R. W. (1989). Is working memory capacity task dependent? *Journal of Memory and Language, 28,* 127–154.

Turvey, M. T. (1973). On peripheral and central processes in vision: Inferences from an information processing analysis of masking with patterned stimuli. *Psychological Review, 80,* 1–52.

Turvey, M. T., Brick, P., & Osborn, J. (1970). Proactive interference in short-term memory as a function of prior-item retention interval. *Quarterly Journal of Experimental Psychology, 22,* 142–147.

Walker, I., & Hulme, C. (1999). Concrete words are easier to recall than abstract: Evidence for a semantic contribution to short-term serial recall. *Journal of Experimental Psychology: Learning, Memory, & Cognition, 25,* 1256–1271.

Watkins, O. C., & Watkins, M. J. (1975). Buildup of proactive inhibition as a cue-overload effect. *Journal of Experimental Psychology: Human Learning and Memory, 104,* 442–452.

Watkins, O. C., & Watkins, M. J. (1980). The modality effect and echoic persistence. *Journal of Experimental Psychology: General, 109,* 251–278.

Wickelgren, W. A. (1967). Rehearsal grouping and hierarchical organization of serial position cues in short-term memory. *Quarterly Journal of Experimental Psychology, 19,* 97–102.

Wickelgren, W. A., Corbett, A. T., & Dosher, B. A. (1980). Priming and retrieval from short-term memory: A speed-accuracy tradeoff analysis. *Journal of Verbal Learning and Verbal Behavior, 19,* 387–404.

Wickens, D. D. (1970). Encoding categories of words: An empirical approach to meaning. *Psychological Review, 77,* 1–15.

Wickens, D. D., Moody, M. J., & Dow, R. (1981). The nature and timing of the retrieval process and of interference effects. *Journal of Experimental Psychology: General, 110,* 1–20.

Wright, A. A., Santiago, H. C., Sands, S. F., Kendrick, D. F., & Cook, R. G. (1985). Memory processing of serial lists by pigeons, monkeys, and people. *Science, 229,* 287–289.

PART SIX

COMPLEX LEARNING AND MEMORY PROCESSES

CHAPTER 16

Semantic Memory and Priming

TIMOTHY P. McNAMARA AND JON B. HOLBROOK

The purpose of this chapter is to review theoretical and empirical developments in the scientific understanding of semantic memory and priming, including both semantic priming and repetition priming. *Semantic memory* is our mental storehouse of knowledge about the world and forms the foundation of our abilities to understand and produce language. *Semantic priming* refers to an effect of context on retrieving information from memory. For example, people can name a word faster if it is paired with a related word (e.g., *lion-tiger*) than if it is paired with an unrelated word (e.g., *table-tiger*). *Repetition priming* refers to an effect of prior experience on retrieving information from memory. For instance, a word can be named faster the second time it appears than the first time it appears. Although these categories of memory phenomena differ in content and scope, they may be related in important ways. Semantic priming is probably produced by fundamental mechanisms of retrieval in semantic memory, and all three have been identified as important components of implicit memory.

The plan of the chapter is as follows: In the first section, we review models of semantic memory proposed in the 1960s and 1970s and the major empirical findings that were used to test these models. We also summarize two contemporary models of semantic memory, distributed network models and high-dimensional spatial models. In the second section of the chapter, we examine semantic priming. We review the most influential models of semantic priming and then summarize empirical developments, focusing in particular on issues that have turned out to be important for testing models of semantic priming. In the final section of the chapter, we look at repetition priming, reviewing both models and major issues and findings. We close with a brief summary of our major conclusions.

SEMANTIC MEMORY

Semantic memory refers to our knowledge about language and facts about the world; it can be thought of as a mental dictionary, encyclopedia, and thesaurus all rolled into one (e.g., E. E. Smith, 1978; Tulving, 1972). A defining characteristic of semantic memories is that we, as introspective observers, do not know where they came from; they are not represented in terms of specific times and places. Semantic memory has traditionally been contrasted with episodic memory (e.g., Tulving, 1983). Episodic memory refers to our knowledge that is tagged temporally or spatially, or identified in some way in terms of personal experiences (see also the chapter in this volume by Roediger & Marsh). Although there are reasons to believe that semantic memory and episodic

Preparation of this chapter was supported in part by NIMH Grant R01-MH57868. The authors are grateful to Derek Besner, Dorothee Chwilla, Alice Healy, Steve Joordens, Margery Lucas, Ken McRae, James Neely, David Plaut, Robert Proctor, and Irving Weiner for their comments on sections or drafts of this chapter.

memory are not independent systems (e.g., McKoon, Ratcliff, & Dell, 1986), the distinction has been extremely influential in the field of memory and is useful for organizing memory phenomena, tasks, and models.

A complete theory of semantic memory should be able to explain the following phenomena (e.g., E. E. Smith, 1978): First, a theory of semantic memory should explain how the meanings of words are mentally represented. It might specify, for example, that meaning is represented as a collection of features, some of which are essential and others of which are just typical (e.g., for *bird, animate,* and *can fly,* respectively). Second, it should be able to explain how the meanings of individual words can be combined to form more complex units. How, for example, is the meaning of a simple noun combination, such as *pet bird,* constructed from the meanings of its constituents, *pet* and *bird*? Third, the theory should specify the permissible inferences that can be made from word and sentence meanings. What can you infer about a grampus if you know that it is a mammal? This goal is, of course, closely tied to the first. Fourth and finally, a theory of semantic memory should explain the connection between word meaning and the world, between semantic representations and perceptual systems. For example, it should explain how we recognize an object from a description, or describe an object based on perceptual input (e.g., vision, taction, etc.).

As a matter of history, theories of semantic memory have dealt primarily with the first goal, specifying how word meanings are mentally represented. There has been a fair amount of research on how word meanings are combined, but it has been carried out under the guise of investigations of concepts and categorization (see the chapter by Goldstone & Kersten). Very little attention has been given to the third and the fourth goals by cognitive psychologists. Our goal in this section of the chapter is to review some of the major theoretical and empirical developments in the field of semantic memory. We begin by summarizing the models developed during the late 1960s and the 1970s, the golden age of semantic memory research. We then turn to a brief review of some of the major empirical challenges posed during that time. We close with a brief review of recent models of semantic memory.

Early Models of Semantic Memory

The early models of semantic memory were of three basic types: network models (e.g., Collins & Loftus, 1975; Collins & Quillian, 1969; Glass & Holyoak, 1974; Quillian, 1967); set-theoretic models (D. E. Meyer, 1970); and feature models (e.g., McCloskey & Glucksberg, 1979; E. E. Smith, Shoben, & Rips, 1974). Two of these models turned out be extremely influential: the spreading-activation theory of Collins and Loftus (1975) and the feature-comparison theory of E. E. Smith et al. (1974). We focus our attention on these two models. For a comprehensive review of the other models, consult E. E. Smith (1978).

Spreading-Activation Theory of Semantic Processing

The spreading-activation theory of semantic processing proposed by Collins and Loftus (1975) is an elaboration of the hierarchical network model proposed by Quillian and Collins (e.g., Collins & Quillian, 1969; Quillian, 1967). A unique feature of the model, at least in the context of psychological models of semantic memory, is that it distinguishes knowledge of the meanings of concepts from knowledge of their names.

The conceptual network is organized according to semantic similarity. Concepts are assumed to be represented as nodes in a network. The more properties two concepts have in common, the more links that exist between the two nodes. For example, *car* and *truck* would have many links between them, whereas *car* and *apple* would have few links. In the original hierarchical network model, several types of links were distinguished (e.g., superordinate and subordinate, modifiers, disjunctive sets, etc.). This rich array of link types allowed the model to account for a wide variety of semantic decisions (e.g., Quillian, 1969). However, the different link types did not play an important role in the elaborated theory.

The names of concepts are stored in a lexical network organized according to phonemic similarity. Thus, for example, several links would exist between the nodes for *car* and *bar,* but no links would exist between the nodes for *car* and *bus*. Each node in the lexical network is connected to at least one node in the conceptual network.

The fundamental retrieval mechanism is spreading activation. Concepts are activated by being mentally processed in some manner; for example, thinking about or seeing apples would activate the corresponding concept in semantic memory. Activation spreads from a concept along links throughout the network and decays with distance in the network; that is, the farther the activation spreads, in terms of number of links traversed, the less arrives at the destination. Activation also requires more time to spread greater distances. Activation is released from a concept as long as it is processed, but only one concept can be actively processed at any one time, and therefore only one concept can be a source of activation. Activation gradually decays with time if no concepts in the network are being processed.

Several ancillary processing assumptions are made to handle particular semantic judgments. One such assumption is that people can control whether to activate the conceptual network or the lexical network. For instance, an individual could try to think of exemplars of *bird,* which involves activating the conceptual network, or think of words that sound like *bird,* which involves activating the lexical network. Another assumption is that semantic decisions, such as verifications of member-category and property statements (e.g., *A robin is an animal* and *A robin has feathers,* respectively), are made by accumulating positive and negative evidence until a positive or a negative criterion is reached. The evidence consists of various kinds of connections that are found during the memory search. For example, for a member-category statement, such as *A robin is an animal,* the superordinate connections from *robin* to *bird* and from *bird* to *animal* would count as positive evidence. These evidence accumulation processes are very similar to the processing assumptions of the feature comparison theory later described.

One of the longest lasting impacts of Collins and Loftus's (1975) model came from its ability to provide an elegant explanation of semantic priming; indeed, this model became the canonical model of semantic priming. According to this model, processing of a prime word causes activation to spread from the prime throughout the conceptual network. More activation will accumulate at concepts close to the prime than at concepts far from the prime. This residual activation then facilitates the semantic decision on the target word. For example, because *bird* and *robin* are closer in memory than are *dog* and *robin,* more activation accumulates at *robin* when *bird* is the prime than when *dog* is the prime, and decision times are correspondingly faster.

Feature-Comparison Theory

The feature-comparison theory (e.g., E. E. Smith et al., 1974) has two major sets of assumptions, those concerning the representation of word meaning and those concerning the processing of word meaning.

The meaning of a word is represented by a set of semantic attributes or features. The features vary continuously on a scale of "definingness": At one end of the scale are features that are essential to the word's meaning; at the other end of the scale are features that are only characteristic of the concept. For example, the concept *mammal* might include as defining features the facts that mammals are animate, have mammary glands, and nurse their young, and as characteristic features the facts that mammals give birth to live young, have four limbs, and live on land.

It is assumed in the model that verification of a statement, such as *A dog is an animal,* involves a two-stage process. In the first stage, a global index of meaning similarity is computed by matching all of the features in the subject and the predicate. If this index of similarity exceeds an upper criterion (e.g., *A dog is an animal*), a rapid *true* decision is made, and if it falls below a lower criterion (e.g., *A dog is furniture*), a rapid *false* decision is made. However, if the similarity index is intermediate in value (e.g., *A dog is a quadruped*), the defining features of the predicate are compared to those of the subject. If all match, the statement is true, whereas if any mismatch, the statement is false.

The basic predictions of the model rely on the assumption that response latencies are faster for statements that can be verified by the first stage than for statements that require both stages. For true statements, the model predicts that statements will be verified faster, on the average, if the subject and the predicate are highly semantically related than if they are not highly related. The reason is that the global index of meaning similarity is more likely to exceed the upper criterion for semantically related subjects and predicates, and therefore processing of the statement is more likely to engage only the first stage. E. E. Smith et al. (1974) assumed that typicality ratings and association norms were reflections of featural similarity between concepts. Hence, the model predicts, in particular, that true statements will be verified faster if the subject is a typical exemplar than if it is an atypical exemplar of the predicate category (e.g., *A robin is a bird* vs. *A penguin is a bird*).

For false statements, the more similar the subject and the predicate, the less likely the statement is to fall below the lower criterion. Therefore, similar false statements (e.g., *A bat is a bird*) should be more likely to engage the second stage of processing, and so take longer to reject, than dissimilar false statements (e.g., *A robin is furniture*). Although this prediction has been confirmed (e.g., E. E. Smith et al., 1974), it has also been disconfirmed for certain types of false statements (Holyoak & Glass, 1975), as discussed below.

Major Issues and Findings

Collins and Loftus's (1975) spreading activation theory is sufficiently complex that it is probably unfalsifiable (but see the section below on semantic priming). In contrast, both the hierarchical network model and the feature comparison model made strong assumptions about how meanings were represented and processed and, therefore, made testable predictions about performance in semantic decision tasks. In the following paragraphs, we summarize two lines of research that were influential in testing these models.

Associative Strength and Typicality

Collins and Quillian's (1969) hierarchical network model made two crucial assumptions: First, noun concepts were assumed to be stored in a hierarchy determined by the logic of class relations. A concept was stored closer to its immediate superordinates than to its more distant ones. For example, *robin* was represented as a *bird,* and *bird* was represented as an *animal,* but *robin* was not directly represented as an *animal.* The second assumption, which was referred to as "cognitive economy" (Conrad, 1972), held that properties were stored at the highest possible semantic level to which they applied. Continuing the example, *feathered* would be stored with *bird* but not with *robin,* because all birds are feathered, whereas *can fly* would be stored with *robin* but not with *bird,* because robins can fly but not all birds can fly.

These assumptions generate two testable predictions: First, member-category statements should be verified faster if the subject is paired with an immediate superordinate, as in *A robin is a bird,* than if the subject is paired with a more distant superordinate, as in *A robin is an animal.* Second, property statements should be verified faster if the subject is paired with a property stored with it, as in *A bird has feathers,* than if the subject is paired with a property stored at a higher semantic level, as in *A bird eats.* Both of these predictions were confirmed (e.g., Collins & Quillian, 1969, 1972).

However, the hierarchical network model soon ran into trouble. Conrad (1972) observed that Collins and Quillian (1969) might have confounded hierarchical distance and associative strength. She argued, for example, that *A bird has feathers* might have been verified faster than *A bird eats* because *bird* and *feathered* are more highly associated than are *bird* and *eats*, not because of a difference in network distance. Conrad independently manipulated (a) the hierarchical distance between concepts and their properties, as determined by the assumptions of hierarchical storage and cognitive economy, and (b) the associative strength between concepts and their properties, as measured by association norms. She found that verification time decreased as associative strength increased, but it was insensitive to hierarchical distance. Rips, Shoben, and Smith (1973) also found that some member-category statements involving immediate superordinates took longer to verify than those involving distant superordinates. For instance, *A dog is a mammal* took longer to verify than *A dog is an animal.* This result conflicts directly with the hierarchical storage assumption.

Subsequent studies (e.g., E. E. Smith et al., 1974) showed that the critical determinant of decision times was the strength of semantic or associative relation between the subject and the predicate. These studies also demonstrated that typical exemplars of a category (e.g., *robin* of *bird*) were verified faster than were atypical exemplars (e.g., *chicken*). The hierarchical network model did not have mechanisms to explain such findings.

False Statements and Similarity

As described earlier, one of the predictions of the feature comparison theory is that false statements containing similar concepts should be more difficult to reject than false statements containing dissimilar concepts. Holyoak and Glass (1975) showed that this prediction was violated for two kinds of statements. In one kind, similar statements expressed contradictions that were assumed to be directly represented in memory (e.g., *All fruits are vegetables, Some chairs are tables*), whereas less similar statements did not (e.g., *All fruits are flowers, Some chairs are beds*). In the other kind of statement, similar statements, but not dissimilar ones, could be disconfirmed by the retrieval of a salient counterexample (e.g., *canary* for *All birds are robins*). The importance of these findings is that they indicate that different kinds of evidence can be used to make semantic decisions. This conclusion does not bode well for models, such as the feature comparison theory, in which a single source of information is the basis of all semantic judgments.

In a comprehensive investigation of the processing of false statements, Ratcliff and McKoon (1982) used a response-signal procedure to trace the time course of processing. An important finding was that performance on category-member statements (e.g., *A bird is a robin*) was nonmonotonic: Early in processing, there was an increasing tendency to respond *true* to these false statements, but, later in processing, there was an increasing tendency to respond correctly. This result indicates that, later in processing, new information became available or a second stage of processing was invoked. The nonmonotonicity is problematic for the network models of semantic memory, but it seems to offer support for feature comparison theory. However, at all points in processing, including the very earliest stages, subjects were more likely to respond *true* to member-category statements (e.g., *A robin is a bird*) than to category-member statements, even though these statements have equal amounts of overall feature overlap. This finding is not consistent with feature-comparison theory.

Contemporary Approaches to Semantic Memory

Research on semantic memory flourished in the late 1960s and 1970s but was already languishing in the early 1980s. Cognitive psychologists did not lose interest in semantic memory phenomena but, rather, migrated to more specialized programs of research, such as word recognition (see chapter by Rayner, Pollatsek, & Starr), language comprehension and production (see chapters by Treiman, Clifton, & Antje and by Butcher & Kintsch), and concepts and categories (see chapter by Goldstone & Kersten). The models developed to account for these phenomena were necessarily more focused than were the original models of semantic memory. In this section of the chapter, we take a quick look at two more recent approaches to understanding knowledge representations.

Distributed Network Models

Distributed network models have a long history (e.g., Hebb, 1949; Rosenblatt, 1962), but they did not become influential in cognitive psychology until the mid-1980s (e.g., McClelland & Rumelhart, 1986; Rumelhart & McClelland, 1986). The development and investigation of distributed network models has become a gigantic enterprise. Our goal will be to summarize the most important characteristics of these models, especially as they apply to semantic memory. According to distributed network models, concepts are represented as patterns of activation across a network of densely interconnected units. Similar concepts are represented by similar patterns of activation. The units can be thought of as representing aspects of the object or event being represented. These aspects, however, need not be nameable or correspond in any obvious way to the features people might list in a description of the entity. Indeed, a traditional feature, such as *has wings,* might itself be a pattern of activation over a collection of units.

Units are typically organized into modules, which correspond to sets of units designed to represent a particular kind of information (e.g., verbal vs. visual) or to accomplish a particular information processing goal (e.g., input vs. output). For example, Farah and McClelland's (1991) model of semantic memory impairment has three modules corresponding to verbal inputs, to visual inputs, and to semantic representations (which are further subdivided into visual units and functional units). Units within a module are richly interconnected with each other, and units in different modules may or may not be connected depending on the architecture of the model. For example, in Farah and McClelland's model, visual input units and verbal input units are connected to semantic representation units but not to each other.

Presenting a stimulus to the network causes an initial pattern of activation across the units, with some units more active than others. This pattern changes as each unit receives activation from the other units to which it is connected. A stable pattern of activation eventually appears across the units. The particular pattern instantiated across a set of units in response to an input, such as seeing an object or hearing a word, is determined by the weights on the connections between the units. Knowledge is therefore encoded in the weights, which constitute the long-term memory of the network.

The feature of distributed network models that may explain more than any other their continuing influence is that they learn. A network can be trained to produce a particular output, such as the meaning of a word, in response to a particular input, such as the orthographic pattern of the word. Training involves incrementally adjusting the weights between units so as to improve the ability of the network to produce the appropriate output in response to an input.

Another important characteristic of distributed network models is that their performance can decay gracefully with damage to the network. This characteristic is a result of having knowledge distributed across many connection weights in the network. For example, even with up to 40% of its visual semantic memory units destroyed, Farah and McClelland's (1991) model was able to correctly associate names and pictures more than 85% of the time.

Distributed network models have been applied to many human behaviors that depend on information traditionally represented in semantic memory, including acquisition of generic knowledge from specific experiences (e.g., McClelland & Rumelhart, 1985), word naming and lexical decision (e.g., Kawamoto, Farrar, & Kello, 1994; Seidenberg & McClelland, 1989), impairments in reading and the use of meaning after brain damage (e.g., Farah & McClelland, 1991; Hinton & Shallice, 1991; Plaut, McClelland, Seidenberg, & Patterson, 1996), and (as discussed later) semantic priming. Although these models have had their critics (e.g., Besner, Twilley, McCann, & Seergobin, 1990; Fodor & Pylyshyn, 1988), their influence on the science of memory has been, and promises to remain, enormous.

High-Dimensional Spatial Models

The idea that concepts can be represented as points in space, such that the dimensions of the space correspond to important dimensions of meaning, has a long history (e.g., Osgood, Suci, & Tannenbaum, 1957). This idea has recently been resurrected in two models of the acquisition and representation of word meaning.

Hyperspace Analog to Language (HAL). HAL (e.g., Burgess & Lund, 2000) is a spatial model of meaning representation in which concepts are represented as points in a very high dimensional space. The semantic similarity between concepts is represented by the distance between corresponding points in the space. As a result of the methodology used, meanings of concepts are represented in terms of their relations to other concepts.

The methodology involves tracking lexical co-occurrences within a 10-word moving window that slides across a corpus of text. The corpus includes approximately 300 million words taken from Usenet newsgroups containing English text. HAL's vocabulary consists of the 70,000 most frequently used symbols in the corpus. About half of these symbols have entries in the standard Unix dictionary; the remainder includes nonwords, misspellings, proper names, and slang. For ease of exposition, we refer to the 70,000 symbols as words. The methodology therefore produces a $70{,}000 \times 70{,}000$ matrix of co-occurrence values.

The co-occurrence matrix is constructed so that entries in each row specify the weighted frequency of co-occurrence of the row word and the words that preceded it in the window; entries in each column specify the weighted frequency of co-occurrence of the column word and the words that followed it in the window. Words that are closer together in the moving window get larger weights. Contiguous words receive a weight of 10; words separated by one intervening word receive a weight of 9; and so forth.

The meaning of a word is captured in the 140,000-element vector obtained by concatenating the row and the column vector for that word. Each vector can be thought of as a point in a 140,000-dimensional space. The similarity in meaning between two words is defined as the Euclidean distance between their corresponding points in the space. An important property of HAL is that two words (e.g., *street* and *road*) can have very similar meanings because they occur in similar contexts and, hence, have similar meaning vectors, not because they appear frequently in the same sentence (cf. McKoon & Ratcliff, 1992).

HAL is a structural model of meaning and has no processing architecture. Hence, most of the evidence on the model consists of qualitative demonstrations or correlations between indices generated by the model and human behavior. For example, when distances between word vectors are computed and submitted to multidimensional scaling, the resulting scaling solutions indicate that words are grouped into sensible categories (e.g., Burgess & Lund, 2000). Other experiments have shown that interword distances computed in HAL predict priming in lexical decision, to a reasonable approximation (e.g., Lund, Burgess, & Audet, 1996).

Latent Semantic Analysis (LSA). The overarching goal of the LSA model (e.g., Landauer, 1998; Landauer & Dumais, 1997; see also the chapter by Butcher & Kintsch) is to explain Plato's paradox: Why do people appear to know so much more than they could have learned from the experiences they have had? Like HAL, LSA is a high-dimensional spatial model of meaning representation. Concepts in LSA are represented by vectors in a space of approximately 300 dimensions. Similarities between meanings of concepts are represented by cosines of angles between vectors.

The input to LSA is a matrix in which rows represent types of events and columns represent contexts in which instances of the events occur. In many applications, for example, the rows correspond to word types and the columns correspond to samples of text (e.g., paragraphs) in which instances of the words appear. Each cell in the matrix contains the number of times that a particular word type appears in a particular context. This matrix is analyzed using singular value decomposition (SVD), which is similar to factor analysis. This analysis allows event types and contexts to be represented as points or vectors in a high-dimensional space. In this new representation, the similarities between any pairs of items can be computed.

In one specific implementation, samples of text were taken from an electronic version of an encyclopedia containing 30,473 articles. From each article, a sample was taken consisting of the first whole text or 2,000 characters, whichever was less. The text data were placed in a matrix of 30,473 columns, each representing a text sample, and 60,768 rows, each representing a word that had appeared in at least two samples. The cells in the matrix contained the frequency with which a word appeared in a particular sample. After transforming the raw cell frequencies, the matrix was submitted to SVD and the 300 most important dimensions were retained. Thus, each word and each context could be represented as a vector in a 300-dimensional space.

LSA has been applied to a varied set of problems. In one application, the model's word knowledge after training was tested using items from the synonym portion of the Test of English as a Foreign Language (TOEFL). Each problem consisted of a target word and four answer options from which the test taker is supposed to choose the one with the most similar meaning to the target. The model's choices were determined by computing cosines between vector representations of the target words in each item and vector representations of the answer options, and choosing the option with the largest cosine. The model performed as well as applicants to U.S. colleges from non-English speaking countries, getting 64.4% correct.

Another application of the model simulated the acquisition of vocabulary by school-aged children. The model gained vocabulary at about the same rate as do seventh-grade students, approximately 10 words per day. This rate greatly exceeds learning rates that have been obtained in experimental attempts to teach children word meanings from context. An important finding in this analysis was that LSA's learning of vocabulary relies heavily on indirect learning: The estimated direct effect of reading a sample of text (e.g., a paragraph) on knowledge of words in the sample was an increase of approximately 0.05 words of total vocabulary, whereas the indirect effect of reading a sample of text on words *not* contained in the sample was an increase of approximately 0.15 words of total vocabulary. Put another way, approximately three fourths of LSA's vocabulary gain from reading a passage of text was in words not even present in the paragraph. This finding helps to explain, according to Landauer and Dumais (1997), why people can have more knowledge than appears to be present in the information to which they have been exposed.

Summary

The first models of semantic memory appeared in the late 1960s, and by the mid-1970s at least half a dozen comprehensive models had been proposed. The two most influential models were the network model proposed by Quillian, Collins, and Loftus (e.g., Collins & Loftus, 1975; Collins & Quillian, 1969; Quillian, 1967) and the feature-comparison model proposed by E. E. Smith et al. (1974). These models became, and largely remain, the canonical models of semantic memory. Although these early models are no longer considered to be viable accounts of semantic memory, they remain influential because they provide useful ways of conceptualizing and categorizing memory phenomena.

Distributed network models offered an entirely different way of thinking about knowledge representations. In traditional models of semantic memory, concepts were represented by localized nodes or features, and the relations between concepts were either stored in the links (network models) or computed on the fly (feature models). In distributed network models, however, concepts are represented by patterns of activation across many units, which participate in representing other concepts, and knowledge about the relations between concepts is represented across many connection weights, which participate in representing other relations. There is no indication that the influence of these models is flagging.

High-dimensional spatial models also use distributed representations. In these models, however, the meaning of a concept is given by the company it keeps, in written and (presumably) spoken language. Concepts are similar to the extent that they are used in similar contexts. A virtue of these models is that they demonstrate how knowledge can be acquired from specific experiences. A significant challenge for the developers of these models will be to incorporate processing architectures that will allow the models to be subjected to rigorous testing. It remains to be seen how influential these high-dimensional spatial models will turn out to be.

SEMANTIC PRIMING

Priming is an improvement in performance in a cognitive task, relative to an appropriate baseline, as a function of context or prior experience. Semantic priming refers to the improvement in speed or accuracy to respond to a stimulus when it is preceded by a semantically related or associated stimulus relative to when it is preceded by a semantically unrelated or unassociated stimulus (e.g., *cat-dog* vs. *table-dog;* D. E. Meyer & Schvaneveldt, 1971). The stimulus to which responses are made is referred to as the *target,* and the preceding stimulus is referred to as the *prime*. The other kind of priming examined in this chapter is repetition priming, which refers to an improvement in speed or accuracy to respond to the second (or subsequent) occurrence of a stimulus relative to the first occurrence of the stimulus. Semantic and repetition priming are probably caused by different mechanisms or by different processing stages (e.g., Durgunoglu, 1988), but because they have been so influential in the study of human memory, we review both areas of research in this chapter.

The *semantic* in *semantic priming* implies that priming is caused by relations of meaning, as exist, for instance, between the concepts *dog* and *goat* (mammals, domesticated, have fur, etc.). In fact, the term has also been used to refer to priming caused by a mixture of semantic and associative relations, as exist between the concepts *dog* and *cat*. These concepts are semantically related, but in addition, if people generate associates to *dog,* they list *cat* with high frequency (and vice versa). In contrast, *goat* almost never comes up as an associate of *dog*. Consistent with usage in the field, we shall use *semantic priming* to refer to both kinds of priming, unless we need to distinguish the two (as in the section "Associative Versus Pure Semantic Priming").

Models of Semantic Priming

Spreading Activation Models

Spreading activation was first incorporated into a model of memory by Quillian (1967); this model was elaborated and extended by Collins and Loftus (1975), as described previously. Spreading activation models were also proposed by Anderson (1976, 1983). Although these models differ in several important ways, they share three fundamental assumptions: (a) Retrieving an item from memory amounts to activating its internal representation; (b) activation spreads from a concept to associated concepts; and (c) residual activation accumulating at a concept facilitates its subsequent retrieval. For example, the visual presentation of a word, such as *lion,* activates its internal representation. This activation spreads to associated concepts, such as *tiger*. If the word *tiger* appears soon after the word *lion,* it can be identified more quickly than normally because it is already partially activated.

Although Collins and Loftus's (1975) model and Anderson's (1983) ACT* model are similar, they differ in important ways. The Collins and Loftus model (as well as Anderson's, 1976, model) assumes that activation takes time to spread from one concept to another. This mechanism is used to explain the effects of hierarchical network distance on verification time. ACT*, in contrast, assumes that activation spreads extremely quickly, reaching asymptote in as little as 50 ms. Effects of network distance are attributed to differences in asymptotic activation levels. Another difference is that Collins and Loftus's model assumes that activation continues to spread (for a while) even when a concept is no longer being processed. In ACT*, however, activation decays very rapidly, within 500 ms, when a concept ceases to be a source of activation. Finally, the Collins and Loftus model assumes that only one concept can be a source of activation at a time, whereas ACT* assumes that the number of possible sources is limited only by the capacity of attention.

The accounts of semantic priming in the two models are really quite different. In the Collins and Loftus model, the prime sends activation to the target, and the target can be in a preactivated state even though the prime is no longer being processed. In ACT*, however, both the prime and the target must be sources of activation—both must be objects of attention—for the association between them to produce heightened activation of the target. Priming occurs in ACT* because the prime is still a source of activation when the target appears.

Two lines of evidence are problematic for the Collins and Loftus (1975) model. Ratcliff and McKoon (1981) showed that priming in item recognition was statistically reliable when the stimulus onset asynchrony (SOA) between the prime and the target was as short as 100 ms (no priming occurred at an SOA of 50 ms). This finding suggests that activation spreads very rapidly. In addition, the magnitude of priming at an SOA of 100 ms was the same for prime-target pairs close in network distance and pairs far in network distance. The effects of network distance appeared in the sizes of priming effects at the longer SOAs: More priming eventually occurred for close pairs than for far pairs. In another line of research, Ratcliff and McKoon (1988) showed that the decay of priming could be very rapid, within 500 ms in some circumstances. These findings contradict basic assumptions of the Collins and Loftus (1975) model, but they are quite consistent with Anderson's (1983) ACT* model.

Compound-Cue Models

Compound-cue models of priming were proposed independently by Ratcliff and McKoon (1988) and by Dosher and Rosedale (1989). The compound-cue model is simply a statement about the contents of retrieval cues. The claim is that the cue to memory contains the target item and elements of the surrounding context. In a lexical decision task, for example, this context could include the prime, or even words occurring before the prime.

The compound-cue model must be combined with a model of memory to make predictions about performance in a task. Models that have figured prominently are the search of associative memory (SAM, Gillund & Shiffrin, 1984), the theory of distributed associative memory (TODAM, Murdock, 1982), and MINERVA 2 (Hintzman, 1986). In all of these models, the familiarity of a cue containing two associated words will be higher than the familiarity of a cue containing two unassociated words. Hence, in a lexical decision task, if the cue contains the target and the prime, familiarity will be higher for a target related to its prime than for a target unrelated to its prime (e.g., *lion-tiger* vs. *table-tiger,* respectively). If familiarity is inversely related to response time, basic priming effects can be explained (e.g., Ratcliff & McKoon, 1988).

Distributed Network Models

Relatively recently, several distributed network models of semantic priming have been proposed. These models fall into two broad categories:

In one category of models, which we refer to as *proximity models,* priming is caused because related primes and targets are closer to each other in a high-dimensional semantic space than are unrelated primes and targets (e.g., Masson, 1995; McRae, de Sa, & Seidenberg, 1997; Moss, Hare, Day, & Tyler, 1994; Plaut & Booth, 2000; Sharkey & Sharkey, 1992). A fundamental assumption in these models is that concepts are represented by patterns of activity over a large number of interconnected units. Related concepts have similar patterns of activity. Semantic priming occurs because in processing a target word the network begins from the pattern created by processing of the prime; this pattern is more similar to the target's representation when the prime is related than when it is unrelated to the target. In effect, the network gets a head start in processing the target when it is preceded by a related prime. A few of these models (e.g., Moss et al., 1994; Plaut & Booth, 2000) are able to distinguish semantic priming, which is attributed to overlapping semantic features, from associative priming. Associative priming occurs in these models because the network learns to make efficient transitions from primes to targets that co-occur frequently during training.

The other category of distributed models, which we refer to as *learning models,* attributes semantic priming to learning that occurs when a word is recognized or is the object of a decision of some kind (e.g., S. Becker, Moscovitch, Behrmann, & Joordens, 1997; Joordens & Becker, 1997). These models also assume that concepts are represented by patterns of activity over a network of units, and that semantically similar concepts have similar patterns of activity. However, in these models semantic priming is caused by incremental learning. Each presentation of a word causes all of the network connections participating in recognition to be altered, so as to increase the probability of producing the same response to the same input. This learning facilitates processing of the word if it reappears, but it also facilitates processing of words with similar representations (e.g., a semantically related target). Learning decays very slowly and is permanent unless undone by additional learning. This class of models, unlike all other models of priming, predicts that semantic priming should occur over very long lags between presentation of the prime and the target. Data relevant to this prediction are reviewed in a subsequent section of the chapter. Proximity may also play a role in these models, especially in explaining priming at short lags.

Major Issues and Findings

Neely (1991) provides the best comprehensive review of research on semantic priming prior to 1991. Our review uses Neely's as a launching point. We focus on empirical issues and findings that have turned out to be especially important for testing models of semantic priming.

Automatic Versus Strategic Priming

Automatic processes are traditionally defined as those having a quick onset, proceeding without intention or awareness, and producing benefits but not costs. Strategic processes are slower acting, require intention or awareness, and produce both benefits and costs (e.g., Posner & Snyder, 1975).

Semantic priming almost certainly is not caused solely by strategic processes (cf. C. A. Becker, 1980). Semantic priming occurs even when there is only one related prime-target pair in the entire test list (Fischler, 1977a). In addition, at short SOAs, semantic priming occurs between a category name prime and exemplars of that category (e.g., *body-leg*) even when subjects are told to expect members of a different category (e.g., parts of buildings) to follow the prime (Neely, 1977). Findings such as these are difficult to reconcile with a purely strategic account of priming. Semantic priming, however, is also not purely automatic. Two types of strategic processes have been identified.

Under the appropriate conditions, semantic priming seems to be affected by an expectancy process (e.g., C. A. Becker, 1980; Neely, 1977). Subjects use the prime to generate explicit candidates for the upcoming target or at least expect primes to be followed by semantically related targets. Priming can be amplified because of a speeding up on related trials or a slowing on unrelated trials. Two factors seem to influence the extent to which expectancy processes are used:

1. The SOA between the prime and the target must be sufficiently long to allow expectations to develop. A commonly used index of expectancy is inhibition, or longer response latencies following unrelated primes than neutral primes (e.g., a row of *x*s, or the words *blank* or *ready*). The reasoning is this: An expectancy process will yield an incongruent outcome on unrelated trials because the target is unrelated to the prime. Responses should therefore be slow in the unrelated condition relative to a condition in which expectancies are not generated. A neutral prime condition should provide such a baseline because neutral primes are repeated many times in the test list and are effectively meaningless in the context of the experiment. It is well documented that inhibition is small or nonexistent for SOAs shorter than 300 ms (e.g., de Groot, 1984; den Heyer, Briand, & Smith, 1985; Neely, 1977). In a direct test of expectancy-based priming, Neely (1977) instructed subjects to generate members of a specified category when given a different category name as the prime; for example, subjects were told to generate parts of the body in response to the prime *building* (and building parts in response to the prime *body*). Expectancy-based priming occurred at a 700-ms but not at a 250-ms SOA.
2. The second factor that influences expectancy is the relatedness proportion (RP), which is typically defined as the proportion of related trials out of all word prime–word target trials (e.g., Neely, Keefe, & Ross, 1989). At long SOAs, semantic priming and inhibition both increase in magnitude as the proportion of related trials increases; at short SOAs, the effects of RP are reduced or eliminated (e.g., de Groot, 1984; den Heyer, Briand, & Dannenbring, 1983; Tweedy, Lapinski, & Schvaneveldt, 1977). Priming in the naming task also increases with the RP (Keefe & Neely, 1990), suggesting that naming is also influenced by expectancy. It is unknown how low the RP must be to eliminate expectancy. Low values of RP in published studies typically range from .10 to .33.

The second type of strategic process is semantic matching (e.g., de Groot, 1983; Forster, 1981; Neely, 1977; Neely et al., 1989; Seidenberg, Waters, Sanders, & Langer, 1984). Under the appropriate conditions, subjects seem to check for a relation between the target and the prime, responding quickly if such a relation is detected, and slowly if no such relation is detected. In the lexical decision task, the existence of a semantic relation is always informative about the lexical status of the target, as only word targets have related primes.

However, the absence of a relation may or may not be informative depending on the construction of the test list. One measure of the informativeness of the absence of a semantic relation is the nonword ratio (NR), which is the conditional probability that the correct response is *nonword* given that the (word) prime and the target are unrelated (Neely et al., 1989). As the nonword ratio deviates from .5, the absence of a semantic relation between the prime and the target becomes increasingly informative, signaling a nonword response when it is above .5 and a word response when it is below .5.

The variables that control semantic matching are not well understood. Neely et al. (1989) manipulated the RP and the NR independently in a lexical decision task in which primes were category names and targets were exemplars. The RP was correlated most strongly with priming for typical exemplars (e.g., *robin* for *bird*). The NR, however, was correlated with priming for both typical and atypical (e.g., *penguin*) exemplars, and with nonword facilitation (defined as faster responses to nonwords primed by words than to nonwords primed by a neutral prime). They argued that the effect of RP on priming for typical exemplars was a true expectancy effect, as subjects would be likely to generate typical but not atypical exemplars to category primes. According to Neely et al., the effect of NR was due to semantic matching. The nonword facilitation effects are especially consistent with this interpretation, as, when NR is high, nonword targets will benefit from a bias to respond *nonword* to targets unrelated to their word primes.

It seems likely that semantic matching is influenced by the RP and the NR. As the RP increases, semantic relations become more noticeable, and as the NR increases, the absence of semantic relations becomes more informative. It is worth pointing out that standard experimental procedures often lead to NRs over .5, as investigators often use equal numbers of word and nonword targets, but only use word primes; hence, the number of word prime–nonword target trials exceeds the number of unrelated word prime–word target trials.

Semantic matching is probably also influenced by the task used. Tasks such as lexical decision that require accumulation of information to make a binary decision are probably more susceptible to semantic matching than are tasks, such as naming, that do not involve an explicit decision (e.g., Seidenberg et al., 1984). McNamara and Altarriba (1988; see also Shelton & Martin, 1992) have argued that semantic matching, as well as expectancy, can be minimized by using a task in which the relations between primes and targets are not apparent to subjects. One method of achieving this goal is to use a sequential or single-presentation lexical decision task. In this task, stimuli are displayed one at a time, and participants respond to each as it appears. Primes precede targets in the test list, but their pairings are not apparent to subjects. Shelton and Martin found that inhibition and backward priming (e.g., prime *hop,* target *bell;* discussed later) did not occur in the single-presentation task.

Neely and Keefe (1989) have proposed a three-process hybrid theory of semantic priming that incorporates expectancy, automatic spreading activation, and semantic matching. Not surprisingly, this theory can account for a greater variety of results than can any one mechanism alone (Neely, 1991). The important contribution of this theory is that it combines a model of automatic, attention-free priming with strategic, attention-laden processes. Viewed in this way, one can see that any of the models of priming outlined earlier in this chapter could be combined with expectancy and semantic matching processes.

In summary, two principal types of strategic processes have been identified, expectancy and semantic matching. Expectancy is minimized at short SOAs and low RPs; semantic matching is minimized with an NR of .5 and, we suspect, low RP as well. Put another way, an investigator interested in the automatic component of priming would be well served by using an SOA less than 300 ms, RP of .20 or less, and NR of .50.

In closing, we should acknowledge that Plaut and Booth (2000) have shown that it may be possible to account for the dependence of inhibition on SOA without invoking an expectancy process. Given all of the evidence implicating the role of strategic processes in semantic priming, it seems likely that any model of priming must incorporate strategic processes of some kind. However, Plaut and Booth's analysis suggests that a single-mechanism account of priming may be able to explain at least some of the phenomena previously attributed to strategic processing.

Associative Versus Pure Semantic Priming

As noted earlier, the term *semantic priming* is a catch-all phrase that includes priming caused by many different kinds of relations, including both associative relations and true relations of meaning. Associatively related words are those produced in response to each other in free-association tasks, and they may be semantically related (e.g., *dog-cat*) or not (e.g., *stork-baby*). Pure semantically related pairs share semantic features or are members of a common category but are not associatively related (e.g., *goose-turkey*).

It is well documented that associatively related words prime each other in lexical decision, naming, and similar tasks. The controversial issue has been whether priming occurs in the absence of association. The evidence is mixed. Fischler (1977b) first investigated priming in the absence of association and reported a reliable pure semantic priming effect. However, several subsequent studies (e.g., Lupker, 1984; Moss, Ostrin, Tyler, & Marslen Wilson, 1995; Shelton & Martin, 1992) failed to find pure semantic priming under certain conditions; indeed, Shelton and Martin (1992) concluded that automatic priming was associative, not semantic. Recent experiments by McRae and Boisvert (1998) indicate that previous failures to find pure semantic priming can be attributed to the use of prime-target pairs that were weakly semantically related.

A recent meta-analysis may bring order to this apparent chaos. Lucas (2000) examined the results of 26 studies in which purely semantically related prime-target pairs were used as stimuli in lexical decision or naming (including Stroop) tasks. Most of these studies also included associatively related primes and targets. The average effect size (J. Cohen, 1977), weighted by the number of subjects in each sample, was .25 for pure semantic priming and .49 for associative priming. There was clear evidence therefore that pure semantic priming was present in the studies reviewed and that associative priming was substantially larger than semantic priming. Because associatively related primes and targets were usually related semantically, the larger effect size is best interpreted as an associative boost to priming. Further analyses indicated that the effect size for pure semantic priming was not influenced by the particular type of lexical decision task used, RP, or SOA, suggesting that pure semantic priming was not strategically mediated.

Lucas (2000) also examined whether pure semantic priming varied with type of semantic relation. Category coordinates (e.g., *bronze-gold*), synonyms, antonyms, and script relations (e.g., *theater-play*) had similar average effect sizes, ranging from .20 to .27. In contrast, functional relationships (e.g., *broom-sweep*) had an average effect size of .55. This result supports the hypothesis that functional relations are central to word meaning (e.g., Tyler & Moss, 1997). Perceptually related prime-target pairs, in which primes and targets share referent shape (e.g., *pizza-coin*), had a very low effect size of .05. This estimate must be treated with caution, however, because only two studies in the corpus examined perceptual priming of this kind.

In summary, although the evidence on pure semantic priming has been mixed, with some studies finding evidence of such priming and others not, Lucas's (2000) meta-analysis shows that pure semantic priming does occur and, moreover, indicates that it may vary as a function of the type of semantic relation. This conclusion is important because distributed network models of priming strongly predict semantic priming. A subset of these models can also explain associative priming (Moss et al., 1994; Plaut & Booth, 2000). Distributed network models that do not include an associative component will need to be modified to account for the associative boost to priming. Spreading-activation and compound-cue models can easily explain both semantic and associative priming as long as the appropriate relations are represented in memory.

Mediated Versus Direct Priming

Mediated priming involves using primes and targets that are not directly associated or semantically related but instead are related via other words. For example, based on free-association norms (e.g., McNamara, 1992b), *mane* and *tiger* are not associates of each other, but each is an associate of *lion*. The associative relation between a prime and a target can be characterized in terms of the number of associative steps or links that separate them: 1-step, or directly related (e.g., *tiger-stripes*), 2-step (e.g., *lion-stripes*), 3-step (e.g., *mane-stripes*), and so on. Models of priming are distinguished based on whether or not they predict priming through mediated relations.

Early experiments suggested that 2-step mediated priming occurred in naming but not in lexical decision (e.g., Balota & Lorch, 1986; de Groot, 1983). Subsequent studies showed that 2-step, and even 3-step, priming could be obtained in lexical decision if the task parameters were selected so as to minimize strategic processing (e.g., McNamara, 1992b; McNamara & Altarriba, 1988; Shelton & Martin, 1992).

Mediated priming is strongly predicted by spreading activation models. Certain versions of compound-cue models can account for 2-step priming, but none predicts 3-step priming (McNamara, 1992a, 1992b). Most distributed network models cannot account for mediated priming of any kind. Possible exceptions are the models proposed by Moss et al. (1994) and by Plaut and Booth (2000). These models learn associative relations between words that co-occur frequently during learning. It is possible that other distributed network models could be augmented with similar mechanisms.

A serious problem exists, however, in interpreting the mediated priming results. Although researchers have made valiant efforts to show that mediated primes and targets are not directly associated and not semantically related (e.g., McNamara, 1992b), there is the nagging possibility that residual associations or semantic relations still exist. This is a big problem because if the primes and targets are directly related in some fashion, all models predict priming between them. The best way to address this issue is in the context of a particular model. For example, McNamara (1992b) showed, using the memory model SAM (Gillund & Shiffrin, 1984), that if direct associations between 3-step primes and targets were high enough to produce priming of the magnitude observed, then these primes and targets would have appeared as mutual associates in a free-association task at a much higher frequency than was observed. This analysis does not prove that the primes and targets were not directly related, and the conclusion is limited to one model of priming (viz., the compound-cue model conjoined with SAM). The contribution exists in demonstrating that a particular model would have difficulty accounting for both the mediated priming and the free-association results. As another example of this approach, Livesay and Burgess (1998) used HAL (discussed in the section on models of semantic memory) to compute semantic distances between the 2-step mediated primes and targets developed by Balota and Lorch (1986) and subsequently used by McNamara and Altarriba (1988). Average semantic distance was *higher* between mediated primes and targets than between unrelated primes and targets. In addition, they found no relation between the magnitude of mediated priming and lexical co-occurrence frequency, contradicting predictions of McKoon and Ratcliff (1992). These results lead us to conclude that mediated priming remains a challenge to many models of semantic priming.

Effects of Lag

Lag refers to the number of items that intervene between the prime and the target. The standard priming paradigm uses a lag of zero; the target immediately follows the prime. Many studies have examined priming at lags of one, two, and even greater. The early literature on lag effects was ambiguous (e.g., Masson, 1991). Subsequent investigations indicated that priming occurred across a lag of one but not two (e.g., Joordens & Besner, 1992; McNamara, 1992b), although Masson (1995) did not obtain lag-1 priming in naming.

Recent experiments indicate that semantic priming may occur over lags much greater than one or two items. For theoretical reasons (discussed in the section on models of semantic priming), S. Becker and Joordens (S. Becker et al., 1997; Joordens & Becker, 1997) hypothesized that semantic priming could be obtained at long lags if the primes and the targets were strongly semantically related and the task engaged semantic processing to a high degree. They constructed prime-target pairs that were semantically similar (e.g., *pontoon-raft, tulip-rose*) and used several methods to increase the semantic processing of target words. S. Becker et al. (1997) used an animacy decision task in which participants were required to decide whether each word referred to a living or a nonliving entity; Joordens and Becker (1997) used a lexical decision task in which nonwords were very word-like (e.g., *brane*). Semantic priming was obtained in these experiments at lags of 4, 8, and even as high as 21.5.

Priming at long lags is predicted by learning models, but it is a serious problem for all other models of priming. In principle, spreading activation models could explain such priming by making the decay of activation very slow, but this assumption would be inconsistent with other findings suggesting that activation decays quickly. Moreover, slow decay would probably leave so much residual activation in memory that basic semantic priming effects could no longer be predicted. Compound-cue models would need cues of between 23 and 24 items to explain priming at a lag of 21.5 (prime + intervening items + target). Cues of this size strain credibility. Proximity models explain priming across intervening items by assuming that the semantic pattern of the prime is not completely replaced by semantic patterns of intervening items (e.g., Masson, 1995; Plaut & Booth, 2000). This mechanism almost certainly will not work with lags greater than one or two items.

There are several reasons to question these findings, however. First, the results are unstable. Joordens and Becker (1997) obtained lag-8 priming in two experiments but did not obtain it in another two experiments. Second, and more important, the priming observed in these studies has peculiar properties. Priming either did not decay with lag or decayed rapidly with lag, and yet priming at the shortest lag did not differ in these situations. For example, in their second experiment, Joordens and Becker varied lag over the values 0, 1, 2, 4, and 8. One condition was designed to produce long-term semantic priming and used a lexical decision task with difficult nonwords (e.g., *brane*). This condition yielded 45 ms of priming at lag 0, and there was no evidence of decay across lags; for example, priming was 41 ms at lag 8. Another condition was designed not to produce long-term semantic priming and used a lexical decision task with easier nonwords (e.g., *brene*). This condition yielded 27 ms of priming at lag 0, which quickly decayed to nonsignificant levels. The 18-ms difference in priming at lag 0 for these two conditions did not approach statistical significance. This pattern of results is difficult to explain even in the learning model. Why should priming of comparable initial magnitude decay slowly in one case but quickly in another?

Joordens and Becker (1997) proposed several explanations of these results that relied on dual mechanisms, but none was compelling. Their preferred model incorporated a quickly decaying associative priming mechanism with a long-term learning mechanism. Priming in the easy nonword condition would be attributed to the associative mechanism alone, whereas priming in the difficult nonword condition would be attributed to the combined effects of both mechanisms. Even this model, however, is not consistent with their findings, as it still predicts some decline in priming with lag: At lag 0, both associative and learning priming would occur, whereas at longer lags, only learning priming would occur.

In summary, if priming at long lags holds up under additional experimental scrutiny, and if the paradoxical results obtained by Joordens, Becker, and their colleagues can be explained, long-term priming will provide compelling evidence in support of distributed-network learning models and virtually insurmountable evidence against other models of semantic priming.

Forward Versus Backward Priming

Associations between primes and targets can be asymmetric. Backward priming refers to the situation in which the association from prime to target is weak, but the association from target to prime is strong (e.g., *baby-stork*). Koriat (1981) was the first to investigate backward priming, and he obtained equal amounts of priming in the forward (e.g., *stork-baby*) and the backward (e.g., *baby-stork*) directions. This result is surprising, because if priming depends on strength of association, it should be larger in the forward than in the backward direction. A perusal of the backward priming literature reveals the following observations and findings.

One of the difficulties in comparing results across studies is that different materials have been used. Several studies have used asymmetrically associated, semantically related primes and targets (e.g., *lamp-light*, *apple-fruit*); other studies have used semantically unrelated compound words (e.g., *fruit-fly, sand-box*); and still others have used a mixture of these types of stimuli. Given the findings reviewed earlier on pure semantic priming, one would expect to find some priming in the forward and in the backward directions for semantically related pairs, regardless of differences in associative strength. In contrast, one wonders why priming would occur at all for semantically unrelated compounds, unless it is strategically mediated. Of the 20 compounds introduced into the literature by Seidenberg et al. (1984), and subsequently used by Shelton and Martin (1992) and by Thompson-Schill, Kurtz, and Gabrieli (1998), 18 prime words appear in the Nelson, McEvoy, and Schreiber (1991) free-association norms. The associative strength in the forward direction (e.g., *fruit-fly*) has a modal value of 0 and a mean of .02! These items are therefore neither semantically related nor associated.

In fact, there is good evidence that forward and backward priming for compounds is produced by strategic processes. Priming does not occur in either direction for compounds when conditions are consistent with automatic priming (Shelton & Martin, 1992; Thompson-Schill et al., 1998). In strategic conditions, processing of forward and backward associations is correlated with physiological indices of strategic processing (Chwilla, Hagoort, & Brown, 1998). Those studies reporting reliable priming for compounds in the forward or the backward directions (Kahan, Neely, & Forsythe, 1999; Seidenberg et al., 1984; Shelton & Martin, 1992) employed task parameters in the strategic regime (e.g., high RP, high NR, or long SOA). We include in this mix experiments using the naming task, as there is evidence that naming is not immune to strategic processing (e.g., Keefe & Neely, 1990).

Asymmetrically associated, semantically related pairs (e.g., *lamp-light*) seem to prime each other in both directions, and there is weak evidence that priming is greater in the forward than in the backward direction. Only three published studies have examined priming in both directions for semantically related pairs (Chwilla et al., 1998; Koriat, 1981; Thompson-Schill et al., 1998), and only one of them has used procedures consistent with automatic priming (Thompson-Schill et al.). Across all three studies, priming was 40% larger, on the average, in the forward than in the backward direction; in the experiments by Thompson-Schill et al., the difference was approximately 30%.

Finally, there is evidence that backward priming in the naming task may depend on the SOA (Kahan et al., 1999; Peterson & Simpson, 1989). For example, Kahan et al. obtained backward priming at an SOA of 150 ms but not at an SOA of 500 ms. These findings are difficult to interpret, however, because the experiments have used RPs of at least .5. In fact, only one experiment (Thompson-Schill et al., 1998) has examined backward priming in naming under near automatic conditions, and it only used one SOA (200 ms). Hence, the apparent dependence of backward priming in naming on SOA may be produced by strategic processing in this task.

In summary, semantic priming does not seem to occur for compounds unless the conditions are ripe for strategic processing, whereas priming occurs in both directions for asymmetrically associated, semantically related pairs, and there is some evidence that the magnitude of priming tracks associative strength. Because only the latter results seem to be caused by automatic processes, only they are crucial for testing models of priming.

Spreading activation models can account for these results as long as appropriate semantic and associative relations exist in memory (e.g., symmetric semantic relations but asymmetric associative strengths). The predictions of compound-cue models depend on which model of memory serves as the base. The two models that have figured most prominently in investigations of priming are SAM (Gillund & Shiffrin, 1984) and TODAM (Murdock, 1982). SAM cannot predict asymmetric priming unless the primes and the targets differ in the strength of the association between the words as cues and their representations in memory. TODAM also has difficulty explaining asymmetric priming because associations are modeled by a commutative operation, convolution. Hence, a demonstration of reliable asymmetric priming with primes and targets of equal word frequency would be problematic for these models. All of the distributed network models predict priming for semantically related primes and targets, but only two (Moss et al., 1994; Plaut & Booth, 2000) have an associative mechanism that would allow them to predict greater priming in the forward than in the backward associative direction.

Subliminal Priming

Several researchers have reported evidence that semantic priming occurs even when the prime is presented under conditions in which it cannot be identified or its presence cannot be detected (e.g., Marcel, 1983). After conducting a comprehensive review of this literature, Holender (1986) concluded that the effects were unreliable and that the stimuli had probably been consciously identified (also see Cheesman & Merikle, 1984). More recent studies addressed many of these problems, but effects were still small and inconsistent (e.g., Greenwald, Klinger, & Schuh, 1995).

Greenwald and his colleagues (e.g., Draine & Greenwald, 1998; Greenwald, Draine, & Abrams, 1996) have recently claimed that robust unconscious priming effects can be obtained under the proper experimental conditions. An important feature of these experiments is that they used evaluative or gender judgments as the priming task rather than standard semantic priming tasks (e.g., lexical decision or naming). For example, in the evaluative judgment task, participants judged whether words had positive or negative meanings (e.g., *happy* vs. *vomit*). Priming was assessed by examining the effect of the prime's category membership (e.g., positive vs. negative) on responses to targets. Greenwald and his colleagues found that under appropriate conditions primes increased the probability of responding in a manner consistent with their category membership even when direct perception of the primes approached zero sensitivity. They attributed this result to the unconscious activation of the meaning of the prime.

There are at least two reasons to question this conclusion, however. First, Klinger, Burton, and Pitts (2000) replicated the priming effects obtained by Greenwald and his colleagues (e.g., Draine & Greenwald, 1998; Greenwald et al., 1996) but also showed that semantic priming of the *lion-tiger* variety did not occur in the same paradigm. Second, Abrams and Greenwald (2000) have shown that the priming obtained in the basic paradigm does not occur unless primes previously occur as targets; the effect may be due to procedural learning in the task (see the chapter in this volume by A. Johnson). Our (admittedly conservative) conclusion is that there is little or no convincing evidence that the meaning of a word can be activated unconsciously.

Prime Task Effects

Given that priming occurs when participants read the prime but make no response to it, one might predict that semantic priming would occur regardless of the task performed on the prime. In fact, this is not true. M. C. Smith, Theodor, and Franklin (1983) showed that semantic priming was eliminated if participants searched the prime for a letter or responded whether or not an asterisk was next to the prime (also see Friedrich, Henik, & Tzelgov, 1991; Henik, Friedrich, & Kellogg, 1983; Henik, Friedrich, Tzelgov, & Tramer, 1994; M. C. Smith, 1979). A general conclusion from these studies is that if attention is directed away from the semantic level early in the processing of the prime, semantic priming is eliminated or attenuated (e.g., Stolz & Besner, 1996). In a related line of research, Besner and Stolz (1999) demonstrated that Stroop interference was reduced in magnitude if attention was directed to individual letters of a word (rather than to the whole word).

These and related findings led Stolz and Besner (1999) to conclude that attentional control is needed to activate the meanings of words. They argue that attention determines how activation is distributed across levels of representation (e.g., letter, word, semantic) during word recognition. The attentional mechanisms implied by this explanation are qualitatively different from those implied by the traditional distinction between automatic and strategic priming (as discussed in a previous section); in particular, they must be fast acting and need not be conscious. Prime-task effects create difficulties for all of the models of priming. The fundamental problems are that the models do not cast the proper roles for attention, or they do not distinguish between levels of representation in a manner that would allow, for instance, attention to be directed to one level (e.g., letter) but not to another (e.g., semantic), or both. These problems are not insurmountable, but they are not trivial to solve either.

Neely and Kahan (2001) have recently argued that prime-task effects may be caused, at least in part, by effects of spatial attention on visual feature integration. The hypothesis is that when attention is directed to individual components of prime words, such as letters, the visual features of unattended letters may not be properly integrated, and hence the primes may not be perceptually encoded as words. Semantic activation of the primes would not be expected under such circumstances. If

Neely and Kahan's hypothesis is correct, then prime-task effects are not so problematic for the models of priming.

Global Context Effects

Recent experiments indicate that the global context established by discourse or by the types of semantic relations appearing in a test list can affect semantic priming. For example, McKoon and Ratcliff (1995) placed a small number of prime-target pairs related in a particular way (e.g., opposites, *close-far*) in a list in which over half of all prime-target pairs were related in a different manner (e.g., synonyms, *mountain-hill*). Semantic priming in lexical decision and in naming was virtually eliminated for the mismatching items. Hess, Foss, and Carroll (1995) obtained similar results by varying the global context established by short vignettes preceding target words.

Although one might be tempted to conclude from these findings that all contextual facilitation is determined by global context (e.g., Hess et al., 1995), this conclusion is not justified. There is just too much evidence that semantic priming occurs between strongly related words in the most infelicitous of conditions (e.g., Fischler, 1977a; Neely, 1977). We suspect that appropriate follow-up studies will show effects of local context in addition to global context. The contribution of these studies is to demonstrate that semantic priming is modulated by relations external to the word pairs. These global context effects are a serious challenge to all existing models of semantic priming.

Summary

Given that we used Neely's (1991) review as a starting point, it is appropriate to ask what has been learned about semantic priming since the publication of that chapter.

First, a new class of models of priming, namely, distributed network models, has been developed. One member of this class of models, the learning models, can explain what may turn out to be the most important new finding on semantic priming, namely, semantic priming over very long lags.

Second, a great deal more has been learned about several important priming phenomena: (a) There is probably a better understanding of the conditions that contribute to automatic versus strategic priming. (b) It is now clear that pure semantic priming occurs, and there is evidence that it is produced by automatic processes. (c) Mediated priming has now been replicated by several investigators using a variety of tasks and procedures. (d) Priming across lags of unrelated intervening items has been replicated in several studies. Moreover, there is new evidence that semantic priming can occur over very long lags. (e) Several new investigations of backward priming have appeared, and the results suggest that backward priming for compounds (e.g., *hop-bell*) is produced by strategic processes, whereas backward priming between asymmetrically associated semantically related words (e.g., *light-lamp*) is caused by semantic overlap. (f) An entirely new line of research on subliminal priming has appeared, and it seems to converge on the conclusion that semantic priming does not occur unconsciously. (g) There is a better understanding of the role of attention in semantic priming. Finally, (h) a new line of research indicates that semantic priming is affected by the global context in which prime-target pairs appear.

Third, although none of the models can account for all of the major priming results, there are reasons to be optimistic about future model development. Assuming, for the moment, that long-term semantic priming turns out to be a robust phenomenon, then distributed-network learning models offer an appealing foundation for model development. If these models can be augmented with associative priming mechanisms and appropriate attentional processes, they will go a long way toward explaining the major findings in the literature.

REPETITION PRIMING

Whereas semantic priming refers to a facilitation in performance between *different* items on the basis of shared meaning or association, repetition priming refers to facilitated performance based on a previous encounter with the *same* stimulus. Essentially, repetition priming reflects the degree to which a single exposure to a stimulus during a study session leads to faster or more accurate processing of that stimulus at a later test (Tulving & Schacter, 1990).

Research on repetition priming has developed largely from studies involving patients with anterograde amnesia. This neurological disorder (or collection of disorders) is characterized by a severely impaired ability to form new explicit memories (for review, see Squire, 1987). This type of amnesia typically accompanies damage to the medial temporal lobes (e.g., for review, see Squire, 1992) or to the diencephalic midline structures (as in Korsakoff's syndrome; for review, see Oscar-Berman, 1984; Shimamura, 1989). Amnesic patients show an impairment of the ability to explicitly recall events that occur after the onset of their amnesia, despite intact intellectual, language, and social skills. In spite of showing severely degraded performance on tests of explicit memory, which require conscious recollection, such as free recall, cued recall, recognition, and paired-associate learning (see also the chapter in this volume by Roediger & Marsh), amnesic patients exhibit intact performance on measures of repetition priming, such as word-stem completion, picture-fragment completion, and picture naming (e.g., Cave & Squire, 1992; N. J. Cohen & Squire, 1980; Graf, Squire, & Mandler, 1984; Shimamura, 1986, 1993; Squire, 1987; Warrington & Weiskrantz, 1968).

In a now-classic study examining repetition priming in amnesic patients, Graf et al. (1984) used a word-stem completion paradigm, in which participants see partially completed words (e.g., ele_____) at test and are asked to fill in the blanks to form the first word that comes to mind. Although no reference is made to an earlier list of words, participants are more likely to complete the string *elephant* if they saw *elephant* during an earlier study session than if they did not. Graf et al. found that normal and amnesic participants showed equal levels of repetition priming on this task. Explicit memory instructions, however, changed the pattern of results. When asked to complete the word stems with study list words, normal participants improved dramatically in their ability to produce study words, whereas amnesic participants did not improve at all. This study and others have shown that robust repetition priming can occur in the absence of explicit memory (for a review, see Shimamura, 1986), and have not only identified areas of the brain crucial to explicit memory but also contributed to the notion that repetition priming may be a form of implicit memory subserved by regions of the brain other than those damaged in amnesia (Cave & Squire, 1992; Schacter, 1990; Squire, 1992; Squire et al., 1993). However, as shall be seen, the notion that repetition priming represents a distinct memory system has been at the center of much controversy. Indeed, not all researchers even acknowledge that repetition priming reflects an aspect of memory.

Models of Repetition Priming

Theories of implicit memory have typically not been concerned with specific processing assumptions, and few research studies have attempted to provide detailed descriptions of the processes underlying repetition priming. As a consequence, model development is not as advanced as in other areas of memory research.

Logogen Model

According to Morton's (1969) model of word recognition, words are mentally represented by feature counters, called *logogens*. An incoming word stimulus causes information to accumulate in the counters for all words that share properties with that stimulus. A word is recognized when the amount of information accumulated in a logogen exceeds the threshold value for that logogen. Repetition priming can be explained as the lowering of the threshold for a previously encountered word (or, equivalently, as the raising of the logogen's resting activation level).

Counter Model

The counter model (Ratcliff & McKoon, 1997) is a variant of the logogen model and was developed to explain repetition priming in perceptual identification. According to the model, each word is represented by a counter, and a decision is made based upon the accumulation of counts. Counts can correspond to perceptual features or to noise (null counts). Null counts are needed to allow the system to respond when there is little or no perceptual information coming from the stimulus. The characteristic of the model that allows it to explain repetition priming is that counters can become attractors of counts. The counter for a previously studied word can steal counts from the counters of similar words. This mechanism produces a pattern of bias in repetition priming because theft of counts is based on similarity and occurs regardless of whether or not the repeated word is the target. Consider, for example, forced-choice perceptual identification in which a target word (e.g., *lied*) is briefly flashed and the subject must then choose between two similar options (e.g., *lied* vs. *died*). If the flashed target is *lied,* prior study of *lied* causes an increase in performance; but if the flashed target is *died,* prior study of *lied* causes a decrement in performance (because its counter steals counts from *died*'s counter). Put another way, people are biased to see the word that was studied previously, even when it is not the target. A potential limitation of the counter model is that it only applies to perceptual identification, which is just one of many tasks in which repetition priming is observed. Of course, this need not present a problem if one takes the view that repetition priming is merely the by-product of the task in which the effect appears (Ratcliff & McKoon, 1997). In this view, repetition priming in perceptual identification may be caused by entirely different mechanisms from those responsible for repetition priming in another task, such as fragment completion. Another problem for the counter model is that there is evidence that prior study can produce increased sensitivity in addition to bias (e.g., Bowers, 1999; Wagenmakers, Zeelenberg, & Raaijmakers, 2000). Although the counter model can be modified to account for these findings (Ratcliff & McKoon, 2000), this change represents a major conceptual shift in the model.

Instance Theory

Logan (1988, 1990) has taken a different approach to elucidating the processes that may underlie repetition priming. In an effort to bridge the gap between research on repetition priming (the effects of *one* prior exposure on performance) and research on automaticity (the effects of *very many* exposures on performance), Logan proposed that repetition priming may be a form of skill acquisition governed by a power function of the number of practice trials. Essentially, Logan has suggested that repetition priming and automaticity may reflect two ends of the same continuum. According to Logan's instance theory, initial performance on a task is determined by a general problem-solving algorithm. As the task progresses, every encounter with a stimulus is stored as a separate instance, even if it is identical to a previous episode. Eventually a level of proficiency with the task may be reached at which the algorithm can be abandoned and responses can be made solely on the basis of instances (i.e., automatically). Presumably, the retrieval of instances can be more efficient than performance of the algorithm. Performance between these two extremes may be automatic for some trials, but not for others. As more instances of a particular stimulus are encoded, the likelihood that the stimulus will receive an automatic response increases. Thus, repetition priming reflects the increased likelihood of an automatic response's following a single prior exposure to a stimulus. A problem for the instance theory is that experiments by Kirsner and Speelman (1996) have provided evidence suggesting that repetition priming can be indifferent to practice and may in fact be a one-shot effect. These findings certainly cast some doubt on the notion that repetition priming and skill acquisition reflect the operation of the same underlying mechanism.

Distributed Network Models

Repetition priming can be explained in distributed network models in much the same way as semantic priming is explained in these models. Indeed, repetition priming can be viewed as an example of semantic priming in which the prime's and the target's semantic representations (as well as orthographic and phonological representations) are identical. Relatively few distributed network models have been applied to repetition priming (but see McClelland & Rumelhart, 1985; Stark & McClelland, 2000), although repetition-priming effects are often interpreted in the context of these models (e.g., Rueckl, Mikolinski, Raveh, Miner, & Mars, 1997). Distributed network models of repetition priming have not been investigated in as much depth as have distributed network models of semantic priming, and little is known about their abilities to account for the major results in the literature.

Major Issues and Findings

As mentioned earlier, research on repetition priming began with studies of patients suffering from impairments of explicit memory. It is not surprising, therefore, that from these earliest observations repetition priming has often been viewed as a form of memory, a type of implicit memory that remains intact in amnesics. Today the term *implicit memory* encompasses a variety of phenomena (e.g., semantic priming, classical conditioning) whose common feature is the influence of prior episodes on behavior without effortful, or explicit, retrieval of those episodes (for reviews, see Richardson-Klavehn & Bjork, 1988; Squire et al., 1993). Repetition priming represents one of the most thoroughly researched of these phenomena. The discussion that follows highlights some of the major findings in the repetition-priming literature, as well as the primary theoretical approaches that have guided the research.

Dissociations from Explicit Memory

If studies of implicit and explicit memory measures produced differences only in an amnesic population, the results of such studies might be of limited interest. However, similar dissociations between implicit and explicit memory performance have been repeatedly demonstrated in normal participants (for a review, see Richardson-Klavehn & Bjork, 1988). Dissociations between implicit and explicit memory performance in normal participants, however, are typically of a different nature. Rather than demonstrating a *presence* of implicit memory and an *absence* of explicit memory as in amnesic patients, dissociations in normal participants are typically demonstrated through differential effects of manipulating an independent variable on measures of implicit and explicit memory.

Levels of Processing. Jacoby and Dallas (1981) demonstrated that manipulating the level of processing of study words did not affect the magnitude of repetition priming in a perceptual identification task (i.e., accuracy of correctly identifying briefly presented stimuli), but it produced large effects on an explicit recognition task (prior semantic processing of words yielded better performance than phonemic or orthographic processing). Insensitivity of repetition priming to level of processing manipulations has also been demonstrated using word fragment completion (e.g., Graf & Mandler, 1984), lexical decision (e.g., Monsell, 1985), perceptual identification of pictures (e.g., Carroll, Byrne, & Kirsner, 1985) and picture naming (e.g., Carroll et al., 1985).

Effects of Delay. Measures of implicit and explicit memory also show differential effects of delay. Several studies manipulating retention interval have found that repetition priming is less affected by delay than explicit memory. For instance, Jacoby and Dallas (1981), Tulving, Schacter, and Stark (1982), and Mitchell and Brown (1988) found that repetition priming persisted with little change across delays of days and weeks (using perceptual identification, word fragment completion, and picture naming tasks, respectively), whereas recognition performance declined sharply across the same delays. Researchers have since demonstrated intact repetition priming for pictures at delays up to 48 weeks (Cave, 1997) and for words at delays up to 16 months (Sloman, Hayman, Ohta, Law, & Tulving, 1988). These findings suggest that repetition priming can be a relatively permanent form of long-term memory rather than a temporary facilitation due to a recent encounter with a stimulus.

Developmental Differences. Research on developmental differences between implicit and explicit memory has been another source of observed dissociations. Many studies have been performed examining developmental dissociations between repetition priming and explicit memory in populations as young as 3 years (e.g., Drummey & Newcombe, 1995; Greenbaum & Graf, 1989), 4 years (e.g., Hayes & Hennessy, 1996), and 5 years (e.g., Carroll et al., 1985). In studies comparing repetition-priming performance of children and adults, equivalent levels of repetition priming were detected across all tested age levels. In contrast, explicit memory performance continued to show developmental improvements up to at least age 12 (e.g., Carroll et al., 1985). Similarly, different developmental trends between explicit and implicit memory have been detected in the aged, with elderly participants typically showing decreases in explicit memory performance relative to younger adults, despite showing equivalent levels of repetition-priming performance (e.g., Graf & Ryan, 1990; Mitchell, 1989); for a discussion of specific implicit memory impairments in elderly participants with Alzheimer's disease, see Gabrieli et al. (1999).

Multiple Systems Versus Processing Theories

Multiple Systems Theories. One way to account for dissociations between implicit and explicit memory has been to postulate separate memory systems in the brain for different types of memory (e.g., N. J. Cohen & Squire, 1980; Schacter, 1990; Squire, 1986; Tulving & Schacter, 1990). Researchers postulating distinct memory systems derive support for this notion in large part from studies with amnesic patients. According to this view, the brain damage in amnesia selectively affects the memory system for conscious recollection, leaving the system (or systems) responsible for other forms of memory intact. Evidence from studies involving amnesic patients suggests that different neural structures underlie performance on tests that rely on different kinds of memory. Because these memory systems operate largely independently of each other, dissociations between performance on tasks that utilize different systems are to be expected. For example, the hippocampus seems to play a crucial role in explicit memory, yet implicit memory performance seems to be unaffected by damage to the hippocampus. The hippocampus, then, must be part of an explicit memory system. Thus, dissociations between different measures of memory are explained by appealing to different memory systems. Based on this view, a taxonomy of memory can be established to classify measures based on the neural mechanisms with which they are associated.

It is important to note, however, that a single (or one-way) dissociation between memory phenomena, such as that observed in amnesics, does not necessarily imply separate memory systems. The data from studies with amnesics could be explained within a single-system framework, for instance, by arguing that explicit memory tasks are more demanding of the neurological resources of a single memory system than implicit tasks. Thus, damage to the memory system, as occurs with amnesia, may leave the system too injured to meet the demands of an explicit memory task, yet not so injured as to affect performance on a less demanding implicit memory task. Many such functional hierarchies might be imagined that incorporate implicit and explicit memory into a single system. Any such structure, however, can only predict the one-way dissociation of intact implicit memory with impaired explicit memory. In the previous example, for instance, implicit memory is more resilient because it is less demanding on the memory system. Thus, if damage to the system were to occur such that implicit memory were impaired, explicit memory would necessarily be impaired because, according to this formulation, the demands on the system are greater for explicit memory tasks than for implicit memory tasks. However, evidence for a *double* dissociation between implicit and explicit memory has been reported by Gabrieli and colleagues (Gabrieli, Fleischman, Keane, Reminger, & Morrell, 1995; Keane, Gabrieli, Mapstone, Johnson, & Corkin, 1995), who have studied patients with occipital lobe lesions. These patients demonstrated impaired repetition-priming performance in a perceptual identification task despite intact explicit memory performance. The results of these studies have been used to support the notion that implicit memory phenomena such as repetition priming are mediated by brain systems separate from those mediating explicit memory. The results of the experiments by Gabrieli and colleagues provide strong evidence that the processes supporting repetition priming do not necessarily contribute to explicit memory performance. Thus, repetition-priming effects should not be interpreted in terms of degraded explicit memory performance. In addition, it should be noted that these patients' ability to perform a perceptual identification task without eliciting repetition priming presents difficulties for models such as the counter model, which assumes that repetition priming occurs as a by-product of performing this task.

On the basis of observed functional and stochastic dissociations between implicit and explicit memory, as well as the evidence from amnesics and other patients with brain damage, theorists have proposed a multiple systems view of memory (e.g., Schacter, 1992; Squire, 1992; Tulving & Schacter, 1990), which holds that neurologically distinct systems subserve different types of memory. The patterns of data have suggested to many that implicit memory is supported by systems distinct from those required for the formation of explicit memories.

The multiple systems view also divides implicit memory into subsystems. Perhaps the best elaborated multiple systems account is that of Tulving and Schacter (1990), who propose a set of neurologically distinct perceptual representation systems (PRS), each of which is designed to encode a particular type of information. Each PRS is presemantic—encoding perceptual information without the necessity for the stimulus to be processed semantically—and supports repetition priming on tasks that use that information. Schacter and his colleagues postulate at least three such systems: a system that encodes information about object parts and their relations in the form of structural descriptions (e.g., Humphreys & Quinlan, 1987; Riddoch & Humphreys, 1987) and supports repetition priming for objects (e.g., Schacter, Cooper, & Delaney, 1990a, 1990b); a visual word-form system that encodes graphemic word information and supports repetition priming for visually presented words (e.g., Marsolek, Kosslyn, & Squire, 1992); and a similar auditory word-form system (e.g., Church & Schacter, 1994). Other systems presumably support repetition priming in more conceptual tasks, although the focus of the multiple systems view has thus far been on perceptual tasks. However, whether implicit and explicit memory are subserved by separate systems at all is a heavily debated issue (cf. Blaxton, 1989; Roediger, 1990; Shimamura, 1990).

Processing Theories. Many researchers have chosen to distinguish memory phenomena on the basis of the different cognitive processes required by the memory tests (e.g., Graf & Mandler, 1984; Roediger & Blaxton, 1987; Roediger, Weldon, & Challis, 1989). Rather than assuming that implicit and explicit tests access separate memory systems, processing theories assume that memory tests are composed of various component processes, and dissociations between performance on memory tests reflect the operation of different processes.

Perhaps the most commonly stated processing account of memory is embodied in the principle of transfer appropriate processing (TAP; e.g., Morris, Bransford, & Franks, 1977; Franks, Bilbrey, Lien, & McNamara, 2000). A primary assumption of TAP is that performance on a memory test benefits to the extent that the cognitive operations at test overlap with those engaged during initial learning. In general, dissociations between performance on explicit and implicit memory tests are characterized in terms of a distinction between *conceptually driven* processes and *data-driven* processes (Roediger et al., 1989). Explicit memory tasks typically (but not always) depend on conceptual processing that is assumed to be sensitive to delay and depth of processing manipulations, whereas implicit memory tests usually depend on data-driven processing that is assumed to be insensitive to these factors. Along the same lines as TAP, Jacoby (1991) has proposed that implicit memory involves automatic processes, whereas explicit memory requires consciously controlled processes. Although Jacoby argues against equating specific memory tests with proposed cognitive processes, he suggests the possibility that special populations, such as amnesics, may show a deficit in intentional processing but preserve automatic or unconscious forms of memory. Jacoby argues that both automatic and controlled processes are always operating, and he has postulated a framework called *process dissociation* that is designed to parse out the relative contributions of each process to performance on a given task.

There has been much debate in recent years concerning the issue of whether memory should be characterized in terms of memory systems or in terms of cognitive processes (e.g., Graf & Ryan, 1990; Mitchell, 1993; Roediger, 1990; Roediger et al., 1989). It is not uncommon for multiple memory systems and processing views to be represented in the implicit memory literature as rival hypotheses. Several researchers, however, have pointed out that these two perspectives are not necessarily incompatible (Schacter, 1990; Shimamura, 1989, 1993). Shimamura (1993) argues that the debate between multiple-systems and TAP views appears to be the result of scientists' working from two different perspectives. Processing views, such as TAP, for instance, are typically championed by researchers in cognitive psychology, whereas multiple-systems views are often forwarded by researchers in neuroscience. The argument for a processing view—in contrast to a multiple-systems view—is often simply a matter of emphasis. Shimamura points out that a processing theory becomes a systems view when it attempts to identify the neural circuitry associated with a process. Likewise, a systems view becomes a processing view when it attempts to identify the process that is subserved by some neural circuitry.

Thus, it may make little theoretical difference whether memory is characterized in terms of multiple brain systems or cognitive processes. Ratcliff and McKoon (1996), however, have pointed out that focusing on multiple memory systems has moved *memory* to the foreground, and put into the background an understanding of the *mechanisms* that mediate memory performance. Likewise, the debate between systems and processing views of memory has moved to the foreground research focused on supporting one view over the other, rather than using the broader perspective afforded by both views taken together to forward our understanding of memory phenomena.

Conceptual Versus Perceptual Priming

Primarily on the basis of the processing demands of a repetition-priming task, researchers have made a distinction between conceptual and perceptual repetition priming (e.g., Roediger & Blaxton, 1987; Roediger et al., 1989). Tasks that involve analysis of stimulus meaning engage conceptual processes, and tasks that involve analysis of stimulus form engage perceptual processes.

Conceptual repetition priming is largely unaffected by changes in the perceptual qualities of a stimulus between study and test, and it is greater following conceptual elaboration at study, such as encoding the meaning of study items. Test tasks that have been used to measure conceptual repetition priming include category exemplar generation and answering general knowledge trivia questions (e.g., Blaxton, 1989; Rappold & Hashtroudi, 1991). Although conceptual processes are thought to also underlie performance on most explicit memory tasks, dissociations between implicit-conceptual and explicit-conceptual tasks have been reported in normal and brain-damaged participants (e.g., Graf, Shimamura, & Squire, 1985; McDermott & Roediger, 1994). Although these results have been taken to suggest that separable processes underlie conceptual implicit and explicit memory, relatively little is known about the processes underlying conceptual priming (Vaidya et al., 1997).

Although the majority of research on perceptual repetition priming has been in the visual domain, repetition priming has also been examined in the auditory domain. For instance, Schacter, Church, and their colleagues (Church & Schacter, 1994; Schacter, Church, & Treadwell, 1994; Schacter, Church, & Bolton, 1995) undertook a systematic investigation of repetition priming across changes in a variety of auditory dimensions. Their participants listened to lists of words recorded from a single speaker. At test, they attempted to identify old and new words embedded in noise. Repetition priming in this paradigm is evidenced by improved accuracy for old words (Jackson & Morton, 1984). They found that repetition priming was reduced (but not eliminated) by changes in speaker, emotional or phrasal intonation, and fundamental frequency, but not by changes in volume (Church & Schacter, 1994). Repetition priming was attributed to the operation of an auditory word-form system specialized to encode frequency information. Whether auditory repetition priming is consistently sensitive to frequency information is still uncertain; the effects of speaker are not observed in amnesic patients (Schacter et al., 1995) and are sometimes not seen in normal participants (Jackson & Morton, 1984).

Perceptual Specificity in Repetition Priming

As mentioned previously, the majority of repetition priming research has focused on perceptual repetition priming in the visual modality. Common tests for visual perceptual repetition priming include word-stem completion, fragment completion (word and picture), lexical decision, perceptual identification (word and picture), and picture naming. Generally, perceptual repetition priming at test is unaffected by conceptual elaboration of study items (e.g., shallow vs. deep processing) but is reduced when perceptual characteristics are changed between study and test. For instance, changes in pictorial exemplar (e.g., from jet to biplane) can reduce perceptual repetition priming, as can changes in symbolic form (e.g., from picture to word) or presentation modality (e.g., from auditory to visual; e.g., Biederman & Cooper, 1991b; Blaxton, 1989; Weldon, 1991).

Interestingly, Easton, Srinivas, and Greene (1997) demonstrated robust repetition priming for words between visual and haptic modalities (words were printed in raised characters that were felt-like to the touch). Easton et al. speculated that vision and haptics may both be adapted for spatial or object discrimination and may share many of the same processing demands and representational characteristics. Specifically, vision and haptics may share geometric representations, unlike the phonological representations in audition. Thus, repetition priming can occur across modalities if the modalities share common representations (or representational characteristics), but repetition priming is attenuated if the representations of a stimulus in different modalities are also different (for additional discussion of visual-haptic interactions, see the chapter by Klatzky & Lederman).

Despite the strong evidence for perceptual specificity in priming, some studies have indicated that repetition priming involving pictorial stimuli may be unaffected by a broad range of perceptual manipulations such as changes in size, location, direction of face, color, and illumination (e.g., Biederman & Cooper, 1991a, 1991b, 1992; Cave, Bost, & Cobb, 1996; Cooper, Schacter, Ballesteros, & Moore, 1992; Srinivas, 1996a). Some of these findings have been interpreted as evidence that object identification is not sensitive to certain stimulus attributes, and therefore priming is not affected by these attributes. However, Srinivas (1996b) has shown that picture priming can be sensitive to size in the context of study and test tasks that required size judgment. This finding suggests that repetition priming may be sensitive to the particular processing demands of the tasks in which the stimuli appear, and may not be a fixed indicator of the stimulus attributes germane to perceptual processing in general. However, this issue has thus far received little attention in the repetition-priming literature.

Purity of Repetition-Priming Measures

Despite the large body of evidence suggesting a distinction between repetition priming and forms of explicit memory, Perruchet and Baveux (1989) demonstrated that performance on certain repetition-priming measures, such as word fragment completion and perceptual clarification (participants identified words that were embedded within a gradually disappearing mask), was correlated with performance on explicit memory tasks, whereas performance on other repetition-priming measures, such as perceptual identification and anagram solution, was not. On this basis, Perruchet and Baveux made a distinction between two classes of repetition-priming tasks. Some tasks may be successfully solved through the use of systematic, controlled procedures (strategic tasks, which may correlate with explicit memory performance). For other tasks, however, the solution seems to pop out from a diffuse, undirected exploration (nonstrategic tasks).

The observations made by Perruchet and Baveux (1989) highlight an important issue in repetition-priming research: To what extent does a particular measure of repetition priming reflect what it is intended to measure? Among measures of perceptual repetition priming, for instance, most include at least some conceptual component. It can be difficult to completely separate facilitation based on perceptual features from facilitation based on meaning when the stimuli themselves have both perceptual and semantic qualities. To control for these effects, some researchers have chosen to use novel stimuli to eliminate the possibility of semantic information contributing to perceptual repetition-priming performance (e.g., Musen & Treisman, 1990; Schacter et al., 1990a).

Likewise, some measures of repetition priming may be open to the use of the same strategies used to make explicit memory decisions. In some instances, the only distinction between a measure of perceptual repetition priming and a measure of explicit memory may be a change in the test instruction. For instance, stem completion and cued recall differ only in that participants in a stem completion task are instructed to complete the stems with the first word that comes to mind, rather than with a previously presented word. Of course, this does not imply that participants are always using explicit memory strategies to perform priming tasks, but it does highlight some of the difficulties in establishing a pure measure of repetition priming in a normal population.

Summary

As should be evident from this survey of repetition priming research, one of the hallmark characteristics of repetition priming is that it is robust. Repetition-priming effects have been demonstrated in patients with neurological disorders as well as in normal populations, and at a wide range of intervals across the lifespan, using a vast array of different measures. Although repetition priming research is still a relatively new science, researchers have amassed a rich data store of knowledge on the subject. Despite the fact that much of what we know about repetition priming comes from research designed to address the multiple-systems versus processing debate, a focus on supporting one view over the other may not be the most fruitful path toward achieving an understanding of the mechanisms that underlie repetition priming and other memory phenomena. The more integrated perspective afforded by both views may allow for a more comprehensive understanding of these mechanisms.

CONCLUSIONS

In this chapter, we tried to provide an historical overview of the major theoretical and empirical advances in our understanding of semantic memory, semantic priming, and repetition priming. Significant progress has been made on both the theoretical and the empirical fronts in each domain.

Although the concept of semantic memory remains heuristic, semantic memory is no longer a coherent domain of inquiry, as nearly all of the phenomena originally associated with semantic memory, such as how word meanings are mentally represented and how language is understood, have become separate research endeavors. The most important recent theoretical advances have been the development of distributed network models and high-dimensional spatial models of knowledge representation. A promising direction for future research is to explore these models in more depth. Another important target of future research is the connection between perceptual systems and semantic representations. This issue is fundamentally important, yet it has received relatively little attention from experimental psychologists (but see A. S. Meyer, Sleiderink, & Levelt, 1998; Tannenhaus, Spivey-Knowlton, Eberhard, & Sedivy, 1995; Zelinsky & Murphy, 2000).

Semantic priming continues to be actively investigated more than 30 years after its discovery by D. E. Meyer and Schvaneveldt (1971). In our opinion, the most important new finding in the past decade is semantic priming over very long lags (e.g., S. Becker et al., 1997; Joordens & Becker, 1997). There are reasons to question the reliability of long-term semantic priming, but if these doubts can be put to rest with independent replications, long-term semantic priming will effectively rule out all existing models of semantic priming with the exception of distributed network learning models. Several other topics are in need of additional empirical or theoretical work, including (a) the variables that control semantic matching, (b) semantic priming for different types of semantic relations, (c) backward priming, and (d) augmenting models of priming with attentional processes that would allow the models to account for prime-task and global context effects.

The evolution of the concept of implicit memory has been one of the most important developments in the cognitive sciences in the past 20 years. Research on implicit memory in general, and repetition priming in particular, continues unabated. We believe that the most important goal for future research is to understand the mechanisms underlying repetition priming. Past research on implicit memory has been dominated by empirical issues or broad theoretical themes rather than by attempts to understand the mental representations and processes involved in repetition priming. A huge literature has now been amassed on various kinds of priming effects; now researchers need to attempt to divine the mechanisms responsible for these effects. An essential component of this endeavor will be the development of models of the sensory, perceptual, and cognitive processes responsible for repetition priming. In our opinion, the recent development of such models (e.g., Ratcliff & McKoon, 1997) represents a major step forward and is an extremely important direction for future research on implicit memory.

REFERENCES

Abrams, R. L., & Greenwald, A. G. (2000). Parts outweigh the whole (word) in unconscious analysis of meaning. *Psychological Science, 11,* 118–124.

Anderson, J. R. (1976). *Language, memory, and thought.* Cambridge, MA: Harvard University Press.

Anderson, J. R. (1983). *The architecture of cognition.* Cambridge, MA: Harvard University Press.

Balota, D. A., & Lorch, R. F. (1986). Depth of automatic spreading activation: Mediated priming effects in pronunciation but not in lexical decision. *Journal of Experimental Psychology: Learning, Memory, and Cognition, 12,* 336–345.

Becker, C. A. (1980). Semantic context effects in visual word recognition: An analysis of semantic strategies. *Memory & Cognition, 8,* 493–512.

Becker, S., Moscovitch, M., Behrmann, M., & Joordens, S. (1997). Long–term semantic priming: A computational account and empirical evidence. *Journal of Experimental Psychology: Learning, Memory, and Cognition, 23,* 1059–1082.

Besner, D., & Stolz, J. A. (1999). What kind of attention modulates the Stroop effect? *Psychonomic Bulletin & Review, 6,* 99–104.

Besner, D., Twilley, L., McCann, R. S., & Seergobin, K. (1990). On the association between connectionism and data: Are a few words necessary? *Psychological Review, 97,* 432–446.

Biederman, I., & Cooper, E. E. (1991a). Priming contour-deleted images: Evidence for intermediate representations in visual object recognition. *Cognitive Psychology, 23,* 393–419.

Biederman, I., & Cooper, E. E. (1991b). Evidence for complete translational and reflectional invariance in visual object priming. *Perception, 20,* 585–593.

Biederman, I., & Cooper, E. E. (1992). Size invariance in visual object priming. *Journal of Experimental Psychology: Human Perception and Performance, 18,* 121–133.

Blaxton, T. A. (1989). Investigating dissociations among memory measures: Support for a transfer-appropriate processing framework. *Journal of Experimental Psychology: Learning, Memory, and Cognition, 15,* 657–668.

Bowers, J. S. (1999). Priming is not all bias: Commentary on Ratcliff and McKoon (1997). *Psychological Review, 106,* 582–596.

Burgess, C., & Lund, K. (2000). The dynamics of meaning in memory. In E. Dietrich & B. Arthur (Eds.), *Cognitive dynamics: Conceptual and representational change in humans and machines* (pp. 117–156). Mahwah, NJ: Erlbaum.

Carroll, M. V., Byrne, B., & Kirsner, K. (1985). Autobiographical memory and perceptual learning: A developmental study using picture recognition, naming latency, and perceptual identification. *Memory & Cognition, 13,* 273–279.

Cave, C. B. (1997). Very long-lasting priming in picture naming. *Psychological Science, 8,* 322–325.

Cave, C. B., Bost, P. R., & Cobb, R. E. (1996). Effects of color and pattern on implicit and explicit picture memory. *Journal of Experimental Psychology: Learning, Memory, and Cognition, 22,* 639–653.

Cave, C. B., & Squire, L. R. (1992). Intact and long-lasting repetition priming in amnesia. *Journal of Experimental Psychology: Learning, Memory, and Cognition, 18,* 509–520.

Cheesman, J., & Merikle, P. (1984). Priming with and without awareness. *Perception & Psychophysics, 36,* 387–395.

Church, B. A., & Schacter, D. L. (1994). Perceptual specificity of auditory priming: Implicit memory for voice intonation and fundamental frequency. *Journal of Experimental Psychology: Learning, Memory, and Cognition, 20,* 521–533.

Chwilla, D. J., Hagoort, P., & Brown, C. M. (1998). The mechanism underlying backward priming in a lexical decision task: Spreading activation versus semantic matching. *Quarterly Journal of Experimental Psychology, 51A,* 531–560.

Cohen, J. (1977). *Statistical power analysis for the behavioral sciences.* New York: Academic Press.

Cohen, N. J., & Squire, L. R. (1980). Preserved learning and retention of pattern-analyzing skill in amnesia: Dissociation of knowing how and knowing that. *Science, 210,* 207–210.

Collins, A. M., & Loftus, E. F. (1975). A spreading-activation theory of semantic processing. *Psychological Review, 82,* 407–428.

Collins, A. M., & Quillian, M. R. (1969). Retrieval time from semantic memory. *Journal of Verbal Learning and Verbal Behavior, 8,* 240–247.

Collins, A. M., & Quillian, M. R. (1972). Experiments on semantic memory and language comprehension. In L. W. Gregg (Ed.), *Cognition in learning and memory* (pp. 117–147). New York: Wiley.

Conrad, C. (1972). Cognitive economy in semantic memory. *Journal of Experimental Psychology, 92,* 149–154.

Cooper, L. A., Schacter, D. L., Ballesteros, S., & Moore, C. (1992). Priming and recognition of transformed three-dimensional objects: Effects of size and reflection. *Journal of Experimental Psychology: Learning, Memory, and Cognition, 18,* 43–57.

de Groot, A. M. (1983). The range of automatic spreading activation in word priming. *Journal of Verbal Learning and Verbal Behavior, 22,* 417–436.

de Groot, A. M. (1984). Primed lexical decision: Combined effects of the proportion of related prime-target pairs and the stimulus-onset asynchrony of prime and target. *Quarterly Journal of Experimental Psychology, 36A,* 253–280.

den Heyer, K., Briand, K., & Dannenbring, G. L. (1983). Strategic factors in a lexical-decision task: Evidence for automatic and attention-driven processes. *Memory & Cognition, 11,* 374–381.

den Heyer, K., Briand, K., & Smith, L. (1985). Automatic and strategic effects in semantic priming: An examination of Becker's verification model. *Memory & Cognition, 13,* 228–232.

Dosher, B. A., & Rosedale, G. (1989). Integrated retrieval cues as a mechanism for priming in retrieval from memory. *Journal of Experimental Psychology: General, 118,* 191–211.

Draine, S. C., & Greenwald, A. G. (1998). Replicable unconscious semantic priming. *Journal of Experimental Psychology: General, 127,* 286–303.

Drummey, A. B., & Newcombe, N. (1995). Remembering versus knowing the past: Children's explicit and implicit memories for pictures. *Journal of Experimental Child Psychology, 59,* 549–565.

Durgunoglu, A. Y. (1988). Repetition, semantic priming, and stimulus quality: Implications for the interactive-compensatory reading model. *Journal of Experimental Psychology: Learning, Memory, and Cognition, 14,* 590–603.

Easton, R. D., Srinivas, K., & Greene, A. J. (1997). Do vision and haptics share common representations? Implicit and explicit memory within and between modalities. *Journal of Experimental Psychology: Learning, Memory, and Cognition, 23,* 153–163.

Farah, M. J., & McClelland, J. L. (1991). A computational model of semantic memory impairment: Modality specificity and emergent category specificity. *Journal of Experimental Psychology: General, 120,* 339–357.

Fischler, I. (1977a). Associative facilitation without expectancy in a lexical decision task. *Journal of Experimental Psychology: Human Perception and Performance, 3,* 18–26.

Fischler, I. (1977b). Semantic facilitation without association in a lexical decision task. *Memory & Cognition, 5,* 335–339.

Fodor, J. A., & Pylyshyn, Z. W. (1988). Connectionism and cognitive architecture: A critical analysis. *Cognition, 28,* 3–71.

Forster, K. I. (1981). Priming and the effects of sentence and lexical contexts on naming time: Evidence for autonomous lexical processing. *Quarterly Journal of Experimental Psychology, 33A,* 465–495.

Franks, J. J., Bilbrey, C. W., Lien, K. G., & McNamara, T. P. (2000). Transfer-appropriate processing (TAP) and repetition priming. *Memory & Cognition, 28,* 1140–1151.

Friedrich, F. J., Henik, A., & Tzelgov, J. (1991). Automatic processes in lexical access and spreading activation. *Journal of Experimental Psychology: Human Perception and Performance, 17,* 792–806.

Gabrieli, J. D. E., Fleischman, D. A., Keane, M. M., Reminger, S. L., & Morrell, F. (1995). Double dissociation between memory systems underlying explicit and implicit memory in the human brain. *Psychological Science, 6,* 76–82.

Gabrieli, J. D. E., Vaidya, C. J., Stone, M., Francis, W. S., Thompson-Schill, S. L., Fleischman, D. A., Tinklenberg, J. R., Yesavage, J. A., & Wilson, R. S. (1999). Convergent behavioral and neuropsychological evidence for a distinction between identification and production forms of repetition priming. *Journal of Experimental Psychology: General, 128,* 479–498.

Gillund, G., & Shiffrin, R. M. (1984). A retrieval model for both recognition and recall. *Psychological Review, 91,* 1–67.

Glass, A. L., & Holyoak, K. J. (1974). Alternative conceptions of semantic theory. *Cognition, 3,* 313–339.

Graf, P., & Mandler, G. (1984). Activation makes words more accessible, but not necessarily more retrievable. *Journal of Verbal Learning and Verbal Behavior, 23,* 553–568.

Graf, P., & Ryan, L. (1990). Transfer-appropriate processing for implicit and explicit memory. *Journal of Experimental Psychology: Learning, Memory, and Cognition, 16,* 978–992.

Graf, P., Shimamura, A. P., & Squire, L. R. (1985). Priming across modalities and priming across category levels: Extending the domain of preserved function in amnesia. *Journal of Experimental Psychology: Learning, Memory, and Cognition, 11,* 386–396.

Graf, P., Squire, L. R., & Mandler, G. (1984). The information that amnesic patients do not forget. *Journal of Experimental Psychology: Learning, Memory, and Cognition, 10,* 164–178.

Greenbaum, J. L., & Graf, P. (1989). Preschool period development of implicit and explicit remembering. *Bulletin of the Psychonomic Society, 27,* 417–420.

Greenwald, A. G., Draine, S. C., & Abrams, R. L. (1996). Three cognitive markers of unconscious semantic activation. *Science, 273,* 1699–1702.

Greenwald, A. G., Klinger, M. R., & Schuh, E. S. (1995). Activation by marginally perceptible ("subliminal") stimuli: Dissociation of unconscious from conscious perception. *Journal of Experimental Psychology: General, 124,* 22–42.

Hayes, B. K., & Hennessy, R. (1996). The nature and development of nonverbal implicit memory. *Journal of Experimental Child Psychology, 63,* 22–43.

Hebb, D. O. (1949). *The organization of behavior.* New York: Wiley.

Henik, A., Friedrich, F. J., & Kellogg, W. A. (1983). The dependence of semantic relatedness effects upon prime processing. *Memory & Cognition, 11,* 366–373.

Henik, A., Friedrich, F. J., Tzelgov, J., & Tramer, S. (1994). Capacity demands of automatic processes in semantic priming. *Memory & Cognition, 22,* 157–168.

Hess, D. J., Foss, D. J., & Carroll, P. (1995). Effects of global and local context on lexical processing during language comprehension. *Journal of Experimental Psychology: General, 124,* 62–82.

Hinton, G. E., & Shallice, T. (1991). Lesioning an attractor network: Investigations of acquired dyslexia. *Psychological Review, 98,* 74–95.

Hintzman, D. L. (1986). "Schema abstraction" in a multiple-trace memory model. *Psychological Review, 93,* 411–428.

Holender, D. (1986). Semantic activation without conscious identification in dichotic listening, parafoveal vision, and visual masking: A survey and appraisal. *Behavioral and Brain Sciences, 9,* 1–66.

Holyoak, K. J., & Glass, A. L. (1975). The role of contradictions and counterexamples in the rejection of false sentences. *Journal of Verbal Learning and Verbal Behavior, 14,* 215–239.

Humphreys, G. W., & Quinlan, P. T. (1987). Normal and pathological processes in visual object constancy. In G. W. Humphreys & M. J. Riddoch (Eds.), *Visual object processing: A cognitive neuropsychological approach* (pp. 43–105). Hillsdale, NJ: Erlbaum.

Jackson, A., & Morton, J. (1984). Facilitation of auditory word recognition. *Memory & Cognition, 12,* 568–574.

Jacoby, L. L. (1991). A process dissociation framework: Separating automatic from intentional uses of memory. *Journal of Memory and Language, 30,* 513–541.

Jacoby, L. L., & Dallas, M. (1981). On the relationship between autobiographical memory and perceptual learning. *Journal of Experimental Psychology: General, 110,* 306–340.

Joordens, S., & Becker, S. (1997). The long and short of semantic priming effects in lexical decision. *Journal of Experimental Psychology: Learning, Memory, and Cognition, 23,* 1083–1105.

Joordens, S., & Besner, D. (1992). Priming effects that span an intervening unrelated word: Implications for models of memory representation and retrieval. *Journal of Experimental Psychology: Learning, Memory, and Cognition, 18,* 483–491.

Kahan, T. A., Neely, J. H., & Forsythe, W. J. (1999). Dissociated backward priming effects in lexical decision and pronunciation tasks. *Psychonomic Bulletin & Review, 6,* 105–110.

Kawamoto, A. H., Farrar, W. T., & Kello, C. T. (1994). When two meanings are better than one: Modeling the ambiguity advantage using a recurrent distributed network. *Journal of Experimental Psychology: Human Perception and Performance, 20,* 1233–1247.

Keane, M. M., Gabrieli, J. D. E., Mapstone, H. C., Johnson, K. A., & Corkin, S. (1995). Double dissociation of memory capacities after bilateral occipital-lobe or medial temporal lobe lesions. *Brain, 118,* 1129–1148.

Keefe, D. E., & Neely, J. H. (1990). Semantic priming in the pronunciation task: The role of prospective prime-generated expectancies. *Memory & Cognition, 18,* 289–298.

Kirsner, K., & Speelman, C. (1996). Skill acquisition and repetition priming: One principle, many processes? *Journal of Experimental Psychology: Learning, Memory, and Cognition, 22,* 563–575.

Klinger, M. R., Burton, P. C., & Pitts, G. S. (2000). Mechanisms of unconscious priming: I. Response competition, not spreading activation. *Journal of Experimental Psychology: Learning, Memory, and Cognition, 26,* 441–455.

Koriat, A. (1981). Semantic facilitation in lexical decision as a function of prime-target association. *Memory & Cognition, 9,* 587–598.

Landauer, T. K. (1998). Learning and representing verbal meaning: The Latent Semantic Analysis Theory. *Current Directions in Psychological Science, 7,* 161–164.

Landauer, T. K., & Dumais, S. T. (1997). A solution to Plato's problem: The latent semantic analysis theory of acquisition, induction, and representation of knowledge. *Psychological Review, 104,* 211–240.

Livesay, K., & Burgess, C. (1998). Mediated priming in high-dimensional semantic space: No effect of direct semantic relationships or co-occurrence. *Brain and Cognition, 37,* 102–105.

Logan, G. D. (1988). Toward an instance theory of automatization. *Psychological Review, 95,* 492–527.

Logan, G. D. (1990). Repetition priming and automaticity: Common underlying mechanisms? *Cognitive Psychology, 22,* 1–35.

Lucas, M. (2000). Semantic priming without association: A meta-analytic review. *Psychonomic Bulletin & Review, 7,* 618–630.

Lund, K., Burgess, C., & Audet, C. (1996). Dissociating semantic and associative word relationships using high-dimensional semantic space. *Proceedings of the Eighteenth Annual Conference of the Cognitive Science Society, 18,* 603–608.

Lupker, S. J. (1984). Semantic priming without association: A second look. *Journal of Verbal Learning and Verbal Behavior, 23,* 709–733.

Marcel, A. (1983). Conscious and unconscious perception: Experiments on visual masking and word recognition. *Journal of Experimental Psychology: Learning, Memory, and Cognition, 12,* 108–115.

Marsolek, C. J., Kosslyn, S. M., & Squire, L. R. (1992). Form-specific visual priming in the right cerebral hemisphere. *Journal of Experimental Psychology: Learning, Memory, and Cognition, 18,* 492–508.

Masson, M. E. J. (1991). A distributed memory model of context effects in word identification. In D. Besner & G. W. Humphreys (Eds.), *Basic processes in reading: Visual word recognition* (pp. 233–263). Hillsdale, NJ: Erlbaum.

Masson, M. E. J. (1995). A distributed memory model of semantic priming. *Journal of Experimental Psychology: Learning, Memory, and Cognition, 21,* 3–23.

McClelland, J. L., & Rumelhart, D. E. (1985). Distributed memory and the representation of general and specific information. *Journal of Experimental Psychology: General, 114,* 159–188.

McClelland, J. L., & Rumelhart, D. E. (Eds.). (1986). *Parallel distributed processing: Explorations in the microstructure of cognition: Vol. 2. Psychological and biological models.* Cambridge, MA: MIT Press.

McCloskey, M., & Glucksberg, S. (1979). Decision processes in verifying category membership statements: Implications for models of semantic memory. *Cognitive Psychology, 11,* 1–37.

McDermott, K. B., & Roediger, H. L. (1994). Effects of imagery on perceptual implicit memory tests. *Journal of Experimental Psychology: Learning, Memory, and Cognition, 20,* 1379–1390.

McKoon, G., & Ratcliff, R. (1992). Spreading activation versus compound cue accounts of priming: Mediated priming revisited. *Journal of Experimental Psychology: Learning, Memory, and Cognition, 18,* 1155–1172.

McKoon, G., & Ratcliff, R. (1995). Conceptual combinations and relational contexts in free association and in priming in lexical decision and naming. *Psychonomic Bulletin & Review, 2,* 527–533.

McKoon, G., Ratcliff, R., & Dell, G. S. (1986). A critical evaluation of the semantic-episodic distinction. *Journal of Experimental Psychology: Learning, Memory, and Cognition, 12,* 295–306.

McNamara, T. P. (1992a). Priming and constraints it places on theories of memory and retrieval. *Psychological Review, 99,* 650–662.

McNamara, T. P. (1992b). Theories of priming: I. Associative distance and lag. *Journal of Experimental Psychology: Learning, Memory, and Cognition, 18,* 1173–1190.

McNamara, T. P., & Altarriba, J. (1988). Depth of spreading activation revisited: Semantic mediated priming occurs in lexical decisions. *Journal of Memory and Language, 27,* 545–559.

McRae, K., & Boisvert, S. (1998). Automatic semantic similarity priming. *Journal of Experimental Psychology: Learning, Memory, and Cognition, 24,* 558–572.

McRae, K., de Sa, V. R., & Seidenberg, M. S. (1997). On the nature and scope of featural representations of word meaning. *Journal of Experimental Psychology: General, 126,* 99–130.

Meyer, A. S., Sleiderink, A. M., & Levelt, W. J. M. (1998). Viewing and naming objects: Eye movements during noun phrase production. *Cognition, 66,* B25–B33.

Meyer, D. E. (1970). On the representation and retrieval of stored semantic information. *Cognitive Psychology, 1,* 242–300.

Meyer, D. E., & Schvaneveldt, R. W. (1971). Facilitation in recognizing pairs of words: Evidence of a dependence between retrieval operations. *Journal of Experimental Psychology, 90,* 227–234.

Mitchell, D. B. (1989). How many memory systems? Evidence from aging. *Journal of Experimental Psychology: Learning, Memory, and Cognition, 15,* 31–49.

Mitchell, D. B. (1993). Implicit and explicit memory for pictures: Multiple views across the lifespan. In P. Graf & M. E. J. Masson (Eds.), *Implicit memory: New directions in cognition, development, and neuropsychology* (pp. 171–190). Hillsdale, NJ: Erlbaum.

Mitchell, D. B., & Brown, A. S. (1988). Persistent repetition priming in picture naming and its dissociation from recognition memory. *Journal of Experimental Psychology: Learning, Memory, and Cognition, 14,* 213–222.

Monsell, S. (1985). Repetition and the lexicon. In A. W. Ellis (Ed.), *Progress in the psychology of language* (pp. 147–196). London: Erlbaum.

Morris, C. D., Bransford, J. D., & Franks, J. J. (1977). Levels of processing versus transfer appropriate processing. *Journal of Verbal Learning and Verbal Behavior, 16,* 519–533.

Morton, J. (1969). Interaction of information in word recognition. *Psychological Review, 76,* 165–178.

Moss, H. E., Hare, M. L., Day, P., & Tyler, L. K. (1994). A distributed memory model of the associative boost in semantic priming. *Connection Science: Journal of Neural Computing, Artificial Intelligence, and Cognitive Research, 6,* 413–427.

Moss, H. E., Ostrin, R. K., Tyler, L. K., & Marslen Wilson, W. D. (1995). Accessing different types of lexical semantic information: Evidence from priming. *Journal of Experimental Psychology: Learning, Memory, and Cognition, 21,* 863–883.

Murdock, B. B. (1982). A theory for the storage and retrieval of item and associative information. *Psychological Review, 89,* 609–626.

Musen, G., & Treisman, A. (1990). Implicit and explicit memory for visual patterns. *Journal of Experimental Psychology: Learning, Memory, and Cognition, 16,* 127–137.

Neely, J. H. (1977). Semantic priming and retrieval from lexical memory: Roles of inhibitionless spreading activation and limited-capacity attention. *Journal of Experimental Psychology: General, 106,* 226–254.

Neely, J. H. (1991). Semantic priming effects in visual word recognition: A selective review of current findings and theories. In D. Besner & G. W. Humphreys (Eds.), *Basic processes in reading: Visual word recognition* (pp. 264–336). Hillsdale, NJ: Erlbaum.

Neely, J. H., & Kahan, T. A. (2001). Is semantic activation automatic? A critical re-evaluation. In H. L. Roediger III, J. S. Nairne, I. Neath, & A. M. Surprenant (Eds.), *The nature of remembering: Essays in honor of Robert G. Crowder* (pp. 69–93). Washington, DC: American Psychological Association.

Neely, J. H., & Keefe, D. E. (1989). Semantic context effects on visual word processing: A hybrid prospective-retrospective processing theory. In G. H. Bower (Ed.), *The psychology of learning and motivation: Advances in research and theory* (Vol. 24, pp. 207–248). New York: Academic Press.

Neely, J. H., Keefe, D. E., & Ross, K. L. (1989). Semantic priming in the lexical decision task: Roles of prospective prime-generated expectancies and retrospective semantic matching. *Journal of Experimental Psychology: Learning, Memory, and Cognition, 15,* 1003–1019.

Nelson, D. L., McEvoy, C. L., & Schreiber, T. A. (1991). *The University of South Florida word association, rhyme, and word fragment norms.* Unpublished manuscript.

Oscar-Berman, M. (1984). Comparative neuropsychology and alcoholic Korsakoff disease. In L. R. Squire & N. Butters (Eds.), *Neuropsychology of Memory* (pp. 194–202). New York: Guilford Press.

Osgood, C. E., Suci, G. J., & Tannenbaum, P. H. (1957). *The measurement of meaning.* Urbana: University of Illinois Press.

Perruchet, P., & Baveux, P. (1989). Correlational analyses of explicit and implicit memory performance. *Memory & Cognition, 17,* 77–86.

Peterson, R. R., & Simpson, G. B. (1989). Effect of backward priming on word recognition in single-word and sentence contexts. *Journal of Experimental Psychology: Learning, Memory, and Cognition, 15,* 1020–1032.

Plaut, D. C., & Booth, J. R. (2000). Individual and developmental differences in semantic priming: Empirical and computational support for a single-mechanism account of lexical processing. *Psychological Review, 107,* 786–823.

Plaut, D. C., McClelland, J. L., Seidenberg, M. S., & Patterson, K. (1996). Understanding normal and impaired word reading: Computational principles in quasi-regular domains. *Psychological Review, 103,* 56–115.

Posner, M. I., & Snyder, C. R. R. (1975). Attention and cognitive control. In R. L. Solso (Ed.), *Information processing and cognition* (pp. 55–85). Hillsdale, NJ: Erlbaum.

Quillian, M. R. (1967). Word concepts: A theory and simulation of some basic semantic capabilities. *Behavioral Science, 12,* 410–430.

Quillian, M. R. (1969). The teachable language comprehender. *Communications of the Association for Computing Machinery, 12,* 459–476.

Rappold, V. A., & Hashtroudi, S. (1991). Does organization improve priming? *Journal of Experimental Psychology: Learning, Memory, and Cognition, 17,* 103–114.

Ratcliff, R., & McKoon, G. (1981). Does activation really spread? *Psychological Review, 88,* 454–462.

Ratcliff, R., & McKoon, G. (1982). Speed and accuracy in the processing of false statements about semantic information. *Journal of Experimental Psychology: Learning, Memory, and Cognition, 8,* 16–36.

Ratcliff, R., & McKoon, G. (1988). A retrieval theory of priming in memory. *Psychological Review, 95,* 385–408.

Ratcliff, R., & McKoon, G. (1996). Bias effects in implicit memory tasks. *Journal of Experimental Psychology: General, 125,* 403–421.

Ratcliff, R., & McKoon, G. (1997). A counter model for implicit priming in perceptual word identification. *Psychological Review, 104,* 319–343.

Ratcliff, R., & McKoon, G. (2000). Modeling the effects of repetition and word frequency in perceptual identification. *Psychonomic Bulletin & Review, 7,* 713–717.

Richardson-Klavehn, A., & Bjork, R. A. (1988). Measures of memory. *Annual Review of Psychology, 39,* 475–543.

Riddoch, M. J., & Humphreys, G. W. (1987). Picture naming. In G. W. Humphreys & M. Riddoch (Eds.), *Visual object processing: A cognitive neuropsychological approach* (pp. 107–143). Hillsdale, NJ: Erlbaum.

Rips, L. J., Shoben, E. J., & Smith, E. E. (1973). Semantic distance and the verification of semantic relations. *Journal of Verbal Learning and Verbal Behavior, 12,* 1–20.

Roediger, H. L., III. (1990). Implicit memory: Retention without remembering. *American Psychologist, 45,* 1043–1056.

Roediger, H. L., III, & Blaxton, T. A. (1987). Effects of varying modality, surface features, and retention interval on priming in word-fragment completion. *Memory & Cognition, 15,* 379–388.

Roediger, H. L., III, Weldon, M. S., & Challis, B. H. (1989). Explaining dissociations between implicit and explicit measures of retention: A processing account. In H. L. Roediger III & F. I. M. Craik (Eds.), *Varieties of memory and consciousness: Essays in honour of Endel Tulving* (pp. 2–41). Hillsdale, NJ: Erlbaum.

Rosenblatt, F. (1962). *Principles of neurodynamics.* New York: Spartan.

Rueckl, J. G., Mikolinski, M., Raveh, M., Miner, C. S., & Mars, F. (1997). Morphological priming, fragment completion, and connectionist networks. *Journal of Memory and Language, 36,* 382–405.

Rumelhart, D. E., & McClelland, J. L. (Eds.). (1986). *Parallel distributed processing: Explorations in the microstructure of cognition: Vol. 1. Foundations.* Cambridge, MA: MIT Press.

Schacter, D. L. (1990). Perceptual representation systems and implicit memory: Toward a resolution of the multiple memory systems debate. *Annals of the New York Academy of Sciences, 608,* 543–571.

Schacter, D. L. (1992). Priming and multiple memory systems: Perceptual mechanisms of implicit memory. *Journal of Cognitive Neuroscience, 4,* 244–256.

Schacter, D. L., Church, B., & Bolton, E. (1995). Implicit memory in amnesic patients: Impairment of voice-specific priming. *Psychological Science, 6,* 20–25.

Schacter, D. L., Church, B., & Treadwell, J. (1994). Implicit memory in amnesic patients: Evidence for spared auditory priming. *Psychological Science, 5,* 20–25.

Schacter, D. L., Cooper, L. A., & Delaney, S. M. (1990a). Implicit memory for unfamiliar objects depends on access to structural descriptions. *Journal of Experimental Psychology: General, 119,* 5–24.

Schacter, D. L., Cooper, L. A., & Delaney, S. M. (1990b). Implicit memory for visual objects and the structural description system. *Bulletin of the Psychonomic Society, 28,* 367–372.

Seidenberg, M. S., & McClelland, J. L. (1989). A distributed, developmental model of word recognition and naming. *Psychological Review, 96,* 523–568.

Seidenberg, M. S., Waters, G. S., Sanders, M., & Langer, P. (1984). Pre- and postlexical loci of contextual effects on word recognition. *Memory & Cognition, 12,* 315–328.

Sharkey, A. J., & Sharkey, N. E. (1992). Weak contextual constraints in text and word priming. *Journal of Memory and Language, 31,* 543–572.

Shelton, J. R., & Martin, R. C. (1992). How semantic is automatic semantic priming? *Journal of Experimental Psychology: Learning, Memory, and Cognition, 18,* 1191–1210.

Shimamura, A. P. (1986). Priming effects in amnesia: Evidence for a dissociable memory function. *Quarterly Journal of Experimental Psychology, 38A,* 619–644.

Shimamura, A. P. (1989). Disorders of memory: The cognitive science perspective. In F. Boller & J. Grafman (Eds.), *Handbook of neuropsychology* (pp. 35–73). Amsterdam: Elsevier Science.

Shimamura, A. P. (1990). Forms of memory: Issues and directions. In J. L. McGaugh, N. M. Weinberger, & G. Lynch (Eds.), *Brain organization and memory: Cells, systems, and circuits* (pp. 159–173). New York: Oxford University Press.

Shimamura, A. P. (1993). Neuropsychological analyses of implicit memory: History, methodology and theoretical interpretations. In P. Graf & M. E. Masson (Eds.), *Implicit memory: New directions in cognition, development, and neuropsychology* (pp. 265–285). Hillsdale, NJ: Erlbaum.

Sloman, S. A., Hayman, C. A. G., Ohta, N., Law, J., & Tulving, E. (1988). Forgetting in primed fragment completion. *Journal of Experimental Psychology: Learning, Memory, and Cognition, 14,* 223–239.

Smith, E. E. (1978). Theories of semantic memory. In W. K. Estes (Ed.), *Handbook of learning and cognitive processes: Vol. 4. Linguistic functions in cognitive theory* (pp. 1–56). Potomic, MD: Erlbaum.

Smith, E. E., Shoben, E. J., & Rips, L. J. (1974). Structure and process in semantic memory: A featural model for semantic decisions. *Psychological Review, 81,* 214–241.

Smith, M. C. (1979). Contextual facilitation in a letter search task depends on how the prime is processed. *Journal of Experimental Psychology: Human Perception and Performance, 5,* 239–251.

Smith, M. C., Theodor, L., & Franklin, P. E. (1983). The relationship between contextual facilitation and depth of processing. *Journal of Experimental Psychology: Learning, Memory, and Cognition, 9,* 697–712.

Squire, L. R. (1986). Mechanisms of memory. *Science, 232,* 1612–1619.

Squire, L. R. (1987). *Memory and brain.* New York: Oxford University Press.

Squire, L. R. (1992). Memory and the hippocampus: A synthesis from findings with rats, monkeys, and humans. *Psychological Review, 99,* 195–231.

Squire, L. R., Zola-Morgan, S., Cave, C. B., Haist, F., Musen, G., & Suzuki, W. A. (1993). Memory: Organization of brain systems and cognition. In D. E. Meyer & S. Kornblum (Eds.), *Attention and performance XIV* (pp. 393–424). Cambridge, MA: MIT Press.

Srinivas, K. (1996a). Contrast and illumination effects on explicit and implicit measures of memory. *Journal of Experimental Psychology: Learning, Memory, and Cognition, 22,* 1123–1135.

Srinivas, K. (1996b). Size and reflection effects in priming: A test of transfer-appropriate processing. *Memory & Cognition, 24,* 441–452.

Stark, C. E. L., & McClelland, J. L. (2000). Repetition priming of words, pseudowords, and nonwords. *Journal of Experimental Psychology: Learning, Memory, and Cognition, 26,* 945–972.

Stolz, J. A., & Besner, D. (1996). Role of set in visual word recognition: Activation and activation blocking as nonautomatic processes. *Journal of Experimental Psychology: Human Perception and Performance, 22,* 1166–1177.

Stolz, J. A., & Besner, D. (1999). On the myth of automatic semantic activation in reading. *Current Directions in Psychological Science, 8,* 61–65.

Tannenhaus, M. K., Spivey-Knowlton, M. J., Eberhard, K., & Sedivy, J. C. (1995). Integration of visual and linguistic information in spoken language comprehension. *Science, 268,* 1632–1634.

Thompson-Schill, S. L., Kurtz, K. J., & Gabrieli, J. D. E. (1998). Effects of semantic and associative relatedness on automatic priming. *Journal of Memory and Language, 38,* 440–458.

Tulving, E. (1972). Episodic and semantic memory. In E. Tulving & W. Donaldson (Eds.), *Organization of memory* (pp. 381–403). New York: Academic Press.

Tulving, E. (1983). *Elements of episodic memory.* New York: Oxford University Press.

Tulving, E., & Schacter, D. L. (1990). Priming and human memory systems. *Science, 247,* 301–306.

Tulving, E., Schacter, D. L., & Stark, H. A. (1982). Priming effects in word-fragment completion are independent of recognition memory. *Journal of Experimental Psychology: Learning, Memory, and Cognition, 8,* 336–342.

Tweedy, J. R., Lapinski, R. H., & Schvaneveldt, R. W. (1977). Semantic-context effects on word recognition: Influence of varying the proportion of items presented in an appropriate context. *Memory & Cognition, 5,* 84–89.

Tyler, L. K., & Moss, H. E. (1997). Functional properties of concepts: Studies of normal and brain-damaged patients. *Cognitive Neuropsychology, 14,* 511–545.

Vaidya, C., Gabrieli, J. D. E., Keane, M. M., Monti, L. A., Gutierrez Rivas, H., & Zarella, M. M. (1997). Evidence for multiple mechanisms of conceptual priming on implicit memory tests. *Journal of Experimental Psychology: Learning, Memory, and Cognition, 23,* 1324–1343.

Wagenmakers, E. J. M., Zeelenberg, R., & Raaijmakers, J. G. W. (2000). Testing the counter model for perceptual identification: Effects of repetition priming and word frequency. *Psychonomic Bulletin & Review, 7,* 662–667.

Warrington, E. K., & Weiskrantz, L. (1968). New method of testing long-term retention with special reference to amnesic patients. *Nature, 217,* 972–974.

Weldon, M. S. (1991). Mechanisms underlying priming on perceptual tests. *Journal of Experimental Psychology: Learning, Memory, and Cognition, 17,* 526–541.

Zelinsky, G. J., & Murphy, G. L. (2000). Synchronizing visual and language processing: An effect of object name length on eye movements. *Psychological Science, 11,* 125–131.

CHAPTER 17

Episodic and Autobiographical Memory

HENRY L. ROEDIGER III AND ELIZABETH J. MARSH

The aim of this chapter is to discuss research on topics of episodic and autobiographical memory. Some researchers have treated these terms as synonyms and written about "episodic or autobiographical memory." Although the concepts are related, we believe there are good reasons to treat them separately because they refer to different psychological constructs, researchers investigating them work in distinct traditions with different techniques, and unique issues of interest arise in these separate (if overlapping) fields of inquiry. Whole books have been written about these topics (e.g., Conway, 1990; Tulving, 1983), so our treatment here will perforce hit only some high points in these areas of inquiry.

Episodic memory was originally defined as memory for events; in retrieval of information from episodic memory the time and place of occurrence of the event must be specified (Tulving, 1972). The query *What did you do on your vacation last summer?* requests information about an episode from life. The request *Recall the pictures and words that I showed you yesterday in the lab* is a laboratory task requiring episodic memory. When Endel Tulving proposed the concept of episodic memory in 1972, he argued that most laboratory tasks that psychologists had used over the past century to study memory could be classified as requiring episodic memory. (We consider these tasks shortly). In 1972, the primary contrast with episodic memory was *semantic memory,* the general store of knowledge that a person has (Tulving, 1972). The definition of the word *elephant,* the meaning of H_2O, the name of the third U.S. president, and myriad other facts are all components of semantic memory. One need not recall the time and place in which these facts or concepts were learned to answer queries asking for this knowledge—hence the notion that these are general or generic memories.

The study of episodic memory has typically occurred in laboratory studies of human memory, but this statement is also true of formal studies of semantic memory. In the past 15–20 years, the concept of episodic memory has not only been treated as a psychological construct useful for heuristic and descriptive purposes, but has been used to refer to a specialized mind-brain system (see Tulving, 2002, and Wheeler, 2000, for recent treatments of the concept). Tulving (2002) provides a compelling case for episodic memory as representing a unique mind-brain system that is (probably) unique to humans and that permits us to travel backward mentally in time to re-experience earlier events through remembering. The system also permits us to think about possible future scenarios and to think about and plan our futures, a capacity that may again be unique to humans and that may have helped pave the way for humans to have developed complex civilizations unlike those of any other animal (Tulving, 1999, 2000). For purposes of this chapter, we concentrate on the more traditional study of episodic memory in laboratory situations.

Writing of this chapter was supported by Grant RO1 AG17481-01A1 from the National Institutes of Aging to the first author, and by an NRSA postdoctoral fellowship from the National Institute of Mental Health, No. 1F32MH12567, to the second author.

Autobiographical memory refers to one's personal history. Memories of one's 5th-grade experiences, of learning to ride a bicycle, of friends one had in college, or of one's grandparents are all autobiographical memories. So, too, are memories of last summer's vacation or of pictures and words presented yesterday in an experiment, which we used as examples of episodic memory (see Conway, 2001, for a discussion of the relation between autobiographical and episodic memory). Therefore, we can think of autobiographical memory as encompassing information from both episodic and semantic memory. It is the knowledge of oneself and the memories surrounding this self-knowledge. We all know what city we were born in and on what date, so these facts are part of autobiographical memory; but we cannot remember the event itself, so it is not part of episodic memory. Autobiographical memories can also represent other types of information, such as *procedural learning* (knowing that we know how to drive, to play tennis, and so on). Therefore, unlike episodic memory, the study of autobiographical memory is not directed to a specific neurocognitive system but to consideration of many different types of memory that are all directed to the self.

Stages in Learning and Memory: Encoding, Storage, and Retrieval

All episodes of remembering involve successful completion of three stages. This is true of both episodic and autobiographical memory. Information must be acquired or encoded, it must be retained across time in the nervous system, and it must be retrieved when needed. These phases are referred to as *encoding* (or *acquisition*), *storage,* and *retrieval* (Melton, 1963). Imagine the situation in which subjects are presented with information to be learned (for example, a list of 50 unrelated words, presented at a rate of 5 s per word) and then are tested 24 hrs later. Subjects receive a blank sheet of paper with the instruction to "recall as many words as possible that were presented yesterday, in any order, without guessing" (a *free recall* test). Let us assume a subject recalled 16 words (thereby forgetting 34). For all items recalled, we can be assured that the encoding, storage, and retrieval phases were successful (if we ignore success by sheer guessing, which is unlikely in recall of unrelated words). Yet, what about the forgotten words? Is there a way to pinpoint at what stage or stages the breakdown occurred?

Let us consider the possibilities. First, perhaps the words were not encoded in the first place. Perhaps the subject closed his or her eyes for 10 s and missed two words entirely. The words were then never encoded. However, in most memory experiments, this cause of poor performance is unlikely because researchers take care to present information under optimal conditions. Still, with fast rates of presentation or a high level of distraction, encoding of information might be minimal. (Ordinarily, we would not refer to someone as forgetting information if the information was never encoded. Encoding is a necessary condition for a later failure to be deemed *forgetting.*)

Encoding essentially refers to accurate perception in the most minimal case. The process of encoding changes the nervous system; every experience one has leaves the nervous system in a different state than before the experience. This change in the nervous system as a function of experience can be referred to as *creation of memory traces*. According to research and theorizing in modern neuroscience, memory traces should not be conceived as tiny packets of neural information stored in discrete locations somewhere in the brain, but rather as an interacting distribution of neural circuits used for registering the events. When the mind-brain system is given a query (e.g., *What were those words you studied yesterday?*), retrieval processes somehow gain access to stored information—the memory traces—and convert (some of it) to forms that can be consciously recalled. Exactly how any of these three processes—encoding, storage, and retrieval—operate is an open question, not yet well explained in either psychological or neural terms. Psychologists and neuroscientists have many theories but there are no definite answers.

Often it is difficult or impossible to separate encoding, storage, and retrieval processes (Watkins, 1990; Roediger & Guynn, 1996). Consider again the 34 words forgotten by our hypothetical subject. Even assuming they were all accurately perceived, how can we know whether their forgetting owes to failures in encoding, in storage, or in retrieval? Here are some possibilities. The words might have been encoded briefly (held in a short-term store or state) but not encoded more permanently. We have all had the experience of looking up a telephone number, being momentarily distracted, and then having no inkling of the number by the time we get to the telephone. Perhaps this experience can be ascribed to a failure of transfer from a short-term to long-term state (see the chapter by Nairne in this volume).

Alternatively, the experience may be stored, but the distributed trace is fragile and has become disorganized or decayed over the 24 hrs; that is, it is "lost" from storage. A further possibility is that the trace is perfectly intact after 24 hrs, but cannot be used or retrieved. Evidence for this last possibility can be obtained by treatments that permit recovery of the seemingly forgotten information. For example, a further test for the 34 forgotten words on a recognition test or another test that used strong retrieval cues might show that people can remember many of the "forgotten" words when tested under better conditions (Tulving & Pearlstone, 1966). That is, many experiments reveal a distinction between information that is available (stored) in memory and information that is accessible (retrievable under a certain set of conditions). Psychologists would like to have measures that faithfully assess availability of information. However, no measure is a faithful measure of information or trace availability. Rather, any test shows only what information is accessible under a particular set of retrieval conditions (Tulving & Pearlstone, 1966; Weiner, 1966).

Although it is difficult to provide a clean separation among encoding, storage, and retrieval processes, making these distinctions is still of critical importance to keep us aware of what kinds of conclusions may be permitted by our experimental procedures. The example we have used, that of remembering a list of words, is an example of an episodic memory task. We could have used a similar example from autobiographical memory. For example, imagine the situation in which a professor insists that he or she told student A about a paper's due date, whereas the student claims to have no memory for this event. Assuming that the event did actually occur (perhaps student B witnessed the event), why does student A fail to remember the event? Perhaps student A was asleep during class or not listening to the professor during the lecture; the due date was then never encoded. Perhaps student A heard the assignment but was then distracted by a joke from a classmate, and thus the due date was not stored more permanently. Alternatively, student A might remember the interaction with the proper retrieval cues, such as a classmate's prompting him or her with other details that were related by the professor at the same time.

In actual practice, experiments on memory may involve manipulations during one or more of four stages in a typical experiment, as shown in Figure 17.1. In order to understand both episodic and autobiographical memory, we need to consider factors (a) prior to the events or episodes to be remembered; (b) during presentation (encoding); (c) during the retention interval between presentation (encoding) and testing (retrieval); and (d) during the test itself. In the following sections, we consider variables operating during these four periods or phases in the learning and memory process. We briefly deal with each phase in turn, beginning with the consideration of some typical manipulations that should illustrate

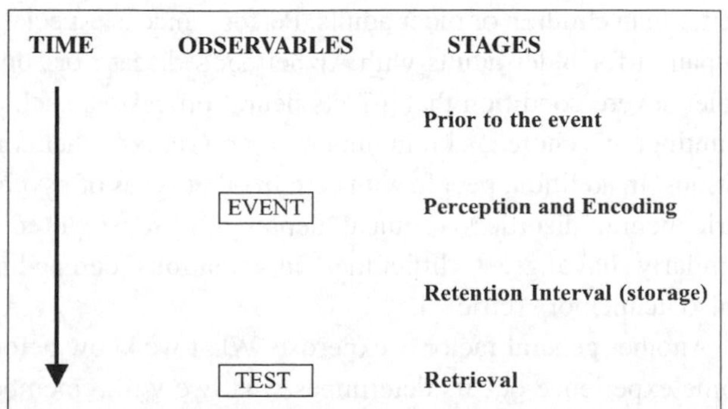

Figure 17.1 The four stages of the learning-memory process that are relevant to understanding how an event is remembered.

issues and problems in the laboratory study of episodic memory. We then do the same for the experimental study of autobiographical memory. The issues overlap, but the standard techniques for study are typically quite different. Ideally, these two research traditions should overlap and inform one another. They should not be seen as being in conflict.

EPISODIC MEMORY

As noted before, *episodic memory* refers to memory for events, and in order to retrieve such memories the time and place of occurrence of the events must be specified (explicitly or implicitly) in the retrieval query (Tulving, 1972). Many of the laboratory techniques developed by psychologists over the years—recall of stories, or pictures, or words learned in the lab—primarily test episodic memory (although some aspect of performance on these tests may reflect the contribution of other memory systems, too). The following nine tasks can all be classified as episodic memory tasks because they require subjects to think back to the time of occurrence of the events in question (Tulving, 1993). (The place is usually given as "in the lab where you are," but outside the lab the place may need to be specified, too).

1. *Free recall.* The person is exposed to a set of words, pictures, or other material and is asked to recall them in any order after a brief delay with no retrieval cues. If the words or pictures are seen once, the test is called *single-trial free recall.* In a variant, the words or pictures can be presented repeatedly (often in a new random order each time) with a test after each presentation trial. Then the task is *multiple-trial ("multitrial") free recall.*
2. *Serial recall.* The person is given a series of digits, words, or pictures and is asked to recall them in the order of occurrence. Variations might include giving one item from the series and asking for the item that appeared before or after it. Either single- or multiple-trial procedures can be used.
3. *Paired-associate recall.* The person learns pairs of items that might be related (e.g., *giraffe-lion*) or unrelated (*tightrope-pickpocket*), and is later given one of the items (e.g., *tightrope-*_____) and is asked to recall the other item. This task measures formation of associations. Again, single- and multiple-trial procedures can be used.
4. *Cued recall.* The person is given a series of words, pictures, or sentences and is then given a cue (often something not presented) and asked to recall a related event from the series. If the person studied sentences such as *The fish attacked the swimmer,* the word *shark* might be given as a cue. Paired-associate learning is a type of cued recall task with the cue item being *intralist,* or coming

from within the list itself. There are many variations on this theme in studies of cued recall.

5. *Recognition.* These tests, as the name implies, require the person to decide whether he or she recognizes an item as being from the studied set. In a typical laboratory paradigm, the subject might study a list of 100 words (under various conditions) and then be given a test with 200 words, half studied and half not studied. The task is to select the previously studied words. If a subject sees the words one at a time, the subject judges whether each one was studied and responds *yes* or *no*. This is called a *free-choice* or *yes-no recognition test.* If a subject is tested with pairs of words, one old and one new, he or she must pick the word that was studied. This is called a *forced-choice recognition test.* Free- and forced-choice recognition tests resemble true-false and multiple choice tests used in educational assessment. Another variation is the *continuous recognition test,* in which a long list of items (words, faces, pictures, etc.) is shown and the subject's task is to judge each item as already seen (*yes*, or old) or not seen (*no,* or new) in the series.
6. *Absolute frequency judgment tasks.* The subject studies items such as words or pictures various numbers of times (say, one to eight times). At test the subject is given the item and has to judge how many times he or she studied it. The task can also be converted for relative frequency judgments. Two pictures can be given during the test, and the subject must judge which one was presented more frequently during the study phase.
7. *Relative recency judgments.* The subject studies items and then is given two and asked which one occurred earlier (or later) in the series. This task captures subjects' estimates of the distance of events in time.
8. *Source judgments.* To-be-remembered information is presented to the subject from a variety of sources (say, spoken or written words, or if all items are spoken, by a male or a female voice). At test the subject is given each item and asked to identify the source—spoken or written? Male or female?
9. *Metamemory judgments.* People can be asked to give other kinds of ratings that are thought to reflect features of episodic memory. Confidence judgments ask for ratings (on, say, a 7-point scale) as to how confident a person is about whether an event occurred, with 7 representing *certain it did* and 1 *certain it did not*. People can also be asked, for items they recall or recognize, to judge whether they remember the moment of occurrence of the item or rather know only that it was presented but cannot remember the moment of actual occurrence (Tulving, 1985). These kinds of remember-know judgments have been extensively studied (e.g., Gardiner & Richardson-Klavehn, 2000) because remember judgments are thought to reflect a pure manifestation of episodic memory: People can mentally travel back in time and re-experience the past (Rajaram, 1993). People can also be asked to evaluate more specifically the sensory, emotional, and contextual characteristics of their retrieved memories (e.g., by using the Memory Characteristics Questionnaire developed by Johnson, Foley, Suengas, & Raye, 1988).

All these tests (and others) tap some aspect of episodic memory by requiring subjects to retrieve from specific times in the past. However, not all performance on the episodic (or explicit) memory tests just listed necessarily reflects "pure" manifestations of episodic memory, because performance from relatively automatic (Jacoby, 1991) or noetic (knowing) states of awareness (Tulving, 1985) might also affect performance, especially on tests with strong retrieval cues. The remember-know judgment task is one way of obtaining a measure that is thought to reflect more purely episodic memory (Tulving, 1985; Gardiner, 1988). Jacoby (1991; Jacoby, Toth, & Yonelinas, 1993) has also developed a procedure for separating conscious recollection from more automatic, nonconscious uses of memory.

The concept of episodic memory has changed over the years since Tulving (1972) first proposed it, but it remains a central organizing concept in cognitive psychology and cognitive neuroscience (see Tulving, 1999, 2000, 2002, for recent treatments). We turn now to discussing some of the research on episodic memory, using the four-stage framework described earlier.

Factors Prior to Encoding of Events

It might seem odd to begin our analysis of how one remembers events with factors that occur before the events in question have occurred. However, these a priori variables are critical determinants of remembering in most situations. First, there are characteristics of the individual rememberer to consider. In general, on episodic memory tests young adults perform better than children or older adults. Performance is especially impaired for older adults with Alzheimer's disease or some other severe condition that affects neural processes, such as Huntington's chorea, a brain tumor, or a myriad of other conditions. In addition, people with certain other types of psychiatric neural disorders (clinical depression, schizophrenia) similarly have great difficulties in situations demanding episodic memory retrieval.

Another general factor is expertise. What we know before some experience occurs determines what we will remember after it. If you know a tremendous amount about baseball and a friend going to a game with you knows nothing, you would both look at the same game—but you would encode and remember it very differently than your friend would. In general, the more expert a person is about a topic domain, the more he or she will remember about an experience in that domain. However, not all prior experiences have positive effects on later memory for events. There can also be *proactive interference,* wherein prior events and activities have interfering effects later on memory for new events. We will consider such proactive interference effects later in the chapter.

Encoding of Events

There is no clear distinction between perception and memory. The perception of an event from the outside world, even such a simple one as seeing a word or picture presented in a list, is extended in time. In many experiments on perception, a stimulus is presented and the researcher asks (essentially) "What did you see?" In memory experiments, the researcher typically shows a larger set of material and asks "What do you remember?" If *kangaroo* is the 15th word presented in a list, however, and immediately after its presentation the procedure is stopped and the experimenter asks for recall of the last word, is the experimenter testing perception or memory? The two processes shade into one another, and the fact that our sensory systems have brief "memories" associated with their operation further clouds any sharp border between perceiving and remembering. (*Iconic memory* is the sensory store for vision and *echoic memory* for audition; see Crowder & Surprenant, 2000, and the chapter by Nairne in this volume.)

Perception is normally thought to be a prerequisite for remembering events. However, the occurrence of false memories shows that this is not necessarily the case, because people can have the full-blown experience of recalling, recognizing, and "remembering" (in the sense of making a "remember" judgment) for events that never happened (Roediger & McDermott, 1995). False memories represent the extreme; but in general, what is encoded does not match exactly what is available for perception. A critically important concept for understanding encoding processes is the distinction between nominal and functional stimuli (Underwood, 1963). The *nominal stimulus* is the event as it happened in the world—all the physical features that might be counted and measured. Imagine walking into a large room containing several people and many objects; the full scene is the nominal stimulus. The *functional stimulus* is that part of the scene to which the individual attends and encodes; these features will be only a subset of the huge number of features and details that could be potentially encoded. Underwood (1963) pointed out that for the understanding of learning and memory it is the functional stimulus that is critical, not the nominal stimulus. That is, when we consider what may be remembered, it is usually the case that an individual will potentially remember only what was originally encoded (if we ignore, for the moment the case of false memories just discussed). Although any situation in the world affords a huge variety of potential features that may be encoded, only a subset will typically be encoded, and this selection during encoding is critical to remembering.

Recoding is a second critical concept for understanding encoding processes; this refers to the conversion of the nominal stimulus of the world into the functional stimulus that can be potentially remembered (Miller, 1956). Miller pointed out that people typically recode information from the world into a form that the cognitive system can more easily handle, and that in fact, for enhancing memory, recoding is often a critical step. (All mnemonic or memory improvement systems provide the rememberer with effective recoding techniques.) Suppose you give a group of people the task of remembering the following 15 digits in order. Try it yourself; read the following series one time aloud and then look away from the book and try to repeat it: 1, 4, 9, 1, 6, 2, 5, 3, 6, 4, 9, 6, 4, 8, 1. Most people get 6 or 7 digits correct when they do try this task, but some people get all 15. That seems impossible to naive listeners (such as bright undergraduates in classes in which we have tried this task). Why do some find it trivially easy and others find it impossible?

The answer to this puzzle is *recoding*. The 15 numbers are the squares of the numbers 1 to 9 ($1 \times 1 = 1$, $2 \times 2 = 4$, $3 \times 3 = 9, \ldots. 9 \times 9 = 81$). If one notices this rule during presentation of the digits (or is told beforehand), then the task becomes trivially easy because the numbers can be easily encoded. If not, and the person tries to remember the sequence like a rote telephone number, then it is impossible.

Consider another example of how past experience and knowledge can lead different people to encode the same scene in quite different ways, with important consequences for later memory. Bartlett relied on

> the old and familiar illustration of the landscape artist, the naturalist, and the geologist who walk in the country together. The one is said to notice the beauty of the scenery, the other details of flora and fauna, and the third the formation of soils and rock. In this case, no doubt, the stimuli, being selected in each instance from what is present, are different for each observer, and obviously the records made in recall are different also. (1932, p. 4)

Again, the same nominal stimulus is recoded in different ways so that the functional stimulus later available to be remembered would be quite different for the three individuals.

The literature on episodic memory is replete with more formal experiments documenting the power of recoding. One of the most famous, and justifiably so, comes from a voluminous literature on the levels of processing effect. Craik and

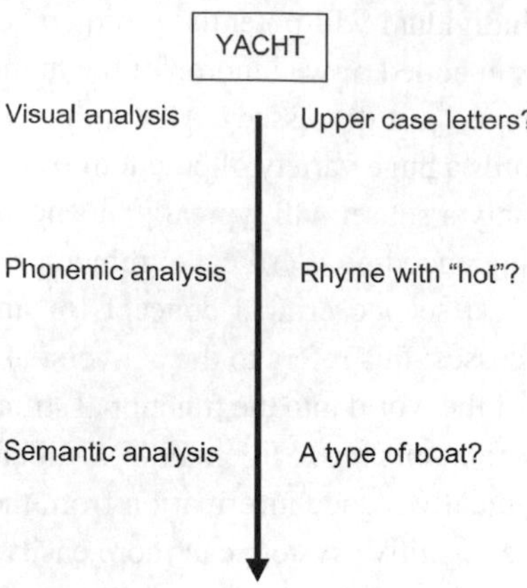

Figure 17.2 The levels-of-processing (LOP) procedure.

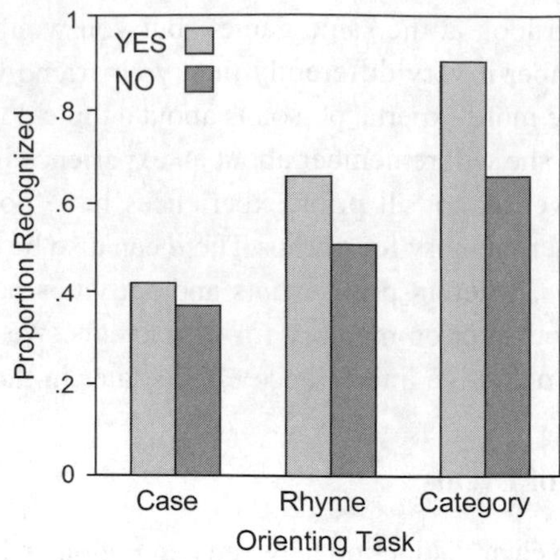

Figure 17.3 The levels-of-processing (LOP) effect. Mean proportion of words recognized as a function of orienting task and type of response to the question (*yes* or *no*). Adapted from Craik and Tulving (1975, Experiment 9B).

Lockhart (1972) proposed that encoding occurred as a byproduct of perception and that perception occurred in a series of stages. For verbal materials, they proposed that people process words through at least three stages: analysis of visual or orthographic features, analysis of the phonemic (sound) properties of words, and analysis of meaning (or semantics) of the words. This set of stages can be considered as occurring to different levels or depths, with *visual features* at the top and *meaning* at the bottom (see the left side of Figure 17.2).

Craik and Tulving (1975) provided an experimental technique for studying the levels of processing approach. People are asked questions before they see words, and the questions are meant to direct attention to a particular level of analysis. For example, for the target word *BEAR,* the questions might be "Is the word in uppercase letters?" or "Does the word rhyme with *CHAIR*?" or "Does the word name an animal?" In each case the answer is *yes,* but the first question directs subjects to a shallow (visual) level of processing of the word, the second question to an intermediate phonemic level, and the third question to a deep, semantic level of analysis. In the actual experiments, Craik and Tulving used many words and questions; half the time the correct answer was *yes* and half the time it was *no,* so subjects had to process the questions and words carefully.

Later, subjects were given a recognition test on which the studied words were intermixed with other, similar words, and the subjects' task was to examine each word and decide whether it had been seen in the earlier (encoding) phase of the experiment. In this particular recognition test, chance performance was 33%. The results are depicted in Figure 17.3 and show a powerful effect of this levels-of-processing manipulation. When people examined the word to answer a question about its visual appearance, performance was barely better than chance. When they answered a question about its meaning, performance was nearly perfect (at least when the answer was *yes*). Therefore, levels of processing strongly determined level of recognition, an outcome that has been replicated many times. The fact that the effect was much stronger for the positive (*yes*) answers than for negative (*no*) answers was not predicted by the levels of processing framework, although it might be explainable by using related concepts such as congruity of the recognition test item with the way the information was encoded for deeply processed questions. For example, if the test word is *bear,* the subject might think "Was I asked about the category of animals?" to help make a decision. If the response were *yes,* this tactic would help, but if *BEAR* had been studied with the question "Does the word name a type of furniture?" then the tactic would fail to aid retrieval of *BEAR*. Although the study of these levels-of-processing effects has continued for more than 30 years, there are still unanswered questions about why the effects arise (Roediger & Gallo, 2002).

The general point for present purposes is that the levels-of-processing effect demonstrates the power of recoding. In all three conditions of the experiment the nominal stimulus is the same—single words presented at slow rates. The question causes the words to be recoded differently, with some types of processing providing for much better recognition than others. Many variables known to affect memory are held constant—the materials used, the knowledge that a test would be given, the individuals tested, and so on. The questions were even all easy ones that could be answered in a fraction of a second. Nonetheless, this split-second difference in encoding of the words created huge differences in recognition.

Many other variables manipulated during encoding phases of experiments have been shown to affect episodic memory performance across a range of tests. Active involvement in learning, such as generating information rather than reading it, promotes retention (Jacoby, 1978; Slamecka & Graf, 1978). This *generation effect,* as it is called, occurs even under conditions in which the generation seems trivially easy. Jacoby (1978) had people either read word pairs (*foot-shoe*) or generate the second word from a word fragment (*foot-s_ _ e*). The fragments were easy (because the words were related) and so the target word could almost always be easily generated. At test subjects were given the first word and asked to respond with the paired word. When subjects had generated the second word they remembered it much better than when they had only read it, even though the generation process involved little effort. Slamecka and Graf (1978) produced similar results in a somewhat different paradigm. Again, this generation effect can disappear under certain conditions, but it has fairly wide generality, especially when the same subjects both read and generate information (that is, when the variable is manipulated within subjects; see Begg, Snider, Foley, & Goddard, 1989; McDaniel, Waddill, & Einstein, 1988; Slamecka & Katsaiti, 1987).

A third variable that reliably affects episodic memory tasks is repetition. In general, and not surprisingly, repeated items are better remembered than items presented only once (the *repetition effect;* see Crowder, 1976, chapter 6). However, less intuitively, the spacing of repetitions matters. *Massed* repetition refers to the situation in which an event is studied twice in succession, whereas *spaced* repetition refers to the case in which time and intervening items occur between repetitions. For tests of long-term retention, spaced presentation almost always leads to better retention than does massed presentation, and, up to some limit, the greater the lag or spacing between two presentations, the better the retention (e.g., Melton, 1970; Dempster, 1988). This *spacing* or *lag effect,* as it is called, occurs on practically all tests and under most conditions. Interestingly, one exception occurs when a test occurs very quickly after the second of two presentations; under that condition, massed presentation leads to better retention than spaced presentation (e.g., Balota, Duchek, & Paullin, 1989).

Fourth, concrete materials generally produce better retention on episodic memory tests than do abstract materials. For example, pictures are better recalled than words (the names of the pictures), a finding which is called the *picture superiority effect* (Paivio & Csapo, 1973; Paivio, Rogers, & Smythe, 1968). Also, words that refer to concrete objects (*umbrella, fingernail*) are better retained than abstract words (*democracy, ambition*) matched on such qualities as word length, part of speech, and frequency of occurrence in the language (Paivio, Yuille, & Rogers, 1969). The same holds true for prose materials (Paivio & Begg, 1971). To generalize, speakers and professors who can explain an abstract theory (e.g., the kinetic theory of gases) by using a concrete analogy or metaphor (molecules of gas behaving like billiard balls on a pool table) can often make their subject matter easier to understand and more memorable. Using imagery is one of the oldest techniques for improving memory, known since the days of the Greeks and Romans, and it relies on the same principle now as then: The mind generally grasps and remembers concrete concepts better than abstract ones.

Finally, distinctive items are generally better remembered on episodic memory tests than is one event in a more or less uniform series (e.g., Hunt, 1995; Hunt & McDaniel, 1993). For example, a picture embedded in a list of words should be better remembered than the same picture embedded in a series of pictures. *Distinctiveness* has been used to explain superior memory for such items as bizarre sentences (McDaniel, Dunay, Lyman, & Kerwin, 1988), unusual faces (Light, Kayra-Stuart, & Hollander, 1979), atypical category members (Schmidt, 1985), and words with unusual orthographies (Hunt & Elliot, 1980). Distinctiveness may increase attention to and processing of an item at study. Distinctive items also provide excellent retrieval cues because no other memories are associated with them; if one picture is embedded in a long list of words, the cue *picture in the list* provokes only one item whereas the cue *word in the list* would lead to many items. Distinctiveness may underlie some of the effects we have already discussed. For example, the better memory associated with pictures and concrete objects may be due to the distinctiveness of their encoding. Similarly, deeper, semantic processing of words leads to more distinctive encoding and retrieval cues than does more shallow phonological or orthographic processing.

The various effects just discussed—the levels-of-processing effect, the generation effect, the picture superiority effect, the spacing (or lag) effect, and the distinctiveness effect—represent merely a sample of important variables that can affect episodic memory performance during encoding or study. However, the fact that these variables are manipulated during learning does not mean they affect only the encoding of memories. As demonstrated in our discussion of why one picture studied amid many words may be well remembered, retrieval processes are critically important in the study of episodic memory. We consider retrieval more fully later in this chapter, but the point here is that many manipulations during the encoding phase of the experiment may have their effects as much during retrieval as during encoding.

Retention of Events

Manipulations occurring between encoding of events and their later test can greatly affect memory, either positively or negatively. After experiences are first encoded, a consolidation process occurs that is extended in time. This process has been known for more than a hundred years and is gradually becoming better understood (see McGaugh & Gold, 1992, for an overview). *Consolidation* refers to the fact that neural processes apparently must persevere for some period of time to permit memories to progress from a labile (easily forgotten) state to one that is more permanent. If a person or animal has an injury to the brain (a concussion) shortly after some experience, forgetting of that experience often occurs. The forgetting of experiences from before the concussive event is called *retrograde amnesia;* the forgetting of events happening after the concussion is called *anterograde amnesia.* The fact of retrograde amnesia implicates a consolidation process: Even though the events in question have already occurred, the brain injury causes their forgetting. Furthermore, retrograde amnesia occurs in a graded fashion, such that events immediately before the injury are remembered less well than older memories. After a period of time following the injury, memories will sometimes gradually recover. However, for severe injuries, the events that occurred just before the concussion usually are never recovered.

Purely psychological manipulations during the retention interval can affect performance on later memory tests. We discuss here only three of the variables that come into play during the retention interval: the passage of time, the rehearsal of to-be-remembered items, and exposure to potentially interfering materials.

Perhaps the most easily manipulated factor that affects retention is simply the passage of *time*. All other things being equal, the longer a test is delayed after encoding, the worse is retention of some experience. Ebbinghaus (1885/1913) discovered this fact in the first experiments on long-term retention, and it has been demonstrated hundreds of times since then. In general, forgetting is rapid at first and then becomes more gradual over time. Of course, "time" per se does not cause forgetting, and most researchers pinpoint some sort of interference as the cause of the forgetting observed over time (McGeoch, 1932; Underwood, 1957). As time passes, people are exposed to more and more information that may impair or interfere with their ability to remember the original target events. We will discuss these kinds of interference effects later in this section.

Repeated covert retrieval of information (*rehearsal*) can increase memory for the retrieved event, but its effectiveness depends on the timing and spacing of rehearsals. The same laws seem to govern rehearsal and the actual repeated presentation of material. That is, massed rehearsals (like massed presentations) have either no effect or a small positive effect on most memory tests. Spaced rehearsals are much more effective in improving recall and recognition. Landauer and Bjork (1978) compared a variety of rehearsal schemes and showed that an expanding retrieval schedule is most effective. For example, if a person were trying to learn the name of a new person, it would be best to rehearse the name just after hearing it to make sure it is encoded. Then the person should wait a slightly longer period and try to rehearse the name again; the third covert retrieval would then be prompted after a somewhat longer interval, and so on, until the new name could easily be retrieved when the face is seen. Of course, in practice, remembering to continue covert retrieval can be a problem, but this expanding retrieval practice has been shown to be quite effective in new learning.

Activities during the retention interval can create interference for learned information. When events that follow some critical event of interest inhibit recall of these critical events, the name applied is *retroactive interference*. Retroactive interference is contrasted with proactive interference (the interfering effects of prior learning on events learned later). Figure 17.4 shows the standard experimental designs for studying proactive and retroactive interference. The minimal conditions for studying retroactive interference are shown at the top; two groups of subjects learn identical material, and then later one group learns a different set of material that may interfere with the original learning. Subjects in the control condition either learn irrelevant items or simply perform a distractor task for the same amount of time. In a typical interference experiment, subjects might learn pairs of words (e.g., *dogwood-giraffe*) in the first phase, and in the second phase of the experimental condition they would learn competing associations (e.g., *dogwood-rhinoceros*). The control group would either perform a distractor task during the second

Retroactive Interference

	Target List	Interference List	Test
Experimental	A-B	A-D	A-B
Control	A-B	rest or learn C-D	A-B

Proactive Interference

	Interference List	Target List	Test
Experimental	A-D	A-B	A-B
Control	rest or learn C-D	A-B	A-B

Figure 17.4 The standard experimental designs for studying retroactive and proactive interference.

phase of the experiment or learn completely unrelated pairs (*record-basketball*). All subjects would then take a memory test that provided the stimulus (left-hand) member of the first pair (*dogwood-*____), and the task would be to recall the paired item (*giraffe*). However, subjects who learned the interfering association (*dogwood-rhinoceros*) would perform worse than subjects in the control condition. Such retroactive interference shows damage created by new learning during the retention interval.

Retroactive interference can change one's memory, often without one's awareness. Loftus, Miller, and Burns (1978) showed this effect in experiments meant to simulate the conditions of an eyewitness to a crime. Students saw a traffic accident in which a car came to an intersection where it should have paused to let another car pass. However, the car proceeded into the intersection and hit another car. Depending on the condition, subjects saw either a stop sign or a yield sign at the intersection. Let us take the case of subjects who saw the stop sign. During a later series of questions the students were asked questions in which the sign was referred to as a *stop sign* (the consistent-information condition), a *yield sign* (the misleading-information condition), or a traffic sign (the neutral-information condition). The question of interest was whether the verbally presented misleading information would be incorporated into the scene and cause the students to misremember the nature of the sign. The students were tested on a forced-choice recognition test in which they were given two scenes (one with a stop sign and the other with a yield sign) and were asked which one had been in the original slides. The results are shown in Figure 17.5, where it can be seen that (relative to the neutral condition) the presentation of consistent information augmented recognition of the

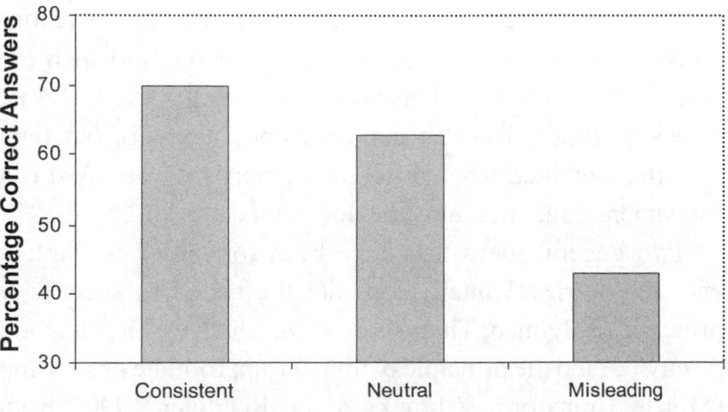

Figure 17.5 The eyewitness suggestibility effect. Exposure to the correct answer during the retention interval increased subjects' ability to answer the critical question at test. However, exposure to misinformation during the retention interval reduced correct answers at test. Adapted from Loftus, Miller, and Burns (1978).

correct sign, but the misleading information decreased correct recognition. This misleading-information effect is a type of retroactive interference and shows how malleable our memories can be (see Ayers & Reder, 1998, for a review of work on this topic).

This section has sampled some manipulations during the retention interval that can have powerful effects on memory. Proper consolidation and repeated covert retrieval can enhance memories, whereas a blow to the head or presentation of interfering material can cause forgetting, making material more difficult to retrieve. We turn now to the retrieval process.

Retrieval Factors

A common experience is to forget some bit of information—the name of an acquaintance, where you left your keys—and then suddenly retrieve the information later. Sometimes the recovered memory seems to occur spontaneously, but in other cases it is prompted by cues. Such recovered memories show that forgetting is not necessarily due to loss of information from memory—degraded memory traces or the like—but rather that the information was available in memory (stored), but not accessible (retrievable) (Tulving & Pearlstone, 1966). Psychologists may wish for a perfect measure of what is stored in memory, but they will never have one; all measures reveal only the information accessible under a particular set of conditions. The study of retrieval processes is therefore a key to understanding episodic memory (Roediger & Guynn, 1996; Roediger, 2000; Tulving, 1974).

One surprising fact of retrieval is that giving the same test repeatedly can increase recall. For example, if subjects study a list of 60 pictures and are given a free recall test on it, they might recall about 25 items. (Subjects usually are asked to recall names of the pictures, if they are simple line drawings.) If a few minutes go by and the subjects are given the same test again, they typically recall more pictures (despite the increased delay until the second test). If a third test is given, recall will increase even more (Erdelyi & Becker, 1974). On each successive test, subjects will forget some pictures from the previous test, but they will also recover pictures on the second test that were not recalled on the first test. This recovery of items is called *reminiscence,* and when the number of items recovered outweighs the number forgotten, to produce an overall increase between tests, the effect is called *hypermnesia*. This hypermnestic effect can continue to expand over a week since original study of material (Erdelyi & Kleinbard, 1978). The phenomenon of hypermnesia is not well understood theoretically, but shows that retrieval phenomena can be quite variable (especially on tests of free recall). Humans seem to have a limited retrieval capacity at any one point in time, so that recall of some items seems to limit other memories from being recalled (Tulving, 1967; Roediger, 1978).

Although repeated attempts at retrieval will usually permit memories to be recovered, providing appropriate retrieval cues can sometimes greatly increase the remembering of past events relative to free recall (Tulving & Pearlstone, 1966; Roediger & Guynn, 1996). The *encoding specificity hypothesis* (or principle) is the basic idea used to guide research in this area. The basic assumption has been discussed already: When an event is encoded, only some of the features in the complex nominal stimulus become functionally encoded. The encoding specificity hypothesis states that, all other things being equal, the more completely features encoded from a retrieval cue overlap (or match) those in the encoded trace, the greater the probability the cue will revive one's memory of the original event. So, for example, if the words *giraffe, elephant, rhinoceros, chimpanzee,* and *lion* were placed in a long list of words, they would be more likely to be recalled if subjects were given the cue *animals* during the test than under conditions of free recall. If subjects were given the cue *African animals,* recall of the words might be even greater. Considerable evidence is consistent with the encoding specificity principle (Tulving, 1983; Roediger & Guynn, 1996).

Often, recognition tests provide powerful retrieval cues because they provide a copy of the event to be remembered. So, if someone studied *chair* in the middle of a 200-word list, the ability to recall the word might be quite low, but the ability to recognize it might still be relatively good if *chair* were presented on a recognition memory test (along with many other distractors). This fact has led some researchers to assume that recognition tests avoid the problem of retrieval and provide a direct measure of the information that is stored. However, this assumption is incorrect. Although retrieval processes are probably quite different in recognition than in recall, recognition memory still involves more than one type of retrieval process (Mandler, 1980; Jacoby, 1991). In fact, sometimes events can be recalled when they cannot be recognized!

Tulving and Thomson (1973) had subjects study pairs of words in which there was a very weak association between the words, as with the pair *glue-CHAIR,* with instructions to remember the capitalized word. Later, subjects were given a free association test in which they were given words like *table* and asked to produce as many as six associates to the word; of course, they quite often wrote down *chair* as a response. In a third phase of the experiment, the subjects were told to use their responses as a recognition test and to go back through all the words they had written down and circle the ones that they recognized as having occurred in the list. When they did this, they correctly circled 24% of the words they had produced. Finally, Tulving and Thomson (1973) gave their subjects a cued recall test with the original left-hand member of the pair as the cue (*glue-*____). Now the subjects recalled 63% of the words. So, surprisingly, subjects did not remember seeing *chair* when they saw the word itself on the recognition test, but they did remember it when they saw the cue *glue!* Here is a case in which subjects could recall the word to a cue (*glue*) better than they could recognize it when provided with the word itself (*chair*). This finding has been replicated many times with all sorts of variations in the conditions used for the testing. Although it is surprising that recall can be greater than recognition under some conditions, the encoding specificity hypothesis can account for the outcome. When *chair* is encoded in the context of *glue,* a specific set of features about *chair* may be encoded (e.g., how chairs are constructed). When *chair* is generated from *table,* the features activated might be quite different. So the cue *chair* in this case might overlap with the features originally encoded from the original *glue-chair* complex less well than in the case of the cue *glue,* which is just what the data suggest.

This example of the recognition failure of recallable words illustrates that recall and recognition measures may not always agree. Let us give one more example, of how a manipulation may differentially affect a recall versus a recognition test. Typically, words that occur in the language with high frequency are better recalled on a free recall test than words that occur with lower frequency (e.g., Hall, 1954). Thus, we might conclude that high-frequency words simply produce stronger or more durable memory traces than do low-frequency words. However, this simple idea is ruled out by recognition experiments. When high- and low-frequency words are presented and then retention is measured by recognition, low-frequency words are better recognized than are high-frequency words (Kinsbourne & George, 1974; Balota & Neely, 1980). The fact that different patterns of outcome are often obtained when different memory tests are used is a fundamental fact that must be understood.

Two general ideas that have been forwarded to explain encoding-retrieval interactions are the encoding specificity principle (Tulving & Thomson, 1973), which we have already discussed, and the principle of transfer-appropriate processing (Morris, Bransford, & Franks, 1977; Roediger, 1990). Both principles maintain that retention is best when the conditions of retrieval match (complement, overlap, recapitulate) the conditions of learning. The transfer-appropriate processing principle states that experiences during learning transfer to a test to the extent that the test requires appropriate cognitive operations to permit expression of what was learned. Tests may be more or less appropriate to tap the knowledge that was learned.

To explicate this, let us revisit the levels of processing effect shown earlier in Figure 17.3. Subjects were best at recognizing words for which they had made category judgments (a "deep" level of processing), next best at recognizing words judged with the rhyme task, and worst at recognizing words for which they had made case judgments (Craik & Tulving, 1975). In all cases, the dependent measure was proportion of items recognized on a standard recognition test. Morris et al. (1977) made the following criticism: On a recognition test containing many semantically unrelated words, subjects presumably decide whether a word was studied based on its meaning rather than on its sound or its physical appearance; thus the standard recognition test best matches the deep, semantic encoding condition. Would performance in the shallow conditions be improved if the test cues better matched the functional stimulus? In their experiment, subjects read words in sentence frames that were designed to promote either phonemic or semantic encodings. For example, some subjects read the word *eagle* in a phonemic sentence frame such as "_____ rhymes with legal," whereas others read the semantic sentence frame "______ is a large bird." Subjects responded *yes* or *no* to each item; of interest is memory for the *yes* responses. There were two different memory tests; a standard semantic yes-no recognition test, and a rhyme test that required subjects to respond *yes* to test items that rhymed with studied words (e.g., "Say *yes* if you studied a word that rhymed with *beagle*"). On the semantic test, the standard levels-of-processing effect was obtained: Performance was better in the deep semantic condition than in the shallow rhyme condition. However, the pattern reversed on the rhyme test: Performance was better in the rhyme condition than in the semantic. Thus, the type of test qualified the interpretation of the levels of processing effect. The larger point—that the match between encoding conditions and test is critical—is supported by much evidence in episodic memory research (see Roediger & Guynn, 1996, for a review) and may hold across all memory tests (Roediger, 1990).

We have discussed at length how finding the appropriate retrieval cues can benefit memory; we turn now to an example of how retrieval cues may mislead the rememberer. In a demonstration of this point, Loftus and Palmer (1974) showed subjects a video of a traffic accident in which two cars collided. Later, subjects were asked a series of questions about the accident, including "How fast were the two cars going when they *contacted* each other?" Other subjects were asked the same question about speed, but with the verb changed to *hit, bumped, collided,* or *smashed.* This simple manipulation affected subjects' speed estimates; the speed of the cars grew from 32 mph (when *contacted* was the verb) to 41 mph (when *collided* was the verb). The wording of the question changed the way subjects conceptualized the accident, and this changed perspective guided the way subjects reconstructed the accident. This example emphasizes the theme of this section: that how a question is asked (or how a memory is tested) can determine what will be remembered, both correctly and incorrectly.

The study of episodic memory is a huge topic, and we can barely scratch the surface in this section. Tulving's (1983) book, *Elements of Episodic Memory,* is a good starting place for further study of this critical topic. Much of episodic memory research has been laboratory based. A somewhat different tradition of research, but one that is also concerned with personal experiences, goes under the rubric of *autobiographical memory,* to which we turn next.

AUTOBIOGRAPHICAL MEMORY

As noted earlier, the term *autobiographical memory* refers to one's personal history. Memories for one's college graduation, learning to ski, and a friend's e-mail address are all autobiographical to some extent. Some autobiographical memories also meet our definition for episodic memory; for example, memories for one's wedding are indeed easily labeled both *memories for events* and part of *one's personal history*. The critical defining feature for autobiographical memory is the importance of the information to one's sense of self and one's life history. The end result is that autobiographical memory consists of many different types of knowledge, and is not limited to episodes but also includes procedures and facts.

The problem of defining autobiographical memory has been discussed elsewhere in depth (e.g., see Conway, 1990). Brewer (1986) distinguished among personal memories, autobiographical facts, and generic personal memories. *Personal memories,* such as memories of one's college graduation, are described as memories for specific life events accompanied by imagery. These would be episodic memories. *Autobiographical facts,* such as memories for e-mail addresses, are memories for self-relevant facts that are unaccompanied by imagery or spatiotemporal context (much like semantic memories, as defined by Tulving, 1972). Other knowledge, such as knowledge of how to ski, are abstractions of events and unaccompanied by specific images. These could be considered procedural memories, but Brewer refers to them as *generic personal memories*. In this section, we will focus on personal memories, with some attention to generic personal memories.

Historically, psychologists have made surprisingly few attempts to capture autobiographical memory. Galton (1879) first attempted to study personal memories; he retrieved and dated personal memories in response to each of a set of 20 cue words. Other early research included Colegrave's (1899) collection of people's memories for having heard the news of Lincoln's assassination, and Freud's clinical investigations of childhood memories (e.g., see Freud 1917/1982). However, experimental psychologists conducted little research on autobiographical memory until the 1970s, when the pendulum swung in favor of more naturalistic research. The 1970s brought the publication of three important methods and ideas: Linton's (1975) diary study of her own memories for six years of her life; the idea that surprising events imprinted vivid "flashbulb memories" on the brain (R. Brown & Kulik, 1977); and the rediscovery of the Galton word-cuing technique (Crovitz & Schiffman, 1974). Urged on by these results and the changing zeitgeist, experimental psychologists turned to the tricky problem of understanding how people come to hold such vivid memories of their own lives. How does one go about understanding how people remember their own lives, especially when one often has no way of knowing what really happened? Autobiographical memory researchers have developed several paradigms of their own, some of which are adaptations of tasks traditionally used to study episodic memory. To allow for comparison with episodic memory tasks, we list here a few of the methods typically used to study autobiographical memory.

1. *Diary studies.* The subject is asked to record events from his or her own life for some time period, and after a fixed interval is given a test on his or her memories for what actually happened. There are many variables of interest; a few common ones include the time interval between recording and testing, the types of to-be-remembered events, the types of retrieval cues provided at test, and the remembered vividness of the events. Variations on diary studies include using randomly set pagers to cue recording of to-be-remembered events (Brewer, 1988a, 1988b) and having roommates select and record events that may be tested at a later point (Thompson, 1982).
2. *Galton word-cuing technique.* The subject is exposed to a list of words and is asked to retrieve and record a personal life event in response to each word. Sometimes the subject is asked to date these memories, or to rate the remembered events on a number of dimensions such as vividness or emotionality. Often reaction times are collected.
3. *Event cuing technique.* As with the Galton word-cuing technique, the subject is asked to recall life events in response to cues; however, the cues may be for specific events such as memories for an assassination or for the subject's first week of college.
4. *Priming paradigms.* Priming paradigms are also a variation on the Galton word-cuing technique; of interest is whether presentation of a semantic or personal prime word affects the speed with which people can retrieve a personal memory in response to a second word, the target word (e.g., Conway & Berkerian, 1987).
5. *Simulated autobiographical events.* All of the autobiographical memory methods described thus far rely on memories for events that were created outside experimental settings. In order to gain control over to-be-remembered events, some researchers have created autobiographical events in the laboratory. For example, the subject might drink a cup of coffee or meet an Indian woman in the laboratory, and later be asked to remember these episodes (e.g., Suengas & Johnson, 1988).

We turn now to a discussion of the research on autobiographical memory. As much as possible, we will use the same framework as we used for our discussion of episodic memory. We will consider (a) factors prior to the events or episodes to be remembered; (b) factors during the to-be-remembered event (encoding); (c) factors occurring in the interval between the event and later testing; and finally (d) factors operating during the memory retrieval phase.

Factors Prior to Event Occurrence

Given that the to-be-remembered autobiographical events themselves are out of the experimenter's control, it may seem far fetched to worry about factors that occur before those events. Just as with episodic memories, however, there are factors that need to be in place before new autobiographical memories can be formed. Perhaps the most obvious requirement is a fully functioning brain; for example, amnesics can not form new autobiographical memories, and patients with frontal lesions often confabulate or have difficulty retrieving autobiographical memories (e.g., Baddeley & Wilson, 1986; Wilson & Wearing, 1995). Children's brains are still developing, and events experienced prior to the development of language are remembered at lower rates than would be predicted from Ebbinghaus forgetting curves (Nelson, 1993). *Childhood amnesia* is the concept capturing the fact that events from early childhood generally cannot be remembered later in life.

Individual differences affect the way people will encode, store, and retrieve memories. For example, depressed individuals show a bias toward studying and encoding sad materials in laboratory studies, they ruminate on negative thoughts, and they are biased toward retrieving sad life events (see Bower & Forgas, 2000, for a review of the effects of mood on memory). They also tend to recall fewer details of events, relying more on the "gist" (e.g., Moffitt, Singer, Nelligan, & Carlson, 1994). Such effects are not limited to clinical populations—simply being in a bad mood will affect what people remember about their lives (see the chapter by Eich and Forgas in this volume).

More generally speaking, how and whether people remember a target event is affected by prior events. As will be described in the next section, unique events are more likely to be remembered (e.g., Wagenaar, 1986). When evaluating forgotten (nonrecognized) events from her own life, Linton (1982) classified many as the "failure to distinguish" the target event from other similar events in memory. Although eating breakfast may seem salient at the time, a week later it may be difficult to distinguish that breakfast from all the similar breakfasts that preceded it. Corresponding to how studying related material in laboratory experiments increases interference effects (e.g., Underwood, 1957), autobiographical memory is not immune to proactive interference effects.

Factors Relating to Events

When reviewing the episodic memory literature, we discussed how some types of events tend to be well remembered (e.g., the picture superiority effect) and how some types of encoding tasks led to better memory (e.g., the levels-of-processing effect). What are the analogous effects and processes for individuals remembering their own lives? That is, what types of life events are better remembered? What type of processing during life events yields the best event memories? Before answering these questions, let us note that the answers will be based mainly on retrospective and more naturalistic methods. That is, experimenters assess people's memories for life events that occurred prior to entry into the laboratory study, and these life events were not manipulated experimentally.

When determining what types of events are typically best remembered, researchers often rely on diary studies. As noted already, Marigold Linton conducted the first major diary study within the experimental tradition. Beginning in 1972, she spent 6 years recording descriptions, dates, and ratings of 5,500 events from her own life. She tested herself for recognition of a semirandom sample of events each month. Although Linton was primarily interested in her ability to date these personal events (e.g., Linton, 1975), she did preliminary analyses of the characteristics associated with remembered versus forgotten events. She argued that remembered events were salient, emotional, and relatively distinctive, and that there was some tendency for positive events to be better remembered (Linton, 1982).

Both White (1982) and Wagenaar (1986) followed up Linton's results, conducting diary studies aimed more specifically at remembering event details rather than dates. Wagenaar collected 2,400 events over a period of 6 years; he recorded the most salient event each day and coded it with four cues: who, what, when, and where. He also rated the salience (distinctiveness) of the event, as well as its pleasantness and his emotional involvement. White recorded one event per day for a year; he haphazardly selected both salient and nonsalient events. For each event, he recorded a description and chose adjective descriptors. He rated each event on a number of dimensions, including how much he had participated in the event, its importance to him, the event's frequency, and its emotionality and physical characteristics (e.g., sights, sounds, smells). Overall, the results from the two studies corresponded well with Linton's observations: Recalled events were unique and, at least in Wagenaar's study, more emotional. In both studies, there was some evidence for the better recall of pleasant events.

Although diary studies provide a rich source of autobiographical memories, such richness comes with methodological costs. Diary studies typically involve only the experimenter as subject, the to-be-remembered events are not randomly selected, and the very act of recording the events probably changes the way they are encoded. As alluded to earlier in this chapter, two different paradigms have been developed to deal with these problems. In one study, Thompson (1982) recruited 16 undergraduates to participate in a diary study; the twist was that the participants recorded events not only from their own lives but also from their roommates' lives. All 32 participants later attempted to retrieve the recorded events and used a 7-point scale to rate how well they remembered them. The critical finding was that memory did not differ between the recorders and their roommates, even though the recorders had selected and recorded the events and had knowledge of the upcoming memory test.

In another clever study, Brewer (1988a) dealt with the event-selection issue by recruiting subjects to carry pagers and record their ongoing events whenever the alarm sounded. Participants also rated their emotional states as well as the frequency, significance, and goal of each event. At test, subjects were given one of five different types of retrieval cues (time, location, both time and location, thoughts, or actions) and were asked to recall the events in question. Compared to events that were not recalled in response to the cues, correctly recalled events were rated as being more associated with remembered sensory details, emotions, and thoughts.

Consistent with the results of earlier diary studies (Wagenaar, 1986; White, 1982), correct recall was associated with exciting, infrequent events occurring in atypical locations. Similar results were also obtained in another beeper study in which the memory test involved recognition rather than cued recall (Brewer, 1988a, 1988b).

We mention here only one of the many other studies that support the idea that vivid memories tend to be for life events that were unique, important, and emotional. Rubin and Kozin (1984) collected data on vivid memories using two paradigms. First, they asked participants to describe their three most vivid memories and then to rate them on a number of scales (e.g., national and personal importance, surprisingness, consequentiality, etc.). Overwhelmingly, participants provided memories of events such as personal injuries or romantic episodes that were rated as high in personal but not national importance (see also Robinson, 1976). Second, participants retrieved autobiographical memories in response to 20 national (e.g., the night President Nixon resigned) and personal (e.g., their own thirteenth birthdays) cues. These cues naturally varied in their ability to elicit vivid memories; vivid memories tended to be associated with consequentiality, surprise, emotional change, and rehearsal (repeated retrieval after the event).

Although vivid personal memories tend to be associated with exciting, emotional, unique, and even surprising life events, we would not want to say that emotional memories are special or different from other memories. It was originally argued that unexpected events (e.g., hearing of an assassination) triggered a special mechanism leading to capture of all event details in a very accurate memory trace (R. Brown & Kulik, 1977). However, a spate of research has appeared arguing to the contrary. The so-called "flashbulb memories" may be particularly vivid, rehearsed at high frequencies, and confidently held—but they are not necessarily accurate. Early investigations of flashbulb memories were retrospective only, in that they did not assess the consistency of participants' stories over time (e.g., Yarmey & Bull, 1978). A different picture emerged from studies that involved the comparison of initial reports to later memories. For example, Neisser and Harsch (1993) compared initial reports of having learned about the space shuttle Challenger explosion to those collected 32–34 months later. Even though their subjects reported high confidence in their memories, just three subjects' (8%) accounts contained only minor discrepancies. Twenty-two subjects were wrong on two out of three major memory attributes (location, activity, and who told them); the remaining 11 subjects were wrong on all three. Other similar studies of disasters such as bombings and assassinations have confirmed that what characterizes flashbulb memories is the confidence with which they are held (e.g., Weaver, 1993) rather than their consistency and accuracy over time (e.g., Christianson, 1989).

The observant reader has noticed two things. First, we have answered the question *What types of events are better remembered?* rather than *What types of processing lead to better memory?* Experimenters do not have a way of manipulating the level of processing during the occurrence of natural life events. In addition, we can assume that the equivalent of "deep processing" for real events (e.g., listening carefully, contributing to the event, attending to as many details as possible) is confounded with event characteristics—a person is more involved with more meaningful, unique, and emotional events. Second, the so-called "encoding variables" that we have just described are likely confounded with processes occurring during other stages in the memory process. For example, a unique emotional event is probably also less susceptible to proactive and retroactive interference, more likely to be talked about during the retention interval, and more likely to be retrieved. With autobiographical memories, it is particularly difficult to pin down the cause of memorability to one particular stage in the process. With that in mind, we turn now to discussing effects occurring during the retention interval.

Factors Occurring During the Retention Interval

In this section, we will discuss four factors: (a) the length of the retention interval, (b) the encountering of new information during the retention interval, (c) the way people continually talk about and retrieve life events over time, and (d) whether people can deliberately avoid thinking about life events.

The Passage of Time

As the retention interval increases, so does forgetting (Linton, 1978). Crovitz and Schiffman (1974) had college students recall and date life events in response to a series of cue words; a logarithmic relation existed between the number of memories recalled and the passage of time, with forgetting being rapid at first and then slowing (see also Rubin, 1982). This is similar to forgetting curves obtained in standard laboratory studies of episodic memory. However, an Ebbinghaus-type forgetting function is obtained only when young adults are recalling memories from the past 10 or 20 years of their lives. A different picture emerges when retention across the entire life span is examined. First, the decline is accelerated for memories from early childhood. Memories from the 1st and 2nd years of life are almost nonexistent, and memories from the first 5 years

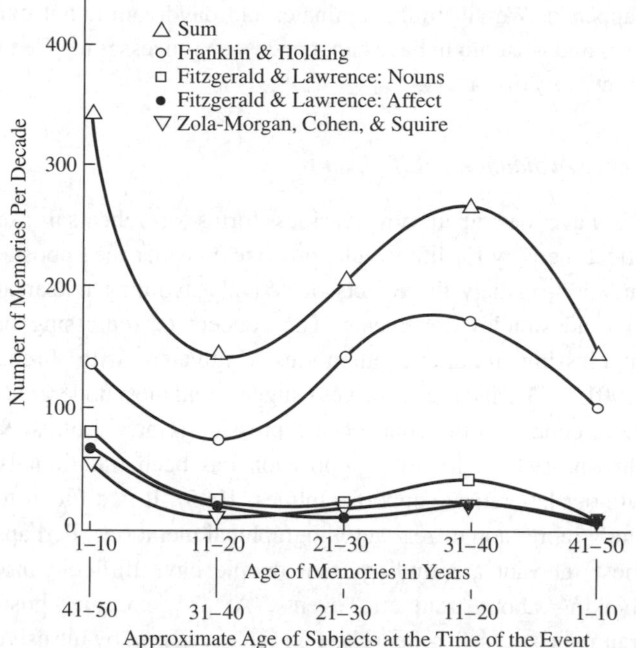

Figure 17.6 Distribution of autobiographical memories across the life span. In four studies, represented by the lower four curves in the figure, 50-year-old subjects remembered and dated life events in response to cue words. The top curve collapses over studies and sums over the lower four curves. Subjects recalled a disproportionate number of events from adolescence and early adulthood (reminiscence bump). *Source:* From Rubin et al. (1986) and reprinted with permission of Cambridge University Press.

of life are infrequent (Freud 1905/1930; Wetzler & Sweeney, 1986). As noted before, this phenomenon is called *childhood* or *infantile amnesia* (Howe & Courage, 1993). Second, a different function occurs for older adults than for college students. When older adults recall and date memories in response to word cues, they still show childhood amnesia and log-linear decline for recent memories. However, as shown in Figure 17.6, they also show what is called the *reminiscence bump:* A greater proportion of retrieved memories are dated to the period of 20–30 years of age than would be expected, given the rest of the distribution (e.g., Rubin & Schulkind, 1997). Numerous reasons have been suggested to account for the so-called reminiscence bump, including a preponderance of "firsts" occurring during the 20-something time period, the importance of that time period for identity formation, and greater rehearsal frequencies for the types of events occurring during one's 20s. The exact reason for the bump remains uncertain.

Exposure to Additional Events

Just as it is not immune to proactive interference, autobiographical memory is susceptible to retroactive interference. An event may be confused with similar events occurring before or afterward. Although one's first few visits to a coffee shop may be discriminable soon afterward, retrieval of specific episodes may become difficult with the passage of time and with continued visits to the coffee shop. This is again Linton's point that unique events are best remembered, and repeated events are susceptible to interference.

People do not exist in a vacuum during the retention interval; as we move through life, we are exposed to sources that provide us with information about our prior experiences. Other people tell us their versions of our shared experiences, we look back at photographs, we reread our diaries, and so on. We have already described how autobiographical memories are susceptible to proactive interference; now we are describing how retroactive interference can affect autobiographical memories just as it does episodic memories created in the laboratory. Although oftentimes this postevent information is correct, it may also be incorrect. Just as in laboratory studies of episodic memory, misleading postevent information can affect how we conceptualize original events and impair our ability to retrieve the original events.

In one clever demonstration of this, Crombag, Wagenaar, and van Koppen (1996) asked Dutch subjects whether they remembered having seen a video of the 1992 crash of an El Al airplane into an apartment building in Amsterdam. There was no actual footage of the moment of impact. However, more than half of participants accepted the suggestion from the interviewer and reported having seen the video. A substantial number of those subjects were then willing to elaborate on their memories, answering questions such as "After the plane hit the building, there was a fire. How long did it take for the fire to start?"

People may be particularly prone to suggestions or postevent information from legitimate sources who might very well have knowledge about their pasts. Elizabeth Loftus and her colleagues developed a procedure using family and friends as confederates to get subjects to misremember entire events. In one version, the trusted confederate asked the subject to repeatedly recall five childhood events for a class experiment; unbeknown to the subject, one of the events had never occurred. Over a series of sessions, participants were willing to describe detailed recollections of the false event, such as being lost in a shopping mall (e.g., see Loftus, 1993). Similar data have been reported by Hyman and Pentland (1996), who found that participants who imagined knocking over a punch bowl at a wedding were more likely to create false memories for having done so. Consistent with the other memory errors described thus far, however, one is more likely to accept a false memory when it is plausible and consistent with the rest of his or her life history. For example, participants were more likely to accept a false memory for a religious event when the ritual was of their own faith (Pezdek, Finger, & Hodge, 1997).

Rehearsal of Life Events

People continue to talk and think about life events long after their occurrence, and such rehearsal will have consequences for the way the events are remembered. In one series of studies, Johnson and colleagues manipulated how subjects talked and thought about events performed in the laboratory (Hashtroudi, Johnson, & Chrosniak, 1990; Johnson & Suengas, 1989; Suengas & Johnson, 1988). Subjects did actions like writing a letter or wrapping a present, and then thought about either the perceptual characteristics of the events or their emotional responses. Subjects who focused on emotional reactions later rated their memories as containing less perceptual detail, an important finding given that people often base source judgments on this type of information (Johnson, Hashtroudi, & Lindsay, 1993).

Whereas laboratory rehearsal instructions typically emphasize accuracy (e.g., "Practice recalling this list so you can repeat the words back to me in order"), no such guidelines constrain the way people talk about their own lives. Subjects' retellings of movies and fictional short stories are veridical only in the standard laboratory context, with accuracy instructions and an experimenter as audience (Hyman, 1994; Wade & Clark, 1993). Storytelling is different when goals and audiences are more realistic, as when one tells a story to friends with the goal of entertaining them. In fact, accuracy appears to be the exception when talking about one's own life. In a recent diary study of people's retellings of events from their own lives, people reported telling "inaccurate" stories almost two thirds of the time! This occurred even though people are likely to underestimate how inaccurate they are in storytelling, due to both ignorance of the inaccuracy and the social desirability of truth-telling (Marsh & Tversky, 2002). The issue is that biased retellings lead to memory distortion in laboratory analogs of the storytelling situation (Tversky & Marsh, 2000). Thus, when people talk about their own lives and take liberties with events in order to entertain or to make a point, memory distortion may result.

Such rehearsal processes may lead to the creation of false memories for entire events. For example, repeatedly imagining an event initially believed not to have happened leads to an increase in one's belief that the event actually occurred (e.g., Garry, Manning, Loftus, & Sherman, 1996; Heaps & Nash, 1999). In these studies, subjects initially rated the likelihood that events had occurred (e.g., *You broke a window with your hand*), and then imagined a subset of events. In the third part of the experiment, subjects again rated the likelihood of events; imagined events were now rated as more likely to have happened. We all think, ruminate, and daydream about our lives and what might have happened; such processes may lead to memory distortion.

Active Avoidance of Life Events

We have described how various forms of rehearsal can affect memory for life events; now we consider the opposite situation, namely the effects of actively avoiding rehearsal of (undesirable) life events. The concept of repressing or suppressing traumatic memories originated with Freud (1901/1971), and recent surveys suggest that most undergraduates believe in the concept of repression (Garry, Loftus, & Brown, 1994). However, repression has been traditionally without laboratory support (Holmes, 1995). It is difficult to study repression of real autobiographical memories. Perhaps most relevant are findings that people have difficulty *not* thinking about traumatic events. At the extreme, posttraumatic stress disorder (PTSD) is characterized by intrusive memories of the precipitating trauma. Similarly, depressed individuals ruminate on negative events (Lyubomirsky, Caldwell, & Nolen-Hoeksema, 1998). Even nonclinical populations such as college undergraduates report that intrusive memories occur commonly (Brewin, Christodoulides, & Hutchinson, 1996). Thus, even though a laboratory demonstration of suppression was recently published (Anderson & Green, 2001), it is not clear that such results will generalize to the emotional memories that people may seek to suppress in real life. In their study, Anderson and Greene (2001) taught students a series of weakly related paired associates (e.g., *ordeal-roach*); the subjects were later instructed to suppress some of the associates when presented with the first word in the pair. The more often subjects attempted to avoid thinking of the target words, the less likely they were to remember them on later memory tests, even when a different cue was used. Although subjects may be trained to suppress thoughts of relatively neutral words (e.g., *roach*), the wealth of data on intrusive memories in normal and depressed individuals makes it questionable as to whether people can force themselves to avoid thinking of painful personal events.

Factors at Retrieval

Much of the research on autobiographical memory is aimed at understanding the factors that affect the retrieval and reconstruction of personal memories. This research emphasis is not surprising given that researchers have little control over the earlier stages, but they can directly manipulate factors during the retrieval phase.

It is critical to note that, as with episodic memories, estimates of forgetting are dependent on the type of retrieval cue utilized. Although diary studies suggest little forgetting of life events, this is probably because they typically provide subjects with excellent retrieval cues, potentially reducing estimates of forgetting. One problem with most diary studies and other early studies was that they did not contain distractor items or other "catch trials" to ensure participants' ability to discriminate between experienced and nonexperienced events. A study by Barclay and Wellman (1986) makes this point nicely. In that study, students took a recognition test on previously recorded life events that included four types of items: duplicates of original diary entries, foils that changed descriptive (surface) details of the original events, foils that changed reactions to original events, and foils that did not correspond to recorded events. Participants were good at recognizing original diary entries (94% correct), but they also accepted a large number of the foils. They incorrectly accepted 50% of modified descriptions and 23% of novel events. These effects increased over a delay such that after a year, subjects were accepting the majority of both semantically related and unrelated foils. Thus, in both autobiographical and episodic memory studies, people falsely recognize events similar to experienced ones, and after a delay may show very little ability to discriminate between what did versus did not occur. However, without the appropriate foils on the recognition test, one would have been tempted to conclude that autobiographical memory was almost perfect.

In general, results from both diary studies and the Galton word-cuing technique suggest that event-content cues are best. Emotion words are not good retrieval cues (e.g., Robinson, 1976), and temporal cues are not as strong as content cues such as *what, who,* and *where* (Wagenaar, 1988; but see Pillemer, Goldsmith, Panter, & White, 1988).

What was experienced may not be what is accessible at retrieval. We already noted how Linton (1982) found better memory for unique events and attributed her failure to recognize events to interference from other, similar events in memory. Due to proactive and retroactive interference, only the gist of events may be available at retrieval (e.g., Bartlett, 1932). Although participants may lose access to specific event memories, they may retain more generic personal memories covering a class of related life events (Brewer, 1986). Barsalou (1988) found that students asked to recall the events from their summer vacations most commonly responded with summaries of events (e.g., *I watched a lot of TV*). Only 21% of responses were classified as corresponding to specific events (e.g., *We had a little picnic*).

Reconstruction of the Past

Even though people may complain about their ability to perform tasks such as remembering a long list of words, it often seems that they feel more confident about their ability to recall events from their own lives. However, although diary studies have suggested that people are sometimes good at recognizing and remembering events that happened to them, they do not prove that people's memories are always accurate. Rather, retrieval times for remembering autobiographical events tend to be slow and variable, suggesting that remembered events are reconstructed. We have already reviewed several mechanisms that may operate during the retention phase to lead to inaccuracy, namely exposure to postevent information, interference, and retelling an event. We now review the literature on reconstructing autobiographical memories at retrieval, beginning with a section on how people date autobiographical memories. As described earlier, temporal cues are not very useful for recollecting events, probably because people do not normally explicitly encode dates of events. Thus, the domain of dating is a perfect example of how people reconstruct memories at the time of a test. After the discussion of dating, we will describe some of the general strategies people have for reconstructing their pasts.

Dating Autobiographical Memories

On what date did you hear about the attempted assassination of Ronald Reagan? On what date did you receive your acceptance letter from the college that you eventually attended? We suspect our readers will be unlikely to answer these questions quickly or accurately. Numerous studies have shown that people have difficulty in dating their autobiographical memories (see Friedman, 1993, for a review), and that this difficulty increases with the passage of time from the target event (Linton, 1975).

However, as introspection quickly reveals, it is not that autobiographical memory lacks all temporal information, which "would be like a jumbled box of snapshots" (Friedman, 1993, p. 44). Although the "snapshots" may lack explicit time-date stamps, we are quite capable of relating, ordering, and organizing the snapshots into a coherent story. The same subjects who cannot date a series of events within a month of their occurrence (3% correct; N. R. Brown, Rips, & Shevell, 1985) can determine the temporal ordering of the events (rank order correlation of .88; N. R. Brown et al., 1985). There is an entire literature on how people accomplish this; due to space constraints, we will describe here only a few of the strategies people use to reconstruct when events occurred.

In general, people make use of what little temporal information was encoded originally. At least two types of temporal information in memory appear relevant: the temporal cycles that regularly occur in people's lives, and temporal landmarks. First, natural *temporal cycles* or structures are encoded that later guide memory; examples include the academic calendar (Kurbat, Shevell, & Rips, 1998; Pillemer, Rhinehart, & White, 1986) and the weekday-weekend cycle (Huttenlocher, Hedges, & Prohaska, 1992). Second, people have a better sense of the dates of consequential landmark events, and thus both public and private *temporal landmarks* can be used to guide date reconstruction (e.g., N. R. Brown, Shevell, & Rips, 1986; Loftus & Marburger, 1983; see Shum, 1998, for a review). Such information about temporal and event boundaries, combined with knowledge of some specific dates, can be used to place a date on a target event. However, people's reconstructed dates tend to be too recent (Loftus & Marburger, 1983).

Other biases come into play when dating autobiographical memories; we will mention only two here. Similar to the availability bias found in decision making, memories for which people have more knowledge are dated as more recent (*the accessibility principle;* N. R. Brown et al., 1985, chapter 24). People also may make rounding errors when they use inappropriately precise standard temporal units (e.g., days, weeks, months; Huttenlocher, Hedges, & Bradburn, 1990).

We turn now to a discussion of more general strategies that people use to reconstruct memories, including implicit theories and motivated searches through memory.

Use of Implicit Theories

Numerous laboratory experiments have shown that people remember their personal histories to be consistent with what they believe should have happened, rather than with what did happen. One way this can happen is via the use of implicit theories of change versus stability.

Ross (1989) has argued that people use their current statuses as benchmarks, and then reconstruct the past based on whether they think changes should have occurred over time. For example, people believe that attitudes and political beliefs remain consistent over time, and so they often overestimate the consistency of the past with the present. In this example, one would assess one's current attitude and then apply a theory of stability to estimate one's attitude in the past. In one study, subjects' attitudes toward toothbrushing were manipulated; subjects exposed to a pro-brushing message overestimated previous brushing reports, whereas participants in an anti-brushing condition underestimated their previous reports (Ross, McFarland, & Fletcher, 1981). Likewise, people may mistakenly remember a nonexistent change if one was expected. In these cases, people also assess their current statuses, but then apply a theory of change inappropriately. For example, in one study participants who took a bogus study skills group (leading to no improvement) misremembered their prior skills as having been worse than they actually were (Conway & Ross, 1984).

Motivated Remembering

People's theories of "how things shoulda been" go beyond simple theories of change over time; rather, people may be motivated to remember things in a particular way. In general, people tend to think of themselves as being better than average, and may engage in downward social comparisons to support such beliefs (Wills, 1981). People are motivated to misremember their past behaviors in a way that supports their self-esteem. Thus, upon learning the norm for a particular domain, people may be motivated to remember their own prior behaviors as better than the norm.

In one study, Klein and Kunda (1993) examined the effect of knowing the norm on subjects' self-reported frequency of health-threatening behaviors such as eating red meat, drinking alcohol, and losing one's temper. Subjects in a control condition simply reported the frequency of their behaviors using a 7-point scale. Subjects in the experimental condition also used 7-point scales; however, the average behavior frequency (established in pretesting) was indicated with an *X* on each of the scales. Subjects given the norms reported engaging in the risky behaviors less often per week (M = 3.18) than the norm established in pretesting (M = 3.52) and than the control subjects (M = 3.78). However, the mechanism underlying this effect remains unclear. Subjects may have misremembered the past, or they may have merely misrepresented or misreported it. It does not appear that subjects were simply changing their reports, because subjects in yet another condition with more extreme norms did not display a more extreme shift in reported behavior frequencies (perhaps because they were constrained by what they did remember). In addition, in the next paragraph we will describe converging experimental evidence from another paradigm that suggests people may selectively search their memories for evidence to support their desired self-concepts.

We may be biased in the way we search memory and the events that we select to remember. In one study, Sanitioso, Kunda, and Fong (1990) made Princeton undergraduates desire a certain trait, and then looked to see whether the students' remembered life experiences exemplified that target trait. In the first phase of the experiment, students read that Stanford psychologists had shown that extraverts (or, in another condition, introverts) performed better in academics and professional settings. In a second (seemingly unrelated) experiment, subjects remembered experiences for each of a series of trait dimensions, including *shy-outgoing*. Of interest was whether subjects tended to list an extraverted or

TABLE 17.1 Motivated Retrieval of Autobiographical Memories

	Success in Academics		Success in Police Force	
First Thought	Extravert-Success	Introvert-Success	Extravert-Success	Introvert-Success
Extraverted	62%	38%	26%	39%
Introverted	38%	62%	73%	61%

Source: Adapted from Sanitioso et al. (1990). The table shows the percentage of subjects in each success condition who listed extraverted and introverted memories first. Motivated retrieval occurred only when the domain was one in which subjects wished to succeed.

introverted memory first. Supporting the idea of motivated memory search, the majority of subjects began recall with a memory relevant to the target trait. This effect is shown in the left-hand panel of Table 17.1. This effect disappeared in a second experiment when the subjects were not motivated to see the trait in themselves. The first phase was modified to involve explaining how introversion-extraversion led to success as a police officer; the second phase remained the same. In this version of the experiment, subjects no longer recruited trait-relevant memories first. These data are shown in the right-hand panel of Table 17.1. Thus, the motivated retrieval effect occurred only when the trait was linked to a success outcome in a domain of interest to the Princeton undergraduates (academic success, not success as a police officer).

CONCLUSIONS

We began by noting that the concepts of episodic and autobiographical memory overlap. Memory for one's experiences during an experiment can be classified as either episodic or autobiographical. Accordingly, the two research traditions often provide converging evidence on how memory works. For example, the principle that *unusual events are well remembered* works to describe the results from both list-learning experiments and studies of autobiographical memory. Similarly, there can be proactive and retroactive interference for both episodic and autobiographical memories, and in both domains retrieval cues can bring back memories that could not be recalled without cues. Both research traditions support the idea that falsely remembered events are often plausible and are similar to actual events. The idea that self-involvement and personal relevance matter is obviously critical to autobiographical memory, but it is also present in the episodic memory literature; experimental psychologists have long known the benefits of elaborative encoding strategies such as generation (Slamecka & Graf, 1978) and encoding items in relation to oneself (Bower & Gilligan, 1979).

Nonetheless, it should not be assumed that results from the two research traditions will always converge, because surprises have occurred and will continue to occur. For example, the distribution of memories over the life span is not exactly as predicted by the logarithmic forgetting function first discovered by Ebbinghaus (1885/1913). In autobiographical memory studies, forgetting is generally logarithmic, but with two major exceptions: There is much forgetting of memories from early childhood (infantile amnesia), and older adults remember more from the years of early adulthood than would be predicted (the reminiscence bump). In addition, the two research traditions have different strengths. Traditional episodic memory experiments allow for manipulations during the encoding phase, whereas this is almost impossible for real-life events. Conversely, there are certain variables that are difficult to investigate within the traditional episodic memory experiment. For example, motivation plays an important role in how we remember ourselves, and it is hard to imagine subjects engaging in meaningful, motivated retrieval and reconstruction in a standard episodic memory experiment. In conclusion, then, we conceptualize episodic and autobiographical memory as overlapping sets that nonetheless may differ, with each domain of inquiry making an important contribution to our larger understanding of human memory.

REFERENCES

Anderson, M. C., & Green, C. (2001). Suppressing unwanted memories by executive control. *Nature, 410,* 366–369.

Ayers, M. S., & Reder, L. M. (1998). A theoretical review of the misinformation effect: Predictions from an activation-based memory model. *Psychonomic Bulletin & Review, 5,* 1–21.

Baddeley, A., & Wilson, B. (1986). Amnesia, autobiographical memory, and confabulation. In D. C. Rubin (Ed.), *Autobiographical memory* (pp. 225–252). Cambridge, UK: Cambridge University Press.

Balota, D. A., Duchek, J. M., & Paullin, R. (1989). Age-related differences in the impact of spacing, lag, and retention interval. *Psychology and Aging, 4,* 3–9.

Balota, D. A., & Neely, J. H. (1980). Test-expectancy and word-frequency effects in recall and recognition. *Journal of Experimental Psychology: Human Learning and Memory, 6,* 576–587.

Barclay, C. R., & Wellman, H. M. (1986). Accuracies and inaccuracies in autobiographical memories. *Journal of Memory and Language, 25,* 93–103.

Barsalou, L. W. (1988). The content and organization of autobiographical memories. In U. Neisser & E. Winograd (Eds.), *Remembering reconsidered: Ecological and traditional approaches to the study of memory* (pp. 193–243). Cambridge, UK: Cambridge University Press.

Bartlett, F. C. (1932). *Remembering: A study in experimental and social psychology.* Cambridge, UK: Cambridge University Press.

Begg, I., Snider, A., Foley, F., & Goddard, R. (1989). The generation effect is no artifact: Generation makes words distinctive. *Journal of Experimental Psychology: Learning, Memory, and Cognition, 15,* 977–989.

Bower, G. H., & Forgas, J. P. (2000). Affect, memory, and social cognition. In E. Eich & J. F. Kihlstrom (Eds.), *Cognition and emotion* (pp. 87–168). New York: Oxford University Press.

Bower, G. H., & Gilligan, S. G. (1979). Remembering information related to one's self. *Journal of Research in Personality, 13,* 420–432.

Brewer, W. F. (1986). What is autobiographical memory? In D. C. Rubin (Ed.), *Autobiographical memory.* Cambridge, UK: Cambridge University Press.

Brewer, W. F. (1988a). Qualitative analysis of the recalls of randomly sampled autobiographical events. In M. M. Gruneberg, P. E. Morris, & R. N. Sykes (Eds.), *Practical aspects of memory: Current research and issues* (pp. 263–268). New York: Wiley.

Brewer, W. F. (1988b). Memory for randomly sampled autobiographical events. In U. Neisser & E. Winograd (Eds.), *Remembering reconsidered: Ecological and traditional approaches to the study of memory* (pp. 21–90). Cambridge, UK: Cambridge University Press.

Brewin, C. R., Christodoulides, J., & Hutchinson, G. (1996). Intrusive thoughts and intrusive memories in a nonclinical sample. *Cognition & Emotion, 10,* 107–112.

Brown, N. R., Rips, L. J., & Shevell, S. K. (1985). The subjective dates of natural events in very-long-term memory. *Cognitive Psychology, 17,* 139–177.

Brown, N. R., Shevell, S. K., & Rips, L. J. (1986). Public memories and their personal context. In D. C. Rubin (Ed.), *Autobiographical memory* (pp. 137–158). Cambridge, UK: Cambridge University Press.

Brown, R., & Kulik, J. (1977). Flashbulb memories. *Cognition, 5,* 73–99.

Christianson, S. A. (1989). Flashbulb memories: Special, but not so special. *Memory & Cognition, 17,* 435–443.

Colegrave, F. W. (1899). Individual memories. *American Journal of Psychology, 10,* 228–255.

Conway, M. A. (1990). *Autobiographical memory: An introduction.* Philadelphia: Milton Keynes.

Conway, M. A. (2001). Sensory-perceptual episodic memory and its context. *Philosophical Transactions of the Royal Society of London, 356,* 1375–1384.

Conway, M. A., & Berkerian, D. A. (1987). Organization in autobiographical memory. *Memory & Cognition, 15,* 119–132.

Conway, M. A., & Ross, M. (1984). Getting what you want by revising what you had. *Journal of Personality and Social Psychology, 47,* 738–748.

Craik, F. I. M., & Lockhart, R. S. (1972). Levels of processing: A framework for memory research. *Journal of Verbal Learning and Verbal Behavior, 11,* 671–684.

Craik, F. I. M., & Tulving, E. (1975). Depth of processing and the retention of words in episodic memory. *Journal of Experimental Psychology: General, 104,* 268–294.

Crombag, H. F. M., Wagenaar, W. A., & van Koppen, P. J. (1996). Crashing memories and the problem of "source monitoring." *Applied Cognitive Psychology, 10,* 95–104.

Crowder, R. G. (1976). *Principles of learning and memory.* Hillsdale, NJ: Erlbaum.

Crowder, R. G., & Surprenant, A. M. (2000). Sensory stores. In A. E. Kazdin (Ed.), *Encyclopedia of psychology* (pp. 227–229). Oxford, UK: American Psychological Association/Oxford University Press.

Crovitz, H. F., & Schiffman, H. (1974). Frequency of episodic memories as a function of their age. *Bulletin of the Psychonomic Society, 4,* 517–518.

Dempster, F. N. (1988). The spacing effect: A case study in the failure to apply the results of psychological research. *American Psychologist, 43,* 627–634.

Ebbinghaus, H. (1913). Memory: A contribution to experimental psychology (H. A. Ruger & C. E. Bussenues, Trans.). New York: Teachers College/Columbia University. (Original work published 1885)

Erdelyi, M. H., & Becker, J. (1974). Hypermnesia for pictures: Incremental memory for pictures but not words in multiple recall trials. *Cognitive Psychology, 6,* 159–171.

Erdelyi, M. H., & Kleinbard, J. (1978). Has Ebbinghaus decayed with time? The growth of recall (hypermnesia) over days. *Journal of Experimental Psychology: Human Learning and Memory, 4,* 275–289.

Freud, S. (1930). Three contributions to the theory of sex (A. A. Brill, Trans.). New York: Nervous and Mental Disease Publishing Co. (Original work published 1905)

Freud, S. (1971). *The psychopathology of everyday life* (A. Tyson, Trans.). New York: W. W. Norton. (Original work published 1901)

Freud, S. (1982). An early memory from Goethe's autobiography. In U. Neisser (Ed.), *Memory observed: Remembering in natural contexts* (pp. 64–72). New York: W. H. Freeman. (Original work published 1917)

Friedman, W. J. (1993). Memory for the time of past events. *Psychological Bulletin, 113,* 44–66.

Galton, F. (1879). Psychometric experiments. *Brain, 2,* 149–162.

Gardiner, J. M. (1988). Functional aspects of recollective experience. *Memory & Cognition, 16,* 309–313.

Gardiner, J. M., & Richardson-Klavehn, A. (2000). Remembering and knowing. In E. Tulving & F. I. M. Craik (Eds.), *The Oxford handbook of memory* (pp. 229–244). New York: Oxford University Press.

Garry, M., Loftus, E. F., & Brown, S. W. (1994). Memory: A river runs through it. *Consciousness & Cognition, 3,* 438–451.

Garry, M., Manning, C. G., Loftus, E. F., & Sherman, S. J. (1996). Imagination inflation: Imagining a childhood event inflates confidence that it occurred. *Psychonomic Bulletin & Review, 3,* 208–214.

Hall, J. F. (1954). Learning as a function of word frequency. *American Journal of Psychology, 67,* 138–140.

Hashtroudi, S., Johnson, M. K., & Chrosniak, L. D. (1990). Aging and qualitative characteristics of memories for perceived and imagined complex events. *Psychology & Aging, 5,* 119–126.

Heaps, C., & Nash, M. (1999). Individual differences in imagination inflation. *Psychonomic Bulletin & Review, 6,* 313–318.

Holmes, D. S. (1995). The evidence for repression: An examination of sixty years of research. In J. L. Singer (Ed.), *Repression and dissociation: Implications for personality theory, psychopathology, and health* (pp. 85–102). Chicago: Chicago University Press.

Howe, M. L., & Courage, M. L. (1993). On resolving the enigma of infantile amnesia. *Psychological Bulletin, 113,* 305–326.

Hunt, R. R. (1995). The subtlety of distinctiveness: What von Restorff really did. *Psychonomic Bulletin & Review, 2,* 105–112.

Hunt, R. R., & Elliot, J. M. (1980). The role of nonsemantic information in memory: Orthographic distinctiveness effects on retention. *Journal of Experimental Psychology: General, 109,* 49–74.

Hunt, R. R., & McDaniel, M. A. (1993). The enigma of organization and distinctiveness. *Journal of Memory & Language, 32,* 421–445.

Huttenlocher, J., Hedges, L. V., & Bradburn, N. M. (1990). Reports of elapsed time: Bounding and rounding processes in estimation. *Journal of Experimental Psychology: Learning, Memory, & Cognition, 16,* 196–213.

Huttenlocher, J., Hedges, L. V., & Prohaska, V. (1992). Memory for the day of the week: A 5 + 2 day cycle. *Journal of Experimental Psychology: General, 121,* 313–325.

Hyman, I. E. (1994). Conversational remembering: Story recall with a peer versus for an experimenter. *Applied Cognitive Psychology, 8,* 49–66.

Hyman, I. E., & Pentland, J. (1996). The role of mental imagery in the creation of false childhood memories. *Journal of Memory and Language, 35,* 101–117.

Jacoby, L. L. (1978). On interpreting the effects of repetition: Solving a problem versus remembering a solution. *Journal of Verbal Learning and Verbal Behavior, 17,* 649–667.

Jacoby, L. L. (1991). A process dissociation framework: Separating automatic from intentional uses of memory. *Journal of Memory & Language, 30,* 513–541.

Jacoby, L. L., Toth, J. P., & Yonelinas, A. P. (1993). Separating conscious and unconscious influences of memory: Measuring recollection. *Journal of Experimental Psychology: General, 122,* 139–154.

Johnson, M. K., Foley, M. A., Suengas, A. G., & Raye, C. L. (1988). Phenomenal characteristics of memories for perceived and imagined autobiographical events. *Journal of Experimental Psychology: General, 117,* 371–376.

Johnson, M. K., Hashtroudi, S., & Lindsay, D. S. (1993). Source Monitoring. *Psychological Bulletin, 114,* 3–28.

Johnson, M. K., & Suengas, A. G. (1989). Reality monitoring judgments of other people's memories. *Bulletin of the Psychonomic Society, 27,* 107–110.

Kinsbourne, M., & George, J. (1974). The mechanism of the word-frequency effect on recognition memory. *Journal of Verbal Learning and Verbal Behavior, 13,* 63–69.

Klein, W. M., & Kunda, Z. (1993). Maintaining self-serving social comparisons: Biased reconstruction of one's past behaviors. *Personality and Social Psychology Bulletin, 19,* 732–739.

Kurbat, M. A., Shevell, S. K., & Rips, L. J. (1998). A year's memories: The calendar effect in autobiographical recall. *Memory & Cognition, 26,* 532–552.

Landauer, T. K., & Bjork, R. A. (1978). Optimum rehearsal patterns and name learning. In M. M. Gruneberg, P. E. Morris, & R. N. Sykes (Eds.), *Practical aspects of memory* (pp. 625–632). London: Academic Press.

Light, L. L., Kayra-Stuart, F., & Hollander, S. (1979). Recognition memory for typical and unusual faces. *Journal of Experimental Psychology: Human Learning and Memory, 5,* 212–228.

Linton, M. (1975). Memory for real-world events. In D. A. Norman & D. E. Rumelhart (Eds.), *Explorations in cognition* (pp. 376–404). San Francisco: W. H. Freeman.

Linton, M. (1978). Real world memory after six years: An *in vivo* of very long term memory. In M. M. Gruneberg, P. E. Morris, & R. N. Skyes (Eds.). *Practical aspects of memory* (pp. 69–76). London: Academic Press.

Linton, M. (1982). Transformations of memory in everyday life. In U. Neisser (Ed.), *Memory observed: Remembering in natural contexts* (pp. 77–91). New York: W. H. Freeman.

Loftus, E. F. (1993). The reality of repressed memories. *American Psychologist, 48,* 518–537.

Loftus, E. F., & Marburger, W. (1983). Since the eruption of Mt. St. Helens, has anyone beaten you up? Improving the accuracy of retrospective reports with landmark events. *Memory & Cognition, 11,* 114–120.

Loftus, E. F., Miller, D. G., & Burns, H. J. (1978). Semantic integration of verbal information into a visual memory. *Journal of Experimental Psychology: Human Learning and Memory, 4,* 19–31.

Loftus, E. F., & Palmer, J. C. (1974). Reconstruction of automobile destruction: An example of interaction between language and memory. *Journal of Verbal Learning and Verbal Behavior, 13,* 585–589.

Lyubomirsky, S., Caldwell, N. D., & Nolen-Hoeksema, S. (1998). Effects of ruminative and distracting responses to depressed mood on retrieval of autobiographical memories. *Journal of Personality and Social Psychology, 75,* 166–177.

Mandler, G. (1980). Recognizing: The judgment of previous occurrence. *Psychological Review, 87,* 252–271.

Marsh, E. J., & Tversky, B. (2002). *Spinning the stories of our lives.* Unpublished manuscript.

McDaniel, M. A., Dunay, P. K., Lyman, B. J., & Kerwin, M. L. (1988). Effects of elaboration and relational distinctiveness of sentence memory. *American Journal of Psychology, 101,* 357–369.

McDaniel, M. A., Waddill, P. J., & Einstein, G. O. (1988). A contextual account of the generation effect: A three-factor theory. *Journal of Memory and Language, 27,* 521–536.

McGaugh, J. L., & Gold, P. E. (1992). Memory consolidation. In L. R. Squire (Ed.), *Encyclopedia of learning and memory* (pp. 395–398). New York: Macmillan.

McGeoch, J. A. (1932). Forgetting and the law of disuse. *Psychological Review, 39,* 352–370.

Melton, A. W. (1963). Implications of short-term memory for a general theory of memory. *Journal of Verbal Learning and Verbal Behavior, 2,* 1–21.

Melton, A. W. (1970). The situation with respect to the spacing of repetitions and memory. *Journal of Verbal Learning and Verbal Behavior, 9,* 596–606.

Miller, G. A. (1956). The magical number seven, plus or minus two: some limits on our capacity for processing information. *Psychological Review, 63,* 81–97.

Moffitt, K. H., Singer, J. A., Nelligan, D. W., & Carlson, M. A. (1994). Depression and memory narrative type. *Journal of Abnormal Psychology, 103,* 581–583.

Morris, C. D., Bransford, J. D., & Franks, J. J. (1977). Levels of processing versus transfer appropriate processing. *Journal of Verbal Learning and Verbal Behavior, 16,* 519–533.

Nelson, K. (1993). The psychological and social origins of autobiographical memory. *Psychological Science, 4,* 7–14.

Neisser, U., & Harsch, N. (1993). Phantom flashbulbs: False recollections of hearing the news about Challenger. In E. Winograd & U. Neisser (Eds.), *Affect and accuracy in recall: Studies of "flashbulb" memories* (pp. 9–31). New York: Cambridge University Press.

Paivio, A., & Begg, I. (1971). Imagery and comprehension latencies as a function of sentence concreteness and structure. *Perception and Psychophysics, 10,* 408–412.

Paivio, A., & Csapo, K. (1973). Picture superiority in free recall: Imagery or dual coding? *Cognitive Psychology, 5,* 176–206.

Paivio, A., Rogers, T. B., & Smythe, P. C. (1968). Why are pictures easier to recall than words? *Psychonomic Science, 11,* 137–138.

Paivio, A., Yuille, J. C., & Rogers, T. B. (1969). Noun imagery and meaningfulness in free and serial recall. *Journal of Experimental Psychology, 79,* 509–514.

Pezdek, K., Finger, K., & Hodge, D. (1997). Planting false childhood memories: The role of event plausibility. *Psychological Science, 8,* 437–441.

Pillemer, D. B., Goldsmith, L. R., Panter, A. T., & White, S. H. (1988). Very long-term memories of the first year in college. *Journal of Experimental Psychology: Learning, Memory, and Cognition, 14,* 709–715.

Pillemer, D. B., Rhinehart, E. D., & White, S. H. (1986). Memories of life transitions: The first year in college. *Human Learning: Journal of Practical Research and Applications, 5,* 109–123.

Rajaram, S. (1993). Remembering and knowing: Two means of access to the personal past. *Memory & Cognition, 21,* 89–102.

Robinson, J. A. (1976). Sampling autobiographical memory. *Cognitive Psychology, 8,* 578–595.

Roediger, H. L., III. (1978). Recall as a self-limiting process. *Memory & Cognition, 6,* 54–63.

Roediger, H. L., III. (1990). Implicit memory: Retention without remembering. *American Psychologist, 45,* 1043–1056.

Roediger, H. L., III. (2000). Why retrieval is the key process in understanding human memory. In E. Tulving (Ed.), *Memory, consciousness, and the brain: The Tallinn conference* (pp. 52–75). Philadelphia: Psychology Press/Taylor & Francis.

Roediger, H. L., III, & Gallo, D. A. (2002). Levels of processing: Some unanswered questions. In M. Naveh-Benjamin, M. Moscovitch, & H. L. Roediger III (Eds.), *Perspectives on Human Memory and Cognitive Aging: Essays in Honour of Fergus Craik* (pp. 28–47). Philadelphia: Psychology Press.

Roediger, H. L., III, & Guynn, M. J. (1996). Retrieval processes. In E. L. Bjork & R. A. Bjork (Eds.), *Memory* (pp. 197–236). San Diego, CA: Academic Press.

Roediger, H. L., III, & McDermott, K. B. (1995). Creating false memories: Remembering words not presented in lists. *Journal of Experimental Psychology: Learning, Memory, and Cognition, 21,* 803–814.

Ross, M. (1989). Relation of implicit theories to the construction of personal histories. *Psychological Review, 96,* 341–357.

Ross, M., McFarland, C., & Fletcher, G. J. (1981). The effect of attitude on the recall of personal histories. *Journal of Personality and Social Psychology, 40,* 627–634.

Rubin, D. C. (1982). On the retention function for autobiographical memory. *Journal of Verbal Learning and Verbal Behavior, 21,* 21–38.

Rubin, D. C., & Kozin, M. (1984). Vivid memories. *Cognition, 16,* 81–95.

Rubin, D. C., & Schulkind, M. D. (1997). The distribution of autobiographical memories across the lifespan. *Memory & Cognition, 25,* 859–866.

Sanitioso, R., Kunda, Z., & Fong, G. T. (1990). Motivated recruitment of autobiographical memories. *Journal of Personality and Social Psychology, 59,* 229–241.

Schmidt, S. R. (1985). Encoding and retrieval processes in the memory for conceptually distinct events. *Journal of Experimental Psychology: Learning, Memory, and Cognition, 11,* 565–578.

Shum, M. S. (1998). The role of temporal landmarks in autobiographical memory processes. *Psychological Bulletin, 124,* 423–442.

Slamecka, N. J., & Graf, P. (1978). The generation effect: Delineation of a phenomenon. *Journal of Experimental Psychology: Learning, Memory, and Cognition, 4,* 592–604.

Slamecka, N. J., & Katsaiti, L. T. (1987). The generation effect as an artifact of selective displaced rehearsal. *Journal of Memory and Language, 26,* 589–607.

Suengas, A. G., & Johnson, M. K. (1988). Qualitative effects of rehearsal on memories for perceived and imagined complex events. *Journal of Experimental Psychology: General, 117,* 377–389.

Thompson, C. P. (1982). Memory for unique personal events: The roommate study. *Memory & Cognition, 10,* 324–332.

Tulving, E. (1967). The effects of presentation and recall of material in free-recall learning. *Journal of Verbal Learning and Verbal Behavior, 6,* 175–184.

Tulving, E. (1972). Episodic and semantic memory. In E. Tulving & W. Donaldson (Eds.), *Organization of memory* (pp. 381–403). New York: Academic Press.

Tulving, E. (1974). Cue-dependent forgetting. *American Scientist, 62,* 74–82.

Tulving, E. (1983). *Elements of episodic memory.* New York: Oxford University Press.

Tulving, E. (1985). Memory and consciousness. *Canadian Journal of Psychology, 26,* 1–12.

Tulving, E. (1993). What is episodic memory? *Current Directions in Psychological Science, 2,* 67–70.

Tulving, E. (1999). On the uniqueness of episodic memory. In L.-G. Nilsson & H. J. Markowitsch (Eds.), *Cognitive neuroscience of memory* (pp. 11–42). Seattle: Hogrefe & Huber.

Tulving, E. (2000). Concepts of memory. In E. Tulving & F. I. M. Craik (Eds.), *The Oxford handbook of memory* (pp. 33–43). New York: Oxford University Press.

Tulving, E. (2002). Episodic memory: From mind to brain. *Annual Review of Psychology, 54,* 1–25.

Tulving, E., & Pearlstone. Z. (1966). Availability versus accessibility of information in memory for words. *Journal of Verbal Learning and Verbal Behavior, 5,* 381–391.

Tulving, E., & Thomson, D. M. (1973). Encoding specificity and retrieval processes in episodic memory. *Psychological Review, 80,* 359–380.

Tversky, B., & Marsh, E. J. (2000). Biased retellings of events yield biased memories. *Cognitive Psychology, 40,* 1–38.

Underwood, B. J. (1957). Interference and forgetting. *Psychological Review, 64,* 49–60.

Underwood, B. J. (1963). Stimulus selection in verbal learning. In C. N. Cofer & B. J. Musgrave (Eds.), *Verbal behavior and learning: Problems and processes* (pp. 33–48). New York: McGraw-Hill.

Wade, E., & Clark, H. H. (1993). Reproduction and demonstration in quotations. *Journal of Memory and Language, 32,* 805–819.

Wagenaar, W. A. (1986). My memory: A study of autobiographical memory over six years. *Cognitive Psychology, 18,* 225–252.

Wagenaar, W. A. (1988). People and places in my memory: A study on cue specificity and retrieval from autobiographical memory. In M. M. Gruneberg, P. E. Morris, & R. N. Sykes (Eds.), *Practical aspects of memory: Current research and issues* (pp. 228–233). New York: Wiley.

Watkins, M. J. (1990). Mediationism and the obfuscation of memory. *American Psychologist, 45,* 328–335.

Weaver, C. A., III. (1993). Do you need a "flash" to form a flashbulb memory? *Journal of Experimental Psychology: General, 122,* 39–46.

Weiner, B. (1966). Motivation and memory. *Psychological Monographs: General and Applied, 80,* 22.

Wetzler, S. E., & Sweeney, J. A. (1986). Childhood amnesia: An empirical demonstration. In D. C. Rubin (Ed.), *Autobiographical memory* (pp. 191–201). Cambridge, UK: Cambridge University Press.

Wheeler, M. A. (2000). Episodic memory and autonoetic awareness. In E. Tulving & F. I. M. Craik (Eds.), *The Oxford handbook of memory* (pp. 597–608). New York: Oxford University Press.

White, R. T. (1982). Memory for personal events. *Human Learning, 1,* 171–183.

Wills, T. A. (1981). Downward social comparison principles in social psychology. *Psychological Bulletin, 90,* 245–271.

Wilson, B. A., & Wearing, D. (1995). Prisoner of consciousness: A state of just awakening following Herpes Simplex Encephalitis. In R. Campbell & M. A. Conway (Eds.), *Broken memories: Case studies in memory impairment* (pp. 15–30). Cambridge, UK: Blackwell.

Yarmey, A. D., & Bull, M. P., III. (1978). Where were you when President Kennedy was assassinated? *Bulletin of the Psychonomic Society, 11,* 133–135.

CHAPTER 18

Procedural Memory and Skill Acquisition

ADDIE JOHNSON

One of the most remarkable things about human performance is the regularity, efficiency, and precision with which it commonly occurs. Despite the fact that we are presented with a complex array of stimuli in a constantly changing environment with a bewildering array of choices, things usually go as planned. Even in the performance of complex tasks, patterns of stimuli in the environment are grouped and reacted to in what appears to be seamless, coordinated ease.

Skilled performance obviously depends on prior experience, but exactly what must be learned and remembered in order to develop and exercise skill? What aspects from learning episodes are important for the development of skill, and what aspects of memory are involved in this learning? These are key issues in understanding the development, maintenance, and exercise of skill. Other issues of importance are the roles of forgetting, the making of mistakes, and attention in the acquisition and execution of skilled performance. In this chapter, the roles of explicit, declarative memory in skilled performance will be considered and contrasted with the role of implicit, procedural memory.

DECLARATIVE MEMORY AND SKILL ACQUISITION

It is probably not too daring to say that all major models of skill acquisition, just as the acquisition of skill, itself, begin with declarative memory. Declarative memory has been described as an episodic or recollective memory system (Squire, 1992), the characterization of which overlaps with descriptions of episodic and semantic memory (see the chapters in this volume by Nairne; McNamara & Holbrook; and Roediger & Marsh). Basically, declarative memory refers to a system that works with verbalizable knowledge. In his influential ACT* (and ACT-R) model of the development of cognitive skill, Anderson (1982, 1983, 1993) calls the first stage in the development of skill the *declarative stage*. Anderson's work will be more fully described in a later section. At this point it is sufficient to note that the declarative stage is one in which verbal mediation is used to maintain facts in working memory so that they can be used to execute the task at hand. In other words, performance at this level depends heavily on declarative memory. Fitts (1962/1990, 1964; Fitts & Posner, 1967) called the first phase of skill acquisition by a different name, but his *cognitive phase* also depends heavily on declarative memory for comprehending instructions and maintaining a description of the cues that must be attended to and the relevance of the feedback that is provided during performance. In the frameworks of both Anderson and Fitts, the development of skill is characterized by reduced dependence on declarative memory.

At least one account of skill acquisition, Logan's (1988, 1990) *instance theory of automaticity,* suggests that memory demands of performance do not qualitatively change as a function of skill, at least not once the basic instructions have been mastered. Logan's theory may not apply to skill acquisition in a broad sense, but it has been to shown to provide a good description of the development of skilled performance in a range of cognitive tasks. Logan describes the development of automaticity as the shift from a dependence on general algorithms that do not rely on previous experience but that are sufficient to produce solutions to problems posed by the task, to a reliance on the retrieval of performance episodes. Memory plays a critical role in this model in which skilled, automatic performance entails a shift from algorithm-based performance to memory-based performance.

The instance theory of automaticity rests on several assumptions. The first of these assumptions is that encoding is obligatory, such that attention to an object or event is sufficient for it to be encoded into memory. The second assumption calls for obligatory retrieval, in which attention to an object or event is sufficient to cause things associated with it to be retrieved. An additional, critical assumption is that each encounter with an object or event is encoded, stored, and retrieved separately, and on every encounter. These encounters are the instances in the instance theory of automaticity. As mentioned above, the instance theory assumes that automaticity involves a transition from performance based on general rules or algorithms for performing a task to performance based on the retrieval of instances. Once performance is instance based, it continues to speed up because the number of instances continues to increase as long as the task is practiced. This speed-up is predicted on the basis of the statistical properties of the distribution of retrieval times for instances: As the number of instances increases, the minimum time to retrieve an instance decreases. Because retrieval is obligatory, according to the theory, performance time will decrease as a function of practice due to this faster retrieval time. An important aspect of the theory is that it predicts that changes in performance will follow a power function. This is consistent with the *power law of practice,* which reflects the finding that performance improvements in many tasks follow a power function (see Figure 18.1).

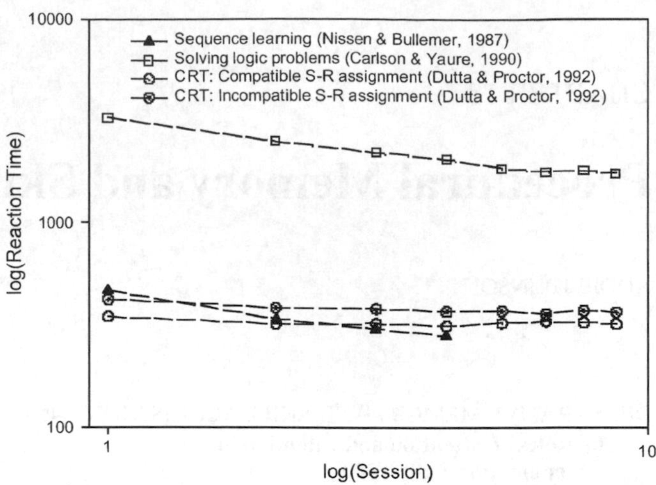

Figure 18.1 Performance speed-up in various tasks illustrating the power law of practice. *Note:* When plotted in log-log coordinates, a power function appears as a straight line. CRT = choice reaction time; S-R = stimulus-response.

It can be argued that the early dependence on an algorithm for task performance can be likened to the declarative or cognitive phase of the frameworks of Fitts (1962/1990, 1964) and Anderson (1982, 1983). At this stage, the rules or guidelines for performing a task presumably must be active in working memory, and performance is relatively deliberative and slow. As a result of experience, and of paying attention to the right things at the right time, a collection of memory traces, or instances, builds up and gradually comes to dominate performance.

The Roles of Attention and Intention in Memory and Skill

Attention has assumed a curious place in the study of skill acquisition. Often, it seems that the goal of researchers has been to show that attention may not be necessary at all once a skill has been learned. The traditional view of attentive processing (or "controlled" processing; Atkinson & Shiffrin, 1968) is that it is relatively slow, requires effort, and involves consciousness of one's actions. Skill is described as a gradual (or abrupt) freeing of resources and shift to a capacity-free, stimulus-driven mode of performance that is not dependent on conscious control. Posner and Snyder (1975) described automatic processes as those that may occur "without intention, without any conscious awareness and without interference with other mental activity" (p. 81). A great deal of research has been directed to exploring and confirming this view of dichotomous processing modes. For example, W. Schneider and Shiffrin (1977; Shiffrin & Schneider, 1977) performed an extensive series of hybrid memory and visual search experiments that seemed to support the idea that there are two different modes of processing and that controlled processing gives way to automatic processing if only enough practice is given.

The view that controlled and automatic processing are qualitatively distinct has, to some extent, fallen out of favor. Within the realm of visual search, where Shiffrin and Schneider (1977) carried out their influential work supporting such a dichotomy, researchers now tend speak about the efficiency of search, rather than pre-attentive and attentive search, and the role of attention in processing remains present across search types. Rather than considering it a form of processing, Neumann (1987) describes automaticity as a phenomenon arising from a conjunction of input stimuli, skill, and the desired action. In his view, it is appropriate to speak of automaticity when all the information for performing a task is present in the input information (stimulus information available in the environment) or in long-term memory. This view is not too different from Logan's (1988, 1990), described above, in which automatic processing is based on memory retrieval, and attention forms the cues necessary for the retrieval processing. Attention remains an important process even in highly practiced tasks.

As will be discussed at more length in the section on training, automatic processing, as assessed by an apparent insensitivity to attentional resources or demands, can develop with learning when the right conditions are provided. The important conditions seem to be the consistency of the discrimination and interpretation of the stimuli, and the stimulus-to-response mapping (W. Schneider & Fisk, 1982). The development of automaticity can be shown for a range of tasks. The idea that it depends more on consistency than on properties of the stimuli, such as perceptual salience, is supported by the finding that automatic processing can also be produced by training with stimuli divided into arbitrary classes (Shiffrin & Schneider, 1977).

According to the instance theory, "attention drives both the acquisition of automaticity and the expression of automaticity in skilled performance" (Logan & Compton, 1998, p. 114). Selected information enters into the instances that come to drive performance, but ignored information does not. Moreover, if attention is not paid to the right cues, associations dependent on those cues will not be retrieved (Logan & Etherton, 1994). Logan and Compton describe attention as an interface between memory and events in the world. The dependence of memory on attention means that knowing (or learning) what to attend to is a critical component in the development of skill. Other authors have emphasized that learning not to attend to irrelevant information is also a component of skill acquisition.

Learning to Ignore Irrelevant Information

One hypothesis about how learning to ignore irrelevant information contributes to performance changes with practice is the *information reduction hypothesis* (Haider & Frensch, 1996). According to this hypothesis, performance improvements can be attributed to learning to distinguish task-relevant information from task-redundant (and, therefore, task-irrelevant) information and then learning to ignore the task-irrelevant information. Evidence for this hypothesis comes largely from tasks in which participants verified alphabetic strings such as E [4] J K L. The task is to determine whether the letters follow in alphabetic order, where the number in brackets corresponds to the number of letters left out of the alphabetic sequence. In most conditions, the length of the string was varied by changing the number of letters following the digit, which always occupied the second position in the string. If there was an error in the stimulus, the error was in the number of letters that was skipped (e.g., E [4] K L M). Early in practice, Haider and Frensch found an effect of string length on performance, such that verification times were slower when the number of letters after the number in brackets was increased. With practice, however, the slope of the function relating performance time to string length decreased. This finding suggests that participants in the study learned that the extra letters were not important for the task and should be ignored. Additional evidence for this hypothesis was found in a transfer condition in which errors *could* occur in the letters to the right of the gap (e.g., E [4] J K M). Consistent with the supposition that participants learned to ignore the extra letters during training, the error rate in detecting these invalid sequences increased as a function of practice. Haider and Frensch also showed that learning in this task was not stimulus specific by demonstrating transfer from one half of the alphabet to the other.

Haider and Frensch (1996) showed that learners were able to distinguish relevant from redundant task information and to limit their processing to the relevant information. They also showed that learning to reduce the amount of information that is processed takes time, developing over the course of practice, and that this ability appears to be largely stimulus independent. Moreover, after finding that speed instructions affect whether or not people learn to ignore irrelevant information, Haider and Frensch (1999) argued that skill acquisition is neither passive nor "low-level," but at least partly under the influence of intention.

It seems obvious that knowing what to attend to will increase the chance that the right events are experienced such that useful instances are created, and that the allocation of attention at encoding and retrieval determines to a large extent both the nature of what is learned and the influence of previous experiences on performance in the present. There is, however, much to be said, and even more to be learned, about the interplay between intention and attention, and about how much we learn without really intending it.

IMPLICIT LEARNING

Learning without intention, and without conscious awareness of what is being learned, is a topic that has received much attention in recent decades. Models of skill typically emphasize early processing of task instructions and goal-directed learning, and paying attention to the correct elements in a task situation is considered crucial to eventual skilled performance. The topic of this section is *implicit learning* (also referred to as *incidental learning*), that is, learning without intention, or the unintended by-product of experience with a task.

Consider a relatively simple task, that of pressing an assigned key whenever a stimulus appears at one of four particular locations on a screen. The instructions are simple: Press the rightmost key when the rightmost stimulus appears, the second key to the right for a stimulus in the corresponding location, and so on. One aspect of performance in such a task is that, despite the simplicity of the task, performance improves as a function of practice. Reaction times become faster and error rates lower (Dutta & Proctor, 1992; Proctor & Dutta, 1993), with improvements in accuracy and reaction time typically following a power function (Newell & Rosenbloom, 1981; see Figure 18.1 and the chapter by Proctor & Vu in this volume). These improvements can be attributed to intentional learning of key and stimulus locations and of the stimulus-response associations. Performance can be considerably improved if elements are repeated within the sequence of trials. One sort of repetition is just that: A particular stimulus may be repeated in two successive trials (see the chapter by Proctor & Vu for a discussion of the basis of such *repetition effects*). However, even when the repetition occurs across a longer sequence of trials, benefits of repetition can occur.

Nissen and Bullemer (1987) provided practice with the task described above, in which keys are pressed according to the spatial location of targets. Within the sequence of trials, certain stimuli were repeated (designating the positions from left to right as A, B, C, and D, the repeating sequence was D-B-C-A-C-B-D-C-B-A). People who practiced this *serial response time* (SRT) task with the 10-element repeating sequence showed vastly more improvement than those who practiced the task with a random presentation of stimuli, even though the participants were not informed that there was a repeating sequence or instructed to look for repetitions while performing the task.

Implicit Learning and Awareness

The participants in Nissen and Bullemer's (1987) study evidently learned something (the repeating sequence) even though they were not instructed to do so. Organizing and making sense of the environment is, however, something that comes naturally to most of us. The question is, then, whether participants in Nissen and Bullemer's study either consciously looked for or somehow noticed that there was a repeating sequence and used this explicit knowledge to improve task performance. In order to separate intentional and incidental learning in this task, and in order to assess the role of awareness in the performance of the task, Nissen and Bullemer asked participants whether they were aware of any sequences in the stimuli. All of the participants in the repeated-sequence condition reported being aware of the sequence. Thus, awareness was coupled with the improvement of performance for this group. In order to address the question of whether awareness was necessary for the performance benefit to occur, Nissen and Bullemer repeated the experiment with a group of individuals characterized by a profound amnesia that prevented them from recognizing and recalling material to which they had been exposed: Korsakoff patients. As predicted, the Korsakoff patients reported no awareness of the repeating sequence. More interesting, their performance showed a degree of learning of the sequence comparable to that of controls (see Figure 18.2). This shows that learning can and does occur without awareness.

Later work (Willingham, Nissen, & Bullemer, 1989) showed that the degree of awareness of the sequence is correlated with performance for normal participants: People who showed more awareness (as indexed by explicit recall of the sequence) also showed more performance improvement. However, when anticipatory responses (i.e., pressing the response key before the next stimulus appeared) were eliminated from the analysis, the difference in performance between those who reported full or partial knowledge of the sequence and those who could evidence no explicit knowledge was minimal.

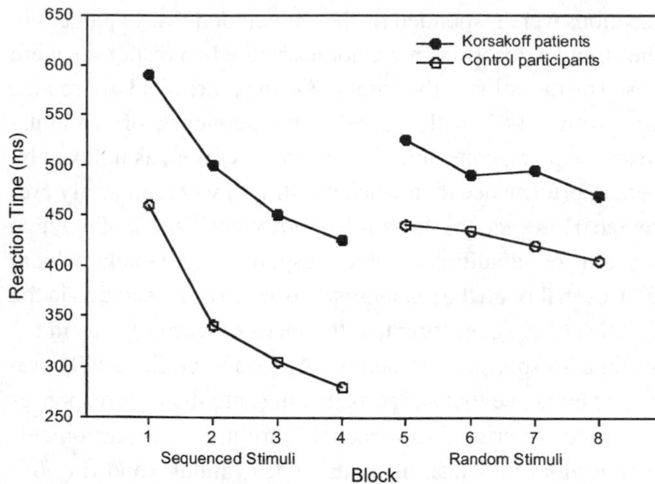

Figure 18.2 Implicit learning in a serial response time task by amnesics and normals. *Source:* Nissen and Bullemer (1987).

Other researchers using different measures of explicit knowledge have shown high correlations between explicit knowledge and performance (e.g., Perruchet & Amorim, 1992), as well as evidence of explicit knowledge of the sequence at the point where performance differences between random and sequential presentation first become evident, casting some doubt on the Willingham et al. (1989) finding of relative independence of the two measures of knowledge. However, given the evidence of sequence learning in Korsakoff amnesics, we see that learning without awareness certainly can occur.

Implicit Learning and Attention

It is interesting to ask whether the learning seen in the SRT task is dependent on the availability of attention to process relations between elements in the task. One way to assess this is to compare learning in a single-task condition, in which only the task to be learned is performed, with a dual-task condition, in which a secondary task is performed. The requirement to perform a secondary task should take attention away from the SRT task. Such an experiment was carried out by A. Cohen, Ivry, and Keele (1990) using a sequence task in combination with distractor tasks of different difficulties. They specially constructed sequences to contain either unique associations, in which each stimulus uniquely specified the following (e.g., A always followed by C), ambiguous associations, such that A might be followed by C in one case and by D in another, or both. They found that ambiguous sequences were not learned under the dual-task conditions but that unique associations were. On the basis of these results, they suggested that sequence learning depends on two processes. The first process is automatic, in that it can occur without attention's being directed to it. This process forms associations between adjacent items. The second process, which requires attention to operate, is proposed to build hierarchical codes based on parsing the sequence at a higher level (i.e., into bigger subsequences) than associations between only two items.

A. Cohen et al. (1990) showed that simple associations could be learned under conditions of distraction, but the amount of learning may nonetheless be affected by attentional load. For example, Frensch, Buchner, and Lin (1994) showed that whereas learning could take place under both single- and dual-task conditions, and for both simple and ambiguous sequences, the amount of learning that took place was reduced when a distractor task was present, suggesting that sequence learning is modulated by attention.

Jiménez and Méndez (1999) attempted to resolve the issue of whether general attentional demands modulate sequence learning by using sequences that were unlikely to be explicitly learned and a secondary task that should produce little disruption. They examined the roles of both selective processing requirements (attending to to-be-associated elements) and generalized mental load (taxing attentional resources by adding a secondary task to the sequence-learning task). An SRT task was used in which the sequences of stimulus locations were generated following a noisy finite-state grammar and response keys were pressed corresponding to the position of the stimuli. In addition, the identity of a stimulus on a given trial gave probabilistic information about where the next stimulus would appear. A single-task condition was contrasted with a dual-task condition in which two of four possible target shapes had to be counted and the total reported at the end of the block. Participants in both single- and dual-task conditions exhibited sequence learning, showing faster reaction times and a lower error rate for practice with grammatical sequences than for random ones. Learning of the predictive relation between a stimulus on one trial and the location of the stimulus on the next trial was assessed by examining the difference between valid (in which the predictive relation held) and invalid (in which the position was not predicted) trials. Only in the dual-task conditions, in which participants had to attend to target identity in order to perform the counting task, were these relations learned. Thus, selective attention does seem to be necessary for such learning to occur, and this learning occurs even though (or precisely because) a secondary task must be performed. In other words, paying attention to a predictive dimension seems to be necessary for this dimension to enter into a predictive relationship.

In summary, sequence learning can occur implicitly, and this learning is at least partly the result of automatic associative processes. Associative processes can be carried out independently of mental load, but only on events that are active in working memory.

The Nature of Implicit Learning

If we accept that learning without intention (and perhaps without awareness) can occur, we can also ask what the nature of the learning is. For example, is one learning relations between stimuli, relations between stimulus-response associations, or the motor sequence? One interesting hypothesis, similar to the idea that prediction is the basis for conditioned learning, is that it is the response-effect relationship that is first implicitly learned and that this might provide the basis for the development of explicit knowledge. To test this hypothesis, Ziessler (1998) modified Nissen and Bullemer's (1987) SRT paradigm so that the location of the stimulus on a particular trial was determined by the response made on the previous trial. Rather than responding to the location of the stimulus, as in Nissen and Bullemer's task, participants in Ziessler's experiments responded to the identity of a target in the presence of distractors. The location of the target was thus not relevant for the response, but knowledge of the location could be used to speed up search and, accordingly, reaction times.

By varying the predictability of the position of the following stimulus (achieved by varying whether all stimuli assigned to a certain key predicted the same position), Ziessler (1998) showed that performance improved more when the response made reliably predicted the position of the next stimulus than when it was only sometimes a valid predictor. Moreover, only the perfectly reliable response-stimulus associations condition showed negative transfer to a condition in which target position was random, as well as showing the largest increase in reaction time when stimulus-response relations were altered. None of the participants in Ziessler's study reported noticing anything predictable in target position. Thus, it seems that knowledge of target position was only implicitly learned.

In the original Nissen and Bullemer (1987) experiments, responses were made to the location of the stimulus. Therefore, it is impossible to say whether performance improvements depended on the learning of perceptual relations (the relation of one stimulus to the next), stimulus-response associations, or response relations (the relation of one response to the next). Willingham et al. (1989) attempted to look separately at the learning of these relations using the SRT task described above in which the locations of the stimuli follow a predictable sequence, but requiring that responses be made to the color of the stimuli, rather than their locations. By assessing performance during practice and in a transfer task in which locations were responded to, they concluded that sequences in the stimulus locations were not learned when responses were based on the color of the stimuli. On the other hand, if practice was with a task with a predictable sequence of stimulus-response pairs, considerable learning occurred, as indexed by better performance than when the stimuli were randomly presented. However, this group also showed no benefit of practice in a transfer condition in which responses were made to location, even though the responses were exactly the same as in the practice task, suggesting that the locus of learning was in the stimulus-response associations. A. Cohen et al. (1990) presented evidence that suggests that the actual motor responses made are not critical to sequence learning: After participants practiced an SRT task using the index, middle, and ring fingers, transfer was virtually perfect in a condition in which only one finger was used to make responses.

The actual responses made may, however, be a locus of learning in some types of tasks. Palmer and Meyer (2000) recently tested the separate contributions that conceptual and motor skill make to the skill of piano playing and found that the relative importance of the effectors used and the movements made changes as a function of skill level. For low- and moderately skilled piano players, transfer was greatest when the motor movements were the same (even though a different part of the keyboard was used) for pieces played in practice and transfer. Skilled players, in contrast, showed the most transfer when conceptual (melody) aspects of the transfer piece corresponded to the practice piece, even when different fingers and hands were used. This suggests that the mental plans for performing an action only become independent of the required movements at an advanced stage of practice. Findings that show independence of learning from the effectors used (e.g., A. Cohen et al., 1990) may be limited to relatively simple motor tasks.

It can be concluded that the research on sequence learning provides evidence that learning can occur without awareness, although attending to the relevant stimulus aspects does seem to be required for this learning to occur. The nature of the learning seems to depend primarily on associations between stimuli and responses (or between responses and stimuli), unless the visual demands are made more complex, in which case perceptual learning also plays a role (see Lewicki, Czyzewska, & Hoffman, 1987; Stadler, 1989).

PROCEDURAL MEMORY

Skill acquisition has been described as a transition from reliance on verbal, declarative knowledge to a reliance on procedures or routines for performing tasks. The distinction between performance based on explicit versus procedural knowledge has led to the conception of different ways of learning and knowing, sometimes described as *knowing that* versus *knowing how*. Explicit memory requires the conscious directing of attention to the act of recall for remembering facts (i.e., knowledge that), whereas the performance of a skilled action (i.e., knowledge how), although it also reflects past experience, does not involve active attention or conscious recall (Squire & Cohen, 1984). Much research indicates that *procedural learning,* indexed by improvements in the execution of task elements, may involve a different system from the declarative learning of facts and instructions. Indeed, it appears that there are different memory systems underlying declarative and procedural learning.

Tulving (1985) described *procedural memory* as a memory system that "enables organisms to retain learned connections between stimuli and responses, including those involving complex stimulus patterns and response chains, and to respond adaptively to the environment" (p. 387). In Tulving's view, procedural memory differs from episodic and semantic memory in the nature of acquiring, representing, and expressing knowledge, as well as in the kind of conscious awareness that characterizes it. Procedural knowledge is available only in the form of overt expression and is not available for conscious introspection. Tulving describes procedural learning as "tuning" (Rumelhart & Norman, 1978), in the sense that procedural memory provides prescriptive knowledge that can be used to guide future action without containing specific information about the past. In this view, procedural learning is abstract in the sense that there is no memory of specific prior events, but it reflects the acquisition, retention, and retrieval of knowledge expressed through experience-induced changes in performance.

Evidence for Procedural Memory

One of the most convincing sources of evidence for a distinction between declarative and procedural memory comes from demonstrations of benefits of practice or learning in amnesic individuals. The observation that amnesic persons sometimes do show good memory performance across long retention intervals was made by Claperède (1911), who remarked that one of his patients' behavior was altered by experience and that this altered behavior outlasted the patient's memory of the experience itself. His patient, a woman with Korsakoff's syndrome, learned not to shake hands with the doctor after he had pricked her with a pin secreted in his hand, but she was unable to tell the doctor why she declined to do so. Such patients can sometimes acquire information at a normal rate and can maintain normal performance across delays. In the absence of the ability to recognize having previously seen a particular stimulus, task, or, in some cases, even the experimenter, many amnesic persons have demonstrated the ability to acquire and retain perceptual-motor skills, such as rotory pursuit and mirror drawing, cognitive skills (e.g., solving jigsaw puzzles or the tower of Hanoi, or using a mathematical rule), and perceptual skill, such as reading mirror-reversed text (N. J. Cohen, 1984) or learning mazes (Corkin, 1965). For example, Nissen and Bullemer's (1987) study, described above, showed that amnesic individuals evidence just as much improvement in the SRT task as do normally functioning individuals (see Figure 18.2).

Brooks and Baddeley (1976) showed that both Korsakoff patients and postencephalitic patients improved in the rotary-pursuit task. Performance of amnesic individuals is often equivalent to that of normal controls in a variety of perceptual-motor tasks; however, they do not benefit as much as normal controls from the repetition of specific items. Although amnesic persons can show preserved memory for particular stimuli, as evidenced by facilitation of certain aspects of test performance based on prior exposure to stimulus materials (i.e., *priming;* e.g., Jacoby & Witherspoon, 1982; Verfaellie, Bauer, & Bowers, 1991), their recognition memory for the stimuli is poor. Thus, amnesic individuals seem to possess normal pattern-analyzing operations or encoding procedures but poor declarative memory for item-specific information that would normally be acquired from applying these operations or procedures.

A Procedural Memory System?

According to Tulving (1985), a memory system consists of memory processes and a supportive structure for those processes. Two important structures for procedural learning seem to be the basal ganglia and the cerebellum. At the moment, there are several different hypotheses about the roles of these two structures. One hypothesis is that learning repetitive motor sequences depends on the basal ganglia, whereas learning new mappings of visual cues to motor responses depends on the cerebellum (Willingham, Koroshetz, & Peterson, 1996). Another hypothesis is that the cerebellum is needed for closed-loop skill learning, in which visual feedback about errors in movement is available and must be used, whereas open-loop skill learning, in which movements are executed without feedback, depends more on the basal ganglia (Gabrieli, 1998). Hikosaka et al. (1999) stress the cerebellum's role in the timing of movements and suggest that the basal ganglia is involved in reward-based evaluation.

Flament and Ebner (1996) propose that the role of the cerebellum as a comparator of desired motor output and actual performance may be most important during learning of a novel motor task. Both positron-emission tomography (PET) and functional magnetic resonance imaging (fMRI) data are compatible with the idea that the cerebellum is heavily involved when movement errors are common and corrective movements must be produced to compensate for them. Cerebellar activity decreases as skill increases, and there is a positive correlation between the number of errors and cerebellar activity. Interestingly, several studies have shown a decrease in cerebellar activity as a function of the learning of finger-movement sequences (e.g., Friston, Frith, Passingham, Liddle, & Frackowiak, 1992). Increased activity in motor cortical areas during motor learning indicates that these areas also contribute to the learning process, and neuroimaging studies point to a role of primary and secondary motor cortex in learning tasks such as the SRT task.

PROCEDURAL MEMORY, IMPLICIT LEARNING, AND SKILL

Most scholars would agree that the distinction between procedural and explicit, episodic memory is a real one, and that different systems underlie implicit and explicit remembering. The exact nature of the relationship between implicit and explicit learning is less clear. Some have argued that implicit knowledge provides the basis for explicit knowledge (Ziessler, 1998), others have argued that explicit knowledge is converted into procedural knowledge (Anderson, 1983), and still others have argued that implicit and explicit knowledge develop independently of each other (Willingham & Goedert-Eschmann, 1999). Studies using PET imaging are consistent with the idea that explicit and implicit learning have separate foundations. Grafton, Hazeltine, and Ivry (1995; Hazeltine, Grafton, & Ivry, 1997), for example, found metabolic changes in primary and supplementary motor cortexes and the putamen that were associated with implicit learning, whereas explicit learning was associated with changes in blood flow in prefrontal and premotor cortices. Willingham and Goedert-Eschmann used transfer tasks to show that the degree of implicit learning in an SRT task did not depend on whether explicit learning instructions were given. This suggests that implicit learning is indeed independent of explicit learning and that performance that is initially dominated by conscious mediation may eventually come to rely on implicit knowledge that has quietly been developing as a direct by-product of task performance. However, further work is necessary to determine the way in which implicit and explicit learning are related.

SKILLED PERFORMANCE

Proctor and Dutta (1995) defined skill as "goal-directed, well-organized behavior that is acquired through practice and performed with economy of effort" (p. 18). Thus, all skills are assumed to be acquired through practice or training, to be the result of goal-directed learning (even though incidental learning may occur as the result of performance), and to be expressed in coordinated, efficient performance. Simple skills, such as performing SRT tasks, consist of only a few basic components (perception, classification, response selection, and response) and are learned after a relatively modest amount of practice. Complex skills, such as solving physics problems, are made up of multiple components that need to be learned and integrated before skill is acquired. Such skills take more time to develop and are more dependent on the nature of training and the background of the performer. Whether the environment is open or closed also affects the acquisition of skill. In a closed environment, the conditions in which the skill is performed are always essentially the same, whereas in open environments conditions are changing and uncertain. In an open environment, the environment itself dictates to some extent how the skill must be performed. For example, given that ice conditions are perfect, a figure skater simply performs the learned skills regardless of where the arena is located. A hockey player, on the other hand, must be aware of the positions of other players in order to appropriately exercise learned skills.

Phases of Skill Acquisition

In the beginning of the chapter, Fitts's (1962/1990, 1964; Fitts & Posner, 1967) framework was mentioned in the context of the role of memory in skilled performance. Fitts did not posit any specific mechanisms that describe changes in the role or importance of memory, attention, or other elementary processes, but his general framework is consistent with a shift from attentive, deliberative processing of the environment and task requirements to a dependence on retrieval from long-term memory, in one form or another. Fitts describes three phases of skill acquisition, the *cognitive, associative* or *fixation,* and *autonomous* phases. As described above, the cognitive phase emphasizes the role of declarative memory and cognitive processes in performance. In the associative, or fixation, phase, "correct patterns of behavior are fixated by continued practice" (Fitts, 1962/1990, p. 286). This phase may last for days or months before the autonomous phase is reached. At this final phase, performance is relatively free from errors (although performance time may continue to improve) and shows increasing resistance to stress and interference from concurrent activities. Fitts suggests that this stage is characterized by a shift from visual to proprioceptive feedback. He also points out that many skills can be described in terms of subskills, and that each of these subroutines may develop at its own rate. This idea provides the basis for part-task training, discussed below.

Anderson's (1982, 1983, 1993) account of skill acquisition also consists of an early *declarative* phase and a later *procedural* phase, with an intermediary process of *knowledge compilation* that enables the learner to move from the declarative to the procedural phase by converting the declarative knowledge of the learner into a procedural form. Procedures, or *productions,* are basically if-then rules. On the basis of productions, even complex environmental conditions (if compiled) can trigger mental or overt actions without the requirement that all relevant aspects of the situation be kept active in working memory for the application of general interpretive mechanisms.

Mechanisms of Change

According to Anderson (1982), practice results in increased speed of processing of component procedures. Procedures may also be compiled or restructured through processes of chunking (Newell & Rosenbloom, 1981). Carlson, Sullivan, and Schneider (1989) investigated the relative contributions of component speed-up and restructuring for the tasks of predicting or verifying the output of logic gates (e.g., "if all inputs are equal to 1, the output is 1; otherwise the output is 0" [*and* gate]). They found that prediction judgments were faster than verification judgments and that both types of judgments were faster when the gate type evaluated whether certain elements were present rather than if they were absent. The same relative ordering of task difficulty was maintained for the full 1,200 trials of practice, suggesting that participants were not able to automatize the procedures used to make the judgments. In order to test whether attentional resources were freed up as a function of practice, a memory load was introduced at two points during practice. The memory load consisted either of irrelevant digits (i.e., digits other than 0 or 1), digits that had to be substituted into the comparisons in order to make the judgments, or digits that could, in principle, be used in logic gate problems, but that were not needed to actually solve the problems. The memory load had an effect on logic gate performance only when it had to be accessed in order to solve the problem, and this effect was the same both early and late in practice. Thus, Carlson et al. did not find evidence for qualitative changes in how the task was performed.

When the task is more complex, requiring the formation of subgoals, evidence for restructuring and speed-up of component processes is sometimes found. Carlson, Khoo, Yaure, and Schneider (1990) devised a task in which complex circuits of logic gates had to be tested. They found that both the number of moves required to troubleshoot a circuit (an indication of the efficiency of the search strategy) and the time per move (the efficiency of operator application) decreased as a function of practice, with especially big improvements early in practice. The pattern of moves also changed with practice, indicating that learners did form subgoals and came to recognize the conditions under which these subgoals could be applied. Retention tests given after 6 months showed retention of both improvements in the speed of component processing and in the restructuring of the component steps.

TYPES OF SKILLS

In order to gain more insight into the nature of learning and the conditions that promote the acquisition of skills, it is necessary to consider performance in a wide range of tasks. Most real-world skills include perceptual, cognitive, and motor components. Although the goal of skills researchers is to understand complex behavior, much can be learned by attempting to isolate these basic information processes and to look at the development of perceptual, cognitive, and motor components of skill.

Perceptual Skill

Perceptual skills are those skills that depend heavily on the ability to discriminate between and to classify stimuli on the basis of perceivable attributes of the stimuli. In some skills, such as wine tasting (Melcher & Schooler, 1996) or determining the sex of baby chicks (Lunn, 1948), the skill to be learned is clearly primarily perceptual. However, often perceptual skills are an important part of other skills. For example, copying high-speed Morse code depends on the perceptual ability to parse the *dit*s and *dah*s that make up the message and to group these symbols into conceptual units, the motor ability to quickly type the message, and the strategic ability to *copy behind,* that is, to allow the typing of the message to lag behind the decoding of the message (Wisher, Sabol, & Kern, 1995). Sports performed in open environments also depend on perceptual skill. For example, it has been shown that skill in volleyball is associated with especially rapid visual search when a volleyball is the target (Allard & Starkes, 1980).

In order for perceptual skill to develop, features that are specific to a particular stimulus and that distinguish it from other stimuli must be learned. One factor that can influence the development of perceptual skill is labeling. Labeling forces observers to attend to the distinctive and unique features of stimuli; having attended to these features, observers can use them to improve performance (e.g., Rabin, 1988). It may be more than a matter of affectation that wine tasters have developed such an elaborate vocabulary for classifying wines. Training that directs the observer's attention to unique features has also been shown to result in better perceptual learning (e.g., Biederman & Shiffrar, 1987).

Sowden, Davies, and Roling (2000) investigated whether improved sensitivity in detecting basic features could be a basis for improvement in reading X-ray images. Experts were found to be more sensitive than novices in detecting dots in X-ray images. Further, novices were found to improve over 4 days of training but to show no transfer to reversed contrast images when these images were simple. When more complicated images were used, transfer (although not perfect) did occur. Sowden et al. interpreted these results as evidence that, in addition to strategic components, stimulus-specific sensory learning is important in learning to read X-ray images.

Perceptual learning leads to improved recognition and classification of stimuli, but it may also reflect improved *processing* of stimuli. Processing may become more efficient because stimuli are unitized in a sort of visual chunking process (LaBerge, 1973), or because observers become more fluent in applying learned operations. Kolers and Roediger (1984) developed the idea that stimuli are not remembered independently of the operations performed on them. That is, learning can be viewed as reflecting both experience with the stimuli and experience processing them. Evidence for this view comes from a series of studies in which observers read geometrically inverted text (i.e., text presented upside down and from right to left; Kolers, 1975a). After about two months of practice, participants became quite proficient in the task. Because different texts were used on different days, the learning was not tied only to the particular stimuli used in the task. In fact, when participants were tested in the same task more than a year later, reading times were only 5% faster when the same passages used in training were read than when completely new passages were used (Kolers, 1976). The advantage for the previously read pages was likely due to specific practice with the analysis of the graphemic patterns and not due to prior exposure to the content of the text. This is suggested by a study from Kolers (1975b) in which prior reading of the same text in a normal orientation did not facilitate reading of inverted text. A similar result was noted by Thorndike and Woodworth (1901a, 1901b, 1901c), who trained people on simple tasks such as estimating areas of geometric shapes or crossing out specific letters in a text, and then transferred them to related tasks. They found that the benefits of practice were restricted in scope, suggesting that the benefits were partly, or even primarily, due to perceptual learning of the training stimuli.

Cognitive Skill

Cognitive skills range from learning to make simple associations between stimuli and responses to solving complex problems or flying fighter planes. Complex skills usually have perceptual or motor components or depend on background knowledge, but much can be gained by examining what is arguably the simplest form of cognitive skill, response-selection skill. Response-selection processes are those processes that are important in determining which response is to be made to which stimulus. Increased facility in response selection is often the most important determinant of improvement in task performance (Teichner & Krebs, 1974; Welford, 1968, 1976), outweighing the importance of making perceptual discriminations or executing motor responses.

Developmental studies have shown that children's improvement as a function of age in a selective-attention task in which one stimulus dimension has to be attended and another ignored is largely attributable to increases in the speed with which stimulus-response translation can occur (Ridderinkhof, van der Molen, Band, & Bashore, 1997). Numerous studies have shown that stimulus-response translation is the locus of performance improvements in choice-reaction tasks among adults. For example, Pashler and Baylis (1991) used a number of practice and transfer conditions to determine the locus of performance improvements in choice-reaction tasks. Participants practiced pressing keys in response to stimulus category (e.g., pressing a key with the index finger if the stimulus was a letter, a middle key with the middle finger for a digit, and a left key with the ring finger for a nonalphanumeric symbol). During practice sessions, a small set of only two stimuli from each category was used. After substantial improvement in performance had occurred, two additional stimuli from each category were added. Importantly, responses were just as fast for new stimuli as for already practiced stimuli, suggesting that the locus of the practice effect was in assigning stimuli to categories and selecting the right category key. Changing the hand used to make the key presses had no effect on performance, ruling out a motor locus for improvements. However, consistent with a response-selection account of performance improvements, reassigning the categories to different keys completely eliminated the benefits of practice.

Although practice effects in choice-reaction tasks are concentrated in response-selection or stimulus-response translation processes, it does not seem to be the case that response selection becomes automatized such that stimuli automatically activate their corresponding responses. Ehrenstein,

Walker, Czerwinski, and Feldman (1997) review evidence from choice-reaction tasks and visual search studies that cast doubt on the idea that, at a fundamental level, performance becomes automatic as a function of practice. For example, it has been shown that one of the variables that most directly affects response selection, stimulus-response compatibility, continues to affect performance even after much practice and after performance seems to have reached an asymptotic level (Dutta & Proctor, 1992; Fitts & Seeger, 1953; see the chapter by Proctor & Vu).

Motor Skill

Motor skills have been extensively studied since the very beginnings of experimental psychology (e.g., Woodworth, 1899; Bryan & Harter, 1897, 1899). Whether one emphasizes "the integration of well-adjusted muscular performance" (Pear, 1948, p. 92) or "continuous interaction of response processes with input and feedback processes" (Fitts, 1962/1990, p. 275), motor performance often plays a central role in definitions of skill. There are three problems to be solved in learning to perform a motor task with skill. The *degrees-of-freedom* problem arises because there are many ways of performing any given action, and the performer is faced with the task of finding the best one. The *serial-order* problem concerns the timing and ordering of sequences of movements. Finally, the *perceptual-motor integration* problem involves coordinating the interactions between the perceptual and motor systems.

The Degrees-of-Freedom Problem

Degrees of freedom are, to put it simply, the dimensions of movement permitted by the joints involved in performing an action. In general, the more complex the movement, the more degrees of freedom there are available (see the chapter by Heuer). A goal of skilled performance is to make optimal use of the available degrees of freedom. Bernstein (1967) suggested that, early in performance, the degrees-of-freedom problem may be solved by simply fixing or "freezing" some of the joints involved in the action. Vereijken, van Emmerik, Whiting, and Newell (1992) showed that as a person masters a skill (in this case, learing to ski on a ski simulator), the degrees of freedom that are initially fixed are gradually freed such that the use of these joints can also enter into performance. As yet, little research has been done on whether fixing degrees of freedom is a general strategy, and results from the studies that have been done are mixed. Broderick and Newell (1999) suggest that both the task and the skill level of the performer must be considered, because the coordination patterns observed seem to depend on an interaction of the task and performer. In some cases, novices seem rigid and stiff (Vereijken et al., 1992). In other cases, novices show much more variability than experts (Broderick & Newell, 1999). Coordination of multiple effectors is more complicated than just a restriction of the range of movement of specific joints.

The Serial-Order Problem

Original ideas about the serial-order problem focused on the relation between one response and the next. In the linear-chain hypothesis of Lashley (1951), the sensory feedback produced by a response initiates the next response in the sequence. Such a process may explain learning when the two responses involved have a unique association such that the second response always follows the first. In such a case, learning might occur automatically, as discussed for unambiguous sequences in the earlier section on sequence learning. However, such a hypothesis cannot explain the learning of ambiguous sequences. Lashley hypothesized that control can also be hierarchical, and this hypothesis is supported by studies that show that the pauses that performers make when carrying out a sequence of finger movements correspond to the hierarchical structure of the sequence (Povel & Collard, 1982).

The Perceptual-Motor Integration Problem

The perceptual-motor integration problem involves the ways perception influences action and action influences perception. Perception provides visual information, as well as sensory input from receptors in the muscles, joints, tendons, and skin. Of these information sources, the role of vision in learning has received the most study. Despite rather extensive research, however, it is difficult to make generalizations about the role of vision in skilled performance. In many cases, if vision does play an important role in performance, it continues to play an important role even after extensive practice. For example, Khan and Franks (2000) showed that a group allowed to view the cursor while performing a cursor positioning task (in which a cursor had to be moved onto a target) performed better than a group that saw the cursor only at the beginning of a trial. When transferred to a no-vision condition, however, the group that practiced with visual feedback performed much worse than the group that had practiced without such feedback.

Some studies have suggested that visual feedback sometimes becomes *more* important with practice (Proteau & Cournoyer, 1990). Such findings are predicted by the *specificity-of-practice hypothesis* (Proteau, 1992; Proteau, Marteniuk, & Levesque, 1992), according to which different sources of sensory information are integrated to form an intermodal sensorimotor representation. Performance suffers if a source of information is removed or added because the incoming sensory information is then no longer compatible with the sensorimotor representation. Because specificity develops with practice, changes in information may result in greater decrements in performance after extensive practice than after moderate levels of practice. Thus, whether reliance on visual information seems to increase could depend on when such reliance is tested. More recently, Proteau, Tremblay, and DeJaeger (1998) have suggested that, with practice, the source of afferent information best suited to ensure optimal performance progressively dominates other sources of sensory information. The withdrawal of this information will lead to a deterioration in performance only when its dominance has been firmly established. Thus, withdrawing such a source of afferent information early in practice will be less detrimental than doing so later.

FACTORS INFLUENCING SKILL ACQUISITION

Coordination of different effectors, hierarchical control, and perceptual-motor integration are all necessary for the development of skill, but what are the factors that can enhance the development of skill? Answering this question requires that we make a distinction between factors that have an effect on the performance of a task and factors that affect learning, as measured by retention of the skill or performance on transfer tasks. Factors that lead to better performance during training do not necessarily lead to better learning. Bjork (1999) has argued that immediate performance is based on the *retrieval strength* of newly made memories, whereas learning is based on what he calls *storage strength*. He warns that training conditions that support performance by providing a short-term basis for ready access to correct responses or procedures may impede the growth of the storage strength necessary to support long-term performance.

A number of factors have been identified that affect the rate and extent of learning of motor tasks, and many of these factors seem to play an equally important role in the learning of cognitive tasks. Although factors such as the motivation and ability of the performer have a big influence on the outcome of practice, the factors that have been most extensively studied are feedback and practice schedules.

Feedback

There are two major sources of feedback: intrinsic and extrinsic. Intrinsic feedback is feedback that is directly produced by the response, and this can include proprioceptive, visual, auditory, and vestibular information. Contrary to an assumption that skilled performance is automatic and therefore increasingly less reliant on feedback, even skilled performance can be dependent on intrinsic feedback. As suggested by Proteau's (1992) specificity-of-practice hypothesis, removing feedback from a task practiced with feedback can disrupt performance, as can adding visual feedback to a task learned without such feedback (Elliott & Jaeger, 1988; Proteau et al., 1992). The important point seems to be that, with practice, a central representation of the relevant feedback is formed and that this representation (like the stimulus-response representations in response-selection tasks) continues to be used in highly skilled performance. It should be noted, however, that some studies have found a decreased reliance on feedback. In one such study, Pew (1966) found evidence that an early reliance on visual information in a higher-order tracking task was replaced by a control strategy that was performed automatically, with only occasional monitoring. One could argue, however, that performers in Pew's study learned to use proprioceptive feedback or other information in place of visual feedback.

Extrinsic feedback is feedback that is added to intrinsic feedback. It might include hearing a beep when a mistake is made or when a target is hit, watching a video of one's own performance, or viewing a plot of movement dynamics. An important distinction is between knowledge of results (KR), in which the outcomes (accuracy or speed) of a movement are conveyed to the performer, and knowledge of performance, in which information about the dynamics of movement (temporal or spatial) is provided to the performer. Knowledge of performance is more effective than KR when the task is more complex than a simple pointing or tracking task.

It seems reasonable to think that KR will be most effective when it is provided immediately and on every trial. However, this is not always the case. For example, Winstein and Schmidt (1990) found that just as much learning occurred when KR was provided on 33% of trials in which a complex movement had to be made as when it was provided on 100% of the trials. Moreover, decreasing the percentage of trials on which KR was provided across the training period led to better learning. It has also been found that providing a summary of performance at the end of a block of trials can be more effective than providing feedback after every trial (Lavery, 1962; Schmidt, Young, Swinnen, & Shapiro, 1989). Schmidt and colleagues have suggested that the function of feedback is to guide the performer toward the performance goal. This *guidance hypothesis* states that when feedback is provided on every trial, performers become too dependent on it, which leads to poorer performance on retention or transfer tests without the feedback. It may be that the important process that underlies the benefit for reduced feedback is a greater reliance on memory. The inclusion of no-KR trials may also lead to the development of the sort of internal representation that is necessary for performers to detect errors on their own. Whether feedback is intrinsic or extrinsic, it takes time to process it: KR provided too soon after a trial can interfere with the processing of intrinsic feedback (Swinnen, 1990; Swinnen, Schmidt, Nicholson, & Shapiro, 1990).

Practice Schedules

The distinction between performance during practice and learning as measured with retention or transfer conditions has proven to be critical in evaluating the results of practice schedules. For example, massing practice, such that only a few sessions with many trials of practice are given in place of more sessions with fewer trials in each session, has been shown to have detrimental effects during acquisition but varying effects on learning. Lee and Genovese (1988) noted that studies with continuous tasks (such as tracking tasks; see chapter by Heuer) show a small but negative effect of massed practice on retention. Discrete tasks actually show more learning when practice is massed.

A dissociation between effects of the scheduling of task conditions on performance during practice and learning is also seen when different variations of a task must be learned. Blocking practice, such that one variation is practiced in one session and another variation in a different one, has been shown to lead to better performance than random practice, in which all variations are possible within a block of practice. However, learning, as assessed by transfer or retention tests, is better for the random conditions (see Figure 18.3;

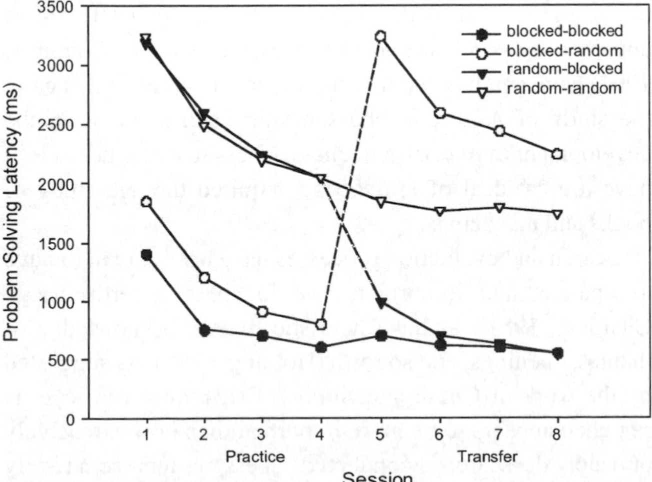

Figure 18.3 Practice and transfer performance in solving logic gate problems as a function of blocked or random problem presentation. *Source:* Carlson and Yaure (1990).

Carlson & Yaure, 1990; V. I. Schneider, Healy, Ericsson, & Bourne, 1995; Shea & Morgan, 1979). It seems that the need to recall task requirements on every trial, as in the random condition, is essential to learning (Battig, 1979; Lee & Magill, 1983).

INDIVIDUAL DIFFERENCES IN SKILLED PERFORMANCE

Individual differences in various abilities have formed the basis of selection and training research as well as a theoretical starting point for characterizing how skill develops. Theoretically, some models make predictions about which abilities should explain the most variance in skilled performance at different levels of skill acquisition. From a practical standpoint, the training and selection literature has focused on determining the abilities that predict success in learning particular skills.

The general progression from cognitive mediation to an associative phase to automatic performance (e.g., Fitts, 1962/1990, 1964) forms the basis for Ackerman's (1988, 1992) account of the relationship between level of skill acquisition and cognitive ability. According to Ackerman, performance in the early, declarative stage of learning a skill is affected more than later stages by the background knowledge and general spatial, verbal, and numeric abilities of the learner. The development of more specific and streamlined procedures in the associative phase leads to less reliance on general declarative knowledge. In this stage, as speed and efficiency develop and the need for conscious mediation lessens, the dependence on general cognitive abilities is reduced and the *perceptual speed* of the learner, as measured by tasks such as letter matching and serial response time, becomes a more important determinant of performance. Finally, in the autonomous stage, in which task components have become more automatic and performance is relatively free of attentional demands, performance will be more subject to the psychomotor ability of the performer.

Ackerman (1992) tested his model by comparing the correlation between performance and ability at different levels of skill acquisition in a complex, computerized air traffic control simulator. The effectiveness of measures of perceptual ability as a predictor of performance was, as predicted, higher at higher levels of skill. However, measures of general ability were also better predictors at high skill levels. It may be that tasks that require the integration of new information never become independent of general ability. One reason for this could be the dependence of such performance on working memory. Another possibility, suggested by Matthews, Jones, and Chamberlain (1992), who found that tests of ability in the context of a mail-coding task showed no trade-off between predictive power of cognitive versus perceptual speed tasks, is that executive control of performance remains important in most complex tasks.

Skilled performance is generally described as being relatively fast and error-free, but in at least some situations, more skilled performers are actually more error-prone than less skilled performers. Bell, Gardner, and Woltz (1997) found individual differences in the rate of making undetected errors on a number reduction task, in which numbers were compared according to a series of rules. After a practice session in which speed was emphasized, participants received a transfer session emphasizing accuracy and the instruction to press a key whenever a performance error was detected. Bell et al. found that the people who were more skilled (as indicated by faster reaction times during the training session) also made more undetected errors in the transfer session. The number of undetected errors was correlated with measures of memory span, with a larger memory span being associated with a lower error rate. Speed of processing was also correlated with the making of undetected errors: Faster processors made fewer undetected errors. Although speed-accuracy trade-off can not be ruled out as an explanation for the finding that latency was negatively correlated with the number of undetected errors made, Bell et al. argue that fluency in a task brings with it an increased chance of making undetected errors. Furthermore, detecting errors seems to require working memory resources, as indicated by the finding that people with a greater memory span were better able to detect errors.

EXPERTISE

Expertise in a particular domain can be viewed as the end product of skill acquisition. Unfortunately, it is an end that most of us do not reach in domains where we are nonetheless active. What enables some people to become expert in their field, whether it be playing tennis, solving physics problems, or playing the viola, and what characteristics distinguish experts and nonexperts?

One of the most debated topics in this field is whether expertise is primarily a result of learning or whether some people are genetically predisposed to become experts. Although it seems obvious that heredity can place constraints on the ability to become an expert, the major factor in developing expertise seems to be a commitment to years of dedicated practice. Newell and Simon (1972) were among the first to suggest that expertise can be explained in terms of the development of knowledge and information-processing abilities (e.g., memory span). Ericsson and Charness (1994) argued that extended training significantly alters both cognitive and physiological processes to an even greater degree than suggested by the work of Newell and Simon. They contend that differences between experts and novices primarily reflect changes brought about by practice rather than differences in aptitude or initial ability. It has even been argued that human expertise can be viewed as the result of circumventing normal limitations on human information processing (e.g., development of parallel processing in typing; Salthouse, 1991).

It may be that prodigious achievements in performance are rare because talent for a specific activity and the necessary environmental support for the development of that talent rarely coincide (Feldman, 1986). Gardner (1983), in particular, has argued that individual differences in aptitude and ability play a much greater role than that assumed by Ericsson and his colleagues. Gardner argues that the deliberate practice account of expertise ignores self-selection and the basis for the ability to engage in the training required to become an expert. However, there are many cases of exceptional performers who did not show any unusual talent early in childhood but, through sustained, intensive practice, nonetheless achieved high performance levels (Ericsson & Charness, 1994).

Chase and Simon (1973; Simon & Chase, 1973) developed both a skill-based account of expertise and methods for studying expertise. Using expertise in chess as an example, they attempted to document the expert's knowledge structures and processes. Their influential work emphasized the roles of perception and memory in expert performance. According to Chase and Simon, the development of expertise in chess relies heavily on chunking. As a result of practice and experience with the game, experts come to recognize configurations of chess pieces as groups or chunks rather than as individual pieces. As chunks develop, increasingly larger configurations are recognized until the game configuration itself can be apprehended as one whole. Other researchers (e.g., Charness, 1991) have emphasized the importance of study, in this case, the study of games of chess masters and strategy, in the development of expertise in chess. Chess masters themselves have a great deal of knowledge acquired through study of books and magazines.

Search and evaluation processes have been shown to have a separate, and important, role in chess expertise (e.g., Charness, 1981), as have heuristic rules and knowledge of themes, openings, and so forth (Holding, 1985). As suggested by the work of Chase and Simon (1973), however, *what* is searched appears to be more important than how extensively or deeply the search is conducted. Chess masters seem to rely more on pattern recognition than search (although very fast search times have not been ruled out). Pattern recognition skills may develop in part because time limits in chess penalize long search times and encourage sacrificing; this factor could limit the generalizability of the characterization of chess expertise to other skills.

Studying Expertise

The original expertise approach consists of three steps. The first step is to produce and observe outstanding performance in the laboratory under relatively standardized conditions using tasks that are representative of the skills possessed by the expert. The second step is to create a detailed picture of expert performance by analyzing and describing the processes critical to the production of an outstanding performance on the tasks. The third and final step is to examine critical cognitive processes and propose explicit learning mechanisms to account for their acquisition. In other words, the object is to develop an account of the expert's knowledge structures and processes.

A variety of knowledge acquisition techniques has been used to analyze expert knowledge structures and processes. Some techniques, such as hierarchical card sorting and general weighted networks, are based on judgments of similarity. In card sorting tasks, cards containing one piece of domain knowledge each are sorted into categories and subcategories. The resulting hierarchical structure is presumed to reflect the way the expert structures his or her actual knowledge. A limitation of this technique is that the requirement to make categories may force the expert to create a different structure from that which actually exists. The Pathfinder algorithm (Schvaneveldt, 1990) poses fewer constraints. Experts simply rate pairs of domain terms for their similarity, and then the algorithm is applied to find the network structure underlying the knowledge. Protocol analysis has also been extensively used to study expert behavior. In its most general application, experts are asked to think aloud while they solve a problem or perform a task. In this method, experts are simply asked to verbalize any thoughts that come to mind as they are performing a task. Ericsson and Simon (1993) maintain that this technique, unlike requiring people to explain their thinking, does not seem to cause any restructuring of the cognitive processes involved in task performance. On the other hand, it is limited to knowledge of which the expert is aware. Actions that are performed automatically or very quickly are likely to escape the notice of the performer.

Characteristics of Expertise

As mentioned above, changes in working memory span for domain information are often cited as a characteristic of expertise. *Skilled memory theory* states that at the time of encoding, experts form a set of retrieval cues that are associated in a meaningful way with the information to be stored. Retrieval then occurs via these cues. Rather than just chunking information so that more information can be stored in short-term memory, experts develop memory skills that enable them to store and retrieve information in long-term memory more quickly and efficiently, thus circumventing the limits of short-term memory (Chase & Ericsson, 1982). Chase and Ericsson thus argue that extensive practice develops skills that lead to qualitative, and not just quantitative, differences in memory performance for the practiced type of information.

In the area of problem solving, several generalizations about expert performance can be made. As Anzai (1991) has shown in studies of physics expertise, experts work forward, novices backward. Novices are also apt to change problem representations more frequently than experts; they seem unable to decide which representation is best for solving a problem. Experts, on the other hand, generate and update a representation of a problem as they read it. By the time a question regarding the problem is presented, they are often able to retrieve a solution plan from memory based on this representation (Larkin, McDermott, Simon, & Simon, 1980). In other words, the representation cues the expert's knowledge. Novices may lack both the organized knowledge base and the ability to build a representation that can act as a cue. Physics experts seem to possess multiple modes of representation for solving problems as well as the procedural knowledge for effective use of these multiple representations. This provides the basis for the formation of abstract or simpler representations from less abstract or more complex ones.

In the area of motor skill expertise, a distinction has been made between knowing and doing (Allard & Starkes, 1991). Knowing, in this context, involves directing the intake of environmental information in the appropriate way. The *doing* component is essential for the execution of actions, sport techniques, and motor-control programs. Knowing (consisting primarily of search processes) dominates in open skills, such as football, in which the environment (often including an opponent) is important and performance is directed toward an external goal. Doing (which can be characterized as skilled memory) predominates in closed skills, such as figure skating, in which the skill is performed in an invariant environment and has the production of a particular motor pattern as its goal.

Skill and Expertise

The fact that practice seems to be the most important determinant of the acquisition of expertise means that learning mechanisms that mediate increasing improvements from repeated practice trials must exist and play important roles in the acquisition of expertise. It is not merely exposure to a task that provides the basis for expert performance, but conscious, deliberate practice in which feedback is sought and used to improve performance. Just as it does in skilled performance in general, memory plays a large role in expertise. As mentioned above, experts have both a large, well-organized knowledge base and, often, specialized procedures for acquiring and storing knowledge. Also noteworthy is the specificity of the skills experts possess. For example, although chess players show an exceptional memory for the positions of chess pieces in various midgame positions, they do not score any higher on general tests of spatial ability than do controls (Doll & Mayr, 1987). As Thorndike and Woodworth (1901a, 1901b, 1901c) argued, there is little evidence for a "doctrine of formal discipline" (see Higginson, 1931) in which practice in one difficult skill leads to generalizable benefits in other domains. The study of expertise allows us to add that there is little evidence that exceptional abilities are a necessary prerequisite for the development of expertise.

TRAINING

Training has been a topic of interest to psychologists for the past hundred years or so. The major question of interest has been how broad the effects of training can be. As suggested by instance accounts of skill acquisition, the effects of training are often quite tightly tied to the training conditions. Therefore, it is necessary to determine what aspects of the target environment need to be included in the training. A related problem is that many skills are too complex to be learned all at once. Effective training can therefore depend on learning only certain aspects of a skill at a time. For these reasons, methods of decomposing skills for training and then recombining them are needed if effective training programs are to be designed.

Effective, efficient training programs depend on the identification of those aspects of the task that are critical for improving skill. These aspects can be identified by interviewing experts, by determining the characteristics that divide good performers and bad performers, and through theoretical analysis of the task. One approach is to emphasize *cue-response relations* (Cormier, 1987) and to determine which cues are necessary for the determination of responses. This approach has been used in designing simulators for training complex or dangerous tasks. Building high-fidelity simulators is expensive, so there is pressure on designers to include only those cues that lead to better transfer to the actual task. If one can determine the relevant cue-response relations, only the cues that are necessary need be incorporated into the simulator. Unfortunately, determining these relations is not always easy. For example, it has been found that motion cues can lead to better performance in a flight simulator (e.g., Perry & Naish, 1964), but not to better transfer to actual flight (e.g., Jacobs & Roscoe, 1975). In order to understand this discrepancy, it is necessary to look at the type of motion cues presented. In general, the presence of disturbance motion cues (cues associated with outside influences) are more important for transfer of simulator training to actual flight. However, for relatively unstable, difficult-to-fly aircraft, maneuver cues (cues associated with control actions) can be important (for a review see Gawron, Bailey, & Lehman, 1995).

Most techniques for analyzing tasks start with a description of the complete human-machine system but focus on the description, analysis, and evaluation of the performance demands placed on the human. For example, the focus might be on decomposing tasks into their constituent information-processing requirements, such as the principles, rules, and goals contained in expert knowledge, the distinction between automatic and controlled processes, or the allocation of attention. An example of one such approach is *principled task decomposition* (Frederiksen & White, 1989). This method was used by Frederiksen and White to develop a training program for the Space Fortress game, a video game developed by researchers to study complex skill acquisition (Mané & Donchin, 1989), and it is based on task decomposition, an analysis of human information-processing requirements, and the characteristics of expert performance. Frederiksen and White first identified the hierarchical relationships between skill and knowledge components that allow the progression from novice to expert performance and then used this task decomposition to construct training activities for the component processes as well as their integration. A comparison of the performance of a group who received componential training and a control group who practiced the Space Fortress game showed an initial deficit for the componential-training group when first transferred to whole-game performance. However, the componential-training group quickly overtook the whole-game training group, suggesting that, after some initial integration of learned skills during their first experience with the whole game, the specific knowledge and heuristics taught in the componential training had benefited learning (see Figure 18.4).

In general, part-task training, such as that used by Frederiksen and White (1989), has been shown to be an effective method of training difficult tasks or tasks with independent components (Holding, 1965; Wightman & Lintern, 1985). Several methods of part-task training have been

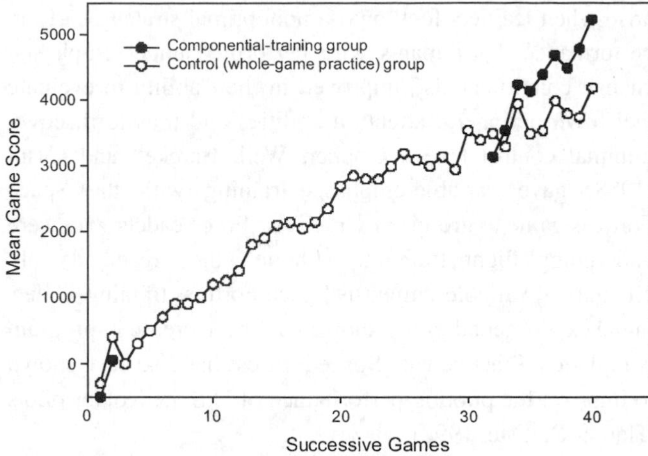

Figure 18.4 Performance of the control and componential-training groups on the Space Fortress game. *Source:* Frederiksen and White (1989).

developed and evaluated. If a task consists of components with clear starting and stopping points, it can simply be segmented into the different components. If the last step in a segmented task is practiced first, with earlier components added later, the procedure is called *backward chaining*. Whether backward chaining is more effective than *forward chaining,* in which segments are trained sequentially, starting with the first one, will depend on the type of feedback needed for performance. For complex tasks in which the initial steps are far removed from the goal, there might be a benefit for backward chaining because this begins by emphasizing the steps closest to the goal. When feedback from one component influences performance on the next, forward chaining might be more effective (Wightman & Lintern, 1985).

Marmie and Healy (1995) showed that the benefits of part-task training using a segmentation and backward-chaining strategy can show long-lasting effects in a simulated tank-gunnery task. In the relevant experiment, participants practiced either the whole task (searching for a target, sighting it, and firing) or, for several sessions, only the sighting and firing components. Performance in whole-task retention sessions given immediately after training or one month later showed no difference between the groups in overall performance (proportion of kills) or in time to identify the target. However, the part-task training group, which was able to devote more resources to the sighting and firing components of the task during training, showed a long-lasting benefit in time to fire.

If different task components are performed in parallel, it is not possible to segment them. In this case, we speak of *fractionation* of the task. This involves practicing some components, such as perceptual skills, in isolation and then combining them with other aspects of the task, such as making responses. It has been argued that fractionation can only be effective if there is relatively little time sharing or interdependence between the components (W. Schneider & Detweiler, 1988). In some cases, such as when multiple-task components must be carried out in parallel, the demands imposed by the need to recombine the separate skills counteract any benefits of part-task training. However, the view that part-task training is ineffective for tasks that must be time shared may be overly pessimistic.

Fabiani et al. (1989) compared the hierarchical training tasks developed by Frederiksen and White (1989) with whole-task training and with a so-called *integrative training,* in which the whole task was practiced, but performers were instructed to emphasize certain of the skills identified by Frederiksen and White. If time sharing must be practiced in order to be learned, one might expect better performance in a whole-task transfer condition for the integrative- than for the hierarchical-training group. However, although the integrative group showed more learning than a control group who practiced the whole task under normal instructions for the same amount of time, they did not do any better than the hierarchical group. A possible benefit for the integrative group was, however, found when a variety of secondary tasks were added to the game. The integrative group proved to be better in coping with these new task demands.

Another method of training is to simplify the task, teach the simplified version, and then release the constraints placed on the task until the task is restored to its original complexity. This method has been used successfully in teaching the use of software and has led to the concept of *minimal training*. Carroll (1997) argues that step-by-step manuals and computer tutorials are often frustrating and ineffective because they do not match the way people approach learning. According to Carroll, learners want to get started fast, which often leads them to omit critical steps, and neglect to plan tasks or predict the outcomes of their explorations. They also prefer not to follow procedures, often reason from inference—even when the similarity to the current situation is only superficial—and, finally, are often poor at recognizing, diagnosing, and recovering from errors. Recognition of these characteristics of learners led Carroll (Carroll & Carrithers, 1984) to develop a training wheels interface for a word processor that restricted what learners could do and, hence, the errors that they could make. They found a substantial benefit for the use of the training wheels interface on transfer to the full word processor. They attributed the benefit to the fact that training wheels users spent less time on error recovery and more time learning useful tasks. The lessons to be learned from Carroll and his colleagues' work on minimalist training (summarized in Carroll, 1997) are that training environments should allow users to get started fast, permit them to think and improvise, embed information in real tasks, relate new information to what people already know, and support error recognition and recovery. In other words, good instruction should enable active learning while providing enough support to keep learners involved in useful tasks.

Skill Acquisition and Attentional Strategies

Skill acquisition depends on paying attention to the right things at the right time. That is, an important aspect of skilled performance is skilled attending. In many tasks, it is important not only to know what to attend to, but *how* to attend to it. Complex, dynamic tasks often require performers to divide attention and processing resources among competing, dynamically changing stimuli or task demands, for which priorities must be established and trade-offs made. Important questions in the training of complex skills concern whether we are aware of attentional investments and can control and allocate attentional resources.

One example of attentional allocation is distributing visual attention across a relatively large area and number of processing items, or focusing it on a small area or number of items (see the chapter by Egeth & Lamy). Learning to focus attention appropriately could well be an important factor in performance of many skills. Most work on the training of attention comes from the study of dual-task performance in which performers had to learn to prioritize their performance of two tasks so that one was performed better at the cost of the other (e.g., Gopher, Brickner, & Navon, 1982). With the provision of augmented feedback, in which details of the nature of the performance are given, people can learn to make performance trade-offs and allocate attention according to instructions (Spitz, 1988).

The training of attentional allocation and prioritization strategies can have a strong and long-lasting influence on performance. Gopher and his colleagues (see Gopher, 1993) have shown that dual-task performance benefits more from training under variable priority settings (e.g., Task 1 priority of 25, 50, or 75%) than from training without priority instructions or with only one priority (e.g., 50%). The higher ability of performers who train under variable priorities seems to stem from an improved ability to detect changes and adjust efforts to cope with changing task demands. Gopher, Weil, and Siegel (1989) implemented variable-priority setting in a training program for the Space Fortress game (Mané & Donchin, 1989). By requiring participants to change their emphasis on different aspects of the game, they forced them to explore different strategies of performance, thus overcoming limitations that arise when learners lock onto a nonoptimal strategy early in performance. Participants who performed under emphasis-change conditions also improved in their ability to evaluate their own peripheral attention abilities and thus to discover minimal control levels. Gopher, Weil, Bareket, and Caspi (1988) gave variable-emphasis training with the Space Fortress game to groups of Israeli Air Force cadets who were undergoing flight training. Although they received only 10 hours of variable-emphasis Space Fortress training, cadets in the experimental group showed a 30% increase in program completion. Practice with Space Fortress has also been shown to improve the piloting performance of U.S. helicopter pilots (Hart & Battiste, 1992).

Automaticity and Training

Attentional strategies can be trained, but to what extent can people be trained to operate without attention? Many complex tasks can only be performed because some task components have become automatized, thus freeing up resources for other components. Several researchers have shown that training in tasks similar to visual search can lead to automatic processing. Such training has been used successfully with air traffic controllers to promote automatic processing of some perceptual information, such as the distances between aircraft, and indications of certain maneuvers, such as the start of turns (W. Schneider, Vidulich, & Yeh, 1982). Shebilske, Goettl, and Regian (1999) have developed a framework for training that emphasizes the development of automaticity in task components. They suggest that by determining the components for which automaticity does not develop, one succeeds in identifying those components that play a controlling, or executive, role in the performance of a task.

Team Training

Many tasks are performed not by individuals working alone but by individuals working in teams. The basic principles of skill acquisition and training apply to the individuals, but teamwork brings with it special concerns. Some of the concerns of teamwork fall within the domain of organizational or social psychology, such as the organizational climate in the cockpit and its contribution to air disasters caused by the reluctance of copilots to contradict or question the pilot's actions. Being a part of a team can also, however, change the way the individual carries out his or her work. Team workers must be able to predict other team members' behavior and must be able to give and receive backup support. The performance of many tasks requires knowledge of what others are doing and of what they know. Salas and colleagues (e.g., Salas & Cannon-Bowers, 1997) refer to this knowledge as a *shared mental model*. They suggest that this knowledge allows team members to anticipate each other's actions and to maintain an accurate, up-to-date picture of the current situation (i.e., *situation awareness*). The question arises whether there are special training procedures that promote such a shared mental model.

Just as in the training of any task, the development of a team-training program starts with task analysis. The communication flow between team members forms an important part of the analysis. One training strategy unique to team training is *cross-training*. In cross-training, team members receive information and training in the tasks of other team members. In addition to providing the team with backup knowledge should a team member be absent, this may also contribute to the development of a shared mental model. Volpe, Cannon-Bowers, Salas, and Spector (1996) showed that 2-person teams who received cross-training used more efficient communication strategies and showed better task performance than teams not provided with this knowledge.

Entin and Serfaty (1999) have argued that cross-training is insufficient as a training method for teams who must function in high-workload environments. They maintain that special strategies are necessary to train team members to recognize high-stress conditions and adapt their behavior accordingly. They found that team performance improved after participating in a training program in which participants learned to recognize signs of stress and to communicate more effectively by anticipating the information needs of other team members.

RETENTION AND TRANSFER OF SKILL

Transfer of Training

According to Logan and Compton (1998), transfer should occur between compatible tasks, where compatibility is defined as a condition in which "traces laid down in one task context can be used to support performance in another" (p. 119). Orthogonal or incompatible traces will be of no use and may even cause confusion if retrieved. This view is consistent with the long-standing view that transfer will occur when elements in the practiced task are also present in the transfer task. This *identical-elements* view of transfer (Thorndike & Woodworth, 1901a, 1901b, 1901c) is elegantly incorporated in production system models of learning (e.g., Singley & Anderson, 1989). Many examples of positive transfer of components of skill are given above. In fact, the presence of transfer is often considered to provide the basis for determining what has been learned in a training session.

Long-Term Retention of Skill

It is an old adage that once you learn to ride a bicycle you will never forget how to do it. In fact, even skills learned in relatively artificial laboratory environments often show surprisingly good retention. One example of this is the Kolers (1976) study mentioned above. After 1 year with presumably no practice, participants were still quite proficient in the skill of reading inverted text, and they even showed some benefit for seeing the same text again. Using the task of visual search of displays with various numbers of elements, Cooke, Durso, and Schvaneveldt (1994) showed retention of skilled search ability, including no loss of visual search rates and a minimal loss of search speed, after a 9-year period of nonuse. Furthermore, the savings were found for both consistent and varied-mapping tasks. The fact that the search rate was maintained suggests that essential elements of the search process were retained. Participants also reported that they still experienced a pop-out effect, in which consistently mapped targets seemed to command attention even though 9 years had elapsed since the development of the search skill.

The retention of skilled performance depends on the conditions of training and the conditions under which retention is tested. In general, as suggested by Kolers and Roediger (1984), performance will be better to the extent that the procedures used by the performers during training are also used in retention testing. Healy et al. (1995) summarize a variety of studies on the learning and retention of simple cognitive skills and conclude that retention will be the greatest when retention requires the procedures employed during training, when information received during training can be related to previous experience and can be retrieved directly, when trained information is made distinctive, and when refresher or practice opportunities are provided (Healy et al., 1993, 1995). In other words, both procedures and information seem to provide the cues necessary for retrieving information even after long periods of nonuse.

The emphasis that Healy et al. (1995) place on direct retrieval fits nicely with instance accounts of skill (e.g., Logan, 1988) in which performance is said to be automatic when performance is governed by retrieval. In other words, if automaticity developed at the time of training, retention of the skill is more likely. This point is illustrated by a comparison of the Cooke et al. (1994) study mentioned above and a study by Fisk and Hodge (1992), which also evaluated retention of visual search skill. Contrary to the results of Cooke et al., Fisk and Hodge did not find good retention of varied-mapping search. The major difference in the two studies is that the performers in the Cooke et al. study showed evidence of automaticity at the end of the initial learning of the task, whereas those in the Fisk and Hodge study did not. It appears that a shift in strategy, or simply the effects of overlearning, has significant consequences for retention.

MODELING SKILL

Although response selection is the locus of learning in many tasks, it was argued above that response selection does not become automatic in the sense that, after learning, stimuli automatically trigger the correct response without regard to the nature of the relationship between stimulus and response. This finding is at odds with one of the most developed models of practice effects, the *chunking hypothesis* of Newell and Rosenbloom (1981; Rosenbloom & Newell, 1987). The model assumes a production-system architecture in which stimuli are related to responses by means of rules (e.g., "if the mapping is incompatible and the right light is on, find the key opposite to the light and press it"). The chunking hypothesis predicts that performance will improve as a function of practice and that the learning curve will follow a power function. Learning occurs by means of pattern-recognition processes whereby increasingly complex patterns of stimuli and responses are learned. In other words, learning is based on the chunking of stimulus and response patterns. Although it predicts the general pattern of improvement in simple tasks quite well, it contains no provision for long-lasting effects of factors such as stimulus-response compatibility.

Many models of learning have been based Anderson's (1982, 1993) production system architecture. Productions have several properties that are consistent with empirical generalizations about skill, such as transfer based on common elements. The independence of productions, the all-or-none learning reflected in their creation and their accrual of strength, and potential abstraction make them an appropriate vehicle for the elements of learning.

Many neural network, or connectionist, models of learning have also been developed, although their scope has usually been rather limited. For example, J. D. Cohen, Dunbar, and McClelland (1990) developed a model of the Stroop effect based on the strength of learning to read words versus name colors. The model provides a demonstration of how the strength of learned associations between stimuli and particular types of responses can produce automatic behavior. Unfortunately, the model has been shown to be rather limited in scope, working in its particulars only when the maximum number of stimuli is two (Kanne, Balota, Spieler, & Faust, 1998).

NEW DIRECTIONS

As in other areas of cognitive psychology, we can expect to see an increasing number of studies devoted to attempts to discover where in the brain learning occurs. We can cxpect that such studies will continue to shed light on issues such as the nature of procedural and episodic memory or whether separate systems underlie implicit and explicit learning. Just as in other areas, the degree to which this knowledge helps us to understand the processes by which skills are acquired remains to be seen. Increasingly, more emphasis is being placed not just on what is learned, but on what is not learned. Ohlsson (1996), for example, has proposed a theory of learning based on making mistakes in which what is not learned at one time becomes the basis for what is learned at another time.

Unskilled performance is characterized by ignorance of what to expect, what to do, or when to do it; lack of knowledge of interrelationships among variables and of what information is relevant; difficulty in combining information; insensitivity to relevant sensory or perceptual discriminations; and a lack of production proficiency. Progress has been made in understanding how these relations, skills, and proficiencies are acquired as a function of experience, and in understanding what sorts of experiences lead to the greatest improvements. The future of research in skill acquisition is as broad and as bright as in all of cognitive psychology. We can expect to see many more questions, and answers, as to the nature of the processes that allow the aforementioned changes to occur.

REFERENCES

Ackerman, P. L. (1988). Components of individual differences during skill acquisition: Cognitive abilities and information processing. *Journal of Experimental Psychology: General, 117,* 288–318.

Ackerman, P. L. (1992). Predicting individual differences in complex skill acquisition: Dynamics of ability determinants. *Journal of Applied Psychology, 77,* 598–614.

Allard, F., & Starkes, J. L. (1980). Perception in sport: Volleyball. *Journal of Sport Psychology, 2,* 22–33.

Allard, F., & Starkes, J. L. (1991). Motor-skill experts in sports, dance, and other domains. In K. A. Ericsson & J. Smith (Eds.), *Toward a general theory of expertise: Prospects and limits* (pp. 126–152). New York: Cambridge University Press.

Anderson, J. R. (1982). Acquisition of cognitive skill. *Psychological Review, 89,* 369–406.

Anderson, J. R. (1983). *The architecture of cognition.* Cambridge, MA: Harvard University Press.

Anderson, J. R. (1993). *Rules of the mind.* Hillsdale, NJ: Erlbaum.

Anzai, Y. (1991). Learning and use of representations for physics expertise. In K. A. Ericsson & J. Smith (Eds.), *Toward a general theory of expertise: Prospects and limits* (pp. 64–92). New York: Cambridge University Press.

Atkinson, R. C., & Shiffrin, R. M. (1968). Human memory: A proposed system and its control processes. In K. W. Spence (Ed.), *The psychology of learning and motivation: Advances in research and theory* (Vol. 2, pp. 89–195). New York: Academic Press.

Battig, W. F. (1979). The flexibility of human memory. In L. S. Cermak & F. I. M. Craik (Eds.), *Levels of processing in human memory* (pp. 23–44). Hillsdale, NJ: Erlbaum.

Bell, B. G., Gardner, M. K., & Woltz, D. J. (1997). Individual differences in undetected errors in skilled cognitive performance. *Learning and Individual Differences, 9,* 43–61.

Bernstein, N. (1967). *The coordination and regulation of movements.* New York: Pergamon Press.

Biederman, I., & Shiffrar, M. M. (1987). Sexing day-old chicks: A case study and expert systems analysis of a difficult perceptual-learning task. *Journal of Experimental Psychology: Learning, Memory, and Cognition, 13,* 640–645.

Bjork, R. A. (1999). Assessing our own competence: Heuristics and illusions. In D. Gopher & A. Koriat (Eds.), *Attention and performance: Vol. 17. Cognitive regulation of performance: Interaction of theory and application* (pp. 435–459). Cambridge, MA: MIT Press.

Broderick, M. P., & Newell, K. M. (1999). Coordination patterns in ball bouncing as a function of skill. *Journal of Motor Behavior, 31,* 165–188.

Brooks, D. N., & Baddeley, A. D. (1976). What can amnesic patients learn? *Neuropsychologia, 14,* 111–122.

Bryan, W. L., & Harter, N. (1897). Studies in the physiology and psychology of the telegraphic language. *Psychological Review, 4,* 27–53.

Bryan, W. L., & Harter, N. (1899). Studies on the telegraphic language. The acquisition of a hierarchy of habits. *Psychological Review, 6,* 345–375.

Carlson, R. A., Khoo, B. H., Yaure, R. G., & Schneider, W. (1990). Acquisition of a problem-solving skill: Levels of organization and use of working memory. *Journal of Experimental Psychology: General, 119,* 193–214.

Carlson, R. A., Sullivan, M. A., & Schneider, W. (1989). Practice and working memory effects in building procedural skill. *Journal of Experimental Psychology: Learning, Memory, and Cognition, 15,* 517–526.

Carlson, R. A., & Yaure, R. G. (1990). Practice schedules and the use of component skills in problem solving. *Journal of Experimental Psychology: Learning, Memory, and Cognition, 16,* 484–496.

Carroll, J. M. (1997). Toward minimalist training: Supporting the sense-making activities of computer users. In M. A. Quiñones & A. Ehrenstein (Eds.), *Training for a rapidly changing workplace: Applications of psychological research* (pp. 303–328). Washington, DC: American Psychological Association.

Carroll, J. M., & Carrithers, C. (1984). Blocking learner errors in a training wheels system. *Human Factors, 26,* 377–389.

Charness, N. (1981). Search in chess: Age and skill differences. *Journal of Experimental Psychology: Human Perception and Performance, 7,* 467–476.

Charness, N. (1991). Expertise in chess: The balance between knowledge and search. In K. A. Ericsson & J. Smith (Eds.), *Toward a general theory of expertise: Prospects and limits* (pp. 39–63). New York: Cambridge University Press.

Chase, W. G., & Ericsson, K. A. (1982). Skill and working memory. In G. H. Bower (Ed.), *The psychology of learning and motivation* (Vol. 16, pp. 1–58). New York: Academic Press.

Chase, W. G., & Simon, H. A. (1973). Perception in chess. *Cognitive Psychology, 4,* 55–81.

Claperède, E. (1911). Recognition et moiité. *Archives de Psychologie, 11,* 79–90.

Cohen, A., Ivry, R. I., & Keele, S. W. (1990). Attention and structure in sequence learning. *Journal of Experimental Psychology: Learning, Memory, and Cognition, 16,* 17–30.

Cohen, J. D., Dunbar, K., & McClelland, J. L. (1990). On the control of automatic processes: A parallel distributed processing account of the Stroop effect. *Psychological Review, 97,* 332–361.

Cohen, N. J. (1984). Preserved learning capacity in amnesia: Evidence for multiple memory systems. In L. R. Squire & N. Butters (Eds.), *The neuropsychology of memory* (pp. 419–432). New York: Guilford.

Cooke, N. J., Durso, F. T., & Schvaneveldt, R. W. (1994). Retention of skilled search after nine years. *Human Factors, 36,* 597–605.

Cormier, S. M. (1987). The structural processes underlying transfer of training. In S. M. Cormier & J. D. Hagman (Eds.), *Transfer of learning: Contemporary research and applications* (pp. 152–182). San Diego, CA: Academic Press.

Doll, J., & Mayr, U. (1987). Intelligenz und Schachleistung—eine Untersuchung an Schachexperten [Intelligence and success in chess playing: An examination of chess experts]. *Psychologische Beiträge, 29,* 270–289.

Dutta, A., & Proctor, R. W. (1992). Persistence of stimulus-response compatibility effects with extended practice. *Journal of Experimental Psychology: Learning, Memory, and Cognition, 18,* 801–809.

Ehrenstein, A., Walker, B. N., Czerwinski, M., & Feldman, E. M. (1997). Some fundamentals of training and transfer: Practice benefits are not automatic. In M. A. Quiñones & A. Ehrenstein (Eds.), *Training for a rapidly changing workplace: Applications of psychological research* (pp. 119–147). Washington, DC: American Psychological Association.

Elliott, D., & Jaeger, M. (1988). Practice and visual control of manual aiming movements. *Journal of Human Movement Studies, 14,* 279–291.

Entin, E. E., & Serfaty, D. (1999). Adaptive team coordination. *Human Factors, 41,* 312–325.

Ericsson, K. A., & Charness, N. (1994). Expert performance: Its structure and acquisition. *American Psychologist, 49,* 725–747.

Ericsson, K. A., & Simon, H. A. (1993). *Protocol analysis.* Cambridge, MA: MIT Press.

Fabiani, M., Buckley, J., Gratton, G., Coles, M. G. H., Donchin, E., & Logie, R. (1989). The training of complex task performance. *Acta Psychologica, 71,* 259–299.

Feldman, D. H. (1986). *Nature's gambit: Child prodigies and the development of human potential.* New York: Basic Books.

Fisk, A. D., & Hodge, K. A. (1992). Retention of trained performance in consistent mapping search after extended delay. *Human Factors, 34,* 147–164.

Fitts, P. M. (1964). Perceptual-motor skill learning. In A. W. Melton (Ed.), *Categories of human learning* (pp. 243–285). New York: Academic Press.

Fitts, P. M. (1990). Factors in complex skill training. In R. Glaser (Ed.), *Training research and education* (pp. 177–197). Pittsburgh, PA: University of Pittsburgh Press. (Reprinted from *Selected readings in human factors,* pp. 275–295, M. Venturino, Ed., 1962, Santa Monica, CA: Human Factors Society)

Fitts, P. M., & Posner, M. I. (1967). *Human performance.* Belmont, CA: Brooks/Cole.

Fitts, P. M., & Seeger, C. M. (1953). S-R compatibility: Spatial characteristics of stimulus and response codes. *Journal of Experimental Psychology, 46,* 199–210.

Flament, D., & Ebner, T. J. (1996). The cerebellum as comparator: Increases in cerebellar activity during motor learning may reflect its role as part of an error detection/correction mechanism. *Behavioral and Brain Sciences, 19,* 447–448.

Frederiksen, J. R., & White, B. Y. (1989). An approach to training based upon principled task decomposition. *Acta Psychologica, 71,* 89–146.

Frensch, P. A., Buchner, A., & Lin, J. (1994). Implicit learning of unique and ambiguous serial transitions in the presence and absence of a distractor task. *Journal of Experimental Psychology: Learning, Memory, and Cognition, 20,* 567–584.

Friston, K. J., Frith, C. D., Passingham, R. E., Liddle, P. F., & Frackowiak, R. S. J. (1992). Motor practice and neurophysiological adaptation in the cerebellum: A positron emission study. *Proceedings of the Royal Society of London, Series B, Biological Science, 248,* 223–228.

Gabrieli, J. D. E. (1998). Cognitive neuroscience of human memory. In J. T. Spence, J. M. Darley, & D. J. Foss (Eds.), *Annual Review of Psychology, 49,* 87–115.

Gardner, H. (1983). *Frames of mind: The theory of multiple intelligences.* New York: Basic Books.

Gawron, V., Bailey, R., & Lehman, E. (1995). Lessons learned in applying simulators to crewstation evaluation. *International Journal of Aviation Psychology, 5,* 277–290.

Gopher, D. (1993). The skill of attention control: Acquisition and execution of attention strategies. In D. E. Meyer & S. Kornblum (Eds.), *Attention and performance: Vol. 14. Synergies in experimental psychology, artificial intelligence, and cognitive neuroscience* (pp. 300–322). Cambridge, MA: MIT Press.

Gopher, D., Brickner, M., & Navon, D. (1982). Different difficulty manipulations interact differently with task emphasis: Evidence for multiple resources. *Journal of Experimental Psychology: Human Perception and Performance, 8,* 146–157.

Gopher, D., Weil, M., Bareket, T., & Caspi, S. (1988). Fidelity of task structure as a guiding principle in the development of skill trainers based upon complex computer games. In *Proceedings of the Human Factors Society 32nd Annual Meeting* (pp. 1266–1270). Santa Monica, CA: Human Factors Society.

Gopher, D., Weil, M., & Siegel, D. (1989). Practice under changing priorities: An approach to training of complex skills. *Acta Psychologica, 71,* 147–177.

Grafton, S. T., Hazeltine, E. & Ivry, R. (1995). Functional mapping of sequence learning in normal humans. *Journal of Cognitive Neuroscience, 7,* 497–510.

Haider, H., & Frensch, P. A. (1996). The role of information reduction in skill acquisition. *Cognitive Psychology, 30,* 304–337.

Haider, H., & Frensch, P. A. (1999). Information reduction during skill acquisition: The influence of task instruction. *Journal of Experimental Psychology: Applied, 5,* 129–151.

Hart, S. G., & Battiste, V. (1992). Field test of video game trainer. In *Proceedings of the Human Factors Society 36th Annual Meeting* (pp. 1291–1295). Santa Monica, CA: Human Factors Society.

Hazeltine, E., Grafton, S. T., & Ivry, R. (1997). Attention and stimulus characteristics determine the locus of motor-sequence encoding: A PET study. *Brain, 120,* 123–140.

Healy, A. F., Clawson, D. M., McNamara, D. S., Marmie, W. R., Schneider, V. I., Rickard, T. C., Crutcher, R. J., King, C. L., Ericsson, K. A., & Bourne, L. E., Jr. (1993). The long-term retention of knowledge and skills. In D. Medin (Ed.), *The psychology of learning and motivation* (Vol. 30, pp. 135–164). New York: Academic Press.

Healy, A. F., King, C. L., Clawson, D. M., Sinclair, G. P., Rickard, T. C., Crutcher, R. J., Ericsson, K. A., & Bourne, L. E., Jr. (1995). Optimizing the long-term retention of skills. In A. F. Healy & L. E. Bourne, Jr. (Eds.), *Learning and memory of knowledge and skills: Durability and specificity* (pp. 1–29). Thousand Oaks, CA: Sage.

Higginson, G. (1931). *Fields of psychology: A study of man and his environment.* New York: Holt.

Hikosaka, O., Nakahara, H., Rand, M. K., Sakai, K., Lu, X., Nakamura, K., Miyachi, S., & Doya, K. (1999). Parallel neural networks for learning sequential procedures. *Trends in Neurosciences, 22,* 464–471.

Holding, D. H. (1965). *Principles of training.* Oxford, UK: Pergamon Press.

Holding, D. H. (1985). *The psychology of chess skill.* Hillsdale, NJ: Erlbaum.

Jacobs, R. S., & Roscoe, S. N. (1975). Simulator cockpit motion and the transfer of initial flight training. *Proceedings of the Human Factors Society 19th Annual Meeting* (pp. 218–226). Santa Monica, CA: Human Factors Society.

Jacoby, L. L., & Witherspoon, D. (1982). Remembering without awareness. *Canadian Journal of Psychology, 36,* 300–324.

Jiménez, L., & Méndez, C. (1999). Which attention is needed for implicit sequence learning? *Journal of Experimental Psychology: Learning, Memory, and Cognition, 25,* 236–259.

Kanne, S. M., Balota, D. A., Spieler, D. H., & Faust, M. E. (1998). Explorations of Cohen, Dunbar, and McClelland's (1990) connectionist model of Stroop performance. *Psychological Review, 105,* 174–187.

Khan, M. A., & Franks, I. M. (2000). The effect of practice on component submovements is dependent on the availability of visual feedback. *Journal of Motor Behavior, 32,* 227–240.

Kolers, P. A. (1975a). Memorial consequences of automatized encoding. *Journal of Experimental Psychology: Human Learning and Memory, 1,* 689–701.

Kolers, P. A. (1975b). Specificity of operations in sentence recognition. *Cognitive Psychology, 7,* 289–306.

Kolers, P. A. (1976). Reading a year later. *Journal of Experimental Psychology: Human Learning and Memory, 2,* 554–565.

Kolers, P. A., & Roediger, H. L., III. (1984). Procedures of mind. *Journal of Verbal Learning and Verbal Behavior, 23,* 425–449.

LaBerge, D. (1973). Attention and the measurement of perceptual learning. *Memory & Cognition, 1,* 268–276.

Larkin, J. H., McDermott, J., Simon, D. P., & Simon, H. A. (1980). Models of competence in solving physics problems. *Cognitive Science, 4,* 317–345.

Lashley, K. S. (1951). The problem of serial order in behavior. In L. A. Jeffress (Ed.), *Cerebral mechanisms in behavior: The Hixon symposium* (pp. 112–131). New York: Wiley.

Lavery, J. J. (1962). Retention of simple motor skills as a function of type of knowledge of results. *Canadian Journal of Psychology, 16,* 300–311.

Lee, T. D., & Genovese, E. D. (1988). Distribution of practice in motor skill acquisition: Learning and performance effects reconsidered. *Research Quarterly for Exercise and Sport, 59,* 277–287.

Lee, T. D., & Magill, R. A. (1983). The locus of contextual interference in motor-skill acquisition. *Journal of Experimental Psychology: Learning, Memory, and Cognition, 9,* 730–746.

Lewicki, P., Czyzewska, M., & Hoffman, H. (1987). Unconscious acquisition of complex procedural knowledge. *Journal of Experimental Psychology: Learning, Memory, and Cognition, 13,* 523–530.

Logan, G. D. (1988). Toward an instance theory of automatization. *Psychological Review, 95,* 492–527.

Logan, G. D. (1990). Repetition priming and automaticity: Common underlying mechanisms? *Cognitive Psychology, 22,* 1–35.

Logan, G. D., & Compton, B. J. (1998). Attention and automaticity. In R. D. Wright (Ed.), *Visual attention: Vancouver studies in cognitive science* (Vol. 8, pp. 108–131). New York: Oxford University Press.

Logan, G. D., & Etherton, J. L. (1994). What is learned during automatization? The role of attention in constructing an instance. *Journal of Experimental Psychology: Learning, Memory, and Cognition, 20,* 1022–1050.

Lunn, J. H. (1948). Chick sexing. *American Scientist, 36,* 280–287.

Mané, A., & Donchin, E. (1989). The space fortress game. *Acta Psychologica, 71,* 17–22.

Marmie, W. R., & Healy, A. F. (1995). The long-term retention of a complex skill. In A. F. Healy & L. E. Bourne, Jr. (Eds.), *Learning and memory of knowledge and skills: Durability and specificity* (pp. 30–65). Thousand Oaks, CA: Sage.

Matthews, G., Jones, D. M., & Chamberlain, A. G. (1992). Predictors of individual differences in mail-coding skills and their variation with ability level. *Journal of Applied Psychology, 77,* 406–418.

Melcher, J. M., & Schooler, J. W. (1996). The misremembrance of wines past: Verbal and perceptual expertise differentially mediate verbal overshadowing of taste memory. *Journal of Memory and Language, 35,* 231–245.

Neumann, O. (1987). Beyond capacity: A functional view of attention. In H. Heuer & A. F. Sanders (Eds.), *Perspectives on perception and action* (pp. 361–394). Hillsdale, NJ: Erlbaum.

Newell, A., & Rosenbloom, P. S. (1981). Mechanisms of skill acquisition and the law of practice. In J. R. Anderson (Ed.), *Cognitive skills and their acquisition* (pp. 1–55). Hillsdale, NJ: Erlbaum.

Newell, A., & Simon, H. A. (1972). *Human problem solving.* Englewood Cliffs, NJ: Prentice-Hall.

Nissen, M. J., & Bullemer, P. (1987). Attentional requirements of learning: Evidence from performance measures. *Cognitive Psychology, 19,* 1–32.

Ohlsson, S. (1996). Learning from performance errors. *Psychological Review, 103,* 241–262.

Palmer, C., & Meyer, R. K. (2000). Conceptual and motor learning in music performance. *Psychological Science, 11,* 63–68.

Pashler, H., & Baylis, G. C. (1991). Procedural learning: 1. Locus of practice effects in speeded choice tasks. *Journal of Experimental Psychology: Learning, Memory, and Cognition, 17,* 20–32.

Pear, T. H. (1948). Professor Bartlett on skill. *Occupational Psychology, 22,* 92–93.

Perruchet, P., & Amorim, M. A. (1992). Conscious knowledge and changes in performance sequence learning: Evidence against dissociation. *Journal of Experimental Psychology: Learning, Memory, and Cognition, 18,* 785–800.

Perry, D. H., & Naish, J. M. (1964). Flight simulation for research. *Journal of the Royal Aeronautical Society, 68,* 645–662.

Pew, R. W. (1966). Acquisition of hierarchical control over the temporal organization of a skill. *Journal of Experimental Psychology, 71,* 764–771.

Posner, M. I., & Snyder, C. R. (1975). Attention and cognitive control. In R. L. Solso (Ed.), *Information processing and cognition: The Loyola symposium* (pp. 55–85). Hillsdale, NJ: Erlbaum.

Povel, D. J., & Collard, R. (1982). Structural factors in patterned finger tapping. *Acta Psychologica, 52,* 107–123.

Proctor, R. W., & Dutta, A. (1993). Do the same stimulus-response relations influence choice reactions initially and after practice? *Journal of Experimental Psychology: Learning, Memory, and Cognition, 19,* 922–930.

Proctor, R. W., & Dutta, A. (1995). *Principles of skill acquisition and human performance.* Newbury Park, CA: Sage.

Proteau, L. (1992). On the specificity of learning and the role of visual information in movement control. In L. Proteau & D. Elliott (Eds.), *Vision and motor control* (pp. 67–103). Amsterdam: North-Holland.

Proteau, L., & Cournoyer, J. (1990). Vision of the stylus in a manual aiming task: The effects of practice. *Quarterly Journal of Experimental Psychology, 42A,* 811–828.

Proteau, L., Marteniuk, R. G., & Levesque, L. (1992). A sensorimotor basis for motor learning: Evidence indicating specificity of practice. *Quarterly Journal of Experimental Psychology, 44A,* 557–575.

Proteau, L., Tremblay, L., & DeJaeger, D. (1998). Practice does not diminish the role of visual information in on-line control of a precision walking task: Support for the specificity of practice hypothesis. *Journal of Motor Behavior, 30,* 143–150.

Rabin, M. D. (1988). Experience facilitates olfactory quality discrimination. *Perception & Psychophysics, 44,* 532–540.

Ridderinkhof, K. R., van der Molen, M. W., Band, G. P. H., & Bashore, T. R. (1997). Sources of interference from irrelevant information: A developmental study. *Journal of Experimental Child Psychology, 65,* 315–341.

Rosenbloom, P. S., & Newell, A. (1987). An integrated computational model of stimulus-response compatibility and practice. In G. H. Bower (Ed.), *The psychology of learning and motivation* (Vol. 21, pp. 1–52). New York: Academic Press.

Rumelhart, D. E., & Norman, D. A. (1978). Accretion, tuning, and restructuring: Three modes of learning. In J. W. Cotton & R. Klatzky (Eds.), *Semantic factors in cognition* (pp. 37–53). Hillsdale, NJ: Erlbaum.

Salas, E., & Cannon-Bowers, J. A. (1997). Methods, tools, and strategies for team training. In M. A. Quinones & A. Ehrenstein (Eds.), *Training for a rapidly changing workplace: Applications of psychological research* (pp. 249–279). Washington, DC: American Psychological Association.

Salthouse, T. A. (1991). Expertise as the circumvention of human processing limitations. In K. A. Ericsson & J. Smith (Eds.), *Toward a general theory of expertise: Prospects and limits.* New York: Cambridge University Press.

Schmidt, R. A., Young, D. E., Swinnen, S., & Shapiro, D. D. (1989). Summary knowledge of results for skill acquisition: Support for the guidance hypothesis. *Journal of Experimental Psychology: Learning, Memory, and Cognition, 15,* 352–359.

Schneider, V. I., Healy, A. F., Ericsson, K. A., & Bourne, L. E., Jr. (1995). The effects of contextual interference on the acquisition and retention of logical rules. In A. F. Healy & L. E. Bourne, Jr. (Eds.), *Learning and memory of knowledge and skills: Durability and specificity* (pp. 95–131). Thousand Oaks, CA: Sage.

Schneider, W., & Detweiler, M. (1988). The role of practice in dual-task performance: Toward workload modeling in a connectionist/control architecture. *Human Factors, 30,* 539–566.

Schneider, W., & Fisk, A. D. (1982). Degree of consistent training: Improvements in search performance and automatic process development. *Perception & Psychophysics, 31,* 160–168.

Schneider, W., & Shiffrin, R. M. (1977). Controlled and automatic human information processing: I. Detection, search, and attention. *Psychological Review, 84,* 1–66.

Schneider, W., Vidulich, M., & Yeh, Y.-Y. (1982). Training spatial skills for air-traffic control. *Proceedings of the Human Factors Society 26th Annual Meeting* (pp. 10–14). Santa Monica, CA: Human Factors Society.

Schvaneveldt, R. W. (Ed.). (1990). *Pathfinder associative networks: Studies in knowledge organization.* Norwood, NJ: Ablex.

Shea, J. B., & Morgan, R. L. (1979). Contextual interference effects on the acquisition, retention, and transfer of a motor skill. *Journal of Experimental Psychology: Learning, Memory, and Cognition, 5,* 179–187.

Shebilske, W., Goettl, B., & Regian, J. W. (1999). Executive control of automatic processes as complex skills develop in laboratory and applied settings. In D. Gopher & A. Koriat (Eds.), *Attention and performance: Vol. 17. Cognitive regulation of performance: Interaction of theory and application* (pp. 401–432). Cambridge, MA: MIT Press.

Shiffrin, R. M., & Schneider, W. (1977). Controlled and automatic human information processing: II. Perceptual learning, automatic attending, and a general theory. *Psychological Review, 84,* 127–190.

Simon, H. A, & Chase, W. G. (1973). Skill in chess. *American Scientist, 61,* 394–403.

Singley, M. K., & Anderson, J. R. (1989). *The transfer of cognitive skill.* Cambridge, MA: Harvard University Press.

Sowden, P. T., Davies, I. R. L., & Roling, P. (2000). Perceptual learning of the detection of features in X-ray images: A functional role for improvements in adult's visual sensitivity? *Journal of Experimental Psychology: Human Perception and Performance, 26,* 379–390.

Spitz, G. (1988). Flexibility in resource allocation and the performance of time-sharing tasks. *Proceedings of the Human Factors Society 32nd Annual Meeting* (pp. 1466–1470). Santa Monica, CA: Human Factors Society.

Squire, L. R. (1992). Declarative and non-declarative memory: Multiple brain systems supporting learning and memory. *Journal of Cognitive Neuroscience, 4,* 232–243.

Squire, L. R. & Cohen, N. J. (1984). Human memory and amnesia. In G. Lynch, J. L. Mc Gaugh, & N. M. Weinberger (Eds.), *Neurobiology of learning and memory* (pp. 3–64). New York: Guilford.

Stadler, M. A. (1989). On learning complex procedural knowledge. *Journal of Experimental Psychology: Learning, Memory, and Cognition, 15,* 1061–1069.

Swinnen, S. P. (1990). Interpolated activities during the knowledge-of-results delay and the post-knowledge-of-results interval: Effects on performance and learning. *Journal of Experimental Psychology: Learning, Memory, and Cognition, 16,* 692–705.

Swinnen, S. P., Schmidt, R. A., Nicholson, D. E., & Shapiro, D. C. (1990). Information feedback for skill acquisition: Instantaneous knowledge of results degrades learning. *Journal of Experimental Psychology: Learning, Memory, and Cognition, 16,* 706–716.

Teichner, W. H., & Krebs, M. J. (1974). Laws of visual choice reaction time. *Psychological Review, 81,* 75–98.

Thorndike, E. L., & Woodworth, R. S. (1901a). The influence of improvement in one mental function upon the efficiency of other functions. I. *Psychological Review, 8,* 247–261.

Thorndike, E. L., & Woodworth, R. S. (1901b). The influence of improvement in one mental function upon the efficiency of other functions. II. The estimation of magnitudes. *Psychological Review, 8,* 384–395.

Thorndike, E. L., & Woodworth, R. S. (1901c). The influence of improvement in one mental function upon the efficiency of other functions. III. Functions involving attention, observation, and discrimination. *Psychological Review, 8,* 553–564.

Tulving, E. (1985). How many memory systems are there? *American Psychologist, 40,* 385–398.

Vereijken, B., van Emmerik, R. E. A., Whiting, H. T. A., & Newell, K. M. (1992). Free(z)ing degrees of freedom in skill acquisition. *Journal of Motor Behavior, 24,* 133–142.

Verfaellie, M., Bauer, R. M., & Bowers, D. (1991). Autonomic and behavioral evidence of "implicit" memory in amnesia. *Brain and Cognition, 15,* 10–25.

Volpe, C., E., Cannon-Bowers, J. A., Salas, E., & Spector, P. E. (1996). The impact of cross-training on team functioning: An empirical investigation. *Human Factors, 38,* 87–100.

Welford, A. T. (1968). *Fundamentals of skill.* London: Methuen.

Welford, A. T. (1976). *Skilled performance: Perceptual and motor skills.* Glenview, IL: Scott Foresman.

Wightman, D. C., & Lintern G. (1985). Part-task training for tracking and manual control. *Human Factors, 27,* 267–283.

Willingham, D. B., & Goedert-Eschmann, K. (1999). The relation between implicit and explicit learning: Evidence for parallel development. *Psychological Science, 10,* 531–534.

Willingham, D. B., Koroshetz, W. J., & Peterson, E. W. (1996). Motor skills have diverse neural bases: Spared and impaired skill acquisition in Huntington's disease. *Neuropsychology, 10,* 315–321.

Willingham, D. B., Nissen, M. J., & Bullemer, P. (1989). On the development of procedural knowledge. *Journal of Experimental Psychology: Learning, Memory, and Cognition, 15,* 1047–1060.

Winstein, C. J., & Schmidt, R. A. (1990). Reduced frequency of knowledge of results enhances motor skill learning. *Journal of Experimental Psychology: Learning, Memory, and Cognition, 16,* 677–691.

Wisher, R.A., Sabol, M. A., & Kern, R. P. (1995). Modeling acquisition of an advanced skill: The case of Morse code copying. *Instructional Science, 23,* 381–403.

Woodworth, R. S. (1899). The accuracy of voluntary movement [Monograph]. *Psychological Review, 3,* 1–119.

Ziessler, M. (1998). Response-effect learning as a major component of implicit serial learning. *Journal of Experimental Psychology: Learning, Memory, and Cognition, 24,* 962–978.

PART SEVEN

LANGUAGE AND INFORMATION PROCESSING

CHAPTER 19

Language Comprehension and Production

REBECCA TREIMAN, CHARLES CLIFTON JR., ANTJE S. MEYER, AND LEE H. WURM

Psychologists have long been interested in language, but psycholinguistics as a field of study did not emerge until the 1960s. It was motivated by Chomsky's work in linguistics and by his claim that the special properties of language require special mechanisms to handle it (e.g., Chomsky, 1959). The special feature of language on which Chomsky focused was its productivity. Possessed with a grammar, or syntax, humans can produce and understand novel sentences that carry novel messages. We do this in a way that is exquisitely sensitive to the structure of the language. For example, we interpret *The umpire helped the child to third base* and *The umpire helped the child on third base* as conveying distinct messages, although the sentences differ in just one small word. We know that *He showed her baby the pictures* and *He showed her the baby pictures* describe quite different events, even though the difference in word order is slight. We can even make some sense of *Colorless green ideas sleep furiously* (Chomsky, 1971), which is semantically anomalous but syntactically well formed. The same kinds of abilities are found at other levels of language. We combine *morphemes* (units of meaning) in systematic ways, and so understand Lewis Carroll's (1871/1977) *slithy toves* to refer to more than one tove that has the characteristics of slithiness. And we can combine *phonemes* (units of sound) according to the patterns of our language, accepting *slithy* but not *tlithy* as a potential English word.

Early psycholinguists described our comprehension and production of language in terms of the rules that were postulated by linguists (Fodor, Bever, & Garrett, 1974). The connections between psychology and linguistics were particularly close in the area of syntax, with psycholinguists testing the psychological reality of various proposed linguistic rules. As the field of psycholinguistics developed, it became clear that theories of sentence comprehension and production cannot be based in any simple way on linguistic theories; psycholinguistic theories must consider the properties of the human mind as well as the structure of the language. Psycholinguistics has thus become its own area of inquiry, informed by but not totally dependent on linguistics.

Although Chomsky and the early psycholinguists focused on the creative side of language, language also has its rote side. For example, we store a great deal of information about the properties of words in our *mental lexicon,* and we retrieve this information when we understand or produce language. According to some views, different kinds of mechanisms are responsible for the creative and the habitual aspects of language, respectively. For example, we may use morpheme-based rules to decompose a complex word like *rewritable* the first few times we encounter it, but after several exposures we may begin to store and access the word as a unit (Caramazza,

Preparation of this chapter was supported by NSF Grant SBR-9807736 to R.T. and NIH Grant HD18708 to C.C.

Laudanna, & Romani, 1988; Schreuder & Baayen, 1995). *Dual-route* views of this kind have been proposed in several areas of psycholinguistics. According to such models, frequency of exposure determines our ability to recall stored instances but not our ability to apply rules. Another idea is that a single set of mechanisms can handle both the creative side and the rote side of language. *Connectionist* theories (see Rumelhart & McClelland, 1986) take this view. Such theories claim, for instance, that readers use the same system of links between spelling units and sound units to generate the pronunciations of novel written words like *tove* and to access the pronunciations of familiar words, be they words that follow typical spelling-to-sound correspondences, like *stove,* or words that are exceptions to these patterns, like *love* (e.g., Plaut, McClelland, Seidenberg, & Patterson, 1996; Seidenberg & McClelland, 1989). According to this view, similarity and frequency both play important roles in processing, with novel items being processed based on their similarity to known ones. The patterns are statistical and probabilistic rather than all-or-none.

Early psycholinguists, following Chomsky's ideas, tended to see language as an autonomous system, insulated from other cognitive systems. In this *modular* view (see J. A. Fodor, 1983), the initial stages of word and sentence comprehension are not influenced by higher levels of knowledge. Information about context and about real-world constraints comes into play only after the first steps of linguistic processing have taken place, giving such models a *serial* quality. In an *interactive* view, in contrast, knowledge about linguistic context and about the world plays an immediate role in the comprehension of words and sentences. In this view, many types of information are used in *parallel,* with the different sources of information working cooperatively or competitively to yield an interpretation. Such ideas are often expressed in connectionist terms. Modular and interactive views may also be distinguished in discussions of language production, in which one issue is whether there is a syntactic component that operates independently of conceptual and phonological factors.

Another tension in current-day psycholinguistics concerns the proper role of linguistics in the field. Work on syntactic processing, especially in the early days of psycholinguistics, was very much influenced by developments in linguistics. Links between linguistics and psycholinguistics have been less close in other areas, but they do exist. For instance, work on phonological processing has been influenced by linguistic accounts of *prosody* (the melody, rhythm, and stress pattern of spoken language) and of the internal structure of syllables. Also, some work on word recognition and language production has been influenced by linguistic analyses of *morphology* (the study of morphemes and their combination). Although most psycholinguists believe that linguistics provides an essential foundation for their field, some advocates of interactive approaches have moved away from a reliance on linguistic rules and principles and toward a view of language in terms of probabilistic patterns (e.g., Seidenberg, 1997).

In this chapter, we describe current views of the comprehension and production of spoken and written language by fluent language users. Although we acknowledge the importance of social factors in language use, our focus is on core processes such as parsing and word retrieval that are not likely to be strongly affected by such factors. We do not have the space to discuss the important field of *developmental psycholinguistics,* which deals with the acquisition of language by children; nor do we cover *neurolinguistics,* how language is represented in the brain, nor *applied psycholinguistics,* which encompasses such topics as language disorders and language teaching.

LANGUAGE COMPREHENSION

Spoken Word Recognition

The perception of spoken words would seem to be an extremely difficult task. Speech is distributed in time, a fleeting signal that has few reliable cues to the boundaries between segments and words. The paucity of cues leads to what is called the *segmentation problem,* or the problem of how listeners hear a sequence of discrete units even though the acoustic signal itself is continuous. Other features of speech could cause difficulty for listeners as well. Certain phonemes are omitted in conversational speech, others change their pronunciations depending on the surrounding sounds (e.g., /n/ may be pronounced as [m] in *lean bacon*), and many words have everyday (or more colloquial) pronunciations (e.g., *going to* frequently becomes *gonna*). Despite these potential problems, we usually seem to perceive speech automatically and with little effort. Whether we do so using procedures that are unique to speech and that form a specialized speech module (Liberman & Mattingly, 1985; see also the chapter by Fowler in this volume), or whether we do so using more general capabilities, it is clear that humans are well adapted for the perception of speech.

Listeners attempt to map the acoustic signal onto a representation in the mental lexicon beginning almost as the signal starts to arrive. The *cohort model,* first proposed by Marslen-Wilson and Welsh (1978), illustrates how this may occur. According to this theory, the first few phonemes of a spoken word activate a set or cohort of word candidates that are consistent with that input. These candidates compete with one another for activation. As more acoustic input is analyzed, candidates that are no longer consistent with the input drop out of the set. This process continues until only one word candidate matches the input; the best fitting word may be chosen if no single candidate is a clear winner. Supporting this view, listeners sometimes glance first at a picture of a candy when instructed to "pick up the candle" (Allopenna, Magnuson, & Tanenhaus, 1998). This result suggests that a set of words beginning with /kæn/ is briefly activated. Listeners may glance at a picture of a handle, too, suggesting that the cohort of word candidates also includes words that rhyme with the target. Indeed, later versions of the cohort theory (Marslen-Wilson, 1987; 1990) have relaxed the insistence on perfectly matching input from the very first phoneme of a word. Other models (McClelland & Elman, 1986; Norris, 1994) also advocate continuous mapping between spoken input and lexical representations, with the initial portion of the spoken word exerting a strong but not exclusive influence on the set of candidates.

The cohort model and the model of McClelland and Elman (1986) are examples of interactive models, those in which higher processing levels have a direct, so-called *top-down* influence on lower levels. In particular, lexical knowledge can affect the perception of phonemes. A number of researchers have found evidence for interactivity in the form of lexical effects on the perception of sublexical units. Wurm and Samuel (1997), for example, reported that listeners' knowledge of words can lead to the inhibition of certain phonemes. Samuel (1997) found additional evidence of interactivity by studying the phenomenon of *phonemic restoration*. This refers to the fact that listeners continue to "hear" phonemes that have been removed from the speech signal and replaced by noise. Samuel discovered that the restored phonemes produced by lexical activation lead to reliable shifts in how listeners labeled ambiguous phonemes. This finding is noteworthy because such shifts are thought to be a very low-level processing phenomenon.

Modular models, which do not allow top-down perceptual effects, have had varying success in accounting for some of the findings just described. The race model of Cutler and Norris (1979; see also Norris, McQueen, & Cutler, 2000) is one example of such a model. The model has two routes that race each other—a prelexical route, which computes phonological information from the acoustic signal, and a lexical route, in which the phonological information associated with a word becomes available when the word itself is accessed. When word-level information appears to affect a lower-level process, it is assumed that the lexical route won the race. Importantly, though, knowledge about words never influences perception at the lower (phonemic) level. There is currently much discussion about whether all of the experimental findings suggesting top-down effects can be explained in these terms or whether interactivity is necessary (see Norris et al., 2000, and the associated commentary).

Although it is a matter of debate whether higher-level linguistic knowledge affects the initial stages of speech perception, it is clear that our knowledge of language and its patterns facilitates perception in some ways. For example, listeners use *phonotactic* information such as the fact that initial /tl/ is illegal in English to help identify phonemes and word boundaries (Halle, Segui, Frauenfelder, & Meunier, 1998). As another example, listeners use their knowledge that English words are often stressed on the first syllable to help parse the speech signal into words (Norris, McQueen, & Cutler, 1995). These types of knowledge help us solve the segmentation problem in a language that we know, even though we perceive an unknown language as an undifferentiated string of sounds.

Printed Word Recognition

Speech is as old as our species and is found in all human civilizations; reading and writing are newer and less widespread. These facts lead us to expect that readers would use the visual representations that are provided by print to recover the phonological and linguistic structure of the message. Supporting this view, readers often access phonology even when they are reading silently and even when reliance on phonology would tend to hurt their performance. In one study, people were asked to quickly decide whether a word belonged to a specified category (Van Orden, 1987). They were more likely to misclassify a homophone like *meet* as a food than to misclassify a control item like *melt* as a food. In other studies, readers were asked to quickly decide whether a printed sentence made sense. Readers with normal hearing were found to have more trouble with sentences such as *He doesn't like to eat meet* than with sentences such as *He doesn't like to eat melt*. Those who were born deaf, in contrast, did not show a difference between the two sentence types (Treiman & Hirsh-Pasek, 1983).

The English writing system, in addition to representing the sound segments of a word, contains clues to the word's stress pattern and morphological structure. Consistent with the view that print serves as a map of linguistic structure, readers take advantage of these clues as well. For example, skilled readers appear to have learned that a word that has more letters than strictly necessary in its second syllable (e.g., *-ette* rather than *-et*) is likely to be an exception to the generalization that English words are typically stressed on the first syllable. In a *lexical decision task,* where participants must quickly decide whether a letter string is a real word, they perform better with words such as *cassette,* whose stressed second syllable is spelled with *-ette,* than with words such as *palette,* which has final *-ette* but first-syllable stress (Kelly, Morris, & Verrekia, 1998). Skilled readers also use the clues to morphological structure that are embedded in English orthography. For example, they know that the prefix *re-* can stand before free morphemes such as *print* and *do,* yielding the two-morpheme words *reprint* and *redo*. Encountering *vive* in a lexical decision task, participants may wrongly judge it to be a word because of their familiarity with *revive* (Taft & Forster, 1975).

Although there is good evidence that phonology and other aspects of linguistic structure are retrieved in reading (see Frost, 1998, for a review), there are a number of questions about how linguistic structure is derived from print. One idea, which is embodied in dual-route theories such as that of Coltheart, Rastle, Perry, Langdon, and Ziegler (2001), is that two different processes are available for converting orthographic representations to phonological representations. A lexical route is used to look up the phonological forms of known words in the mental lexicon; this procedure yields correct pronunciations for exception words such as *love*. A nonlexical route accounts for the productivity of reading: It generates pronunciations for novel letter strings (e.g., *tove*) as well as for regular words (e.g., *stove*) on the basis of smaller units. This latter route gives incorrect pronunciations for exception words, so that these words may be pronounced slowly or erroneously (e.g., *love* said as /lov/) in speeded word-naming tasks (e.g., Glushko, 1979). In contrast, connectionist theories claim that a single set of connections from orthography to phonology can account for performance on both regular words and exception words (e.g., Plaut et al., 1996; Seidenberg & McClelland, 1989).

Another question about orthography-to-phonology translation concerns its grain size. English, which has been the subject of much of the research on word recognition, has a rather irregular writing system. For example, *ea* corresponds to /i/ in *bead* but /ε/ in *dead*; *c* is /k/ in *cat* but /s/ in *city*. Such irregularities are particularly common for vowels. Quantitative analyses have shown, however, that consideration of the consonant that follows a vowel can often help to specify the vowel's pronunciation (Kessler & Treiman, 2001; Treiman, Mullennix, Bijeljac-Babic, & Richmond-Welty, 1995). The /ε/ pronunciation of *ea,* for example, is more likely before *d* than before *m*. Such considerations have led to the proposal that readers of English often use letter groups that correspond to the syllable *rime* (the vowel nucleus plus an optional consonantal coda) in spelling-to-sound translation (see Bowey, 1990; Treiman et al., 1995, for supporting evidence). In more regular alphabets, such as Dutch, spelling-to-sound translation can be successfully performed at a small grain size and rime-based processing may not be needed (Martensen, Maris, & Dijkstra, 2000).

Researchers have also asked whether a phonological form, once activated, feeds activation back to the orthographic level. If so, a word such as *heap* may be harder to process than otherwise expected because its phonological form, /hip/, would be consistent with the spelling *heep* as well as with the actual *heap*. Some studies have found evidence for feedback of this kind (e.g., Stone, Vanhoy, & Van Orden, 1997), but others have not (e.g., Peereman, Content, & Bonin, 1998).

Because spoken words are spread out in time, as discussed earlier, spoken word recognition is generally considered a sequential process. With many printed words, however, the eye takes in all of the letters during a single fixation (Rayner & Pollatsek, 1989). The connectionist models of reading cited earlier maintain that all phonemes of a word are activated in parallel. Current dual-route theories, in contrast, claim that the assembly process operates in a serial fashion such that the phonological forms of the leftmost elements are delivered before those for the succeeding elements (Coltheart et al., 2001). Still another view (Berent & Perfetti, 1995) is that consonants, whatever their position, are translated into phonological form before vowels. These issues are the subject of current research and debate (see Lee, Rayner, & Pollatsek, 2001; Lukatela & Turvey, 2000; Rastle & Coltheart, 1999; Zorzi, 2000).

Progress in determining how linguistic representations are derived from print will be made as researchers move beyond the short, monosyllabic words that have been the focus of much current research and modeling. In addition, experimental techniques that involve the brief presentation of stimuli and the tracking of eye movements are contributing useful information. These methods supplement the naming tasks and lexical decision tasks that are used in much of the research on single-word reading (see chapter by Rayner, Pollatsek, & Starr in this volume for further discussion of eye movements and reading). Although many questions remain to be answered, it is clear that the visual representations provided by print rapidly make contact with the representations stored in the mental lexicon. After this contact has been made, it matters little whether the initial input was by eye or by ear. The principles and processing procedures are much the same.

The Mental Lexicon

So far, in discussing how listeners and readers access information in the mental lexicon, we have not said much about the nature of the information that they access. It is to this topic that we now turn. One question that relates to the trade-off between computation and storage in language processing is whether the mental lexicon is organized by morphemes or by words. According to a word-based view, the lexicon contains representations of all words that the language user knows, whether they are single-morpheme words such as *cat* or polymorphemic words such as *beautifully.* Supporting this view, Tyler, Marslen-Wilson, Rentoul, and Hanney (1988) found that spoken-word recognition performance was related to when the word began to diverge from other words in the mental lexicon, as predicted by the cohort model, but was not related to morphemic predictors of where recognition should take place. According to a morpheme-based view, in contrast, the lexicon is organized in terms of morphemes such as *beauty, ful,* and *ly.* In this view, complex words are processed and represented in terms of such units.

The study by Taft and Forster (1975) brought morphological issues to the attention of many psychologists and pointed to some form of morpheme-based storage. As mentioned earlier, these researchers found that nonwords such as *vive* (which is found in *revive*) were difficult to reject in a lexical decision task. Participants also had trouble with items such as *dejuvenate* which, although not a real word, consists of genuine prefix together with a genuine root. Taft and Forster interpreted their results to suggest that access to the mental lexicon is based on root morphemes and that obligatory decomposition must precede word recognition for polymorphemic words.

More recent studies suggest that there are in fact two routes to recognition for polymorphemic words, one based on morphological analysis and the other based on whole-word storage. In one instantiation of this dual-route view, morphologically complex words are simultaneously analyzed as whole words and in terms of morphemes. In the model of Wurm (1997, Wurm & Ross, 2001), for instance, the system maintains a representation of which morphemes can combine, and in what ways. A potential word root is checked against a list of free roots that have combined in the past with the prefix in question. In another instantiation of the dual-route view, some morphologically complex words are decomposed and others are not. For example, Marslen-Wilson, Tyler, Waksler, and Older (1994) argued that semantically opaque words such as *organize* and *casualty* are treated by listeners and readers as monomorphemic and are not decomposed no matter how many morphemes they technically contain. Commonly encountered words may also be treated as wholes rather than in terms of morphemes (Caramazza et al., 1988; Schreuder & Baayen, 1995). Although morphological decomposition may not always take place, the evidence we have reviewed suggests that the lexicon is organized, in part, in terms of morphemes. This organization helps explain our ability to make some sense of *slithy* and *toves*.

Ambiguous words, or those with more than one meaning, might be expected to cause difficulties in lexical processing. Researchers have been interested in ambiguity because studies of this issue may provide insight into whether processing at the lexical level is influenced by information at higher levels or whether it is modular. In the former case, comprehenders would be expected to access only the contextually appropriate meaning of a word. In the latter case, all meanings should be retrieved and context should have its effects only after the initial processing has taken place. The original version of the cohort model (Marslen-Wilson & Welsh, 1978) adopts an interactive view when it states that context acts directly on cohort membership. However, later versions of cohort theory (Marslen-Wilson, 1987; 1990; Moss & Marslen-Wilson, 1993) hold that context has its effects at a later, integrative stage.

Initially, it appears, both meanings of an ambiguous morpheme are looked up in many cases. This may even occur when the preceding context would seem to favor one meaning over the other. In one representative study (Gernsbacher & Faust, 1991), participants read sentences such as *Jack tried the punch but he didn't think it tasted very good.* After the word *punch* had been presented, an upper-case letter string was presented and participants were asked to decide whether it was a real word. Of interest were lexical decision targets such as *hit* (which are related to an unintended meaning of the ambiguous word) and *drink* (which are related to the intended meaning). When the target was presented immediately after the participant had read *punch,* performance was speeded on both *hit* and *drink.* This result suggests that even the contextually inappropriate meaning of the ambiguous morpheme was activated. The initial lack of contextual effects in this and other studies (e.g., Swinney, 1979) supports the idea that lexical access is a modular process, uninfluenced by higher-level syntactic and semantic constraints.

Significantly, Gernsbacher and Faust (1991) found a different pattern of results when the lexical decision task was delayed by a half second or so but still preceded the following word of the sentence. In this case, *drink* remained active but *hit* did not. Gernsbacher and Faust interpreted these results to mean that comprehenders initially access all meanings of an ambiguous word but then actively suppress the meaning (or meanings) that does not fit the context. This suppression process, they contend, is more efficient in better comprehenders than in poorer comprehenders. Because the inappropriate meaning is quickly suppressed, the reader or listener is typically not aware of the ambiguity.

Although all meanings of an ambiguous word may be accessed initially in many cases, this may not always be so (see Simpson, 1994). For example, when one meaning of an ambiguous word is much more frequent than the other or when the context very strongly favors one meaning, the other meaning may show little or no activation. It has thus been difficult to provide a clear answer to the question of whether lexical access is modular.

The preceding discussion considered words that have two or more unrelated meanings. More common are *polysemous* words, which have several senses that are related to one another. For example, *paper* can refer to a substance made of wood pulp or to an article that is typically written on that substance but that nowadays may be written and published electronically. Processing a polysemous word in one of its senses can make it harder to subsequently comprehend the word in another of its senses (Klein & Murphy, 2001). That one sense can be activated and the other suppressed suggests to these researchers that at least some senses have separate representations, just as the different meanings of a morpheme like *punch* have separate representations.

Problems with ambiguity are potentially greater in bilingual than in monolingual individuals. For example, *leek* has a single sense for a monolingual speaker of English, but it has another meaning, *layperson,* for one who also knows Dutch. When asked to decide whether printed words are English, and when the experimental items included some exclusively Dutch words, Dutch-English bilinguals were found to have more difficulty with words such as *leek* than with appropriate control words such as *pox* (Dijkstra, Timmermans, & Schriefers, 2000). Such results suggest that the Dutch lexicon is activated along with the English one in this situation. Although optimal performance could be achieved by deactivating the irrelevant language, bilinguals are sometimes unable to do this. Further evidence for this view comes from a study in which Russian-English bilinguals were asked, in Russian, to pick up objects such as a *marku* (*stamp;* Spivey & Marian, 1999). When a marker was also present—an object whose English name is similar to *marku*—people sometimes looked at it before looking at the stamp and carrying out the instruction. Although English was not used during the experimental session, the bilinguals appeared unable to ignore the irrelevant lexicon.

Information about the meanings of words and about the concepts that they represent is also linked to lexical representations. The chapter in this volume by Goldstone and Kersten includes a discussion of conceptual representation.

Comprehension of Sentences and Discourse

Important as word recognition is, understanding language requires far more than adding the meanings of the individual words together. We must combine the meanings in ways that honor the grammar of the language and that are sensitive to the possibility that language is being used in a metaphoric or nonliteral manner (see Cacciari & Glucksberg, 1994). Psycholinguists have addressed the phenomena of sentence comprehension in different ways. Some theorists have focused on the fact that the sentence comprehension system continually creates novel representations of novel messages, following the constraints of a language's grammar, and does so with remarkable speed. Others have emphasized that the comprehension system is sensitive to a vast range of information, including grammatical, lexical, and contextual, as well as knowledge of the speaker or writer and of the world in general. Theorists in the former group (e.g., Ford, Bresnan, & Kaplan, 1982; Frazier & Rayner, 1982; Pritchett, 1992) have constructed modular, serial models that describe how the processor quickly constructs one or more representations of a sentence based on a restricted range of information, primarily grammatical information, that is guaranteed to be relevant to its interpretation. Any such representation is then quickly interpreted and evaluated, using the full range of information that might be relevant. Theorists in the latter group (e.g., MacDonald, Pearlmutter & Seidenberg, 1994; Tanenhaus & Trueswell, 1995) have constructed parallel models, often of a connectionist nature, describing how the processor uses all relevant information to quickly evaluate the full range of possible interpretations of a sentence (see Pickering, 1999, for discussion).

Neither of the two approaches just described provides a full account of how the sentence processing mechanism works. Modular models, by and large, do not adequately deal with how interpretation occurs, how the full range of information relevant to interpretation is integrated, or how the initial representation is revised when necessary (but see J. D. Fodor & Ferreira, 1998, for a beginning on the latter question). Parallel models, for the most part, do not adequately deal with how the processor constructs or activates the various interpretations whose competitive evaluation they describe (see Frazier, 1995). However, both approaches have motivated bodies of research that have advanced our knowledge of language comprehension, and new models are being developed that have the promise of overcoming the limitations of the models that have guided research in the past (Gibson, 1998; Jurafsky, 1996; Vosse & Kempen, 2000).

Structural Factors in Comprehension

Comprehension of written and spoken language can be difficult, in part, because it is not always easy to identify the *constituents* (phrases) of a sentence and the ways in which they relate to one another. The place of a particular constituent within the grammatical structure may be temporarily or permanently ambiguous. Studies of how people resolve grammatical ambiguities, like studies of how they resolve lexical ambiguities, have provided insights into the processes of language comprehension. Consider the sentence *The second wife will claim the inheritance belongs to her*. When *the inheritance* first appears, it could be interpreted as either the direct object of *claim* or the subject of *belongs*. Frazier and Rayner (1982) found that readers' eyes fixated for longer than usual on the verb *belongs*, which disambiguates the sentence. They interpreted this result to mean that readers first interpreted *the inheritance* as a direct object. Readers were disrupted when they had to revise this initial interpretation to the one in which *the inheritance* is subject of *belongs*. Following Bever (1970), Frazier and Rayner described their readers as being led down a garden path. Readers are led down the garden path, Frazier and Rayner claimed, because the direct-object analysis is structurally simpler than the other possible analysis. These researchers proposed a principle, *minimal attachment,* which defined the phrase *structurally simpler,* and they claimed that structural simplicity guides all initial analyses. In this view, the sentence processor constructs a single analysis of a sentence and attempts to interpret it. The first analysis is the one that requires the fewest applications of grammatical rules to attach each incoming word into the structure being built; it is the automatic consequence of an effort to get some analysis constructed as soon as possible. Many researchers have tested and confirmed the minimal attachment principle for a variety of sentence types (see Frazier & Clifton, 1996, for a review).

Minimal attachment is not the only principle that has been proposed as governing how readers and listeners use grammatical knowledge in parsing. Another principle that has received substantial support is *late closure* (Frazier, 1987a). Frazier and Rayner (1982) provided some early support for this principle by showing disruption on the phrase *seems like* in *Since Jay always jogs a mile seems like a very short distance to him.* Here, *a mile* is first taken to be the direct object of *jogs* because the processor tries to relate it to the phrase currently being processed. Reading is disrupted when *a mile* must be reanalyzed as the subject of *seems*.

Another principle is some version of *prefer argument* (e.g., Abney, 1989; Konieczny, Hemforth, Scheepers, & Strube, 1997; Pritchett, 1992). Grammars often distinguish between *arguments* and *adjuncts*. An argument is a phrase whose relation to a verb or other argument assigner is lexically specified; an adjunct is related to what it modifies in a less specific fashion (see Schütze & Gibson, 1999). With the sentence *Joe expressed his interest in the car,* the prefer argument principle predicts that a reader will attach *in the car* to the noun *interest* rather than to the verb *express,* even though the latter analysis is structurally simpler and preferred according to minimal attachment. *In the car* is an argument of *interest* (the nature of its relation to *interest* is specified by the word *interest*) but an adjunct of *express* (it states the location of the action just as it would for any action). Substantial evidence suggests that the argument analysis is preferred in the end (Clifton, Speer, & Abney, 1991; Konieczny et al., 1997; Schütze & Gibson, 1999). However, some evidence suggests a brief initial preference for the minimal attachment analysis (Clifton et al., 1991).

Long-distance dependencies, like ambiguities, can cause problems in the parsing of language. Language gains much of its expressive power from its recursive properties: Sentences can be placed inside sentences, without limit. This means that related phrases can be distant from one another. Many linguists describe constructions like *Who did you see t at the zoo* and *The girl I saw t at the zoo was my sister* as having an empty element, a *trace* (symbolized by *t*), in the position where the moved element (*who* and *the girl*) must be interpreted. Psycholinguists who have adopted this analysis ask how the sentence processor discovers the relation between the moved element (or *filler*) and the trace (or *gap*). One possibility, J. D. Fodor (1978) suggested, is that the processor might delay filler-gap assignment as long as possible. However, there is evidence that the processor actually identifies the gap as soon as possible, an *active filler* strategy (Frazier, 1987b).

The active filler strategy is closely related to minimal attachment, for both strategies attempt to find some grammatical analysis of a sentence as soon as possible (see De Vincenzi, 1991). But the active filler strategy may not be the whole story. Pickering and Barry (1991) and Boland, Tanenhaus, Garnsey, and Carlson (1995) proposed what the latter called a *direct assignment* strategy, according to which a filler is semantically interpreted as soon as a reader or listener encounters the verb to which it is related, without waiting for the gap position. Evidence for this strategy comes from a study in which Boland et al. presented sentences word by word, asking readers to indicate when and if a sentence became unacceptable. An implausible sentence like *Which public library did John contribute some cheap liquor to t last week* tended to be rejected right on the word *liquor,* before the position of the gap.

Lexical and Contextual Factors in Comprehension

Most of the phenomena discussed so far show that preferences for certain structural relations play an important role in sentence comprehension. However, as syntactic theory has shifted away from describing particular structural configurations and toward specifying lexical information that constrains possible grammatical relations, many psycholinguists have proposed that the human sentence processor is primarily guided by information about specific words that is stored in the lexicon. The research on comprehenders' preference for arguments discussed earlier is one example of this move, as is the research by Boland et al. (1995) on long-distance dependencies (see Tanenhaus, Boland, Mauner, & Carlson, 1993, for further discussion).

Spivey-Knowlton and Sedivy (1995) demonstrated effects of particular categories of lexical items, as well as effects of discourse structure, in the comprehension of sentences like *The salesman glanced at a/the customer with suspicion/ripped jeans*. The prepositional phrases *with suspicion* or *with ripped jeans* could modify either the verb *glance* or the noun *customer*. Minimal attachment favors the former analysis, but Spivey-Knowlton and Sedivy showed that this held true only for action verbs like *smash down,* not for perception verbs like *glance at*. The researchers further noted that an actual preference for noun phrase modification only appeared when the noun had the indefinite article *a.* This outcome, they suggested, points to the importance of discourse factors (such as whether an entity is newly referred to or not) in sentence comprehension.

Some theorists (e.g., Altmann & Steedman, 1988) have proposed that contextual appropriateness guides parsing and indeed is responsible for the effects that have previously been attributed to structural factors such as minimal attachment. The basic claim of their *referential theory* is that, for a phrase to modify a definite noun phrase, there must be two or more possible referents of the noun phrase in the discourse context. For instance, in the sentence *The burglar blew open a safe with the dynamite,* treatment of *with the dynamite* as modifying *a safe* is claimed to presuppose the existence of two or more safes, one of which contains dynamite. If multiple safes had not been mentioned, the sentence processor must either infer the existence of other safes or must analyze the phrase in another way, for example as specifying an instrument of *blow open.* Supporters of referential theory have argued that the out-of-context preferences that have been taken to support principles like minimal attachment disappear when sentences are presented in appropriate discourse contexts. In one study, Altmann and Steedman examined how long readers took on sentences like *The burglar blew open the safe with the dynamite/new lock and made off with the loot* in contexts that had introduced either one safe or two safes, one with a new lock. The version containing *with the dynamite* was read faster in the one-safe context, in which the phrase modified the verb and thus satisfied minimal attachment. The version containing *with the new lock* was read faster in the two-safe context, fitting referential theory.

Many studies have examined effects like the one just described (see Mitchell, 1994, for a summary). It is clear that the use of a definite noun phrase when the discourse context contains two possible referents disrupts reading. This result shows once again that interpretation is nearly immediate and that reading is disrupted when unambiguous interpretation is blocked. A context that provides two referents can eliminate the disruption observed out of context when a phrase must modify a noun, at least when the out-of-context structural preference is weak (Britt, 1994). When the out-of-context bias is strong (as in the case of reduced relative clauses, like Bever's *The horse raced past the barn fell;* 1970), a context that satisfies the presumed referential presuppositions of a modifier reduces the amount of disruption rather than eliminating it.

Given the wide variety of factors that seem to affect sentence comprehension, some psycholinguists have developed lexicalist, constraint-based theories of sentence processing (e.g., MacDonald et al., 1994; Tanenhaus & Trueswell, 1995). These theories, which are described and sometimes implemented in connectionist terms, assume that multiple possible interpretations of a sentence are available to the processor. Each possible interpretation receives activation (or inhibition) from some knowledge sources, as well as (generally) being inhibited by the other interpretations. Competition among the interpretations eventually results in the dominance of a single one. Increased competition is responsible for the effects that the theories discussed earlier have attributed to the need to revise an analysis. Constraint-based theories can accommodate influences of specific lexical information, context, verb category, and many other factors, and they have encouraged the search for additional influences. However, they may not be the final word on sentence processing. These theories correctly predict that a variety of factors can reduce or eliminate garden-path effects when a temporarily ambiguous sentence is resolved in favor of an analysis that is not normally preferred (e.g., nonminimal attachment). But the constraint-based theories also predict that these factors will create garden paths when the sentence is resolved in favor of its normally preferred analysis. This may not always be the case (Binder, Duffy, & Rayner, 2001).

Competitive constraint-based theories, like other connectionist theories, grant a major role to frequency. Frequent constructions should be more readily activated by appropriate sources of information than less common constructions are. Supporting this view, readers understand sentences like *The award accepted by the man was very impressive* more readily when the first verb is frequently used as a passive participle, as *accept* is, than when the verb is not frequently used as a passive particle, as with *search* (Trueswell, 1996). Also, reduced relative-clause sentences, such as *The rancher could see that the nervous cattle pushed/moved into the crowded pen were afraid of the cowboys,* are read more rapidly when the verb of the complement sentence is more often used as a transitive verb (*push*) than when it is more often used as an intransitive verb (*move;* MacDonald, 1994). The frequency of particular constructions may not always predict comprehension preferences and comprehension difficulty (Gibson, Schütze, & Salomon, 1996; Kennison, 2001; Pickering, Traxler, & Crocker, 2000). However, theorists such as Jurafsky (1996) have made a strong case that the frequency of exposure to certain constructions is a major factor guiding sentence comprehension.

Competitive constraint-based theories have also emphasized discourse and situational context as constraints on sentence comprehension. Researchers have taken advantage of the fact that listeners quickly direct their eyes to the referents of what they hear, as shown by the Allopenna et al. (1998) study mentioned in the earlier discussion of spoken word recognition, to study how comprehension is guided by situational context. Spivey, Tanenhaus, Eberhard, and Sedivy (in press) found that, when a listener hears a command like *Put the cup on the napkin under the book,* the eyes move quickly to an empty napkin when the context contains just one cup, even if the cup had been on a napkin. This result suggests that *on the napkin* was taken as the goal argument of *put*. However, when the context contains two cups, only one on a napkin, the eyes do not move to an empty napkin. This result suggests that the situational context overrode the default preference to take the *on*-phrase as an argument. Related work explores how quickly knowledge of the roles objects typically play in events is used in determining the reference of phrases. In one study, people observed a scene on a video display and judged the appropriateness of an auditory sentence describing the scene (Altmann & Kamide, 1999). Their eyes moved faster to a relevant target when the verb in the sentence was commonly used with the target item. For instance, when people heard *The boy will eat the cake* their eyes moved more quickly to a picture of a cake than when they heard *The boy will move the cake*.

Comprehension of Text and Discourse

The research just described shows how quickly listeners integrate grammatical and situational knowledge in understanding a sentence. Integration is also important across sentence boundaries. Sentences come in texts and discourses, and the entire text or discourse is relevant to the messages conveyed. Researchers have examined how readers and listeners determine whether referring expressions, especially pronouns and noun phrases, pick out a new entity or one that was introduced earlier in the discourse. They have studied how readers and listeners determine the relations between one assertion and earlier assertions, including determining what unexpressed assertions follow as implications of what was heard or read. Many studies have examined how readers and listeners create a nonlinguistic representation of the content, one that supports the functions of determining reference, relevance, and implications (see the several chapters on text and discourse comprehension in Gernsbacher, 1994, and also Garnham, 1999, and Sanford, 1999, for summaries of this work).

Much research on text comprehension has been guided by the work of Kintsch (1974; Kintsch & Van Dijk, 1978; see chapter in this volume by Butcher & Kintsch), who has proposed a series of models of the process by which the propositions that make up the semantic interpretations of individual sentences are integrated into such larger structures. His models describe ways in which readers could abstract the main threads of a discourse and infer missing connections, constrained by limitations of short-term memory and guided by how arguments overlap across propositions and by linguistic cues signaled by the text.

One line of research explores how a text or discourse makes contact with knowledge in long-term memory (e.g., Kintsch, 1988), including material introduced earlier in a discourse. Some research emphasizes how retrieval of information from long-term memory can be a passive process that occurs automatically throughout comprehension (e.g., McKoon & Ratcliff, 1998; Myers & O'Brien, 1998). In the Myers and O'Brien *resonance* model, information in long-term memory is automatically activated by the presence in short-term memory of material that apparently bears a rough semantic relation to it. Semantic details, including factors such as negation that drastically change the truth of propositions, do not seem to affect the resonance process. Other research has emphasized a more active and intelligent search for meaning as the basis by which a reader discovers the conceptual structure of a discourse. Graesser, Singer, and Trabasso (1994) argued that a reader of a narrative text attempts to build a representation of the causal structure of the text, analyzing events in terms of goals, actions, and reactions. Another view (Rizzella & O'Brien, 1996) is that a resonance process serves as a first stage in processing a text and that reading objectives and details of text structure determine whether a reader goes further and searches for a coherent goal structure for the text.

Modality-Specific Factors

The theories and phenomena that we have discussed so far apply to comprehension of both spoken language and written language. One challenge that is specific to listening comes from the evanescent nature of speech. People cannot relisten to what they have just heard in the way that readers can move their eyes back in the text. However, the fact that humans are adapted through evolution to process auditory (vs. written) language suggests that this may not be such a problem. Auditory sensory memory can hold information for up to several seconds (Cowan, 1984; see chapter by Nairne in this volume), and so language that is heard may in fact persist for longer than language that is read, permitting effective revision. In addition, auditory structure may facilitate short-term memory for spoken language. Imposing a rhythm on the items in a to-be-remembered list can help people remember them (Ryan, 1969), and prosody may aid memory for sentences as well (Speer, Crowder, & Thomas, 1993). Prosody may also guide the parsing and interpretation of utterances (see Warren, 1999). For example, prosody can help resolve lexical and syntactic ambiguities, it can signal the importance, novelty, and contrastive value of phrases, and it can relate newly heard information to the prior discourse. If readers translate visually presented sentences into a phonological form, complete with prosody, these benefits may extend to reading (Bader, 1998; Slowiaczek & Clifton, 1980).

Consider how prosody can permit listeners to avoid the kinds of garden paths that have been observed in reading (Frazier & Rayner, 1982). Several researchers (see Warren, 1999) have demonstrated that prosody can disambiguate utterances. In particular, an *intonational phrase boundary* (marked by pausing, lengthening, and tonal movement) can signal the listener that a syntactic phrase is ending (see Selkirk, 1984, for discussion of the relation between prosodic and syntactic boundaries). Recent evidence for this conclusion comes from a study by Kjelgaard and Speer (1999) that examined ambiguities like *When Madonna sings the song it's/is a hit*. Readers, as mentioned earlier, initially take the phrase *the song* as the direct object of *sings*. This results in a garden path when the sentence continues with *is,* forcing readers to reinterpret the role of *the song*. Kjelgaard and Speer found that such difficulties were eliminated when these kinds of sentences were supplied with appropriate prosodies. The relevant prosodic property does not seem to be simply the occurrence of a local cue, such as an intonational phrase break (Schafer, 1997). Rather, the effectiveness of a prosodic boundary seems to depend on its relation to certain other boundaries (Carlson, Clifton & Frazier, 2001), even the global prosodic representation of a sentence.

Written language carries some information that is not available in the auditory signal. For example, word boundaries are explicitly indicated in many languages, and readers seldom have to suffer the kinds of degradation in signal quality that are commonly experienced by listeners in noisy environments. However, writing lacks the full range of grammatically relevant prosodic information that is available in speech. Punctuation has value in that it restores some of this information (see Hill & Murray, 1998). For instance, readers can use the comma in *Since Jay always jogs, a mile seems like a very short distance to him* to avoid misinterpretation. Readers also seem to be sensitive to line breaks, paragraph marking, and the like. Their comprehension improves, for example, when line breaks in a text correspond to major constituent boundaries (Clark & Clark, 1977, pp. 51–52).

LANGUAGE PRODUCTION

As we have discussed, comprehenders must map the spoken or written input onto entries in the mental lexicon and must generate various levels of syntactic, semantic, and conceptual structure. In language production, people are faced with the converse problem. They must map from a conceptual structure to words and their elements. In this section, we first discuss how people produce single words and then turn to the production of longer utterances. Our discussion concentrates on spoken language production, which has been the focus of most of the research on language production. We then consider how the representations and processes involved in writing differ from those involved in speaking.

Access to Single Words in Spoken Language Production

To give an overview of how speakers generate single words, we first summarize the model of lexical access proposed by Levelt, Roelofs, and Meyer (1999; see Roelofs, 1997, for a computational model implementing key parts of the theory). Like most other models of word production, this model claims that words are planned in several processing steps. Each step generates a specific type of representation, and information is transmitted between representations via the spreading of activation. The first processing step, called conceptualization, is deciding what notion to express. For instance, a speaker can say "the baby," "Emilio," "Her Majesty's grandson," or simply "he" to refer to a small person in a highchair. In making such a choice, the speaker considers a variety of things, including whether the person has been mentioned before and whether the listener is likely to know the proper name of the person being discussed (see Clark, 1996; Levelt, 1989, for discussions of conceptualization and the role of social factors therein).

The next step is to select a word that corresponds to the chosen concept. In the view of Levelt et al. (1999), the speaker first selects a *lemma,* or syntactic word unit. Lemmas specify the syntactic class of the word and often additional syntactic information, such as whether a verb is intransitive (e.g., *sleep*) or transitive (e.g., *eat*) and, if transitive, what arguments it takes. Lemma selection is a competitive process. Several lemmas may be activated at the same time because several concepts are more or less suitable to express the message, and because lemmas that correspond to semantically similar concepts activate each other via links to shared superordinate concepts or conceptual features. A lemma is selected as soon as its activation level exceeds the summed activation of all competitors. A checking mechanism ascertains that the selected lemma indeed maps onto the intended concept.

The following processing step, morphophonological encoding, begins with the retrieval of the morphemes corresponding to the selected lemma. For the lemma *baby* there is only one morpheme to retrieve, but for *grandson* or *walked* two morphemes must be retrieved. Evidence that speakers access morphological information comes from a variety of sources. For instance, people sometimes make speech errors such as "imagine getting your model renosed," in which stems exchange while affixes remain in place (Fromkin, 1971). Other evidence shows that morphologically related primes have different effects on the production of target words than do semantically or phonologically related primes (e.g., Roelofs, 1996; Zwitserlood, Boelte, & Dohmes, 2000). Priming experiments have also shown that morphemes are accessed in sequence, according to their order in the utterance (e.g., Roelofs, 1996).

In the model of Levelt et al. (1999), the next processing step is the generation of the phonological form of the word. Word forms are not simply retrieved as units, but are first decomposed into individual segments (or perhaps segments and certain groups of segments, such as /st/), which are subsequently mapped onto prosodic patterns. The most convincing evidence for phonological decomposition stems from studies of speech errors (e.g., Fromkin, 1971). Speakers sometimes make errors in which they replace or misorder single phonemes, as in *perry pie* instead of *cherry pie.* These errors show that the words' segments constitute processing units; if word forms were retrieved as units, such errors could not occur. Thus, for the word *baby,* the segments /b/, /e/, /b/, /i/ are retrieved. In the model of Levelt et al., the string of segments is subsequently syllabified following the syllabification rules of the language and is assigned stress. Many words are stressed according to simple default rules: For example, bisyllabic English words are usually stressed on the first syllable. For words that deviate from these rules, stress information is stored in the lexicon. During phonological encoding, the segmental and stress information are combined. Results from a large number of experiments using various types of priming and interference paradigms suggest that all phonemes of a word may be activated at the same time, but that the formation of syllables is a sequential process, proceeding from the beginning of the word to the end (e.g., Meyer, 1991; Meyer & Schriefers, 1991; O'Seaghdha & Marin, 2000).

The phonological representation of a word is abstract in that it consists of discrete, nonoverlapping segments, which define static positions of the vocal tract or states of the acoustic signal to be attained, and in that the definitions of the segments are independent of the contexts in which they appear. However, actual speech movements overlap in time, and they are continuous and context-dependent. The final planning step for a word is the generation of a phonetic representation, which specifies the articulatory gestures to be carried out and their timing. There may be syllable-sized routines for frequent syllables that can be retrieved as units and unpacked during articulation (e.g., Levelt & Wheeldon, 1994). The chapter by Fowler in this volume discusses the generation and execution of articulatory commands.

All current models of word production distinguish among conceptual processes, word retrieval processes, and articulatory processes. The models differ in the types of representations they postulate at each level and in their assumptions about processing. One important representational issue is whether it is useful to assume lemmas as purely syntactic units and to postulate separate units representing word forms, or whether there are lexical units that encompass both syntactic and word-form information. Relevant evidence comes from experiments that use reaction times and measures of brain activity to trace how syntactic and form information is retrieved across time (e.g., van Turennout, Hagoort, & Brown, 1998). Also relevant are analyses of *tip-of-the-tongue states,* in which speakers can only retrieve part of the information pertaining to a word—for example, its grammatical gender but not its form (e.g., Vigliocco, Antonini, & Garrett, 1997). How these findings should be interpreted is still a matter of debate (see Caramazza & Miozzo, 1997; Roelofs, Meyer, & Levelt, 1998). Representational issues also arise at the phonological level. In the model of Levelt et al. (1999), segments are associated to unitary syllable nodes without internal structure. In other models, syllables are frames with slots corresponding to subsyllabic units (onset and rime, or onset, nucleus, and coda; see Dell, 1986) or consonantal and vocalic positions (Dell, 1988; O'Seaghdha & Marin, 2000).

Models of language production also differ in the emphasis that they place on storage versus computation. Levelt et al. (1999) emphasize computation. In their view, stress is computed rather than stored when possible. Also, even common forms like *walked* are derived by the combination of stems and affixes. Other models assume that some information that could in principle be computed is stored in the lexicon. For example, stress may be stored for all entries, and forms such as *walked* may be retrieved as wholes (e.g., Stemberger & MacWhinney, 1986).

In all models of language production, the main direction of processing is from the conceptual level to articulation. Some production models, like some comprehension models, assume serial processing stages such that processing at one level must finish before processing at the next level can begin. Other models assume *cascaded* processing, whereby each activated unit immediately spreads activation to its subordinate units (e.g., Humphreys, Price, & Riddoch, 2000; MacKay, 1987). Some cascading models permit feedback from lower to higher levels of processing (e.g., Dell, 1986, 1988; Dell, Schwartz, Martin, Saffran, & Gagnon, 1997). In serial stage models, in which higher-level processing is completed before lower-level processing begins, lower-level information cannot affect higher-level processing.

In the model of Levelt et al. (1999), there is feedback between the conceptual and lemma levels. Because these levels are shared between production and comprehension, information would be expected to flow in both directions. Processing at the lemma and word-form levels is strictly sequential. Thus, in this model, word-form retrieval only begins after a lemma has been selected. In cascaded models, by contrast, each lemma that receives some activation from the conceptual level spreads some of its activation to the corresponding word form, so that several word forms may be active at once. In priming experiments, Levelt, Schriefers, Vorberg, Meyer, Pechmann, and Havinga (1991) found no evidence for simultaneous activation of the forms of competing lemmas. However, Peterson and Savoy (1998) showed that near-synonyms such as *couch* and *sofa* may simultaneously activate their forms. Levelt et al. proposed that in such cases, speakers may have failed to unambiguously select one lemma. An important argument for feedback from lower to higher levels of processing is that speech errors in which the target and outcome are related in both form and meaning (as in *cat* for *rat*) occur far more often than would be expected if lemma and word form were selected independently (e.g., Dell, 1986, 1988). To account for this finding within a serial stage model, Levelt et al. proposed that people are particularly likely to overlook such errors when they monitor their speech.

Generation of Sentences in Spoken Language Production

We now consider how speakers generate longer utterances, such as descriptions of scenes or events. The first step is again conceptual preparation—deciding what to say. Evidently, conceptual preparation is more complex for longer than for shorter utterances. To make a complicated theoretical argument or to describe a series of events, the speaker needs a global plan (see Levelt, 1989). Each part of the plan must be elaborated, perhaps via intermediate stages, until a representational level is reached that consists of lexical concepts. This representation, the message, forms the input to linguistic planning. Utterances comprising several sentences are rarely laid out entirely before linguistic planning begins. Instead, all current theories of sentence generation assume that speakers prepare utterances incrementally. That is, they initiate linguistic planning as soon as they have selected the first few lexical concepts and prepare the rest later, either while they are speaking or between parts of the utterance. Speakers can probably choose conceptual planning units of various sizes, but the typical unit for many situations appears to correspond roughly to a clause (Bock & Cutting, 1992).

When speakers plan sentences, they retrieve words as described earlier. However, because sentences are not simply sets of words but have syntactic structure, speakers must apply syntactic knowledge to generate sentences. Following Garrett (1975), models of sentence production generally assume that two distinct sets of processes are involved in generating syntactic structure (Bock & Levelt, 1994; Levelt, 1989). The first set, often called functional planning processes, assigns grammatical functions, such as subject, verb, or direct object, to lemmas. These processes rely primarily on information from the message level and the syntactic properties of the retrieved lemmas. The second set of processes, often called positional encoding, uses the retrieved lemmas and the functions to which they have been assigned in order to generate syntactic structures that capture the dependencies among constituents and their order. In English, the mapping from the functional to the positional level is usually quite straightforward: The subject usually precedes the verb, and the direct object and indirect object follow it. However, inversions can occur, as in *I don't mind bikes; cars I hate.*

Evidence for the distinction between functional and positional processes comes from the finding that some speech errors (e.g., exchanges of words from different phrases, as in *put the tables on the plate*) can best be explained as errors of functional encoding. Other errors with different properties (e.g., shifts of morphemes within phrases, as in *the come homing of the queen*) can best be explained as errors of positional encoding. The distinction is further supported by the results of structural priming studies. In such studies, people first hear or say a sentence such as *The woman shows the man the dress.* They later see a picture that can be described using the same kind of structure (e.g., *The boy gives the teacher the flowers*) or a different one (*The boy gives the flowers to the teacher*). Speakers tend to repeat the structure used on previous trials, even when the words featured in prime and target sentences are different and even when the events are unrelated. The results of many such studies strongly suggest that the priming effect arises during the positional encoding processes (Bock, 1986; Bock & Loebell, 1990; Chang, Dell, Bock, & Griffin, 2000).

As we have noted, grammatical encoding begins with the assignment of lemmas to grammatical functions. This mapping process is largely determined by conceptual information. In studies of functional encoding, speakers are often asked to describe pictures of scenes or events or to recall sentences from memory; the recall task involves the reconstruction of the surface structure of the utterance on the basis of stored conceptual information. Many such studies have focused on the question of which part of the conceptual structure will be assigned the role of grammatical subject (e.g., McDonald, Bock, & Kelly, 1993). The results show that function assignment is strongly affected by the relative availability or salience of concepts. If a concept is very salient—for example, because it has recently been referred to or because it is the only concrete or animate entity to be mentioned—it is likely to become the sentence subject. As soon as the subject role has been filled, the positional processes can generate the corresponding fragment of the phrase structure and the retrieval of the phonological form of the subject noun phrase can begin.

Events or actions are often encoded in a verb. As noted earlier, verb lemmas specify the arguments that the verbs require. Pickering and Branigan (1998) proposed to represent this information in nodes, which receive activation from verb lemmas. For instance, the lemma for *give* is connected to two syntactic nodes, one representing the NP-NP (noun phrase–noun phrase) node and the other the NP-PP (noun phrase–prepositional phrase) node. Selection of the NP-NP node results in a double object construction such as *the baby gives the dog a cookie*. Selection of the NP-PP node yields a prepositional phrase structure, as in *the baby gives a cookie to the dog*.

Many verbs, such as *give*, license more than one syntactic structure. Speeded sentence production experiments carried out by Ferreira (1996) show that the alternative syntactic structures associated with verb lemmas do not compete with each other but instead represent different options for generating sentences. This explains why, under certain conditions, speakers are faster to complete sentences with alternator verbs (e.g., *to give*) than sentences with nonalternator verbs (e.g., *to donate*). Ferreira proposed that a speaker's choice among the structures permitted by an alternator verb depends, in part, on the salience of the lemmas assigned to the patient and recipient roles. If the patient is very salient, the corresponding fragment of the sentence will be built early. This encourages the generation of an NP-NP construction in which the patient is expressed early (*give the dog a cookie*). If the direct object is highly activated, an NP-PP construction will be more likely (*give the cookie to the dog*). Ferreira and Dell (2000) proposed that in general, the choice of syntactic structure may depend largely on the availability of lemmas filling different thematic roles. If a lemma is highly available, it will be processed early at the functional and positional levels and will thus appear early in the sentence. Whether lemma availability by itself is sufficient to explain how speakers choose between alternative word orders remains to be determined.

Certain elements within well-formed sentences must agree with one another. In English, subject and verb must agree in number, as must pronouns and their noun antecedents. In languages such as German, Dutch, Italian, and French, nouns have grammatical gender, and there is gender agreement between nouns and determiners, adjectives, and pronouns. Number agreement and grammatical gender agreement differ in that number information usually stems from the conceptual level, whereas grammatical gender is specified as part of the noun lemma. Consequently, different mechanisms are likely to be involved in generating the two types of agreement. We briefly consider each type of agreement, beginning with English number agreement.

In most cases, the mapping from conceptual number onto the lemma level is straightforward: The singular form of a noun is chosen to refer to one entity, and the plural form to refer to two or more entities. Because number is coded at both the conceptual and grammatical levels, speakers could use either or both types of information to generate agreement. What information do speakers actually use? According to a strictly modular theory of language production, the grammatical coding process should be sensitive only to grammatical information. A more interactive theory would permit grammatical encoding processes to be affected by both grammatical and conceptual information. To examine this issue, researchers have studied agreement for *collective* nouns such as *fleet* and *gang,* which are exceptions to the straightforward mapping between conceptual and grammatical number. For example, *fleet* is grammatically singular but refers to a group of ships. The studies have often used sentence completion tasks, in which speakers hear the beginnings of sentences (e.g., *The condition of the ship/ships/fleet/fleets . . .*; Bock & Eberhard, 1993), repeat the fragments, and then complete them to form full sentences. When the two nouns in the fragment differ in number, speakers sometimes make agreement errors (*The condition of the ships* were *poor*).

Most studies using sentence completion tasks like those just described have found that speakers rely primarily on grammatical information to generate subject-verb agreement. For instance, agreement errors appear to be no more likely for *the condition of the fleet* than for *the condition of the ship,* but such errors are more common for *the condition of the ships* (Bock & Eberhard, 1993; Bock & Miller, 1991; but see Vigliocco, Butterworth, & Garrett, 1996). In contrast, studies of noun-pronoun agreement in American English have shown that this type of agreement is primarily based on conceptual number information (Bock, 1995; Bock, Nicol, & Cutting, 1999). Thus, speakers are likely to say, *The gang with the dangerous rival armed themselves,* using the plural pronoun *themselves* to refer to a collective (Bock et al., 1999).

Whereas number information usually originates at the conceptual level, grammatical gender is lexical information and gender agreement can therefore be achieved only by consulting grammatical information. For determiner-noun agreement (as in Dutch *het huis;* the house, neuter gender, and *de kerk;* the church, nonneuter gender), most theories invoke a mechanism of indirect selection. In the model proposed by Jescheniak and Levelt (1994) for Dutch, each noun lemma is connected to one of two gender nodes (neuter or nonneuter). Each gender node is connected to the lemma for the determiner that is appropriate for that gender. Activation flows from a selected noun lemma to the gender node and from there to the determiner lemma, which can then be selected as well (see Miozzo & Caramazza, 1999, for a model for Italian, in which determiner-noun agreement is more complex).

Determiners are special in that their choice is governed exclusively by the grammatical gender of the noun. Other forms of agreement involve independently selected words. For instance, the lemmas of adjectives are selected on the basis of conceptual information and are then, in some languages, marked depending on the grammatical gender of the noun to which they refer. In French and Italian, agreement errors between adjectives and nouns—such as the French *la sortie* (f) *du tunnel* (m) *glissant* (m) instead of *la sortie* (f) *du tunnel* (m) *glissante* (f), *the way out of the slippery tunnel*—are less likely for animate subjects, which have natural gender in addition to grammatical gender, than for inanimate subjects, which have grammatical gender alone (Vigliocco & Franck, 1999). Such results suggest that agreement processes, although primarily guided by syntactic information, can get support from the conceptual level if gender is marked there as well.

When the positional representation for an utterance fragment has been generated, the corresponding phonological form can be built. For each word, phonological segments and, when necessary, information about the word's stress pattern are retrieved from the mental lexicon as described earlier. But the phonological form of a phrase is not just a concatenation of the forms of words as pronounced in isolation. Instead, the stored word forms are combined into new prosodic units (Nespor & Vogel, 1986; Wheeldon, 2000). We have already discussed the syllable, a small prosodic unit. The next larger unit is the *phonological word.* Phonological words often correspond to lexical words. However, a morphologically complex word may comprise several phonological words, and unstressed items such as conjunctions and pronouns combine with preceding or following content words into single phonological words. Phonological words are the domain of syllabification. Thus, when a speaker says *find it,* two morphemes are retrieved, and these are combined to form one phonological word. In line with the tendency for the onsets of English syllables to contain as much material as possible, /d/ is assigned to the second syllable, yielding [fain] [dɪt]. Thus syllables can, and often do, straddle the boundaries of lexical words.

The next level in the prosodic hierarchy is the *phonological phrase*. Phonological phrases often correspond to syntactic phrases, but long syntactic phrases may be divided into several phonological phrases. Like the phonological word, the phonological phrase is a domain of application for certain phonological rules. These include the rule of English that changes the stress patterns of words to generate an alternating pattern (as in the typical pronunciation of the phrase *Chinese menu*) and the rule that lengthens the final syllable of the phrase. Finally, phonological phrases combine into intonational phrases, which were mentioned in the discussion of spoken language comprehension.

Earlier, we discussed the decomposition of morphemes into segments. This may have appeared to be a vacuous process. Why should morphemes first be decomposed into segments that are later reassembled into syllables? The likely answer is that the same morpheme can be pronounced in different ways depending on the context. For instance, *hand* may lose its final consonant in *put your hand down* and may gain a final [m] in *handbag. Hand* corresponds to a syllable in *I hand you the book* but not in *I am handing you the book.* There are phonological rules governing how words are pronounced in different environments. For these rules to apply, the individual segments must be available to the processor. In connected speech, the decomposition of morphemes and the reassembly into phonological forms is not a vacuous process but yields phonological forms that differ from those stored in the mental lexicon.

Written Language Production

Many of the steps in the production of written language are similar to those in the production of spoken language. A major difference is that after a lemma and its morphological representation have been accessed, it is the orthographic rather than the phonological form that must be retrieved and produced. Phonology plays an important role in this process, just as it does in the process of deriving meaning from print in reading. Support for this view comes from a study in which speakers of French were shown drawings of such objects as a seal (*phoque*) and a pipe (*pipe*) and were asked to write their names as quickly as they could (Bonin, Peereman, & Fayol, 2001). The time needed to initiate writing was longer for items such as *phoque,* for which the initial phoneme has an unusual spelling (/f/ is usually spelled as *f* in French), than for items such as *pipe,* for which the initial phoneme is spelled in the typical manner. Thus, even when a to-be-spelled word is not presented orally, its phonological form appears to be involved in the selection of the spelling.

A number of the same issues that were raised earlier about the derivation of phonology from orthography in reading arise with respect to the derivation of orthography from phonology in spelling. For instance, issues about grain size apply to spelling as well as to reading. Kessler and Treiman (2001) have shown that the spelling of an English segment becomes more predictable when neighboring segments are taken into account. The largest effects involve the vowel and the coda, suggesting that rimes play a special role in English spelling. Feedback between production and comprehension is another issue that arises in spelling as well as in reading: We may read a spelling back to check whether it is correct.

Writing differs from speaking in that writers often have more time available for conceptual preparation and planning. They may have more need to do so as well, as the intended reader of a written text is often distant in time and space from the writer. Monitoring and revising, too, typically play a greater role in writing than in speaking. For these reasons, much of the research on writing (see Kellogg, 1994; Levy & Ransdell, 1996) has concentrated on the preparation and revision processes rather than on the sentence generation and lexical access processes that have been the focus of spoken language production research.

CONCLUSIONS

We have talked about language comprehension and language production in separate sections of this chapter, but the two processes are carried out in the same head, presumably using many of the same representations and processes. In some cases, there have been strong claims that each of these two aspects of language relies heavily on the other. For example, some theories of speech perception (Liberman & Mattingly, 1985) maintain that listeners perceive speech sounds by making unconscious reference to the articulatory gestures of the speaker in a process referred to as *analysis by synthesis.* As another example, speech production researchers have described how speakers can listen to their own speech and correct themselves when necessary, and how speakers can even monitor an internal version of their speech and interrupt themselves before an anticipated error occurs (see Levelt, 1983; Postma, 2000).

Although researchers have described how comprehension and production may interact in particular tasks, the two areas of research have not always been closely connected. One reason for this separation is that different methods traditionally have been used to study comprehension and production. Language comprehension researchers have often measured how long it takes people to carry out tasks such as word naming, lexical decision making, or reading for comprehension. These experimental paradigms are designed to tap the time course of processing. Language production research has traditionally focused on product rather than process, as in analyses of speech errors and written productions. However, researchers in the area of language production are increasingly using reaction time paradigms (e.g., the structural priming technique mentioned earlier) to yield more direct evidence about the time course of processing. Stronger connections between the two areas are expected to develop with the increasing similarity in the research tools and the increasing interest in time-course issues in the production arena.

Another reason that production research and comprehension research have been somewhat separate from one another is that researchers in the two areas have sometimes focused on different topics and talked about them in different ways. For example, the concept of a lemma or syntactic word unit plays a central role in some theories of language production, with theorists such as Levelt et al. (1999) assuming that lemmas are shared between production and comprehension. However, most researchers in the area of comprehension have not explicitly used the concept of a lemma in discussing the structure of the mental lexicon and have not considered which of the representations inferred through comprehension experiments might also play a role in production. An important direction for the future will be to increase the links between theories of comprehension and production.

Despite these gaps, it is clear that both comprehension and production are strongly driven by the mental lexicon. When listeners hear utterances, they rapidly map the speech stream onto entries in the lexicon. As each word is identified, semantic and syntactic information becomes available. This information is immediately used to begin constructing the syntactic structure and meaning of the utterance. Similarly, when speakers generate utterances, they select words from the lexicon. Each word brings with it syntactic and morphological properties, and these properties are taken into account when additional words are chosen. A theory based on analysis by synthesis is probably not appropriate for syntactic comprehension, but there may be strong similarities between the routines involved in parsing and those involved in grammatical encoding in language production (Vosse & Kempen, 2000). Given the importance of the lexicon in all aspects of language processing, the nature and organization of the stored information and the processes that are involved in accessing this information are likely to continue as major topics of research.

In addition to developing closer ties between comprehension and production, it will be important to build bridges between studies of the processing of isolated words and studies of sentences and texts. For example, theories of word recognition have focused on how readers and listeners access phonological and, to a lesser extent, morphological information. They have paid little attention to how people access the syntactic information that is necessary for sentence processing and comprehension. Further work is needed, too, on the similarities and differences between the processing of written language and the processing of spoken language. Given the importance of prosody in spoken language comprehension, for example, we need to know more about its possible role in reading.

Many of the theoretical debates within the field of psycholinguistics apply to both comprehension and production and to both spoken language and written language. For example, issues about the balance between computation and storage arise in all of these domains. Clearly, a good deal of information must be stored in the mental lexicon, including the forms of irregular verbs such as *went*. Are forms that could in principle be derived by rule (e.g., *walked*) computed each time they are heard or said, are they stored as ready-made units, or are both procedures available? Such issues have been debated in both the comprehension and production literatures, and will be important topics for future research. Another broad debate is that between interactive and modular views. As we have seen, there is no clear resolution to this debate. It has been difficult to determine whether there is a syntactic component in language production that operates independently of conceptual and phonological factors. Similarly, comprehension researchers have found it difficult to determine whether an initial analysis that considers a restricted range of information is followed by a later and broader process, or whether a wide range of linguistic and nonlinguistic information is involved from the start. The speed at which language is produced and understood may make it impossible to resolve these questions. However, asking the questions has led researchers to seek out and attempt to understand important phenomena, and this may be the best and most lasting outcome of the debate.

The debate between rule-based and statistical views of language processing provides a good example of how theoretical tensions and the research they engender has furthered progress in psycholinguistics. Statistical approaches, as embodied in connectionist models, have served the field well by emphasizing that certain aspects of language involve probabilistic patterns. In reading, for example, *-ove* is often pronounced as /ov/ but is sometimes pronounced as /ʌv/ (as in *love*) or /uv/ (as in *move*). People appear to pick up and use statistical information of this kind in reading and other areas of language processing. In such cases, we do well to go beyond the notion of all-or-none rules. We must keep in mind, however, that many linguistic patterns are all-or-none. For example, nouns and adjectives in French always agree in gender. Our ability to follow such patterns, as well as our ability to make some sense of sentences like *Colorless green ideas sleep furiously,* suggests that Chomsky's notion of language as an internalized system of rules still has an important place to play in views of language processing.

REFERENCES

Abney, S. (1989). A computational model of human parsing. *Journal of Psycholinguistic Research, 18,* 129–144.

Allopenna, P. D., Magnuson, J. S., & Tanenhaus, M. K. (1998). Tracking the time course of spoken word recognition using eye movements: Evidence for continuous mapping models. *Journal of Memory and Language, 38,* 419–439.

Altmann, G. T. M., & Kamide, Y. (1999). Incremental interpretation at verbs: Restricting the domain of subsequent reference. *Cognition, 73,* 247–264.

Altmann, G. T. M., & Steedman, M. (1988). Interaction with context during human sentence processing. *Cognition, 30,* 191–238.

Bader, M. (1998). Prosodic influences on reading syntactically ambiguous sentences. In J. Fodor & F. Ferreira (Eds.), *Reanalysis in sentence processing* (pp. 1–46). Dordrecht, The Netherlands: Kluwer.

Berent, I., & Perfetti, C. A. (1995). A rose is a REEZ: The two-cycles model of phonology assembly in reading English. *Psychological Review, 102,* 146–184.

Bever, T. G. (1970). The cognitive basis for linguistic structures. In J. R. Hayes (Ed.), *Cognition and the development of language* (pp. 279–352). New York: Wiley.

Binder, K. S., Duffy, S. A., & Rayner, K. (2001). The effects of thematic fit and discourse context on syntactic ambiguity resolution. *Journal of Memory and Language, 44,* 297–324.

Bock, J. K. (1986). Meaning, sound, and syntax: Lexical priming in sentence production. *Journal of Experimental Psychology: Learning, Memory, and Cognition, 12,* 575–586.

Bock, K. (1995). Producing agreement. *Current Directions in Psychological Science, 4,* 56–61.

Bock, K., & Cutting, J. C. (1992). Regulating mental energy: Performance units in language production. *Journal of Memory and Language, 31,* 99–127.

Bock, K., & Eberhard, K. M. (1993). Meaning, sound, and syntax in English number agreement. *Language and Cognitive Processes, 8,* 57–99.

Bock, K., & Levelt, W. (1994). Language production: Grammatical encoding. In M. A. Gernsbacher (Ed.), *Handbook of psycholinguistics* (pp. 945–985). New York: Academic Press.

Bock, K., & Loebell, H. (1990). Framing sentences. *Cognition, 35,* 1–39.

Bock, K., & Miller, C. A. (1991). Broken agreement. *Cognitive Psychology, 23,* 45–93.

Bock, K., Nicol, J., & Cutting, J. C. (1999). The ties that bind: Creating number agreement in speech. *Journal of Memory and Language, 40,* 330–346.

Boland, J. E., Tanenhaus, M. K., Garnsey, S. M., & Carlson, G. N. (1995). Verb argument structure in parsing and interpretation: Evidence from wh-questions. *Journal of Memory and Language, 34,* 774–806.

Bonin, P., Peereman, R., & Fayol, M. (2001). Do phonological codes constrain the selection of orthographic codes in written picture naming? *Journal of Memory and Language, 45,* 688–720.

Bowey, J. A. (1990). Orthographic onsets and rimes as functional units of reading. *Memory & Cognition, 18,* 419–427.

Britt, M. A. (1994). The interaction of referential ambiguity and argument structure in the parsing of prepositional phrases. *Journal of Memory and Language, 33,* 251–283.

Cacciari, C., & Glucksberg, S. (1994). Understanding figurative language. In M. A. Gernsbacher (Ed.), *Handbook of psycholinguistics* (pp. 447–477). San Diego, CA: Academic Press.

Caramazza, A., Laudanna, A., & Romani, C. (1988). Lexical access and inflectional morphology. *Cognition, 28,* 297–332.

Caramazza, A., & Miozzo, M. (1997). The relation between syntactic and phonological knowledge in lexical access: Evidence from the tip-of-the-tongue phenomenon. *Cognition, 64,* 309–343.

Carlson, K., Clifton, C., Jr., & Frazier, L. (2001). Prosodic boundaries in adjunct attachment. *Journal of Memory and Language, 45,* 58–81.

Carroll, L. (1977). *Through the looking-glass, and what Alice found there.* New York: St. Martin's Press. (Original work published 1871)

Chang, F., Dell, G. S., Bock, K., & Griffin, Z. M. (2000). Structural priming as implicit learning: A comparison of models of sentence production. *Journal of Psycholinguistic Research, 29,* 217–230.

Chomsky, N. (1959). Review of Skinner's Verbal Behavior. *Language, 35,* 26–58.

Chomsky, N. (1971). *Syntactic structures.* The Hague, The Netherlands: Mouton.

Clark, H. H. (1996). *Using language.* New York, NY: Cambridge University Press.

Clark, H. H., & Clark, E. V. (1977). *Psychology and language.* New York: Harcourt Brace.

Clifton, C., Jr., Speer, S., & Abney, S. (1991). Parsing arguments: Phrase structure and argument structure as determinants of initial parsing decisions. *Journal of Memory and Language, 30,* 251–271.

Coltheart, M., Rastle, K., Perry, C., Langdon, R., & Ziegler, J. (2001). DRC: A dual route cascaded model of visual word recognition and reading aloud. *Psychological Review, 108,* 204–258.

Cowan, N. (1984). On short and long auditory stores. *Psychological Bulletin, 96,* 341–370.

Cutler, A., & Norris, D. G. (1979). Monitoring sentence comprehension. In W. E. Cooper & E. C. T. Walker (Eds.), *Sentence processing: Psycholinguistic studies presented to Merrill Garrett* (pp. 113–134). Hillsdale, NJ: Erlbaum.

De Vincenzi, M. (1991). *Syntactic parsing strategies in Italian.* Dordrecht, The Netherlands: Kluwer.

Dell, G. S. (1986). A spreading-activation theory of retrieval in sentence production. *Psychological Review, 93,* 283–321.

Dell, G. S. (1988). The retrieval of phonological forms in production: Tests of predictions from a connectionist model. *Journal of Memory and Language, 27,* 124–142.

Dell, G. S., Schwartz, M. F., Martin, N., Saffran, E. M., & Gagnon, D. A. (1997). Lexical access in normal and aphasic speech. *Psychological Review, 104,* 801–838.

Dijkstra, T., Timmermans, M., & Schriefers, H. (2000). On being blinded by your other language: Effects of task demands in interlingual homograph recognition. *Journal of Memory and Language, 42,* 445–464.

Ferreira, V. S. (1996). Is it better to give than to donate? Syntactic flexibility in language production. *Journal of Memory and Language, 35,* 724–755.

Ferreira, V. S., & Dell, G. S. (2000). Effect of ambiguity and lexical availability on syntactic and lexical production. *Cognitive Psychology, 40,* 296–340.

Fodor, J. A. (1983). *The modularity of mind: An essay on faculty psychology.* Cambridge, MA: MIT Press.

Fodor, J. A., Bever, T. G., & Garrett, M. F. (1974). *The psychology of language: An introduction to psycholinguistics and generative grammar.* New York: McGraw-Hill.

Fodor, J. D. (1978). Parsing strategies and constraints on transformations. *Linguistic Inquiry, 9,* 427–474.

Fodor, J. D., & Ferreira, F. (Eds.). (1998). *Sentence reanalysis.* Dordrecht, The Netherlands: Kluwer.

Ford, M., Bresnan, J., & Kaplan, R. (1982). A competence-based theory of syntactic closure. In J. Bresnan (Ed.), *The mental representation of grammatical relations* (pp. 727–796). Cambridge, MA: MIT Press.

Frazier, L. (1987a). Sentence processing: A tutorial review. In M. Coltheart (Ed.), *Attention and performance: The psychology of reading* (pp. 559–586). Hillsdale, NJ: Erlbaum.

Frazier, L. (1987b). Syntactic processing: Evidence from Dutch. *Natural Language and Linguistic Theory, 5,* 519–559.

Frazier, L. (1995). Constraint satisfaction as a theory of sentence processing. *Journal of Psycholinguistic Research, 24,* 437–468.

Frazier, L., & Clifton, C., Jr. (1996). *Construal.* Cambridge, MA: MIT Press.

Frazier, L., & Rayner, K. (1982). Making and correcting errors during sentence comprehension: Eye movements in the analysis of structurally ambiguous sentences. *Cognitive Psychology, 14,* 178–210.

Fromkin, V. A. (1971). The non-anomalous nature of anomalous utterances. *Language, 47,* 27–52.

Frost, R. (1998). Toward a strong phonological theory of visual word recognition: True issues and false trails. *Psychological Bulletin, 123,* 71–99.

Garnham, A. (1999). Reference and anaphora. In S. Garrod & M. J. Pickering (Eds.), *Language processing* (pp. 335–362). Hove, UK: Psychology Press.

Garrett, M. F. (1975). The analysis of sentence production. In G. H. Bower (Ed.), *The psychology of learning and motivation* (Vol. 9, pp. 133–177). New York: Academic Press.

Gernsbacher, M. A. (Ed.). (1994). *Handbook of psycholinguistics.* San Diego, CA: Academic Press.

Gernsbacher, M. A., & Faust, M. (1991). The role of suppression in sentence comprehension. In G. B. Simpson (Ed.), *Understanding word and sentence* (pp. 97–128). Amsterdam: North-Holland.

Gibson, E. (1998). Linguistic complexity: Locality of syntactic dependencies. *Cognition, 68,* 1–76.

Gibson, E., Schütze, C. T., & Salomon, A. (1996). The relationship between the frequency and the processing complexity of linguistic structure. *Journal of Psycholinguistic Research, 25,* 59–92.

Glushko, R. J. (1979). The organization and activation of orthographic knowledge in reading aloud. *Journal of Experimental Psychology: Human Perception and Performance, 5,* 674–691.

Graesser, A. C., Singer, M., & Trabasso, T. (1994). Constructing inferences during narrative text comprehension. *Psychological Review, 101,* 371–395.

Halle, P. A., Segui, J., Frauenfelder, U., & Meunier, C. (1998). Processing of illegal consonant clusters: A case of perceptual assimilation? *Journal of Experimental Psychology: Human Perception and Performance, 24,* 592–608.

Hill, R. L., & Murray, W. S. (1998, March). *Commas and spaces: The point of punctuation.* Poster session presented at the CUNY Conference on Human Sentence Processing, New Brunswick, NJ.

Humphreys, G. W., Price, C. J., & Riddoch, M. J. (2000). On the naming of objects: Evidence from cognitive neuroscience. In L. Wheeldon (Ed.), *Aspects of language production* (pp. 143–163). Hove, UK: Psychology Press.

Jescheniak, J. D., & Levelt, W. J. M. (1994). Word frequency effects in speech production: Retrieval of syntactic information and of phonological form. *Journal of Experimental Psychology: Language, Memory, and Cognition, 20,* 824–843.

Jurafsky, D. (1996). A probabilistic model of lexical and syntactic access and disambiguation. *Cognitive Science, 20,* 137–194.

Kellogg, R. T. (1994). *The psychology of writing.* New York: Oxford University Press.

Kelly, M. H., Morris, J., & Verrekia, L. (1998). Orthographic cues to lexical stress: Effects on naming and lexical decision. *Memory & Cognition, 26,* 822–832.

Kennison, S. M. (2001). Limitations on the use of verb information during sentence comprehension. *Psychonomic Bulletin & Review, 8,* 132–138.

Kessler, B., & Treiman, R. (2001). Relationships between sounds and letters in English monosyllables. *Journal of Memory and Language, 44,* 592–617.

Kintsch, W. (1974). *The representation of meaning in memory and knowledge.* New York: Wiley.

Kintsch, W. (1988). The use of knowledge in discourse processing. *Psychological Review, 95,* 163–182.

Kintsch, W., & van Dijk, T. A. (1978). Toward a model of text comprehension and production. *Psychological Review, 85,* 363–394.

Kjelgaard, M. M., & Speer, S. R. (1999). Prosodic facilitation and interference in the resolution of temporary syntactic closure ambiguity. *Journal of Memory and Language, 40,* 153–194.

Klein, D. E., & Murphy, G. L. (2001). The representation of polysemous words. *Journal of Memory and Language, 45,* 259–282.

Konieczny, L., Hemforth, B., Scheepers, C., & Strube, G. (1997). The role of lexical heads in parsing: Evidence from German. *Language and Cognitive Processes, 12,* 307–348.

Lee, H-W., Rayner, K., & Pollatsek, A. (2001). The relative contribution of consonants and vowels in word recognition in reading. *Journal of Memory and Language, 47,* 189–205.

Levelt, W. J. M. (1983). Monitoring and self-repair in speech. *Cognition, 14,* 41–104.

Levelt, W. J. M. (1989). *Speaking: From intention to articulation.* Cambridge, MA: MIT Press.

Levelt, W. J. M., Roelofs, A., & Meyer, A. S. (1999). A theory of lexical access in speech production. *Behavioral and Brain Sciences, 22,* 1–75.

Levelt, W. J. M., Schriefers, H., Vorberg, D., Meyer, A. S., Pechmann, T., & Havinga, J. (1991). The time course of lexical access in speech production: A study of picture naming. *Psychological Review, 98,* 122–142.

Levelt, W. J. M., & Wheeldon, L. (1994). Do speakers have access to a mental syllabary? *Cognition, 50,* 239–269.

Levy, C. M., & Ransdell, S. (Eds.). (1996). *The science of writing: Theories, methods, individual differences, and applications.* Mahwah, NJ: Erlbaum.

Liberman, A. M., & Mattingly, I. G. (1985). The motor theory of speech perception revised. *Cognition, 21,* 1–36.

Lukatela, G., & Turvey, M. T. (2000). An evaluation of the two-cycles model of phonological assembly. *Journal of Memory and Language, 42,* 183–207.

MacDonald, M. C. (1994). Probabilistic constraints and syntactic ambiguity resolution. *Language and Cognitive Processes, 9,* 157–201.

MacDonald, M. C., Pearlmutter, N. J., & Seidenberg, M. S. (1994). Lexical nature of syntactic ambiguity resolution. *Psychological Review, 101,* 676–703.

MacKay, D. G. (1987). *The organization of perception and action: A theory for language and other cognitive skills.* Berlin: Springer-Verlag.

Marslen-Wilson, W. D. (1987). Functional parallelism in spoken word-recognition. *Cognition, 25,* 71–102.

Marslen-Wilson, W. D. (1990). Activation, competition, and frequency in lexical access. In G. T. M. Altmann (Ed.), *Cognitive models of speech processing* (pp. 148–172). Cambridge, MA: MIT Press.

Marslen-Wilson, W. D., Tyler, L. K., Waksler, R., & Older, L. (1994). Morphology and meaning in the English mental lexicon. *Psychological Review, 101,* 3–33.

Marslen-Wilson, W., & Welsh, A. (1978). Processing interactions and lexical access during word recognition in continuous speech. *Cognitive Psychology, 10,* 29–63.

Martensen, H., Maris, E., & Dijkstra, T. (2000). When does inconsistency hurt? On the relation between phonological consistency effects and the reliability of sublexical units. *Memory & Cognition, 28,* 648–656.

McClelland, J. L., & Elman, J. L. (1986). The TRACE model of speech perception. *Cognitive Psychology, 18,* 1–86.

McDonald, J. L., Bock, K., & Kelly, M. H. (1993). Word and world order: Semantic, phonological, and metrical determinants of serial position. *Cognitive Psychology, 25,* 188–230.

McKoon, G., & Ratcliff, R. (1998). Memory-based language processing: Psycholinguistic research in the 1990s. *Annual Review of Psychology, 49,* 25–42.

Meyer, A. S. (1991). The time course of phonological encoding in language production: Phonological encoding inside a syllable. *Journal of Memory and Language, 30,* 69–89.

Meyer, A. S. & Schriefers, H. (1991). Phonological facilitation in picture-word interference experiments: Effects of stimulus onset asynchrony and types of interfering stimuli. *Journal of Experimental Psychology: Language, Memory, and Cognition, 17,* 1146–1160.

Miozzo, M., & Caramazza, A. (1999). The selection of determiners in noun-phrase production. *Journal of Experimental Psychology: Learning, Memory, and Cognition, 25,* 907–922.

Mitchell, D. C. (1994). Sentence parsing. In M. A. Gernsbacher (Ed.), *Handbook of psycholinguistics* (pp. 375–410). New York: Academic Press.

Moss, H. E., & Marslen-Wilson, W. D. (1993). Access to word meanings during spoken language comprehension: Effects of sentential semantic context. *Journal of Experimental Psychology: Learning, Memory, and Cognition, 19,* 1254–1276.

Myers, J. L., & O'Brien, E. J. (1998). Accessing the discourse representation while reading. *Discourse Processes, 26,* 131–157.

Nespor, M., & Vogel, I. (1986). *Prosodic phonology.* Dordrecht, The Netherlands: Foris.

Norris, D. (1994). Shortlist: A connectionist model of continuous speech recognition. *Cognition, 52,* 189–234.

Norris, D., McQueen, J. M., & Cutler, A. (1995). Competition and segmentation in spoken-word recognition. *Journal of Experimental Psychology: Learning, Memory, and Cognition, 21,* 1209–1228.

Norris, D., McQueen, J. M., & Cutler, A. (2000). Merging information in speech recognition: Feedback is never necessary. *Behavioral and Brain Sciences, 23,* 299–370.

O'Seaghdha, P., & Marin, J. W. (2000). Phonological competition and cooperation in form-related priming: Sequential and nonsequential processes in word production. *Journal of Experimental Psychology: Human Perception and Performance, 26,* 57–73.

Peereman, R., Content, A., & Bonin, P. (1998). Is perception a two-way street? The case of feedback consistency in visual word recognition. *Journal of Memory and Language, 39,* 151–174.

Peterson, R. R., & Savoy, P. (1998). Lexical selection and phonological encoding during language production: Evidence for cascaded processing. *Journal of Experimental Psychology: Language, Memory, and Cognition, 24,* 539–557.

Pickering, M. J. (1999). Sentence comprehension. In S. Garrod & M. J. Pickering (Eds.), *Language processing* (pp. 123–153). Hove, UK: Psychology Press.

Pickering, M. J., & Barry, G. (1991). Sentence processing without empty categories. *Language and Cognitive Processes, 6,* 229–259.

Pickering, M. J., & Branigan, H. P. (1998). The representation of verbs: Evidence from syntactic priming in language production. *Journal of Memory and Language, 39,* 633–651.

Pickering, M. J., Traxler, M. J., & Crocker, M. W. (2000). Ambiguity resolution in sentence processing: Evidence against frequency-based accounts. *Journal of Memory and Language, 43,* 447–475.

Plaut, D. C., McClelland, J. L., Seidenberg, M. S., & Patterson, K. (1996). Understanding normal and impaired word reading:

Computational principles in quasi-regular domains. *Psychological Review, 103,* 56–115.

Postma, A. (2000). Detection of errors during speech production: A review of speech monitoring models. *Cognition, 77,* 97–131.

Pritchett, B. L. (1992). *Grammatical competence and parsing performance.* Chicago: University of Chicago Press.

Rastle, K., & Coltheart, M. (1999). Serial and strategic effects in reading aloud. *Journal of Experimental Psychology: Human Perception and Performance, 25,* 482–503.

Rayner, K., & Pollatsek, A. (1989). *Psychology of reading.* Englewood Cliffs, NJ: Prentice-Hall.

Rizzella, M. L., & O'Brien, E. J. (1996). Accessing global causes during reading. *Journal of Experimental Psychology: Learning, Memory, and Cognition, 22,* 1208–1218.

Roelofs, A. (1996). Serial order in planning the production of successive morphemes of a word. *Journal of Memory and Language, 35,* 854–876.

Roelofs, A. (1997). The WEAVER model of word-form encoding in speech production. *Cognition, 64,* 249–284.

Roelofs, A., Meyer, A. S., & Levelt, W. J. M. (1998). A case for the lemma-lexeme distinction in models of speaking: Comment on Caramazza and Miozzo (1997). *Cognition, 69,* 219–230.

Rumelhart, D., & McClelland, J. L. (Eds.). (1986). *Parallel distributed processing: Explorations in the microstructure of cognition* (Vol. 1). Cambridge, MA: MIT Press.

Ryan, J. (1969). Grouping and short-term memory: Different means and patterns of grouping. *Quarterly Journal of Experimental Psychology, 21,* 137–147.

Samuel, A. G. (1997). Lexical activation produces potent phonemic percepts. *Cognitive Psychology, 32,* 97–127.

Sanford, A. (1999). Word meaning and discourse processing: A tutorial review. In S. Garrod & M. J. Pickering (Eds.), *Language processing* (pp. 301–334). Hove, UK: Psychology Press.

Schafer, A. (1997). *Prosodic parsing: The role of prosody in sentence comprehension.* Unpublished doctoral dissertation, University of Massachusetts, Amherst.

Schreuder, R., & Baayen, R. H. (1995). Modeling morphological processing. In L. B. Feldman (Ed.), *Morphological aspects of language processing* (pp. 131–154). Hillsdale, NJ: Erlbaum.

Schütze, C. T., & Gibson, E. (1999). Argumenthood and English prepositional phrase attachment. *Journal of Memory and Language, 40,* 409–431.

Seidenberg, M. S. (1997). Language acquisition and use: Learning and applying probabilistic constraints. *Science, 275,* 1599–1603.

Seidenberg, M. S., & McClelland, J. L. (1989). A distributed, developmental model of word recognition and naming. *Psychological Review, 96,* 523–568.

Selkirk, E. (1984). *Phonology and syntax: The relation between sound and structure.* Cambridge, MA: MIT Press.

Simpson, G. B. (1994). Context and the processing of ambiguous words. In M. A. Gernsbacher (Ed.), *Handbook of psycholinguistics* (pp. 359–374). San Diego, CA: Academic Press.

Slowiaczek, M. L., & Clifton, C., Jr. (1980). Subvocalization and reading for meaning. *Journal of Verbal Learning and Verbal Behavior, 19,* 573–582.

Speer, S. R., Crowder, R. G., & Thomas, L. M. (1993). Prosodic structure and sentence recognition. *Journal of Memory and Language, 32,* 336–358.

Spivey, M. J., & Marian, V. (1999). Cross talk between native and second languages: Partial activation of an irrelevant lexicon. *Psychological Science, 10,* 281–284.

Spivey, M. J., Tanenhaus, M., Eberhard, K. M., & Sedivy, J. C. (in press). Eye movements and spoken language comprehension: Effects of visual context on syntactic ambiguity resolution. *Cognitive Psychology.*

Spivey-Knowlton, M., & Sedivy, J. C. (1995). Resolving attachment ambiguities with multiple constraints. *Cognition, 55,* 227–267.

Stemberger, J. P., & MacWhinney, B. (1986). Frequency and the lexical storage of regularly inflected forms. *Memory & Cognition, 14,* 17–26.

Stone, G. O., Vanhoy, M., & Van Orden, G. C. (1997). Perception is a two-way street: Feedforward and feedback phonology in visual word recognition. *Journal of Memory and Language, 36,* 337–359.

Swinney, D. A. (1979). Lexical access during sentence comprehension: (Re)consideration of context effects. *Journal of Verbal Learning and Verbal Behavior, 18,* 645–659.

Taft, M., & Forster, K. I. (1975). Lexical storage and retrieval of prefixed words. *Journal of Verbal Learning and Verbal Behavior, 14,* 638–647.

Tanenhaus, M. K., Boland, J. E., Mauner, G., & Carlson, G. N. (1993). More on combinatory lexical information: Thematic structure in parsing and interpretation. In G. Altmann & R. Shillcock (Eds.), *Cognitive models of speech processing: The second Sperlonga meeting* (pp. 297–319). Hillsdale, NJ: Erlbaum.

Tanenhaus, M. K., & Trueswell, J. C. (1995). Sentence comprehension. In J. Miller & P. Eimas (Eds.), *Handbook of perception and cognition: Speech, language, and communication* (2nd ed., Vol. 11, pp. 217–262). San Diego, CA: Academic Press.

Treiman, R., & Hirsh-Pasek, K. (1983). Silent reading: Insights from second-generation deaf readers. *Cognitive Psychology, 15,* 39–65.

Treiman, R., Mullennix, J., Bijeljac-Babic, R., & Richmond-Welty, E. D. (1995). The special role of rimes in the description, use, and acquisition of English orthography. *Journal of Experimental Psychology: General, 124,* 107–136.

Trueswell, J. C. (1996). The role of lexical frequency in syntactic ambiguity resolution. *Journal of Memory and Language, 35,* 566–585.

Tyler, L. K., Marslen-Wilson, W., Rentoul, J., & Hanney, P. (1988). Continuous and discontinuous access in spoken word-recognition: The role of derivational prefixes. *Journal of Memory and Language, 27,* 368–381.

Van Orden, G. C. (1987). A ROWS is a ROSE: Spelling, sound, and reading. *Memory & Cognition, 15,* 181–198.

van Turennout, M., Hagoort, P., & Brown, C. M. (1998). Brain activity during speaking: From syntax to phonology in 40 milliseconds. *Nature, 280,* 572–574.

Vigliocco, G., Antonini, T., & Garrett, M. F. (1997). Grammatical gender is on the tip of Italian tongues. *Psychological Science, 8,* 314–317.

Vigliocco, G., Butterworth, B., & Garrett, M. F. (1996). Subject-verb agreement in Spanish and English: Differences in the role of conceptual constraints. *Cognition, 61,* 261–298.

Vigliocco, G., & Franck, J. (1999). When sex and syntax go hand in hand: Gender agreement in language production. *Journal of Memory and Language, 40,* 455–478.

Vosse, T., & Kempen, G. (2000). Syntactic structure assembly in human parsing: A computational model based on competitive - inhibition and lexicalist grammar. *Cognition, 75,* 105–143.

Warren, P. (1999). Prosody and language processing. In S. Garrod & M. J. Pickering (Eds.), *Language processing* (pp. 155–188). Hove, UK: Psychology Press.

Wheeldon, L. (2000). Generating prosodic structure. In L. Wheeldon (Ed.), *Aspects of language production* (pp. 249–274). Hove, UK: Psychology Press.

Wurm, L. H. (1997). Auditory processing of prefixed English words is both continuous and decompositional. *Journal of Memory and Language, 37,* 438–461.

Wurm, L. H., & Ross, S. E. (2001). Conditional root uniqueness points: Psychological validity and perceptual consequences. *Journal of Memory and Language, 45,* 39–57.

Wurm, L. H., & Samuel, A. G. (1997). Lexical inhibition and attentional allocation during speech perception: Evidence from phoneme monitoring. *Journal of Memory and Language, 36,* 165–187.

Zorzi, M. (2000). Serial processing in reading aloud: No challenge for a parallel model. *Journal of Experimental Psychology: Human Perception and Performance, 26,* 847–856.

Zwitserlood, P., Boelte, J., & Dohmes, P. (2000). Morphological effects on speech production: Evidence from picture naming. *Language and Cognitive Processes, 15,* 563–591.

CHAPTER 20

Reading

KEITH RAYNER, ALEXANDER POLLATSEK, AND MATTHEW S. STARR

Reading is a vast topic to which entire textbooks are devoted (Crowder & Wagner, 1992; Just & Carpenter, 1987; Rayner & Pollatsek, 1989). We have selected five topics within the field of reading that seem particularly relevant in the context of the present volume (see also the chapters by Butcher & Kintsch; Treiman, Clifton, Meyer, & Wurm in this volume for topics relevant to reading). The topics we have chosen, and think are central to understanding skilled reading (as opposed to understanding language comprehension in general) are (a) visual word identification, (b) the role of sound coding in word identification and reading, (c) eye movements during reading, (d) word identification in context, and (e) eye movement control in reading.

Before discussing each of these five topics, we would like to place them in context by listing what we see as the central questions in the psychology of reading:

1. How are printed words identified?
2. How does the speech processing system interact with word identification and reading?
3. Are printed words identified differently in isolation than in text?
4. How does the fact that readers typically make about four to five eye movements per second affect the reading process?
5. How does the reader go beyond the meaning of individual words? This question relates to how sentences are parsed, how the literal meaning of a sentence is constructed, how anaphoric links are established, how inferences are made, and so on.
6. What is the end product of reading? What new mental structures are formed or retained as a result of reading?
7. How does the skill of reading develop?
8. How can we characterize individual differences among readers in the same culture and differences in readers across cultures?
9. How can we characterize reading disabilities?
10. Can we improve on so-called normal reading? Is speed-reading possible?

These 10 questions typically represent the chapters in textbooks on the psychology of reading (Crowder & Wagner, 1992; Just & Carpenter, 1987; Rayner & Pollatsek, 1989). The topics we discuss here have been studied extensively by experimental psychologists for the past 25 years. Prior to discussing word identification per se, we briefly review the primary methods that have been used to study word identification. In most word identification experiments, words are presented in isolation and subjects are asked to make some type of response to them. However, because one of the primary goals in studying word identification is to make inferences about how words are identified during reading, we go beyond isolated word identification in much of our discussion and discuss word identification in the context of reading.

METHODS USED TO STUDY WORD IDENTIFICATION

In this section, we focus on three methods used to examine word identification: (a) tachistoscopic presentations, (b) reaction time measures, and (c) eye movements. Although various other techniques, such as letter detection (Healy, 1976), visual search (Krueger, 1970), and Stroop interference (MacLeod, 1991) have been used to study word identification, we think it is incontrovertible that the three methods we discuss in the following section have been most widely used to study word identification and reading. More recently, investigators in cognitive neuroscience have been using brain imaging and localization techniques—especially event-related potentials (ERP), functional magnetic resonance imaging (fMRI) and positron-emission tomography (PET)—to study issues related to which parts of the brain are activated when different types of words are processed. However, in our view, these techniques have not yet advanced our understanding of word identification per se and are thus beyond the scope of this chapter.

Perhaps the oldest paradigm used to study word identification is tachistoscopic (i.e., very brief) presentation of a word (often followed by some type of masking pattern). Although tachistoscopes per se have been largely replaced by computer presentations of words on a video monitor, we use the term *tachistoscopic presentation* for convenience throughout this chapter. With tachistoscopic presentations, words are presented for a very brief time period (on the order of 30–60 ms) followed by a masking pattern, and subjects either have to identify the word or make some type of forced-choice response. Accuracy is therefore the major dependent variable with tachistoscopic presentations.

The most common method used to study word identification is some type of response time measure. The three types of responses to words typically used are (a) naming, (b) lexical decision, and (c) categorization. With *naming,* subjects name a word aloud as quickly as they can; with *lexical decision,* they must decide whether a letter string is a word or a nonword as quickly as they can; and with *categorization,* they must decide whether a word belongs to a certain category (usually a semantic category). Naming responses typically take about 400–500 ms, whereas lexical decisions typically take 500–600 ms and categorization takes about 650–700 ms. Although response time is the primary dependent variable, error rates are also recorded in these studies: Naming errors are typically rare (1% or less), whereas errors in lexical decision times are typically about 5% and error rates in categorization tasks may be as high as 10–15%.

The third major technique used to study word identification (particularly in the context of reading) is *eye movement monitoring:* Participants are asked to read either single sentences or longer passages of text as their eye movements are recorded. One great advantage of eye tracking (i.e., eye movement monitoring), other than the fact that participants are actually reading, is that a great deal of data is obtained (so that not only measures associated with a given target word can be obtained, but measures of processing time for words preceding and following the target word are also available). The three most important dependent variables for examining word identification in reading are first-fixation duration (the duration of the first fixation on a word), gaze duration (the sum of all fixations on a word prior to moving to another word), and the probability of skipping a word.

WORD IDENTIFICATION

Surprisingly, one of the problems in experimental psychology on which researchers have made little headway is understanding how objects are recognized. We still have very little understanding of how one can easily recognize a common object like a dog or chair in spite of seeing it from varying viewpoints and distances, and in spite of that fact that different exemplars of these categories are quite different visually. Basically, models that have tried to understand object identification, often called *models of pattern recognition* (Neisser, 1967; Uhr, 1963), fall into two classes.

In the first class, *template models,* wholistic memory representations of object categories, called *templates,* are compared to the visual input that comes in, and the template that best matches the visual input signals what the object is. An immediate question that comes to mind is what form these templates would have to be in order for this scheme to work. In one version, there is only one template per category; this assumption, however, does not work very well because a template that matches an object well seen from one viewpoint is not likely to match well when the same object is seen from a different viewpoint. In an attempt to remedy this problem, some versions of the template model posit a so-called preprocessing stage, in which the image is normalized to the template before the comparison; however, so far no particularly plausible normalization routines have been suggested because it is not clear how a person could normalize an image without prior knowledge of what the object is. Another possibility is that many templates exist for each object category; however, it is not clear whether memory could store all of these object templates, nor how all of the templates would have been stored in the first place.

The other class of models are called *feature models*. They differ in their details, but essential to all of these models is that objects are defined by a set of visual features. Although this kind of formulation sounds more reasonable than the template model to most people, it may not be any better a solution to the general problem because it is not at all clear what the defining visual features are for most real-world objects. In fact, most of the more successful artificial intelligence (AI) pattern recognition devices use some sort of template model. Their success, however, relies heavily on the fact that they are typically only required to distinguish among at most a few dozen objects rather than the many thousands of objects with which humans must cope.

This rather pessimistic introduction to object identification, in general, would suggest that we have learned little about how words are identified; however, that is not the case. Even though visual words are clearly artificial stimuli that evolution has not programmed humans to identify, there are several ways in which the problem of identifying words is simpler than that of identifying objects in general. The first is that, with a few exceptions, we do not have to deal with identifying words from various viewpoints: We almost always read text right side up. (It is quite difficult to read text from unusual angles.) Second, if we confine ourselves to recognizing printed words, we do not encounter that much variation from one exemplar to another. Most type fonts are quite similar, and those that are unusual are in fact difficult to read, indicating that they are indeed poor matches to our mental representations of the letters. Thus, the problem of understanding how printed words are identified may not be as difficult as understanding how objects are identified. One possibility is that we have several thousand templates for words we know. Or perhaps in alphabetic languages, all we need are a set of templates for each letter of the alphabet (more likely, two sets of templates—one for uppercase letters and one for lowercase letters).

Do We Recognize Words Through the Component Letters?

The previous discussion hints at one of the basic issues in visual word recognition: whether readers of English identify

Fixation Marker	*	*	*
Target Stimulus	word	d	owrd
Mask and Forced Choice	d xxxx k	d xxxx k	d xxxx k

Figure 20.1 Example of the Reicher-Wheeler paradigm. In the condition on the left, a fixation marker is followed by the target word, which in turn is followed by a mask and two forced-choice alternatives. In the conditions in the center and on the right, the sequence of events is the same, except that either a single letter or a scrambled version of the word (respectively) is the target stimulus.

words directly through a visual template of a word, or whether they go through a process in which each letter is identified and then the word as a whole is identified through the letters (we discuss encoding of nonalphabetic languages shortly). In a clever tachistoscopic paradigm, Reicher (1969) and Wheeler (1970) presented participants (see Figure 20.1) with either (a) a four-letter word (e.g., *word*); (b) a single letter (e.g., *d*); or (c) a nonword that was a scrambled version of the word (e.g., *orwd*). In each case, the stimulus was masked and, when the mask appeared, two test letters, (e.g., a *d* and a *k*) appeared above and below the location where the critical letter (*d* in this case) had appeared. The task was to decide which of the two letters had been in that location. Note that either of the test letters was consistent with a word—*word* or *work*—so that participants could not be correct in the task merely by guessing that the stimulus was a word. The exposure duration was adjusted so that overall performance was about 75% (halfway between chance and perfect).

Quite surprisingly, the data showed that participants were about 10% more accurate in identifying the letter when it was in a word than when it was a single letter in isolation! This finding certainly rules out the possibility that the letters in words are encoded exclusively one at a time (presumably in something like a left-to-right order) in order to enable recognition. This superiority of words over single letters (at least superficially) may seem to be striking evidence for the assertion that words (short words at least) are encoded through something like a visual template. However, there is another possibility: that words are processed through their component letters, but the letters are encoded in parallel, and somehow their organization into words facilitates the encoding process. In fact, several lines of evidence indicate that this parallel-letter encoding model is a better explanation of the data than is the visual template model. First, all the words in this experiment were all uppercase; it seems unlikely that people would have visual templates of words in uppercase, because words rarely appear in that form. Second, performance in the scrambled-word condition was about the same as it was in the single-letter condition. Thus, it appears that letters, even in nonpronounceable nonwords, are processed in parallel. Third, subsequent experiments (e.g., Baron & Thurston, 1973; Hawkins, Reicher, Rogers, & Peterson, 1976) showed that the *word superiority* effect extends to *pseudowords* (i.e., orthographically legal and pronounceable nonwords like *mard*): that is, letters in pseudowords are also identified more accurately than are letters in isolation. (In fact, many experiments found virtually no difference between words and pseudowords in this task.) Because it is extremely implausible that people have templates for pseudowords, they cannot merely have visual templates of words unconnected to the component letters. Instead, it seems highly likely that all short strings of letters are processed in parallel and that for words or wordlike strings, there is mutual facilitation in the encoding process.

Although the above explanation in terms of so-called mutual facilitation may seem a bit vague, several successful and precise quantitative models of word encoding have accounted very nicely for the data in this paradigm. The two original ones were by McClelland and Rumelhart (1981) and Paap, Newsome, McDonald, and Schwaneveldt (1982). In both of these models, there are both word detectors and letter detectors. In the McClelland and Rumelhart model, there is explicit feedback from words to letters, so that if a stimulus is a word, partial detection of the letters will excite the word detector, which in turn feeds back to the letter detectors to help activate them further. In the Paap et al. model, there is no explicit feedback; instead, a decision stage effectively incorporates a similar feedback process. Moreover, both of the models successfully explain the superiority of pseudowords over isolated letters. That is, even though a pseudoword like *mard* has no *mard* detector, it has quite a bit of letter overlap with several words (e.g., *card, mark, maid*). Thus, its component letters will get feedback from all of these word detectors, which for the most part will succeed in activating the detectors for the component letters in *mard*. Although this verbal explanation might seem to indicate that the facilitation would be significantly less for pseudowords than for words because there is no direct match with a single word detector, both models in fact quantitatively gave a good account of the data.

To summarize, the aforementioned experiments (and many related ones) all point to the conclusion that words (short words, at least) are processed in parallel, but through a process in which the component letters are identified and feed into the word identification process. Above, we have been vague about what *letter detector* means. Are the letter detectors that feed into words *abstract letter detectors* (i.e., case- and font-independent) or specific to the visual form that is seen? (Needless to say, if there are abstract letter detectors, they would have to be fed by case-specific letter detectors, as it is unlikely that a single template or set of features would be able to recognize *a* and *A* as the same thing.) As we have mentioned, the word superiority experiments chiefly used all uppercase letters, and it seems implausible that there would be prearranged hook-ups between the uppercase letters and the word detectors. Other experiments using a variety of techniques (e.g., Besner, Coltheart, & Davelaar, 1984; Evett & Humphreys, 1981; Rayner, McConkie, & Zola, 1980) also indicate that the hook-up is almost certainly between abstract letter detectors and the word detectors. One type of experiment had participants either identify individual words or read text that was in MiXeD cAsE, like this. Even though such text looks strange, after a little practice, people can read it almost as fast as they read normal text (Smith, Lott, & Cronnell, 1969). Among other things, this research indicates that word shape (i.e., the visual pattern of the word) plays little or no part in word identification.

These word superiority effect experiments, besides showing that letters in words are processed in parallel, suggest that word recognition is quite rapid. The exposure durations in these experiments that achieved about 75% correct recognition was typically about 30 ms, and if the duration is increased to 50 ms, word identification is virtually perfect. This does not necessarily mean, however, that word identification only takes 50 ms—it merely shows that some initial visual encoding stages are completed in something like 50 ms. However, after 50 ms or so, it may just be that the visual information is held in a short-term memory buffer, but it has not yet been fully processed. In fact, most estimates of the time to recognize a word are significantly longer than that (Rayner & Pollatsek, 1989). As we have previously noted, it takes about 500 ms to begin to name a word out loud, but that is clearly an upper estimate because it also includes motor programming and execution time. Skilled readers read about 300 words per minute or about 5 words per second, which would suggest that one fifth of a second or 200 ms might not be a bad guess for how long it takes to identify a word. Of course in connected discourse, some words are predictable and can be identified to the right of fixation in parafoveal vision, so that not all words need to be fixated. On the other hand, readers have to do more than identify words to understand the meaning of text. However, most data point to something like 150–200 ms as a ballpark estimate of the time to encode a word.

Automaticity of Word Encoding

One surprising result from the word encoding literature is that encoding of words seems to be automatic; that is, people can't help encoding words. The easiest demonstration of this is called the *Stroop effect* (Stroop, 1935; see MacLeod, 1991 for a comprehensive review). There is actually some controversy about how strongly automatic the Stroop effect is (see Besner, Stolz, & Boutilier, 1997, and the chapter by Proctor and Vu in this volume). That is, it may not be the case that people always process a word when they are trying their best not to process it. However, it appears that even in some cases when they are trying not to process it, they still do. In the Stroop task, people see words written in colored ink (e.g., they see *red* in green ink) and their task is to ignore the word and name the color (in this case, they should say *green*). The standard finding is that when the word is a different color name, participants are slowed down considerably in their naming and make considerable errors compared to a control condition (e.g., something like *&&&&* written in colored ink). In fact, even color-neutral words (i.e., noncolor names such as *desk*) slow down naming times. Such findings suggest that people are just unable to ignore the words. Moreover, these effects persist even with days of practice. The effect is not limited to naming colors; one gets similar slowing of naming times if one is to name a common object that has a name superimposed on it—for example, a picture of a cat with the word *dog* superimposed on the middle of the cat (Rayner & Posnansky, 1978; Rayner & Springer, 1986; Rosinski, Golinkoff, & Kukish, 1975).

Another way in which word processing appears to be automatic is that people encode the meaning of a word even though they are not aware of it. This has been demonstrated using the *semantic priming* paradigm (Meyer & Schvaneveldt, 1971). In this paradigm, two words, a *prime* and a *target,* are seen in rapid succession. The details of the experiments differ, but in some, participants just look at the prime and name the target. The phenomenon of semantic priming is that naming times are approximately 30 ms faster when the prime is semantically related to the target (e.g., *dog–cat*) than when it is not (e.g, *desk–cat*). The most interesting version of this paradigm occurs when the prime is presented *subliminally* (Balota, 1983; Carr, McCauley, Sperber, & Parmelee, 1982; Marcel, 1983). Usually this is achieved by a very brief presentation of the prime (about 10–20 ms) followed by a pattern mask and then the target. The amazing finding is that a priming effect (often almost as strong as when the prime is visible) occurs even in cases where the subject can not reliably report whether anything appeared before the pattern mask, let alone what the identity of the prime was. Thus, individuals are encoding the meaning of the prime even though they are unaware of having done so.

Word Encoding in Nonalphabetic Languages

So far, we have concentrated on decoding words in alphabetic languages, using experiments in English as our guide. For all the results we have described so far, there is no reason to believe that the results would come out differently in other languages. However, some other written languages use different systems of orthography. Space does not permit a full description of all of these writing systems nor what is known about decoding in them (see Rayner & Pollatsek, 1989, chapter 2, for a fuller discussion of writing systems).

Basically, there are two other systems of orthography, with some languages using hybrids of several systems. First, the Semitic languages use an alphabetic system, but one in which few of the vowels are represented, so that the reader needs to supply the missing information. In Hebrew, there is a system with *points* (little marks) that indicate the vowels that are used for children beginning to read; in virtually all materials read by adult readers, however, the points are omitted. The other basic system is exemplified by Chinese, which is sometimes characterized as so-called picture writing, although that term is somewhat misleading because it oversimplifies the actual orthography. In Chinese, the basic unit is the *character,* which does not represent a word, but a *morpheme,* a smaller unit of meaning, which is also a syllable. (In English, for instance, compound words such as *cow/boy* would be two morphemes, as would prefixed, suffixed, and inflected words such as *re/view, safe/ty,* and *read/ing.*) The characters in Chinese are, to some extent, pictographic representations of the meaning of the morpheme; in many cases, however, they have become quite schematic over time, so that a naive reader would have a hard time guessing the meaning of the morpheme merely by looking at the form of the character. In addition, characters are not unitary in that a majority are made up of two *radicals,* a semantic radical and a phonetic radical. The semantic radical gives some information about the meaning of the word and the phonetic radical gives some hint about the pronunciation, although it is quite unreliable. (In addition, the Chinese character system is used to represent quite widely diverging dialects.)

A hybrid system is Japanese, which uses Chinese characters (called *Kanji* in Japanese) to represent the roots of most *content words* (nouns, verbs, and adjectives), which are not usually single syllables in Japanese. This is supplemented by a system of simpler characters, called *Kana,* in which each Kana character represents a syllable. One Kana system is used to represent *function words* (prepositions, articles, conjunctions) and inflections; another Kana system is used to represent loanwords from other languges, such as *baseball.* Another fairly unique system is the Korean writing system, *Hangul.* In Hangul, a character represents a syllable, but it is not arbitrary, as in Kana. Instead, the component "letters" are represented not in a left-to-right fashion, but rather are all superimposed in the same character. Thus, in some sense, Hangul is similar to an alphabetic language.

The obvious question for languages without alphabets is whether encoding of words in such languages is more like learning visual templates than encoding is in alphabetic languages. However, as we hope the previous discussion indicates, thinking of words as visual templates even in Chinese is an oversimplification, as a word is typically two characters, and each character typically has two component radicals. Nonetheless, the system is different from an alphabetic language in that one has to learn how each character is pronounced and what it means, as opposed to an alphabetic language in which (to some approximation) one merely has to know the system in order to be able to pronounce it and know what it means (up to homophony). In fact, the Chinese orthography is hard for children to learn. One indication of this is that Chinese children are typically first taught a Roman script (*Pin yin*), which is a phonetic representation of Chinese, in the early grades. They are only taught the Chinese characters later, and then only gradually—a few characters at a time. It thus appears that having an alphabet is indeed a benefit in reading, and that learning word templates is difficult—either because it is easier to learn approximately 50 templates for letters than to learn several thousand templates for words, or because the alphabetic characters allow one to derive the sound of the word (or both).

SOUND CODING IN WORD IDENTIFICATION AND READING

So far, we have discussed word identification as if it were a purely visual process. That is to say, the prior section tacitly assumed that a process of word identification involves detectors for individual letters (in alphabetic languages), which feed into a word detector, in which the word is defined as a sequence of abstract letters. (In fact, one detail that was glossed over in the discussion of the parallel word-identification models is that the positions of individual letters need to be encoded precisely; otherwise people could not tell *dog* from *god.*) However, given that alphabets are supposed to code for the sounds of the words, it seems plausible that the process of identifying words is not a purely visual one, and that it also involves accessing the sounds that the letters represent and possibly assembling them into the sound of a word. Moreover, once one thinks about accessing the sound of a word, it becomes less clear what the term *word identification* actually means. Is it accessing a sequence of abstract letters, accessing the sound of the word, accessing the meaning of the word, or some combination of all three? In addition, what is the causal relationship between accessing the three types of codes? One possibility is that one merely accesses the visual code—more or less like finding a dictionary entry—and then looks up the sound of the word and the meaning in the "dictionary entry." (This must be an approximation of what happens in orthographies such as Chinese.) Another relatively simple possibility is that for alphabetic languages, the reader *must* first access the sound of the word and can only then access the meaning. That is to say, according to this view, the written symbols merely serve to access the spoken form of the language, and a word's meaning is tied only to the spoken form. On the other hand, the relationship may be more complex. For example, the written form may start to activate both the sound codes and the meaning codes, and then the three types of codes send feedback to each other to arrive at a solution as to what the visual form, auditory form, and meaning of the word are. There are probably few topics in reading that have generated as much controversy as this: what the role of sound coding is in the reading process.

As mentioned earlier, naming of words is quite rapid (within about 500 ms for most words). Given that a significant part of this time must be taken up in programming the motor response and in beginning to execute the motor act of speaking, it certainly seems plausible that accessing the sound code *could be* rapid enough to be part of the process of getting to the meaning of a word. But even if the sound code is accessed at least as rapidly as the meaning, it may not play any causal role. Certainly, there is no logical necessity for involving the sound codes, because the sequence of letters is sufficient to access the meaning (or meanings) of the word; in the McClelland and Rumelhart (1981) and Paap et al. (1982) models, access to the lexicon (and hence word meaning) is achieved via a *direct look-up* procedure, which only involves the letters which comprise a word. However, before examining the role of sound coding in accessing the meanings of words, let us first look at how sound codes themselves are accessed.

The Access of Sound Codes

There are three general possibilities for how we could access the pronunciation of a letter string. Many words in English have irregular pronunciations (e.g., *one*), such that their pronunciations cannot be derived from the spelling-to-sound rules as defined by the language. In these cases, it appears that the only way to access the sound code would be via a direct access procedure by which the word's spelling is matched to a lexical entry within the lexicon. In the above example, the letters *o-n-e* would activate the visual word detector for *one,* which would in turn activate the subsequent lexical entry. After this entry is accessed, the appropriate pronunciation for the word (/wun/) could be activated. In contrast, other words have regular pronunciations (e.g., *won*). Such words' pronunciations could also be accessed via a direct route, but their sound codes could also be constructed through the utilization of spelling-to-sound correspondence rules or by analogy to other words in the language. Finally, it is of course possible to pronounce nonwords like *mard.* Unless all possible pronounceable letter strings have lexical entries (which seems unlikely), nonwords' sound codes would have to be constructed.

Research on patients with *acquired dyslexia,* who were previously able to read normally but suffered a stroke or brain injury, has revealed two constellations of symptoms that seem to argue for the existence of both the direct and the constructive routes to a word's pronunciation (Coltheart, Patterson, & Marshall, 1980). In one type, *surface dyslexia,* the patients can pronounce both real words and nonwords but they tend to regularize irregularly pronounced words (e.g., pronouncing *island* as *iz-land*). In contrast to those with surface dyslexia, individuals with *deep* and *phonemic dyslexia* can pronounce real words (whether they are regular or irregular), but they cannot pronounce nonwords. Researchers initially believed that individuals with surface dyslexia completely relied on their intact constructive route, whereas those with deep dyslexia completely relied on their direct route. However, researchers now realize that these syndromes are somewhat more complex than had been first thought, and the descriptions of them here are somewhat oversimplified. Nonetheless, they do seem to argue that the two processes (a direct look-up process and a constructive process) may be somewhat independent of each other.

Assuming that these two processes exist in normal skilled readers (who can pronounce both irregular words and nonwords correctly), how do they relate to each other? Perhaps the simplest possibility is that they operate independently of each other in a race, so to speak. Whichever process finishes first would presumably win, determining the pronunciation. Thus, because the direct look-up process cannot access pronunciations of nonwords, the constructive process would determine the pronunciations of nonwords. What would happen for words? Presumably, the speed of the direct look-up process would be sensitive to the frequency of the word in the language, with low-frequency words taking longer to access. However, the constructive process, which is not dependent on lexical knowledge, should be largely independent of the word's frequency. Thus, for common (i.e. frequent) words, the pronunciation of both regular and irregular words should be determined by the direct look-up process and should take more or less the same time. For less frequent words, however, both the direct and constructive processes would be operating because the direct access process would be slower. Thus, for irregular words, there would be conflict between the pronunciations generated by the two processes; therefore one would either expect irregular words to be pronounced more slowly (if the conflict is resolved successfully), or there would be errors if the word is regularized.

The data from many studies are consistent with such a model. A very reliable finding (Baron & Strawson, 1976; Perfetti & Hogaboam, 1975) is that regular words are pronounced (named) more quickly than are irregular words. However, the difference in naming times between regular and irregular words is a function of word frequency: For high-frequency words there is little or no difference, but there is a large difference for low-frequency words. However, the process of naming is likely to be more complex than a simple race, as people usually make few errors in naming, even for low-frequency irregular words. Thus, somehow, it appears that the two routes cooperate in some way to produce the correct pronunciation, but when the two routes conflict in their output, there is slowing of the naming time (Carr & Pollatsek, 1985). It is worth noting, however, that few words are totally irregular. That is to say, even for quite irregular words like *one* and *island,* the constructive route would produce a pronunciation that had some overlap with the actual pronunciation.

Before leaving this section, we must note that there is considerable controversy at the moment concerning exactly how the lexicon is accessed. In the traditional *dual route* models that we have been discussing (e.g., Coltheart, 1978; Coltheart, Curtis, Atkins, & Haller, 1993; Coltheart, Rastle, Perry, Langdon, & Ziegler, 2001), there are two pathways to the lexicon, one from graphemic units to meaning directly, and one from graphemic units to phonological units, and then to meaning (the phonological mediation pathway). A key aspect of these models is that (a) the direct pathway must be used to read exception words (e.g., *one*) for which an indirect phonological route would fail and (b) the phonological route must be used to read pseudowords (e.g., *nufe*) that have no lexical representation. Another more recent class of models, often termed *connectionist models,* takes a different approach. These models take issue with the key idea that we actually have a mental lexicon. Instead, they assume that processing a word (or pseudoword) comes from an interaction of the stimulus and a mental representation which represents the past experience of the reader. However, this past experience is not represented in the form of a lexicon, but rather from patterns of activity that are *distributed* in the sense that one's total memory, in some sense, engages with a given word, rather than a single lexical entry. In addition, this memory is nonrepresentational, in that the elements are just relatively arbitrary features of experience rather than being things like words or letters (Harm & Seidenberg, 1999; Plaut, McClelland, Seidenberg, & Patterson, 1996; Seidenberg & McClelland, 1989). For this process to work rapidly enough for one to recognize a word in a fraction of a second, these models all assume that this contact between the current stimulus and memory must be *in parallel* across all these features. For this reason, these models are often termed *parallel distributed processing* (PDP) models. *Resonance models* (Stone & Van Orden, 1994; Van Orden & Goldinger, 1994) are a similar class of models that posit a somewhat different type of internal memory structure. Because these models are complex and depend on computer simulation in which many arbitrary assumptions need to be made in order for the simulations to work, it is often hard to judge how well they account for various phenomena. Certainly, at our present state of knowledge, it is quite difficult to decide whether this nonrepresentational approach is an improvement on the more traditional representational models (see Besner, Twilley, McCann, & Seergobin, 1990; Coltheart et al., 1990; Seidenberg & McClelland, 1990). For the purposes of our present discussion, a major difference in emphasis between the models is that for the connectionist models, processes that would look like the phonological route in the more traditional models enter into the processing of regular words, and processes that would look like direct lexical look-up enter into the processing of pseudowords.

Sound Codes and the Access of Word Meanings

In the previous section we discussed how readers access a visual word's sound codes. However, a much more important question is how readers access a visual word's meaning (or meanings). As previously indicated, this has been a highly contentious issue on which respected researchers have stated quite differing positions. For example, Kolers (1972) claimed that processing during reading does not involve readers' formulating articulatory representations of printed words, whereas Gibson (1971) claimed that the heart of reading is the decoding of written symbols into speech. Although we have learned a great deal about this topic, the controversy represented by this dichotomy of views continues, and researchers' opinions on this question still differ greatly.

Some of the first attempts to resolve this issue involved the previously discussed lexical decision task. One question that was asked was whether there was a difference between regularly and irregularly spelled words, under the tacit assumption that the task reflects the speed of accessing the meaning of words (Bauer & Stanovich, 1980; Coltheart, 1978). These data unfortunately tended to be highly variable: Some studies found a regularity effect whereas others did not. Meyer, Schvaneveldt, and Ruddy (1974) utilized a somewhat different paradigm and found that the time for readers to determine whether *touch* was a word was slower when it was preceded by a word such as *couch* (which presumably primed the incorrect pronunciation) as compared to when it was preceded by an unrelated word. However, there is now considerable concern that the lexical decision task is fundamentally flawed as a measure of so-called lexical access that is related to accessing a word's meaning. The most influential of these arguments was that this task is likely to induce artificial checking strategies before making a response (Balota & Chumbley, 1984, 1985).

A task that gets more directly at accessing a word's meaning is the categorization task. As noted earlier, in this task, participants are given a category label (e.g., *tree*) and then are given a target word (e.g., *beech, beach,* or *bench*) and have to decide whether it represented a member of the preceding category (Van Orden, 1987; Van Orden, Johnston, & Hale, 1988; Van Orden, Pennington, & Stone, 1990). The key finding was that participants had difficulties rejecting homophones of true category exemplars (e.g. *beach*). Not only were they slow in rejecting these items, they typically made 10–20% more errors on these items than on control items that were visually similar (e.g., *bench*). In fact, these errors persisted even when people were urged to be cautious and go slowly. Moreover, this effect is not restricted to word homophones. A similar, although somewhat smaller effect was reported with pseudohomophones (e.g., *brane*). Moreover, in a similar semantic relatedness judgment task (i.e., decide whether the two words on the screen are semantically related), individuals are slower and make more errors on *false homophone* pairs such as *pillow-bead* (Lesch & Pollatsek, 1998). (Bead is a false homophone of pillow because *bead* could be a homophone of *bed,* analogously to *head*'s rhyming with *bed.*) These findings with pseudohomophones and false homophones both indicate that it is unlikely that such results are merely due to participants' lack of knowledge of the target words' spelling, and that assembled phonology plays a significant role in accessing a word's meaning.

Still, in order for sound codes to play a crucial role in the access of word meaning, they must be activated relatively early in word processing. In addition, these sound codes must be activated during natural reading, and not just when words are presented in relative isolation (as they were in the aforementioned studies). To address these issues, Pollatsek, Lesch, Morris, and Rayner (1992) utilized a *boundary* paradigm (Rayner, 1975) to examine whether phonological codes were active before words were even fixated (and hence very early in processing). Although we discuss the boundary paradigm in more detail later in this chapter, it basically consists of presenting a parafoveal preview of a word or a letter string to the right of a boundary within a sentence. When readers' eyes move past the boundary and toward a parafoveal target word, the preview changes. In the Pollatsek et al. study, the preview word was either identical to the target word (*rains*), a homophone of it (*reins*), or an orthographic control word that shared many letters with the target word (*ruins*). That is, participants often see a different word in the target word location before they fixate it, although they are virtually never aware of any changes. The key finding was that reading was faster when the preview was a homophone of the target than when it was just orthographically similar; this indicates that in reading text, sound codes are extracted from words even before they are fixated, which is quite early in the encoding process. In fact, data from a similar experiment indicate that Chinese readers also benefit from a homophone of a word in the parafovea (Pollatsek, Tan, & Rayner, 2000).

Some other paradigms, however, have come up with less convincing evidence for the importance of sound coding in word identification. One, in fact, used a manipulation in a reading study similar to the preview study with three conditions: correct homophone, incorrect homophone, and spelling control (e.g., "Even a cold bowl of *cereal/serial/verbal*. . . ."). However, in this study, when a wrong word appeared (either the wrong homophone or the spelling control) it remained in the text throughout the trial. People read short passages containing these errors, and the key question was whether the wrong homophones would be less disruptive than the spelling controls because they "sounded right." In these studies (Daneman & Reingold, 1993, 2000; Daneman, Reingold, & Davidson, 1995) there was a disruption in the reading process (measured by examining the gaze duration on the target word) for both types of wrong words, but no significant difference between the wrong homophones and the spelling control (although they did find more disruption for the spelling control slightly later in processing). This finding is consistent with a view in which sound coding plays only a backup role in word identification. On the other hand, Rayner, Pollatsek, and Binder (1998) found greater disruption for the spelling control than for the wrong homophone even on immediate measures of processing. However, even in the Rayner et al. study, the homophone effects were relatively subtle (far more so than in Van Orden's categorization paradigm). Thus, it appears that sentence and paragraph context may interact with word processing to make errors (be they phonological or orthographical) less damaging to the reading process. Finally, we should note that at the moment there is some controversy about the exact nature of the findings in these homophone substitution studies (Jared, Levy, & Rayner, 1999) and with respect to the use of such substitutions to study sound coding in reading (Starr & Fleming, 2001). However, for the most part, the results obtained from studies using homophone substitutions are broadly consistent with other studies examining sound coding in which homophones are not used.

Summary

Although it does seem clear that phonological representations are used in the reading process, it is a matter of controversy how important these sound codes are to accessing the meaning of a word. Certainly, the categorical judgment studies make clear that sound coding plays a large role in getting to the meaning of a word, and the parafoveal preview studies indicate that sound codes are accessed early when reading text. However, the data from the wrong-homophone studies in reading seem to indicate that the role of sound coding in accessing word meanings in reading may be a bit more modest. In contrast, most cognitive psychologists do agree that phonological codes are activated in reading and play an important role by assisting short-term memory (Kleiman, 1975; Levy, 1975; Slowiaczek & Clifton, 1980).

EYE MOVEMENTS IN READING

The experiments we have discussed thus far have mainly studied individuals who are viewing words in isolation. However, fluent reading consists of much more than simply processing single words—it also involves the integration of successive words into a meaningful context. In this section, we discuss a number of factors that seem to influence the ease or difficulty with which we read words embedded in text. Ultimately, one could view the research within the realm of reading as an attempt to formulate a list of all the variables that have an influence on reading processes. Ideally, if we had an exhaustive list of each and every constituent factor in reading (and, of course, how each of these factors interacted with one another), we could develop a complete model of reading. Although quite a bit of work needs to be done in order to accomplish such an ambitious endeavor, a great deal of progress has been made. In particular, as the potential for technical innovation has improved, researchers have developed more accurate and direct methodologies for studying the reading process. One of these innovations, which has been used extensively for the past 25 years, has involved using readers' eye movements in order to uncover the cognitive processes involved in reading.

Basic Facts About Eye Movements

Although it may seem as if our eyes sweep continuously across the page as we read, our eyes actually make a series of discrete jumps between different locations in the text, more or less going from left to right across a line of text (see Huey, 1908; Rayner, 1978, 1998). More specifically, typical eye movement activity during reading consists of sequences of *saccades,* which are rapid, discrete, jumps from location to location, and *fixations,* during which the eyes remain relatively stable for periods that last, on average, about a quarter of a second. The reason that continual eye movements are necessary during reading is that our visual acuity is generally quite limited. Although the retina itself is capable of detecting stimuli from a relatively wide visual field (about 240° of visual angle), high-acuity vision is limited to the *fovea,* which consists of only the center 2° of visual angle (which for a normal reading distance consists of approximately six to eight letters). As one gets further away from the point of fixation (toward the *parafovea* and eventually the *periphery*), visual acuity decreases dramatically and it is much more difficult to see letters and words clearly.

The purpose of a saccade is to focus a region of text onto foveal vision for more detailed analysis, because reading on the basis of only parafoveal-peripheral information is generally not possible (Rayner & Bertera, 1979; Rayner, Inhoff, Morrison, Slowiaczek, & Bertera, 1981). Saccades are relatively fast, taking only about 20–50 ms (depending on the distance covered). In addition, because their velocity can reach up to 500°/s, visual sensitivity is reduced to a blur during an eye movement, and little or no new information is obtained while the eye is in motion. Moreover, one is not aware of this blur due to *saccadic suppression* (Dodge, 1900; Ishida & Ikeda, 1989; Matin, 1974; Wolverton & Zola, 1983). Eye movements during reading range from less than one character space to 15–20 character spaces (although such long saccades are quite rare and typically follow *regressions,* see below), with the eyes typically moving forward approximately eight character spaces at a time. As words in typical English prose are on average five letters long, the eyes thus move on average a distance that is roughly equivalent to the length of one and one-half words.

Although (perhaps not surprisingly) the eyes typically move from left to right (i.e., in the direction of the text in English), about 10–15% of eye movements shift backwards in text and are termed *regressions* (Rayner, 1978, 1998; Rayner & Pollatsek, 1989). For the most part, regressions tend to be short, as the eyes only move a few letters. Readers often make such regressions in response to comprehension difficulty (see Rayner, 1998, for a review), but regressive eye movements may also occur when the eyes have moved a little too far forward in the text and a small backwards correction is needed in order for us to process a particular word of interest. Longer regressions do occur occasionally, and when such movements are necessary in order to correctly comprehend the text, readers are generally accurate at moving their eyes back to the location within the text that caused them difficulty (Frazier & Rayner, 1982; Kennedy & Murray, 1987).

Given the blur of visual information during the physical movement of the eyes, the input of meaningful information takes place during fixations (Ishida & Ikeda, 1989; Wolverton & Zola, 1983). As we discuss later in the chapter, readers tend to fixate on or near most words in text, and the majority of words are only fixated once (Just & Carpenter, 1980). However, some words are skipped (Ehrlich & Rayner, 1981; Gautier, O'Regan, & LaGargasson, 2000; O'Regan, 1979, 1980; Rayner & Well, 1996). Word skipping tends to be related to word length: Short words (e.g., function words like *the* or *and*) are skipped about 75% of the time, whereas longer words are rarely skipped. More specifically, as length increases, the probability of fixating a word increases (Rayner & McConkie, 1976): Two- to three-letter words are fixated around 25% of the time, but words with eight or more letters are almost always fixated (and are often fixated more than once before the eyes move to the next word). However, as we discuss later, longer content words that are highly predictable from the preceding context are also sometimes skipped.

Fixation durations are highly variable, ranging from less than 100 ms to over 500 ms, with a mean of about 250 ms (Rayner & Pollatsek, 1989). One important question is whether this variability in the time readers spend fixating on words is only due to low-level factors such as word length or whether such variability may also be due to higher level influences as well. As the prior sentence suggests, it is clear that low-level variables are important. Word length in particular has been found to have a powerful influence on the amount of time a reader fixates on a word (Kliegl, Olson, & Davidson, 1982; Rayner & McConkie, 1976; Rayner, Sereno, & Raney, 1996): As word length increases, fixation times increase as well. The fact that readers tend to fixate longer words for longer periods of time is perhaps not surprising—such an effect could simply be the product of the mechanical (i.e., motor) processes involved in moving and fixating the eyes. What has been somewhat more controversial is whether eye movement measures can also be used to infer moment-to-moment cognitive processes in reading such as the difficulty in identifying a word.

There is now a large body of evidence, however, that the time spent fixating a word is influenced by word frequency: Fixation times are longer for words of lower frequency (i.e., words less frequently seen in text) than for words of higher frequency, even when the low-frequency words are the same length as the high-frequency words (Hyönä & Olson, 1995; Inhoff & Rayner, 1986; Just & Carpenter, 1980; Kennison & Clifton, 1995; Rayner, 1977; Rayner & Duffy, 1986; Rayner & Fischer, 1996; Raney & Rayner, 1995; Rayner & Raney, 1996; Rayner et al., 1996; Sereno & Rayner, 2000; Vitu, 1991). As with words in isolation, this is presumably because the slower direct access process for words of lower frequency increases the time to identify them. Furthermore, there is a *spillover effect* for low-frequency words (Rayner & Duffy, 1986; Rayner, Sereno, Morris, Schmauder, & Clifton, 1989). When the currently fixated word is of low frequency, cognitive processing may be passed downstream in the text, leading to longer fixation times on the next word. A corollary to the spillover effect is that when words are fixated multiple times within a passage, fixation durations on these words decrease, particularly if they are of low frequency (Hyönä & Niemi, 1990; Rayner, Raney, & Pollatsek, 1995). Finally, the nature of a word's morphology also has a mediating effect on fixation times. Lima (1987), for example, found that readers tend to fixate for longer periods of time on prefixed words (e.g., *revive*) as compared to pseudoprefixed words (e.g., *rescue*). More recently Hyönä and Pollatsek (1998) found that the frequency of both the morphemes of compound words influenced fixation time on the word for compound words that were equated on the frequency of the word. However, the timing was different; the first morpheme influenced the duration of the initial fixation on the word, whereas the second morpheme only influenced later processing on the word. Similarly, Niswander, Pollatsek, and Rayner (2000) found that the frequency of the root morpheme of suffixed words (e.g. *govern* in *government*) affected the fixation time on the word. Thus, at least some components of words, in addition to the words themselves, are influencing fixation times in reading.

The Perceptual Span

A central question in reading is how much information we can extract from text during a single fixation. As mentioned earlier, the data show that our eyes move approximately once every quarter of a second during normal reading, suggesting that only a limited amount of information is typically extracted from the text on each fixation. This, coupled with the physical acuity limitations inherent in the visual system, suggests that the region of text on the page from which useful information may be extracted on each fixation is relatively small.

Although a number of different techniques have been used in attempts to measure the size of the effective visual field (or *perceptual span*) in reading, most of them have rather severe limitations (see Rayner, 1975, 1978 for a discussion). One method which has proven to be effective, however, is called the *moving window technique* (McConkie & Rayner, 1975; Rayner, 1986; Rayner & Bertera, 1979; N. R. Underwood & McConkie, 1985). This technique involves presenting readers with a window of normal text around the fixation point on each fixation, with the information outside that window degraded in some manner. In order to accomplish this, readers' eye movements and fixations are continuously monitored and recorded by a computer while they read text presented on a computer monitor, and, when the eyes move, the computer changes the text contingent on the position of the eyes. In a typical experiment, an experimenter-defined window of normal text is presented around the fixation point, while all the letters outside the window are changed to random letters. The extent of the perceptual span may be examined by manipulating the size of the window region. The logic of this technique is that if reading is normal for a window of a particular size (i.e., if people read both with normal comprehension and at their normal rate), then information outside this window is not used in the reading process.

Figure 20.2 illustrates a typical example of the moving window technique. In this example, a hypothetical reader is presented with a window of text that consists of 4 letters to the left of fixation and 14 letters to the right of fixation (fixation points are indicated by asterisks). As can be seen in the

Moving Window Paradigm

```
xx xxample of a moving xxxxxx pxxxxxxx   (fixation 1)
        *
xx xxxxxxx xx a moving window paxxxxxx   (fixation 2)
                 *
```

Boundary Paradigm

```
an example of the previous paradigm   (fixation 1)
        *
an example of the boundary paradigm   (fixation 2)
                     *
```

Figure 20.2 Examples of the moving window and boundary paradigms. The moving window example consists of a window that extends 4 characters to the left of fixation and 14 characters to the right of fixation on the two fixations shown (fixation locations are marked by asterisks). In the boundary paradigm example, a word (in this case, the word *previews*) is present in a target location prior to a reader's moving over an invisible boundary location (the letter *e* in *the*). When the eyes cross this boundary location, the preview word is replaced by the target word (in this case, the word *boundary*).

figure, the window of normal text follows the reader's fixation points—if the eyes make a forward saccade, the window moves forward, but if the eyes make a backward saccade (a regression), the window moves backward as well.

Studies using this technique have consistently shown that the size of the perceptual span is relatively small. For readers of alphabetical languages such as English, French, and Dutch, the span extends from the beginning of the currently fixated word or about three to four letters to the left of fixation (McConkie & Rayner, 1976; Rayner, Well, & Pollatsek, 1980; N. R. Underwood & McConkie, 1985) to about 14–15 letters to the right of fixation (DenBuurman, Boersma, & Gerrissen, 1981; McConkie & Rayner, 1975; Rayner, 1986; Rayner & Bertera, 1979). Thus, the span is asymmetric to the right for readers of English. Interestingly, for written languages such as Hebrew (which are printed from right to left), the span is asymmetric to the left of fixation (Pollatsek, Bolozky, Well, & Rayner, 1981).

The perceptual span is influenced both by characteristics of the writing system and characteristics of the reader. Thus, the span is considerably smaller for Japanese text (Ikeda & Saida, 1978; Osaka, 1992). For Japanese text written vertically, the effective visual field is five to six character spaces in the vertical direction of the eye movement (Osaka & Oda, 1991). More recently, Inhoff and Liu (1998) found that Chinese readers have an asymmetric perceptual span extending from one character left of fixation to three character spaces to the right. (Chinese is now written from left to right.) Furthermore, Rayner (1986) found that beginning readers at the end of the first grade had a smaller span, consisting of about 12 letter spaces to the right of fixation, than did skilled readers, whose perceptual span was 14–15 letter spaces to the right of fixation. Thus, it seems that the size of the perceptual span is defined by not only our physical limitations (our limited visual acuity), but also by the amount and difficulty of the information we need to process as we read. As text density increases, our perceptual span decreases, and we are only able to extract information from smaller areas of text.

Another issue regarding the perceptual span is whether readers acquire information from below the line which they are reading. Inhoff and Briihl (1991; Inhoff & Topolski, 1992) examined this issue by recording readers' eye movements as they read a line from a target passage while ignoring a distracting line of text (taken from a related passage) located directly below target text. Initially, readers' answers to multiple-choice questions suggested that they had indeed obtained information from both attended and unattended lines. However, when readers' eye movements were examined, that data showed that they occasionally fixated the distractor text. When these extraneous fixations were removed from the analysis, there was no indication that readers obtained useful semantic information from the unattended text. Pollatsek, Raney, LaGasse, and Rayner (1993) more directly examined the issue by using a moving window technique. The line the reader was reading and all lines above it were normal, but the text below the currently fixated line was altered in a number of ways (including replacing lines of text with other text and replacing the letters below the currently fixated line with random letters). Pollatsek et al. (1993) found that text was read most easily when the normal text was below the line and when there were *X*s below the line. None of the other conditions differed from each other, which suggests that readers do not obtain semantic information from below the currently fixated line.

Although the perceptual span is limited, it does extend beyond the currently fixated word. Rayner, Well, Pollatsek, and Bertera (1982) presented readers with either a three-word window (consisting of the fixated word and the next two words), a two-word window (consisting of the fixated word and the next word), or a one-word window (consisting only of the currently fixated word). When reading normal, unperturbed text (the baseline), the average reading rate was about 330 words per minute (wpm), and the same average reading rate was found in the three-word condition. However, in the two-word window condition, when the amount of text available to the reader was reduced to only two words, the average reading rate fell to 300 wpm, and the reading rate slowed to 200 wpm in the one-word window condition. So, it seems that if skilled readers are allowed to see three words at a time, reading may proceed normally, but if the amount of text available for processing is reduced to only the currently fixated word, they can read reasonably fluently, but at only two-thirds of normal speed. Hence, although readers may extract information from more than one word per fixation, the area of effective vision is no more than three words.

One potential limitation of the moving window technique is that reading would be artifactually slowed if readers could see the display changes occurring outside the window of unperturbed text and are simply distracted by them. If this were the case, one could argue that data obtained using the moving window technique are confounded—slower reading rates in the one-word condition mentioned above could either be due to readers' limited perceptual span or to the fact that readers are simply distracted by nonsensical letters in their peripheries. In some instances this is true: When the text falling outside the window consists of all *X*s, the reader is generally aware of where the normal text is and where the *X*s are. In contrast, if random letters are used instead of *X*s, readers are generally unaware of the display changes taking place in their peripheries, although they may be aware that they are reading more slowly and may have the impression that something is preventing them from reading normally. More directly, however, readers' conscious awareness of display changes are not related to reading speed in that participants in moving window experiments can actually read faster when the text outside of the window is *X*s as opposed to random letters. This is most likely the case because random letters are more likely to lead to misidentification of other letters or words, whereas *X*s are not.

The Acquisition of Information to the Right of Fixation

So far we have discussed the fact that when readers are not allowed to see letters or words in the parafovea, reading rates are slowed, indicating that at least some characteristics of the information from the parafovea are necessary for fluent reading. Another important indication that readers extract information from text to the right of fixation is that we do not read every word in text, indicating that words to the right of fixation can be partially (or fully) identified and skipped (incidentally, in cases where a word is skipped, the duration of the fixation prior to the skip tends to be inflated; Pollatsek, Rayner, & Balota, 1986). As mentioned earlier, short function words (e.g., conjunctions and articles) and words that are highly predictable or constrained by the preceding context are also more likely to be skipped than are long words or words that are not constrained by preceding context. Such a pattern in skipping rates indicates that readers obtain information from both the currently fixated word and from the next (parafoveal) word, but it also seems to indicate that the amount of information from the right of fixation is limited (e.g., because longer words tend not to be skipped). This suggests that the major information used in the parafovea is the first few letters of the word to the right of the fixated word.

Further evidence for this conclusion comes from an additional experiment conducted by Rayner et al. (1982). In this experiment, sentences were presented to readers in which there was either (a) a one-word window; (b) a two-word window, or (c) the fixated word, visible together with partial information from the word immediately to the right of fixation (either the first one, two, or three letters; the remaining letters of the word to the right of fixation were replaced by letters that were either visually similar or visually dissimilar to the ones they replaced). The data showed that as long as the first three letters of the word to the right of fixation were normal and the others were replaced by letters that were visually similar to the letters that they replaced, reading was as fast as when the entire word to the right was available. However, the other letter information is not irrelevant, because when the remainder of the word was replaced by visually dissimilar letters, reading rates were slower as compared to when the entire word to the right was available, indicating that more information is processed than just the first three letters of the next word (see also Lima 1987; Lima & Inhoff, 1985).

In addition to the extraction of partial word information from the right of fixation, word length information is also obtained from the parafovea, and this information is used in computing where to move the eyes next (Morris, Rayner, & Pollatsek, 1990; O'Regan, 1979, 1980; Pollatsek & Rayner, 1982; Rayner, 1979; Rayner, Fischer, & Pollatsek, 1998; Rayner & Morris, 1992; Rayner et al., 1996). Word length information may also be utilized by readers to determine how parafoveal information is to be used—sometimes enough parafoveal letter information can be obtained from short words that they can be identified and skipped. In contrast, partial word information extracted from a longer parafoveal word may not usually allow full identification of the word but may facilitate subsequent foveal processing when the parafoveal word is eventually fixated (Blanchard, Pollatsek, & Rayner, 1989).

Integration of Information Across Fixations

The extraction of partial word information from the parafovea suggests that it is integrated in some fashion with information obtained from the parafoveal word when it is subsequently fixated. A variety of experiments have been conducted to determine the kinds of information that are involved in this synthesis. One experimental method that has been used to investigate this issue, the *boundary paradigm* (Rayner, 1975), is a variation of the moving window technique discussed earlier. Similar to the moving window paradigm, text displayed on a computer screen is manipulated as a function of where the eyes are fixated, but in the boundary paradigm, only the characteristics of a specific target word in a particular location within a sentence are manipulated. For example, in the sentence *The man picked up an old map from the chart in the bedroom,* when readers' eyes move past the space between *the* and *chart,* the target word *chart* would change to *chest.* (The rest of the sentence remains normal throughout the trial.) By examining how long readers fixate on a target word as a function of what was previously available in the target region prior to fixation, researchers can make inferences about the types of information that readers obtained from the target word prior to fixating upon it.

Two different tasks have been used to examine the integration of information across saccades: reading and word naming. In the reading studies, fixation time on the target word is the primary dependent variable. In the naming studies (Balota & Rayner, 1983; McClelland & O'Regan, 1981; Rayner, 1978; Rayner, McConkie, & Ehrlich, 1978; Rayner et al., 1980), a single word or letter string is presented in the parafovea, and when the reader makes an eye movement toward it, it is replaced by a word that is to be named as quickly as possible. The influence of the parafoveal stimulus is assessed by measuring the effect of the parafoveal stimuli on naming times. Surprisingly, in spite of the differences in procedure (text vs. single words) and dependent variables (eye movement measures vs. naming latency), virtually identical effects of the parafoveal stimulus have been found in the reading and naming studies.

Findings from the naming task indicate that if the first two or three letters of the parafoveal word are retained following the eye movement and subsequent boundary display change (i.e., if the first few letters of the to-be-fixated parafoveal word are preserved across the saccade), naming times are facilitated as compared to when these letters change across the saccade. Parafoveal processing is spatially limited, however, in that this facilitation was found when the parafoveal word was presented 3° or less from fixation, but not when the parafoveal stimulus was 5° from fixation (i.e., about 15 character spaces). Furthermore, when the parafoveal stimulus was presented 1° from fixation, naming was faster when there was no change than when only the first two or three letters were preserved across the saccade, but when the parafoveal stimulus was presented farther away from fixation (2.3 or 3°), naming times were virtually identical regardless of whether only the first two to three letters or all of the letters are were preserved across the saccade.

Hence, it is clear that readers can extract partial word information on one fixation to use in identification of a word on a subsequent fixation, but precisely what types of information may be carried across saccades? One possibility is that this integration is simply a function of the commonality of visual patterns from two fixations, such that the extraction of visual codes from the parafovea facilitates processing via an image-matching process. McConkie and Zola (1979; see also Rayner et al., 1980) tested this prediction by asking readers to read text in alternating case such that each time they moved their eyes, the text in the parafovea shifted from one alternated case pattern to its inverse (e.g., *cHaNgE* shifted to *ChAnGe*). Counter to the prediction that visual codes are involved in the integration of information across fixations, readers didn't notice the case changes and reading behavior was not different from the control condition in which there were no case changes from fixation to fixation. Because changing visual features did not disrupt reading, it appears that visual codes are not combined across saccades during reading. However, readers extract abstract (i.e., case-independent) letter information from the parafovea (Rayner et al., 1980).

A number of other variables have been considered. One possibility is that some type of phonological (sound) code is involved in conveying information across saccades. As we discussed earlier, Pollatsek et al. (1992; see also Henderson, Dixon, Petersen, Twilley, & Ferreira, 1995) utilized both a naming task and a reading task; they found that a homophone of a target word (e.g., *beach-beech*) presented as a preview in the parafovea facilitated processing of the target word seen on the next fixation more than did a preview of a word that was visually similar to the target word (e.g., *bench*). However, they also found that the visual similarity of the preview to the target played a role in the facilitative effect of the preview so that abstract letter codes are also preserved across saccades.

Morphemes, or the smallest units of meaning, have also been examined as a possibility for facilitating information processing across saccades, but the evidence for this suggestion has thus far been negative. In another experiment Lima (1987) used words that contained true prefixes (e.g., *revive*) and words that contained pseudoprefixes (e.g., *rescue*). If readers extract morphological information from the parafovea, then a larger *preview benefit* (the difference in fixation time between when a parafoveal preview of the target was available to the reader as compared to when a preview was not available) should be found for the prefixed words. Lima, however, found an equal benefit in the prefixed and pseudoprefixed conditions, indicating that prefixes are not involved in the integration of information across saccades. Furthermore, in a similar study, Inhoff (1989) presented readers with either the first morpheme of a true compound word such as *cow* in *cowboy* or the first morpheme of a pseudocompound such as *car* in *carpet,* and the study found no differences in the sizes of the parafoveal preview benefits.

Finally, it has been suggested that semantic (meaning) information in the parafovea may aid in later identification of a word (G. Underwood, 1985), but studies examining this issue have generally been negative. Rayner, Balota, and Pollatsek (1986) reported a boundary experiment in which readers were shown three possible types of parafoveal previews prior to fixating on a target word. For example, prior to fixating on the target word *tune,* readers could have seen a parafoveal preview of either *turc* (orthographically similar), *song* (semantically related), or *door* (semantically unrelated). In a simple semantic priming experiment (with a naming response), semantically similar pairs (*tune-song*) resulted in a standard priming effect. However, when these targets were embedded in sentences, a parafoveal preview benefit was found only in the orthographically similar condition (supporting the idea that abstract letter codes are involved in integrating information from words across saccades), but there was no difference in preview benefit between the related and unrelated conditions (see also Altarriba, Kambe, Pollatsek, & Rayner, 2001). Thus, readers apparently do not extract semantic information from to-be-fixated parafoveal words.

The research we have reported here has focused on the fact that information extracted from a parafoveal word decreases the fixation time on that word when it is subsequently fixated. However, recently, a number of studies have examined whether information located in the parafovea influences the processing of the currently fixated word or, in similar terms, whether readers may process two or more words in parallel.

Murray (1998) designed a word comparison task in which readers were to asked to detect a one-word difference in meaning between two sentences. Fixation times on target words were shorter when the parafoveal word was a plausible continuation of the sentence as compared to when it was an implausible continuation. In another study, Kennedy (2000) instructed subjects to discriminate whether successively fixated words were identical or synonymous to each other, and found that fixation times on fixated (foveal) words were longer when the parafoveal word had a high frequency of occurrence as compared to a low frequency of occurrence.

It is possible, however, that the nature of attentional allocation is different in word comparison tasks than it is in more naturalistic reading tasks. In fact, several studies have demonstrated that the frequency of the word to the right of fixation during reading does not influence the processing of the fixated word (Carpenter & Just, 1983; Henderson & Ferreira, 1993; Rayner et al., 1998). To examine more closely whether properties of parafoveal words may have an effect on the viewing durations of the currently fixated word during natural reading, Inhoff, Starr, and Shindler (2000) constructed sentence triplets in which readers were allowed one of three types of parafoveal preview. In the related condition, when readers fixated on a target word (e.g., *traffic*), they saw a related word (e.g., *light*) in the parafovea. In the unrelated condition, when readers fixated on the target word (e.g., *traffic*), they saw a semantically unrelated word (e.g., *smoke*) in the parafovea. Finally, in the dissimilar condition, upon fixating a target word, readers saw a series of quasi-random letters in the parafovea (e.g., *govcq*). Readers' fixation times on target words were shortest in the related condition (though not different from the unrelated word) and longest in the dissimilar condition, suggesting that they at least processed some degree of abstract letter information from the parafoveal stimuli in parallel with the currently fixated word. However, semantic properties (i.e., meaning) of the parafoveal word had little effect on the time spent reading the target word.

Summary

The relative ease with which we read words is influenced by a number of variables, which include both low-level factors such as word length and high-level factors such as word frequency. The region of text from which readers may extract useful information on any given fixation is limited to the word being fixated and perhaps the next one or two words to the right. Moreover, the information that may be obtained to the right of fixation is generally limited to abstract letter codes (McConkie & Zola, 1979; Rayner et al., 1980) and phonological codes (Pollatsek et al., 1992), both of which may play a role in integrating information from words across saccades. Although there is no evidence that indicates that visual, morphological, or semantic information extracted from the parafovea aids later word identification, there is some controversy as to whether words may (under some circumstances and to some extent) be processed in parallel.

WORD IDENTIFICATION IN CONTEXT

There are many studies measuring either accuracy of identification in tachistoscopic (i.e., very brief) presentations (Tulving & Gold, 1963), naming latency (Becker, 1985; Stanovich & West, 1979, 1983), or lexical decision latency (Fischler & Bloom, 1979; Schuberth & Eimas, 1977) that have also demonstrated contextual effects on word identification. These experiments typically involved having subjects read a sentence fragment like *The skiers were buried alive by the sudden. . . .* The subjects were then either shown the target word *avalanche* very briefly and asked to identify it or the word was presented until they made a response to it (such as naming or lexical decision). The basic finding in the brief exposure experiments was that people could identify the target word at significantly briefer exposures when the context predicted it than when it was preceded either by neutral context, inappropriate context, or no context. In the naming and lexical decision versions of the experiment, a highly constraining context facilitated naming or lexical decision latency relative to a neutral condition such as the frame *The next word in the sentence will be*. We should note that there has been some controversy over the appropriate baseline to use in these experiments, but that is beyond the scope of this chapter. We turn now to a discussion of context effects when readers are reading text.

In the previous section we discussed a number of variables that influence the ease or difficulty with which a word may be processed during reading. As we have pointed out, much of the variation in readers' eye fixation times can be explained by differences in word length and word frequency. In addition, a number of variables involved in text processing at a higher level have also been found to affect the speed of word identification. For example, we have already mentioned that a parafoveal word is more likely to be skipped if it is predictable from prior sentence context (Ehrlich & Rayner, 1981; O'Regan, 1979). Moreover, such predictable words are also fixated for shorter periods of time (Balota, Pollatsek, &

Rayner, 1985; Binder, Pollatsek, & Rayner, 1999; Inhoff, 1984; Rayner, Binder, Ashby, & Pollatsek, 2001; Rayner & Well, 1996; Schustack, Ehrlich, & Rayner, 1987).

Before moving on, we should clarify what we mean when we talk about *predictability.* In the studies we discuss in this section, predictability is generally assessed by presenting a group of readers with a sentence fragment up to, but not including, the potential target word. They are then asked to guess what the next word in the sentence might be. In most experiments, a target word is operationally defined as predictable if more than 70% of the readers are able to guess the target word based on prior sentence context, and unpredictable if fewer than 5% of the readers are able to guess the target word. We should note that during this norming process, readers generally take up to several seconds to formulate a guess, whereas during natural reading, readers only fixate each word in the text for about 250 ms. This makes it unlikely that predictability effects in normal silent reading are due to such a conscious guessing process. Moreover, most readers' introspection is that they are rarely if ever guessing what the next word will be as they read a passage of text. Hence, although we talk about predictability extensively in this section, we are certainly not claiming the effects are due to conscious prediction. They may be due to something like an unconscious process that is somewhat like prediction, although it would likely be quite different from conscious prediction.

Although these predictability effects on skipping rates are quite clear, there is some controversy as to the nature of these effects. One possibility is that contextual influences take place relatively early on during processing and, as such, affect the ease of processing a word (i.e., *lexical access*). An alternative view is that contextual influences affect later stages of word processing, such as the time it takes to integrate the word into ongoing discourse structures (i.e., *text integration*). One stumbling block in resolving this issue is that some evidence suggests that fixation time on a word is at least in part affected by higher level text integration processing. For example, O'Brien, Shank, Myers, and Rayner (1988) constructed three different versions of a passage that contained one of three potential phrases early in the passage (e.g., *stabbed her with his weapon, stabbed her with his knife,* or *assaulted her with his weapon*). When the word *knife* appeared later in the passage, readers' fixation times on *knife* were equivalent for *stabbed her with his weapon* and *stabbed her with his knife,* presumably because readers had inferred when reading the former phrase that the weapon was a knife (i.e., it is unlikely that someone would be stabbed with a gun). In contrast, when the earlier phrase was *assaulted her with his weapon,* fixation durations on the later appearance of *knife* were longer. That is, in this last case, the fixation duration on *knife* reflected not only the time to understand the literal meaning of the word, but also to infer that the previously mentioned weapon was a knife.

Thus, a major question about these effects of predictability is whether the effect occurs because the manipulation actually modulates the extraction of visual information in the initial encoding of the word, or whether the unpredictable word is harder to integrate into the sentence context, just as *knife* is harder to process in the above example if it is not clear from prior context that the murder weapon is a knife. Balota et al. (1985) examined this question by looking at the joint effects of predictability of a target word and the availability of the visual information of the target word. Participants were given two versions of a sentence—one that was highly predictable from prior sentence context or one that was not predictable (e.g., *Since the wedding day was today, the baker rushed the wedding* cake/pies *to the reception*). The availability of visual information was manipulated by changing the parafoveal preview. Prior to when a reader's eyes crossed a boundary in the text (e.g., the *n* in *wedding*), the parafoveal preview letter string was either identical to the target (e.g., *cake* for *cake* and *pies* for *pies*), visually similar to the target (*cahc* for *cake* and *picz* for *pies*), identical to the alternative word (*pies* for *cake* and vice versa), or visually similar to the alternative word (*picz* for *cake* and *cahc* for *pies*). The results replicated earlier findings that predictable words are skipped more often than are unpredictable words, but more importantly, visually similar previews facilitated fixation times on predictable words more than on unpredictable words. Moreover, there was a difference in the preview benefit for *cake* and *cahc,* but there was no difference in the benefit for *pies* and *picz,* so that readers were able to extract more visual information (i.e., ending letters) from a wider region of the parafovea when the target was predictable as compared to unpredictable. The fact that predictability interacts with these visual variables indicates that at least part of the effect of predictability is on initial encoding processes. If it merely had an effect after the word was identified, one would have no reason to expect it to interact with these orthographic variables.

Resolution of Ambiguity

The studies we have discussed up to this point clearly show that there are powerful effects of context on word identification in reading. However, they don't make clear what level or levels of word identification are influencing the progress of the eyes through the text. For example, virtually all the phenomena discussed so far could merely be reflecting the identification of the orthographic or phonological form of a word.

The studies we discuss in the following section have tried to understand how quickly the meaning of a word is understood and how the surrounding sentential context interacts with the this process of meaning extraction. Two ways in which researchers have tried to understand these processes are (a) resolution of lexical ambiguity and (b) resolution of syntactic ambiguity.

There are now a large number of eye movement studies (see Binder & Rayner, 1998; Duffy, Morris, & Rayner, 1988; Kambe, Rayner, & Duffy, 2001; Rayner & Duffy, 1986; Rayner & Frazier, 1989; Rayner, Pacht, & Duffy, 1994; Sereno, Pacht, & Rayner, 1992) that have examined how lexically ambiguous words (like *straw*) are processed during reading. Such lexically ambiguous words potentially allow one to understand when and how the several possible meanings of a word are encoded. That is, the orthographic and phonological forms of a word like *straw* do not allow you to determine what the intended meaning of the word is (e.g., whether it is a drinking straw or a dried piece of grass). Clearly, for such words, there is no logical way to determine which meaning is intended if the word is seen in isolation, and the determination of the intended meaning in a sentence depends on the sentential context. As indicated previously, of greatest interest is how quickly the meaning or meanings of the word are extracted and at what point the sentential context comes in and helps to disambiguate between the two (or more generally, several) meanings of an ambiguous word. To help think about the issues, consider two extreme possibilities. One is that all meanings of ambiguous words are always extracted, and only then does the context come in and help the reader choose which was the intended meaning (if it can). The other extreme would be that context always enters the disambiguation process early and that it blocks all but the intended meaning from being activated. As we will see in the following discussion, the truth is somewhere between these extremes.

Two key variables that experimenters have manipulated to understand the processing of lexically ambiguous words are (a) whether the information in the context prior to the ambiguous word allows one to disambiguate the meaning and (b) the relative frequencies of the two meanings. To make the findings as clear as possible, the manipulations on each of the variables are fairly extreme. In the case of the prior context, either it is *neutral* (i.e., it gives no information about which of the two meanings is intended) or it is strongly biasing (i.e., when people read the part of the sentence up to the target word and are asked to judge which meaning was intended, they almost always give the intended meaning). In the sentences in which the prior context does not disambiguate the meaning, however, the following context does. Thus, in all cases, the meaning of the ambiguous word should be clear at the end of the sentence. For the relative frequencies of the two meanings, experimenters either choose words that are *balanced* (like *straw*), for which the two likely meanings are equally frequent in the language, or they chose ones for which one of the meanings is highly *dominant* (such as *bank,* for which the *financial institution* meaning is much more frequent than the *slope* meaning). To simplify exposition, in this discussion we assume that these ambiguous words have only two distinct meanings, although many words have several shades of meaning, such as slight differences in the *slope* meaning of bank.

The basic findings from this research indicate that both meaning dominance and contextual information influence the processing of such words. When there is a neutral prior context, readers look longer at balanced ambiguous words (like *straw*) than they do at control words matched in length and word frequency. This evidence suggests that both meanings of the ambiguous word have been accessed and that the conflict between the two meanings is causing some processing difficulty. However, when the prior context disambiguates the meaning that should be instantiated, fixation time on a balanced ambiguous word is no longer than it is on the control word. Thus, for these balanced ambiguous words, the contextual information helps readers choose the appropriate meaning quickly—apparently before they move on to the next word in the text. In contrast, for ambiguous words for which one meaning is much more dominant (i.e., much more frequent) than the other, readers look no longer at the ambiguous word than they do at the control word when the prior context is neutral. Thus, it appears in these cases that only the dominant meaning is fully accessed and that there is little or no conflict between the two meanings. However, when the following parts of the sentence make it clear that the less frequent meaning should be instantiated, fixation times on the disambiguating information are quite long and regressions back to the target word are frequent (also indicating that the reader incorrectly selected the dominant meaning and now has to reaccess the subordinate meaning). Conversely, when the prior disambiguating information instantiates the less frequent meaning of the ambiguous word, readers' gaze durations on the ambiguous word are lengthened (relative to an unambiguous control word). Thus, in this case, it appears that the contextual information increases the level of activation for the less frequent meaning so that the two meanings are in competition (just as the two meanings of a balanced ambiguous word are in competition in a neutral context).

In sum, the data on lexically ambiguous words make clear that the meaning of a word is processed quite rapidly: The meaning of an ambiguous word, in at least some cases, is apparently determined before the saccade to the next word is programmed. Moreover, it appears that context, at least in some cases, enters into the assignment of meaning early: It can either shorten the time spent on a word (when it boosts the activation of one of two equally dominant meanings) or prolong the time spent on a word (when it boosts the activation of the subordinate meaning). For a more complete exposition of the theoretical ideas in this section (the reordered access model), see Duffy et al., 1988, and Duffy, Kambe, and Rayner, 2001.

A second type of ambiguity that readers commonly encounter is syntactic ambiguity. For example, consider a sentence like *While Mary was mending the sock fell off her lap.* When one has read the sentence up to *sock* (i.e., *While Mary was mending the sock*), the function of the phrase *the sock* is ambiguous: It could either be the object of *was mending* or it could be (as it turns out to be in the sentence) the subject of a subordinate clause. How do readers deal with such ambiguities? Similar types of question arise with this type of ambiguity as with lexical ambiguity. One obvious question is whether readers are constructing a syntactic representation of the sentence on line, so to speak, or whether syntactic processing lags well behind encoding individual words. For example, one possibility is that there is no problem with such ambiguities because they are temporary—that is, if the reader waits until the end of the sentence before constructing a parse of the sentence, then there may be no ambiguity problem. In contrast, if such ambiguities cause readers problems, then one has evidence that syntactic processing, like meaning processing, is more on line and closely linked in time to the word identification process.

The data on this issue are quite clear, as many studies have demonstrated that such temporary ambiguities do indeed cause processing difficulty; furthermore, data indicate that these processing difficulties often can occur quite early (i.e., immediately when the eyes encounter the point of ambiguity). For example, Frazier and Rayner (1982) used sentences like the *While Mary was mending the sock fell off her lap* example previously cited. They found that when readers first came to the word *fell*, they either made very long fixations on it or they regressed back to an earlier point in the sentence (where their initial parse would have gone astray). A full explanation of this phenomenon would require going into considerable detail on linguistic theories of parsing, a topic that is beyond the scope of this chapter (see the chapter by Treiman, Clifton, Meyer, & Wurm in this volume for a fuller treatment on this subject). However, the explanation, in one sense, is similar to the lexical ambiguity situation in which one meaning is dominant—that is, in many cases one syntactic structure is dominant over the other. In this case, assigning the direct object function to *the sock* is highly preferred. From the data, it thus becomes clear that readers initially adopt this incorrect interpretation of the sentence (are led up the garden path, so to speak), and only then can construct the correct parse of the sentence with some difficulty. The phenomenon is somewhat different from lexical ambiguity because (a) the dominance of one interpretation over another is not easily modified by context manipulations, and (b) it appears that the reinterpretation needs to be constructed rather than accessed, as is the case with a different meaning of an ambiguous word (Binder, Duffy, & Rayner, 2001).

Summary

As discussed in this section, the ease or difficulty with which readers process words is affected not only by lexical factors such as word frequency and word length, but also by higher level, postlexical factors (such as those involved in text integration) as well. It has been argued that many variables, such as word frequency, contextual constraint, semantic relationships between words, lexical ambiguity, and phonological ambiguity influence the time it takes to access a word. However, it seems unlikely that syntactic disambiguation effects (e.g., the fact that fixation times on syntactically disambiguating words are longer than fixation times on words that are not syntactically disambiguating) are due to the relatively low-level processes involved in lexical access. One plausible framework for thinking about these effects (see Carroll & Slowiaczek, 1987; Hyönä, 1995; Pollatsek, 1993; Rayner & Morris, 1990; Reichle, Pollatsek, Fisher, & Rayner, 1998) is that lexical access is the primary engine driving the eyes forward, but that higher level (postlexical) processes may also influence fixation times when there is a problem (e.g., a syntactic ambiguity).

MODELS OF EYE MOVEMENT CONTROL

Earlier in this chapter we outlined some models of word identification. However, these models only take into account the processing of words in isolation and are not specifically designed to account for factors that are part and parcel of fluent reading (e.g., the integration of information across eye movements, context effects, etc.). In the past, modelers have tended to focus on one aspect of reading and have tended to neglect others. The models of LaBerge and Samuels (1974) and Gough (1972), for example, focused on word encoding, whereas Kintsch and van Dijk's (1978) model mainly addressed integration of text. Although having such a narrow focus on a model of reading is perhaps not ideal, there is some logic behind such an approach. Models that are broad in scope tend to suffer from a lack of specificity. The reader model of Just and Carpenter (1980; see also Thibadeau, Just, & Carpenter, 1982) illustrates one example of this difficulty. It attempted to account for the reading comprehension processes ranging from individual eye fixations to the integration of words into sentence context (e.g., clauses). Although it was a comprehensive and highly flexible model of reading, its relatively nebulous nature made it difficult for researchers to use the model to make specific predictions about the reading process.

In the past few years, however, a number of models have been proposed that have been generally designed to expand upon models of word perception and specifically designed to explain and predict eye movement behavior during fluent reading. Because these models are based upon the relatively observable behavior of the eyes, they allow researchers to make specific predictions about the reading process. However, as with many issues in reading, the nature of eye movement models is a matter of controversy. Eye movement models can be separated into two general categories: *oculomotor* models (e.g., O'Regan, 1990, 1992), which posit that eye movements are primarily controlled by low-level mechanical (oculomotor) factors and are only indirectly related to ongoing language processing; and *processing* models (Morrison, 1984; Henderson & Ferreira, 1990; Just & Carpenter, 1980; Pollatsek, Reichle, & Rayner, in press; Reichle et al., 1998; Reichle, Rayner, & Pollatsek, 1999), which presume that lexical and other moment-to-moment cognitive processing are important influences on when the eyes move. Although space prohibits an extensive discussion of the pros and cons of each of these models, in this section we briefly delineate some of the more influential contributions to the field.

According to oculomotor models, the decision of where to move the eyes is determined both by visual properties of text (e.g., word length, spaces between words) and by the limitations in visual acuity that we discussed in a previous section. Furthermore, the length of time spent actually viewing any given word is postulated to be primarily a function of where the eyes have landed within the word. That is to say, the location of our fixations within words is not random. Instead, there is a *preferred viewing location*—as we read, our eyes tend to land somewhere between the middle and the beginning of words (Radach & McConkie, 1998; Rayner, 1979). Vitu (1991) also found that although readers' eyes tended to land on or near this preferred viewing location, when they viewed longer words (101 letters), readers initially fixated near the beginning of the word and then made another fixation near the end of the word (Rayner & Morris, 1992).

One of the more prominent oculomotor models is the *strategy-tactics model* (O'Regan, 1990, 1992; Reilly & O'Regan, 1998). The model accounts for the aforementioned landing position effects by stipulating that words are most easily identified when they are fixated just to the left of the middle of the word, but that readers may adopt one of two possible reading strategies—one riskier, so to speak, than the other. According to the risky strategy, readers can just try to move their eyes so that they fixate on this optimal viewing position within each word. In addition, readers may also use a more careful strategy, so that when their eyes land on a nonoptimal location (e.g., too far toward the end of the word), they can refixate and move their eyes to the other end of the word.

Without going into too much detail, the strategy-tactics models make some specific predictions about the nature of eye movements during reading. For example, they predict that the probability of a reader's refixating a word should only be a function of low-level visual factors (such as where the eyes landed in the word) and that it should not be influenced by linguistic processing. However, Rayner et al. (1996) found that the probability of a refixation was higher for words of lower frequency than for words of higher frequency even when the length of the two words was matched. Due to this and other difficulties, many researchers believe that oculomotor models are incomplete and that, although they do give good explanations of how lower level oculomotor factors influence reading, they largely ignore the influence of linguistic factors such as word frequency and word predictability.

As we discussed earlier, readers' eye movements are influenced by factors other than just word frequency (e.g., predictability, context, etc.). Given the influence of these linguistic variables, some researchers have developed models that are based upon the assumption that eye movements are influenced by both lexical (linguistic) factors and by moment-to-moment comprehension processes. It should be noted that these models generally do not exclude the influence of the low-level oculomotor strategies inherent in oculomotor models, but they posit that this influence is small relative to that of cognitive factors. Overall, then, processing theorists posit that the decision of when to move the eyes (fixation duration) is primarily a function of linguistic-cognitive processing, and the decision of where to move the eyes is a function of visual factors.

Although a number of models (e.g., Morrison, 1984) have utilized such a framework, the most recent and extensive attempt to predict eye movement behavior during reading is the E-Z Reader model (Reichle & Rayner, 2001; Reichle et al., 1998; Reichle et al., 1999). Currently, E-Z reader includes a number of variables that have been found to influence both fixation durations and fixation locations. Importantly, its computational framework has been used to both simulate and predict eye movement behavior. Although the E-Z Reader model is complex, it essentially consists of four processes: a familiarity check, the completion of lexical access (i.e., word recognition), the programming of eye movements, and the eye movements themselves. When a reader first attends to a word, (which is usually before the reader fixates the word) lexical access of the fixated word begins. However, before lexical access is complete, a rougher familiarity check is completed first. The familiarity check is a function of the word's frequency in the language, its contextual predictability, and the distance of the word from the center of the fovea. (It may be the point at which a reasonable match is made with either the orthographic or phonological entry in the lexicon.) After the familiarity check has been completed, an initial eye-movement program to the next word is initiated and the lexical access process continues (in parallel), either of which may be completed first. Finally, lexical access is completed (perhaps this reflects when the meaning of the word is encoded).

The model has been able to account successfully for many of the findings from the eye movement literature. However, it is admittedly incomplete, as the only cognitive processes that are posited to influence eye movements relate to word identification, whereas phenomena such as the syntactic ambiguity studies we briefly discussed earlier indicate that language processes of a somewhat higher order influence eye movements as well. One way to think of the E-Z reader model is that it explains the mechanisms that drive the eyes forward in reading and that higher order processes, such as syntactic parsing and constructing the meanings of sentence and paragraphs, lag behind this process of comprehending words and do not usually intervene in the movement of the eyes. Given that these higher order processes lag behind word identification, it would probably slow skilled reading appreciably if the eyes had to wait for successful completion of these processes. We think that a more likely scenario is that these higher order processes intervene in the normal forward movement of the eyes (driven largely by word identification, as in the E-Z reader model) only when a problem is detected (such as an incorrect parse of the sentence in the syntactic ambiguity example discussed earlier); then the so-called normal processing is interrupted and a signal goes out either not to move the eyes forward, to execute a regression back to the likely point of difficulty and begin to recompute a new syntactic or higher-order discourse structure, or both (see chapter by Treiman, Clifton, Meyer, & Wurm in this volume).

CONCLUSIONS

For the past century, researchers have struggled to understand the complexities of the myriad cognitive processes involved in reading. In this chapter we have discussed only a few of these processes, and we have primarily focused on the visual processes that are responsible for word identification during reading, both in isolation and in context. Although many issues still remain unresolved, a growing body of experimental data have emerged that has allowed researchers to develop a number of models and computer simulations to better explain and predict reading phenomena.

So what do we really know about reading? Many researchers would agree that words are accessed through some type of abstract letter identities (Coltheart, 1981; Rayner et al., 1980), and that letters (at least to some extent) may be processed in parallel. It is also clear that sound codes are somehow involved in word identification, but the details involved in this process are not clear. We do know, for example, that words' phonological representations are activated relatively early (perhaps within 30–40 ms and most likely even before a word is fixated). The time course of phonological processing would seem to indicate that sound codes are used to access word meaning, but studies that have attempted to study this issue directly have been criticized for a variety of reasons. Overall, it seems likely that there are two possible routes to word meaning: a direct letter-to-meaning lookup and an indirect constructive mechanism that utilizes sound codes and the spelling-to-sound rules of a language. However, the internal workings of these two mechanisms are underspecified, and researchers are still speculating on the nature of words' sound codes (e.g., are they real or abstract?).

Although we may get the subjective impression that we are able to see many words at the same time when we read, the amount of information we can extract from text is actually quite small (though we may realize that there are multiple lines of text or that there are many wordlike objects on the page). Furthermore, the process by which we extract information from this limited amount of text is somewhat complex. We are able to extract information from more than one word in a fixation, and some information that is obtained during one fixation may be used on the next fixation. Hence, the processing of words during reading is both a function of the word being fixated as well as the next word or two within the text.

The time spent looking at a word is a function of a variety of factors including its length, frequency, sound characteristics, morphology, and predictability. However, even before a word is fixated, some information has already been extracted from it. On some occasions, a word can be fully identified and skipped. Most of the time, however, partial information is extracted and integrated with the information seen when it is fixated. The extent to which parafoveal processing aids identification of a word on the next fixation is still under examination, but readers are at least able to integrate abstract letter information and some sound information across the two fixations. In addition, the predictability of a word within a sentence context has an effect on the speed of word identification, with predictable words processed faster than are unpredictable words. The reasons for this are a matter of debate. However, effects of context on word identification are generally small, and much of the work on word perception suggests that visual information can be processed quickly even without the aid of context. Thus, predictability and other contextual factors may actually only play a limited role in word processing in reading. More specifically, as Balota et al. (1985) have shown, context primarily influences the amount of information that may be extracted from the parafovea and thus, more generally, context may become increasingly important when visual information is poor.

REFERENCES

Altarriba, J., Kambe, G., Pollatsek, A., & Rayner, K. (2001). Semantic codes are not used in integrated information across eye fixations in reading: Evidence from fluent Spanish-English bilinguals. *Perception & Psychophysics, 63,* 875–890.

Balota, D. A. (1983). Automatic semantic activation and episodic memory encoding. *Journal of Verbal Learning and Verbal Behavior, 22,* 88–104.

Balota, D. A., & Chumbley, J. I. (1984). Are lexical decisions a good measure of lexical access? The role of word frequency in the neglected decision stage. *Journal of Experimental Psychology: Human Perception and Performance, 10,* 340–357.

Balota, D. A., & Chumbley, J. I. (1985). The locus of word-frequency effects in the pronunciation task: Lexical access and/or production? *Journal of Memory and Language, 24,* 89–106.

Balota, D. A., Pollatsek, A., & Rayner, K. (1985). The interaction of contextual constraints and parafoveal visual information in reading. *Cognitive Psychology, 17,* 364–390.

Balota, D. A., & Rayner, K. (1983). Parafoveal visual information and semantic contextual constraints. *Journal of Experimental Psychology: Human Perception and Performance, 9,* 726–738.

Baron, J., & Strawson, C. (1976). Use of orthographic and word-specific knowledge in reading words aloud. *Journal of Experimental Psychology: Human Perception and Performance, 2,* 386–393.

Baron, J., & Thurston, I. (1973). An analysis of the word superiority effect. *Cognitive Psychology, 4,* 207–228.

Bauer, D., & Stanovich, K. E. (1980). Lexical access and the spelling-to-sound regularity effect. *Memory & Cognition, 8,* 424–432.

Becker, C. A. (1985). What do we really know about semantic context effects during reading? In D. Besner, T. G. Waller, & G. E. MacKinnon (Eds.), *Reading research: Advances in theory and practice* (pp. 125–166). New York: Academic Press.

Besner, D., Coltheart, M., & Davelaar, E. (1984). Basic processes in reading: Computation of abstract letter identities. *Canadian Journal of Psychology, 38,* 126–134.

Besner, D., Stolz, J. A., & Boutilier, C. (1997). The Stroop effect and the myth of automaticity. *Psychonomic Bulletin & Review, 4,* 221–225.

Besner, D., Twilley, L., McCann, R. S., & Seergobin, K. (1990). On the association between connectionism and data: Are a few words necessary? *Psychological Review, 97,* 432–446.

Binder, K. S., Duffy, S. A., & Rayner, K. (2001). The effects of thematic fit and discourse context in syntactic ambiguity resolution. *Journal of Memory and Language, 44,* 297–324.

Binder, K. S., Pollatsek, A., & Rayner, K. (1999). Extraction of information to the left of the fixated word in reading. *Journal of Experimental Psychology: Human Perception and Performance, 25,* 1142–1158.

Binder, K. S., & Rayner, K. (1998). Contextual strength does not modulate the subordinate bias effect: Evidence from eye fixations and self-paced reading. *Psychonomic Bulletin & Review, 5,* 271–276.

Blanchard, H. E., Pollatsek, A., & Rayner, K. (1989). The acquisition of parafoveal word information in reading. *Perception & Psychophysics, 46,* 85–94.

Carpenter, P. A., & Just, M. A. (1983). What your eyes do while your mind is reading. In K. Rayner (Ed.), *Eye movements in reading: Perceptual and language processes* (pp. 275–307). New York: Academic Press.

Carr, T. H., McCauley, C., Sperber, R. D., & Parmelee, C. M. (1982). Words, pictures, and priming: On semantic activation, conscious identification, and the automaticity of information processing. *Journal of Experimental Psychology: Human Perception and Performance, 8,* 757–777.

Carr, T. H., & Pollatsek, A. (1985). Recognizing printed words: A look at current models. In D. Besner, T. G. Waller, & G. E. MacKinnon (Eds.), *Reading research: Advances in theory and practice* (Vol. 5, pp. 2–82). Orlando, FL: Academic Press.

Carroll, P. J., & Slowiaczek, M. L. (1987). Models and modules: Multiple pathways to the language processor. In J. L. Garfield (Ed.), *Modularity in knowledge representation and natural-language understanding* (pp. 221–248). Cambridge, MA: MIT Press.

Coltheart, M. (1978). Lexical access in simple reading tasks. In G. Underwood (Ed.), *Strategies of information processing* (pp. 151–216). San Diego, CA: Academic Press.

Coltheart, M. (1981). Disorders of reading and their implications for models of normal reading. *Visible Language, 15,* 245–286.

Coltheart, M., Curtis, B., Atkins, P., & Haller, M. (1993). Models of reading aloud: Dual-route and parallel-distributed-processing approaches. *Psychological Review, 100,* 589–608.

Coltheart, M., Patterson, K., & Marshall, J. (1980). *Deep dyslexia.* London: Routledge & Kegan Paul.

Coltheart, M., Rastle, K., Perry, C., Langdon, R., & Ziegler, J. (2001). DRC: A dual route cascaded model of visual word recognition and reading aloud. *Psychological Review, 108,* 204–256.

Crowder, R. G., & Wagner, R. K. (1992). *The Psychology of reading*. New York: Oxford University Press.

Daneman, M., & Reingold, E. M. (1993). What eye fixations tell us about phonological recoding during reading. *Canadian Journal of Experimental Psychology, 47,* 153–178.

Daneman, M., & Reingold, E. M. (2000). Do readers use phonological codes to activate word meanings? Evidence from eye movements. In A. Kennedy, R. Radach, D. Heller, & J. Pynte (Eds.), *Reading as a perceptual process* (pp. 447–474). Amsterdam: North Holland.

Daneman, M., Reingold, E. M., & Davidson, M. (1995). Time course of phonological activation during reading: Evidence from eye fixations. *Journal of Experimental Psychology: Learning, Memory, and Cognition, 21,* 884–898.

DenBuurman, R., Boersma, T., & Gerrissen, J. F. (1981). Eye movements and the perceptual span in reading. *Reading Research Quarterly, 16,* 227–235.

Dodge, R. (1900). Visual perception during eye movement. *Psychological Review, 7,* 454–465.

Duffy, S. A., Kambe, G., & Rayner, K. (2001). The effect of prior disambiguating context on the comprehension of ambiguous words: Evidence from eye fixations. In D. Gorfein (Ed.), *On the consequences of meaning selection* (pp. 27–43). Washington, DC: American Psychological Association.

Duffy, S. A., Morris, R. K., & Rayner, K. (1988). Lexical ambiguity and fixation times in reading. *Journal of Memory and Language, 27,* 429–446.

Ehrlich, S. F., & Rayner, K. (1981). Contextual effects on word perception and eye movements during reading. *Journal of Verbal Learning and Verbal Behavior, 20,* 641–655.

Evett, L. J., & Humphreys, G. W. (1981). The use of abstract graphemic information in lexical access. *Quarterly Journal of Experimental Psychology, 33A,* 325–350.

Fischler, I., & Bloom, P. (1979). Automatic and attentional processes in the effects of sentence context on word recognition. *Journal of Verbal Learning and Verbal Behavior, 18,* 1–20.

Frazier, L., & Rayner, K. (1982). Making and correcting errors during sentence comprehension: Eye movements in the analysis of structurally ambiguous sentences. *Cognitive Psychology, 14,* 178–210.

Gautier, V., O'Regan, J. K., & LaGargasson, J. F. (2000). 'The skipping' revisited in French: programming saccades to skip the article 'les'. *Vision Research, 40,* 2517–2531.

Gibson, E. J. (1971). Perceptual learning and the theory of word perception. *Cognitive Psychology, 2,* 351–368.

Gough, P. B. (1972). One second of reading. In J. F. Kavanagh & I. G. Mattingly (Eds.), *Language by ear and by eye* (pp. 331–358). Cambridge, MA: MIT Press.

Harm, M. W., & Seidenberg, M. S. (1999). Phonology, reading acquisition, and dyslexia: Insights from connectionist models. *Psychological Review, 106,* 491–528.

Hawkins, H. L., Reicher, G. M., Rogers, M., & Peterson, L. (1976). Flexible coding in work recognition. *Journal of Experimental Psychology: Human Perception and Performance, 2,* 380–385.

Healy, A. F. (1976). Detection errors on the word *the*: Evidence for reading units larger than letters. *Journal of Experimental Psychology, 2,* 235–242.

Henderson, J. M., Dixon, P., Petersen, A., Twilley, L. C., & Ferreira, F. (1995). Evidence for the use of phonological representations during transsaccadic word recognition. *Journal of Experimental Psychology: Human Perception and Performance, 21,* 82–97.

Henderson, J. M., & Ferreira, F. (1990). Effects of foveal processing difficulty on the perceptual span in reading: Implications for attention and eye movement control. *Journal of Experimental Psychology: Learning, Memory, and Cognition, 16,* 417–429.

Henderson, J. M., & Ferreira, F. (1993). Eye movement control during reading: Fixation measures reflect foveal but not parafoveal processing difficulty. *Canadian Journal of Experimental Psychology, 47,* 201–221.

Huey, E. B. (1908). *The psychology and pedagogy of reading.* New York: Macmillan.

Hyönä, J. (1995). Do irregular letter combinations attract readers' attention? Evidence from fixation locations in words. *Journal of Experimental Psychology: Human Perception and Performance, 21,* 68–81.

Hyönä, J., & Niemi, P. (1990). Eye movements in repeated reading of a text. *Acta Psychologica, 73,* 259–280.

Hyönä, J., & Olson, R. K. (1995). Eye movement patterns among dyslexic and normal readers: Effects of word length and word frequency. *Journal of Experimental Psychology: Learning, Memory, and Cognition, 21,* 1430–1440.

Hyönä, J., & Pollatsek, A. (1998). Reading Finnish compound words: Eye fixations are affected by component morphemes. *Journal of Experimental Psychology: Human Perception and Performance, 24,* 1612–1627.

Ikeda, M., & Saida, S. (1978). Span of recognition in reading. *Vision Research, 18,* 83–88.

Inhoff, A. W. (1984). Two stages of word processing during eye fixations in the reading of prose. *Journal of Verbal Learning and Verbal Behavior, 23,* 612–624.

Inhoff, A. W. (1989). Parafoveal processing of words and saccade computation during eye fixations in reading. *Journal of Experimental Psychology: Human Perception and Performance, 15,* 544–555.

Inhoff, A. W., & Briihl, D. (1991). Semantic processing of unattended text during selective reading: How the eyes see it. *Perception & Psychophysics, 49,* 289–294.

Inhoff, A. W., & Liu, W. (1998). The perceptual span and oculomotor activity during the reading of Chinese sentences. *Journal of*

Experimental Psychology: Human Perception and Performance, 24, 20–34.

Inhoff, A. W., & Rayner, K. (1986). Parafoveal word processing during eye fixations in reading: Effects of word frequency. *Perception & Psychophysics, 40,* 431–439.

Inhoff, A. W., Starr, M. S., & Shindler, K. (2000). Is the processing of words during a fixation of text strictly serial? *Perception & Psychophysics, 62,* 1474–1484.

Inhoff, A. W., & Topolski, R. (1992). Lack of semantic activation from unattended text during passage reading. *Bulletin of the Psychonomic Society, 30,* 365–366.

Ishida, T., & Ikeda, M. (1989). Temporal properties of information extraction in reading studied by a text-mask replacement technique. *Journal of the Optical Society A: Optics and Image Science, 6,* 1624–1632.

Jared, D., Levy, B., & Rayner, K. (1999). The role of phonology in the activation of word meanings during reading: Evidence from proofreading and eye movements. *Journal of Experimental Psychology: General, 128*(3), 219–264.

Just, M. A., & Carpenter, P. A. (1980). A theory of reading: From eye fixations to comprehension. *Psychological Review, 87,* 329–354.

Just, M. A., & Carpenter, P. A. (1987). *The psychology of reading and language comprehension.* Newton, MA: Allyn & Bacon.

Kambe, G., G., Rayner, K., & Duffy, S. A. (2001). Global context effects on processing lexically ambiguous words. *Memory & Cognition, 29,* 363–372.

Kennedy, A. (2000). Parafoveal processing in word recognition. *Quarterly Journal of Experimental Psychology, 53A,* 429–455.

Kennedy, A., & Murray, W. S. (1987). The components of reading time: Eye movement patterns of good and poor readers. In J. K. O'Regan & A. Levy-Schoen (Eds.), *Eye movements: From physiology to cognition* (pp. 509–520). Amsterdam: North Holland.

Kennison, S. M., & Clifton, C. (1995). Determinants of parafoveal preview benefit in high and low working memory capacity readers: Implications for eye movement control. *Journal of Experimental Psychology: Learning, Memory, and Cognition, 21,* 68–81.

Kintsch, W., & van Dijk, T. A. (1978). Toward a model of text comprehension and production. *Psychological Review, 85,* 363–394.

Kleiman, G. M. (1975). Speech recoding in reading. *Journal of Verbal Learning and Verbal Behavior, 14,* 323–339.

Kliegl, R., Olson, R. K., & Davidson, B. J. (1982). Regression analyses as a tool for studying reading processes: Comments on Just and Carpenter's eye fixation theory. *Memory & Cognition, 10,* 287–296.

Kolers, P. (1972). Experiments in reading. *Scientific American, 227,* 84–91.

Krueger, L. (1970). Visual comparison in a redundant display. *Cognitive Psychology, 1,* 341–357.

LaBerge, D., & Samuels, J. (1974). Toward a theory of automatic information processing in reading. *Cognitive Psychology, 6,* 293–323.

Lesch, M. F., & Pollatsek, A. (1998). Evidence for the use of assembled phonology in accessing the meaning of printed words. *Journal of Experimental Psychology: Learning, Memory and Cognition, 24,* 573–592.

Levy, B. A. (1975). Vocalization and suppression effects in sentence memory. *Journal of Verbal Learning and Verbal Behavior, 14,* 304–316.

Lima, S. D. (1987). Morphological analysis in sentence reading. *Journal of Memory and Language, 26,* 84–99.

Lima, S. D., & Inhoff, A. W. (1985). Lexical access during eye fixations in reading: Effects of word-initial letter sequences. *Journal of Experimental Psychology: Human Perception and Performance, 11,* 272–285.

MacLeod, C. (1991). Half a century of research on the Stroop effect: An integrative review. *Psychological Bulletin, 109,* 163–203.

Marcel, A. J. (1983). Conscious and unconscious perception: Experiments on visual masking. *Cognitive Psychology, 15,* 197–237.

Matin, E. (1974). Saccadic suppression: A review. *Psychological Bulletin, 81,* 899–917.

McClelland, J. L., & O'Regan, J. K. (1981). Expectations increase the benefit derived from parafoveal visual information in reading words aloud. *Journal of Experimental Psychology: Human Perception and Performance, 7,* 634–644.

McClelland, J. L., & Rumelhart, D. E. (1981). An interactive activation model of context effects in letter perception: Part 1. An account of basic findings. *Psychological Review, 88,* 375–407.

McConkie, G. W., & Rayner, K. (1975). The span of the effective stimulus during a fixation in reading. *Perception & Psychophysics, 17,* 578–586.

McConkie, G. W., & Rayner, K. (1976). Asymmetry of the perceptual span in reading. *Bulletin of the Psychonomic Society, 8,* 365–368.

McConkie, G. W., & Zola, D. (1979). Is visual information integrated across successive fixations in reading? *Perception & Psychophysics, 25,* 221–224.

Meyer, D. E., & Schvaneveldt, R. W. (1971). Facilitation in recognizing pairs of words: Evidence of a dependence between retrieval operations. *Journal of Experimental Psychology, 90,* 227–234.

Meyer, D. E., Schvaneveldt, R. W., & Ruddy, M. G. (1974). Functions of graphemic and phonemic codes in visual word-recognition, *Memory & Cognition, 2,* 309–321.

Morris, R. K., Rayner, K., & Pollatsek, A. (1990). Eye movement guidance in reading: The role of parafoveal letter and space information. *Journal of Experimental Psychology: Human Perception and Performance, 16,* 268–281.

Morrison, R. E. (1984). Manipulation of stimulus onset delay in reading: Evidence for parallel programming of saccades. *Journal of Experimental Psychology: Human Perception and Performance, 10,* 667–682.

Murray, W. S. (1998). Parafoveal pragmatics. In G. Underwood (Ed.), *Eye guidance in reading and scene perception* (pp. 181–200). Oxford, UK: Elsevier.

Neisser, U. (1967). *Cognitive psychology.* New York: Appleton-Century-Crofts.

Niswander, E., Pollatsek, A., & Rayner K. (2000) The processing of derived and inflected suffixed words during reading. *Language and Cognitive Processes, 15,* 389–420.

O'Brien, E. J., Shank, D. M., Myers, J. L., & Rayner, K. (1988). Elaborative inferences during reading: Do they occur on-line? *Journal of Experimental Psychology: Learning, Memory, and Cognition, 14,* 410–420.

O'Regan, J. K. (1979). Eye guidance in reading: Evidence for linguistic control hypothesis. *Perception & Psychophysics, 25,* 501–509.

O'Regan, J. K. (1980). The control of saccade size and fixation duration in reading: The limits of linguistic control. *Perception & Psychophysics, 28,* 112–117.

O'Regan, J. K. (1990). Eye movements and reading. In E. Kowler (Ed.), *Eye movements and their role in visual and cognitive processes* (pp. 395–453). Amsterdam: Elsevier.

O'Regan, J. K. (1992). Optimal viewing position in words and the strategy-tactics theory of eye movements in reading. In K. Rayner (Ed.), *Eye movements and visual cognition: Scene perception and reading* (pp. 333–354). New York: Springer-Verlag.

Osaka, N. (1992). Size of saccade and fixation duration of eye movements during reading: Psychophysics of Japanese text processing. *Journal of the Optical Society of America A, 9,* 5–13.

Osaka, N., & Oda, K. (1991). Effective visual field size necessary for vertical reading during Japanese text processing. *Bulletin of the Psychonomic Society, 29,* 345–347.

Paap, K. R., Newsome, S. L., McDonald, J. E., & Schvaneveldt, R. W. (1982). An activation-verification model for letter and word recognition: The word superiority effect. *Psychological Review, 89,* 573–594.

Perfetti, C. A., & Hogaboam, T. W. (1975). The relationship between single word decoding and reading comprehension skill. *Journal of Educational Psychology, 67,* 461–469.

Plaut, D. C., McClelland, J. L., Seidenberg, M. S., & Patterson, K. (1996). Understanding normal and impaired word reading: Computational principles in quasi-regular domains. *Psychological Review, 103,* 56–115.

Pollatsek, A. (1993). Eye movements in reading. In D. M. Willows, R. S. Kruk, & E. Corcos (Eds.), *Visual processes in reading and reading disabilities* (pp. 105, 125–157). Hillsdale, NJ: Erlbaum.

Pollatsek, A., Bolozky, S., Well, A. D., & Rayner, K. (1981). Asymmetries in the perceptual span for Israeli readers. *Brain and Language, 14,* 174–180.

Pollatsek, A., Lesch, M., Morris, R. K., & Rayner, K. (1992). Phonological codes are used in integrating information across saccades in word identification and reading. *Journal of Experimental Psychology: Human Perception and Performance, 18,* 148–162.

Pollatsek, A., Raney, G. E., LaGasse, L., & Rayner, K. (1993) The use of information below fixation in reading and in visual search. *Canadian Journal of Experimental Psychology, 47,* 179–200.

Pollatsek, A., & Rayner, K. (1982). Eye movement control in reading: The role of word boundaries. *Journal of Experimental Psychology: Human Perception and Performance, 8,* 817–833.

Pollatsek, A., Rayner, K., & Balota, D. A. (1986). Inferences about eye movement control from the perceptual span in reading. *Perception & Psychophysics, 40,* 123–130.

Pollatsek, A., Reichle, E., & Rayner, K. (in press). Modeling eye movements in reading. In J. Hyönä, R. Radach, and H. Denbel (Eds.), *The mind's eyes: Cognitive and applied aspects of eye movements.* Oxford, UK: Elsevier.

Pollatsek, A., Tan, L.-H., & Rayner, K. (2000). The role of phonological codes in integrating information across saccadic eye movements in Chinese character identification. *Journal of Experimental Psychology: Human Perception and Performance, 26,* 607–633.

Radach, R., & McConkie, G. W. (1998) Determinants of fixation positions in words during reading. In G. Underwood (Ed.), *Eye guidance in reading and scene perception* (pp. 77–100). Oxford, UK: Elsevier.

Raney, G. E., & Rayner, K. (1995). Word frequency effects and eye movements during two readings of a text. *Canadian Journal of Experimental Psychology, 49,* 151–172.

Rayner, K. (1975). The perceptual span and peripheral cues in reading. *Cognitive Psychology, 7,* 65–81.

Rayner, K. (1977). Visual attention in reading: Eye movements reflect cognitive processes. *Memory & Cognition, 4,* 443–448.

Rayner, K. (1978). Eye movements in reading and information processing. *Psychological Bulletin, 85,* 618–660.

Rayner, K. (1979). Eye guidance in reading: Fixation locations within words. *Perception, 8,* 21–30.

Rayner, K. (1986). Eye movements and the perceptual span in beginning and skilled readers. *Journal of Experimental Child Psychology, 41,* 211–236.

Rayner, K. (1998). Eye movements in reading and information processing: 20 years of research. *Psychological Bulletin, 124,* 372–422.

Rayner, K., Balota, D. A., & Pollatsek, A. (1986). Against parafoveal semantic preprocessing during eye fixations in reading. *Canadian Journal of Psychology, 40,* 473–483.

Rayner, K., & Bertera, J. H. (1979). Reading without a fovea. *Science, 206,* 468–469.

Rayner, K., Binder, K., Ashby, J., & Pollatsek, A. (2001). Eye movement control in reading: Word predictability has little influence on initial landing positions in words. *Vision Research, 41,* 943–954.

Rayner, K., & Duffy, S. A. (1986). Lexical complexity and fixation times in reading: Effects of word frequency, verb complexity, and lexical ambiguity. *Memory & Cognition, 14,* 191–201.

Rayner, K., & Fischer, M. H. (1996). Mindless reading revisited: Eye movements during reading and scanning are different. *Perception & Psychophysics, 58,* 734–747.

Rayner, K., Fischer, M. H., & Pollatsek, A. (1998). Unspaced text interferes with both word identification and eye movement control. *Vision Research, 38,* 1129–1144.

Rayner, K., & Frazier, L. (1989). Selection mechanisms in reading lexically ambiguous words. *Journal of Experimental Psychology: Learning, Memory, and Cognition, 15,* 779–790.

Rayner, K., Inhoff, A. W., Morrison, R., Slowiaczek, M. L., & Bertera, J. H. (1981). Masking of foveal and parafoveal vision during eye fixations in reading. *Journal of Experimental Psychology: Human Perception and Performance, 7,* 167–179.

Rayner, K., & McConkie, G. W. (1976). What guides a reader's eye movements. *Vision Research, 16,* 829–837.

Rayner, K., McConkie, G. W., & Ehrlich, S. F. (1978). Eye movements and integrating information across fixations. *Journal of Experimental Psychology: Human Perception and Performance, 4,* 529–544.

Rayner, K., McConkie, G. W., & Zola, D. (1980). Integrating information across eye movements. *Cognitive Psychology, 12,* 206–226.

Rayner, K., & Morris, R. K. (1990). Do eye movements reflect higher order processes in reading? In R. Groner, G. d'Ydewalle, & R. Parnham (Eds.), *From eye to mind: Information acquisition in perception, search, and reading* (pp. 170–190). Amsterdam: North Holland.

Rayner, K., & Morris, R. K. (1992). Eye movement control in reading: Evidence against semantic preprocessing. *Journal of Experimental Psychology: Human Perception and Performance, 18,* 163–172.

Rayner, K., Pacht, J. M., & Duffy, S. A. (1994). Effects of prior encounter and global discourse bias on the processing of lexically ambiguous words: Evidence from eye fixations. *Journal of Memory and Language, 33,* 527–544.

Rayner, K., & Pollatsek, A. (1989). *The psychology of reading.* Englewood Cliffs, NJ: Prentice-Hall.

Rayner, K., Pollatsek, A., & Binder, K. S. (1998). Phonological codes and eye movements in reading. *Journal of Experimental Psychology: Learning, Memory and Cognition, 24,* 476–497.

Rayner, K., & Posnansky, C. (1978). Stages of processing in word identification. *Journal of Experimental Psychology: General, 107,* 64–80.

Rayner, K., & Raney, G. E. (1996). Eye movement control in reading and visual search: Effects of word frequency. *Psychonomic Bulletin & Review, 3,* 238–244.

Rayner, K., Raney, G. E., & Pollatsek, A. (1995). Eye movements and discourse processing. In R. F. Lorch & E. J. O'Brien (Eds.), *Sources of coherence in reading* (pp. 9–36). Hillsdale, NJ: Erlbaum.

Rayner, K., Sereno, S. C., Morris, R. K., Schmauder, A. R., & Clifton, C. (1989). Eye movements and on-line language comprehension processes. *Language and Cognition Processes, 4*(Special issue), 21–49.

Rayner, K., Sereno, S. C., & Raney, G. E. (1996). Eye movement control in reading: A comparison of two types of models. *Journal of Experimental Psychology: Human Perception and Performance, 22,* 1188–1200.

Rayner, K., & Springer, C. J. (1986). Graphemic and semantic similarity effects in the picture-word interference task. *British Journal of Psychology, 77,* 207–222.

Rayner, K., & Well, A. D. (1996). Effects of contextual constraint on eye movements in reading: A further examination. *Psychonomic Bulletin & Review, 3,* 504–509.

Rayner, K., Well, A. D., & Pollatsek, A. (1980). Asymmetry of the effective visual field in reading. *Perception & Psychophysics, 27,* 537–544.

Rayner, K., Well, A. D., Pollatsek, A., & Bertera, J. H. (1982). The availability of useful information to the right of fixation in reading. *Perception & Psychophysics, 31,* 537–550.

Reicher, G. M. (1969). Perceptual recognition as a function of meaningfulness of stimulus material. *Journal of Experimental Psychology, 81,* 275–280.

Reichle, E., Pollatsek, A., Fisher, D. L., & Rayner, K. (1998). Towards a model of eye movement control in reading. *Psychological Review, 105,* 125–157.

Reichle, E., & Rayner, K. (2001). Cognitive processing and models of reading. In G. K. Hung & K. J. Ciuffreda (Eds.), *Models of the visual system* (pp. 565–604). New York: Kluwer Academic/ Plenum Publishers.

Reichle, E., Rayner, K., & Pollatsek, A. (1999). Eye movement control in reading: Accounting for initial fixation locations and refixations within the E-Z Reader model. *Vision Research, 39,* 4403–4411.

Reilly, R., & O'Regan, J. K. (1998). Eye movement control in reading: A simulation of some word-targeting strategies. *Vision Research, 38,* 303–317.

Rosinski, R. R., Golinkoff, R. M., & Kukish, K. (1975). Automatic semantic processing in a picture-word interference task. *Child Development, 46,* 243–253.

Schuberth, R. E., & Eimas, P. D. (1977). Effects of context on the classification of words and nonwords. *Journal of Experimental Psychology: Human Perception and Performance, 3,* 27–36.

Schustack, M. W., Ehrlich, S. F., & Rayner, K. (1987). The complexity of contextual facilitation in reading: Local and global influences. *Journal of Memory and Language, 26,* 322–340.

Seidenberg, M. S., & McClelland, J. L. (1989). A distributed, developmental model of word recognition and naming. *Psychological Review, 96,* 523–568.

Seidenberg, M. S., & McClelland, J. L. (1990). More words but still no lexicon: Reply to Besner et al. (1990). *Psychological Review, 97,* 447–452

Sereno, S. C., Pacht, J. M., & Rayner, K. (1992). The effect of meaning frequency on processing lexically ambiguous words: Evidence from eye fixations. *Psychological Science, 3,* 296–300.

Sereno, S. C., & Rayner, K. (2000). Spelling-sound regularity effects on eye fixations in reading. *Perception & Psychophysics, 62*(2), 402–409.

Slowiaczek, M. L., & Clifton, C., (1980). Subvocalization and reading for meaning. *Journal of Verbal Learning and Verbal Behavior, 19,* 573–582.

Smith, F., Lott, D., & Cronnell, B. (1969). The effect of type size and case alternation on word identification. *American Journal of Psychology, 82,* 248–253.

Stanovich, K. E., & West, R. F. (1979). Mechanisms of sentence context effects in reading: Automatic activation and conscious attention. *Memory & Cognition, 7,* 77–85.

Stanovich, K. E., & West, R. F. (1983). On priming by a sentence context. *Journal of Experimental Psychology: General, 112,* 1–36.

Starr, M. S., & Fleming, K. K. (2001). A rose by any other name is not the same: The role of orthographic knowledge in homophone confusion errors. *Journal of Experimental Psychology: Learning, Memory, and Cognition, 27,* 744–760.

Stroop, J. R. (1935). Studies of interference in serial verbal reactions. *Journal of Experimental Psychology, 18,* 643–662.

Stone, G. O., & Van Orden, G. (1994). Building a resonance framework for word recognition using design and system principles. *Journal of Experimental Psychology: Human Perception and Performance, 20,* 1248–1268.

Thibadeau, R., Just, M. A., & Carpenter, P. A. (1982). A model of the time course and content of human reading. *Cognitive Science, 6,* 101–155.

Tulving, E., & Gold, C. (1963). Stimulus information and contextual information as determinants of tachistoscopic recognition of words. *Journal of Experimental Psychology, 66,* 319–327.

Underwood, G. (1985). Eye movements during the comprehension of written language. In A. W. Ellis (Ed.), *Progress in the psychology of language* (Vol. 2, pp. 45–71). London: Erlbaum.

Underwood, N. R., & McConkie, G. W. (1985). Perceptual span for letter distinctions during reading. *Reading Research Quarterly, 20,* 153–162.

Uhr, L. (1963). "Pattern recognition" computers as models for form perception. *Psychological Bulletin, 60,* 40–73

Van Orden, G. C. (1987). A rows is a rose: Spelling, sound, and reading. *Memory & Cognition, 15,* 181–198.

Van Orden, G. C., & Goldinger, S. D. (1994). Interdependence of form and function in cognitive systems explains perception of printed words. *Journal of Experimental Psychology: Human Perception and Performance, 20,* 1269–1291.

Van Orden, G. C., Johnston, J. C., & Hale, B. L. (1988). Word identification in reading proceeds from spelling to sound to meaning. *Journal of Experimental Psychology: Learning, Memory, and Cognition, 14,* 371–386.

Van Orden, G. C., Pennington, B. F., & Stone, G. O. (1990). Word identification in reading and the promise of subsymbolic psycholinguistics. *Psychological Review, 97,* 488–522.

Vitu, F. (1991). The influence of parafoveal processing and linguistic context on the optimal landing position effect. *Perception & Psychophysics, 50,* 58–75.

Wheeler, D. D. (1970). Processes in word recognition. *Cognitive Psychology, 1,* 59–85.

Wolverton, G. S., & Zola, D. (1983). The temporal characteristics of visual information extraction during reading. In K. Rayner (Ed.), *Eye movements in reading: Perceptual and language processes* (pp. 41–52). New York: Academic Press.

CHAPTER 21

Text Comprehension and Discourse Processing

KIRSTEN R. BUTCHER AND WALTER KINTSCH

Psychology is a newcomer to discourse analysis, which has been practiced for a long time by other disciplines. Indeed, discourse analysis in the form of rhetoric was among the first disciplines studied in our culture. This tradition continues strongly into our days, but it has spawned many offshoots, both within philosophy and beyond: Formal semantics has a long tradition (e.g., Seuren, 1985); within linguistics, text linguistics became important in the 1970s (Halliday & Hasan, 1976; van Dijk, 1972); natural language processing by computers and computational linguistics became prominent in the 1980s (e.g., Jurafsky & Martin, 2000); and, at about the same time, models of how discourse is processed were developed through cooperation of linguists, computer scientists, and psychologists (e.g., W. Kintsch & van Dijk, 1978; Schank & Abelson, 1977) as a branch of the new cognitive science. Research of the latter type is the concern of this chapter.

Before we focus on psychological process models of discourse comprehension, a comment is required on the two major issues that have existed throughout the long history of discourse analysis and that are still unresolved. The first controversy has to do with a difference in viewpoint. Some discourse analysts view language essentially as a means for information transmission. A speaker or writer intends to transmit information to a listener or reader. Information is factual, propositional. Researchers in this tradition focus on story understanding, memory for factual material presented in texts, learning from texts, and the inferences involved in this process. Examples of this approach are, for instance, the psychological work of W. Kintsch and van Dijk (1978) and the linguistic work reviewed by Lyons (1977). However, information transmission is only one function of language. Social interaction is another, and a competing research tradition focuses on this aspect of discourse. Language is often used not to transmit information, but rather to establish social roles, to regulate social interactions, to amuse, and to entertain. Labov (1972) or H. H. Clark (1996) exemplify this research tradition. Although most students of language would agree that both approaches are legitimate and valuable, the obviously desirable integration of these fields of research has not yet been achieved.

Since the days of Aristotle and Plato, some have viewed language as basically orderly and logical, at least in its underlying essence, while others have claimed that language is messy and anomalous by its very nature. The former tradition has tended to develop logical and mathematical theories of language. Such theories can be both elegant and highly informative (e.g., Barwise & Perry, 1983, for semantics; Chomsky, 1965, for syntax). However, the opposing tradition has always delighted in pointing out the gap between theory and reality, as well as the seemingly boundless irrationality of language and language use. Although this conflict continues unabated today, an intermediate position has emerged in recent years that may yet alter the nature of this debate. Connectionist models of language (Elman et al., 1996; also hybrid models like W. Kintsch, 1998) are formal, with all the advantages that mathematical models provide, but they do not employ the concept of logical rules. Thus, connectionist models may be better able to account for the disorderly part of language while retaining the important advantages of a mathematical model.

The comprehension processes involved in reading a text and in listening to spoken discourse are essentially the same (reading and listening comprehension are also discussed in this volume in the chapter by Rayner, Pollatsek, & Starr). Texts and conversations are very different in their properties and structure, task demands, and contextual constraints, but the comprehension processes are similar. That is, both make demands on working memory, both require relevant background knowledge, and both are constructive processes in which inferences and construction play a crucial role. We describe the features that set apart reading comprehension and comprehension of conversations, but most of what we have to say in this chapter holds for both.

In this chapter we first discuss the role of memory in text comprehension, focusing on short-term working memory and long-term working memory. Then we review studies that are concerned with what people remember from reading a text, and how they learn from reading a text. Of particular importance here is what a reader has to already know in order to be able to acquire new knowledge from a text, and the role of constructive processes in comprehension and learning. We then turn to a consideration of current models of comprehension and knowledge representations. Finally, we discuss experiments investigating the factors that influence comprehension, making comprehension easier or making it more difficult.

MEMORY AND TEXT COMPREHENSION

Working Memory

Text comprehension is a task that requires processing and integration of a sequential series of symbols; as such, memory processes—especially working memory, due to its storage and computational abilities—are strongly implicated in comprehension ability (Carpenter, Miyake, & Just, 1994; Just & Carpenter, 1987; also see the chapter in this volume by Nairne). Unlike early characterizations of working memory as a storage system used to hold a few chunks of information, working memory has come to be seen as a limited resource for which processing and storage demands compete. Working memory can be seen as a sort of attentional work space that keeps information active for short-term use while it directs cognitive resources for task performance.

It is easy to see how the demands required by text comprehension should draw heavily on working memory resources. At the same time text is decoded and processed, important ideas or current propositions must be maintained in memory and retrieved at key points in the comprehension process. Maintaining ideas or propositions from a text at the same time new text is analyzed is necessary to form inferences, develop an understanding of text coherence, recognize inconsistencies, and so on. Accordingly, researchers have come to regard working memory as a key component of comprehension processes and the possible source of individual differences in comprehension.

Daneman and Carpenter (1980; 1983) theorized that individual differences in working memory capacity could explain individual differences in reading comprehension. They argued that reading processes of poor readers make heavy demands on working memory that result in a trade-off compromising the working memory capacity for maintaining text information. As a result, poor readers are unable to make the appropriate connections between text necessary to recognize inconsistencies and, presumably, to link text and form inferences necessary for expert comprehension. To measure the functional capacity of working memory for reading, Daneman and Carpenter developed a measure called the reading-span test. This test requires readers to read aloud a series of unrelated sentences at the same time that they memorize the final word in each sentence. Sentences are presented in sets containing varied numbers of sentences, and the largest number of sentences for which a participant can recall all memorized final words in at least 60% of the sets of that size is defined as the reading span. Reading span differs among individuals—from about 2 to 5.5 for college students (Just & Carpenter, 1992)—but can also be influenced by text complexity or other demanding types of text processing (e.g., linguistic ambiguity or text distance).

When reading span is consistently tested, empirical evidence demonstrates that working memory capacity is a reliable predictor of proficiency in text processing. Daneman and Carpenter (1980, 1983) have linked reading spans to various tests of reading comprehension (including the verbal SAT) and have demonstrated that reading span can reliably predict the likelihood of a reader discovering inconsistencies in a text. In a series of experiments, Carpenter et al. (1994) demonstrated that reading span accounted for systematic differences in the way college students processed text. These authors argue that individuals with limited working memory capacity are disproportionately affected by manipulations that increase the demand on working memory resources during comprehension. The decline in performance by low-span individuals occurs regardless of whether the increase in demand is integrated into the comprehension task (for example, increasing syntactic complexity or introducing ambiguity into a text) or represents a demand external to the comprehension process (for example, a set of unrelated memory items).

Regardless of the source of memory demand, it is important to note that working memory capacity does not just affect the amount of information that can be retained during reading of a text. In fact, many of the systematic comprehension differences associated with working memory capacity reflect higher-level processes of text integration and representation. For example, Carpenter et al. (1994) found that high-span readers were more likely to keep multiple representations of a homograph active until context could be determined; they also found that high-span readers were better able to integrate text information that was separated by increasing amounts of intervening text than low-span readers. Similarly, Whitney, Ritchie, and Clark (1991) found that individuals with high working memory capacity were better able to maintain ambiguous interpretations of a text, whereas low-span individuals were much more likely to choose specific text interpretations earlier in their reading. Consistent with all these findings, calculation of the demands a text is likely to have on working memory has been shown to predict the actual comprehensibility of the text (Britton & Gulgoz, 1991; J. R. Miller & Kintsch, 1980).

Empirical evidence also ties working memory capacity directly to comprehension processes. Singer and Ritchot (1996) found that individuals with high reading spans were better able to verify bridging inferences about a text. Singer, Andrusiak, Reisdorf, and Black (1992) found that higher working memory capacity supported inference processing. Other studies have confirmed that working memory consistently predicts inference making and text learning (Haenggi & Perfetti, 1994; Myers, Cook, Kambe, Mason, & O'Brien, 2000). Finally, research has demonstrated that known components of working memory can be tied to specific types of inferential processes. Friedman and Miyake (2000) demonstrated that maintaining the spatial and causal aspects of a situation model—a type of cognitive representation of comprehended text that is discussed later in this chapter—could be tied to the visuospatial and verbal components, respectively, of working memory.

The implications of these studies are clear: Working memory has important and measurable ties to comprehension processes and, all else remaining equal, individuals with high working memory capacity are at a comprehension advantage. However, it should be noted that although working memory capacity has been shown to have a reliable influence on measures of inference and learning, other factors can be equally important in predicting comprehension skills. For example, domain knowledge can strongly influence the amount of learning an individual takes from a text; high domain knowledge can compensate for poor decoding skills, low working memory capacity, very demanding texts, and so on. As we discuss later in the chapter, many factors can influence the ultimate comprehension performance of an individual, and no single factor is sufficient to predict success or failure in comprehension.

Long-Term Working Memory in Discourse Comprehension

Working memory, as previously discussed, is our name for the information that is active and available in consciousness. Whereas text comprehension clearly depends upon active processing, storage, and retrieval of information, working memory is strictly limited in sheer capacity and in the duration for which items are kept active. Working memory limitations cannot explain empirical evidence that shows capable readers to be relatively insensitive to interruptions, to be resistant to interference, and to have accurate recall that far exceeds the capacity of working memory (for a summary, see W. Kintsch, 1998). Thus, working memory is clearly insufficient to manage the heavy demands of comprehension. Discourse comprehension requires ready access to a large amount of information, significantly more than laboratory measurements of the capacity of working memory indicate is available. Van Dijk and Kintsch (1983, p. 347) list the following memory requirements for discourse comprehension—information that must be available for analysis and reanalysis; graphemic and phonological information; words and phrases, often whole sentences; the propositional structure of the text, microstructure as well as the macrostructure (The concepts of text microstructure and macrostructure will be discussed later in this chapter; for now, consider the macrostructure to represent the high-level gist of a text and the microstructure to represent the detailed content of a text.); the emerging situation model; lexical knowledge and general world knowledge; and goals, subgoals, and the general task context. Each of these components of the memory system involved in text comprehension could exceed the capacity of short-term working memory—but they are all required for the process of comprehension, and are demonstrably used in that process. How can these facts about memory demands in comprehension be reconciled with the strong laboratory evidence for a strictly limited working memory capacity of three or four chunks?

Psychologists have sometimes despaired in the face of this puzzle, asserting that real-life memory is totally different from memory studied in the laboratory. Laboratory results have been claimed to be unnatural, irrelevant, and hence useless (Jenkins, 1974). Recalling information read in the daily paper at breakfast or retelling the complicated plot of a novel is quite easy; however, it takes an hour of hard work to memorize a list of 100 random words in the laboratory! An individual cannot repeat more than about nine digits on a digit span test, but the experienced physician keeps in mind seemingly endless chunks of patient information, laboratory data, relevant disease knowledge, alternative diagnoses, and so on. Such information can be shown to influence the physician's reasoning and decision processes—but how could it fit into the limited capacity working memory we have identified in laboratory research?

Ericsson and Kintsch (1995) have provided an answer to these questions, and were able to successfully reconcile everyday memory phenomena with the results of laboratory studies of memory since the days of Ebbinghaus. Their argument is based on a distinction between short-term working memory and long-term working memory. Short-term working memory is what has typically been studied in the laboratory; it plays an important role in discourse comprehension, as discussed in the previous section. Long-term working memory (LTWM) is different: It is not capacity limited, but it only functions under certain rather restrictive conditions. Nevertheless, these are the conditions under which we observe prodigious feats of memory in real life.

Long-term working memory (see also W. Kintsch, 1998; W. Kintsch, Patel, & Ericsson, 1999; LTWM is also discussed in this volume in the chapter by Leighton & Sternberg) is a skill experts acquire. In fact, becoming an expert in any cognitive task involves the acquisition of LTWM skills. The skill consists in the ability to access information in long-term memory via cues in short-term working memory without time-consuming and resource-demanding retrieval operations. Experts can access relevant information in their long-term memory quickly (in about 400 ms) and effortlessly. This accessible portion of their long-term memory becomes part of their working memory—their LTWM. How much information can be accessed depends on the nature and efficiency of the retrieval structures experts have formed, but there are no capacity limitations. Thus, experts retrieve task relevant knowledge and experiences quickly and without effort, and recall what they did with ease. Examples of such expert memory are the physician making a medical diagnosis, the chess master playing blindfold chess (for further discussion on development of expertise, see the chapter in this volume on Procedural Memory and Skill Acquisition by Johnson)—and all of us when we use our expertise in reading familiar materials, such as a story or the typical newspaper article.

Long-term working memory cannot be used in traditional laboratory experiments. Ebbinghaus wanted to study what he saw as pure memory unaffected by our daily experience; hence he invented the nonsense syllable. And although modern psychologists no longer use the nonsense syllable, they have followed Ebbinghaus's lead in excluding or controlling the role of experience in their experiments as carefully as is possible. The types of tasks used in traditional laboratory experiments thus remove the essential component of LTWM—experience. When it comes to repeating a string of digits or memorizing a list of words, we are all novices, and we cannot use whatever LTWM skills we might possess. However, when we read an article or participate in a conversation on a familiar topic, a lifetime of experiences and a rich store of knowledge become relevant. We comprehend as experts and remember as experts. Of course, our expertise is limited to certain familiar, frequently experienced topics, or to some restricted professional domain. If we read or listen outside our domain of expertise, we immediately become aware of our inability to comprehend what we read because we cannot activate the required background knowledge. In unfamiliar domains, our recall is equally limited because we do not have the knowledge that would allow the proficient and easy recall that occurs with familiar texts. Unfamiliar domains restrict the use of experience just as in the laboratory, where the experimenters carefully design their experiments in such a way to prevent us from using whatever knowledge we might have.

For the remainder of this section, assume someone is reading a simple text in a familiar domain—a straightforward story, for example. Alternatively, one could assume that someone is listening to a story, for example a soap opera. Although soap opera stories are rarely straightforward, they (like most stories we encounter) are about human affairs (no pun intended), motivations, actions, character—things we have experienced throughout our lives. We are familiar with these concepts in the form of texts, but primarily we understand them through our actions and interactions in the social world. Thus, we are highly familiar with most stories in general, with the words and syntax used in the story, and with the schematic structure of the story itself. In other words, the reader is an expert. In reading such a text, LTWM comes into play in two ways.

First of all, the reader activates relevant knowledge automatically. The necessary concepts, frames, scripts, schemata (Schank & Abelson, 1977), and personal experiences immediately link information in the text held in working memory to the reader's general knowledge and episodic memory. That does not mean that this knowledge enters into short-term working memory, or becomes conscious; it only means that it is available to be used, should there be any reason to use it. Text comprehension researchers have described this process as one of *making inferences* (W. Kintsch, 1993). This is not always an accurate description, if we mean by *making an inference* that some statement not directly contained in the text is derived from the text with the help of relevant background knowledge and becomes part of the mental representation of the text. That happens, or can happen, but knowledge activation does not necessarily imply an explicit inference. Activated knowledge simply becomes available for further use—if there is further use. There is a definite need for knowledge activation in many experiments, when the experimenter asks a question or presents a relevant word in a lexical decision task. In uncontrived situations the need for knowledge activation may arise spontaneously, as when a reader detects a gap in his or her understanding that can only be filled through some problem-solving activity involving that knowledge. But in the normal course of automatic reading comprehension, activated knowledge merely stands by in LTWM. For example, consider the bridging inference involved in the well-known sentence pair of Haviland and Clark (1974):

> We checked the picnic supplies. The beer was warm.

Understanding this sentence does not involve the inference *Picnic supplies normally include beer,* in the sense that this inference statement becomes an explicit part of the mental representation of this text. Rather, *picnic supplies* as well as *beer* both make strongly associated information, such as *beer is frequently a part of picnic supplies,* available in LTWM. This requires a little extra processing time; 219 ms in this experiment, in comparison with a control sentence pair in which *beer* was explicitly mentioned in the first sentence. This knowledge activation suffices to establish the coherence between the two sentences and allows the comprehension process to proceed without the reader ever becoming conscious of a bridging problem. Note that this use of LTWM entirely depends on the availability of strong automatic retrieval links between the words of the sentence and the contents of long-term memory. Consider a different example:

> The weather was calm. Connors used Kevlar sails.

Anyone but an expert sailor will not automatically find this to be coherent text, because there is nothing in our long-term memory that strongly links *calm weather* either to *Connors* or to *Kevlar sails*. We might figure out that perhaps Kevlar sails are good for calm weather—but that is not an automatic processes. Rather, it is a controlled problem-solving process with significant time and resource demands. Long-term working memory functions only in those situations in which we can rely on strongly overlearned knowledge: that is, in domains where we are experts.

A second way in which LTWM plays a role in text comprehension is by ensuring that the mental representation of the text that already has been constructed remains readily accessible as reading continues. If we read something, it is not only necessary to link what we read with our long-term store of knowledge and experiences, but it is also necessary that we link what we read now with relevant earlier portions of the text. These portions cannot be held in short-term working memory. We know from our own experience as well as from experimental studies (e.g. Jarvella, 1971) that no more than the current sentence—if it is not too long—is held in the focus of attention during reading. We also know that we effortlessly retrieve referents and relevant propositions from earlier portions of the text when needed to construct the meaning of the current sentence. Comprehending a text implies linking its various parts effectively in such a way as to permit easy retrieval. That is to say, comprehension implies the construction of a new network in LTWM. Of course, unlike the well-established links between text and long-term knowledge, the newly generated textbase is subject to forgetting.

Thus, LTWM during text comprehension includes short-term working memory—the sentence currently in the focus of attention—plus relevant knowledge activated from long-term memory that is directly linked via strong retrieval structures to the current contents of short-term working memory. It also includes the textbase (including contextual information, such as reading goals) that has already been generated, of which the presently worked-on sentence is a continuation.

Long-term working memory as previously described is incidental, an inherent by-product of the process of text comprehension. This is also the case for the physician and chess master. The chess master learns to play chess—not to memorize chess boards. It is worth noting, however, that LTWM can be intentional—as in the case of the runner who invented an encoding and retrieval system that allowed him to memorize long sequences of random digits (Ericsson, Chase, & Faloon, 1980), or the waiter who learned to use retrieval structures to memorize the orders of his customers (Ericsson & Polson, 1988). However, what we all do naturally in text comprehension is functionally equivalent to the memorial strategies employed in these cases.

ASPECTS OF COMPREHENSION

Previously in this chapter, multiple facets of comprehension have been alluded to, but not discussed. Comprehension is a complex process. Multiple factors influence the comprehension of individuals; these factors include characteristics of the text as well as those of the reader or comprehender. Further, the goal of comprehension—whether memory for information or true understanding of such—can be influenced by factors both internal and external to the learner.

Memory for Text

Often when people talk about learning from a text, they speak about recalling information from that text. It is not surprising that many students equate learning from a text with memorizing its content, because traditional tests of learning have focused primarily on the recall of information. Multiple-choice, fill-in-the blank, and true-or-false components from standard educational tests typically require only surface memory for the source information. However, there is a distinction to be made between memory for a text and learning from a text (W. Kintsch, 1998). Three levels of text representation have been identified by van Dijk and Kintsch (1983): *the surface level, the textbase,* and *the situation model.* The surface level and textbase relate to memory for a text, whereas the situation model concerns learning from a text. Memory for a text reflects superficial recognition or recall of information, whereas true learning from a text, as discussed in the next section, involves integration of text material with prior knowledge.

Memory for a text can exist at several levels and typically is demonstrated by recognition or recall tasks. Being able to identify or verify exact passages, sentences, or words that appeared in a text involves surface-level knowledge of the text. This type of task involves recognition of previously read text and is the most superficial type of text processing in that it requires no understanding of the text's meaning. One can memorize a sentence or learn to recite a poem without ever really understanding the contents (W. Kintsch, 1998). But when most individuals attempt to memorize a text, they are not really trying to faithfully encode the surface-level representation of the text. Normally they are attempting to create a textbase representation of the text.

Creation of a textbase differs from surface-level knowledge of a text in that the textbase does not necessarily represent the exact words or sentences used in the text. Instead, the textbase contains a representation of the ideas or propositions contained within a text. The information contained in the textbase can be tied directly to the information derived from the text, without any additional knowledge or inferences that the reader might contribute to such information (W. Kintsch, 1998). Thus, it is entirely possible for a textbase representation to be incomplete or incoherent. This is especially true because texts often are not completely explicit and require the reader to make inferences to connect ideas in the text. A textbase representation, then, requires readers to generate a faithful representation of the information contained in a text, but does not require them to form more than a superficial level of understanding about that information (McNamara, Kintsch, Songer, & Kintsch, 1996).

As previously noted, text memory generally is tested using recognition and recall methods. Sentence recognition tasks reveal that most individuals have surprisingly good and long-lasting memory for what they read (W. Kintsch, 1998). Interestingly, various studies have found that the recognizability of a sentence is related to its importance to the text: Major text propositions are recognized more easily than minor, detail-oriented propositions (C. I. Walker & Yekovich, 1984). Not only are the text-relevant characteristics of the target sentence important, but characteristics of the distractor sentences also influence the likelihood that a reader will incorrectly "recognize" it as a sentence from the text. Distractors that are more relevant to the reader's representation of the text tend to be confused with the actual text. Paraphrases are most likely to be mistaken as original text, followed by inferences, then topic-relevant distractors and, finally, topic-irrelevant distractors (W. Kintsch, Welsch, Schmalhofer, & Zimny, 1990). W. Kintsch et al. (1990) not only identified the pattern by which distractors are confused with original text, but also they analyzed the extent to which different text representations—surface level, textbase, or situation model (an integrated representation of text information and background knowledge)—are negatively affected by delay. Recognition tested before and after a 4-day delay demonstrated no decline in recognition memory for the situation model, a substantial decline (50% loss of strength) for the textbase, and a complete loss of surface information.

Thus, recognition memory depends not only on the strength of text representation formed during reading, but also upon the type of representation formed and the degree to which distractor sentences approach this representation. In general, recognition memory is quite good and long lasting but does not offer the learner much in the way of useful, transferable knowledge.

Another way to test text memory is through methods that focus on the recall of text. Commonly, summarization is used to assess recall of text, especially because longer texts lend themselves to reproduction of their macrostructure but not their microstructure (Bartlett, 1932). Presumably this result occurs because recall of a text progresses in a top-down, hierarchical manner through a text representation (e.g., W. Kintsch & van Dijk, 1978; Lorch & Lorch, 1985). Indeed, evidence does demonstrate that facilitating text organization produces better recall. An extensive literature on advance organizers (Corkill, 1992; see also Ausubel, 1960) suggests that use of advance organizers presented before learning may facilitate recall and organization of knowledge. Studies on expository text (e.g., Lorch & Lorch, 1995; Lorch, Lorch, & Inman, 1993) have found that text components that signaled the structure of a text produced better memory for text ideas and their organization. In a study that included writing quality as an independent variable, Moravcsik and Kintsch (1993) found that well-written, organized texts facilitated recall.

Well-written texts may offer another advantage to students other than the ease with which text macrostructure is identified and encoded—these texts also may require less background knowledge and facilitate more complete understanding than poorly written texts. It is important to recognize that the recall of a text is only as good as the individual's representation of the text. Thus, in cases in which an individual develops an incomplete or erroneous representation of the text, the summary of the text will reflect those problems. Especially in cases when individuals lack requisite background knowledge or when the subject matter is technical, well-written and well-organized texts may be critical to encourage complete, accurate representations of text. Again, although recall memory for a text can be quite good depending upon the quality of the textbase representation, recall memory is limited in use to tests of knowledge rather than applications of it.

Inferences

Inferences in text comprehension play a crucial role in comprehension. The total information that is necessary for a true understanding of a text is rarely stated explicitly in the text. Much is left unsaid, with the expectation that a well-informed and motivated reader will fill it in. Indeed, texts that aspire to be fully explicit, like some legal documents, are very hard and boring to read. For most texts, readers must construct the meaning of a text—although this task requires sufficient clues for processing, overwhelming readers with redundant and superfluous cues is not to their advantage at all. How people infer what is not stated explicitly in a text has been an active topic of investigation among text researchers. It also has been a fairly confused issue, because researchers have not always distinguished adequately between different types of inferences.

Inferences are often directed toward linking different parts of a text. One distinction that must be made in this respect is between the cohesion and coherence of a text. *Cohesion* (Halliday & Hasan, 1976) refers to the linguistic signals that link sentences in a passage; that is, it is a characteristic of the linguistic surface structure of a text. Typical cohesive devices, for instance, are sentence connectives, such as *but* or *however*. *Coherence* (van Dijk & Kintsch, 1983) refers to linkages at the propositional level, which may or may not be signaled linguistically. For instance,

(a) The weather was sunny all week. But on Sunday it snowed.

is both cohesive and coherent, whereas

(b) The weather was sunny all week. On Sunday it snowed.

lacks the cohesive *but,* but is nevertheless coherent because of our knowledge that *Sunday* is a day of the *week*. Although linguists typically study cohesion, most of the psychological research concerns coherence. In general, explicit cohesive markers in a passage allow for faster processing but do not affect recall if coherence can be inferred without them (Sanders & Noordman, 2000).

Bridging inferences are necessary to establish coherence when there is no explicit link between two parts of a passage, as in (b). Bridging inferences have been studied extensively (Haviland & Clark, 1974; Myers et al., 2000; Revlin & Hegarty, 1999). They are necessary for true understanding, because otherwise the two parts of the passage would be unrelated in the mental representation of the text.

However, not all inferences have to do with coherence. Elaborative inferences do not link pieces of text, but rather enrich the text through the addition of information from the reader's knowledge, experience, or imagination. Thus, elaborations link a text with the reader's background, fulfilling a very important function, as is further discussed in the section on learning from texts.

Much of what is called inferencing has already been discussed in this chapter's section on long-term working memory. For instance, the so-called inference in (b) is not a true inference at all, but represents automatic knowledge activation. Readers do not have to actively infer that *Sunday* and *week* are related in a certain way—they know it automatically and their long-term working memory provides them with the necessary coherence link. We are dealing here not with true inferences, but rather with automatic knowledge retrieval.

There are other types of automatic inferences, however, that are not purely a question of knowledge retrieval. For instance, readers of

(c) Three turtles sat on a log. A fish swam under the log.

automatically infer

(d) The turtles were above the fish. (*Bransford, Barclay, & Franks, 1972.*)

This inference is an automatic consequence of forming an appropriate situation model, for example an image of the situation described in (c).

Strategic inferences are a controlled process, as opposed to automatic inferences (W. Kintsch, 1993, 1998). Strategic inferences may involve knowledge retrieval, but in the absence of long-term working memory structures, so that the retrieval process is resource consuming and often quite difficult. Or they can be true inferences, not just retrieving preexisting knowledge, as in logical inferences such as *modus ponens,* which require special training for most people (see the chapter in this volume by Leighton & Sternberg). Predicting when strategic inferences will be made is quite difficult. It depends on a host of factors such as reading goals, motivation, and background knowledge. For instance, in reading a story, readers sometimes but by no means always make forward or predictive inferences (Klin, Guzman, & Levine, 1999). Indeed, text researchers disagree strongly as to the prevalence of strategic inferences. Some minimalists (McKoon & Ratcliff, 1992) find very little evidence for such inferences, while others (Graesser, Singer, & Trabasso, 1994) disagree. The question is when such inferences are made—spontaneously, as an integral part of reading a text (like bridging inferences), or in response to special task demands such as a question or verification test afterwards. It seems clear that this is not an issue that is capable of a general resolution. Rather, the answer must depend on the exact condition of reading because this kind of inference process is under strategic control of the reader.

Learning From Text

Learning from a text means that the reader understands the content and is able to use the information in ways that are not specific to the text. Thus, learning involves much more than storage of a text for recall. Unlike memory for a text, actual learning from the text requires integration of information into the reader's existing knowledge and creates a flexible and powerful representation of the new information. This integrated representation of text information is called the situation model.

Development of a situation model has many benefits for learners. Individuals who have created powerful situation models are able to transfer their knowledge and apply it to new domains or situations. The situation model is not just a more flexible representation, it is the longest lasting of the text representations. Because it integrates text information with a reader's existing knowledge, it offers the long-term potential to be transferred to other situations and to be incorporated into other learning situations. Thus, construction of the situation model represents true learning from a text (W. Kintsch, 1994; Zwaan & Radvansky, 1998).

A variety of methods have been used to assess the strength of the situation model that an individual constructs. Ideally, the method used to assess the situation model must differentiate between a textbase representation and the situation model. Tasks that adequately assess the situation model above and beyond the textbase generally require the learner to transfer or generalize the information from a text in a new situation. Short-answer questions requiring inferences and transfer, concept-key word sorting tasks (McNamara et al., 1996; Wolfe et al., 1998), and changes in knowledge mapping before and after reading a text (Ferstl & Kintsch, 1999) all have been used to asses the strength of the situation model after learning.

Although it may seem that the situation model is a more desirable goal of reading than a textbase representation is, the purpose for which a text is being studied should be considered when comparing the effectiveness of the textbase and the situation model. Because traditional academic tests (such as multiple-choice recognition) often emphasize textbase learning, students seeking a peak performance on such exams may do well to emphasize textbase learning during their study. At the least, when text memory will be assessed, students should prevent emphasizing the situation model at the expense of textbase learning. However, students who desire long-term benefits from text learning are best aided by emphasizing situation model development.

To some extent, the situation model is dependent upon construction of an accurate and complete textbase. Without this foundation, integration with background knowledge is prone to error, misconceptions, and gaps. However, just as central to the situation model is the presence of adequate and appropriate domain knowledge with which text information can be integrated. Thus, it is essential for comprehension that texts be matched appropriately to readers who have the background knowledge necessary to comprehend them. Wolfe et al. (1998) demonstrated that matching readers to texts that are suited to their levels of background knowledge can result in substantial comprehension benefits. Understanding the role of domain knowledge in comprehension is a key aspect of predicting the success of text comprehension for an individual reading a certain text.

Domain Knowledge

Clearly, domain knowledge is a very powerful variable that affects situation model development and, thus, learning from text. Because development of a situation model requires adequate prior knowledge, it is logical to assume that level of domain knowledge is important in determining the extent to which individuals will learn from a text. Empirical evidence in the experimental literature supports the idea that domain knowledge is exceedingly important in predicting comprehension (Recht & Leslie, 1988; Schneider, Körkel, & Weinert, 1989; C. H. Walker, 1987; Wolfe et al., 1998). The results overwhelmingly demonstrate that high domain knowledge improves comprehension performance, even when experiments control for factors such as IQ (W. Kintsch, 1998). To some extent, high domain knowledge can also compensate for poor reading skill. Of course, domain knowledge cannot compensate for complete lack of reading skill or deficient decoding skills. However, for individuals who have basic but low-level reading skills, high levels of domain knowledge can cancel out such disadvantages under the right circumstances (e.g., given a text that utilizes the domain of expertise). For example, Adams, Bell, and Perfetti (1995) demonstrated that domain knowledge and reading skill can trade off in order to equate reading comprehension.

Domain knowledge has been shown to impact comprehension at a deeper level than that of factors external to the individual. Moravcsik and Kintsch (1993) investigated the interactive effects of domain knowledge, text quality (good vs. poor writing and organization), and participants' reading ability in comprehension. Results demonstrated that without appropriate domain knowledge, readers could not form appropriate inferences about the text. Although high- and low-knowledge readers generated about the same global number of inferences, most of the those created by low-knowledge readers were erroneous. In contrast, high-quality texts (with good, organized writing) facilitated recall of a text but not formation of a situation model. Thus, although good writing can help readers, it does not compensate for lack of adequate domain knowledge when learning is the goal.

Text Factors

Although text factors cannot overcome factors internal to the individual (adequate and appropriate domain knowledge), they can influence a reader's comprehension. In order to create a situation model from text, readers must form a coherent textbase that can be integrated with prior knowledge. For low-knowledge readers, texts with a clear macrostructure (e.g., texts with embedded headings or clear topic sentences) facilitate both memory for and learning from text. Empirical evidence supports this claim. Brooks, Dansereau, Spurlin, and Holley (1983) compared the comprehension performance of individuals after reading a text containing embedded headings versus a text without these embedded headings. A comprehension test administered immediately after reading showed only small benefits for the text with headings, but a test 2 days later revealed significant benefits for readers exposed to the embellished text. In a second experiment, however, Brooks et al. found that headings were not well used by students unless accompanied by instructions on using the headings as processing aids. Thus, the extent to which students spontaneously attend to and make use of text headings may predict the headings' effectiveness.

Other manipulations of text components also have been successful in promoting reader comprehension. Britton and Gulgoz (1991) improved comprehension of texts unfamiliar to students by identifying and repairing coherence gaps in a text (according to the method proposed by J. R. Miller & Kintsch, 1980). The effect of this manipulation is explicit presentation of text structure achieved by connecting information that normally requires bridging inferences (W. Kintsch, 1998). Thus, removing coherence gaps and making the text more fully explicit has the effect of reducing the number of inferences the reader must make, thereby facilitating comprehension. Other research has supported the conclusion that making text macrostructure clear has comprehension benefits (Beck, McKeown, Sinatra, & Loxterman, 1991; Lorch & Lorch, 1995; Lorch et al., 1993; McNamara et al., 1996). As discussed earlier, clear presentation of text macrostructure facilitates the recall of text information and the organization of text representations.

However, some evidence suggests that when readers have ample domain knowledge, texts that do not require inferencing or active processing are not ideal for facilitating comprehension (W. Kintsch, 1998; McNamara et al., 1996). Surprisingly, high-knowledge readers actually can learn more (as indicated by situation model measures) from text with relatively low coherence (McNamara & Kintsch, 1996; McNamara et al., 1996). The interpretation of this effect is that high-knowledge readers must work harder to make sense out of a low coherence text; this text-relevant processing results in formation of a better-developed situation model, whereas recall is not influenced. Other methods that encourage active text processing have similar benefits; these include frequent self-explanations or use of advance outlines that do not match the structure of the text (W. Kintsch, 1998).

Although active processing is a powerful determinant of text learning, it is important to remember that increasing the difficulty of text is fruitful only for the reader with adequate knowledge. Further, increasing text difficulty often is problematic and time consuming. This may explain the large number of instructional programs that have been designed to teach active strategies for comprehension. The effectiveness of such strategies is unclear; some research shows clear benefits after teaching strategies and some does not. For example, Palincsar and Brown (1984) found that training children on general comprehension processes results in strong and generalizable improvements in text understanding. Yet in a study with 6- to 8-year-olds Cain (1999) found that although poor comprehenders did have poorer knowledge of metacognitive strategies for reading when compared to readers their own age, their comprehension performance was worse even when compared to that of younger readers with the same level of metacognitive ability. These mixed results probably stem from the difficulty of ensuring that children and adult readers use the strategy in the absence of continual monitoring, together with individual differences in the efficiency with which the strategy is performed.

Conversation

Conversation is an interesting case for comprehension. Clearly, understanding a speaker's meaning during conversation is essential to the successful progression and conclusion of communication. For the most part, comprehension of oral discourse follows the same principles as text-based comprehension. However, conversation is a unique form of comprehension in several ways. First, the purposes of conversational comprehension and text comprehension usually differ. Conversations can be used to transmit information, but often serve more human, social roles. Conversations involve exchange of information and may seek to amuse, entertain, or punish. Consistent with these aspects of social interaction, conversations are also unique in the process by which information is added to conversation and the extent to which frequent comprehension checks are made by both the speaker and the comprehender during communication. Interestingly, conversation requires frequent checks for comprehension before it can proceed; individuals contributing to a conversation repeatedly and continually check understanding before continuing along a conversational path (H. H. Clark & Schaefer, 1989).

Just as background knowledge facilitates comprehension of text, conversation involves what H. H. Clark and Schaefer (1989) call common ground among participants. *Common ground* describes the personal beliefs and knowledge that a participant brings to the conversation. However, common ground is not exactly like background knowledge, which remains stable even as readers make connections between a text and background knowledge and integrate text ideas into the knowledge. Common ground is a more flexible entity—it changes, is added to, or is destroyed and rebuilt during the course of a conversation (H. H. Clark & Schaefer, 1989). Comprehension checks called *grounding* (H. H. Clark, 2000; H. H. Clark & Schaefer, 1989) continually assess the state of common ground. Various techniques for grounding exist, but they all elucidate the extent a speaker's communicative intent is clear to the listener. If grounding reveals a problem, a repair is initiated to reestablish common ground before the rest of the conversation can ensue.

Speakers do not ignore a listener's background knowledge when contributing to a conversation, but rather attempt to modify their contributions based on their assessment of the other's knowledge. Isaacs and Clark (1987) studied experts and novices participating in a conversation requiring knowledge of New York City. These researchers found that the participants were able to assess each other's level of expertise and modify their conversation accordingly. In their study, experts modified their contributions to be more explicit, and during the task novices acquired specialized knowledge, which could be used subsequently. Thus, the comprehension of each utterance is not only evaluated, but the degree to which common ground must be improved for successful communication is also assessed and modified. Unlike text comprehension, this assessment allows some potential comprehension problems to be avoided before they are encountered.

According to H. H. Clark and Schaefer (1989), contributions in conversation serve not only to highlight misunderstandings for clarification, but also to offer essential evidence of successful understanding during the course of an exchange. By the process of repeatedly checking understanding, the common ground between participants in a conversation is both established and added to in the course of the conversation. However, conversation can lack explicit links between contributions and can require inferences by the other participants. H. H. Clark and Schaefer call the inferential processes of conversation *bridging* and *accommodation.* Analogous to text inferences, these conversational processes rely upon knowledge and experience: Inferential processes add to the understanding of the contribution just offered, and the interpretation created by the inference often is made explicit by a contribution from the participant making the inference.

Amazingly, participants pursue conversational goals, establish common ground, repeatedly check understanding, make inferences, and continue to advance the conversation more or less smoothly without noticeable lapses for processing or planning. Certainly, contributions to conversations occasionally fail and repairs must be made, for example, by repetition or rephrasing. However, a surprisingly large portion of conversation is involved in demonstrating positive understanding and, considering the multiple processes involved in each exchange, conversation proceeds with remarkable ease.

Clearly, conversation benefits from the continuous efforts of participants to establish that comprehension of contributions has been successful. Conversation also is highly practiced and individuals can be considered experts in contributing to discourse. Normally, participants also benefit from an inherent interest in the conversation at hand. Interest and motivation have long been presumed to be important factors in comprehension, but the manner in which they influence conversational or text comprehension is not well understood.

Purpose and Interest

Clearly, factors internal to the comprehender can have as much or more influence on ultimate learning as do text or conversational factors that either promote or hinder comprehension. Generally, factors such as the goals or purpose of the reader and his or her interest in the text at hand have been considered to be quite important in understanding comprehension. However, it is difficult to specify methods by which such factors can be objectively measured. Further, it is unclear by what mechanisms purpose and interest may affect comprehension processes. It has been suggested that increased interest in a text frees up attentional resources, leading to increased processing of the text; indeed, recent research has found that individuals perform a secondary task faster when reading an interesting as opposed to less interesting text (McDaniel, Waddill, Finstad, & Bourg, 2000). However, McDaniel et al.'s study did not find a recall benefit related to text interest, despite the general finding that increased interest results in increased recall for text material (for a review, see Alexander, Kulikowich, & Jetton, 1994). The difficulty of reconciling these results simply highlights the fact that the interactions between purpose, interest, and other variables internal to the comprehender and their influence on comprehension is only poorly understood at this point.

The purpose of text processing is somewhat easier to manipulate than text interest in that researchers may specify specific outcomes or products that the comprehender will be asked to produce after the reading task. Research has demonstrated that the nature of some educational tasks can promote certain types of comprehension. For example, requiring students to write arguments about information promotes construction of situation models and understanding of information (Wiley & Voss, 1999). Regardless of the type of product that readers must produce after comprehension, different purposes during learning may change or influence behaviors directly related to comprehension performance. Narvaez, van den Broek, and Ruiz (1999) found that simply manipulating whether readers had a study or entertainment purpose changed on-line reading behaviors as well as metacognitive checks on comprehension. In this study, students who read expository texts with a study purpose were more likely to repeat sections of the text, were more likely to evaluate the text during reading, and were more likely to acknowledge comprehension difficulties related to gaps in the background knowledge. However, it is interesting to note that some effects of reader purpose appear to depend upon the type of text. For example, Narvaez et al. found that strategic behaviors for comprehension were weaker for narrative as compared to expository texts.

Regardless of an individual's purpose in pursuing a text, interest in the text is clearly relevant to comprehension processes. Research on this topic varies widely on the type of interest manipulated (e.g., whether texts are matched to individual interests and knowledge, or texts are manipulated to include details that appeal more generally to readers), but for the most part has demonstrated that increased interest leads to increased memory for and comprehension of texts. In a review of research manipulating both reader background knowledge and interest, Alexander et al. (1994) argued that most studies find that interest is positively related to learning from text. However, they acknowledge that stronger and more consistent effects are found when interest is predicted by a reader's prior knowledge of and long-term interest in a topic rather than by the specific characteristics of an individual text.

This is not to argue that interest-related characteristics of an individual text are not influential in text processing. The effects of seductive details—bits of information in a text that are considered intrinsically interesting but unimportant to the major text ideas—are an interesting case. In general, studies have found that seductive details are well remembered and sometimes are recalled better than main text ideas (e.g., Alexander et al., 1994; Schraw, 1998). Although Schraw (1998) found that seductive details were remembered better than main text ideas, he also found that seductive details did not interfere with recall for global text information. Thus, enhancing a text with seductive details may increase interest and promote memory for such intrinsically interesting information, but may do little to improve overall memory for the topic at hand.

Other types of text manipulations may affect interest without adding unnecessary information to text. Sadoski, Goetz, and Rodriguez (2000) found that the concreteness of a text was a strong predictor of interest in a text. Manipulating a text to use concrete descriptions may enhance interest in a text and promote recall. However, not all texts or concepts can be expressed in a concrete way and doing so may compromise abstract or complex relationships in certain texts. For these types of texts, it is difficult to envision modifications that would increase text interest without sacrificing the rigor of the text.

Certainly the factors previously discussed and other factors a reader brings to the text (e.g., emotion) are important to comprehension performance, and the influence of such factors should be included in a complete model of comprehension. We are confident that cognitive psychology will continue to explore these issues and will be able to describe the ways in which the individual interacts with a text during comprehension. The current and future challenge for research in text comprehension will be to continue to uncover individual factors and text variables that influence and support learning from texts and to integrate such knowledge into the already complex picture of what factors predict what and how much an individual will learn from a text.

MODELS OF COMPREHENSION

Schema-Based Models

Early comprehension models heavily emphasized the role of top-down processes. Comprehension was thought to involve (a) schema activation through key words or phrases in the text, followed by (b) filling the slots of the schema with relevant information from the text (Anderson & Pichert, 1978; Rumelhart & Ortony, 1977; Schank & Abelson, 1977). An extreme version of such a theory was the artificial intelligence (AI) program FRUMP (DeJong, 1979), which actually attempted to understand news reports in this way. It was never meant as a psychological theory, but it illustrates nicely both the strengths and weaknesses of a schema-based approach. FRUMP was equipped with a large number of schemas relevant to news reports (e.g., a schema for accidents). A schema could be activated by appropriate key words in the text (e.g., *crash*). Once activated, it serves as a guide for searching the text for schema-relevant information: What sort of vehicle crashed? How many people? Killed? Wounded? Causes of the crash?

The comprehension problem was thereby greatly simplified. One did not have to fully understand a text, but merely find certain well-specified items of information. As an AI program, FRUMP turned out to be fatally limited. The main difficulty was that the schema often did not fit the facts of a text. Even for something as well-structured as an accident report, one needs to look for different information in stories about a car crash, a plane crash, or a skier crashing into a tree. It is simply not possible to predefine adequate schemas for all (or even most) texts. Schank (1982) realized this and modified his approach accordingly by introducing memory organization packets—building blocks from which to construct a schema. It was clear that a simple schema-based approach would not work, neither in AI nor as a psychological model.

Nevertheless, schemas play a major role in comprehension, and every psychological model of comprehension uses schemas in one way or another (Whitney, Budd, Bramucci, & Crane, 1995). However, schemas are no longer regarded as the sole or even the most important control structure in comprehension. Instead, prior knowledge and expectations—some in the form of schemas—are top-down influences that interact with a variety of bottom-up processes to yield what we call comprehension.

A Psychological Process Model

Comprehension has many facets and there are many ways to model comprehension: Rhetoric and linguistics represent an ancient and important tradition, whereas artificial intelligence programs are a recent innovation. Psychological process models take a different approach yet. They build on the constraints provided by our knowledge of the perceptual and cognitive processes involved in comprehension: word perception and recognition, attention, short- and long-term memory, retrieval processes, sentence comprehension, knowledge representation and activation, and the like. Of course, psychological process models cannot neglect the constraints imposed by the text to be comprehended, and indeed, it may be the case that textual constraints dominate the comprehension process, relegating cognitive aspects to a minor role—which is the premise of purely linguistic or AI approaches. However, the recent research on psychological models of comprehension suggests otherwise.

The attempt to analyze comprehension in psychological terms began with the model of W. Kintsch and van Dijk (1978; van Dijk & Kintsch, 1983). The model is based on the assumption that the limitations of working memory force readers (or listeners) to decode one sentence at a time. *Decoding* consists of translating the sentence from natural language to a general and universal mental language—a propositional representation. In spite of its name, this propositional structure is not a full semantic representation of the meaning of a sentence or a text; rather, it is designed merely to capture the core idea—how people understand a sentence when they are not analyzing it in all its detail. This sort of representation is useful mainly because it allows the psychologist to count so-called idea units in the comprehension as well as reproduction of a text. Counting words is not very useful with texts. In a list of random words, whether a subject recalls 12 or 15 words is a meaningful statistic. The exact number of words someone recalls from a text, on the other hand, is not necessarily directly related to either comprehension or memory; for most purposes, the number of ideas matters, rather than the words expressing them. Thus, the propositional representation of the sentence *John read the old book in the library* is

Predicate: READ
  Agent: JOHN
  Object: BOOK
  Modifier: OLD
Location: LIBRARY

Paraphrasing this sentence as *The book, which was old, was read by John in the library* does not change this propositional representation. For purposes of scoring a recall protocol, one can count either sentence as one complex proposition, or as one core proposition, one modifier, and one location, depending on the grain of the analysis that is desired.

The W. Kintsch and van Dijk model assumes that understanding a text means constructing a propositional representation of the text. This representation consists of a network of propositions. Propositions that share a common argument are linked (in the example above, the proposition would be linked to other propositions containing one or more of the arguments *John, book,* or *library*). However, propositions can be linked only if they reside in the reader's working memory at the same time. The capacity of this working memory is limited (estimates usually range between three to five propositions). A spreading activation process among the propositions in working memory determines their activation level. As the next sentence in a text is read, working memory is cleared: The propositions from the previous processing cycle are added to long-term memory and the propositions from the current sentence(s) are added to working memory. However, to ensure continuity, the most activated proposition(s) from the last cycle is retained in a short-term buffer, so that it can be linked with the propositions of the current sentence. In this way, a connected textbase is gradually constructed as the text is processed sentence by sentence. This textbase is called the *microstructure* of the text. It represents the meaning of all the sentences of a text in terms of a propositional network, as an ideal reader would construct it. The links in this structure are determined jointly by the nature of the text and by the capacity limits of working memory and the short-term buffer. Furthermore, those propositions that are most strongly interlinked in this network will gain the greatest memory strength in the spreading activation process.

In addition, the W. Kintsch and van Dijk model also constructs a *macrostructure* representation of a text. Schemas play a role at this level: They allow the reader to identify the structurally most important propositions in a text and their interrelationships, thus providing a basis for the formation of a macrostructure. Intuitively, the macrostructure represents the gist of a text, whereas the microstructure represents all of its detailed content.

In a large number of studies, the W. Kintsch and van Dijk model has been shown to predict the data from psychological experiments with texts quite well—comprehension as well as memory (e.g., Graesser, Millis, & Zwaan, 1997; W. Kintsch, 1974; W. Kintsch & van Dijk, 1978; van Dijk & Kintsch, 1983). The model thus justified the basic premise of the psychological processing approach to text comprehension: that cognitive constraints as well as linguistic constraints must be taken into account in modeling text comprehension.

The Construction-Integration Model

The mental representation that results from reading a text is, however, only in part determined by the content and structure of the text itself—the process that the van Dijk and Kintsch (1983) model attempts to describe. The reader's goals and prior knowledge are equally important factors. Schema theory provided the first account of how prior knowledge influences comprehension. An alternative account, which leaves room for the top-down effects of schemas but relies more heavily on bottom-up processes, has been developed by W. Kintsch (1988, 1998) within the general framework of the van Dijk and Kintsch processing model.

Consider what happens when a reader encounters a homonym in a discourse context. Almost always, only the context-appropriate meaning of the word comes to mind. However, experimental studies, using both lexical decision and eye movement methods, suggest for a very brief period of time, about 350 ms, both meanings of a homonym are activated under certain conditions (Rayner, Pacht, & Duffy, 1994; Swinney, 1979; also see the chapter in this volume by Rayner, Pollatsek, Starr, & Wurm). This observation suggests that it is not a top-down process, such as a schema, that primes the context-appropriate meaning or filters out the inappropriate ones, but that all meanings are activated and that the context then suppresses the activation of inappropriate meanings. The construction-integration model is based on this idea. It assumes that construction processes during comprehension—both at the word level as well as at the syntactic and discourse levels—are context independent and unconstrained. Thus, they are inherently promiscuous. However, context quickly imposes its constraints. Constructions that are consistent with each other support each other in a spreading activation process, and inconsistent and irrelevant constructions become deactivated. According to this model, the construction process results in an incoherent mental representation. An integration process is needed to turn this contradictory tangle of hypotheses into a coherent mental representation. This integration is essentially a process of constraint satisfaction. It works quickly enough so that inappropriate initial hypotheses do not reach the level of consciousness. According to experimental results (e.g., Till, Mross, & Kintsch, 1988) it takes about 300–350 ms for word meanings to become fixated in a discourse context, and 500–700 ms for topic inferences.

Schemas play an important role in the construction-integration model, because they are likely to be activated in the construction phase of the process, just like many other knowledge structures. However, once activated, an appropriate schema will most likely become the central unit in the integration phase, attracting relevant pieces of information and thereby deactivating schema-irrelevant constructions.

W. Kintsch (1998) describes how this model can account for a wide variety of experimental findings, such as the construction of word meanings in discourse, priming in discourse, syntactic parsing, macrostructure formation, generating inferences, and the construction of situation models. The construction-integration model has also been successfully applied to how people solve mathematical word problems, and beyond the sphere of text comprehension, to action planning, problem solving, and decision making (for more information on human performance in these tasks, see the chapter in this volume by Leighton & Sternberg). In other words, the model aspires to be a general theory of comprehension, not just of text comprehension.

The Collaborative Activation-Based Production System Architecture

The bottom-up, spreading activation component of the construction-integration model is quite successful and has been included in most subsequent models of text comprehension. Models of comprehension can be broadly described as attempts to instantiate activation-based theories of comprehension within limitations suggested by other cognitive processes. Given the importance of working memory resources for comprehension, it is not surprising that many models have focused on constraints surrounding comprehension processes when developing simulations. Just and Carpenter (1992) developed a model of sentence comprehension that attempted to account for characteristics of comprehension based on a flexible but limited capacity system simulating the constraints of working memory. It should be noted that although the capacity-constraints of the collaborative action-based production system (CAPS) are based on working memory characteristics, they relate to theoretically based, higher-level activation limits rather than to modality-specific buffers commonly thought to exist within working memory (e.g., Baddeley, 1986; also see the chapter in this volume by Nairne).

The CAPS architecture is a combination of a production system and an activation-based connection system that Just and Carpenter (1992) used to produce a simulation of their theory. According to the theory, activation is responsible both for storage and processing components of language comprehension. In CAPS, an element is activated either by being constructed from text (written or spoken), constructed by a process, or retrieved from long-term memory. Like the construction-integration model, CAPS does not neglect the influence of top-down effects of context. In fact, CAPS assumes that activation of text propositions and background knowledge proceeds similarly to the construction-integration model. However, the difference in CAPS appears when the comprehension processes approach capacity limits.

Although elements with above-threshold activation are available to comprehension processes, complications occur when the amount of activation required for elements exceeds the total activation available in the system. Capacity limits in CAPS do not necessarily result in deactivation of weak elements, but rather in an overall decrease of system activation. In CAPS, activation for maintaining elements as well as for processing these elements is shared. Thus, capacity limits on activation can lead to forgetting of old elements as well as decreased processing of current elements.

Just and Carpenter's (1992) model is quite successful at modeling comprehension differences produced by texts with differing working memory demands as read by individuals with varying working memory capacity. Interestingly, Just and Carpenter (1992) argue that their evidence suggests that activation capacity is a single resource. They assert that because increasing demand by a variety of methods—for example, increasing text distance or ambiguity, reducing available working memory capacity—produces consistent effects on comprehension, it is reasonable to assume that the same mechanisms underlie diverse types of comprehension processing. Clearly, cognitive processes are subject to capacity limits, and the power of this model lies in the dynamic manner in which it accounts for such limits in comprehension.

The Capacity-Constrained Construction-Integration Model

Inclusion of working memory constraints in comprehension models offers some clear benefits to explaining individual differences in comprehension. Both the construction-integration model and the CAPS architecture are quite successful in explaining some aspects of comprehension. Given that construction-integration seeks to model comprehension in general (rather than stopping with text comprehension) but CAPS provides a successful account of individual differences in text comprehension based on working memory constraints, could the two models be combined as a capacity-limited model of general comprehension? The capacity-constrained construction integration model (CCCI; Goldman & Varma, 1995) attempts to combine the ways in which knowledge is constructed, represented, and integrated in the construction-integration (CI) model within the more flexible capacity-constrained CAPS system. Instantiating construction-integration in a working-memory limited system has the effect of changing the way in which propositions are held over for additional processing cycles. Whereas the CI model uses a buffer of fixed size to simulate limitations of working memory in text processing, Goldman and Varma's (1995) CCCI model retains all propositions not exceeding capacity limitations for further processing. When capacity limits are reached (as in CAPS), new propositions may draw activation away from retained elements, which gracefully fall below threshold.

The main strength of the CCCI model is that it reproduces the major, successful comprehension results of the construction-integration model at the same time as it automatically produces stronger weights for propositions representing main points from a text passage instead of assigning initial weights to reflect differences in text importance. Thus, providing the construction-integration model with working memory limits may help us understand how comprehension processes arrive at different representation strengths for different text elements.

The Landscape Model

The landscape model (van den Broek, Risden, Fletcher, & Thurlow, 1996) also assumes that patterns of activation work within constraints during a cyclical process of comprehension. However, the landscape model deals more specifically with the process by which coherence is computed and represented during comprehension. In this model, activation strengths during each processing cycle are set on a 5-point scale determined by the degree to which the concept is necessary to establish coherence in the text. Accordingly, concepts that are explicitly defined are assigned the highest weights, whereas inferences that are not necessary to establish coherence receive the lowest activation weights. Concepts that contribute to coherence are weighted to varying degrees along this continuum as a function of their degree of contribution to the coherence.

The landscape model draws its name from the patterns of activations seen for text concepts across all processing cycles during comprehension. That is, an activation map of all concepts across cycles is constructed and graphically demonstrates the degree to which concepts are activated during the progression of the story, as well as the number of concepts that are concurrently activated in each cycle of comprehension. According to van den Broek et al., the topography of activation suggests the way in which comprehended text becomes encoded as a stable, coherent representation. Further, van den Broek et al. argue that the total activation of a concept across cycles predicts the importance of the concept to the story and that concepts activated together during a processing cycle will be linked in memory.

Testing by van den Broek et al. (1996) suggests that the activation of concepts during processing cycles can predict patterns of human recall for story concepts. In their research, nearly all (94%) concepts first recalled by participants were the concepts that demonstrated greatest overall activation during the course of reading. Further, the pattern of subsequent concepts recalled was predicted by the degree to which the prior and subsequent concepts were coactivated during reading. The landscape model, then, provides a description of and a general methodology for testing the ways concepts are emphasized and linked in a text. However, the landscape model falls short of offering a theoretical rationale for the ways in which humans construct, represent, and integrate their knowledge. In general, models of comprehension reflect similar assumptions about the way in which knowledge is represented, but it is valid to question the precise nature of such representations.

MODELS OF KNOWLEDGE REPRESENTATION

One of the central problems in cognitive science is how to model human knowledge. How can we define *knowledge?* The word *know* is used in so many ways; is what we know always knowledge? Consider this list, selected from the 11 senses of *know* listed in WordNet (http://www.cogsci.princeton.edu/~wn/):

1. I know who is winning the game.

2. She knows how to knit.

3. Galileo knew that the earth moved around the sun.

4. Do you know my sister?
5. I know the feeling!
6. His greed knew no limits.
7. I know Latin.
8. This child knows right from wrong.

Examples 3, 4, and 7 would seem to be clear examples of knowledge, but how does one draw the line? But suppose we knew what knowledge was. What, then, is its structure, how is it organized? Semantic hierarchies, feature systems, schemas, and scripts, or one huge associative net? All of these possibilities and several more have had their sponsors, as well as their critics. But once again, suppose we had a workable model of what human knowledge structures are like. How could we then determine what the content of these structures actually is? There are two ways to do this: One can hand-code all knowledge, as it is done in a dictionary or encyclopedia, except more systematically and more complete, or one can build a system that learns all it needs to know. We discus an example of both approaches, both of which have proven their usefulness for psychological research on discourse comprehension.

WordNet

WordNet is what a dictionary should be. Unlike most dictionaries, WordNet aspires to be a complete and exhaustive list of all word meanings or senses in the English language; it defines these meanings with a general phrase and some illustrative examples, and lists certain semantically related terms (Fellbaum, 1998; G. A. Miller, 1996). This is all done by hand coding. Each word in the language has an internal structure in WordNet, consisting of the syntactic categories of the word and, for each category, the number of different semantic senses (together with informal definitions and examples). Thus, the word *bank* is both a noun and a verb. For the noun, 10 senses are listed (the first two are *familiar financial institution* and *river bank;* the 10th is *a flight maneuver*). The verb *bank* has seven senses in WordNet. Furthermore, each word (actually, each word sense) is related to other words by a number of semantic relationships that are specified in WordNet: synonymy (e.g. *financial institution* is a synonym of *bank-1*), coordinate relationship (*lending institution* is a coordinate term for *bank-1*), hyponymy (*. . . is a kind of bank*), holonymy (*bank is part of . . .*), and meronymy (*parts of bank*). Thus, a detailed, explicit description of the lexicon of the English language is achieved, structured by certain semantic relations.

WordNet is a useful and widely used tool for psycholinguists and linguists. Nevertheless, it has certain limitations, some of which arise from the need for hand coding. WordNet is the reified intuition of its coders, limited by the chosen format (e.g., the semantic relations that are made explicit). But language changes, there are individual differences, and people can use words creatively in novel ways and be understood (E. V. Clark, 1997). The mental lexicon may not be static, as WordNet necessarily must be, but may evolve dynamically, and the context dependency of word meanings may be so strong as to make a listing of fixed senses illusory.

The task of hand coding a complete lexicon of the English language is certainly a daunting one. Hand coding all human knowledge presents significant additional difficulties. Nevertheless, the CYC (CYC is a very large database in which human knowledge is formally represented by a language called CycL. CYC is a registered trademark of Cycorp. The interested reader is directed to http://www.cyc.com/tech.html for more information.) system of Lenat and Guha (1990) attempts just that. CYC postulates that all human knowledge can be represented as a network of propositions. Thus, it has a local, propositional structure, as well as global structure—the relations among propositions and the operations that these relations afford. Like WordNet, however, CYC is a static structure, always vulnerable because some piece of human knowledge has not been coded or acts in an unanticipated way in a new context.

Therefore, some authors have argued for knowledge representations that learn what they need to know and thus are capable of keeping up with the demands of an ever-changing context. One such proposal is reviewed in the following section.

Latent Semantic Analysis

Latent semantic analysis (LSA) is a machine learning procedure that constructs a high-dimensional semantic space from an input consisting of a large amount of text (LSA is also discussed in this volume in the chapter by Treiman, Clifton, Meyer, & Wurm and in the chapter by Goldstone & Kersten). LSA analyzes the pattern of co-occurrences among words in many thousands of documents, using the well-known mathematical technique of singular value decomposition. This technique allows one to extract 300–500 dimensions of meaning that are capable of representing human semantic intuitions with considerable accuracy. LSA generates a semantic space in which words as well as sentences or whole texts are represented as mathematical vectors. The angle between two vectors (as measured by their cosine) provides a useful, fully automatic measure of the semantic similarity between the words they represent. Thus, we can compute the semantic similarity between any two word pairs or any two texts.

Randomly chosen word pairs tend to have an average cosine very near zero ($M = .02$, $SD = .06$), whereas a sample of 100 singular and plural word pairs (e.g., house, houses) have much higher, but not perfect, average cosines ($M = .66$, $SD = .15$). What is computed here is not word overlap or word co-occurrence, but something entirely new: a semantic distance in a high-dimensional space that was constructed from such data.

The distinction between measurement of word overlap and semantic content as measured by LSA is illustrated in the following example taken from Butcher and Kintsch (2001). Two students learn a text containing the following statement: *The phonological loop responds to the phonetic characteristics of speech but does not evaluate speech for semantic content.* In a summary, Student A writes "The rehearsal loop that practices speech sounds does not pick up meaning in words. Rather, it just reacts whenever it hears something that sounds like language." Student B writes, "The loop that listens to words does not understand anything about the phonetic noises that it hears. All it does is listen for noise and then responds by practicing that noise." As human comprehenders, we can see that Student A has a better understanding of the text and has constructed a more appropriate summary of that bit of information. Using LSA to compare each student's summary with the learned text, we find that Student A's text has a cosine of .62 with the original text, whereas Student B's text has a cosine of only .40 with the original text (Only the relative values of cosines generated for equivalent types of text can be compared. Cosines for word pairs and sentence pairs, for instance, are not comparable.). Note that this result is not due to overlapping words in the text and summaries; Student A repeats two words from the original sentence but Student B repeats three words from the original sentence. Using the relative values of the cosines, LSA tells us what we have concluded by reading the texts: Student A's summary is a closer semantic match to the original text than that of Student B. The differences between the texts are subtle but clear; although Student B is not completely confused, his summary does reflect a less thorough understanding of the original content than does Student A's summary. For more detailed descriptions of LSA, see Landauer (1998), Landauer and Dumais (1997), and Landauer, Foltz, and Laham (1998).

Before examining the achievements of LSA, its limitations must be discussed, for LSA is by no means a complete semantic theory; rather, it provides a strong basis for building such a theory. First, LSA disregards syntax and syntax obviously plays a role in determining the meaning of sentences. Second, LSA can learn only from written text, whereas human experience is based on perception, action, and emotion—the real world, not just words—as well. Third, LSA starts with a tabula rasa, whereas the acquisition of human knowledge is subject to epigenetic constraints that determine its very character. Surprisingly, neither of these problems is fatal. Much can be achieved without syntax, and it is possible to bring syntactic information to bear within the LSA framework, at least to some extent, as we discuss later in this chapter. Words are not all of human knowledge, but language has evolved to talk about all human affairs—action, perception, emotion. Thus, words mirror the nonverbal aspects of human experience—not with complete accuracy, but enough to make LSA useful. Finally, LSA does not learn from scratch but from language. Thus its input already incorporates the epigenetic rules that structure human knowledge.

LSA makes semantic judgments that are humanlike in many ways, but it can only perform correctly when it has been trained on an appropriate textual corpus. One of the semantic spaces that has been constructed represents the knowledge of a typical American high-school graduate: It is based on a text of more than 11 million words, comprising over 90,000 different words and over 36,000 documents. It is a model of what a high-school student would know if all his or her experience were limited to reading these texts. In one respect this is not much, but in another it is a considerable achievement. It will, for instance, pass the TOEFL test of English as foreign language: Given a rare word (like *abandoned*) and several alternatives (like *forsake, aberration,* and *deviance*) it will choose the correct one, because *forsake* has a higher cosine (.20) with the target word than the other alternatives (.09 and .09). On the other hand, it will fail an introductory psychology multiple-choice exam, because the high-school reading material does not contain enough psychology texts. If we create a new space by teaching LSA psychology with a standard introductory text, however, it will pass the test: Asked to match *attention* to the alternatives *memory, selectivity, problem solving,* and *language,* it will correctly choose *selectivity,* because the cosine between *attention* and *selectivity* is .52 and the cosines between *attention* and the other alternatives are only .17, .05, and .07, respectively.

LSA is a powerful tool for the simulation of psycholinguistic phenomena. Landauer and Dumais (1997) have discussed vocabulary acquisition as the construction of a semantic space, modeled by LSA; Laham (2000) investigated the emergence of natural categories from the LSA space; Foltz, Kintsch, and Landauer (1998) have used LSA to analyze textual coherence; and Butcher and Kintsch (2001) have used LSA as an analytic tool in the study of writing. LSA has also been used effectively in a number of applications that depend on an effective representation of verbal meaning. To mention just some of the practical applications, there is first the use of LSA to select instructional texts that are appropriate to a student's level of background knowledge (Wolfe et al., 1998). Second, LSA provides feedback about their writing to 6th-grade students summarizing science or social science texts (E. Kintsch et al., 2000). And last but not least, LSA has been successfully employed for essay grading. LSA grades the content of certain types of essays as well and as reliably as human professionals (Landauer, Laham, & Foltz, 2000). The humanlike performance of LSA in these areas strongly suggests that the way meaning is represented in LSA is closely related to the way humans operate.

Again, LSA does a very good job of representing semantic meaning, but it does not represent all the components of language that humans may use in comprehension. For one thing, people use syntax in the construction of meaning, whereas LSA does not. However, it might be possible to combine LSA with other psychological process theories, thereby expanding the scope of an LSA-based theory of meaning. W. Kintsch (2001) has combined an LSA knowledge base with a spreading activation model of comprehension, thereby offering a solution to the problem of how word senses might be generated in a discourse context—instead of being prelisted, as in WordNet.

According to LSA, word meanings are vectors in a high-dimensional semantic space. The meaning of a two-word sentence in LSA is the centroid of the two-word vectors. Thus, for *The horse runs* and *The color runs,* we compute the vectors {*horse, runs*} and {*color, runs*}. However, there is a problem, for the meaning of *run* in the two contexts is somewhat different; two different senses of the verb *run* are involved.

In the CI model of discourse comprehension (W. Kintsch, 1988, 1998), mental representations of a text are constructed via a constraint satisfaction process, computationally realized via a spreading-activation mechanism: The semantic relations among the concepts and propositions of a text are strengthened if they fit into the overall context and deactivated if they do not. This idea can be extended to the predication problem. Those aspects of the predicate (*run* in our example) that are appropriate for its argument are strengthened and the others are de-emphasized. This is achieved by means of a constraint satisfaction process in the manner of the CI model, in which the argument is allowed to select related relevant terms from the neighborhood of the predicate, which are then used to modify the predicate vector appropriately (W. Kintsch, 2001).

This turns out to be a powerful algorithm. It correctly computes that *The bridge collapsed* is related to *failure* and that *The runner collapsed* is related to *race*. It differentiates appropriately between *A pelican is a bird* and *The bird is a pelican*. It also correctly computes the meaning of metaphors—for example, that *My lawyer is a shark* is more related to *viciousness* than to *fish* (W. Kintsch, 2000). Furthermore, it computes that *The student washed the table* is more related to *The table is clean* than *The student is clean*. And it mirrors many of the well-documented asymmetries and context effects in human similarity judgments (W. Kintsch, 2001).

LSA by itself models the associative foundation of meaning. Together with the spreading-activation mechanism of the CI theory, it allows us to model a broad range of additional phenomena, but we still fall short of a complete semantic theory. We need to explore other psychological process theories of human thought processes that can be combined with an LSA knowledge base to further broaden the scope of an LSA-based semantic theory. Research on LSA is still new, but one can expect that it will have an increasingly large impact on the way we think about comprehension and the way we do research on language in the coming years.

CONCLUSIONS

Overall, cognitive psychology has made great strides in understanding the factors that predict individual differences in comprehension. We have learned about both factors internal to the learner (such as background knowledge) and external to the individual (such as text organization or conversational coherence) that determine comprehension. The variables influencing comprehension performance interact in quite complex ways; as discussed earlier, readers who are knowledgeable about a subject learn better from a difficult text, whereas readers with less prior knowledge about a topic learn better from a more coherent, organized text. Thus, no single factor can be shown to be sufficient to ensure adequate comprehension by a learner, and no single prescription can be recommended for all learners in all situations.

The practical applications of comprehension research are obvious; with adequate understanding of the variables that influence reading and listening comprehension, educators can manipulate situations to maximize learning for an individual in a set of particular circumstances. Even though cognitive psychologists understand many of the variables that influence learning, unfortunately we are far from developing a complete model of comprehension. There currently is no exact recipe for creating comprehension in a learner. We know about some key ingredients of the comprehension recipe and how they contribute to a successful performance, but we do not fully understand the extent to which changes in these factors exert a direct influence on comprehension and the extent to which they impact other variables in the learning situation. In addition, we have a lot to learn about the individual variables that are difficult to quantify (e.g., motivation, persistence, interest) but undoubtedly are critical in a full model of comprehension. The current and future challenge for research in comprehension is to continue to uncover variables in input and individual factors that influence and support learning and to integrate such knowledge into the already complex picture of what makes a good learner.

REFERENCES

Adams, B. C., Bell, L. C., & Perfetti, C. A. (1995). A trading relationship between reading skill and domain knowledge in children's text comprehension. *Discourse Processes, 20,* 307–323.

Alexander, P. A., Kulikowich, J. M., & Jetton, T. L. (1994). The role of subject-matter knowledge and interest in the processing of linear and nonlinear texts. *Review of Educational Research, 64,* 201–252.

Anderson, R. C., & Pichert, J. W. (1978). Recall of previously unrecallable material following a shift in perspective. *Journal of Verbal Behavior and Verbal Learning, 17,* 1–12.

Ausubel, D. P. (1960). The use of advance organizers in the learning and retention of meaningful verbal material. *Journal of Educational Psychology, 51,* 267–272.

Baddeley, A. (1986). *Working Memory.* New York: Oxford University Press.

Bartlett, F. C. (1932). *Remembering.* Cambridge, UK: Cambridge University Press.

Barwise, J., & Perry, J. (1983). *Situations and attitudes.* Cambridge, MA: MIT Press.

Beck, I. L., McKeown, M. G., Sinatra, G. M., & Loxterman, J. A. (1991). Revising social studies texts from a text-processing perspective: Evidence of improved comprehensibility. *Reading Research Quarterly, 27,* 251–276.

Bransford, J. D., Barclay, J. R., & Franks, J. J. (1972). Sentence memory: A constructive versus interpretive approach. *Cognitive Psychology, 3,* 193–209.

Britton, B. K., & Gulgoz, S. (1991). Using Kintsch's computational model to improve instructional text: Effects of repairing inference calls on recall and cognitive structures. *Journal of Educational Psychology, 83,* 329–345.

Brooks, L. W., Dansereau, D. F., Spurlin, J. E., & Holley, C. D. (1983). Effects of headings on text processing. *Journal of Educational Psychology, 75,* 292–302.

Butcher, K. R., & Kintsch, W. (2001). Support of content and rhetorical processes of writing: Effects on the writing process and the written product. *Cognition and Instruction, 19,* 277–322.

Cain, K. (1999). Ways of reading: How knowledge and use of strategies are related to reading comprehension. *British Journal of Developmental Psychology, 17,* 293–312.

Carpenter, P. A., Miyake, A., & Just, M. A. (1994). Working memory constraints on the resolution of lexical ambiguity: Maintaining multiple interpretations in neutral contexts. *Journal of Memory and Language, 33,* 175–202.

Chomsky, N. (1965). *Aspects of the theory of syntax.* Cambridge, MA: MIT Press.

Clark, E. V. (1997). Conceptual perspective and lexical choice in acquisition. *Cognition, 64,* 1–37.

Clark, H. H. (1996). *Using language.* Cambridge, UK: Cambridge University Press.

Clark, H. H. (2000). Conversation. In A. E. Kazdin (Ed.), *Encyclopedia of psychology* (pp. 292–294). New York: Oxford University Press.

Clark, H. H., & Schaefer, E. R. (1989). Contributing to discourse. *Cognitive Science, 13,* 259–294.

Corkill, A. J. (1992). Advance organizers: Facilitators of recall. *Educational Psychology Review, 4,* 33–67.

Daneman, M., & Carpenter, P. A. (1980). Individual differences in working memory and reading. *Journal of Verbal Learning and Verbal Behavior, 19,* 450–466.

Daneman, M., & Carpenter, P. A. (1983). Individual differences in integrating information between and within sentences. *Journal of Experimental Psychology: Learning, Memory, and Cognition, 9,* 561–584.

DeJong, G. F. (1979). Prediction and substantiation: A new approach to natural language processing. *Cognitive Science, 3,* 251–272.

Elman, J. L., Bates, E. A., Johnson, M. H., Karmiloff-Smith, A., Parisi, D., & Plunkett, K. (1996). *Rethinking innateness: A connectionist perspective on development.* Cambridge, MA: MIT Press.

Ericsson, K. A., Chase, W. G., & Faloon, S. (1980). Acquisition of a memory skill. *Science, 208,* 1181–1182.

Ericsson, K. A., & Kintsch, W. (1995). Long-term working memory. *Psychological Review, 102,* 211–245.

Ericsson, K. A., & Polson, P. (1988). An experimental analysis of the mechanisms of a memory skill. *Memory and Cognition, 14,* 305–316.

Fellbaum, C. (Ed.). (1998). *WordNet: An electronic lexical database.* Cambridge, UK: Cambridge University Press.

Ferstl, E., & Kintsch, W. (1999). Learning from text: Structural knowledge assessment in the study of discourse comprehension. In H. V. Ostendorp & S. Goldman (Eds.), *The construction of mental representations during reading* (pp. 247–278). Mahwah, NJ: Erlbaum.

Foltz, P. W., Kintsch, W., & Landauer, T. K. (1998). The measurement of textual coherence with Latent Semantic Analysis. *Discourse Processes, 25,* 285–308.

Friedman, N. P., & Miyake, A. (2000). Differential roles for visuospatial and verbal working memory in situation model construction. *Journal of Experimental Psychology: General, 129,* 61–83.

Goldman, S. R., & Varma, S. (1995). CAPing the construction-integration model of discourse comprehension. In C. A. Weaver III, S. M. Mannes, & C. R. Fletcher (Eds.), *Discourse comprehension: Essays in honor of Walter Kintsch* (pp. 337–358). Hillsdale, NJ: Erlbaum.

Graesser, A. C., Millis, K. K., & Zwaan, R. A. (1997). Discourse comprehension. *Annual Review of Psychology, 48,* 163–189.

Graesser, A. C., Singer, M., & Trabasso, T. (1994). Constructing inferences during narrative text comprehension. *Psychological Review, 101,* 371–395.

Haenggi, D., & Perfetti, C. A. (1994). Processing components of college-level reading comprehension. *Discourse Processes, 17,* 83–104.

Halliday, M. A. K., & Hasan, R. (1976). *Cohesion in English.* London: Longman.

Haviland, S. E., & Clark, H. H. (1974). What's new? Acquiring new information as a process in comprehension. *Journal of Verbal Behavior and Verbal Learning, 13,* 512–521.

Isaacs, E. A., & Clark, H. (1987). References in conversation between experts and novices. *Journal of Experimental Psychology: General, 116,* 26–37.

Jarvella, R. J. (1971). Syntactic processing of connected speech. *Journal of Verbal Learning and Verbal Behavior, 10,* 409–416.

Jenkins, J. J. (1974). Remember that old theory of memory? Well, forget it! *American Psychologist, 29,* 785–795.

Jurafsky, D., & Martin, J. H. (2000). *Speech and language processing.* Upper Saddle River, NJ: Prentice-Hall.

Just, M. A., & Carpenter, P. A. (1987). *The psychology of reading and language comprehension.* Boston: Allyn & Bacon.

Just, M. A., & Carpenter, P. A. (1992). A capacity theory of comprehension: Individual differences in working memory. *Psychological Review, 99,* 122–149.

Kintsch, E., Steinhart, D., Stahl, G., Matthews, C., Lamb, R., & the LSA Research Group. (2000). Developing summarization skills through the use of LSA-backed feedback. *Interactive Learning Environments, 8,* 87–109.

Kintsch, W. (1974). *The representation of meaning in memory.* Hillsdale, NJ: Erlbaum.

Kintsch, W. (1988). The use of knowledge in discourse processing: A construction-integration model. *Psychological Review, 95,* 163–182.

Kintsch, W. (1993). Information accretion and reduction in text processing: Inferences. *Discourse Processes, 16,* 193–202.

Kintsch, W. (1994). Text comprehension, memory, and learning. *American Psychologist, 49,* 294–303.

Kintsch, W. (1998). *Comprehension: A paradigm for cognition.* New York: Cambridge University Press.

Kintsch, W. (2000). Metaphor comprehension: A computational theory. *Psychonomic Bulletin & Review, 7,* 257–266.

Kintsch, W. (2001). Predication. *Cognitive Science, 25,* 173–202.

Kintsch, W., Patel, V. L., & Ericsson, K. A. (1999). The role of long-term working memory in text comprehension. *Psychologia, 42,* 186–198.

Kintsch, W., & van Dijk, T. A. (1978). Towards a model of text comprehension and production. *Psychological Review, 85,* 363–394.

Kintsch, W., Welsch, D., Schmalhofer, F., & Zimny, S. (1990). Sentence memory: A theoretical analysis. *Journal of Memory and Language, 29,* 133–159.

Klin, C. M., Guzman, A. E., & Levine, W. H. (1999). Prevalence and persistence of predictive inferences. *Journal of Memory and Language, 40,* 593–604.

Labov, W. (1972). *Sociolinguistic patterns.* Philadelphia: University of Pennsylvania Press.

Laham, R. D. (2000). *Automated content assessment of text using Latent Semantic Analysis to simulate human cognition.* Unpublished doctoral dissertation, University of Colorado, Colorado.

Landauer, T. K. (1998). Learning and representing verbal meaning: Latent Semantic Analysis theory. *Current Directions in Psychological Science, 7,* 161–164.

Landauer, T. K., & Dumais, S. T. (1997). A solution to Plato's problem: The Latent Semantic Analysis theory of acquisition, induction and representation of knowledge. *Psychological Review, 104,* 211–240.

Landauer, T. K., Foltz, P. W., & Laham, D. (1998). An introduction to Latent Semantic Analysis. *Discourse Processes, 25,* 259–284.

Landauer, T. K., Laham, D., & Foltz, P. (2000). The Intelligent Essay Assessor. *IEEE Intelligent Systems,* 27–31.

Lenat, D., & Guha, R. (1990). *Building large knowledge-based systems.* Reading, MA: Addison-Wesley.

Lorch, R. F., & Lorch, E. P. (1985). Topic structure representation and text recall. *Journal of Educational Psychology, 77,* 137–148.

Lorch, R. F., & Lorch, E. P. (1995). Effects of organizational signals on text-processing strategies. *Journal of Educational Psychology, 87,* 537–544.

Lorch, R. F., Lorch, E. P., & Inman, W. E. (1993). Effects of signaling topic structure on text recall. *Journal of Educational Psychology, 85,* 281–290.

Lyons, J. (1977). *Semantics.* Cambridge, UK: Cambridge University Press.

McDaniel, M. A., Waddill, P. J., Finstad, K., & Bourg, T. (2000). The effects of text-based interest on attention and recall. *Journal of Educational Psychology, 92,* 492–502.

McKoon, G., & Ratcliff, R. (1992). Inference during reading. *Psychological Review, 99,* 440–466.

McNamara, D. S., Kintsch, E., Songer, N. B., & Kintsch, W. (1996). Are good texts always better? Text coherence, background knowledge, and levels of understanding in learning from text. *Cognition and Instruction, 14,* 1–43.

McNamara, D. S., & Kintsch, W. (1996). Learning from text: Effect of prior knowledge and text coherence. *Discourse Processes, 22,* 247–288.

Miller, G. A. (1996). *The science of words.* New York: Freeman.

Miller, J. R., & W. Kintsch (1980). Readability and recall for short passages: A theoretical analysis. *Journal of Experimental Psychology: Human Learning and Memory, 6,* 335–354.

Moravcsik, J. E., & Kintsch, W. (1993). Writing quality, reading skills, and domain knowledge as factors in text comprehension. *Canadian Journal of Experimental Psychology, 47,* 360–374.

Myers, J. L., Cook, A. E., Kambe, G., Mason, R., & O'Brien, E. J. (2000). Semantic and episodic effects on bridging inferences. *Discourse Processes, 29,* 179–199.

Narvaez, D., van den Broek, P., & Ruiz, A. B. (1999). The influence of reading purpose on inference generation and comprehension in reading. *Journal of Educational Psychology, 91,* 488–496.

Palincsar, A. S., & Brown, A. L. (1984). Reciprocal teaching of comprehension-fostering and comprehension-monitoring activities. *Cognition and Instruction, 1,* 117–175.

Rayner, K., Pacht, J. M., & Duffy, S. A. (1994). Effects of prior encounter and global discourse bias on the processing of lexically ambiguous words: Evidence from eye fixations. *Journal of Memory and Language, 33,* 527–544.

Recht, D. R., & Leslie, L. (1988). Effect of prior knowledge on good and poor readers. *Journal of Educational Psychology, 80,* 16–20.

Revlin, R., & Hegarty, M. (1999). Resolving signals to cohesion: Two models of bridging inference. *Discourse Processes, 27,* 77–102.

Rumelhart, D. E., & Ortony, A. (1977). The representation of knowledge in memory. In R. C. Anderson, R. J. Spiro, & W. E. Montague (Eds.), *Schooling and the acquisition of knowledge* (pp. 99–135). Hillsdale, NJ: Erlbaum.

Sadoski, M., Goetz, E. T., & Rodriguez, M. (2000). Engaging texts: Effects of concreteness on comprehensibility, interest, and recall in four text types. *Journal of Educational Psychology, 92,* 85–95.

Sanders, T. J. M., & Noordman, L. G. M. (2000). The role of coherence relations and their linguistic markers in text processing. *Discourse Processes, 29,* 37–60.

Schank, R. C. (1982). *Dynamic memory.* Cambridge, UK: Cambridge University Press.

Schank, R. C., & Abelson, R. P. (1977). *Scripts, plans, goals, and understanding.* Hillsdale, NJ: Erlbaum.

Schneider, W., Körkel, J., & Weinert, F. (1989). Domain-specific knowledge and memory performance: A comparison of high- and low-aptitude children. *Journal of Educational Psychology, 81,* 306–312.

Schraw, G. (1998). Processing and recall differences among selective details. *Journal of Educational Psychology, 90,* 3–12.

Seuren, P. A. M. (1985). *Discourse semantics.* New York: Basil Blackwell.

Singer, M., Andrusiak, P., Reisdorf, P., & Black, N. L. (1992). Individual differences in bridging inference processes. *Memory & Cognition, 20,* 539–548.

Singer, M., & Ritchot, K. F. M. (1996). The role of working memory capacity and knowledge access in text inference processing. *Memory & Cognition, 24,* 733–743.

Swinney, D. A. (1979). Lexical access during sentence comprehension: (Re)consideration of context effects. *Journal of Verbal Learning and Verbal Behavior, 18,* 645–659.

Till, R. E., Mross, E. F., & Kintsch, W. (1988). Time course of priming for associate and inference words in a discourse context. *Memory & Cognition, 16,* 283–298.

van den Broek, P., Risden, K., Fletcher, C. R., & Thurlow, R. (1996). A "landscape" view of reading: Fluctuating patterns of activation and the construction of a stable memory representation. In B. K. Britton & A. C. Graesser (Eds.), *Models of understanding text* (pp. 165–187). Hillsdale, NJ: Erlbaum.

van Dijk, T. A. (1972). *Some aspects of text grammars.* The Hague, The Netherlands: Mouton.

van Dijk, T. A., & Kintsch, W. (1983). *Strategies of discourse comprehension.* New York: Academic Press.

Walker, C. H. (1987). Relative importance of domain knowledge and overall aptitude on acquisition of domain-related knowledge. *Cognition and Instruction, 4,* 25–42.

Walker, C. I., & Yekovich, F. R. (1984). Script based inferences: Effects of text and knowledge variables on recognition memory. *Journal of Verbal Learning and Verbal Behavior, 23,* 357–370.

Whitney, P., Budd, D., Bramucci, R. S., & Crane, R. S. (1995). On babies, bathwater, and schemata: A reconsideration of top-down processes in comprehension. *Discourse Processes, 20,* 135–166.

Whitney, P., Ritchie, B. G., & Clark, M. B. (1991). Working-memory capacity and the use of elaborative inferences in text comprehension. *Discourse Processes, 14,* 133–145.

Wiley, J., & Voss, J. F. (1999). Constructing arguments from multiple sources: Tasks that promote understanding and not just memory for text. *Journal of Educational Psychology, 91,* 301–311.

Wolfe, M. B. W., Schreiner, M. E., Rehder, B., Laham, D., Foltz, P., Kintsch, W., & Landauer, T. K. (1998). Learning from text: Matching readers and texts by Latent Semantic Analysis. *Discourse Processes, 25,* 309–336.

Zwaan, R. A., & Radvansky, G. A. (1998). Situation models in language comprehension and memory. *Psychological Bulletin, 123,* 162–185.

PART EIGHT

THINKING AND APPLICATIONS

CHAPTER 22

Concepts and Categorization

ROBERT L. GOLDSTONE AND ALAN KERSTEN

Issues related to concepts and categorization are nearly ubiquitous in psychology because of people's natural tendency to perceive a thing as something. We have a powerful impulse to interpret our world. This act of interpretation, an act of "seeing something as X" rather than simply seeing it (Wittgenstein, 1953), is fundamentally an act of categorization.

The attraction of research on concepts is that an extremely wide variety of cognitive acts can be understood as categorizations. Identifying the person sitting across from you at the breakfast table involves categorizing something as (for example) your spouse. Diagnosing the cause of someone's illness involves a disease categorization. Interpreting a painting as a Picasso, an artifact as Mayan, a geometry as non-Euclidean, a fugue as baroque, a conversationalist as charming, a wine as a Bordeaux, and a government as socialist are categorizations at various levels of abstraction. The typically unspoken assumption of research on concepts is that these cognitive acts have something in common. That is, there are principles that explain many or all acts of categorization. This assumption is controversial (see Medin, Lynch, & Solomon, 2000), but is perhaps justified by the potential payoff of discovering common principles governing concepts in their diverse manifestations.

The desirability of a general account of concept learning has led the field to focus its energy on what might be called generic concepts. Experiments typically involve artificial categories that are (it is hoped) unfamiliar to the subject. Formal models of concept learning and use are constructed to be able to handle any kind of concept irrespective of its content. Although there are exceptions to this general trend (Malt, 1994; Ross & Murphy, 1999), much of the mainstream empirical and theoretical work on concept learning is concerned not with explaining how particular concepts are created, but with how concepts in general are represented and processed.

One manifestation of this approach is that the members of a concept are often given an abstract symbolic representation. For example, Table 22.1 shows a typical notation used to describe the stimuli seen by a subject in a psychological experiment or presented to a formal model of concept learning. Nine objects belong to two categories, and each object is defined by its value along four binary dimensions. In this notation, objects from Category A typically have values of 1 on each of the four dimensions, whereas objects from Category B have values of 0. The dimensions are typically unrelated to each other, and assigning values of 0 and 1 to a dimension is

The authors are grateful to Alice Healy, Robert Proctor, Brian Rogosky, and Irving Weiner for helpful comments on earlier drafts of this chapter. This research was funded by NIH Grant MH56871, NSF Grant 0125287, and a Gill fellowship to the first author.

TABLE 22.1 A Common Category Structure, Originally Used by Medin and Schaffer (1978)

		Dimension			
Category	Stimulus	D1	D2	D3	D4
Category A	A1	1	1	1	0
	A2	1	0	1	0
	A3	1	0	1	1
	A4	1	1	0	1
	A5	0	1	1	1
Category B	B1	1	1	0	0
	B2	0	1	1	0
	B3	0	0	0	1
	B4	0	0	0	0

arbitrary. For example, for a color dimension, red may be assigned a value of 0 and blue a value 1. The exact category structure of Table 22.1 has been used in at least 30 studies (reviewed by J. D. Smith & Minda, 2000), instantiated by stimuli as diverse as geometric forms (Nosofsky, Kruschke, & McKinley, 1992), cartoons of faces (Medin & Schaffer, 1978), yearbook photographs (Medin, Dewey, & Murphy, 1983), and line drawings of rocket ships (Nosofsky, Palmeri, & McKinley, 1994). These authors are not particularly interested in the category structure of Table 22.1 and are certainly not interested in the categorization of rocket ships per se. Instead, they choose their structures and stimuli so as to be (a) unfamiliar (so that learning is required), (b) well controlled (dimensions are approximately equally salient and independent), (c) diagnostic with respect to theories, and (d) potentially generalizable to natural categories that people learn. Work on generic concepts is very valuable if it turns out that there are domain-general principles underlying human concepts that can be discovered. Still, there is no a priori reason to assume that all concepts will follow the same principles, or that we can generalize from generic concepts to naturally occurring concepts.

WHAT ARE CONCEPTS?

Concepts, Categories, and Internal Representations

A good starting place is Edward E. Smith's (1989) characterization that a concept is "a mental representation of a class or individual and deals with what is being represented and how that information is typically used during the categorization" (p. 502). It is common to distinguish between a concept and a category. A concept refers to a mentally possessed idea or notion, whereas a category refers to a set of entities that are grouped together. The concept **dog** is whatever psychological state signifies thoughts of dogs. The category **dog** consists of all the entities in the real world that are appropriately categorized as dogs. The question of whether concepts determine categories or vice versa is an important foundational controversy. If one assumes the primacy of external categories of entities, then one will tend to view concept learning as the enterprise of inductively creating mental structures that predict these categories. One extreme version of this view is the exemplar model of concept learning (Estes, 1994; Medin & Schaffer, 1978; Nosofsky, 1984; see also Capaldi's chapter in this volume), in which one's internal representation for a concept is nothing more than the set of all of the externally supplied examples of the concept to which one has been exposed. If one assumes the primacy of internal mental concepts, then one tends to view external categories as the end product of applying these internal concepts to observed entities. An extreme version of this approach is to argue that the external world does not inherently consist of rocks, dogs, and tables; these are mental concepts that organize an otherwise unstructured external world (Lakoff, 1987).

Equivalence Classes

Another important aspect of concepts is that they are equivalence classes. In the classical notion of an equivalence class, distinguishable stimuli come to be treated as the same thing once they have been placed in the same category (Sidman, 1994). This kind of equivalence is too strong when it comes to human concepts because even when we place two objects into the same category, we do not treat them as the same thing for all purposes. Some researchers have stressed the intrinsic variability of human concepts—variability that makes it unlikely that a concept has the same sense or meaning each time it is used (Barsalou, 1987; Thelen & Smith, 1994). Still, it is impressive the extent to which perceptually dissimilar things can be treated equivalently, given the appropriate conceptualization. To the biologist armed with a strong **mammal** concept, even whales and dogs may be treated as equivalent in many situations related to biochemistry, child rearing, and thermoregulation. Even sea lions may possess equivalence classes, as Schusterman, Reichmuth, and Kastak (2000) have argued that these animals show free substitution between two entities once they have been associated together.

Equivalence classes are relatively impervious to superficial similarities. Once one has formed a concept that treats all skunks as equivalent for some purposes, irrelevant variations among skunks can be greatly deemphasized. When subjects are told a story in which scientists discover that an animal that looks exactly like a raccoon actually contains the internal organs of a skunk and has skunk parents and skunk children, they often categorize the animal as a skunk (Keil, 1989;

Rips, 1989). People may never be able to transcend superficial appearances when categorizing objects (Goldstone, 1994a), nor is it clear that they would want to (Jones & Smith, 1993). Still, one of the most powerful aspects of concepts is their ability to make superficially different things alike (Sloman, 1996). If one has the concept Things to remove from a burning house, even children and jewelry become similar (Barsalou, 1983). The spoken phonemes /d/ /o/ /g/, the French word chien, the written word dog, and a picture of a dog can all trigger one's concept of **dog** (Snodgrass, 1984), and although they may trigger slightly different representations, much of the core information will be the same. Concepts are particularly useful when we need to make connections between things that have different apparent forms.

WHAT DO CONCEPTS DO FOR US?

Fundamentally, concepts function as filters. We do not have direct access to our external world. We have access to our world only as filtered through our concepts. Concepts are useful when they provide informative or diagnostic ways of structuring this world. An excellent way of understanding the mental world of an individual, group, scientific community, or culture is to find out how they organize their world into concepts (Lakoff, 1987; Medin & Atran, 1999; Wolff, Medin, & Pankratz, 1999).

Components of Thought

Concepts are cognitive elements that combine to generatively produce an infinite variety of thoughts. Just as a finite set of building blocks can be constructed into an endless variety of architectural structures, so can concepts act as building blocks for an endless variety of complex thoughts. Claiming that concepts are cognitive elements does not entail that they are primitive elements in the sense of existing without being learned and without being constructed from other concepts. Some theorists have argued that concepts such as **bachelor**, **kill**, and **house** are primitive in this sense (Fodor, 1975; Fodor, Garrett, Walker, & Parkes, 1980), but a considerable body of evidence suggests that concepts typically are acquired elements that are themselves decomposable into semantic elements (McNamara & Miller, 1989).

Once a concept has been formed, it can enter into compositions with other concepts. Several researchers have studied how novel combinations of concepts are produced and comprehended. For example, how does one interpret the term buffalo paper when one first hears it? Is it paper in the shape of buffalo, paper used to wrap buffaloes presented as gifts, an essay on the subject of buffalo, coarse paper, or something like fly paper but used to catch bison? Interpretations of word combinations are often created by finding a relation that connects the two concepts. In Murphy's (1988) concept specialization model, one interprets noun-noun combinations by finding a variable that the second noun has that can be filled by the first noun. By this account, a robin snake might be interpreted as a snake that eats robins once **robin** is used to the fill the **eats** slot in the **snake** concept. Wisniewski (1997, 1998; Wisniewski & Love, 1998) has argued that properties from one concept are often transferred to another concept, and that this is more likely to occur if the concepts are similar, with parts that can be easily aligned. By this account, a robin snake may be interpreted as a snake with a red belly, once the attribute **red breast** from the robin is transferred to the snake.

In addition to promoting creative thought, the combinatorial power of concepts is required for cognitive systematicity (Fodor & Pylyshyn, 1988). The notion of systematicity is that a system's ability to entertain complex thoughts is intrinsically connected to its ability to entertain the components of those thoughts. In the field of conceptual combination, this has appeared as the issue of whether the meaning of a combination of concepts can be deduced on the basis of the meanings of its constituents. On the one hand, there are some salient violations of this type of systematicity. When adjective and noun concepts are combined, there are sometimes emergent interactions that cannot be predicted by the "main effects" of the concepts themselves. For example, the concept **gray hair** is more similar to **white hair** than to **black hair**, but **gray cloud** is more similar to **black cloud** than to **white cloud** (Medin & Shoben, 1988). Wooden spoons are judged to be fairly large (for spoons), even though this property is not generally possessed by wooden objects or spoons in general (Medin & Shoben, 1988). On the other hand, there have been notable successes in predicting how well an object fits a conjunctive description based on how well it fits the individual descriptions that comprise the conjunction (Hampton, 1987, 1997; Storms, De Boeck, Hampton, & Van Mechelen, 1999). A reasonable reconciliation of these results is that when concepts are combined the concepts' meanings systematically determine the meaning of the conjunction, but emergent interactions and real-world plausibility also shape the conjunction's meaning.

Inductive Predictions

Concepts allow us to generalize our experiences with some objects to other objects from the same category. Experience with one slobbering dog may lead one to suspect that an unfamiliar dog may have the same proclivity. These inductive generalizations may be wrong and can lead to unfair stereotypes if inadequately supported by data, but if an organism is to survive in a world that has some systematicity, it must "go beyond the information given" (Bruner, 1973) and generalize what it has learned. The concepts we use most often are useful because they allow many properties to be predicted inductively. To see why this is the case, we must digress slightly and consider different types of concepts. Categories can be arranged roughly in order of their grounding by similarity: natural kinds (**dog** and **oak tree**), man-made artifacts (**hammer, airplane,** and **chair**), ad hoc categories (**things to take out of a burning house,** and **things that could be stood on to reach a lightbulb**), and abstract schemas or metaphors (e.g., **events in which a kind action is repaid with cruelty, metaphorical prisons,** and **problems that are solved by breaking a large force into parts that converge on a target**). For the latter categories, members need not have very much in common at all. An unrewarding job and a relationship that cannot be ended may both be metaphorical prisons, but the situations may share little other than this.

Unlike ad hoc and metaphor-based categories, most natural kinds and many artifacts are characterized by members that share many features. In a series of studies, Rosch (Rosch, 1975; Rosch & Mervis, 1975; see also the chapters in this volume by Palmer and by Treiman, Clifton, Meyer, & Wurm) has shown that the members of natural kind and artifact "basic-level" categories such as chair, trout, bus, apple, saw, and guitar are characterized by high within-category overall similarity. Subjects listed features for basic-level categories, as well as for broader superordinate (e.g., furniture) and narrower subordinate (e.g., kitchen chair) categories. An index of within-category similarity was obtained by tallying the number of features listed by subjects that were common to items in the same category. Items within a basic-level category tend to have several features in common, far more than items within a superordinate category and almost as many as items that share a subordinate categorization. Rosch (Rosch & Mervis, 1975; Rosch, Mervis, Gray, Johnson, & Boyes-Braem, 1976) argues that categories are defined by family resemblance; category members need not all share a definitional feature, but they tend to have several features in common. Furthermore, she argues that people's basic-level categories preserve the intrinsic correlational structure of the world. All feature combinations are not equally likely. For example, in the animal kingdom, flying is correlated with laying eggs and possessing a beak. There are "clumps" of features that tend to occur together. Some categories (e.g., ad hoc categories) do not conform to these clumps, but many of our most natural-seeming categories do.

These natural categories also permit many inductive inferences. If we know something belongs to the category **dog,** then we know that it probably has four legs and two eyes, eats dog food, is someone's pet, pants, barks, is bigger than a breadbox, and so on. Generally, natural-kind objects, particularly those at Rosch's basic level, permit many inferences. Basic-level categories allow many inductions because their members share similarities across many dimensions or features. Ad hoc categories and highly metaphorical categories permit fewer inductive inferences, but in certain situations the inferences they allow are so important that the categories are created on a "by-need" basis. One interesting possibility is that all concepts are created to fulfill an inductive need, and that standard taxonomic categories such as **bird** and **hammer** simply become automatically triggered because they have been used often, whereas ad hoc categories are created only when specifically needed (Barsalou, 1982, 1991). In any case, evaluating the inductive potential of a concept goes a long way toward understanding why we have the concepts that we do. The single concept **peaches, llamas, telephone answering machines, or Ringo Starr** is an unlikely concept because belonging in this concept predicts very little. Several researchers have been formally developing the notion that the concepts we possess are those that maximize inductive potential (Anderson, 1991; Heit, 2000; Oaksford & Chater, 1998).

Communication

Communication between people is enormously facilitated if the people can count upon sharing a set of common concepts. By uttering a simple sentence such as "Ed is a football player," one can transmit a wealth of information to a colleague, dealing with the probabilities of Ed's being strong, having violent tendencies, being a college physics or physical education major, and having a history of steroid use. Markman and Makin (1998) have argued that a major force in shaping our concepts is the need to communicate efficiently. They find that a person's concepts become more consistent and systematic over time in order to establish reference unambiguously for another individual with whom they need to communicate (see also Garrod & Doherty, 1994).

Cognitive Economy

We can discriminate far more stimuli than those for which we have concepts. For example, estimates suggest that we can perceptually discriminate at least 10,000 colors from each other, but we have far fewer color concepts than this. Dramatic savings in storage requirements can be achieved by encoding concepts rather than entire raw (unprocessed) inputs. A classic study by Posner and Keele (1967) found that subjects code letters such as **A** by a raw, physical code, but that this code rapidly (within 2 s) gives way to a more abstract conceptual code that **A** and **a** share. Huttenlocher, Hedges, and Vevea (2000) develop a formal model in which judgments about a stimulus are based on both its category membership and its individuating information. As predicted by the model, when subjects are asked to reproduce a stimulus, their reproductions reflect a compromise between the stimulus itself and the category to which it belongs. When a delay is introduced between seeing the stimulus and reproducing it, the contribution of category-level information relative to individual-level information increases (Crawford, Huttenlocher, & Engebretson, 2000). Together with studies showing that, over time, people tend to preserve the gist of a category rather than the exact members that constitute it (e.g., Posner & Keele, 1970), these results suggest that through the preservation of category-level information rather than individual-level information, efficient long-term representations can be maintained.

From an information-theory perspective, storing a category in memory rather than a complete description of an individual is efficient because fewer bits of information are required to specify the category. For example, Figure 22.1 depicts a set of objects (shown by circles) described along two dimensions. Rather than preserving the complete description of each of the 19 objects, one can create a reasonably faithful representation of the distribution of objects by storing only the positions of the four triangles in Figure 22.1. This kind of information reduction is particularly significant because computational algorithms exist that can automatically form these categories when supplied with the objects (Kohonen, 1995). For example, the competitive learning algorithm (Rumelhart & Zipser, 1985) begins with random positions for the triangles, and when an object is presented, the triangle that is closest to the object moves its position even closer to the object. The other triangles move less quickly, or do not move at all, leaving them free to specialize for other classes of objects. In addition to showing a way in which efficient category representations can be created, this algorithm has been put forth as a model of how a person creates categories even when there is no teacher, parent, or label that tells the person what, or how many, categories there are.

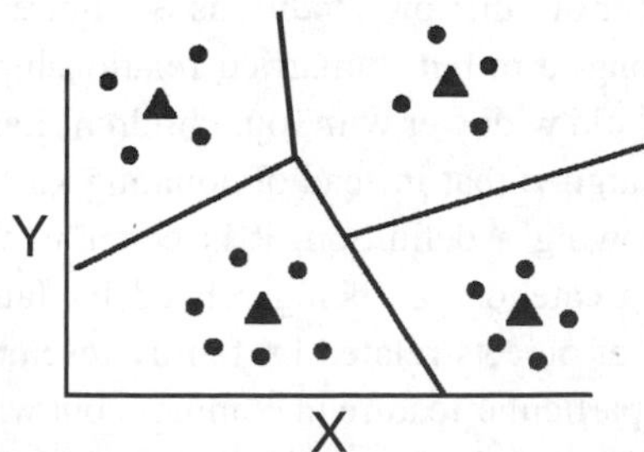

Figure 22.1 Alternative proposals have suggested that categories are represented by the individual exemplars in the categories (the circles), the prototypes of the categories (the triangles), or the category boundaries (the lines dividing the categories).

The above argument suggests that concepts can be used to conserve memory. An equally important economizing advantage of concepts is to reduce the need for learning (Bruner, Goodnow, & Austin, 1956). An unfamiliar object that has not been placed in a category attracts attention because the observer must figure out how to think of it. Conversely, if an object can be identified as belonging to a preestablished category, then less cognitive processing is typically necessary. One can simply treat the object as another instance of something that is known, updating one's knowledge slightly, if at all. The difference between events that require altering one's concepts and those that do not was described by Piaget (1952) in terms of accommodation (adjusting concepts on the basis of a new event) and assimilation (applying already known concepts to an event). This distinction has also been incorporated into computational models of concept learning that determine whether an input can be assimilated into a previously learned concept. If it cannot, then reconceptualization is triggered (Grossberg, 1982). When a category instance is consistent with a simple category description, then an individual is less likely to store a detailed description of it than if it is an exceptional item (Palmeri & Nosofsky, 1995), consistent with the notion that people simply use an existing category description when it suffices.

HOW ARE CONCEPTS REPRESENTED?

Much of the research on concepts and categorization revolves around the issue of how concepts are mentally represented. As with all discussion of representations, the standard caveat must be issued—mental representations cannot be determined or used without processes that operate on these representations (Anderson, 1978). Rather than discussing the representation of a concept such as **cat,** we should discuss a representation-process pair that allows for the use of this concept. Empirical results interpreted as favoring a particular representation format should almost always be interpreted as supporting a particular representation given particular processes that use the representation. As a simple example, when trying to decide whether a shadowy figure briefly glimpsed was a cat or fox, one needs to know more than how one's **cat** and **fox** concepts are represented. One needs to know how the information in these representations is integrated to make the final categorization. Does one wait for the amount of confirmatory evidence for one of the animals to rise above a certain threshold (Busemeyer & Townsend, 1993)? Does one compare the evidence for the two animals and choose the more likely (Luce, 1959)? Is the information in the candidate animal concepts accessed simultaneously or successively? Probabilistically or deterministically? These are all questions about the processes that use conceptual representations. One reaction to the insufficiency of representations alone to account for concept use has been to dispense with all reference to independent representations, and instead to frame theories in terms of dynamic processes alone (Thelen & Smith, 1994; van Gelder, 1998). However, some researchers feel that this is a case of throwing out the baby with the bath water, and insist that representations must still be posited to account for enduring, organized, and rule-governed thought (Markman & Dietrich, 2000).

Rules

There is considerable intuitive appeal to the notion that concepts are represented by something like dictionary entries. By a rule-based account of concept representation, to possess the concept cat is to know the dictionary entry for it. A person's **cat** concept may differ from Webster's Dictionary entry: "a carnivorous mammal (Felis catus) long domesticated and kept as a pet and for catching rats and mice." Still, this account claims that a concept is represented by some rule that allows one to determine whether an entity belongs within the category (see also the chapter by Leighton & Sternberg in this volume).

The most influential rule-based approach to concepts may be Bruner, Goodnow, and Austin's (1956) hypothesis-testing approach. Their theorizing was, in part, a reaction against behaviorist approaches (Hull, 1920) in which concept learning involved the relatively passive acquisition of an association between a stimulus (an object to be categorized) and a response (such as a verbal response, key press, or labeling). Instead, Bruner et al. argued that concept learning typically involves active hypothesis formation and testing. In a typical experiment, their subjects were shown flash cards that had different shapes, colors, quantities, and borders. The subjects' task was to discover the rule for categorizing the flash cards by selecting cards to be tested and by receiving feedback from the experimenter indicating whether the selected card fit the categorizing rule. The researchers documented different strategies for selecting cards, and a considerable body of subsequent work (e.g., Bourne, 1970) showed large differences in how easily acquired are different categorization rules. For example, a conjunctive rule such as **white and square** is more easily learned than a conditional rule such as **if white, then square,** which is in turn more easily learned than a biconditional rule such as **white if and only if square**.

A parallel development to these laboratory studies of artificial categories was Katz and Fodor's (1963) semantic marker theory of compositional semantics within linguistics. In this theory, a word's semantic representation consists of a list of atomic semantic markers such as +Male, +Adult, +Physical, and −Married for the word bachelor. These markers serve as the components of a rule that specifies when a word is appropriately used. Each of the semantic markers for a word is assumed to be necessary for something to belong to the word category, and the markers are assumed to be jointly sufficient to make the categorization.

The assumptions of these rule-based models have been vigorously challenged for several decades now (see the chapter by Treiman et al. in this volume). Douglas Medin and Edward E. Smith (Medin & Smith, 1984; E. E. Smith & Medin, 1981) dubbed this rule-based approach "the classical view," and characterized it as holding that all instances of a concept share common properties that are necessary and sufficient conditions for defining the concept. At least three criticisms have been levied against this classical view.

First, it has proven to be very difficult to specify the defining rules for most concepts. Wittgenstein (1953) raised this point with his famous example of the concept **game**. He argued that none of the candidate definitions of this concept, such as activity engaged in for fun, activity with certain rules, or competitive activity with winners and losers, is adequate to identify Frisbee, professional baseball, and roulette as games, while simultaneously excluding wars, debates, television viewing, and leisure walking from the game category. Even a seemingly well-defined concept such as **bachelor** seems to involve more than its simple definition of unmarried male. The counterexample of a 5-year-old child (who does not really seem to be a bachelor) may be solved by adding an adult precondition to the unmarried male condition, but an indefinite number of other preconditions is required to exclude a man in a long-term but unmarried relationship, the Pope, and a 80-year-old widower with four children (Lakoff, 1987). Wittgenstein argued that instead of equating knowing a concept with knowing a definition, it is better to think of the members of a category as being related by family resemblance. A set of objects related by family resemblance need not have any particular feature in common, but will have several features that are characteristic or typical of the set.

Second, the category membership for some objects is unclear. People may disagree on whether a starfish is a fish, a camel is a vehicle, a hammer is a weapon, or a stroke is a disease. By itself, this is not too problematic for a rule-based approach. People may use rules to categorize objects, but different people may have different rules. However, it turns out that people not only disagree with each other about whether a bat is mammal—they also disagree with themselves! McCloskey and Glucksberg (1978) showed that subjects give surprisingly inconsistent category membership judgments when asked the same questions at different times. Either there is variability in how to apply a categorization rule to an object, people spontaneously change their categorization rules, or (as many researchers believe) people simply do not represent objects in terms of clear-cut rules.

Third, even when a person shows consistency in placing objects in a category, he or she might not treat all the objects as equally good members of that category. By a rule-based account, one might argue that all objects that match a category rule would be considered equally good members of the category (but see Bourne, 1982). However, when subjects are asked to rate the typicality of animals such as a robin and an eagle for the category bird, or a chair and a hammock for the category furniture, they reliably give different typicality ratings for different objects. Rosch and Mervis (1975) were able to predict typicality ratings with respectable accuracy by asking subjects to list properties of category members, and measuring how many properties possessed by a category member were shared by other category members. The magnitude of this so-called "family resemblance measure" is positively correlated with typicality ratings.

Despite these strong challenges to the classical view, the rule-based approach is by no means moribund. In fact, in part due to the perceived lack of constraints in neural network models that learn concepts by gradually building up associations, the rule-based approach experienced a rekindling of interest in the 1990s after its low point in the 1970s and 1980s (Marcus, 1998). Nosofsky and Palmeri (1998; Nosofsky et al., 1994; Palmeri & Nosofsky, 1995) have proposed a quantitative model of human concept learning that learns to classify objects by forming simple logical rules and remembering occasional exceptions to those rules. This work is reminiscent of earlier computational models of human learning that created rules such as **if white and square, then Category 1** from experience with specific examples (Anderson, Kline, & Beasley, 1979; Medin, Wattenmaker, & Michalski, 1987). The models have a bias to create simple rules, and are able to predict entire distributions of subjects' categorization responses rather than simply average responses.

In defending a role for rule-based reasoning in human cognition, E. E. Smith, Langston, and Nisbett (1992) proposed eight criteria for determining whether people use abstract rules in reasoning. These criteria include the following: "Performance on rule-governed items is as accurate with abstract as with concrete material"; "performance on rule-governed items is as accurate with unfamiliar as with familiar material"; and "performance on a rule-governed item or problem deteriorates as a function of the number of rules that are required for solving the problem." Based on the full set of criteria, they argue that rule-based reasoning does occur, and that it may be a mode of reasoning distinct from association-based or similarity-based reasoning. Similarly, Pinker (1991) argued for distinct rule-based and association-based modes for determining linguistic categories. Neurophysiological support for this distinction comes from studies showing that rule-based and similarity-based categorization involve anatomically separate brain regions (Ashby, Alfonso-Reese, Turken, & Waldron, 1998; Ashby & Waldron, 2000; E. E. Smith, Patalano, & Jonides, 1998).

In developing a similar distinction between similarity-based and rule-based categorization, Sloman (1996) introduced the notion that the two systems can simultaneously generate different solutions to a reasoning problem. For example, Rips (1989; see also Rips & Collins, 1993) asked subjects to imagine a 3 in. (7.62 cm) round object, and then asked whether the object is more similar to a quarter or a pizza, and whether the object is more likely to be a pizza or a quarter. There is a tendency for the object to be judged as more similar to a quarter, but as more likely to be a pizza. The rule that quarters must not be greater than 1 in. plays a larger role in the categorization decision than in the similarity judgment, causing the two judgments to dissociate. By Sloman's analysis, the tension we feel about the categorization of the 3-in. object stems from the two different systems' indicating incompatible categorizations. Sloman argues that the rule-based system can suppress the similarity-based system but cannot completely suspend it. When Rips's experiment is repeated with a richer description of the object to be categorized, categorization again tracks similarity, and people tend to choose the quarter for both the categorization and similarity choices (E. E. Smith & Sloman, 1994).

Prototypes

Just as the active hypothesis-testing approach of the classical view was a reaction against the passive stimulus–response association approach, so the prototype model was developed as a reaction against what was seen as the overly analytic, rule-based classical view. Central to Eleanor Rosch's development of prototype theory is the notion that concepts are organized around family resemblances rather than features that are individually necessary and jointly sufficient for categorization (Mervis & Rosch, 1981; Rosch, 1975; Rosch &

Mervis, 1975; see also the chapters in this volume by Capaldi, by Palmer, and by Treiman et al.). The prototype for a category consists of the most common attribute values associated with the members of the category, and can be empirically derived by the previously described method of asking subjects to generate a list of attributes for several members of a category. Once prototypes for a set of concepts have been determined, categorizations can be predicted by determining how similar an object is to each of the prototypes. The likelihood of placing an object into a category increases as it becomes more similar to the category's prototype and less similar to other category prototypes (Rosch & Mervis, 1975).

This prototype model can naturally deal with the three problems that confronted the classical view. It is no problem if defining rules for a category are difficult or impossible to devise. If concepts are organized around prototypes, then only characteristic (not necessary or sufficient) features are expected. Unclear category boundaries are expected if objects are presented that are approximately equally similar to prototypes from more than one concept. Objects that clearly belong to a category may still vary in their typicality because they may be more similar to the category's prototype than to any other category's prototype, but they still may differ in how similar they are to the prototype. Prototype models do not require "fuzzy" boundaries around concepts (Hampton, 1993), but prototype similarities are based on commonalities across many attributes and are consequently graded, and lead naturally to categories with graded membership.

A considerable body of data has been amassed that suggests that prototypes have cognitively important functions. The similarity of an item to its category prototype (in terms of featural overlap) predicts the results from several converging tasks. Somewhat obviously, it is correlated with the average rating the item receives when subjects are asked to rate how good an example the item is of its category (Rosch, 1975). It is correlated with subjects' speed in verifying statements of the form "An [item] is a [category name]" (E. E. Smith, Shoben, & Rips, 1974). It is correlated with subjects' frequency and speed of listing the item when asked to supply members of a category (Mervis & Rosch, 1981). It is correlated with the probability of inductively extending a property from the item to other members of the category (Rips, 1975). Taken in total, these results indicate that different members of the same category differ in how typical they are of the category, and that these differences have a strong cognitive impact. Many natural categories seem to be organized not around definitive boundaries, but by graded typicality to the category's prototype.

The prototype model described previously generates category prototypes by finding the most common attribute values shared among category members. An alternative conception views a prototype as the central tendency of continuously varying attributes. If the four observed members of a lizard category had tail lengths of 3, 3, 3, and 7 in., the former prototype model would store a value of 3 (the modal value) as the prototype's tail length, whereas the central tendency model would store a value of 4 (the average value). The central tendency approach has proven useful in modeling categories composed of artificial stimuli that vary on continuous dimensions. For example, Posner and Keele's (1968) classic dot-pattern stimuli consisted of nine dots positioned randomly or in familiar configurations on a 30×30 invisible grid. Each prototype was a particular configuration of dots, but during categorization training, subjects never saw the prototypes themselves. Instead, they saw distortions of the prototypes obtained by shifting each dot randomly by a small amount. Categorization training involved subjects' seeing dot patterns, guessing their category assignment, and receiving feedback indicating whether their guesses were correct or not. During a transfer stage, Posner and Keele found that subjects were better able to categorize the never-before-seen category prototypes than they were to categorize new distortions of those prototypes. In addition, subjects' accuracy in categorizing distortions of category prototypes was strongly correlated with the proximity of those distortions to the never-before-seen prototypes. The authors interpreted these results as suggesting that prototypes are extracted from distortions, and used as a basis for determining categorizations (see also Homa, Sterling, & Trepel, 1981).

Exemplars

Exemplar models deny that prototypes are explicitly extracted from individual cases, stored in memory, and used to categorize new objects. Instead, in exemplar models, a conceptual representation consists of only those actual, individual cases that one has observed. The prototype representation for the category **bird** consists of the most typical bird, or an assemblage of the most common attribute values across all birds, or the central tendency of all attribute values for observed birds. By contrast, an exemplar model represents the category **bird** by representing all of the instances (exemplars) that belong to this category (Brooks, 1978; Estes, 1986, 1994; Hintzman, 1986; Kruschke, 1992; Lamberts, 1998, 2000; Logan, 1988; Medin & Schaffer, 1978; Nosofsky, 1984, 1986; see also the chapter by Capaldi in this volume).

Although the prime motivation for these models has been to provide good fits to results from human experiments, computer scientists have pursued similar models with the aim to exploit the power of storing individual exposures to stimuli in a relatively raw, unabstracted form. Exemplar, instance-based (Aha, 1992), view-based (Tarr & Gauthier, 1998), case-based (Schank, 1982), nearest neighbor (Ripley, 1996), configural cue (Gluck & Bower, 1990), and vector quantization (Kohonen, 1995) models all share the fundamental insight that novel patterns can be identified, recognized, or categorized by giving the novel patterns the same response that was learned for similar, previously presented patterns. By creating representations for presented patterns, not only is it possible to respond to repetitions of these patterns; it is also possible to give responses to novel patterns that are likely to be correct by sampling responses to old patterns, weighted by their similarity to the novel patterns. Consistent with these models, psychological evidence suggests that people show good transfer to new stimuli in perceptual tasks only to the extent that the new stimuli superficially resemble previously learned stimuli (Kolers & Roediger, 1984; Palmeri, 1997).

The frequent inability of human generalization to transcend superficial similarities might be considered evidence for either human stupidity or laziness. To the contrary, if a strong theory about which stimulus features promote valid inductions is lacking, the strategy of least commitment is to preserve the entire stimulus in its full richness of detail (Brooks, 1978). That is, by storing entire instances and basing generalizations on all of the features of these instances, one can be confident that one's generalizations are not systematically biased. It has been shown that in many situations, categorizing new instances by their similarity to old instances maximizes the likelihood of categorizing the new instances correctly (Ashby & Maddox, 1993; McKinley & Nosofsky, 1995; Ripley, 1996). Furthermore, if information later becomes available that specifies which properties are useful for generalizing appropriately, then preserving entire instances will allow these properties to be recovered. Such properties might be lost and unrecoverable if people were less "lazy" in their generalizations from instances.

Given these considerations, it is understandable that people often use all of the attributes of an object even when a task demands the use of specific attributes. Doctors' diagnoses of skin disorders are facilitated when they are similar to previously presented cases, even when the similarity is based on attributes that are known to be irrelevant for the diagnosis (Brooks, Norman, & Allen, 1991). Even when subjects know a simple, clear-cut rule for a perceptual classification, performance is better on frequently presented items than rare items (Allen & Brooks, 1991). Consistent with exemplar models, responses to stimuli are frequently based on their overall similarity to previously exposed stimuli.

The exemplar approach assumes that a category is represented by the category exemplars that have been encountered, and that categorization decisions are based on the similarity of the object to be categorized to all of the exemplars of each relevant category. As such, as an item becomes more similar to the exemplars of Category A (or less similar to the exemplars of other categories), then the probability that it will be placed in Category A increases. Categorization judgments may shift if an item is approximately equally close to two sets of exemplars, because probabilistic decision rules are typically used. Items will vary in their typicality to a category as long as they vary in their similarity to the aggregate set of exemplars.

The exemplar approach to categorization raises a number of questions. First, once one has decided that concepts are to be represented in terms of sets of exemplars, the obvious question remains: How are the exemplars to be represented? Some exemplar models use a featural or attribute-value representation for each of the exemplars (Hintzman, 1986; Medin & Schaffer, 1978). Another popular approach is to represent exemplars as points in a multidimensional psychological space. These points are obtained by measuring the subjective similarity of every object in a set to every other object. Once an $N \times N$ matrix of similarities between N objects has been determined by similarity ratings, perceptual confusions, spontaneous sortings, or other methods, a statistical technique called multidimensional scaling (MDS) finds coordinates for the objects in a D-dimensional space that allow the $N \times N$ matrix of similarities to be reconstructed with as little error as possible (Nosofsky, 1992). Given that D is typically smaller than N, a reduced representation is created in which each object is represented in terms of its values on D dimensions. Distances between objects in these quantitatively derived spaces can be used as the input to exemplar models to determine item-to-exemplar similarities. These MDS representations are useful for generating quantitative exemplar models that can be fit to human categorizations and similarity judgments, but these still beg the question of how a stand-alone computer program or a person would generate these MDS representations. Presumably, there is some human process that computes object representations and can derive object-to-object similarities from them, but this process is not currently modeled by exemplar models (for steps in this direction, see Edelman, 1999).

A second question for exemplar models is, If exemplar models do not explicitly extract prototypes, how can they account for results that concepts are organized around prototypes? A useful place to begin is by considering Posner and Keele's (1968) result that the never-before-seen prototype is categorized better than new distortions based on the prototype. Exemplar models have been able to model this result because a categorization of an object is based on its summed similarity to all previously stored exemplars (Medin & Schaffer, 1978; Nosofsky, 1986). The prototype of a category will, on average, be more similar to the training distortions than are new distortions because the prototype was used to generate all of the training distortions. Without our positing the explicit extraction of the prototype, the cumulative effect of many exemplars in an exemplar model can create an emergent, epiphenomenal advantage for the prototype.

Given the exemplar model's account of prototype categorization, one might ask whether predictions from exemplar and prototype models differ. In fact, they typically do, in large part because categorizations in exemplar models are not simply based on summed similarity to category exemplars, but to similarities weighted by the proximity of an exemplar to the item to be categorized. In particular, exemplar models have mechanisms to bias categorization decisions so that they are more influenced by exemplars that are similar to items to be categorized. In Medin and Schaffer's (1978) context model, this is achieved through computing the similarity between objects by multiplying rather than adding their similarities on each of their features. In Hintzman's (1986) Minerva model, this is achieved by raising object-to-object similarities to a power of 3 before summing them together. In Nosofsky's Generalized Context Model (1986), this is achieved by basing object-to-object similarities on an exponential function of the objects' distance in an MDS space. With these quantitative biases for close exemplars, the exemplar model does a better job of predicting categorization accuracy for Posner and Keele's experiment than the prototype model because it can also predict that familiar distortions will be categorized more accurately than novel distortions that are equally far removed from the prototype (Shin & Nosofsky, 1992).

A third question for exemplar models is, In what way are concept representations economical if every experienced exemplar is stored? It is certainly implausible with large real-world categories to suppose that every instance ever experienced is stored in a separate trace. However, more realistic exemplar models may either store only part of the information associated with an exemplar (Lassaline & Logan, 1993), or only some of the exemplars (Aha, 1992; Palmeri & Nosofsky, 1995). One particularly interesting way of conserving space that has received empirical support (Barsalou, Huttenlocher, & Lamberts, 1998) is to combine separate events that all constitute a single individual into a single representation. Rather than passively registering every event as distinct, people seem naturally to consolidate events that refer to the same individual. If an observer fails to register the difference between a new exemplar and a previously encountered exemplar (e.g., two similar-looking chihuahuas), then he or she may combine the two, resulting in an exemplar representation that is a blend of two instances.

Category Boundaries

Another notion is that a concept representation describes the boundary around a category. The prototype model would represent the four categories of Figure 22.1 in terms of the triangles. The exemplar model represents the categories by the circles. The category boundary model would represent the categories by the four dividing lines between the categories. This view has been most closely associated with the work of Ashby and his colleagues (Ashby, 1992; Ashby et al., 1998; Ashby & Gott, 1988; Ashby & Maddox, 1993; Ashby & Townsend, 1986; Maddox & Ashby, 1993). It is particularly interesting to contrast the prototype and category boundary approaches, because their representational assumptions are almost perfectly complementary. The prototype model represents a category in terms of its most typical member—the object in the center of the distribution of items included in the category. The category boundary model represents categories by their periphery, not their center.

An interesting phenomenon to consider with respect to whether centers or peripheries of concepts are representationally privileged is categorical perception. According to this phenomenon, people are better able to distinguish between physically different stimuli when the stimuli come from different categories than when they come from the same category (see Harnad, 1987, for several reviews of research; see also the chapters in this volume by Fowler and by Treiman et al.). The effect has been best documented for speech phoneme categories. For example, Liberman, Harris, Hoffman, and Griffith (1957) generated a continuum of equally spaced consonant-vowel syllables going from /be/ to /de/. Observers listened to three sounds—A followed by B followed by X—and indicated whether X was identical to A or B. Subjects performed the task more accurately when syllables A and B belonged to different phonemic categories than when they were variants of the same phoneme, even when physical differences were equated.

Categorical perception effects have been observed for visual categories (Calder, Young, Perrett, Etcoff, & Rowland, 1996) and for arbitrarily created laboratory categories (Goldstone, 1994b). Categorical perception could emerge from either prototype or boundary representations. An item to be categorized might be compared to the prototypes of two candidate categories. Increased sensitivity at the category boundary would exist because people represent items in terms of the prototypes to which they are closest. Items that fall on different sides of a boundary would have very different representations because they would be closest to different prototypes (Liberman et al., 1957). Alternatively, the boundary itself might be represented as a reference point, and as pairs of items move closer to the boundary, it becomes easier to discriminate between them because of their proximity to this reference point (Pastore, 1987).

Computational models have been developed that operate on both principles. Following the prototype approach, Harnad, Hanson, and Lubin (1995) describe a neural network in which the representation of an item is "pulled" toward the prototype of the category to which it belongs. Following the boundaries approach, Goldstone, Steyvers, Spencer-Smith, and Kersten (2000) describe a neural network that learns to strongly represent critical boundaries between categories by shifting perceptual detectors to these regions. Empirically, the results are mixed. Consistent with prototypes' being represented, some researchers have found particularly good discriminability close to a familiar prototype (Acker, Pastore, & Hall, 1995; McFadden & Callaway, 1999). Consistent with boundaries' being represented, other researchers have found that the sensitivity peaks associated with categorical perception heavily depend on the saliency of perceptual cues at the boundary (Kuhl & Miller, 1975). Rather than being arbitrarily fixed, a category boundary is most likely to occur at a location where a distinctive perceptual cue, such as the difference between an aspirated and unaspirated speech sound, is present. A possible reconciliation is that information about either the center or periphery of a category can be represented, and that boundary information is more likely to be represented when two highly similar categories must be frequently discriminated and there is a salient reference point for the boundary.

Different versions of the category boundary approach, illustrated in Figure 22.2, have been based on different ways of partitioning categories (Ashby & Maddox, 1998). With independent decision boundaries, category boundaries must be perpendicular to a dimensional axis, forming rules such as Category A items are larger than 3 cm, irrespective of their color. This kind of boundary is appropriate when the dimensions that make up a stimulus are difficult to integrate (Ashby & Gott, 1988). With minimal distance boundaries, a Category A response is given if and only if an object is closer to the Category A prototype than the Category B prototype. The decision boundary is formed by finding the line that connects the two categories' prototypes, and creating a boundary that bisects and is orthogonal to this line. The optimal boundary is the boundary that maximizes the likelihood of correctly categorizing an object. If the two categories have the same patterns of variability on their dimensions, and people use information about variance to form their boundaries, then the optimal boundary will be a straight line. If the categories differ in variability, then the optimal boundary will be described by a quadratic equation (Ashby & Maddox, 1993, 1998). A general quadratic boundary is any boundary that can be described by a quadratic equation.

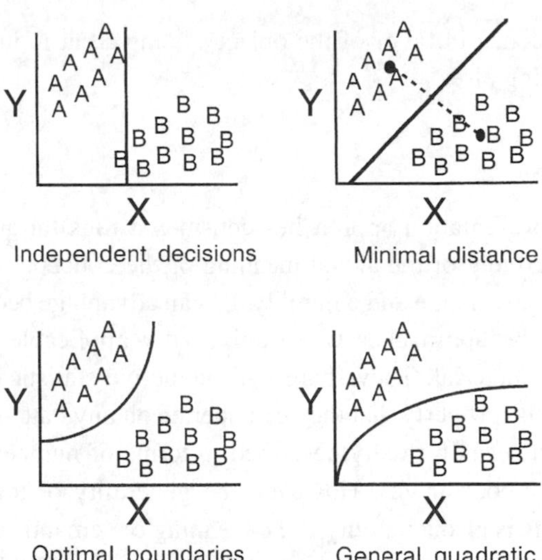

Figure 22.2 The notion that categories are represented by their boundaries can be constrained in several ways. Boundaries can be constrained to be perpendicular to a dimensional axis, to be equally close to prototypes for neighboring categories, to produce optimal categorization performance, or (loosely constrained) to be a quadratic function.

One difficulty with representing a concept by a boundary is that the location of the boundary between two categories depends on several contextual factors. For example, Repp and Liberman (1987) argue that categories of speech sounds are influenced by order effects, adaptation, and the surrounding speech context. The same sound that is halfway between [pa] and [ba] will be categorized as /pa/ if preceded by several repetitions of a prototypical [ba] sound, but categorized as /ba/ if preceded by several [pa] sounds. For a category boundary representation to accommodate this, two category boundaries would need to hypothesized—a relatively permanent category boundary between /ba/ and /pa/, and a second boundary that shifts depending upon the immediate context. The relatively permanent boundary is needed because the contextualized boundary must be based on some earlier information. In many cases, it is more parsimonious to hypothesize representations for the category members themselves, and to view category boundaries as side effects of the competition between neighboring categories. Context effects are then explained simply by changes to the strengths associated with different categories. By this account, there may be no reified boundary around one's **cat** concept that causally affects categorizations. When asked about a particular object we can decide whether it is a cat, but this is done by comparing the evidence in favor of the object's being a cat to its being something else.

Theories

The representation approaches considered thus far all work irrespectively of the actual meaning of the concepts. This is both an advantage and a liability. It is an advantage because it allows the approaches to be universally applicable to any kind of material. They share with inductive statistical techniques the property that they can operate on any data set once the data set is formally described in terms of numbers, features, or coordinates. However, the generality of these approaches is also a liability if the meaning or semantic content of a concept influences how it is represented. While few would argue that statistical t-tests are appropriate only for certain domains of inquiry (e.g., testing political differences, but not disease differences), many researchers have argued that the use of purely data-driven, inductive methods for concept learning are strongly limited and modulated by the background knowledge one has about a concept (Carey, 1985; Gelman & Markman, 1986; Keil, 1989; Medin, 1989; Murphy & Medin, 1985).

People's categorizations seem to depend on the theories they have about the world (for reviews, see Komatsu, 1992; Medin, 1989). Theories involve organized systems of knowledge. In making an argument for the use of theories in categorization, Murphy and Medin (1985) provide the example of a man jumping into a swimming pool fully clothed. This man may be categorized as drunk because we have a theory of behavior and inebriation that explains the man's action. Murphy and Medin argue that the categorization of the man's behavior does not depend on matching the man's features to those of the category **drunk**. It is highly unlikely that the category **drunk** would have such a specific feature as **jumps into pools fully clothed**. It is not the similarity between the instance and the category that determines the instance's classification; it is the fact that our category provides a theory that explains the behavior.

Other researchers have empirically supported the dissociation between theory-derived categorization and similarity. In one experiment, Carey (1985) observes that children choose a toy monkey over a worm as being more similar to a human, but that when they are told that humans have spleens, are more likely to infer that the worm has a spleen than that the toy monkey does. Thus, the categorization of objects into spleen and no-spleen groups does not appear to depend on the same knowledge that guides similarity judgments. Carey argues that even young children have a theory of living things. Part of this theory is the notion that living things have self-propelled motion and rich internal organizations. Children as young as 3 years of age make inferences about an animal's properties on the basis of its category label even when the label opposes superficial visual similarity (Gelman & Markman, 1986; see also the chapter by Treiman et al. in this volume).

Using different empirical techniques, Keil (1989) has come to a similar conclusion. In one experiment, children are told a story in which scientists discover that an animal that looks exactly like a raccoon actually contains the internal organs of a skunk and has skunk parents and skunk children. With increasing age, children increasingly claim that the animal is a skunk. That is, there is a developmental trend for children to categorize on the basis of theories of heredity and biology rather than on visual appearance. In a similar experiment, Rips (1989) shows an explicit dissociation between categorization judgments and similarity judgments in adults. An animal that is transformed (by toxic waste) from a bird into something that looks like an insect is judged by subjects to be more similar to an insect, but is also judged to be a bird still. Again, the category judgment seems to depend on biological, genetic, and historical knowledge, whereas the similarity judgments seems to depend more on gross visual appearance.

Researchers have explored the importance of background knowledge in shaping our concepts by manipulating this knowledge experimentally. Concepts are more easily learned when a learner has appropriate background knowledge, indicating that more than "brute" statistical regularities underlie our concepts (Pazzani, 1991). Similarly, when the features of a category can be connected through prior knowledge, category learning is facilitated (Murphy & Allopenna, 1994; Spalding & Murphy, 1999). Even a single instance of a category can allow one to form a coherent category if background knowledge constrains the interpretation of this instance (Ahn, Brewer, & Mooney, 1992). Concepts are disproportionately represented in terms of concept features that are tightly connected to other features (Sloman, Love, & Ahn, 1998).

Forming categories on the basis of data-driven, statistical evidence and forming them based upon knowledge-rich theories of the world seem like strategies fundamentally at odds with each other. Indeed, this is probably the most basic difference between theories of concepts. However, these approaches need not be mutually exclusive. Even the most outspoken proponents of theory-based concepts do not claim that similarity-based or statistical approaches are not also needed (Murphy & Medin, 1985). Moreover, some researchers have suggested integrating the two approaches. Heit (1994, 1997) describes a similarity-based, exemplar model of categorization that incorporates background knowledge by storing category members as they are observed (as with all exemplar models), but also storing never-seen instances that are consistent with the background knowledge. Choi, McDaniel, and Busemeyer (1993) described a neural network model of concept learning that does not begin with random or neutral connections between features and concepts (as is typical), but begins with theory-consistent connections that are relatively strong. Both approaches allow domain-general category learners to also have biases toward learning categories consistent with background knowledge.

Summary to Representation Approaches

One cynical conclusion to reach from the preceding alternative approaches is that a researcher begins with a theory, then tends to find evidence consistent with the theory (a result that is meta-analytically consistent with a theory-based approach!). Although this state of affairs is typical throughout the field of psychology, it is particularly rife in concept-learning research because researchers have a significant amount of flexibility in choosing what concepts they will experimentally use. Evidence for rule-based categories tends to be found with categories that are created from simple rules (Bruner, Goodnow, & Austin, 1956). Evidence for prototypes tends to be found for categories made up of members that are distortions around single prototypes (Posner & Keele, 1968). Evidence for exemplar models is particular strong when categories include exceptional instances that must be individually memorized (Nosofsky & Palmeri, 1998; Nosofsky et al., 1994). Evidence for theories is found when categories are created that subjects already know something about (Murphy & Kaplan, 2000). The researcher's choice of representation seems to determine the experiment that is conducted, rather than the experiment's influencing the choice of representation.

There may be a grain of truth to this cynical conclusion, but our conclusions are instead that people use multiple representational strategies, and can flexibly deploy these strategies based upon the categories to be learned. From this perspective, representational strategies should be evaluated according to their trade-offs and for their fit to the real-world categories and empirical results. For example, exemplar representations are costly in terms of storage demands, but are sensitive to interactions between features and adaptable to new categorization demands. There is a growing consensus that at least two kinds of representational strategy are both present but separated—rule-based and similarity-based processes (Erickson & Kruschke, 1998; Pinker, 1991; Sloman, 1996). Other researchers have argued for separate processes for storing exemplars and extracting prototypes (Knowlton & Squire, 1993; J. D. Smith & Minda, 2000). Even if one holds out hope for a unified model of concept learning, it is important to recognize these different representational strategies as special cases that must be achievable by the unified model given the appropriate inputs.

CONNECTING CONCEPTS

Although knowledge representation approaches have often treated conceptual systems as independent networks that gain their meaning by their internal connections (Lenat & Feigenbaum, 1991), it is important to remember that concepts are connected to both perception and language. Concepts' connections to perception serve to ground them (Harnad, 1990), and their connections to language allow them to transcend direct experience and to be transmitted easily.

Connecting Concepts to Perception

Concept formation is often studied as though it were a modular process (in the sense of Fodor, 1983). For example, participants in category-learning experiments are often presented with verbal feature lists representing the objects to be categorized. The use of this method suggests an implicit assumption that the perceptual analysis of an object into features is complete before one begins to categorize that object. This may be a useful simplifying assumption, allowing a researcher to test theories of how features are combined to form concepts. There is mounting evidence, however, that the relationship between the formation of concepts and the identification of features is bidirectional (Goldstone & Barsalou, 1998). In particular, not only does the identification of features influence the categorization of an object, but also the categorization of an object influences the interpretation of features (Bassok, 1996).

In this section of the chapter, we will review the evidence for a bidirectional relationship between concept formation and perception. Evidence for an influence of perception on concept formation comes from the classic study of Heider (1972). She presented a paired-associate learning task involving colors and words to the Dani, a population in New Guinea that has only two color terms. Participants were given a different verbal label for each of 16 color chips. They were then presented with each of the chips and asked for the appropriate label. The correct label was given as feedback when participants made incorrect responses, allowing participants to learn the new color terms over the course of training.

The key manipulation in this experiment was that 8 of the color chips represented English focal colors, whereas 8 represented colors that were not prototypical examples of one of the basic English color categories. Both English speakers and Dani were found to be more accurate at providing the correct label for the focal color chips than for the nonfocal color chips, where focal colors are those that have a consistent and strong label in English. Heider's (1972) explanation for this finding was that the English division of the color spectrum into color categories is not arbitrary, but rather reflects the sensitivities of the human perceptual system. Because the Dani share these same perceptual sensitivities with English speakers, they were better at distinguishing focal colors than nonfocal colors, allowing them to learn color categories for focal colors more easily.

Further research provides evidence for a role of perceptual information not only in the formation but also in the use of concepts. This evidence comes from research relating to Barsalou's (1999) theory of perceptual symbol systems. According to this theory, sensorimotor areas of the brain that are activated during the initial perception of an event are reactivated at a later time by association areas, serving as a representation of one's prior perceptual experience. Rather than preserving a verbatim record of what was experienced, however, association areas only reactivate certain aspects of one's perceptual experience, namely those that received attention. Because these reactivated aspects of experience may be common to a number of different events, they may be thought of as symbols, representing an entire class of events. Because they are formed around perceptual experience, however, they are perceptual symbols, unlike the amodal symbols typically employed in symbolic theories of cognition.

Barsalou's (1999) theory suggests a powerful influence of perception on the formation and use of concepts. Evidence consistent with this proposal comes from property verification tasks. Solomon and Barsalou (1999) presented participants with a number of concept words, each followed by a property word, and asked participants whether each property was a part of the corresponding concept. Half of the participants were instructed to use visual imagery to perform the task, whereas half were given no specific instructions. Despite this difference in instructions, participants in both conditions were found to perform in a qualitatively similar manner. In particular, reaction times of participants in both conditions were predicted most strongly by the perceptual characteristics of properties. For example, participants were quicker to verify small properties of objects than to verify large properties. Findings such as this suggest that detailed perceptual information is represented in concepts and that this information is used when reasoning about those concepts.

There is also evidence for an influence of concepts on perception. Classic evidence for such an influence comes from research on the previously described phenomenon of categorical perception. Listeners are much better at perceiving contrasts that are representative of different phoneme categories (Liberman, Cooper, Shankweiler, & Studdert-Kennedy, 1967). For example, listeners can hear the difference in voice onset time between the words bill and pill, even when this difference is no greater than the difference between two /b/ sounds that cannot be distinguished. One may simply argue that categorical perception provides further evidence of an influence of perception on concepts. In particular, the phonemes of language may have evolved to reflect the sensitivities of the human perceptual system. Evidence consistent with this viewpoint comes from the fact that chinchillas are sensitive to many of the same sound contrasts as are humans, even though chinchillas obviously have no language (Kuhl & Miller, 1975; see also the chapter by Treiman et al. in this volume). There is evidence, however, that the phonemes to which a listener is sensitive can be modified by experience. In particular, although newborn babies appear to be sensitive to all of the sound contrasts present in all of the world's languages, a 1-year-old can hear only those sound contrasts present in his or her linguistic environment (Werker & Tees, 1984). Thus, children growing up in Japan lose the ability to distinguish between the /l/ and /r/ phonemes, whereas children growing up in the United States retain this ability (Miyawaki, 1975). The categories of language thus influence one's perceptual sensitivities, providing evidence for an influence of concepts on perception.

Although categorical perception was originally demonstrated in the context of auditory perception, similar phenomena have since been discovered in vision. For example, Goldstone (1994b) trained participants to make a category discrimination in terms of either the size or the brightness of an object. He then presented those participants with a same-different task, in which two briefly presented objects were either the same or varied in terms of size or brightness. Participants who had earlier categorized objects on the basis of a particular dimension were found to perform better at telling objects apart in terms of that dimension than were control participants who had been given no prior categorization training. Moreover, this sensitization of categorically relevant dimensions was most evident at those values of the dimension that straddled the boundary between categories.

These findings thus provide evidence that the concepts that one has learned influence one's perceptual sensitivities, in the visual as well as in the auditory modality. Other research has shown that prolonged experience with a domain such as dogs (Tanaka & Taylor, 1991) or faces (Levin &

Beale, 2000; O'Toole, Peterson, & Deffenbacher, 1995) leads to development of a perceptual system that is tuned to these domains. Goldstone et al. (2000) review other evidence for conceptual influences on visual perception. Concept learning appears to be effective both in combining stimulus properties to create perceptual chunks that are diagnostic for categorization (Goldstone, 2000), and in splitting apart and isolating perceptual dimensions if they are differentially diagnostic for categorization (Goldstone & Steyvers, 2001).

The evidence reviewed here suggests that there is a strong interrelationship between concepts and perception, with perceptual information influencing the concepts that one forms and conceptual information influencing how one perceives the world. Most theories of concept formation fail to account for this interrelationship. They instead take the perceptual attributes of a stimulus as a given and try to account for how these attributes are used to categorize that stimulus.

One area of research that provides an exception to this rule is research on object recognition. As pointed out by Schyns (1998), object recognition can be thought of as an example of object categorization, with the goal of the process being to identify what kind of object one is observing. Unlike theories of categorization, theories of object recognition place strong emphasis on the role of perceptual information in identifying an object.

Interestingly, some of the theories that have been proposed to account for object recognition have characteristics in common with theories of categorization. For example, structural description theories of object recognition (e.g., Biederman, 1987; Hummel & Biederman, 1992; Marr & Nishihara, 1978; see also the chapter by Palmer in this volume) are similar to prototype theories of categorization in that a newly encountered exemplar is compared to a summary representation of a category in order to determine whether the exemplar is a member of that category. In contrast, multiple-views theories of object recognition (e.g., Edelman, 1998; Tarr & Bülthoff, 1995; see also Palmer's chapter in this volume) are similar to exemplar-based theories of categorization in that a newly encountered exemplar is compared to a number of previously encountered exemplars stored in memory. The categorization of an exemplar is determined either by the exemplar in memory that most closely matches it or by a computation of the similarities of the new exemplar to each of a number of stored exemplars.

The similarities in the models proposed to account for categorization and object recognition suggest that there is considerable opportunity for cross-talk between these two domains. For example, theories of categorization could potentially be adapted to provide a more complete account for object recognition. In particular, they may be able to provide an account of not only the recognition of established object categories, but also the learning of new ones, a problem not typically addressed by theories of object recognition. Furthermore, theories of object recognition could be adapted to provide a better account of the role of perceptual information in concept formation and use. The rapid recent developments in object recognition research, including the development of detailed computational, neurally based models (e.g., Perrett, Oram, & Ashbridge, 1998), suggest that a careful consideration of the role of perceptual information in categorization can be a profitable research strategy.

Connecting Concepts to Language

Concepts also take part in a bidirectional relationship with language. In particular, one's repertoire of concepts may influence the types of word meanings that one learns, whereas the language that one speaks may influence the types of concepts that one forms.

The first of these two proposals is the less controversial. It is widely believed that children come into the process of vocabulary learning with a large set of unlabeled concepts. These early concepts may reflect the correlational structure in the environment of the young child, as suggested by Rosch et al. (1976). For example, a child may form a concept of dog around the correlated properties of four legs, tail, wagging, slobbering, and so forth. The subsequent learning of a word's meaning should be relatively easy to the extent that one can map that word onto one of these existing concepts.

Different kinds of words may vary in the extent to which they map directly onto existing concepts, and thus some types of words may be learned more easily than others. For example, Gentner (1981, 1982; Gentner & Boroditsky, 2001) has proposed that nouns can be mapped straightforwardly onto existing object concepts, and that nouns are thus learned relatively early by children. The relation of verbs to prelinguistic event categories, on the other hand, may be less straightforward. The nature of children's prelinguistic event categories is not very well understood, but the available evidence suggests that they are structured quite differently from verb meanings. In particular, research by Kersten and Billman (1997) demonstrated that when adults learned event categories in the absence of category labels, they formed those categories around a rich set of correlated properties, including the characteristics of the objects in the event, the motions of those objects, and the outcome of the event. Research by Cohen and Oakes (1993) has similarly demonstrated that 10-month-old infants learned unlabeled event categories involving correlations among different aspects of an event, in this case between the agent in an event and the outcome of a causal interaction involving that agent. These unlabeled event categories learned by children and adults differ markedly from verb meanings. Verb meanings tend to have limited correlational structure, instead picking out only a small number of properties of an event (Huttenlocher & Lui, 1979; Talmy, 1985). For example, the verb collide involves two objects moving into contact with one another, irrespective of the objects involved or the outcome of this collision.

Verbs thus cannot be mapped directly onto existing event categories. Instead, language-learning experience is necessary to determine which aspects of an event are relevant and which aspects are irrelevant to verb meanings. Perhaps as a result, children learning a variety of different languages have been found to learn verbs later than nouns (Au, Dapretto, & Song, 1994; Gentner, 1982; Gentner & Boroditsky, 2000; but see Gopnik & Choi, 1995, and Tardif, 1996, for possible exceptions). More generally, word meanings should be easy to learn to the extent that they can be mapped onto existing concepts.

There is greater controversy regarding the extent to which language may influence one's concepts. Some influences of language on concepts are fairly straightforward, however. For example, whether a concept is learned in the presence or absence of language (e.g., a category label) may influence the way in which that concept is learned. When categories are learned in the presence of a category label, a common finding is one of competition among correlated cues for predictive strength (Gluck & Bower, 1988; Shanks, 1991). In particular, more salient cues may overshadow less salient cues, causing the concept learner to fail to notice the predictiveness of the less salient cue (Gluck & Bower, 1988; Kruschke, 1992; Shanks, 1991).

When categories are learned in the absence of a category label, on the other hand, there is facilitation rather than competition among correlated predictors of category membership (Billman, 1989; Billman & Knutson, 1996; Cabrera & Billman, 1996; Kersten & Billman, 1997). The learning of unlabeled categories has been measured in terms of the learning of correlations among attributes of a stimulus. For example, one's knowledge of the correlation between a wagging tail and a slobbering mouth can be used as a measure of one's knowledge of the category **dog**. Billman and Knutson (1996) used this method to examine the learning of unlabeled categories of novel animals. They found that participants were more likely to learn the predictiveness of an attribute when other correlated predictors were also present.

The key difference between these two concept-learning situations may be that in the learning of labeled categories, one piece of information, namely the category label, is singled out as being important to predict. Thus, when participants can adequately predict the category label on the basis of a single attribute, they need not look to additional attributes. On the other hand, when no one piece of information is singled out, as in the case of unlabeled categories, participants who have learned one predictive relation cannot be sure that they have learned all that they need to learn. As a result, they may continue looking for additional predictive relations. In doing so, they may preferentially attend to those attributes that have already been discovered to be useful, resulting in facilitated learning of further relations involving those attributes (Billman & Heit, 1988).

There is thus evidence that the presence of language influences the way in which a concept is learned. A more controversial suggestion is that the language that one speaks may influence the types of concepts that one is capable of learning. This suggestion, termed the linguistic relativity hypothesis, was first made by Whorf (1956) on the basis of apparent dramatic differences between English and Native American languages in their expressions of ideas such as time, motion, and color. For example, Whorf proposed that the Hopi have no concept of time because the Hopi language provides no mechanism for talking about time. Many of Whorf's linguistic analyses have since been debunked (see Pinker, 1994, for a review), but his theory remains a source of controversy.

Early experimental evidence suggested that concepts were relatively impervious to linguistic influences. In particular, Heider's (1972) finding that the Dani learned new color concepts in a similar fashion to English speakers, despite the fact that the Dani had only two color words, suggested that concepts were determined by perception rather than by language. More recently, however, Roberson, Davies, and Davidoff (2000) attempted to replicate Heider's findings with another group of people with a limited color vocabulary, the Berinmo of New Guinea. In contrast to Heider's findings, Roberson et al. found that the Berinmo performed no better at learning a new color concept for a focal color than for a nonfocal color. Moreover, the Berinmo performed no better at learning a category discrimination between green and blue (a distinction not made in their language) than they did at learning a discrimination between two shades of green. This result contrasted with the results of English-speaking participants, who performed better at the green-blue discrimination. It also contrasted with superior Berinmo performance on a discrimination that was present in their language. These results suggest that the English division of the color spectrum may be more a function of the English language and less a function of human color physiology than was originally believed.

Regardless of one's interpretation of the Heider (1972) and Roberson et al. (2000) results, there are straightforward reasons to expect at least some influence of language on one's concepts. Homa and Cultice (1984) have demonstrated that people are better at learning concepts when category labels are provided as feedback. Thus, at the very least, one may expect that a concept will be more likely to be learned when it is labeled in a language than when it is unlabeled. Although this may seem obvious, further predictions are possible when this finding is combined with the evidence for influences of concepts on perception reviewed earlier. In particular, on the basis of the results of Goldstone (1994b), one may predict that when a language makes reference to a particular dimension, thus causing people to learn concepts around that dimension, people's perceptual sensitivities to that dimension will be increased. This, in turn, will make people who learn this language more likely to notice further contrasts along this dimension. Thus, language may influence people's concepts indirectly through one's perceptual abilities.

This proposal is consistent with L. B. Smith's (1999) account of the apparent shape bias in children's word learning. Smith proposed that children learn over the course of early language acquisition that the shapes of objects are important in distinguishing different nouns. As a result, they attend more strongly to shape in subsequent word learning, resulting in an acceleration in subsequent shape-word learning. Although this proposal is consistent with an influence of language on concepts, languages do not seem to differ very much in the extent to which they refer to the shapes of objects (Gentner, 1982; Gentner & Boroditsky, 2001), and thus one would not expect speakers of different languages to differ in the extent to which they are sensitive to shape.

Languages do differ in other respects, however, most notably in their use of verbs (Gentner & Boroditsky, 2001; Kersten, 1998). In English, the most frequently used class of verbs refers to the manner of motion of an object (e.g., running, skipping, sauntering), or the way in which an object moves around (Talmy, 1985). In other languages (e.g., Spanish), however, the most frequently used class of verbs refers to the path of an object (e.g., entering, exiting), or its direction with respect to some external reference point. In these languages, manner of motion is relegated to an adverbial, if it is mentioned at all. If language influences one's perceptual sensitivities, it is possible that English speakers and Spanish speakers may differ in the extent to which they are sensitive to motion attributes such as the path and manner of motion of an object.

Suggestive evidence in this regard comes from a study by Naigles and Terrazas (1998). They found that English speakers were more likely to generalize a novel verb to an event involving the same manner of motion and a different path than to an event involving the same path and a different manner of motion, whereas Spanish speakers showed the opposite tendency. One possible account of this result is that English speakers attended more strongly to manner of motion than did Spanish speakers, causing English speakers to be more likely to map the new verb onto manner of motion. If this were the case, it would have important implications for learning a second language. In particular, one may have difficulty attending to contrasts in a second language that are not explicitly marked in one's native language.

Thus, although the evidence for influences of language on one's concepts is mixed, there are reasons to believe that some such influence may take place, if only at the level of attention to different attributes of a stimulus. Proponents of the universalist viewpoint (e.g., Pinker, 1994) may argue that this level of influence is a far cry from the strongest interpretation of Whorf's hypothesis that language determines the concepts that one is capable of learning. A more fruitful approach, however, may be to stop arguing about whether a given result supports Whorf's theory and start testing more specific theories regarding the relationship between language and concepts.

THE FUTURE OF CONCEPTS AND CATEGORIZATION

The field of concept learning and representation is noteworthy for its large number of directions and perspectives. Although the lack of closure may frustrate some outside observers, it is also a source of strength and resilience. With an eye toward the future, we describe some of the most important avenues for future progress in the field.

First, as the previous section suggests, we believe that much of the progress of research on concepts will be to connect concepts to other concepts (Goldstone, 1996; Landauer & Dumais, 1997), to the perceptual world, and to language. One of the risks of viewing concepts as represented by rules, prototypes, sets of exemplars, or category boundaries is that one can easily imagine that one concept is independent of others. For example, one can list the exemplars that are included in the concept **bird**, or describe its central tendency, without making recourse to any other concepts. However, it is likely that all of our concepts are embedded in a network in which each concept's meaning depends on other concepts as well as on perceptual processes and linguistic labels. The proper level of analysis may not be individual concepts, as many researchers have assumed, but systems of concepts. The connections between concepts and perception on the one hand and between concepts and language on the other hand reveal an important dual nature of concepts. Concepts are used both to recognize objects and to ground word meanings.

Working out the details of this dual nature will go a long way toward understanding how human thinking can be both concrete and symbolic.

A second direction is the development of more sophisticated formal models of concept learning. Progress in neural networks, mathematical models, statistical models, and rational analyses can be gauged by several measures: goodness of fit to human data, breadth of empirical phenomena accommodated, model constraint and parsimony, and autonomy from human intervention. The current crop of models is fairly impressive in terms of fitting specific data sets, but there is much room for improvement in terms of their ability to accommodate rich sets of concepts and to process real-world stimuli without relying on human judgments or hand coding.

A final important direction will be to apply psychological research on concepts (see also the chapter by Nickerson & Pew in this volume). Perhaps the most important and relevant application is in the area of educational reform. Psychologists have amassed a large amount of empirical research on various factors that impact the ease of learning and transferring conceptual knowledge. The literature contains excellent suggestions on how to manipulate category labels, presentation order, learning strategies, stimulus format, and category variability in order to optimize the efficiency and likelihood of concept attainment. Putting these suggestions to use in classrooms, computer-based tutorials, and multimedia instructional systems could have a substantial positive impact on pedagogy. This research can also be used to develop autonomous computer diagnosis systems, user models, information visualization systems, and databases that are organized in a manner consistent with human conceptual systems. Given the importance of concepts for intelligent thought, it is not unreasonable to suppose that concept learning research will be equally important for improving thought processes.

REFERENCES

Acker, B. E., Pastore, R. E., & Hall, M. D. (1995). Within-category discrimination of musical chords: Perceptual magnet or anchor? *Perception & Psychophysics, 57,* 863–874.

Aha, D. W. (1992). Tolerating noisy, irrelevant and novel attributes in instance-based learning algorithms. *International Journal of Man Machine Studies, 36,* 267–287.

Ahn, W.-K., Brewer, W. F., & Mooney, R. J. (1992). Schema acquisition from a single example. *Journal of Experimental Psychology: Learning, Memory, and Cognition, 18,* 391–412.

Allen, S. W., & Brooks, L. R. (1991). Specializing the operation of an explicit rule. *Journal of Experimental Psychology: General, 120,* 3–19.

Anderson, J. R. (1978). Arguments concerning representations for mental imagery. *Psychological Review, 85,* 249–277.

Anderson, J. R. (1991). The adaptive nature of human categorization. *Psychological Review, 98,* 409–429.

Anderson, J. R., Kline, P. J., & Beasley, C. M., Jr. (1979). A general learning theory and its application to schema abstraction. *Psychology of Learning and Motivation, 13,* 277–318.

Ashby, F. G. (1992). *Multidimensional models of perception and cognition.* Hillsdale, NJ: Erlbaum.

Ashby, F. G., Alfonso-Reese, L. A., Turken, A. U., & Waldron, E. M. (1998). A neuropsychological theory of multiple systems in category learning. *Psychological Review, 10,* 442–481.

Ashby, F. G., & Gott, R. (1988). Decision rules in perception and categorization of multidimensional stimuli. *Journal of Experimental Psychology: Learning, Memory, and Cognition, 14,* 33–53.

Ashby, F. G., & Maddox, W. T. (1993). Relations among prototype, exemplar, and decision bound models of categorization. *Journal of Mathematical Psychology, 38,* 423–466.

Ashby, F. G., & Maddox, W. T. (1998). Stimulus categorization. In M. H. Birnbaum (Ed.), *Measurement, judgment, and decision making: Handbook of perception and cognition* (pp. 251–301). San Diego, CA: Academic Press.

Ashby, F. G., & Townsend, J. T. (1986). Varieties of perceptual independence. *Psychological Review, 93,* 154–179.

Ashby, F. G., & Waldron, E. M. (2000). The neuropsychological bases of category learning. *Current Directions in Psychological Science, 9,* 10–14.

Au, T. K., Dapretto, M., & Song, Y. K. (1994). Input vs. constraints: Early word acquisition in Korean and English. *Journal of Memory and Language, 33,* 567–582.

Barsalou, L. W. (1982). Context-independent and context-dependent information in concepts. *Memory & Cognition, 10,* 82–93.

Barsalou, L. W. (1983). Ad hoc categories. *Memory & Cognition, 11,* 211–227.

Barsalou, L. W. (1987). The instability of graded structure: Implications for the nature of concepts. In U. Neisser (Ed.), *Concepts and conceptual development* (pp. 101–140). New York: Cambridge University Press.

Barsalou, L. W. (1991). Deriving categories to achieve goals. In G. H. Bower (Ed.), *The psychology of learning and motivation: Advances in research and theory* (Vol. 27, pp. 1–64). New York: Academic Press.

Barsalou, L. W. (1999). Perceptual symbol systems. *Behavioral and Brain Sciences, 22,* 577–660.

Barsalou, L. W., Huttenlocher, J., & Lamberts, K. (1998). Basing categorization on individuals and events. *Cognitive Psychology, 36,* 203–272.

Bassok, M. (1996). Using content to interpret structure: Effects on analogical transfer. *Current Directions in Psychological Science, 5,* 54–58.

Biederman, I. (1987). Recognition-by-components: A theory of human image understanding. *Psychological Review, 94,* 115–147.

Billman, D. (1989). Systems of correlations in rule and category learning: Use of structured input in learning syntactic categories. *Language and Cognitive Processes, 4,* 127–155.

Billman, D., & Heit, E. (1988). Observational learning from internal feedback: A simulation of an adaptive learning method. *Cognitive Science, 12,* 587–625.

Billman, D., & Knutson, J. F. (1996). Unsupervised concept learning and value systematicity: A complex whole aids learning the parts. *Journal of Experimental Psychology: Learning, Memory, and Cognition, 22,* 458–475.

Bourne, L. E., Jr. (1970). Knowing and using concepts. *Psychological Review, 77,* 546–556.

Bourne, L. E., Jr. (1982). Typicality effect in logically defined categories. *Memory & Cognition, 10,* 3–9.

Brooks, L. R. (1978). Non-analytic concept formation and memory for instances. In E. Rosch & B. B. Lloyd (Eds.), *Cognition and categorization* (pp. 169–211). Hillsdale, NJ: Erlbaum.

Brooks, L. R., Norman, G. R., & Allen, S. W. (1991). Role of specific similarity in a medical diagnostic task. *Journal of Experimental Psychology: General, 120,* 278–287.

Bruner, J. S. (1973). *Beyond the information given: Studies in the psychology of knowing.* New York: Norton.

Bruner, J. S., Goodnow, J. J., & Austin, G. A. (1956). *A study of thinking.* New York: Wiley.

Busemeyer, J. R., & Townsend, J. T. (1993). Decision field theory: A dynamic-cognitive approach to decision making in an uncertain environment. *Psychological Review, 100,* 432–459.

Cabrera, A., & Billman, D. (1996). Language-driven concept learning: Deciphering "Jabberwocky." *Journal of Experimental Psychology: Learning, Memory, and Cognition, 22,* 539–555.

Calder, A. J., Young, A. W., Perrett, D. I., Etcoff, N. L., & Rowland, D. (1996). Categorical perception of morphed facial expressions. *Visual Cognition, 3,* 81–117.

Carey, S. (1985). *Conceptual change in childhood.* Cambridge, MA: Bradford Books.

Choi, S., McDaniel, M. A., & Busemeyer, J. R. (1993). Incorporating prior biases in network models of conceptual rule learning. *Memory & Cognition, 21,* 413–423.

Cohen, L. B., & Oakes, L. M. (1993). How infants perceive a simple causal event. *Developmental Psychology, 29,* 421–433.

Crawford, L. J., Huttenlocher, J., & Engebretson, P. H. (2000). Category effects on estimates of stimuli: Perception or reconstruction? *Psychological Science, 11,* 284–288.

Edelman, S. (1998). Representation is representation of similarities. *Behavioral and Brain Sciences, 21,* 449–498.

Edelman, S. (1999). *Representation and recognition in vision.* Cambridge, MA: Bradford Books/MIT Press.

Erickson, M. A., & Kruschke, J. K. (1998). Rules and exemplars in category learning. *Journal of Experimental Psychology: General, 127,* 107–140.

Estes, W. K. (1986). Array models for category learning. *Cognitive Psychology, 18,* 500–549.

Estes, W. K. (1994). *Classification and cognition.* New York: Oxford University Press.

Fodor, J. A. (1975). *The language of thought.* New York: Thomas Y. Crowell.

Fodor, J. A. (1983). *The modularity of mind: An essay on faculty psychology.* Cambridge, MA: MIT Press.

Fodor, J. A., Garrett, M., Walker, E., & Parkes, C. M. (1980). Against definitions. *Cognition, 8,* 263–367.

Fodor, J. A., & Pylyshyn, Z. W. (1988). Connectionism and cognitive architecture: A critical analysis. *Cognition, 28,* 3–71.

Garrod, S., & Doherty, G. (1994). Conversation, co-ordination and convention: An empirical investigation of how groups establish linguistic conventions. *Cognition, 53,* 181–215.

Gelman, S. A., & Markman, E. M. (1986). Categories and induction in young children. *Cognition, 23,* 183–209.

Gentner, D. (1981). Some interesting differences between verbs and nouns. *Cognition and Brain Theory, 4,* 161–178.

Gentner, D. (1982). Why nouns are learned before verbs: Linguistic relativity versus natural partitioning. In S. A. Kuczaj (Ed.), *Language development: Vol. 2. Language, thought, and culture* (pp. 301–334). Hillsdale, NJ: Erlbaum.

Gentner, D., & Boroditsky, L. (2001). Individuation, relativity, and early word learning. In M. Bowerman & S. Levinson (Eds.), *Language acquisition and conceptual development* (pp. 215–256). Cambridge, UK: Cambridge University Press.

Gluck, M. A., & Bower, G. H. (1988). From conditioning to category learning: An adaptive network model. *Journal of Experimental Psychology: General, 117,* 227–247.

Gluck, M. A., & Bower, G. H. (1990). Component and pattern information in adaptive networks. *Journal of Experimental Psychology: General, 119,* 105–109.

Goldstone, R. L. (1994a). The role of similarity in categorization: Providing a groundwork. *Cognition, 52,* 125–157.

Goldstone, R. L. (1994b). Influences of categorization on perceptual discrimination. *Journal of Experimental Psychology: General, 123,* 178–200.

Goldstone, R. L. (1996). Isolated and Interrelated Concepts. *Memory & Cognition, 24,* 608–628.

Goldstone, R. L. (2000). Unitization during category learning. *Journal of Experimental Psychology: Human Perception and Performance, 26,* 86–112.

Goldstone, R. L., & Barsalou, L. (1998). Reuniting perception and conception. *Cognition, 65,* 231–262.

Goldstone, R. L., & Steyvers, M. (2001). The sensitization and differentiation of dimensions during category learning. *Journal of Experimental Psychology: General, 130,* 116–139.

Goldstone, R. L., Steyvers, M., Spencer-Smith, J., & Kersten, A. (2000). Interactions between perceptual and conceptual learning. In E. Diettrich & A. B. Markman (Eds.), *Cognitive dynamics: Conceptual change in humans and machines* (pp. 191–228). Mahwah, NJ: Erlbaum.

Gopnik, A., & Choi, S. (1995). Names, relational words, and cognitive development in English and Korean speakers: Nouns are not always learned before verbs. In M. Tomasello & W. E. Merriman (Eds.), *Beyond names for things: Young children's acquisition of verbs* (pp. 62–94). Hillsdale, NJ: Erlbaum.

Grossberg, S. (1982). Processing of expected and unexpected events during conditioning and attention: A psychophysiological theory. *Psychological Review, 89,* 529–572.

Hampton, J. A. (1987). Inheritance of attributes in natural concept conjunctions. *Memory & Cognition, 15,* 55–71.

Hampton, J. A. (1993). Prototype models of concept representation. In I. V. Mecheln, J. Hampton, R. S. Michalski, & P. Theuns (Eds.), *Categories and concepts: Theoretical views and inductive data analysis* (pp. 67–95). London: Academic Press.

Hampton, J. A. (1997). Conceptual combination: Conjunction and negation of natural concepts. *Memory & Cognition, 25,* 888–909.

Harnad, S. (1987). *Categorical perception.* Cambridge, UK: Cambridge University Press.

Harnad, S. (1990). The symbol grounding problem. *Physica D, 42,* 335–346.

Harnad, S., Hanson, S. J., & Lubin, J. (1995). Learned categorical perception in neural nets: Implications for symbol grounding. In V. Honavar & L. Uhr (Eds.), *Symbolic processors and connectionist network models in artificial intelligence and cognitive modelling: Steps toward principled integration* (pp. 191–206). Boston: Academic Press.

Heider, E. R. (1972). Universals in color naming and memory. *Journal of Experimental Psychology, 93,* 10–20.

Heit, E. (1994). Models of the effects of prior knowledge on category learning. *Journal of Experimental Psychology: Learning, Memory, and Cognition, 20,* 1264–1282.

Heit, E. (1997). Knowledge and concept learning. In K. Lamberts & D. Shanks (Eds.), *Knowledge, concepts, and categories* (pp. 7–41). Hove, UK: Psychology Press.

Heit, E. (2000). Properties of inductive reasoning. *Psychonomic Bulletin and Review, 7,* 569–592.

Hintzman, D. L. (1986). "Schema abstraction" in a multiple-trace memory model. *Psychological Review, 93,* 411–429.

Homa, D., & Cultice, J. C. (1984). Role of feedback, category size, and stimulus distortion on the acquisition and utilization of ill-defined categories. *Journal of Experimental Psychology: Learning, Memory, and Cognition, 10,* 234–257.

Homa, D., Sterling, S., & Trepel, L. (1981). Limitations of exemplar-based generalization and the abstraction of categorical information. *Journal of Experimental Psychology: Human Learning and Memory, 7,* 418–439.

Hull, C. L. (1920). Quantitative aspects of the evolution of concepts. *Psychological Monographs, 28* (Whole No. 123).

Hummel, J. E., & Biederman, I. (1992). Dynamic binding in a neural network for shape recognition. *Psychological Review, 99,* 480–517.

Huttenlocher, J., Hedges, L. V., & Vevea, J. L. (2000). Why do categories affect stimulus judgment? *Journal of Experimental Psychology: General, 129,* 220–241.

Huttenlocher, J., & Lui, F. (1979). The semantic organization of some simple nouns and verbs. *Journal of Verbal Learning and Verbal Behavior, 18,* 141–162.

Jones, S. S., & Smith, L. B. (1993). The place of perception in children's concepts. *Cognitive Development, 8,* 113–139.

Katz, J., & Fodor, J. (1963). The structure of a semantic theory. *Language, 39,* 170–210.

Keil, F. C. (1989). *Concepts, kinds and development.* Cambridge, MA: Bradford Books/MIT Press.

Kersten, A. W. (1998). A division of labor between nouns and verbs in the representation of motion. *Journal of Experimental Psychology: General, 127,* 34–54.

Kersten, A. W., & Billman, D. O. (1997). Event category learning. *Journal of Experimental Psychology: Learning, Memory, and Cognition, 23,* 638–658.

Kolers, P. A., & Roediger, H. L. (1984). Procedures of mind. *Journal of Verbal Learning and Verbal Behavior, 23,* 425–449.

Kohonen, T. (1995). *Self-organizing maps.* Berlin: Springer-Verlag.

Komatsu, L. K. (1992). Recent views of conceptual structure. *Psychological Bulletin, 112,* 500–526.

Knowlton, B. J., & Squire, L. R. (1993). The learning of categories: Parallel brain systems for item memory and category knowledge. *Science, 262,* 1747–1749.

Kruschke, J. K. (1992). ALCOVE: An exemplar-based connectionist model of category learning. *Psychological Review, 99,* 22–44.

Kuhl, P. K., & Miller, J. D. (1975). Speech perception by the chinchilla: Voice-voiceless distinction in alveolar plosive consonants. *Science, 190,* 69–72.

Lakoff, G. (1987). *Women, fire and dangerous things: What categories reveal about the mind.* Chicago: University of Chicago Press.

Lamberts, K. (1998). The time course of categorization. *Journal of Experimental Psychology: Learning, Memory, and Cognition, 24,* 695–711.

Lamberts, K. (2000). Information-accumulation theory of speeded categorization. *Psychological Review, 107,* 227–260.

Landauer, T. K., & Dumais, S. T. (1997). A solution to Plato's problem: The Latent Semantic Analysis theory of the acquisition, induction, and representation of knowledge. *Psychological Review, 104,* 211–240.

Lassaline, M. E., & Logan, G. D. (1993). Memory-based automaticity in the discrimination of visual numerosity. *Journal of*

Experimental Psychology: Learning, Memory, and Cognition, 19, 561–581.

Lenat, D. B., & Feigenbaum, E. A. (1991). On the thresholds of knowledge. *Artificial Intelligence, 47,* 185–250.

Levin, D. T., & Beale, J. M. (2000). Categorical perception occurs in newly learned faces, other-race faces, and inverted faces. *Perception & Psychophysics, 62,* 386–401.

Liberman, A. M., Cooper, F. S., Shankweiler, D. P., & Studdert-Kennedy, M. (1967). Perception of the speech code. *Psychological Review, 74,* 431–461.

Liberman, A. M., Harris, K. S., Hoffman, H. S., & Griffith, B. C. (1957). The discrimination of speech sounds within and across phoneme boundaries. *Journal of Experimental Psychology, 54,* 358–368.

Logan, G. D. (1988). Toward an instance theory of automatization. *Psychological Review, 95,* 492–527.

Luce, R. D. (1959). *Individual choice behavior.* New York: Wiley.

Maddox, W. T., & Ashby, F. G. (1993). Comparing decision bound and exemplar models of categorization. *Perception & Psychophysics, 53,* 49–70.

Malt, B. C. (1994). Water is not H_2O. *Cognitive Psychology, 27,* 41–70.

Marcus, G. F. (1998). Rethinking eliminativist connectionism. *Cognitive Psychology, 37,* 243–282.

Markman, A. B., & Dietrich, E. (2000). In defense of representation. *Cognitive Psychology, 40,* 138–171.

Markman, A. B., & Makin, V. S. (1998). Referential communication and category acquisition. *Journal of Experimental Psychology: General, 127,* 331–354.

Marr, D., & Nishihara, H. K. (1978). Representation and recognition of the spatial organization of three-dimensional shapes. *Proceedings of the Royal Society of London, 200B,* 269–294.

McCloskey, M., & Glucksberg, S. (1978). Natural categories: Well defined or fuzzy-sets? *Memory & Cognition, 6,* 462–472.

McFadden, D., & Callaway, N. L. (1999). Better discrimination of small changes in commonly encountered than in less commonly encountered auditory stimuli. *Journal of Experimental Psychology: Human Perception and Performance, 25,* 543–560.

McKinley, S. C., & Nosofsky, R. M. (1995). Investigations of exemplar and decision bound models in large, ill-defined category structures. *Journal of Experimental Psychology: Human Perception and Performance, 21,* 128–148.

McNamara, T. P, & Miller, D. L. (1989). Attributes of theories of meaning. *Psychological Bulletin, 106,* 355–376.

Medin, D. L. (1989). Concepts and conceptual structure. *American Psychologist, 44,* 1469–1481.

Medin, D. L., & Atran, S. (1999). *Folkbiology.* Cambridge, MA: MIT Press.

Medin, D. L., Dewey, G. I., & Murphy, T. D. (1983). Relationships between item and category learning: Evidence that abstraction is not automatic. *Journal of Experimental Psychology: Learning, Memory, and Cognition, 9,* 607–625.

Medin, D. L., Lynch. E. B., & Solomon, K. O. (2000). Are there kinds of concepts? *Annual Review of Psychology, 51,* 121–147.

Medin, D. L., & Schaffer, M. M. (1978). Context theory of classification learning. *Psychological Review, 85,* 207–238.

Medin, D. L., & Shoben, E. J. (1988). Context and structure in conceptual combination. *Cognitive Psychology, 20,* 158–190.

Medin, D. L., & Smith, E. E. (1984). Concepts and concept formation. *Annual Review of Psychology, 35,* 113–138.

Medin, D. L., Wattenmaker, W. D., & Michalski, R. S. (1987). Constraints and preferences in inductive learning: An experimental study of human and machine performance. *Cognitive Science, 11,* 299–339.

Mervis, C. B., & Rosch, E. (1981). Categorization of natural objects. *Annual Review of Psychology, 32,* 89–115.

Miyawaki, K. (1975). An effect of linguistic experience. The discrimination of (r) and (l) by native speakers of Japanese and English. *Perception & Psychophysics, 18,* 331–340.

Murphy, G. L. (1988). Comprehending complex concepts. *Cognitive Science, 12,* 529–562.

Murphy, G. L., & Allopenna, P. D. (1994). The locus of knowledge effects in category learning. *Journal of Experimental Psychology: Learning, Memory, and Cognition, 20,* 904–919.

Murphy, G. L., & Kaplan, A. S. (2000). Feature distribution and background knowledge in category learning. *Quarterly Journal of Experimental Psychology: Human Experimental Psychology, 53A,* 962–982.

Murphy, G. L., & Medin, D. L. (1985). The role of theories in conceptual coherence. *Psychological Review, 92,* 289–316.

Naigles, L. R., & Terrazas, P. (1998). Motion-verb generalizations in English and Spanish: Influences of language and syntax. *Psychological Science, 9,* 363–369.

Nosofsky, R. M. (1984). Choice, similarity, and the context theory of classification. *Journal of Experimental Psychology: Learning, Memory, and Cognition, 10,* 104–114.

Nosofsky, R. M (1986). Attention, similarity, and the identification-categorization relationship. *Journal of Experimental Psychology: General, 115,* 39–57.

Nosofsky, R. M. (1992). Similarity scaling and cognitive process models. *Annual Review of Psychology, 43,* 25–53.

Nosofsky, R. M., Kruschke, J. K., & McKinley, S. C. (1992). Combining exemplar-based category representations and connectionist learning rules. *Journal of Experimental Psychology: Learning, Memory, and Cognition, 18,* 211–233.

Nosofsky, R. M., & Palmeri, T. J. (1998). A rule-plus-exception model for classifying objects in continuous-dimension spaces. *Psychonomic Bulletin and Review, 5,* 345–369.

Nosofsky, R. M., Palmeri, T. J., & McKinley, S. K. (1994). Rule-plus-exception model of classification learning. *Psychological Review, 101,* 53–79.

Oaksford, M., & Chater, N. (1998). *Rationality in an uncertain world: Essays on the cognitive science of human reasoning.* Hove, UK: Psychology Press/Erlbaum.

O'Toole, A. J., Peterson, J., & Deffenbacher, K. A. (1995). An 'other-race effect' for categorizing faces by sex. *Perception, 25,* 669–676.

Palmeri, T. J. (1997). Exemplar similarity and the development of automaticity. *Journal of Experimental Psychology: Learning, Memory, and Cognition, 23,* 324–354.

Palmeri, T. J., & Nosofsky, R. M. (1995). Recognition memory for exceptions to the category rule. *Journal of Experimental Psychology: Learning, Memory, and Cognition, 21,* 548–568.

Pastore, R. E. (1987). Categorical perception: Some psychophysical models. In S. Harnad (Ed.), *Categorical perception* (pp. 29–52). Cambridge, UK: Cambridge University Press.

Pazzani, M. J. (1991). Influence of prior knowledge on concept acquisition: Experimental and computational results. *Journal of Experimental Psychology: Learning, Memory, and Cognition, 17,* 416–432.

Perrett, D. I., Oram, M. W., & Ashbridge, E. (1998). Evidence accumulation in cell populations responsive to faces: An account of generalization of recognition without mental transformations. *Cognition, 67,* 111–145.

Piaget, J. (1952). *The origins of intelligence in children.* New York: International Universities Press.

Pinker, S. (1991). Rules of language. *Science, 253,* 530–535.

Pinker, S. (1994). *The language instinct.* New York: W. Morrow.

Posner, M. I., & Keele, S. W. (1967). Decay of visual information from a single letter. *Science, 158,* 137–139.

Posner, M. I., & Keele, S. W. (1968). On the genesis of abstract ideas. *Journal of Experimental Psychology, 77,* 353–363.

Posner, M. I., & Keele, S. W. (1970). Retention of abstract ideas. *Journal of Experimental Psychology, 83,* 304–308.

Repp, B. H., & Liberman, A. M. (1987). Phonetic category boundaries are flexible. In S. R. Harnad (Ed.), *Categorical perception* (pp. 89–112). New York: Cambridge University Press.

Ripley, B. D. (1996). *Pattern recognition and neural networks.* Cambridge, UK: Cambridge University Press.

Rips, L. J. (1975). Inductive judgments about natural categories. *Journal of Verbal Learning and Verbal Behavior, 14,* 665–681.

Rips, L. J. (1989). Similarity, typicality, and categorization. In S. Vosniadu & A. Ortony (Eds.), *Similarity, analogy, and thought* (pp. 21–59). Cambridge, UK: Cambridge University Press.

Rips, L. J., & Collins, A. (1993). Categories and resemblance. *Journal of Experimental Psychology: General, 122,* 468–486.

Roberson, D., Davies, I., & Davidoff, J. (2000). Color categories are not universal: Replications and new evidence from a stone-age culture. *Journal of Experimental Psychology: General, 129,* 369–398.

Rosch, E. (1975). Cognitive representations of semantic categories. *Journal of Experimental Psychology: General, 104,* 192–232.

Rosch, E., & Mervis, C. B. (1975). Family resemblances: Studies in the internal structure of categories. *Cognitive Psychology, 7,* 573–605.

Rosch, E., Mervis, C. B., Gray, W., Johnson, D., & Boyes-Braem, P. (1976). Basic objects in natural categories. *Cognitive Psychology, 8,* 382–439.

Ross, B. H., & Murphy, G. L. (1999). Food for thought: Cross-classification and category organization in a complex real-world domain. *Cognitive Psychology, 38,* 495–553.

Rumelhart, D. E., & Zipser, D. (1985). Feature discovery by competitive learning. *Cognitive Science, 9,* 75–112.

Schank, R. C. (1982). *Dynamic memory: A theory of reminding and learning in computers and people.* Cambridge, UK: Cambridge University Press.

Schusterman, R. J., Reichmuth, C. J., & Kastak, D. (2000). How animals classify friends and foes. *Current Directions in Psychological Science, 9,* 1–6.

Schyns, P. G. (1998). Diagnostic recognition: Task constraints, object information, and their interactions. *Cognition, 67,* 147–179.

Shanks, D. R. (1991). Categorization by a connectionist network. *Journal of Experimental Psychology: Learning, Memory, and Cognition, 17,* 433–443.

Shin, H. J., & Nosofsky, R. M. (1992). Similarity-scaling studies of dot-pattern classification and recognition. *Journal of Experimental Psychology: General, 121,* 278–304.

Sidman, M. (1994). *Equivalence relations and behavior: A research story.* Boston: Authors.

Sloman, S. A. (1996). The empirical case for two systems of reasoning. *Psychological Bulletin, 119,* 3–22.

Sloman, S. A., Love, B. C., & Ahn, W.-K. (1998). Feature centrality and conceptual coherence. *Cognitive Science, 22,* 189–228.

Smith, E. E. (1989). Concepts and induction. In M. I. Posner (Ed.), *Foundations of cognitive science* (pp. 501–526). Cambridge, MA: MIT Press.

Smith, E. E., Langston, C., & Nisbett, R. (1992). The case for rules in reasoning. *Cognitive Science, 16,* 1–40.

Smith, E. E., & Medin, D. L. (1981). *Categories and concepts.* Cambridge, MA: Harvard University Press.

Smith. E. E., Patalano, A. L., & Jonides, J. (1998). Alternative strategies of categorization. *Cognition, 65,* 167–196.

Smith, E. E., Shoben, E. J., & Rips, L. J. (1974). Structure and process in semantic memory: A featural model for semantic decisions. *Psychological Review, 81,* 214–241.

Smith, E. E., & Sloman, S. A. (1994). Similarity- versus rule-based categorization. *Memory & Cognition, 22,* 377–386.

Smith, J. D., & Minda, J. P. (2000). Thirty categorization results in search of a model. *Journal of Experimental Psychology: Learning, Memory, and Cognition, 26,* 3–27.

Smith, L. B. (1999). Children's noun learning: How general processes make specialized learning mechanisms. In B. MacWhinney

(Ed.), *The emergence of language* (pp. 277–304). Mahwah, NJ: Erlbaum.

Snodgrass, J. G. (1984). Concepts and their surface representations. *Journal of Verbal Learning and Verbal Behavior, 23,* 3–22.

Solomon, K., & Barsalou, L. W. (1999). *Grounding concepts in perceptual simulation: Vol. 2. Evidence from property verification.* Manuscript submitted for publication.

Spalding, T. L., & Murphy, G. L. (1999). What is learned in knowledge-related categories? Evidence from typicality and feature frequency judgments. *Memory & Cognition, 27,* 856–867.

Storms, G., De Boeck, P., Hampton, J. A., & Van Mechelen, I. (1999). Predicting conjunction typicalities by component typicalities. *Psychonomic Bulletin and Review, 6,* 677–684.

Talmy, L. (1985). Lexicalization patterns: Semantic structure in lexical forms. In T. Shopen (Ed.), *Language typology and syntactic description: Vol. 3. Grammatical categories and the lexicon* (pp. 97–149). New York: Cambridge University Press.

Tardif, T. (1996). Nouns are not always learned before verbs: Evidence from Mandarin speakers' early vocabularies. *Developmental Psychology, 32,* 492–504.

Tanaka, J., & Taylor, M. (1991). Object categories and expertise: Is the basic level in the eye of the beholder? *Cognitive Psychology, 23,* 457–482.

Tarr, M. J., & Bülthoff, H. H. (1995). Is human object recognition better described by geon-structural-descriptions of by multiple-views? *Journal of Experimental Psychology: Human Perception and Performance, 21,* 1494–1505.

Tarr, M. J., & Gauthier, I. (1998). Do viewpoint-dependent mechanisms generalize across members of a class? *Cognition, 67,* 73–110.

Tennenbaum, J. B. (1999). Bayesian modeling of human concept learning. *Advances in Neural Information Processing Systems, 11,* 251–257.

Thelen, E., & Smith, L. B. (1994). *A dynamic systems approach to the development of cognition and action.* Cambridge, MA: MIT Press.

van Gelder, T. (1998). The dynamical hypothesis in cognitive science. *Behavioral and Brain Sciences, 21,* 615–665.

Werker, J. F., & Tees, R. C. (1984). Cross-language speech perception: Evidence for perceptual reorganization during the first year of life. *Infant Behavior and Development, 7,* 49–63.

Whorf, B. L. (1956). The relation of habitual thought and behavior to language. In J. B. Carroll (Ed.), *Language, thought, and reality: Essays by B. L. Whorf* (pp. 35–270). Cambridge, MA: MIT Press.

Wisniewski, E. J. (1997). When concepts combine. *Psychonomic Bulletin and Review, 4,* 167–183.

Wisniewski, E. J. (1998). Property instantiation in conceptual combination. *Memory & Cognition, 26,* 1330–1347.

Wisniewski, E. J., & Love, B. C. (1998). Relations versus properties in conceptual combination. *Journal of Memory and Language, 38,* 177–202.

Wittgenstein, L. (1953). *Philosophical investigations* (G. E. M. Anscombe, Trans.). New York: Macmillan.

Wolff, P., Medin, D. L., & Pankratz, C. (1999). Evolution and devolution of folkbiological knowledge. *Cognition, 73,* 177–204.

CHAPTER 23

Reasoning and Problem Solving

JACQUELINE P. LEIGHTON AND ROBERT J. STERNBERG

The winged sphinx of Boeotian Thebes terrorized men by demanding an answer to a riddle taught to her by the Muses: *What is it that walks on four feet and two feet and three feet and has only one voice, and when it walks on most feet it is the weakest?* The men who failed to answer this riddle were devoured until one man, Oedipus, eventually gave the proper answer: *Man, who crawls on all fours in infancy, walks on two feet when grown, and leans on a staff in old age.* In amazement, the sphinx killed herself and, from her death, the story of her proverbial wisdom evolved. Although the riddle describes a person's life stages in general, the sphinx is considered wise because her riddle specifically predicted the life stage Oedipus would ultimately endure. Upon learning that he married his mother and unknowingly killed his father, Oedipus gouges out his eyes and blinds himself, thereby creating the need for a staff to walk for the rest of his life.

How did Oedipus solve a problem that had led so many to an early grave? Is there any purpose in knowing that he solved the problem by inferring the conclusion, applying a strategy, or experiencing an insight into its resolution? Knowing how Oedipus arrived at his answer might have saved the men before him from death as sphinx fodder. Most of the problems that we face in everyday life are not as menacing as the one Oedipus faced that day. Nevertheless, the conditions under which Oedipus resolved the riddle correspond in some ways to the conditions of our own everyday problems: Everyday problems are solved with incomplete information and under time constraints, and they are subject to meaningful consequences. For example, imagine you need to go pick up a friend from a party and you realize that a note on which you wrote the address is missing. How would you go about recovering the address or the note on which you wrote the address without being late? If there is a way to unlock the mysteries of thinking and secure clever solutions—to peer inside Oedipus's mind—then we might learn to negotiate answers in the face of uncertainty.

It might be possible to begin unraveling Oedipus's solution by considering how Oedipus approached the riddle; that is, did he approach the riddle as a *reasoning* task, in which a conclusion needed to be deduced, or did he approach the riddle as a *problem-solving* task, in which a solution needed to be found? Is there any purpose in distinguishing between the processes of *reasoning* and *problem solving* in considering how Oedipus solved the riddle? There is some purpose in distinguishing these processes, at least at the outset, because psychologists believe that these operations are relatively distinct (Galotti, 1989). Reasoning is commonly defined as the process of drawing conclusions from principles and from evidence (Wason & Johnson-Laird, 1972). In contrast, problem solving is defined as the goal-driven process of overcoming obstacles that obstruct the path to a solution (Simon, 1999a;

Sternberg, 1999). Given these definitions, would it be more accurate to say that Oedipus resolved the riddle by reasoning or by problem solving? Knowing which operation he used might help us understand which operations we should apply to negotiate our own answers to uncertain problems.

Unfortunately, we cannot peer inside the head of the legendary Oedipus, and it is not immediately obvious from these definitions which one—the definition of reasoning or that of problem solving—describes the set of processes leading to his answer. If we are to have any hope of understanding how Oedipus negotiated a solution to the riddle and how we might negotiate answers to our own everyday riddles, then we must examine reasoning and problem solving more closely for clues.

GOALS OF CHAPTER

The goals of the present chapter are to cover what is known about reasoning and problem solving, what is currently being done, and in what directions future conceptualizations, research, and practice are likely to proceed. We hope through the chapter to convey an understanding of how reasoning and problem solving differ from each other and how they resemble each other. In addition, we hope that we can apply what we have learned to determine whether the sphinx's riddle was essentially a reasoning task or a problem-solving task, and whether knowing which one it was helps us understand how Oedipus solved it.

REASONING

During the last three decades, investigators of reasoning have advanced many different theories (see Evans, Newstead, & Byrne, 1993, for a review). The principal theories can be categorized as *rule theories* (e.g., Cheng & Holyoak, 1985; Rips, 1994), *semantic theories* (e.g., Johnson-Laird, 1999; Polk & Newell, 1995), and *evolutionary theories* (e.g., Cosmides, 1989). These theories advance the idea of a *fundamental reasoning mechanism* (Roberts, 1993, 2000), a hardwired or basic mechanism that controls most, if not all, kinds of reasoning (Roberts, 2000). In addition, some investigators have proposed *heuristic theories* of reasoning, which do not claim a fundamental reasoning mechanism but, instead, claim that simple strategies govern reasoning. Sometimes these simple strategies lead people to erroneous conclusions, but, most of the time, they help people draw adequate conclusions in everyday life. According to rule theorists, semantic theorists, and evolutionary theorists, however, reasoning is better described as a basic mechanism that, if unaltered, should always lead to correct inferences.

Rule Theories

Supporters of rule theories believe that reasoning is characterized by the use of specific rules or commands. Competent reasoning is characterized by applying rules properly, by using the appropriate rules, and by implementing the correct sequence of rules (Galotti, 1989; Rips, 1994). Although the exact nature of the rules might change depending on the specific rule theory considered, all rules are normally expressed as propositional commands such as (*antecedent or premise*) → (*consequent or conclusion*). If a reasoning task matches the antecedent of the rule, then the rule is elicited and applied to the task to draw a conclusion. Specific rule theories are considered below.

Syntactic Rule Theory

According to syntactic rule theory, people draw conclusions using formal rules that are based on natural deduction and that can be applied to a wide variety of situations (Braine, 1978; Braine & O'Brien, 1991, 1998; Braine & Rumain, 1983; Rips, 1994, 1995; Rumain, Connell, & Braine, 1983). Reasoners are able to use these formal rules by extracting the logical forms of premises and then applying the rules to these logical forms to derive conclusions (Braine & O' Brien, 1998).

For example, imagine Oedipus trying to answer the sphinx's riddle, which makes reference to something walking on two legs. In trying to make sense of the riddle, Oedipus might have remembered an old rule stating that *If it walks on two legs, then it is a person*. Combining part of the riddle with his old rule, Oedipus might have formed the following premise set in his mind:

If it walks on two legs, then it is a person. (Oedipus' rule A) (1)

<u>It walks on two legs.</u> (Part of riddle)

Therefore ?

The conclusion to the above premise set can be inferred by applying a rule of logic, *modus ponens,* which eliminates the *if,* as follows:

If A then B.

<u>A.</u>

Therefore B.

Applying the *modus ponens* rule to premise set (1) would have allowed Oedipus to conclude "person."

Another feature of syntactic theory is the use of *suppositions,* which involve assuming additional information for the sake of argument. A supposition can be paired with other premises to show that it leads to a contradiction and, therefore, must be false. For example, consider the following premise set:

a. If it walks on three legitimate legs, then it is not a person. (Oedipus' rule B) (2)

b. It is a person. (Conclusion from premise set (1) above)

c. <u>It walks on three legitimate legs.</u> (*A supposition*)

d. Therefore it is not a person (Modus ponens applied to a and c)

As can be seen from premise set (2), there is a contradiction between the premise *It is a person* and the conclusion derived from the supposition, *It is not a person.* According to the rule of reductio ad absurdum, because the supposition leads to a contradiction, the supposition must be negated. In other words, we reject that *it walks on three legitimate legs.* Because this so-called *modus tollens* inference is not generated as simply as is the *modus ponens* inference, syntactic rule theorists propose that the *modus tollens* inference relies on a series of inferential steps, instead of on the single step associated with *modus ponens.* If Oedipus considered the line of argument above, it might have led him to reject the possibility that the sphinx's riddle referred to anything with three legitimate legs.

In an effort to validate people's use of reasoning rules, Braine, Reiser, and Rumain (1998) conducted two studies. In one of their studies, 28 participants were asked to read 85 reasoning problems and then to evaluate the conclusion presented with each problem. Some problems were predicted to require the use of only one rule for their evaluation (e.g., *There is an O and a Z; There is an O?*), whereas other problems were predicted to require the use of multiple rules or deductive steps for their evaluation (e.g., *There is an F or a C; If there's not an F, then there is a C?*). Participants were asked to evaluate the conclusions by stating whether the proposed conclusion was true, false, or indeterminate. The time taken by each participant to evaluate the conclusion was measured. In addition, after solving each problem, participants were asked to rate the difficulty of the problem using a 9-point scale, with 1 indicating a very easy problem and 9 indicating a very difficult problem. These difficulty ratings were then used to estimate difficulty weights for the reasoning rules assumed to be involved in evaluating the problems. The estimated difficulty weights were then used to predict how another group of participants in a similar study rated a set of new reasoning problems. Braine et al. (1998) found that the difficulty weights could be used to predict participants' difficulty ratings in the similar study with excellent accuracy (correlations ranged up to .95). In addition, the difficulty weights predicted errors and latencies well; long reaction times and inaccurate performance indicated people's attempts to apply difficult and long rule routines, whereas short reaction times and accurate performance indicated people's attempts to apply easy and short rule routines (see also Rips, 1994). Braine et al. (1998) concluded from these results that participants do in fact reason using the steps proposed by the syntactic theory of mental-propositional logic. Outside of these results, other investigators have also found evidence of rule use (e.g., Ford, 1995; Galotti, Baron, & Sabini, 1986; Torrens, Thompson, & Cramer, 1999).

Supporters of syntactic theory use formal or logical reasoning tasks in their investigations of reasoning rules. According to syntactic theorists, errors in reasoning arise because people apply long rule routines incorrectly or draw unnecessary *invited conclusions* from the task information. *Invited,* or simply plausible (but not logically certain), conclusions can be drawn in everyday discourse but are prohibited on formal reasoning tasks, in which information must be interpreted in a strictly logical manner. Because the rules in syntactic theory are used to draw logically certain conclusions, critics of the theory maintain that these rules appear unsuitable for reasoning in everyday situations, in which information is ambiguous and uncertain and additional information must be considered before any *reasonable* conclusion is likely to be drawn (see the chapter by Goldstone & Kersten in this volume for a discussion of rule-based reasoning as it relates to categorization). In defense of the rule approach, it is possible that people unknowingly interject additional information in order to make formal rules applicable. However, it is unclear how one would know what kind of additional information to include. Dennett (1990) has described the uncertainty of what additional information to consider as the *frame problem* (see also Fodor, 1983).

The frame problem involves deciding which beliefs from a multitude of different beliefs to consider when solving a task or when updating beliefs after an action has occurred (Dennett, 1990; Fodor, 1983). The ability to consider different beliefs can lead to insightful and creative comparisons and solutions, but it also raises the question: How do human beings select from among all their beliefs those that are relevant to generating a conclusion in a reasoning problem? The frame problem is a perplexing issue that has not been addressed by syntactic rule theorists.

If it were possible to ask Oedipus how he reached the answer to the riddle, would he be able to say how he did it? That is, could he articulate that he used a rule of some sort to generate his conclusion, or would this knowledge be outside of his awareness? This question brings up a fundamental issue that arises when discussing theories of reasoning: Is the theory making a claim about the *strategies* that a person in particular might use in reasoning or about something more basic, such as how the mind in general processes information, that is, the mind's *cognitive architecture* (Dawson, 1998; Johnson-Laird, 1999; Newell, 1990; Rips, 1994)? The mind's cognitive architecture is thought to lie outside conscious awareness because it embodies the most basic non-physical description of cognition—the fundamental information processing steps underlying cognition (Dawson, 1998; Newell, 1990). In contrast, strategies are thought to be accessible to conscious awareness (Evans, 2000).

Some theories of reasoning seem to pertain to the nature of the mind's cognitive architecture. For example, Rips (1994) has proposed a *deduction-system hypothesis,* according to which formal rules do not underlie only deductive reasoning, or even only reasoning in general, but also the mind's cognitive architecture. He argues that his theory of rules can be used as a *programming* language of general cognitive functions, for example, to implement a production system: a routine that controls cognitive actions by determining whether the antecedents for the cognitive actions have been satisfied (Simon, 1999b; see below for a detailed definition of production systems). The problem with this claim is that production systems have already been proposed as underlying the cognitive architecture and as potentially used to derive syntactic rules (see Eisenstadt & Simon, 1997). Thus, it is not clear which is more fundamental: the syntactic rules or the production systems. Claims have been staked according to which each derives from the other, but both sets of claims cannot be correct.

Another concern with Rips's (1994) deductive-system hypothesis is that its claim about the mind's cognitive architecture is based on data obtained from participants' performance on reasoning tasks, tasks that are used to measure controlled behaviors. Controlled behavior, according to Newell (1990), is not where we find evidence for the mind's architecture, because this behavior is slow, load-dependent, and open to awareness; it can be inhibited; and it permits self-terminating search processes. In contrast, immediate behavior (e.g., as revealed in choice reaction tasks) "is the appropriate arena in which to discover the nature of the cognitive architecture" (Newell, 1990, p. 236). The swiftness of immediate, automatic responses exposes the mind's basic mechanism, which is revealed in true form and unregulated by goal-driven adaptive behavior.

Determining at what level a theory is intended to account for reasoning is important in order to assess the evidence presented as support for the theory. If syntactic rule theory is primarily a theory of the mind's cognitive architecture, then we would not think, for example, of asking Oedipus to think aloud as to how he solved the riddle in an effort to confirm syntactic rule theory. Think-aloud reports would be inadequate evidence in support of the theory. Our question would be fruitless because, although Oedipus might be able to tell us about the strategies he used and the information he thought about in solving the riddle, he presumably would not be able to tell us about his cognitive architecture; he would not have access to it.

Pragmatic Reasoning Theory

Another theory that invokes reasoning rules is pragmatic reasoning theory (Cheng & Holyoak, 1985, 1989; Cheng & Nisbett, 1993). Pragmatic reasoning theorists suggest that people reason by mapping the information they are reasoning about to information they already have stored in memory. In particular, these theorists suggest that this mapping is accomplished by means of *schemas,* which consist of sets of rules related to achieving particular kinds of goals for reasoning in specific domains.

Cheng and Holyoak (1985) have proposed that in domains where permission and obligation must be negotiated, we activate a permission schema to help us reason. The permission schema is composed of four production rules, "each of which specifies one of the four possible antecedent situations, assuming the occurrence or nonoccurrence of the action and precondition" (p. 396). The four possible antecedent situations along with their corresponding consequences are shown below:

> Rule 1: If the action is to be taken, then the precondition must be satisfied.
>
> Rule 2: If the action is not to be taken, then the precondition need not be satisfied.
>
> Rule 3: If the precondition is satisfied, then the action may be taken.
>
> Rule 4: If the precondition is not satisfied, then the action must not be taken.

To understand how these rules are related to reasoning, we first need to discuss how pragmatic reasoning theory grew out of tests of the Wason selection task (Wason, 1966). The selection task is a hypothesis-testing task in which participants are given a conditional rule of the form *If P then Q* and four cards, each of which has either a *P* or a *not-P* on one side and either a *Q* or a *not-Q* on the other side. As shown in Figure 23.1, each of the cards is placed face down so that participants can see only one side of a given card. After participants read the conditional rule, they are asked to select the cards that test the truth or falsity of the rule. According to propositional logic, only

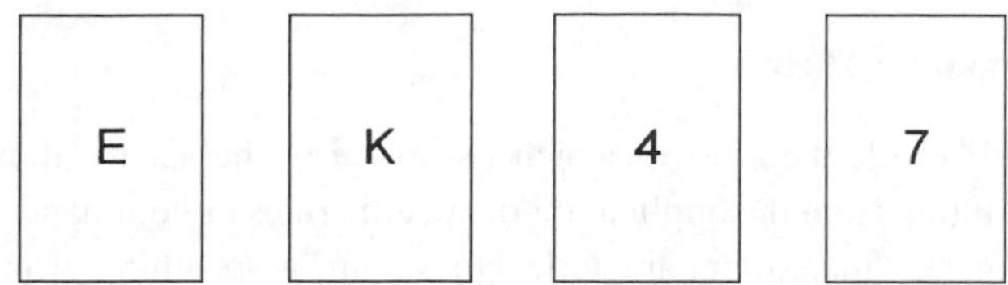
Conditional Rule: "If there is a vowel on one side of the card, then there is an even number on the other side of the card."
E
K
4
7

Figure 23.1 Example of the Wason selection task.

two cards can conclusively test the conditional rule: The *P* card can potentially test the truth or falsity of the rule because when flipped it might have a *not-Q* on its other side, and the *not-Q* card can test the rule because when flipped it might have a *P* on its other side. The actual conditional rule used in the Wason selection task is *If there is a vowel on one side of the card, then there is an even number on the other side of the card,* and the actual cards shown to participants have an exemplar of either a vowel or a consonant on one side and an even number or an odd number on the other side. As few as 10% of participants choose both the *P* and *not-Q* cards (the logically correct cards), with many more participants choosing either the *P* card by itself or both the *P* and *Q* cards (Evans & Lynch, 1973; Wason, 1966, 1983; Wason & Johnson-Laird, 1972; for a review of the task see Evans, Newstead, et al., 1993).

Cheng and Holyoak (1985, 1989) have argued that people perform poorly on the selection task because it is too abstract and not meaningful. Their pragmatic reasoning theory grew out of studies showing that it was possible to improve significantly participants' performance on the selection task by using a meaningful, concrete scenario involving permissions and obligations. *Permission* is defined by Cheng and Holyoak (1985) as a regulation in which, in order to undertake a particular action, one first must fulfill a particular precondition. An *obligation* is defined as a regulation in which a situation requires the execution of a subsequent action. In a test of pragmatic reasoning theory, Cheng and Holyoak (1985) presented participants with the following permission scenario as an introduction to the selection task:

> You are an immigration officer at the International Airport in Manila, capital of the Philippines. Among the documents you must check is a sheet called Form H. One side of this form indicates whether the passenger is entering the country or in transit, and the other side of the form lists inoculations the passenger has had in the past 6 months. You must make sure that *if the form says ENTERING on one side, then the other side includes cholera among the list of diseases*. This is to ensure that entering passengers are protected against the disease. Which of the following forms would you have to turn over to check? (pp. 400–401)

TABLE 23.1 Percentage Correct on Selection Task (Experiment 3)

	Rule Type		
Given Form	Permission	Arbitrary	Mean
If-then	67	17	42
Only-if	56	4	30
Mean	62	11	

Source: From "Pragmatic Reasoning Schemas" by P. W. Cheng and K. J. Holyoak (1985), *Cognitive Psychology, 17,* 407. Copyright 1985 by Academic Press. Reprinted by permission.

The above introduction was followed by depictions of four cards in a fashion similar to that shown in Figure 23.1. The first card depicted the word TRANSIT, another card depicted the word ENTERING, a third card listed the diseases "cholera, typhoid, hepatitis," and a fourth card listed the diseases "typhoid, hepatitis." Table 23.1 shows that participants were significantly more accurate in choosing the correct alternatives, *P and not-Q*, for the permission task (62 %) than for the abstract version of the task (11%). In addition, Table 23.1 indicates that the effect of the permission context generalized across corresponding connective forms; that is, participants' performance improved not only for permission rules containing the connective *if . . . then,* but also for permission rules containing the equivalent connective *only if.*

According to Cheng and Holyoak (1985), the permission schema's production rules,

(1) If the action is to be taken, then the precondition must be satisfied; and

(2) If the pre-condition is not satisfied, then the action must not be taken,

guided participants' correct selection of cards by highlighting the cases where the action was taken (i.e., *if the person is entering,* then the person must have been inoculated against cholera) and where the precondition was not satisfied (i.e., *if the person has not been inoculated,* then the person must not enter). According to the theory, reasoning errors occur when a task's content fails to elicit an appropriate pragmatic reasoning schema. The content of the task must be meaningful and not arbitrary, however; otherwise, participants perform as poorly on concrete as on abstract versions of the selection task (e.g., Manktelow & Evans, 1979).

Despite its success in improving performance on the selection task, pragmatic reasoning theory has been criticized on a number of grounds. For instance, some investigators have charged that pragmatic reasoning schemas are better conceptualized as an undeveloped collection of *deontic* rules, which are invoked in situations calling for *deontic reasoning.* Manktelow and Over (1991) describe deontic reasoning as reasoning about what we are allowed to do or what we should do instead of what is actually the case. In other words, deontic reasoning involves reasoning about permissions and obligations. Deontic reasoning is moderated by subtle considerations of semantic, pragmatic, and social information that influence a person's assessment of the utilities of possible actions. Assessing the utilities of possible actions involves thinking about whether pursuing an action will lead to a desired goal (i.e., does the action have utility for me?) and whether it is justifiable to pursue the action given the value of the outcome. Manktelow and Over (1991) have suggested that although Cheng and Holyoak's (1985, 1989) schemas are deontic in character, they fail to include how people assess utilities when reasoning about permissions. Furthermore, they have pointed out that the very production rules that make up the permission schema incorporate deontic terms such as *may* and *must* that need to be decoded by a more basic schema that deciphers deontic terms.

Other critics of pragmatic reasoning theory have also claimed that the theory is too closely connected with a single task to offer an account of human reasoning generally (e.g., Rips, 1994). Although pragmatic reasoning schemas have been used to explain reasoning about permissions, obligations, and causes and effects, it is unclear if equivalent schemas, whatever form they might take, can also be used to explain other forms of reasoning, such as reasoning about classes or spatial relationships (Liberman & Klar, 1996). The ambiguity of how pragmatic reasoning schemas are applied in unusual or novel situations is one reason why, for example, it is unlikely that Oedipus reasoned according to pragmatic reasoning theory in deriving a conclusion to the sphinx's riddle. The riddle represents an unusual problem, one for which a schema might not even exist. In addition, even if it were possible to map the riddle's information onto a schema, how would the schema be selected from the many other schemas in the reasoner's repertoire?

Finally, although Cheng and Holyoak (1985, 1989) have described how the permission schema helps reasoners infer conclusions in situations involving permissions (see paragraph above), they do not specify how reasoners actually implement the schemas. Schemas serve to represent or organize declarative knowledge, but how does someone proceed from having this representational scheme to knowing when and how to apply it? Does application happen automatically, or is it under our control? If it is under our control, then it seems critical to explore the strategies that people use in deciding to apply a schema. If it is not under our control, then what are the processes by which ineffective schemas are disregarded in the search for the proper schema? The latter issue of how schemas are applied and disregarded is another example of the frame problem (Dennett, 1990). The frame problem in this case involves deciding which schemas—from a possible multitude of schemas—to consider when solving a task.

Semantic Theories

Unlike rule theories, in which reasoning is characterized as resulting from the application of specific rules or commands, semantic theories characterize reasoning as resulting from the particular interpretations assigned to specific assertions. Rules are not adopted in semantic theories because reasoning is thought to depend on the meaning of assertions and not on the syntactic form of assertions.

Mental Model Theory

According to the theory of mental models, reasoning is based on manipulating meaningful concrete information, which is representative of the situations around us, and is not based on deducing conclusions by means of abstract logical forms that are devoid of meaning (Johnson-Laird, 1999). Two mental model theorists, Phil Johnson-Laird and Ruth Byrne (1991), have proposed a three-step procedure for drawing necessary inferences: First, the reasoner constructs an initial model or representation that is analogous to the state of affairs (or information) being reasoned about (Johnson-Laird, 1983). For example, consider that a reasoner is given a conditional rule *If there is a circle then there is a square* plus an assertion *There is a circle* and is asked then to draw a conclusion. The initial model or representation he or she might construct for the conditional would likely include the salient cases of the conditional, namely a circle and a square, as follows:

❍ ❑

The reasoner might also recognize the possibility that the antecedent of the conditional (i.e., *If there is a circle*) could be false, but this possibility would not be normally represented explicitly in the initial model. Rather, this possibility would be represented implicitly in another model, whose presence is defined by an ellipsis attached to the explicit model as follows:

❍ ❑
. . .

The second step in the procedure involves drawing a conclusion from the initial model. For example, from the foregoing initial model of the rule, *If there is a circle then there is a square,* and the assertion, *There is a circle*, the reasoner can conclude immediately that *there is a square* alongside the circle. Third, in some cases, the reasoner constructs alternative models of the information in order to verify (or disprove) the conclusion drawn (Johnson-Laird, 1999; Johnson-Laird & Byrne, 1991). For example, suppose that the reasoner had been given a different assertion, such as that *There is not a circle* in addition to the rule *If there is a circle then there is a square*. This time, in order to verify the conclusion to be drawn from the conditional rule plus this new assertion, the reasoner would need to flesh out the implicit model indicated in the ellipsis of the initial model. For example, according to a material implication interpretation of the conditional rule, he or she would need to flesh out the implicit model as follows:

~❍ ❑
~❍ ~❑

where ~ refers to negation.

By using the fleshed out model above, the reasoner would be able to conclude that there is no definite conclusion to be drawn about the presence or absence of a square given the assertion *There is not a circle* and the rule *If there is a circle then there is a square*. There is no definite conclusion that can be drawn because in the absence of a circle (i.e., ~ ❍), a square may or may not also be absent. The first two steps in mental model theory—the construction of an initial explicit model and the generation of a conclusion—involve primarily comprehension processes. The third step, the search for alternative models or the fleshing out of the implicit model, defines the process of reasoning (Evans, Newstead, et al., 1993; Johnson-Laird & Byrne, 1991).

The theory of mental models can be further illustrated with *categorical syllogisms,* which form a standard task used in reasoning experiments (e.g., Johnson-Laird, 1994; Johnson-Laird & Bara, 1984; Johnson-Laird & Byrne, 1991; Johnson-Laird, Byrne, & Schaeken, 1992). Categorical syllogisms consist of two quantified premises and a quantified conclusion. The premises reflect an implicit relation between a subject (S) and a predicate (P) via a middle term (M), whereas the conclusion reflects an explicit relation between the subject (S) and predicate (P). The set of statements below is an example of a categorical syllogism.

ALL S are M
ALL M are P
―――――
ALL S are P

Each of the premises and the conclusion in a categorical syllogism takes on a particular form or mood such as *All S are M, Some S are M, Some S are not M,* or *No S are M*. The validity of syllogisms can be proven using either proof-theoretical methods or, more commonly, a model-theoretical method. According to the model-theoretical method, a valid syllogism is one whose premises cannot be true without its conclusion also being true (Garnham & Oakhill, 1994). The validity of syllogisms can also be defined using proof-theoretical methods that involve applying rules of inference in much the same way as one would in formulating a mathematical proof (see Chapter 4 in Garnham & Oakhill, 1994, for a detailed description of proof-theoretical methods).

Mental model theory has been used successfully to account for participants' performance on categorical syllogisms (Evans, Handley, Harper, & Johnson-Laird, 1999; Johnson-Laird & Bara, 1984; Johnson-Laird & Byrne, 1991). A number of predictions derived from the theory have been tested and observed. For instance, one prediction suggests that participants should be more accurate in deriving conclusions from syllogisms that require the construction of only a single model than from syllogisms that require the construction of multiple models for their evaluation. An example of a single-model categorical syllogism is shown below:

Syllogism: ALL S are M
ALL M are P
―――――
ALL S are P
Model: S = M = P

where = refers to an identity function.

In contrast, a multiple-model syllogism requires that participants construct at least two models of the premises in order to deduce a valid conclusion or determine that a valid conclusion cannot be deduced. Johnson-Laird and Bara (1984) tested the prediction that participants should be more accurate in deriving conclusions from single-model syllogisms than from multiple-model syllogisms by asking 20 untrained volunteers to make an inference from each of 64 pairs of categorical premises randomly presented. The 64 pairs of premises included single-model and multiple-model problems. An analysis of participants' inferences revealed that valid conclusions declined significantly as the number of models that needed to be constructed to derive a conclusion increased (Johnson-Laird & Bara, 1984, Table 6). Although numerous studies have shown that performance on multiple-model categorical syllogisms is inferior to performance on single-model categorical syllogisms, Greene (1992) has suggested that inferior performance on multiple-model syllogisms may have little to do with constructing multiple models. Instead, Greene has suggested that participants may find the conclusions from valid, multiple-model categorical syllogisms awkward to express because they have the form

Some A are not B, a form not frequently used in everyday language.

According to Johnson-Laird and Byrne (1991), however, errors in reasoning have three main sources: First, reasoning errors can occur when people fail to verify that the conclusion drawn from an initial model is valid; that is, people fail to search alternative models. Second, reasoning errors can occur when people prematurely end their search for alternative models because of working memory limitations. Third, reasoning errors can occur when people construct an inaccurate initial model of the task information. In this latter case, the error is not so much a reasoning error as it is an encoding error.

Recent research suggests that people may not search for alternative models spontaneously (Evans et al., 1999). In one study in which participants were asked to endorse conclusions that followed only *necessarily* from sets of categorical premises, Evans et al. (1999) found that participants endorsed conclusions that followed *necessarily* from the premises as frequently as conclusions that followed *possibly* but *strongly* from the premises (means of 80 and 79%, respectively). Evans et al. (1999) defined *possible strong* conclusions as conclusions that are unnecessary given their premises but that are regularly endorsed as necessary. Assuming that participants had taken seriously the instruction to endorse only necessary conclusions, Evans et al. (1999) had expected participants to endorse the necessary conclusions more frequently than the possible strong conclusions. Unlike necessary conclusions, possible strong conclusions should be rejected after alternative models of the premises are considered. Participants, however, endorsed necessary and possible strong conclusions equally often. Evans et al. (1999) explained the equivalent endorsement rates by suggesting that participants were not searching for alternative models of the premises but, instead, were using an initial model of the premises to evaluate both necessary and possible strong conclusions. Evans et al. (1999) suggested that if participants were constructing a single model of the premises, then possible strong conclusions should be endorsed as frequently as necessary conclusions because, in both cases, an initial model of the premises would support the conclusion. Participants, however, did not frequently endorse conclusions that followed *possibly* but *weakly* from the categorical premises (mean of 19%), that is, conclusions that are unnecessary given their premises and that are *rarely* endorsed as necessary. In this case, according to Evans et al. (1999), an initial model of the premises would not likely support the conclusion. Evans et al. concluded from this study that although previous research has shown that people can search for alternative models in some circumstances (e.g., the Newstead and Evans, 1993, study indicated that participants were highly motivated to search for alternative models of unbelievable conclusions from categorical syllogisms), people do not necessarily employ such a search in all circumstances.

Although mental model theory has been used successfully to account for a number of different results (for a review see Schaeken, DeVooght, Vandierendonck, & d'Ydewalle, 2000), it has been criticized for not detailing clearly how the process of model construction is achieved (O'Brien, 1993). For instance, it might be useful if the process of model construction was mapped onto a series of stages of information processing, such as the stages—encoding, combination, comparison, and response—outlined in Guyote and Sternberg (1981; Sternberg, 1983). In addition, the theory is unclear as to whether models serve primarily as strategies or whether models should be considered more basic components of the mind's cognitive architecture.

Oedipus might have employed mental models to solve the sphinx's riddle. For example, Oedipus could have constructed the following models of the riddle:

$$\begin{array}{l} X = a,\ b\ b\ b\ b \\ X = a,\ b\ b \\ X = a,\ b\ b\ b \\ \hline X = ? \end{array}$$

where X represents the same something or someone over time, a represents voice, and b represents feet.

In the models above, X is the unknown entity whose identity needs to be deduced. Each line of the display above reflects a different model or state of time. For example, X = a, b b b b is the first model of the unknown entity at infancy when it has one voice and four feet (crawls on all fours). An examination of the models above, however, does not suggest what conclusion can be deduced. The answer to the riddle is far from clear. The models might be supplemented with additional information, but what other information might be incorporated? Failing to deduce a conclusion from the models above, Oedipus could have decided to construct additional models of the information presented in the riddle. But how would Oedipus go about selecting the additional information needed to construct additional models? This is the same problem that was encountered in our discussion of syntactic rule theory: When one is reasoning about uncertain problems, additional information is a prerequisite to solving the problems, but how this additional information is selected from the massive supply of information stored in memory is left unspecified. It is not an easy problem, but it is one that makes the theory of mental models as difficult to use as syntactic rule theory in explaining Oedipus's response, even though the theories are general ones that, in principle, can be applied to any task, regardless of content.

Verbal Comprehension Theory

This theory is similar to the theory of mental models in the initial inference steps a reasoner is expected to follow in interpreting a reasoning task (i.e., constructing an initial model of the premises and attempting to deduce a conclusion from the initial model). Unlike the theory of mental models, however, verbal comprehension theory does not propose that people search for alternative models of task information.

Polk and Newell (1995), the originators of verbal comprehension theory, have proposed that people draw conclusions *automatically* from information as part of their everyday efforts at communication. In deductive reasoning tasks, however, when a conclusion is not immediately obvious, Polk and Newell have suggested that people attempt to interpret the task information differently until they are able to draw the proper conclusion. Interpretation and reinterpretation define reasoning, according to verbal comprehension theory, and not the search for alternative models, as in mental model theory. In spite of this alleged dissimilarity between verbal comprehension theory and mental model theory, it is not entirely clear how the iterative interpretation process differs from the search for models.

Polk and Newell (1995) have suggested that people commit errors on deductive tasks because "linguistic processes cannot be adapted to a deductive reasoning task instantaneously" (p. 534). That is, reasoning errors occur because people's comprehension processes are adapted to everyday situations and tasks and not to deductive tasks that require specific and formal interpretations.

Polk and Newell (1995) have presented a computational model of categorical syllogistic reasoning based on verbal comprehension theory that accounts for some standard findings in the psychological literature. The computational model, VR, produces regularities commonly and robustly observed in human studies of syllogistic reasoning. For example, whereas people, on average, answer correctly 53% of categorical syllogism problems, VR generates correct answers to an average of 59% of such problems. Also, whereas people, on average, construct valid conclusions that match the *atmosphere* or surface similarities of the premises on 77% of categorical syllogism problems, VR generates similar conclusions on 93% of the problems.

Verbal comprehension theory can only be used to account for reasoning on tasks that supply the reasoner with all the information he or she will need to reach a conclusion (Polk & Newell, 1995). For this reason, this theory cannot be used to explain how Oedipus might have solved the sphinx's riddle, unless we can find out what additional information Oedipus used to solve the riddle. If we assume that Oedipus supplied additional information, then how did Oedipus select the additional information? This is the same question we asked when considering syntactic rule theory and mental model theory. The sphinx's riddle, as with so many of the problems people face in everyday situations, requires the consideration of information beyond that presented in the problem statement. Any theory that fails to outline how this search for additional information occurs is hampered in its applicability to everyday reasoning.

Verbal comprehension theory has additional limitations. One criticism of the theory is that it fails to incorporate findings that show the use of nonverbal methods of reasoning, such as spatial representations, to solve categorical and linear syllogisms (Evans, 1989; Evans, Newstead, et al., 1993; Ford, 1995; Galotti, 1989; Sternberg, 1980a, 1980b, 1981). For example, Ford (1995) found that some individuals used primarily verbal methods to solve categorical syllogisms, whereas other individuals used primarily spatial methods to solve categorical syllogisms. Individuals employing spatial methods constructed a variant of Euler circles to evaluate conclusions derived from categorical syllogisms. Moreover, in studies of linear syllogisms (i.e., logical tasks about relations between entities), researchers reported that participants created visual, mental arrays of both the items and the relations in the linear syllogisms in the process of evaluating conclusions (for a review see Evans, Newstead, et al., 1993). Verbal comprehension theory is also ambiguous as to whether verbal comprehension operates at the level of strategies or at the level of cognitive architecture. Polk and Newell (1995) described verbal reasoning as a strategy that involves the linguistic processes of encoding and reencoding, but some linguistic processes are more automatic than controlled (see Evans, 2000). If verbal reasoning is to be viewed as a strategy, then future treatments of the theory might need to identify the specific linguistic processes that are controlled by the reasoner and how this control is achieved.

Evolutionary Theories

According to evolutionary theories, domain-specific reasoning mechanisms have evolved to help human beings meet specific environmental needs (Cosmides & Tooby, 1996).

Social Contract Theory

Unlike most of the previous theories discussed that advance domain-general methods of reasoning, social contract

Your job is to enforce the following law

If you take the benefit, then you must pay the cost.

The cards below have information about four people. Each card represents one person. One side of the card tells whether a person accepted the benefit, and the other side of the card tells whether that person paid the cost. Indicate only those card(s) that you definitely need to turn over to see if any of these people are breaking the law.

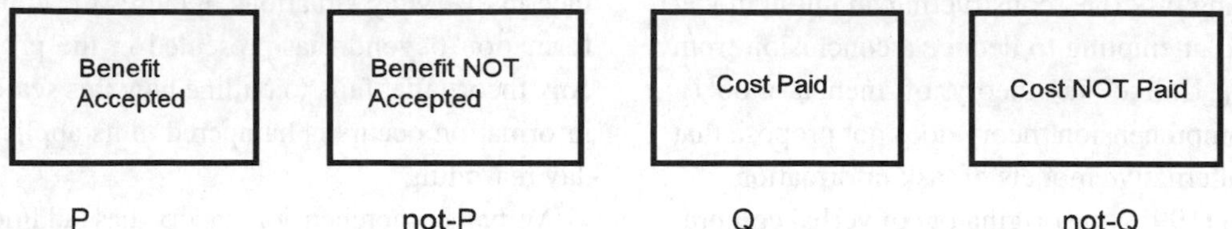

Figure 23.2 The cost-benefit structure of a social-contract version of the Wason selection task (adapted from Cosmides, 1989).

theory advances domain-specific algorithms for reasoning (Cosmides, 1989). These Darwinian algorithms are hypothesized to focus attention, organize perception and memory, and invoke specialized procedural knowledge for the purpose of making inferences, judgments, and choices that are appropriate for a given domain. According to Cosmides (1989), one domain that has cultivated a specialized reasoning algorithm involves situations in which individuals must exchange services or objects contingent on a contract. It is hypothesized that when individuals reason in a social-exchange domain, a *social-contract algorithm* is invoked.

The social-contract algorithm is an example of a Darwinian algorithm that allegedly developed out of an evolutionary necessity for "adaptive cooperation between two or more individuals for mutual benefit" (Cosmides, 1989, p. 193). The algorithm is induced in situations that reflect a cost-benefit theme and involve potential cheaters—individuals who might take a benefit without paying a cost. The algorithm includes a look-for-cheaters procedure that focuses attention on anyone who has *not* paid a cost but might have *taken* a benefit.

Social contract theory was initially proposed as a rival to Cheng and Holyoak's (1985) pragmatic reasoning theory. The two theories are very similar, leading some investigators to view social contract theory as simply a more specific version of pragmatic reasoning theory: a version that focuses on contracts specifically instead of obligations and permissions generally (Pollard, 1990). Cosmides's (1989) social contract theory has been used to account for participants' poor performance on abstract versions of the selection task. According to the theory, reasoning errors occur whenever the context of a reasoning task fails to induce the social-contract algorithm. Cosmides has claimed that the social-contract algorithm is induced in concrete, thematic versions of the Wason selection task and that this is the reason for participants' improved performance on thematic versions of the task. Figure 23.2 illustrates a social-contract representation of the Wason selection task.

Many of the same weaknesses identified in pragmatic reasoning theory can also be identified in social contract theory. First, social contract theory lacks generality because it was developed primarily to explain performance on thematic versions of the selection task. Second, the status of the social-contract algorithm is unclear. On the one hand, the algorithm is described as a strategy that is induced in cost-benefit contexts, but it is unclear whether participants select this strategy or whether the strategy is induced automatically. If it is induced automatically, then its status as a strategy is questionable because strategies are normally under an individual's control (Evans, 2000). If it is not induced automatically, then one needs to inquire how it is selected from among all available algorithms. On the other hand, the algorithm's proposed evolutionary origin would suggest that it might be a fundamental mechanism used to represent specific kinds of contextual information. In other words, if an algorithm has evolved over time to facilitate reasoning in particular contexts (e.g., social-exchange situations), then one would expect most, if not all, human beings to have the algorithm as part of their cognitive architecture. One would not expect such a basic algorithm to have the status of a strategy.

Cheating Detection Theory

Cheating detection theory (Gigerenzer & Hug, 1992) is similar to social contract theory. However, unlike social contract theory, it explores how a reasoner's perspective influences reasoning performance. Gigerenzer and Hug (1992) have maintained the view that individuals possess a reasoning algorithm for handling social contracts. However, unlike

Cosmides (1989), they have proposed that the algorithm yields different responses, depending on the perspective of the reasoner; that is, the algorithm leads participants to generate different responses depending on whether the participant is the recipient of the benefit or the bearer of the cost. For instance, in the following conditional permission rule originally used by Manktelow and Over (1991) in a thematic version of the selection task (see also Manktelow, Fairley, Kilpatrick, & Over, 2000), the perspective of the reasoner determines who and what defines *cheating* and, therefore, what constitutes potentially violating evidence:

If you tidy your room, then you may go out to play.

This rule, which was uttered by a mother to her son, was presented to participants along with four cards. Each card had a record on one side of whether the boy had tidied his room and, on the other, whether the boy had gone out to play, as follows: room tidied (*P*), room not tidied (*not-P*), went out to play (*Q*), or did not go out to play (*not-Q*). Participants were then asked to detect possible violations of the rule either from the mother's perspective or from the son's perspective. Participants who were asked to assume the son's perspective selected the *room tidied* (*P*) and *did not go out to play* (*not-Q*) cards most frequently as instances of possible violations of the rule. These instances correspond to the correct solution sanctioned by standard logic. Participants who were asked to assume the mother's perspective, however, selected the *room not tidied* (*not-P*) and *went out to play* (*Q*) cards most frequently as instances of possible violations—the mirror image of the standard correct solution. From these responses, it seems that participants are sensitive to perspective in reasoning tasks (e.g., Gigerenzer & Hug, 1992; Light, Girotto, & Legrenzi, 1990).

As is the case with social contract theory, cheating detection theory grew out of an attempt to understand performance on thematic versions of the selection task. As with social contract theory, facilitated performance on the selection task is believed to be contingent on the task's context. If the context of the task induces the cheating-detection algorithm, then performance is facilitated, but if the context of the task fails to induce the algorithm, then performance suffers. Thus, cheating detection theory can be criticized for having the same weaknesses as social contract theory; in particular, its scope is too narrow to account for reasoning in general.

Heuristic Theories

A heuristic is a rule of thumb that often but not always leads to a correct answer (Fischhoff, 1999; Simon, 1999a). Some researchers (e.g., Chater & Oaksford, 1999) have proposed that heuristics are used instead of syntactic rules or mental models to reason in everyday situations. Because everyday inferences are often uncertain and can be easily overturned with knowledge of additional information (i.e., everyday inferences are *defeasible* in this sense), some investigators have proposed that heuristics are well adapted for reasoning in everyday situations (e.g., Holland, Holyoak, Nisbett, & Thagard, 1986). Chater and Oaksford (1999) have illustrated the uncertainty of everyday inferences with the following example: Knowing *Tweety is a bird* and *Birds fly* makes it possible to infer that *Tweety can fly,* but this conclusion is uncertain or can be overturned upon learning that *Tweety is an ostrich*. According to Chater and Oaksford (1999), defeasible inferences are problematic for syntactic rule theory and mental model theory because these theories offer mechanisms for how inferences are generated but not for how inferences are overturned, if at all. Consequently, other approaches need to be considered to explain how individuals draw defeasible inferences under everyday conditions.

Judgment Under Uncertainty

Tversky and Kahneman (1974, 1986) outlined several heuristics for making judgments under uncertainty. For example, one of the heuristics they discovered is displayed when people are asked to answer questions such as *What is the probability that John is an engineer?* According to Tversky and Kahneman (1974), many people answer such a question by evaluating the degree to which John resembles or is *representative* of the constellation of traits associated with being an engineer. If participants consider that John shares many of the traits associated with being an engineer, then the probability that he is an engineer is judged to be high. Evaluating the degree to which A is *representative* of B in order to answer questions about the probability that A originated with or belongs to B might often lead to correct answers, but it can also lead to systematic errors. In order to improve the likelihood of generating accurate answers, Tversky and Kahneman (1974) suggested that participants consider the *base rate* of B (e.g., the probability of being an engineer in the general population) before determining the probability that A belongs to B.

Another heuristic that is used to make judgments under uncertainty can be observed when people are asked to assess the probability of an event, for example, the probability that it will rain tomorrow. In this case, many people might assess the probability that it will rain by the ease with which they generate or make *available* thoughts of last week's rainy days. This heuristic can lead to errors if people cannot generate any instances of rain or if people employ a biased search, in which they ignore all of last week's sunny days and focus only on the rainy days in assessing the probability of rain tomorrow (see the chapter by Nickerson & Pew for a fuller discussion of heuristics). Tversky and Kahneman (1974, 1986) considered that people's reliance on heuristics undermined the view of people as rational and intuitive statisticians. Other investigators disagree.

Fast and Frugal Heuristics

Gigerenzer, Todd, and their colleagues from the ABC research group (1999) have suggested that people employ fast and frugal heuristics that take a minimum amount of time, knowledge, and computation to implement, and yield outcomes that are as accurate as outcomes derived from normative statistical strategies. Gigerenzer et al. (1999) have proposed that people use these simple heuristics to generate inferences in everyday environments. One such heuristic exploits the efficiency of *recognition* to draw inferences about unknown aspects of the environment. In a description of the recognition heuristic, Gigerenzer et al. stated that in tasks in which one must choose between two alternatives and only one is recognized, the recognized alternative is chosen. As this statement suggests, the recognition heuristic can be applied only when one alternative is less recognizable than the other alternative.

In a series of experiments, Gigerenzer et al. (1999) showed that people use the recognition heuristic when reasoning about everyday topics. For example, in one experiment, 21 participants were shown pairs of American cities plus additional information about each of the cities and asked to choose the larger city of each pair. The results showed that participants' choices of large cities tended to match those cities they had selected in a previous study as being more recognizable. The recognition heuristic can often lead to accurate inferences because objects or places that score very high (or very low) on a particular criterion are normally made salient in our environment; their atypical characteristics make them stand out.

The recognition heuristic also yields accurate inferences in business situations such as those that involve stock market transactions. In one study, 480 participants were grouped into one of four categories of stock market expertise—American laypeople, American experts, German laypeople, and German experts—and asked to complete a company recognition task of American and German companies (Gigerenzer et al., 1999). Participants then monitored the progress of two investment portfolios, one consisting of companies they recognized highly in the United States and the other consisting of companies they recognized highly in Germany. Participants analyzed the performance of the investment portfolios for a period of 6 months. Results showed that the recognition knowledge of laypeople turned out to be only slightly less profitable than the recognition knowledge of experts. For instance, the investment portfolio of German stocks based on the recognition of the German experts gained 57% during the study; however, German stocks based on the recognition of the German laypeople gained 47% during the same period—only 10% less than the gains made by means of expert advice! The investment portfolios of U.S. stocks based on the recognition of American laypeople and experts did not make such dramatic gains (13 vs. 16%, respectively). However, in all cases, portfolios consisting of recognized stocks yielded average returns that were 3 times as high as the returns from portfolios consisting of unrecognized stocks. These findings indicate that when one is investing, a simple heuristic might be a worthwhile strategy.

Probability Heuristic Model

Another heuristic approach to reasoning is Chater and Oaksford's (1999) probability heuristic model (PH model) of syllogistic reasoning (see also Oaksford & Chater, 1994). According to Chater and Oaksford, simple heuristics can account for many of the findings in syllogistic reasoning studies without the need to posit complicated search processes. In the PH model, quantified statements such as *All birds are small* or *Most apples are red* are ordered based on their informational value. Using convex regions of a similarity space to model informativeness, Chater and Oaksford showed mathematically that different quantified statements vary in how much space they occupy in the similarity space. Categories such as *all* and *most* in quantified statements occupy a *small* proportion of the similarity space and overlap greatly, and are thus considered *more* informative than those quantified statements whose categories occupy a *larger* proportion of the similarity space and do not overlap greatly (see their Appendix A, p. 242). In other words, quantified statements considered to be high in informational value are those "that surprise us the most if they turn out to be true" (Chater & Oaksford, 1999, p. 197) because we perceive them as unlikely. In Chater and Oaksford's (1999) computational analysis, quantifiers are ordered as follows:

All > Most > Few > Some . . . are > No . . . are >> Some . . . are not

where > stands for *more informative than.*

Thus, statements containing the quantifier *all,* such as *All people are tall,* are considered more informative than statements containing the quantifier *most,* such as *Most people are tall.*

One informational strategy based on this ordering is the *min-heuristic,* which involves choosing a conclusion to a premise set that has the same quantifier as that of the least informative premise (*the min-premise*). Thus, if the first premise contains the quantifier *all* and the second premise contains the quantifier *some,* the min-heuristic would suggest selecting *some* as the quantifier for the conclusion as follows:

All Y are X
Some Z are Y (min-premise)
———————————
Some X are Z

Chater and Oaksford (1999) showed that the min-heuristic could be used to predict the conclusions participants generated to valid categorical syllogisms with almost perfect accuracy. The min-heuristic predicted correctly conclusions of the form *All A are B, No A are B,* and *Some A are B* but failed slightly to predict conclusions of the form *Some A are not B* (see their Appendix C, p. 247). The min-heuristic also accounted for the conclusions participants generated incorrectly to invalid syllogisms.

Chater and Oaksford's (1999) PH model fares well against other accounts of syllogistic reasoning. For example, when the PH model was used to model Rips's (1994) syllogistic reasoning results, it obtained as good a fit as Rips's model but with fewer parameters. Moreover, Chater and Oaksford showed that the PH model predicts the differences in difficulty between single-model syllogisms and multiple-model syllogisms described in mental model theory. According to the PH model, participants might be more inclined to solve single-model syllogisms correctly because they lead to more informative conclusions than those arising from multiple-model syllogisms.

Although the heuristics described in Chater and Oaksford's (1999) PH model account for many of participants' responses to categorical syllogisms, the application of their model to other reasoning tasks is unclear. It is unclear how their heuristics can be extended to everyday reasoning tasks in which people must generate conclusions from incomplete and often imprecise information. In addition, these heuristics need to be embedded in a wider theory of human reasoning.

Theorists who promote the fast and frugal heuristic approach to reasoning maintain that heuristics are adaptive responses to an uncertain environment (Anderson, 1983; Chater & Oaksford, 1999; Gigerenzer et al., 1999). In other words, heuristics should not be viewed as irrational responses (even when they do not generate standard logical responses) but as reflections of the way in which human behavior has come to be adaptive to its environment (see also Sternberg & Ben Zeev, 2001). Although the heuristic approach reminds us of the efficiency of rules of thumb in reasoning, it does not explain how people reason when fast and simple heuristics are eschewed. For example, what are the strategies that reasoners invoke when they have decided they want to expend the time and effort to search for the best alternative? It is hard to imagine that heuristics characterize all human reasoning, because factors such as context, instructions, effort, and interest might cue more elaborate reasoning processes.

Factors that Mediate Reasoning Performance

Context

Context can facilitate or hinder reasoning performance. For example, if the context of a reasoning task is completely meaningless to a reasoner, then it is unlikely that the reasoner will be able to use previous experiences or background knowledge to generate a correct solution to the task. It might be possible for a reasoner to generate a logical conclusion to a nonsensical syllogism if the reasoner is familiar with logical necessity but not if he or she is unfamiliar with logical necessity. If a task fails to elicit any background knowledge, logical or otherwise, it is difficult to imagine how someone might establish a sensible starting point in his or her reasoning. For instance, some critics of the abstract version of the Wason selection task have argued that participants perform poorly on the task because the task's abstract context fails to induce a domain-specific reasoning algorithm (e.g., Cheng & Holyoak, 1985, 1989; Cosmides, 1989).

That participants' reasoning performance improves on thematic (or concrete) versions of the selection task, however, does not demonstrate participants' understanding of logic. Recall that depending on the perspective the reasoner assumes, a reasoner will choose the *not-P* and *Q* cards as easily as the *P* and *not-Q* cards in the selection task (see the section titled "Cheating Detection Theory"; Gigerenzer & Hug, 1992; Manktelow & Over, 1991; Manktelow et al., 2000). The facility with which reasoners can change their card choices depending on the perspective they assume suggests that logical principles are not guiding their performance, but, rather, the specific details of the situation. It appears that contextual factors, outside of logic, have a significant influence upon participants' reasoning.

Instructions

The instructions participants receive prior to a reasoning task have been shown to influence their performance. For instance, instructing participants about the importance of searching for alternative models has been shown to improve their performance on categorical syllogisms (Newstead &

Evans, 1993). Additionally, in thematic versions of the selection task, Pollard and Evans (1987) found that instructing participants to *enforce* a rule led to better performance than did instructing them to *test* a rule.

Rule enforcement is what Cheng and Holyoak (1985) and Cosmides (1989) asked participants to do in their studies of thematic versions of the selection task. Cheng and Holyoak asked participants to *enforce* the rule—*If the form says ENTERING on one side, then the other side includes cholera among the list of diseases*—by selecting those cards that represented possible violations of the rule. In contrast, traditional instructions to the selection task have involved asking participants to select cards that will *test the truth or falsity* of the conditional rule. Liberman and Klar (1996) have claimed that asking participants to enforce a rule, by searching for violating instances, is not the same as asking participants to test a rule, by searching for falsifying instances; the latter task is more difficult than the former task because participants must reason *about* a rule instead of *from* a rule.

Reasoning *about* a rule is considered to be a more difficult task than reasoning *from* a rule. Reasoning about a rule requires the metacognitive awareness underlying the hypothetico-deductive method of hypothesis testing; that is, participants reasoning about a rule must test the epistemic status or reliability of the rule (Liberman & Klar, 1996). In contrast, participants reasoning *from* a rule do not test the reliability of the rule but, instead, assume the veracity of the rule and then check for violating instances. Critics of thematic versions of the selection task have argued that enforcer instructions induce participants to think of counterexamples to the rule without understanding the logical structure of the task (Wason, 1983).

The existence of perspective effects provides some evidence that enforcer instructions change the demands of the selection task from that of logical rule *testing* to that of simple rule *following*. The perspective of the participant is a contextual variable that leaves the logical structure of the task unchanged. Thus, if participants are aware of the task's underlying logical structure, then their perspective of the task should not influence their choice of cards—the *P* and *not-Q* remain the correct card choices regardless of perspective. However, recall that asking participants to assume different perspectives in a thematic version of the selection task influenced their choice of cards. Sometimes participants chose the *P* and *not-Q* cards as violating instances of the conditional rule, and sometimes they chose the *not-P* and *Q* cards as violating instances of the conditional rule (see the section titled "Cheating Detection Theory"; Gigerenzer & Hug, 1992). The ease with which participants altered their card choices suggests that their reasoning was influenced more by contextual variables than by logic. The improved performance obtained with the use of enforcer instructions has led some investigators to doubt that these results should be compared with results obtained using traditional instructions (e.g., Griggs, 1983; Liberman & Klar, 1996; Manktelow & Over, 1991; Noveck & O'Brien, 1996; Rips, 1994; Wason, 1983).

Although enforcer instructions might alter the purpose of the abstract selection task, the results obtained with these instructions are significant. That participants manifest a semblance of logical reasoning with enforcer instructions seems to point to the specificity of competent reasoning. This specificity does not refer to the specific brain modules that, according to some researchers, have evolved to help people reason in particular domains (e.g., Cosmides, 1989; Cosmides & Tooby, 1996). Rather, this specificity might be more indicative of the specific background knowledge needed to reason competently (e.g., Chi, Glaser, & Farr, 1988). One reason that enforcer instructions might facilitate reasoning on thematic versions of the selection task is that they cue very specific knowledge about rule enforcement. Most people learn extensively about rule enforcement from an early age. Enforcer instructions might induce the use of specific knowledge about rule enforcement. In short, enforcer instructions might facilitate reasoning performance by permitting participants to use their background knowledge.

Relevance

It is reasonable to assume that individuals will be motivated to solve tasks that are relevant to their lives. The sphinx's riddle must have had immediate relevance for the men who tried to answer it; indeed, the riddle provoked a situation that constituted a life-or-death affair. Sperber, Cara, and Girotto (1995) have proposed that people gauge the relevance of a task to themselves by determining its *cognitive effect* (i.e., the benefits of the task) and its *processing effort* (i.e., the costs of performing the task). According to Sperber et al., a relevant task is one that requires minimal processing effort or whose solution is beneficial, or both. For instance, a task that requires significant processing effort might be considered relevant if its benefits are great (e.g., going to college).

Assessments of task relevance are related to an individual's knowledge, however. For example, being knowledgeable about a task might reduce the reasoner's perception of the processing efforts required to solve it. Conversely, a task that promises great rewards might inspire the reasoner to become knowledgeable about the task's contextual domain. According to Cosmides (1989), for example, the promise of benefits (and the fear of loss) inspired a social-contract algorithm to evolve to help human beings negotiate goods in social-exchange situations. Sperber et al. (1995) have claimed that tasks in any conceptual domain can achieve relevance.

Reasoners who can solve tasks within a contextual domain with little processing effort and who view these tasks as beneficial are likely to be those who have some domain-specific knowledge about the tasks. Because a person's domain-specific knowledge seems to be closely linked to how task relevance is assessed and, therefore, to the person's motivation for solving the task, domain-specific knowledge appears fundamental to performance on reasoning tasks. If knowledge is fundamental to reasoning, then how did Oedipus solve the sphinx's riddle? He had little domain-specific knowledge about the riddle. Perhaps Oedipus did not resolve the riddle by reasoning after all. Perhaps he resolved it by problem solving.

PROBLEM SOLVING

Problem solving is defined as the goal-driven process of overcoming obstacles that obstruct the path to a solution (Simon, 1999a; Sternberg, 1999). Problem solving and reasoning are alike in many ways. For example, in both problem solving and reasoning, the individual is creating new knowledge, albeit in the form of a solution needed to reach a goal or in the form of a conclusion derived from evidence, respectively. Problem solving and reasoning seem to differ, however, in the processes by which this new knowledge is created. In problem solving, individuals use strategies to overcome obstacles in pursuit of a solution (Newell & Simon, 1972). In reasoning, however, the role of strategies is not as clear. It was mentioned earlier that reasoning theories, such as syntactic rule theory, pragmatic reasoning theory, and mental model theory, do not explicitly specify if syntactic rules, pragmatic reasoning schemas, and mental models, respectively, should be viewed as strategies or, more fundamentally, as forms of *representing* knowledge. *Representation* refers to the way in which knowledge or information is formalized in the mind, whereas *strategy* refers to the methods by which this knowledge or information is manipulated to reach a goal. Although individuals may be consciously aware of the strategies they choose to solve problems, individuals are believed to be unaware of how they represent knowledge, which is considered to be part of the mind's cognitive architecture.

It is possible that strategies are unimportant in reasoning because the objective in reasoning is not to reach a goal so much as it is to infer what follows from evidence; the conclusion is meant perhaps to fall out of the set of premises without too much work on the part of the reasoner. Although some reasoning tasks do require goal-oriented conclusions that are not easily deduced—or directly deduced at all—from the premises, it might be more accurate to describe such reasoning tasks as more akin to problem-solving tasks (Galotti, 1989; Evans, Over, & Manktelow, 1993). For instance, reasoning tasks leading to inductive inferences—inferences that go beyond the information given in the task—might be considered more akin to problem-solving tasks. Strategies, however, are clearly important in problem solving because the goal in problem solving is to reach a solution, which is not always derived deductively or even solely from the problem information.

Knowledge Representation and Strategies in Problem Solving

Production Systems

The distinction between representation and strategy is made explicit in the problem-solving literature. For example, some investigators propose that knowledge is represented in terms of *production systems* (Dawson, 1998; Simon, 1999b; Sternberg, 1999). In a production system, instructions (called productions) for behavior take the following form:

IF<<conditions> , THEN<<actions>.

The form above indicates that if certain conditions are met or satisfied, then certain actions can be carried out (Simon, 1999b). The conditions of a production involve propositions that "state properties of, or relations among, the components of the system being modeled" (Simon, 1999b, p. 676). A production system is normally implemented following a match between the conditions of the production and elements stored in working memory. The production is implemented when the conditions specified in the production's IF clause are satisfied or met by the elements of working memory. Following the satisfaction of the production system's IF clause with the elements of working memory, an action is initiated (as specified in the production system). The action may take the form of a motor action or a mental action such as the elimination or creation of working memory elements (Simon, 1999b).

The elements of working memory may satisfy the conditions of numerous productions at any given time. One way in which all the productions that are executable at a given moment can be restrained from overwhelming the problem solver is through the presence of goals. A *goal* can be defined simply as a symbol or representation that must be present both in the conditions of the production and in working memory before that production is activated. In other words, a goal provides a more stringent condition that must be met by an element in working memory before the production is activated (Simon, 1999b). In the following example of a production system, the goal is to determine if a particular sense of the word *knows* is to be applied (taken from Lehman, Lewis, & Newell, 1998, p. 156):

IF comprehending *knows,* and
  there's a preceding word, and
  that word can receive the subject role, and
  the word refers to a person, and
  the word is third person singular,
THEN use sense 1 of *knows.*

The antecedent or the condition of the production consists of a statement of the goal (i.e., comprehending *knows*), along with additional conditions that need to be met before the consequent or action is applied (i.e., use sense 1 of *knows*). Although the above production system might look like a strategy, it is not because knowledge has not been manipulated.

Parallel Distributed Processing (PDP) Systems

Other theories of knowledge representation exist outside of production systems. For example, some investigators propose that knowledge is represented in the form of a parallel distributed processing (PDP) system (Bechtel & Abrahamsen, 1991; Dawson, 1998; Dawson, Medler, & Berkeley, 1997). A PDP system involves a network of inter-connected, processing units that learn to classify patterns by attending to their specific features. A PDP system is made up of simple processing units that communicate information about patterns by means of weighted connections. The weighted connections inform the recipient processing unit whether a to-be-classified pattern includes a feature that the recipient processing unit needs to attend to and use in classifying the pattern. According to PDP theory, knowledge is represented in the layout of connections that develops as the system learns to classify a set of patterns. In Figure 23.3, a PDP representation of the Wason (1966) selection task is shown. This representation illustrates a network that has learned to select the *P* and *Q* in response to the selection task (Leighton & Dawson, 2001). The conditional rule and set of four cards are coded as *1*s and *0*s and are presented to the network's input unit layer. The network responds to the task by turning on one of the four units in its output unit layer, which correspond to the set of four cards coded in the input unit layer. The layer of hidden units indicates the number of cuts or divisions in the pattern space required to solve the task correctly (i.e., generate the correct responses to the task). Training the network to

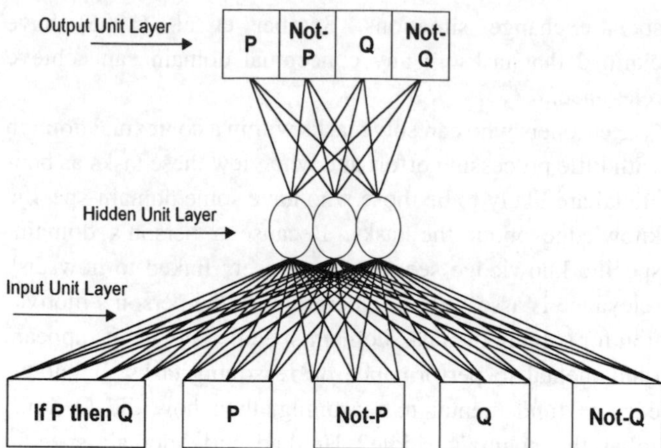

Figure 23.3 Illustration of a PDP network, including layer of input units, hidden units, and output units (adapted from Leighton & Dawson, 2001).

generate the *P* response required a minimum of three hidden units.

Strategies can be extracted from a PDP system. The process by which strategies are identified in a PDP system is laborious, however, and requires the investigator to examine the specific procedures used by the system to classify a set of patterns (Dawson, 1998).

Algorithms

The representation of knowledge provides the language in which cognitive processes in models of cognitive systems can be described. An *algorithm* is one cognitive process for accomplishing an explicit outcome. More specifically, an algorithm is made up of a finite set of operations that is straightforward and unambiguous and, when applied to a set of objects (e.g., playing cards, chess pieces, computer parts), leads to a specified outcome (Dietrich, 1999). The initial state of the set of objects constitutes the input to the algorithm, and the final state of the objects constitutes the output of the algorithm. The initial state of objects is transformed into a final state by implementing the operations of the algorithm that correspond to state transitions. Algorithms can be described more specifically when the context of the algorithm is defined because an algorithm's clarity and simplicity are relative to the context in which it is being applied (Dietrich, 1999). An example of an algorithm might be the instructions included with a new desktop computer (at least, such instructions are supposed to be algorithms). If one follows the instructions for installing all the parts of the computer, the outcome is certain: a working computer. Algorithms are sometimes unavailable for accomplishing certain outcomes; under these circumstances, heuristics can be implemented to *approximate* the desired outcome.

Heuristics

A problem-solving *heuristic* is a rule of thumb for approximating a desired outcome. As with reasoning heuristics, problem-solving heuristics sometimes produce desired outcomes and sometimes not. Heuristics are imperfect strategies (Fischhoff, 1999). Examples of heuristics are considered below in the context of Newell and Simon's model of problem solving.

Theories of Problem Solving

Newell and Simon's Model of Problem Solving

Even after 25 years, Newell and Simon's (1972) model of problem solving remains influential today. Newell and Simon's model of problem solving was generated from computer simulations and from participants' think-aloud responses as they worked through problems. According to the model, the problem solver perceives both the *initial state,* the state at which he or she originally is, and the *goal state,* the state that the problem solver would like to achieve. Both of these states occupy positions within a *problem space,* the universe of all possible actions that can be applied to the problem, given any constraints that apply to the solution of the problem (Simon, 1999a; Sternberg, 1999).

In the ongoing process of problem solving, a person decomposes a problem into a series of intermediate steps with the purpose of bringing the initial state of the problem closer to the goal state. At each intermediate step prior to the goal state, the subgoal is to achieve the next intermediate step that will bring the problem solver closer to the goal state. Each step toward the goal state involves applying an operation or rule that will change one state into another state. The set of operations is organized into a program, including sublevel programs. The program can be a heuristic or an algorithm, depending on its specific nature. In short, according to Newell and Simon's (1972) model, problem solving is a search through a series of states within a problem space; the solution to a problem lies in finding the correct sequence of actions for moving from one (initial) state to another (goal) state (Newell & Simon, 1972; Simon, 1999a; Sternberg, 1999).

A variety of heuristics can be used for changing one state into another. For example, the *difference-reduction method* involves reducing the difference between the initial state and goal state by applying operators that increase the surface similarity of both states. If an operator cannot be directly applied to reduce the difference between the initial state and goal state, then the heuristic is discarded. Another method that is similar to the difference-reduction method is Newell and Simon's (1972) *means-ends analysis,* a heuristic Newell and Simon studied extensively in a computer simulation program (i.e., General Problem Solver [GPS]) that modeled human problem solving. Means-end analysis is similar to the difference-reduction method, with the exception that if an operator cannot be directly applied to reduce a difference between the initial state and goal state, then, instead of the strategy's being discarded, a sub-goal is set up to make the operator applicable (Simon, 1999a).

Analogy is another heuristic. Under this heuristic, the problem solver uses the structure of the solution to an analogous problem to guide his or her solution to a current problem. The main focus in research on analogy is in how people interpret or understand one situation in terms of another; that is, how it is that one situation is *mapped* onto another for problem-solving purposes (Gentner, 1999). Two main subprocesses are proposed to mediate the use of analogy. According to Gentner's structure-mapping theory (1983), an unfamiliar situation can be understood in terms of another familiar situation by aligning the representational structures of the two situations and projecting inferences from the familiar case to the unfamiliar case. The alignment must be structurally consistent such that there is a one-to-one correspondence between the mapped elements in the familiar and unfamiliar situations. Inferences are then projected from the familiar to the unfamiliar situation so as to obtain structural completion (Gentner, 1983, 1999). Following this alignment, the analogy and its inferences are *evaluated* by assessing (a) the structural soundness of the alignment between the two situations; (b) the factual validity of the inferences, because the use of analogy does not guarantee deductive validity; and (c) whether the inferences meet the requirements of the goal that prompted the use of the analogy in the first place (Gentner, 1999).

Recent research suggests that use of analogy in real-world contexts is based on structural or deep underlying similarities, instead of surface or superficial similarities, between the unfamiliar situation and the familiar situation (Dunbar, 1995, 1997). For example, Dunbar (1997) found that over 50% of analogies that scientists generated at weekly meetings in a molecular biology lab were based on deep, structural features between problems, rather than on surface features between problems. In previous studies, however, investigators (e.g., Gentner, Rattermann, & Forbus, 1993) have found that participants in laboratory experiments sometimes rely on superficial features when using analogy. According to Blanchette and Dunbar (2000; see also Dunbar, 1995, 1997), participants' reliance on superficial features when using analogy might be due to the kind of paradigm used to study analogy. For example, Blanchette and Dunbar indicated that previous studies have used a *reception paradigm* to study analogy use. Under the reception paradigm, participants are provided with both a target (less familiar) and a source (familiar) analog and then asked to indicate the relationships between both rather than being asked to generate their own source analogs. In a series of studies aimed at evaluating participants' analogies, Blanchette and Dunbar found that when participants were given a target problem and asked to *generate* their own source analog, most of the analogies (67%) generated by participants did not exhibit superficial similarities with the target but, instead, exhibited deeper similarities with the target. The proportion of these deep analogies increased to 81% when participants worked individually. These results suggest that participants, like scientists, can generate analogies based on deep, structural features when laboratory conditions are more akin to real-world contexts, that is, when participants are free to generate their own source analogs.

Error is always a possibility when heuristics are used. Not only might a chosen heuristic be inappropriate for the problem under consideration, but a heuristic might be inappropriately used, resulting in unsuccessful problem solving. Heuristics such as the difference-reduction method, means-end analysis, analogy, and others (e.g., see Anderson, 1990, for further descriptions of the generate and test method, working forward method, and working backward method) are only general rules of thumb that work most of the time but not necessarily all of the time (Fischhoff, 1999; Holyoak, 1990; Simon, 1999a). They represent general problem-solving methods that can be applied with relative success to a wide range of problems across domains.

According to Newell and Simon (1972), the use of heuristics embodies problem solving because of the cognitive limitations or *bounded rationality* that characterizes human behavior (see also Sternberg & Ben Zeev, 2001). Simon (1991) described bounded rationality as involving two central components: the limitations of the human mind and the structure of the environment in which the mind must operate. The first of these components suggests that the human mind is subject to limitations, and, due to these limitations, models of human problem solving, decision making, and reasoning should be constructed around how the mind actually performs instead of on how the mind should perform from an engineering point of view. Foolproof strategies do not exist in everyday cognition because the ill-defined structure of our environment makes it unlikely that people can identify perfect heuristics for solving imperfect, uncertain problems. The second of these components suggests that the structure of the environment shapes the heuristics that will be most successfully applied in problem solving endeavors. If the environment is ill defined (in the sense that it reflects numerous uncertain tasks), then general heuristics that work most of the time and do not overburden the cognitive system will be favored (see also Brunswick, 1943; Gigerenzer et al., 1999; Shepard, 1990). Heuristics, however, are only one of the kinds of tools that facilitate problem solving. Investigators have also found that *insight* is an important variable that aids some forms of problem solving (Davidson & Sternberg, 1984; Metcalfe & Wiebe, 1987; Sternberg & Davidson, 1995).

Problem Solving by Means of Insight

Insightful problem solving can be defined as problem solving that is significantly assisted by the awareness of a key piece of information—information that is not necessarily obvious from the problem presented (Sternberg, 1999). It is believed that insight plays a role in the solution of *ill-defined problems*. Ill-defined problems are problems whose solution paths are elusive; the goal is not immediately certain. Because the solution path is elusive, ill-defined problems are challenging to represent within a problem space. Ill-defined problems are often termed *insight problems* because they require the problem solver to perceive the problem in a new way, a way that illuminates the goal state and the path that leads to a solution. Insight into a solution can manifest itself after the problem solver has put the problem aside for hours and then comes back to it. The new perspective one gains on a problem when coming back to it after having put it aside is known as an *incubation effect* (Dominowski & Jenrick, 1973; Smith & Blankenship, 1989).

Metcalfe and Wiebe (1987; see also Metcalfe, 1986, 1998) have shown that insightful problem solving seems to differ from ordinary (noninsightful) problem solving. For example, these investigators have shown that participants who are highly accurate in estimating their problem-solving success with ordinary problems are not as accurate in estimating their success with insight problems. The processes that might be responsible for these differences are not yet detailed, making this account more representative of a performance-based account than a process-based account of problem solving (for a fuller discussion of insight, see Sternberg & Davidson, 1995).

In a more process-oriented theory of insight, however, Davidson and Sternberg (1984) have offered a three process view of insight. These investigators have proposed that insightful problem solving manifests itself in three different forms: (a) *Selective encoding* insights involve attending to a part of the problem that is relevant to solving the problem, (b) *selective comparison* insights involve novel comparisons of information presented in the problem with information stored in long-term memory, and (c) *selective combination* insights involve new ways of integrating and synthesizing new and old information. Insight gained in any one of these three forms can facilitate insightful problem solving.

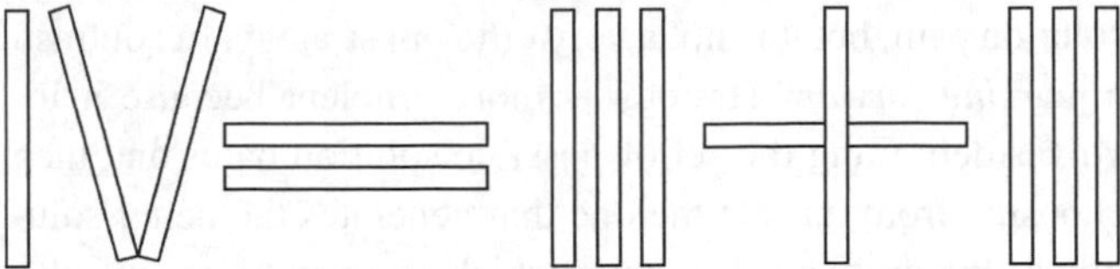

Figure 23.4 Example of matchstick problem (adapted from Knoblich, Ohlsson, Haider, & Rhenius, 1999).

In addition, Knoblich, Ohlsson, Haider, and Rhenius (1999) have characterized insightful problem solving as overcoming *impasses,* states of mind in which the thinker is unsure of what to do next. These investigators have proposed that impasses are overcome by changing the problem representation by means of two hypothetical processes or mechanisms. The first mechanism involves *relaxing* the constraints imposed upon the solution, and the second mechanism involves decomposing the problem into *perceptual chunks*. In a series of four studies aimed at examining insightful problem solving, Knoblich et al. (1999) asked participants to solve insight problems called "match-stick arithmetic" problems. As shown in Figure 23.4, match-stick arithmetic problems involve false arithmetic statements written with Roman numerals (e.g., I, II, IV), arithmetic operations (e.g., −, +), and equal signs constructed out of matchsticks. The goal in matchstick problems is to move a single stick in such a way that the initial false arithmetic statement is transformed into a true statement. A move can be made on a numerical value or an operator and can consist of grasping a stick and moving it, rotating it, or sliding it.

According to Knoblich et al. (1999), matchstick problems can be solved by relaxing the constraints on how numerical values are represented, how operators are represented, and how arithmetic functions are supposed to be formed—for example, form of X = f(Y, Z). In particular, the numerical value constraint in arithmetic suggests that a numerical value on one side of an equation cannot be changed unless an equivalent change is made to the numerical value on the other side of the equation, such as when the same quantity is added to or subtracted from both sides of an equation. Relaxing the constraint on how numerical values are represented would involve accepting the possibility that a numerical value on one side of an equation can be changed without changing the other side of the equation as well (e.g., if 1 is subtracted from one side of the equation, this same operation need not be performed on the other side of the equation). Note that numerical value constraints do not include constraints on how the numerical quantities are perceived. For example, the numerical value constraint does not include constraints on whether the number 4 is perceived as *IV* or as *IIII* or some other representation. According to Knoblich et al. (1999), how numbers are perceived in the context of the matchstick task is better explained by considering the process of chunking.

Knoblich et al. (1999) suggest that decomposing elements of matchstick problems into perceptual chunks can also help to solve the problems. Perceptual decomposition involves, for instance, recognizing that the Roman numeral *IV* can be decomposed into the elements *I* and *V,* and that the resulting elements can be moved independently of each other to generate a true matchstick arithmetic equation. Roman numerals cannot, however, be decomposed into elements that are not used in constructing the numerals. For instance, the Roman numeral *IV* could not be decomposed into *IIII* because four vertical lines were not used to construct the numeral *IV*.

In an effort to examine how constraint relaxation and chunking mediated insightful problem solving, Knoblich et al. (1999) asked participants to solve matchstick problems of varying difficulty. After an initial training phase, participants were presented with two blocks of six matchstick problems on a computer screen and given 5 minutes to respond to each problem. Each block of problems contained instances of easy matchstick problems (i.e., Type A) and difficult matchstick problems (i.e., Type C and D). Results from their four studies revealed, as expected, that participants were more successful at solving problems that required the relaxation of lower order constraints (e.g., relaxing constraints on numerical value representation) than problems that required the relaxation of higher order constraints (e.g., relaxing constraints on arithmetic function representation). For example, after an average of 5 minutes, almost all participants solved problems requiring the relaxation of low-order constraints (Type A), whereas fewer than half of all participants solved problems requiring the relaxation of high-order constraints (Type C). In addition, participants were more successful at solving problems that required the decomposition of loose chunks (e.g., decomposing *IV* into *I* and *V*) than problems that required the decomposition of tight chunks (e.g., decomposing *V* into \ and /). After an average of 5 minutes, almost all participants solved problems requiring the decomposition of loose chunks (Type A), whereas only 75% of participants solved problems requiring the decomposition of tight chunks (Type D). Overcoming impasses in solving insight problems exemplifies a general need to override *mental sets* or fixed ways of thinking about problems generated from past experience with similar problems. The encumbrance of mental sets highlights the existence of factors such as how the problem is interpreted that can influence problem-solving success.

It is very likely that Oedipus solved the sphinx's riddle by experiencing an insight into its solution. The riddle can certainly be labeled an ill-defined problem—one whose solution required the awareness of a key piece of information. What are the processes by which Oedipus gained the insight necessary to solve the riddle? This is an important question, but one whose answer remains a mystery. On the one hand, that any belief or thought can, in principle, be brought to bear on problem-solving endeavors permits the possibility of creative or insightful problem solving. On the other hand, because any belief or thought can be brought to bear on problem-solving endeavors, understanding how individuals select specific beliefs and thoughts as they solve problems remains a challenge—a challenge that we earlier identified as the frame problem (Fodor, 1983).

Factors that Mediate Problem Solving

Definition of Problem: Mental Set

A mental set involves thinking about a problem, its context, and its possible solution from a single perspective (Luchins, 1942; Sternberg, 1999). Such a limited perspective can hinder problem solving if a successful solution can be achieved only by viewing the problem from a novel angle. Setting the problem aside momentarily can foster insight or a new perspective (see earlier discussion of *incubation effect*) and help break the mental set. For example, misreading a word in an essay or misreading a variable in a mathematical proof can lead to a mental set and block understanding. In these cases, putting the material aside even for an hour and then coming back to it can break the mental set.

Past experience can be beneficial to problem solving, but it can also foster mental sets by biasing the way in which the problem solver ventures to reach a solution. In particular, *expertise* in the domain of the problem can actually disrupt problem solving, especially if the problem calls for a creative solution (Wiley, 1998). Although experts are generally able to solve problems in their domains more effectively than novices because their well-structured, easily activated knowledge permits an efficient search of the problem space, sometimes this knowledge can be disadvantageous. For example, Wiley (1998) has suggested that a large amount of domain knowledge can bias problem-solving efforts by confining the search space and therefore excluding the portion of the space in which the solution resides. That is, expertise can actually constrain creative problem solving by foreclosing the problem space prematurely (see also Bedard & Chi, 1992; Frensch & Sternberg, 1989).

Strategy Selection and Knowledge

Selecting the right strategy in response to a problem can determine whether a problem's solution will be found and, if so, whether it will be found expeditiously. For example, the *generate and test* heuristic (Newell & Simon, 1972), which involves arbitrarily generating solution paths until the correct path is found, may ultimately lead one down the correct solution path, but it is not a very efficient strategy. In contrast, a *working forward* strategy is more efficient because it involves delimiting the set of possible solution paths and then choosing from this set the one that generates the better solution to the problem. Knowing which strategy to use in solving a given problem, however, is dependent on the problem solver's level of expertise in the problem domain.

Not all strategies are used equally often by all problem solvers. Strategy selection depends on the problem domain and on the level of expertise of the problem solver within that domain (Chi et al., 1988). Expertise plays a pivotal role in strategy selection because greater domain knowledge in the domain of the problem influences the way in which the problem is interpreted, how the solution is envisioned, and hence the strategy that is ultimately selected to solve the problem. Bedard and Chi (1992), in a review of studies of expert problem solving, concluded that, in general, experts are better problem solvers than are novices because (a) they know more about their domain than do novices; (b) their knowledge is better organized in ways that make that knowledge more accessible, functional, and efficient; (c) they perform better than novices in domain-related tasks on the basis of their greater knowledge and better organization; and (d) their skills are domain specific. In short, experts select strategies and solve problems more efficiently than do novices.

EXPERT PROBLEM SOLVING AND REASONING

The influential role of knowledge in successful problem solving has led investigators to examine closely the attributes of expert problem solvers (e.g., Charness & Schultetus, 1999; Ericsson, 1996; Ericsson & Charness, 1994; Ericsson & Smith, 1991; Sternberg, 1999). In contrast to the popular opinion that superior performance within a contextual domain originates solely from innate ability, research on expertise suggests that exceptional performance develops largely, although not exclusively, from intense preparation (Ericsson & Charness, 1994; see also the chapter by Johnson in this volume). Studies of expertise are intriguing because they suggest that human cognitive abilities are flexible and can adapt to meet increasingly higher expectations. Although research on expertise is integrated into the literature on problem solving (e.g., Chase & Simon, 1973; Chi et al., 1988; de Groot, 1965; Gobet, 1997; Holding, 1992), it is interesting that research on expertise has not been integrated into the literature on reasoning. As we will examine shortly, the absence of this integration may be a shortcoming in the field of reasoning.

Expertise is defined by Charness and Schultetus (1999) as "consistently superior performance on a set of representative tasks for the domain that can be administered to any subject" (p. 58). Studies of expertise suggest that expert performance is a reliable phenomenon that can be measured using standard tasks or conditions for competition in laboratory settings (for a review, see Ericsson, 1996). Identified experts within a domain seem to share a cluster of features about their training and performance. First, peak performance results after many years of intense preparation and practice within the domain: 10,000 hours, for example, are normally required to reach top-level performance within a domain (Charness & Schultetus, 1999). Second, experts do not simply spend more leisure time in their respective domain in comparison to others but, rather, spend more hours engaging in *deliberate* practice (Ericsson & Charness, 1994). Deliberate practice normally involves solitary study with the purpose of improving performance.

Expertise is associated with the ability to recognize important problem features quickly (Allard & Starkes, 1991; Chase & Simon, 1973; de Groot, 1965; Gobet, 1997; Gobet & Simon, 1996). For example, Gobet and Simon (1996) found that champion chess players could recall more than nine chess positions that had been presented to the players briefly and without breaks between presentations (see also the chapter by Butcher & Kintsch in this volume, in which experts' memory skills are discussed). Likewise, Allard and Starkes (1991) found that elite athletes were able to abstract and recall more information about game situations after a brief exposure than nonelite athletes. In sum, experts recognize meaningful relations or patterns in their domains of expertise (Gobet, 1997). Distilling such patterns allows experts to form complex representations of the problem situation, representations that integrate task information with background knowledge to select and evaluate actions and to consider alternative actions (Ericsson, 1996; Ericsson & Kintsch, 1995).

The Neglect of Expertise in Reasoning Theories

Although studies of expertise have been integrated into the problem-solving literature, these studies have not been integrated into the reasoning literature. For example, in tests of syntactic rule theory and mental model theory, participants who have training in logic or are considered expert reasoners on categorical and conditional syllogisms are excluded from participating. It is not entirely clear why participants with training in logic are excluded from participating in reasoning studies, but one reason seems to involve the belief that participants' training will bias the study's results. Participants without any training in logic (i.e., novices in logic) are usually included in studies of reasoning.

The systematic exclusion of expert reasoners from reasoning studies has likely obscured the rich variety of reasoning strategies available to individuals of different knowledge levels. Studying only how novices reason on a specific task makes it impossible to assess the full set of strategies available to reasoners with different knowledge levels: The full spectrum of responses is restricted. We know from research in expert problem solving that it is not uncommon for novices to resemble each other in their problem solving endeavors within a specific domain (e.g., Priest & Lindsay, 1992). However, that novices employ a single strategy on task X does not suggest that individuals with expertise on task X will use the same strategy or that novices will not use an alternate strategy on task Y. When both a restricted sample of participants (e.g., novices) and a restricted sample of tasks (e.g., categorical syllogisms) are used in reasoning studies, participants' strategies and responses might appear much more alike and consistent than they really are.

The neglect of expertise in reasoning studies might be a source of some ambiguity in theories of reasoning. Recall that at the beginning of the chapter we suggested that some ambiguity beset reasoning theories such as syntactic rule theory and mental model theory as to how syntactic rules and mental models should be conceptualized: that is, whether syntactic rules and mental models should be viewed as reasoning strategies or, more fundamentally, as mechanisms that comprise the cognitive architecture of the mind. Both syntactic rule theory and mental model theory propose that syntactic rules and mental models, respectively, comprise a fundamental mechanism in reasoning. In both theories, either rules or models are proposed to underlie reasoning, but not both. However, Stenning and Yule (1997) have indicated that rule-based and model-based theories are essentially similar in their underlying logic but differ only as *algorithms* (cf. Falmagne & Gonsalves, 1995; Roberts, 1993; for a contrasting view see Over & Evans, 1999). Thus, rules and models are not mutually exclusive. We propose that some of the confusion regarding the cognitive status of syntactic rules and mental models—whether rules and models represent strategies or a fundamental reasoning mechanism—might be due to the nature of the participants and the tasks included in reasoning studies. When participants with no training in logic are tested on a restricted set of logical reasoning tasks (e.g., categorical and conditional syllogisms), results from reasoning studies show far more consistency in participants' performance than there might be if participants with varying levels of training were included. The consistency in participants' performance might, mistakenly, lead syntactic rule supporters (or mental model supporters) to view rules (or models) as comprising a fixed or hard-wired mechanism in reasoning instead of a simple strategy.

Thematic Reasoning Tasks as Expert Tasks

Although participants with training in logic have been excluded from participating in reasoning studies, the influence of *everyday* expertise has not altogether been excluded. Paradoxically, the power of expertise in reasoning can be illustrated by examining performance on thematic reasoning tasks. Although the tasks in reasoning studies generally fail to reflect a substantive content domain, it is possible to view *thematic* reasoning tasks (e.g., thematic versions of the selection task) as reflecting a nominal, everyday content domain. When they are viewed thus, it is possible to consider thematic reasoning tasks as tests of *everyday expertise*—tests of everyday knowledge that most people possess in order to function successfully in everyday life. If we view thematic tasks as tests of everyday expertise, then it is not surprising that participants generally perform quite well on these tasks. Individuals might perform substantially better on thematic reasoning tasks than on abstract reasoning tasks because thematic tasks might cue their "expert" background knowledge, knowledge that is useful to their functioning in everyday life (e.g., Cosmides, 1989; Cummins, 1995). For example, most adults could easily be labeled experts at deontic reasoning—reasoning that involves knowing how to enforce a rule, catch rule violators, or understand what permissions and obligations entail.

Viewing competent performance on thematic reasoning tasks as evidence of everyday expertise is consistent with Cosmides's (1989) social contract theory and Gigerenzer and Hug's (1992) cheating detection theory. In fact, these theories might be better termed theories of everyday expertise without the need to incorporate post-hoc evolutionary claims. Social contract theory and cheating detection theory advance the idea that human beings are experts in domains that are essential to their survival (e.g., social exchange). These investigators claim that some domains are so fundamental to our survival that specific Darwinian algorithms have evolved to help us reason in those domains. In other words, in domains in which human beings must be knowledgeable in order to adapt and survive, expert algorithms have developed to guarantee successful reasoning. In short, it is possible that the facilitated performance observed on thematic versions of the selection task might serve as a clue that knowledge is power in reasoning as it is in problem solving and as early work on expert systems has made clear in the field of artificial intelligence (see Feigenbaum, 1989).

Because it appears that knowledge is power in reasoning, more studies need to explore how individuals with different knowledge levels perform on reasoning tasks that reflect a substantive content domain. In studying individuals with a range of knowledge, it will be possible to identify the strategies employed in reasoning and to determine whether myriad strategies characterize the reasoning of different groups of participants or whether a single strategy is employed by all participants on a specific task. It is premature at this stage to state that people reason primarily with mental models or mental rules or according to any other theory, given that a sizable group of participants (e.g., experts in logic) is excluded from reasoning studies of abstract categorical syllogisms and conditional syllogisms. If experts are included in reasoning studies, new evidence might illuminate the nature of reasoning. For example, new evidence for the use of rules in reasoning might be found by studying experts.

If neither rules nor models at present describe a fundamental reasoning mechanism or, alternatively, the representational mechanism in reasoning, then in what other form might reasoning be formalized? Borrowing from the literature on expertise, patterns might exemplify the representational mechanism in reasoning. The notion of patterns as a possible representational mechanism is not a new idea. For instance, Bechtel and Abrahamsen (1991) have suggested this idea, and numerous studies employing a connectionist methodology support the idea of patterns underlying reasoning. Patterns underlie reasoning in the sense that the pattern of connectivity in a PDP network produces reliable responses to reasoning problems. Although it is beyond the scope of this chapter to review the role of patterns in reasoning, the interested reader is referred to studies in which connectionist methodology is used to model reasoning performance (e.g., Langston & Trabasso, 1999; Park & Robertson, 1997; Stenning & Oaksford, 1993; Stenning & Oberlander, 1995).

SUMMARY AND CONCLUSION

We will never know how the legendary Oedipus solved the sphinx's riddle, but from our discussion thus far it is possible to speculate. First, it is unlikely that Oedipus either reasoned or problem solved exclusively in his search for a solution. He probably used a combination of methods. Having said this, however, we must add that it is likely that Oedipus used more problem solving techniques than reasoning techniques to generate the answer. In particular, because a riddle can be characterized as an ill-defined problem, it is likely that Oedipus experienced an insight into its solution. Of course, it is always possible that he used some kind of strategy.

It seems trite to say that investigators of reasoning and problem solving have a great deal to learn from each other. It is true, however, and it is especially relevant as we attempt to further our understanding of how knowledge influences—for better or for worse—our reasoning on everyday tasks. Research on expertise offers an optimistic view that thinking, problem solving, reasoning, and other activities are not controlled solely by innate abilities. Deliberate practice and training can improve our performance. Expertise, the idea that performance evolves with practice, should be incorporated into theories of reasoning so as to delineate fully how individuals reason at different times with different levels of knowledge. One risk of excluding expert reasoners, as has been the case in studies of logical reasoning, is that participants' performance on reasoning tasks might appear to be overly consistent. The apparent consistency in participants' performance might be illusory and misleading, leading to the ambiguity and entanglement of reasoning strategies with a fundamental reasoning mechanism. Because the responses of untrained logical reasoners appear consistent, investigators might mistakenly attribute these responses to a fundamental reasoning mechanism, when in fact they might only represent the application of strategies. Stenning and Yule (1997) have suggested that rules and models should be viewed as algorithms and not as anything more fundamental than that. Failing to test participants who reflect a range of knowledge levels on reasoning tasks constrains the likelihood of capturing and examining the full range of strategies and solutions generated to reasoning tasks. Ultimately, our understanding is also constrained.

The literature on expertise, furthermore, leads us to conclude that pattern recognition might serve as a representational mechanism in reasoning. Connectionist studies of reasoning exemplify a pattern-recognition approach, but the challenge is to interpret precisely how connectionist architectures solve reasoning problems (Dawson, 1998). Only by interpreting connectionist models can we validate that their algorithms for solving problems are psychologically plausible (Berkeley, Dawson, Medler, Schopflocher, & Hornsby, 1995; Dawson, 1998; Oaksford & Chater, 1993).

The future challenge for investigators of reasoning, more so than for investigators of problem solving, is to (a) clarify how strategies differ from representational mechanisms in reasoning and (b) further our understanding of how knowledge mediates reasoning. If the goal of experimental laboratory studies of reasoning and problem solving is to gain a better understanding of how people reason and problem solve in everyday contexts, then background knowledge must be a fundamental variable in studies of reasoning and problem solving. In the end, a more solid understanding of how everyday reasoning and problem solving operate has tremendous social benefits in a variety of contexts—educational, professional, political, legal, and medical—in which we aim to improve performance. Indeed, knowledge is power.

REFERENCES

Allard, F., & Starkes, J. L. (1991). Motor-skill experts in sports, dance, and other domains. In K. Anders Ericsson & Jacqui Smith (Eds.), *Toward a general theory of expertise: Prospects and limits* (pp. 126–152). New York: Cambridge University Press.

Anderson, J. R. (1983). *The architecture of cognition.* Cambridge, MA: Harvard University Press.

Anderson, J. R. (1990). *Cognitive psychology and its implications* (3rd ed.). New York: W. H. Freeman.

Bechtel, W., & Abrahamsen, A. (1991). *Connectionism and the mind.* Cambridge, MA: Blackwell.

Bedard, J., & Chi, M. T. (1992). Expertise. *Current Directions in Psychological Science, 1,* 135–139.

Berkeley, I. S. N., Dawson, M. R. W., Medler, D. A., Schopflocher, D. P., & Hornsby, L. (1995). Density plots of hidden value unit activations reveal interpretable bands. *Connection Science, 7,* 167–186.

Blanchette, I., & Dunbar, K. (2000). How analogies are generated: The role of structural and superficial similarity. *Memory & Cognition, 28,* 108–124.

Braine, M. D. S. (1978). On the relation between the natural logic of reasoning and standard logic. *Psychological Review, 85,* 1–21.

Braine, M. D. S., & O'Brien, D. P. (1991). A theory of *If:* A lexical entry, reasoning program, and pragmatic principles. *Psychological Review, 98,* 182–203.

Braine, M. D. S., & O'Brien, D. P. (1998). The theory of mental-propositional logic: Description and illustration. In M. D. S. Braine & D. P. O'Brien (Eds.), *Mental logic* (pp. 79–89). Mahwah, NJ: Erlbaum.

Braine, M. D. S., Reiser, B. J., & Rumain, B. (1998). Evidence for the theory: Predicting the difficulty of propositional logic inference problems. In M. D. S. Braine & D. P. O'Brien (Eds.), *Mental logic* (pp. 91–144). Mahwah, NJ: Erlbaum.

Braine, M. D. S., & Rumain, B. (1983). Logical reasoning. In P. H. Mussen (Series Ed.) & J. H. Flavell & E. M. Markman (Vol. Eds.), *Handbook of child psychology: Vol. 3. Cognitive development* (4th ed., pp. 263–340). New York: Wiley.

Brunswick, E. (1943). Organismic achievement and environmental probability. *Psychological Review, 50,* 255–272.

Charness, N., & Schultetus, R. S. (1999). Knowledge and expertise. In F. T. Durso, R. S. Nickerson, R. W. Schvaneveldt, S. T. Dumais, D. S. Lindsay, & M. Chi (Eds.), *Handbook of applied cognition* (pp. 57–81). Chichester, England: Wiley.

Chase, W. G., & Simon, H. A. (1973). Perception in chess. *Cognitive Psychology, 4,* 55–81.

Chater, N., & Oaksford, M. (1999). The probability heuristics model of syllogistic reasoning. *Cognitive Psychology, 38,* 191–258.

Cheng, P. W., & Holyoak, K. J. (1985). Pragmatic reasoning schemas. *Cognitive Psychology, 17,* 391–416.

Cheng, P. W., & Holyoak, K. J. (1989). On the natural selection of reasoning theories. *Cognition, 33,* 285–313.

Cheng, P. W., & Nisbett, R. E. (1993). Pragmatic constraints on causal deduction. In R. E. Nisbett (Ed.), *Rules for reasoning* (pp. 202–227). Hillsdale, NJ: Erlbaum.

Chi, M. T. H., Glaser, R., & Farr, M. J. (Eds.). (1988). *The nature of expertise.* Hillsdale, NJ: Erlbaum.

Cosmides, L. (1989). The logic of social exchange: Has natural selection shaped how human reason? Studies with the Wason selection task. *Cognition, 31,* 187–276.

Cosmides, L., & Tooby, J. (1996). Are humans good intuitive statisticians after all? Rethinking some conclusions from the literature on judgement under uncertainty. *Cognition, 58,* 1–73.

Cummins, D. D. (1995). Naïve theories and causal deduction. *Memory & Cognition, 23,* 646–658.

Davidson, J., & Sternberg, R. J. (1984). The role of insight in intellectual giftedness. *Gifted Child Quarterly, 28,* 58–64.

Dawson, M. R. W. (1998). *Understanding cognitive science.* Malden, MA: Blackwell.

Dawson, M. R. W., Medler, D. A., & Berkeley, I. S. N. (1997). PDP networks can provide models that are not mere implementations of classical theories. *Philosophical Psychology, 10,* 25–40.

de Groot, A. D. (1965). *Thought and choice in chess.* The Hague, The Netherlands: Mouton.

Dennett, D. (1990). Cognitive wheels: The frame problem of AI. In M. Boden (Ed.), *The philosophy of artificial intelligence: Oxford readings in philosophy* (pp. 147–170). Oxford, UK: Oxford University Press.

Dietrich, E. (1999). Algorithm. In R. A. Wilson & F. C. Keil (Eds.), *The MIT encyclopedia of the cognitive sciences* (pp. 11–12). Cambridge, MA: MIT Press.

Dominowski, R. L., & Jenrick, R. (1973). Effects of hints and interpolated activity on solution of an insight problem. *Psychonomic Science, 26,* 335–338.

Dunbar, K. (1995). How scientists really reason: Scientific reasoning in real-world laboratories. In R. J. Sternberg & J. E. Davidson (Eds.), *The nature of insight* (pp. 365–395). Cambridge, MA: MIT Press.

Dunbar, K. (1997). How scientists think: On-line creativity and conceptual change in science. In T. B. Ward & S. M. Smith (Eds.), *Creative thought: An investigation of conceptual structures and processes* (pp. 461–493). Washington, DC: American Psychological Association.

Eisenstadt, S. A., & Simon, H. A. (1997). Logic and thought. *Minds & Machines, 7,* 365–385.

Ericsson, K. A. (1996). The acquisition of expert performance. In K. A. Ericsson (Ed.), *The road to excellence.* Mahwah, NJ: Erlbaum.

Ericsson, K. A., & Charness, N. (1994). Expert performance: Its structure and acquisition. *American Psychologist, 49,* 725–747.

Ericsson, K. A., & Kintsch, W. (1995). Long-term working memory. *Psychological Review, 102,* 211–245.

Ericsson, K. A., & Smith, J. (1991). Prospects and limits in the empirical study of expertise: An introduction. In K. A. Ericsson & J. Smith (Eds.), *Toward a general theory of expertise: Prospects and limits* (pp. 1–38). Cambridge, UK: Cambridge University Press.

Evans, J. St. B. T. (1989). *Bias in human reasoning: Causes and consequences.* Hillsdale, NJ: Erlbaum.

Evans, J. St. B. T. (2000). What could and could not be a strategy in reasoning. In W. Schaeken, G. De Vooght, A. Vandierendonck, & G. d'Ydewalle (Eds.), *Deductive reasoning and strategies* (pp. 23–48). Mahwah, NJ: Erlbaum.

Evans, J. St. B. T., Handley, S. J., Harper, C. N. J., & Johnson-Laird, P. N. (1999). Reasoning about necessity and possibility: A test of the mental model theory of deduction. *Journal of Experimental Psychology: Learning, Memory, and Cognition, 25,* 1495–1513.

Evans, J. St. B. T., & Lynch, J. S. (1973). Matching bias in the selection task. *British Journal of Psychology, 64,* 391–397.

Evans, St. B. T., Newstead, S. E., & Byrne, R. M. (1993). *Human reasoning: The psychology of deduction.* Hillsdale, NJ: Erlbaum.

Evans, J. St. B. T., Over, D. E., & Manktelow, K. I. (1993). Reasoning, decision making, and rationality. *Cognition, 49,* 165–187.

Falmagne, R. J., & Gonsalves, J. (1995). Deductive inference. *Annual Review of Psychology, 46,* 525–559.

Feigenbaum, E. A. (1989). What hath Simon wrought? In D. Klahr & K. Kotovsky (Eds.), *Complex information processing: The impact of Herbert A. Simon* (pp. 165–182). Hillsdale, NJ: Erlbaum.

Fischhoff, B. (1999). Judgement heuristics. In R. A. Wilson & F. C. Keil (Eds.), *The MIT encyclopedia of the cognitive sciences* (pp. 423–425). Cambridge, MA: MIT Press.

Fodor, J. A. (1983). *The modularity of mind.* Cambridge, MA: MIT Press.

Ford, M. (1995). Two models of mental representation and problem solving in syllogistic reasoning. *Cognition, 54,* 1–71.

Frensch, P. A., & Sternberg, R. J. (1989). Expertise and intelligent thinking: When is it worse to know better? In R. J. Sternberg (Ed.), *Advances in the psychology of human intelligence* (Vol. 5, pp. 157–188). Hillsdale, NJ: Erlbaum.

Galotti, K. M. (1989). Approaches to studying formal and everyday reasoning. *Psychological Bulletin, 105,* 331–351.

Galotti, K. M., Baron, J., & Sabini, J. P. (1986). Individual differences in syllogistic reasoning: Deduction rules or mental models? *Journal of Experimental Psychology: General, 115,* 16–25.

Garnham, A., & Oakhill, J. (1994). *Thinking and reasoning.* Cambridge, MA: Blackwell.

Gentner, D. (1983). Structure-mapping: A theoretical framework for analogy. *Cognitive Science, 7,* 155–170.

Gentner, D. (1999). Analogy. In R. A. Wilson & F. C. Keil (Eds.), *The MIT encyclopedia of the cognitive sciences* (pp. 17–19). Cambridge, MA: MIT Press.

Gentner, D., Rattermann, M. J., & Forbus, K. D. (1993). The roles of similarity in transfer: Separating retrievability from inferential soundness. *Cognitive Psychology, 25,* 524–575.

Gigerenzer, G., & Hug, K. (1992). Domain-specific reasoning: Social contracts, cheating, and perspective change. *Cognition, 43,* 127–171.

Gigerenzer, G., Todd, P. M., & the ABC Research Group. (Eds.). (1999). *Simple heuristics that make us smart.* New York: Oxford University Press.

Greene, S. B. (1992). Multiple explanations for multiply quantified sentences: Are multiple models necessary? *Psychological Review, 99,* 184–187.

Griggs, R. A. (1983). The role of problem content in the selection task. In J. St. B. T. Evans (Ed.), *Thinking and reasoning: Psychological approaches* (pp. 16–43). London: Routledge and Kegan Paul.

Gobet, F. (1997). A pattern-recognition theory of search in expert problem solving. *Thinking and Reasoning, 3,* 291–313.

Gobet, F., & Simon, H. A. (1996). Templates in chess memory: A mechanism for recalling several boards. *Cognitive Psychology, 31,* 1–40.

Guyote, M. J., & Sternberg, R. J. (1981). A transitive-chain theory of syllogistic reasoning. *Cognitive Psychology, 13,* 461–525.

Holding, D. H. (1992). Theories of chess skill. *Psychological Research, 54,* 10–16.

Holland, J. H., Holyoak, K. J., Nisbett, R. E., & Thagard, P. R. (1986). A framework for induction. *Induction: Processes of inferences, learning, and discovery* (pp. 1–28). Cambridge, MA: MIT Press.

Holyoak, K. J. (1990). Problem solving. In D. N. Osherson & E. E. Smith (Eds.), *Thinking: An invitation to cognitive science* (Vol. 3, pp. 117–146). Cambridge, MA: MIT Press.

Johnson-Laird, P. N. (1983). *Mental models. Towards a cognitive science of language, inference, and consciousness.* Cambridge, MA: Harvard University Press.

Johnson-Laird, P. N. (1994). Mental models and probabilistic thinking. *Cognition, 50,* 189–209.

Johnson-Laird, P. N. (1999). Deductive reasoning. *Annual Review of Psychology, 50,* 109–135.

Johnson-Laird, P. N., & Bara, B. G. (1984). Syllogistic inference. *Cognition, 16,* 1–61.

Johnson-Laird, P. N., & Byrne, R. M. J. (1991). *Deduction.* Hillsdale, NJ: Erlbaum.

Johnson-Laird, P. N., Byrne, R. M. J., & Schaeken, W. (1992). Propositional reasoning by model. *Psychological Review, 99,* 418–439.

Knoblich, G., Ohlsson, S., Haider, H., & Rhenius, D. (1999). Constraint relaxation and chunk decomposition in insight problem solving. *Journal of Experimental Psychology: Learning, Memory, and Cognition, 25,* 1534–1555.

Langston, M., & Trabasso, T. (1999). Modeling causal integration and availability of information during comprehension of narrative texts. In H. van Oostendorp & S. Goldman (Eds.), *The construction of mental representations during reading* (pp. 29–69). Mahwah, NJ: Erlbaum.

Lehman, J. F., Lewis, R. L., & Newell, A. (1998). Architectural influences on language comprehension. In Z. Pylyshyn (Ed.), *Constraining cognitive theories* (pp. 141–163). Stamford, CT: Ablex Publishing.

Leighton, J. P., & Dawson, M. R. W. (2001). A parallel distributed processing model of Wason's selection task. *Cognitive Systems Research, 2,* 207–231.

Liberman, N., & Klar, Y. (1996). Hypothesis testing in Wason's selection task: Social exchange, cheating detection, or task understanding. *Cognition, 58,* 127–156.

Light, P., Girotto, V., & Legrenzi, P. (1990). Children's reasoning on conditional promises and permissions. *Cognitive Development, 5,* 369–383.

Luchins, A. S. (1942). Mechanization in problem solving—the effect of Einstellung. *Psychological Monographs, 54* (Serial No. 6, 95).

Manktelow, K. I., & Evans, J. St. B. T. (1979). Facilitation of reasoning by realism: Effect or non-effect? *British Journal of Psychology, 70,* 477–488.

Manktelow, K. I., Fairley, N., Kilpatrick, S. G., & Over, D. E. (2000). Pragmatics and strategies for practical reasoning. In W. Schaeken, G. De Vooght, & G. d'Ydewalle (Eds.), *Deductive reasoning and strategies* (pp. 23–48). Mahwah, NJ: Erlbaum.

Manktelow, K. I., & Over, D. E. (1991). Social roles and utilities in reasoning with deontic conditionals. *Cognition, 39,* 85–105.

Metcalfe, J. (1986). Premonitions of insight predict impending error. *Journal of Experimental Psychology: Learning, Memory, and Cognition, 12,* 623–634.

Metcalfe, J. (1998). Insight and metacognition. In G. Mazzoni & T. Nelson (Eds.), *Metacognition and cognitive neuropsychology: Monitoring and control processes* (pp. 181–197). Mahwah, NJ: Erlbaum.

Metcalfe, J., & Wiebe, D. (1987). Intuition in insight and noninsight problem solving. *Memory & Cognition, 3,* 238–246.

Newell, A. (1990). *Unified theories of cognition.* Cambridge, MA: Harvard University Press.

Newell, A., & Simon, H. A. (1972). *Human problem solving.* Englewood Cliffs, NJ: Prentice-Hall. .

Newstead, S. E., & Evans, J. St. B. T. (1993), Mental models as an explanation of belief bias effects in syllogistic reasoning. *Cognition, 46,* 93–97.

Noveck, I., & O'Brien, D. P. (1996). To what extent do pragmatic reasoning schemas affect performance on Wason's selection task? *Quarterly Journal of Experimental Psychology: Human Experimental Psychology, 49A,* 463–489.

O'Brien, D. P. (1993). Mental logic and human irrationality: We can put a man on the moon, so why can't we solve those logical-reasoning problems? In K. I. Manktelow & D. E. Over (Eds.), *Rationality: Psychological and philosophical perspectives* (pp. 110–135) London: Routledge.

Oaksford, M., & Chater, N. (1993). Reasoning theories and bounded rationality. In K. I. Manktelow & D. E. Over (Eds.), *Rationality: Psychological and philosophical perspectives* (pp. 31–60). London: Routledge.

Oaksford, M., & Chater, N. (1994). A rational analysis of the selection task as optimal data selection. *Psychological Review, 101,* 608–631.

Over, D. E., & Evans, J. St. B. T. (1999). The meaning of mental logic. *Cahiers de Psychologie, 18,* 99–104.

Park, N. S., & Robertson, D. (1997). A localist network architecture for logical inference. In R. Sun & F. Alexandre (Eds.), *Connectionist-symbolic integration: From unified to hybrid approaches* (pp. 245–263). Mahwah, NJ: Erlbaum.

Polk, T. A., & Newell, A. (1995). Deduction as verbal reasoning. *Psychological Review, 102,* 533–566.

Pollard, P. (1990). Natural selection for the selection task: Limits to social-exchange theory. *Cognition, 36,* 195–204.

Pollard, P., & Evans, J. St. B. T. (1987). Content and context effects in reasoning. *American Journal of Psychology, 100,* 41–60.

Priest, A. G., & Lindsay, R. O. (1992). New light on novice-expert differences in physics problem solving. *British Journal of Psychology, 83,* 389–405.

Rips, L. J. (1994). *The psychology of proof.* Cambridge, MA: MIT Press.

Rips, L. J. (1995). Deduction and cognition. In E. E. Smith & D. N. Osherson (Eds.), *Thinking: Vol. 3. An invitation to cognitive science* (2nd ed., pp. 297–343). Cambridge, MA: MIT Press.

Roberts, M. J. (1993). Human reasoning: Deduction rules or mental models, or both? *Quarterly Journal of Experimental Psychology, 46A,* 569–589.

Roberts, M. J. (2000). Individual differences in reasoning strategies: A problem to solve or an opportunity to seize? In W. Schaeken, G. De Vooght, A. Vandierendonck, & G. d'Ydewalle (Eds.), *Deductive reasoning and strategies* (pp. 23–48). Mahwah, NJ: Erlbaum.

Rumain, B., Connell, J., Braine, M. D. S. (1983). Conversational comprehension processes are responsible for reasoning fallacies in children as well as adults: *If* is not the biconditional. *Developmental Psychology, 19,* 471–481.

Schaeken, W., De Vooght, G., Vandierendonck, A., & d'Ydewalle, G. (Eds.). (2000). *Deductive reasoning and strategies.* Mahwah, NJ: Erlbaum.

Shepard, R. N. (1990). *Mind sights.* New York: W. H. Freeman.

Simon, H. A. (1991). Cognitive architectures and rational analysis: Comment. In K. VanLehn (Ed.), *Architectures for intelligence* (pp. 25–39). Hillsdale, NJ: Erlbaum.

Simon, H. A. (1999a). Problem solving. In R. A. Wilson & F. C. Keil (Eds.), *The MIT encyclopedia of the cognitive sciences* (pp. 674–676). Cambridge, MA: MIT Press.

Simon, H. A. (1999b). Production systems. In R. A. Wilson & F. C. Keil (Eds.), *The MIT encyclopedia of the cognitive sciences* (pp. 676–677). Cambridge, MA: MIT Press.

Smith, S. M., & Blankenship, S. E. (1989). Incubation effects. *Bulletin of the Psychonomic Society, 27,* 311–314.

Sperber, D., Cara, F., & Girotto, V. (1995). Relevance theory explains the selection task. *Cognition, 57,* 31–95.

Stenning, K., & Oaksford, M. (1993). Rational reasoning and human implementations of logic. In K. I. Manktelow & D. E. Over (Eds.), *Rationality: Psychological and philosophical perspectives* (pp. 136–176). Florence, KY: Taylor & Francis/Routledge.

Stenning, K., & Oberlander, J. (1995). A cognitive theory of graphical and linguistic reasoning: Logic and implementation. *Cognitive Science, 19,* 97–140.

Stenning, K., & Yule, P. (1997). Image and language in human reasoning: A syllogistic illustration. *Cognitive Psychology, 34,* 109–159.

Sternberg, R. J. (1980a). Representation and process in linear syllogistic reasoning. *Journal of Experimental Psychology: General, 109,* 119–159.

Sternberg, R. J. (1980b). The development of linear syllogistic reasoning. *Journal of Experimental Child Psychology, 29,* 340–356.

Sternberg, R. J. (1981). Reasoning with determinate and indeterminate linear syllogisms. *British Journal of Psychology, 72,* 407–420.

Sternberg, R. J. (1983). Components of human intelligence. *Cognition, 15,* 1–48.

Sternberg, R. J. (1999). *Cognitive psychology* (2nd ed.). Ft. Worth, TX: Harcourt Brace.

Sternberg, R. J., & Ben Zeev, T. (2001). *Complex cognition: The psychology of human thought.* New York: Oxford University Press.

Sternberg, R. J., & Davidson, J. E. (Eds.). (1995). *The nature of insight.* Cambridge, MA: MIT Press.

Torrens, D., Thompson, V. A., & Cramer, K. M. (1999). Individual differences and the belief bias effect: Mental models, logical necessity, and abstract reasoning. *Thinking and Reasoning, 5,* 1–28.

Tversky, A., & Kahneman, D. (1974). Judgement under uncertainty: Heuristics and biases. *Science, 185,* 1124–1131.

Tversky, A., & Kahneman, D. (1986). Judgment under uncertainty: Heuristics and biases. In H. R. Arkes & K. R. Hammond (Eds.), *Judgment and decision making: An interdisciplinary reader* (pp. 38–55). Cambridge, UK: Cambridge University Press.

Wason, P. C. (1966). Reasoning. In B. M. Foss (Ed.), *New horizons in psychology* (pp. 135–151). Harmondsworth, Middlesex, England: Penguin.

Wason, P. C. (1983). Realism and rationality in the selection task. In J. St. B. T. Evans (Ed.), *Thinking and reasoning: Psychological approaches* (pp. 44–75). London: Routledge & Kegan Paul.

Wason, P. C., & Johnson-Laird, P. N. (1972). *Psychology of reasoning: Structure and content.* Cambridge, MA: Harvard University Press.

Wiley, J. (1998). Expertise as mental set: The effects of domain knowledge in creative problem solving. *Memory & Cognition, 26,* 716–730.

CHAPTER 24

Psychological Experimentation Addressing Practical Concerns

RAYMOND S. NICKERSON AND RICHARD W. PEW

Unlike other chapters in this book, this one does not focus on a psychological process or a specific area of psychological research; it deals instead with research that is defined by its methodology and its applicability to practical ends rather than by its subject matter. One might reasonably question whether such a chapter belongs in a handbook of experimental psychology. As the fundamental method by which theoretical hypotheses are tested, experimentation is essential to psychology, no less than to other areas of science. The goal of all scientific activity is the discovery of regularities of nature and their representation in theories from which predictions can be made. Theories that have proved to be robust—to have stood up under rigorous testing by experimentation—have often, perhaps usually, proved also to be useful to practical ends, sometimes in unanticipated and surprising ways. So, one might argue, any well-designed experimentation aimed at testing a theory has the potential of being useful in a practical sense, even if none of the eventual applications of the theory is of interest to, or even known by, the experimenter.

We think that this argument, with some qualifications, has considerable force, and we do not wish to contest it here. We note, however, that experimenters differ in the degree to which applied interests motivate their work and that experiments differ with respect to the immediacy of the applicability of their results to practical ends. In this chapter we focus on experimentation that has been motivated explicitly by practical concerns or that has yielded results whose practical implications are relatively direct.

BASIC AND APPLIED RESEARCH

The Distinction

The distinction between basic and applied research is a familiar one, not only within psychology but in science generally. Within the psychological research community some investigators are seen primarily as basic scientists and others as explicitly applications oriented. The perception of a cultural divide (Herrmann, Raybeck, & Gruneberg, 1997) is reinforced by association of theoretically oriented researchers mainly with the academy and of those who are more applications oriented mainly with industry or government laboratories. The perception is further strengthened by the fact that some research journals emphasize the theoretical implications of research findings whereas others focus more on practical implications.

Prominent among the properties that are usually mentioned as distinguishing between basic and applied research is motivation: Basic research is said to be motivated primarily by questions of a theoretical nature, whereas applied research is motivated by an interest in solving practical problems. This is not always an easy criterion to apply in specific instances because researchers' motivations are generally more complex than this simple dichotomy suggests. Many psychologists who do research have both types of interest, although individuals undoubtedly differ with respect to the relative strengths of the influence of theoretical and practical concerns on their choices of problems on which to work.

We believe that basic and applied should not be thought of as two mutually exclusive categories, into one or the other of which all instances of research can be placed unambiguously. Even thinking of basic and applied as representing ends of a continuum is an oversimplification because research often yields results that have both theoretical and practical implications. We view the distinction as better considered a matter of emphasis than as representing a true dichotomy; and although our focus is on work for which the practical motivation is relatively strong, we believe that much of the best research in psychology (as in other areas) is motivated by both theoretical and practical concerns.

History of Distinction in Psychology

Identifying the origin of the distinction between basic and applied research in psychology and tracking its history would prove an interesting study. We make no effort to do this here, but we do note that the distinction was well established by the second decade of the twentieth century. It was recognized explicitly by G. Stanley Hall in an address prepared for the 25th anniversary of the American Psychological Association (APA) in 1916 and later published as the lead article in the first issue of the *Journal of Applied Psychology* (Hall, 1917). Geissler (1917b), in the same issue, contrasted pure and applied psychology this way:

> The ultimate aim of pure psychology is . . . to extend and improve our knowledge of mental life with regard to its structural, functional, genetic, and social aspects. . . . On the other hand, applied psychology aims to investigate and improve those conditions and phases of human life and conduct which involve mental life, especially in its social aspects, since practically all human activity is nowadays carried on as a function of social intercourse. (p. 49)

In the foreword to the same issue of the *Journal of Applied Psychology,* the editors, Hall, Baird, and Geissler (1917), in explaining the need for a journal focusing on applied psychology, noted that at the time there already existed several journals and associations that had been established to serve the interests of psychology, but that "none of the existing journals devote themselves to the task of gathering together the results of workers in the various fields of applied psychology, or of bringing these results into relation with pure psychology" (p. 6). They implied that applied psychology did not command the same level of respect as did pure psychology, at least among some members of the profession: "The psychologist finds that the old distinction between pure and applied science is already obscured in his domain; and he is beginning to realize that applied psychology can no longer be relegated to a distinctly inferior plane" (p. 6). Unfortunately, contention about the relative merits of basic and applied work did not end with this observation; many researchers in psychology and other sciences as well have continued to project attitudes of superiority with respect to their own approach to research, whether it is driven primarily by theoretical or practical concerns.

Current Interest in Applications

We believe that interest among research psychologists—and among organizations that represent them—in seeing the results of psychological research applied to practical problems has been on the increase recently and is unusually high at the present time. In saying this, we are mindful of the fact that the founders of the *Journal of Applied Psychology* noted "an unprecedented interest in the extension of the application of psychology to various fields of human activity" when they introduced the new journal (Hall et al., 1917, p. 5), so possibly our belief is illusory—a consequence of the greater salience of recent than of more remote events and possibly of some wishful thinking on our part.

One indication of the currently high interest in applying psychology to real-world problems is the effort to inform policy makers and the general public of practical implications of psychological research through presentations (e.g., Science and Public Policy Seminars) by psychologists to members of Congress and congressional staffers arranged by the Federation of Behavioral, Psychological, and Cognitive Sciences (Farley & Null, 1987). Talks given at these seminars, which began in 1982 and have been held at the rate of approximately six per year, have dealt with the applicability of the results of psychological research to education, legal processes, effects of television on behavior, family violence, human error in medicine, and many other topics of general interest and relevance to public policy making. A complete list of the talks that have been given can be obtained at the federation's Web site, http://www.thefederationonline.org. Many, though not all, of the talks have been published by the federation; information regarding whether specific talks exist in print can be obtained either from authors or by an e-mail request to federation@apa.org.

Further evidence of current interest in drawing attention to the practical applications of the results of psychological research is the APA's recently established practice of issuing press releases regarding research findings that have been published in APA journals and that are deemed to be of public interest. Recent releases mention findings regarding the effects of emotion suppression on cognitive functioning, the effects of insufficient sleep on preteen children's physical and mental performance, the relationship between the playing of violent video games and aggressive behavior, effects of a cognitively demanding secondary task on driving performance, and personal and environmental barriers to exercise by older women. Copies of the releases can be accessed at http://www.apa.org/releases.

In response to requests from experimentalists who wanted a journal dedicated to the publication of theoretically grounded experimental studies addressed to practical problems, in 1995 the APA launched the *Journal of Experimental Psychology: Applied.* This journal is like the other *Journals of Experimental Psychology* in publishing articles that report experimentation and like the *Journal of Applied Psychology* in publishing those that address practical concerns, but it is unlike these in that it requires experimental methodology and applied orientation in combination. Articles published during the first few years of the journal's existence have addressed a wide variety of topics, including education and training, communication and information presentation, decision making, health care and maintenance, driving and highway safety, pilot performance, aging, computer interface design, stress management, eye- and earwitness testimony, consumer behavior, and many others.

In May 2000 the American Psychological Society published the first issue of *Psychological Science in the Public Interest* as a supplement to *Psychological Science.* The hope expressed by the founding coeditors of this journal, which is scheduled to appear with one major article twice a year, is that the reports that appear in it, all of which are to be commissioned by its editorial board, "will come to be seen as definitive summaries of research on nationally important questions, much like the reports commissioned by the National Research Council, but focused on issues for which psychological research plays a central role" (Ceci & Bjork, 2000, p. 178). The first issue describes ways—well researched by psychologists over many years—in which the accuracy of diagnostic decisions, which are constantly being made with serious consequences in a wide variety of real-world situations, can be enhanced (Swets, Dawes, & Monahan, 2000b; see also Swets, Dawes, & Monahan, 2000a). In the second issue, Lilienfeld, Wood, and Garb (2000; see also Lilienfeld, Wood, & Garb, 2001) critically reviewed research on projective testing instruments often used in clinical and forensic settings (Rorschach inkblot test, thematic apperception test, and human figure drawings).

Among other topics for which *Psychology in the Public Interest* has commissioned papers are the relationship between academic achievement and class size, the question of whether certain herbal products affect cognitive functioning, the relationship of self-esteem to academic performance and social adjustment, the effectiveness of coaching for the Scholastic Achievement Test, and the best ways to teach reading to different types of learners. One of the stated considerations that motivated the establishment of this journal and the approach it represents to publicizing findings from psychological research that are deemed to be of public interest was the concern that psychologists too often have presented research findings to the public prematurely and in conflicting ways.

There are other reasons for believing that interest in applications of psychological research is relatively high at the present (Nickerson, 1998). We note here the American Psychological Society's identification, under the "Human Capital Initiative," of six priority areas for psychological research: productivity in the workplace, schooling and literacy, the aging society, drug and alcohol abuse, health, and violence in America ("Human Capital," 1992). To date the society has issued six reports as follow-ups to the announcement of this initiative: "The Changing Nature of Work," "Vitality for Life: Research for Productive Aging," "Reducing Mental Disorders: A Behavioral Science Research Plan for Psychopathology," "Doing the Right Thing: A Research Plan for Healthy Living," "Reducing Violence: A Research Agenda," and "Basic Research in Psychological Science: A Human Capital Initiative Report." These reports are available from the communications office of the American

Psychological Society, or they can be downloaded from http://www.psychologicalscience.org/newsresearch.

HISTORICAL ROOTS OF APPLIED EXPERIMENTAL PSYCHOLOGY

Perhaps the first stimulus for applied experimental psychology is to be found in the work of astronomers in the late 1700s. Before the development of accurate chronoscopes, the British Astronomer Royal, Nevil Maskelyne, required a procedure by which he could accurately measure the time of transit of a star. According to Sanford (1888), he used the "eye and ear" method, attributed to Bradley:

> When the star is about to make its transit, the observer reads off the time from his clock and then, while he watches the star in the telescope, continues to count the second beats. He fixes firmly in mind (as the moving image approaches the wire) its place at the last beat before it crosses the wire, and its place at the first beat after, and from the distances of these two points from the wire, estimates by eye the time of the crossing in tenths of a second. The role of the mind in observations by this method is fixing the exact place of the star at the first beat, the holding of the same in memory, the fixing of the place of the second beat, the comparison of the two and the expression of their relation in tenths. (p. 7)

The story goes that Maskelyne fired his assistant, David Kinnebrook, because the latter's star measurements differed by as much as 0.8 s from those of his supervisor. The result of this event, 30 or more years later, was a series of behavioral experiments to study individual differences in what became known as the *personal equation.* It was this very practical problem that motivated the initial studies of human reaction time. Over the next 100 years investigators of the personal equation continued to modify their measurement methodology to take advantage of the improved technology for measuring and recording events in time.

Despite, or perhaps because of, the prevailing belief that the conduction velocity of nerves was infinitely short, or at least not measurable, several nineteenth-century scientists showed interest in the possibility of measuring the speed of neurological and mental processes. The mid-nineteenth-century experiments of Hermann Helmholtz on the speed of transmission of the neural impulse in frogs are widely recognized as outstanding examples of pioneering research in this area. It was Frans Donders (1868/1969), however, who, building on the work of Helmholtz, firmly established the measurement of human reaction times and the taking of reaction-time differences as a means of measuring the speed of mental processes. The approach that Donders developed was quickly adopted as a primary investigative tool by researchers for use in both theoretically and practically motivated experiments, and it remains so to this day. (For more on the Kinnebrook incident and reaction-time research, see chapter by Proctor & Vu in this volume.) Extensive accounts of the earliest days of experimental psychology include Boring (1929/1950), Heidbreder (1935), Woodworth (1938), and Woodworth and Schlosberg (1954).

Early Experimental and Applied Journals

The *Journal of Experimental Psychology* and the *Journal of Applied Psychology* were established at about the same time, the first issue of the former appearing in 1916 and that of the latter in 1917. The *Journal of Experimental Psychology* was established under the auspices of the APA; the *Journal of Applied Psychology* began as a private journal, financed by its editors, and became an APA journal in 1943.

The scope of the *Journal of Applied Psychology,* as described in the front material of the first issue, was to include the following:

> (a) The application of psychology to vocational activities, such as law, art, public speaking, industrial and commercial work, and problems of business appeal. (b) Studies of individual mentalities, such as types of character, special talents, genius, and individual differences, including the problems of mental diagnosis and vocational prognosis. (c) The influence of general environmental conditions, such as climate, weather, humidity, temperature; also such conditions as nutrition, fatigue, etc. (d) The psychology of everyday activities, such as reading, writing, speaking, singing, playing games or musical instruments, sports, etc. (pp. i, ii)

Contributors of original articles to the journal were admonished that emphasis was to be laid on "clear and accurate statement of results, together with their practical applications" (iii).

There is no editorial or front matter in the first issue of the *Journal of Experimental Psychology,* so we could not make a direct comparison of the stated objectives of the two journals. However, the main difference between them appears to have been that articles to be published in the *Journal of Experimental Psychology* were to report experiments but did not have to be applied (although they could be), whereas those to be published in the *Journal of Applied Psychology* had to be applied but did not have to report experiments (although they could).

To get an idea of the overlap between the two journals, we scanned the first two volumes of each looking especially for applied studies in the *Journal of Experimental Psychology* and for experimental studies in the *Journal of Applied*

Psychology. Of course, not everyone will agree on what constitutes an applied or an experimental study, so our estimates are subjective, but we considered roughly 10% of the 62 articles (not counting discussions) published in the first two volumes of the *Journal of Experimental Psychology* to be applied in the sense that the authors appeared to have been motivated, at least in part, by an interest in some practical problem and discussed how their results might be applied to it. The majority of articles lack any explicit mention of the relevance of the findings to any practical ends; this is not to suggest that the investigators had no interest in practical issues, but only to note that they did not emphasize them in reporting their experiments. Examples of studies we classified as applied for purposes of this exercise are shown in Table 24.1.

"Experimental" was given a relatively broad connotation for determining appropriateness for the *Journal of Experimental Psychology*. Many of the articles in the first two volumes of the journal did not report experimentation in the strict sense of involving controlled manipulation of variables, use of control groups, and so on. Several of the reported experiments were relatively informal. About one quarter of the articles focused on methodology; some described puzzles designed for testing purposes; and several others involved mental testing.

TABLE 24.1 Examples of Articles with an Emphasis on Applications in the First Two Volumes of the *Journal of Experimental Psychology* (1916–1917)

Author	Title	Subject
Kent (1916)	A graded series of geometric puzzles.	Evaluation of geometric puzzles for use in a nonverbal test of intelligence.
Haines (1916)	Relative values of point-scale and year-scale measurements of 1,000 minor delinquents.	Exploration of the utility of a modified Binet-Simon intelligence test for identifying mental deficiency among delinquent minors.
Burtt (1916)	The effect of uniform and nonuniform illumination upon attention and reaction times, with special reference to street illumination.	Evaluation of safety implications of an experimental street lighting system in the field and in the laboratory, as indexed by reaction time to an auditory stimulus.
H. F. Adams (1917)	The memory value of mixed sizes of advertisements.	Investigation of dependence of memorability of ad on its size and one's frequency of exposure to it.
Marston (1917)	Systolic blood pressure symptoms of deception.	Investigation of effects on systolic blood pressure of "lying" or telling the truth in an experimental situation.

TABLE 24.2 Examples of Experimental Articles in the First Two Volumes of the *Journal of Applied Psychology* (1917–1918)

Author	Title	Subject
Geissler (1917a)	Association-reactions applied to ideas of commercial brands of familiar articles.	Investigation of reasons for differential recall of common brand names.
Downey (1917)	Handwriting disguise.	Investigation of ability of people to disguise their handwritings and of judges to match disguised and undisguised hands.
Stevenson (1918)	Correlation between different forms of sensory discrimination.	Study of correspondence between judgments of tactile pressure, line length, auditory intensity, and brightness.
Wembridge (1918)	Obscurities in voting upon measures due to double-negative.	Demonstration of ease with which expressions using double or complex negatives are misinterpreted.

Of 67 articles published in the first two volumes of the *Journal of Applied Psychology*, a large majority would not be considered experimental in the narrowest sense of the term (but as we have noted, many of the articles appearing in the early issues of the *Journal of Experimental Psychology* probably would not pass that test either). We estimate that not more than 10% would be considered experimental in a sense that would make them appropriate for any of the *Journals of Experimental Psychology* today. Articles included observational studies, anecdotal reports, essays, position papers, and descriptions of tests, training courses, and research plans. Examples of studies that we consider most likely to be judged by experimentalists to be experimental are shown in Table 24.2.

Experimental Psychology in World War II

Controlled experimentation was being used to investigate the effects of various situational factors on human performance before World War II—examples of this work include studies by McFarland (1932) on the effects of oxygen deprivation and those by Fletcher and Munson (1933, 1937) on the masking properties of auditory noise—but the war presented a need for many more studies of these sorts, and research efforts were mobilized on both sides of the Atlantic. In Great Britain well-known experimental psychologists, including Sir Frederic Bartlett, Norman Mackworth, and J. K. W. (Kenneth) Craik, played leading roles in this effort. The main centers of activity were first at Cambridge University, under Bartlett, and later at the newly established Applied Psychology Research Unit (APRU) of the Medical Research Council, also in Cambridge, under Craik. The APRU went on to become a leading establishment in Great Britain for the scientific study of problems relating to the human use of technology. Bartlett (1943, 1948) studied the effects of fatigue on human performance. Mackworth developed the first laboratory tests designed to simulate the requirements for sustained attention when monitoring a radar screen and spawned the field of vigilance research (Mackworth, 1950). Craik abstracted the requirements of antiaircraft gunnery into laboratory tracking tasks and, through experiments using a simulated cockpit that he built, advanced understanding of perceptual-motor performance generally. Not only did Craik (1947, 1948) contribute as an experimentalist, but his theoretical ideas, some of which were published after his untimely death in 1945, also were influential both in psychology and in the emerging area of feedback systems or cybernetics.

In the United States, S. S. Stevens collected at the Harvard Psychoacoustics Laboratory a cadre of psychologists who soon would become well known, including James Egan, Karl Kryter, J. C. R. Licklider, George Miller, and Irwin Pollack. Among other achievements, this group improved intelligibility-testing techniques and explored methods for improving the understanding of speech in aircraft cockpits (Egan, 1944; Miller, 1947). Licklider (1946) experimentally investigated peak clipping and discovered that he could enhance the intelligibility of speech in a radio transmission system by using signal power to increase the signal amplitude even though the system amplitude-handling capability was limited and peak clipping would result.

Harvard University had a broader contract with the National Defense Research Committee (NDRC) that included funding for the Electro-Acoustics Laboratory and the Radio Research Laboratory, as well as subcontracts with other university laboratories that were working on human-machine interaction. In early 1945, just before the end of the war, the NDRC was asked to fund a new activity examining behavioral issues in naval combat information centers. Immediately after the war, this work was turned over to Johns Hopkins University, where Clifford Morgan, Alphonse Chapanis, Wendell Garner, John Gebhard, and Robert Sleight became key contributors in a laboratory that identified with most of the psychological issues associated with the design of large-scale systems with which people had to interact (Chapanis, 1999). The creation of this laboratory led to publication of "Lectures on Men and Machines: An Introduction to Human Engineering," by Chapanis, Garner, Morgan, and Sanford in 1947, and then to the first text to use the title, *Applied Experimental Psychology,* by Chapanis, Garner, and Morgan in 1949.

Another distinguished team, which included Paul Fitts and Arthur Melton, was assembled in Washington, DC, by J. R. Flanagan to develop improved methods for selecting and training Army Air Force pilots. At the time, all testing was done with paper and pencil. This group developed the first reliable apparatus tests for evaluating the skills associated with flying (Bray, 1948; Fitts, 1947a, 1947b). Psychological testing was also used in connection with the selection of officers and key military personnel in Germany at least during the early days of the war; however, test results served primarily to guide the clinical judgment of those responsible for personnel assignments. "Concepts of objectivity, standardization, reliability and validity were almost entirely lacking" (Fitts, 1946, p. 160). The psychological testing program was inexplicably abandoned in Germany in 1942.

Postwar Developments

The contributions of psychologists to the war effort in the United States were widely recognized; as a result, each military service set up a laboratory for the continued study of the behavioral and psychological issues relevant to equipment design. In 1945 Paul Fitts became the first director of the Army Air Force Psychology Branch of the Aeromedical Laboratory at Wright Patterson Field in Ohio, while Arthur Melton became head of an Army Air Force program on personnel selection and training in San Antonio, TX. In the same year, Franklin V. Taylor, with the assistance of Henry Birmingham, established the first Navy human engineering program at the Naval Research Laboratory. The following year, the Human Engineering Division of the Naval Electronics Laboratory was established in San Diego under Arnold Small. The army's Human Engineering Laboratory was formed by the Army Ordnance Corps at Aberdeen Proving Ground near Baltimore in 1952, initially under the direction of Ben Ami Blau. In each of these establishments, the focus was on designing military equipment to make it easier for operational personnel to use and on improving the availability and readiness of the military forces through personnel selection and training. In the military sphere human performance is pushed to its limits, and there is a need to understand what those limits are and how to design to take account of them. It is significant that all the military services recognized the importance of human performance capacities and limitations in the operation of their equipment and began in-depth experimental investigations of them soon after World War II ended.

The desire among researchers with special interests in applied problems to be affiliated with associations that represented specifically those interests found expression in the establishment in Great Britain of the Ergonomics Research

Society in 1949. In 1957 both Division 21 of the APA (then known as the Society of Engineering Psychologists, and now known as the Division of Applied Experimental and Engineering Psychology) and the Human Factors Society (now known as the Human Factors and Ergonomics Society) came into existence. There now are numerous associations and societies of a similar sort in several countries, as well as organizations and journals, that represent more focused interests within applied experimental psychology broadly defined. Although researchers who affiliate with these organizations continue to focus attention on implications of human capabilities and limitations for system and equipment design and operation, interests have broadened into process control, transportation systems, health systems, human-computer interaction (HCI), design for the aging population, and many other areas.

During the 1960s and 1970s the most significant stimuli to further growth in the field in the United States were associated with initiatives of various government regulatory organizations. Many of these initiatives were stimulated by one or more levels of advocacy from the public sector. For example, Ralph Nader's 1965 book *Unsafe at Any Speed* and related advocacy led to the establishment of the National Highway Safety Bureau (NHSB) to carry out safety programs under the National Traffic and Motor Vehicle Safety Act of 1966 and the Highway Safety Act of 1966. In 1970 the National Highway Transportation Safety Administration was created as the successor to the NHSB. The critical incident at the Three Mile Island nuclear power generation plant in 1979 marshaled the public support that led the Nuclear Regulatory Commission to establish a Division of Human Factors Safety in 1980. These agencies, which focused predominantly on issues of safety, recognized that accidents are seldom exclusively physical in origin—that they almost always involve human error and that an understanding of human sensory, cognitive, and motor processes is essential to reducing that error.

In the 1980s and 1990s, although safety was still an important focus, the emphasis shifted somewhat to questions of ease of use of products of technology, and increased attention was given to the user interface in computer software design. Computers have become ubiquitous in the workplace and in the home. Not only are desktop computers commonplace, but most modern appliances and workplace systems, from videocassette recorders and hospital patient monitors to automated teller machines and vehicle navigation systems, also have one or more computers embedded in them somewhere. Usability has become a major objective of effective software design and evaluation, and many of the methods of experimental psychology have been adapted to respond to this need.

STATUS OF THE FIELD TODAY

How should we think of applied experimental psychology as it exists today? As a discipline (like high-energy physics or biochemistry)? An occupational specialty (like forensic psychology or vocational counseling)? A topical focus (like vision or working memory)? A methodology (like eye-movement tracking or evoked-potential recording)? We think it is none of these, but rather a domain of psychological research defined as experimentation with a practical purpose; it encompasses that work within experimental psychology that is motivated to a significant degree by practical concerns. We say "to a significant degree" because we do not wish to suggest that it is driven only by practical concerns; as already noted, we believe that much of the best applied work is motivated by, and contributes substantively to, both practical and theoretical interests.

Practical but Not Atheoretical

The last point deserves emphasis. Sometimes applied work is assumed necessarily to be atheoretical. We take issue with this view. It is possible for work to be motivated by the desire to answer an immediate practical question and to be atheoretical, and it is possible for work to be motivated by a purely theoretical question that has no obvious relevance to any real-world problem; but it is not essential that practical work be atheoretical or that theoretical work be divorced from applications.

Of special relevance to the focus of this chapter are numerous examples of theoretical ideas and constructs that have been put forth and developed by investigators who were keenly interested in practical problems and who were motivated to help solve them. Among the names that come immediately to mind in this regard are Frederic Bartlett (1932, 1943, 1948), Paul Fitts (1951, 1954; Fitts & Seeger, 1953), and Donald Broadbent (1957, 1958, 1971). These and many other investigators who could be mentioned did work that simultaneously addressed theoretical and practical interests. Among the theoretical ideas that have been closely associated with applied work—sometimes guiding that work and sometimes being informed by it—are theories of human motor skills, information theory (and communications theory more generally), detection and decision theory, and game theory.

An Interdisciplinary Field

Much applied experimentation is interdisciplinary in the sense that addressing applied problems in specific domains requires knowledge of those domains. If, for example, one wishes to do research on teaching or learning for the express purpose of helping to increase the effectiveness of classroom instruction, one must know more than a little about education from a practitioner's point of view. Or if one wants to work on the objective of decreasing the frequency of human error in the operating room or in the delivery of medical services more generally, one needs to know a lot—or to work with someone who knows a lot—about medical procedures and systems.

Many psychological researchers who work in highly applied areas, such as the human factors of aviation, nuclear power plant control, or manufacturing, have training both in psychology and in their area of application. Others work as members of research teams that depend on domain specialists to contribute the domain-specific knowledge to the operation, but even here the psychologist is likely to need a more-than-passing acquaintance with the relevant disciplines in order to ensure a smoothly functioning and productive team endeavor.

Laboratory and Field Experimentation

Experimentation, as we are using the term, includes both laboratory and field studies. People doing applied research are keenly aware of the considerable differences that typically characterize laboratory and field work. Variables are easier to control in the laboratory than in the field; as a consequence, the results of laboratory experiments typically are easier to interpret. However, the increased control usually comes at the expense of less realism than one has in operational real-world situations, so while the laboratory results may be easier to interpret, they are likely to be harder to apply without qualification to the real-world situations of interest.

A strategy that has been recommended for applied research involves both laboratory and field research. Hypotheses can be tested in a preliminary fashion in simplified or abstracted laboratory simulations of real-world situations, perhaps using students as participants, and then the findings can be checked with people functioning in their normal real-world contexts. This approach is illustrated by the work of Gopher, Weil, and Bareket (1994) in checking the extent to which effects of training with a simulation of certain aspects of flight control transfer to performance in an actual flight situation. Unfortunately, too often only the first step is taken, and the assumption is made that the results obtained will transfer to the operational situations of interest. We believe that the development of a trustworthy store of psychological knowledge that can be applied in confidence to real-world problems requires a continuing interplay between laboratory and field experimentation where what is learned in each context is informing further work in the other, and theory is being refined by the outcomes of both types of research.

Closely Related Disciplines

Defined as psychological experimentation that is explicitly addressed to practical concerns, applied experimental psychology overlaps considerably with several other disciplines. Most obviously, it has much in common with human-factors psychology (which for purposes of this chapter can be considered synonymous with ergonomics or engineering psychology, although for some purposes somewhat different connotations are given to these terms; Nickerson, 1999; Pew, 2000; Wogalter, Hancock, & Dempsey, 1998). It intersects also with many subfields in psychology that are defined by a focus on an area of application, such as organizational/industrial psychology, military psychology, aviation psychology, forensic psychology, consumer psychology, and the psychology of aging, among several others. Researchers in each of these and other subfields conduct experimental studies addressed to practical questions of special interest to people involved in these areas and hence provide many examples of applied experimental psychology.

Employment

The kinds of settings in which applied experimental psychologists work are as varied as are the fields of activity. Many applied experimentalists work in universities, and their work is frequently associated with institutes or other organizations that specialize in applied work, perhaps with a specific focus, such as transportation, education, aging, disabilities, or computer technology. Major employers of experimentalists are the various branches and research laboratories of the federal government. Notable among these are the laboratories of the military services, the National Aeronautics and Space Administration, the Department of Transportation, and the National Institutes of Health.

Several for-profit and nonprofit companies provide opportunities for applied experimentalists. These include the American Institutes of Research, Anacapa Sciences, and CHI Systems. Many large corporations have human-factors groups that either work on their own in-house research and development programs or on systems-development projects done under contract for the government or other organizations. Boeing and Lockheed-Martin in the aerospace industry and Ford and General Motors in the automotive industry are examples of such companies in the United States. Product-development projects may involve experimentation during design or concept development stages as well as during product test and evaluation.

Many organizations in the computer and communications industries, especially the software side of these industries, have vested interests in research on HCI and in the evaluation of product usability. IBM, Xerox, Microsoft, and Sun Microsystems are notable among large companies that provide opportunities for research and development in this area. However, while controlled experimentation has played, and continues to play, an important role in providing results that inform the design of user-friendly products, much of the testing and evaluation that is done is limited by cost-effectiveness concerns to heuristic analyses or other shortcut methods based on the expert judgment of one or a few specialists (Nielson, 1994).

The National Research Council's Committee on Human Factors issued a report in 1992 that provides demographic information, including employment information, on human factors specialists, many of whom are applied experimentalists (VanCott & Huey, 1992). Other sources of information regarding where applied experimental psychologists work include P. J. Woods (1976), Super and Super (1988), and Nickerson (1997).

EXAMPLES OF RECENT APPLIED EXPERIMENTAL WORK

Applied experimental work is performed in essentially all areas of psychology. Here our intent is to illustrate, by reference to specific studies, the range of subjects addressed. We focus primarily on relatively recent work, but there is no paucity of comparable examples from earlier times, a few of which were mentioned in the section on the historical roots of applied experimental psychology. It will be obvious from the examples given that applications of experimental psychology are not limited to the design of devices or systems that people use or with which they interact. This is a major focus of human-factors or engineering psychology, but experimental psychology has many applications that do not fall in this category.

Memory Enhancement

Interest in the development of devices and procedures for enhancing memory (mnemonics) predates the emergence of experimental psychology as a discipline by many centuries, and the search for ways to improve memory continues to the present day (McEvoy, 1992; Wenger, & Payne, 1995; see also chapter by Roediger & Marsh in this volume). Recent experimentation in this area is illustrated by the method of *expanding practice* first investigated by Landauer and Bjork (1978), and subsequently by Cull, Shaughnessy, and Zechmeister (1996). The method involves increasing the spacing between successive rehearsals of any given item in the list to be recalled, and it has proved to be effective in various contexts.

Another focus of research has been the *keyword mnemonic* of associating visual images with words that are to be learned. Since it was originally proposed by Atkinson (1975), the method has been studied and applied in many contexts, including the learning of foreign-language vocabulary (Atkinson & Raugh, 1975), state capitals (Levin, Shriberg, Miller, McCormick, & Levin, 1980), and science vocabulary (King-Sears, Mercer, & Sindelar, 1992). Interest in determining the strengths and limitations of the method continues to motivate research (Thomas & Wang, 1996).

The ability to associate names with faces—to remember the names of people to whom one has recently been introduced—is a sufficiently valuable social asset to have motivated many efforts to find ways to improve it (e.g., McCarty, 1980; Morris & Fritz, 2000). Morris and Fritz demonstrated that recall of the names of the members of a group of modest size can be enhanced by a simple game that applies the principle of expanding practice to the process of making introductions. Other experimentally developed techniques for enhancing memory for names, often involving the use of imagery or word-image associations, have also proved to be effective (Furst, 1944; Morris, Jones, & Hampson, 1978).

Researchers have shown great interest in the development of ways and devices to aid people—especially elderly people, but also people who maintain full and tight schedules—to remember to carry through on plans and intentions (e.g., to keep appointments, take medications, and perform time-critical tasks; J. E. Harris, 1978; Herrmann, Brubaker, Yoder, Sheets, & Tio, 1999; Kapur, 1995). The desirability of such aids is evidenced by the ease with which many people forget to keep appointments, take medications, and so on, without them. Identification of the determinants of the effectiveness of proposed approaches and devices intended to aid prospective memory has been the focus of some experimentation (Herrmann, Sheets, Wells, & Yoder, 1997).

Eyewitness and Earwitness Testimony

Much experimentation has been done on eyewitness (Sobel & Pridgen, 1981; Wells, 1993) and earwitness (Bull & Clifford, 1984; Read & Craik, 1995; Olsson, Juslin, & Winman, 1998) testimony in recent years; these topics are of considerable practical interest because of their relevance to court proceedings. What factors contribute to the accuracy (or inaccuracy) of such testimony? How is the accuracy of testimony influenced by methods of interrogation? What makes eyewitness or earwitness testimony more or less credible to jurors? What special considerations are necessary when the eyewitness or earwitness is a young child, and especially when the child is the alleged victim of abuse? These and many related questions have been subjects of experimental research.

Lineup procedures have been the focus of many studies (R. C. L. Lindsay & Wells, 1980; Malpass & Devine, 1984; Wells & Lindsay, 1980). One question that has received attention is whether sequential lineups are more or less effective than simultaneous lineups; sequential lineups appear to be superior to simultaneous lineups at least in the sense that they are less likely to yield false identifications (R. C. L. Lindsay & Wells, 1985). How the confidence with which identifications are made relates to the accuracy of those identifications has been another question of interest; overconfidence is not an unusual finding (Juslin, Olsson, & Winman, 1996; Loftus, Donders, Hoffman, & Schooler, 1989; Wells & Bradfield, 1998), and some data show that confidence may increase as a result of interrogation without a corresponding increase in accuracy (Shaw, 1996). A related question has to do with the degree to which the confidence expressed by a witness determines the credence that is given by jurors to the witness's testimony; it appears that more confident witnesses tend to be seen as more credible (Cutler, Penrod, & Stuve, 1988; R. C. L. Lindsay, Wells, & O'Connor, 1989).

The reliability of testimony of very young children (Ceci & Bruck, 1993, 1995; Dent & Flin, 1992; Poole & Lindsay, 2001) and of very elderly people (Bornstein, 1995; Yarmey, 1984; Yarmey & Kent, 1980) has been studied experimentally. Experimentation has shown that having children draw pictures relating to experiences, especially emotional experiences, can facilitate their verbal recall of those experiences (Butler, Gross, & Hayne, 1995; Gross & Hayne, 1998, 1999). Especially relevant to the assessment of the reliability of testimony is the finding of the possibility of eliciting "memories" of events in one's past that did not occur (Hyman & Kleinknecht, 1999; Loftus, 1997; Pezdek, Finger, & Hodge, 1997). Such results are especially relevant to reports by adults of having recovered lost memories of molestation or other forms of abuse as children. The problem of suggestibility more generally has motivated some experimentation (Gudjonsson, 1992; D. S. Lindsay, 1990; Tomes & Katz, 1997), as has interest in the effects of sleep deprivation on suggestibility in interrogation procedures (Blagrove, 1996; Blagrove & Akehurst, 2000).

A topic closely related to eyewitness testimony is that of face recognition, which has also been the focus of much experimentation. How reliable is the recognition of faces captured by a high-quality video camera relative to that of faces in photographs? Some work suggests that recognition based on video shots is not very reliable (Bruce et al., 1999; Henderson, Bruce, & Burton, 2001)—an important finding in view of the widespread use of closed-circuit TV systems for security surveillance.

Human-Computer Interaction

There are few, if any, areas that have stimulated more experimental work in recent years than that of HCI. Interest has grown sufficiently rapidly to have stimulated the establishment of several new journals focused on the subject. Topics investigated within this domain include e-mail and other computer-mediated human communication (Kiesler, Siegel, & McGuire, 1984; Kiesler, Zubrow, Moses, & Geller, 1985), computer-supported work by groups or teams (special issues of *Human-Computer Interaction,* 1992, and *Interacting with Computers,* 1992; Sproull & Kiesler, 1991), interface design (Fisher, Yungkurth, & Moss, 1990; Norman, 1991; Paap & Roske-Hofstrand, 1986), and a host of others (Helander, Landauer, & Prabhu, 1997).

Work in this general area has been spurred by a rapid increase in the number of people who use computers more or less daily for professional or personal purposes. The first heavy users of computers, during the middle of the twentieth century, were for the most part technically oriented people. Many of them were working on the development of computer technology itself or were specialists who were applying it to computationally intensive tasks. With the production of affordable desktop computers and the proliferation of computer networks, more and more people who were not trained in computer science or related technical areas became computer users, and the need for the design of interfaces and software with their requirements in mind became increasingly important.

Much of the early experimental work focused on the design of input-output devices. Efforts to design keyboards that improve on the standard QWERTY layout predate modern computer technology by many years, but the proliferation of computer users for whom the keyboard is the main input device has increased interest not only in the possibility of alternative key arrangements but in other aspects of keyboard design (e.g., split keyboards and chord keyboards; Lewis, Potosnak, & Magyar, 1997). Questions of what should appear on a visual interface and how the display should be laid out motivated much experimentation on the design of option menus and icons (Norman, 1991; Paap & Cooke, 1997) and on the management of objects that sometimes are (at least partially) visible and sometimes not (Marcus, 1997).

Making computer technology accessible to people with various types of disabling conditions represents a special challenge that has also motivated research (Elkind, Nickerson, Van Cott, & Williges, 1995; Newell & Gregor, 1997). Experimentation with natural language and speech for communicating with computer systems has been ongoing for several years; these technologies are sufficiently mature that they are beginning to be applied in practical situations (Makhoul, Jelinek, Rabiner, Weinstein, & Zue, 1990; Ogden & Bernick, 1997). The research that has brought these technologies to their current state of development has revealed much about human language and speech understanding (see chapter by Fowler in this volume).

The short history of computing technology has been one of a steady increase in the amount of computing power that can be packaged in a given space and that can be obtained for a given cost. Although there are limits to what can be accomplished by advances in miniaturization, they have not yet been realized. Already the state of the art provides people with access (in a physical though not necessarily a psychological sense) to enormous amounts of information via the Internet and the World Wide Web, and it makes possible the embedding of computing power into the instruments and objects of everyday life. Research challenges for the future are likely to have less to do with questions of the design of input-output devices and more with questions of how to help people interact effectively with extremely large information repositories and with objects and environments that have increasingly cognition-like capabilities (Nickerson, 1995).

Part-Task Training

Training of certain types—especially for tasks involving interaction with complex machines that are costly to build and operate, such as aircraft—is a very expensive undertaking. For this reason there has long been interest in the possibility of doing training of some aspects of such tasks with much less costly devices. Whether such part-task training is effective in any particular case is an empirical question and is best answered by experiment. Many years of research on the topic have yielded mixed results (Lintern & Gopher, 1980; Stammers, 1982; Wightman & Lintern, 1985).

Illustrative of recent work in the area is that of several investigators who have been successful in showing that practice with Space Fortress, a computer game that is intended to capture some aspects of flying tasks, can facilitate subsequent training of pilots of both fixed- and rotary-wing aircraft (Gopher et al., 1994; Hart & Battiste, 1992). Space Fortress was used in a coordinated set of studies sponsored by the U.S. Advanced Research Projects Agency to investigate the relative effectiveness of a variety of training strategies, most of which involved part-task training. The composite task—doing well at the Space Fortress game—was the same for all participants, but the variety of training regimens used reflected experimenters' differing ideas about how best to break down the composite task and train people on the components. The set of studies is described in a special volume of *Acta Psychologica* (Donchin, Fabiani, & Sanders, 1989).

The use of simulation for training purposes constitutes a part-task approach to training, inasmuch as any simulator faithfully represents only some subset of the characteristics of the real-world situation of interest. A great deal of experimentation has been required to bring the state of the art of simulation to the point where it can be the primary means of training people to perform many complex tasks, piloting and other aviation tasks being perhaps the most notable examples. How realistic a simulation must be in order to be effective for training purposes is a perennial question (Hays & Singer, 1989), and the answer appears to depend on the specifics of the task that must be learned.

Aviation Psychology

As we have already noted, many of the problems that engaged experimental psychologists during World War II had to do with military aviation. Much research continued this focus after the war, but attention began to be given to problems within commercial and civil aviation as well. Today the problems encountered in aviation psychology are considerably broader in range than are those that occupied researchers in the early days of the field. The development of multifunction glass-cockpit displays—cathode ray tubes, liquid crystal plasma displays—that have less resolution but much greater flexibility than dedicated traditional instruments or paper maps has raised a host of questions about how to make the best use of the new technologies. Heads-up displays projected on an aircraft's windscreen provide new challenges to the visual system (Wickens & Long, 1995). They have received extensive research attention in the aviation context and are beginning to be examined for potential use in automotive systems as well (Weintraub, 1992). There remain unresolved questions regarding how best to match displays to pilots' preferred ways of conceptualizing an airspace (Wickens & Prevett, 1995). Helmet-mounted displays are also receiving attention from experimenters because of their potential uses in aviation, especially in nighttime flight (Seagull & Gopher, 1997).

Over the past 20 years, flying, especially of commercial and military transport aircraft, has changed from being predominately a task of perceptual motor control to being one of supervisory management of automated avionics systems, from computer-controlled artificial stability systems to flight-management computers (Billings, 1996). The applied psychology questions often concern the relationship between the aircrew and the automated systems. Does the introduction of automation actually reduce mental workload? Does it lead to complacency on the part of the aircrew? Under what conditions does the aircrew establish trust in the automation (Parasuraman & Riley, 1997)? What are the training implications of introducing high levels of automation?

Flight training has been a major interest of aviation psychologists from the beginnings of the field; the rapidly changing technology has brought new challenges to this problem area as well (Salas, Bowers, & Prince, 1998). The use of simulation and the part-task approach in the training of piloting was noted in the preceding section. In recent years there has been great interest in the study of the training and performance of aircrew teams and of individuals as members of teams (Prince & Salas, 1993; Salas & Cannon-Bowers, 1997). Interpersonal team factors involving the captain and first officer, and, when present, the engineer are considered critical determinants of aviation safety (Helmreich & Foushee, 1993). This concern has led to research by psychologists in the area that has been called *cockpit resource management,* a goal of which is to help members of aircrews interact with greater sensitivity and respect for each other without violating the requisite authority relationships. Commercial airlines have widely adopted such programs and are showing interest in applying similar methods in air traffic control, training of crew operations, and other critical team activities.

Planning is currently underway to introduce advanced technology and major procedure revisions in the management of the national airspace by the Federal Aviation Administration. With research support from the National Aeronautics and Space Administration, researchers are exploring concepts of free flight in which aircrews and airline operations centers are given more opportunity to select the routes they fly. The success of such procedural modifications will depend on how well human factors are taken into account in the development and implementation of these plans (Wickens, Mavor, & McGee, 1997). We can expect continued applied experimental psychological research in support of these developments.

Highway Safety

Work relating to highway safety has been going on since the early 1930s, although a special impetus for it was provided by the establishment of the National Highway Traffic Safety Administration in 1970. There has been a sustained interest in research concerning the head and rear lighting of automobiles; the design, location, coding, and standardization of vehicle controls, especially as the number and variety of secondary controls has increased; the design, location, coding, and standardization of vehicle displays; driver performance and its role as a causal or preventive agent for accidents, and especially the problem of driving under the influence of alcohol; safety education and driver training programs; and the effects of aging on driving performance (Peacock & Karwowski, 1993). Behavioral research led to the recommendation that rear brake lights be located in a different position than running lights (Crosley & Allen, 1966; Nickerson, Baron, Collins, & Crothers, 1968) and eventually to the practice of locating them above the vehicle's trunk. Most studies of the effectiveness of the high location have concluded that it has reduced the incidence of rear-end collisions, but the magnitude of the reduction appears to be considerably less than was originally assumed (Mortimer, 1998). Much attention has been given to the problem of driving at night or under generally poor lighting conditions (Leibowitz & Owens, 1977; Owens & Tyrell, 1999); this attention is well-deserved in view of the high incidence of traffic fatalities in industrialized countries (Evans, 1991) and the fact that a large percentage of these fatalities occurs at nighttime (Owens, Helmers, & Sivak, 1993).

In 1991 two major programs impacting behavioral science research were initiated. The first was the Intelligent Transportation Systems Program, which includes a number of initiatives directed at improving traffic flow and traffic management for commercial and private vehicles. One component of this program, the Intelligent Vehicle Initiative, aims to accelerate the development and availability of advanced safety and information systems applied to all types of vehicles. The goal is to integrate driver assistance and motorist information functions so that vehicles operate more safely and efficiently. It includes in-vehicle navigation, traffic advisory, and emergency response functions. There is currently concern about the best ways to communicate this information to the vehicle driver. Government contractors and commercial companies are conducting studies to evaluate alternative approaches, such as heads-up displays and speech, and the impact on vehicle safety of introducing such systems (Kantowitz, Lee, & Kantowitz, 1997).

The second notable program is the development of a major high-fidelity driving simulator, the National Advanced Driving Simulator, which is intended to be a national asset. Nearing completion at the University of Iowa, the simulator will provide an experimental resource, including a scientific staff of engineers and behavioral scientists, for a wide variety of experimental studies relating to highway safety. It is expected to be used in both government and commercial research and development efforts, particularly in support of such projects as the Intelligent Transportation Systems Program. On the basis of these developments, continued growth can be expected in the application of psychological research methods and data to national driver-highway-system problems (Bloomfield et al., 1995; Kantowitz et al., 1997).

In this and the preceding section we have focused on research relating to aviation and highway safety. We should note that although most of the psychological work pertaining to transportation safety has in fact dealt with airspace operations or highway traffic, work has also been done on rail and maritime safety as well. Multiple-fatality accidents have occurred with disturbing frequency in both contexts, and human error has often been implicated as the major causal factor (Secretary of State for Transport, 1989; Wilson, 1992). Ship disasters claiming the lives of 200 or more people are not uncommon; the *World Almanac* (1998) lists twelve such incidents between 1981 and 1997. It seems clear that transportation safety will deserve the attention of applied researchers for the foreseeable future.

Medicine and Health

Both the rapid increase in the elderly population and the constant development of new medicines and technological devices for use in outpatient treatment of various types of illnesses and impairments have motivated concern among psychologists regarding the adequacy of the design of medical devices from a user's point of view (Klatzky & Ayoub, 1995). Devices that are intended to be used by people without medical training in the home need to be designed not only so that they serve the function that they are intended to serve when properly used, but also so that proper use is easy, the possibility of incorrect use is minimized, and the consequences are not disastrous when the latter occurs. The question of what can be done through training to help people who are chronically ill cope more effectively with their medical problems has stimulated some research (McWilliam et al., 1999).

The identification of factors that influence the likelihood that people will voluntarily get medical examinations or take disease-prevention measures has been the focus of some experimentation (Chapman, & Coups, 1999; Chapman & Sonnenberg, 2000; Klatzky & Messick, 1995; Klatzky, Messick, & Loftus, 1992). Efforts have been made to determine the relative effectiveness of various methods of promoting self-examination and participation in medical screening for skin cancer (Mickler, Rodrigue, & Lescano, 1999), prostate cancer (Davidson, Kirk, Degner, & Hassard, 1999), and breast and cervical cancer (Holden, Moore, & Holiday, 1998), among other diseases.

Interest in the question of how to design and deliver messages that will motivate health maintenance and illness-prevention activities has stimulated experimental work (Wright, 1999). Some researchers have found that health messages are likely to be more effective in evoking risk-reducing behavior changes if tailored to meet recipients' individual needs than if presented in more generic form (Kreuter, Bull, Clark, & Oswald, 1999); others have begun to explore the possibility of applying computer technology to the production of such individually tailored messages (DeVries & Brug, 1999; Dijkstra & DeVries, 1999).

Human error has been mentioned several times already as a focus of experimental work in various contexts. Interest in the subject stems in large part from the fact that such errors can have severe consequences, as when they lead to industrial accidents, airplane crashes, or train wrecks (Reason, 1990; Senders & Moray, 1991; D. D. Woods & Cook, 1999). Notable among the contexts in which such human error has been studied are transportation and process control; recently, however, much attention has been focused on human error in medical contexts. Although errors that occur in the operating room—as when a surgeon performs the right operation on the wrong limb—are likely to get more press than those that occur in more mundane settings, serious consequences can occur when medicine is misprescribed, interactions among medicines are overlooked, a prescription is misread, printed instructions are misunderstood, or medications are not taken as prescribed. Identifying the various types of medical errors that occur and finding ways to eliminate them or decrease their frequency of occurrence have become important objectives for experimental research (Bogner, 1994).

Sensory, Motor, and Cognitive Aids for Disabled People

The number of people in the United States who have physical or mental disabilities that constitute serious impediments to employment or daily living is not known precisely but is unquestionably large. Elkind (1990) has estimated that about 40% of the 30% of the U.S. population that reports having some type of disability (i.e., about 12% of the entire population) has a disability that can be considered severe. A 1997 report of the U.S. Census Bureau gives a lower figure (19.7%) as the percentage of the U.S. population with some level of disability, but essentially the same (12.3%) as the percentage having a severe disability. The 1999 *Statistical Abstract* (U.S. Census Bureau, 1999, Table 627) gives about 17 million as the number of people between 16 and 64 years of age with "work disability," which is about 10% of the population in this age group. This figure is also consistent with the earlier estimates if we assume that the percentage of children with comparable disabilities is similar whereas that of older people is undoubtedly higher. In any case, the percentage of the population that experiences nontrivial difficulties because of physical or mental disabilities is large enough to represent a major national concern for both economic and humanitarian reasons. The situation may be assumed to be comparable in other countries as well.

Much experimentation has been driven by an interest in developing aids for people who have disabilities of various sorts. Many devices have been developed to help people function effectively despite one or another type of handicap; these include mechanical limbs, automatic readers that will output speech or a tactile representation of what is read, tactile maps, sonar canes, and navigation systems for visually impaired people (Loomis, Golledge, Klatzky, 1998; Redden & Stern, 1983; Stern & Redden, 1982; see also chapter by Klatzky & Lederman in this volume). Generally a great deal of experimentation with potential users of such systems is required to determine whether they will be effective in operational situations, or how they might be made so. As Mann (1982) has noted, there is going to be no shortage of hardware in the future—the ability to package ever larger amounts of computer power in very small spaces ensures that there will be many attempts to build sophisticated devices to help meet the needs of people with disabilities—but much experimentation will be required to ensure the utility of the inventions. Many of the questions that need to be addressed are psychological: "How do you organize and present information to the 'wrong' sense, so that it is logical to the blind person or the deaf person? . . . How do you operate a sort of mechanical organ player so that it modulates sensations on the skin and in the ear and projects a sense of what this room looks like and how to negotiate it?" (Mann, 1982, p. 73).

The Psychology of Aging

Between 1890 and 1990, the average life expectancy at birth increased by about 75% for Whites and just about doubled for non-Whites in the United States (Johnson, 1997). Spectacular increases have been realized also in other industrialized countries. It is not surprising that as the percentage of the population that lives far beyond conventional retirement age has been steadily increasing, more and more attention has been paid by researchers to questions of special relevance to the elderly (Fisk & Rogers, 1996; Rogers & Fisk, 2000).

Research has been motivated by concern for understanding and meeting special needs that many elderly people are likely to have with respect to transportation (Barr & Eberhard, 1991; Eberhard & Barr, 1992; Kostyniuk & Kitamura, 1987), communication (Czaja, Guerrier, Nair, & Landauer, 1993), work performance (Czaja & Sharit, 1998; Salthouse, Hambrick, Lukas, & Dell, 1996; Salthouse & Maurer, 1996), and health care (Gardner-Bonneau & Gosbee, 1997; Klatzky & Ayoub, 1995), among other aspects of living. Many researchers have been seeking ways to enhance the cognitive functioning of the elderly; much of this work has focused on memory, which often tends to show decreasing functionality with increasing age (Verhaeghen, Marcoen, & Goossens, 1992; West, 1989; Yesavage, Rose, & Bower, 1983).

The question of how the ability to perform complex tasks may change with advancing age has been given some attention, as has that of what can be done to compensate for typical losses in sensory acuity and motor strength and dexterity. Airplane piloting and automobile driving are two such tasks that have been the focus of research on aging (Hardy & Parasuraman, 1997). Interest in the effects of aging on automobile driving has been fueled by the changing demographics of the driving population. As the general population's age distribution continues to shift to the right, the percentage of all automobile drivers who are elderly should continue to increase proportionately; some difficulties might be expected simply from the fact that highways have typically been designed on the basis of data collected with young male drivers (Waller, 1991). The effects on driving performance of decreases in visual acuity—especially for night vision—that may be so gradual that they go unnoticed illustrates one focus of experimental work in this area (Leibowitz, 1996).

Difficulties that some elderly people have in using high-tech devices have also stimulated experimental research. Elderly people often can benefit from specially designed interfaces, and optimal approaches to training in their use may differ from those that are more effective with younger people. These observations pertain to personal computers (Charness, Schuman, & Boritz, 1992; Czaja, 1997; Czaja & Sharit, 1998), automated teller machines (Mead & Fisk, 1998; Rogers, Fisk, Mead, Walker, & Cabrera, 1996), and home-based medical devices (Klatzky & Ayoub, 1995). The implications that declining sensory acuity with increasing age has for such activities as reading Braille has also stimulated experimental research (Stevens, Foulke, & Patterson, 1996).

We have mentioned a few problem areas in which applied psychological experimentation has been done to good effect. Many more could be mentioned. Several are discussed in other chapters of this book. A desire to address practical problems motivated much of the earliest work in experimental psychology and has continued to play a major role in setting the research agenda for many experimentalists to the present day.

FUTURE CHALLENGES FOR APPLIED EXPERIMENTAL PSYCHOLOGY

Practical challenges for experimental psychology come from many quarters. Without any claim of exhaustiveness, we mention three major (not entirely independent) categories—psychological, social, and technological—and give some examples of each. Many of the examples could be placed in more than one category. A better understanding of aging, for example, is desirable for individuals who must deal with its effects in their personal lives, for institutions that must respond to the social implications of an aging populace, and for technologists who want their products to be usable by elderly people. A similar comment could be made with respect to the problem of designing devices and environments to increase accessibility of resources for people with various types of disabilities, or with respect to many other topics. For convenience, however, we place each example in only one category, even when it requires a bit of arbitrariness to do so.

Psychological

A better understanding of basic cognitive processes of learning, thinking, decision making, problem solving, and the like is important for both theoretical and practical reasons. Much research on these topics is motivated primarily by an interest in advancing psychological theory—broadening and deepening the knowledge base represented by psychology as a science. But each of these topics is important also from a practical point of view. Educational goals and techniques, for example, need to be informed by a clear understanding of how children learn and of what facilitates or inhibits learning.

Can experiments be done that will shed light on why people do things (smoke, intentionally expose themselves to excessive sunlight, take illicit drugs, engage in risky driving, etc.) that are known to be harmful to them or to have a high probability of being so? Can such experiments reveal effective ways of decreasing the likelihood of high-risk behavior? Essentially, any form of unnecessarily risky behavior represents a challenge to research to explain it and perhaps to find a way to modify it. Consider, for illustrative purposes, risky driving. Automobile accidents remain a major cause of accidental death in the United States and most other industrialized countries, and this despite the considerable improvements that have been made in automobiles and highways from a safety point of view over the last few decades. It is clear that many automotive deaths are the direct result of risky driving—driving too fast, driving while drinking, following leading vehicles too closely, running traffic lights, passing with insufficient forward vision, failing to use seat belts, driving vehicles that are in ill repair, and purposefully using a vehicle as a weapon (road rage).

In any particular case of risky driving, it could be either that the driver underestimates the magnitude of the risk that is being taken or that he or she is fully aware of the risk and is taking it willingly. The driver in the first situation is analogous to a person who skates on thin ice believing it to be thick; the one in the second to a person who willingly skates on ice that he or she knows to be thin. The distinction is important for practical purposes because the two cases call for different approaches to modifying the risky behavior: The first calls for finding a way to make the driver aware of the risk that is being taken; the second requires something more than effecting this awareness, which the driver already has.

Documented egocentric biases of various sorts may be causal factors in risky behavior. Many investigators have found that people tend to consider specified positive events to be more likely to happen to themselves than to another person, and to consider specified negative events to be more likely to happen to someone else than to themselves (Dunning, 1993; D. M. Harris & Guten, 1979; Linville, Fischer, & Fischhoff, 1993). People appear to be likely to discount the seriousness of a risk if they believe themselves to be especially susceptible to it (Block & Keller, 1995; Ditto, Jemmott, & Darley, 1988; Ditto & Lopez, 1992; Kunda, 1987). Such egocentric biases have shown up in the tendency of drivers to consider themselves more expert and safer than average (Svenson, 1981; Svenson, Fischhoff, & MacGregor, 1985) and in people judging their chances of being involved in an automobile accident to be higher when they are a passenger in an automobile than when driving it themselves (Greening & Chandler, 1997; McKenna, 1993; McKenna, Stanier & Lewis, 1991). The question of how people can be made better aware of the real risks that they are taking in specific cases is a major challenge for future research.

Social

In 1998 representatives from more than 90 organizations concerned with scientific psychology convened a summit that became known as the 1998 Summit of Psychological Science Societies. Emerging from this meeting was a resolution composed of six recommendations, the fourth of which called upon "psychological scientists to equip themselves and their students and to educate the public to address the issues of importance to society" ("Summit '98," 1998, p. 14). This resolution is in keeping with other evidences, mentioned earlier in this chapter, of the currently strong interest among research psychologists and organizations that represent them in seeing the results of psychological research applied to practical problems.

Many of the most pressing problems that society faces have their roots in human behavior. These include problems of violence and crime, of drug addiction and substance abuse, of lifestyles that work against the maintenance of health, and of behavior that causes detrimental environmental change. There is a need for the development and use of more effective approaches to education, conflict resolution, wellness maintenance, and protection of the environment.

The nature of work has changed drastically for many people in the recent past, especially with the infusion of information technology in many workplaces. More and more jobs involve the hands-on use of this technology. Changes in job opportunities and job requirements are driven primarily by the market and not by considerations of workers' satisfaction with what they do. A better understanding is needed of what makes the difference between jobs and avocational pursuits that people find fulfilling and deeply satisfying and those that they find meaningless or acceptable only as a means of making a living.

Changing demographics brings some research challenges as well. The percentage of the U.S. population that is over 65 grew steadily from about 4% in 1900 to about 13% by the end of the century. The most rapidly growing age group in terms of percentage is the 85 and older group, which has been predicted to increase from 1.6% of the U.S. population in 2000 to about 4.6% by 2050 (*World Almanac,* 1998). Such changes in population statistics harbor a host of research challenges, many of which have barely begun to be addressed (Czaja, 1990).

The increasing concentration of the population in and around major cities is a worldwide phenomenon (Vining, 1985). Changing immigration patterns (Kasarda, 1988) are rapidly modifying the ethnic and cultural composition of many cities and increasing the importance of developing a better understanding of how best to maintain social stability and coherence in an increasingly diverse society. Finding more effective ways to promote understanding and tolerance of individual differences is a continuing challenge.

How to foster cooperation and the pursuit of win-win strategies in interpersonal dealings is another important question for research. It would be good to know more about how altruism relates to personal and social mores and to what extent it can be cultivated (Schwartz, 1977). How to deal with social dilemmas and the "tragedy of the commons" (Hardin, 1968; Glance & Huberman, 1994; Platt, 1973) is a question on which considerable research has been done but on which much more is needed. Hardin (1968) illustrated the conflict that can occur between self-interest and the common good with a metaphor of a herdsman who can realize a substantial personal benefit at little personal cost by adding an animal to his herd that is grazing on common land. The benefit that comes from having an additional animal is his alone, whereas the cost, in terms of slightly less grazing land per animal, is shared by all users of the common. When every herdsman sees the situation the same way, and each works in what appears to be his own best short-term interest, they collectively ruin the land. The commons tragedy plays itself out in many forms, and the challenge is to find ways to motivate behaviors that contribute to the common good.

Technological

Applied experimental psychologists have an important role to play in helping to ensure that the products of technology are well matched not only to the needs but also to the capabilities and limitations of their users. For years the complaint has been heard that the development of new technologies has been outstripping the knowledge required to incorporate them usefully into applications. Landauer (1995), for example, discussed the productivity paradox and came to the conclusion that much of computer technology is being used for purposes that, in and of themselves, are unlikely to show productivity gains. He argued that lack of attention to design for human users is at the heart of the productivity problems that the world is experiencing with respect to computer applications.

It is widely recognized that many people have difficulties with setting the clocks on their automobile dashboards, recording programs on their VCRs, using their telephone answering machines to receive messages from remotely located phones, and availing themselves of other conveniences that modern technology provides (Nussbaum & Neff, 1991). With the continuing introduction of new technological devices, such as personal digital assistants capable of receiving e-mail through wireless connections, these problems are likely to get worse. Again, here is a challenge to applied experimentalists to contribute to an understanding of how to make specific products of technology compatible with the needs, capabilities, and limitations of their everyday users.

Engineers are introducing automation into large-scale systems with confidence that the systems' performance will be better as a result. In many cases this expectation has turned out to be wrong. Early attempts to introduce flight management computers into airplane cockpits led to many instances in which the workload associated with monitoring and controlling them was greater than the workload involved in conducting the same operations without them (Billings, 1996). The introduction of automation raises questions of trust: Which aspects of the design of automated systems result in users' trusting that they will accomplish their intended purposes (M. J. Adams, Tenney, & Pew, 1991; Parasuraman & Riley, 1997)? Such systems take the human operator out of the loop. Operators tend to lose situation awareness concerning the state of the system and the environment in which it is operating (Endsley, 1996; Endsley & Kiris, 1995). If not designed properly, automated systems can lead to complacency; if the computer is managing one's system, one is no longer responsible for what goes wrong. Human-centered design that takes account of the user from the initial stages of system conceptualization is required if this kind of misuse of automation is to be prevented.

The introduction of computers and telephone call routers into our communication infrastructure is imposing a cold, impersonal, automated intermediary—and in some cases not just an intermediary, but an ultimate adjudicator in control of the information resources one is trying to tap. Machines are performing more and more of the communication functions that in the past have involved person-to-person connections. Applied psychologists need to challenge the ways in which these systems are designed. We need to create ways to achieve the same level of efficiency without resorting to such uncommunicative alternatives.

Work on these kinds of problems can take place within an academic, government, or industrial setting. Progress is not likely to be made by the social planner, the economist, the political scientist, or even by the engineer who is focused solely on technology. Progress will be made by individuals who understand human behavior and are motivated to improve the human use of technology by providing objective data showing how improvements could be made and by influencing the design process directly at the interface between the human user and the technology itself.

With the rapidly expanding use of the internet for business purposes, many jobs have come into existence that were unheard of a short time ago. Most of these jobs require the use of computers for one or another purpose, and many of them involve working with geographically distributed groups. The need for new tools to support the performance of the new tasks and to facilitate collaboration among dispersed members of a team, for techniques to coordinate distributed work, for approaches to management that work well with distributed groups, for effective methods of information finding and resource sharing—these and many other needs associated with jobs being created by information technology represent opportunities for applied experimental work (Attewell, Huey, Moray, & Sanderson, 1995; Gould, 1995).

The Internet and associated technologies are affecting us in many ways in addition to their effects on business and work. They have profound implications as well for education, entertainment, interperson communication, and many other aspects of our lives. An especially noteworthy development is the rapid increase in the amount of information that is available to the computer user through resources epitomized by the World Wide Web, which has been growing by approximately 1 million electronic pages a day (Members of the *Clever* Project, 1999). The Web contains information on every conceivable subject, and what it contains covers the full range with respect to intelligibility and accuracy.

A major challenge relating to the future of technology, from a user's point of view, is to provide tools and methods that will make it easy for one to get quickly to information one wants without having to attend to an excess of material in which one has no interest. A variety of search engines currently exist, but while they are unquestionably useful for many purposes, their operation is often frustratingly slow, and the ratio of false positives to hits in their returns is unacceptably high. As Bosak and Bray (1999) put it, the "Internet is a speed-of-light network that often moves at a crawl; and although nearly every kind of information is available online, it can be maddeningly difficult to find the one piece you need" (p. 89).

These problems will become increasingly severe as the number of sites continues to grow at an exponential rate. Addressing them effectively will require advances on several fronts, including the design of languages for organizing information (Bosak & Bray, 1999) and the development of more efficient search techniques (Members of the *Clever* Project, 1999). The value of any technological advance in this area resides, however, in the extent to which it helps people interact effectively with extremely large databases; the design and evaluation of tools to facilitate that interaction deserve more attention from psychological researchers than they have received, and the importance of these topics as possible foci of research can only increase.

Although for convenience we have organized these comments under the topics "psychological," "social," and "technological," the limitations of this partitioning are apparent when one considers the challenges that information (computer and communication) technology represents to psychological research in the future. Many visions of what the future holds in this regard have been published; one readily accessible example is *Scientific American*'s special report on MIT's Oxygen Project (1999). The vision motivating this effort includes not only powerful information resources in the hands of nearly everyone and the potential of a manifold increase in human productivity but also, as conditions of realization, great increases in the ease of use of the devices that connect people with the networked resources (Dertouzos, 1999). Ease of use includes better utilization of speech for communication between person and computer (Zue, 1999) and the development of handheld devices capable of great versatility (Guttag, 1999). The forces driving the continuing information revolution are psychological and social as well as technological, and its effects are of all three types as well.

Communicating and Effecting the Practical Implications of Experimentation

It should perhaps go without saying that researchers who do experiments that are explicitly addressed to practical questions should make clear in the reporting of their results what the practical implications of their findings are. However, our experience suggests that many researchers whose work is motivated by practical concerns have difficulty in describing, in terms that intelligent lay readers will find easy to understand, precisely why an experiment they have done is important from a practical point of view and how the results might be applied.

Sometimes the problem is vagueness. Pointing out that a particular finding is relevant to a specified problem is much less helpful than giving examples of how the finding might be applied. The reader would like to know who, not counting other researchers, would benefit from being aware of the finding, and how they might make use of it. Because the abstract of a journal article is usually the first (and often the only) thing a reader sees, abstracts of applied experimental articles should state explicitly what the author believes are the most important practical implications of the reported results.

Another common problem is overstatement. In this case, claims are made regarding real-world relationships that go beyond what the experimental results will support. Sometimes results obtained with college students performing artificial tasks after minutes, or at best hours, of experience with them, and for the purpose of fulfilling a psychology course requirement, are generalized without qualification to the performance of motivated experienced professionals in operational contexts. We are not suggesting that the results of laboratory experiments with college students can have no relevance to real-world situations, but simply noting that it is easy to extrapolate from the one situation to the other in an insufficiently guarded way. Generally speaking, what the laboratory experiments produce is suggestive evidence of relationships that need to be verified in the applied contexts of interest. We think it very important that the implications of experimental results be stated with appropriate qualifications; overstatement contributes negatively to the credibility of the field.

We believe that experimentation motivated strictly by theoretical questions often yields results that have practical implications that are never made explicit. Researchers whose primary interests are theoretical are generally more likely to develop and communicate the theoretical implications of their findings than any practical applications they may have, and they may not be the best equipped to spell out the latter. Psychology and society could be well served by psychologists who are interested in and capable of explicating (in lay terms) ways in which the results of theoretically motivated experimentation could be applied to real-world problems to good effect.

Finally, we need to recognize that having practical implications—even practical implications that have been spelled out—does not necessarily mean having practical impact. In order to have impact, an actual application must be made. Many results of experiments have practical implications that have not been applied to full advantage in practical situations, despite having been recognized for what they are. One may question, for example, whether the results from experimentation on learning have had the impact they should have had on education, or whether the results of studies of negotiation and conflict resolution have been applied to maximum effect to actual conflict situations, or whether what has been discovered about human error has been applied as extensively and effectively as it could be to reduce the consequences of such error in industrial, medical, and other contexts that have implications for public safety.

Ensuring impact requires different skills than does spelling out implications. Consideration of how this can be done is beyond the scope of this chapter, but we do want to support a point made by Geissler (1917b), who argued that applications are best made by experts in the fields in which the findings are believed to apply. This means that psychologists who would like to have a role in seeing that the results of research are actually applied to real-world problems need either to work with experts in the relevant fields or to become experts themselves. However well intentioned, efforts to apply the findings of experimentation to real-world problems by researchers who have only a superficial knowledge of areas of application can result in harm both to psychology and to the areas of interest.

SOURCES OF ADDITIONAL INFORMATION

Many journals publish applied experimental work. Examples are given in Table 24.3. There are several professional organizations with which researchers doing applied experimental work in psychology tend to affiliate. Notable among them in the United States are the APA's Divisions 21 (Applied Experimental and Engineering Psychology), 3 (Experimental

TABLE 24.3 Examples of Journals That Publish Applied Experimental Research

Applied experimental research (nearly) exclusively
- *Journal of Experimental Psychology: Applied*

Experimental research that may or not be applied
- *Acta Psychologica*
- *Cognition*
- *Cognitive Psychology*
- *Journal of Experimental Social Psychology*
- Other *Journals of Experimental Psychology*
- *Quarterly Journal of Experimental Psychology*
- *Thinking and Reasoning*

Applied research that may or may not be experimental
- *Applied Cognitive Psychology*
- *Cognitive Technology*
- *Ergonomics*
- *Human Factors and Ergonomics*
- *International Journal of Cognitive Ergonomics*
- *Journal of Applied Psychology*
- *Journal of Applied Social Psychology*

Applied experimental research (though not necessarily exclusively) in specific areas
- *Behavior and Information Technology*
- *Cognition and Instruction*
- *Human-Computer Interaction*
- *International Journal of Aviation Psychology*
- *Journal of the Acoustical Society of America*
- *Journal of Behavioral Decision Making*
- *Journal of Conflict Resolution*
- *Law and Human Behavior*
- *Military Psychology*
- *Organizational Behavior and Human Performance*
- *Transportation Human Factors*

Psychology), 14 (Industrial and Organizational), and 19 (Military), among others; the American Psychological Society; the Human Factors and Ergonomics Society; and the Society for Applied Research in Memory and Cognition. Each of these organizations publishes one or more refereed journals, and most publish a magazine or newsletter containing timely information of interest to its membership as well. Parsons (1999) published a historical account of the APA's division of Applied Experimental and Engineering Psychology. A collection of biographies of distinguished members of this division was edited by Taylor (1994).

Textbooks and reviews that emphasize applied experimental work in psychology include, in order of publication, Wickens (1984/2000), Barber (1988), Lave (1988), Izawa (1993), and Harper and Branthwaite (2000). Examples of books that discuss applications of experimental work in specific areas include Baddeley (1982) on memory and mnemonics; McGilly (1994) on education; Ceci and Bruck (1995) on childhood memory and testimony; Baron (1998) on public decision making; Foddy, Smithson, Schneider, and Hogg (1999) on resolving social dilemmas; Gärling, Kristensen, Ekehammar, and Wessells (2000) on international negotiations; and Durso et al. (1999) on a variety of applied topics. More of the history of applied experimental psychology and extensive reviews of work that has been done in many of its subfields can be found in chapters of the *Annual Review of Psychology*.

CONCLUDING COMMENTS

Experimental research may be motivated by theoretical or practical interests, or both. Independently of its motivation, it may have theoretical or practical implications, or both. And the implications it has may or may not have been made explicit. In this chapter we have focused on experimental research that has been motivated by practical interests or that has produced results with obvious practical implications.

Are there major success stories in applied experimental psychology? Are there examples of individual experiments that have had great practical impact? We cannot point to examples of such experiments, but we think that these may not be the right questions to ask. It is not easy to find many examples in any experimental science of isolated experiments that have had major practical effect. More appropriate, we think, is the question of whether there are practical matters for which the cumulative effects of experimentation have made a difference. What is reasonable to hope for as a consequence of applied experimentation is not major practical impact from single studies, but a gradual increase in understanding of phenomena and relationships that can be applied to practical ends. As to whether this goal has been realized to a significant degree, the answer is undoubtedly yes.

About 30 years ago, Deutsch, Platt, and Senghaas (1971) identified what they considered to be 62 major advances in the social sciences (anthropology, economics, mathematical statistics, philosophy, politics, psychology, and sociology) that had occurred during the first six-and-a-half decades of the twentieth century. Of special interest in the present context is the conclusion to which Deutsch, Platt, and Senghaas's analysis led them: "that practical demands or conflicts *stimulated* about three-fourths of all contributions between 1900 and 1965. In fact, as the years went on, their share rose from two-thirds before 1930 to more than four-fifths thereafter" (pp. 458). Further, they noted that "major social science advances were *applied* to social practice in almost exactly the same proportion as they were stimulated by it, and they showed considerable practical importance" (pp. 458).

Although we cannot report comparably specific figures for experimental psychology, the history of the domain contains many examples of findings that are applicable to real-world practical problems. Some of these findings have been applied to good effect; more have the potential to be so applied. Perhaps more important, opportunities for psychological experimentation addressed to practical concerns abound in the psychological, social, and technological challenges of modern life.

REFERENCES

Adams, H. F. (1917). The memory value of mixed sizes of advertisements. *Journal of Experimental Psychology, 2,* 448–465.

Adams, M. J., Tenney, Y. J., & Pew, R. W. (1991). *Strategic workload and the cognitive management of advanced multi-task systems. CSERIAC SOAR 91-6.* Wright-Patterson Air Force Base, OH: Crew Systems Ergonomics Information Analysis Center.

Atkinson, R. (1975). Mnemotechnics in second language learning. *American Psychologist, 30,* 821–828.

Atkinson, R., & Raugh, M. R. (1975). An application of the mnemonic keyword method to the acquisition of a Russian vocabulary. *Journal of Experimental Psychology: Human Learning and Memory, 104,* 126–133.

Attewell, P. A., Huey, B. M., Moray, N. P., & Sanderson, P. M. (1995). Emerging technologies in work design. In R. S. Nickerson (Ed.), *Emerging needs and opportunities for human factors research* (pp. 220–240). Washington, DC: National Academy Press.

Baddeley, A. (1982). *Your memory: A user's guide.* New York: Macmillan.

Barber, D. (1988). *Applied cognitive psychology.* London: Methuen.

Baron, J. (1998). *Judgment misguided: Intuition and error in public decision making*. New York: Oxford University Press.

Barr, R. A., & Eberhard, J. W. (1991). Safety and mobility of elderly drivers: Part I. *Human Factors, 33,* 583–595.

Bartlett, F. C. (1932). *Remembering.* Cambridge, UK: Cambridge University Press.

Bartlett, F. C. (1948). Fatigue following highly skilled work. *Proceedings of the Royal Society, 131B,* 247–257.

Bartlett, F. C. (1947). The measurement of human skill. *Occupational Psychology, 23,* 31–38 and 83–91.

Billings, C. E. (1996). *Aviation automation: The search for a human-centered approach.* Mahwah, NJ: Erlbaum.

Blagrove, M. (1996). Effects of length of sleep deprivation on interrogative suggestibility. *Journal of Experimental Psychology: Applied, 2,* 48–59.

Blagrove, M., & Akehurst, L. (2000). Effects of sleep loss on confidence-accuracy relationships for reasoning and eyewitness memory. *Journal of Experimental Psychology: Applied, 6,* 59–73.

Bogner, M. S. (Ed.). (1994). *Human error in medicine.* Hillsdale, NJ: Erlbaum.

Bloomfield, J. R., Buck, J. R., Carroll, S. A., Booth, M. S., Romano, R. A., McGehee, D. V., & North, R. A. (1995). *Human factors aspects of the transfer of control from the automated highway system to the driver. Report No. FHWA-RD-96-114.* McLean, VA: Federal Highway Administration.

Boring, E. G. (1950). *A history of experimental psychology.* New York: Appleton-Century. (Original work published 1929)

Bornstein, B. H. (1995). Memory processes in elderly eyewitnesses: What we know and what we don't know. *Behavioral Sciences and the Law, 13,* 337–348.

Bosak, J., & Bray, T. (1999). XML and the second-generation web. *Scientific American, 280*(5), 89–93.

Bray, C. W. (1948). *Psychology and military proficiency.* Princeton, NJ: Princeton University Press.

Broadbent, D. E. (1957). Effects of noise on behavior. In C. M. Harris (Ed.), *Handbook of noise control* (pp. 1–33). New York: McGraw-Hill.

Broadbent, D. E. (1958). *Perception and communication.* London: Pergamon Press.

Broadbent, D. E. (1971). *Decision and stress.* London: Academic Press.

Bruce, V., Henderson, Z., Greenwood, K., Hancock, P. J. B., Burton, A. M., & Miller, P. (1999). Verification of face identities from images captured on video. *Journal of Experimental Psychology: Applied, 5,* 339–360.

Bull, R., & Clifford, B. R. (1984). Earwitness voice recognition accuracy. In G. L. Wells & E. F. Loftus (Eds.), *Eyewitness testimony: Psychological perspectives* (pp. 92–123). New York: Cambridge University Press.

Burtt, H. E. (1916). The effect of uniform and non-uniform illumination upon attention and reaction-times, with especial reference to street illumination. *Journal of Experimental Psychology, 1,* 155–182.

Butler, S., Gross, J., & Hayne, H. (1995). The effect of drawing on memory performance in young children. *Developmental Psychology, 31,* 597–608.

Ceci, S. J., & Bjork, R. A. (2000). Psychological science in the public interest: The case for juried analyses. *Psychological Science, 11,* 177–178.

Ceci, S. J., & Bruck, M. (1993). The suggestibility of the child witness: A historical review and synthesis. *Psychological Bulletin, 113,* 403–439.

Ceci, S. J., & Bruck, M. (1995). *Jeopardy in the courtroom: A scientific analysis of children's testimony.* Washington, DC: American Psychological Association.

Chapanis, A. (1999). *The Chapanis chronicles: 50 years of human factors research, education, and design.* Santa Barbara, CA: Aegean.

Chapanis, A., Garner, W. R., & Morgan, C. T. (1949). *Applied experimental psychology: Human factors in engineering design.* New York: Wiley.

Chapanis, A., Garner, W. R., Morgan, C. T., & Sanford, F. H. (1947). *Lectures on men and machines: An introduction to human engineering.* Baltimore: Systems Research Laboratory.

Chapman, G. B., & Coups, E. J. (1999). Time preferences and preventive health behavior: Acceptance of the influenza vaccine. *Medical Decision Making, 19,* 307–314.

Chapman, G. B., & Sonnenberg, F. A. (Eds.). (2000). *Decision making in health care.* Cambridge, UK: Cambridge University Press.

Charness, N., Schuman, C. E., & Boritz, G. A. (1992). Training older adults in word processing: Effects of age, training technique, and computer anxiety. *International Journal of Aging and Technology, 5,* 79–106.

Craik, K. J. W. (1947). Theory of the human operator in control systems, I. *British Journal of Psychology, 38,* 56–61.

Craik, K. J. W. (1948). Theory of the human operator in control systems, II. *British Journal of Psychology, 38,* 142–148.

Crosley, J., & Allen, M. J. (1966). Automobile brake light effectiveness: An evaluation of high placement and accelerator switching. *American Journal of Optometry and Archives of American Academy of Optometry, 43,* 299–305.

Cull, W. L., Shaughnessy, J. J., & Zechmeister, E. B. (1996). Expanding understanding of the expanding-pattern-of-retrieval mnemonic: Toward confidence in applicability. *Journal of Experimental Psychology: Applied, 2,* 365–378.

Cutler, B. L., Penrod, S. D., & Stuve, T. E. (1988). Jury decision making in eyewitness identification cases. *Law and Human Behavior, 12,* 41–56.

Czaja, S. J. (Ed.). (1990). *Human factors research needs for an aging population.* Panel on Human Factors Research Issues for an Aging Population. Committee on Human Factors, National Research Council. Washington, DC: National Academy Press.

Czaja, S. J. (1997). Computer technology and the older adult. In M. G. Helander, T. K. Landauer, & P. V. Prabhu (Eds.), *Handbook of human-computer interaction* (pp. 797–812). New York: Elsevier.

Czaja, S. J., Guerrier, J., Nair, S. N., & Landauer, T. K. (1993). Computer communication as an aid to independence for older adults. *Behavior and Information Technology, 12,* 197–207.

Czaja, S. J., & Sharit, J. (1998). Ability-performance relationships as a function of age and task experience for a data entry task. *Journal of Experimental Psychology: Applied, 4,* 332–351.

Davidson, B. J., Kirk, P., Degner, L. F., & Hassard, T. H. (1999). Information and patient participation in screening for prostate cancer. *Patient Education and Counseling, 37,* 255–263.

Dent, R., & Flin, R. (Eds.). (1992). *Children as witnesses.* Chichester, UK: Wiley.

Dertouzos, M. L. (1999). The future of computing. *Scientific American, 281*(2), 52–55.

Deutsch, K. W., Platt, J., & Senghaas, D. (1971). Conditions favoring major advances in social sciences. *Science, 171,* 450–459.

DeVries, H., & Brug, J. (1999). Computer-tailored interventions motivating people to adopt health promoting behaviours: Introduction to a new approach. *Patient Education and Counseling, 36,* 99–192.

Dijkstra, A., & DeVries, H. (1999). The development of computer-generated tailored interventions. *Patient Education and Counseling, 36,* 193–203.

Ditto, P. H., Jemmott, J. B., & Darley, J. M. (1988). Appraising the threat of illness: A mental representational approach. *Health Psychology, 7,* 183–201.

Ditto, P. H., & Lopez, D. F. (1992). Motivated skepticism: Use of differential decision criteria for preferred and nonpreferred conclusions. *Journal of Personality and Social Psychology, 63,* 568–584.

Donchin, E., Fabiani, M., & Sanders, A. (1989). The learning strategies program: An examination of the strategies in skill acquisition. *Acta Psychologica, 71.*

Donders, F. C. (1969). On the speed of mental processes. In W. G. Koster (Ed.), *Attention and performance* (Vol. 2, pp. 412–431). Amsterdam: North Holland. (Original work published 1968)

Downey, J. E. (1917). Handwriting disguise. *Journal of Applied Psychology, 1,* 368–379.

Dunning, D. (1993). Words to live by: The self and definitions of social concepts and categories. In J. Suls (Ed.), *Psychological perspectives on the self* (pp. 99–126). Hillsdale, NJ: Erlbaum.

Durso, F. (Ed.), Nickerson, R. S., Schvaneveldt, R. W., Dumais, S. T., Lindsay, D. S., & Chi, M. T. H. (Assoc. Eds.). (1999). *Handbook of applied cognition.* New York: Wiley.

Eberhard, J. W., & Barr, R. A. (1992). Safety and mobility of elderly drivers: Part 2. *Human Factors, 34,* 1–2.

Egan, J. P. (1944). Articulation testing methods: Part 2. Office of Scientific Research and Development Report No. 3802. U.S. Department of Commerce Report PB 22848.

Elkind, J. I. (1990). The incidence of disabilities in the United States. *Human Factors, 32,* 397–405.

Elkind, J. I., Nickerson, R. S., Van Cott, H. P., & Williges, R. C. (1995). Employment and disabilities. In R. S. Nickerson (Ed.), *Emerging needs and opportunities for human factors research* (pp. 106–130). Washington, DC: National Academy Press.

Endsley, M. R. (1996). Automation and situation awareness. In R. Parasuraman & M. Mouloua (Eds.), *Automation and human performance: Theory and applications* (pp. 163–200). Hillsdale, NJ: Erlbaum.

Endsley, M. R., & Kiris, E. O. (1995). The out-of-loop performance problem and level of control in automation. *Human Factors, 37,* 381–394.

Evans, L. (1991). *Traffic safety and the driver.* New York: Van Nostrand Reinhold.

Farley, F., & Null, C. E. (Eds.). (1987). *Using psychological science: Making the public case.* Washington, DC: Psychological and Cognitive Sciences.

Fisher, D. L., Yungkurth, E. J., & Moss, S. M. (1990). Optimal menu hierarchy design: Syntax and semantics. *Human Factors, 32,* 665–683.

Fisk, A. D., & Rogers, W. A. (Eds.). (1996). *Handbook of human factors and the older adult.* San Diego, CA: Academic Press.

Fitts, P. M. (1946). German applied psychology during World War II. *American Psychologist, 1,* 151–160.

Fitts, P. M. (1947a). Psychological research on equipment design. *The aviation psychology research program of the Army Air Forces.* Washington, DC: Government Printing Office.

Fitts, P. M. (1947b). Psychological research on equipment design in the AAF. *American Psychologist, 2,* 93–98.

Fitts, P. M. (1951). Engineering psychology and equipment design. In S. S. Stevens (Ed.), *Handbook of experimental psychology* (pp. 1287–1340). New York: Wiley.

Fitts, P. M. (1954). The information capacity of the human motor system in controlling the amplitude of movement. *Journal of Experimental Psychology, 47,* 81–88.

Fitts, P. M., & Seeger, D. M. (1953). S-R compatibility: Spatial characteristics of stimulus and response codes. *Journal of Experimental Psychology, 46,* 199–210.

Fletcher, H., & Munson, W. A. (1933). Loudness, its definition, measurement and calculation. *Journal of the Acoustical Society of America, 5,* 82–108.

Fletcher, H., & Munson, W. A. (1937). Relation between loudness and masking. *Journal of the Acoustical Society of America, 9,* 1–10.

Foddy, M., Smithson, M., Schneider, S., & Hogg, M. (1999). *Resolving social dilemmas.* Philadelphia, PA: Psychology Press.

Furst, B. (1944). *How to remember.* New York: Greenberg.

Gardner-Bonneau, D., & Gosbee, J. (1997). Health care and rehabilitation. In A. D. Fisk & W. A. Rogers (Eds.), *Handbook of human factors and the older adult* (pp. 321–255). San Diego, CA: Academic Press.

Gärling, T., Kristensen, H., Ekehammar, B, & Wessells, M. G. (2000). *Psychological contributions to international negotiations, conflict prevention, and world peace.* Philadelphia: Psychology Press.

Geissler, L. R. (1917a). Association-reactions applied to ideas of commercial brands of familiar articles. *Journal of Applied Psychology, 1,* 275–290.

Geissler, L. R. (1917b). What is applied psychology? *Journal of Applied Psychology, 1,* 46–60.

Glance, N. S., & Huberman, B. A. (1994). The dynamics of social dilemmas. *Scientific American, 279*(3), 76–81.

Gopher, D., Weil, M., & Bareket, T. (1994). Transfer of a skill from computer game trainer to flight. *Human Factors, 36,* 387–405.

Gould, J. D. (1995). Aiding intellectual work. In R. S. Nickerson (Ed.), *Emerging needs and opportunities for human factors research* (pp. 291–321). Washington, DC: National Academy Press.

Greening, L., & Chandler, C. C. (1997). Why it can't happen to me: The base rate matters, but overestimating skill leads to underestimating risk. *Journal of Applied Psychology, 27,* 760–780.

Gross, J., & Hayne, H. (1998). Drawing facilitates children's verbal reports of emotionally laden events. *Journal of Experimental Psychology: Applied, 4,* 163–179.

Gross, J., & Hayne, H. (1999). Drawing facilitates children's verbal reports after long delays. *Journal of Experimental Psychology: Applied, 5,* 265–283.

Gudjonsson, G. H. (1992). *The psychology of interrogations, confessions and testimony.* Chichester, UK: Wiley.

Guttag, J. V. (1999). Communication chameleons. *Scientific American, 281*(2), 58–59.

Haines, T. H. (1916). Relative values of point-scale and year-scale measurements of one thousand minor delinquents. *Journal of Experimental Psychology, 1,* 51–82.

Hall, G. S. (1917). Practical relations between psychology and the war. *Journal of Applied Psychology, 1,* 5–7.

Hall, G. S., Baird, J. W., & Geissler, L. R. (1917). Foreword. *Journal of Applied Psychology, 1,* 5–7.

Hardin, G. (1968). The tragedy of the commons. *Science, 162,* 1243–1248.

Hardy, D. J., & Parasuraman, R. (1997). Cognition and flight performance in older pilots. *Journal of Experimental Psychology: Applied, 3,* 313–348.

Harper, J., & Branthwaite, A. (2000). *The applied psychologist* (2nd ed.). Philadelphia: Open University Press.

Harris, D. M., & Guten, S. (1979). Health protective behavior: An exploratory study. *Journal of Health and Social Behavior, 20,* 17–29.

Harris, J. E. (1978). External memory aids. In P. E. Grunegerg, P. E. Morris, & R. N. Sykes (Eds.), *Practical aspects of memory* (pp. 172–179). London: Academic Press.

Hart, S. G., & Battiste, V. (1992). Flight test of a video game trainer. In *Proceedings of the Human Factors Society 36th Annual Meeting* (pp. 1291–1295). Santa Monica, CA: Human Factors Society.

Hays, R., & Singer, M. (1989). *Simulation fidelity in training system design: Bridging the gap between reality and training.* New York: Springer-Verlag.

Heidbreder, E. (1935). *Seven psychologies.* New York: Appleton-Century.

Helander, M., Landauer, T., & Prabhu, P. (Eds.) (1997). *The handbook of human-computer interaction.* Amsterdam: Elsevier Science.

Helmreich, R. I., & Foushee, H. C. (1993). Why crew management? In E. L. Weiner, B. G. Kanki, & R. L. Helmreich (Eds.), *Cockpit resource management* (pp. xxx). San Diego, CA: Academic Press.

Henderson, Z., Bruce, V., & Burton, A. M. (2001). Matching the faces of robbers captured on video. *Applied Cognitive Psychology, 14,* 445–464.

Herrmann, D., Brubaker, B., Yoder, C., Sheets, V., & Tio, A. (1999). Devices that remind. In F. T. Durso, R. S. Nickerson, R. W. Schvanaveldt, R. W. Dumais, S. T. Lindsaly, & M. T. H. Chi

(Eds.), *The handbook of applied cognition* (pp. 377–407). Chichester, UK: Wiley.

Herrmann, D., Raybeck, D., & Gruneberg, M. (1997). *A clash of scientific cultures: The relationship between basic and applied research.* Terre Haute: Indiana State University Press.

Herrmann, D., Sheets, V., Wells, J., & Yoder, C. (1997). Palmtop computerized reminding devices: The effectiveness of the temporal properties of warning signals. *AI and Society, 11,* 71–84.

Holden, J. J., Moore, K. S., & Holiday, J. L. (1998). Health education for a breast and cervical cancer screening program: Using the exological model to assess local initiatives. *Health Education Research, 13,* 293–299.

Human capital initiative: Report of the National Behavioral Science Research Agenda Committee. (1992, February). [Special Issue]. *APS Observer.*

Hyman, I. E., Jr., & Kleinknecht, E. E. (1999). False childhood memories: Research, theory, and applications. In L. M. Williams & V. L. Banyard (Eds.), *Trauma and memory* (pp. 175–188). Thousand Oaks, CA: Sage.

Izawa, C. (1993). *Cognitive psychology applied.* Hillsdale, NJ: Erlbaum.

Johnson, O. (Ed.). (1997). *Information please almanac.* Boston: Houghton-Mifflin.

Juslin, P., Olsson, N., & Winman, A. (1996). Calibration and diagnosticity of confidence in eyewitness identification: Comments on what can be inferred from the low confidence-accuracy correlation. *Journal of Experimental Psychology: Learning, Memory, and Cognition, 22,* 1–13.

Kantowitz, B. H., Lee, J. D., & Kantowitz, S. C. (1997). *Development of human factors guidelines for advanced traveler information systems and commercial vehicle operations: Definitions and prioritization of research studies. Report No. FHWA-RD-96-177.* McLean, VA: Federal Highway Administration.

Kapur, N. (1995). Memory aids in the rehabilitation of memory disordered patients. In A. D. Baddeley, B. A. Wilson, & F. N. Watts (Eds.), *Handbook of memory disorders* (pp. 533–556). New York: Wiley.

Kasarda, J. D. (1988). Population and employment change in the United States: Past, present, and future. In *A look ahead: Year 2020,* Special report 220. Washington, DC: Transportation Research Board, National Research Council.

Kent, G. H. (1916). A graded series of geometrical puzzles. *Journal of Experimental Psychology, 1,* 40–50.

Kiesler, S., Siegel, J., & McGuire, T. W. (1984). Social psychological aspects of computer-mediated communication. *American Psychologist, 39,* 1123–1134.

Kiesler, S., Zubrow, D., Moses, A. M., & Geller, V. (1985). Affect in computer-mediated communication: An experiment in synchronous terminal-to-terminal discussion. *Human-Computer Interaction, 1,* 77–104.

King-Sears, M. E., Mercer, C. D., & Sindelar, P. T. (1992). Toward independence with keyword mnemonicsjj: A strategy for science vocabulary instruction. *Remedial and Special Education, 13,* 22–33.

Klatzky, R. L., & Ayoub, M. M. (1995). Health care. In R. S. Nickerson (Ed.), *Emerging needs and opportunities for human factors research* (pp. 131–157). Washington, DC: National Academy Press.

Klatzky, R. L., & Messick, D. M. (1995). Curtailing medical inspections in the face of negative consequences. *Journal of Experimental Psychology: Applied, 1,* 163–178.

Klatzky, R. L., Messick, E. M., & Loftus, J. (1992). Heuristics for determining the optimal interval between checkups. *Psychological Science, 3,* 279–284.

Kostyniuk, L. P., & Kitamura, R. (1987). *Effects of aging and motorization on travel behavior: An exploration.* Transportation Research Record, 1135. Washington, DC: Transportation Research Board, National Research Council.

Kreuter, M. W., Bull, F. C., Clark, E. M., & Oswald, D. L. (1999). Understanding how people process health information: A comparison of tailored and non-tailored weight-loss materials. *Health Psychology, 18,* 487–494.

Kunda, Z. (1987). Motivation and inference: Self-serving generation and evaluation of evidence. *Journal of Personality and Social Psychology, 53,* 636–647.

Landauer, T. K. (1995). *The trouble with computers: Usefulness, usability, and productivity.* Cambridge, MA: MIT Press.

Landauer, T. K., & Bjork, R. A. (1978). Optimum rehearsal patterns and name learning. In M. M. Gruneberg, P. E. Morris, & R. N. Sykes (Eds.), *Practical aspects of memory* (pp. 625–632). London: Academic Press.

Lave, J. (1988). *Cognition in practice.* Hillsdale, NJ: Erlbaum.

Leibowitz, H. W. (1996). The symbiosis between basic and applied research. *American Psychologist, 51,* 366–370.

Leibowitz, H. W., & Owens, D. A. (1977). Nighttime driving accidents and selective visual degradation. *Science, 197,* 422–423.

Levin, J. R., Shriberg, L. K., Miller, G. E., McCormick, C. B., & Levin, B. (1980). The keyword method in the classroom: How to remember the states and their capitals. *Elementary School Journal, 80,* 185–191.

Lewis, J. R., Potosnak, K. M., & Magyar, R. L. (1997). Keys and keyboards. In M. G. Helander, T. K. Landauer, & P. V. Prabhu (Eds.), *Handbook of human-computer interaction* (pp. 1285–1316). New York: Elsevier.

Licklider, J. C. R. (1946). Effects of amplitude distortion upon the intelligibility of speech. *Journal of the Acoustical Society of America, 18,* 429–434.

Lilienfeld, S. O., Wood, J. M., & Garb, H. N. (2000). The scientific status of projective techniques. *Psychological Science in the Public Interest, 1,* 25–66.

Lilienfeld, S. O., Wood, J. M., & Garb, H. N. (2001). What's wrong with this picture? *Scientific American, 284*(5), 80–87.

Lindsay, D. S. (1990). Misleading suggestions can impair eyewitnesses' ability to remember event details. *Journal of Experimental Psychology: Learning, Memory, and Cognition, 16,* 1077–1083.

Lindsay, R. C. L., & Wells, G. L. (1980). What price justice? Exploring the relationship of lineup fairness to identification accuracy. *Law and Human Behavior, 4,* 303–313.

Lindsay, R. C. L., & Wells, G. L. (1985). Improving eyewitness identifications from lineups: simultaneous versus sequential lineup presentation. *Journal of Applied Psychology, 70,* 556–564.

Lindsay, R. C. L., Wells, G. L., & O'Connor, F. (1989). Mock juror belief of accurate and inaccurate eyewitnesses: A replication. *Law and Human Behavior, 13,* 333–340.

Lintern, G., & Gopher, D. (1980). Adaptive training of perceptual-motor skills: Issues, results, and future directions. *International Journal of Man-Machine Studies, 10,* 521–551.

Linville, P. W., Fischer, G. W., & Fischhoff, B. (1993). AIDS risk perceptions and decision biases. In J. B. Pryor & G. D. Reeder (Eds.), *The social psychology of HIV infection* (pp. 5–38). Hillsdale, NJ: Erlbaum.

Loftus, E. F. (1997). Creating false memories. *Scientific American, 277*(3), 70–75.

Loftus, E. F., Donders, K., Hoffman, H. G., & Schooler, J. W. (1989). Creating new memories that are quickly accessed and confidently held. *Memory & Cognition, 17,* 607–616.

Loomis, J. M., Golledge, R. G., & Klatzky, R. L. (1998). Navigation system for the blind: Auditory display modes and guidance. *Presence, 7,* 193–203.

Mackworth, N. H. (1950). *Researches in the measurement of human performance.* MRC Special Report Series No. 268. London: Her Majesty's Stationary Office.

Makhoul, J., Jelinek, F., Rabiner, L., Weinstein, C., & Zue, V. (1990). Spoken language systems. *Annual Review of Computer Science, 4,* 481–501.

Malpass, R. S., & Devine, P. G. (1984). Research on suggestion in lineups and photospreads. In G. L. Wells & E. F. Loftus (Eds.), *Eyewitness testimony: Psychological perspectives* (pp. 64–91). New York: Cambridge University Press.

Mann, R. W. (1982). From concept to commercial use: A history of aids for the visually impaired. In V. W. Stern & M. R. Redden (Eds.), *Technology for independent living* (pp. 62–73). Washington, DC: American Association for the Advancement of Science.

Marcus, A. (1997). Graphical user interfaces. In M. G. Helander, T. K. Landauer, & P. V. Prabhu (Eds.), *Handbook of human-computer interaction* (pp. 423–440). New York: Elsevier.

Marston, W. (1917). Systolic blood pressure symptoms of deception. *Journal of Experimental Psychology, 2,* 117–163.

McCarty, D. L. (1980). Investigation of a visual imagery mnemonic device for acquiring face-name associations. *Journal of Experimental Psychology: Human Learning and Memory, 6,* 145–155.

McEvoy, C. (1992). Memory improvement in context: Implications for the development of memory improvement theory. In D. J. Herrmann, H. Weingartner, A. Searleman, & C. McEvoy (Eds.), *Memory improvement: Implications for memory theory* (pp. 210–231). New York: Springer-Verlag.

McFarland, R. A. (1932). The psychological effects of oxygen deprivation on human behavior. *Archives of Psychol.* N. Y., No. 145.

McGilly, K. (Ed.). (1994). *Classroom lessons: Integrating cognitive theory and classroom practice.* Cambridge, MA: MIT Press.

McKenna, F. P. (1993). It won't happen to me: Unrealistic optimism or illusion of control? *British Journal of Psychology, 84,* 39–50.

McKenna, F. P., Stanier, R. A., & Lewis, C. (1991). Factors underlying illusory self-assessment of driving skill in males and females. *Accident Analysis and Prevention, 23,* 45–52.

McWilliam, C. L., Stewart, M., Brown, J. B., McNair, S., Donna, A., Desai, K., Coderre, P., & Galajda, J. (1999). Home based health promotion for chronically ill older persons: Results of a randomized controlled trial of a critical reflection approach. *Health Promotion International, 14,* 27–41.

Mead, S., & Fisk, A. D. (1998). Measuring skill acquisition and retention with an ATM simulator: The need for age-specific training. *Human Factors, 40,* 516–523.

Members of the *Clever* Project (1999). Hypersearching the Web. *Scientific American, 280*(6), 54–60.

Mickler, T. S., Rodrigue, J. R., & Lescano, C. M. (1999). A comparison of three methods of traching skin self-examination. *Journal of Clinical Psychology in Medical Settings, 6,* 273–286.

Miller, G. A. (1947). The masking of speech. *Psychological Bulletin, 44,* 105–129.

Morris, P. E., & Fritz, C. O. (2000). The name game: Using retrieval practice to improve the learning of names. *Journal of Experimental Psychology: Applied, 6,* 124–129.

Morris, P. E., Jones, S., & Hampson, P. J. (1978). An imagery mnemonic for the learning of people's names. *British Journal of Psychology, 69,* 335–336.

Mortimer, R. G. (1998). The high mounted brake lamp—The 4% solution. Society of Automotive Engineers Report PC-16.

Nader, R. (1965). *Unsafe at any speed.* New York: Grossman.

Newell, A. F., & Gregor, P. (1997). Human computer interfaces for people with disabilities. In M. G. Helander, T. K. Landauer, & P. V. Prabhu (Eds.), *Handbook of human-computer interaction* (pp. 813–824). New York: Elsevier.

Nickerson, R. S. (1995). Human interaction with computers and robots. *International Journal of Human Factors in Manufacturing, 5,* 5–27.

Nickerson, R. S. (1997). Designing for human use: Human-factors psychologists. In R. J. Sternberg (Ed.), *Career paths in psychology* (pp. 213–243). Washington, DC: American Psychological Association.

Nickerson, R. S. (1998). Applied experimental psychology. *Applied Psychology: An International Review, 47,* 155–173.

Nickerson, R. S. (1999). Engineering psychology and ergonomics. In E. C. Carterette & M. Friedman (Eds.), *Human performance and ergonomics: Vol. 17. Handbook of perception and cognition* (pp. 1–45). San Diego, CA: Academic Press.

Nickerson, R. S., Baron, S., Collins, A. M., & Crothers, C. G. (1968). *Investigation of some of the problems of vehicle rear lighting.* Cambridge, MA: Bolt Beranedz & Newman Inc. Report 1586.

Nielson, J. (1994). *Usability inspection methods.* New York: Wiley.

Norman, K. (1991). *The psychology of menu selection: Designing cognitive control of the human/computer interface.* Norwood, NJ: Ablex.

Nussbaum, B., & Neff, R. (1991, April 29). I can't work this thing. *Business Week,* pp. 58–66.

Ogden, W. C., & Bernick, P. (1997). Using natural language. In M. G. Helander, T. K. Landauer, & P. V. Prabhu (Eds.), *Handbook of human-computer interaction* (pp. 137–161). New York: Elsevier.

Olsson, N., Juslin P., & Winman, A. (1998). Realism of confidence in earwitness versus eyewitness identification. *Journal of Experimental Psychology: Applied, 4,* 101–118.

Oskamp, S. (1984). *Applied social psychology.* Englewood Cliffs, NJ: Prentice-Hall.

Owens, D. A., Helmers, G., & Sivak, M. (1993). Intelligent vehicle highway systems: A call for user-centered design. *Ergonomics, 36,* 363–369.

Owens, D. A., & Tyrell, R. A. (1999). Effects of luminance, blur, and age on nighttime visual guidance: A test of the selective degradation hypothesis. *Journal of Experimental Psychology: Applied, 5,* 115–128.

The Oxygen Project. (1999). *Scientific American, 281*(2), 52–63.

Paap, K. R., & Cooke, N. J. (1997). Design of menus. In M. G. Helander, T. K. Landauer, & P. V. Prabhu (Eds.), *Handbook of human-computer interaction* (pp. 533–572). New York: Elsevier.

Paap, K. R., & Roske-Hofstrand, R. J. (1986). The optimal number of menu options per panel. *Human Factors, 28,* 377–385.

Parasuraman, R., & Riley, V. A. (1997). Humans and automation: Use, misuse, disuse, and abuse. *Human Factors, 39,* 230–253.

Parsons, H. M. (1999). A history of Division 21 (Applied experimental and engineering psychology). In D. A. Dewsbury (Ed.), *Unification through division: Histories of the divisions of the American Psychological Association* (Vol. 3, pp. 43–72). Washington, DC: American Psychological Association.

Peacock, B., & Karwowski, W. (1993). *Automotive ergonomics.* London: Taylor and Francis.

Pew, R. W. (2000). Human factors psychology. In A. E. Kazdin (Ed.), *Encyclopedia of psychology* (pp. 179–186). Washington, DC: American Psychological Association.

Pezdek, K., Finger, K., & Hodge, D. (1997). Planting false childhood memories: The role of event plausibility. *Psychological Science, 8,* 437–441.

Platt, J. (1973). Social traps. *American Psychologist, 28,* 641–651.

Poole, D. A., & Lindsay, D. S. (2001). Children's eyewitness reports after exposure to misinformation from parents. *Journal of Experimental Psychology, 7,* 27–50.

Prince, C., & Salas, E. (1993). Training and research for teamwork in the military aircrew. In E. L. Weiner, B. G. Kanki, & R. L. Helmreich (Eds.), *Cockpit resource management* (pp. 337–366). San Diego, CA: Academic Press.

Read, D., & Craik, F. I. (1995). Earwitness identification: Some influences on voice recognition. *Journal of Experimental Psychology: Applied, 1,* 6–18.

Reason, J. (1990). *Human error.* New York: Cambridge University Press.

Redden, M. R., & Stern, V. W. (Eds.). (1983). *Technology for independent living: Vol. 2.* Washington, DC: American Association for the Advancement of Science.

Rogers, W. A., & Fisk, A. D. (2000). Human factors, applied cognition, and aging. In F. I. M. Craik & T. A. Salthouse (Eds.), *The handbook of aging and cognition* (2nd ed., pp. 559–591). Hillsdale, NJ: Erlbaum.

Rogers, W. A., Fisk, A. D., Mead, S. E., Walker, N., & Cabrera, E. F. (1996). Training older adults to use automatic teller machines. *Human Factors, 38,* 425–433.

Salas, E., Bowers, C. A., & Prince, C. (Guest Eds.). (1998). *The International Journal of Aviation Psychology, 8,* 195–317.

Salas, E., & Cannon-Bowers, J. A. (1997). Methods, tools, and strategies for team training. In M. A. Quiñones & A. Ehrenstein (Eds.), *Training for a rapidly changing workplace: Applications of psychological research* (pp. 249–279). Washington, DC: American Psychological Association Press.

Salthouse, T. A., Hambrick, D. Z., Lukas, K. E., & Dell, T. C. (1996). Determinants of adult age differences on synthetic work performance. *Journal of Experimental Psychology: Applied, 2,* 305–329.

Salthouse, T. A., & Maurer, T. J. (1996). Aging, job performance, and career development. In J. E. Birren & K. W. Schaie (Eds.), *Handbook of the psychology of aging* (4th ed.), 353–364. San Diego, CA: Academic Press.

Sanford, E. C. (1888). Personal equation. *American Journal of Psychology, 2,* 6–16.

Schwartz, S. H. (1977). Normative influences on altruism. In L. Berkowitz (Ed.), *Advances in experimental social psychology* (Vol. 10, pp. 221–279). New York: Academic Press.

Seagull, F. J., & Gopher, D. (1997). Training head movement in visual scanning: An embedded approach to the development of piloting skills with helmet-mounted displays. *Journal of Experimental Psychology: Applied, 3,* 163–180.

Secretary of State for Transport. (1989, November). *Investigation into the Clapham Junction railway accident.* London: Her Majesty's Stationary Office.

Senders, J., & Moray, N. (Eds.). (1991). *Human error: Cause, prediction, and reduction.* Hillsdale, NJ: Erlbaum.

Shaw, J. S. III (1996). Increases in eyewitness confidence resulting from postevent questioning. *Journal of Experimental Psychology: Applied, 2,* 126–146.

Sobel, N. R., & Pridgen, D (1981). *Eyewitness identification: Legal and practical problems.* New York: Clark Boardman.

Sproull, L., & Kiesler, S. (1991). *Connections: New ways of working in the networked organization.* Cambridge, MA: MIT Press.

Stammers, R. B. (1982). Part and whole practice in training for procedural tasks. *Human Learning, 1,* 185–207.

Stern, V. W., & Redden, M. R. (Eds.). (1982). *Technology for independent living.* Washington, DC: American Association for the Advancement of Science.

Stevens, J. C., Foulke, E., & Patterson, M. Q. (1996). Tactile acuity, aging, and Braille reading in long-term blindness. *Journal of Experimental Psychology: Applied, 2,* 91–106.

Stevenson, J. A. (1918). Correlation between different forms of sensory discrimination. *Journal of Applied Psychology, 2,* 26–42.

Summit '98: Consensus on the future of psychological science. (1998, May/June). *APS Observer,* pp. 1, 14–16, 18, 20–21.

Super, C., & Super, D. (1988). *Opportunities in psychology careers.* Lincolnwood, IL: VGM Career Horizons.

Svenson, O. (1981). Are we all less risky and more skillful than our fellow drivers? *Acta Psychologica, 47,* 143–148.

Svenson, O., Fischhoff, B., & MacGregor, D. (1985). Perceived driving safety and seatbelt usage. *Accident Analysis and Prevention, 17,* 119–133.

Swets, J. A., Dawes, R. M., & Monahan, J. (2000a). Better decisions through science. *Scientific American, 283*(4), 82–87.

Swets, J. A., Dawes, R. M., & Monahan, J. (2000b). Psychological science can improve diagnostic decisions. *Psychological Science in the Public Interest, 1,* 1–26.

Taylor, H. L. (Ed.). (1994). *Division 21 members who made distinguished contributions to engineering psychology.* Washington, DC: American Psychological Association.

Thomas, M. H., & Wang, A. Y. (1996). Learning by the keyword mnemonic: Looking for the long-term benefits. *Journal of Experimental Psychology: Applied, 2,* 330–342.

Tomes, J. L., & Katz, A. N. (1997). Habitual susceptibility to misinformation and individual differences in eyewitness memory. *Applied Cognitive Psychology, 11,* 233–251.

U.S. Census Bureau (1997). *Americans with disabilities.* Washington, DC: U.S. Department of Commerce.

U.S. Census Bureau (1999). *Statistical abstract of the United States 1999.* Washington, DC: U.S. Department of Commerce.

VanCott, H. P., & Huey, B. M. (1992). *Human factors specialists' education and utilization.* Washington, DC: National Academy Press.

Verhaeghen, P., Marcoen, A., & Goossens, L. (1992). Improving memory performance in the aged through mnemonic training: A meta-analytic study. *Psychology and Aging, 7,* 242–251.

Vining, D. R., Jr. (1985). The growth of core regions in the third world. *Scientific American, 252*(4), 42–49.

Waller, P. F. (1991). The older driver. *Human Factors, 22,* 499–505.

Weintraub, D. J. (1992). *Human factors issues in head-up display design: The book of HUD.* Dayton, OH: Crew Systems Ergonomics Information Analysis Center.

Wells, G. L. (1993). What do we know about eyewitness identification? *American Psychologist, 48,* 553–571.

Wells, G. L., & Bradfield, A. L. (1998). "Good, you identified the suspect:" Feedback to eyewitnesses distorts their reports of the witnessing experience. *Journal of Applied Psychology, 83,* 360–376.

Wells, G. L., & Lindsay, R. C. L. (1980). On estimating the diagnosticity of eyewitness nonidentifications. *Psychological Bulletin, 88,* 776–784.

Wembridge, E. R. (1918). Obscurities in voting upon measures due to double-negative. *Journal of Applied Psychology, 2,* 156–163.

Wenger, M. J., & Payne, D. G. (1995). On the acquisition of mnemonic skill: Application of skilled memory theory. *Journal of Experimental Psychology: Applied, 1,* 194–215.

West, R. L. (1989). Planning and practical memory training for the aged. In L. W. Poon, D. C. Rubin, & B. A. Wilson, (Eds.), *Everyday cognition in adulthood and late life* (pp. 573–597). New York: Cambridge University Press.

Wickens, C. D. (2000). *Engineering psychology and human performance* (3rd ed.). New York: Harper Collins. (Original work published 1984)

Wickens, C. D., & Long, J. (1995). Object versus space-based models of visual attention: Implications for the design of head-up displays. *Journal of Experimental Psychology: Applied, 1,* 179–193.

Wickens, C. D., Mavor, A. S., & McGee, J. P. (1997). *Flight to the future: Human factors in air traffic control.* Washington, DC: National Academy Press.

Wickens, C. D., & Prevett, T. T. (1995). Exploring the dimensions of egocentricity in aircraft navigation displays. *Journal of Experimental Psychology: Applied, 1,* 110–135.

Wightman, D. C., & Lintern, G. (1985). Part-task training for tracking and manual control. *Human Factors, 27,* 267–283.

Wilson, M. B. (1992, September). *Human factors: An initiative in the U.S. Coast Guard.* Paper presented at the Ship Production Symposium, New Orleans, LA.

Wogalter, M. S., Hancock, P. A., & Dempsey, P. G. (1998). On the description and definition of human factors/ergonomics. *Proceedings of the Human Factors and Ergonomics Society 42nd Annual Meeting* (pp. 671–674). Santa Monica, CA: Human Factors and Ergonomics Society.

Woods, D. D., & Cook, R. I. (1999). Perspectives on human error: Hindsight biases and local rationality. In F. T. Durso, R. S. Nickerson, R. W. Schvanaveldt, R. W. Dumais, S. T. Lindsaly, & M. T. H. Chi (Eds.), *The handbook of applied cognition* (pp. 143–171). Chichester, UK: Wiley.

Woods, P. J. (Ed.). (1976). *Career opportunities for psychologists: Expanding and emerging areas.* Washington, DC: American Psychological Association.

Woodworth, R. S. (1938). *Experimental psychology.* New York: Henry Holt.

Woodworth, R. S., & Schlosberg, H. (1954). *Experimental psychology.* New York: Henry Holt.

World Almanac. (1998). *The world almanac and book of facts.* Mahwah, NJ: K-III Reference Corporation.

Wright, P. (1999). Designing healthcare advice for the public. In F. T. Durso, R. S. Nickerson, R. W. Schvanaveldt, R. W. Dumais, S. T. Lindsaly, & M. T. H. Chi (Eds.), *The handbook of applied cognition* (pp. 695–723). Chichester, UK: Wiley.

Yarmey, A. D. (1984). Age as a factor in eyewitness memory. In G. L. Wells & E. F. Loftus (Eds.), *Eyewitness testimony: Psychological perspectives* (pp. 142–154). New York: Cambridge University Press.

Yarmey, A. D., & Kent, J. (1980). Eyewitness identification by elderly and young adults. *Law and Human Behavior, 4*, 359–371.

Yesavage, J. A., Rose, T. L., & Bower, G. H. (1983). Interactive imagery and affective judgments improve face-name learning in the elderly. *Journal of Gerontology, 38,* 197–203.

Zue, V. (1999). Talking with your computer. *Scientific American, 281*(2), 56–57.

Author Index

Subject Index